THE OXFORD HANDBOOK OF

MODERN AND CONTEMPORARY AMERICAN POETRY

THE OXFORD HANDBOOK OF

MODERN AND CONTEMPORARY AMERICAN POETRY

Edited by
CARY NELSON

OXFORD
UNIVERSITY PRESS

OXFORD
UNIVERSITY PRESS

Oxford University Press is a department of the University of Oxford.
It furthers the University's objective of excellence in research, scholarship,
and education by publishing worldwide.

Oxford   New York
Auckland   Cape Town   Dar es Salaam   Hong Kong   Karachi
Kuala Lumpur   Madrid   Melbourne   Mexico City   Nairobi
New Delhi   Shanghai   Taipei   Toronto

With offices in
Argentina   Austria   Brazil   Chile   Czech Republic   France   Greece
Guatemala   Hungary   Italy   Japan   Poland   Portugal   Singapore
South Korea   Switzerland   Thailand   Turkey   Ukraine   Vietnam

Oxford is a registered trade mark of Oxford University Press
in the UK and certain other countries.

Published in the United States of America by
Oxford University Press
198 Madison Avenue, New York, NY 10016

© Oxford University Press 2012

First issued as an Oxford University Press paperback, 2014.

Library of Congress Cataloging-in-Publication Data
The Oxford handbook of modern and contemporary American poetry / edited by Cary Nelson.
p. cm. — (Oxford handbooks)
Includes bibliographical references and index.
ISBN 978-0-19-539877-9 (hardcover : alk. paper); 978-0-19-020415-0 (paperback : alk. paper)
1. American poetry—20th century—History and criticism.   I. Nelson, Cary.
PS323.5.O94 2011
811'.5409—dc220
2011003460

Contents

....

Acknowledgments

The authors would like to thank the following for providing permission to quote their works in this volume.

Gwendolyn Brooks: "The Last Quatrain of the Ballad of Emmett Till," from *Blacks* by Gwendolyn Brooks. Reprinted by consent of Brooks permissions.

Carlos Bulosan: "These Are Also Living," from *Letter from America* by Carlos Bulosan, copyright © 1942 by Carlos Bulosan. Reprinted by Permission of Ateneo de Manila University Press.

Countee Cullen: "Yet Do I Marvel," published in *On These I Stand* by Countee Cullen, copyright © Harper & Bros., NY, NY. Copyrights held by Amidstad Research Center, Administered by Thompson and Thompson, New York, NY.

Shaikh Abdurraheem Dost, from *Poems From Guantanamo: The Detainees Speak*, ed. By Mark Falkoff, copyright © 2007. Reprinted by permission of the University of Iowa Press.

Kenneth Fearing: "Aphrodite Metropolis II," from *Complete Poems*, 1997. Reprinted by the permission of Russell & Volkening, Inc., as agents for the author. Copyright © 1994 by Jubal Fearing and Phoebe Fearing.

Randall Jarrell: "The Death of the Ball Turret Gunner," from *Randall Jarrell: Complete Poems* by Randall Jarrell. Copyright © 1969, renewed 1997 by Mary von S. Jarrell. Reprinted by permission of Farrar, Straus & Giroux, L.L.C., and Faber and Faber.

Lawrence Joseph: "News Back Even Further Than That," from *Into It* by Lawrence Joseph, copyright © 2007 by Farrar, Straus & Giroux. Reprinted by permission of Farrar, Straus & Giroux, L.L.C.

Adrian Louis: "Looking for Judas," from *Vortex of Indian Fevers* by Adrian Louis, copyright © 1995 by Northwestern University Press/Triquarterly Books. Reprinted by permission of Northwestern University Press.

Etheridge Knight: "Eastern guard tower," "Making Jazz swing in," and "Two hours I've walked" from *The Essential Etheridge Knight*, by Etheridge Knight, copyright © 1986. Reprinted by permission of the University of Pittsburgh Press.

Yusef Komunyakaa: "We Never Know" and "Facing It" from *Pleasure Dome: New and Collected Poems*, copyright © 2001 by Yusef Komunyakaa. Reprinted by permission of Wesleyan University Press.

Lynn Riggs: "A Letter," from *The Iron Dish* by Lynn Riggs, copyright © 1930 by Lynn Riggs. Used by permission of Doubleday, a division of Random House, Inc.

Muriel Rukeyser: "Poem," from *Collected Poems* by Muriel Rukeyser, copyright © 1968 by Muriel Rukeyser. Copyright © 1994 by Jan Heller Levi and William Rukeyser. Reprinted by permission of International Creative Management, Inc.

Albert Saijo: "A SYLLOGISM NO DOUBT," from *Outspeaks: A Rhapsody* by Albert Saijo, copyright © 1997 by Albert Saijo. Reprinted by permission of Bamboo Ridge and the author.

Gary Snyder: "Surrounded by Wild Turkeys" from *No Nature* by Gary Snyder, copyright © 1992 by Gary Snyder. Used by permission of Pantheon Books, a division of Random House, Inc.

Brian Turner: "Here, Bullet," from *Here, Bullet*. Copyright © 2005 by Brian Turner. Reprinted with the permission of Bloodaxe Books and Alice James Books, www.alicejamesbooks.org.

Jose Garcia Villa: "Elegy for the Airplane," from *Doveglion: Collected Poems* by Jose Garcia Villa, edited by John Edwin Cowen, copyright © 2008 by John Edwin Cowen, Literary Executor of the Jose Garcia Cowen Estate. Used by permission of Penguin, a division of Penguin Group (USA) Inc.

William Carlos Williams: "To Elsie," from *The Collected Poems: Volume 1, 1909–1939*, copyright © 1938 by New Directions Publishing Corp. Reprinted by permission of New Directions Publishing Corp. and Carcanet Press.

John Yau: "Sam Spade Haiku," from *Radiant Silhouette: New and Selected Work*, copyright © 1994 by John Yau. Reprinted by permission of the author.

LIST OF CONTRIBUTORS

Charles Altieri teaches modern American poetry and related topics at the University of California, Berkeley. His most recent books have been *The Particulars of Rapture* and *The Art of Modern American Poetry*. He is working on a book about Wallace Stevens and the concept of value.

Edward Brunner is a professor at Southern Illinois University, Carbondale. His most recent study is *Cold War Poetry*. He teaches courses in modern poetry, popular culture, and graphic novels.

Mike Chasar is Assistant Professor of English at Willamette University in Salem, Oregon. His articles have appeared in *PMLA* and *American Literature*, and he is the coeditor of *Poetry after Cultural Studies* (forthcoming from University of Iowa Press).

Michael Davidson is Distinguished Professor of Literature at the University of California, San Diego. His most recent books are *Ghostlier Demarcations: Modern Poetry and the Material Word, Guys Like Us: Citing Masculinity in Cold War Poetics*, and *Concerto for the Left Hand: Disability and the Defamiliar Body. On the Outskirts of Form: Practicing Cultural Poetics* is forthcoming from Wesleyan University Press.

Rachel Blau DuPlessis, Professor Emerita, Temple University, is the author of *Genders, Races and Religious Cultures in Modern American Poetry* (Cambridge, 2001) and of the long poem *Drafts*, begun in 1986 and collected most recently in two books published by Salt Publishing—*Pitch: Drafts 77–95* (2010) and *The Collage Poems of Drafts* (2011). Her newest critical book (2012) is *Purple Passages: Pound, Eliot, Zukofsky, Olson, Creeley and the Ends of Patriarchal Poetry* from University of Iowa Press. In 2006, two books of her innovative essays were published: *Blue Studios: Poetry and Its Cultural Work* (2006) and the ground-breaking *The Pink Guitar: Writing as Feminist Practice* ([1990] 2006), both from University of Alabama Press. She has written several other critical books, co-edited three anthologies, and edited *The Selected Letters of George Oppen* (1990). Her websites are http://rachelblauduplessis.com and http://wings.buffalo.edu/epc/authors/duplessis.

Al Filreis is the Kelly Professor, Director of the Center for Programs in Contemporary Writing, Faculty Director of the Kelly Writers House, Co-Director (with Charles Bernstein) of the digital poetry archive PennSound, and Publisher of *Jacket2* magazine at the University of Pennsylvania. He is the author of many articles, editions, and books, including *Counter-Revolution of the Word: The Conservative Attack on Modern Poetry, 1945–1960* and *Modernism from Right to Left*.

Karen Jackson Ford is Professor of English at the University of Oregon, where she teaches poetry and poetics. She has published *Gender and the Poetics of Excess*, *Split-Gut Song: Jean Toomer and the Poetics of Modernity*, and essays on American poetry. She is currently working on a book about race and poetic form in the United States.

Melissa Girard is Assistant Professor of English at the University of Wisconsin—Eau Claire. Her articles have appeared in the *Journal of Modern Literature* and the critical collection *Kenneth Burke and His Circles*.

Walter Kalaidjian is Professor of English at Emory University. His research and teaching focus on transnational modernism, cultural studies, and psychoanalysis. He has authored four books about twentieth-century American literature, including *The Edge of Modernism: American Poetry and the Traumatic Past*, *American Culture between the Wars: Revisionary Modernism and Postmodern Critique*, and *Languages of Liberation: The Social Text in Contemporary American Poetry*. In addition, he is the editor of the *Cambridge Companion to American Modernism*.

Lynn Keller is the author of *Re-Making It New: Contemporary American Poetry and the Modernist Tradition*, *Forms of Expansion: Recent Long Poems by Women*, and *Thinking Poetry: Readings in Contemporary Women's Exploratory Poetics*. With Cristanne Miller, she edited *Feminist Measures: Soundings in Poetry and Theory*. She is the poetry editor for the journal *Contemporary Literature* and is coeditor with Dee Morris and Alan Golding of the University of Iowa Press Contemporary North American Poetry Series. She teaches at the University of Wisconsin–Madison.

Linda A. Kinnahan is Professor of English at Duquesne University. Her publications include numerous articles and book chapters on modernist and contemporary poets, along with two books on twentieth-century poetry, *Poetics of the Feminine: Literary Tradition and Authority in William Carlos Williams, Mina Loy, Denise Levertov, and Kathleen Fraser* and *Lyric Interventions: Feminist Experimental Poetry and Contemporary Social Discourse*. She is currently working on a book entitled *Modernist Poetry and the Gendering of Economics*, which focuses on modernist women poets (Marianne Moore, Mina Loy, and Lola Ridge) in relationship to the interactive dynamics of economics and visual culture in the early twentieth century.

John Marsh is Assistant Professor of English at Pennsylvania State University. He is the editor of *You Work Tomorrow: An Anthology of American Labor Poetry, 1929–1941* and the author of two forthcoming books, *Hog Butchers, Beggars, and Busboys: Poverty, Labor, and the Making of Modern American Poetry* and *Class Dismissed: Why We Can't Teach or Learn Our Way Out of Inequality*.

Philip Metres is Associate Professor of English at John Carroll University in Cleveland, Ohio. He is also the author of *To See the Earth, Come Together: Imagine Peace*, and *Behind the Lines: War Resistance Poetry on the American Homefront Since 1941*, among others. His work has appeared in *Best American Poetry* and has garnered an NEA, a Watson Fellowship, two Ohio Arts Council Grants, and the Cleveland Arts Prize.

Adalaide Morris is Professor of English at the University of Iowa. The frame of her recent writing is the expanded field of modern and contemporary poetics, including sound art, the documentary, and the digital. Her books include *How to Live/ What to Do: H.D.'s Cultural Poetics*; an edited collection of essays, *Sound States: Innovative Poetics and Acoustical Technologies*; and a coedited collection, *New Media Poetics: Contexts, Technotexts, and Theories*.

Cary Nelson is Jubilee Professor of Liberal Arts and Sciences and Professor of English at the University of Illinois at Urbana-Champaign. From 2006 to 2012, he was also the national president of the American Association of University Professors. He is the author or editor of more than 20 books. *When Death Rhymed: Poem Cards and Poetry Panics of the Great Wars* is forthcoming.

John Timberman Newcomb is Associate Professor of English at the University of Illinois at Urbana-Champaign. He is the author of *Wallace Stevens and Literary Canons* and *Would Poetry Disappear? American Verse and the Crisis of Modernity*.

Peter Nicholls is Professor of English at New York University. His publications include *Ezra Pound: Politics, Economics and Writing, Modernisms: A Literary Guide, George Oppen and the Fate of Modernism*, and many articles and essays on literature and theory. He coedited (with Laura Marcus) *The Cambridge History of Twentieth-Century English Literature* and (with Gianni Cianci) *Ruskin and Modernism*. He is the U.S. editor of *Textual Practice*.

Josephine Park is Associate Professor of English and Asian American Studies at the University of Pennsylvania. She is the author of *Apparitions of Asia: Modernist Form and Asian American Poetics*.

Robert Dale Parker is the James M. Benson Professor in English at the University of Illinois. He is the author of *The Invention of Native American Literature* and *How to Interpret Literature: Critical Theory for Literary and Cultural Studies* as well as books on Faulkner and Elizabeth Bishop. He has also published an edition of the works of Jane Johnston Schoolcraft and *Changing Is Not Vanishing: A Collection of American Indian Poetry to 1930*.

Jahan Ramazani is Edgar F. Shannon Professor of English at the University of Virginia. He is the author of *A Transnational Poetics,* winner of the ACLA's Harry Levin Prize; *The Hybrid Muse: Postcolonial Poetry in English*; *Poetry of Mourning: The Modern Elegy from Hardy to Heaney*; and *Yeats and the Poetry of Death*. He is a coeditor of the most recent editions of *The Norton Anthology of English Literature* and *The Norton Anthology of Modern and Contemporary Poetry.*

Susan Rosenbaum is Associate Professor of English at the University of Georgia. She is the author of *Professing Sincerity: Modern Lyric Poetry, Commercial Culture, and the Crisis in Reading,* and she is currently writing a book about surrealism, American poetry, and the Museum of Modern Art in New York City.

Lytle Shaw is Associate Professor of English at New York University. His books include *Frank O'Hara: The Poetics of Coterie, 19 Lines: A Drawing Center Writing Anthology,* and *Fieldworks: From Place to Site in Postwar Poetics.*

James Smethurst teaches Afro-American Studies at the University of Massachusetts, Amherst. He authored *The New Red Negro: The Literary Left and African American Poetry, 1930–1946, The Black Arts Movement: Literary Nationalism in the 1960s and 1970s,* and *The African American Roots of Modernism: From Reconstruction to the Harlem Renaissance.* He coedited *Left of the Color Line: Race, Radicalism and Twentieth-Century Literature of the United States* and *Radicalism in the South Since Reconstruction.*

Michael Thurston is Professor of English and Director of the American Studies Program at Smith College. He is the author of *Making Something Happen: American Political Poetry between the World Wars* and *The Underworld Descent in Twentieth-Century Poetry: From Pound and Eliot to Heaney and Walcott.* He is also the coeditor, with Jani Scandura, of *Modernism, Inc: Body, Memory, Capital.* An editor of the *Massachusetts Review,* he is currently at work on two books: a volume on reading postwar British and Irish poetry, and a study of changing representations of Cape Cod.

Mark W. Van Wienen is Professor of English at Northern Illinois University. He is the editor of *Rendezvous with Death: American Poems of the Great War* and the author of *Partisans and Poets: The Political Work of American Poetry in the Great War.* His *American Socialist Tryptich: Charlotte Perkins Gilman, Upton Sinclair, W. E. B. Du Bois* is forthcoming.

Timothy Yu is Associate Professor of English and Asian Studies at the University of Wisconsin–Madison. He is the author of *Race and the Avant-Garde: Experimental and Asian American Poetry Since 1965.* His current research focuses on the poetry created by those within the Asian diaspora around the Pacific Rim.

THE OXFORD HANDBOOK OF

MODERN AND CONTEMPORARY AMERICAN POETRY

PART I

....

CHAPTER 1

A CENTURY OF INNOVATION: AMERICAN POETRY FROM 1900 TO THE PRESENT

....

CARY NELSON

HISTORIANS are well aware that the past never stays the same. New documents are discovered. Events lost to contemporary memory are recovered and adjustments ripple through accounts of past actors, key episodes, and entire periods alike. Despite a misleading popular image of the arts and humanities—one in which literature faculty are notably thought to conserve and transmit a stable tradition—the dynamic within fields like literature and history is not actually so different. For a time, to be sure, modern American poetry scholars thought that all that really mattered were the careers of half a dozen major poets whose canonical status was largely established by the 1960s or, in some cases, earlier: T. S. Eliot, Robert Frost, Wallace Stevens, Ezra Pound, and William Carlos Williams. Pound's status had to survive his wartime radio broadcasts for Mussolini's Italy. Williams did not receive full academic recognition until the 1970s. Frost was long partly outside the fold because he never embraced modernist experimentalism. Yet, though their individual fortunes varied, these five white, male poets constituted the core of the academy's story of the development and major achievements of twentieth-century American poetry. Neither Marianne Moore nor Langston Hughes, both now fully canonical and present throughout this book, was frequently to be found. Scores and scores of poets once widely read had dropped out of academic scholarly and classroom conversation.

That is not to say that the poets canonized early on were not major voices. They certainly were. Pound's collage techniques, for example, have inspired many other poets who have no patience with his politics. Rather, the narrow academic canon offered an inadequate account of a much richer and more diverse literary history. This Handbook seeks simultaneously to recognize major voices and to bring many other poets into our conversations about modern poetry. Eliot, Pound, and Williams, among others, appear in many of the chapters that follow. Indeed, this collection was assembled on the principle that no contributor bore sole responsibility for discussing any given poet. Although I avoided commissioning chapters that covered the same general topic, writers were free to discuss any poets they chose. There are thus multiple perspectives on a number of poets. We will encounter quite different T. S. Eliots and Ezra Pounds.

Though there was a time when William Carlos Williams was not a central figure for poetry scholars, this book makes that hard to understand. Williams's "To Elsie" receives an elaborate psychoanalytic reading from Walter Kalaidjian in this collection, while Michael Davidson views the same poem through the lens of disability studies. Charles Altieri places Williams's "Spring and All" in a provocative relationship with Cézanne as part of an effort to move beyond the conventional collage terminology I use myself and to urge a deeper understanding of the relationship between poetry and painting in American modernism. Jahan Ramazani focuses on Williams's incorporation of news events and local information into his early and late poetry. Edward Brunner looks at Williams's musical references and tracks the musical component in his improvisations. Tim Newcomb analyzes Williams's attitude toward sports spectators in "At the Ball Game." And Susan Rosenbaum discusses Williams's interest in surrealism.

Born in Rutherford, New Jersey, a town near the city of Paterson, Williams (1883–1963) made the city his home for most of his life. He would mix cosmopolitan experience with a commitment to local American life. His father, of British birth and West Indies upbringing, was a perfume company salesman; his mother, of mixed Spanish, French, Dutch, and Jewish ancestry, was born in Puerto Rico and had studied art in Paris. After two years of study in Switzerland and Paris, Williams returned to earn an M.D. at the University of Pennsylvania. From then on, he would maintain a remarkable dual career. One of the most prolific and versatile writers of the period, he was also a full-time doctor serving poor and middle-class patients in northern New Jersey, delivering over a thousand babies in the course of his career.

From his medical practice, Williams would draw characters who appeared in his fiction and poetry; he would also remain deeply committed to his patients' lives, to the struggles they underwent and to their sustaining humor. His class sympathy helped him understand the relationship between radical artistic innovation and radical politics in the 1920s and 1930s. As a result, for decades he was a fellow traveler on the Left, publishing in communist journals, supporting the Spanish Republic, and earning enough of a progressive reputation to be turned down for a position as poetry consultant at the Library of Congress a year after the anticommunist witch hunts started in 1947. Many literary scholars during the McCarthy period of the

next decade avoided Williams out of fear of his politics and revulsion at his conver-
sational idiom and working-class commitments. But Williams had been immensely
influential for other poets all along.

Williams had met Pound and H.D. (Hilda Doolittle, 1886–1961) at Penn; he
would later become friends with Moore and Stevens and a number of avant-garde
painters based in New York. His first poems were somewhat derivatively romantic,
but by 1916 he was writing short lyrics in a decidedly American idiom that drew
on several modernist impulses. They remain among his masterpieces. *Spring and
All* (1923) and *The Descent of Winter* (1928) were breakthrough volumes, radical col-
lages of poetry and prose that mix flawless, crafted, and rather minimalist texts with
passages of almost automatic writing.

In the 1940s he would begin publishing portions of his book-length poetic epic,
Paterson. It was the fulfillment of his impassioned sense of place, of a commitment
to American culture that was never merely celebratory but rather the witness of a
devoted and attentive critic, a critic seeking a redemptive idiom amidst crass mate-
rialism and violence. *Paterson* was also the culmination of his lifelong rejection of
the Eliot/Pound expatriate impulse, and its mix of letters, documents, and lyrics
was a further realization of the collage experiments of the 1920s. In his last years he
devised a triadic, or step-down, form that he called a "variable foot." It is employed
in "Asphodel, That Greeny Flower," a three-part love poem to his wife Florence.

The slow process of recovering Williams and other poets has occupied several
decades. As this collection will demonstrate, it is by no means complete. Indeed,
there is no longer any reason to think it ever will be. A specialist in modern poetry is
never fundamentally more than a student of the field. No matter how long you read
and study and think, you will never fully master modern American poetry. True
expertise means accepting and accounting for the necessarily limited and partial
nature of your knowledge. It means realizing you cannot even entirely name what
you do not know. The opening chapter by Robert Parker is a telling and extreme
example of that phenomenon. Of the thirty Native American poets he names, I was
aware of only three of them before reading his chapter, and most modern poetry
scholars would only have known of one. As Parker points out, virtually all modern
poetry specialists were unaware of the whole existence of a rich half century of Native
American poetry. That ignorance, moreover, speaks volumes about what we do and
do not treasure and continue to disseminate. Parker, however, was helped by the
ambitious and ongoing bibliography produced by Daniel F. Littlefield (Cherokee),
whose Sequoyah Research Center and Native American Press Archives also house
many of the poems as part of their massive effort to archive as much Indian writ-
ing as possible. The bibliography by Littlefield and James M. Parins is a great, vastly
underused, and under-known resource.

Recovery itself, moreover, is not simply a neutral work of investigation and accu-
mulation. The work has had to be theorized in order for it to be coherent and effec-
tive. The acquisition of important poetic traditions engaged with social life in ways
apparently very different from that of the traditional canon has meant broadening
and complicating our understanding of poetry's social functions. New understand-

ings of the relation between text and context, of poets' engagements with history and of the historical witness possible through metaphor have had to be developed in tandem with an expanded canon. Rachel Blau DuPlessis's opening chapter clarifies many of those developments.

Part of the work of theorizing modern poetry is the work of exploring the conceptual, aesthetic, and historical categories that will help us see patterns, connections, and trends in the literary record. We have always had such categories in the form of schools, movements, periods, and nationalities. The last of these categories, as Timothy Yu shows in his contribution on transnationalism and James Smethurst demonstrates in his analysis of the multinational phenomenon of hip hop poetry, has been the most disabling. One of the aims of this handbook is to show that these categories do not have to be mutually exclusive: they can overlap to produce coexisting alternative maps of the modern poetry terrain.

Thinking about the relationship between poetry and psychoanalysis, as Walter Kalaidjian does here, provides one telling map of the last century's poetry. Looking at the influence of surrealism, even in the absence of an official roster of surrealist poets, as Susan Rosenbaum does, produces yet another grouping. But the surrealists were, in effect, devoted to the unconscious, so the maps overlap. To the extent that narratives about schools and movements suggest active organization and collaboration, they may be deceptive. Yet identifying aesthetic, rhetorical, and political trends in poetry does help us recognize influence, motivation, and cultural impact. Unless we put such categories into play, key features of the landscape will remain invisible. Thus, Mike Chasar uses a few examples to open up what is a vast and continuing terrain of popular poetry, work that remains invisible until we look at literary history from that vantage point and until we venture into the extensive archive of newspaper poetry, something few literary scholars have been willing to do. Ignorance about poems published only in newspapers has also hampered the recovery of Native American poetry. Mark Van Wienen reconfigures a portion of our history with the category of prison poetry and thereby makes a potentially invisible social dynamic visible. Linda Kinnahan puts early modern poetry by women in dialogue with economic theory and thus opens unacknowledged intersections for discussion. Tim Newcomb highlights interactions with mass culture and John Marsh identifies poets' engagements with material problems of manual labor that a more elitist critical aesthetic had preferred to ignore. Edward Brunner's comprehensive survey of the role that jazz and the blues have played in the development of modern poetry reveals a complex multiracial history. Karen Ford's powerful rereading of the whole history of African American poetry convincingly shows that the tensions between traditional and alternative forms do not represent mutually exclusive political and aesthetic commitments but rather the key defining dialectic of black poetry in the United States. Michael Davidson's overview of disability poetics addresses not only poets associated with the movement but also a wide range of poets not typically associated with their disabilities. As new categories and cultural possibilities emerge, the past itself is reconfigured. Evidence of that is strikingly evident in Adalaide Morris's concluding chapter, as Whitman's

claim to "sing the body electric" is put in dialogue with the mechanically ampli-
fied and computerized bodies and poems of the new millennium. Like the work of
recovery and interpretation, the work of theorizing the cultural status of modern
poetry is ongoing.

This handbook to modern and contemporary American poetry thus disavows
any pretense at comprehensiveness. It consolidates two interwoven features of
the last generation of scholarship—textual recovery and critical rereading—but
it also looks to the future in an effort to identify emerging areas of research. It is
intended not only as a partial record of what we have learned but also as a com-
panion to and inspiration for the work students of the field will be doing in years
to come.

The gaps, erasures, and misconceptions in our historical knowledge are of
several kinds. One may begin with faulty conceptions of individual poets' careers.
Consider "Spring in the Naugatuck Valley," first published in the progressive peri-
odical *The Survey* in 1915 and introduced with a factual epigraph:

> News item: "Brass, copper and wire mills in the Naugatuck Valley are shipping nearly
> a thousand tons of war material daily. One mill is turning out 200 tons a day of
> shrapnel 'fillers' of lead and other metals."

> Spring comes back to the winding valley,
> The dogwood over the hill is white,
> The meadow-lark from the ground is piping
> His notes like tinkling bells of light;
> Peace, clear peace in the pearly evening,
> Peace on field and sheltered town—
> But why is the sky so wild and lurid
> Long, long after the sun goes down?

> They are making ammunition,
> Blow on blow and spark on spark,
> With their blasting and their casting
> In the holy April dark.
> They have fed their hungry furnaces
> Again and yet again,
> They are shaping brass and bullets
> That will kill their fellow-men;
> Forging in the April midnight
> Shrapnel fillers, shot and shell,
> And the murderers go scatheless
> Though they do the work of hell.

Unless you happen to have read the 2009 essay by Melissa Girard (one of this
handbook's contributors) in which the poem was reprinted for the first time in
nearly a hundred years, you are unlikely to guess that "Spring in the Naugatuck
Valley" is by Sara Teasdale (1884–1933), now almost universally ridiculed as a sen-
timental love poet. Teasdale herself contributed to her subsequent denigration,

leaving most of her antiwar poems either unpublished or uncollected. As Girard writes, "The genteel tropes scattered throughout the poem's first stanza—'tinkling bells of light' and 'pearly evening'—are undercut sharply by the clandestine operations that occur 'long, long after the sun goes down.' These genteel epithets are ultimately exposed as a kind of idyllic front masking the mills' murderous business. Rather than a genteel poem, 'Spring in the Naugatuck Valley' belongs to a vital tradition of popular anti-war poetry, which collectively radicalized the conventions of the so-called 'genteel' lyric in response to WWI" (48). Girard concludes: "Teasdale succeeded in suppressing many of her most controversial political poems....The record of this anxious struggle with modern politics and aesthetics has been largely effaced within Teasdale's critical legacy. Over the last half-century, we have reduced Teasdale to a caricature of her previous self. Rather than a complex, divided figure, she has been remembered as a stereotypical 'poetess': timid, genteel, and decidedly 'un-modern'" (42–43). Girard's chapter within this handbook is a rethinking of the whole sentimental tradition that combines recovered texts with a new critical and theoretical orientation to a segment of modernity that has been persistently belittled even as others have sought to recover it. Girard breaks with that critical tradition and urges new directions for future research.

What is increasingly clear as scholars recover the work of forgotten poets and read more widely in original sources, among them not just books but also newspapers and magazines that regularly published poetry, is that American poetry of roughly the first half of the twentieth century is remarkable in its richness, inventiveness, and diversity. The variety of poetry written and published in the United States in the last century represents a great period that was marked by an explosion of literary creativity. Its range of forms, styles, and preoccupations are in a fundamental sense uncontainable. They exceed any single story we might try to tell about them. The overview I offer here is thus inevitably partial, but it will help contextualize the chapters that follow.

It also enables me to provide more biographical information about some of the poets who are discussed in this handbook. As we have learned from expanding the canon, biography does matter, despite a sometimes programmatic New Critical determination to exclude it from consideration. To the extent that New Critics bracketed biography so as to focus attention on the poems themselves, the effect was salutary. But we have always kept some biographical differences in mind. Philip Metres reminds us that it makes sense to distinguish between soldier and civilian poets in wartime. It is certainly important to keep in mind that most contemporary American Holocaust poetry has been written by post-Holocaust generations. Poems written by writers who participated in or witnessed key social movements or traumas—from McCarthyism to Black power to antiwar protests to feminism—carry somewhat different inflections and implications than poetry written at a significant historical distance.

Most disciplinary histories, to be sure, have omitted such considerations. In the most familiar account of when modern American poetry arrived on the scene, the Imagist revolution of the century's second decade played a key role. The Imagist movement's emphases were on extreme concision and on a certain neutrality of description. Ezra Pound's (1885–1972) "In a Station of the Metro" (1913) and William

Carlos Williams's "The Red Wheelbarrow" (1923) remain two of its defining texts. Pound's poem is only two lines long, three with the title:

In A Station at the Metro
The apparition of these faces in the crowd;
Petals on a wet, black bough. (204)[1]

Williams's poem gets much of its effect from its line breaks and its careful placement of words on the page:

so much depends
upon

a red wheel
barrow

glazed with rain
water

beside the white
chickens (170)

Yet Imagism from the outset never quite held to the model of concision and descriptive neutrality. John Gould Fletcher (1886–1950) is a clear example of Imagism's less widely recognized, loosely descriptive, and impressionistic mode. His subjects in *Irradiations* (1915) include "the swirling of the seamews above the sullen river" (5), "the iridescent vibrations of midsummer light" (6), the "trees, like great jade elephants" that "chained, stamp and shake 'neath the gadflies of the breeze" (12) and

Flickering of incessant rain
On flashing pavements:
Sudden scurry of umbrellas:
Bending, recurved blossoms of the storm. (9)

He was also capable of indulging himself in "lacquered mandarin moments" (7) and "crimson placques of cinnabar" (13). Fletcher was echoing Imagism's precursors, among them Sadakichi Hartmann, whose work is commemorated here in Josephine Park's chapter on Asian American poetry. Fletcher himself is discussed by Tim Newcomb. With his tendency to echo the writerly excesses of the 1890s, Fletcher is already outside the tradition of Imagist precision and restraint. But the group title of Imagist is even more problematic for Amy Lowell, and H.D.'s work, which soon became too diverse to be classified in any single movement.

With H.D., even in her early poems there is too much throttled self-expression displaced onto nature, too much rhythmic invention, for her work to fit easily within Imagism's more regularly anthologized mode of pictorial detachment. As Walter

Kalaidjian reminds us, H.D. went through analysis with Freud himself. "Hurl your green over us," she calls to the sea in "Oread" (1914), "cover us with your pools of fir" (233). The presence of the speaker here, calling up a force out of nature and intensifying it, enlisting descriptive imagery in a vatic psychological demand, removes "Oread" from any of the conventional paradigms of Imagism. Passages like these in H.D.'s work provoke a whole series of displacements and reversible oppositions. If nature is sexualized, psychologized, and placed in a dynamic, transformative relation with the speaking subject here, the same images invoke demands made of a lover and of the subject's own unconscious. Yet the dynamic psychological torque in this work does not justify assimilating H.D. to the expressive subjectivity we have long associated with lyric poetry. We are not simply in the presence here of a discourse of resplendent or imperiled identity. It hearkens toward an anonymous, sacralized voice, a ritual incantation, in which a transgressive otherness breaks through the discourse of identity. That is partly how we can understand the sense in "Oread" that the body is an animate landscape of vital forces. We cannot choose between such readings in H.D.; these semantic possibilities are simultaneously concentrated in and disseminated by her language. What is clear, however, is that we cannot cast her poetry in the mold of disinterested description. That becomes even clearer in some of her mythological poems. Her 1924 poem "Helen" is a succinct and telling indictment of the relationship between frustrated idealization and misogyny. Though it appears to be exclusively about an earlier age, "Helen" in fact also addresses its own historical moment, not just the period of the Trojan War. It describes the anger some in the culture feel now that women are not simply beautiful objects. "Remembering past enchantments," Greece now "hates / the still eyes in the white face." Only death, it seems, can relieve this tension and recompense the culture for the changes women have wrought:

> Greece sees unmoved,
> God's daughter, born of love,
> the beauty of cool feet
> and slenderest knees,
> could love indeed the maid,
> only if she were laid,
> white ash amid funereal cypresses. (240)

The most famous promoter of Imagism was Amy Lowell (1874–1925), but disinterested description was not her chosen mode either. Lowell's series of poems from 1919—including "Decade," "Opal," "Madonna of the Evening Flowers," and "Venus Transiens"—are among the most elegantly passionate love poems in modern American poetry. As we can tell from its first stanza, "The Weather-Cock Points South" is remarkable for the way it fuses an eroticized spirituality with explicit physical references:

> I put your leaves aside,
> One by one:
> The stiff, broad outer leaves;

> The smaller ones,
> Pleasant to touch, veined with purple;
> The glazed inner leaves.
> One by one
> I parted you from your leaves,
> Until you stood up like a white flower
> Swaying slightly in the evening wind. (47)

The leaves are put aside at once by a disrobing and by a probing embrace. The poem involves a pursuit of psychic intimacy—a drive to know and celebrate another's inwardness—and an explicit vaginal caress. The flower with its petals and bud is thus both body and spirit, but there is no severing the two. And the woman she describes seems both the object of her gaze and the flower of her own unfolding affection. The flower is both the center of the lover's body and the center of the self, for it becomes the site from which the subject seems to speak. It is also the center of the gardens coalescing in the poem and, implicitly, of nature as a whole. Her unwavering concentration on it gives it the transience of wax and the permanence of stone—"of jade, of unstreaked agate; / Flower with surfaces of ice." Despite her groundbreaking erotic work, Lowell herself, as Melissa Girard recounts, was not sympathetic to the most popular women poets of her day.

Also appropriately linked with Imagism, if once again idiosyncratically, is the early work of Wallace Stevens (1879–1955). Had Stevens not existed—as a lifelong insurance executive who wrote some of his country's most insistently metaphysical poetry—it would hardly be plausible to invent him. Yet Stevens had actually committed himself to writing poetry before taking a position with the Hartford Accident and Indemnity Company; the job was a way to earn a living. He was born and grew up in Reading, Pennsylvania, and was educated at Harvard and at the New York University Law School. He began publishing poems in magazines in 1914, but his first book, *Harmonium*, did not appear until 1923.

The book was organized to open with a number of his short, exquisite lyrics, rather than with the longer and more abstract poems that have become the focus of extended critical analysis. Although Stevens lived and worked in Connecticut, a number of his poems drew on the Florida landscape he saw on regular business trips:

> And deck the bananas in leaves
> Plucked from the Carib trees,
> Fibrous and dangling down
> Oozing cantankerous gum
> Out of their purple maws,
> Darting out of their purple craws
> Their musky and tingling tongues. (130)

Indeed, the sheer riotous excess and profusion of Florida's flora and fauna often gave him a perfect analogue for the mental life he used nature to evoke. The poems are thus at once referential and devoted to elaborate rhetorical invention that creates a world of its own. In comments in letters that are less than fully trustworthy or definitive, Stevens sometimes denied the poems this double life, but readers should judge for themselves.

The poems are so captivating in their rhetorical inventiveness—the play of words deployed for their sound, the almost palimpsestic thickness of imagery, the wit—that one can easily miss Stevens's regular (if abstract) engagement with the issues of his day, but it is nonetheless a continual feature of his work. Debates both with the world of public events and between contrasting philosophical or cultural positions occur throughout the poems. In "Sunday Morning" (1915), a woman wonders whether her sensual pleasures amount to a belief system that is comparable to Christianity's obsession with mortality:

> Complacencies of the peignoir, and late
> Coffee and oranges in a sunny chair,
> And the green freedom of a cockatoo
> Upon a rug mingle to dissipate
> The holy hush of ancient sacrifice. (135)

To some degree, such philosophical issues crowd out the sensuous surfaces and the rich music in Stevens's later poems. Some critics also find many of the late lyrics too similar to one another. Yet their obsessive circling around related themes of emptiness is a large part of their interest:

> Yet the absence of the imagination had
> Itself to be imagined. The great pond,
> The plain sense of it, without reflections, leaves,
> Mud, water like dirty glass, expressing silence
>   (from "The Plain Sense of Things," 143)

> Today the air is clear of everything.
> It has no knowledge except of nothingness
> And it flows over us without meanings,
> As if none of us had ever been here before
> And are not now: in this hallow spectacle,
> This invisible activity, this sense.
>   (from "A Clear Day and No Memories," 144)

Stevens's late poems form a single, driven project that anticipates postmodern work like W. S. Merwin's poetry of Vietnam war despair.

In the case of Imagism, therefore, we have a founding movement in modern American poetry that is richer and more diverse than we have been inclined to think. But what if there are alternative beginnings that literary historians have largely ignored? One major preoccupation for American poets has been race, the country's longest-running social trauma. In the standard account of modern American poetry, the issue animates the poetry produced during the mid-nineteenth-century abolitionist debates but then largely disappears until the Harlem (or New Negro) Renaissance of the 1920s. Yet the twentieth century began for many Americans with a debate precisely over race, and poets were a vocal part of the conflict.

In 1900, Morrison I. Swift (1856–1946), a well-known pamphleteer on Left issues, published *Advent of Empire*, a book of poems devoted substantially to America's genocidal war in the Philippines. An Anti-Imperialist League met in Boston in November 1898, but such sentiments were swept aside in widespread national enthusiasm for this first overseas adventure. Literally hundreds of prowar poems were published in newspapers across the country that year. Echoing the notorious cry "Remember the Maine!" they certified the principle of manifest destiny and sanctified the use of military force. Meanwhile, the British poet Rudyard Kipling urged us on in his notorious poem "The White Man's Burden," and in February 1899 the United States embarked on a major war of conquest against the Filipino independence movement. Some 4,000 Americans and over 200,000 Filipinos would eventually die in a war that became increasingly brutal as it shifted from large-scale battles to guerrilla tactics. As Robert Parker informs us in his chapter, the Native American poet J. C. Duncan wrote a bitter rejoinder to Kipling titled "The Red Man's Burden."

Late in 1901 public sentiment shifted against the war. By then, antiwar poetry would open out into a mass movement. But there were also poets, like Swift, who were in the vanguard of anti-imperialist politics, issuing effective poems highlighting the war's racist politics and economics. As Philip Metres reminds us, Mark Twain wrote a parody of "Battle Hymn of the Republic" in order to critique the war. In satiric and polemical poems like "Imperial Sam," "Go Die for the President King," "American Love," "Butcher McKinley," "Might and Right," and "The Primitive Races Shall Be Cultured," Swift attacks capitalism and exposes imperialism's hidden logic. Here is Swift, in the midst of the Philippine war, borrowing some of his diction and rhythms from Shakespeare and speaking in the persona of President McKinley. The poem, "Butcher McKinley," 130 lines long, is composed at the turning point of the centuries and driven deep into the rhetoric of its own time. But Swift also reaches back and forward to indict the whole history of imperialism as a form of sanctified racism:

> Sweet friends, sweet fellowmen, sweet voters,
> Call not murder murder if God wills.
> 'Tis blasphemy, abortion, miscontent, abomination,
> Hell's own self, to charge dear God with crime.
> I must as many Filipinos kill as shall appease
> God's wrath at them for spurning my decree . . .
> I am a pious man, a holy man, and member of a church.
> Did I not tell the damned blacks
> To ground their arms? . . .

Fiends, monsters, toads, green lizards, scorpions,
snakes . . .
They must submit. For mean and weak and black
There is no virtue but submission.
After submission,—well, we'll see . . .
It is a law of mine
That niggers must submit to my sublimity . . .
And how I love them! God! Everyone that dies
In disobedience penetrates my soul! . . .
Send him across the brine to cleave the skulls
Of those foul imps of mud the Filipinos.
(Nelson, Revolutionary Memory, 23)

In its condemnation of pious racism, "Butcher McKinley" draws on the history of the abolitionist movement and also looks forward to poems like Langston Hughes's (1902–1967) "Christ in Alabama" (1931). But the poem readily challenges more recent imperialist ventures as well. Part of what is so startling about the poem is the contemporaneity of its insights. The knowledge that racism underlies and underwrites international relations is knowledge we often suppress. Apparently it must be relearned by each generation. American poets had earlier protested slavery. Now some began to realize racism was also a component of our international adventures. There were several interesting volumes by other poets as well, but the most notable anti-imperialist anthology is, no doubt, Liberty Poems, issued by the New England Anti-Imperialist League in June 1900.

There are a number of reasons to remember the moment of 1900 and to give it a place in a history of modern American poetry. It holds a key position in a 150-year history of American poets writing about race. It helps us recognize that the history of American antiracist poetry is itself multiracial. Finally, as I shall argue later, it is with poems protesting racism and political repression that American modernity comes to an end in the 1950s. So the moment of 1900 helps frame the first half of the twentieth century in a particularly instructive way.

That makes for a different and quite unconventional starting point for a history of modern poetry. Yet the longstanding consensus about what poetry most mattered—the best that American poets had thought and said—still stands as a reference point for every effort to rethink and deepen our heritage. For decades, the single most defining moment of American modernism was taken to be the publication in 1922, by an American then living in London, of T. S. Eliot's (1888–1965) The Waste Land. Part of what The Waste Land did was to establish collage as a central technique of modern poetry; it also placed radical formal experimentation at the forefront of modernist technique. It was not the first work to adapt visual collage to a literary text. Indeed, Agnes Ernst Meyer's and Marius De Zayas's "Mental Reactions," published in the journal 291 in 1915, made much more radical and disruptive use of the space of the page than Eliot's poem did, and it even used graphic forms to make the connection with artistic movements like cubism explicit. But "Mental

Reactions" was a one-shot experiment in a very small-circulation journal. Moreover, though aimed at once for a pop-cultural celebration and parody of female stereo-types, it could hardly claim the cultural ambitions *The Waste Land* appeared to embody. Eliot's poem was published in the aftermath of World War I, and it evoked for many readers the ruined landscape left to them after the historically unique devastation of trench warfare and mass slaughter: "A crowd flowed over London bridge, so many, / I had not thought death had undone so many" (288). The poem's fragments mirrored a shattered world, and its allusions, however erudite, recalled a civilized culture many felt they had lost:

> What are the roots that clutch, what branches grow
> Out of this stony rubbish? Son of man,
> You cannot say, or guess, for you know only
> A heap of broken images ... (286)

Even its tendency to taunt readers with failed possibilities of spiritual rebirth, rein-forced by Eliot's own notes to the poem, along with its glimpses of a religious route to joining the pieces of a dismembered god and a broken culture, struck a chord. Eliot was one of many major modernist writers to yearn for a mythic synthesis remaining out of reach.

Years later, with hindsight, the benediction at the poem's end—"Shantih shantih shantih" (301) (The peace which passeth understanding)—could seem to fore-shadow the more explicit religiosity of the *Four Quartets* (1936–1942). But that was not apparent in 1922, and Eliot's monarchist political conservatism and his reac-tionary social and racial prejudices were not yet in evidence. So readers and writ-ers from all points of the political spectrum found inspiration in Eliot's technical innovations. In a surprisingly short period of time, *The Waste Land* became the preeminent poem of modernism, the unquestioned symbol of what was actually a much more diverse movement. Eventually, as its shadow came to hide other kinds of modernism—from more decisively vernacular language to poems strongly identi-fied with race or revolution—*The Waste Land* gathered a set of compensatory ambi-tions and resentments. Of course, it was hardly Eliot's aim to make adulation of *The Waste Land* into a justification for ignoring the Harlem Renaissance, a movement barely under way when the poem was written, but conservative literary scholars turned the poem into a weapon with that sort of cultural power.

Meanwhile, the poem itself remains available to be reread. Its mix of multiple voices, its fusion of personal anguish with historical experience, its fragments of narrativity, its riveting imagery and layered allusiveness: all of these remain hall-marks of the literary response to modernity. *The Waste Land* is among a tiny hand-ful of poems that define Eliot's career, something that cannot be said of Robert Frost, Langston Hughes, Wallace Stevens, or William Carlos Williams, all of whom wrote large numbers of short poems from which people will choose different favor-ites. Eliot, on the other hand, has a career that runs more definitively from "The Love Song of J. Alfred Prufrock" (1915) through *The Waste Land* to *Four Quartets*.

As John Marsh shows in his chapter, Eliot's own diversity has been partly obscured by the shadow of *The Waste Land* and the dominant perspectives of modern poetry scholarship.

At the same time that experimental modernism was under way, however, other American poets were dramatically transforming traditional forms. Robert Frost (1874–1963) regularly worked with traditional forms, using rhyme, meter, and regular stanzas, but he undermined every consolation we might have been led to expect from regularity. Frost cultivated his public image of a New England sage, and the poems, read carelessly in search of platitudes, often seem to support that view. In English classes in American high schools, Frost's poems continue to be misread to teach little moral lessons that the poems themselves actually decisively undercut. "Take the road less traveled by," students are urged, in a sentimentalized promotion of individual initiative; or, even more crudely, "don't turn like most toward sin or self-gratification; take the road less traveled by." About the only certainty "The Road Not Taken" (1915) may be said to offer is that of self-deception, for the poem makes it clear there is really no difference to be discerned:

> Two roads diverged in a yellow wood,
> And sorry I could not travel both
> And be one traveler, long I stood
> And looked down one as far as I could
> To where it bent in the undergrowth;
> Then took the other, as just as fair,
>
> And having perhaps the better claim,
> Because it was grassy and wanted wear;
> Though as for that the passing there
> Had worn them really about the same,
>
> And both that morning equally lay
> In leaves no step had trodden black.
> Oh, I kept the first for another day!
> Yet knowing how way leads on to way,
> I doubted if I should ever come back.
>
> I shall be telling this with a sigh
> Somewhere ages and ages hence:
> Two roads diverged in a wood, and I—
> I took the one less traveled by,
> And that has made all the difference. (90)

Frost's poems can be corrosively sardonic, offering a menacing nature or human cruelty as the only alternatives to emptiness. That the voice is so crisp, folksy, and pithy only adds to the underlying sense of terror. Over and over again the poems drain human choices of any meaning, yet they do so in straightforward images, colloquial diction, and rhythms that evoke natural speech. His dark view of human nature would also, remarkably, help him in poems like "The Hill Wife" (1916) to write some of American modernism's most sensitive portraits of women. It is only in the last generation, however, that Frost's uncanny, effectively feminist, poems have been recognized for what they are. Meanwhile, rereadings of Frost continue. In his chapter here, John Marsh grounds some of Frost's early work in the specifics of early twentieth-century rural labor relations.

The centrality of revolutionary changes in traditional forms, however, is especially clear in the transformation that two poets—Claude McKay (1889–1948) and Edna St. Vincent Millay (1892–1950)—worked in the sonnet. Raised in Jamaica and familiar with the history of English poetry, McKay chose the sonnet as the vehicle for his shock and rage at the racism he encountered when he came to the United States. His work gets attention here from Karen Ford in her major rereading of twentieth-century African American poetry, but it also gets repositioned by Timothy Yu as a notable example of transnational poetry. McKay's "Outcast" (1922) is one culmination of several years of his effort to produce capsule indictments of all aspects of race in America:

> For the dim regions whence my fathers came
> My spirit, bondaged by the body, longs.
> Words felt, but never heard, my lips would frame;
> My soul would sing forgotten jungle songs.
> I would go back to darkness and to peace,
> But the great western world holds me in fee,
> And I may never hope for full release
> While to its alien gods I bend my knee.
> Something in me is lost, forever lost,
> Some vital thing has gone out of my heart,
> And I must walk the way of life a ghost
> Among the sons of earth, a thing apart.
>
> For I was born, far from my native clime,
> Under the white man's menace, out of time. (318)

Haunted by a past they never knew, exiled to an impossible present, blacks in America may be doubly imperiled. They exist apart from the ordinary social space of lived time and yet are urgently endangered. McKay took the romance and the consolations of the historical sonnet and replaced them with a hand grenade of protest. Compressed and rhetorically proficient anger would now be among the sonnet's resources and its cultural aims; the form would never be quite the same again. Together with Millay, whose antiromantic sonnets positioned the form in an about-face, McKay reconceived the meaning of a centuries-long tradition. Millay's achievements in the sonnet—despite being disparaged, as Melissa Girard reminds us, by several male contemporaries—are perhaps most fully realized in

Millay's 1923 sequence of 17 "Sonnets from an Ungrafted Tree." The final number in the sequence opens as the speaker sits at her dead husband's bedside:

> Gazing upon him now, severe and dead,
> It seemed a curious thing that she had lain
> Beside him many a night in that cold bed (327)

and closes in an antiromantic flourish as she

> ... sees a man she never saw before—
> The man who eats his victuals at her side,
> Small, and absurd, and hers: for once, not hers, unclassified. (327)

This sort of dramatic rethinking of gender relations in fact takes place across both rethought traditional forms and innovative experimental ones. If there is one signal example of a recently recovered work of experimental modernism predating *The Waste Land* it is probably Mina Loy's (1882–1966) elliptical and minimalist poem sequence "Love Songs" (1915–1917). In her "Feminist Manifesto," discussed by Linda Kinnahan in this volume, Loy argues that "woman must destroy in herself the desire to be loved" and urges that "honor, grief, sentimentality, pride and consequently jealousy must be detached from sex." Employing a form of collage that is primarily conceptual, rather than both conceptual and visual, the "Love Songs" accomplish that and more. Loy concludes that all the values embedded in masculinity and femininity are perilous and destructive. Idealization of female purity and virtue, for example, is "the principle instrument of her subjugation."

As the sequence begins, the speaker has already failed at conventional romance—steeped in all the drama of stereotyped emotions—and opts instead not for unreflective animal sexuality but for something like a verbally inventive biological union. The sequence repeatedly offers up the illusory dramas of gender ("I am the jealous storehouse of the candle-ends / That lit your adolescent learning" [152]) only to reject them; repeatedly, in their place, Loy offers us versions of intercourse that invent figures for bodily fluids and anatomy:

> ... laughing honey
>
> And spermatozoa
> At the core of Nothing
> In the milk of the Moon (152)
>
> Shuttle-cock and battle-door
> A little pink-love
> And feathers are strewn (153)

Some critics have concluded that these are images of degraded lust; they seem instead to be antiromantic but celebratory. Moreover, their variety and surprising capacity to recode the rhetoric of romance ("honey," "the milk of the Moon," "pink-love," and "feathers" all reposition romance tropes) demonstrate that a degendered human sexuality—one that is freed of cultural clichés about men and women—need not be impoverished. Loy's experimental form is wedded to a cultural project of rethinking the nature of human sexuality.

Yet the other clear masterpiece of experimental modernism grounded in a collage aesthetic is no doubt Ezra Pound's major lifetime project. Perhaps no other major modern American poet's work is so deeply and irreducibly conflicted. Pound was at once the impresario of high modernism—promoting the work of those contemporaries he admired, among them H.D., Marianne Moore, and James Joyce; editing T. S. Eliot's *The Waste Land* so drastically he is almost its coauthor; defining the Imagist movement and making metrical innovation and metaphoric concision central to modernist poetics—and its most tragic figure, undermined by his own arrogance and eventually allied with the worst political impulses of the century. One may compare two early poems, "Portrait d'une Femme" (1912) and "The River-Merchant's Wife: A Letter" (1915), to get a glimpse of how divided his impulses can be; the first is arguably misogynist, the second almost a sympathetic interior portrait. Decades later he would leave *The Cantos* officially unfinished, but for all practical purposes complete, a major poem sequence torn between utopianism and bestiality.

Born in Idaho and raised in Pennsylvania, he earned an M.A. in Romance languages at the University of Pennsylvania, taught briefly, and then departed for Europe. But he remained interested in America for years and put himself in direct conflict with his country during World War II. Pound's major poetic achievement, and the focus of decades of his life, is *The Cantos* (1915–1969), a booklength sequence of more than 116 poems that is unquestionably one of the most influential and most controversial documents of twentieth-century literature. The poems' learning and system of unexplained references are immense; like all passionate learning, is the poems are also periodically idiosyncratic. No one save Pound himself is likely to have at hand both the range of classical references and the unconventional economic and cultural theories he cites. Pound himself is effectively the only reader fully prepared to read his poem. Unlike Eliot or Melvin Tolson, moreover, he published no notes with *The Cantos*, though when he read Canto 46 over shortwave radio from Mussolini's Italy in World War II, he did preface it with some glosses, so he was clearly aware that the ordinary reader would either need a course of study or a handbook. Pound pioneered the distribution of what one critic liked to call "radiant gist" (a phrase coined by William Carlos Williams) throughout *The Cantos*, brief allusions that are designed to invoke a whole historical and emotional context for the reader.

Pound called *The Cantos* "a poem containing history," and in that deceptively neutral, if potentially grandiose, formulation inheres the poem's great challenge. For *The Cantos* is history as Pound saw it; to some degree the poem sequence is also history as he participated in it, albeit in a modest but unforgettable way. Some critics have tried to separate Pound's political views from his art—among them were those who supported his receipt of the first Bollingen prize for his "Pisan Cantos" in 1949, an award that sparked a firestorm of debate at the time—but only a casual or self-deceptive reader of *The Cantos* can manage that trick. The poems are replete with Pound's enthusiasm for and defense of the nightmare of European fascism; over 50 million people died in World War II, and Pound believed the wrong side won. Moreover, as Pound looked over history he decided that all the arts were at their best when allied with absolute political power. He made such an alliance himself in Italy, and *The Cantos* repeatedly urges it on us as one route to a new Golden Age. None of this makes the poems easier to deal with, but none of it makes them less critical to understanding modern culture or human temptation either. The relationship between poetry and power receives its most compromising realization in *The Cantos*, as one of our most accomplished poets decides the century's most evil means served glorious ends.

Pound was initially contemptuous of Adolf Hitler; instead, Mussolini was his contemporary hero. Yet Pound gradually became an admirer of the Nazis, and in a wartime radio broadcast from Rome he announced that in *Mein Kampf* (1925), Hitler's anti-Semitic and megalomaniac manifesto, history is "keenly analyzed." Certainly Pound's racial theories found more reinforcement in Hitler than in Mussolini. Yet Pound's anti-Semitism was firmly in place early on; as early as his 1914 *Blast* poem "Salutation the Third," Pound had written, "Let us be done with Jews and Jobbery, / Let us SPIT upon those who fawn on the JEWS for their money." Pound's decades-long jeremiad against usury, or money lending (see Canto 45) was for him also a denunciation of world Jewry. In his 1941–1943 wartime radio broadcasts, published as *"Ezra Pound Speaking": Radio Speeches of World War II* (1978) he rails against the Jews unceasingly, against them and their fantasized allies, "Jews, Jews-playfellows, and the bedfellows of Jews and of Jewesses" (113). He also stated that "the danger to the United States as a system of government is NOT from Japan, but from Jewry" (86). Pound sometimes called President Franklin D. Roosevelt "Rosen-feld" to suggest his fantasized dominance by Jewish interests. In Canto 73, published in an Italian military journal in 1945, Pound calls Roosevelt and Churchill "bastards and small Jews." He warned us in the radio broadcasts that "any man who submits to Roosevelt's treason to the Republic commits breech of citizen's duty" (104). Meanwhile, from time to time he tried to persuade American troops that they would lose the war. For an American citizen to give aid and comfort to the enemy in the midst of a declared war is a capital offense. When Pound was captured by American troops in 1945 he was headed toward a U.S. trial for treason; government agencies had recorded his broadcasts. As Mark Van Wienen points out here, Pound's work on the *Pisan Cantos* behind bars earns him a place among America's prison poets. The likely verdict was not in doubt, but a group of friends intervened and had him declared insane. It was a ruse, because he was no more insane than some millions of Germans who shared his beliefs, but it kept him alive. The price he paid was to be confined to St. Elizabeths Hospital in Washington, DC, from 1946 to 1958.

Despite this anguished history, *The Cantos* remains the primary model for an ambitious American poem based on collage and historical and literary citation. It has also, as Peter Nicholls points out here, proven influential because of its elaborate mix of rhetoric and musicality. Poets at the opposite end of the political spectrum from Pound, including Charles Olson and Robert Duncan, were deeply influenced by Pound's technique. The Cantos are richly conflicted texts—at once lyrical and polemical, visionary and demonic—that well reward the investment required to read them carefully. It is possible also to identify what amounts to the spine of the sequence, a selection that highlights the entanglement of aesthetics and politics, that emphasizes the compromised ambitions that make the poem compelling reading. Canto I gives us Pound's epic ambitions at their most pure.

Canto 9 presents the fatal allure of aestheticized power that would haunt Pound for the rest of his life. It is the second of the four 1923 Malatesta Cantos (8–11), which are at the core of Pound's whole project. They concern Sigismundo Pandolfo Malatesta (1417–1468), a famous *condottiere* (Italian leader of mercenary soldiers), military engineer, and patron of the arts. Malatesta grew up in the age when Italian city-states, formally subservient to the Pope, warred with one another and competed for power and papal recognition. Malatesta became Lord of Rimini, Fano, and Cesena at age 15, but he would have to defend his domain for the rest of his days, and his means were sometimes ruthless. Yet he also patronized poets and painters (who often took Malatesta himself as their subject) and employed the greatest artists of his day to design and build a temple at Rimini. The Tempio, honoring Malatesta and his mistress Isotta, was never quite finished and thus remained in part a "monumental failure." For Pound, these aesthetic ends justify Malatesta's sometimes murderous means. He is the prototype for Pound of a leader who kills with warrant in the service of a purported ideal of achievement; Mussolini for Pound would be a contemporary Malatesta. As Pound noted in Canto 80, Malatesta's Tempio was damaged by Allied bombers during World War II in the effort to "cwuth Mutholini" (crush Mussolini). Toward the end of the war, Pound thought the Tempio had been entirely destroyed. In effect, *The Cantos* became Pound's own unfinished, ruined Tempio.

Canto 45 (1936) is Pound's towering brief against usury:

> With usura hath no man a house of good stone
> each block cut smooth and well fitting . . .
> WITH USURA
> wool comes not to market . . .
> Usura slayeth the child in the womb . . . (218–219)

Canto 81 (1948) juxtaposes apologies for fascism with lyrical invocations of nature; for a moment he verges on humility—"Pull down thy vanity"—then rejects it and denies that vanity defined either his ambitions or Mussolini's: "But to have done instead of not doing / this is not vanity." Finally, in a mixture of multilinguistic collage and counterpointed arguments, Canto 116 and the unfinished fragments give us the competing tensions in Pound's life and work in their most condensed form:

> Tho' my errors and wrecks lie about me,
> And I am not a demigod,
> I cannot make it cohere. (227)

Consistently both conceptual and visual, Pound's lifelong project in *The Cantos* traverses much of the modern period and provides one continuing model for a modernist aesthetic. Yet it is not the only major strain in experimental American poetry. Loy's work, notably, is both conceptually and linguistically experimental and its relentlessly innovative verbal character places it simultaneously in that linked experimental tradition, but she does not adopt the distinctly visual form of collage that Pound would use in *The Cantos*. The major figure in linguistically experimental modernism, the inspiration to a whole generation of poets in the second half of the century, is, without question, Gertrude Stein (1874–1946).

Born in Allegheny, Pennsylvania, Stein studied art and medicine before moving to France in 1902 and establishing what would become a famous Paris salon. By the end of the decade Stein had met her lifelong companion and collaborator, a fellow American expatriate named Alice B. Toklas. Increasingly influenced by the visual arts and by experimental modernism, Stein wrote both recognizable narratives like *Three Lives* (1909) and playful experimental texts like *Tender Buttons* (1914). In her experimental mode she was arguably the most radical and forward looking of all modernists. "Patriarchal Poetry" (55–83) is a 1927 prose poem that did not make its way into print until decades later. Yet it may be the only fully realized and rigorous deconstructive poem in American modernism. Can the poem, the title implicitly asks, be *about* patriarchal poetry, or is it to be an instance *of* patriarchal poetry? The parameters of that question are immediately ruptured. For the "poetry" referred to here is not just a literary genre but rather the poetics of everyday thought. "Patriarchal poetry" is the metaphoric logic ruling the meanings that make our culture what it is. The ambiguity of the title thus reflects Stein's judgment that everything one writes will be in some ways patriarchal. A critique of patriarchal poetry cannot be mounted from a position outside it. The only strategy for demolition is a defamiliarizing burlesque from within: "Patriarchal Poetry in pieces."

Using witty and strategically staged repetition, variation, and rhyme, Stein exposes hierarchical and gendered biases built into the most unassuming usages. Repetition short-circuits the expectation that words and phrases can function as neutral syntactic units and frees us to recognize patterns of semantic association that all language carries with it in use: "They said they said they said when they said men. / Men many men many how many many many men men men said many here" (280). "Men," we hear here, is always a statement, always an assertion, always a cultural imprimatur. In patriarchal poetics "they said" always means "men said." Patriarchy's differences are really the repetition of the same: the honorific imposition of the law of male priority, "patriarchal poetry as signed."

Repetition and variation let Stein place a variety of words, phrases, and concepts under philosophical and cultural pressure, so that all the components of a statement are shown to be permeated with the assumptions of patriarchal poetry. This technique also isolates and decontextualizes words and phrases, seeming at first to turn them into unstable echolalic nonsense, but thereby severing them from their syntactical functionalism and making it possible to see them as counters in a very different semantic game. The "Language" poetry that flourished in the work of Ron Silliman, Barrett Watten, Charles Bernstein, Bob Perelman, Lyn Hejinian, and others in the 1980s and 1990s drew on some of the same techniques and made explicit the political implications of exposing the indirect ideological work that rhetoric can do. On the other side of nonsense is the worldview that patriarchal poetics continually reinforces: "Patriarchal poetry makes no mistake"; "Patriarchal poetry is the same as Patriotic Poetry."

Patriarchal poetry is the poetics of unreflective reason and order, of officious segmentation and classification—often to comic effect: "Patriarchal poetry and not meat on Monday patriarchal poetry and meat on Tuesday. Patriarchal poetry and venison on Wednesday Patriarchal poetry and fish on Friday Patriarchal poetry and birds on Sunday." Patriarchal poetry is therefore a poetics of marching: "One Patriarchal Poetry. / Two Patriarchal Poetry. / Three Patriarchal Poetry." It is the signature of the authority of the nation-state and of the corollary authority of the individual male person: "signed by them. / Signed by him."

Stein's poem does not proceed in a linear way; that would be to adopt the armature she wants to disavow. So she works by indirection. But the poem does have signal moments of disruption and revelation. The first of these occurs as a serial eruption of the phrases "Let her be," "Let her try," and "Let her be shy." These are pleas for space for women's freedom and commands, disseminating women's differences through the language. "Let her be" is also the letter "b," whose additive and secondary character Stein offers in place of patriarchal claims for priority, origin, and power.

Equally—and relentlessly—experimental, though, like other modernists, in her own distinctive way, is Marianne Moore (1887–1972). Born in Kirkwood, Missouri, and raised in Carlisle, Pennsylvania, Moore shared a house with her mother all her life, much of it working at a series of jobs in the New York area, but always focusing on writing. Notably, her use of quotation in her poems is as elaborate as that of T. S. Eliot, but to quite different purposes. If Eliot aimed for magisterial allusiveness, Moore aimed for something more complex and subversive, to model the cultural constitution of knowledge and understanding. Her poems braided of multiple sources are, at their most ambitious, social and philosophical investigations of great subtlety. "Marriage" (1924) and "An Octopus" (1924) are the most important poems of this impulse. She also had continuing political and historical interests, as two poems about Ireland—"Sojourn in the Whale" (1921) and "Spenser's Ireland" (1941)—make clear.

On one level, Moore's "Marriage" (256–263) is a strikingly even-handed demolition of the illusion that either party to a marriage can so divest himself or herself of self-absorption and self-interest to make a union possible. "He loves himself so much," she writes, "he can permit himself / no rival in that love." But the poem is much more than an analysis of the pitfalls in gender relations. It actually moves centripetally and centrifugally at the same time, treating marriage not only as a site on which individuals and the culture as a whole act out their contradictory investments in independence and community but also as a figural resource that informs all compromised institutions in the culture. Thus, the poem is at once about the marriage two people make and about the marriage the states made to form one country—"Liberty and union / now and forever." Both require "public promises / of one's intention / to fulfill a private obligation" and both "can never be more / than an interesting impossibility." Marriage is an institution constructed by contractualized idealization and a model for comparably problematic institutions of other sorts. Marriage in the poem is effectively thus both victim and purveyor of illusions within the culture. Until the last generation, "Marriage" and "An Octopus" took second stage in critical conversation to Moore's better-known shorter poems. But the Moore canon is expanded still further here, as Linda Kinnahan takes a fresh look at other early Moore work and Al Filreis makes an extended case for her late and often belittled poetry.

At just under 300 lines, "Marriage" is a relatively long poem. *The Waste Land* was just over 400. They are both dwarfed by *The Cantos*, but all of these works exemplify the modern American interest in the long poem that is formally and verbally experimental. Though equally linked to the lyric tradition, Hart Crane's *The Bridge* (1930) is also an experimental long poem. Born in a small Ohio town, Crane (1899–1932) grew up in Cleveland. He went to New York after leaving high school, but he ended up returning to Cleveland until 1923, along the way accumulating work experience in advertising agencies, at a newspaper, and in his father's businesses. He faced continual difficulty and much stress supporting himself and he had to rely on relatives and a benefactor. The first phase of his career includes such Imagist poems as "October-November" (1916) and the remarkable "Episode of Hands" (1920), one of the most beautiful of explicitly homosexual poems from the modernist period, but his major legacy is *The Bridge*.

The sheer ambition of this booklength project frustrated Crane's attempts to begin it from 1923 to 1926. A change of location from New York City to a summer cottage on the Isles of Pines off the Cuban coast resulted in an outburst of new writing, and all but 4 of the poem's 15 sections were substantially complete when an October 1926 hurricane devastated the island. The poem sequence takes its title and the focus of its opening and closing poems, "Proem" and "Atlantis," from a much-celebrated piece of New York architecture and engineering, the Brooklyn Bridge. Widely considered both an aesthetic triumph and a highly successful technical project, Crane reasonably takes it as a symbol of American ambition and spirit combined. By reaching back into American history to Columbus's return voyage from the New World ("Ave Maria"), traveling through the Mississippi River region by train in the present day ("The River"), and then imaginatively flying by plane over the East Coast of the United States ("Cape Hatteras"), Crane attempts to articulate a unifying vision of America.

Yet if the bridge is a transcendent and ecstatic symbol, the airplane in "Cape Hatteras" is sometimes a demonic one, given over to war rather than cultural poetry. The conflict is resolved, if at all, in the controversial bravado performance of "Atlantis," the final poem, which is one of the most rhetorically flamboyant texts among American long poems:

> So to thine Everpresence, beyond time,
> Like spears ensanguined of one tolling star
> That bleeds infinity—the orphic strings,
> Sideral phalanxes, leap and converge:
> —One Song, one Bridge of Fire! Is it Cathay,
> Now pity steeps the grass and rainbows ring
> The serpent with the eagle in the leaves …?
> Whispers antiphonal in azure swing. (407)

Like Muriel Rukeyser's *The Book of the Dead* published eight years later, *The Bridge* chooses commercial enterprises and construction projects as images of both greed and transcendence. Like her poem, too, it creates a unifying myth out of the most resistant materials. Reacting to Eliot's *The Waste Land*, both Crane and Rukeyser wrote long poem sequences that were American rather than international. Crane also wished to substitute cultural optimism for Eliot's bleak pessimism and to imagine that collaborative human work could offer some hope for the future. At the end, Crane saw little hope for his own; at only 33 years old, he jumped overboard from a boat returning from Mexico and drowned.

Unlike Crane, from the outset, Rukeyser (1913–1980), whose work is a touchstone in several of the chapters that follow, was at once a political activist and a visionary. At times, as at points in *The Book of the Dead* (1938, 656–687), those qualities were intensified and in those moments she was simultaneously a revolutionary and a mystic. But to grasp the forces that drive her work—through a career that spanned five decades of American history—we have to come to terms with a visionary impulse rooted in time, embedded in a struggle with lived history. Consider as a case in point the rhapsodic images she crafts to voice the mother's anguish at the death of her sons in "Absalom" from *The Book of the Dead*." To understand her work we must also embrace the larger, wiser notion of politics that underlies all her poetry. For she understood early on what so many Americans could not: politics encompasses all of the ways that social life is hierarchically structured and made meaningful. Politics is not only the large-scale public life of nations. It is also the advantages and inequities and illusions that make daily life very different for different groups among us. Thus, Rukeyser understood that race and gender are integral parts of our social and political lives. Never officially a feminist, she nonetheless devoted herself, as she does in "Rite," to voicing women's distinctive experience throughout her career.

Although Rukeyser wrote numerous short, tightly controlled poems like "The Minotaur" and "Poem," the latter analyzed here by Philip Metres, it may well be that her most rich and suggestive accomplishments are her poem sequences. *The Book of the Dead* is one of the major poem sequences of American modernism. Based on Rukeyser's own research in West Virginia, it combines historical background, congressional testimony, and the voices of a number of victims in telling the story of a 1930s industrial scandal: a company building a tunnel for a dam decided to double its profit by rapidly mining silica at the same time (without any of the necessary precautions). A great many workers died of lung disease as a result. *The Book of the Dead* is thus also one of Rukeyser's many poems that reflect and contribute to her political activism.

Rukeyser was born and raised in New York City. During the 1930s she regularly wrote for Communist Party publications like *New Masses*. She was in Spain in 1936 to cover the antifascist Olympics in Barcelona when the Spanish Civil War broke out. She described that experience in the long poem "Mediterranean" and returned to the subject throughout her life. Years later, in 1975, she went to South Korea to protest the poet Kim Chi-Ha's imprisonment and anticipated execution; the poem sequence "The Gates" grew out of that trip.

Although *The Book of the Dead* is self-evidently an ambitious experimental long poem, it is usually omitted from accounts of American modernism. There is little question why. Because *The Book of the Dead* is one of the highlights of our most pervasively radical political decade, the 1930s, and many scholars, steeped in the anxieties of the cold war, have preferred to ignore this most overtly political poetry. As the Depression deepened in the early 1930s, large numbers of Americans, including both young and established writers, Rukeyser among them, were increasingly drawn to the Left or to the Communist Party. There was a widespread conviction that capitalism had failed, that the old order could not be restored, and that only the most thoroughgoing social and political change could bring about social and economic justice. A number of active poets had already been writing from that perspective in the 1920s. For one thing, the much heralded "roaring twenties" had not brought economic health to everyone. Not only agriculture but also the entire rural economy had remained depressed throughout the decade; moreover, several major industries were already in recession before the stock market crash of 1929. Especially in the South and in depressed areas in the north, working-class and labor poets, along with poets affiliated with socialism, had been writing about economic inequities for years. Subcultural traditions of protest poetry stretched back into the nineteenth century, and some of the poets in those traditions felt themselves to be not only individual voices but also participants in movements for social change.

The Depression's impact on poverty, combined with the continuing influence of the Harlem Renaissance of the 1920s and the resurgence of violent racism in the same decade, would lead to intensified protests against racism from numerous poets. Langston Hughes would open the decade with one of his most compressed and searing indictments of America's founding betrayal of its ideals in his poem "Christ in Alabama":

> Christ is a Nigger
> Beaten and black—
> *O, bare your back.*
>
> Mary is His Mother—
> *Mammy of the South.*
> *Silence your mouth.*

God's His father—
White Master above.
Grant us your love.

Most holy bastard
Of the bleeding mouth:
Nigger Christ
On the cross of the South. (1232)

Two hundred years of racial trauma are driven full force into this 13-line, 47-word poem. Cast out, vilified, and crucified, the historical Christ returns to earth in serial fashion—in the person of every black man "beaten and black," every slave, every lynching victim, every post–Civil War black man denied the full rights of citizenship. It asks a contemporary American reader to understand the black man as the Christ of our time. Of course the archetypal black victim is the product of rape, especially the white rape of a black woman, for then the white father can repress his paternity by murdering his own son. The South's omnipresent and universally denied trinity—white father, black mother, and ostracized black son—form the background for the South's repeated crucifixion scene: "*Nigger Christ / On the cross of the South.*"

It is a poem that calls out to waken the world and change it. For a brief moment in American literary history, writing poetry became a credible form of revolutionary action. Reading poetry, in turn, became a way of positioning one's self in relation to the possibility of basic social change. Earlier, the poems of the Industrial Workers of the World (IWW) set to music had been among the IWW's most successful recruitment devices. Now, to read a poem like Langston Hughes's "Let America Be America Again" (1936) was to find more than an echo of one's own sense of cultural crisis and necessity. It was to find a place to stand ideologically, a concise discursive perspective on America's history and engagement with its contemporary culture. It was also to find a voice one could temporarily take up as one's own. Poetry at once gave people a radical critique and a visionary aspiration, and it did so in language fit for the speaking voice. It strengthened the beliefs of those already radicalized and helped to persuade some who were not yet decided. It was thus a notable force in articulating and cementing what was a significant cultural and political shift toward the Left. To write poetry under these conditions of readership was therefore to ask not only what one wanted to say but also what other people wanted to read; the sense of audience was pressing, immediate. A revolutionary poem in a magazine or newspaper could be taken up and used by an audience only days or weeks after it was written. Thus when Angelo Herndon, a black communist unconstitutionally charged with "attempting to incite insurrection" for helping to organize a Georgia hunger march, was released on bail in 1934, poems celebrating his August 7 arrival in New York were written and published within days. Alfred Hayes's "Welcome to Angelo Herndon" appeared in *The Daily Worker* on August 9; Michael Blankfort's "Angelo Herndon's Bail" was published in the same newspaper on August 15; and

Edwin Rolfe's "Homecoming" was in the August 21 issue of *New Masses*. When such poems offered readers politically committed speaking voices with which they could identify, moreover, the poems were in a sense a gift to prospective readers, a text whose authorship was inherently transferable. To publish a poem that might prove politically persuasive was, in effect, to ask readers to live by way of these words as if they were their own.

The mass audience for poetry in the Depression was, paradoxically, one of the triumphs of a time of widespread suffering. To begin to understand what it meant to be a poet on the Left in the Depression, it is necessary to extend that recognition to the whole cultural field and accept it as a general paradox that typifies life in that period. Hand in hand with hunger and unemployment and the many difficulties of everyday life went a sense of impending revolutionary change. For those poets who participated in the mass movement of the 1930s, the period combined sometimes desperate hardship with something like utopian exhilaration. Writing poetry often meant helping to articulate and dramatize both the period's suffering and its characteristic yearnings for change. To write poetry was not only to comment on these cultural processes but also to help shape them. And you were not alone. Down the street, across town, and in towns and cities across the country other poets were contributing to the cultural climate in much the same way.

One of the more symptomatic changes brought about by the culture's redefinition of poetry's mission was in the concept of authorship, a corollary to a shift away from an emphasis on self-expressive subjectivity. We would see the same impulse derive from different cultural forces again in the "Language" poetry that emerged in the late 1980s and in the recent computer-generated poetry that Adalaide Morris discusses. It is perhaps the worker's correspondence poem of the 1930s, the found poem of that era, that most clearly displaced notions of authorship and originality in that period. Tillie Olsen (1912–2007), who was then writing under her maiden name Lerner, wrote the poem "I Want You Women Up North to Know" (1934), based on a letter that had been published in the January 9, 1934, issue of *New Masses*, under the heading "Where the Sun Spends the Winter," a version of the slogan adopted by a Texas Chamber of Commerce as the motto for a tourist campaign. The letter describes the impossible lives of four women who survive by hand-embroidering children's dresses for a few pennies each. The author of the letter, Felipe Ibarro, may well have been a journalist or a social worker or perhaps simply an activist, so the letter is not the direct testimony of the workers described but reported testimony that is already self-consciously rhetorical. Nonetheless, it offers one interesting version of this distinctive 1930s genre. It is worth comparing the opening two paragraphs of the letter with the first three stanzas of the poem. Here is the opening of the letter:

> I want the women of New York, Chicago and Boston who buy at Macy's, Wannamaker's, Gimbel's and Marshall Field to know that when they buy embroidered children's dresses labeled "hand made" they are getting dresses made in San Antonio, Texas, by women and girls with trembling fingers and broken backs.

These are bloody facts and I know, because I've spoken to the women who make them. Catalina Rodriguez is a 24-year-old Mexican girl but she looks like 12. She's in the last stages of consumption and works from six in the morning till midnight. She says she never makes more than three dollars a week. I don't wonder any more why in our city with a population of 250,000 the Board of Health has registered 800 professional "daughters of joy" and in addition, about 2,000 *Mujeres Alegres* (happy women), who are not registered and sell themselves for as little as five cents.

Here are the opening stanzas of the poem:

> i want you women up north to know
> how those dainty children's dresses you buy
> at macy's, wannamaker's, gimbels, marshall fields,
> are dyed in blood, are stitched in wasting flesh,
> down in San Antonio, "where sunshine spends the winter."

> I want you women up north to see
> the obsequious smile, the salesladies trill
> "exquisite work, madame, exquisite pleats"
> vanish into a bloated face, ordering more dresses,
> gouging the wages down,
> dissolve into maria, ambrosa, catalina,
> stitching these dresses from dawn to night,
> in blood, in wasting flesh.

> Catalina Rodriguez, 24,
> body shrivelled to a child's at twelve,
> catalina rodriguez, last stages of consumption,
> works for three dollars a week from dawn to midnight.
> A fog of pain thickens over her skull, the parching heat
> breaks over her body.
> and the bright red blood embroiders the floor of her room.
> White rain stitching the night, the bourgeois poet would say,
> white gulls of hands, darting, veering,
> white lightning, threading the clouds,
> this is the exquisite dance of her hands over the cloth,
> and her cough, gay, quick, staccato,
> like skeleton's bones clattering,
> is appropriate accompaniment for the esthetic dance
> of her fingers
> and the tremulo, tremulo when the hands tremble with pain.
> Three dollars a week,
> two fifty-five,
> seventy cents a week,
> no wonder two thousands eight hundred ladies of joy
> are spending the winter with the sun after he goes down ... (652–654)

Olsen works with Ibarro's letter to draw out its drama and intensify the metaphoric power of the suffering it recounts. The poem's title, drawn from the letter, serves as a refrain line that becomes a paradigm for North-South relations and for those who benefit, often indifferently and sometimes in ignorance, from economic exploitation. Olsen uses her own metaphors as well as Ibarro's, but her poem remains nonetheless an inventive extension of the original letter. Keeping true to Ibarro's wish to have women up north understand the economic and social relations that are hidden within the clothing they buy, Olsen adds a passage describing a department store where the children's dresses are sold. Notably, however, the poem's most explicit challenge—a challenge built into the original letter—is not to the businessmen who hire the dressmakers or to the department store owners who sell them but to the consumers who buy them and thus fuel the entire set of transactions. Olsen is not alone in focusing on how ordinary people's actions help sustain economic exploitation. Kenneth Fearing, who Tim Newcomb examines in detail, often satirizes the ways that people's illusions reinforce the ideology of the marketplace. However, attacks on industrialists were certainly more common during the period in which Olsen was writing.

The primary change from Ibarro's text to Olsen's, as with most poems based on worker correspondence, is the generic shift itself, the move from prose to poetry. This is a shift Olsen embraces, but with uneasiness, as her effort to emulate (and thereby critique) a bourgeois poet's lyrical evocation of Catalina Rodriguez's dying efforts at embroidery suggests: "White rain stitching the night, the bourgeois poet would say, / white gulls of hands, darting." Yet Olsen cannot actually cast out the imagined bourgeois poet's literariness without casting out her own as well. She would reject an obfuscating metaphoricity that substitutes fantasies of birds on the wing for hand movements that are actually painful. Yet one could also take the line as celebrating a deft beauty in the midst of suffering. The poem in short puts forward an argumentative dichotomy that the poem itself simultaneously destabilizes and undermines, making the reader examine his or her own relationship to the moral and political implications of figurative language.

Such motives animate much of the political poetry of the 1930s, which often focuses on economic hardship and revolutionary change, on general social conditions rather than private experience. Even when individual experience is recounted, it is often recounted because of its representative character, its simultaneous enabling and determination by current history. With individual poets each offering alternative versions of life in the Depression and with poets hearing one another's work at group poetry readings and reading each other's work in books and magazines, it is not difficult to see how one is led not merely to read comparatively but to read chorally, to see these poems not as entries in a competition but as mutually responsive contributions to an emerging revolutionary consensus. That increases the impact of the poems, at least for those reading them as part of a movement. To read or write a 1930s political poem properly, then, is to be continually hailed by other voices. Here, for example, is a collage of quotations from poetry of the period that suggests both a collaborative critique of Depression-era capitalism and a collective call for revolutionary change:

> The mills are down
> The hundred stacks
> are shorn of their drifting fume.
> The idle tracks
> rust . . .
> Smeared red with the dust
> of millions of tons of smelted ore
> the furnaces loom—
> towering, desolate tubes—
> smokeless and stark in the sun . . .
>
> (John Beecher)

> Flanking the freightyards: alleys, wooden shacks,
> And hovels: a grim battalion
> Of crouching rats covered down by the waters
> Of fog that trickles down their slimy backs.
> Near these: the blackened sheds
> Of foundries, smelting furnaces,
> And forges flanking the grey backs of the river
>
> (Stanley Burnshaw)

> the earth smoked and baked;
> stones in the field
> marked the dead land:
> coins taxing the earth.
>
> (Sol Funaroff)

> In these days of marking time,
> While the whole tense land marks time
>
> (Burnshaw)

> Where there is no life, no breath, no sound, no touch, no warmth,
> no light but the lamp that shines on a trooper's drawn and
> ready bayonet
>
> (Kenneth Fearing)

> Our age has Caesars though they wear silk hats
>
> (Joseph Freeman)

> men, pig-snouted, puff
> and puke at the stars
>
> (Herman Spector)

They burn the grain in the furnace while men go hungry.
They pile the cloth of the looms while men go ragged.
(Stephen Vincent Benét)

Under the sign of the coin and the contract,
under the mask of the two-faced double-dealing dollar,
under the fetish of the document, stocks and bonds,
the parchment faces trade in securities.
(Funaroff)

Men of paper, robbing by paper, with paper faces.
(Benét)

The friend of caesar's friend murders the friend
who murders caesar. The juggler of knives
slits his own throat. Tight-rope walkers
find democracy in public urinals.
Black robed ministers stand with hatchet crosses;
the headsman hacks a worker's life to bone.
(Funaroff)

Then an end, an end to this. Say enough . . .
(Genevieve Taggard)

The west is dying like a brood of aged birds
In the nests of their decay.
(Norman Macleod)

America today; its fields plowed under . . .
its wide avenues blistered by sun and poison gas
(Rolfe)

And no lilacs bloom, Walt Whitman.
(Mike Gold)

There is a rust on the land
(Benét)

an unseen hand
Weaving a filmy rust of spiderwebs
Over . . . turbines and grinding gears.
(Joseph Kalar)

Oh Capital! even in your palaces of learning,
as in your streets and factories,
there is one constant study.
Escape!
(Isidor Schneider)

We've eaten tin-can stew, tin-can java, tin-can soup
Inside the jungles of America!
We've slept in rain soaked gondolas, across ice-caked bars,
On top of wind-beaten boxes.

(Robert Gessner)

I'm not too starved to want food
not too homeless to want a home not too dumb
to answer questions come to think of it it'll take a hell
of a lot more than you've got to stop what's
going on deep inside us when it starts out
when it starts wheels going worlds growing
and any man can live on earth when we're through with it.

(Kenneth Patchen)

The million men and a million boys,
Come out of hell

(Horace Gregory)

From harvest fields rise up
Bone-aching and flesh-sore
Bondsmen

(Ruth Lechlitner)

and crawling back,
maybe they don't know what they're saying,
maybe they don't dare,
but they know what they mean:
Knock down the big boss . . .
hit him again, he cut my pay, Dempsey.

(Horace Gregory)

Awake and sing, you that dwell in the dust.

(Funaroff)

Brothers, Comrades, pool the last strength of men
in party, in mass, boil into form, and strike.

(Taggard)

let the workers storm from the factories,
the peasants from the farms;
sweep the earth clean of this nightmare.

(Freeman)

you shall rise in the dust of their cities
as a people of grass,
as roots out of dry ground.

(Funaroff)

If the dispossessed should rise,
Burning anger in their eyes ...
Oh my brothers in the mire,
Clothe with lightning, shoe with fire ...
                                   (Henry George Weiss)

I am black and I have seen black hands
Raised in fists of revolt, side by side with the white fists of
    white workers
                                   (Richard Wright)

Fists tight-clenched around a crimson banner
                                   (Rolfe)

Banners of rebellion, surging to the storm,
Rousing men to vision, turning cold blood warm
                                   (Lucia Trent)

And we think
Of barricades in some red dawn
On the East Side of New York City
                                   (Norman Macleod)

Split by a tendril of revolt
stone cedes to blossom everywhere
                                   (Muriel Rukeyser)

The blood's unvoiced rebellion brooding under
This sorrow, this despair.
                                   (Burnshaw)

We shall rise up, create our own new lands,
For the last frontiers are taken
                                   (Lechlitner)

Poets, pickets
Prepare for dawn
                                   (Rukeyser)

Red in the sky our torches write
Resurgence over death
                                   (Lechlitner)

The red train starts and nothing shall stop it
                         (Louis Aragon/ E. E. Cummings)

Scarlet seas surge
exultant upon new shores
                                   (Funaroff)

into the red fields of sunrise

(Funaroff)

to grind the streets into the single lens
of revolution, and converge their massing thunder
to the one pure bolt of proletarian red.

(Ben Maddow)

Listen, Mary, Mother of God, wrap your new born babe in
the red flag of Revolution.
Now, the red revolution comes.

(Isidor Schneider)
(all from Nelson, *Revolutionary Memory*, 166–173)

In the early 1930s it was partly the sense that capitalism had run its course and failed that led many of these poets to embrace the possibility of revolutionary change and to join a collective mode of writing. But with Hitler's rise to power in 1933, Japan's invasion of Manchuria, and Italy's invasion of Ethiopia, a new force entered the picture, a threat more terrible than unprincipled exploitation and severe inequity—the threat of fascism. The Communist International, or Comintern, called for a worldwide alliance between revolutionaries and progressives, a Popular Front to defeat fascism, in 1935, but many writers were not entirely ready to heed the call. Even the Communist Party's *Daily Worker* published revolutionary poems up through the early months of 1936. That winter the American Left celebrated a Popular Front victory in Spain, one that seemed destined to grant real relief to Spain's impoverished workforce. Then in July 1936 a group of right-wing army officers allied with conservative clergy and reactionary politicians to stage a revolt against the democratically elected government. The people themselves rose up in Madrid and Barcelona to crush the revolt, and the whole insurgency might well have ended within weeks. But Hitler and Mussolini intervened on the side of the rebel generals. What might have been a brief internal conflict turned into a two-and-a-half-year war with wide international implications. Thousands of volunteers joined the Comintern-organized International Brigades to help defend the Spanish Republic against its own army and German and Italian forces. And the choral poetry of revolution was transformed almost immediately into the still more coherent and more powerfully collective poetry of antifascism.

For a number of modern American poets, the period of the Spanish Civil War was a period when they were no longer primarily *American* writers; they were part of an international political struggle and an international community of writers. Part of what is important about American poets' contributions to the dialogue about Spain, therefore, is that a number of them figuratively gave up nationhood as the ground of their being. It is thus the very reverse of projects like Hart Crane's poem sequence *The Bridge* and William Carlos Williams's critical book *In the American Grain* (1925). If a number of American poets had earlier wondered how to give modernist experimentalism an American inflection, how to interleave collage with

American sights and sounds, how to construct a myth that would enable uniquely American identities, now, in the shadow of fascism, the challenge was to enter the international arena seamlessly. My answer to one of my opening questions—what distinguishes American poetry and justifies giving it partial autonomy?—is precisely its continuing obsession with American identity and its ongoing engagement with American history. But Spain is the exception that proves the rule.

Perhaps the quintessential American poem about the Spanish Civil War—because it captures both the idealism of the cause and the sense of loss and exile that followed the Spanish Republic's loss—is Edwin Rolfe's (1909–1954) "First Love" (1943):

> Again I am summoned to the eternal field
> green with the blood still fresh at the roots of flowers,
> green through the dust-rimmed memory of faces
> that moved among the trees there for the last time
> before the final shock, the glazed eye, the hasty mound.
>
> But why are my thoughts in another country?
> Why do I always return to the sunken road through corroded hills,
> with the Moorish castle's shadow casting ruins over my shoulder,
> and the black-smocked girl approaching, her hands laden with grapes?
>
> I am eager to enter it, eager to end it.
> Perhaps this will be the last one.
> And men afterward will study our arms in museums
> and nod their heads, and frown, and name the inadequate dates
> and stumble with infant tongues over the strange place-names.
>
> But my heart is forever captive of that other war
> that taught me first the meaning of peace and of comradeship
>
> and always I think of my friend who amid the apparition of bombs
> saw on the lyric lake the single perfect swan. (610)

The couplet that ends "First Love" is based upon the experience of one of Rolfe's friends in Spain, but it is also an echo—with an insistence on historical specificity—of Pound's "In a Station at the Metro." This "apparition" is in counterpoint with political history.

A decade later, as Michael Thurston reminds us here, the Popular Front consensus would be under sustained assault in the midst of the McCarthy period. For many of the revolutionary poets of the 1930s, 1954 would be a key year. Aaron Kramer (1921–1997) and Edwin Rolfe would each write a series of bleak but sometimes sardonic poems attacking the culture of the witch hunts. In Rolfe's "Little Ballad for Americans—1954" the wit is inseparable from rage and anguish:

> Brother, brother, best avoid your workmate—
> Words planted in affection can spout a field of hate.

Housewife, housewife, never trust your neighbor—
A chance remark may boomerang to five years at hard labor.

Student, student, keep mouth shut and brain spry—
Your best friend Dick Merriwell's employed by the F.B.I.

Lady, lady, make your phone calls frugal—
The chief of all Inquisitors has ruled the wire-tap legal.

Daughter, daughter, learn soon your heart to harden—
They've planted stoolies everywhere; why not in kindergarten?

Lovers, lovers, be careful when you're wed—
The wire-tap grows in living-room, in auto, and in bed.

Give full allegiance only to circuses and bread;
No person's really trustworthy until he's dead. (619)

For progressive poets writing in the early 1950s, the repressive culture of McCarthyism also renewed their anger at American racism. In 1952 Aaron Kramer published "Denmark Vesey," a long poem sequence—described more thoroughly here by Michael Thurston—about an 1821 South Carolina slave revolt that is a masterpiece of American modernism and the single most ambitious poem about race and African American history ever written by a white American. His portrait of slaveowner culture culminates in a nightmare vision:

The lovely brocade their ladies wore
had once been Negro grandmothers' hair.
The gems that blinked on their arms like stars
were bright Negro eyes that had lately shed tears. (Kramer, 50)

Nature meanwhile is indifferent:

Perhaps the free winds and the unbound waves
rendered the lamentation of the slaves
in language that the sky might understand . . .
But from the sky's red mouth no answer came. (Kramer, 44–45)

The only solution is resistance. A year later, Melvin Tolson (1900–1966) published his dense, allusive masterpiece *The Libretto for the Republic of Liberia*:

Liberia?
No side-show barker's bio-accident,
    No corpse of a soul's errand
To the Dark Continent:
 You are
   The lightning rod of Europe, Canaan's key,

> The rope across the abyss,
> *Mehr licht* for the Africa-To-Be! (418–419)

> *Liberia?*
> No haply black man's X
> Fixed to a Magna Charta without a magic-square
>   By Helon's leprous hand, to haunt and vex:
> You are
> The Orient of Colors everywhere
>   The oasis of Tahoua, the salt bar of Harrar,
> To trekkers in saharas, in sierras, with Despair! (419)

As rich with literary and historical allusions as *The Waste Land*, Tolson's *Libretto*, which is 770 lines long with its own set of footnotes, instead reflected on the history of slavery and the potential for liberation while the memory of European fascism was still fresh and the ravages of McCarthyism ongoing.

In 1956 Allen Ginsberg (1926–1997) published "Howl" and looked back on recent history, fusing autobiography with political and cultural analysis: "I saw the best minds of my generation destroyed by madness." Three years later, Robert Lowell (1917–1977) issued *Life Studies*. Uncannily, it, too, came out of a telling conjunction between personal anguish and historical experience, not unlike *The Waste Land*. But Eliot's mask of impersonality was altogether abandoned. Autobiography was now in the forefront of the poem. American modernism had come to an end.

Lowell grew up in Boston, Massachusetts, as part of a family with a distinguished literary heritage. The poets James Russell Lowell and Amy Lowell were among his ancestors. This heritage no doubt made his own father's limitations—he was a business failure after his retirement from the U.S. Navy—seem more severe. Lowell enrolled at Harvard, much as the family expected, but after the first of his lifelong series of emotional breakdowns and periods of manic behavior—a history that brings him into Walter Kalaidjian's chapter—he transferred to Kenyon College in 1937. There he met the poet and critic John Crowe Ransom, one of the leaders of American New Criticism, who introduced Lowell to preferences for rhetorically intricate and ironic poems. Lowell also broke with his Protestant family history by converting to Catholicism in 1940. Opposed to some of America's World War II policies, he served a year in prison as a conscientious objector and thus is included as one of the prisoner poets Mark Van Wienen discusses.

Lowell's first books, biblical and apocalyptic in tone, gave way in *Life Studies* (1959) to a new style that would guarantee his reputation. Accompanied by an autobiographical essay and written in a far more open and personal style, the poems came to herald what would be called the "confessional" school of poetry. Yet from the outset of his career Lowell had actually been drawn to a more complex subject, one that Walter Kalaidjian documents: the intersection of public history and autobiographical experience. Though later work like *The Dolphin* (1973) would sometimes mine his personal experience remorselessly, his poems overall are a remarkable testament to

how a reflective person lives and internalizes both the historical record and the pub-
lic life of his time. As Philip Metres makes clear, the "confessional" label, which was
more comfortable for critics who preferred poetry to be apolitical, has thus obscured
the degree to which Lowell is a powerful critic of American culture and history.

Ginsberg was at once one of the major poets of the second half of the twentieth
century and a public figure who entreated his country by way of his poetry to realize
its full democratic potential. No one who saw and heard Ginsberg stand on a flatbed
truck before thousands of U.S. army troops at the Pentagon during the famous 1968
demonstration against the Vietnam War either could or would wish altogether to
separate his work from its reception. With rifles bristling at him, Ginsberg read his
Pentagon exorcism poem in defiance of imperialist military power and in a plea that
the demons of war would quit the building. A rather modest poem, it nonetheless
made for an unforgettable occasion. Yet Ginsberg was never actually militant or
aggressive. Learned in Zen Buddhism and western mysticism, his presence exuded
rather an expansive and insistent gentleness.

He was born and grew up in New Jersey, but it was the emerging Beat genera-
tion in New York City that shaped his vision and that he helped to define. He was
educated at Columbia University, though his degree was delayed when he was
expelled for what would now constitute no more than a prank: placing obscene
messages on his grimy dormitory window to draw attention to the need to clean
the room. As he became friends with William Burroughs, Jack Kerouac, and other
figures in the Beat literary and drug scene, a more serious infraction arose when
he let Herbert Huncke use his dorm room to store the stolen goods he employed to
support his heroin habit. In exchange for avoiding prosecution, Ginsberg pleaded
insanity and spent eight months in the Columbia Psychiatric Institute.

By then he had worked a series of odd jobs, including service on merchant
tankers, but he had also had an auditory vision of William Blake reading his poems
aloud one day in Harlem. He also soon met and was befriended by William Carlos
Williams. Then he was on his way to San Francisco and *Howl and Other Poems*
was published in 1956. Buoyed by the publicity that accompanied its obscenity trial,
"Howl" would become perhaps the most widely known poem of the era. Ginsberg
had become a twentieth-century incarnation of Walt Whitman.

The mix of moods in his work would remain consistent throughout his career—
prophetic, elegiac, ecstatic. He would write triumphant poems of political protest,
lamentations about death, celebratory poems about homosexuality, and affirmations
of visionary transformation. He chanted his poems to the accompaniment of finger
cymbals, sang them with rock groups, and intoned them in a high resonant voice
that made his poetry a form of contemporary prophecy.

Some of the other writers associated with the Beats—notably Amiri Baraka
(at the time still known as LeRoi Jones) and Gary Snyder—evolved in other direc-
tions. Baraka became the central theorist and a leading practitioner of the Black Arts
Movement. Born Everett Leroy Jones in 1934 to a middle-class family in Newark,
New Jersey, as the son of a postal employee and social worker, Baraka was educated
at Rutgers, Howard, and Columbia universities. His work and his system of beliefs

have gone through several distinct phases. In the late 1950s and early 1960s he was active among Beat writers on New York's Lower East Side, writing his own poetry and plays and editing two period magazines, *Yugen* and *Floating Bear*. Yet he was also increasingly impatient with what he saw as the political irrelevance of the Beats and the gradualism of the civil rights movement. In Baraka, the Beats' scorn for material-ism was gradually being transformed into a more aggressive and politically focused critique of capitalism. Race was also becoming more central to his view of American culture. His center of operations moved from the Lower East Side to Harlem, and he became a founding figure of the Black Arts Movement of the late 1960s and early 1970s. "Black Art" (998–999) was essentially the ars poetica of the movement. He had first published as LeRoi Jones; he then became Amiri Baraka. For several years he was a stunningly forceful advocate of black cultural nationalism, but by 1975 he was finding its racial exclusivity confining. He thus embraced the revolutionary forms of international socialism. Baraka's poetry, plays, and essays have been defining docu-ments for African American culture for nearly four decades. His view of Christianity in "When We'll Worship Jesus" (1972; 999–1001), a poem that should be read aloud, may be compared with that of Langston Hughes in "Goodbye Christ" and contrasted with that of Carolyn Rodgers (1945–). Baraka receives treatment in this handbook in several chapters. Karen Ford sets Baraka's work within the long history of African American aesthetics, James Smethurst contextualizes it within the Black Arts Move-ment, and Lytle Shaw links the phases of Baraka's career to a poetics of place.

Gary Snyder's career went in a distinctly different direction, though both Lytle Shaw and Lynn Keller in their chapters here successfully identify his work with an aesthetics of place as well. Born in 1930 in San Francisco and raised on a farm north of Seattle, Washington, Snyder was educated at Reed College, where he studied lit-erature, Buddhist philosophy, and Native American mythology. He then worked as a logger and spent summers as a forest-fire lookout in Oregon, Washington, and Cali-fornia. Involved with the Beat writers in San Francisco in the mid-1950s, he made a major change in his life in 1956 by moving to Japan to study Zen Buddhism. Except for some shipboard work, he remained there for 12 years. He returned to the United States in 1968, and a few years later he built a home in a remote community in the foothills of the Sierra Mountains in California.

Although Snyder has adopted different forms over the years, he generally pre-fers a direct, simple diction over intricate metaphor and allusion. In "Riprap" (956), he uses words like material objects to refine and teach us a mental discipline. One may hear Thoreau and Whitman behind such an impulse, along with his Zen stud-ies, but the ecological imperative includes an anguish that we only fully earned in the twentieth century. Against the errors of industrial civilization Snyder sets not only a reverence for nature but also a vital celebration of human sexuality. More recently, Snyder has borrowed shamanistic effects from oral poetry and has experi-mented with field effects and the space of the page.

If Snyder is a central poet for the whole ecological movement, it is notable that several other poets who began work in the 1950s became key figures in loosely orga-nized literary movements in the following decade as well. The New York School claims Frank O'Hara (1926–1966) and, to a lesser degree, John Ashbery (1927–). Born in Baltimore, Maryland, and raised in Grafton, Massachusetts, O'Hara served in the U.S. Navy in the South Pacific from 1944 to 1946. He was educated at Harvard and the University of Michigan, after which he served as associate curator at New York's Museum of Modern Art and editor of *Art News*. Like John Ashbery, O'Hara mixes high and low cultural allusions with a certain effortless glee; he also manages abrupt shifts of tone that mimic the erratic, associational paths of a consciousness stimulated by external events and images. The poems skate easily over surfaces, light on objects, absorb variations in mood, and register the cultural and political temper of the times with a grace that makes them immensely pleasurable, but an oblique sense of tragedy also gives them a haunting gravity. Jahan Ramazani examines some of O'Hara's key poems here in detail. As with the painters he admired, O'Hara's poems are also chronicles of the process of their composition. He was often casual about his output, sometimes not even keeping copies of his poems; O'Hara's work survives today in part because he sent poems to friends that were later collected posthumously. Widely imitated, his voice remains exceptional. He was accidentally run over and killed by a jeep on New York's Fire Island.

O'Hara's career was thus violently cut short. His friend John Ashbery, however, has lived to have a long and rich career. Ashbery was born in Rochester, New York. He grew up on a farm in nearby Sodus and was educated at Harvard and Columbia. After a Fulbright fellowship that took him to France, he stayed on and worked as an art critic for several newspapers and magazines, finally returning to become executive editor of *Art News* from 1965 to 1972. His long poem "Self-Portrait in a Convex Mirror" (1975) mixes critical analysis of a Renaissance painting by Parmigianino with reflections on his own mental process, though it lacks the cheerful surrealism and aggressive disjunctiveness of many of his shorter poems. In his early work his approach sometimes seemed antirepresentational, with a focus on linguistic events and the structures of thought. As a result, he was often associated with abstract expressionist painting of the 1940s and 1950s. But as his witty incorporation of linguistic commonplaces and public speech was matched by the use of multiple references to popular culture, his work became more accessible and his project more distinctive. Rapid changes in focus and mood still marked his poems, but he was now questioning how a commodified world might shape human consciousness. He is thus perhaps the poet who has thought most deeply about the mental life that mass culture grants to us. In the process he came to doubt the plausibility of any coherent selfhood or the credibility of a conventionally coherent narrative.

No poet of the period, however, is more central to a literary movement than Sylvia Plath (1932–1963), though she did not live to see the movement—contemporary feminism—come to fruition. Born in Boston, Massachusetts, Plath grew up in Winthrop. She was raised by her mother after her father died of complications from diabetes when she was eight. Plath was educated at Smith College and at Newnham College of Cambridge University. Even before attending college she had published poems and journalism; her academic and literary achievements, however, were in conflict with the traditional view of women's roles that prevailed in the 1950s, and she was unable to live comfortably with the contradictions. In 1953, after serving a month as a college guest editor at the New York fashion magazine *Mademoiselle*, she had a breakdown, was unwisely subjected to electric shock therapy, and then attempted suicide and was hospitalized for six months, events she later adapted for her novel *The Bell Jar* (1963). It was while in England two years later, from 1955 to 1956, that she met her husband, the British poet Ted Hughes, who has been the controversial shepherd of her posthumous career.

Plath and Hughes came to the United States in 1957, and she taught at Smith for a year, while also taking a poetry writing seminar offered by Robert Lowell at Boston University; Anne Sexton was enrolled as well. Plath and Hughes returned to England in 1959 and she published her first book of poems, *The Colossus*, the following year, but the marriage was in difficulty, with their individual ambitions sometimes putting them at odds with one another despite willingness to support each other's careers. In the fall of 1962, after Plath learned that Hughes had been unfaithful, they separated.

It was a brutally cold winter and not easy to maintain a household. Yet the freedom had an impact on her. That fall she began writing with an astonishing intensity, shaping nearly overwhelming emotions into flawlessly crafted poems. Into a crucible went details of her own life and the horrors of modern history; she fused them into a harrowing, ironic persona, an archetype of a modern woman in an ecstatic crisis of gendered self-recognition amidst the ruins of history. In a few short months these astonishingly lucid poems—furious, sardonic, defiant, and exquisitely musical—established a benchmark against which every American poet wishing to tell a brutal truth would have to measure himself or herself:

> I was ten when they buried you.
> At twenty I tried to die
> And get back, back, back to you,
> I thought even the bones would.
>
> But they pulled me out of the sack,
> And they stuck me together with glue.
> And then I knew what to do.
> I made a model of you,
> A man in black with a Meinkampf look
>
> And a love of the rack and the screw,
> And I said I do, I do,
> So daddy, I'm finally through,
> The black telephone's off at the root,
> The voices just can't worm through.
>
> If I've killed one man, I've killed two—
> The vampire who said he was you
> And drank my blood for a year,
> Seven years, if you want to know.
> Daddy, you can lie back now.

> There's a stake in your fat black heart
> And the villagers never liked you,
> They are dancing and stamping on you.
> They always *knew* it was you.
> Daddy, daddy, you bastard, I'm through.
>   (from "Daddy," 986)

Then, apparently, Plath broke through into a kind of icy calm, or so some of the final poems suggest. In December she moved from Devon to a London apartment with her two children. The whole experience had overwhelmed her, and she took her own life in February 1963. Much more than with male poets who committed suicide—Crane, Berryman, among others—critics have tended to read Plath's poems in the light of her death, as though she were writing against some inexorable deadline. Yet the poems are a personal and cultural triumph, not funeral ornaments. Her suicide comes afterwards and tells us nothing about the poems; for they are about all of us, not about her alone.

Although nothing in contemporary feminist poetry would be possible without Plath, it is, above all, Adrienne Rich (1929–) whose poetry and poetics have shaped the movement. She grew up in Baltimore and was educated at Radcliffe College. After early work that had the controlled elegance and formality characteristic of some poets in the first years of the 1950s, she began to adapt the open forms that have been central to the American tradition since Whitman. Since then, she has become one of the most widely read and influential poets of the second half of the century. That impact has grown not only from her poetry but also from a number of groundbreaking essays, including "When We Dead Awaken: Writing as Re-Vision" and "Compulsory Heterosexuality and Lesbian Existence." "Twenty-one Love Poems" (1974–1976) remains one of her triumphs and a sequence that helped belatedly highlight the tradition of lesbian and gay poetry. The opening poem invokes a couple outside heterosexual norms:

> No one has imagined us. We want to live like trees,
> Sycamores blazing through the sulfuric air,
> Dappled with scars, still exuberantly budding,
> Our animal passion rooted in the city. (945)

Later she inserts "The Floating Poem, Unnumbered" with its breakthrough explicit sexuality:

> Whatever happens with us, your body
> Will haunt mine—tender, delicate
> Your lovemaking, like the half-curled frond
> Of the fiddlehead fern in forests
> … Your traveled, generous thighs
> between which my whole face has come and come— (950)

Rich's position now is in many ways unique. She is our foremost feminist poet and an important theorist of the social construction of gender, but that dual status sometimes overshadows, and even obscures, the range of her most ambitious work. She has written a number of unforgettable short poems, variously visionary, historical, political, and polemical. Some of these, along with longer poems like "Diving into the Wreck" have helped to define the personal and social understanding of a generation. Yet her many long poem sequences are inevitably more complex aesthetically and philosophically, and they demand extended reading and reflection.

It is in these poem sequences especially that her recurring topic of several decades—the relationship between individual experience, contemporary political and social life, and historical memory—receives its most innovative treatment. Devoted like so many other poets to understanding the burdens of national identity, she has tried to uncover at once the texture and the governing principles of the lesson Americans are least willing to learn: that we are intricately embedded in and shaped by social life. Other poets, to be sure, have dealt with the intersection of personal and public life. It was Robert Lowell's lifetime theme. But Rich is unusual in tracking these intersections with a keen sense for their temporal intricacy; in Rich's work, social life and politics and the lives of earlier women (like that of Marie Curie in Rich's poem "Power") are registered on the pulses.

The 1960s and 1970s saw not only a new renaissance of feminist poetry with Rich at its center but also the first signs of a multicultural resurgence across the spectrum of minority poetries. Reimagining poetry as a public and popular form, a group of Puerto Rican poets performed their work at the Nuyorican Poets' Café in Manhattan. Miguel Algarín, Miguel Piñero, and Victor Hernández Cruz are among the poets of the Puerto Rican diaspora who developed distinctive voices. But perhaps the most accomplished poet with a Puerto Rican heritage now is Martín Espada (1957–), most well known for his witty and devastating poems of political protest. "Federico's Ghost" (1990) tells the story of a young migrant whose death inspires the other workers to acts of modest sabotage. Here is its opening stanza:

> The story is
> that whole families of fruitpickers
> still crept between the furrows
> of the field at dusk,
> when for reasons of whiskey or whatever
> the cropduster plane sprayed anyway,
> floating a pesticide drizzle
> over the pickers
> who thrashed like dark birds
> in a glistening white net,
> except for Federico,

> a skinny boy who stood apart
> in his own green row,
> and, knowing the pilot
> would not understand in Spanish
> that he was the son of a whore,
> instead jerked his arm
> and thrust an obscene finger. (1212)

Yet another strain of Hispanic American poetry emerged among Chicano or Mexican American poets. That tradition—embracing such diverse figures as José Montoya, Gloria Anzaldúa, Cherríe Moraga, Sandra Cisneros, Lorna Dee Cervantes, Alberto Ríos, and Gary Soto—ranges from poems of protest to poems recapturing historical mythology to poems of personal meditation. In her poem "Refugee Ship" (1981), Cervantes (1954–) writes

> Mama raised me without language.
> I'm orphaned from my Spanish name.
> The words are foreign, stumbling
> On my tongue . . .
> I feel I am captive
> Aboard the refugee ship.
> The ship that will never dock.

Her "*Poema para los Californios Muertos*" (1981) affirms the connection:

> I run my fingers
> Across this brass plaque.
> Its cold stirs in me a memory
> Of silver buckles and spent bullets,
> Of embroidered shawls and dark rebozos.

Ríos (1952–) sometimes manages poetry that edges into surrealism with a casual, factual rhetoric that is both convincing and uncanny. "Madre Sofía" (1982) recounts a childhood visit to a gypsy fortuneteller:

> She looked at me but spoke to my mother
> Words dark, smoky like the small room,
> Words coming like red ants stepping occasionally
> From a hole on a summer day in the valley,
> Red ants from her mouth, her nose, her ears,
> tears from the corners of her cinched eyes. . (26)

In her chapter, Josephine Park traces the parallel renaissance among Asian American poets, while Edward Brunner, Walter Kalaidjian, Karen Ford, Philip Metres, and

James Smethurst describe the inventive new work being done by a new generation
of African American poets. Michael Davidson meanwhile reveals the collective phe-
nomenon of disability poetry made visible both by political activism and a newly
focused body of theory.

These minority traditions are all, of course, emerging ones. They are developing
and changing before our eyes. But the new is always, as Adalaide Morris shows, in
an intricate dialogue with the past. As Karen Ford demonstrates, that is notably true
of African American poetry. But at least one other minority poetry deserves special
recognition. Neither its readers nor its practitioners have had the more full aware-
ness of its history that Robert Parker has brought to us. The new Native American
poetry nonetheless catapults an earlier unnamable genocide into contemporary
articulation, with some writers now grafting protest to satire and humor. That said,
different minority and ethnic literatures have suffered very different fates within
the dominant culture's institutions. Investment by a largely white professoriate in
African American literature did not really begin to flourish until the 1970s. The long
history of black institutions meanwhile facilitated preservation of some cultural
work. The continuing effects of history and linguistic difference have also impacted
the differential dissemination and interpretation of ethnic and minority literatures.
That said, the will to cherish Native American literature remains more fragile. It will
require greater investment both by Indian communities and the non-Indian profes-
soriate for it to win the attention it deserves.

Born and raised in Nevada, Adrian Louis (1946–) is an enrolled member of
the Lovelock Paiute Indian tribe. He was educated at Brown University, where he
also went on to receive an M.A. in creative writing. A former journalist, he edited
four tribal newspapers and was a founder of the Native American Press Associa-
tion. Since 1984, he has taught English at Oglala Lakota College on the Pine Ridge
Reservation of South Dakota, where he lives. Louis, who writes both poetry and
fiction, is at the forefront of a new generation of Native American writers. Having
abandoned the celebratory lyricism of some of his predecessors, he opts instead
to tell harsh truths about both white and Indian cultures. Frank about alcoholism,
frank about self-pity, he also displays an articulate bitterness about the humiliation
and demoralization his people continue to suffer. His primary focus is not the past
but the present life of Native Americans, but it is a present at once redolent with his-
tory and destabilized by moments of magical revelation. Here is his 1995 "Looking
for Judas" in its entirety:

> Weathered gray, the wooden walls
> Of the old barn soak in the bright
> Sparkling blood of the five-point mule
> Deer I hang there in the moonlight.
> Gutted, skinned, and shimmering in eternal
> Nakedness, the glint in its eyes could
> Be stolen from the dry hills of Jerusalem.
> They say before the white man

> Brought us Jesus, we had honor.
> They say when we killed the Deer People,
> We told them their spirits
> Would live in our flesh.
> We used bows of ash, no spotlights, no rifles,
> And their holy blood became ours,
> Or something like that. (1131)

Louis often discovers uncanny instances of transfiguration amidst loss and the ordinary routines of daily life. Like Sherman Alexie (1966–), his work mixes uncompromising social criticism with an unforgettable and nearly disabling irony, but Louis is unique in turning that irony on himself as often as he turns it on the world around him.

Alexie's visibility and reputation have increased so rapidly since the 1990s that at times he seems more a natural phenomenon, like a summer thunderstorm, than a mere writer. But he is an astonishingly inventive writer. The son of a Spokane father and a part Coeur d'Alene mother, Alexie grew up on the Spokane Indian Reservation in Wellpinit, Washington. He was educated first at Gonzaga University in Spokane and then at Washington State University in Pullman; he now lives in Seattle. His first book of poems and prose poems, *The Business of Fancydancing*, was selected as a Notable Book of the Year by the *New York Times Book Review* in 1992. His next poetry collection, *First Indian on the Moon*, appeared the following year, along with a volume of his short fiction, *The Lone Ranger and Tonto Fistfight in Heaven*. Alexie has since reworked the short story collection into a film script, which was released as a major motion picture, *Smoke Signals*, in 1998. That same year he appeared on public television in a panel discussion about race with the U.S. president. And he has continued to be a prolific writer of poetry and fiction, while simultaneously exploring other media.

Proficient at adapting traditional stanzaic forms, Alexie writes poetry notable for its fusion of cultural criticism and a highly focused irreverence. He has an exuberant, inventive imagination that generates continual surprises and gives him the courage to try almost anything in his writing. Not all his experiments succeed, but no writer as productive as Alexie could succeed all the time. Meanwhile, he has followed Adrian Louis's example of writing poetry of astonishing frankness about both the Native American world and the surrounding dominant culture. The ninth section of "The Native American Broadcasting System" (1993) opens with a portrait of a commercialized, commodified, and degraded contemporary powwow:

> I am the essence of powwow. I am
> Toilets without paper, I am fry bread
> On rodeo grounds at the All-Indian
> Rodeo and Horse Show . . . (1218)

"Tourists" (1996) is a three-part poem with a section each about James Dean, Janis Joplin, and Marilyn Monroe individually engaging with Indian culture. Monroe's section ends in a sweat lodge:

> Cold water is splashed on hot rocks
> and steam fills the lodge. There is no place like this.
> At first, Marilyn is self-conscious, aware
> of her body and face, the tremendous heat, her thirst,
> and the brown bodies circled around her.
> But the Indian women do not stare. It is dark
> inside the lodge. The hot rocks glow red
> and the songs begin. Marilyn has never heard
> these songs before, but she soon sings along.
> Marilyn is not Indian. Marilyn will never be Indian
> but the Indian women sing about her courage.
> The Indian women sing for her health.
> The Indian women sing for Marilyn.
> Finally she is no more naked than anyone else. (1223)

Other notable Native American poets include Anita Endrezze (Yaqui), Louise Erdrich (Chippewa), Joy Harjo (Creek), Wendy Rose (Hopi/Miwok), Leslie Marmon Silko (Laguna Pueblo), and Ray A. Young Bear (Mesquakie). N. Scott Momaday remains the towering figure from an earlier generation. Endrezze has been highly successful at finding linguistic equivalents of Native American views of nature. Erdrich has written protests against the indignities historically imposed on Native Americans, and she has castigated the dominant culture for its racism. Momaday has written about Native American culture with Imagist precision and economy. Whatever generalizations one might be inclined to make about the new Native American poetry, however, are likely to be undone by the next generations of poets. Much the same, oddly enough, can be said of the digitized poetry Morris describes. Both represent key elements of poetry's future. They are guaranteed to surprise us. In the process poems will become what they have not altogether been before. We will assess them and use them differently. And we may become different in their company.

NOTE

1 Except as noted, poems in this chapter are quoted from my *Anthology of Modern American Poetry*. The contributors to the book generally cite the most accessible source, so that readers can readily consult the full poem, rather than the place of first publication.

REFERENCES

Cervantes, Lorna Dee. *Emplumada*. Pittsburgh: University of Pittsburgh Press, 1981.

Doob, Leonard W., ed. *"Ezra Pound Speaking": Radio Speeches of World War II*. Westport, CT: Greenwood Press, 1978.

Fletcher, John Gould. *Irradiations: Sand and Spray*. Boston: Houghton Mifflin, 1915.

Girard, Melissa. "'How autocratic our country is becoming': The Sentimental Poetess at War." *Journal of Modern Literature* 32.2 (Winter 2009): 41–64.

Kramer, Aaron. *Wicked Times: Selected Poems*. Ed. Cary Nelson and Donald Gilzinger Jr. Urbana: University of Illinois Press, 2004.

Littlefield, Daniel F., and James M. Parins. *American Indian and Native Newspapers and Periodicals, 1826–1924*. Westport, CT: Greenwood Press, 1984.

Nelson, Cary, ed. *Anthology of Modern American Poetry*. New York: Oxford University Press, 2000.

———. *Revolutionary Memory: Recovering the Poetry of the American Left*. New York: Routledge, 2001.

Rios, Alberto, "Madre Sofia," *Whispering to Fool the Wind*. Riverdale-on-Hudson, New York: Sheep Meadow Press, 1982, pp. 25–6.

PART II

CHAPTER 2

SOCIAL TEXTS AND POETIC TEXTS: POETRY AND CULTURAL STUDIES

RACHEL BLAU DUPLESSIS

CRITICAL intersections between cultural studies questions and the poetic text have often been considered suspect. This gets structured as a debate between the historical and the aesthetic, as if cultural studies lined up on one side, and poetry on the other. For those lined up on the "side" of history, reading or studying poetry did not (apparently) contribute to understanding hegemony or its torquing, to unpacking ideology or making critique, to understanding social contradictions and their real or imaginary resolutions. That this is hardly accurate or plausible was irrelevant. Indeed, poetry ideology, the exemption of "the poetic" from critical scrutiny, and investments in that exceptionalism are themselves attitudes for cultural studies to examine.

Further, the universalizing, taming, humanizing claims of poetry and the silvery aura around the word "poetic" (symptoms of poetry ideology) have meant that some debates on social location—class, gender, sexualities, national origins and meanings, subcultures, religious cultures, ethnicity, political adhesion, and their various intersections and syncretisms—and debates on specific community-based uses of texts, both so crucial to cultural studies, were felt either as implausible for the poetic text or, banally, all too plausible as if some artworks were simply delivery mechanisms for easily extracted social protest and affirmative empowerment ideas.

Researchers within cultural studies examine objects, discourses, and practices in order to analyze the meanings, ideologies and social-political functions associated with these in their time and across time.[1] This is a general definition, applicable to many objects, both artistic products and commodities in general. Although this definition won't illuminate poetry exclusively, literary-critical analyses of the poem, the poet, and poetic oeuvres can begin here.

PRACTICES AND DISCOURSES

Production, dissemination, and reception are well-known categories for examining poetry and its social life. A critic might investigate the historical and institutional origins of poets, their economic and writing situations and supports, and their social subject positions. All these have rippling impacts on careers, oeuvres, and reception. Critics might study institutions of poetic production, the conventions and accidents of editorial dissemination and textual presentation, and the vagaries of reception.

All exchanges and negotiations around the circulation of artifacts, discourses, and practices have serious impacts on careers and canonicity within the categories of poet and poem. What constitutes a successful poetic text may differ for various communities of production and use. And—this is central—there are many "refractions" of specific and large-scale ideological and historical debates in poems, but how these get textually manifested is a major topic for analysis (Bourdieu, *Field*, 14, 182). Further, the category "poems" does not necessarily cover all artful, lineated texts. The verbal materials of popular song, slogans and deturned or torqued slogans, vispo (visual and concrete poetries), advertising jingles, manifestos, and visual artworks using words may be on a functional spectrum with poems.

Under the cultural studies rubric of practices and discourses, one can study artistic groups, coteries or cohorts, their formations and filiations, and the invested agency of poets putting themselves and their familiars on the cultural map. Critical study of the accumulation of cultural power seen by Pierre Bourdieu as analogous by homology to economic power has been a fruitful territory to explore for cultural studies; current criticism includes analyses of questions of "career" focused via performance, archive building, formations of "tactical community," allusions/citation, publication strategies, positional moves in reception, and various nodes of promotion (Bourdieu, *Rules*; Rifkin, 37). Ezra Pound's "Hugh Selwyn Mauberley" exposes and thematizes these tactics; Timothy Materer's essay "Make It Sell!" investigates Pound's own stakes and strains (Materer in Dettmar and Watt). Cohort study is critically fruitful as a sociology—or ethnography—of literary production, functioning like a tribal biography of group interactions, of mutual artistic challenges, dialogues, friction, and specific collaborations that illuminate the functions and poetics of a text (Epstein; Shaw; M. Nelson). In evoking the "densely interwoven cultural, intertextual, interpersonal spaces," Andrew Epstein's repetition of those three "inter's" indicate the critical desire emphatically to articulate the cross-hatched density and passions of community and affiliation (Epstein, 5).[2]

Such studies of production, dissemination, and reception acknowledge the soci-
ality of artistic production by scrutinizing the impact of personal interactions and
communities on the making of poets, on the fabrication of their artifacts, even on
the material form and economic underpinnings of these activities (Silliman, Blog).
Here, too, one may see practices around exclusion of practitioners (female artists
and their fates are a notorious sore point in some groups), and one may analyze
uses of career support systems (friends, family, helper figures, muses, publishers,
publicizing mechanisms, interested critics). A critic might comment on the poets'
various motivations (micro-political, macro-political, economic, ideological, stylis-
tic, biographical, interactive) for producing a particularly inflected object at a par-
ticular temporal juncture (Harrington). Contemporary poets and poet-critics who
are, like critics and readers, social actors in the literary field may also weigh in var-
iously with remarks and interventions about the social stakes and cultural work of
poetic praxes, particularly their oppositional, insubordinate imperatives (this short
list is skewed to the contemporary: Rich, *Human Eye, What Is Found*; Bernstein;
Mackey; Watten, *Constructivist*; Retallack).

Among relevant practices, one may ask how the social coordinates of an author
(among them gender, sexuality, religious culture, race/ethnicity, class, and status
within a nation-state) affect the production of, the circulation of, and even the
nature—or definition—of the text. Is a given work "folk poetry"—a disparaging term
historically deployed for minority or specifically classed practitioners, or is a work
in the realm of the hegemonically assimilable "literary" (Neigh)? Has the rubric
"avant-garde" become dysfunctionally formalist, neglecting the "social outsider"
locations of many of its practitioners and their embedded social critiques (Damon,
vii, x–xi)? Have New Critical, Agrarian, formalist reception rubrics—such as those
developed upholding a post-Reconstruction (but unreconstructed) Southern public
sphere—"served politically as a strategy of containment" of lively cultural work on
the left, by African Americans and women, as Cary Nelson and Walter Kalaidjian
have argued (C. Nelson 1989; 1996; Kalaidjian in Dettmar and Watt, 299)?

The economic basis for poetic work includes the question of patronage, the
marketing of the rare, the role of literary magazines as real means of support
(for paying literary journalism), as well as dissemination and cohort affirmation
(Rainey). Also included are the issue of political repression and the blacklisting
of poetries and poetic movements (Smethurst; C. Nelson, *Revolutionary*). One
can study the appreciation and propulsion of texts (by reviewing, poetics writing,
blogging, marketing) in ongoing nexus formations of reception across generations.
One can study the building of critical reception in several eras, the discourses used,
the debates such as reception occasion, and the sociocultural interventions made
by the institutions of judgment, particularly as it settles, if unevenly and with
many material constraints, in the contemporary university and the contemporary
anthology (Guillory; C. Nelson, "Murder").

There are also general cultural debates that have both political and aesthetic
resonance. In the United States from the 1920s onward, critically and artistically
producing the "Americanness" of U.S. literature was a concern that led to certain

representations and certain arguments within reception. In the world of the 1970s and 1980s, producing a female, feminine, or woman-inflected writing was a political goal and (interested) social good in key cultural arenas. When a cultural category is available for use, often one finds the self-conscious construction of new work fitting the boundaries of this category. These efforts generally lead to recalibrated critical lenses for the reception of prior work.

Cultural and social changes are reflected, magnetized, and projected in literary texts. General historical changes on all scales absolutely make their mark on themes and trends in writing—and many critics have noted the impress of social materials on texts, including poems. Attending at least to specific thematic and topical readings, there is much "postformalist" work taking the "formal features of a text, matters of style, [as] indices to larger intellectual and cultural matters" (Strier, cited in Levinson, 565). The uses of poetic texts as indices or refractions of social and ideological materials do not necessarily depend on a work's being "occasional," or tied directly to a particular historical or political event, but they do depend on analyzing the interfaces of cultural materials with their ideological layers and historical allusions as these saturate texts and are specified within them. There are many examples of this mode of "indexical" work with poetry (Davidson, *Ghostlier, Guys, San Francisco*; Kalaidjian, *American, Edge, Languages*; Thomas; Lowney; Keenaghan are only some examples).

In these readings, a poem as well as other literary works might be characterized variously as a "*reflection*" or a refraction of the socioeconomic, a "*symptom*" of it, "a characteristic *manifestation* of it," a "*by-product*," a "*coming to consciousness*" of it, and "an imaginary or symbolic *resolution*" of real forces in literary form. This suggestive list is provided by Fredric Jameson (*Marxism*, 5), but in each case the particularities of these general possibilities need specific articulation.

Historical and cultural studies focus attention on all varieties of poetry. Critics examine sentimental traditions; "schoolroom" poets formerly important to primary and secondary education; poems used for recitation, elocution, and civic lessons; overtly political poetry (like war resistance poetry); popular poetry (like cowboy poetry); advertising slogans that deploy poetry; and poetry by ambiguously nonhegemonic or even subaltern groups whose production was previously ignored given the assumptions or regimes of "greatness" and complexity (Clark; Rubin; C. Nelson, *Revolutionary*; Metres; Chasar, *Poetry*). Thinking "*historically* about aesthetic judgment," about social forms of poetry and their multiple functions, Joseph Harrington proposes that literature departments should "take popular tastes in poetry" seriously (in a sociology of literature mode); former and contemporary institutions of poetic practice like newspaper verse, poetry slams, and local, nonuniversity workshops and writing groups are, for him, a vital restorative of "public culture" (Harrington, 159–186; citations, 3, 186). The question of social uses of poetry in advertising (doggerel for Burma-Shave advertising), in greeting cards, in occasional verse and satire, in comic or parodic modes, in children's literature (for both pedagogy and pleasure) and in places where it is not now "normative" (as in the daily paper) are all zones for research and theorizing (Chasar, "Business").

How people use poetry, what kinds of poetries are supported in a variety of communities, how poetry functions, and how rhythmic, conventionalized explosions of the signifier occur and garner meaning—all this may be studied with attention to rhetorics and forms, and to the formation and propulsion of subjectivity and community, not only to overt statements. Because an artwork can be productive as well as refractive or indexical of social materials, it may open a pathway, via reading or via a community constructed in reception for debates among assumptions and values or for intellectual, affective destabilizations of known categories (Retallack). Further, the uses of intense rhythms, rhyming, and even semi-sensical materials for children's verbal pleasure (Mother Goose, nonsense syllables, invented languages ["Pig Latin"], tongue-twisters, proverbs, the alphabet song, jump-rope and other play-time rhymes, cheers, counting-out rhymes and chants) all suggest the importance of poetry and poeticity in the acquisition of literacy by children.

Talking about categories of poetry involves genre or the varieties of genre-traces in works: this is an enormously fruitful zone for cultural studies. In his discussion of the prose poem as an emergent genre, Jonathan Monroe implicitly raises the enlarged possibility of reading encoded social debates in debates and struggles around genre choices. Understanding of the mobile uses of genre enriches analyses of the linkage between the literary and the social. Genre is one site at which "social evaluation," in the sense that Mikhail Bakhtin and Pavel Nikolaevich Medvedev use this phrase, takes precise shape (Bakhtin and Medvedev, 118–140).

Further examples under this general complex of practices and discourses might extend or transform the current canon of the read, the critically legible, or the critically considerable by attention to works or genres that have fallen out of favor or out of discussion. This canon-expanding critical enterprise has been undertaken by a number of feminist critics for women's poetry, by a number of ethnic critics for poetry of underrepresented racial groups, by people interested in social class and in movements of struggle and rectification, all activities with an implicit cultural politics. The recoveries spearheaded by Cary Nelson for the multiple traditions of Left poetry, by Aldon Nielsen of African American experimentalisms, by Alan Golding of specific institutional mechanisms in canon formation bring poetries of overt statement into consideration by studies of their practices and their "languages," as Nielsen says (C. Nelson, *Revolutionary*; Nielsen; Golding). Poems and poetic practices might serve political-cultural functions for a community, or they might be provoked by an intersection of several communities; in the cases that Chris Green analyzes there were publisher interest, educational uplift movements, and radical politics in Appalachia (Green). Sometimes an aspect of poetry's rhetoric is taken as a symptom of decay and decline, as Al Filreis argues in an account of conservative attacks in a Red Scare mode made on modernist poetry and its stylistic markers.

In cases where "canon" is under debate, reconstructed, probed, and widened, there is a double question: what does it say about our reception strategies and ideologies that any particular (missing or under-read) work has been ignored? And what does it say that we are at this (or whatever) moment "rediscovering" it? Examples from 2010 include the revival of attention to poets theater (Killian and Brazil) and the interest in transnational poetry and poetics in all Anglophone communities and nations (Ramazani). In the 1970s and 1980s the exhilarating attention to the recovery of poetry by women made past generations of women writers the contemporaries of the present. The problematic of any recovery would be a corollary assumption: it is impossible that such work is automatically and necessarily subversive and critical, as if the work itself were positioned as protesting its long under-read status and came out swinging at hegemony. Of course, any understudied work might be a work of protest, but it might also "transmit dominant ideological positions," because there is no "necessary identity of political and aesthetic value" or an identity of the under-read and the automatically critical (Felski, 175, 176).

Value, one must remind oneself, is contingent, mobile, and situational, not perfectly absolute. Who supports, who disseminates, and how affiliations are made and unmade all contribute to value; other contributing factors are career options, publishing struggles, commercial conditions, and cohorts and competitors. Some institutions uphold the norms of correct, legitimate, proper, or rewardable poetry, and then proceed (surprise!) to offer those rewards. And who or where is the reader? The constructs of reception depend on the reader—the reader's socialization, practices, analyses of needs, demands, social situations, and training for how to receive any given work. The reader's subject position, too, exists inside material conditions. Ron Silliman summarizes: "Thus one cannot define value without specifying the reader at stake: valuable for whom? to what end?" ("Canons," 153). These are questions about the social life of the poem.

Practices around poetry can also fall away and become inactive across time. Memorization and recitation in schools, verse recitation classes in settlement houses, group choral performances of poems often for affirmative bonding, socialization to national pride, and verse recited to provide the secular uplift of civic values ("I Hear America Singing") are not now current practices in the United States although they have been serious pursuits (Rubin). A use of poetry as a bearer of dominant values harnessed the rhythmic and rhyming swing of such works as Henry Wadsworth Longfellow's "Psalm of Life," "Excelsior," and "Evangeline" to teach history and heroism (Sorby). (The cultural use of these poems may also be measured by their parodies.) The public speaking of poetry did reemerge recently, in poetic competitions, poetry slams, and spoken word performance that are often counter-hegemonic or at least boldly frank, but with specific values, conventions, and rhetorical appeals (Somers-Willett; Wheeler).

This question of what is read when, and for what complex of reasons, will eventually evoke the terms "major" and "minor," a distinction both potentially so spurious as to be meaningless as a judgment pronounced on something, but, as received ideology, a significant filtering device. Categorizing a writer as "minor" (negligible, low-impact, culturally unproductive) may have its origins in many intersecting institutions (archives, schools, anthologies, warring coteries, political climate) and in social location. The categories of female, gay, left, or "minority" poet had once automatically functioned that way but perhaps do not any longer.

Another contested term marginalizing certain poetic communities, functions, and objects is "political" poetry, or work invested in and drawing energy from political movements. This is a key site at which the aesthetic/formal and the social/statement slang each other with binarist weapons. Or, particularly, where "modernism" is seen as "serious" and "universal," while left-interested literature is seen as "hack," "provincial," "naïve," or even "deluded"—to use terms and scare quotes from James Smethurst's work on African American poetry in the 1930s and 1940s (6). There is a good deal one might say polemically here—the assimilability of Pound's "time-less" peasants unquestioning hierarchy being culturally legitimated (Canto XLIX), but the general poetic theme after 1939 mourning the loss of Spain to fascism being harder to credit as culturally powerful? (C. Nelson, *Revolutionary*, 224–225). A recu-perative move in cultural studies might be simply to track institutions and practices of exclusion and their larger cultural functions (Berke; Thurston). A contemporary journal that both exemplifies and studies political poetry among other cultural texts is *XcP: Cross Cultural Poetics* (edited by Mark Nowak).

Cultural legibility is a learned practice: that is, cultural legibility and ascriptions of value are fundamentally social and institutionally based. However, this learning process occurs both in hegemonically enforced ways (university exam lists, "seri-ous" journalism, poetry prizes, the awarding of national or prestigious grants) and in the creation and sustaining of counter-publics. These counter-publics may, in their turn, be simply alternatives to the norm or may be clearly counter-hegemonic and critical. The fact that cultural legibility is learned and culturally reinforced, and the fact that institutions (including counter-hegemonic ones) manage social and aesthetic responses to poetry mean that modification, debate, and cultural struggle or reaffirmation are (even if muted and veiled) the permanent condition of cul-ture. Because canon forming, deforming, and reforming are constant and perpetual activities, the only dangers of canon talk are reification, solidification for all-time universals, and any claim of an ahistorical final word on the subject.

Other social practices with their attendant discourses have many implica-tions for poetry and the poem. The first is "genius" as a historical subject position with variable propositions (but always power claims) (Perelman; Battersby). The poetess might be its (structural) antitype (Boym). Mentor-aspirant relations exist within sociocultural institutions of poetic formation. Among practices central to poetry, the muse as an imagined—and real—figure has had a lively function (DuPlessis, 2006).

In their 2009 anthology *Poetry and Cultural Studies*, Maria Damon and Ira Livingston trace two prongs or traditions in the general field of cultural studies and poetry: a Birmingham School sociology of literature and a Frankfurt School interest in form and its cultural work. Their anthology tilts toward the Birmingham School, if only because that is the nature of the work to date available to anthologize. (Presumably, the nature of the scholarship to date explains the total lack of poetry in Jean Franco's synoptic essay on "cultural studies" in a recent MLA guide to scholar-ship and method.) A synthesis of Birmingham and Frankfurt is plausible, if difficult. It would mean accepting both a range of practitioners (including popular/populist poets and uses of poetry) and concerted investigation of the rhetorics, genres, and aesthetic practices of a variety of communities (Damon and Livingston, 5–7).

The potential for braiding the sociohistorical and aesthetic for poetry criticism can also draw on such semi-aestheticizing, yet socially investigative critics as Roman Jakobson and Theodor Adorno. Specific traits and structures of poems, their dictions, conventions, and formal play, their "poeticity" have to figure in the discussion of their politics, social tasks, and historical representations (Jakobson, 378). Jonathan Arac invites study of "how poetry relates to socio-cultural codes," given the fact that the "same" rhetorical figure is not the same functionally over time (351). This rejection of any transhistorical mode of thinking about poetry as a practice is very important, because, for some, to say "poetry" is precisely to evoke the zone of the sublime (i.e., the transhistorical). The ability to keep things in motion, to suggest a dynamic field of practices and discourses, and to track the transactions accomplished by poetic objects are essential to effective readings of poetry in cultural studies modes.

Thus in thinking about a poetic text, one cannot be limited to the social information about it, to the social information it appears to present, or to the surface attitudes it seems to convey; in addition, a critic must focus on articulating the complex relationships that may be constructed among statement and mode. "Both the domain of art and its relationship to the other constituents of the social structure are in constant dialectical flux" (Jakobson, 377–378). So the problem of interpretation becomes one of articulating the dynamic variables, making adequate readings of social texts, rhetorics, and poetics; the problem is actually riding those waves and pulses of dialectical flux.

Objects

The segregation of poetry from the social may also be attributable to poetry's formalist and stylized condensations, constituting more acute barriers to a relatively innocent reader than parallel conventions in novels (or even films), which may well be consumed almost as if "the real" itself. Because poetry is a language use inflected with the music of excess and the remainder, not (or not only) the frames of information and attitude, one cannot take it as "true to life"—which is, anyway, an innocent position ignoring all conventions of stylized representations in writing.

The current exclusion of poetry from many professional zones of "cultural studies" (such as American literature and culture) is a product of a bolus of assumptions and is also institutionalized as a learned social and intellectual practice. However, to move to a more inclusive kind of cultural studies practice, the rhetorics and embedded histories of poetry as a practice would need serious attention. Scanting the aesthetic, generic, and conventional aspects of poetry limits criticism to an extractive reading strategy that reduces a text to a message (even an apparently "accessible" one with an apparently clear speaking subject that looks "devoid" of rhetoric—that last is always a myth).[3]

Cultural studies readings often resist purely aesthetic strategies of formal analysis, yet to address the text successfully, readings evoking cultural studies methods need to assimilate formalist readings dialectically, making sure that a poem gets treated as an art object saturated with aesthetic choices (even banal ones). To ignore the formal issues in a poem, to ignore the signifier (the material, textual, poetic matter), to limit "cultural studies" to opinions, situations, and rhetorics in the signified (content, semantic meaning, extractable ideas, ideologemes, historically active political power relations and their representation) result in lopsided readings. To accomplish full analyses, one needs "reading strategies to help mediate between what is said *in* poetry and what is said *as* poetry" (DuPlessis, *Blue*, 122). To articulate the performative structuring of political agency or the social statements in the enounced (the signified content) without understanding the subjectivity created in the enunciation and the poet's textual choices would be inadequate to both text and context.

What then distinguishes a poem? All art objects in words—novels, drama, poems, film—use meaningful sequencing: they have an arrangement of parts, order, a pace of disclosure, unrolling in imagined time (and in reading time). These modes have in common the potential for hyper-saturations of verbal plenitude and for linguistic, sonic, grammatical intricacy. So if poets (like novelists and dramatists and filmmakers) make meaningful sequences, and if they have an exacerbated awareness of language choices (and all certainly use imagery, metaphor, sonority, and so on), then what *fundamentally* distinguishes a poem as a construction? Simply put, *a poem is a formed object of/in language in lines and segments that is culturally received as a poem.*

"Segmentivity" constitutively distinguishes the poem. This means poems are formed by their uses of segments—gaps at the turn of every line break; segments counted as regular rhythm; caesura or the intralinear use of page space; gaps between stanzas; leaps and gaps in the grammatical ordering; interesting clashes when sentences (one kind of segment) articulate across lines (another kind of segment). The traditional line markers, rhyme and repeated meter, are emphases of segmentivity; poetic syntax (skewed word order) may be a result of those segmentivities. The "disjunctive" strategies of some modern and contemporary poetry (juxtaposition, anacoluthon, fragmentation; a-logical vectors) are thoroughly consistent with segmentivity; even if challenging, they still conform to this basic feature of the poetic text.

If sequence is a property of all temporally unrolling art objects, and segment is central to poems, the construction of subjectivity is pertinent to poems in a specific way. It is plausible to divide subjectivity in three parts, like Gaul. First, there is the writing poet as authorial agent. Using a number of historically determinate and tempting tools, for many reasons, and by various acts of choosing and half-choosing, a specific person puts together a specific text, thereby announcing his or her literary presence (the announced). This is not the biographical person in the world, but what that person "announces" of his or her formal, ideological, and discursive agency at the writing table. Second, there is the subjectivity of the enunciation (loosely, the fabrication of formal strategies for a specific text—this is linked to genre, verbal choices, and rhetoric). Finally, there are the speaking subject(s) of the enounced (the speaker, as a specific character, pronoun, or created voice inside the poem, along with other pronouns). Holding these subject positions apart analytically is very difficult. For one thing, such a reading practice seems unsympathetic, mechanistic, and cold; it blocks identification. As Antony Easthope has argued, we are invested in the fusion of those three positions to propel the humanist illusion of presence—a real poet/a person really sincerely and authentically speaking to us directly.[4] This yearning is a decisive part of our reception strategies for poems: we want to feel feeling and even personality—and we don't always understand that we have also felt language, rhetoric, sound, pace, and line. The intense artifice of poems often collides with our desire (and even some authors' desires) for authentic presence in the poem, as if every poem were to be taken as autobiography or memoir, or at least the performance of autobiography.

So poems are texts that use segmentivity of the word and line, as defined by meter and/or rhyme, by rhetorical rhythms, by the line break and its attendant white space, and by segmentivity of the sentence or paragraph (in the case of the prose poem) as the main elements. Poetry is, then, the practice of writing in lines (or, in prose-poem variants, in segmented sentences) where syntax and the chosen signifiers are deployed in ways that extend, super-saturate, and possibly overrun the semantic, message-bearing functions of language.[5]

Theodor Adorno's essay will stand here for a number of possible Frankfurt School and Russian formalist claims about the poetic text. Yet while many of these theorists call for social-formalist readings of the poetic text and justify such readings, many methodological questions remain.[6] Adorno's now classic, oblique, suggestive essay about the lyric proposes that this apparently slight, apparently personal, and most "poetic" of modes bespeaks the social realm. Social situations are "imprinted in reverse on the poetic work"—the more a lyric poem seems to have no social meaning, the more social meaning it has (Adorno, 39). Fredric Jameson, dismissively but with comic panache, speaks of this as "betting on both sides at once," a Marxist form of Pascal's wager (*Marxism*, 34). Does poetry seem to be distant from the social world? Yes, because the social world is distasteful and alienating; poetry thus expresses utopian longings for a better world. The lyric is not only embedded in the social, but the demand that it *not* be is "itself social in nature"—a false consciousness that needs to be demystified. This cunning dialectical argument is a ready-made meta-narrative.

Anything one desires to find may be found in this negative dialectics of reading-for-the-reverse. For Adorno, that imprint of the social is often macro-historical, drawing on generalizations around *longue durée*. When this essay is disappointing, it is here that one feels a loss. Adorno's readings of both the poems he selects concern alienation in modernity, an alienation shown (in reverse) by the utopian yearnings depicted in both poems used as illustrations. These yearnings are expressed through lyric affirmation of wonder itself, through hearing the trace-voice of a female muse, and through love for an idealized male ephebe, all yearned for by a male poet. Fundamentally, the utopian urges that we feel when faced with the predations of our

society get retranslated in modes of erotic and/or spiritual longing that then repre-
sent "the idea of a free humankind." These erotic and muse-inflected yearnings are
mechanisms treated as self-evident, without having gender, sexuality, desire, and
eros be problematized—or even viewed by Adorno as themselves socially inflected
and historically constructed.

Adorno also has a particular (peculiar) definition of ideology as false con-
sciousness, a cover story, a mystificatory idea package that needs unmasking. For
Adorno, delusional collective beliefs are ripped away by great and good art (39).
The postulate that important art ruptures false consciousness—that this is its most
vital social function—parallels Julia Kristeva's idea that great art is *ipso facto* trans-
gressive. Both view art as an automatic critique—an inspiring if circular argument.
Important (great) art performs a critique of ideology; the art that performs such a
critique is great. A more useful definition from Raymond Williams proposes ide-
ology's hegemonic—yet conflictual—saturations of consciousness in three modes
themselves in contestation: the dominant, residual, and emergent (121–127). Why
are these ideas important? They carry out an Adorno-esque or Jakobsonian reading
in order to involve attentiveness to the "medium of language," subjectivity, to ideo-
logical conventions and their transposition (Adorno, 43).

Methods of analysis and practices of scrutiny appropriate to cultural studies and
poetry, the discourses and practices in Adorno and Jakobson on the one hand, and
Birmingham School readers on the other, wobble between the macro-historical and
the micro-ethnographic. It is difficult to get a balance of claims, attentive to both
social and aesthetic realms, where texts are exemplary of historical moments, or
where the language of texts condense social debates, but where the critic also analyzes
a text's aesthetic acuity and elaborates the sociopolitical by describing how language
materials function. Social poetics, socio-poesis, a social philology, cultural poetics,
"ideology of form," and "social formalism" are all terms indicating critical posi-
tions intent on analyzing social and aesthetic issues together (Jameson, *Political*, 98;
Watten, "Social"; Davidson, *Ghostlier*; DuPlessis, *Genders*; Milne).

A reading practice that engages the poem as a specific kind of object will first
attend to the physical and material (and historical) "bibliographic codes" at work
(font choice, page presentations, bindings), because these choices make ideological
claims even before the book or poem is read (McGann, 16). Parallel material forms
may evoke related political engagements; Janet Lyon proposes a socio-aesthetic
comparison between the feminist-political and modernist-aesthetic manifestos
during the struggles for woman suffrage.

There are also notable readings of the same textual objects set at or used in dif-
ferent historical moments, and this shows how, without changing a word, the objects
are seen differently, with different features emphasized at different times. George
Bornstein argues that Marianne Moore's poem "The Fish," in its original periodical
publication would have been read as an antiwar poem, and he marks the moment "at
which the original bibliographic and contextual codes disappeared, to be replaced by
ones that emphasize formalism and aesthetics over social engagement and politics"
(Bornstein, 99). Peter Middleton proposes two versions of "Burnt Norton." With

a bibliographic turn, he argues that the placement of "Burnt Norton" in the *Four Quartets* (eight years after its original publication in 1936) refigured that poem's "perversity," "diminished masculinity," "erotic longing and contemporary vacuity." The recontexturalized "Burnt Norton" becomes a war work about the public world of men, noble causes, social speech, and Christian authority, in which the poet/speaker "must exercise manly virtues of courage, vigilance, initiative, and fortitude," and "disavow same sex affects, especially 'feminized' feelings" (Middleton, 194, 206, 214).

One might ask (in a cultural studies mode) how and why a particular exemplary poem functions to galvanize and focus a social community of reception that is aroused precisely by that work and its politics or message. T. S. Eliot's *Four Quartets*, Allen Ginsberg's "Howl," and Adrienne Rich's "Diving into the Wreck" all have (quite variously) served this function. Such inquiry involves not only the statements they propose but also the formal moves and the rhetorics of their appeals to the audiences organized by and through these texts.

The cunning array of apparently random vignettes in Langston Hughes's "Montage of a Dream Deferred" (1951), presented in casual, conversational diction, tell varied community stories with a chosen directness so that readers will discover (for instance) that both races are similar in yearnings, desires, and mistakes; that blacks have as much to "teach" whites as whites do blacks (the latter being the usual claim, with its bizarre vestiges of "civilizing"). This mutually interactive understanding is proposed by a black student to his white teacher ("Theme for English B"). The ambiguous, unachieved status of social equality is indicated by Hughes's careful semantic image "a part." The lines "You are white— / yet a part of me, as I am a part of you" evoke but resist the encrypted homonym "apart"—the palpable apartheid of segregation, eroding a little, yet still active historically (410). "But I guess I'm what / I feel and see and hear, Harlem, I hear you: / hear you, hear me—we two—you, me, talk on this page. / (I hear New York, too.) Me—who?" (410). Given the general plainness and temperate tone, this insistently rhymed, stammering moment of incoherence in the speaker (you, two, too, who) can be attributed to the tensions of performing a "Du Bois-ian" double consciousness: the speaker is simultaneously addressing two things as "you": Harlem (his culture of identification) and New York (the white instructor, his culture of aspiration and ambivalence).

The formal evocation of the mode of "montage" implies motion, but the word "deferred" announces that the end or goal also keeps on moving and is never reached. Thus the whole poem is in suspension: a precise statement made by the serial form as well as the semantic content. Situations pile up without solution, without any breaking of the logjam of racial containment; the interplay of stasis, depression, and hope; and the deferral of progress toward social justice. Narrative without progress contradicts the sense of telos in filmic montage. Hughes was aware enough that the title term had a radical history of use and called up Soviet cinema and the theories of Eisenstein (whom Hughes had met in 1932); "montage" might therefore be a guarded social justice allusion via genre (Shoptaw, 118).

Another social reading via poetic practices could examine "Howl, Part 1" (1955–1956), with its enumeration of acts of rage, lust, beatitude, self-destruction, dada critique, and ecstasy. "Howl" produces its impression of a now-existing plethora of active marginals by bringing them into being by the rhetorical techniques of catalog, anaphora, and repetition. The expansiveness of the list and its inclusive length has the effect (parallel to Whitman) of hailing the reader as part of that tempting cohort, "the best minds of my generation." That effect draws on such generic traces from religious culture as sermon, prophecy, jeremiad, with their arousals of subjective agency and rhetorical cues for joining the right side and exorcising the wrong side.

Ginsberg sporadically employs particular grammar-shifting tactics, so that social displacement is signaled by bits of syntax that are "mis"-used, parallel to the "mis"-fits being accumulated in being enumerated; the energy of nouns used as adjectives is particularly notable. Any given verset of this work has a vast number of appositives and descriptors, many of which are plausibly realistic if extreme, but one of which will suddenly step over the line into irreality, ecstatic vision, surrealist *combinatoire*. This has the effect of naturalizing, again and again, the step into vision. The poetic-formal cues are vital both to the sociopolitical critique and to the excited reception that the poem received. This reception (given Ginsberg's own paratextual dedication as reading list) seems part of the "intentional production of literary communities" (Rifkin, 6). The poem appeared to be a documentary of an existing movement, but in fact, the poem is proleptic; until the poem (and until the Kerouac novel *On the Road* [pub. 1957]), there was no Beat Movement, although there might have been random "beat" people.

In "Burbank with a Baedeker: Bleistein with a Cigar" (1920), one of Eliot's quatrain poems, the distinctive placement of one family name at the head of the last stanza—"Klein," isolated after a line break and after a stanza break—is a unique moment in Eliot's quatrain poems overall and a rare rhetorical move of double segmentivity. This placement pointedly calls attention to the Jewishness of the figure, something with many implications and manipulations (Eliot, 43). The inference from poetic form was that Klein, the Jewish banker, was at the bottom of everything. This functioned as a nudge and a wink to those in the know, linking the Jewish "menace" and cultural, spiritual, even physical decline—the proposition of this poem (DuPlessis, *Genders*, 145–150).

Where and how, then, do contemporaneous idea systems and sociopolitical statements get expressed in a given poem's linguistic and rhetorical strategies? Answer: *In any poetic function that can be made visible*: genre, line break, placement of words, rhyme, diction, sound, or syntax. This kind of reading strategy emphatically calls attention to the detail. But poetry is often a question of the detail. Understanding how poetic mechanisms (placement on a line, form of a stanza, specific imagery, genre allusions in a title, and so on) express particular historical moments, ideological materials, and debates can constitute ways of "viewing forms in ideological space" (Felski, 175).

Methodologically, what these bits of analysis exemplify is a close reading ethos with a commitment to uncovering, in poetic texts, the inflection of social materials and ideologies, along with some plausible historical and political meanings. This is done not simply by reading the text for content, but by interpreting the text via the formal modes and practices of poetry. These materials can be traced in individual poems as bibliographic code and context, as language, as structure, as genre, as diction, as convention. In a poem, surface *is* depth, and all formal choices are potentially part of the argument of the poem. This reading method (what I have elsewhere called social philology or socio-poesis) thus respects the verbal complexities, formal particularities, and aesthetic intricacy of the poetic text while analyzing the ideologies and social meanings that are condensed in and propelled by these linguistic and rhetorical choices.

NOTES

1 This formulation is modified from Robert S. DuPlessis. My thanks to Libbie Rifkin for a head-clearing reading of this essay.
2 The lists of practitioners under certain rubrics here must not be taken as a review of the literature, but as constellations of critical readings of suggestive interest.
3 My division of this chapter should not suggest that critics who are placed under the rubric "practices and discourses" never discuss "objects."
4 Based on Easthope's encapsulation of Benveniste (Easthope).
5 I follow Roman Jakobson in rejecting definitions of poetry that are based on its subject matter, on its devices or rhetorics, on emotional validity (as in, he really suffered, she is really good). Jakobson also resists all ethical criteria—the true, the natural, the real, the sincere, and the verifications of the poetic from nobility of sentiment, as these might be performances, conventions, or even hoaxes. He also resists biographically reductive readings of texts (Jakobson).
6 For example, Pierre Bourdieu seems to put full confidence in the Lucien Goldman model of homology: "The science of cultural works has as its object the correspondence between two homologous structures, the structure of the works (i.e., of genres, forms and themes) and the structure of the literary field, a field of forces that is unavoidably a field of struggle" (Bourdieu *Field*, 183).

REFERENCES

Adorno, Theodor W. "On Lyric Poetry and Society" (1959). In *Notes to Literature* (vol. I), ed. Rolf Tiedemann. Trans. Shierry Weber Nicholsen. New York: Columbia University Press, 1991. 37–54.

Arac, Jonathan. "Afterword: Lyric Poetry and the Bounds of New Criticism." In *Lyric Poetry: Beyond New Criticism*, ed. Chaviva Hosek and Patricia Parker. Ithaca: Cornell University Press, 1985. 345–355.

Bakhtin, M. M., and P. N. Medvedev. *The Formal Method in Literary Scholarship: A Critical Introduction to Sociological Poetics* [1928]. Trans. Albert J. Wehrle. Baltimore: Johns Hopkins University Press, 1978.

Battersby, Christine. *Gender and Genius: Towards a Feminist Aesthetics*. Bloomington: Indiana University Press, 1990.

Berke, Nancy. *Women Poets on the Left: Lola Ridge, Genevieve Taggard, Margaret Walker*. Gainesville: University Press of Florida, 2001.

Bernstein, Charles, ed. *The Politics of Poetic Form: Poetry and Public Policy*. New York: Roof Books, 1990.

Bornstein, George. *Material Modernism: The Politics of the Page*. Cambridge: Cambridge University Press, 2001.

Bourdieu, Pierre. *The Rules of Art: Genesis and Structure of the Literary Field* [1992]. Trans. Susan Emanuel. Stanford: Stanford University Press, 1995.

———. *The Field of Cultural Production*. Ed. Randal Johnson. New York: Columbia University Press, 1993.

Boym, Svetlana. *Death in Quotation Marks: Cultural Myths of the Modern Poet*. Cambridge: Harvard University Press, 1991.

Chasar, Mike. *Poetry and Popular Culture*. http://mikechasar.blogspot.com, n.d.

———. "The Business of Rhyming: Burma-Shave Poetry and Popular Culture." *PMLA* 125(1) (January 2010): 29–47.

Clark, Suzanne. *Sentimental Modernism: Women Writers and the Revolution of the Word*. Bloomington: Indiana University Press, 1991.

Damon, Maria. *The Dark End of the Street: Margins in American Vanguard Poetry*. Minneapolis: University of Minnesota Press, 1993.

Damon, Maria, and Ira Livingston, eds. *Poetry and Cultural Studies: A Reader*. Urbana: University of Illinois Press, 2009.

Davidson, Michael. *The San Francisco Renaissance: Poetics and Community at Mid-Century*. Berkeley: University of California Press, 1989.

———. *Ghostlier Demarcations: Modern Poetry and the Material Word*. Berkeley: University of California Press, 1997.

———. *Guys Like Us: Citing Masculinity in Cold War Poetics*. Chicago: University of Chicago Press, 2004.

Dettmar, Kevin J. H., and Stephen Watt, eds. *Marketing Modernisms: Self-Promotion, Canonization, Rereading*. Ann Arbor: University of Michigan Press, 1996.

DuPlessis, Rachel Blau. *Genders, Races and Religious Cultures in Modern American Poetry, 1908–1934*. Cambridge: Cambridge University Press, 2001.

———. *Blue Studios: Poetry and Its Cultural Work*. Tuscaloosa: University of Alabama Press, 2006.

DuPlessis, Robert. "Textiles and Imperial Cultures in the Early Modern Atlantic." Colloque/Conference "Cultures d'empires? Circulations, échanges et affrontements culturels en situations coloniales et impériales," Paris, October 22–24, 2009.

Easthope, Antony. *Poetry as Discourse*. London: Methuen, 1983.

Eliot, T. S. "Burbank with a Baedeker: Bleistein with a Cigar." In *Collected Poems 1909–1962*. London: Faber and Faber, 1963. 42–43.

Epstein, Andrew. *Beautiful Enemies: Friendship and Postwar American Poetry*. New York: Oxford University Press, 2006.

Felski, Rita. *Beyond Feminist Aesthetics*. Cambridge: Harvard University Press, 1989.

Filreis, Alan. *Counter-Revolution of the Word: The Conservative Attack on Modern Poetry 1945–1960*. Chapel Hill: University of North Carolina Press, 2008.

Franco, Jean. "Cultural Studies." In *Introduction to Scholarship in Modern Languages and Literatures*, ed. David G. Nicholls. New York: Modern Language Association, 2007. 209–224.

Ginsberg, Allen. "Howl [1955–56]." In *Collected Poems, 1947–1980*. New York: Harper & Row, 1984. 126–134.

Golding, Alan. *From Outlaw to Classic: Canons in American Poetry*. Madison: University of Wisconsin Press, 1995.

Green, Chris. *The Social Life of Poetry: Appalachia, Race, and Radical Modernism*. New York: Palgrave Macmillan, 2009.

Guillory, John. *Cultural Capital: The Problem of Literary Canon Formation*. Chicago: University of Chicago Press, 1993.

Harrington, Joseph. *Poetry and the Public: The Social Form of Modern U.S. Poetics*. Middletown, CT: Wesleyan University Press, 2002.

Hughes, Langston. "Montage of a Dream Deferred [1951]." In *The Collected Poems of Langston Hughes*, ed. Arnold Rampersad. New York: Alfred A. Knopf, 1994. 387–429.

Jakobson, Roman. "What Is Poetry?" In *Language in Literature*, ed. Krystyna Pomorska and Stephen Rudy. Cambridge: Harvard University Press, 1987. 368–378. [First delivered 1933–1934; first English translation, 1976.]

Jameson, Fredric. *Marxism and Form: Twentieth-Century Dialectical Theories of Literature*. Princeton: Princeton University Press, 1971.

———. *The Political Unconscious: Narrative as a Socially Symbolic Act*. Ithaca: Cornell University Press, 1981.

Kalaidjian, Walter. *Languages of Liberation: The Social Text in Contemporary American Poetry*. New York: Columbia University Press, 1989.

———. *American Culture between the Wars: Revisionary Modernism and Postmodern Critique*. New York: Columbia University Press, 1993.

———. *The Edge of Modernism: American Poetry and the Traumatic Past*. Baltimore: Johns Hopkins University Press, 2006.

———. "Marketing Modern Poetry and the Southern Public Sphere." In Dettmar and Watts 1996. 297–319.

Keenaghan, Eric. *Queering Cold War Poetry: Ethics of Vulnerability in Cuba and the United States*. Columbus: Ohio State University Press, 2009.

Killian, Kevin, and David Brazil, eds. *The Kenning Anthology of Poets Theater: 1945–1985*. Chicago: Kenning Editions, 2010.

Kristeva, Julia. "From One Identity to an Other." In *Desire in Language: A Semiotic Approach to Literature and Art*. New York: Columbia University Press, 1980. 125–147.

Levinson, Marjorie. "What Is New Formalism?" *PMLA* 122(2) (2007): 558–569.

Lowney, John. *History, Memory, and the Literary Left: Modern American Poetry, 1935–1968*. Iowa City: University of Iowa Press, 2006.

Lyon, Janet. *Manifestoes: Provocations of the Modern*. Ithaca: Cornell University Press, 1999.

Mackey, Nathaniel. *Discrepant Engagement: Dissonance, Cross-Culturality, and Experimental Writing*. Tuscaloosa: University of Alabama Press, 2000.

Materer, Timothy. "Make It Sell! Ezra Pound Advertises Modernism." In Dettmar and Watt 1996. 17–36.

McGann, Jerome. *The Textual Condition*. Princeton: Princeton University Press, 1991.

Metres, Philip. *Behind the Lines: War Resistance Poetry on the American Homefront Since 1941*. Iowa City: University of Iowa Press, 2007.

Middleton, Peter. "The Masculinity behind the Ghosts of Modernism in Eliot's *Four Quartets*." In *Gender, Desire, and Sexuality in T. S. Eliot*, ed. Cassandra Laity and Nancy K. Gish. Cambridge: Cambridge University Press, 2004. 83–104.

Milne, Drew. "Politics and Modernist Poetics." In *Teaching Modernist Poetry*, ed. Peter Middleton and Nicky Marsh. Houndmills: Palgrave Macmillan, 2010. 25–44.

Monroe, Jonathan. *A Poverty of Objects: The Prose Poem and the Politics of Genre*. Ithaca: Cornell University Press, 1987.

Neigh, Janet. "Rhythmic Literacy: Poetry, Reading and Public Voices in Black Atlantic Poetics." Unpublished dissertation, Temple University, 2010.

Nelson, Cary. *Repression and Recovery: Modern American Poetry and The Politics of Cultural Memory, 1910–1945*. Madison: University of Wisconsin Press, 1989.

——. "The Fate of Gender in Modern American Poetry." In Dettmar and Watt, 1996. 321–360.

——. *Revolutionary Memory: Recovering the Poetry of the American Left*. New York: Routledge, 2001.

——. "Murder in the Cathedral: Editing a Comprehensive Anthology of Modern American Poetry." *American Literary History* 14(2) (June 2002): 311–327.

Nelson, Maggie. *Women, the New York School, and Other True Abstractions*. Iowa City: University of Iowa Press, 2007.

Nielsen, Aldon Lynn. *Integral Music: Languages of African American Innovation*. Tuscaloosa: The University of Alabama Press, 2004.

Nielsen, Aldon Lynn, and Lauri Ramey, eds. *Every Goodbye Ain't Gone: An Anthology of Innovative Poetry by African Americans*. Tuscaloosa: University of Alabama Press, 2006.

Perelman, Bob. *The Trouble with Genius: Reading Pound, Joyce, Stein, and Zukofsky*. Berkeley: University of California Press, 1994.

Rainey, Lawrence. "The Price of Modernism: Publishing *The Waste Land*." In *T. S. Eliot: The Modernist in History*, ed. Ronald Bush. Cambridge: Cambridge University Press, 1991. 91–133.

Ramazani, Jahan. *A Transnational Poetics*. Chicago: University of Chicago Press, 2009.

Retallack, Joan. *The Poethical Wager*. Berkeley: University of California Press, 2003.

Rich, Adrienne. *What Is Found There: Notebooks on Poetry and Politics*. New York: W. W. Norton, 1993.

——. *A Human Eye: Essays on Art in Society, 1996–2008*. New York: W. W. Norton, 2009.

Rifkin, Libbie. *Career Moves: Olson, Creeley, Zukofsky, Berrigan and the American Avant-Garde*. Madison: University of Wisconsin Press, 2000.

Rubin, Joan Shelley. *Songs of Ourselves: The Uses of Poetry in America*. Cambridge: Belknap, 2007.

Silliman, Ron. *Silliman's Blog*. ronsilliman.blogspot.com, n.d.

——. "Canons and Institutions: New Hope for the Disappeared." In Bernstein, 1990. 149–174.

Shaw, Lytle. *Frank O'Hara: The Poetics of Coterie*. Iowa City: University of Iowa Press, 2006.

Shoptaw, John. "Lyric Incorporated: The Serial Object of George Oppen and Langston Hughes." *Sagetrieb* 12(3) (Winter 1993): 105–124.

Smethurst, James Edward. *The New Red Negro: The Literary Left and African American Poetry, 1930–1946*. New York: Oxford University Press, 1999.

Somers-Willett, Susan B. A. *The Cultural Politics of Slam Poetry: Race, Identity and the Performance of Popular Verse in America*. Ann Arbor: University of Michigan Press, 2009.

Sorby, Angela. *Schoolroom Poets: Childhood, Performance, and the Place of American Poetry, 1865–1917*. Lebanon: University of New Hampshire Press, 2005.

Thomas, Lorenzo. *Extraordinary Measures: Afrocentric Modernism and Twentieth-Century American Poetry*. Tuscaloosa: University of Alabama Press, 2000.

Thurston, Michael. *Making Something Happen: American Political Poetry between the World Wars*. Chapel Hill: University of North Carolina Press, 2001.

Watten, Barrett. *The Constructivist Moment: From Material Text to Cultural Poetics*. Middletown, CT: Wesleyan University Press, 2003.

——. "Social Formalism: Zukofsky, Andrews, & Habitus in Contemporary Poetry." *North Dakota Quarterly* 55(4) (Fall 1987): 365–382.

Wheeler, Lesley. *Voicing American Poetry: Sound and Performance from the 1920s to the Present*. Ithaca: Cornell University Press, 2008.

Williams, Raymond. *Marxism and Literature*. Oxford: Oxford University Press, 1977.

CHAPTER 3

....

AMERICAN INDIAN POETRY AT THE DAWN OF MODERNISM

....

ROBERT DALE PARKER

SCHOLARS and readers of American poetry in general and American Indian poetry in particular generally assume, implicitly or explicitly, that American Indian poetry begins in the late 1960s with the American Indian Renaissance. Even among scholars of American Indian literature, let alone scholars of American poetry in general, few readers can name more than, at most, a few American Indian poets before N. Scott Momaday. But indigenous people in what is now the United States have written poetry since the time of Anne Bradstreet, and the 1890s and the early twentieth century brought an effusion of Indian-written poetry. I have found poems by more than ninety different American Indians writing from 1900 to 1930 (plus a good many from earlier years), and I put together an anthology, *Changing Is Not Vanishing: A Collection of American Indian Poetry to 1930*, that showcases the work of eighty-three poets and provides a bibliography that lists almost 150 Indian poets up to 1930. (The anthology includes all the poems addressed in this chapter.) While Indian poets wrote about the same range of topics as non-Indian poets, they also brought their interests and experiences as Indians to bear on their poems. Here I will discuss how these poems address colonialism and the federal government, land, the condition of the world in general, nature, Christianity, love, war, other Indian peoples, and the temptation to internalize anti-Indian ways of thinking.

Most of the surviving Indian-written poetry from these years appeared in local newspapers published for predominantly Indian audiences, in Indian magazines, or in the closely supervised publications of government boarding schools that published the work of their own students, partly for publicity and partly to discipline Indian boys through vocational training as printers. Without a national audience and without readers in the hallowed halls where literary reputations were made, Indian-written poetry soon disappeared from cultural memory. But the poems have not quite disappeared from the archive, and their recovery opens the possibility of a reverberating new chapter in the history of American poetry.

Two clarifications are in order. First, for present purposes, I am distinguishing poems from song lyrics. While in many contexts, there is much to gain from blurring the boundary between poetry and song, the tendency to see Indian song lyrics as poetry has contributed to the invisibility of poems written as poetry rather than as lyrics. Second, the Indian-written poems I have found from these years were all written in English. It seems likely that some poets wrote in Indian languages, but poems in Indian languages were less likely to reach print and survive. Still, many of the poets spoke their languages, often fluently, and some of them use words or phrases from those languages in predominantly English-language poems. That they nevertheless concentrated their writing of poetry in English tells us that the Indians who wrote poetry and who had the most access to the concept of writing poetry and to the conditions that foster writing it were also fluent in English. Those who had the kind of education that came with English fluency were less likely to be fluent in Indian languages (even though many of them were). In most cases, Indian poets who published relied on non-Indian editors who did not speak Indian languages. Indian poets, moreover, tended to associate Indian languages with orality rather than with writing and to associate poetry with English rather than with Indian languages. Indian poets no doubt also understood that English could serve Indian readers of different nations who spoke different Indian languages.

POEMS ABOUT COLONIALISM, THE FEDERAL GOVERNMENT, AND INDIAN LAND

Indian poets often wrote about the federal government that so regularly intruded into their lives and politics. In the late nineteenth century and early twentieth century, the United States government and many non-Indian Americans continued to focus on driving Indian people away from their lands and traditions, expecting that Indian people would mostly die off or assimilate. Instead of disappearing, Indian poets responded with unease or anger when they saw the sovereignty of Indian nations threatened. In Indian Territory, as the pressure increased to sacrifice sovereignty in favor of statehood, most Indians in the region wanted Indian Territory to become the Indian state of Sequoyah—a name that highlights Indian literacy—but in 1907 Oklahoma Territory and Indian Territory were merged into the new state of Oklahoma.

Many of the poems are fervently critical, even scornful, of white colonialism and the federal government. Mabel Washbourne Anderson's "Nowita, the Sweet Singer" (1900) tells the tale of a white teacher at the Cherokee Male Seminary who trifles with the gullible emotions of Nowita, a student at the Female Seminary. Anderson draws an analogy between the teacher's abuse of Nowita and the federal government's theft of Cherokee lands and obliviousness to Cherokee sovereignty. The heartbroken Nowita, who expected to marry her sweetheart, ends up wedded only to her memories. In effect, Anderson's poem warns Indians against committing to or depending on whites. In "Poor Lo," Wenotah (Irene Campbell Beaulieu [Sioux]) catalogs a long list of outrages, the buffalo "driven…away forever, / By white man's avarice," "wigwams burned," land stolen, "graves…looted, then forsaken," and treaties "diverted / With motives low, unjust, and base / To benefit only the alien race" (1916). ("Poor lo" was a slang and often derogatory term for American Indians, playing off the famous passage in Alexander Pope's *An Essay on Man*, "Lo! the poor Indian, whose untutor'd mind / Sees God in the clouds or hears him in the wind," epistle 1, line 99, p. 508.) Leta V. Meyers Smart (Omaha) expresses astonishment that the word "Liberty" appears "directly in front / Of the Indian face" on a nickel, with "the Indian /…looking toward it, / With hopeful expression me thought," though

> the Indian
> Has not known it
> Since he became a ward,
> A subject
> Or a prisoner of war
> Of the Government,—
> Or a supposed part of it,—
> The Indian Bureau.
> ("On a Nickel," 1921)

In other poems, Smart makes fun of the federal commissioners of Indian Affairs, even turning them into spooky spirits like something out of a poem by Stephen Crane.

Lawyer poets Richard C. Adams and Too-qua-stee (DeWitt Clinton Duncan) give their outrage a legal turn. Adams explains the closed, circular logic of colonialism:

> If the Indian seeks the Government, there his grievance to relate,
> He must first obtain permission from those who rule the State!
> If his rights are there denied him and an attorney he would seek,
> He is sternly then reminded he has no right to speak!
> "For under section so and so, which guides your legal move,
> "You see no attorneys can appear for you, except if we approve;
> "And if, in our opinion, your claim does not adhere
> "To the interests of the public, then your cause we cannot hear."
> ("To the Delaware Indians," 1899)

Adams conveys how the U.S. government drove the Delawares, like many other Indian nations, into a Kafkaesque house of bureaucratic mirrors, so that whatever they did to deserve their rights or get their rights recognized, the ground beneath them still shifted and the bureaucracy tipped against them. In "Cherokee Memories" (1900), Too-qua-stee recalls an idyllic interlude between the brutality of removal to Indian Territory and the later encroachment onto Indian Territory of white people and culture with their laws and statutes. He envisions an outraged Lord upbraiding white men for their misguided sense of legal entitlement:

> Go tell those white men, I, the Lord of Hosts,
> Have marked their high presumption, heard their boasts.
> Observe their laws; their government is might
> Enthroned to rule, instead of perfect right.
> Could I have taught them such gross heresy,
> As "Greatest good to greatest number" be?
> Has shipwrecked crew, with gnawing famine pressed,
> A right to slaughter one to feed the rest?
> Should just minorities be made to yield
> That wrong majorities may be upheld?
> In nature, is this not the rule that brutes
> Observe in settling up their fierce disputes?

Too-qua-stee/Duncan sees whites as violating the larger principles of their own law and of legal and ethical principles too broad to belong to any one group.

In less legal domains, Too-qua-stee's Lord is no less stunned by white presumption and vanity:

> Go tell those white men not to be so proud;
> 'Twas I that hid the lightning in the cloud.
> That twice ten thousand years, or thereabout,
> Should pass ere they could find the secret out,
> Shows dullness quite enough to chill their pride
> And make their swelling vanity subside.
> Steam, too, I made; its power was nothing hid;
> From age to age it shook the kettle's lid
> Full in their view; but never could they see it,
> Till chance vouchsafed from mystery to free it.
> The art of printing, too, is all my own,
> Lo! every foot of living thing had shown,
> (I ordered so) as long as time had run,
> How easily the printing job was done;
> Yet time's last grain of sand had well nigh sped,
> Ere their dull wit these signs correctly read;

> Ere Gutenberg, by chance, could take the hint,
> And fumbling set a thought in clumsy print.
>   ("The White Man's Burden," 1899)

These dull white wits, who can read clumsy print on a page (as Too-qua-stee haugh-tily shows that he can too) but cannot read the footprints of living things, are the same who think it the inherent right of their supposed superiority to drive Indians from their land and take away Indians' right to rule themselves.

Whites have company in their colonialist abuse of Indians, for they sometimes encourage or recruit corrupt Indians. In "The Indian Game" (1922), Wa Wa Chaw (Payomkowishum, Luíseño) spoofs corrupt Indian leaders who join corrupt whites to play the "Indian game" and take the whites' payoffs. Government officials abuse Indian friendships, and "Heap-chiefs share the Pale-face leaf" (meaning greenbacks for bribes), she complains, in her satirical take-off on clichéd, non-Indian ideas of Indian speech.

Carlos Montezuma (Yavapai), who was probably the first Indian graduate of my own university, the University of Illinois, takes on the United States government with special fury. In "Indian Office" (1916), he offers a long list of travesties from the Office of Indian Affairs (now called the Bureau of Indian Affairs), including "Keep-ing the Indians as wards," "caging the Indians on reservations," "opening Indians' land for settlers," "Reimbursement Funds (Government Mortgage)," "dams built on reservations," "Giving five or ten acres of irrigation land to the Indian and taking the rest of his land away for land-grabbers," "selling the Indians' surplus (?) land," disposing "of the Indians' mineral lands," "selling the timber land of the Indians," sending children away to schools, and generally discriminating and "doing every-thing for the Indians without their consent." Montezuma's question mark between "surplus" and "land" rejects the concept of surplus land, a category designed to paint communally owned land as extra, since no individual owned it, and thus to make it seem destined for sale to the supposedly natural and inevitable buyers, white people. As Montezuma puts it—patriarchally—in another poem, "Steady, Indians, Steady!" (1917):

> They have taken your country,
> They have taken your manhood,
> They have imprisoned you,
> They have made you wards,
> They have stunted your faculties.

Taking the country comes first on Montezuma's list. If there is one particular issue in Indian-white conflict that comes up most often and most passionately across Indian-written poems from the early nineteenth century onward, it is "removal," a euphemism for the forced expulsion of Indian nations from their lands. Numer-ous poems lament removal, including passionate poems by poets who suffered through removal themselves, not only on the notorious Cherokee Trail of Tears but through other expulsions as well, as the relentless white hunger for other people's land pushed Indian nations from one promised refuge to another. In 1848, Te-con-ees-kee poured forth his agony over the forced removal from his Georgia home:

> Georgia, o Georgia there is a stain on thy name!
> And ages to come will yet blush for thy shame,
> While the child of the Cherokee exile unborn,
> The results of thy violence deeply will mourn....
> For this comes the name of the land of my birth,
> On my ear as the sound of a curse on the earth.
>
> ("Though far from thee Georgia in exile I roam")

Nearly eighty-five after the Trail of Tears, Cherokee Ruth Margaret Muskrat, the "child of the Cherokee exile" foreseen by Te-con-ees-kee, lives up to his anguished prophecy as she recalls "The Trail of Tears" (1922):

> In the night they shriek and moan,
> In the dark the tall pines moan
> As they guard the dismal trail.
> The Cherokees say it is the groan,
> Every shriek an echoed groan
> Of their forefathers that fell
> With broken hopes and bitter fears
> On that weary trail of tears.

Through repetition where we might expect rhyme, and repetition combined with rhyme—moan and moan, groan and groan—Muskrat burns in the memory of a suffering that the surrounding non-Indian world would rather see as inevitable, inconsequential. But for Muskrat and the Cherokee communal remembrance she insists on, even the pine trees uphold the scalding memory.

The despair and anger over removal draws on and contributes to a larger pattern of Indian people's cultural and emotional commitment to their land. In that context, even poems that might sound like routinely Romantic evocations of landscape take on a specially Indian meaning. To Alfred C. Gillis, for example, the rivers are not mere rivers. In "Where Sleep the Wintoon Dead" (1924), the Sacramento and McCloud Rivers in Northern California, "Far from the white man's tread," mark the graves where his ancestors "sleep the sleep of the dead."

The fight over land came to another crisis late in the nineteenth century and early in the twentieth century when Congress passed the Dawes Act and the federal government gradually began to follow through on the act's provisions to break up communally held lands, "allot" portions to each Indian, and sell the rest as "surplus." The controversy over allotment divided many Indian communities. On the one hand, greedy or would-be reformist whites couched allotment as the path to a future of United States citizenship and equality. On the other hand, it threatened Indian community, tradition, cultural identity, and—not least—political sovereignty. As Muskogee (Creek) Alex Posey put the question in 1894, with his characteristic humor playing off Hamlet's famous soliloquy,

> To allot, or not to allot, that is the
> Question; whether 'tis nobler in the mind to
> Suffer the country to lie in common as it is,
> Or to divide it up and give each man
> His share pro rata, and by dividing
> End this sea of troubles? To allot, divide,
> Perchance to end in statehood;
> Ah, there's the rub!
>
> ("To allot, or not to allot")

Posey's "On the Capture and Imprisonment of Crazy Snake, January, 1901" and Too-qua-stee's "Truth Is Mortal" (1901) lament the arrest of Chitto Harjo (in English, Crazy Snake), the legendary Muskogee (Creek) anti-allotment leader. In Posey's words:

> Down with him! chain him! bind him fast!
>   Slam to the iron door and turn the key!
> The one true Creek, perhaps the last
>   To dare declare, "You have wronged me!"

It is one thing when Posey romanticizes the world of birds, flowers, and rivers in his nature poems, poems dedicated to finding lyricism in the lands that were about to be allotted. It is something else when he romanticizes a person, Chitto Harjo, as "the one true Creek," another in the ironically endless line of the last of the Mohicans, as if Chitto Harjo's heroic objection to specific changes meant that he somehow lived outside the inevitable world of change that everyone lives in. Even so, at least for this reader, the romanticizing cliché fades amid the high drama and emphatic rhythms in Posey's sarcastic mockery. Colonialist violence and power finally sound petty next to the heroic courage of those who stand up against all odds for what they believe.

In "Indian Territory at World's Fair" (1904), Too-qua-stee, like Posey, finds the changes in Indian country driving him to sarcasm. He laments the impending loss of Indian Territory as Oklahoma was about to be granted statehood, a change closely tied to allotment, and a change that, as we have noted, forfeited the sovereignty of Indian nations, including their sovereignty over land. With his bitterest sarcasm, he maternalizes Indian Territory and congratulates her for supplanting her (implicitly Indian) children with a second set of (implicitly mostly white) children, who can join "that mighty group" of mostly white states:

Thy charms shall be by other loves caressed;
A new-born race shall revel on thy breast. . . .
Ah! grandest glories wait upon thy touch,
When thou becom'st a state, or something such.

The move to statehood went hand in hand with wild speculation over Indian lands newly put up for purchase. In that context, Joseph M. La Hay's "Consolation" (1905) pokes fun at a white friend, a speculator who covets the land of a Cherokee freedman (that is, a black Cherokee)—both of them actual, nonfictional people. The freedman defies the speculator by selling his land to someone else. La Hay seems to think it funny that someone he calls a "coon" outsmarts a powerful white law-yer. Compared to the sneering fury of Too-qua-stee, La Hay's poem takes capitalist speculation and statehood merely as an occasion for amusement. If for Too-qua-stee the world has turned upside down, for La Hay—a Cherokee who left only this one poem—a black man's ascendancy seems funny, as if to suggest that it is only fleeting and cannot challenge the accustomed hierarchy of power, which La Hay does not question. Too-qua-stee's anger, however, seems more typical of those poets who directly address politics and economics.

POEMS ABOUT THE CONDITION OF THE WORLD AND POEMS ABOUT NATURE

The poets speak not only to the local topics of tribal and Indian relations with whites. They also speak to international culture and controversies. Posey, DeWitt Clinton Duncan/Too-qua-stee, and J. C. Duncan (Cherokee) allude to the wars in Cuba and the Philippines, with Posey proclaiming in 1896 that "Cuba shall be free" and with the others, a few years later in the fighting, looking skeptically at the onset of American imperialism. Posey sees an analogy between the federal treatment of American Indians and the United States' betrayal of its promise to support Phil-ippine independence: "the Filipino looks; / The vow not kept is in that doubting stare" ("The Fall of the Redskin," 1901). For Olivia Ward Bush-Banks, by contrast, the only poet I have found who was certainly African American as well as Indian (Montaukett), the Spanish-American War provoked a patriotic poem ("A Hero of San Juan," 1899) celebrating the "glory" and "honor" of African American troops who triumphed and often died in the famous charge up San Juan Hill (more popu-larly credited to Theodore Roosevelt). J. C. Duncan, seemingly an unpracticed poet, responded to the spread of American imperialism from Indian lands to lands across the waters more in the outraged manner of Posey and Too-qua-stee. When Rudyard Kipling published his famous "The White Man's Burden," with its now often forgot-ten subtitle "The United States and the Philippine Islands," while the United States was reaching its disastrous decision to make the Philippines an American colony in

1899, J. C. Duncan felt so incensed that he wrote "The Red Man's Burden" (the x's indicate words illegible in the only copy I have found):

> Behold the white man's burden
> Of gold and silver bullion,
> Of Redmen's scalps and broken vows
> By hundreds, yes by millions.
> Yet fill their mouths of famine xxx,
> With bombshells and with grape,
> For that's the way all "Christians" do
> Like Shafter did of late.
>
> From Florida to Havana
> One stride the goddess made,
> To cheer the word "expansion,"
> And in seas of blood to wade;
> The xxxxxxx Philippine xxxxxx
> In less than half a stride,
> And spread the eagle's wing o'er
> The world xx in style to xxxxx.

Shafter was the general who led American troops in Cuba during the Spanish-American War. For the angry Duncan, American Indians, Cubans, and Filipinos all alike get shafted by the United States.

Indeed, in terms not always pointed to conflict between Indians and whites, the political poems often take a broadly oppositional stance, protesting cultural habits and assumptions that came to dominate American culture, perhaps afflicting Indians especially but also burdening the nation at large. "In UNCLE SAM'S dominion," Posey laments, "A few own all the 'dust.' / They rule by combination / And trade by forming trusts" (1895). Less concretely, but more grimly, James Roane Gregory, a brilliant Yuchi whose poetry sometimes gets tangled in awkward and marginally intelligible syntax, wrote a poem at the turn of the century, in 1900, that bears comparison to Thomas Hardy's famously grim yet mysterious "The Darkling Thrush." "The land's sharp features seemed to be / The Century's corpse outleant," Hardy writes (2001: 150). Gregory's poem, called "Nineteenth Century Finality," begins powerfully and then grows hard to untangle. Here it is in its entirety:

> Nineteen hundred and it rains fire and blood,
> Fast filling up hell and the grave;
> A million lives trampled in gory mud,
> They kill to kill—killing to save.
>
> Great wars fought for paradise by the lost,
> Hark! Widows' cries and orphans' wails!
> God of Love! Pierce our hearts with cold death frost!
> Crown Jesus Christ a stone, God Baal!

> The love of God for man deified him,
>   The gentiles glorified his name.
> The Roman and the Jew crucified him,
>   Science covers His love with shame.

To Gregory's thinking, apparently, people have crowned Jesus with a stone—or like a stone?—and conflated him with Baal, even while God deifies man in the form of Jesus. While Christians glorify Jesus, Gregory blames "the Roman and the Jew" for crucifying Jesus and in effect figuring the terrible future of a science that teaches how to rain fire and blood. Gregory sees scientific modernity as corrupting the desire to save, converting the compassion of saving grace into a rationalization of modern brutality. No less apocalyptic, at the end of the century, is Too-qua-stee/Duncan's 1899 "A Vision of the End," a scathing, almost Swiftian nightmare of catastrophe that begins:

> I once beheld the end of time!
>   Its stream has ceased to be.
> The drifting years, all soiled with crime,
>   Lay in a filthy sea.

At the inverse of Duncan's filthy apocalypse of "reeking waste" where "all that men were wont to prize.../ In slimy undulations roiled," where "government, a monstrous form.../ On grimy billows rode," and where "all the monsters ever bred.../ Lay scattered, floating, dead," other Indian poets, especially Posey, wax lyrical over nature in the familiar tradition of Euro-American Romantic poetry about flowers, birds, rivers, and so on. But there are variations. When the Wyandot Hentoh takes up the genre of dialect poems, perhaps building on Posey's dialect writing (a misleading term, because all language comes in dialect), his speakers let the habits of Wyandot grammar inflect their English:

> What sed it Ol' Injuns 'bout a summa-time?
>   Oh it's good woman followed that girl,
> An' it's dress like a nice, jus' all kin' a green.
>   He don' dance, jus' kin' a float,
>   Like on wata', seen it, boat,
>   An' jus' smile 'roun' eva-wha' goes,
>   ("The Seasons," 1924)

Drawing on Wyandot grammar, the "it" of "it's dress" and the "he" of "he don' dance" match what speakers of English usually render as "she." In similarly oral fashion, and again in dialect, Hen-toh addresses nature through an animal story:

> Say, you know that time that Ol' Otta'
> He's slide down that mount'in from th' sky?
> Well, he's wored it jus' all a fur off his tail,
> Jus' smoof, an' skin looks ugly an' a' dry.
>   ("A Borrowed Tale," 1924)

Far from the usual verbal tick, the "you know" irons in its knowledge as a shared communal repertoire, not news to the ostensible listeners so much as an occasion for enjoyable and instructive repetition and variation on the shared and the familiar. The animals share in that community as well. Hen-toh speaks to the coyote as an equal who can speak back in turn: "Yo-ho, Little Medicine Brother in gray, / Yo-ho, I am list'ning to your call" ("Coyote," 1924). While dialect writing is not specifically Indian, these are Indian variations on the form, and collectively such variations provide a partly indigenous take on Native lyricism and, in these examples, the poetry of nature.

At times, in Indian poetry as elsewhere, the lyricism in nature poems may seem forced, as in Gillis's "The Shasta Lily" (1923):

> Fragrant, perfumed, rich and rare,
> Wondrous sweet beyond compare,
> I fain would pluck thee from thy stem,
> O, thou priceless mountain gem.

The heavily end-stopped lines complete themselves by butting into a wall of one-syllable end rhymes that Gillis calls up to fill out the rhyme and the rough meter, comparing the Shasta lily to other flowers by resorting, paradoxically, to the cliché that it lies beyond comparison. Yet the rough meter (beginning the generally iambic pattern with trochees in lines 1, 2, and 4) has its own version of grace, arguably more lyrical than the neatly iambic tetrameter third line, and Gillis places his poem in a specifically local and tribal context. He follows the title, "The Shasta Lily," with the name of the lily in the Wintun language, the Den-Hu-Luly, and he follows the poem with a note telling how the Wintu people identify this flower with their land and history.

D'Arcy McNickle's "The Mountains" (Cree, Confederated Salish and Kootenai, 1925) makes no direct reference to anything Indian, but readers of his great novel *The Surrounded* (1936) will recognize the mountain setting from the novel. They will also recall how, for the Salish characters in *The Surrounded,* the mountain scenes reverberate with Salish memory and tradition and with a sense of continuing but eventually dashed hopes for a refuge from aggressive white settlers and federal officials. In that sense, a wider context from McNickle's writing helps populate the locally Indian meanings of his poem's mountain landscape.

While "April Will Come" (1928) by Choctaw Mary Cornelia Hartshorne does not call on the same local meaning, she deftly handles the language of nature poetry:

> April will come, and with it April rain
> Singing among young oak leaves; the refrain
> Of it will lie upon the opalescent mist
> Like bells of Angelus. Green bugle vine will twist
> And coil itself around the trunks of trees long dead;
> And moistened grasses, crushed beneath one's tread,

> Will fill the hazy air with pungent scents,
> Stirring the dream-fraught earth from somnolence.

Opening a predominantly iambic pattern with insistent trochees (April, Singing), as Gillis did earlier, Hartshorne deftly blends enjambed rhythms (as in lines 1–4) with caesuras (as in lines 2 and 4). Sometimes, she rhymes single-syllable words with multisyllable words, and she lets a caesura anchor internal rhyme (the near rhyme of mist and twist with angelus). Such language has a flexibility that can speak over the fence dividing an age that expects rhyme and meter from an age that often finds them off-puttingly artificial.

Cherokee Lynn Riggs's style perhaps comes the closest to patterns familiar to dedicated readers of contemporary poetry, partly because he is among the most recent poets under consideration here (the poems quoted below were all published in 1930) and more because he is the one who did the most to join mainstream, elite literary culture, associating with mainstream writers, publishing in elite, mainstream journals, and moving on to a distinguished career as a playwright. Riggs works with traditional forms, especially rhyme, but with the lightly carried touch of a later age, as in his conclusion to a poem about the moon rising over the hilly and mountainous horizon outside Santa Fe:

> A light in the *portales* of the hill
> Opened the earth. A cricket shook the air.
> On Monte Sol guitars of gold, too still
> For music, said a silver prayer.
>   ("Moon")

The counterpoint of flowingly enjambed lines with a line ("Opened the . . .") that, though short, manages to fit into its short space a verb, then an object, then a strong caesura, and then a complete, end-stopped sentence paces the irony of watching the moon rise over Sun Mountain (Monte Sol). In "A Letter," partly another poem of nature and partly a poem of culture, the natural, figurative guitars of "Moon" emerge less completely as metaphors, while remaining metaphors nevertheless:

> I don't know why I should be writing to you,
> I don't know why I should be writing to anyone:
> Nella has brought me yellow calendulas,
> In my neighbor's garden is sun.
>
> In my neighbor's garden chickens, like snow,
> Drift in the alfalfa. Bees are humming;
> A pink dress, a blue wagon play in the road;
> Guitars are strumming.

> Guitars are saying the same things
> They said last night—in a different key.
> What they have said I know—so their strumming
> Means nothing to me.
>
> Nothing to me is the pale pride of Lucinda
> Washing her hair—nothing to anyone:
> Here in a black bowl are calendulas,
> In my neighbor's garden, sun.

Riggs sets a base of simple, vernacular vocabulary without a conspicuously poetic sound, and then, perhaps in an echo of Wallace Stevens, he rotates on the vernacular axis and turns to the suddenly lyrical calendulas and the sudden appearance and disappearance of Nella and Lucinda, draped in the lyrically liquid ells of their names and the artful splashes of yellow, pink, blue, and black, complete with the background of strumming guitars. In unmetered stanzas, Riggs offers the familiarity of repetition paced by rhyme: abcb, dede, fgfg, hbcb. With a few near rhymes (snow with road and things with strumming) and a pattern that slaloms beyond the predictable just enough to keep fresh while staying within the predictable just enough to suggest completion and recognition, each line from the first stanza meets its match or its near match elsewhere in the poem (lines 1 and 2, lines 3 and 15, and lines 4, 5, and 16), while the last line of a stanza finds an echo in the first line of the next stanza.

In "The Vandals," Riggs turns the lyricism of nature in an environmentalist direction, lamenting the way that miners scrape and blast the landscape. Against such devastation, the motions of bird and beast may sound "Like protestation shrunk to song," he concludes, "Yet all that horde were without tears / Or cognizance of any wrong." The birds and beasts, like the oblivious spider in Robert Frost's "Range-Finding," cannot comprehend the scale of human destruction and are not up to the task of calling it to a halt. With his typical indirectness, Riggs thus seems to ask whether humanity itself has any hope of staunching the devastation it wreaks. In "Change," he sees a far wider devastation. "This is the way of things in this mad world," he begins. "Summer is wrenched at its bright root and whirled / ... Cones bleed and fall; ... / ... the tawny river / Breaks from its bed to scar the sand by night." "Change" is Riggs's version of W. B. Yeats's prophecy in "The Second Coming," as finally Riggs steps aside from his characteristic gentleness and indirection to proclaim that "all form / Crumbles like stones of cities."

At such a moment, Riggs takes on the apocalyptic sound of Too-qua-stee and James Roane Gregory. More typically, and unlike most of the other poets under discussion here, Riggs favors the indirection that suits an audience already committed to poetry, especially to Modernist poetry. His poems are like the shadow he compares himself to in "Shadow on Snow": "I, a shadow, thinking as I go, / ... I, a shadow, moving across the snow."

POEMS ABOUT LOVE AND WAR

Besides nature poems, there are poems about heterosexual love of many kinds, and here and there a comic poem. While readers might notice a closeted feeling in some of Riggs's poems (for a reading of Riggs's plays and life as closeting his gay desire, see Womack 1999: 271–303), I have found at most one uncloseted same-sex love poem, the quirky Wa Wa Chaw's "In Memory of My Homosexual Friend: Imaginary Love. . . ." (date uncertain):

> What mystery is the seat of personality
> > Whose beautiful form has neither Love
> > > Nor the sentiment of a rose. . . .
> Do not imprison My immodest Spirit.
> > Is there not an ear that can hear Thy Voice.
> Has not Nature linked My Manly form
> > With a Womanly passion. . . .
> Crying from beneath My hidden thoughts
> > are memories.
> Lo, though I walk through the valley of Life
> I Fear only the things of the Mind.
> > Love smothers the Womanly passion
> > > which was conquered by time.
> Maybe I am but a Man in form.
> > My Womanly passion is admitted
> > > to feast on the open spaces.
> Thy being craves and raves.
> > Thy Manly form refuses to respond.
> Am I not the Victim of imaginary Love.

Do the references to "manly form" mean that the friend is a man, or is the manly form a part of herself? Is it lesbian desire that feels imprisoned? Is the womanly passion a passion from women for men, or is it from and for women? Are the feared things of the mind the same things as the smothered passion that somehow still cries out, craving and raving? It is hard to tell how the cryptic obscurity mediates and masks the passions and memories and how, in a less mediated way, surely queer whether or not lesbian, the obscurity enacts and expresses them.

More conventionally, Muskrat concludes a love poem in the following lines:

> > No lover's art
> Can lift full, heavy sorrow from my view
> Or still my restless longing, purge my hate,
> Because I learned I loved you, dear, too late.

Muskrat signals that her poem fits into a tradition of English poetry—and signals her variation on that tradition—by using the sonnet form and by titling her set of sonnets "Sonnets from the Cherokee" and then adding "(May Mrs. Browning Pardon Me)," flagging her playful homage to Elizabeth Barrett Browning's *Sonnets from the Portuguese* (1850). Muskrat walks us through the requisite series and lexicon of love's emotions, recognizing (almost but not quite with a knowing wink) how convention—the "lover's art"—mediates and in some sense produces what it might seem merely to report.

McNickle might seem equally beholden to convention and tradition when he ends each in a series of three stanzas about love and the seasons with an artfully rhyming "My lover will come when summer is nigh" and then varies the pattern to conclude the fourth and final stanza:

> Spring brings the thaw and brant cleave the sky,
> My lover will come when summer is nigh.
>
> Rich be the cargo he brings from the north,
> Beaver and fox skins, a king's ransom's worth;
> Then we will wed, my lover and I,—
> I pray he returns when summer is nigh!
> ("Sweet Is the Prairie," 1934)

But the cultural setting can hint at other ways to read the repetition. In a note, McNickle marks the poem as his effort to reconstruct a French-Canadian song he cannot remember, presumably a song from the world of his childhood on the Flathead reservation in Montana among his mother's Métis family, who fled Canada after the defeat of the Riel rebellions. In short, this is the fur trade culture—with its "cargo" of "Beaver and fox skins"—where white male fur traders and their Métis sons depended on Indian and Métis women. The men married or promised to marry the women and then often, after getting what they wanted, never came back. The Métis of McNickle's childhood (a distinct Indian and white culture—Métis is French for mixed), like their music of fiddle and song, descended through the fur trade, however much or little they continued to reenact its patterns of gender (which of course varied) as the fur trade died out, victim of its environmental devastation, and as its cultural legacy evolved over the generations. Repetition leads both to variation and in some ways to more repetition, so that the confident refrain of "My lover will come when summer is nigh" transforms into "I pray he returns," which eventually means that she knows her lover, like the treacherous white lover of Nowita, the sweet singer, will never return and may never truly have meant to return. Colonialism, misogyny, and the use-and-discard ethic of environmental exploitation all inflect and overdetermine each other, until the small space of one woman's sadness can end up figuring continental and global devastation and tragedy.

Meanwhile, as war gets coded through ideologies of vulnerable or needy masculinity and nationhood, poetry about war invites a variety of emotional investments. We have already seen responses to the Spanish-American War ranging from indignation to pride. Poems about World War I sometimes evoke pride in the strong tradition of military service in many Indian communities. For Choctaw Thomas Dewey Slinker, joining the army offers a chance for men across the races to bond together in masculine self-respect: "We're not ashamed of the uniform, / . . . / For we have an honored calling, / As our garments plainly show" ("Our Side of It," 1918). In "The Doughboy" (1925), another Choctaw, Ben D. Locke, takes a similar pride in continuing a warrior tradition, yet he believes that the Indian soldier "Stands as a hero undaunted / To a race fast fading from sight." Locke buys into the myth that Indians are vanishing, "on the brink of the abyss," and so for him the tradition he celebrates has run to the end of its course. For Hen-toh, by contrast, the interruption of war cannot threaten Indian continuities. In Hen-toh's "My Fren'" (1924), the speaker's point is not to glorify the male camaraderie of the military that Slinker celebrates so much as to insist that going off to war cannot destroy the camaraderie his friend will return to when the war is over:

> If you go flat bust, an' I got one dime,
> I know wha' you could fin' nickel, I bet,
>   Or mebbe ten cent.
>
> It's jus' that way all time, me an' you,
> We bin know'd each otha' how you say, well.
> I don' care fo' hundred snakes what you do;
> Even you tell it me: "You go to hell,"
>   I could do it, e-a-s-y.

Mildly teasing the speaking friend's lingo, Hen-toh exchanges military pride for comic affection. Tlingit Francis L. Verigan takes up the topic of war in more broadly comic tones. Verging on mock epic, he writes about a cat named Funny-Face who dies after getting caught "between the attic floor and downstairs ceiling" while fighting not to save democracy but, more prosaically, to save Carlisle seed corn from squirrels.

> When he was drafted to the attic war,
>   He called on himself not to slack.
> He adopted a war hymn instead of a purr
>   And he rubbed the fur wrong on his back.

"He took prisoner after prisoner," Verigan explains in a note, "until in one Verdun-like battle he was compelled to retreat" ("The Martyrdom of Funny Face," 1918).

In another poem, Gillis looks on the war with scorn:

> God pity us all, for our hands are red,
> With the wars we've made, the blood we've shed,
> As we battle to death, for greed and gain,
> Red are our hands, with the thousands slain.
>   ("My Prayer," 1924)

The ironies that Gillis spins on the color red show no patience with Indian tradi-
tions of warfare and military service. Similarly, for Carlos Montezuma, the war is no
happy chance for camaraderie or amusement. He sees the war and its slaughter as
proof that the vaunted "civilization" is "the worst savagery." "Civilization," he writes,
"thou art great, thou canst raise millions to slaughter, / Tear to pieces thy brother
in the air," but it all comes down to "the Almighty dollar," to "might and not right"
("Civilization," 1917). Writing to Indian readers, Montezuma warns:

> The War Craze is on.
> If you want to fight—fight—
> But let no one force you in. . . .
> They have taken your country,
> They have taken your manhood,
> They have imprisoned you,
> They have made you wards. . . .
> You are not an American citizen—
> You are an Indian;
> You are nothing and that is all. . . .
> Redskins, *true Americans*, you have a fight with those whom you wish
>   to fight for.
>
> ("Steady, Indians, Steady!" 1917)

Montezuma's polarizing repetition (the anaphora of "They…, They…, They . . ."
versus "You…, You…, You . . .") calls up Indian pride, and in that way it matches
the work of soldier poets like Slinker and Locke. But Montezuma recruits Indian
pride not to defend federal authority but instead to resist it.

POEMS ABOUT CHRISTIANITY

In something like the same way that some poets take pride in World War I while
others cast it in doubt, some of the poets take pride in Christianity while others
look at it with skepticism. Still others, however, hedge their bets and take both
stances, more or less subtly but in line with widespread patterns of Native religious
syncretism. Indian people, like other people, have always built their own cultures
from what they find around them as well as from what they imagine and believe
on their own, without necessarily seeing a division between those two paths. Some
poems fit snugly in traditional Christian patterns, as when Hartshorne addresses
Christ directly to say that "within your eyes / The tender mercy of your Father lies"
("Three Poems of Christmas Eve"). On the other hand, the irrepressible DeWitt
Clinton Duncan/Too-qua-stee, who ends "The Dead Nation" by rhyming "Christ"
with "priced," proclaims that he would "drive old Claus with his load of cheap goods

/ If I could, to the place where he ought to go— / To freeze to death in the cold polar woods" ("A Christmas Song"). For the place where St. Nicholas ought to go, Too-qua-stee's pause allows us to fill in the name of the hot place before he rounds out the stanza with a hardly less forbidding cold place. J. C. Duncan is less jocular and, if less eloquent, nevertheless more direct when he tells the "White man" to

> Return our land and moneys,
>   Then Christianity take,
> Return us to our innocence,
>   We never burned at stakes.
> ("The Red Man's Burden," 1899)

It is hard to tell whether the last line means that Indians never burned their innocence, that Cherokees never burned Christians, or, as the syntax but not the sense seems to suggest, never burned themselves, never, in effect, cooperated with what amounts to an inquisition.

Some poets blame white Christians for not living up to the Christianity they preach. In "The Dead Nation," Too-qua-stee says wryly that the Cherokee Nation will have to give way to civilization—"And so did Socrates and Jesus Christ" ("The Dead Nation"). Richard C. Adams might seem to want it both ways, demurring that "I do not blame the Christians, if Christians true they be," but he uses his accusation of false Christianity as a passport to decry Christians more largely. He sees Christians as hypocrites: " 'This is a Christian Nation,' they oft with pride maintain, / And even on their money their faith they do proclaim." But he also sees Christians, if not Christianity itself, as complicit with colonialism from the get-go, in part because, as so often, it comes down to land:

> …there came some pilgrims from a far and distant shore,
> As they said "with Christian motives," our country to explore;
> For us, "a poor heathen nation," their hearts were truly sad;
> And to save us from "the infernal powers" they'd be very glad.
> But to provide the daily bread of those who laid the plan,
> Well, of course, we'd be expected to give them plenty of land.
> ("To the Delaware Indians," 1899)

When Indian poets criticize whites' theft of land, white civilization, or white Christianity, they step outside their colonially assigned roles as ethnographic representatives of their own cultures. Instead, as participant observers in the surrounding white-majority world, they offer their own ethnographic account of the dominant culture, but without the usual pose of ethnographic neutrality. Given the routine of ethnographic thinking when it comes to representing Indian cultures, that is, the sense of obligation to explain Indian cultures more or less from scratch to an audience that knows little about the topic, it may seem remarkable that Indian poets typically refuse to take up the role of what Mary Louise Pratt has called auto-ethnographers, writers who explain their own cultures from the privi-leged position of insiders, reproducing or mimicking the way that anthropologists, journalists, and travel writers typically described Indian cultures. Instead of writing to serve colonialist curiosity, Indian poets write for their own purposes, both politi-cally and aesthetically.

Poems about Other Indian Peoples and Poems about Internalized Racism

Occasionally, though, when the poets write about another Indian culture besides their own, they approach the task ethnographically. "Whence comes this mystic night-song?" asks the Wyandot Hen-toh, to prompt his metrical explanation that " 'Tis the An-gu, the Kat-ci-na, 'tis the Hopi's song of prayer" ("A Desert Memory," 1906). Similarly, Hen-toh adopts the voice of a Navajo weaver who explains who Navajos are, prompting a narrative of Navajo origins and beliefs ("The Song of a Navajo Weaver," 1906). In a later, almost Imagist style, the more restrained Riggs, an Oklahoma Cherokee who lived for a while in Santa Fe, describes a corn dance at Santo Domingo Pueblo in New Mexico, with Koshari (sacred Pueblo clowns) who "glide, halt, grimace, grin, / And turn" while

> Beyond
> The baking roofs,
> A barren mountain points
> Still higher, though its feet are white
> With bloom.
>   ("Santo Domingo Corn Dance," 1930)

Typically, then, in a pattern that might provoke a smile of amused recogni-tion from many Indian readers, in these relatively early years of Indian poetry, the poets who write about Indian peoples other than their own are displaced South-easterners from Indian Territory (later Oklahoma) writing about peoples from the Southwest. Robbed of the lands that anchored their heritage, and forced to move to what eventually became Oklahoma, the still prideful Southeasterners often feel self-conscious about their racially mixed heritage and cultures. In that context, they can cast romanticizing eyes on the culturally more conservative peoples of the South-west, peoples more successful at retaining their lands, languages, homes, and reli-gions. They can see the Southwestern peoples as icons of a genuine Indianness that the surrounding colonialist thinking may lead Oklahoma Indians to see as more genuine or more authentic, even when such comparisons trade on oversimplifying clichés about both Southwestern and Southeastern traditions. Such clichés would be hard to resist. "Where the breezes blow full of invigoration / There lies an Indian reservation," explains Muskrat, as if writing for people who need to be introduced to the fact of the reservation in the first place, though—unlike Hen-toh or Riggs—as Muskrat goes on to linger lyrically over an Apache reservation she does not get into matters that ring specifically as Southwestern. Instead, she describes generic Indians with teepees, papooses, and, in perhaps the stubbornest cliché, a yearning "for the tale to be told / Of a race that is dying" ("The Apache Reservation," 1922).

Such clichés run widely through these poems and can raise obstacles and questions for later readers. Depending on their experience, to be sure, later readers often subscribe to the same clichés, more or less unwittingly, but many readers now respond to clichés about Indians with resentment or scorn. These poems can help us look—perhaps sympathetically, perhaps not always or only sympathetically—at the history of how Indian people can get drawn into anti-Indian ways of thinking from the general culture and find themselves taking those ways of thinking for granted, even against what today we might see as Indian people's own best interests. Even a proud poem like Hen-toh's homage to Pontiac can refer to Indian people as "primitive" or describe Pontiac—the famous eighteenth-century Odawa (Ottawa) leader—as "untaught" ("Pontiac"). While recognizing Pontiac's vast knowledge, Hen-toh—in the usual way of the dominant culture—writes as if only school learning counts as education. Perhaps the most pervasive cliché, however, echoed in Muskrat's and Locke's laments for "a race that is dying" or "fading from sight," Hen-toh's reference to Pontiac's people as "scattered remnants of thy valiant race," and Bush-Banks's reference to a "scattered remnant" that "Sinks beneath Oblivion's Wave" ("On the Long Island Indian," 1890) is the stubborn myth of the vanishing Indian, immortalized in James Fenimore Cooper's *The Last of the Mohicans.*

In a variety of ways, some poets see Indian people as disappearing but use the language of disappearance to describe what sometimes sounds more like change than like disappearance. Thus when Bush-Banks's fellow Montaukett James E. Waters refers to "Montauk's children, scattered tho' they be" ("Montauk," 1919), he refers not so much to the notion that his people are disappearing as to the problem that real estate developers had pushed most of the Montaukett people away from their homeland at the eastern tip of Long Island, making it harder to keep up their traditions and sense of community. As elected chief, Waters's focus on reintegrating the widely dispersed Montaukett diaspora made him a controversial figure (Strong 2001). Bush-Banks herself, some twenty-five years after writing about Long Island Indians as "scattered remnants" sinking "beneath Oblivion's Wave," was active in the revival of the Montaukett diaspora that Waters tried to lead.

In another variation on the dialogue between disappearance and changing continuity, Muskrat's "Sentenced (*A Dirge*)" (1921) draws on powerfully repetitive rhythms to drum a resignation to vanishing into an outrage at the colonialist conquest:

> They have come, they have come,
> Out of the unknown they have come;

> Out of the great sea they have come;
> Dazzling and conquering the white man has come
> To make this land his home.

Perhaps the word "dazzling" sneers at the white man's vanity, but amid the drumbeat of resignation it is hard to tell. By the last stanza, though, Muskrat leaves no uncertainty about whether she likes the conquest she feels resigned to:

> They have won, they have won,
> Thru fraud and thru warfare they have won,
> Our council and burial grounds they have won,
> Our birthright for pottage the white man has won,
> And the red man must perish alone.

With its whiff of a sneer and its insistently rhythmical witnessing, Muskrat's lyrical testimony gives the lie to her claim about perishing, but only barely.

In "The Conquered Race" (1927), Sunshine Rider (one of several pen or stage names for a Cherokee artist, performer, and writer whose family name was Rider) describes "an aged chieftain" mourning—at sunset, no less—that "the White Man's ways" have led to the Indians' demise, but in response, a "Paleface spoke with sympathy," arguing that because Indian "young will learn" and take on the role of citizens, "the modern Redman" will rise "wide awake!" His pride stirred by the Paleface's response, the chieftain "leaped to life," only then to fall "foremost on the earth-beaten sod," as if to suggest that, proud though he may be, he and the time he represents are irrevocably doomed. In a sense, then, for Sunshine Rider, Indians may seem conquered and ready to vanish into the past, but from our later perspective we might reinterpret the point as suggesting that one kind of Indian will fade into the past but another kind will live on. Montezuma seems to understand the point exactly, if less melodramatically, when he insists in the title of one of his poems that "Changing Is Not Vanishing." Poets like Sunshine Rider are more typical. They negotiate a fraught position between, on one hand, the sense of a dying "race fast fading from sight," a position that, without realizing it, gives in to what we today call internalized racism, and, on the other hand, Montezuma's defiance, which likely rings more accurately to Indian readers in the twenty-first century.

When Anderson calls Nowita "this child of nature," Gillis calls Indian toddlers "nature's children" ("To the Wenem Mame River," 1924), or Blue Feather describes Indians as "Happy and free, just children of nature" ("The Lone Tee-Pee," 1921), their characterizations are casual and their condescension unwitting, sometimes even meant as praise. Not so for Verigan's "Be a Carlisle Student" (1917):

> Say Chief: Just a minute of your time is all I pray. . . .
> Tho I know you'll scorn these verses, it is just the talk you loathe.
> But take it for it's something that must come—
> Be a Carlisle Student, not a reservation bum. . . .

Look your best you'll then feel better, there's noble blood in all your veins,
You're the hope of all your people—show them something for their pains.
Don't be helpless, hopeless, useless, getting by with old time bluff,
Strike a gait with business to it, if there's evil treat it rough.
Take a bulldog grip—make something come—
Be a Carlisle Student, not a reservation bum.

Probably Verigan is joking with his fellow students, at least a little, when he begins with "Chief," the pet name that many non-Indians apply to Indian men, trying to make Indian people and culture fit the colonizers' need to oversimplify Indian variety and Indian leadership. But the poem then funnels its slippery energies into the astonishing refrain that fills out the title and ends each stanza with its snappy conclusive rhyme: "Be a Carlisle Student, not a reservation bum." To live up to Verigan's ideal, and presumably the ideal of the Carlisle authorities who allowed his poem to appear in *The Carlisle Arrow and Red Man*, apparently means not to mope around in hopeless idleness and instead to take up the world of energetic business. In that way, Verigan abides by a common stereotype that runs widely through American culture and even through Indian-written fiction: the stereotype of restless young Indian men with nothing to do who supposedly waste away their lives by refusing to go along with the colonialist business ethic. That stereotype draws on the at least questionable assumption that colonization removed the pre-colonial roles of Indian men without producing anything like the same displacement for Indian women. (For a discussion of this stereotype in Indian writing, see Parker, *Invention*.) From such a perspective, Indians' own ways of doing are invisible. And therefore, from such a perspective, when young Indians do not go along with colonialist expectations, they look as if they're doing nothing at all. From such a perspective, an Indian without a job and a business gait that fits standard-issue white aspirations is simply a bum.

Yet we might wonder what makes Verigan write this poem, besides the ordinary student desire to say and perhaps to believe what students hear from their teachers. He must have a sense that some of the Carlisle students want to be what he reads—or misreads—as a reservation bum. He may believe that many Carlisle students, after leaving Carlisle, turn into reservation bums. After all, if some students embrace what their teachers tell them, other students resent what their teachers say and even rebel against it, either in school or after they leave school. Verigan addresses his fellow students directly as "you," realizing that some of the other Carlisle students will see his sentiments as "just the talk you loathe." Maybe the students who loathe Verigan's ideas and the ideas of the Carlisle authorities simply follow the familiar, and familiarly adolescent, path of resisting authority. Or maybe some of them think through the issue more programmatically and see Verigan's sentiments not merely as encouraging responsibility but also, at least partly, as colonialist. As cultural studies scholars have argued, we might be wary of seeing adolescent and political models of resistance as at odds with each other. Sometimes, adolescent recalcitrance can encourage programmatic, theorized resistance.

In these lights, I hope that we can look at the internalized racism in many of the poems with thoughtfulness about the poets' uncertain position and the history that it helps make visible. I hope that we can view the poets without harsh judgment and with, instead, a sense of the contradictions and pressures swirling around and within them. But difficult as it may have been for many of these poets to see their way entirely outside internalized racism, some of them saw right through it. Broken Wing Bird, echoing Shakespeare's Shylock's perplexity at anti-Semitism, asks "Why? Why? Why?" do people suppose that Indians must be irresponsible with "eyes, but not for seeing," "feet, but not for walking," and "a tongue, but not for talking" (1921). In "Changing Is Not Vanishing" (1916), Montezuma, though he was a friend of Carlisle and worked there as a physician for two and a half years, programmatically attacks the colonialist assumptions that underlie many of the other poets' internalized racism:

> Who says the Indian race is vanishing?
> The Indians will not vanish.
> The feathers, paint and moccasin will vanish, but the Indians,—never! . . .
> He has changed externally but he has not vanished.
> He is an industrial and commercial man, competing with the world; he
>   has not vanished. . . .
> The Indian race vanishing? No, never! The race will live on and prosper
>   forever.

In long lines reminiscent of Walt Whitman but with rhetoric like a stump speech, Montezuma finds a way to extol industry and commerce without chastising Indians whose idea of industry and commerce might not match the business gait, the colonialist control of the body and its actions, that looms so large for Carlisle's authorities. Implicitly addressing a touchy topic, he recognizes that a steadily increasing number and proportion of Indian people will have non-Indian as well as Indian ancestors: "Just as long as there is a drop of human blood in America, the Indians will not vanish." More to the point, he recognizes that for Indians to have non-Indian ancestors does not make them less Indian, a concept that remains difficult for many non-Indians to process and that Indians themselves are sometimes pressured to deny. Indeed, it would be impossible to live without change, but the dominant culture typically supposes that change threatens the authenticity of the rest of the world (but not of the dominant culture), not recognizing that the static signifiers of authenticity (concepts and expressions like nature's children, "Chief," or scattered remnants fading into the sunset) are constructions of the colonizers' fantasies. The colonizers project those static models of authenticity onto colonized peoples as a way of denying the colonized peoples' ongoing life and resistance to colonialist authority.

Such burdens lay heavily on Indian poetry even from its early years, well before the upsurge of writing in the late nineteenth century and early twentieth century. Both the Cherokee John Rollin Ridge, for example, one of the major early Indian

poets (and one of the great American poets of his time, little known though he
remains), and the much later and, thus far, completely unknown Yuma Arsenius
Chaleco lament the vanishing of Indians by discovering the remains of Indians past.
Ridge sees the era of Indians as irrevocably in the past and gone:

> A thousand cities
> Stand, where once thy nation's wigwams stood,—
> And num'rous palaces of giant strength
> Are floating down the streams where long ago
> Thy bark canoe was gliding. All is changed.
> ("An Indian's Grave," 1847)

For Ridge, whose grandiloquent rhythms and laments sometimes make him sound
like an American Shelley, the message of Shelley's "Ozymandias" and "Mutability"
speaks of the transience of Indians but not the transience of whites. For Ridge, at
least in this poem, the world of whites has conquered. The steamboat palaces seem
like the pinnacle of civilization, free from the winds of mortality that sweep Indians
off into the dusty mutabilities of time. Chaleco, by contrast, can take the critical
skepticism he brings to Indians and turn it back on whites. He laments the vanish-
ing of Indians, lingering lyrically over a colonialist plow that churns up the "mould-
ering bone[s]" of a warrior and his mourners, including his wife and their child,
who "little thought…/ That through their graves would cut the plow." But then
Chaleco faces the conquering wielders of the plow and points the myth of vanishing
Indians back at them:

> But I behold a fearful sign
> To which the white man's eyes are blind,
> Their race may vanish hence like mine
> And leave no trace behind,
>
> Save ruins o'er the region spread,
> And tall white stones above the dead.
> And realms our tribes were crushed to get
> May be our barren desert yet.
> ("The Indian Requiem," 1924)

Chaleco may continue to think from within the myth of vanishing, but he takes
it outside internalized racism by turning it back on the conquerors. In effect, he
accuses the colonizers of vanity and self-delusion to go along with their habit of
stealing land. Releasing Indians from the special burden that colonialism imagines
for indigenous peoples, he proposes that no people escapes change, that no people
escapes the mutability of time.

Thus, if some of these poets sometimes get snared in the self-defeating lingo
of disrespect for Indian people that they find around them, they can stand up to it

as well. In "Fallen Leaves" (1927), Hartshorne recalls how she has "heard the white sages" say that her people have lost "their hour / Of dominion," that their "brief time of blooming" has "shattered; / Like the leaves of the oak tree its people are scattered." But she also sees that leaves have a rhythm, that they come and go as the seasons change. In effect, she agrees with Montezuma that changing is not vanishing. In that light, like so many of these poets, both those who expect Indian people to vanish and those who expect better things, Hartshorne risks predicting the future. In the "leaves, soon to be crumpled and broken," she also sees "the gradual unfolding / Of brilliance and strength."

REFERENCES

Hardy, Thomas. *Thomas Hardy: The Complete Poems*. London: Macmillan, 2001.

Parker, Robert Dale. *The Invention of Native American Literature*. Ithaca, NY: Cornell University Press, 2003.

———, ed. *Changing Is Not Vanishing: A Collection of American Indian Poetry to 1930*. Philadelphia: University of Pennsylvania Press, 2011.

Pope, Alexander. *The Poems of Alexander Pope*. Ed. John Butt. New Haven: Yale University Press, 1963.

Pratt, Mary Louise. *Imperial Eyes: Travel Writing and Transculturation*. London: Routledge, 1992.

Strong, John A. *The Montaukett Indians of Eastern Long Island*. Syracuse: Syracuse University Press, 2001.

Womack, Craig S. *Red on Red: Native American Literary Separatism*. Minneapolis: University of Minnesota Press, 1999.

CHAPTER 4

"JEWELED BINDINGS": MODERNIST WOMEN'S POETRY AND THE LIMITS OF SENTIMENTALITY

MELISSA GIRARD

"The epithet 'sentimental' is *always* stamped in indelible ink."
—Eve Kosofsky Sedgwick (152)

IN December 1923, the *New Republic* devoted a special issue to American poetry. In the marquee essay, "Two Generations in American Poetry," Amy Lowell articulates—for perhaps the first time—what has become a paradigmatic vision of modernist women's poetry. She begins by rehearsing a familiar narrative: with the founding of *Poetry* magazine in October 1912 and its subsequent publication of "H.D., *Imagiste*," she writes, a "revolution" occurred in modern poetry (2). Lowell reflects proudly on the achievements of H.D., Ezra Pound, Gertrude Stein, and T. S. Eliot—her so-called first generation in American poetry (2). However, she also warns her readers that their aesthetic progress—the progress, that is, of modernism—is now being threatened by a "reactionary," "second generation" who had recently risen to national prominence (3). "While the older movement was innately masculine," Lowell writes, "the new one is all feminine. It is, indeed, a feminine movement, and remains such even in the work of its men." She cites Edna St. Vincent Millay and Elinor Wylie as the most prominent representatives of this new "feminine movement" in which "emotion is the chief stock in trade" and poets concern themselves primarily with "the perennial theme of love." Although Lowell admires their technical "expertness," she cautions her readers that they "should not expect a high degree of intellectual content." "It is a fact that the younger group deliberately seeks the narrow, personal note," she concludes. "It is a symptom, I suppose, a weariness of far horizons, a breath-taking before a final leap" (3).

Lowell's "feminine movement" is the tradition we now call "sentimental modernism." As Lowell accurately recounts, in the early twenties—in the wake of war, in celebration of women's suffrage—a group of white women poets centered in New York City came to dominate the field of American poetry. Along with Millay and Wylie, other prominent members of this group include Louise Bogan, Genevieve Taggard, and Sara Teasdale—whose bold love poetry, published throughout the teens, paved the way for Millay, in particular, and lived on well into the twenties. These influential women writers were the immediate inheritors of poetic modernism; they studied not only symbolism and decadence, but also "new" poetic strategies like Imagism and impersonality. They wrote out of and alongside that innovation, but, as Lowell rightly suggests, they did not take its lessons directly to heart. Their challenges to and departures from "high" modernism confounded their poetic contemporaries—many of whom, like Lowell, dismissed them as merely conventional. Now, nearly a century later, these false aesthetic presumptions remain deeply embedded within our contemporary field. Why do we still believe that so many modernist women poets had no aesthetic ambitions?

This chapter will chart the making-conventional of modernist women's poetry: a critical and institutional process that began in the modernist era, accelerated with the New Criticism, and, I will argue, persists stubbornly into our present moment. Lowell provides an early example of this problematic when she claims that the "feminine movement" "deliberately seeks the narrow, personal note" (3). In this single statement, which will echo across the twentieth century, she cordons these poets off from modernism's formal aesthetic ambitions and cedes them to a diffusely misconceived nineteenth century. This is a reductively Romantic reading of modernist women's poetry, which undoubtedly does a disservice to Romanticism as well. However, in terms of aesthetics, it could not be more damaging. Lowell is claiming, like countless critics who have followed, that the "feminine movement" has no aesthetics—no poetics—of its own. By "poetics," I mean a formal theory or method that reveals itself within and through the poetry—as Charles Bernstein puts it, "some 'complex' beyond an accumulation of devices and subject matters" (9). In contrast to their high modern and avant-garde contemporaries, these poets have been seen as all "devices and subject matters," no formal poetics. This is a crucial misreading, which has done far more than simply devalue these poetries. Beginning at least as far back as Lowell, we have suppressed—indeed, refused to read—everything that is "new" and innovative about their work. "They proclaim no tenets," Lowell insists, wrongly, emphasizing what she considers to be the poets' "willfully restricted limits" (3).

More recently, sentimentality has served as the primary lens through which we have viewed the "feminine movement." This paradigm arose as a recuperative strategy in the work of feminist scholars such as Suzanne Clark and Cheryl Walker, who sought to revalue this vital tradition of women's poetry that had been utterly denigrated by the New Critics. Importantly, in the modernist era, none of these poets were considered to be—nor considered themselves to be—"sentimental." The category of "sentimental modernism" emerged in the 1980s and 1990s—not in the 1920s or 1930s—as a way of giving form and meaning to a poetry that was perceived as having none. This methodological move, I will argue, skirted but did not resolve a foundational problematic that inhered within the New Criticism regarding gender and poetic form.

For instance, it is not unusual to find within this "sentimental" scholarship foundational aesthetic concessions regarding modernist women's poetry. Walker, who surveys a broad field of popular women poets, including Millay, Teasdale, Bogan, Lowell, and H.D., argues that only H.D. qualifies as a "true modernist" (105). Walker is right that H.D.'s poetry—her early Imagist experiments, at least—more closely resembles the tenets of high modernism than, say, Teasdale's. But Walker's designation evinces much more than a mere stylistic affinity. As a "true modernist," H.D. is also afforded a true poetics: in this case, an innovative, formal theory of time and temporality, which is identified within her poetry. In contrast, Walker positions the other figures within her study as minor technicians. Even Bogan, who spent most of her career authoring literary criticism, is limited in terms of aesthetic ambition. Walker, in fact, dismisses Bogan's prose as an "exhausting" and "debilitating" distraction from her primary lyric craft (190). "All we can say with certainty," she concludes, "is that Louise Bogan succeeded in creating some superb lyrics" (190).

Clark's landmark study, *Sentimental Modernism*, has had a similarly de-aestheticizing effect on modernist women's poetry. Deeply indebted to the sentimental model established by Jane Tompkins, Clark recirculates antebellum sentimental literature's social and political capital throughout a modernist milieu. As she announces at the outset of her work, "The sentimental is here connected loosely to a version of liberal humanism: valuing the individual, intrinsic value, emotion or pathos, the endorsement of niceness and cooperation, and the family farm" (12). She argues that these nineteenth-century values place "modernist sentimental poetry" at odds with high modernism. In her reading of Millay, for example, Clark assesses, "In the age of Eliot, defined by the failure of relationship and the antiheroics of the poetic loner, Millay was writing most of all about love…she was writing in a way…that invites the reader in, that makes community with the reader and tries to heal alienation" (69). Clark thus transposes the adhesive facility that nineteenth-century scholars frequently attribute to antebellum sentimental literature onto the aesthetic field of poetic modernism. Millay "may shock her audience," Clark writes, "but she does not separate herself from them" (69). As a result of this historical transference, Millay's poetry is rendered as a vague, half-remembered cultural inheritance. A "sentimental modernism" excludes or diminishes the significance of any and all aesthetic and political developments that are not immediately recognizable as being derived from a specific genre of nineteenth-century American sentimental texts.

Lauren Berlant has famously characterized sentimentality as a "love affair with conventionality" (2). She means that it is a place subjects go to be rather than to become—a form that confirms rather than (re)constitutes subjectivity. To Berlant, sentimentality is comprised of a structural relation—a form of belonging—that she calls an "intimate public" (viii). "What makes a public sphere intimate," she explains, "is an expectation that the consumers of its particular stuff *already* share a worldview and emotional knowledge that they have derived from a broadly common historical experience" (viii, emphasis in original). It is because of this belated status—a desire on the part of the sentimental consumer to have her already-constituted self and her preexisting store of feelings, thoughts, and fears, reflected back—that Berlant categorizes sentimentality as a "juxtapolitical" formation: these are "aesthetic worlds" that hang around the political but that ultimately foreclose the possibility of effective political action (3). Sentimental literature, in Berlant's influential conception, is not only a highly emotional discourse, as it is popularly thought to be, but is also one that taunts its subjects with the possibility of political and aesthetic agency that it always ultimately denies.

With the possible exceptions of H.D., Mina Loy, Marianne Moore, and Gertrude Stein—and, indeed, even this list is debatable—modernist women poets continue to face charges of sentimentality and, hence, conventionality even today. African American women poets, too, including Angelina Weld Grimké, Georgia Douglas Johnson, and Anne Spencer, routinely confront these aesthetic accusations, in part due to their historical affiliation with the so-called feminine movement. Alain Locke, for instance, in 1928, likened Johnson's love poetry to Teasdale's in order to market it to white audiences (196). More than seventy-five years later, in 2007, Clark ratifies these aesthetic connections when she constitutes Grimké, Millay, Bogan, and Kay Boyle as part of the same domestic, "sentimental" tradition (in *Gender in Modernism*). A "sentimental modernism" thus unites a disparate group of women poets across two centuries—through the Civil War, the abolition of slavery, Reconstruction and post-Reconstruction America, World War I, women's achievement of suffrage, and beyond—through their purported adherence to the literary and political discourse of sentimentality. While there are undeniably threads of continuity that connect the early nineteenth and early twentieth centuries, categorizing so much of American women's poetry as "sentimental" has effaced the aesthetic and political distinctions that matter.[1] Although my chapter focuses on Bogan, Millay, Taggard, and Wylie, I will suggest that we need to take a decidedly unsentimental look at a much broader field of modernist women's poetries. Sentimentalism, in this modernist context, is a compromise position. It has given us a language for revaluing this poetry, but one that never quite fit. To correct these longstanding misconceptions, we need to restore to these poets the distinctively modernist discourses that they produced and that once surrounded their poetries.

"A MANNER THAT VERY JUSTLY ENCLOSES OUR MATTER"

We don't need to look very far to find evidence that contradicts Lowell's claims. In the same issue of the *New Republic*, in December 1923, both Wylie and Bogan published essays—and proclaimed tenets—of their own. Wylie's "Jeweled Bindings," which has been completely overlooked by modernist scholars, offers a sophisticated reflection on the changing status of women's lyric poetry in the age of *vers libre*. When the essay appeared, Wylie was one of the most celebrated and widely read poets in America. An earlier collection, *Nets to Catch the Wind*, had been awarded the Poetry Society's prize for the best book of 1921, and its follow-up, *Black Armour*, had recently appeared to equal, if not greater, acclaim. In a 1922 review, Millay hailed the publication of *Nets to Catch the Wind* as "an event in the life of every poet and every lover of poetry" ("Review," 379). "Such lines as these," she writes, "will not easily be erased" (379). Between 1921 and her death in 1928, Wylie produced four volumes of poetry and four novels, all of which were best-sellers, and she regularly placed her writing in prestigious magazines, including *Poetry*, *Vanity Fair*, the *Nation*, and the *New Yorker*. Yet, despite her indisputable centrality to the literary scene of the American 1920s, she has been almost completely forgotten. Her *Collected Poems*, for instance, which appeared in 1932, has never been reissued.[2]

The concept of "jeweled bindings," which Wylie outlines provocatively in her essay, is meant to serve as a grounding metaphor for her own poetry as well as the broader tradition of women lyric poets writing in the wake of World War I. The practice of embellishing books with precious gems and metals dates to at least the Middle Ages, but Wylie has a more recent history in mind. She explains that she "purloined" the title of her essay from an advertisement announcing the sale of "Superb Jeweled Bindings" at the Anderson Galleries on Park Avenue, which was owned by the influential modernist publisher and art dealer Mitchell Kennerley. (Kennerley, it is worth noting, published Millay's verse drama *Aria da Capo* and the first edition of *Second April* in 1921.) The particular volume that caught Wylie's eye was a collection of poems by John Keats, which had been encased by "a large wreath of laurel, tied with a mauve ribbon, and studded with fifty-eight pearls set in gold," all surrounded by hundreds of other jewels and precious stones (14). Wylie likens the contemporary lyric to this complex collision of literary, artistic, and economic value: "In the curious museum of our own time some, nay many, poems by eminent young lyricists appear, if not similarly tied with mauve ribbon, at least painstakingly inlaid with seven moonstones and twelve blue chalcedonies." She claims that these "exquisite" bindings are destroying the lyric: "They are the spiritual bonds, the sharp and delicately turned shapes and forms which so decoratively constrict the essence of contemporary lyric verse."

In one of the few scholarly essays devoted to Wylie, Anna Shannon Elfenbein and Terence Allan Hoagland observe that the complexity of Wylie's poetry "has been obscured less by neglect than by superficial appreciation" (387). Her writing, in fact, invites these misreadings, through its coy fascination with pretty surfaces, as she herself admits in the poem "Unfinished Portrait": "I have been accused / Of gold and silver trickery, infused / With blood of meteors, and moonstones which / Are cold as eyeballs in a flooded ditch" (lines 4–7). In "Jeweled Bindings," she tricks the reader with these same glimmering materials. It is an essay that demands a kind of careful attention that she has rarely received. Millay, however, always an insightful reader, saw through the ruse:

> The material from which [*Nets to Catch the Wind*] is made is not the usual material. They are not about love, not about death, not about war, not about nature, not about God, not exclusively about Elinor Wylie. They are not pourings forth. There is not a groan or a shout contained between the covers. They are carefully and skillfully executed works of art, done by a person to whom the creation of loveliness and not the expression of a personality through the medium of ink and paper is the major consideration.
>
> ("Review," 379)

In "Jeweled Bindings," it is significant that, tropically, the same materials that burden modernist women poets are the ones that will set them free. Wylie characterizes herself and her fellow lyricists as "dwindled to the jewel brightness of the picture in a camera obscura, hunched over our filing and fitting, careful lapidaries, clever goldsmiths, excellent workmen for the most part, but a thought too intent upon the binding." "Careful" and "clever," "dwindled" and "hunched," Wylie seems to be playing into Lowell's stereotypical portrait of a technically accomplished but artistically limited "feminine movement."

However, the materials with which Wylie casts these familiar figures are substantially new. Celeste Wright Turner, writing in 1980, notes, for instance, that Wylie's cold, hard metaphors—images of jewels, porcelain, Venetian glass, and crystal run throughout her corpus—evoke the quasi-Imagist landscapes of both H.D. and Marianne Moore (159). There is, as Turner suggests, more than a touch of Imagism in Wylie's desire to forge "short lines, clear small stanzas, brilliant and compact," and her vision of modernist women poets, "enchanted by a midas-touch or a colder silver madness into workers in metal and glass, in substances hard and brittle, in crisp and sharp-edged forms." But to read Wylie's poetics as strictly Imagist is to miss the greater part of her innovation. Wylie is criticizing not only the decorous effusions of nineteenth-century verse, but also high modernism, a tradition she describes as "all persons whose poetry the *Dial* will publish, whether their lines rhyme or no." The inscrutability of "Jeweled Bindings," like so many of the writings produced by Wylie, Bogan, Millay, and Taggard arises from this complex dialectic—a desire to carve out a space between the nineteenth and twentieth centuries, Romanticism and modernism.

The essay's final cascade of metaphors brings the distinctiveness of Wylie's poetics into sharp relief. Into her densely populated metaphoric landscape, she introduces the image of the nightingale, which has served as a powerful symbol for lyricism since at least the Enlightenment. Wylie charts the trope's evolution from the eighteenth century—when "gilded birds" were confined to musical snuffboxes—toward the increasing freedoms of "stone dovecotes," "wicker cages," and the "groves of Academe," where nightingales perch high above the crowds. The shifting imagery highlights the subtlety and sophistication of Wylie's lyric vision; rather than a simplistic subjective/objective divide—personal versus impersonal poetries—she conceives of expressivity on a continuum. This is, as I will discuss later in this chapter, an important rejoinder to Eliot, in particular, whose influential theory of impersonality fails to account for the complexity and varied nature of subjective poetic experiments. Wylie is also accusing her high modern contemporaries of forgetting their history. Of her own metaphorical bird, she writes, "I should let him out into freedom, but not necessarily into free verse. I should try to remember that he was born in a snuff-box, and be prepared to build him another house."

These varied motifs come together in the essay's final paragraph. I quote the conclusion of "Jeweled Bindings" in its entirety:

> But the question remains unanswered, in my opinion at least, as to whether we have shut up any eagles or nightingales in our snuff-boxes. And I believe we are good workmen, dexterous and clean in our handling of gold and silver and precious—or even semi-precious—stones. I believe we are careful and conscientious, but not so much as our detractors declare. I think rather that we have a manner which very justly encloses our matter, a letter which very nicely defines our spirit. As to the decoration, the setting of words transparent or opaque in a pattern upon our jeweled bindings, I am by no means ready to discard it. It is a deliberate art, perhaps, but as such it is a discipline and a struggle not to be too impetuously scorned. If our spirit is greater than the thing that holds it, it will go free of its own accord; our work is notoriously brittle, and I have no fear that its forms will ever imprison an authentic genius. And, in the remote possibility that some of us are not geniuses, but only adroit and talented young people with a passion for writing verse, it may be an excellent thing after all that we have cultivated a small clean technique. A number of minor poets are far better employed at being brittle and bright and metallic than in being soft and opulently luscious. It keeps the workshop tidier, and leaves a little elbow-room in which the very great may move their hammers and chisels in serenity.

Despite her veneer of modesty, Wylie captures the newness of this generation of lyric poets perfectly. Her imagery posits a fundamental openness toward the lyric poetries of the past—both Romanticism as well as sentimentalism. Although "detractors" like Lowell dismissed this lyric impulse as evidence of their "willfully restricted limits," Wylie locates in these "deliberate" structures the potential for a new "discipline."

In her recent study of Emily Dickinson, Virginia Jackson notes that by the modernist era the image of the nightingale had become profoundly debased. Earlier in the nineteenth century, as in Coleridge, Keats, and Shelley, the trope of the nightingale had represented an impossible ideal of pure romantic expressivity. Nineteenth-century poets, including Dickinson, had appropriated this metaphor for "inhuman lyricism" in order to plumb lyric and subjective boundaries and to mark "a pure expressive capacity the human poet cannot own" (27). Jackson writes, "In the early

nineteenth century, birdsong was not poetic personification but lyric antipersonifi-
cation (Keats could not become the nightingale, Shelley could not pretend to be the
skylark), yet by the time of Dickinson's publication at the end of the century, birds
and poets were often conflated with one another" (27). When modernist critics char-
acterized a poet—particularly, a female poet—as a "nightingale," which they so often
did, they meant that she was a purely, unconsciously expressive singer. A nightin-
gale, in this later critical vernacular, was compelled to sing; she neither reflected on
nor theorized her song. This critical move collapsed the distance between the poet
and her poem, and, in so doing, it denied women ownership over their poetry and
profoundly de-aestheticized their productions.

Wylie restores this debased modernist trope to its earlier complexity. She inserts
a formal space between the woman poet and the nightingale—the "soft and opu-
lently luscious" singing of nineteenth-century sentimentality—so that the control
she exerts over her expressions, or her craft, is made visible. Women poets, in Wylie's
conception, labor at their trades: they are lapidaries, goldsmiths, workers, builders.
This is an importantly professional vision of women poets and is one modeled from
the same rhetoric that high modernists were using to advance their professional
standing. "Il miglior fabbro," "the better craftsman," is the single compliment Eliot
chose for Pound in dedicating The Waste Land to him. One also hears echoes of
Lorine Niedecker's Objectivist statement, "Poet's Work"—"No layoff / from this /
condensery"—which borrowed from the same Imagist and post-Imagist stuff that
Wylie had inherited a decade earlier. If Lowell and other high modernist critics
considered Wylie and Millay to be too deliberate, Wylie responded directly in "Jew-
eled Bindings" by showing them that their vigilance—a carefully cultivated disci-
pline—was necessary due to the highly specialized, precarious nature of their work.
Notice that by the end of the essay poetry is no longer being confined or obscured
by "jeweled bindings"; the poet is now inscribing her writing upon them: "the set-
ting of words transparent or opaque in a pattern upon our jeweled bindings." This is
a powerful challenge to the limits that Lowell had tried to impose upon the "femi-
nine movement," which simultaneously produces a provocatively new assemblage.
Wylie's conception of modernist poetry begins with Keats; she binds him tightly
in metal, covers him in jewels and stones, and sets new words, "transparent and
opaque," upon him. Like her high modernist contemporaries, Wylie was therefore
borrowing and utterly reinventing her lyric inheritance, using a diversity of forms,
techniques, and materials. One of her most acclaimed poems, "The Eagle and the
Mole," evokes a similar condition of historical and artistic promiscuity, which, she
suggests, is constitutive of the modernist lyric:

> If in the eagle's track
> Your sinews cannot leap,
> Avoid the lathered pack,
> Turn from the steaming sheep.
>
> If you would keep your soul
> From spotted sight or sound,

Live like the velvet mole;
Go burrow underground.

And there hold intercourse
With roots of trees and stones,
With rivers at their source,
And disembodied bones. (lines 13–24)

"Little-girl Things"

Two years after the publication of Lowell's essay, her reductive reading of the "femi-nine movement" had begun to catch on. As a result, in 1925, Genevieve Taggard issued a formal rejoinder in the feminist periodical *Equal Rights*, in which she defended Millay and her lyric contemporaries against the charge that they were conventional, unambitious poets.[3] Taggard writes,

> Because in the English lady's past her poetry was often like her embroidery, we have an audience now that minimizes this lyricism. In an article a year ago in the *New Republic* Miss Amy Lowell lamented that the new school of poetry, of which Miss Millay is the chief figure, was essentially a feminine and minor affair, claiming for her own the adjectives major and masculine. Subjective poetry for Miss Lowell is, according to the article, always, or usually, minor. (35)

Given Lowell's sophisticated gender and sexual politics, evinced famously in poems such as "The Sisters," "Venus Transiens," and "The Weather-Cock Points South," as well as her advocacy for women poets, this debate with Taggard highlights how aesthetics often cut across political alliances in the 1920s. These essays do not ask whether gender and sexuality should form the stuff of modernist poetry, but rather how that essential material should be given shape. In their discord, these essays productively destabilize the category of "modernist women's poetry" and illustrate the rich variety of aesthetic conversations taking place in modernist periodicals. Recovering this divergent criticism in fact confirms Lowell's insight that "Taking us by and large, we're a queer lot / We women who write poetry" ("The Sisters," lines 1–2).

Taggard identifies within Lowell's logic a categorical devaluation of women's lyric productions. Specifically, she accuses Lowell of domesticating the "feminine movement"—that is, of conflating their poetry with its domestic predecessors. Interestingly, this is the precise move that many critics today continue to make. The poet Amy Clampitt, for instance, sounds virtually indistinguishable from Lowell when she likens Millay's poetry to "the art of the cameo":

> The effects produced by [Millay's poetry] are limited. The bewilderments clutched at and grappled with by [William Carlos] Williams are beyond the ordering of any-

thing so brittle. There is hardly room for ambiguity of thought or feeling—for anything that critical analysis might take hold of or take apart. (46)

Rather than Wylie's complexly layered mode of poetic inscription, Clampitt and Lowell deploy domestic metaphors like embroidery and the cameo to mark the artistic and intellectual limits of this poetry. Taggard notes, for instance, that Lowell only professionalizes the supposedly masculine endeavors of high modern poets. "Their object is science rather than art," Lowell writes, "or perhaps it is fairer to say that to them art is akin to mathematics. They are much intrigued by structure, in a sense quite other than that in which it is usually employed in poetry" (3). Unlike scientists and mathematicians, the labor of the feminine movement is utterly invisible to Lowell—secreted away like the employments of an English lady, trapped in a domestic economy outside the reach of a professional market. Taggard argues, rightly, that this is an antiquated vision of the woman poet. She also claims, presciently, that subjective poetry lies at the heart of the problem.

A decade later, when the New Critics launched their hysterical campaign against Millay, her status as a purely subjective, expressive poet would play a primary role in their collective devaluation. Following Lowell, the New Critics argued repeatedly and convincingly that Millay was a "personal" and, hence, "minor" poet. Prior to their influential misreadings, there was nothing minor about Millay. Along with Lowell, Robert Frost, and Edwin Arlington Robinson, Millay was indisputably one of America's leading poets. This is why she features so prominently within the New Criticism: in order to install Eliot and Pound at the head of "modernism," they had to unseat Millay. Ransom's notorious essay "The Poet as Woman" was in fact occasioned by the publication of Elizabeth Atkins's *Edna St. Vincent Millay and Her Times* (1936). The appearance of this full-length critical study threatened to increase Millay's literary and cultural capital significantly. Ransom thus sets out to limit Millay's sphere of influence, and he does so in a reprehensible manner: by reminding his readers that Millay is not only a poet, but also, more importantly, a woman. "No poet ever registered herself more deliberately in that light," he writes. "She therefore fascinates the male reviewer but at the same time horrifies him a little too" (77). Ransom goes on to argue that Millay's identity as a woman fundamentally limits the value of her poetry: "Miss Millay is rarely and barely very intellectual, and I think everybody knows it" (78).

However, critics who would never conscience Ransom's gender politics often still support his aesthetic assessment of Millay. In the less hysterical portion of his essay, Ransom argues against what was then a common aesthetic equation between Millay and John Donne. Atkins had recently relied on this analogy in her study of Millay, and it provoked Ransom's ire. Donne's metaphysical poetry was, of course, crucial to the modernist and/or New Critical re-conceptualization of form. In the preceding decade, Eliot had popularized the metaphysical poets—Donne, in particular—through his Clark and Trumbull Lectures, delivered at Trinity College, Cambridge University, and Johns Hopkins University, as well as in a series of six broadcasts about seventeenth-century poetry for the BBC.[4]

Millay's close affiliation with Donne thus presented a valuative crisis for the New Critics; they had to disentangle his "serious," "intellectual" poetry from her "little-girl things," as Ransom derisively terms them (82). Millay's poetry emerges in Ransom's influential assessment as a "pretty," "lovely" surface, completely lacking in material substance (82).

Like Ransom, Cleanth Brooks also placed key aesthetic limits on Millay's poetry, which have had lasting implications for her literary reputation. His essay "Miss Millay's Maturity" makes plain the fact that Millay posed a serious aesthetic problem for the New Critics. At the outset, he concedes that her poems "invite and demand criticism as major poetry" (1). It is this and only this—her status as a major poet—that he purports to challenge:

> Miss Millay fails at major poetry—that is, at poetry which makes major predic-
> tions about life. Her distinction lies in a poetry of narrower limits and on a lower
> plane....So successful are these sonnets that the narrowness of their range has
> been somewhat disguised. But the limitations are really very strict. (4)

Brooks equates "major" poetry with a diffuse characteristic he terms "maturity." As he explains, the "failure" of Millay's poetry is "not because she is a woman, and not because she is a love poet. The failure springs from an essential immaturity." "Miss Millay," he continues, "has not grown up" (2).

It is tempting to dismiss such aesthetic accusations as mere rationalizations—simplistic screens for a more primary gender bias. Brooks is, after all, calling Millay a little girl, and Ransom is chiding her for allowing sex to spill provocatively onto the page. But there is an aesthetic method that emerges from this madness. Brooks's charge of "immaturity," for instance, resonates with Freud and his fundamentally passive conception of femininity. According to this patriarchal logic, Millay's love poems could never achieve maturity, because female sexuality itself is considered to be fundamentally stunted.[5] But Brooks's charge is also importantly aesthetic: he is aligning body with poetry, sexuality with form, and claiming that both have failed to develop.

This is in fact why Allen Tate classifies Millay as a poet of "sensibility" rather than "intellect" (121). He condemns her use of "shopworn materials" and argues that a distinctive "personal idiom" is her sole accomplishment: "She has been able to use the vocabulary of the previous generation to convey an emotion peculiar to her own" (120). Tate continues: "Of her it may be said, as of the late Elinor Wylie, that properly speaking she has no style, but has subtly transformed to her use the indefin-able average of poetic English" (123). These personal, regressive qualities supposedly position Millay in stark contrast to high modernism: "Her poetry does not define the break with the nineteenth century. This task was left to the school of Eliot" (120). Despite their myriad insults, the New Critics' winning point, here and through-out their criticism of Millay, is not their devaluation of her poetry, but rather this polarization of the historical field of poetic modernism. The real problem with their formulation is not their devaluation of "sensibility" or "sentimentality," so much as their redeployment of these categories as the perfect counter to a newly legitimated, "intellectual" field of "high modernism." Their thesis and the terms through which it reconstructs the field of poetic modernism, namely as a struggle between Millayan "sentimentality" and Eliotic "modernism," personal versus impersonal poetries, has been profoundly influential. However, when we read the writings of Bogan, Millay, Taggard, and Wylie, we see that they fiercely contested these foundational aesthetic presumptions. Poetic innovation, these women repeatedly insist, does not reside solely within high modernist forms.

In her response to Lowell, Taggard does not argue, as many scholars since the 1920s have done, that subjective poetry is just as good as objective poetry. She does not attempt, in other words, to revalue the feminine movement as a countervailing but equally "major" modernist tradition. Instead, Taggard claims, like Wylie and Millay before her, that the new lyric turn in American poetry isn't subjective at all. In her critique of Lowell, Taggard suggests that the constitution and subsequent consolidation of the "feminine movement" has obscured the objective substance of their lyric poetry. She thus accuses Lowell and likeminded critics of misrecognizing "the driving force behind the whole lyric impulse":

> An eternal feud between centripetal and centrifugal forces sunders and reunites all magical expression. There is one impulse for control and its antagonistic impulse for abandon, one pressing inward, the other exploding at the center. This battle holds the little atom of creative intensity almost quiet because of its balance. If either gain the upper hand entirely, the moment of creation is destroyed. To despise lyric poetry or call it personal—and this, I think, is what many people are doing when they say subjective—is to miss the point of its being uttered at all.
>
> (*Equal Rights*, 35)

In appropriating the "masculine" discourse of science, Taggard forges yet another metaphor for this new lyric tradition. This is not the "soft and opulently luscious" embroidery Lowell suggests, but a new formalism held in the balance between a nineteenth-century subjective tradition ("centripetal forces") and the objective poetics of Imagism and impersonality ("centrifugal forces"). (The word "atom" is, in fact, derived from an ancient Greek word meaning "indivisible" or "incapable of further division.") The new lyric poetry thus represents the essence of both subjective and objective poetries. "A sharp lyric cry," Taggard writes, "may sum up all the slow-moving objective meanings and purposes" (*Equal Rights*, 35).

"Beyond the Will"

Taggard's emphasis on the "lyric cry" is a direct reference to Bogan, whose essay "The Springs of Poetry" had also appeared in the *New Republic* alongside Lowell and Wylie, as well as Vachel Lindsay, Alfred Kreymborg, Witter Bynner, Joseph Auslander, and Archibald MacLeish, all of whom contributed to this landmark modernist issue. In "The Springs of Poetry," Bogan had criticized the "synthetic" poetry

being produced by some of her contemporaries (9). A "synthetic" poem, accord-
ing to Bogan, is a chemically induced objectivity, an artificial method for creating
(or destroying) emotion within the poem. Her description resonates with Eliot's
famously chemical metaphor in "Tradition and the Individual Talent": "The mind of
the mature poet differs from that of the immature one not precisely in any valuation
of 'personality,' not being necessarily more interesting, or having 'more to say,' but
rather by being a more finely perfected medium into which special, or very varied,
feelings are at liberty to enter into new combinations" (40–41). Indeed, Bogan both
conversed with and critiqued Eliot's influential doctrine of impersonality through-
out her career. Like Eliot, Bogan acknowledges that direct, unmediated expression is
neither desirable nor possible—poetry, she says, must always "be the mask, not the
incredible face." However, she also worries that too many of her contemporaries had
begun producing emotionally sterile poetry—poetry like "a veil dropped before a
void" (9). She cites, as a cautionary tale, the example of the contemporary poet

> determined to take a holiday from any emotion at all, being certain that to hear, see,
> smell and touch, merely, is enough. His hand has become chilled, from being held
> too long against the ground to feel how it is cold; his mind flinches at cutting down
> once again into the dark with the knife of irony or analysis.

This "synthetic" poetry, she writes, "may sound . . . in ears uninitiate to the festival, but
never to those, who, having once heard, can recognize again, the maenad cry."

Against "synthetic" poetry, Bogan posits an organic solution, a formal poetic
strategy she terms "reticence." Reticence, she says, is modeled on the silence of the
Old Testament prophets, who spoke infrequently but, when they did, spoke with
tongues of fire. This is a poetics, she explains, "in which passion is made to achieve
its own form, definite and singular," "as though the very mind had a tongue," and
"in which the hazy adverbial quality has no place, built of sentences reduced to the
bones of nouns, verb, and preposition" (9). "This is the further, the test simplic-
ity," Bogan concludes, "the passion of which every poet will always be afraid, but
to which he should vow himself forever" (9). Years later, it was this distinctively
organic formalism that Marianne Moore hailed in Bogan's poetry: "Emotion with
[Bogan], as she has said of certain fiction, is 'itself form, the kernel which builds
outward form from inward intensity'" (61).

Bogan's poem "The Alchemist," which appeared in her 1923 collection, *Body
of This Death*, illustrates the sophistication of her thinking regarding emotion and
poetic form. Although Bogan's theories are not entirely in line with her high mod-
ernist contemporaries, they are certainly not "sentimental" either:

> I burned my life, that I might find
> A passion wholly of the mind,
> Thought divorced from eye and bone,
> Ecstasy come to breath alone.
> I broke my life, to seek relief
> From the flawed light of love and grief.

> With mounting beat the utter fire
> Charred existence and desire.
> It died low, ceased its sudden thresh.
> I had found unmysterious flesh—
> Not the mind's avid substance—still
> Passionate beyond the will. (19)

Bogan is not the first modern poet to have dabbled in the magical science of emotional alchemy. As Diane Middlebrook observes, "The Alchemist" tropes a long line of poetic speakers who embarked on similar quests for spiritual and aesthetic purity, including Shelley's Alastor, Byron's Manfred, Arnold's Scholar Gypsy, and, in a modernist context, William Butler Yeats's speaker in "Sailing to Byzantium" (Middlebrook, 176). "Sick with desire," Yeats's speaker craves the purifying influence of "God's holy fire." "Consume my heart away," he begs, "and gather me / into the artifice of eternity" (lines 17–24). Byzantium thus serves as a metaphor for the spirit's transcendence of the body—that "dying animal" that impedes the speaker's communion with eternity (line 22).

Yeats's spiritual yearning—to transcend a decaying body and a heart that refuses to die—finds its aesthetic complement in Eliot's "Tradition and the Individual Talent." Here, as in "Sailing to Byzantium," the "bodily form" is tempered or purified through an alchemic process; for Yeats, it is the spirit that transcends, and, for Eliot, the mind that "transmutes" a baser, bodily substance. In Eliot's quasi-scientific language, the poet's mind functions as a catalyst, digesting and transmuting the raw stuff of emotion into a new, more "perfect" compound. "The more perfect the artist," Eliot writes, "the more completely separate in him will be the man who suffers and the mind which creates; the more perfectly will the mind digest and transmute the passions which are its material" (41). Eliot's impersonality is not, as it is sometimes mistakenly thought to be, a method for creating an "unemotional" form of poetry. It is, however, a method for intellectualizing the emotions or "passions"—managing them, consciously, through poetic form.

At the outset of "The Alchemist," Bogan's poetic speaker seems to have taken Eliot's advice to heart. "I burned my life," she begins, proudly documenting the lengths to which she was willing to go in pursuit of an impersonal poetics, "a passion wholly of the mind." Yet, rather than a new compound—"the mind's avid substance"— Bogan's alchemy has produced only "unmysterious flesh." By attempting to separate her intellect from her body, to transmute the base material of emotion into a finer substance, the speaker has not only destroyed her life, but also, ironically, discovered that emotion is fundamentally more pure than intellect: "still / Passionate beyond the will."

There is no transcendence to be found in Bogan's poem, only the keen insight that emotions and the body cannot be managed fully by the conscious mind. Notice, for instance, the rhythmic breaks that disrupt the poem's meter in the second stanza. From the heavily stressed tetrameter of lines 7 and 8—a "mounting beat" created by the use of iambs and trochees—the poem moves into the less regular rhythms of "unmysterious" and "passionate," both of which contain dactyls that fundamentally alter the meter of those lines. In this rhythmic shift, Bogan models the unruliness of emotion—a trace of affective or bodily agency that has exceeded the subject's best attempts at formal discipline. In contrast to both Eliot and Yeats, Bogan's alchemy eschews a Western, masculine ideal of the mind, in favor of an embodied formalism. "Expression is molded by feeling," Bogan writes, "as the liquid in a glass is shaped by the glass itself" (*Achievement*, 25).

"A Vehicle of Me"

Sentimentalism, in the sense we typically mean it, cannot account for the distinctiveness of these modernist discourses. It should be clear, even from this limited sampling, that these poets were invested fundamentally in challenging the subjective limits of the traditional lyric. They each sought innovative, objective strategies for formalizing their affective, expressive inheritance. They were also frequently critical of nineteenth-century sentimentalism. Bogan, for instance, mocked the form of romantic effusiveness she playfully called "Ella Wheeler Wilcoxism." "Never shall I give the feminine sonneteers any competition," she insisted (Letter to JHW, 127). Nevertheless, it would be a mistake to believe that these aesthetic criticisms represented a wholesale rejection of nineteenth-century sentimental discourse. In her essay "The Heart and the Lyre," which focuses explicitly on her nineteenth-century female predecessors, Bogan suggests that a "nightingale" tradition might help to remedy the emotional "void" present in contemporary American poetry:

> The great importance of keeping the emotional channels of a literature open has frequently been overlooked. The need of the refreshment and the restitution of feeling, in all its warmth and depth, has never been more apparent than it is today, when cruelty and fright often seem about to overwhelm man and his world. For women to abandon their contact with, and their expression of, deep and powerful emotional streams, because of contemporary pressures or mistaken self-consciousness, would result in an impoverishment not only of their own inner resources but of mankind's at large. Certainly it is not a regression to romanticism to remember that women are capable of perfect and poignant song. (341)

By "keeping the emotional channels" open, Bogan argues for the need to conserve the "warmth and depth" of nineteenth-century sentimental poetry, while simultaneously challenging its aesthetic limits. In the 1930s, she passed these crucial lessons on to Theodore Roethke, her one-time lover and lifelong friend. Early in his poetic career, Bogan warned Roethke not to invest too heavily in form at the expense of emotional expression: "The difficulty with you now, as I see it, is that you are afraid to suffer, or to feel in any way, and that is what you'll have to get over, lamb pie, before you can toss off the masterpieces." A poem "cannot be written by technique alone," she continues. "It is carved out of agony, just as a statue is carved out of marble" (Letter to TR, 130). She advises Roethke to let out a "lyric cry," one that would be "heart-rendering" (131).

The model for this newly hybridized aesthetics, which would later be embraced by "confessional" poets like Roethke, Robert Lowell, and Sylvia Plath, is undoubtedly Millay. Even more than Wylie, Taggard, or Bogan, Millay embodied—quite literally, as we will see—the reformed emotions of nineteenth-century lyric poetry. By the mid-1920s, Millay was one of the most well-regarded and highly visible poets in America. Writing in 1924, Taggard asks, "Can there be any doubt that two hundred years hence (unless the language is Chinese, and even then perhaps in translation) old men and children, young men and maidens will be repeating [Millay's poem] *God's World*?" ("Classics," 620–621). Taggard, in particular, considered Millay to be the most important poet of her generation, calling her "the first woman poet to take herself seriously as an artist" (*Equal Rights*, 137). If we can forgive Taggard's historical shortsightedness—surely, Millay was not the *first* such woman poet—her case for the "seriousness" of Millay's poetry proves to be remarkably sophisticated.

Since the nineteenth century, Taggard writes, "Women have borne poets and evoked poetry, but how few of them have written it! And for the simplest possible reason. We are coming to know that you cannot separate the creative fiber" (*Equal Rights*, 137). Taggard had addressed the theme of women's "creative fiber" before, notably in her poem "With Child," which appeared in *The Liberator* in December 1921, and then in *For Eager Lovers* in 1922:

> Now I am slow and placid, fond of sun,
> Like a sleek beast, or a worn one,
> No slim and languid girl—not glad
> With the windy trip I once had,
> But velvet-footed, musing of my own,
> Torpid, mellow, stupid as a stone.
>
> You cleft me with your beauty's pulse, and now
> Your pulse has taken body. Care not how
> The old grace goes, how heavy I am grown,
> Big with this loneliness, how you alone
> Ponder our love. Touch my feet and feel
> How earth tingles, teeming at my heel!
> Earth's urge, not mine, —my little death, not hers;
> And the pure beauty yearns and stirs. (lines 1–14)

Taggard's speaker is profoundly divided by her pregnancy: "You cleft me with your beauty's pulse, and now / Your pulse has taken body" (lines 7–8). She is at once compelled toward this new "beauty" and, at the same time, haunted by the "old grace" that has been "taken" from her (line 9). She refers to the pregnancy as "Earth's urge, not mine," a testament to the complexity of her desires, which are not entirely her own (line 13). Moreover, the poem persistently conflates the unborn child and "beauty"—

reproduction and aesthetic production. The use of the objective pronoun "it" in the poem's final stanza makes this ambiguity complete:

> It does not heed our ecstasies, it turns
> With secrets of its own, its own concerns,
> Toward a windy world of its own, toward stark
> And solitary places. In the dark,
> Defiant even now, it tugs and moans
> To be untangled from these mother's bones. (lines 15–20)

"With Child" is a remarkable poem, written on the eve of women's suffrage, and, yet, it is marked still by the ambivalence of freedom—or, at least, its incompleteness. Read literally, the poem documents the experience of pregnancy from the viewpoint of a decidedly modern woman. A woman, that is, like Taggard herself—a feminist, suffragist, and "free love" advocate—confronted, suddenly, with the necessity of ceding control of her body. Or, perhaps, what is so haunting about the poem is that the speaker seems to realize that that control was always already ceded. Read figuratively, as a meta-poem reflecting on the creative process, these complexities redouble. This is no one's muse, but a woman artist, "musing of my own" (line 5). At the same time, she is "cleft" by text—her "own" agency interrupted by the secret life of an artistic object, struggling to be born.[6]

In her reading of Millay's poetry, Taggard identifies a similar entanglement of women's bodies and creative labors, as in this stanza that she cites from Millay's poem "The Poet and His Book":

> Women at your toil,
> Women at your leisure
> Till the kettle boil,
> Snatch of me your pleasure,
> Where the broom straw marks the leaf;
> Women quiet with your weeping
> Lest you wake a workman sleeping,
> Mix me with your grief! (lines 89–96)

The stanza confirms the two poets' shared investment in the corporealization of women's writing. When Millay commands her female audience to "Mix me with your grief!" there is no distance separating the poem from the poet's body—"it" from "me"—just as with Taggard's "defiant" beauty, coming "untangled from these mother's bones."

As a whole, "The Poet and His Book" addresses the proto-Shakespearean question of poetic immortality. Faced with "personal death," the decaying of her mortal body, Millay's speaker wants to live on in the pages of her books: "From the dust of ages / Lift this little book, / Turn the tattered pages, / Read me, do not let me die!" (lines 42–45). As the poem progresses, her imperative, "Read me," takes on a decidedly sexual charge:

> Bear me to the light,
> Flat upon your bellies
> By the webby window lie,
> Where the little flies are crawling,
> Read me, margin me with scrawling,
> Do not let me die! (lines 107–112)

Millay's use of the verb "margin" forges an explicit intimacy between the physical body and the physical text. "Margin me with scrawling" evokes a sexual fantasy of "scrawling" on the female poet's body, while also conjuring the expressive myth of having a real-life poet living in the margins of the page. This is not Shakespeare's metonymic immortality—where language safely stands in for the poet's body. Millay is attempting to reconceive poetic form as an even more intimately embodied form—what she refers to as "a vehicle of me" (line 88).

This is not the naïve romanticism that the New Critics and many subsequent scholars have presumed. As Taggard suggests, the gendered body represents a complex material through which Millay manipulates the expressive and auto-biographical conventions of the traditional lyric. Like Wylie, Millay plays with "pretty" surfaces—in this case, beauty and body—to challenge the superficiality typically associated with this feminine stuff. "Beauty is not enough," she famously declares at the outset of *Second April*, and, yet, ironically, she continues to draw upon her own beauty as a source of aesthetic innovation throughout her poetry ("Spring," 1). Even her most seemingly flippant, "light" verse participates in this mode of lyric experimentation. Consider, for instance, her wildly popular "First Fig": "My candle burns at both ends; / It will not last the night; / But ah, my foes, and oh, my friends— / It gives a lovely light." The poem has typically been read as an emblem of the bohemian ethos that dominated Greenwich Village in the late teens and early twenties. While this is undoubtedly true, the proem—which arrives on the opening page of Millay's landmark volume, *A Few Figs from Thistles*—also performs an important meta-poetic function. As we are dazzled by that brilliant, double-burning candle—a powerful metaphor for Millay's body—the speaker addresses us directly, "Ah, my foes, and oh, my friends," and commands us to watch: "It gives a lovely light!" We are positioned explicitly as voyeurs rather than readers, by a coy speaker who seems to revel in that objectification. Moreover, unlike the solitary, expressive conceit of writing by candlelight, this spectacular mode of poetic production can be witnessed and enjoyed by all.

This power dynamic, in which a visually arresting speaker captivates her audience and manipulates our desire to watch and follow, develops across Millay's poetry into a formal aesthetic logic. We see it, for instance, in some of her most famous sonnets. In "[Oh, oh, you will be sorry for that word!]," the speaker protests against the gendered insult "'What a big book for such a little head!'" "Give back my book and take my kiss instead," she calmly proffers:

> Come, I will show you my newest hat,
> And you may watch me purse my mouth and prink!
> Oh, I shall love you still, and all of that.
> I never again shall tell you what I think.
> I shall be sweet and crafty, soft and sly;
> You will not catch me reading any more:
> I shall be called a wife to pattern by (lines 5–11)

A "sentimental modernism" can help us identify what is importantly familiar within this poem. Politically, it participates in a long line of "sweet and crafty" domestic protests. Like many of her nineteenth-century predecessors, the female speaker locates a subversive space within the confines of marriage, which enables her to assert her intellectual and political independence. But there is also important formal work happening within this poem. When the speaker says of her husband that she will love him "still," she means that she will immobilize him through her performance of femininity: "And some day when you knock and push the door, / Some sane day, not too bright and not too stormy, / I shall be gone, and you may whistle for me" (lines 12–14). In the poem's final lines, it is the husband who is trapped within a cloistered domestic space—watching, waiting, and whistling—while the female speaker has moved on and out. This is politically progressive, but it is also a powerful demonstration of the female poet's ability to push beyond the domestic confines of the conventional lyric.

Borrowing from Wylie's "gold and silver trickery," we might call this postsentimental aesthetic strategy "enchantment." While there is, at first glance, much that is familiar about it—Romantic and sentimental tropes, inherited forms like the sonnet, "a wife to pattern by"—it is, as Millay said of Wylie's poetry, not made of the "usual material." What I have begun to chart textually, in just a few, representative instances, develops throughout Millay's poetry and also well beyond it. For Millay was not only one of the twentieth century's most celebrated poets, but also among its most dynamic performers. In recent years, critics have begun to attach new significance to this long-neglected archive of extra-textual material that once surrounded her poetry. Derek Furr, for instance, has studied recordings of Millay's popular poetry broadcasts to argue for their significance in the history of American radio; Lesley Wheeler has similarly claimed that Millay's poetry readings, which drew huge audiences throughout the twenties, revolutionized the technology of poetry performance. In Furr and Wheeler's compelling visions, Millay sets the stage for a century of newly mediated lyric experiments, in which sound and body, listening and watching, would push poetry beyond the page. The only danger inherent in these otherwise sophisticated readings is that they might, paradoxically, ossify Millay's reputation as a conventional poet. The New Critics, for instance, were fully acquainted with Millay's media power: they dismissed it, claiming that she used photographs and performances, beauty and body, to prop up an otherwise weak aesthetic. Following Wylie, Taggard, and Bogan, I am arguing that the same strategies Millay used to motivate cultural and political change formed the basis of her poetic innovations. Just as she challenged conventional gender politics, so too did she seek to open the traditionally closed lyric form. As Taggard rightly suggests, a complex play of beauty and body distinguishes Millay's poetry fundamentally from the subjective, expressive lyrics of the past. Although she borrows from an American sentimental tradition, her new mode of poetic "enchantment" also takes sentimentality as its target. Knowing that her sophisticated modernist readers expected intimacy, Millay delivered that sentimental illusion. "My heart is what it was before," she writes. "A house where people come and go" ("Alms," lines 1–2).

"Home-made Critics"

If it seems difficult to place Wylie's, Taggard's, Bogan's, and Millay's theories, it is because we have become so accustomed to our impoverished landscape of modernist poetics. To high modernists like Lowell and, later, the New Critics, a poet was either "modernist" or, well, nothing. However, in the early twenties, American poetry was a capacious, unruly field of debate and experimentation, characterized by a diversity of aesthetic theories. These influential women poets borrowed heavily from the emotional language of the nineteenth century—as well as an ancient tradition of the lyric—to criticize the new poetries being forged in the twentieth century. They spoke, moreover, with authority: they were not only successful poets but were also editors and critics affiliated with respected literary journals and magazines. Bogan, for instance, served as the poetry reviewer at the *New Yorker* for thirty-eight years. Across a critical career spanning nearly a half-century, Bogan published more than three hundred reviews in the *New Yorker* alone, while also contributing frequently to a host of other journals and magazines, including the *Nation*, *Partisan Review*, and *Poetry*. In 1951, Bogan also published a book-length study, *Achievement in American Poetry, 1900–1950*, which departs importantly from the dominant New Critical methodology of its age. "The Springs of Poetry" was merely the first in a long line of critical and theoretical publications, which demand far greater scholarly attention than they have yet to receive.

In the early 1920s, Bogan, Taggard, and Wylie began their critical careers by serving on the editorial board of *Measure* (1921–1926), a now largely forgotten little magazine that Taggard helped to found along with Maxwell Anderson as a formal corrective to high modern and avant-garde poetics. In their inaugural issue, Anderson announced that modern poetry was becoming too "minor." To fight that trend, *Measure* would favor "musical and rounded forms" over "half-said, half-conceived whimsicalities," "impassioned utterances" over the merely "suggestive" or "telegraphic" ("Thunder," 23). Its opening essay focused exclusively on Millay, whom it termed "the most interesting person in American poetry"—a noteworthy, early accolade for the poet still awaiting celebrity (Hill, "Edna," 25). Reading *Measure*, one realizes not only that a lyric tradition competed alongside high modernism in

America, but also that this alternative group of poets maintained a fierce allegiance to an entirely disparate poetic legacy extending from the nineteenth century through to the 1920s. It is not at all surprising that Bogan, Millay, Taggard, and Wylie should have chosen to align themselves with *Measure*, because its artistic philosophies read much like their own. Their tenure at the journal also indicates that there was a much broader community of writers and publishing professionals who shared their fundamental distrust of high modernism.

The New Critics did not simply devalue the lyric productions of these modernist women poets. Beginning in the mid-1930s, they sealed them off fundamentally from the newly professionalized space of the literary academy. They did so, in large part, by inserting a wedge between "literary criticism" and the critical and theoretical writing being produced outside the academy in popular journals and magazines. For instance, in his seminal 1938 essay "Criticism, Inc.," Ransom mocks what he calls "home-made critics": "Naturally, they are not too wise, these amateurs who furnish our reviews and critical studies" (337). Criticism, he writes, "must be developed by the collective and sustained efforts of learned persons—which means that its proper seat is in the universities" (329). This consolidation of criticism in the academy may not have been motivated exclusively or even primarily by gender bias, but it had profoundly gendered ramifications. As we have seen, the popular periodicals of the 1920s provided women with opportunities to publish creative writing and to participate actively in the production of critical discourse, which would be unmatched in the literary academy for at least a generation. When the New Critics professionalized literary criticism, they simultaneously deprofessionalized a rich critical and aesthetic discourse produced by women poets in the modernist era. When we followed the New Critics and left Bogan, Millay, Taggard, and Wylie behind, we lost a canon of once prominent modernist poets. But this canonical thinning, however significant, is only one aspect of our impoverishment. More fundamentally, I am arguing, we lost an aesthetic method—a set of theories, values, and strategies for reading that arose from within that poetry, that made sense and meaning out of it. We lost, in other words, its poetics.

NOTES

1   Domesticity and sentimentality are not necessarily coextensive with one another, although they are deeply and complexly entangled. For an excellent examination of these critical issues, see June Howard, "What Is Sentimentality?" *American Literary History* 11.1(Spring 1999): 63–81. In Clark and Walker's work, sentimentality is often used as a synonym for domesticity, a characterization I contest in my readings of Millay's poetry. Howard's work is important because it highlights the contested, variable nature of sentimentality across the eighteenth and nineteenth centuries and beyond. Following Howard, many scholars of sentimentality have embraced a more flexible historical and cultural frame. Paula Bernat Bennett, for instance, charts a remarkably diverse aesthetic and political field of sentimentality in *Poets in the Public Sphere: The Emancipatory*

Project of American Women's Poetry, 1800–1900 (Princeton: Princeton University Press, 2003); as do Glenn Hendler and Mary Chapman, eds., in Sentimental Men: Masculinity and the Politics of Affect in American Culture (Berkley: University of California Press, 1999), and Michael Bell in Sentimentalism, Ethics, and the Culture of Feeling (New York: Palgrave, 2000), which productively distinguishes continental varieties of sentimentality from their American counterparts. I want to mark the significance of this scholarship and my own support for a more elastic conception of sentimentality. It is the rigidity of our current paradigm for reading modernist women's poetry—be it "feminine," "sentimental," or "domestic"—that I will challenge.

2   One can hope that two recent publications by Evelyn Helmick Hively, the critical biography, A Private Madness: The Genius of Elinor Wylie (Kent, OH: Kent State University Press, 2003), and the accompanying anthology, Selected Works of Elinor Wylie (Kent, OH: Kent State University Press, 2005), can begin to remedy this shocking neglect.

3   Equal Rights was published by the National Woman's Party (NWP), of which Millay was a member. See J. Stanley Lemons, The Woman Citizen: Social Feminism in the 1920s (Urbana: University of Illinois Press, 1973) 183. As Lemons explains, the NWP was among the era's most radical feminist organizations: "From its inception, the National Woman's Party attracted women who were impatient with piecemeal, compromise approaches" (183). Founded by Alice Paul, the NWP focused exclusively on suffrage campaigns in its early years. Later, they applied "the same intense energy" to the pursuit of an equal rights amendment (183).

4   These lectures are collected in T. S. Eliot, The Varieties of Metaphysical Poetry, ed. Ronald Schuchard (San Diego: Harvest Books, 1993).

5   The psychosexual dimensions of Brooks's critique form the basis of Suzanne Clark's re-reading of Millay in Chapter 3 of Sentimental Modernism. Via the feminist psychoanalysis of Teresa de Lauretis, Julia Kristeva, Hélène Cixous, and Luce Irigaray, Clark restores to Millay's texts a play of desire and jouissance—a distinctly "grown-up" form of pleasure, grounded in a "mature" female subjectivity. Despite the de-aestheticization that I have identified in Sentimental Modernism, this reading is an excellent example of how politically generative Clark's work has been and will continue to be.

6   For extended treatments of Taggard's complex feminism, see Nina Miller, Making Love Modern (New York: Oxford University Press, 1998), which devotes two chapters to Taggard, and Nancy Berke, Women Poets on the Left: Lola Ridge, Genevieve Taggard, Margaret Walker (Gainesville: University Press of Florida, 2001). Berke, it is worth noting, frequently highlights Taggard's radical politics as a means of distancing her from "sentimental" poets such as Millay and Teasdale. While it is true that Taggard's poetry became increasingly political in the 1930s, eliding her connections to this earlier tradition diminishes the complexity of her (and their) poetics.

REFERENCES

Anderson, Maxwell. "Thunder in the Index." Measure: A Journal of Poetry (March 1921): 23–25.

Atkins, Elizabeth. Edna St. Vincent Millay and Her Times. Chicago: University of Chicago Press, 1936.

Berlant, Lauren. The Female Complaint: The Unfinished Business of Sentimentality in American Culture. Durham, NC: Duke University Press, 2008.

Bogan, Louise. *Achievement in American Poetry, 1900–1950.* Chicago: Henry Regnery
    Company: 1951.
——. "The Alchemist." In *Body of This Death.* New York: R. M. McBride, 1923. 19.
——. "The Heart and the Lyre." *A Poet's Prose: Selected Writings of Louise Bogan.* Ed. Mary
    Kinzie. 1947; Athens, OH: Ohio University Press, 2005. 335–342.
——. Letter to John Hall Wheelock. 1 July 1935. In *A Poet's Prose: Selected Writings of
    Louise Bogan.* Ed. Mary Kinzie. 1947; Athens, OH: Ohio University Press, 2005.
    126–127.
——. Letter to Theodore Roethke. 23 August 1935. In *A Poet's Prose: Selected Writings
    of Louise Bogan.* Ed. Mary Kinzie. 1947; Athens, OH: Ohio University Press, 2005.
    130–131.
——. "The Springs of Poetry." *New Republic* 37 (5 December 1923): suppl. 9.
Bernstein, Charles. *A Poetics.* Cambridge: Harvard University Press, 1992.
Brooks, Cleanth. "Miss Millay's Maturity." Book Review Section, *Southwest Review* 20.2
    (January 1935): 1–5.
Clampitt, Amy. "Two Cheers for Prettiness." *New Republic* 106.1–2 (6–13 January 1992):
    44–46.
Clark, Suzanne. *Sentimental Modernism: Women Writers and the Revolution of the Word.*
    Bloomington: Indiana University Press, 1991.
——. "Sentimental Modernism." In *Gender in Modernism: New Geographies, Complex
    Intersections.* Ed. Bonnie Kime Scott. Urbana: University of Illinois Press, 2007.
    125–159.
Elfenbein, Anna Shannon, and Terence Allan Hoagland. "'Wild Peaches': Landscapes of
    Desire and Deprivation." *Women's Studies* 15 (1988): 387–397.
Eliot, T. S. "Tradition and the Individual Talent." In *Selected Prose of T.S. Eliot,* ed. Frank
    Kermode. 1919; San Diego: Harvest Book, 1975. 45–49.
Furr, Derek. "Listening to Millay." *Journal of Modern Literature* 29.2 (Winter 2006): 94–110.
Hill, Frank Ernest. "Edna St. Vincent Millay." *Measure: A Journal of Poetry* (March 1921):
    25–26.
Jackson, Virginia. *Dickinson's Misery: A Theory of Lyric Reading.* Princeton: Princeton
    University Press, 2005.
Locke, Alain. *An Autumn Love Cycle.* By Georgia Douglas Johnson. 1928. In *Selected Works
    of Georgia Douglas Johnson.* New York: G. K. Hall & Co., 1997. 193–197.
Lowell, Amy. "The Sisters." In *The Complete Poetical Works of Amy Lowell.* Boston:
    Houghton Mifflin, 1955. 459–461.
——. "Two Generations in American Poetry." *New Republic* 37 (5 December 1923):
    suppl. 1–3.
Middlebrook, Diane. "The Problem of the Woman Artist: Louise Bogan, 'The Alchemist.'"
    In *Critical Essays on Louise Bogan.* Ed. Martha Collins. Boston: G. K. Hall & Co., 1984.
    174–180.
Millay, Edna St. Vincent. "Alms." In *Second April.* New York: Harper & Brothers, 1921. 36.
——. "First Fig." In *A Few Figs from Thistles.* New York: Harper & Brothers, 1922. 1.
——. "[Oh, oh, you will be sorry for that word!]." In *The Harp-Weaver and Other Poems.*
    New York: Harper and Brothers, 1923. 60.
——. "The Poet and His Book." In *Second April.* New York: Harper & Brothers, 1921. 30–35.
——. "Review of *Nets to Catch the Wind* by Elinor Wylie." *The Literary Review, New York
    Evening Post* (28 January 1922): 379.
——. "Spring." In *Second April.* New York: Harper & Brothers, 1921. 1.

Moore, Marianne. "Compactness Compacted." 1941; In *Critical Essays on Louise Bogan*. Ed. Martha Collins. Boston: G. K. Hall & Co., 1984. 61–63.

Niedecker, Lorine. "Poet's Work." In *The Selected Poems of Lorine Niedecker*. Ed. Cid Corman. Frankfort, KY: Gnomon Press, 1996. 60.

Ransom, John Crowe. "Criticism, Inc." In *The World's Body*. New York: Charles Scribner's Sons, 1938. 327–350.

———. "The Poet as Woman." In *The World's Body*. New York: Charles Scribner's Sons, 1938. 76–110.

Sedgwick, Eve Kosofsky. *Epistemology of the Closet*. Berkeley: University of California Press, 1990.

Taggard, Genevieve. "Classics of the Future." *American Review* 2 (1924): 620–630.

———. "Review of Edna St. Vincent Millay." *Equal Rights* (14 March 1925): 35.

———. *For Eager Lovers*. New York: Thomas Seltzer. 1922.

Tate, Allen. "Miss Millay's Sonnets: A Review of *Fatal Interview* by Edna St. Vincent Millay." *New Republic* (6 May 1931): 335–336. Rpt. in *The Poetry Reviews of Allen Tate, 1924–1944*, ed. Ashley Brown and Frances Neel Cheney (Baton Rouge: Louisiana State University Press, 1983): 119–123.

Walker, Cheryl. *Masks Outrageous and Austere: Culture, Psyche, and Persona in Modern Women Poets*. Bloomington: Indiana University Press, 1991.

Wheeler, Lesley. *Voicing American Poetry: Sound and Performance from the 1920s to the Present*. Ithaca: Cornell University Press, 2008.

Wright, Celeste Turner. "Elinor Wylie: The Glass Chimaera and the Minotaur." *Women's Studies* 7 (1980): 159–170.

Wylie, Elinor. "The Eagle and the Mole." In *Nets to Catch the Wind*. New York: Harcourt Brace and Company, 1921. 4–5.

———. "Jeweled Bindings." *New Republic* 37 (5 December 1923): suppl. 14.

———. "Unfinished Portrait." In *Black Armour: A Book of Poems*. New York: George H. Doran Company, 1923. 58.

Yeats, William Butler. "Sailing to Byzantium." In *The Collected Poems of W.B. Yeats*. Ed. Richard J. Finneran. New York: Scribner Paperback Poetry, 1996. 193–194.

CHAPTER 5

HIRED MEN AND HIRED WOMEN: MODERN AMERICAN POETRY AND THE LABOR PROBLEM

JOHN MARSH

In March 2002, Larry J. Griffin and Maria Tempenis published the results of a study of articles that appeared in the leading American studies journal *American Quarterly* over the past fifty-year period (1949–1999). They concluded that gender and multicultural approaches to the field of American studies had not, as some critics had charged, displaced class analysis.[1] That is not because gender and multicultural approaches now merrily shared space with class analysis but, rather, because class analysis had never been present and therefore could not be displaced. As Griffin and Tempenis observed, "American studies…has never much 'done' class," and "class…has never really had its 'particular moment' in the field" (93). Their conclusion echoed many other complaints about American literary criticism and its aversion to class analyses. As Paul Lauter and Ann Fitzgerald (among others) have noted, often in similar language, "class remains the unaddressed member of that now-famous trio, 'race, gender, class'" (*Literature*, 2).

While those complaints may have once had merit, they have grown weaker with each conference and publishing season. In the last decade, class *has* begun to have, if not its particular moment in the field, nevertheless *a* moment in the field, as evidenced by numerous panels, conferences, books, and even book series. For the most part, however, that class moment has been strictly a prose moment; poetry, to put it another way, has not had its moment within that class moment. Today, whole books that promise class-devoted re-readings of American literary history usually go by without a line of verse examined.[2] While these critical interventions have offered invaluable insight into how questions of class have informed literature and vice versa, they have done a mostly dreadful job of incorporating poetry into their literary histories.[3]

The problem, then, may no longer be that Americanists shy away from class but, rather, that class-conscious Americanists shy away from poetry.

As with most everything else that scholars regret about the discipline, this continuing critical predilection for prose (or indifference to poetry) can be laid at the steps of the New Critics. Under their tutelage, Joseph Harrington argues, "poetry constituted the most autonomous form of literature, an alternative to the public, the popular, and the mass" (504). That reputation for autonomy, however, did not endear poetry to a discipline newly committed to cultivating the historical contexts of works. Rather than reject or revise the supposed autonomy of poetry, however, critics, speaking very broadly, tended to grant it and turn instead to other, supposedly more historicized genres, namely prose. In short, as Harrington summarizes the conventional critical wisdom, "we go to novels to find historical reality because novelists represent historical reality" (509), and we go to poetry, as the New Critics bid us to, to escape history. The result casts "prose narrative as the bearer of historical value…and poetry as the repository of aesthetic value" (509).[4] And while the scholarly wisdom has changed since Harrington's article, and (obviously) much historicizing poetry criticism has appeared, scholars of modern American poetry still live with the legacy and the gaps of this critical sensibility.

One of the largest of those gaps is modern American poetry and its relationship to what, beginning in the late 1870s and continuing through the 1930s, a generation of writers, reformers, and economists almost invariably referred to as "the labor problem." By the labor problem, these writers meant more than just the infamous strikes and labor violence that occurred during this period. Instead, the labor problem included, as one 1914 textbook outlined it, the "evils and abuses" of woman and child labor, immigration, sweatshops, poverty, and unemployment, to name but the most prominent (Adams and Sumner, 3). Nevertheless, the periodic violence of strikes, more than the background noise of poverty or other problems, gave the labor problem its urgency, especially when, beginning in 1909, it seemed like those strikes would become a permanent rather than periodic phenomenon. (The best known of these—in Lawrence, Paterson, and Ludlow—have acquired iconic status, although they represent the tip of the labor violence iceberg.)[5] "We live in a revolutionary period," the journalist Walter Lippmann wrote in the aftermath of the Lawrence textile strike of 1914, "and nothing is so important as to be aware of it" (317). Nor did industrial unrest—and its underpinning labor problems—cease in the years to come. If anything, workers grew even more restless, until, in the period just before and after World War I, the number of strikes and workers participating in them rivaled the more famously turbulent years of the 1930s.[6] Specifically, the period from 1912 to 1922—the decade of the birth of modern American poetry—coincided with what has been called "one of the most tumultuous periods of labor conflict in American history" (Stromquist, 168).

Yet to judge from most histories of modern American poetry, it would seem that, disappointing Lippmann, modern American poets, with the exception of some forgotten left-wing and proto-proletarian poets, remained decidedly unaware of this "revolutionary period." A closer look, though, reveals that modern American poets were keenly aware of the labor problem and, perhaps even more so, the laborers and working poor who constituted it. In fact, before and after World War I, the poets who incorporated the poor and working class into their verse read like a who's who of canonical modernism. Supposedly, Ezra Pound's first published poem (titled "Ezra and the Strike") adopted the persona of a farmer praising then-President Theodore Roosevelt for settling a coal miner's strike (Stock, 34–35). T. S. Eliot's first poem to appear in Harriet Monroe's *Poetry* ("Morning at the Window") claimed to be "aware" of cooks "rattling breakfast plates in basement kitchens" (1) and offered the arresting image of a working girl moving through the early-morning city streets. Among Wallace Stevens's early poems is one entitled "A Window in the Slums." In "Episode of Hands," Hart Crane recounts the binding of a factory worker's injured hand. William Carlos Williams's first poem in *Poetry* pretended to be the song of a Sicilian emigrant upon arriving in the United States; Williams would later write of the Paterson silk strike of 1913 and, repeatedly, about the poor and working class, who were also, of course, Dr. Williams's patients. Most of Carl Sandburg's first volume of poetry, *Chicago Poems* (1916), is devoted to documenting the city's labor problem: poverty, unemployment, vampire-like factories—one poem even purports to be an interview (over dinner, no less) with a dreaded dynamiter. Some of Robert Frost's earliest unpublished poems depict his brief stints working in and living near New England textile mills; he would later write about isolated and overworked farmers' wives and hired laborers. Even Edna St. Vincent Millay's infamous early poem, "Recuerdo," ends with its bohemian merry ferry-goers giving away all their money to an old beggar. And Langston Hughes, Claude McKay, and other Harlem Renaissance poets would compose dozens of poems about waiters, busboys, elevator operators, porters, servants, cabaret dancers, and other Harlem service workers.

As this brief survey attests, when many modern American poets began writing poems, they began by writing about the poor and working class. Indeed, at its foundational moment in the early twentieth century, modern American poetry, like the rest of the culture at large, was haunted by the labor problem. Despite all the recent work done in the field of new modernism and modern American poetry, however, this history of modern poetry and the labor problem has gone untold.

But why the history has gone untold matters less than the history itself. So what might a class-conscious approach to modern American poetry, especially canonical modern American poetry, look like? In what follows, I offer readings of two of the mostly frequently anthologized poems in the modern American poetry canon: Robert Frost's "The Death of the Hired Man" and T. S. Eliot's "Preludes." Each can suggest the integral but long-neglected role that the labor problem and those who lived it—that is, the poor and working class—would play in the formation of canonical modern American poetry. Although they confront vastly different labor problems—hired laborers versus urban slums and prostitutes—both poems nevertheless wrestle with the claims such problems (and the human figures behind such problems) should make upon observers' sympathies.

Hired Men

In his 1858 essay "Farming," Ralph Waldo Emerson extols the independence made possible by farming, whether independence from the ravages of poverty or independence from political corruption. Like Thomas Jefferson before him, Emerson praises farming because it is largely self-reliant work; it does not require the presence of, as Jefferson might have put it, morally dubious, politically corrupting laborers.[7] "Who are the farmer's servants?" Emerson asks. "Not the Irish, nor the coolies, but Geology and Chemistry, the quarry of the air, the water of the brook, the lightning of the cloud, the castings of the warm, the plough of the frost" (676). "The earth works for him," Emerson adds, "the earth is a machine which yields gratuitous service to every application of intellect" (676). Thus served by nature and not workers, farmers—and a nation of farmers—need not depend on dangerous, foreign labor.

Unlike how Emerson imagined it, though, farmers, especially those who grew large crops for a market, could not rely on geology and chemistry to do all of their work. Occasionally, as Emerson put it, the Irish or coolies (or other workers) had to be employed. In fact, even as Emerson was writing, and even more so in the decades that followed, farmers typically hired outside labor, either for the whole year or, more commonly, during the harvest season when crops needed to be gathered in a fairly short window of time.

On the surface, these hired workers posed a crisis for the supposed independence of farmers. On the one hand, farmers depended on their labor, and on the other, hired laborers worked at the whim of and for the wages of those farmers. Originally, however, these mutual dependencies did not entail any lasting sacrifice of independence. Rather, seasonal workers and hired laborers were supposed to be merely pausing on what was called "the agricultural ladder." Just starting out, many young men could not afford to buy a farm—or did not have a father who could give them land—and therefore they had to hire themselves out for a couple of seasons or years until they had earned enough to buy their own. As no less a figure than Abraham Lincoln put it, "Many independent men everywhere in these states, a few years back in their lives, were hired laborers. The prudent, penniless beginner in the world, labors for wages awhile, saves a surplus with which to buy tools or land for himself; then labors on his own account another while, and at length hires another new beginner to help him" (296–297). In other words, farmers were not exploiting desperate workers. Instead, they were giving others a hand up. Meanwhile, hired laborers were not the wage slaves of tyrannical landowners but were climbing the ladder to economic independence. Or so the story went.

So long as farm land was relatively affordable and remunerative, the agricultural ladder Lincoln celebrated held steady. Yet the industrialization of agriculture in the late nineteenth and early twentieth centuries would change everything. That transformation had several effects. First, it shifted production from small-scale, diversified farming in the East to large-scale, specialized farming in the West. Second, because of the increase in scale and specialization, there followed an increased demand for hired farm labor across the country, but especially in the East, for reasons detailed below. Third, the industrialization of agriculture created a permanent class of hired men—the agricultural proletariat—whose presence threatened to turn the farm from a site of independence and apprenticeship independence into a site of dependence, wage labor, and exploitation.

The industrialization of agriculture, however, had specific effects for farming in the northeast. Because of increased competition out West, many New England farmers either had to scale up or, more commonly, simply abandon farming altogether. As the Connecticut Board of Agriculture put it in 1890, "The New England farmer has found his products selling at lower prices because of the new, fierce, and rapidly increasing competition. One by one he has had to abandon the growing of this or that crop because the West crowded him beyond the paying point" (qtd. in Shannon, 246). "In the East, particularly," the agrarian Bolton Hall observed in 1907, "the competition of Western lands, aided by discriminating freight rates, now so notorious, has resulted in the abandonment to the mortgage of vast areas in New York, Connecticut, New Hampshire, Maine, and to some extent New Jersey" (20). In Maine in 1890, for example, nearly 3,400 farms had been abandoned. And in order to attract would-be farmers, nearly every New England state published, as Massachusetts titled theirs, *A Descriptive List of Farms…Abandoned or Partially Abandoned* (Hahamovich, 20).

One of the most pernicious effects of farmers abandoning their farms was that it decreased the supply of seasonal labor needed by those who remained on their land. Because other farmers and the sons of other farmers frequently supplied that seasonal labor force, fewer farmers meant fewer potential laborers. "What was lost," Cindy Hahamovich observes, "was a rural population available for temporary employment" (28). As the *Report of the Commission on Country Life* put it in 1911, "There is a general, but not a universal, complaint of scarcity of farm labor" (91). Less qualifiedly, the authors of the volume asserted that "there is not sufficient good labor available in the country to enable us to farm our lands under present systems of agriculture and to develop our institutions effectively" (93). "The man whom I engaged to begin work today has not come," the Back-to-the-Land farmer Alice Dinsmoor noted in her diary for March 9, 1908. On March 12, she wrote, "In city to find man for outside work; woman for indoor. Engaged two—brought woman with me. Man promised to come, but didn't" (61).

The scarcity—the disappearance, nonappearance, and, to be sure, sudden reappearance—of farm labor is the context for one of Robert Frost's most frequently reprinted poems, "The Death of the Hired Man," yet it is a context that, so far as I know, has received relatively little commentary. The poem has more often than not been read as a contest between masculine and feminine ethics, between justice and mercy, with various critics applauding or regretting its supposed sentimental-ism. It certainly is all those things, yet the poem also demonstrates how much the origins of modern American poetry lie in its borrowings from contemporary labor problems, in this case, the industrialization of agriculture and the agricultural pro-letariat it gave birth to. As such, one must pay as much attention to the background incident of the poem—the broken contract between Warren and Silas—as to the debate between Warren and Mary about the definition of home and what, as a result, they owe their hired labor. According to this way of reading the poem, the dialogue between Warren and Mary is not only (or even primarily) one between two types of people, two models of human character. Rather, it is a dialogue about changing economic conditions and how to respond to them.

As the poem opens, Mary sits "musing on the lamp-flame at the table / Waiting for Warren" (40), and when Warren arrives, Mary "meet[s] him in the doorway with the news" (40) that "Silas," their aged hired hand, "is back" (40). Their exchange follows:

> "Be kind," she said.
> She took the market things from Warren's arms
> And set them on the porch, then drew him down
> To sit beside her on the wooden steps.
>
> "When was I ever anything but kind to him?
> But I'll not have the fellow back,' he said.
> 'I told him so last haying, didn't I?
> If he left then, I said, that ended it.
> What good is he? Who else will harbor him
> At his age for the little he can do?
> What help he is there's no depending on.
> Off he goes always when I need him most.
> He thinks he ought to earn a little pay,
> Enough at least to buy tobacco with,
> So he won't have to beg and be beholden.
> 'All right,' I say, 'I can't afford to pay
> Any fixed wages, though I wish I could.'
> 'Someone else can.' 'Then someone else will have to.'
> I shouldn't mind his bettering himself
> If that was what it was. You can be certain,
> When he begins like that, there's someone at him
> Trying to coax him off with pocket money,—
> In haying time, when any help is scarce.
> In winter he comes back to us. I'm done." (40–41)[8]

In the opening stanza quoted above, Mary bids Warren to "be kind" (40) and then takes "the market things from Warren's arms" (40), implicitly setting one set of ethics (kindness) against another (the market and its things). Warren's response, "When was I ever anything but kind to him?" (40) depends on a certain definition of kindness, namely, one of contracts and fair-dealing. From Warren's perspective, however, Silas has violated their agreement and has thus forfeited his right to kindness. Warren offers two reasons why he will "not have the fellow back" (40). The first is that Silas is no longer of use, can no longer perform sufficient labor to merit his pay or room and board. "What good is he?" Warren asks. "Who else will harbor him / At his age for the little he can do?" (40). Yet Silas is not totally useless—otherwise, he would not have left Warren during the harvest season. Obviously, someone found Silas useful enough to want to employ him. The second, related reason for Warren's refusal to take Silas back, then, is because Silas has broken a contract. After agreeing to work for Warren during the harvest season, Silas has run off to work elsewhere for better pay.

What emerges in the poem is a conflict between two modes of hired labor employment. Moreover, the conflict the poem represents was not especially new—discussions of it date to the 1840s—but it was, as Frost was writing in the early 1910s, and because of the changes in farming detailed above, approaching a crisis. Like Warren, many small farmers who could not pay regular, monthly wages to their hired labor instead offered them room and board for the entire year and, at the end of the harvest season, after farmers themselves had turned their harvest into cash, would pay laborers their back wages. Other, more large-scale farmers, however, employed laborers for only two or three months during the harvest season—but paid them immediately, monthly. Each situation had advantages and disadvantages for hired laborers. If employed year-round, laborers generally made less in wages than they would by working seasonally, and, as Silas objects, in the interval had no or little money. ("He thinks he ought to earn a little pay," Warren explains. "Enough at least to buy tobacco with, / So he won't have to beg and be beholden" [40].) In contrast, if men hired themselves out strictly for a few months during harvest season, they would make decent money and have (as Warren calls it) "fixed wages" (41) but, come winter, they would be left without employment, room, or board. Some farmers, like Warren, took advantage of this situation. "By employing a man for several months or the entire year," the agricultural historian David E. Schob notes, "the farmer in effect guaranteed himself a permanent harvest hand during July and August" (73). Because he has employed him throughout the year, Warren expects Silas to remain throughout the harvest season.

But changes in agricultural production began to undermine this already unstable situation. As Cindy Hahamovitch puts it, "Dwindling were the days of the 'hired man' who took most of his pay in room and board and shared the table with the family who employed him" (35). New England farmers who tried to survive by shifting toward large-scale, concentrated production had to rely even more on "just-in-time" seasonal labor to harvest their crops, thus driving up demand in an already strained hired labor market, where, as Warren puts it, "any help is scarce" (41). And that is precisely the opportunity that leads Silas to abandon Warren. Even though Silas is "good" for little, during harvest season his labor is nevertheless in demand. "You can be certain," Warren says, "When he begins like that, / there's someone at him / Trying to coax him off with pocket money" (41). In fact, hired laborers frequently left year-round employment for temporary though better-paid harvest work, betraying the farmers who had thought that they had guaranteed themselves harvest labor. Unlike Silas, however, few of those who jumped these formal or informal contracts had the audacity to return to the farmers whom they had abandoned. As Warren puts it, rightly angered, "What help he [Silas] is there's no depending on. / Off he goes always when I need him most" (40), and "In winter time he comes back to us. I'm done" (41).

The situation was made worse by the collapse of the agricultural ladder that was supposed to make this problem, at least for hired laborers, temporary. As Warren tells Mary, "I shouldn't mind his bettering himself / If that was what it was" (41). In other words, Warren could understand Silas's going off "always when I need him most" (41) if in going off and earning wages he put those wages to "bettering himself" (41), that is, climbing the agricultural ladder and using the money he earned as seasonal harvest labor to buy his own land and start his own farm. Silas, however, does no such thing. Either by choice or by necessity, and by the time the poem is published, this was increasingly a matter of necessity, Silas remains a hired man, dependent, in his later years, on the kindness of employer-farmers who, according to the practices of the time, bore little to no responsibility for their hired labor. As the radical agronomist Abner E. Woodruff put it in 1919, "when the farm hand was really an apprentice to the trade"—that is, when the cost of taking up farming (land and tools) remained comparatively low—"the relations of the farmer and his hired man were, therefore, those of social equals" (69). "But with the introduction of machinery on the farms," Woodruff observed, "and the development of commercial or competitive farming, the farm hand was forced to remain longer at his apprenticeship" (69) or, like Silas, give up on apprenticeship altogether and settle into what Abner called "the agricultural proletariat" (68). "The price of farm land and the cost of farm equipment has advanced to such a figure," Woodruff argued, "that the farm wage worker, with an average wage of less than $35 per month (1918), has a remarkably slim chance to become a farmer on his own account and that chance growing slimmer" (72). As a result, Woodruff added, "The farm hand of today is no longer the potential equal of his employer" (72). "Economically the line of cleavage between the farmer and the farm laborer has widened into a gulf," he concluded, "across which they glare at each other in uncompromising hostility" (57). Although uncompromising hostility may not fairly describe Warren's relationship with Silas, even so, the terms of their relationship have been affected by the industrialization of agriculture. For example, if hired workers got sick, as Silas does, David E. Schob explains, "Their employers"— and note the change in terminology—"might provide some immediate help but were not expected to assume long-term burdens or obligations" (230).

Thus, when Silas returns to Warren and Mary's farm after leaving them during the harvest season, he has violated two principles of the farmer-hired labor contract: he jumped his contract, leaving Warren without much-needed harvest help, and yet he still expects room and board over the winter; moreover, and although he is still under the impression that he will earn his room and board, Silas has become a responsibility and a burden to a family who, by rights, was no longer obliged to accept that responsibility. This context makes the debate about home between Warren and Mary so pointed:

> "Warren," she said, "he has come home to die:
> You needn't be afraid he'll leave you this time."
>
> "Home," he mocked gently.
>   "Yes, what else but home?
>
> It all depends on what you mean by home.
> Of course he's nothing to us, any more
> Than was the hound that came a stranger to us
> Out of the woods, worn out upon the trail."
>
> "Home is the place where, when you have to go there,
> They have to take you in."
>   "I should have called it
>
> Something you somehow haven't to deserve." (43)

Warren's definition of home is suitably cynical. It is "the place where, when you have to go there, / They have to take you in" (43). While on the surface still offering harbor, Warren's definition of home implicitly objects to the fact that it is a functionally a-moral place. Regardless of how one has treated those at home, one can nevertheless expect to be taken in there. Or, rather, it is not quite that the home is an a-moral place but that one moral, hospitality, trumps all others, including justice.

Mary, of course, offers a different definition of home. "I should have called it," she tells Warren, "Something you somehow haven't to deserve" (43), and the poem puts a lot of pressure on that word "deserve." Warren insists on an ethics ruled by exchange and contract: labor (or service) for wages, room, and board. When that contract is violated, or when one party (Silas) has no labor to exchange, then that marks the end of the relationship and responsibilities—even if sentimentalists will insist that home remains a place where one will have to take someone in regardless of the latter's sins. Mary, in contrast, wants an ethics—her definition of home— that transcends that calculated system of exchange. Home, for her, is something you haven't to "deserve," in the sense of deserve in its original Latin (*deservire*), "to serve diligently." In other words, as in so much nineteenth-century discourse, the "home" stands as an asylum from and even an implicit rebuke to the public, economic sphere of use and exchange.

While some debate remains alive, most readers of the poem have concluded that Warren comes around to Mary's way of thinking. Critics of "Death of the Hired

Man," therefore, tend to read the poem as a triumph of, as Karen Kilcup puts it, "the ethic of connection and nurturing" over an ethic of the market. Mary's "most important task in the poem," Kilcup writes, "is to teach Warren and, by extension, the reader, especially the masculine reader, the value of sustaining relationships" (85). Moreover, "Warren's transformation mirrors the reader's own, as the dialogue of the poem teaches us to value relationships over autonomy, compassion over economics, and feeling over thinking" (86). In addition, and perhaps because of Frost's own comments on the poem, in which he identified Mary's view of home as the "feminine way of it, the mother way" ("*Paris Review* Interview," 885) and Warren's, by contrast, as "the male one," critics have argued that these ethics—economics over against compassion—are also gendered, and that the triumph of the one (compassion) over the other (economics) also signals the triumph of one perspective (female) over another (male).

Yet that reading ignores a slight irony, one that emerges not in the poem itself but in the poem as it stands in relation to other poems in the collection, *North of Boston* (1914), in which "Death of the Hired Man" appears. If Silas had not died, and Warren had agreed to let him stay, the care of Silas would in all likelihood have fallen to Mary. In other words, as Frost in other poems like "Home Burial," "The Fear," "The Hill Wife," "The Witch of Coos," and "The Housekeeper" makes disturbingly evident, women were, far more frequently than men, providers (and occasionally victims) of an ethic of compassion and an ethic of home grounded in compassion and not service. In short, home might be something you somehow haven't to deserve, but someone—usually women—had to serve the undeserved. Indeed, another Frost poem, "A Servant to Servants," turns on the irony that women had to serve those who served—that is, all those hired laborers like Silas that made the newly industrialized farms go.

Because so many of Frost's poems take place in some unmarked pastoral landscape, the temptation, which Frost himself cultivated, is to view him as some sort of rural isolate. Yet it is surprising how often the various rural dramas and epiphanies (like "The Death of the Hired Man") that play out in the course of *North of Boston* do not occur in isolation but, as the title also rather deliberately announces, also in relation to the political, financial, and industrial center of Boston specifically or modernity more generally. The nation's farms and fields, Frost shows, tend to mirror, rather than solve or provide a haven from, the labor problems playing out in factories and cities.

The labor problem, that is, did not stop at the outposts of cities, the fences of farms, or, even, at the doors of farmhouses. Rather, it penetrated into modernity's very crevices, into the habits and routines of men and women everywhere. "The earth works for him," Emerson wrote of farmers, but by the first decades of the twentieth century, the farmer required more than just earthly labor. He required human laborers, too, men and women alike, and more than ever before. Moreover, the presence of these laborers created new problems, both for the laborers and, as "The Death of the Hired Man" suggests, for their employers. They also created, as Frost's book of poems suggests, opportunities for new kinds of poetry to be written.

HIRED WOMEN

Unlike "The Death of the Hired Man," which ultimately grants the claim that Silas and other workers make upon observers inclined—or persuaded—to sympathize, another canonical modern American poem, T. S. Eliot's "Preludes," struggles to resist and recast such claims for sympathy, even going so far as to enlist French metaphysical philosophy to do so.

Beginning in early 1910, a still in his early-twenties T. S. Eliot devoted a notebook to recording what he ambitiously called "the Complete Poems of/ T.S. Eliot," afterward changing the title to "Inventions of the March Hare." In 1917, Eliot would draw on these poems to compile *Prufrock and Other Observations*, his first published volume of verse, although many of the notebook poems remained unpublished until Christopher Ricks's edition in 1996. Intriguingly, among the first poems Eliot collected in that notebook—and, based on Eliot's dating, the first poems he composed and chose to preserve—are a series of poems set in the slums of North Cambridge that he wrote between late 1909 and 1911. As these and other poems from this period suggest, his efforts as a serious poet appear to coincide with his discovery of the urban poor.

That phrase, "the slums of Cambridge," may sound off to contemporary ears, but Cambridge, Massachusetts, circa 1909 differed notably from the Cambridge of today. Then as now, Harvard University dominated the part of the city adjacent to the Charles River, but the remainder of Cambridge and its adjoining neighborhoods (Dorchester, Roxbury) constituted a whole other world. As Samuel Atkins Eliot observed in his *A History of Cambridge, Massachusetts* (1913), Cambridge had grown because "many of the leading merchants and professional men of Boston make their homes" there, and also, of course, because of "the presence of the University" (120). Yet the city's "growth had also," Eliot notes, "been expedited by the establishment of numerous factories" and "great manufacturing plants" (120). This Cambridge, as the authors of *Massachusetts: A Guide to Its People and Places* (1937) later put it, unconsciously echoing lines from T. S. Eliot's *The Waste Land*, was the "Unknown City." "This Unknown City," the 1937 guidebook declared, "is the second in Massachusetts in the value of goods manufactured; it is third in all New England, outranked only by Boston and Providence" (184). As a result of this industrial expansion, workers, many of them immigrants, settled in Cambridge, especially the North Cambridge of Eliot's poems, close to the factories where they worked.

Inevitably, overcrowding and slums attended their arrival. Samuel Atkins Eliot's otherwise relentlessly upbeat *History of Cambridge, Massachusetts* ends on the disquieting note that "there is one peril which Cambridge is likely to encounter" because of its "increasing density of population," namely, "tenements housing," which, if left unchecked, would lead, as it had in other cities and had begun to in Cambridge, to the "evils" of "unhealthy premises, dark rooms, overcrowding, excessive rents, and other deplorable manifestations of the social life of modern cities" (150). The citizens of Cambridge, Eliot asserts, "must prevent the growth of slums,"

and the "housing evils that exist today are a reflection"—and not a positive one—
"upon the intelligence and right-mindedness of the community" (152).

  While Samuel Atkins Eliot may have sought to prevent the further growth of
slums, his namesake, Thomas Stearns Eliot, seems to have taken a decidedly dif-
ferent attitude toward them. As an undergraduate at Harvard from 1906 to 1909,
Eliot trolled the immigrant and working-class neighborhoods that ringed Cam-
bridge proper. His most thorough biographer, Lyndall Gordon, locates in these
walks through North Cambridge the beginnings of Eliot's work as a poet. "Failing
to find life amongst his own class," Gordon observes, "Eliot sought out the slum
areas."

> In Roxbury, then, and North Cambridge, Eliot deliberately courted squalor, but
> found that as life-destroying as the well-to-do Boston squares. He was physically
> repelled by smells and depressed by slums. In St. Louis the darker and grimmer
> aspects of the city had passed him by; in Boston, for the first time, he conceived
> a horror of the commercial city, its cluster and the sordid patience of its dwellers.
> [...] He was both horrified and, in a way, engaged. It seemed a far world from his
> studies, the neat definitions and laws he was piling up at college, but it touched him
> as Harvard did not. It was his first image of a waste land, a scene he was to make
> his own. (18–19)

That last phrase, "a scene he was to make his own," is particularly apt because, as
these early poems demonstrate, Eliot would take what had become a fairly stock
phenomenon, and a symbol of the labor problem, the urban slum, and transform
it—or one's attitude toward it—into something altogether unusual.

  Although many of these slum poems would remain buried in Eliot's note-
book for decades, "Preludes," written in the period between October 1910 and
November 1911, would later appear in *Prufrock and Other Observations* (1917).
"Preludes," from its setting to its musical title, shares much with the earlier poems.
Instead of studies of Cambridge, though, "Preludes," as Eliot's notebook indicates,
occurs in Dorchester and Roxbury, other down-at-the-heels neighborhoods across
the river from Cambridge. While most of the elements of these early poems—vacant
lots, expressive animals, the wreckage of civilization—would also appear in this first
section of "Preludes," the poem differs in the tension it cultivates between singular
and regular action, between things that happen once and things that happen or are
happening often, multiply:

> The winter evening settles down
> With smell of steaks in passage ways.
> Six o'clock.
> The burnt out ends of smoky days.
> And now a gusty shower wraps
> The grimy scraps
> Of withered leaves around your feet,
> And newspapers from vacant lots.

> The showers beat
> On broken blinds and chimney pots,
> And at the corner of the street
>
> A lonely cab horse steams and stamps.
> And then the lighting of the lamps. (1–13)

The opening line, for example, describes a single winter evening settling down. Yet it settles down with the smell of multiple people cooking multiple steaks in multiple passageways. Similarly, the next line names a specific time of day, "Six o'clock" (3), yet it—that time—represents the "burnt out ends" of all "smoky days" (4). It is not *a* time but the usual time. The following line, beginning "And now" (5), seems to describe an isolated incident of a gusty shower wrapping leaves and newspapers around "your feet" (7). (A shower, by the way, that threatens to entrap the speaker in a scene he would prefer merely to observe.) Yet by the following line this same shower is now plural, "showers" (9), which beat, habitually, on multiple "broken blinds and chimney pots" (10). Similarly, the penultimate image ("a lonely cab horse steams and stamps" [12]) seems to be singular, breaking the habitual action of showers that repeatedly beat, yet the "And then" (13) language of the final image makes the cab horse—and every previous incident in the poem—seem like one in a series of repeated, cheerlessly predictable events, so much so that it goes far toward robbing what should be a redemptive image ("the lighting of the lamps" [13]) of its redemption. If the lamps must be lighted every night, they cannot have done much—and will not do much—to dispel the darkness.

In other words, Eliot depicts the slum as a static, repeating space, where even incidents that seem to promise hope or development are instead revealed to be part of a recurring pattern. In the language of Prufrock, the speaker has known the slums already, known them all, because they do not change, they only repeat. The second section of "Preludes" depicts a similar relationship between incident and repetition:

> The morning comes to consciousness,
> Of faint stale smells of beer
> From the sawdust trampled street
> With its muddy feet that press
> To early coffee stands.
>
> With the other masquerades
> That time resumes
> One thinks of all the hands
> That are raising dingy shades
> In a thousand furnished rooms. (14–23)

What starts out singular—the morning coming to consciousness—quickly turns multiple, or, rather, part of what the morning (and the poem) comes to consciousness of is multiplicity: smells (plural) of beer and the many, muddy feet pressing to many, early coffee stands. Whereas the first section of "Preludes" describes what habitually happens in the evening, the second section describes what habitually happens in the morning, "the other masquerades / That time resumes" (19–20)—that time is always resuming. Furthermore, just as at the outset of the poem the morning comes to consciousness of multiplicity, in the final image of the poem "one thinks" as well of multiplicity, "of all the hands / That are raising dingy shades / In a thousand furnished rooms" (21–23). And while that powerful image—especially when it is framed as one of many "masquerades" (19)—suggests the loneliness and anomie of those who live in the thousand furnished rooms, much as the lonely cab horse concludes the previous section of the poem, that sense of loneliness seems to be overwhelmed by the aura of monotony, the habitual actions of an undifferentiated mass of slum dwellers, anonymous and interchangeable as their furniture, resuming another anonymous and interchangeable day. In other words, Eliot seems to be impressed by what he calls in an early notebook poem, "First Caprice in North Cambridge," the "sordid patience" of slum dwellers, with hands—not even people but dissociated hands—that rouse their owners to yet another round of raising dingy shades and other ritualized masquerades.

Because of their strict focus on routine, on the undifferentiated mass, the first two sections of "Preludes" make the third section all the more surprising. As many critics have noted, the section reflects Eliot's reading of the French novelist Charles-Louise Philippe, particularly his 1901 novel *Bubu de Montparnasse*. Philippe's novel tracks the lives of a syphilitic prostitute, her pimp, and a sympathetic but spiritually and sexually conflicted low-level clerk through the red light districts of turn-of-the-century Paris. In both the novel and Eliot's poem, a prostitute, Berthe, awakes late in a hotel room after a night of sex, alcohol, and "torpid-sleep" (49). "This bed of hotel rooms," Philippe writes, "where the bodies are dirty and the souls are as well" (49). While Philippe merely describes Berthe's sense of "disorder" and "degradation" as she wakes—"her thoughts lay heaped confusedly in her head" (49)—Eliot, in adapting novel to poem, delves into her consciousness:

> You tossed a blanket from the bed,
> You lay upon your back, and waited;
> You dozed, and watched the night revealing
> The thousand sordid images
> Of which your soul was constituted.
> They flickered against the ceiling.
> And when all the world came back
> And the light crept up between the shutters
> And you heard the sparrows in the gutters,
> You had such a vision of the street
> As the street hardly understands;
> Sitting along the bed's edge, where

> You curled the papers from your hair,
> Or clasped the yellow soles of feet
> In the palms of both soiled hands. (24–38)

According to Eliot's dating, almost a full year separates the composition of the third section of "Preludes" from the first two, and the difference is striking. When they do in fact concern themselves with people and not furniture or vacant lots, the first two sections of "Preludes" are concerned with the parts of many people—feet, hands—and not whole or even individual people. In the third section of "Preludes," however, Eliot unexpectedly takes up the soul of a single, discrete individual. Moreover, the soul he examines is capable of epiphanies that remain unavailable to the dismembered, consciousless slum dwellers whose hands and feet Eliot depicts in other poems. When the woman of the poem hears "the sparrows in the gutter," an image Eliot had used in "First Caprice in North Cambridge" to represent the "sordid patience" of slum dwellers, she, unlike them, achieves "such a vision of the street / As the street hardly understands" (33–34).

As Eric Schocket asserts, apparently forgetting this section of the "Preludes," "deeply intersubjective moments" with "the class Other" "is a road not taken" (165) in Eliot's poetry, but here Eliot decisively takes that road. To be sure, this poem reads like the exception that proves the rule, both of Eliot avoiding intersubjective moments with class Others and class Others having subjects and mind that Eliot could, however briefly, occupy. Still, it is a revealing exception. This section of the poem suggests, as John T. Mayer aptly puts it, "that ordinary unpromising individuals may be touched to vision by suffering that releases them from the blindness of mechanical, routinized lives" (90). Of course, the conclusion of the poem returns to a world where people are known by their parts—hair, feet, palms, hands—and not by their being, where they are known by their soles and not their souls, but that last pun distinguishes this instance of fragmentation from the typical Eliot dismemberment. By its end, the poem not only credits the woman with visionary insights into her soul unavailable to the street and its inhabitants but also with a desire for redemption. Instead of her sordid "soul," the woman clasps the "yellow soles of feet / In the palms of both soiled hands" (37–38), praying, it seems, to be freed from the life that imposes so many sordid, soul-constituting images on her.

Crucially, this moment of intersubjectivity with the class Other, as Schocket might put it, threatens the emotional detachment that the poem (and others like it) so carefully cultivates. Indeed, you can watch the fourth. final section of "Preludes" deliberately pulling back from the sympathy such a close identification with the soul and visions of another would demand. From the start, this final section of the poem returns to images of mechanical, routinized lives from which the soul of the previous poem had been released:

> His soul stretched tight across the skies
> That fade behind a city block,
> Trampled by insistent feet

> At four and five and six o'clock.
> And short square fingers stuffing pipes,
> And evening newspapers, and eyes
> Assured of certain certainties:
> The conscience of a blackened street
> Impatient to assume the world.
>
> I am moved by fancies that are curled
> Around these images and cling:
>
> The notion of some infinitely gentle
> Infinitely suffering thing.
>
> Wipe your hand across your mouth, and laugh;
> The worlds revolve like ancient women
> Gathering fuel in vacant lots. (39–54)

Again, the poem returns to a dismembered world of feet and to the regular, clockwork return of workers from their jobs. So that even though "his soul" (the speaker's?) is "stretched tight across the skies" (39), it still feels trampled by the insistency, the monotony of life among the urban working poor who periodically and predictably make their way home. Unsurprisingly, the poem resumes being bothered by multiplicity, in this case by the "short square fingers stuffing pipes" (43), "evening newspapers" (44) and "eyes / Assured of certain certainties" (44–45), a phrase that captures the fixed and even predetermined patterns of the slum. Nor does the street—or its inhabitants—seem to regret these "certain certainties." Unlike the previous section of the poem, in which a conscience suffering through a long night of the soul achieves a vision of the street the street hardly understands, here the darkened street is merely "impatient to assume the world" (47), to take the world, that is, and its "certain certainties" for granted.

The final stanzas of the section, however, mark yet another shift in the poem, this time toward an acknowledgment of suffering and, albeit interrupted, an expression of sympathy, a shift that can be tracked in Eliot's use of pronouns. Throughout the previous sections of the poem, the pronouns drift closer and closer to the first person. The first section briefly occupies the second person ("the shower wraps leaves around your feet"), for example, while the second section settles for the impersonal "one" who "thinks." The third section abandons the impersonal for an identifiable "you," a real you, that is, and not an impersonal "you" or a "one" that elsewhere seems to mask the speaker. The fourth section gets to "his," and whether that soul belongs to the speaker or another "you"—the prostitute's companion, perhaps— remains unclear. In any case, by the final stanzas of the final section of the poem, the speaker of the poem at last assumes an "I," an "I," moreover, that is capable of being "moved" by what it sees in ways that its previous incarnation as a "you" or a "one" or a "his" was not—or would not admit to. (Eliot's original phrasing—"I am wrought" instead of "I am moved" (48)—conveys even more strongly the sense that the speaker is created by what he witnesses.) This drift toward the personal suggests that the poem is finally ready to admit the claims such scenes might make on the observer's (or any observer's) sympathy. His use of the word "curled" (48) too, to describe the fancies around these images, recalls the woman from the third stanza who, in the moment of her epiphany, curls the paper from her hair. She, then, seems to be the "infinitely gentle / Infinitely suffering thing" (40–41) that moves the speaker. (Christ on the Cross is another possibility.) Either way, the poem admits the existence of undeserved ("gentle") suffering, whether in the redeemer (Christ) or those (the woman from the previous poem) who desire redemption. In either case, the poem returns to the singular—*some* suffering and gentle thing—and not, say, the systematic loneliness that characterizes (and therefore minimizes) the suffering present in the thousand furnished rooms of the second section of the poem and which one rather dispassionately "thinks of" (44).

Yet the poem, even these same lines, does not settle for such a redemptive, humane reading. The speaker, for example, is not moved by suffering per se but by "fancies" (48), a word that seems to distance him from the suffering he imagines, as does referring to what he witnesses as "images." In other words, what moves him is not real: they are illusions, delusions even, and in any case merely images and not realities.[9] Furthermore, the speaker is not moved by some infinitely gentle, infinitely suffering thing but by the "notion" (49) of such a thing. Needless to say, too, the speaker entertains a notion not of some infinitely gentle, infinitely suffering *soul* or *person* but instead a "thing" (51). The poem, then, when it risks coming closest to the suffering it earlier acknowledges, retreats to abstractions.

Even so, these fancies, the notion of this thing, however abstracted, does seem, as Eliot wrote of a similar scene in another early notebook poem, "Second Caprice in North Cambridge," to "demand your pity" (5). The final stanza of "Preludes," however, deliberately undermines that pity. The pronouns retreat to "you," the speaker seems to urge himself to abandon his pity for laughter, and in its final image, a somewhat forced simile, the poem returns to seeing the world in terms of multiplicity and habit. "The worlds"—plural—"revolve like ancient women / Gathering fuel in vacant lots" (53–54), and the image recalls the poem squarely to the "sordid patience" of slum dwellers, the inevitable, immutable, and literally cyclical routine of suffering.

Another notebook poem from this period that would later appear in *Prufrock and Other Poems*, "Rhapsody on a Windy Night," reveals the philosopher Henri Bergson's influence on Eliot. Yet the retreat from feeling to laughter at the conclusion of "Preludes" suggests his influence as well. In his later years, Eliot admitted to "a temporary conversion to Bergsonism" (*Sermon*, 5), and that "I was certainly very much under Bergson's influence during the year 1910–11, when I both attended his lectures and gave close study to the books he had then written" (qtd. in Kumar, 154). One of the books Eliot would have read, although few critics have noted it, was Bergson's *Laughter: An Essay on the Meaning of the Comic* (1900). In it, Bergson argues two points about laughter that bear on the conclusion of "Preludes." First, laughter is accompanied by "the *absence of feeling*" (4, emphasis in original); second, laughter originates in, as Bergson repeatedly puts it, "some-thing mechanical encrusted upon the living" (39). As to the first, laughter and the absence of feeling, Bergson argues that "laughter has no greater foe than emotion" and, consequently, "indifference is its natural environment" (4). In other words, we cannot laugh at what (or those whom) we sympathize with, at least not in the moment of our laughter. "Highly emotional souls," Bergson writes, "in tune and unison with life, in whom every event would be sentimentally prolonged and re-echoed, would neither know nor understand laughter" (4). "To produce the whole of its effect, then," he concludes, "the comic demands something like a momentary anesthesia of the heart" (5). The conclusion of "Preludes" takes this principle and assumes that effects will follow from causes, that laughter, rather than reflecting a "momentary anesthesia of the heart," will deliver that anesthetic. For an observer who feels too much, as the speaker of the final lines of "Preludes" does, the command to "Wipe your hand across your mouth, and laugh" may res-cue the speaker from sentiment, may bring about the desired apathy. "Look upon life as a disinterested spectator," Bergson continues, and "many a drama will turn into a comedy" (5). Rather like the hope that smiling, regardless of one's mood, will make one happier, the speaker here assumes that laughing, regardless of one's feelings, will cultivate one's indifference. Not because the scene has changed but because one's attitude toward it has. If I laugh at something, I cannot, by Bergson's definition, feel emotion about it.

But the poem does not settle for the dubious strategy of merely commanding one to laugh at suffering; rather, it recasts that suffering as something that should legitimately inspire laughter, which, for Bergson, means showing that suffering to be essentially mechanical. For Bergson, laughter arises when something or some-one exhibits what he calls "a certain *mechanical elasticity*" (10, emphasis in original), when individuals fail to respond adequately to their environment. His example is "a man, who, running along the street, stumbles and falls," whereupon "passers-by burst out laughing" (8). They would not have laughed, Bergson supposes, if the man had chosen to sit on the ground. Rather, they laugh, Bergson argues,

> because his sitting down is involuntary. Consequently, it is not his sudden change of attitude that raises a laugh, but rather the involuntary element in this change,— his clumsiness, in fact. Perhaps there was a stone on the road. He should have altered his pace or avoided the obstacle. Instead of that, through lack of elasticity, through absentmindedness and a kind of physical obstinacy, *as a result, in fact, of rigidity or of momentum*, the muscles continued to perform the same movement when the circumstances of the case called for something else. That is the reason of the man's fall, and also of people's laughter.
>
> (8–9, emphasis in original)

In sum, for Bergson, as the example of the clumsy runner suggests, "*The attitudes, gestures and movements of the human body are laughable in exact proportion as that body reminds us of a mere machine*" (29, emphasis in original). In contrast, Bergson claims, "a really living life should never repeat itself" (34) and, it goes without say-ing, would also never be laughed at.

Eliot does not merely urge his observer to laugh at "fancies" that previously moved him, then, but, rather, makes those fancies—that infinitely gentle, infinitely suffering thing—into something laughable. In order to do that, the speaker must make it into a thing in the first place, which a shift in diction accomplishes, but he also must emphasize that thing's mechanical inelasticity by, say, highlighting its similarities to a mere machine. Hence the simile that concludes the poem: "The worlds revolve like ancient women / Gathering fuel in vacant lots," and the key words here seem to be "revolve" and "ancient." The worlds revolve like ancient women walking around in a vacant lot and, like ancient women, do not stop because of anything as inconsequential as suffering, just as the ancient women have not stopped gathering fuel in all their lifetimes. Both women and worlds display a certain mechanical inelasticity; both repeat, fail to adapt, or fail to protest, and both, according to Bergson and, it seems, the poem, are therefore laughable. The world resembles a mere machine by resembling women who themselves act in machinelike ways. From a close-up view of some infinitely gentle, infinitely suffering thing, the poem pulls back to reveal worlds in motion, suffering multiplied but also as a result made routine, inevitable, and therefore unremarkable—except perhaps when it is laughable. The laughter may seem forced, but that may also be the point. The poem is trying, a little desperately, to turn a tragedy into a comedy. And while the equation that allows it to do so only emerges at the conclusion of the poem, that equation has operated throughout. Individual things, and individuals, as in the third section of "Preludes," inspire pity, while anything that repeats, anything that is repeated, or both—that is, "short square fingers stuffing pipes" or "muddy feet that press / To early coffee stands"—does not. Such things—and they are mere things—in their very multiplicity and inelasticity actively repulse sympathy.

In repulsing sympathy, Eliot strains to shed the "problem" part of the labor problem discourse. In the early decades of the twentieth century, when slums and prostitution were the peculiar obsession of most social reformers and middle-class women's magazines, Eliot does not use his poetic representation of those problems to advance any explicit social program. By casting such scenes as laughable rather than, say, tear-stained, Eliot could further taunt those in his culture—and, even closer to home, those in his family—who could only see these problems through the lens of social reform. (In St. Louis, for example, Eliot's mother, Charlotte C. Eliot, was the second vice president of the Humanity Club. Eliot's older sister, Ada Eliot Sheffield, was a graduate of the New York School of Philanthropy and was "an eminent social work leader" [Tice 52], as a contemporary historian has called her, first as a probation officer in New York City and later as a leader of various charitable associations and social work bureaus in Boston.) So Eric Schocket is right to insist that Eliot belongs to the school of "American modernists" who abstract the worker "from a sentimental system of affect" and who, as Schocket says of "First Caprice in North Cambridge," disarticulate "working-class forms from their previous symbolic systems" in order "to vitalize new aesthetic structures" (152). Hence Eliot's infinitely gentle, infinitely suffering things, not to mention all the hands raising dingy shades in a thousand furnished rooms, whose perpetual toil and suffering, perhaps too conveniently, become the occasion to cultivate a stoic, laughing attitude toward suffering. What Schocket underestimates, however, is how reluctantly, and therefore awkwardly, Eliot undertakes that abstraction and disarticulation from a sentimental system of affect. As in the conclusion of "Preludes," Eliot, it seems, has to laugh to keep from crying.

Awkward or not, having freed workers and the poor—and himself—from a discourse of pity and social reform, Eliot could put them to other uses, as he does throughout *The Love Song of J. Alfred Prufrock* and *The Waste Land*. Although Eliot's attitude toward them will change, workers in these poems never cease to be essentially mechanical, often enough mindlessly driven by their sexuality, which, at times, also makes them animal. For Eliot, however, as for Frost and countless other modern American poets, the question was not whether to include workers and the poor in modern poems—one searches in vain for a modern American poet who did not take them up—but what roles they would play in that poetry. Some poets, like Eliot, made that process into modern poetry itself.

In this contest over how much sympathy to expend upon workers and the poor, both "The Death of the Hired Man" and "Preludes" embody the larger culture out of which they come. This culture struggled to grasp, and respond to, the problems posed by the advent of modern industrial and global capitalism. In contrast to the critical conventional wisdom, then, far from muting or distancing itself from history generally or the labor problem specifically, poetry may have been the genre in which these struggles most intensely played out.

NOTES

1 Parts of this chapter, mostly the material on T. S. Eliot, is adapted from a book, *Hog Butchers, Beggars, and Busboys: Poverty, Labor, and the Making of Modern American Poetry*, forthcoming from the University of Michigan Press. I am grateful to the press for the opportunity to share that research here.

2 Of only the most recent publications, consider Eric Shocket's *Vanishing Moments: Class and American Literature* (2006), Gavin Jones's *American Hungers: The Problem of Poverty in U.S. Literature, 1840–1945* (2007), Patrick Chura's *Vital Contact: Downclassing Journeys in American Literature from Herman Melville to Richard Wright* (2005), Peter Conn's *The American 1930s: A Literary History* (2009), or Morris Dickstein's *Dancing in the Dark: A Cultural History of the Great Depression* (2009). With the exception of Schocket, who devotes an uneven chapter to T. S. Eliot, and Dickstein, who briefly considers William Carlos Williams, Robert Frost, and Wallace Stevens, all of these authors form their arguments around readings of prose works.

3 One recent exception to this rule is John Lowney's *History, Memory, and the Literary Left: Modern American Poetry, 1935–1968*, but it remains an exception. As James Smethurst pointed out in his review of Lowney's book, even "in the comparative boom of scholarship on the American artistic Left of the 1930s and 1940s over the last fifteen or twenty years," "poetry has received short shrift" (787).

4 As Alan Golding wrote in 1995, "much 'New Americanist' work reflects "the critical
  neglect of poetry [in the academy] in favor of prose forms (usually fiction) that have
  a superficially more 'direct' connection to social and historical reality" (xiii). One
  obvious exception to this literary history has been the research of Cary Nelson and those
  influenced by his work. (In particular, see Nelson's *Repression and Recovery* [1992] and
  Revolutionary Memory [2002].) More often than not, however, this work is devoted to
  recovering forgotten poets or offering criticism about recovered poets.

5 A quick, admittedly partial survey may nevertheless illuminate the extent of this
  dissatisfaction. In November 1909, some twenty thousand mostly female workers
  picketed the shirtwaist manufacturers in and around Manhattan. The strike quickly
  turned violent. Picketers assaulted strikebreakers, and police—both those from the city
  and those hired by the manufacturers—attacked and arrested picketers. In July 1910,
  the mostly male cloak-and-suit makers followed suit. As in the 1909 strike, as Graham
  Adams notes, "both adversaries"—strikers and manufacturers—"employed belligerent
  methods" (114), including, unlike in 1909, workers storming factories and destroying
  property. In addition to the 1909 IWW-led strike at the Pressed Steel Car Company
  in McKees Rock, Pennsylvania, in which dozens of workers were injured and a dozen
  killed, in December of that year, a strike among streetcar workers in Philadelphia
  quickly turned into a citywide general strike, one marred by rioting, violence, and death
  (Dubofsky, 114–121; Adams, 181–188). A few months later, in February 1910, workers
  struck the Bethlehem Steel Company in Bethlehem, Pennsylvania. In the course of
  that strike, police shot and killed one striking worker and wounded another (Adams,
  189–192). Throughout the latter half of 1911 and into 1912, the "timber wars" between
  sawmill workers and lumber barons raged in east Texas and west Louisiana, culminating
  on July 7, 1912, with a riot between workers and hired gunmen that left four dead and
  forty wounded (Dubofsky, 121–127).

6 "For the seven years following 1915," the labor historian David Montgomery writes,
  "the ratio of strikers to all industrial and service employees remained constantly on a
  par with the more famous strike years of 1934 and 1937" (95). "Tight labor markets, an
  improving economy, and the consequent rise in union militancy," Joseph A. McCartin
  observes, "combined to unleash a mammoth strike wave" (39). The year 1919 seemed
  especially harrowing. It was, as Regin Schmidt writes, "one of those dramatic years, like
  1968, filled with unrest, protest, and a clashing of social and political forces, when, for a
  short moment, the future of the nation seemed to hang in the balance" (24). In January
  of that year, Seattle workers participated in a citywide general strike. After Seattle, the
  situation grew even more desperate. By August 1919, 400,000 coal miners, 120,000 textile
  workers, 50,000 garment workers, and 300,000 steel workers had all gone out on strike.
  All told, by the end of 1919, nearly one out of every five workers—millions of them—had
  participated in a strike (Gerstle, 229). All these strikes played out, of course, against the
  backdrop of the Bolshevik Revolution in Russia in 1917, where there but for the grace
  of the newly formed Federal Bureau of Investigation it appeared the United States was
  heading, especially once the bombs started going off. In April 1919, two mail bombs
  exploded at the office of the mayor of Seattle and the home of a U.S. senator. In the
  coming days, another thirty-four bombs were discovered, either at post offices (where
  they lingered because of, of all things, insufficient postage) or already headed to their
  targets, who were capitalists such as John D. Rockefeller, J. P. Morgan, and others that
  were, as one pamphlet found with a bomb called them, "class enemies" (Gerstle, 229).
  In June, bombs exploded in eight cities, and the next year, 1920, witnessed the deadliest
  terror attack in U.S. history. At mid-day on September 16, a horse-drawn carriage

carrying dynamite and window sash-weights parked across the street from the Wall Street headquarters of J. P. Morgan. This bomb killed thirty-eight people and injured some four hundred others.

7 In a much-quoted sentence from his *Notes on the State of Virginia*, Jefferson asserted that "Those who labour in the earth are the chosen people of God, if he ever had a chosen people, whose breasts he has made his peculiar deposit for substantial and genuine virtue" (176). For Jefferson, farmers were the chosen people of God because they supposedly remained immune from corruption. Unlike manufacturers and handicraftsman, who must serve their customers and the market, farmers depended upon "their own soil and industry...for their subsistence" (176). In other words, farmers could, if need be, exist independently of the market, whereas manufacturers and handicraftsmen always depended on it. And dependence, Jefferson formulated, "begets subservience and venality, suffocates the germ of virtue, and prepares fit tools for the designs of ambition" (176). ("Ambition," in Jefferson's view, was plainly bad.) "While we have land to labour, then," Jefferson concluded, "let us never wish to see our citizens occupied at a workbench, or twirling a distaff" (176). "Let our workshops," Jefferson asserts, "remain in Europe" (176).

8 Because The Library of America edition of Frost's *Collected Poems, Prose, and Plays* does not include line numbers for poems, and many Frost poems are hundreds of lines long, all references are to page numbers.

9 From a Bergsonian perspective, it should be noted, "images" may not connote unreality; rather, for Bergson, all memories and all perceptions are images, and, as in Imagist poetry, may therefore have more and not less effect on those who perceive them.

REFERENCES

Adams, Thomas Sewell, and Helen L. Sumner. *Labor Problems: A Text Book*. 8th ed. New York: Macmillan, 1914.

Bergson, Henri. *Laughter: An Essay on the Meaning of the Comic*. 1911. Trans. Cloudesley Brereton and Fred Rothwell. New York: Macmillan, 1928.

Dinsmoor, Alice. "Three Acres and Chains." *The Craftsman* 18 (April–September 1910): 59–66.

Eliot, Samuel Atkins. *A History of Cambridge, Massachusetts, 1630–1913*. Cambridge, MA: The Cambridge Tribune, 1913.

Eliot, T.S. *Inventions of the March Hare: Poems 1909–1917*. Ed. Christopher Ricks. San Diego, CA: Harcourt Brace, 1996.

———. "Preludes." In *Collected Poems, 1909–1962*. San Diego: Harcourt Brace & Co., 1963. 13–15.

———. *A Sermon Preached in Magdalene College*. Cambridge: Cambridge University Press, 1948.

Emerson, Ralph Waldo. "Farming." 1858. In *Essential Writings*. Ed. Brooks Atkinson. New York: Modern Library, 2000. 673–681.

Frost, Robert. "The Death of the Hired Man." In *Collected Poems, Prose, and Plays*. New York: Library of America, 1995. 40–45.

———. "*Paris Review* Interview, with Richard Poirier." In *Collected Poems, Prose, and Plays*. New York: Library of America, 1995. 873–893.

Gordon, Lyndall. *Eliot's Early Years*. Oxford: Oxford University Press, 1977.

Griffin, Larry J., and Maria Tempenis. "Class, Multiculturalism, and the *American Quarterly*." *American Quarterly* 54.1 (2002): 67–99.

Hahamovitch, Cindy. *The Fruits of Their Labor: Atlantic Coast Farmworkers and the Making of Migrant Poverty, 1870–1945.* Chapel Hill: University of North Carolina Press, 1997.

Hall, Bolton. *Three Acres and Liberty.* 1907. Middlesex: Echo Library, 2006.

Harrington, Joseph. "Why American Poetry Is Not American Literature." *American Literary History* 8.3 (1996): 496–515.

Kilcup, Karen. *Robert Frost and the Feminine Literary Tradition.* Ann Arbor: University of Michigan Press, 1999.

Kumar, Shiv V. *Bergson and the Stream of Consciousness Novel.* New York: New York University Press, 1963.

Lauter, Paul and Ann Fitzgerald. *Literature, Class, Culture: An Anthology.* New York: Longman, 2000.

Lincoln, Abraham. "Annual Message to Congress, December 3, 1861." In *Speeches and Writings, 1859–1865.* New York: Library of America, 1989.

Lippmann, Walter. *A Preface to Politics.* Mitchell Kennerley: New York, 1914.

Massachusetts: A Guide to Its People and Places. Boston: Houghton Mifflin, 1937.

Mayer, John T. *T. S. Eliot's Silent Voices.* New York: Oxford University Press, 1989.

Philippe, Charles-Louise. *Bubu of Montparnasse.* 1901. New York: Shakespeare House, 1951.

Report of the Commission on Country Life. New York: Sturgis and Walton, 1911.

Schob, David E. *Hired Hands and Plowboys: Farm Labor in the Midwest, 1815–60.* Urbana: University of Illinois Press, 1975.

Schocket, Eric. *Vanishing Moments: Class and American Literature.* Ann Arbor: University of Michigan Press, 2006.

Shannon, Fred Albert. *The Farmer's Last Frontier: Agriculture 1860–1897.* New York: Farrar & Rinehart, 1945.

Stromquist, Shelton. *Reinventing "The People": The Progressive Labor Movement, the Class Problem, and the Origins of Modern Liberalism.* Urbana: University of Illinois Press, 2006.

Tice, Karen Whitney. *Tales of Wayward Girls and Immoral Women: Case Records and the Professionalization of Social Work.* Urbana: University of Illinois Press, 1998.

Woodruff, Abner E. *Evolution of American Agriculture.* N.p.: Agricultural Workers Industrial Union, 1919.

CHAPTER 6

ECONOMICS AND GENDER IN MINA LOY, LOLA RIDGE, AND MARIANNE MOORE

LINDA A. KINNAHAN

THE American economist Simon Patten claimed, in 1908, that "so popular has economic thinking become that it seems a natural state of affairs that must always have existed.... Today economics is in everyone's thoughts and on every one's tongue" (Patten in Leach, 231).[1] The socioeconomics of gender played an important part in debates and discussions about the "new economy" of corporate consumer capitalism, fueled by the rise of the "new woman" and the vigor of twentieth-century's first-wave feminist movement. As women moved toward fuller civic and economic participation in the opening decades of the century, popular and intellectual venues examined the position of women within the modern economy, and women themselves contributed significantly to an economic rethinking of gender.

In its early years, American modernist poetry emerged within a context of interactive discursive fields, keenly aware of the socioeconomic language "on every one's tongue" and the ruptures wrought by what Alan Trachtenburg aptly calls "the incorporation of America." When, in the mid-forties, William Carlos Williams urged a "new measure" for poetry, he specified a "new way of measuring that will be commensurate with the social, economic world" (Williams, 283), a world in which the "culture of purchase...has become predominant" (147).[2] His call for a "new measure" galvanized, in many respects, a longstanding concern with economics in modernist poetry, evident in its earliest years and particularly heightened in relation to gender during feminism's most vocal period, from the 1890s until the 1920s. The poets Mina Loy, Marianne Moore, and Lola Ridge all participated in these poetic energies by bringing economics, poetry, and gender into animated relation during the first two decades of the century. Rather than anomalies, as women speculating about economic forces they joined a multitude of women activists, reformers, researchers, and theorists who insisted upon the relevance of gender to the "new economy." Women's engagement with economics in this period can be approached in a number of ways, such as labor or social work histories; however, both the role of women in theorizing about economics and the role that the figure of the woman plays in theories of economics help reveal how gender ideologies shaped powerful assumptions about the "new economy" and its cultural consequences. That these assumptions were not limited to ivory-tower theorizing but grew from and filtered in to popular forums sustains the economist Anna Jennings's comment that "theory is a potent expression of cultural belief and practice" (Jennings, 126).

In looking at the early poetry of Mina Loy, Lola Ridge, and Marianne Moore in relation to economics, it is important to recognize not only that economic theory mattered to a wide public in the early years of the twentieth century but that the economic field was itself a gendered site of contention as it transitioned into a centrally defining system of modernity. Not only did these three poets circulate in the same avant-garde crowds in New York during the late teens and publish in many of the same little magazines, they also shared feminist sentiments concurrent with the first-wave movement, including challenges to male-dominated economies and institutions. Within their work, economic arrangements of gender are not only challenged but connected to modern ideas of value, work, desire, and need; subsequently, the tension between an economy of consumption and an economy of social provisioning finds expression in a distinctively feminist poetics concerned with capitalism's degradation of both work and human need.

By the late nineteenth century, mass production, enabled by new technologies, made goods more accessible and affordable, and the consumer and the act of consuming took on new importance. The traditional status of work lessened as production, or the experience of work and labor, was reshaped to meet the final goal of consumption as quickly and efficiently as possible. Taylorism, part of the "scientific management" of the workplace, promoted a mechanistic analysis of the laborer to eliminate wasted time and motion, breaking up and recombining component parts of a task in ways favorable to factory production. What T. J. Jackson Lears terms the "rationalization of economic life—the drive for maximum profits through the adoption of the most efficient forms of organization" quickly began to dominate business.

Alongside the growth of corporate capitalism, the international development of economics as an academic discipline valuing scientific objectivity distinguished the field from earlier forms of political economy, notably reversing the significance of production and consumption in theorizing modern capitalism. As Lawrence Birken points out, the "transition from a productivist to a consumerist ideology among intellectuals on both sides of the Atlantic was evidenced first of all by the transformation of economic thought in the closing decades of the nineteenth century," signaling "the partial emergence of a new complex of values"(22). Earlier forms of classical or political economy, from Adam Smith forward, understood the function of economics as the increase (production) of the wealth of nations, attended by the "faith that labor is the genuinely creative source of value" in producing wealth. Classical economy valued "on the one hand, *productivity*, and, on the other hand, the *neediness*, of human beings," paying attention to the relationship of material goods and human survival (Birken, 27, emphasis in original). Subsequently, the neoclassical or "marginal" school of economics dominating Western thought after the 1870s regarded consumption as the central economic activity and goal. Economists such as J. B. Clark, Leon Walras, W. Stanley Jevons, Alfred Marshall, and Karl Menger viewed production not as an end in itself but as the deferral of consumption. They defended property ownership, free competition, a concept of desire as natural, and the importance of "natural" desires in creating utility and value. Their thinking focused on "want" or idiosyncratic desire, often to the neglect of "need" or social good.

Economy became defined as the movement of markets motivated by individualistic desires rather than the social provisioning of needs. Within the neoclassical scheme, "the idea of need was abolished.... [And] in the new science, it was not that useful things were desired but that desired things were useful" (J. Nelson, 31). Julie Nelson, along with other recent feminist economists critiquing the neoclassical model's continued dominance, argues that the "primacy within market-oriented economics of the focus on 'want' to the neglect of any consideration of the provisioning-related concept of 'need' suggests ... [a masculine] interpretation of the world as a world of scarcity, hostile to human purposes," while the "admittance of a category of 'need' implies the recognition of an inescapable dependence of human bodies on their physical environment that is lacking in the modern view." As Nelson contends, the "deprecation of need" is tied to the "deprecation of the feminine" as passive and dependent (J. Nelson, 34).

Most obviously, the figure of Economic Man, the model for economic subjectivity central to neoclassical theory, privileges socially understood concepts of masculinity. Economic Man is "radically separate from other humans and from nature: the emphasis is on separation, distance, demarcation, autonomy, independence of self" (J. Nelson, 31). Within the neoclassical worldview, "women are dependents who cannot stand on their own," defined only as "wives, daughters, mothers," while "men make economic decisions ... [and] they circulate freely in the market sphere" (Pujol, 29). Individual agency forms within and in conjunction with the market, a failure to recognize either the self's relation to the world or the range of identities and work shaped by social constructions such as gender, race, and class. While neoclassical theory promotes itself as a scientific, objective, and rational approach—ideas that maintain disciplinary currency to this day—its cultural biases have been well documented, especially by late twentieth century feminists. However, at the turn of the twentieth century and during its first decades, as economics fought to define itself in scientific terms, what constituted "economics" was similarly contested, especially in its relationship to social issues, prominently including issues of gender. First-wave feminists, women activists and reformers, and oppositional economic schools of thought maintained a vital focus on women, gendering economics in the modern era's first decades.

For first-wave feminists, the position of women within modern capitalism intersected with issues of labor, social reform, power, patriarchal institutions, citizenship, and education. As women entered the work force in large numbers, the emergence of unions by the late nineteenth century fueled workers demanding reforms through protests, strikes, and riots.[3] Supporters of the labor, socialist, and feminist movements, centered in New York City, interacted and overlapped. Although individual male socialists like Max Eastman, the editor of the leftist journal *The Masses*, demonstrated support for feminist causes, women's issues were often subordinated within the male-dominated labor and socialist movements. Early unions excluded women, who subsequently formed their own unions, and the emergence of the Women's Trade Union League galvanized issues of women's labor to fight for equal wages, better working conditions, child labor laws, and protective legislation for women. Between 1909 and 1914, women's involvement in a "strike wave" across the country "announced to the world women's wage-earning presence" (Cott, 23).

In the face of capitalism's forceful growth, women took on increasingly prominent public roles, beginning in the Progressive era to contribute "to both the theory and practice of the [Progressive] movement" (Eisenach, xvi). A generation of reform-minded women, among the first to attend colleges and universities newly opened to women in the 1880s and 1890s, promoted a "provisioning view" of economics, in which needs for survival and health sustenance emphasized the "socially and materially situated human being" rather than the increasingly disembodied, abstracted Economic Man of mainstream theory. Many feminists absorbed socialist ideas popular at the time, and the "socialist critiques of the inequities inherent in industrial capitalism organized on a competitive and individualist basis" provided a "major intellectual seedbed" for women of the nineteenth-century Woman Movement, who drew upon various "utopian socialist visions" more so than upon a Marxian model of history and class conflict (Cott, 17).[4] This brand of socialism prompted alternative models of economics in the activism of women like Lillian Wald and Jane Addams, who established settlement houses to help counteract poverty in New York and Chicago. Wald also worked in New York in 1908 to help develop the free lunch program in public schools, and women like Mary Richmond, as the head of the Charity Organization Society, advanced the cause of the poor.

By the turn of the century and into its early years, economic thought focusing on need drew explicitly upon feminist frameworks. While social work and social issues were increasingly bracketed as the economics field developed a mathematical and scientific emphasis, women academics established programs stressing the interrelation of social provisioning and economic theory, such as Bryn Mawr's Graduate Department of Social Economy and Social Research (established in 1915), or through publications and studies of women's relationship to economic systems authored by women themselves. By 1920, the percentage of women granted a PhD in economics peaked at the highest level it would reach until the late 1970s, reflective of the early energy of women researchers and of their subsequent marginalization within increasingly competitive economics programs (Olson and Emami, 5).[5] Research forums devoted to gender and economics prominently included the Women's

Education and Industrial Union (WEIU), founded in Boston in 1877 to support the city's working women and instituting a Department of Research in 1905 to publish studies on women, labor, and social reform over the next fifteen years. As women progressed toward universal suffrage, the struggle for economic citizenship generated new research about working women. The founding of the federal government's Women's Bureau in 1920, charged by Congress to "formulate standards and policies which shall promote the welfare of wage-earning women," led to investigations and reports that appeared in popular publications such as the *New York Times*, *Atlantic Monthly*, and *Ladies' Home Journal*, as well as more specialized labor and economic journals on labor conditions in American industry and the integral role that women workers played in the modern economy (Hendrickson, 483). As feminist economic historians have uncovered, "Women in the United States have a long history in economics, dating back before its inception as an academic discipline," producing "early contributions to the development of economic thought" (Olson and Emami, 5). However, as Dora Madden notes, "many women with economics training [between 1890 and 1920] and/or economics in mind" wrote on topics taboo or unrecognized within standard classifications of economic research by the teens (6); nonetheless, women contributed "a substantial number of writings on economics in the first few decades of the twentieth century," especially on race, gender, children, religion, suffrage, and the "domestic sector" (2–3).[6]

With the advance of the "new woman," a stream of feminist economic theory and thought also reached a wide popular audience through economic treatises and lectures by women and through well-known forms of activism. Charlotte Perkins Gilman, speaking all over the country and vigorously spreading her economic theories developed in *Women and Economics* (1898), influenced critiques of economic systems privileging men. Her analysis of women's position in marriage as an economic arrangement, sustained by the importance of a woman's appearance in gaining a husband and displaying his pecuniary power (the "oversexed woman"), dovetailed with Veblen's analysis of women (proffered a year later) in patriarchal capitalism; moreover, her theory of women's domestic labor disputed the privatization of the home and the organization of women's work within the family. Her later involvement with the Greenwich Village feminist group Heterodoxy (begun in 1912 and including many of the leading women in professions, activism, and education at the time, such as Loy's friend Mabel Dodge), her feminist fictions, including the utopian *Herland*, and her editorial work with the feminist magazine she founded, *The Forerunner*, continued her economic arguments throughout the teens. Olive Schreiner's *Woman and Labor* (1911) advocated economic freedom and sexual liberation for women, citing female "parasitism" as woman's position of dependence and subordination within capitalism. During the prewar years, women like Crystal Eastman and Emma Goldman promoted improvement in labor conditions, while critiquing the military-industrial complex through their efforts in the peace movement. Marriage, as well, was seen as an economically shaped institution rather than a natural alignment. Goldman spoke of marriage as an economic arrangement, viewing the wife's body as "capital to be exploited and manipulated," thus causing the wife to "look on success as the size of her husband's income" (Drinnon, 149–150). Margaret Sanger's birth control movement and her radical feminist journal *Woman Rebel* garnered international attention in challenging the economic basis of male control of women's bodies.

MINA LOY: FEMINIST MODERNISM
AND ECONOMICS

Mina Loy's feminist modernism gained attention with her first publications, underscoring the impact of her poetry on avant-garde formations as integral to rethinking gender norms.[7] Publishing her first poems in 1914 in little American magazines, Loy arrived in the United States in 1916. Her early avant-garde work, so striking to her American readers, coincides with feminist thinking about economic matters coalescing around the "new woman." Economics mattered to Loy throughout the whole of her life and her poetry. Beginning during her student years in Paris at the end of the nineteenth century, she demonstrated a proclivity for alternative forms of purchase and exchange, haunting the flea markets or scavenging urban streets for second-hand or cast-off goods to use in her home and artwork; as a business woman, she designed and sold lamps in Paris during the twenties and continued to design new products as possible business ventures.[8]

Her poems and prose writings from the teens and twenties, heavily influenced by first-wave feminist thought, read economic and gender equality in vexed relation, declaiming to the New Woman in her 1914 Feminist Manifesto that "[p]rofessional and commercial careers are opening up to you. *Is that all you want?*" For Loy, until deeply engrained attitudes about women that sustain masculine power and privilege were demolished, women would not be truly free to experience selfhood. Loy's early concern with gender economies locates a tradition of patriarchal practices and attitudes that precedes capitalism but continues within it. Linking economic contexts older than but shaping modern capitalism, Loy's gender analysis coincides with sociological approaches to women's constructed position within capitalism. From the "Virgins for sale" in her early poetry to the "pockets of the Father—- / invisible /.../ from which spring riches / and a sullen / economic war" in her epic auto-mythology of the twenties, to the "cocotte" wandering the department stores of urban scenes and the vagabonds haunting the Bowery of her late poetry, Mina Loy returns again and again to the structural consequences of economic systems upon human beings.

From the earliest manuscripts, women's pecuniary circumstances provided a way to explore modern subjectivity. An early unpublished poem, "The Prototype," figures a "half-broken mother" in criticizing religion's collusion with forces that keep women and children oppressed by poverty.[9] Troubled by Christianity's hypocritical idealizing of the Christ child, the poem's speaker rejects the "perfect" but "cold wax baby" born on Christmas Eve and worships instead a "horrible little / baby" born the same night, but of "half warm flesh; / flesh that is covered with sores—carried / by a half-broken mother." This figure of poverty is the real Christ figure and the speaker, "called heretic," is "the only follower in Christ's foot-steps / among this crowd adoring a wax doll." The "I" is alone in "worshipping the poor / sore baby— the child of sex igno- / rance & poverty" (Loy, *Lost,* 221). Margaret Sanger's vocal recognition of the class dimensions of America's Comstock Law's ban on birth control and reproductive information drew public attention to the impact of high birth rates on the poor, transforming a moral issue into an issue of social justice involving women's rights and an environmental view of poverty. This feminist insistence on relationships between class and gender refuses to see poverty as a moral flaw. The "New Gospel" promoted by the poem's final stanzas evokes, either coincidentally or purposefully, the Social Gospel movement's attempts at that time to transform attitudes toward the poor and to consider poverty not as a character weakness but as a systemic, environmentally produced social condition.[10]

Loy's interest in American feminism and related reform efforts, such as the birth control movement, developed while she was beginning to write poetry in Florence and coming to know American expatriots like Mabel Dodge. Dodge's Florence salons introduced Loy to a variety of writers, artists, and intellectuals, including Gertrude Stein, and when Dodge returned to America in 1912, she and Loy continued to correspond. Dodge, hosting salons in Greenwich Village that included Margaret Sanger and Havelock Ellis, would send Loy news of feminist discussions and agitation. Intrigued by the ideas coming from America, Loy wrote a Feminist Manifesto in 1914, in which she critiqued the "value of woman" as determined by "'virtue'" and "physical purity" (Loy, *Lost,* 154). The manifesto resonates with contemporaneous critiques of patriarchal womanhood, such as Charlotte Perkins Gilman's figure of the "oversexed woman" who has been culturally constructed to attract men through adornment and display. This system of attributing value to woman, Loy insists, renders her "lethargic in the acquisition of intrinsic merits of character by which she could obtain a concrete value" (154). Somewhat sardonically, Loy recommends the "unconditional surgical destruction of virginity" at puberty, deploying the manifesto form's signature strategy of using shock as radical persuasion. Repeatedly, "value" is invoked as a constructed difference between men and women: "The value of man is assessed entirely according to his use or interest to the community," while "the value of woman, depends entirely on chance, her success or insuccess [sic] in manoeuvering a man into taking the life-long responsibility of her" (155). Because the "ample" advantages of marriage outweigh those of most "trades," a woman's virginity remains her most important economic asset even in "modern conditions," when "a woman can accept preposterously luxurious support from a man... as a thank offering for her virginity," sarcastically labeling marriage as an "advantageous bargain" (155).

Within this system of exchange, the married woman is not unlike the prostitute, and indeed she has the choice "as conditions are at present constituted" between "**Parasitism, & Prostitution—or Negation**."[11] Loy's collapse of marriage and prostitution echoes the "equation of marriage with trade and even with prostitution" that "emerged in the late nineteenth century in the writings of social and political thinkers such as Friedrich Engels, Thorstein Veblen, August Bebel" (Scuriatti, 78). Gilman's feminist analysis of the "mercenary marriage [as] a perfectly natural consequence of the economic dependence of women" (C. Gilman, 47) deplored the "sex-relation for sale" hypocritically approved in modern marriage but condemned in prostitution (49). For Gilman, emerging consumer capitalism intensifies this sexual-economic problem and constructs woman as a "non-productive consumer" (58). Loy calls for women to reject confining ideas about marriage, maternity, and sexuality that serve this economy, urging women to rid themselves of the romantic "illusion" that confuses an economically motivated transaction with love (Loy, Lost, 156).

Although never published, the Feminist Manifesto's economic analysis of gender finds poetic form in "Virgins Plus Curtains Minus Dots," published in Rogue in 1915. "Houses hold virgins" who are "without dots" or dowries. The "men pass" and are "going somewhere," while the virgins offer themselves to "the mirror" (Loy, Lost, 21) to confirm their capacity to attract through display, even as they wait under the illusion of a love that will never come to pass in the real world of marriage as finance. They are "indoctrinated with a myth of Romance," trapped in the "double bind of dominant ideology and economic hegemony" (Goody, 108):

> We have been taught
> Love is a god
> White with soft wings
> Nobody shouts
> Virgins for sale
> (Loy, Lost, 22)

Virginity "is revealed as the ultimate commodity fetish; though endowed with supposed essential value…, its actual value is purely monetary" (Goody, 108). Trapped behind a door bolted by "Somebody who was never / a virgin" (Loy, Lost, 21), the virgins' eyes "look out" on a world they cannot move through as freely as men (22).

The image of virgins' eyes to signify woman's commodification appears also in "Three Moments in Paris." Also published in Rogue a few months earlier in 1915, the poem's three sections capture a small vignette of Parisian commerce—the café and the modern department store. The first two sections take place among couples late at night in cafés, centering on women who understand "nothing of man / But mastery" (Loy, Lost, 16) and, "As usual," smile "bravely/ As it is given to her to be brave" (15, sic). The third section, "Magasins du Louvre," names the Parisian department store founded in the mid-nineteenth century and expanded in 1877 to occupy an entire hotel building, abundantly full of consumer goods of all kinds. As the first modern consumer city, Paris invented the department store as a distinct space for enticing consumer desire with intricate displays and abundant goods of all kinds. The poem describes "Long lines of boxes / Of dolls" and "composite babies with arms extended" that "Hang from the ceiling" (17). The dolls are compared to virgins, as "All the virgin eyes in the world are made of glass," and the comparison suggests that real girls are like a mass-manufactured commodity, ordered, dissected, and reassembled for the customer's desire. Two women, each described as a"cocotte" wander the aisles, and their eyes meet one another's in a surreptitious moment of contact that suggests both the relative freedom for women to wander publicly that the department store offered and the concurrent constrictions of commodified femininity on the desire—ambiguously suggestive of lesbian desire—of the young women catching each other's glance amidst the "virgin eyes" of glass.

The gendering of space, like the space of the department store, is contingent upon a masculine economy in Loy's poems. The space of the marriage house organizes "The Effectual Marriage, or *The Insipid Narrative of Gina and Miovanni,*" a satirical poem featuring herself and the Futurist Giovanni Papini, with whom she had an affair. Also involved with the Futurist leader Filippo Tomasso Marinetti, Loy encountered the movement's glorification of masculine aggression and disdain for women as weak. Written in 1915 and published in the *Others* anthology of 1917, the poem mocks the radical movement's retention of regressive gender roles that see man as "ego" and as "magnificently man" (Loy, *Lost,* 37). By the end of the nineteenth century, earlier assumptions that "housewives were gainful workers [and producers] was gradually displaced" by the "concept of the unproductive housewife" defined within a "new distinction between market and nonmarket labor" (Folbre, 464). Coalescing within popular thinking and assisted by theoretical devaluations of women's work in capitalism, the housewife was seen to operate "outside the realm of economics and therefore did not contribute to economic growth" (Folbre, 466). Loy's poem reflects this gendered bias infusing economic thought by the turn of the century. Miovanni spends his time in the library, "Outside time and space," while Gina wanders among "pots and pans" (Loy, *Lost,* 37) in her kitchen, tending to the "Pet simplicities of her Universe" with "devotional fingers" (39). As Laura Scuriatti observes, "The literary tropes of domesticity, faithful love, and docile femininity are exposed as the product of a ruthless economic system of exchange" that "also informs the architectural spaces of daily life," perpetuating "the conditions through which gender identity is essentialised and conceived as 'natural,' while its economic roots may remain unspoken" (Scuriatti, 73).

The status of woman as a commodity within marriage is one of the "tatters of tradition" that Loy sees lingering into the modern era, bearing with it "our forebear's excrements" and "subconscious archives" (Loy, *Lost,* 71). A short poem appearing in the initial issue of *Contact* in December 1920, "O Hell" imagined the modern self as "a covered entrance to infinity / Choked with the tatters of tradition" (71). Linked semantically by the shared use of the phrase, "covered entrance to infinity," to a prose polemic written during the same period, the poem suggests the "unconscious" habits of thought that, in "International Psycho-Democracy," are squarely rooted in a capitalist, militaristic, and masculine economy. Subtitled "Mina Loy's Tenets," it refutes Marinetti's "War, the Only Hygiene" and Futurism's glorification of military might.[12] Loy encourages the reader to

> Invest Your Consciousness
>
> in
>
> My Idea-Market

of "*Psycho-Democracy*," a "psychological gauge applied to all social problems, for the interpretation of political, religious and financial systems" (Loy, *Last*, 277, emphasis in original). Claiming that the "one class distinction is between the dominator and the dominated" (279), Loy places the "Capitalist" at the center of modern social existence. It is the Capitalist

> For whom the politician legislates
> The army fights,
> The church collects. (278)

Modern industry creates a system by which workers' bodies are sacrificed to the production of military might, which then destroys more bodies in a dehumanizing cycle of industrial profit making: it is "*Criminal lunacy*" that "millions of men and women...wear out their organisms with no reward but the maintenance of those organisms, imperfectly functioning, and that this social condition should be safeguarded and preserved by the blowing up of other millions of human organisms" (279, emphasis in original). Pointing to the power of ideology in regulating the masses, Loy asserts that "*Power* is a secret society of the minority, whose hold on the majority lies in the esoteric or actual value of social ideas" (280, emphasis in original). The "advantage of the minority" is conferred with the "consent of the majority" (280), whose "habits" are shaped by the "Dominator's standard" (281).

However, "class evolution" must "democratize the Dominator's standard" through shifting from a profit motive to a provisioning motive, fulfilling needs of the "self" and the collective: "Man's desire is for Self," attainable only with a new "standard" recognizing that "The earth offers super-abundance for All" (Loy, *Last*, 281). The "*belligerent masculine* social ideal" underlying capitalism and militarism is nonetheless "*psychically magnetic*" because it has "created certain formulae figuring largely in our social pleasures" of possession and consumption (281, emphasis in original). Like Gilman, imagining an evolutionary shift in human consciousness is possible, and believing that "man has the conceptual power to create a substitute for war," Loy calls for "a concerted effort to evolve and establish *a new social symbolism, a new social rhythm*" to replace the "hypnotic war lust" of militaristic capitalism (282, emphasis in original).

Appearing first as a pamphlet in Florence in 1920, and subsequently reprinted in *The Little Review* in 1921, the concurrence of "Psycho-Democracy" with "O Hell" moreover joins with a short prose piece that accompanied the poem in *Contact's* inaugural issue. In "Summer Night in a Florentine Slum," depictions of class, family, and gender observed by the English-identified speaker of the piece concretize, through the frame of gender, the economic/sociopolitical critiques of forces hindering selfhood in the other two pieces. As the speaker leans out of her window, she can see and hear the poor Italian families in the neighborhood surrounding her. A juxtaposed set of tiny vignettes depicts women struggling within patriarchal sexual economies—the women burdened with too many babies; a baby "dead of starvation" (Loy, *Last,* 82); the "handsome half of a lady…born without legs" that "groups of grey soldiers watched—their eyes intrigued" (81); the wife whose carpenter husband "pawed his young wife's breast—the table he had beaten her with the same morning" (83). The piece ends as the speaker withdraws into her room, pulling the "English chintz curtains scattered with prevaricating rosebuds" (83) to suggest her nationalistically class-defined difference as a British woman. Yet she too is part of a patriarchal system shaping both class and gender. With a sly gesture to the British woman's position within modern empire—a position of display, a signifier of a masculine and national wealth—the final image seen by the speaker is a print in her room of "Beardsley's Mademoiselle De Maupin," fashionably drawing "on her gloves" (83). Such reference prefigures "Anglo-Mongrels and the Rose"(1923–1925), Loy's long poem—her "auto-mythology"—which foregrounds the economic roots connecting marriage, family, and nation through the interdependent economies of domestic and global male dominance sustaining British empire.

Contemplating her British class roots in the 1920s as she composed her long poem, Loy's American experience nonetheless colored her thinking about poetry. Her essay "Modern Poetry," published in 1925, identifies a distinctively economic measure for a modernist "renaissance of poetry" in America's emergence as an industrial and commercial power, swelling its cities with new immigrants and migrants. In America's modern cities, she wrote, English and its poetic measure have been remade, as "latterly a thousand languages have been born, and each one, for purposes of communication at least, English—English enriched and variegated with the grammatical structure and voice-inflection of many races, in novel alloy with the fundamental *time-is-money idiom* of the United States" (Loy, *Lost,* 158, emphasis added). America's modern industrial needs had drawn new waves of immigrants to its cities,[13] and Loy points specifically to "the baser avenues of Manhattan," where "every voice swings to the triple rhythm of its race, its citizenship and its personality" as foundation for the poetry renaissance (159). Their richly "unclassifiable speech" counterpoints the staleness of class-privileged language, which "professors of Harvard and Oxford labored to preserve" as " 'God's English,' " while "the muse of modern literature arose, and her tongue had been loosened in the melting-pot" of America's poor urban streets (159). Loy goes on to argue that a strong "relationship of expression between the high browest modern poets and an adolescent Slav who has speculated in a wholesale job-lot of mandarines and is trying to sell them in a retail market on First Avenue" develops on the city streets in America. The "time-is-money idiom" of both poet and immigrant marketer "have…adapted to a country where the mind has to put on its verbal clothes at terrific speed if it would speak in time; where no one will listen if you attack him twice with the same missile of argument" (159).

Rather than one of the avant-garde magazines that routinely included Loy's poetry, "Modern Poetry" was published in *Charm,* an "eclectic magazine published in the 1920s, devoted to women's fashion and clothing" (Conover, in Loy, *Lost,* 217,

n. 53). Appropriate to the cross-vectors of economics, modern subjectivity, and poetry in Loy's work, this discussion of poetry, written by a woman who had gained notoriety in the teens for her sexually frank poetry and her iconic status as a "new woman," took place within a magazine geared toward the woman as consumer and produced within the context of a booming consumer culture. However, her faith in America's diversity as a source for poetic language stands in tension with the growing imperative to engage in consumption as a way of conforming and standardizing the American masses. New technologies created a bounty of cheap, disposable goods, in sync with the "new American tempo" described in 1926 by the advertiser Robert Updegraff, whose ideas about stimulating rapid fluctuations in consumer desire influenced the advertising world's message to routinely buy, replace, and dispose of goods rather than value frugality or durability (in McGovern, 122). The seeming abundance of cheap goods naturalized the concept of ownership as a particularly American quality, linking acquisition to freedom in overtly nationalistic language. Both advertisers and economists also regarded consumer activity as a way to Americanize and assimilate waves of new immigrants, and consumption took on a nationalistic slant in ad copy as well as in economic treatises such as Simon Patten's *The Consumption of Wealth* (1908), which advocated the assimilative powers of consumption for the migrant masses who would become Americanized through spending or what he called "socialized consumption." In a 1911 address to social scientists, Franklin Giddens, a co-founder of the American Economic Association, called standardized consumption the "assimilative force" that would create conformity and greater social solidarity (Sklansky, 179).

Taking a different tact, Thorstein Veblen and the American Institutional School that developed from his thinking distrusted the standardizing impulse of modern business as a profit-generating ploy in which customers themselves were manufactured and "required to conform to the uniform gradations imposed upon consumable goods" (McGovern, 146). The "modern tempo" of rapid change and continual newness aggravated tension between consumption and social provisioning as primary economic concerns in the new capitalist economy occupying the attention of Americans.

THE AMERICAN INSTITUTIONAL SCHOOL AND THE FIGURE OF "WOMAN"

In America, one of the most sustained and influential theories of women's position within capitalism evolved from the work of Thorstein Veblen, beginning with his *Theory of the Leisure Class* in 1899 and pursued by his followers who constituted the American Institutional School. Fellow intellectuals in Greenwich Village generally considered him to share feminist convictions.[14] His "awareness of women's central role in the new consumer civilization" to ultimately function "as a marker of her husband's pecuniary prowess" led him to resist the masculine bias of purportedly neutral economic theories of the marketplace, showing instead that "in a patriarchal society where women 'belonged' to men, every act of consumption by a woman served to increase the prestige of her possessing male," and, therefore, "women's consumption worked to glorify the men who provided them with the means to consume" (N. Gilman, 5). Further, for Veblen, man's claim to possession of a woman arose from the seizure of property, including women, in ancient dynamics of war. Individual ownership, or the "right to exclusive consumption," followed the "subjugation of women…[as] the foundational act, one might say, of a consumer society" (N. Gilman, 686). Marriage, as the exchange of women, historically linked private property and patriarchy; indeed, within consumer culture, "the institution of display remained most embedded…through the unreconstructed role of women" (688) as possessions of their husbands and, consequently, as important signs of masculine wealth through unfettered display—by means of clothing, jewelry, domestic goods, and a myriad of consumer items. Indeed, the popular notion of women as "natural" (and even liberated) consumers, fostered by new modes and representations of consumer activity, cloaked the subjugation of women that Veblen's social constructivist theory sought to expose as foundational to modern economic theories and systems.

Women's work with social provisioning, either in research or in practice, coincided with the values espoused by Veblen and his followers. Veblen saw economics as "a social provisioning process," reacting against neoclassical and capitalist concepts of economy, exchange, and agency, alongside concepts of private property, individualism, and competition (Jennings, 113). His first major work, *The Theory of the Leisure Class*, offered a scathing critique of corporate, consumer capitalism that continued until his death in the 1920s. Veblen critically observed that modern status depended upon the ability to consume, especially without the demeaning activity of labor. Thus, the display of pecuniary strength through "conspicuous consumption," or the display of wealth through unnecessary (or wasteful, for Veblen) acquisition, depended upon the degradation of work and productivity. For Veblen, adhering to a productivist view, the "instinct for work" enabling creative workmanship (as opposed to the drudgery of mechanical labor) constituted an essential human quality endangered by consumer capitalism. The relegation of women's work to the category of "unproductive labor" alongside the enforced leisure of middle and upper-class women "enraged" Veblen, for "the exclusion of women from the workplace…prevented the instinct of workmanship from flourishing" and inhibited women's advancement (N. Gilman, 13).[15]

LOLA RIDGE: WOMEN AS WORKERS AND WOMEN AS WASTE

Figures of women within economic capitalism garner particular notice in Lola Ridge's 1918 book, *The Ghetto and Other Poems*, a collection that presents the New York's

Lower East Side through its markets, commerce, and labor while also extending a critique of capitalism beyond the city to consider the plight of workers in America and other issues of social injustice. Active within poetic, intellectual, and activist circles in New York in the teens, Ridge's leftist and feminist convictions shaped her modernist experiments with the long poem and lyric forms, while influencing her editorial work with the important avant-garde journals *Others* and *Broom*. Hosting salons for the New York avant-garde attended by poets that included Moore and Loy and social justice advocates like Dorothy Day (committed to justice issues even in her preconversion years) and Floyd Dell, Ridge distinguished herself early on as a modernist "proletarian poet," attentive to poverty, injustice, and capitalist abuses.[16] Like the reporter Jacob Riis before her, whose 1899 book *How the Other Half Lives* recorded conditions of tenement slums through photographic images and words, she sought to make the city visible to itself through capturing the material effects on the poor and working classes of New York's dramatic emergence as a center of commerce and capital.

The visibility of women's bodies in these poems is striking in suggesting the circulation of concurrent, dual feminized associations: the association of use and need with women's work, both degraded within an ideology of consumer desire; and the association of women with consumer activities and display. "The Ghetto," a nine-part poetic sequence, figures women as laboring both within capitalism's mechanistic drudgery and in more creative ways uniting mind and body while perpetuating cultural continuity within the ghetto's diversity. At the same time, particularly in the section *Manhattan*, which offers a more pessimistic view of the city, women's bodies are the very sites of conspicuous consumption and display that Veblen, Gilman, and others theorized.

The opening long poem "The Ghetto" adopts the speaking voice of a woman residing in the Lower East Side tenements. Voluntarily embracing poverty, Ridge lived in Greenwich Village, around Hester Street where she interacted with an immigrant population diverse in language, religion, and ethnicity.[17] "The Ghetto" reflects the confluence of the labor movement, socialism, and an expanding immigrant population in New York City. The poem's interest in women within the street market and as factory workers distinctively casts issues of labor in relation to gender. The garment workers, three of whom live in the speaker's tenement, are part of an industry employing large numbers of women and giving rise to the first women's labor unions in America.

On Hester Street, the heat of the crowded tenements renders the "cool" air of the night "inaccessible" (Ridge, 3), echoing voices of housing reform arguing against tenement crowding, poor lighting, and insufficient ventilation.[18] In the poem, the ghetto is felt both *as* a body and *on* the body, as the heat is like a "beast pressing its great steaming belly close" to the bodies in the tenements, a "hot tide of flesh" (3, 4). The close attention to bodies comes early in the first section's panoramic view of the streets as "Bodies dangle from the fire escapes / Or sprawl over the stoops," with pallid and "Herring-yellow faces, spotted as with a mold / . . . And infants' faces with open parched mouths / that suck at the air as at empty teats" (3). This first view of bodies presents them as sites of unmet need, struggling to survive among the "garbage of the world" (3).

Another kind of body appears, however, an "enduring flesh" of communities of women. In this first section, women form images of collectivity, linked to possibilities of freedom fought for in the present and to virtues of endurance carried from the past. On the street, "Young women pass in groups / Converging to the forums and meeting halls, / Surging indomitable, slow." Like the modern new woman, "Their heads are uncovered to the stars, / And they call to the young men and to one another / With a free camaraderie" (Ridge, 4). Moving freely through public spaces with a sense of gender equality semantically associated with socialist politics (camaraderie), these women also embody a particularly female and maternal wisdom, figured by the poem through their "ancient" eyes and "vision" and "enduring flesh," a flesh associated with Jewishness and a history of Jewish enslavement. In the final two stanzas of the first section, the word "flesh" is repeated four times, transfiguring the bodily crowdedness of the urban street into an embodied, inherited, and specifically feminized vision of endurance through oppression. The word "flesh" signifies both the oppressed body and the body of resistance in a stanza that moves from a wide-angle view of the street to a focus on the "ancient mothers": the street's "Heavy surges of flesh" are the "Flesh of this abiding / Brood of those ancient mothers who saw the dawn break over Egypt" and continue the century's old "march of their enduring flesh" (4).

The market activity of vendors and shoppers, the display of goods, and the crush of "herded stalls / In dissolute array" (Ridge, 12) all communicate the energy and diversity of New York's new immigrants.[19] The street commerce involves "All who come and go" within a local space of exchange that includes multiple generations and ethnicities of women, children, babies, and men (15). The poem unabashedly celebrates this market scene as a "great bazaar" full of the "garbled majesty" of "glitter and...jumbled finery / And strangely juxtaposed / Cans, paper, rags / And colors decomposing" (12). The market is an "ancient tapestry of motley weave / Upon the open wall of this new land," in contrast with modern forms of market commerce (13). That contrast is most sharply drawn at the end of the fourth section, following a long description of an older merchant, "an old grey scholar" who "fingers lovingly each calico" he displays for sale, "As though it were a gorgeous shawl, / Or costly vesture" (13). His goods connect him with his homeland that is now "dwindling in remembrance." In one of numerous generational contrasts drawn in the poem, the younger generation of men or the "raw young seed of Israel /. . . have no backward vision in their eyes" (14). Instead, like the street market's "young trader," the vision of the younger merchants is "tape-ruled," or more akin to the seemingly rational measures of efficiency, value, and profit one sees as he "Looks Westward where the trade-lights glow." His vision symbolically rises to the structures of commerce, "Some fifty stories to the skies" that dwarf the street market and measure economic selfhood within the strictures of capitalism's drive for profit (15).

The laboring bodies enabling this "Westward" vision of selfhood and market exchange are nonetheless elided from its frame. The poem, however, offers particularly keen attention to the impact of labor upon the workers' bodies. That the most particularized attention is paid to women bespeaks Ridge's feminist commitment to rendering women's lives visible and recognizing the significant presence of women within the work force in the early twentieth century, while bemoaning industry's mechanistic labor. The loss of a creative form of labor, in which the worker experiences a connection with the product of his or her labor, is figured through Old Sodos, a saddle maker in the old country who has now "forgotten how" (Ridge, 5). A younger generation's factory work further denies labor's creative potential through shaping the body as a machine part. Sadie, Old Sodo's daughter, works in a garment factory, her body "keyed to the long day" of sewing machines (7), as "All day the power machines / Drone in her ears" in the hot, foul air of the garment factory (6). Presenting a vivid picture of industrialized factory work, Sadie's movements are regulated by the repetitive labor that makes her "One with her machine," the "biting steel—that twice / Has nipped her to the bone" (6). When the body tires, Sadie fights fatigue to keep up with the machine, driving her body to compete to the point that she is described in gearlike, mechanical terms, a part of the industrial machine. She "quivers like a rod.../ A thin black piston flying / One with her machine," as she "stabs the piece-work with her bitter eye." She is a "fiery static atom, / Held in place by the fierce pressure all about" as she "Speeds up the driven wheels / And biting steel" (6). Taylorism's virtues of efficiency, speed, and high productivity render the body's well-being negligible. The worker's relationship with her material is hostile, stabbing the "piece-work" and becoming like the machine that constricts and regulates her. However, she finds freedom in the labor of the mind, reading at night "Those books that have most unset thought, / New-poured and malleable." Unlike the body's constraint within the factory, her mind is active and "her thought / Leaps fusing at white heat" that fuels her revolutionary energy. She "spits her fire out" at a "protest meeting on the Square / Her lit eyes kindling the mob." Although she awakens "a little whiter... Alert, yet weary," her strength is a source of rebellion against the economic molding of both body and mind (7).

The speaker's focus on the tenement environment, in which her "little fifth floor room" is low-ceilinged and bare, with "coppery stains / Left by seeping rains," and "roaches, sepia-brown" that "consort" at night (Ridge, 15), pointedly clashes with America's ideal of a prosperous nation unburdened by a system of class division, despite the presence of poverty. Until the late nineteenth century, the dominant American attitudes toward poverty regarded the poor as responsible for their status because of inherent weakness or immorality. Arguing instead that systemic, material conditions promoted poverty, the environmental view of poverty emerged around the turn of the century, drawing from and disseminated within a combination of new social sciences (especially sociology), the Social Gospel movement, and the progressive era's reform movements. The speaker's care in detailing the tenement environment, as well as the cramped urban streets, pointedly emphasizes the environmental view of poverty and makes possible the affirmation of the humanity of the poor.

Within the tenement, an older woman bears upon her body the devastation of living and working conditions while also holding forth a community ethos pervading the environment. She is an "old stooped mother," carrying the "uneven droopiness that women know / who have suckled many young" (Ridge, 16). As she shakes out her rugs, "Her thews are slack / And curved the ruined back / And flesh empurpled like old meat" (16). Yet, like the "ancient mothers" in this "dismal house" of noise and crowdedness, the old woman nurtures human spiritual connections by lighting candles each Friday night that connect, like "Infinite fine rays / To other windows" (16–17). The conjoined candle lights link "the tenements / Like an endless prayer" (17). The wretchedness of the domestic tenement space, unsparingly detailed as oppressing the body, does not suppress the spirit or minds of the women within or, in the case of the old woman, the communities they enable.

The poem ends with an image of Hester Street as being such a woman. Awakening at dawn, the street is "Like a forlorn woman over-born / By many babies at her teats, / Turns on her trampled bed to meet the day" (Ridge, 24). As if giving birth, this maternal image brings forth the word "LIFE!" that begins the next stanza and the ode-like celebration of the Ghetto's life energy coursing through the final nine stanzas, printed in italicized type: "*Startling, vigorous life, / That squirms under my touch*" (24); "*Life leaping in the shaken flesh*" and "*Seething as in a great vat*" (25); vital as "*Electric currents of life, / Throwing off thoughts like sparks, / Glittering, disappearing, / Making unknown circuits*" (25). In a final cascade of active verbs, economic terms suggest a kind of new economy that can come out of the "*bitter wine*" of tenements and wage labor, out of the "*bloody stills of the world*" (26). The Ghetto market of "*Bartering, changing, extorting*," is also the market of "*Dreaming, debating, aspiring*" that sustains the "*Astounding, indestructible / Life of the Ghetto*," the "*Strong flux of life*" made sacred as the "*Passion eternal*" (26). The combined discourses of economics and Christianity evoke a particularly spiritual reading of human economics within a larger frame of human dignity and life, a humanity the poem views as threatened by industrial capitalism's greed.

The poems that follow "The Ghetto" reframe a more pessimistic view of the city, less about a vital life force and more about the modern systems of commerce changing the cityscape and dehumanizing its inhabitants. In poems like "Manhattan," "Broadway," and "Promenade," the modern city of light burns endlessly with neon lights of display and the glitter of wealth. Generated by money, light robes the city in "Manhattan", just as "Diaphonous gold" is "Veiling the Woolworth" department store (29). "Flaring and multiplying" with a force uncontrolled and unpredictable (29), the city is addressed as "You of unknown voltage / Whirling on your axis…/ Scrawling vermillion signatures / Over the night's velvet hoarding. . . ." (30, ellipses included). The red neon "signatures" on the night sky inscribe the power of the city's looming towers of commerce as both dominating and unstable: the axis whirls "Insolent, towering spherical / To apices ever shifting" (30). In "Broadway" the imagery of "serpent", "eunuch lights," and the "slow suction of her breath" that bewitch the "multitudes" link the "light" of commercialism to a kind of soul-crushing by the "unsubtle courtezan," the prostitute emerging from "towers rampant" (32). The commerce of consumption, figured as female and degenerate, echoes through other poems.

"Promenade" pointedly highlights the city's conspicuous consumption. Like Veblen, Ridge sees this gendering of consumerism as an entrapment of women, most blatantly evident in women's fashions: "Undulant rustlings, / Of oncoming silk, / Rhythmic, incessant" open the poem, training our vision on "Glimpses of green / And blurs of gold / And delicate mauves / That snatch at youth." The hint of life—or youth—being snatched away is compounded by the immediate description of objectified bodies on display in the promenade: "And bodies all rosily / Fleshed for the airing / In warm velvety surges / Passing imperious, slow" (Ridge, 39). That the use of the woman's body as a display of male wealth is a form of death finds overt expression as "Women drift into the limousines / that shut like silken caskets / On gems half weary of their glittering" (39).

The woman's body in "The Woman with Jewels" grotesquely parodies the Renaissance catalog form, gazing on body parts inscribed by a system of conspicuous consumption: "The woman with jewels sits in the café" with diamonds that "glitter on her bulbous fingers / And on her arms, great as thighs, / Diamonds gush from her ear-lobes over the goitrous throat" (83). Alone, she is on the prowl for companionship in her "black satin dress...a little lifted, showing the dropsical legs in their silken fleshings," her "mountainous breasts" trembling beneath the "agitation in her gems" that "quiver incessantly, emitting trillions of fiery rays" (83, ellipses added). She is the body of excess and display that collapses wealth and sexual availability, as though the body of the wealthy wife is no different from the prostitute in a male-dominated market that positions "woman" as a commodity for display and exchange. The speaker queries "Why does she come alone to this obscure basement / She who should have a litter and hand-maidens to support her on either side?" The poem suggests that, as a wealthy but lost soul, she has been violated by the system of exchange in which she participates. Sexually loaded images describing her face equate a deromanticized sex act with this exchange: her eyes are like "little pools of tar, spilled by a sailor in mad haste for the shore," and her mouth is "scarlet and full—only a little crumpled—like a flower that has been pressed apart" (83). The images of lips "pressed apart" and "spillage" suggest a sexual economy of waste and violence. The woman's body, in essence, is violated repeatedly by this ideology of display and consumption, a form of social wastage.

Ridge's images of women as workers and women as waste resonate with a "sketchy but discernible portrait of consumption [that] had thus emerged in American social thought by the 1920s" (McGovern, 161), in which the figure of woman played a central role, just as her image would dominate the explosion of visual advertising aimed at the (feminized) consumer. Veblen's followers, including Wesley Clair Mitchell and Hazel Kyrk, continued in the teens and twenties to analyze "modern consumption as a woman's issue" within an Institutional commitment to ideas about "managing the economy for social betterment" (McGovern, 151).[20] Lorine Pruette, whose *Women and Leisure: A Study of Social Waste* appeared in 1923, reiterated Veblen's endorsement of the work instinct as a remedy for women's enforced (and unhealthy) leisure. An example of a "Veblenian text" from the modernist era that associates the "feminine body with conspicuous consumption, since it is given over to leisure, to display," Pruette "develops Veblen's stress on femininity as display and, extending his support for the 'new woman,' argues for a countervailing involvement of women in the workforce" (Armstrong, 60).[21] Against a postwar sense of an "obligation to consume" in the 1920s (Armstrong, 61), Pruette (who held a PhD in economics) argues the "uselessness" and "from a social standpoint...actual menace" of women's enforced leisure: "They are a mark, not only of their husbands' ability to keep them in comfort, not only of 'vicarious consumption,' but of social inefficiency, of society's failure adequately to make use of its human material" (Pruette, xiii). Pruette criticizes commodity capitalism for denying women a full range of creative work and for deeming housework "unproductive" because it is not wage-earning, although it sustains society through forms of provisioning labor. To talk about women and work, therefore, meant revising official definitions of "work" while challenging and complicating the gendered associations of femininity and consumerism.

MARIANNE MOORE: NEED OR DESIRE?

When Marianne Moore's long poem "Marriage" appeared in a 1923 limited edition chapbook in Monroe Wheeler's *Manikin* series (and reappeared in her first American book *Observations* a year later), her language is strikingly unromantic and indeed economic in referring to "This institution, / perhaps one should say enterprise" of modern marriage (Moore, 73).[22] Laden with quoted materials, sinewy movements, and rapid juxtapositions, the poem's complicated discourse on gender difference pointedly includes the economics of consumption and display operating within the "institution" of marriage. The importance of the conspicuous display of pecuniary acquisition underscores the quoted observation found midway through the poem, that " 'Men are monopolists / of stars, garters, buttons / and other shining baubles' " (78). Moore's note indicates that she merges the words of M. Thomas Carey, a feminist and President Emeritus of Bryn Mawr College (attributed with the comment that "Men are monopolists"), with a second feminist moment, coming almost a century earlier in the 1821 founder's address of Mount Holyoke College.[23] Moore's note includes a substantial excerpt from that address that stresses the preserves of male power unavailable to women and circulated through forms of display:

> Men practically reserve for themselves stately funerals, splendid monuments, memorial statutes, membership in academies, medals, titles, honorary degrees, stars, garters, ribbons, buttons and other shining baubles, so valueless in themselves and yet so infinitely desirable because they are symbols of recognition by their fellow craftsmen of difficult work well done. (104)

Including specific material drawn from women educators important to Moore thickens the poem's notion that gender is taught, not natural, and that women have been mistaught (as have men) through the institutions controlled by men. The woman "loves herself so much, / she cannot see herself enough—," a self-delusion that is "the logical last touch / to an expansive splendor / *earned as wages for work done*" (79, emphasis added). Thus, the institution or enterprise requires "all one's criminal ingenuity / to avoid!" (73).

As a college student at Bryn Mawr from 1905 through 1909 and a young adult, teaching business and commercial courses at the Carlisle Indian School[24] and then moving to Manhattan in 1918, Marianne Moore gained exposure to a breadth of ideas about economics as she developed as a poet. At Bryn Mawr, she encountered socialist, feminist, and progressive ideas reacting against capitalism's forceful growth. Her intrigue with the urban environment of commerce, fashion, and diversity during her Philadelphia years and her numerous travels and eventual move to New York City, bolstered by her copious consumption of culture and the arts, suggest how the modern energies of the city coincided with Moore's emerging poetics. The economic energies of production and consumption, and the debates about them, were not lost on Moore. The poems of her first American book, *Observations* (1924), gathered from throughout her young writing career, reflect the historio-economic contexts of their production, weaving a language of exchange, labor, value, display, and consumption in poems that often explore how these concepts shaping modern life relate to the creative process and to the common good. Most notably evoked and explored within the poem "New York," Moore's economic concerns develop through strategies of indirection, inflection, and suggestive association rather than direct treatment of economic topics as in Loy or Ridge.

Nonetheless, Moore probably understood economic theory more systematically than her fellow two poets, learning about the discipline within a stronghold of women's education and taught by women of the first substantial generation to enter higher education. The school's consciousness of its mission to educate women and to model rigorous female intellectualism across all fields—even those traditionally deemed masculine—was bolstered by the feminist convictions of the institution's president, M. Carey Thomas, and of many of the faculty.[25] Attending suffrage meetings and talks on the settlement movement, Moore engaged the heady combination of socialism and feminism, expressing an attraction to socialism tempered by a pragmatic endorsement of incremental change. Visiting New York City in 1909, her senior year, she writes back to her family of attending a suffrage meeting at the Cooper Institute, which was "a joy," and references the settlement house movement led by Jane Addams (Costello, 61).

In another letter to her family during the same visit, she reports on a conversation with the host family's father in which he asks, "Are you a Socialist?" (Costello, 56).[26] Her response—"I said I was, but not a Marxian"—and the ensuing conversation about the ideas of prominent socialist thinkers, social reform activists, and economists (she references R. F. Hunter's *Socialists at Work*) includes discussion of "the German insurance and labor commissions and democracy vs. monarchy or communism." In part flip and in part serious, Moore concludes: "Of course we all [Bryn Mawr girls] are Socialists, (I say this to you) in so far as we know economics and are halfway moral and want clean politics." She goes on, though, reflecting upon her status as a nonvoter despite clear political ideas, claiming that, given the vote, she would "have voted for Taft...should have voted for Roosevelt, if I could have, however the socialist cause might have been booming." Her reasons convey her incipient pragmatism, for Moore has crossed out part of the sentence that reads "for I believe in gradual adaptation to new policy as most do," rewriting it to say that she can be in favor of "no goose scheme with everything turned upside down when we need old dogs for present difficulties" (Costello, 56).[27]

Moore's formal education included modern economic theory as a social science major in history, economics, and politics (an early version of political science), taking a series of economics courses from instructors newly and internationally educated in modern theories. Moore's Bryn Mawr undergraduate catalog specifically speaks of economics as a "science" and lists course descriptions clearly focused upon neoclassical economics, attentive in particular to German and Austrian theorists. A number of Bryn Mawr's economics professors were trained at the University of Austria and at Columbia University (where Simon Patten was a faculty member). Marion Parris, a Bryn Mawr doctoral student who had studied at the University of Vienna—a center of neoclassical theory—taught political economy and political science to Moore in her junior and senior years while completing her dissertation on modern economic theory and ethics.[28] Taking the doctoral degree in 1909 from Bryn Mawr,[29] with a minor in ethics, Parris undertook in her dissertation to investigate the field's shift to the "subjective" nature of the desiring individual, entering the "debated borderlines between economics, ethics and psychology whose boundaries have remained undefined since economic theory annexed a subjective province to its former realm of 'scarce natural objects' and 'exchangeable goods'" (Parris, 17). While Moore would not likely have read Parris's dissertation, her instructor's enthusiasm about ethics and her historical understanding of social reform and the idea of the social good, as recounted in her study, would certainly have entered the classroom.

Moreover, Parris's feminist sensibility prompted her subsequent research into women's issues that contributed to the period's feminist gendering of economic discourse, both in her research and pedagogy. Publishing a piece on women's work within the research series of the WEIU in Boston, Parris also codirected a dissertation on the millinery trade for women that appeared in 1916 in the series, authored by her doctoral student Lorinda Parry, one of the first students in Bryn Mawr's Graduate Department of Social Economy and Social Research. Founded in 1915, this interdisciplinary program, unique for its time, combined academic research and social work practice for social workers and for social researchers. Parris's courses "focused on economic reform movements and legislation," intertwining social justice issues and economic theory to consider areas of economy not recognized by neoclassical paradigms (Dzuback, 584, 590), interests informing her classes even before the graduate program started. In Moore's senior year, for example, the course catalog described Parris's class in "Theoretical Sociology" (not taken by Moore) that linked social problems and economic systems to study "social problems confronting the modern state...such as the congestion of population, housing and transportation problems in...cities, immigration and race problems in America, the standard of living among various economic groups, etc." (Bryn Mawr, 92).

Alongside an awareness of the socially embedded and even gendered dimensions of economy, Moore's Bryn Mawr years introduced her to the new economic theories. Frank A. Fetter's The Principles of Economics, the major economics textbook in use at the time and listed in the Bryn Mawr course catalog, claimed to use the "language of recent [neoclassical] economists" in asserting that "[h]uman activity is directed to shaping and arranging things so as to increase want-gratifying power" and that "labor is not the origin of value" (219, 223, 224).[30] Fetter, an American economist of the Austrian school, instructs his student readers that "[s]carcity of things *desired* is the one objective condition of value" (225, emphasis added); indeed, a primary tactic for increasing value within capitalism is to create scarcity. Almost a decade later, but echoing ideas he had espoused since the 1890s, Thorstein Veblen's *Dial* articles (in issues that Moore owned) argued that the capitalist practice of restricting production for the owner's gain sacrificed the "common good": "In one way and another...the net production of goods serviceable for human use falls considerably short of the gross output, and the gross output is always short of the productive capacity of the available plant and man power" ("The Modern Point of View," Nov. 30, 1918, 483). This "deliberate waste and confusion...for private gain," argues Veblen, is to the detriment of human need. Moore's education in economics at Bryn Mawr would have equipped her to follow Veblen's arguments in a particularly informed manner.

Indeed, during the teens, *The Dial* brought multiple discourses together with poetry. Before the journal was taken over by Scofield Thayer in 1920, the well-respected publication was dominated more by cultural commentary than by literature, a ratio that is later reversed. Commentaries on feminism, the war, economics, foreign policy, and the like proliferated, including a standing series of articles by Veblen in 1918 and 1919. In these articles, Veblen advanced his pacifist stance, analyzing the growing industrial-military complex sustained by capitalist business and criticizing the passivity of profit making through investment systems rampant in business. Ridge and Moore would be reading *The Dial*, certainly, in these years, and Ridge's labor poems appear concurrently with Veblen's pieces.[31] Loy would have been aware of *The Dial* as one of the avant-garde magazines increasingly important to the New York avant-garde she joined in 1916, and her work began to appear there in 1921. Moore's first poems were published in *The Dial* in 1920, a few months after Veblen's final article. Her tour de force "New York" appeared in December 1921, regarded by many as celebrating an American embrace of progress, ingenuity, and power. Read in the light of the consumer ethos saturating American society by the 1920s, however, the poem's picture of the "savage's romance, / accreted where we need the space for commerce" layers a history of economic might and "plunder" with concerns over a modern consumer culture hostile to social provisioning (Moore, 65).

To my reading, Moore's "New York" echoes what Veblen criticized as the "new order" of modernity throughout his *Dial* articles. Whether or not Moore read or directly endorsed Veblen's ideas is a matter of speculation, although she was an avid reader of *The Dial* and would surely be cognizant of its interest in economic topics during the teens. What I want to suggest is not that Moore is responding to any particular economic thinker or theory but that the prevalence of economic discourse within American society in general was at a high pitch, that she was equipped to follow it knowledgeably, and that it makes up a part of the historical fabric during which her early work is produced. In short, I want to imagine something of a conversation between Moore's "New York" and Veblenian thought as a way of accessing a deeper layer of feminist concern for the economic good.

A main theme of Veblen's late *Dial* articles is the modern-day adherence to principles of individualism developed during the Enlightenment period. In essence, he sees the move from production to consumption as perverting the democratic impetus of American individualism by benefiting only the most powerful and wealthy. Most conspicuously for Veblen, the predatory instinct central to earlier stages of "barbarian civilization" continues to ground the modern "pecuniary impulse." For Veblen, emulation—the desire to copy others in habits of consumption—girded modern forms of ownership, encouraging patterns of consumption.

From the start of "New York," the woman as consumer haunts the evocation of New York's history as "the centre of the wholesale fur trade," initially in the subtle metaphoric transformation of "the ground dotted with deer-skins" into a feminized image of "'satin needlework'"—included in the poem's first use of an external quote—as though the feminization of commodity goods covers over the slaughter (or in the poem's later language, the "plunder" of "shooting-irons and dogs"). This kind of feminized presence emerges more explicitly midway through the poem as an expressive desire for luxury goods, in phrases voicing the emulative consumerist ethos:

> It is a far cry from the "queen full of jewels"
> and the beau with the muff,
> from the gilt coach shaped like a perfume bottle,
> to the conjunction of the Monongahela and the Allegheny,
> and the scholastic philosophy of the wilderness (Moore, 65)

The gender-inflected commodity language in the first three lines *seems* to contrast with the rather masculine, rough-and-ready individualism of the wilderness, while the grammatical ambiguity of the antecedent for "It," which starts the entire series of lines, throws any clear-cut opposition into doubt. Indeed, the luxuries of jewels, muffs, and perfumes are, in a philosophical sense, *not* a "far cry" from the bustling industry of the Pittsburgh the poem implicitly references, an industry that (like the opening lines) displaces a "romance" of eighteenth-century wilderness with the nineteenth-century might of the Kings of Capitalism—the Carnegies, Fricks, Mellons, Claytons, and others whose wealth stunned the late nineteenth and early twentieth centuries. Sustained by the ideals of individualism and ownership, the revolutionary eighteenth-century "scholastic philosophy of the wilderness" that helped settle the colonies and liberate the country is both distant from a modern consumerist ethos and yet ironically bound up in it. Indeed, for Veblen, Enlightenment individualism—reshaped by the rise of industry—is the foundation for corporate gain. Therefore, the consumer ethos *is* a far cry from the *historically* situated philosophy marking the country's early years; at the same time, that philosophy, detached from its history, gives rise to the consumer ethos and the intertwined impulses of the predatory and the pecuniary expansion of the "space for commerce."[32]

However, the gendering of that space requires continuing the myth of the wilderness, or the "savage's romance," and to continue the masculine subjectivity that attends it, in part by projecting upon a feminine sphere and subject the more passive, pleasure-seeking role of the consumer. The next few lines again set up a seeming opposition between gendered activities, generating a listing of things that "it" is not, while suspending any clear idea of what "it" is: "It is not the dime-novel exterior, / Niagara Falls, the calico horses and the war canoe." Continuing a thread of references to the fur trade, the feminized voice of the fur-wearer, rather than the fur-trader or hunter, culminates this paratactic sequence, inserted as a quote: "it is not that 'if the fur is not finer than such as one sees / others wear, / one would rather be without it.'" Moore's notes attribute this quote to Frank Alvah Parsons's 1920 study of fashion, *The Psychology of Dress*, who is himself quoting Isabell, Duchess of Gonzaga. Moore's note provides Isabell's full comment, quoted in Parsons and oddly different from the phrase in the poem: "I wish black cloth even if it costs ten ducats a yard. If it is only as good as that which I see other people wear, I had rather be without it" (Parsons, 100). Moore, in effect, changes the quote while alerting us to the change in the notes. In a sense, this change helps to modernize and Americanize the sentiment, linking it to the fur trade (in Parsons, Isabell actually is talking about cloth, not fur) in the same oxymoronic process that connects the jewels and muff with a wilderness philosophy. The deliberate misquote also suggests the role of representation in mediating reality and, by extension, calls attention to the ideological implications upholding prevalent representations of women as consumers and fashion as disabling women for "useful activity" (Veblen, *Theory*, 181). The very instability of fashion furthers consumer desire and the role of display imposed upon women in consumer culture. In Moore's tampered quote, the fur is valuable in creating a class distinction—what Veblen termed an "invidious distinction"—between the wearer and others that must necessarily be conspicuous.

In Moore's poem, the *consumptive* desire for fur is stunningly followed and countered by reference to an alternatively *productive* system in a line ruminating "that estimated in raw meat and berries, we could feed the universe." Distinct from the poem's references to consumerism as a fuel for "commerce," this line enigmatically imagines the centrality of "need" to systems of production rather than "want" or the desire that sustains consumerism. Formally, the line stands alone, without the qualifying "it is not" that begins the other lines in question. Under an alternate economic system, what "is" could be a shared abundance, in which exchange would recognize human need as foundational to economic systems, paralleling a key Institutional (and feminist) principle that emphasizes the "life-process" promoted by "nurture and purposeful activity, [which] by its very nature takes account of labor outside the market" (Greenwood, 675). The introduction of bodily need accomplished by Moore's reference to "meat and berries" asserts this alternate notion of need and of a provisioning labor, countering the consumerist emphasis on desire while also suggesting that the "savage's romance" underlying the "space for commerce" cannot admit such a reading of abundance. Indeed, to sustain the romance, it is necessary to cover over a history of plunder ("It is not the plunder") and the development of a consumerist ideology ("it is not that 'if the fur is not finer than such as one sees others wear)'". That the potential for a nondesire-based exchange—to regard abundance as a way to "feed the universe"—inserts itself within the poem's litany of commerce, presents a sentiment grounded in feminist thought, countering the (patriarchally produced) feminized consumer with the feminist economic philosophy of social provisioning.

Even the poem's final assertion, quoting Henry James, that "it is the 'accessibility to experience,'" provides no clear division between America's space of commerce and its consumerist ideology. Grammatically, as with the listing of items throughout the poem, the "it" goes back to the "romance," or the illusion obscuring commerce's plunder. However, even "accessibility to experience" is repackaged in consumer culture—as are many forms of democratic idealism—to help sell products. Well underway by the 1920s, the advertising world's emphatic drive to convince the buying public of the "authentic" nature of goods or of the authenticity of experience that consumption promises is most tellingly demonstrated by the marketing campaign for Coca-Cola, "the real thing."[33] Moore's marked quotation of James's words, formally re-presenting someone else's words in a new context as did the advertising discourse that surrounded her in the 1920s, simultaneously pays homage to the writer while also signaling the recycling of ideals to urge authentic experience through consuming more and more goods.

Moore's poem sits uneasily within the growing absenteeism of the body from experience as both body and experience are particularly constructed by a modern discourse of consumerism. Modernity, in the broad sweep of its twentieth-century manifestations, threw into doubt the capacity for tangible experience as the world seemed more and more constructed to alienate, reduce, or erase the human bodily presence through new vistas, forces, and powers exceeding and eclipsing the human dimension. And while consumer desire, as one of the most dominant discourses of modernity, would seem to insist upon the body as a site of pleasure, it simultaneously removes the laboring body from the process of determining value and generating profit. Susan Feiner, offering a recent feminist critique of neoclassical economics, articulates this concern: "The elevation of exchange in modern economics displaces classical concerns for concrete, embodied activities like labor and production. These inescapably physical activities—some would even say womanly—vanish, replaced by autonomous, rational choosing minds . . ." (158).

Moore's "New York" questions the "romance" of such a promise of either commerce or "experience," suggesting in its attention to forces of plunder and desire what Daniel Horowitz describes as a fundamental direction of the modern economy: "a world of commercialism and mass consumption" and human "lives influenced by advertising, disposable consumer goods, and instant, artificial experiences" (316). This is the economic world of New York that Ridge's poetry begins to condemn in the late teens and that Mina Loy's Depression-era poetry explicitly depicts. In the late thirties and early forties, Loy responded to both the poverty of her Bowery environment (where she moved in 1936) and the consumer culture defining the commercial streets. In poems like "On Third Avenue," "Mass-Production on 14th Street,"

"Chiffon Velours," "Property of Pigeons," and "Hot Cross Bum," Loy continues her modernist experiments with language and form to join with other more direct Depression-era voices in pointed consideration of the mechanisms of American consumer capitalism and its underlying ideologies of selfhood, unfolding in poems focused on systemic poverty kept in place by the dynamics of the consumer capitalist engine. In her attention to consumerism's animating relationship to poverty, the construction of woman as consumer becomes particularly important. As Loy's late work exemplifies, alongside work in the thirties and forties by Muriel Rukeyser, Genevieve Taggard, and Moore herself, the vitality of women's modernism in carving out gendered ways of thinking economically continues beyond the limited time span this chapter treats, although the debates and discourses emerging alongside consumer capitalism lay a rich foundation for reconsidering women's poetic labors as they bring women, modernism, and economics into "new" relations.

NOTES

1 See Patten, "The Conflict Theory of Distribution," for original text.
2 See Marsh for an extensive and excellent discussion of Williams and economics. Although scholars, such as Sieberth and Surette, have provided extensive study of Pound and economics, and to a lesser degree of Williams, little substantial work has been done to consider women writers or issues of gender in regard to economics and modernism. For exceptions, see discussions of economics in Armstrong, Scuriatti, and Goody.
3 See Cary Nelson, *Revolutionary Memory*, for an extended discussion of labor poetry and its repression within literary histories of the twentieth century. See Berke for extended discussions of modernist poetry and the working-class body.
4 Cott lists that "the utopian socialist visions of Henri St. Simon and Charles Fourier early in the century, the ideals for a cooperative commonwealth held by the Knights of Labor after the Civil War, and the effortlessly harmonious corporatist proposals of Edward Bellamy's Nationalism at the end of the century supplied models of alternative social organization taken up by women in the United States" (17).
5 Olson and Emami go on to claim that, by 1920, as "economics began to define the boundaries of the discipline...women were simultaneously excluded," and the "adoption of a positivist methodology rendered feminist, institutionalist, and radical analysis as 'not economics' "(5).
6 Madden has identified "2,264 works with an economic content in the period 1900–1940," most of which are American and European (4). She has discovered 332 PhDs granted to women in this period and 124 MAs; her study charts publication topics and venues for women economists during these years.
7 See Burke, "New Poetry."
8 See Burke, *Becoming Modern*. In editorial notes to Loy's *Lost*, Conover writes that Loy was always "preoccupied with income-producing schemes and brought to bear her considerable esoteric knowledge of art, technology, and human nature to advance practical experiments, test entrepreneurial ideas, and promote business strategies to pay the rent and support her children" (Loy, *Lost*, 218n55).
9 "The Prototype" was probably drafted in 1914, according to Conover in Loy, *Lost*.

10 See Finnegan for an excellent discussion of the period's changing views on poverty.

11 Loy makes use of typographical variety in the manifesto, changing font sizes and creating emphasis through bold and underlined words, as with the highlighted and underlined words in this quote.

12 See Conover's note on this poem in Loy, *Lost*, 194.

13 See C. Miller on New York, immigration, and women modernists.

14 For discussions of Veblen, American Institutionalist economics, and feminism, see N. Gilman, E. Miller, Greenwood, and Jennings.

15 See N. Gilman and Jennings for persuasively informative arguments linking Veblen's thinking and first-wave feminism.

16 Tobin uses the term "proletarian poet." See Tobin and Berke for useful discussions of Ridge's poetry and politics.

17 For a fuller discussion of the impact of immigrant communities upon Ridge's poetry, see Cristanne Miller, who also discusses Moore and Loy in this regard.

18 Jacob Riis's work argued vociferously for housing reform in the Lower East End.

19 The largest populations of immigrants came from eastern and southern Europe at this time, as distinct from earlier waves of European immigration from northern and western countries and bringing a new diversity of language and religion. Jewish and Catholic immigrants entered the country in larger numbers than ever before.

20 Also see Hutchinson for a discussion of the importance of women's issues to the Social Credit Movement emerging just after World War I and influenced by both Institutional and feminist thought.

21 See Armstrong's excellent discussion of Veblenian associations of feminine body, consumption, and waste as they run through literary and cultural texts. Armstrong mistakenly spells Pruette's name as "Prunette."

22 All quotes are from the 1924 edition of *Observations*. The *Manikin* version appears in *Becoming Marianne Moore*, ed. Schulze, along with a listing of linguistic variations between versions. All references to Moore's poetry are from the 1924 edition of *Observations*, reprinted in facsimile form in Schulze. Page numbers for Moore's poems reference those in her original edition.

23 Interestingly, the 1923 version separates with punctuation the quotes taken, respectively, from Thomas and the Mount Holyoke address, while the 1924 version eliminates quotation marks to make the two quotes appear as one; nonetheless, the fact that she is drawing on two quotes is stipulated in her note in *Observations* for these lines. See Schulze, 307.

24 After taking a year of courses in "typing, shorthand, and stenography at Carlisle Commercial college," Moore "obtained a position teaching bookkeeping, stenography, commercial law, commercial arithmetic, and English at Carlisle Indian School," where she taught until 1914 (Costello, 72).

25 See Hicok.

26 Letter dated February 1, 1909, to Mary Warner Moore and John Warner Moore, her mother and brother.

27 Once she obtained the vote as a woman in 1921, Moore tended to vote with the Republican Party. During the Depression, to Morton Zabel in 1933, she expressed her support for Hoover as a man who "cares for another man's good." "Whether his political economy is the best, I am not wise enough to say" (Costello, 299; Feb. 22, 1933). She opposed FDR in 1936, preferring Alfred Mossman Landon, a liberal Republican who supported government's support for social issues and partially endorsed the New Deal. To Bryher, Moore cast Landon similarly to her earlier remarks about Hoover, the common good, and human need: "his ideal of sacrifice on the part of those who have

something, so that those who have nothing might live, would not have been popular"
(Costello, 369, to Bryher, Nov. 7, 1936). See Carson for a full discussion of Moore's
Republican politics during the 1930s.

28 Moore's course record for her years at Bryn Mawr (1905–1909) is printed in the
Marianne Moore Newsletter, 13–14.

29 Bryn Mawr was among the top five institutions to grant PhDs in economics to women
in the first decades of the century (Madden, 6).

30 Fetter's textbook was included in the course description for "Introduction to Economics"
in the Bryn Mawr undergraduate catalog during Moore's years there. Situating itself
squarely within the neoclassical camp, it demonstrates the rapidity with which the
marginal revolution in economics became, and remains, mainstream. Despite claims to
scientific neutrality, Fetter demonstrates blatantly the privileging of the white male as
model for Economic Man. For example, in discussing theories of value, Fetter admits to the
"enjoyment of free goods, as in the case of the care-free darky basking in the sun" (223).

31 Ridge's "Kreymborg's Marionettes," an article on Alfred Kreymborg's book of poem-
plays (that included *Lima Beans*, subsequently performed by William Carlos Williams
and Mina Loy) and reviews of her first two books appeared in the same issue as articles
by Veblen. Moore had unsuccessfully submitted work to *The Dial* before 1920, when her
first publication did appear, while Ridge's work appeared a number of times in the late
teens, including poems urging labor revolt.

32 See Donahue on the changing gender identity of the consumer in the 1890s. Examining
the discourse attending debates over "the proper political role for the consumer," she
argues that "[t]hose who wanted to establish the consumer as an active and pivotal player
in the political sphere defined him as male. Those who wanted to establish the consumer
as a passive and marginal political identity coded her female" (Donahue, 20). Donahue
offers a useful reading of Veblen within this gendered discourse and its cultural contexts.

33 See Orvell for an astute analysis of the discourse of authenticity in early-century
advertising. Orvell discusses James in this context, claiming that the "question of
ownership is a key one in his work throughout his career, and his fiction offers a
powerful critique of the upper end of the consumer world . . . [offering] a psychological
investigation of ownership that brings us inside the mentality of consumption" (65).

REFERENCES

Armstrong, Tim. *Modernism, Technology, and the Body: A Cultural Study*. New York:
    Cambridge University Press, 1998.
Berke, Nancy. *Women Poets on the Left: Lola Ridge, Genevieve Taggard, Margaret Walker*.
    Gainesville: University Press of Florida, 2002.
Birken, Lawrence. *Consuming Desire: Sexual Science and the Emergence of a Culture of
    Abundance, 1870–1914*. Ithaca: Cornell University Press, 1988.
Bryn Mawr College Calendar, 1908. Volume 1, Part 1. Philadephia: Johan C. Winston Co.,
    March 1908.
Burke, Carolyn. *Becoming Modern: The Life of Mina Loy*. Berkeley: University of California
    Press, 1997.
———. "The New Poetry and the New Woman: Mina Loy." In *Coming to Light: American
    Women Poets in the Twentieth Century*. Ed. Diane Middlebrook and Marilyn Yalom,
    37–57. Ann Arbor: University of Michigan Press, 1985.

Carson, Luke. "Republicanism and Leisure in Marianne Moore's Depression." *Modern Language Quarterly* 63, no. 3 (2002): 315–342.

Costello, Bonnie, general ed., Celeste Goodridge, and Cristanne Miller, associate eds. *The Selected Letters of Marianne Moore*. New York: Alfred A. Knopf, 1997.

Cott, Nancy. *The Grounding of Modern Feminism*. New Haven: Yale University Press, 1989.

Donahue, Kathleen G. "What Gender Is the Consumer? The Role of Gender Connotations in Defining the Political." *Journal of American Studies* 33, no.1 (1999): 19–44.

Drinnon, Richard. *Rebel in Paradise: A Biography of Emma Goldman*. Chicago: University of Chicago Press, 1982.

Dzuback, Mary Ann. "Women and Social Research at Bryn Mawr College, 1915–1940." *History of Education Quarterly* 33, no. 4 (1993): 579–608.

Eisenach, Eldon J., ed. *The Social and Political Thought of American Progressivism*. Indianapolis: Hackett Publishing Co., 2006.

Feiner, Susan F. "Reading Neoclassical Economics: Toward an Erotic Economy of Sharing." In *Out of the Margin: Feminist Perspectives on Economics*. Ed. Edith Kuiper and Jolande Sap. London: Routledge, 1995.

Fetter, Frank A. *The Principles of Economics*. New York: The Century Co., 1905.

Finnegan, Cara A. *Picturing Poverty: Print Culture and FSA Photographs*. Washington and London: Smithsonian Books, 2003.

Folbre, Nancy. "The Unproductive Housewife: Her Evolution in Nineteenth-Century Economic Thought." *Signs* 16, no. 3 (1991): 463–484.

Gilman, Charlotte Perkins. *Women and Economics: A Study of the Economic Relation Between Men and Women as a Factor in Social Evolution*. New York: Dover, 1997.

Gilman, Nils. "Thorstein Veblen's Neglected Feminism." *Journal of Economic Issues* 33, no. 3 (1999): 689–711.

Goody, Alex. *Modernist Articulations: A Cultural Study of Djuna Barnes, Mina Loy and Gertrude Stein*. New York: Palgrave Macmillan, 2007.

Greenwood, Daphne. "The Economic Significance of 'Woman's Place' In Society: A New-Institutionalist View." *Journal of Economic Issues* 28, no. 3 (1984): 663–695.

Hendrickson, Mark. "Gender Research as Labor Activism: The Woman's Bureau in the New Era." *Journal of Policy History* 20, no. 4 (2008): 482–515.

Hicok, Bethany. "To Work 'Lovingly': Marianne Moore at Bryn Mawr, 1905–1909." *Journal of Modern Literature* 23, no. 3/4 (2000): 483–501.

Horowitz, Daniel. "Consumption and Its Discontents: Simon N. Patten, Thorstein Veblen, and George Gunton." *Journal of American History* 67, no. 2 (1980): 301–317.

Hutchinson, Frances. "A Heretical View of Economic Growth and Income Distribution." In *Out of the Margins: Feminist Perspectives on Economics*. Ed. Edith Kuiper and Jolande Sap. New York: Routledge, 1995.

Jennings, Ann L. "Public or Private? Institutional Economics and Feminism." In *Beyond Economic Man: Feminist Theory and Economics*. Ed. Marianne A. Ferber and Julie A. Nelson, 111–129. Chicago: University of Chicago Press, 1993.

Leach, William. *Land of Desire: Merchants, Power, and the Rise of a New American Culture*. New York: Vintage, 1994.

Lears, T. J. Jackson. *No Place of Grace: Antimodernism and the Transformation of American Culture, 1880–1920*. Chicago: University of Chicago Press, 1981.

Loy, Mina. *The Last Lunar Baedeker*. Ed. Roger Conover. Winston-Salem, NC: Jargon, 1982.

———. *The Lost Lunar Baedeker, Poems*. Ed. Roger Conover. New York: Farrar, Straus, and Giroux, 1996.

McGovern, Charles S. *Sold American: Consumption and Citizenship, 1890–1945*. Chapel Hill: University of North Carolina Press, 2006.

Madden, Kristen Kara. "Female Contributions to Economic Thought, 1900–1940." *History of Political Economy* 34, no. 1 (2002): 1–30. *Marianne Moore Newsletter* 5, no.1 (1981).

Marsh, Alec. *Money and Modernity: Pound, Williams, and the Spirit of Jefferson.* Tuscaloosa: University of Alabama Press, 1998.

Miller, Cristanne. "Tongues 'loosened in the melting pot': The Poets of *Others* and the Lower East Side." *Modernism/Modernity* 14, no. 3 (2007): 455–476.

Miller, Edyth S. "Veblen and Women's Lib: A Parallel." *Journal of Economic Issues* 6, no. 2 (1972): 75–86.

Moore, Marianne. "Marriage." In *Manikin Number Three.* New York: Monroe Wheeler, 1923.

———. *Observations.* New York: Dial Press, 1924.

Nelson, Cary. *Revolutionary Memory: Recovering the Poetry of the American Left.* New York: Routledge, 2003.

Nelson, Julie A. "The Study of Choice or the Study of Provisioning? Gender and the Definition of Economics." In *Beyond Economic Man: Feminist Theory and Economics.* Ed. Marianne A. Ferber and Julie A. Nelson, 23–35. Chicago: University of Chicago Press, 1993.

Olson, Paulette, and Zohren Emami. *Engendering Economics: Conversations with Women Economists in the United States.* New York: Routledge, 2002.

Orvell, Miles. *The Real Thing: Imitation and Authenticity in American Culture, 1880–1940.* Chapel Hill: University of North Carolina Press, 1989.

Parris, Marion. "Total Utility and the Economic Judgment Compared with Their Ethical Counterparts." PhD diss., Bryn Mawr, 1909.

Parsons, Frank Alvah. *The Psychology of Dress.* New York: Doubleday, Page & Company, 1920.

Patten, Simon. *The Consumption of Wealth.* Philadelphia: University of Pennsylvania, 1889.

———. "The Conflict Theory of Distribution." In *Essays in Economic Theory.* Ed. Rexford Tugwell. New York, 1924.

Pruette, Lorine. *Women and Leisure: A Study of Social Waste.* New York: E. P. Dutton, 1924.

Pujol, Michéle. "Into the Margin!" Introduction to *Out of the Margin: Feminist Perspectives on Economics.* Ed. Edith Kuiper and Jolande Sap. New York and London: Routledge, 1995.

Ridge, Lola. *The Ghetto and Other Poems.* New York: B. W. Huebsch, 1918.

———. "Kreymborg's Marionettes." *The Dial* LXVI, No. 781 (1919): 29–31.

Schulze, Robin G. *Becoming Marianne Moore, The Early Poems, 1907–1924.* Berkeley: University of California Press, 2002.

Scuriatti, Laura. "Negotiating Boundaries: The Economics of Space and Gender in Mina Loy's Early Poems." *Femnismo/s* no. 5 (2005): 71–84.

Sieburth, Richard. "In Pound We Trust: The Economy of Poetry/The Poetry of Economics." *Critical Inquiry* no. 14 (1987): 142–172.

Sklansky, Jeffrey. *The Soul's Economy: Market Society and Selfhood in American Thought, 1820–1920.* Chapel Hill: University of North Carolina Press, 2002.

Surette, Leon. *Pound in Purgatory: From Economic Radicalism to Anti-Semitism.* Urbana: University of Illinois Press, 2003.

Tobin, Daniel. "Modernism, Leftism, and the Spirit: The Poetry of Lola Ridge." *New Hibernia Review* 8, no. 3 (2004): 65–85.

Trachtenburg, Alan. *The Incorporation of America: Culture and Society in the Gilded Age.* New York: Hill and Wang, 1982.

Veblen, Thorstein. *The Theory of the Leisure Class.* London: Oxford University Press, 2008.

———. "The Modern Point of View and the New Order, IV." *The Dial* (Nov. 30, 1918): 482–488.

Williams, William Carlos. *Selected Essays.* New York: New Directions, 1969.

CHAPTER 7

POETRY AND RHETORIC: MODERNISM AND BEYOND

PETER NICHOLLS

In Melville's chilly masterpiece "Bartleby, the Scrivener," the "pale plaster-of-paris" bust of Cicero that presides over the lawyer's office is a pointed reminder of the final stage of rhetoric's decline in the second half of the nineteenth century (Melville, 21). The Ciceronian tradition is a mere shadow of its former self (the head alone and not the heart remains) and the legal practice overlooked by the bust is occupied not with feats of forensic artistry but with the purely mechanical business of textual transcription.[1] The ancient rhetor surveys a scene in which the art of speaking does little more than support a deviously self-serving philanthropy, the lawyer pondering whether by befriending Bartleby he "might cheaply purchase a delicious self-approval" (Melville, 23). At the time Melville writes, classical rhetoric is witnessing its final decline or "reduction," as Gerard Genette calls it, a process begun in the Middle Ages as once crucial parts of the rhetorical curriculum gradually fell into disuse: "next [to be lost was] the balance between the 'parts' (*inventio, dispositio, elocutio*), because the rhetoric of the *trivium*, crushed between grammar and dialectic, soon came to be confined to the study of *elocutio*, the ornaments of discourse, *colores rhetorici*" (104).[2]

Bartleby, with his formulaic disengagement and his previous experience of the Dead Letter Office, is arguably the prophet of literature's failure as an authentic public form and of *its* consequent reduction to empty repetition.[3] Both he and Cicero are described as "pale" and fragile, and when the lawyer confronts him with questions about his past, Bartleby, says the lawyer, "kept his glance fixed upon my bust of Cicero" (30), an object no longer inspiring eloquence but now prompting instead an enigmatic reluctance to speak (" 'At present I prefer to give no answer,' he said"). The "ancient empire" of rhetoric, as Roland Barthes once called it, has become a land of tombs and spectral presences; Melville's own later foray into the rhetoric of public memory—the poems of *Battle-Pieces* (1866)—would similarly seem to many readers lifeless and marmoreal, witness both to the disaster of the war and to the inadequacy of the stylistic figures through which the nation's losses might now be remembered and mourned.[4]

By the middle of the nineteenth century, then, the once-rich rhetorical tradition had dwindled to a "mechanical typology of figures of speech," tricked out with cumbrous Latin labels (Naremore, par. 4). More than ever, "rhetoric" denoted not just the deception with which it had long been associated but an empty formalism that was opposed to the very purpose of imaginative literature. "Rhetoric" would for this reason constitute the pole against which modernism would aggressively define itself. For Ezra Pound, arguably the key mover in this break with the past, Victorianism represented a culture of "the opalescent word, the rhetorical tradition" (*Literary Essays*, 371); in a piece called "A Retrospect" (published in 1918), he called for a "harder and saner" poetry, one freed from the previous century's "rhetorical din, and luxurious riot," "austere, direct, free from emotional slither" (*Literary Essays*, 12).

While Pound's assault on his literary predecessors has seemed tough-minded and generally convincing, we also need to remember that for many Victorian poets, rhetoric was inextricably bound up with the art of poetry. Some twenty years after Melville's bleak novella, Gerard Manley Hopkins, for example, wrote the following to Robert Bridges:

> [Sprung rhythm] is the nearest to the rhythm of prose, that is the native and natural rhythm of speech, the least forced, the most rhetorical and emphatic of all possible rhythms, combining, as it seems to me, opposite and, one wd. have thought, incompatible excellences, markedness of rhythm—that is rhythm's self—and naturalness of expression.... My verse is less to be read than heard, as I have told you before; it is oratorical, that is the rhythm is so.
>
> (Hopkins, in Mariani, 89–90)

Leaving aside the more idiosyncratic features of Hopkins's poetics, we may note his association of "the natural rhythm of speech" with "rhetorical" rhythm and his frank aspiration toward poetry as an "oratorical" art. For Hopkins, the very purpose of poetry is rhetorical: "To do [my poem] the Eurydice any kind of justice," he explains, "you must not slovenly read it with the eyes but with your ears, as if the paper were declaring it at you" (Hopkins in Marucci, 25).[5] For Hopkins, what is "declared" by the poem is something that exceeds the words on the page; poetry, he says, is "speech wholly or partially repeating some kind of figure which is over and above meaning, at least the grammatical, historical, and logical meaning"(Hopkins, 289). A performative element is vital to Hopkins's poetic and it is ironic indeed, given that none of his major work was published until after his death, that one of its defining features is its assumption of an audience (one critic observes that "Hopkins's poetry presupposes, postulates, and demands an addressee, *real* though *virtual*" [Marucci, 22, emphasis in original]).[6]

Pound was little interested in Hopkins, and in a rare comment on his work he dismissed it as a mere "technical exercise" (Pound, *Guide to Kulchur*, 293). Yet like Hopkins, Pound also discerned a dimension of poetry precisely as being in excess of directly communicable meaning, though when his theorizing took a self-consciously "modern" turn with the poetics of Imagism he tended to appeal to the visual as a model for an emotional "pattern" capable of curbing the unfocused expression of emotion he associated with the backwash of Romanticism (Pound, *Gaudier-Brzeska*, 87).[7] It was here that the term "rhetoric" was constantly invoked as the enemy or the "other" of modernism. The Imagist program, with its call for "direct treatment of the 'thing,'" verbal economy, and rhythms determined by "the sequence of the musical phrase" (*Literary Essays*, 4), was underpinned by both the Kantian criticism of rhetoric as "the art of persuasion, i.e., of deceiving by a beautiful show (*ars oratoria*)" (Kant, 171)[8] and by the assumption that rhetoric trafficked in some sort of supplementary excess. "The 'image,'" declared Pound, "is the furthest possible remove from rhetoric. Rhetoric is the art of dressing up some unimportant matter so as to fool the audience for the time being" (*Gaudier-Brzeska*, 83). Rhetoric, then, makes the work of art a kind of confidence trick, a sleight of hand in which one thing appears in the guise of another: "The Renaissance sought a realism and attained it. It rose in a search for precision and declined through rhetoric and rhetorical thinking, through a habit of defining things always 'in terms of something else'" (*Gaudier-Brzeska*, 117).[9] Pound's concept of rhetoric has, in fact, something in common with what Jacques Derrida has termed the logic of the "supplement": it *adds* to what had seemed already complete, "dressing up" an originally naked truth, but in so doing it simultaneously *diminishes* its meaning, surrendering originality to mere "habit" (Derrida, 144–145).[10] It is in these terms that Pound speaks of "rhetoric, or the use of *cliché* unconsciously, or a mere playing with phrases" (*Literary Essays*, 283).[11]

This hostility to ornamentation has, of course, little of novelty about it: we can trace it as least as far back as the eighteenth-century denunciation of "luxury" and on into Wordsworth's 1802 preface to *Lyrical Ballads* with its rejection of "transitory and accidental ornaments" as the means by which a writer, says Wordsworth, "endeavour[s] to excite admiration of himself by arts, the necessity of which must manifestly depend upon the assumed meanness of his subject" (168–169).[12] Wordsworth's way of associating disruptive "accidental ornaments" with the breaking in of an artistic egotism recalls in its turn Aristotle's advice to trust the speech rather than the speaker: "This kind of persuasion, like the others, should be achieved by what the speaker says, not by what people think of his character before he begins to speak" (*Rhetoric*, 1356a, 6–8). This is, however, an implicitly circular argument that smuggles evidence of the speaker's character back into the equation by deducing it from the ethical rectitude (or otherwise) of his words.[13] We may take Pound's belief in "technique as the test of a man's sincerity" (*Literary Essays*, 9) as a way of breaking that rhetorical bond between audience and speaker, and leaving the poetic text, a text now apparently purged of residual voice and presence, as the sole "test" of emotional integrity. Sincerity, then, will be discerned in the writing's self-sufficiency, in the "irreplaceability" of its constituent elements, and in its eschewal of any dependence on rhetorical figuration to register and inflate authorial "intention." Eliot wrote in a similar vein that rhetoric comprised "any adornment or inflation of speech which is *not done for a particular effect* but for a general impressiveness" (Eliot, " 'Rhetoric,' " 77, emphasis in original).[14]

By the time Pound was propagandizing for Imagism, much of this antirhetorical argument was quite familiar, with similar-sounding statements having already issued from a variety of different quarters. Herbert Spencer, for example, in his crudely instrumental *Philosophy of Style* (1852), had expanded on the need "to express an idea in the smallest number of words" (6) and to focus writing on the particular and concrete: "we do not think in generals but in particulars" (10), he wrote, and "the succession [in the arrangement of sentences] should be from the less specific to the more specific—from the abstract to the concrete" (13). Spencer reminds us of the extended tradition lying behind such literary protocols when he quotes Hugh Blair's classic *Lectures on Rhetoric and Belles Lettres* (1783): "every needless part of a sentence 'interrupts the description and clogs the image' " (3), a turn of phrase that cannot but make us hear Pound's much later warning that abstraction "dulls the image" (*Literary Essays*, 5). *Brevitas* and *claritas* are Spencer's watchwords; well in advance of Pound's speculations he is keen to claim poetry's potential economy of statement as an ideal of communicational precision.[15]

While Pound might well have warmed to Spencer's no-nonsense view that "the aim must be to convey the greatest quality of thoughts with the smallest quantity of words" (Spencer, 24), Walter Pater's more subtly nuanced expression of some similar ideas probably had a more direct effect on Pound's thinking. In the key essay "Style" (in the collection *Appreciations, with an Essay on Style*, 1888), Pater had defined "ornament" as "what is in itself non-essential" and as "removable decoration" (15), turning (like Pound after him) to prose models (Flaubert, Stendhal) for examples of what he called "composition[s] utterly unadorned" (15–16). The task of the writer, then, says Pater, "consist[s] in the removal of surplusage," much as Michelangelo works on "the rough-hewn block of stone" to release the form already lodged there (16), an old fantasy that would flourish again in Pound's *Cantos*. The continuity in thinking between Pater and Pound looks clear, then, but Pater, we should note, is not quite as ready as Pound to attribute the effect of "surplusage" simply to verbal inflation:

> While half the world is using figure unconsciously, [the lover of words] will be fully aware not only of all that latent figurative texture in speech, but of the vague, lazy, half-formed personification—a rhetoric, depressing, and worse than nothing because it has no really rhetorical motive—which plays so large a part there. (17)

Pater may seem to be about to lambaste "rhetoric" in true modernist fashion, but his criticism is actually leveled at "dead" figures of speech ("half-formed personification" and so on), figures that are unmotivated by what he regards as genuine rhetorical purpose.

The distinction is important, for while Pater's aesthetic contains many features soon to be met with in a modernist poetics—his emphasis on the focusing power of the visual image, for example, and his appeal to the sculptural analogy—his concept of "style" remains closely intertwined with a concept of "rhetoric"; in fact, the project of aesthetic criticism is rhetorical in its very origins. In "Style," for example, Pater meditates on

> how difficult [it is] to define the point where, from time to time, argument which, if it is to be worth anything at all, must consist of facts or groups of facts, becomes a pleading—a theorem no longer, but essentially an appeal to the reader to catch the writer's spirit, to think with him, if one can or will. (4–5)

Pater had already considered the matter of rhetoric in much more detail in *Marius the Epicurean* (1885),[16] and the discussion of "fact" in the "Style" essay exhibits a clearly developed sense of an affective relation between writer and reader. Poetry and rhetoric would actually part company not in Pater's work but in that of his disciple Arthur Symons. In his influential *The Symbolist Movement in Literature* (1899), Symons would unashamedly appropriate the cadenced contours of Pater's style ("Our only chance, in this world, of a complete happiness") (93)[17] while at the same time celebrating that introverted turn that Pater had chafed against in his "Conclusion" to *The Renaissance* ("the whole scope of observation is dwarfed into the narrow chamber of the individual mind"). Symons adapts Pater's aestheticism as the basis for a much more direct denigration of all forms of "rhetoric," observing that the Symbolist movement "is all an attempt to spiritualise literature, to evade the old bondage of rhetoric, the old bondage of exteriority" (Symons, 5).

This in turn would be the "bondage" of which Pound would so often complain, echoing as he does the antirhetorical stance of some of his fellow modernists: Yeats, for example, with his much quoted dictum that "we make out of the quarrel with others, rhetoric, but of the quarrel with ourselves, poetry" (Yeats, 331),[18] and Wallace Stevens claiming that "the nobility of rhetoric is, of course, a lifeless nobility" (Stevens, 35). Those two poets' dislike of "rhetoric" did not, however, mean that they were able to write a defiantly nonrhetorical poetry; in fact, as Charles Altieri has observed, "we see that despite their abiding hatred of 'rhetoric' their poetry frequently turns to the figure of the orator as a figure for the powers of idealization they project for their imaginative labors" ("Rhetoric," 474).

This way of challenging rhetoric by pitting its own figurative maneuvers against its parallel claims for truth and identification would affect one major line of poetic endeavour in the twentieth century and beyond. In some cases—Eliot's *Four Quartets* provides a major example—the poem's claim rests on a testing of different rhetorics, seeking "the word neither diffident nor ostentatious" that might express poetry's aspiration to a genuinely spiritual language (Eliot, *Little Gidding*, 193). Then again, poets writing with a more clearly political intent might appropriate traditional literary rhetoric for polemical ends: Claude McKay's early sonnets, with their frequent use of Shakespearean motifs, are a case in point.[19] Such practices, which tended to expose rather than to conceal the workings of rhetoric, could also be managed with a deliberately lighter touch. Altieri observes of W. H. Auden, for example, that he "shows how rhetoric can become so self-conscious and visibly playful that it can bear even our imaginary investments with a lightness that simply

forecloses any effort at 'sincere' identification" (*Art*, 152). In our own time, this way
with rhetoric has become the hallmark of John Ashbery's style: as Altieri also notes,
Ashbery "thinks that the most serious danger in poetry is not that it will be too rhe-
torical but that it will not insist enough on the rhetorical theater it establishes" (*Art*,
202). Ashbery's habit—early and late—has been to bracket rhetorical objectives and
to revel in forms of periphrasis that defer and often undermine a propositional out-
come. Frequently, the urgency of rhetorical address is precisely a measure of mean-
ing's failure:

> Yes, friends, these clouds pulled along on invisible ropes
> Are, as you have guessed, merely stage machinery,
> And the funny thing is it knows we know
> About it and still wants us to go on believing
> In what it so unskilfully imitates, and wants
> To be loved not for that but for itself . . .
> . . . so we may know
> We too are somehow impossible, formed of so many
>   different things,
> Too many to make sense to anybody.
>   (Ashbery, 50)

If that way with rhetoric typifies one main line of development in American
poetry after modernism, another might be seen to originate with Imagism and with
Pound's development of its poetics after his exposure to Ernest Fenollosa's essay on
the Chinese written character in 1913. As is well known, Fenollosa advanced the
proposition that the Chinese language was inherently disposed toward imaginative
dynamism and a "natural" syntactic order. Fenollosa seems to have mistaken the
ideogram for a simple pictogram, and in the process he arguably overemphasized
the function of active verbs in Chinese writing.[20] The Chinese written character thus
came to represent what he called "vivid shorthand picture[s] of actions or processes"
(Fenollosa and Pound, 45). The rightness or wrongness of this interpretation—
mainly wrongness, it has been thought—is not, however, especially important to my
argument here (Fenollosa himself stressed that his "concern is poetry, not language"
[43]). For what was crucial to Pound were the directness and verbal dynamism that
Fenollosa attributed to the Chinese language; the essay, said Pound, dealt ultimately
with "Style, that is to say, limpidity, as opposed to rhetoric" (44). "Limpidity" is the
thing clearly seen, that is, rather than being "dressed up" in the grandiloquent garb
of rhetoric. Ideograms seemed to dispense with the Western dependence on the
copula; where we would say "the tree is green," the Chinese, according to Fenollosa,
would render this as "the tree greens itself" (49), with an active verb thus replacing
the passive. Where Western languages deal with abstractions, with "concepts drawn
out of things by a sifting process" (47), the ideogram is said to follow "the actual
and entangled lines of forces as they pulse through things" (47). Here we encounter
not "bloodless adjectival abstraction" but "concrete" verbs (52). In fact, in contrast

to what Fenollosa calls, in a fortuitous echo of Melville's bust of Cicero, the West's dependence on "the dead white plaster of the copula" (59), the ideogram seems to preserve *things* rather than to develop *concepts* from them—so the character for "east," for example, seems to show quite literally "the sun entangled in the branches of a tree" (60). Such characters gesture toward natural relations rather than logical ones. Fenollosa thus explains that "two things added together do not produce a third thing but suggest some fundamental relation between them" (46).

It's not hard to see how Fenollosa's essay could be readily recruited to support Pound's campaign against rhetoric. Yet it's here that we can also begin to gauge the consequences of the denigration of the rhetorical tradition that, for all its excesses, had always assumed the social locatedness of verbal expression. Take one of Fenollosa's prize exhibits: three ideograms that make up the sentence "Farmer pound[s] rice" (48), a sentence in which no word can be designated "ornamental" and where the transmission of "force" is unimpeded by any hint of "rhetoric." Yet while both Fenollosa and Pound look to Chinese as a language that pictographically preserves the sensuous particular, this sentence actually draws what "force" it has from its generic simplicity rather than from its capacity to bring "language close to *things*," as Fenollosa claims.[21] "Farmer pound[s] rice": as soon as we add even minimal rhetorical coloring to this sentence, we begin to enter a world of social relations that Fenollosa's emphasis on "nature" effectively suppresses.[22] To stress the first word of the sentence, "*Farmer* pounds rice," suggests not only that farmers always do this, but also that *only* farmers do it (pounding rice is the task of the rural poor). Again, "Farmer *pounds* rice" indicates the degree of manual labor involved in this process, while "Farmer pounds *rice*" might suggest that this is the only food crop available to the lower orders.[23] Stripped of any such emphasis, however, the sentence in question reminds us of the abstractness of Pound's early sense of "China" as a culture possessing unchanging, universal qualities (even though Pound wrote to John Quinn in 1916 that "China is the coming nation!" neither then nor later did he display any real interest in China as a contemporary nation) (Fenollosa and Pound, 3).[24]

While this idealized version of "China" was common at the time, in another respect Fenollosa's and Pound's theory of the ideogram also broke with a fundamental Western view of the Chinese writing system as a major obstacle to modern thinking; as Christopher Bush observes, with Fenollosa's essay, what had so frequently been castigated as "an emblem of cultural stagnation" has here become "a model of literary modernity" (Bush, 32). At the same time, though, it is precisely the assumed capacity of the ideogram to impede the rationalizing tendencies of modern thinking that makes it so important to Fenollosa and Pound. *The Chinese Written Character* thus finds in the ideogram a means of resisting the customary movement of Western thought as it ascends from things to concepts. Says Fenollosa, "At the basis of the pyramid lie *things*, but stunned, as it were.... We take a concept of lower attenuation, such as 'cherry'; we see that it is contained under one higher, such as 'redness'" (56, emphasis in original).

It may be helpful to consider these familiar modernist arguments in relation to a later and differently inflected criticism of Western thought. I have in mind

T. W. Adorno's attack on "identity thinking," which interestingly shadows the Fenollosa/Pound critique but with some revealing differences. J. M. Bernstein summarizes Adorno's view as follows:

> Rationalized reason produces a compulsion to identify, a compulsion to make (practically) or to construe (theoretically) each sensuous particular to be the token of some context-independent, immaterial type: exchange value, scientific law, law of reason, a priori procedure. One expression of this process is the duality between art and science.
>
> ("Mimetic Rationality," 7)

Pound shares this hostility to identity thinking: in his essay on Guido Cavalcanti, for example, he rejects any "attempt to unify different things, however small the difference" (*Literary Essays*, 185). *The Chinese Written Character*, as we have seen, is similarly critical of hypotaxis, finding in the ideogram a model of writing that is valued precisely because it is context-*dependent* and "material." The divergence of science from the arts is also a key issue here: Fenollosa declares that "poetry agrees with science and not with logic" (57) and this preference is fully endorsed by Pound, for whom "science" also deals in the currency of empirical "facts" while "logic" is understood as the means by which sensuous particulars are subordinated to "immaterial types."[25] Pound and Adorno both, in their different ways, want to tip the balance against "rationalized reason" or "logic" and toward a material context that resists subordination of the particular to some general "type." Yet they also differ in one crucial respect, which is that for Adorno the affective properties that provide this resistance are defined as "rhetoric." Adorno acknowledges that rhetoric "is incessantly corrupted by persuasive purposes" (so much again he shares with Pound), but he goes on to observe that without such purposes "the thought act would no longer have a practical relation" (55). Indeed, in *Negative Dialectics* Adorno insists that what is needed to save us from "rationalized reason" is "a critical rescue of the rhetorical element, a mutual approximation of thing and expression, to the point where the difference fades" (56). Since Plato, Adorno argues, philosophers have tried to forget the dependence of thought on language, hence the centuries-old denigration of rhetoric that Pound inherits.

Now we can begin to see the problem, or rather, perhaps, the maneuver that differentiates Poundian modernism from Adornian dialectics: for it is not that Pound wishes to outlaw the expressive and performative features that Adorno calls "rhetoric"—Pound is, after all, preeminently a poet of sound, rhythm, echo, phrasal parallelism, and so on, all devices used, of course, to persuade. What is notable, though, is that he will not define these features as "rhetorical" because to do so would be to concede the priority of some sort of obligation to an audience, that "appeal to the reader to catch the writer's spirit, to think with him" of which we have heard Pater speak. Pound, in contrast, derides "that infamous remark of Whitman's about poets needing an audience," thus underlining his assumption that the literary avant-garde comes into being only by disavowing such rhetorical dependencies (Pound, *Selected Letters*, 107).[26] Yet this, of course, is only half the story, for committed as he was to avant-gardism, Pound was also increasingly certain that (as he put it in a 1922 letter) "it's all rubbish to pretend that art isn't didactic" (*Selected Letters*, 180).[27] But how to create a didactic poetry with no rhetorical features? This conundrum Pound would solve in a time-honored, if not essentially modernist way, by transferring the affective properties of language that Adorno designated as "rhetorical" to an ideal of poetic musicality. While the more demotic sections of *The Cantos* would assemble the "facts," the patently musical or "melopoeic" sequences would engage the reader at the affective level.

The term "melopoeia" is one of three announced in Pound's 1931 pamphlet *How to Read*: there we have logopoeia, "the dance of the intellect among words"; phanopoeia, the "casting of images upon the visual imagination"; and finally melopoeia, wherein, Pound, says, "the words are charged, *over and above their plain meaning, with some musical property*, which directs the bearing or trend of that meaning" (170, emphasis added). We might recall Hopkins's talk of poetry as the repetition of "some kind of figure which is over and above meaning, at least the grammatical, historical, and logical meaning." But where Hopkins sees this affective surplus as the momentum behind the poet's direct oratorical address to the reader, Pound goes on to note that melopoeia amounts to "a force tending often to lull, or to distract the reader from the exact sense of the language. It is poetry on the borders of music, and music is perhaps the bridge between consciousness and the unthinking sentient or even insentient universe" (171–172). The last sentence of this passage works hard to conceal the fact that this ostensibly un-Poundian poetics of "lull[ing]" and "distract[ing] the reader from the exact sense of the language" is thoroughly rhetorical in purpose.

As we move through Pound's *Cantos*, in fact, we are increasingly aware of the didactic weight borne by its lyrical sequences. Pound will still inveigh against "rhetoric" but he is quite ready to affirm the pedagogical purpose of his poem. It's curious that in the 1938 *Guide to Kulchur*, Pound roundly denounced Plato's tendency to "prose rhapsody" as a kind of illegitimate "inebriety" or intoxication, for many passages in the later Cantos have precisely this quality, marking themselves off from the more demotic and prosaic parts of the poem that deal with "facts" by their seductive musicality (*Guide to Kulchur*, 222). This fusion of music and rhetoric is actually what Plato was arguing *against* in *The Republic*, so runs Eric Havelock's argument in his *Preface to Plato*. Plato's dismissal of the poets from *The Republic* is to be understood, Havelock suggests, in terms of a rejection of the old, oral culture based on sound, rhythm, repetition, and association. Plato was attempting nothing less, says Havelock, than the complete reconfiguration of the old paideia, with its dependence on acoustic patterning as a mnemonic and pedagogical device; in its place he put the "idea" or "form" that transcended the oral world of repetition and outlawed the sensual pleasure it brought to the business of instruction. In the Homeric culture, as Havelock put it, listeners had to submit "to the paideutic spell. You allowed yourself to become 'musical' in the functional sense of the Greek term" (159).[28] From the vantage point of a society acquiring the skills of literacy, such "musicality" amounted, of course, to little more than an enchantment we would call indoctrination; hence, Plato's condemnation of that kind of "rhetoric."

This particular fusion of rhetoric and musicality in *The Cantos* has made that poem a sort of watershed for younger American poets. From the troubled reception of *The Pisan Cantos* onward, the association of lyric beauty with didacticism has triggered various forms of poetic reaction.[29] Elizabeth Bishop, for example, wrote to Robert Lowell on the appearance of Pound's *Thrones*: "How is THRONES? I refused to buy ROCKDRILL [sic]. Pound criticism is wildly confused, don't you think, but I agree with D[udley] Fitts that poetry is *not* to be drilled into you, nor is music, and that's one of P[ound]'s—oh well—I'll skip it" (Bishop and Lowell, 320, emphasis in original).[30] It's a shame that Bishop breaks off there, but her point is clear enough: in *The Cantos* poetic "music" is somehow making an undue rhetorical claim. Other poets—Robert Duncan, for example—valued and sought to perpetuate Pound's visionary music but only by separating it out from the politics that underwrite it.[31] Others, like the Objectivist George Oppen, recoiled from what he regarded as Pound's lofty aestheticism. "A hypnotic art," Oppen called it, "a dithyrambic art protected by its special vocabulary etc.—It produces such a destitute world, such a destroyed world when that music stops" (*Selected Prose*, 67). For Oppen, the great rhythmic set pieces of *The Cantos* are beautiful, but in a *negative* way, a paean of praise to art rather than an affirmation of being in the world. Indeed, in his own late poems, Oppen might be seen to take his revenge on the ascending rhythms of the visionary sequences of the late Cantos, with their rich musicality and signature end-stopped lines. It's almost as if Oppen wants to disfigure the poetic line by subjecting it to a kind of internal rupture. One poem demonstrates this at both thematic and prosodic levels. In "Song, the Winds of Downhill," Oppen defines the diction to which his poem lays claim as "impoverished // of tone of pose that common / wealth // of parlance" (*New Collected Poems*, 220). "Tone" is not, in fact, effaced and survives in the regular iambic patterning of this line, though this is fractured and counter-stressed by the poem's lineation and by the heavily marked caesura that would become a distinctive feature of Oppen's later work.[32] "Rhetorical," he observes in his notes, "it means a flowing speech, it means a deluge of speech," and in another passage he defines his objective as "to slow down, that is, to isolate the words. Clatter, chatter is extreme rapidity of the words" (Oppen, in Nicholls, *George Oppen*, 138). Smoothness and rhetoric: these are routes to an illusory success in fluency and certainty. Ironically, the antirhetorical Pound is now viewed himself as a source of damaging rhetorical effects.

We find the same suspicion of "flowing speech" in the work of Susan Howe who programmatically rejects what she calls the "fluent language of fanaticism" for one that enlists the alleged inchoateness of women's speech as precisely a strength rather than a weakness (*Articulation*, 31). "This tradition that I hope I am part of," writes Howe, "has involved a breaking of boundaries of all sorts. It involves a fracturing of discourse, a stammering even. Interruption and hesitation used as a force. A recognition that there is an other voice, an attempt to hear and speak it. It's this brokenness that interests me" ("Encloser," 192). Much is contained for Howe in that idea of hesitation, a word, as she notes, "from the Latin meaning to stick. Stammer. To

hold back in doubt, have difficulty in speaking" (Howe, *My Emily Dickinson*, 21).[33]
None of which is to suggest that the characteristic viscosity of Howe's writing is a
bar to musicality but that its sonic and rhythmic features are typically assigned to
an "other voice" that in its "brokenness" and incompleteness can enchant but not, in
the usual sense, persuade. To this end, Howe's intricate patterns of echo and repeti-
tion constantly insist on the evanescence of meaning:

> I have loved come veiling
> Lyrist come veil come lure
> echo remnant sentence spar
> never never form wherefor
> Wait some recognition you
> Lyric over us unclothe
> Never forever whoso move
>
> (Howe, *Pierce-Arrow*, 144)

The characteristic injunction to "Wait some recognition" is coupled with a sense
of phantasmal presence and dispersal, as Howe weaves together a complex mesh
of /o/ and /v/ sounds that creates a shimmering uncertainty around "never" and
"for(ever)," so that, for example, we hear "whoso*ever*" even though we do not actu-
ally read it.

   Howe is perhaps unusual among contemporary poets in her continuing
fascination with such prosodic effects. More generally, it seems, poets are suspi-
cious of the temptations of their medium; in the face of Pound's refusal to surren-
der the musical sublime, they can be seen cultivating instead a poetry of limitation,
of the demotic, even, perhaps, of the bathetic (the New York School, and espe-
cially the poems of James Schuyler provide examples).[34] Even when the influence
of a modernist precursor is welcomed as benign and productive, its appropriation
tends to require a censoring out of qualities I have been defining here as "musical"
ones. Gertrude Stein's style, for example, undoubtedly survives in contemporary
Language poetry but it usually does so in a quite rebarbative form that is hostile to
the seductively sensual "music," which often motivated it in the first place. Here,
the wheel might be thought to come full circle, for what we currently call Language
writing is motivated by a recognition of rhetoric as an inescapable horizon of con-
temporary poetry. As Charles Bernstein puts it, "poetry is a form of rhetoric, not
a form of subjectivity" (Bernstein et al., "Poetry," 199), by which he means that, as
fellow poet Bob Perelman observes, "the word 'rhetoric' acknowledges the fact that
language is always socially, multiply, situated" (Nicholls, "A Conversation," 537).
Perelman is using the word "rhetoric," he says, in "a Bahktinian sense" to desig-
nate "speech genres, writing in a social situation. It's not exactly persuasion," he
continues. "What about a rhetoric that reveals its persuasive, identificatory powers
to the addressee? And invites the addressee to notice these powers of language to
interpellate and to stir up emotion? That's what I'm aiming for: an in-front-of-the-
scenes mutually pedagogic rhetoric" (538).[35] In contrast to Poundian pedagogy,

the type envisaged here openly acknowledges the designs particular usages of language may have upon us. Much Language writing is thus characterized by those very features that Pound had condemned as "rhetorical": by various kinds of verbal excess, of cliché, redundancy, duplicity, opacity, un-musicality. Here, discourse is seen always to involve some sort of "dressing up" in its capacity as a medium of social exchange; Pound's "ideology of accuracy," as Perelman calls it, yields to Bernstein's fondness for, in his words, "certain kinds of pratfalls...slipping on a banana; or throwing a pie in my own face" (Bernstein, in Perelman, 82). Slipping or slippage neatly defines Bernstein's own way with rhetoric, as poems typically skid between idioms and registers in a way that recalls familiar verbal formulations even as it seeks to frame them ideologically through crafty distortion. The much-maligned cliché is frequently here the motor of the poem: "There is an emptiness that fills / Our lives" (Bernstein, *All the Whiskey,* 72). "Time wounds all heals, spills through / with echoes neither idea nor lair / can jam" (73); "Poetry is like a swoon, with this difference: / it brings you to your senses" (84).[36]

Pound had condemned rhetoric for its intention to deceive, and while Language writing rejects much of his legacy, in its own way it too is founded in a sort of hermeneutics of suspicion, albeit suspicion often mitigated by playfulness and humor. In the last and most recent tendency I want to notice here—what is currently called "conceptual writing"—it is not so much "rhetoric" as a practice of deception that is at issue as "rhetoricality" conceived as an all-embracing cultural condition.[37] The term "conceptual writing" is designedly unoriginal, borrowing from 1960s and 1970s art theory and particularly from statements by Sol LeWitt and Joseph Kosuth.[38] One of the leading practitioners of the form, Kenneth Goldsmith, rewrites LeWitt's "Paragraphs on Conceptual Art" (first published in 1967 in *Artforum*) by replacing visual art terms with ones relevant to writing:

> I will refer to the kind of writing in which I am involved as conceptual writing. In conceptual writing the idea or concept is the most important aspect of the work. When an author uses a conceptual form of writing, it means that all of the planning and decisions are made beforehand and the execution is a perfunctory affair. The idea becomes a machine that makes the text. This kind of writing is not theoretical or illustrative of theories; it is intuitive, it is involved with all types of mental processes and it is purposeless. It is usually free from the dependence on the skill of the writer as a craftsman. It is the objective of the author who is concerned with conceptual writing to make her work mentally interesting to the reader, and therefore usually she would want it to become emotionally dry. There is no reason to suppose, however, that the conceptual writer is out to bore the reader. It is only the expectation of an emotional kick, to which one conditioned to Romantic literature is accustomed, that would deter the reader from perceiving this writing.
>
> ("Paragraphs on Conceptual Writing," 98)

The absence of "an emotional kick" in this avowedly "uncreative" writing might suggest that Goldsmith is proposing texts with a minimum of rhetorical features. Indeed, the primacy accorded the "concept" effectively seems to play down aspects of writing we would normally think of as "literary" or "poetic":

> Conceptual writing is made to engage the mind of the reader rather than her ear or emotions. The physicality of the work can become a contradiction to its non-emotive intent. Rhyme, meter, texture, and enjambment only emphasize the physical aspects of the work. Anything that calls attention to and interests the reader in this physicality is a deterrent to our understanding of the idea and is used as an expressive device.
>
> ("Paragraphs on Conceptual Writing," 101)[39]

This writing, then, is designedly nonexpressive, substituting transcription for invention, and the "conceptual" for the aural.[40] In feats of labor that might recall those of Melville's copyists, Goldsmith has produced booklength transcriptions of "every word I spoke for a week unedited" (*Soliloquy*, 2001), of "every move my body made over the course of a day" (*Fidget*, 2000), of a year's worth of radio traffic reports (*Traffic*, 2007), and so on; he has even transcribed the whole of one day's issue of the *New York Times* (*Day*, 2003) to make "a 900 page book" ("Being Boring," par. 11). Yet while Goldsmith emphasizes "concept" at the expense of text, the works themselves amount to "great chunks" of speech and writing that digitization makes it possible to transport effortlessly from one context and format to another.[41] And because the technique is that of transcription, of "simply retyping existing texts" as Goldsmith candidly describes their "general concept" (par. 1–2), the expressive force of rhetoric is absorbed into the repetitive loops of seemingly endless commentary (on the weather, on the traffic flow, on baseball, whatever).

Transcription reveals nothing;[42] as a process it is without the "suspicion" that motivates the Language writer's play with rhetorical forms. Nor is there any anxiety about eloquence or its false claims on our attention. Describing his transcription of the *New York Times* in *Day*, Goldsmith says,

> Everywhere there was a bit of text in the paper, I grabbed it. I made no distinction between editorial and advertising, stock quotes or classified ads. If it could be considered text, I had to have it. Even if there was, say, an ad for a car, I took a magnifying glass and grabbed the text off the license plate.
>
> ("Being Boring," par. 13)

Speech and text amaze by their sheer volume and are everywhere waiting to be "grabbed." Here, finally, there is no distrust of rhetoric—Goldsmith is, he says, interested "in quantifying and concretizing the vast amount of 'nutrionless' language; I'm also interested in the process itself being equally nutrionless" ("Uncreativity," par. 6).[43] Language—generally other people's language—spills on to the page in huge swathes, transcribed with all its hesitations and phatic markers—"well," "um," "like"—but with no real motive other than to provide commentary on a society already awash with it. The linguistic "surplus" that Pound had seen as such a threat to clarity and precision is here precisely what fascinates; where Bartleby had preferred neither to speak nor to copy, Goldsmith is addicted to both: "I love speech," he declares in a studied reversal of Language Poetry's talismanic "I hate speech";[44] and "There's nothing I love more than transcription" ("Being Boring," par. 3).

Many of the tensions we have seen arising from different poets' conceptions of "rhetoric" and their ways of situating their work in relation to them may be focused in an intriguing book published in 1941 by the French critic and philosopher Jean Paulhan. In *Les Fleurs de Tarbes, ou, La Terreur dans les lettres*, Paulhan defines two main types of thinking about literary expression: the first is "Rhetoric," and the second is "Terror."[45] "Rhetoric" is characterized by an essentially rule-based regard for language and its capacity to express the commonplace; "Terror," on the other hand, represents a desire to break not just with rules and conventions but with language itself. This second view of literature prioritizes originality and is founded in the belief that "the presence of the commonplace expression betrays servitude and submission at every turn" (*Flowers of Tarbes*, 34). What looks like a stark antithesis, however, actually conceals a relation of tricky intimacy, for while the literary terrorist might seem to value thought above the formal constraints of language, "no writer is more preoccupied with words than the one who at every point sets out to get rid of them, to get away from them, or to reinvent them" (76).[46] As Maurice Blanchot remarks in a penetrating reading of Paulhan's text, literature's pursuit of authenticity and originality is an impossible one, given that it is always preempted by rhetoric, with "poetic language" inevitably shadowed by the language of the "commonplace" from which it strives constantly to distinguish itself (Blanchot, 58).[47]

In the foregoing pages, "rhetoric" has proved itself, not surprisingly, a multivalent term, encompassing deliberate deception, false fluency, redundancy, and inflated self-emphasis. As Paulhan's treatise shows, it is a deeply unstable term, with one writer's meat invariably being another one's poison. Defined as cliché, commonplace, and unoriginal, though, rhetoric becomes a sort of inescapable ground against which literary innovation struggles constantly and "impossibly" (Syrotinski, Introduction, 3).[48] Ezra Pound, we recall, had defined "rhetoric" as "the use of cliché unconsciously" (*Literary Essays*, 283), thereby perhaps leaving room for his own late invention of a *consciously* commonplace language of ethical injunction derived from Confucianism.[49] Pound, we may safely assume, would not have seen the point of today's conceptual writing, though in one sense Goldsmith's work, with its blunt rejection of originality—"Why use your own words when you can express yourself just as well by using someone else's?"(Goldsmith, "Introduction to Flarf," par. 3)—might be read as a programmatic and perhaps inevitable embrace of a rhetoric that was, for modernism, both a threat and a temptation.

NOTES

1 None of which is meant to suggest that interest in Cicero declined but rather that its focus changed. See Rosner, 166: "when the status of rhetoric and the classical system of education declined, interest in Cicero did not, for the nineteenth century also met him in the broader context of popular histories and biographies." Rosner notes also that "most of these non-academic works questioned the value and sincerity of orators" (171).

The silent bust of Cicero may also register the contemporary move from oral practice to written composition (see Rosner, 164).

2   As Hayden White observes, "the suppression of rhetoric was a necessary precondition for the separation of literary from other forms of writing" (22). See also Barthes (92) for the claim that Aristotelian rhetoric has come to seem in "stubborn agreement" with "an ideology of the 'greatest number', of the majority-as-norm, of current opinion." The arduous process of copying would gradually be replaced not only by reprographic media but by more clearly functionalist means of interoffice communication (see Guillory).

3   On Bartleby's "I would prefer not to," see Deleuze.

4   See, for example, the review in *The Atlantic Monthly*, excerpted in Leyda, 685: "Is it possible...that there has really been a great war, with battles fought by men and bewailed by women? Or is it only that Mr. Melville's inner consciousness has been perturbed, and filled with the phantasms of enlistments, marches, fights in the air, parenthetic bulletin-boards, and tortured humanity shedding, not words and blood, but words alone?" Rogin offers perhaps the bleakest view of Melville's turn toward a kind of "formalism" in his political thinking of his later years.

5   The reference here is to Hopkins's poem "The Loss of the *Eurydice*." Marucci also argues that it is a mistake to understand Hopkins's rhetoric "as prevalently *expressive* (i.e., an expression of the writer's emotion) and not also as *impressive* (i.e., provoking the emotion of the listener)" (15). See also Hopkins, 267 for the paper entitled "Rhythm and Other Structural Parts of Rhetoric—Verse." The original working title was "Rhythm and the Other Structural Parts of Oratory and Poetry—Verse--."

6   See also Von Hallberg, who notes that in Hopkins's poetry, "Syntactically artful writing not only presses a claim to authority...; it alludes to a distinctive way of constructing authority: namely by negotiation between parties within the constraints of recognized rules" (32). My account of Hopkins's "oratorical" ambitions is not meant to blink the fact that the period also saw a completely antithetical tendency (Von Hallberg terms it "orphic") that would more directly influence modernist writing and that is announced in John Stuart Mill's "Thoughts on Poetry and Its Varieties": "Poetry and eloquence are both alike the expression or utterance of feeling: but, if we may be excused the antithesis, we should say that eloquence is *heard*; poetry is *overheard*. Eloquence supposes an audience. The peculiarity of poetry appears to us to lie in the poet's utter unconsciousness of a listener" (Mill, 70–71, emphasis in original).

7   See Pound's account of his best-known Imagist poem "In a Station of the Metro" in *Gaudier-Brzeska*: "I found, suddenly, the expression. I do not mean that I found words, but there came an equation...not in speech, but in little splotches of colour. It was just that—a 'pattern', or hardly a pattern, if by 'pattern' you mean something with a 'repeat' in it" (87).

8   Pound, "A Retrospect" (1918), in *Literary Essays*, 3. This collection of early pieces includes Pound's famous "A Few Don'ts" (4); Immanuel Kant, *Critique of Judgment*, trans. J. H. Bernard (New York: Hafner Press, 1951), 171.

9   Pound, *Gaudier-Brzeska*, 117. Pound is probably thinking of Aristotle's definition of metaphor in the *Poetics*: "Metaphor is the application of a word that belongs to another thing" (1457b, 7-8).

10 See Jacques Derrida, *Of Grammatology*, trans. Gayatri Chakravorty Spivak (Baltimore: Johns Hopkins University Press, 1976), 144–145.

11 As Jean Paulhan observes in *The Flowers of Tarbes*, "In terms of writing conventions, we should also mention the italics, the quotation marks and the parentheses, which we

see proliferate in Romantic writers as soon as rhetoric is invalidated" (80n3). Pound's handling of cliché in *Hugh Selwyn Mauberley* is a notable modernist example. Paulhan's account of rhetoric is considered later in this chapter.

12 In "Cavalcanti," Pound distinguishes "ornament" negatively conceived from the "irreplaceable ornament" he associates with Cavalcanti (*Literary Essays*, 154).

13 Noted in Moore, 434.

14 Eliot's view of "rhetoric" is considerably more nuanced than Pound's, admitting of both "good" and "bad" kinds. In the same essay, he suggests that we "avoid the assumption that rhetoric is a vice of manner, and endeavour to find a rhetoric of substance also, which is right because it issues from what it has to express" ("'Rhetoric,'" 72). See also Gage, 32.

15 As Guillory remarks, "The evidence for this point is the extreme compression of poetic language, particularly figurative language; but Spencer has confused compression, which might very well tax the reader's attention by producing ambiguity, with a concept of brevity that would seem to resist ambiguity as an impediment to communication" (125). The search for a model of "pure" communication was as persistent as the quest for the "universal characteristic" to which it was, of course, related. Later, Pound would show interest in the Basic English program of Ogden and Richards, but he may also have been aware of the extraordinary attack on Woodrow Wilson's political rhetoric in Hale, *The Story of a Style*. Hale there lambastes Wilson's "talent for copious eloquence rather than clear thought" (4), associating his excessively "ornamental language" (95) with the economics of conspicuous consumption (106).

16 For a commentary, see Jarratt.

17 Compare, of course, Pater's "Conclusion" to *The Renaissance*: "Our one chance lies in expanding that interval, in getting as many pulsations as possible into the given time."

18 However, as Pound recalled Yeats saying, "I have spent the whole of my life trying to get rid of rhetoric....I have got rid of one kind of rhetoric and have merely set up another." Characteristically and rather missing the point, Pound adds, "Being a serious character, at least along certain lines, he set about getting rid of THAT" (*Make It New*, 245).

19 See, for example, Baker, 85.

20 It is worth noting that Fenollosa added the following qualification to his account of the Chinese language: "Such a pictorial method, whether the Chinese exemplified it or not, would be the ideal language of the world" (59). One customary view has, of course, been that while some ideograms may have had a pictographic origin, they are nonetheless construed by Chinese readers as conventionalized symbols. For a subtle reconsideration of the graphic nature of the Chinese character that carefully distinguishes between imitative representation and semiotic iconicity, see de Campos.

21 See also the following cautionary comment in Jarvis: "The stripping down of poetry, the removal of everything which is adventitious to a description, all this does not in the end leave us with the impossible dead letter, with perfected literalness, but rather forces us right up against that in language which will not be made absolutely literal: the way in which under the steadiest description still sounds a prescription, the way in which a norm, or a value, or a meaning, echoes in what is apparently the most naked and simple 'is'" (29).

22 Compare Fenollosa's complaint about Western grammar: "The sentence according to this definition is not an attribute of nature but an accident of man as a conversational animal" (47).

23 Cf. Fenollosa: " 'Farmer' and 'rice' are mere hard terms which define the extremes of the pounding. But in themselves, apart from this sentence-function, they are naturally verbs. The farmer is one who tills the ground, and the rice is a plant which grows in a special way" (52).

24 On "orientalist" constructions of China, see, for example, Bush and Hayot. Haroldo de Campos proposes that "according to Fenollosa's reading, ideograms are rooted deep down in history or rather in a quasi-paradisiacal arche-history" (292).

25 Cf. Fenollosa's manuscript note: "Poetry is akin to Modern Science / task of Science is to undermine Logic" (200n).

26 The "remark" drew Pound's attention because it was a running feature on the cover of *Poetry* magazine. Specifically, Pound objected to *Poetry*'s habit of genuflecting to its audience in its concern with "christianizing all poems they print, [and in] their concessions to local pudibundery" (*Selected Letters*, 107).

27 "It's all rubbish to pretend that art isn't didactic. A revelation is always didactic. Only the aesthetes since 1880 have pretended the contrary, and they aren't a very sturdy lot" (*Selected Letters*, 180).

28 See also Jaeger on the early Greeks' "educational conception of poetry" (1:133) and on Plato's "criticism of poetry as paideia" (2:222).

29 A case in point is the famous passage in Canto LXXXI, "Pull down thy vanity," initially read in terms of a supposed "recantation" on Pound's part but now increasingly construed as an exhortation to the reader. For a fine account of the prosodic ingenuity of the sequence of which this passage is part, see Kenner.

30 The reference is to Fitts, "Music Fit for the Odes."

31 See Nicholls, "Beyond *The Cantos*," 146–148.

32 For more on the function of the caesura in Oppen's late work, see Nicholls, *George Oppen and the Fate of Modernism*, 191–192.

33 On the association of a "rhetoric of obscuration" with prophecy in the biblical tradition, see Marks.

34 See Wilkinson.

35 Nicholls, "A Conversation with Bob Perelman," is reprinted with "Coda" in *Jacket* no. 39.

36 From "Stove's Out," "You," and "The Kluptzy Girl," respectively.

37 See also Bender and Wellbery: "Our historical thesis leads us to this conclusion: *Modernism is an age not of rhetoric, but of rhetoricality*, the age, that is, of a generalized rhetoric that penetrates to the deepest levels of human experience.... Rhetoric is no longer the title of a doctrine or a practice, nor a form of cultural memory; it becomes instead something like the condition of our existence" (25, emphasis in original).

38 For introductory accounts of conceptual writing, see, for example, Perloff, "A Conversation with Kenneth Goldsmith"; Dworkin; and Place and Fitterman, Perloff's *Unoriginal Genius* has an intriguing chapter-length account of Goldsmith's *Traffic*.

39 Place and Fitterman argue accordingly that "all conceptual writing is allegorical writing" (15).

40 So Goldsmith writes that "literature that is meant for the sensation of the ear primarily would be called aural rather than conceptual. This would include most poetry and certain strains of fiction" ("Paragraphs on Conceptual Writing," 99). LeWitt's original is as follows: "Art that is meant for the sensation of the eye primarily would be called

perceptual rather than conceptual. This would include most optical, kinetic, light, and color art" ("Paragraphs on Conceptual Art," 80).

41 Cf. Goldsmith, "Being Boring": "The simple act of moving information from one place to another today constitutes a significant act in and of itself.... Some of us call this writing" (par. 2).

42 See also on "transcription" as deployed in Julianna Spahr's *LIVE*: "The transcriber writes down only language that is not his or her own, but language which has already been put forth.... Transcription thus involves a relationship to language that is *inherently* one of belatedness or redundancy. The relationship between transcription and language is also one of labor, and in a form few would describe as intellectually or aesthetically 'rewarding'" (Ngai, 324–325, emphasis in original).

43 Compare Michael Fried's account of Tony Smith's *Die*, a six-foot black-painted steel cube: "[It] is *always* of further interest; one never feels that one has come to the end of it; it is inexhaustible. It is inexhaustible, however, not because of any fullness—that is the inexhaustibility of art—but because there is nothing there to exhaust. It is endless the way a road might be: if it were circular, for example" (qtd. in J. M. Bernstein, *Against Voluptuous Bodies*, 132).

44 The poet and artist Robert Grenier used the phrase in the first issue of *This* magazine (1971) which he edited with Barrett Watten.

45 Paulhan's thought on this subject is further developed in "Rhetoric Rises from Its Ashes" and "Young Lady with Mirrors," in Paulhan, *On Poetry and Politics*.

46 For a reading that speaks more simply of the "return of rhetoric," see Compagnon, 98.

47 See also Syrotinski, *Defying Gravity*, 73.

48 Syrotinski notes that "it is ultimately impossible to determine whether a given word or expression is 'original' or not" (Introduction, 3).

49 The tendency is pronounced in the late sequence *Thrones*, especially where Pound draws on *The Sacred Edict of K'ang Hsi* for examples of proverbial folk wisdom ("There is worship in plowing / and equity in the weeding hoe" ["Canto XCIX"]).

REFERENCES

Adorno, Theodor. *Negative Dialectics*. Translated by E. B. Ashton. New York: Continuum, 1973.

Altieri, Charles. *The Art of Twentieth-Century American Poetry*. Oxford: Blackwell, 2006.

———. "Rhetoric and Poetics: How to Use the Inevitable Return of the Repressed." In *A Companion to Rhetoric and Rhetorical Criticism*, edited by Walter Jost and Wendy Olmsted, 473–493. Oxford: Blackwell, 2004.

Aristotle. *Poetics*. Translated by W. Rhys Roberts. New York: Dover, 2004.

———. *Rhetoric*. Translated by W. Rhys Roberts. New York: Dover, 2004.

Ashbery, John. "The Wrong Kind of Insurance." In *Houseboat Days*, 50. Harmondsworth, UK: Penguin, 1977.

Baker, Houston. *Modernism and the Harlem Renaissance*. Chicago: University of Chicago Press, 1987.

Barthes, Roland. "The Old Rhetoric: An Aide-Memoire." In *The Semiotic Challenge*, translated by Richard Howard, 11–94. New York: Hill and Wang, 1988.

Bender, J., and D. E. Wellbery. "Rhetoricality." In *The Ends of Rhetoric: History, Theory, Practice*, edited by J. Bender and D. E. Wellbery, 3–42. Stanford: Stanford University Press, 1990.

Bernstein, Charles. *All the Whiskey in Heaven: Selected Poems*. New York: Farrar, Straus, and Giroux, 2010.

Bernstein, Charles, et al. "Poetry, Community, Movement: A Conversation." *Diacritics* 26, no. 3/4 (Fall/Winter 1996): 196–210.

Bernstein, J. M. *Against Voluptuous Bodies: Late Modernism and the Meaning of Painting*. Stanford: Stanford University Press, 2006.

———. "Mimetic Rationality and Material Inference: Adorno and Brandom."*Revue internationale de philosophie* no. 227 (2004): 7–23.

Bishop, Elizabeth, and Robert Lowell. *Words in Air: The Complete Correspondence between Elizabeth Bishop and Robert Lowell*, edited by Thomas Travisano with Saskia Hamilton. New York: Farrar, Straus, and Giroux, 2010.

Blanchot, Maurice. "How Is Literature Possible?" In *The Blanchot Reader*, edited by Michael Holland, 49–60. Cambridge, MA: Blackwell, 1995.

Bush, Christopher. *Ideographic Modernism: China, Writing, Media*. Oxford: Oxford University Press, 2010.

Compagnon, Antoine. "L'arrière-garde, de Peguy à Paulhan et Barthes." In *Les arrière-gardes au XX siècle: L'autre face de la modernité esthétique*, edited by William Marx, Paris: PUF, 2004.

de Campos, Haroldo. "Poetic Function and Ideogram/The Sinological Argument." In *Novas: Selected Writings of Haroldo de Campos*, edited and introduced by. Antonio Sergio Bessa and Odile Cisneros, 287–311. Evanston, IL: Northwestern University Press, 2007.

Deleuze, Gilles. "Bartleby; or, The Formula." In *Essays Critical and Clinical*, translated by Daniel W. Smith and Michael A. Greco, 68–90. Minneapolis: University of Minnesota Press, 1997.

Derrida, Jacques. *Of Grammatology*. Translated by Gayatri Chakravorty Spivak. Baltimore: Johns Hopkins University Press, 1976.

Dworkin, Craig. Introduction to *The Ubuweb Anthology of Conceptual Writing*, edited by Craig Dworkin. http://www.ubu.com/concept/.

Eliot, T. S. *Little Gidding*. In *The Complete Poems and Plays of T. S. Eliot*. London: Faber and Faber, 1969.

———. " 'Rhetoric' and Poetic Drama." In *The Sacred Wood*. New York: Alfred A. Knopf, 1921.

Fenollosa, Ernest, and Ezra Pound. *The Chinese Written Character as a Medium for Poetry: A Critical Edition*. Edited by Haun Saussy, Jonathan Stalling, and Lucas Klein. New York: Fordham University Press, 2008.

Fitts, Dudley. "Music Fit for the Odes." *The Hound and Horn* 4, no. 2 (1931): 278–289.

Gage, John. *In the Arresting Eye: The Rhetoric of Imagism*. Baton Rouge: Louisiana State University Press, 1981.

Genette, Gerard. "Rhetoric Restrained." In *Figures of Discourse*, translated by Alan Sheridan. Oxford: Basil Blackwell, 1982.

Goldsmith, Kenneth. "Being Boring." http://epc.buffalo.edu/authors/goldsmith/goldsmith_boring.html.

———. "Introduction to Flarf vs. Conceptual Writing." http:/epc.buffalo.edu/authors/goldsmith/whitney-intro.html.

———. "Paragraphs on Conceptual Writing." *Open Letter* 12, no. 7 (2005)

———. "Uncreativity as Creative Practice." http://epc.buffalo.edu/authors/goldsmith/
    uncreativity.html.
Guillory, John. "The Memo and Modernity." *Critical Inquiry* 31, no. 1 (2004): 108–131.
Hale, William Bayard. *The Story of a Style*. New York: B. W. Huebsch, 1920.
Havelock, Eric. *Preface to Plato*. Oxford: Basil Blackwell, 1963.
Hayot, Eric. *Chinese Dreams: Pound, Brecht, and Tel Quel*. Ann Arbor: University of
    Michigan Press, 2004.
Hopkins, Gerard Manley. "Rhythm and Other Structural Parts." In *The Journals and Papers
    of Gerard Manley Hopkins*, edited by Humphrey House. Oxford: Oxford University
    Press, 1959.
Howe, Susan. *Articulation of Sound Forms in Time*. In *Singularities*, 1–38. Hanover:
    Wesleyan University Press and University Press of New England, 1990.
———. "Encloser." In *The Politics of Poetic Form: Poetry and Public Policy*, edited by Charles
    Bernstein. New York: Roof Books, 1990.
———. *My Emily Dickinson*. Berkeley: North Atlantic, 1985.
———. *Pierce-Arrow*. New York: New Directions, 1999.
Jaeger, Werner. *Paideia: The Ideals of Greek Culture*. Vols. 1 and 2. Translated by Gilbert
    Highet. Oxford: Basil Blackwell, 1965.
Jarratt, Susan. "Walter Pater and the Sophistication of Rhetoric." *College English* 51, no. 1
    (1989): 73–87.
Jarvis, Simon. *Wordsworth's Philosophic Song*. Cambridge: Cambridge University Press,
    2007.
Kant, Immanuel. *Critique of Judgment*. Translated by J. H. Bernard. New York: Hafner
    Press, 1951.
Kenner, Hugh. *The Pound Era*. Berkeley: University of California Press, 1971.
LeWitt, Sol. "Paragraphs on Conceptual Art." *Artforum* 5 no.10 (Summer 1967): 79–83.
Leyda, Jay, ed. *The Melville Log: A Documentary Life of Herman Melville*. Vol. 2. New York:
    Gordian Press, 1969.
Mariani, Paul L. *A Commentary on the Complete Poems of Gerard Manley Hopkins*. Ithaca,
    NY: Cornell University Press, 1970.
Marks, Herbert. "On Prophetic Stammering." *Yale Journal of Criticism* 1, no.1 (1987): 1–19.
Marucci, Franco. *The Fine Delight That Fathers Thought: Rhetoric and Medievalism in
    Gerard Manley Hopkins*. Washington, DC: Catholic University of America Press,
    1994.
Melville, Herman. "Bartleby, the Scrivener." In *The Piazza Tales and Other Prose Pieces,
    1839–1860*, edited by Harrison Hayford et al., 13–45. Evanston, IL: Northwestern
    University Press, 1987.
Mill, John Stuart. "Thoughts on Poetry and Its Varieties." In *Dissertations and Discussions*,
    Vol. 1, 63–94. New York: Haskell House, 1973.
Moore, Arthur K. "Lyric Voices and Ethical Proofs." *Journal of Aesthetics and Art Criticism*
    23, no. 4 (1965): 429–439.
Naremore, James. "The Death and Rebirth of Rhetoric." http//archive.sensesofcinema.com/
    contents/00/5/rhetoric.html.
Ngai, Sianne. *Ugly Feelings*. Cambridge, MA: Harvard University Press, 2005.
Nicholls, Peter. "Beyond *The Cantos*: Pound and American Poetry." In *The Cambridge
    Companion to Ezra Pound*, edited by Ira Nadel, 139–160. Cambridge: Cambridge
    University Press, 1999.
———. "A Conversation with Bob Perelman." *Textual Practice* 12, no. 3 (1998): 525–544.
———. *George Oppen and the Fate of Modernism*. Oxford: Oxford University Press, 2007.

Oppen, George. *New Collected Poems*. Edited by Michael Davidson. New York: New Directions, 2008.

———. *Selected Prose, Daybooks, and Papers*. Edited by Stephen Cope. Berkeley: University of California Press, 2008.

Pater, Walter. *Appreciations, with an Essay on Style*. London: Macmillan, 1931.

Paulhan, Jean. *The Flowers of Tarbes, or, Terror in Literature*. Translated and introduced by Michael Syrotinski. Urbana: University of Illinois Press, 2006.

———. *Les Fleurs de Tarbes, ou, La Terreur dans les lettres*. Paris: Gallimard, 1941.

———. "Rhetoric Rises from Its Ashes." In *On Poetry and Politics*, edited by Jennifer Bjorek and Eric Trudel, and translated by Charlotte Mandell, 44–56. Urbana: University of Illinois Press, 2008.

———. "Young Lady with Mirrors." In *On Poetry and Politics*, edited by Jennifer Bjorek and Eric Trudel, and translated by Charlotte Mandell, 57–69. Urbana: University of Illinois Press, 2008.

Perelman, Bob. *The Marginalization of Poetry: Language Writing and Literary History*. Princeton, NJ: Princeton University Press, 1996.

Perloff, Marjorie. "A Conversation with Kenneth Goldsmith." *Jacket* no. 21 (2003): http://jacketmagazine.com/21/perl-gold-iv.html.

———. *Unoriginal Genius: Poetry by Other Means in the New Century*. Chicago: University of Chicago Press, 2010.

Place, Vanessa, and Robert Fitterman. *Notes on Conceptualisms*. Brooklyn: Ugly Duckling Presse, 2009.

Pound, Ezra. "Canto XCIX." In *Thrones: 96–109 de los cantares*. New York: New Directions, 1959.

———. *Gaudier-Brzeska: A Memoir*. Hessle, East Yorkshire: The Marvell Press, 1960 (original, 1916).

———. *Guide to Kulchur*. London: Peter Owen, 1966 (original, 1938).

———. *How to Read*. In *Polite Essays*. Plainview, NY: Books for Libraries Press, 1966 (original, 1937).

———. *Literary Essays*. Edited by T. S. Eliot. London: Faber, 1968.

———. *Make It New*. London: Faber and Faber, 1934.

———. *The Selected Letters of Ezra Pound 1907–1941*. Edited by D. D. Paige. London: Faber and Faber, 1971.

Rogin, Michael Paul. *Subversive Genealogy: The Politics and Art of Herman Melville*. Berkeley: University of California Press, 1983.

Rosner, Mary. "Cicero in Nineteenth-Century England and America." *Rhetorica* 4, no. 2 (1986): 153–182.

Spencer, Herbert. *The Philosophy of Style*. Whitefish, MT: Kessinger Publishing, 2004 (original, 1852).

Stevens, Wallace. *The Necessary Angel*. New York: Random House, 1951.

Symons, Arthur. *The Symbolist Movement in Literature*. New York: E. P. Dutton and Co., Inc., 1958 (original, 1899).

Syrotinski, Michael. *Defying Gravity: Jean Paulhan's Interventions in Twentieth-Century French Intellectual History*. Albany, NY: SUNY Press, 1998.

———. Introduction to *The Power of Rhetoric, the Rhetoric of Power: Jean Paulhan's Fiction, Criticism, and Editorial Activity*. *Yale French Studies* no. 106 (2004): 1–7.

Von Hallberg, Robert. *Lyric Powers*. Chicago: University of Chicago Press, 2008.

White, Hayden. "The Suppression of Rhetoric in the Nineteenth Century." In *The Rhetoric Canon*, edited by Brenda Dean Schildgen, 21–32. Detroit: Wayne State Press, 1997.

Wilkinson, John. "Jim the Jerk: Bathos and Loveliness in the Poetry of James Schuyler." In *On Bathos: Literature, Music, Art,* edited by Sara Crangle and Peter Nicholls, 71–89. London: Continuum, 2010.

Wordsworth, William. "Preface of 1800, with a Collation of the Enlarged Preface of 1802." In William Wordsworth and Samuel Taylor Coleridge, *Lyrical Ballads 1798,* edited by W. J. B. Owen. Oxford: Oxford University Press, 1967.

Yeats, W. B. *Mythologies.* London: Macmillan, 1959.

CHAPTER 8

CÉZANNE'S IDEAL OF "REALIZATION": A USEFUL ANALOGY FOR THE SPIRIT OF MODERNITY IN AMERICAN POETRY

CHARLES ALTIERI

> However various the directions in which different groups are exploring the newly-found regions of expressive form they all alike derive in some measure from the great originator of the whole idea, Cézanne.... One must always refer to him to understand the origin of these ideas.
>
> Roger Fry, "The French Group" (1912, 191)

The actual fact is that in Cézanne modern French art make its first tiny step back to real substance, to objective substance.... Van Gogh's earth was still subjective earth, himself projected into earth.... Cézanne's great effort was... to shove the apple away from him, and let it live of itself.... It is the first real sign that man has made for several thousand years that he is willing to admit that matter *actually* exists.... And then, the moment it is done, and we realize that matter is

only a form of energy...that...exists absolutely, since it is
compact energy itself.

D. H. Lawrence, *The Paintings of D.H. Lawrence*
(London, 1929, 17)

My epigraphs embody the challenge that thinkers faced in interpreting how paint-
ing succeeded in defining a distinctively modernist spirit. I want to elaborate what
American modernist poets shared as they tried to appropriate aspects of the paint-
ers' projects while refusing slavish imitation and visible envy of the painters' cen-
trality. There is much more at stake than learning how to adapt painterly collage.
To adapt to a modernism defined primarily in the visual arts, they would have rec-
onciled on their own terms the contrast in the epigraphs between Fry's formalism
and Lawrence's sense of Cézanne's introducing a new relationship to matter and to
energy. The formalism stemmed primarily from the need for an art that could take
on manifest force as a sensuous particular while refusing all representational ideals,
either of accurate description or of discursive moral exemplarity. But the rhetoric
of formalism simply could not encompass either the tremendous intensities with
which the new painting engaged the world or the sense that finally art could rival
science in exploring matter as a form of energy. A modernist poetry would also
have to develop new lines of relation to the material world. Because I think the
best and most influential grappling with these issues takes place in the later work
of Cézanne, I will concentrate on the implicit theorizing that frames his use of the
term "réalization" for his painterly quest. This concern puts the energies that form
carries into dialogue with the possibilities of an artist providing a new yet plausible
sense of the real, despite rejecting traditional representational paths to realist ends.
Modernist poets, I will argue, adapt virtually the same strategies for their grappling
with how a different medium might provide its own convincing access to what it
could treat as reality.[1]

There are many storylines for making form into a vehicle for soliciting a sense
of matter. Western modernism is unthinkable without Manet's mastery of tones that
stage self-consciousness but do not settle for straightforward ironic reversals. And
the art's capacities to embody affective states seem in continual dialogue with the
expressionism of *Die Brucke* and Kandinsky's theorizing that emerged from that con-
text. But Cézanne provides the greatest scope, in part because he manages to have
achieved immense influence on the future by reformulating the mobility of hand,
eye, and mind fostered within Impressionism, the movement dominating the spirit of
experiment in which his styles developed. Both Cubism and non-iconic abstraction
manifestly pursued aspects of perspective and conversions of matter into energy only
incipiently present in his work. And by 1914 most ambitious poets in the United States
and Europe were exploring how they could develop that Cézannian heritage by taking
it over into their medium and developing an art that repudiates ideals of imitation.

I act as if this connection between form and content were widely accepted by
readers and critics. Yet critics with a theoretical bent now seem much in need of

reminders of what "realization" promised because they tend to make a series of problematic moves. The first move is accepting Greenberg's analysis of the turn by artists to emphasizing the power of their medium. Greenberg sees that shift as motivated primarily by the modernists' hatred of kitsch and the commodity culture that it exemplified. Art then becomes primarily a purification of kitsch by treating the basic content of the work as a structure of internal relations elaborating the artist's sense of the powers of the medium. But then it becomes difficult to avoid corollary claims that this purification aspires to an autonomous position separating art from claims about truth and social responsibility. And then, lacking any positive language for anything but the work of the medium, it becomes far too easy to envision that the energies of modernism are primarily devoted to critique of modernity. Critique becomes the extension of the spirit of modernism, and, conversely, modernist writing is mined for its powers as critique.[2]

Such thinking seems to me anachronistic and costly. It is anachronistic because in fact modernist poets do not talk about form as separable from experiments with the delivery of something they can consider a version of the real. Greenberg's arguments apply at best to abstract expressionism and the minimalist responses it provoked. Moreover, it is rare to find poets or even painters before World War II who use the term autonomy to echo nineteenth-century cries for the separation of art from life. If they use the concept at all it is to carve a space where they can resist claims about the authority of tradition so that they can develop new ways in which form intensifies content and provides it with new imaginative sites in which to dwell.[3]

And these developments are costly because they largely ignore the constructive and idealizing dimensions of modernist art and modernist poetics. Cézanne on realization will help us keep one powerful idealization in mind, an idealization that expanded to give a motive for modernist art to attempt extending its parameters well beyond formalism. Modernist abstraction was devoted to imagining how abstraction could participate in elemental forces that underlie perception, thereby carrying a sense that the work was actually bringing into the real rhythms and balances that embodied fundamental structural relations that underlie appearance. What could not be represented as real could at least be modeled and exemplified. And these experiences in turn could make people see how their individuality had immense capacities for connection with other agents. It might require a critique of modernity to free these energies; but it would then take a self-confident art to embody them and exemplify what their significance might be. Even as dour a presence as Eliot argued that art could modify the consequences of dissociated sensibility.

A final advantage to pursuing the concept of realization is that the concept helps us explain why the reign of modernism could not last. Realization obviously provides a term for what art objects can establish. But in stressing this, critics tend to forget how important ideals of subjective intensity become as measures both of what needs to be objectified and of the triumph over subjectivity that this involves. I will argue that this model makes it difficult for modernists to appreciate any art based in rhetoric or politics where the motives are social interests rather than subjective intensities. Similarly, bonding the subject to the object makes it difficult to explore ways of cutting the subject free of objects to explore its own unrepresentable intricacies. Intimations of these new possibilities began during World War I with Dada and surrealism. But because the war was a long way from the United States and because poetry in America turned to Eliot's struggles against dissociated sensibility, with all its attendant conservative values, these painterly movements began to have their full effect on American poetry only after World War II, when poets like O'Hara and Ashbery sought relief from the authority of high modernism.[4]

1

Ezra Pound put best the dream of early modernist poetry—that it combine the virtues of Impressionism and Symbolism while refusing their vices of subjectivist sensualism and abstract spirituality (*Gaudier*-Brzeska, 84; cf. Altieri, *Painterly Abstraction*, 295–303). And this is precisely what Cézanne offered when he spoke of "the obstinacy with which I pursue the realization of that part of nature, which coming into our line of vision, gives the picture."[5]

Then he added the psychological correlate inseparable from the material aspect of his quest:

> The thesis to develop—whatever our temperament or form of power in the presence of nature—is to give the image of what we see, forgetting everything that appears in front of us. Which I think should permit the artist to give all of his personality, large or small.

Cézanne's principle of realization offered a release from the nineteenth century's constitutive oppositions between arrogantly reductive versions of realism and vaguely earnest spiritualism seeking alternatives to traditional religion. Equally important, realization foregrounds the activities possible in articulating the powers of the medium as the vehicle for a renewed sense of the worldliness art could carry, so it played a major role in establishing the sense that art was first of all a means of labor and only secondarily, by accepting the demands of labor, a continuation of aristocratic privilege by other means.

When Cézanne repeatedly expressed this ideal of realization he was close to death and preoccupied by a sense that such "realization of my sensations" was always painful because he could not "attain the intensity which unfolds to my senses."[6] But even the 1905 letter's comment on giving the personality suggests that the ideal of realization is not always haunted by the feeling of failure. At times, visual intensity could find a home in the relations among objects and there could be this giving up to the image of one's whole personality. Therefore, while I recognize the potential for tragedy in any quest for self-transcendence, I want to take the idea of realization as covering the full range of Cézanne's paintings from 1890 to his death, so that this ideal can stand for what in fact his successors perceived as the core legacy of his aesthetics.[7] Then I can demonstrate what constitutes realization and isolate five principles within it that clarify the ambitions of a significant range of modernist writerly projects, in part because they provide touchstones by which writers could with some confidence identify as distinctively modernist.

But first let me briefly explain this ideal by pointing to features that make Cézanne's landscapes so distinctive. My favorite example is *Pines and Rocks (Fontainebleau?)* (1894) because it interprets realization as a clear repudiation of classical landscape for its failures to capture how one might see reality actually emerge in the immediacy of seeing.[8] In the painting, the trees and rocks bleed into another, and the erasing of the vanishing point makes air part of the substance of the scene rather than a transparent medium. Varying color intensities and harmonies refuse to let the eye settle or sustain any division between matter and energy, and the trees seem to provide gravity for the eye while the rocks become weightless visual masses, as if any more substantial sense of mass were an inference not actually present in vision and a lazy substitute for capturing how rocks both ground color and are released into it. Cézanne's manifest refusal to paint in accord with realistic conventions becomes his launch pad for a new realism where matter is inseparable from force and the artist's mind and hand inseparable from the appearance of intricate substantial structures displaying what can be seen for the eye willing to commit itself to the adventure of looking.

2

I will attend more carefully to another painting by Cézanne in a few moments. But just this description should remind readers of his work sufficiently to test the adequacy of the five principles I propose as a summary of what realization involves— for poets as well as for painters.

1) Art as actuality. Art is primarily a process of expression in which the subject manages to objectify impressions into a living structure that transcends the partiality of the point of view making it possible. I call this objective expressionism because the focus is not on the subjectivity of the artist but on its overcoming. Realizing the intensity of apperception within a work of art requires that the decisions of the mind operating on that sensibility be overtly transferred to the operations of the hand (Schapiro, 70). Only then will the object come to express a sense of the artist's engagement within the play of forces that renders a reality at least approximating the energy inspiring the painting in the first place. This is obviously a painfully abstract definition. But I need the abstraction because I want to be able to show how many competing visions of force and reality can be located within the same general vision of what matters about art.

This first principle provides a significant theoretical means of explaining a sense of reality for art despite that artists' refusing to consider themselves as representing something objective or according with social convention. Art is composed by sharpening and composing sensations into structures so that the structuring or suturing literally builds an experience out of manifest decision making. The intensity of sensation secures that the object will not be subordinated to the understanding. Yet the understanding feels itself called upon to track the intricate relations the sensations form—whether the result be triumphant understanding or a tragic sense of the ultimate inadequacy of such understanding. Cézannian realization affords imaginative space then for moments of satisfaction and for moments of tragic striving in which we know nature by the painting's doomed effort to honor the sense of force that elicits it. (Lacan is not the first figure to posit reality in what emerges as the limits of our symbolic structures.) What matters is how the work foregrounds the constant process of decision making and compositional labor involved in constructing states that can approximate these limits.

2) Creative Forgetting. Such art can dismiss the understanding as an adequate vehicle for grasping the sense of reality possible in art because it is constantly reminding its audience that one aspect of decision making for the artist is continual vigilance against habits of representation emphasized by previous generations. Art can emphasize compositional powers largely because those powers become inseparable from the demonstration of how forgetting can be a powerful productive principle. It is crucial for Cézanne that his landscapes and still lives appear as if the artist has come upon a mode of vision that is intensely shaped by present forces and indebted to the past only for the structural vocabulary of volumetric forms. This forgetting proved especially important in relation to perspective because Cézanne could begin to experiment with reversing the limits of monocular perspective and the idea that the painting must represent only one moment of vision. Then the Cubists could push this principle much further. Why not treat perspective as itself a compositional principle capable of merging object directly into a kind of concrete ideality, exploring the possibility that one important sense of reality might be inseparable from how imagination can configure points of view? (Surrealism is a strange extension of this configuration of perspectives, freed from any responsibility to visual relations that can be characterized as features of the actual world.)

3) Absoluteness. Because Cézanne tries to make what takes place in his painting separable from habit and modes of instruction, it appears ridiculous to attempt to contextualize these presences in any language borrowed from such habits or modes of instruction. The visual event takes on a kind of absoluteness, freed from narrative or argument or anything else that might confuse the satisfactions of the eye with satisfactions deriving from other sources of desire. And the work must educate audiences to accept this absoluteness as a condition of modernist seeing. To Rilke, it seemed as if color in Cézanne's paintings was wholly used up in becoming things (Cachin, 45). And, as Meyer Schapiro observed, no one would desire to eat an apple painted by Cézanne. In fact Cézanne fantasized that he could "astonish Paris with

an apple" (Baumann et al., 82) precisely because he understood that he was the first painter to isolate modes of visual desire and treat them as absolute, as breeching no compromise with what binds desire to the world of action and opinion.

One has to be careful here not to equate absoluteness with any sense of mastering what is presented. Mastery is itself a practical ideal, far from Cézanne's sense that the image becomes a reality in itself as an effort to be responsive to and responsible for what the world gives to the eye. Absoluteness here is both a celebration of power and an admission of humility about what generates the effort in the first place. As my epigraph from Lawrence shows, the combination was taken to have substantial ethical force because Cézanne treats his objects as having rights to be seen as fully as possible without being relegated to categories of use or need or even the pleasures of association or consumption.

4) Form as a record of decision making. Cézanne's absoluteness brings a new level of self-consciousness into the manifest features of art that generates a new attitude toward form. Rather than rely on analogies to organic nature, form comes to derive primarily from culture. The creative intensity of the artist's refusals is seen as shaping the particular decisions that give a distinctive presence to the work. And, positively, that decision making becomes the overt taking of responsibility for the labor of making something important because of its difference from traditional painting. Form must try to replace ideology and sentiment as the basic indicator of the human significance for what is seen or said. So the absoluteness of the art image goes hand in hand with the desire to manifest formal choices as intrinsic to the object. Yet, pace Clive Bell, form is not significant primarily because it becomes an object in its own right. Rather, form becomes the manifest structuring of the painter's decisions so that they constitute a distinctive complement dynamizing and thickening the visual event.[9]

Jay Bernstein speaks for a growing number of critics who treat modernist focus on form as necessarily representing the loss of "orientational" forces once derived from perception but banished by Kant from philosophical treatments of "nature." Yet this seems oversimplified, especially in dealing with Cézanne, because it is through the work of form that one becomes self-consciousness about what satisfactions it seeks from the nature eliciting the artist's effort in the first place.[10] Form matters because it can reflect and resolve the difficulties encountered by the mind and hand as they work. Conversely, the seamless relation between form and content that makes for the absoluteness of the image provides a powerful psychological goal for the artist. The fullest measure of realization is the sense idealized by Nietzsche that there are no subjective needs or illusions that have not taken objective form in the work.

5) The overcoming of personality. It is important to connect the desire for absoluteness to the widespread modernist idealization of impersonality because that helps us see how this ideal is not primarily a fiction created to compensate for artists and writers losing a sense of the importance of personality and personhood and so preferring to escape the messy dynamics of social relationships. Rather, impersonality for these figures was a profound psychological ideal that could be

seen as the finest development of personality, and so it was the fullest means available of projecting how art could enter society. Impersonality becomes a measure of what agents can become when they absorb themselves in their labor and trust to the intricacy of form as the fulfillment of personality. Cézanne is a perfect illustration here because his career so visibly moved from an art haunted by subjective energies that overdetermined scenes with unrecoverable depths of private emotional significance to the vision that through realization one can give all of one's personality to the realized object. In effect impersonality is the achievement of managing to organize personality so that it can be absorbed by love and expressed in the effort to make visible the immediate grounds for how the art object seems worthy of that love.

3

I hope this account is sufficiently clear that it will justify very brief indications of how each principle pervades and helps to justify the imaginative projects of modernist poetry. First, we find the opposition to representation everywhere in modernist poetry as it explores the possibilities of expressive freedoms won by the Impressionist tradition. But we also find the recurrent need to have the work of these artists negotiate a world in ways that can become exemplary for audiences. Therefore, like Cézanne, modernist poets foregrounded how grappling with the medium might replace confident assertions about the real. Now what could claim to be real depended manifestly on the artist's labor: the real was something one had to work to reveal, and it had to be pursued in accord with the paths that the work established.

Let me take as my example the poem "Spring and All" by William Carlos Williams. One might say that this apparently innocuous "all" in the title is Williams's most Cézannian gesture because then so much depends upon getting something right about spring. Yet there is one sense in which the poem merely announces that spring is coming. No respectable Victorian writer would so reduce this motif and so minimize lyrical expressiveness. But Williams is committed to an expressiveness that is not so dependent on the writer's demonstration of personal involvement. He wants an involvement that is constitutive for the scene and capable of serving as evidence that the poet has worked to establish a moment of discovery significant for all readers, whatever their personal memories.

The poem begins with fourteen lines that try to render the feel of "dazed spring" just coming out of winter. No verbs are allowed in this sequence presenting flat particulars linked only by adjacency. The poem's first verb in line fifteen is merely the abstract "approaches" that only indicates further adjacency. Then, the first "now" changes the level of activity because it forces spatial wandering into a sense of temporal possibility for change. "Now" proves more of a verb than "approaches," generating in turn a series of verbs that gather the diverse space into an overall "it." Now there can be a sense of the whole in which the adjacent elements participate:

> One by one objects are defined—
> It quickens: clarity, outline of leaf
>
> But now the stark dignity of
> entrance—Still, the profound change
> has come upon them: rooted, they
> grip down and begin to awaken. (*Collected Poems*, 182)

Williams is careful here to make everything asserted about spring literally happen within what proves a complex set of choices. "Now" is also given the grammatical task of a verb, this time predicating the austere collective state of the "stark dignity of entrance." That state develops "it" as the relevant agency here, since there is certainly no human source responsible for the action. Instead this mode of agency can correlate "now" and "still"—no mean feat, especially because "still" serves as both an adjective giving action to the substance and an adverb measuring the increasing focus engaged by the observing consciousness. More important, "now" and "still" are totalizing atmospheric conditions shared by all the particulars and intensified by the ability of the final verbs to mobilize that general state by adapting unobtrusive partial personifications. Here personification seems to go outward rather than inward by suggesting actions that persons share with natural processes.

Williams is also very careful in his decisions about how to present the sequence of verbs. "Rooted" begins the series with a past participle, a reminder of what allows for life and what prepares for the ensuing verbs in the present tense. And then the present-tense verbs are intricately related: "grip down" becomes a precondition for growing up. Two other aspects of tense emerge with the phrase "begin to awaken" because it combines a sense of continuing action with a sense of the timelessness or at least undefined temporality of the infinitive. The state of matter here becomes inseparable from the verbs that transfer energy and bring the activity of nature into ineluctable proximity with the desires of the situated impersonal mind.

This poem seems to me unthinkable without what Cézanne accomplished. Compare it to Wordsworth's equally intelligent rendering in "Tintern Abbey" of mind in nature. Wordsworth's poem also foregrounds stylistic decisions as fundamental to the experience of nature. But these decisions are emphatically rhetorical ones: they stem less from the objects of attention that from the subject's need to construct a certain kind of ethos capable of responding to the world and responding to what he sees about himself seeing the world in this way. Wordsworth's rhetoric is naturalized as dialectical, for it enables the poet to see the increase in his own power and attribute that to "a spirit and a power that rolls through all things." This realization in turn allows the poet to stage a spiritual growth that can project himself at the end as a potential example for showing the way from youth to maturity. Williams, in contrast, is insistently not dialectical, at least in relation to the embodied speaker. In fact he refuses to stage any self-reflexive subject apart from the consciousness that manages to attune its decision making to the possible significance of what it engages as event. The relevant powers are not aspects of self-expression so much as those of sheer compositional possibility for the scene to which the artist has given his whole personality.

Second, Williams also relies in "Spring and All" on a Cézannian forgetting to clear that consciousness of any traces of habit that might get between its decision making and what it sees as defining how spring may be experienced. It is not a question of this spring or that spring: forgetting is also abstracting toward what can claim to be conditions any spring must meet to engage fully the energies of consciousness. In fact one might say this correlation of forgetting, abstracting, and essentializing for the imagination is an important distinguishing quality of modernist poetry in general. The best Imagist and Objectivist poems are not at all modest, despite their limited focus, because the limitations in scope become vehicles of concentration and a means of shedding all inherited habits (including those that invoke a rhetoric of modesty) so that the building blocks of experience become at once transparent and vitally engaged with each other.

These poems take on a monumental task of having constantly to produce value for perceptions by the naked force of working compositional intelligence. But even the most ambitious modernist poems use this nakedness as a means of foregrounding what can be discovered when one walks "barefoot into reality." *The Cantos* is a great example of how a poet uses the necessity to forget a deeply flawed immediate inheritance in order to find what is worth remembering in voices responding to experiences of beauty, even though these experiences have been suppressed by decadent economic and poetic practices. And Eliot's *Waste Land* takes on the unenviable chore of literally disentangling from the seductions of cultural memory the vague hope that there is at the core of those memories mythical patterns that can at least preserve the space where foregrounded patterns of juxtaposition can still plausibly claim a meaningfulness not absorbed into the poles of critique and kitsch.

Third, the appearance of absoluteness is clearly a corollary of the demand for forgetting. The poem must stand alone with its only possible justification its capacity to convince an audience of its capacities to make experience significant. I think of Loy's intricate diction and radical lucidity, all offered without scenic context or apology or justification. The justification can only be developed by those who are willing to let themselves find their emotional ways with only the poets' decisions as guides. Similarly one might take Pound's short lyrics engaging the presence of the gods as modes of imaginative literalness providing a powerful contrast to the way his satires mire him in the social world. (One might say that proximity to the gods is a constant in Pound because he wants the fullest form of emotions, purified of all historical contingencies.) But for me the fullest lyric version of absoluteness takes place in the opening poems of Stevens's *Harmonium*. These poems plunge us into imaginative states where we do not even have the consolation of identifying with any recognizable human subject. Instead the poems present their own investments in being taken directly and literally as states worthy of attention in their own right. So the volume begins by posing the Nietzschean challenge to engage without defensiveness these unfamiliar demands to try a fullness of imaginative being not defaced by all the compromises of the social theater. Even the lyric "I" in "Domination of Black" seems not the source of emotion but the object of intensities for which there are no empirical correlates:

> Out of the window,
> I saw how the planets gathered
> Like the leaves themselves
> Turning in the wind.
> I saw how the night came,
> Came striding like the color of the heavy hemlocks.
> I felt afraid.
> And I remembered the cry of the peacocks.
>
> (*Collected Poetry and* Prose, 7)

Fourth, Cézanne is especially useful in helping us think about form in the lyric because he shows a way to avoid identifying form with technical constraints while also not positing Romantic ideals of participating organically in natural forces. Form is for him the evidence that one's decision-making can produce an event in which patterns emerge that complement and deepen the work's claims to be treated as a distinctive aspect of reality—not about the real but realized as one aspect of shapes being can take. Form is the imaginative body established by allowing self-awareness about choices to establish a sense of second-order substance created by internal relations.

I hope my reading of how Williams structures his verbs can save me the extended development necessary to make good on those claims about form. There, realization is a matter of visibly making choices about syntax, about pacing, and ultimately about the force of different kinds of verbs. From Williams we are led directly back to Pound, and from Pound to the very idea of a modernist poetry in English:

> It is no more ridiculous that a person should receive or convey an emotion by means of an arrangement of shapes or planes or colours, than that they should receive or convey such emotion by an arrangement of musical notes.... There comes a time when one is more deeply moved by that form of intelligence which can present "masses in relation" than by that combination of patience and of trickery which can make marble chains with free links and spin out bronze until it copies the feathers on a general's hat.
>
> (*Gaudier-Brzeska*, 81, 93)

Fifth, all of these values depend on the manifest impersonality of the artist because they have to make visible the force of the work as work, rather than as the activity of a personality that imposes its particular version of the human on what is objective. If the art succeeds in being convincing as art, as a structure where internal relations shape significance, then anything not carried by those internal relations is excessive and destructive. As Eliot insisted, in impersonal art one does not lose the self but transcends its tendencies to let self-contradiction and fear limit what can be successfully expressed.[11]

No poet quite has Cézanne's view of impersonality in art as enabling the giving of the whole personality because it can see what is objectively demanded of it. Eliot's, Pound's, and even Moore's explicit stances were more Nietzschean: one who can bend the self to the forces that actually determine the shape of experiences can escape the neediness that accompanies any desire to be recognized for one's "personality." Yet on a more abstract level Cézanne exemplifies a struggle common to the poets—how can the will accept a demystified world and still find complete satisfaction? How can it put aside the Augustinian model insisting that our hearts are restless until they can rest in God? The only possible measure of peace in art is that there is no longer a striving to go beyond the object. So the poets strive to avoid work like *Hamlet* that exceeds what the artist can compose as an objective correlative for its emotional intensities. To realize fully is also to accommodate oneself to these particulars as defining one's reality and challenging the will not to try to evade it by either idealism or endless negation.

We tend to forget the great range of impersonal stances in modernist poetry. They range from the simple image realizing elemental states that virtually have to be shared by all conscious beings to the intricate indirection of Marianne Moore's treatments of exemplary figures like her father in "Silence" to the steeplejack "placing danger signs by the church / while he is gilding the solid- / pointed star, which on a steeple, stands for hope" (*Poems of Marianne Moore*, 184). But probably the richest realization is Eliot's own *Waste Land*, where there emerge several possible persons and tones, now features of an impersonal rendering that makes them all participants in a vision of objectively rendered subject conditions. Here the only positive value might be finding a way to acknowledge how personality is doomed to constant frustration and disillusion. We encounter many facets of a world that will only manifest itself in the form of objective conditions that have to be understood in terms of how they refuse our desires for subjective satisfactions.

4

Each of these fiercely achieved principles was critical to the modernist dream of making a truly new poetry capable of replacing rhetorical gestures toward the world with activities that gave readers intimate senses of how the imagination might hold on to real presences experienced with a direct intensity capable of modifying their values. But each principle would also contribute to modernism's eventual failure to hold the cultural stage. Some of the reasons for this failure are attributable to external pressures like changes in social attitudes and simple desires to try something new. But some were internal, involving limitations trapping modernism within somewhat narrow values that were prone to sponsoring contradictory pursuits. In order to elaborate this sense of internal limitations I have to develop one more feature that the poets shared with Cézanne—this time, an aspect of aesthetics with direct political implications.

This feature is clearest in Cézanne's portraits after about 1888. When Cézanne applies principles of forgetting he adapts in landscapes also to portraits, he finds himself in a strange situation. For then the artist must forget all the social distinctions and rhetorics that make portraiture matter in the first place. Without traditional notions of rank and merit or their inversions in radical politics, portraits just become material for the eye, just like landscapes and still lives. But suppose the painter willingly accepts that reduction because it has an intriguing evaluative dimension. Perhaps the artist can use the logic of realization to win for portrait subjects the sense of dignity and significance provided usually by ideas and received ways of noting class and status? Then the achievement of human dignity would not depend on conceptual backgrounds and inherited practices but could become manifest simply by the perceptual acumen of the artist.

Such ambitions cannot be satisfied by a formalist approach. Rather, they involve something like a labor theory for determining human values: the work demanded of the painter shows why the portrait subject is worthy of respect, and painting becomes an exemplary state of consciousness because of its capacity to make the link visible between conditions of labor and realizing what can count as terms for conferring human dignity. Conversely when objects of vision fail to compel, one has to look first toward the qualities of one's own involvement. States of consciousness determine how value can be conferred because there is such a gap between the activity of realization and the merely objective.

No modernist would quite be this bold in stating a labor theory for valuing human beings, in part because this exposes a major vulnerability in the traditions that Cézanne sponsored. While the end is realization, the means has to be intensely subjective. The artist does not copy or imitate. Rather, the artist labors to get his or her sensations and feelings into objective form. The only possible means to objectivity on the model of realization is intense subjective labor. Such states are evident in the ways that many major modernists, most visibly Pound and the Cubist Picasso, talk about the social value of the objective states the artist realizes. Their rhetoric here is much less about the value of the object than about the defense of the artist's individuality as the necessary condition for bringing such art into the world. Their aesthetics stressed the object while their ethics emphasized the development of individual powers and responsibilities. Impersonality, it turned out, left the artist no choice but to make subjective measures for the intensity of experience the norm for attributing values to what would become objective subject matter. Everything else doomed the subject to the rhetorical postures carried by the marketplace.

There are two basic ways to criticize this tendency within modernism, both of which were developed in the 1930s. First, one could follow a version of the arguments developed by Cary Nelson. Painters and poets can seek versions of objective presence in art that do not depend on the intense subjective labors insisted upon by Cézanne. Artists did not have to realize some intensely held state of private apprehension. Rather they could consider themselves fully alive in the twentieth century simply by expressing social interests or interpreting what seemed to be given as objective social conditions that seemed oppressive, as if they were too perfect for the realization of class interests. And then they need not resist rhetorical stances in the name of some more authentic subjective intensities. Instead they felt they had to use the resources of rhetoric in the attempt to change the actual world rather than realize its inadequacies in objective forms.

Because this critique of modernism has been receiving a good deal of attention, I am content to show how my story opens into it, then move on to my second, stranger mode of resistance that would eventually become more influential on the poets who have come to matter most to the academy. The first model of resistance sought an alternative version of the aesthetic object, free of dependency on subjective intensities. The second shares the modernist cult of the creative subject but makes it more self-conscious and more radical than it can be when it has to be subordinated to ideals of realization. Suppose the arts could do away with all claims to objectivity, even those subtle models like Cézanne's that have managed to break from representational ideals. Surrealism made just this assertion: artists could organize their imaginative energies to emphasize what could not be "realized" but had to remain unrepresentable. These redirected energies would carry painting and writing into what has to be defined as the domain of the unreal, that is, the domain of what are irreducibly subjective overdeterminations of what can become objective. Then the way would be clear to an artistic politics based on principles of de-realization. Minimally, this politics could release utopian energies without which the entrenched forces of respectability would inevitably impose their own deadening habits and interests on the political situation. And there might be more complicated efforts to provide psychological analogues to political states based not on reception but on production (and on what elicits production like states of enigma or Bataille's "informe" or the Situationist's "derive"). The arts could provide a model for full democratic agency because all participants would be defining and pursuing their own desires and building communities on their own terms. Art would elaborate the politics of imaginative excess.

5

This point probably does not need illustrating but I will take any excuse to write about Cézanne's paintings. And in this case my elaborating a group portrait, the

Card Players (1890–1892) at the Barnes Collection, enables us to reflect on how it differs from Picasso's *Three Musicians* (1921) in ways that have political implications. Cézanne's painting combines a remarkable sense of respect for the individuals involved with a strikingly bleak insistence on surroundings that offer no other enticements that might expand the horizons of these characters. This sense of respect emerges from an intricate balancing act that harmonizes what individuates these characters, deprived of the overt rhetorical signs of nobility that pervade Millet's and Pissarro's laboring peasants, and what establishes their common humanity, primarily through their shared concentration on their game. Perhaps the respect is based on their capacity to find a means of living actively within this encompassing sense of the narrowness of their lives.

But the respect is based even more on the ways the characters challenge the painter to render what in them seems to invite realization. Cézanne reinforces the sense of common humanity sharing attention to the game by adding several synthesizing horizontal connections. There are parallels between the table, game board, row of hats, and heads adjusting them to the line from the shelf through the row of pipes. The horizontals stretch the canvas to create a productive tension with the three-dimensional forces established by the half-circle of the aligned arms and capacious shoulders of the seated card players. By playing these linked forms against the horizontals, Cézanne establishes a significant sense of shared, substantial being.

But stressing common humanity alone would be a version of the rhetorical piety Cézanne rejects. So he produces strong individual differences that develop a counterforce resisting and complementing that commonness. While most painters would rely on straightforward realism to produce this sense of uniqueness for each character, Cézanne seems to think such realism would offer only variations on the level of appearance. Instead he abstracts from appearances and highlights isolated painterly differences that seem instant signs of character. It helps here to imagine this abstract particularity as analogous to the rendering of each fruit in his still lives as a distinctive event of seeing. Distinction is not a matter of how the painting reflects what is observable but rather of how painterly choices make visible significant textures within an overall color scheme.

Each of the five agents represented seems a response to a separate demand on the artist's capacity to make color complement character and to make attention an intense physical state. The visual key is the play among the hands that position the elemental ways each person takes in the scene. It is as if each set of hands functioned the way the apical point does in his still lives as an index of where each piece of fruit most fully takes its shading from how the light strikes it. And each player sits at a different angle to the table, as if character were inseparable from both how the body concentrates and how that stance sponsors the painter's specific color harmonies. Plays of light and shadow and intricate textures of brown, blue, and off-white produce a sense of substance sufficiently active for the audience to feel the thinking and willing involved in the game.

All of these differences culminate in each face, defining powers to make the self present while also withdrawing something of appearance into a kind of privacy (or perhaps a blankness mirroring the setting). The man in beige is painted frontally, but he sets his gaze resolutely on his cards and offers no clue about what he will make of them. The man on the left is brightly lit but he offers only half a face. The other player offers the opposite side view, but his much rounder features (and much larger ear) are in shadows that even cover his eyes. How he will act is probably even a mystery to himself.

This painting stages an adventure in becoming a spectator, so it should be no surprise that it includes two actual spectators who become surrogates for the viewing audience. But these are not typical stand-ins. Their different ways of being interested confirm the power of the player's concentration and provide a figure for how the self-consciousness of the painter-witness can be included within the painting. Each observer is given in full frontal view, perhaps an emblem of what is required for full witnessing. Yet these two faces are very different, in size, in age, and in the kind of attention each pays. The boy's simple spherical head has no distinguishing features, probably because he is content to be utterly caught up in the game. The observing man, in contrast, is built up of many levels of clothing and color, all self-contained by his folded arms and his face's complacent self-possession. These differences between the observers in turn are emphasized by the structural roles they play in the overall painting. They are forces of intricate destabilization of the visual scene. The boy helps to form a triangle with two playing figures on the right; the man forms a larger yet proportionate triangle with the players on the left. But these triangles themselves are disjunctive. The boy's triangle recedes into deep space, intensifying the gap between the players. The man comes forward so that his triangle pushes back against the viewer. Then the discrepancy between the heights of the observers establishes a transition to the flattening pressure of the wall while also making the space jumpy and intricate, so that the players' static focus is nonetheless visually fluid and unsettled.

These discrepancies make the viewer work hard to stabilize the relation between recession and availability. One might say that the painting activates for the viewer the position left open at the front of the canvas—an ideal position to observe what there is to see, as well as to imagine what here requires our going beyond the objects of sight. These card players are not just concentrating on what can be observed. They are projecting possible strategies and so embody conative powers that extend imagination into action. Realizing these card players requires making visible a potential for multiple further actions. The task of achieving painterly satisfaction proves inseparable from the understanding of what unseen powers these agents might possess to use their common humanity for individual purposes.

6

I think we should not dismiss this subjective labor politics of portraiture. There is no dependency on abstract ideas that easily become materials for self-righteous rhetorics, and there is possible a concrete realization of one's powers to give up personality to other interests. More important, there is an implicit democratic politics because every person calls upon the artist to make their differences conditions for realization. Yet without realization, without the heroic labors of the artist, they have no significant existence, nor does the audience, who needs to be taught to appreciate the relation between realization and the granting of what empowers individuals.

Picasso's *Three Musicians* implies a very different politics. The painting does not criticize Cézanne's or Picasso's earlier works for their reliance on intense subjective states that serve as preconditions for an impersonal art. But it does lead me to ask if perhaps the ideal of realization produces an unnecessary and limiting task for these intense subjective endeavors. For this painting, in either of its two versions, seems deliberately to be repudiating any principles of objectification. (The fact of two versions of the image may be one aspect of this critique because each seems in part a commentary on the other, as if Picasso were suggesting that when art becomes this engaged in mortality no one interpretive stance can suffice.) If I am right, the crucial question is not how we can realize what we see but how we can interpret and ground emerging surrealist efforts to seek freedom from the obligations imposed by the objective world. In this respect the paintings resist any sense that individual expressive acts can respond adequately to all that music suggests. These monumental paintings have something like a collective dream subject. Yet they do not offer typical surrealist dream images. It is better to see the musicians as variants of Picasso's neoclassical figures but developed for some unknown culture that we are invited to project as its audience.

These paintings also differ from garden-variety surrealism in their basing so much of their power on complexity of tone, especially if one takes the two paintings together. The Philadelphia version combines a witty reduction of the body to weirdly expressive elements with a sinister sense that foreground and background each presents indecipherable but imposing threats to any audience seduced by this playing. And yet what else can we do in relation to this aura of threat than to try to enjoy the music? And the version at the Museum of Modern Art darkens and simplifies the images to make more mysterious both the pressure on the musicians and the relation between bright surface and melancholy background (with the suggestion of depth on the floor to the viewer's left a remarkably affecting slip beyond what any surface can capture).

As I try to describe the painting, I am painfully aware that I quickly run out of objective features that I can confidently interpret. Here, Picasso equates emotional power with the capacity quickly to get beyond even descriptive language so that viewers must stake themselves on what they each imagine to be the overall situation. Where Cézanne wants to realize a world to which he can give himself, Picasso experiments with de-realizing any imposition of a common order that might limit the projective scope of his image. Picasso's sense of mysterious agency makes a pseudo-metaphysics of surrealism's pseudo-psychology. ("Pseudo" here has to have a positive sense.)

And to do that Picasso also has to remake Cézanne. Notice that there are traces of the horizontal forces in Cézanne's *Card Players*. The wonderful eyes in both paintings almost align—that is part of the wit and part of the spooky sense that these musicians inhabit a world that refuses our senses of stable order. One sees also that the hats and the table make gestures toward horizontal stability that the painting refuses to carry out because it wants the possibility of order to be the stage for more intricate and strange and indecipherable shapes. Rather than move toward a grasp of the real, the viewers are confronted with their individual responsibilities toward the unreal that frames mortality on every side. One cannot represent death or even fear or the conjunctions that occur when fear and pleasure meet. One can represent agents who engage such states but the states themselves remain on the edges of what audiences can share.

It should not be surprising then that there are no audience figures here that might compare to the audiencing in *Cardplayers*. Making music involves a quite different kind of concentration from what card players do and offer to observers. Making music is both forming a world and undoing an observable world into this relation where background imposes on foreground and the human figures become inseparable from the rhythms and sharp, contrasting colors that pervade how their eyes and limbs and torsos might actually appear on the stage. Realization for Picasso in this painting involves making concrete the forces that push us into having to accept how the unreality of imaginary construction pervades our encounters with this synthesis of intense pleasure and pervasive threat. And that means what might be represented as audience or as common humanity simply pales before the need for individuals to activate their own senses of how the unreal pervades what matters in their lives. Cézanne's dream of giving the personality now becomes a call for individual differences in interpretation that in effect produce the kind of music that continues to disrupt and to haunt.

NOTES

1 This also gives me a way of returning to the issue of modernist poetry and modernist painting without repudiating or fundamentally repeating my previous three engagements with this topic. My *Painterly Abstraction* emphasized how the painters foreground the syntax of art making so that whatever semantic force the work sustains derives from the painterly activity without detours into narrative or thematic argument. Then my *Art of Modernist American Poetry* develops links between artists and the "new realism" promoted by Bergson and others. Recently I have also emphasized how Cézanne breaks from an ideal of contemplative unity to make tension itself the organizing force of the artwork and therefore indicates how categories of author, audience, work, and world are best seen as mutually defining interrelated forces rather than as independent sets of expectations ("Why Modernist"). Seen this way, autonomy becomes the artists' license to elaborate these mutually defining structures while insisting on new interconnections between art and life.

2 My dismay was focused by Ross's *Modernism and Theory: A Critical Debate*. I admire
the intelligence and earnestness of the authors but I am mystified by statements like
the following that pervade the book and require response: "Critique—particularly
the critique of modernity—is essential to those continuities and remains the core of
the affinities between modernism and theory" (12). The authors collected here also
seem to agree that modernist writers are insufficiently negative so that they must
provide a supplemental negativity: "Theory's recognition and embrace of critique as
a fundamentally negative energy, a process of disruption and challenge rather than
synthesis, allowed it to avoid for the most part the modernist mistake of proffering
concrete alternatives to what was being critiqued" (10). But by what standard is that
practice a "mistake"? Modernism was not adequate in its critique but felt critique was
inadequate to what they wanted—to construct plausible idealizations for artworks as loci
for imaginative energies that might provide scenes of instruction capable of changing
audiences' taste and judgment. Cézanne's idealizations seem to me particularly important
because realization depends on a sharp contrast between imaginative and imaginary.
This is well worth remembering in this age when basic versions of Lacan shape so much
of our thinking.

3 See my essay on autonomy as relationality, "Why Modernist Claims for Autonomy
Matter."

4 I discuss this shift in painterly influence in my "Surrealism as a Living Modernism." It is
crucial that the New York poets argued for a very general spirit of surrealism (capable
of appropriating Pollock) that went far beyond efforts to develop images that might
somehow represent the unconscious. They saw in this enlarged surrealism the possibility
of a different kind of subject and different kind of object. Idealizations of the new
subject tried to replace the maker of formal intensities by the producer or performer
of compositional mobility on every level of the psyche. Idealizations of the new object
replaced realization by the quest for eliciting an endless chain of creative responses, each
becoming a disruptive event creating conditions for further transformations of what
could count as real. There is a similar shift to emphasize productive energies that takes
place among contemporary heirs of Williams and the Objectivists, but here I think the
sharp break from their models to stress the free participating reader stems largely from
internalizing that work as avatars of an experimental spirit, because it is difficult to stress
the spirit of experiment and not confer that same spirit on readers.

5 This letter is dated October 23, 1905 (*Letters*, 251–252). Stevens cites this letter in his
"The Figure of the Youth as Virile Poet" (671–672) but omits the sentence on giving the
personality from the citation, probably because it sounded embarrassingly self-heroizing.

6 *Letters*, 262.

7 How "realization" might figure into Cézanne's career is most evident in how his
contemporaries saw his work as a synthesis of Courbet and Impressionism. See Cachin
et al., 35–37, 45–48.

8 I borrow my remarks from my own *Painterly Abstraction in Modernist American
Poetry*, 187–191, partially because I think Cézanne's achievement in this painting is not
sufficiently appreciated.

9 Obviously this is a matter of degree. Painters like Giorgone, Raphael, and Caravaggio
foreground the decisions that produce modes of balance and thematic emphasis. But
they paint as if the formal structures were aspects of the planning of the painting
that then are realized in the labor. For Cézanne it is the labor that affords paths for
the realizing, and form is what makes present the interrelations that emerge as labor
becomes conscious of what it has wrought.

10 The best example of how form might become constitutive for experiences of life is Pound's use of the analogue of analytic geometry in *Gaudier-Brzeska*, 91.

11 Eliot's famous passage is still worth quoting: "Poetry is not a turning loose of emotion, but an escape from emotion; it is not the expression of personality but an escape from personality. But, of course, only those who have personality and emotions know what it means to want to escape from these things" (*Selected Essays*, 10–11).

REFERENCES

Altieri, Charles. *The Art of Modernist American Poetry*. Oxford: Blackwell, 2005.

———. *Painterly Abstraction in Modernist American Poetry*. Cambridge: Cambridge University Press, 1989.

———. "Surrealism as a Living Modernism: What the New York Poets Learned from Two Generations of New York Painting." In a forthcoming collection edited by Jennifer Ashton for Cambridge University Press.

———. "Why Modernist Claims for Autonomy Matter." *Journal of Modern Literature* 32, no. 3 (2009): 1–21.

Baumann, Felix, et al., eds. *Cézanne and the Dawn of Modern Art*. Ostfildern-Ruit: Hatje Cantz Verlag, 2004.

Cachin, Francoise, et al. *Cézanne*. Philadelphia: Philadelphia Museum of Art, 1996.

Cézanne, Paul. *Paul Cézanne Letters*. 4th ed. Edited by John Rewald. New York: Da Capo Press, 1976.

Eliot, T. S. *Selected Essays*. New York: Harcourt, Brace, 1950.

Moore, Marianne. *The Poems of Marianne Moore*. Edited by Grace Shulman. New York: Penguin, 2005.

Pound, Ezra. *Gaudier-Brzeska*. New York: New Directions, 1970.

Ross, Stephen, ed. *Modernism and Theory: A Critical Debate*. Abingdon, UK: Routledge, 2009.

Schapiro, Meyer. "The Apples of Cézanne: An Essay on the Meaning of Still Life." In Schapiro, *Modern Art: Nineteenth and Twentieth Centuries*. New York: Braziller, 1979. 1–38.

Stevens, Wallace. *Collected Poetry and Prose*. Edited by Frank Kermode and Joan Richardson. New York: Library of America, 1997.

Williams, William Carlos. *The Collected Poems of William Carlos Williams*. Volume 1: 1909–1939. Edited by A. Walton Litz and Christopher McGowan. New York: New Directions, 1986.

CHAPTER 9

STEPPING OUT, SITTING IN: MODERN POETRY'S COUNTERPOINT WITH JAZZ AND THE BLUES

EDWARD BRUNNER

MODERN poetry would not sound, move, or look the way it does were it not for jazz and the blues. Especially in the first half of the twentieth century, these arts evolved in tandem. The combination was explosive. The "new poetry" of the young practiced an art responsive to the vernacular, capable of registering fleeting moments inventively, and eager to address an audience ready to play against expectations. But when poetry aligned itself with jazz and the blues, it also embraced a minority culture in the process of defining its own history, its values, and its place. This conjoining led not simply to material with a straightforward political activism, though political activism was never remote. More important, the dissonance, unexpected pauses, and off-rhythms that are staples of jazz and the blues gave rise, in poetry, to practices that not only helped de-center the meditative lyric from its position at the center of modern poetry but also re-described avant-garde practices as plausible tactics for engaging with everyday crises. When the twentieth century began, jazz and the blues were rogue music, and young poets of privilege could flaunt their modernity by investigating alien activity and associating with sites marked as dangerous. When the twenty-first century began, poetry had so incorporated tenets of jazz and the blues it was no longer possible to discern where the influence of one left off and another began.

Recalling the poet Kevin Young's elegant distinction—"with the blues the form fights the feeling, with jazz the form is the feeling" ("Foreword," 15)—this chapter will also distinguish jazz from the blues as exerting subtly different pressures on modern poetry. The representation of jazz in the earliest years of modernism by young white poets envisioned it as a raw force of disruption, a chaotic intruder in need of containment. Jazz traces in a new poetic language signaled a release of linguistic energy in the 1910s and early 1920s in the works of Carl Sandburg, Vachel Lindsay, and William Carlos Williams. Only late in the 1920s, in work by Hart Crane, Mina Loy, and Sterling Brown, did "Jazz Age" moments began to thicken around issues of social justice and a jazz text begin to emerge—a poem that engages with jazz not as a novelty or as a daring stunt but as a complicated site of biracial exchange that, as it worked through elements of history, also confronted misrepresentation.

By contrast, the poem that formally resembles a blues lyric takes a different turn, largely due to the seminal volume by Langston Hughes, *Fine Clothes to the Jew* (1927), which recasts the blues as a viable poetic form. Blues form in poetry evolves into a discourse that remains indelibly a part of African American tradition even as it provides a sympathetic position for others to inhabit. To have transferred a popular musical style into a poetic form is a remarkable achievement: the blues poem is accessible to all, used by so many that it can be examined as a kind of "indigenous" sonnet, an attractive form whose flexibility recommends it for wide circulation. So various are the occasions for responding with melancholy as the twentieth century turns into the twenty-first that the influence of the blues is likely to be found anywhere; it is a form that crosses generation, gender, ethnic, and racial barriers.

Poetry as a jazz text, by contrast, has resisted popularization, despite the achievement of another volume by Hughes, *Montage of a Dream Deferred* (1948). Yet Hughes's postwar homage to the opposed musical styles of boogie-woogie and bebop reveals music that, like African American ambitions, remains still a work in progress. The improvisational energy of jazz, with its voracious appetite for experiment, endlessly postpones closure. But if it is a music that addresses issues still deferred, it is also a music whose repertory taps into a rich and eclectic archive. Even as the blues poem has become broadly diffused in recent years, the improvisational poem about jazz has been taken up in various situations, from the simple rhapsody in celebration of a jazz performer that prompts an imitative verbal style in homage to the intricate allusive performance that moves dialectically to engage portions of a forgotten African American history. This esoteric jazz text anticipates postmodern aesthetics: it draws on a discursive community of forerunners, requires attentive and even specialized listening skills, and represents the improvisational as an activity that redistributes artifacts as archival treasures.

"Jazz Age" Jazz

Jazz and the blues, as they emerge from New Orleans after the turn of the century, thus represent divergent poles of a vernacular response to modernity. At their simplest, jazz and the blues are a record of black Americans talking among themselves about what matters to them, including whether they really need the white culture that oppresses them—but talking in a way that they know will be overheard by whites. For young poets overhearing this intense and complex conversation in the 1910s and early 1920s after this new music had circulated through gramophone recordings, cabaret performances, and silent film accompaniment, the works they wrote in response were not just signs of their openness to experimental writing, but also an awareness of a world of uncertainty and even violence in which justice was remote and persons had to fall back on their own enterprise and ingenuity. In one sense, that world was generally unfamiliar to poets coming of age around 1900, who were likely to be sons and daughters of upper- or middle-class professionals, raised in comfortable surroundings, and multilingual and well educated. In another sense, though, the isolated realms in which ethnic and racial groups were clustered in the nineteenth century disguised the numerous interrelationships that brought different classes and social groups into contact—as servants or as occasional workers, as carnivalesque figures glimpsed in celebration on holidays, as exotics appreciated while deliberately traveling away from home, as sexual partners in an underground economy of pleasure, and as subjects in the popular "local color" tales that flooded the newspapers and weekly magazines that penetrated middle-class homes at the time as pervasively as today's cable TV. Some in these marginalized groups used jazz and the blues to register their sharp awareness of both the threats and opportunities opened by modernity: their music not only entertained themselves and others but sharply conveyed an awareness of the divides that were spoken and unspoken as well as the connections that were made but denied. Out of this tangle of occasional, semicovert interconnections, young American poets were able to glimpse—and just as often, deny—a rich culture that was both oppositional and alternative, a culture that had evolved from a marginal group whose existence was ostensibly mysterious and alluring even as it actually was familiar and intimate. If the previous generation of young poets from the 1890s, as John Timberman Newcomb has noted, turned for inspiration to the weekly magazine and the daily newspaper—a veritable anthology of multiple registers—the next generation had available a convenient distillation of modernity in the discordance of path-breaking music (234–235).

It was no coincidence that African Americans contributed most to this new music: the tactics of resistance they had been honing ever more finely, over decades of practice, were the most recent stage in a collective effort necessarily undertaken to survive in a climate bent upon eradicating their history, their values, and their sense of place. Unlike the affable "coon songs" popularized by minstrel shows or the ragtime whose jaunty syncopation invoked the wind-up toys of childhood, jazz and the blues were vivid, harsh registers of experience. It can be no surprise that new trends in African American vernacular music began to emerge in the 1890s; as Jim Crow laws legitimated separation by racial traits, a new music arose that acknowledged that widening gap even as it derided it. This offered abundant evidence that dissolving barriers, crossing boundaries, and inhabiting new realms was the kind of thrilling experience that would always attract the bold. The new music was designed to make an indelible impression, to leave a mark, to inscribe presence, to resist facile duplication. Its production, moreover, was shaped as a one-of-a- kind experience that emerged from a fleeting moment. This music was not to be directly imitated or easily reproduced—its "bent" notes and odd inflections eluded transcription. Poet Sterling A. Brown began his 1946 essay "Stray Notes on Jazz" with a (perhaps apocryphal) anecdote from 1916 in which black New Orleans trumpeter Freddie Keppard refused to record his Original Creole Band for Victor: "We won't put our stuff on records for everybody to steal" (265; see Baraka, 145). This position was defended by Sidney Bechet: if "every Tom, Dick, or Harry who could ever blow a note would be making records" then it would "get so the music wasn't where it belonged" (qtd. in Ogren, 95). Jazz as performance was asserted to be beyond duplication, even as its example of free expression was a powerful encouragement and provocation for others to respond in kind.

In vernacular African American music, jazz and the blues began as being intricately entwined. Jazz and the blues share the same harmonic inclinations—the flatted third, fifth, and seventh notes in the diatonic scale—but jazz improvisation escapes both the formal regularity of the blues and its interest in the refrain. Unlike the emphasis in the blues on the communal possibilities of a repeated set of phrases, jazz performance ultimately highlights the isolation and daring of the individual, encouraged to self-present as a virtuoso. Jazz is always on the run, escaping from the restrictions of regularization even as its route of escape is woven through the protective cover of standard harmonic progressions (that may be manifest, in another virtuosic achievement, through ingenious substitutions). The blues, by contrast, embraces repetition, in an invitation extended to others to anticipate and thus join in a refrain, though a well-marked point in its pattern always makes space for the individual to have a say, to remark on what everyone has heard. If the harmonies and rhythms of jazz tend to startle and surprise, the harmonies and rhythms of the blues are old friends, familiar and stylized.

These distinctions between jazz and the blues were only amplified in the writings of young poets. Although both branches of African American music were condemned vociferously from the pulpit and the newspaper as the latest signs of a civilization in rapid decay, when young poets sought lines of affinity with this new music, it was jazz that most often caught attention. As Bryan Wagner has recently argued, black music, whether packaged by entrepreneurs or examined by ethnographers in the 1920s, was consistently aligned with qualities that legal authorities attributed to criminality and vagrancy (15–41). The improvisational daring of jazz, its willingness to break rules and cross lines, coincided with aspects of the free verse, its dangerous unmarked pathways that had been slowly emerging as the advance guard of poetry after 1900. The rapid-fire pace of jazz performance aligned itself with such emblems of machine-age modernity as the automobile and airplane, which poets were eager to take into their writing, while the blues, with its mournful cadences that issued forth rhymed couplets, too closely resembled either conventional song or the sober dirge of the spiritual. Thus the new poetry was especially accommodating to moments of improvisation: it identified linguistic clashing as a source of unpremeditated but unerring insight, it delighted in a structure that amplified fleeting moments, and it addressed a new reading public that sought plea-sure in disruption and novelty. The *New York Times* editorialist who lamented in 1924 that jazz "is to real music exactly what most of the 'new poetry,' so-called, is to real poetry" (Levine, 179) inadvertently confirmed the primary value to young poets of an alliance that imported an aura of danger into an art of versifying that was struggling to shake off the onus of versification.

Such "danger" is on display, however, in early poems about jazz that stage a cautiously disruptive performance, usually through shifting linguistic registers that embrace slang or portray this new music as noise. Vachel Lindsay's "The Jazz Bird," in its 1918 version recovered by Mark Van Wienen, opens with a description of African American vernacular music as a tangle of unlikely noises—"A cock-a-doodle bray, / A jungle bells, a boiler works, / A he-man's roundelay"—but it also associates those sounds with a retrograde setting that places them outside moder-nity: "The Jazz Bird," Lindsay asserts, "sings a barnyard song" (229). To present Afri-can American jazz sounds as primitive and premodern was, in this early jazz poetry, to claim that poetry's modernity was its ability to identify and contain primitive elements. The 1917 sheet music for the "Tiger Rag," a hit recording by the Original Dixieland Jazz Band, evoked the animal roaring of that song not so much in its pub-lished transcriptions—the song's sensational breakaway chorus of "hold that tiger!" as performed by the band appears nowhere in the sheet music, which transcribes only the tune's several jiglike dance formations—but in the design of its cover, which featured sketches of a mule, a pig, a cow, a rabbit, a hen and rooster, and several birds singing notes, appearing below a photograph of the five white musicians who composed the group. In this setup, the interplay between animal and human tilted toward the animalistic or perhaps mechanistic: the bodies of three of the five musi-cians were, through a photo-montage, physically embedded in a piano—a relation that was both disturbing and delimiting (see La Rocca, 114).

An even better example of such contained disruption is a four-line passage from Ellen Coit Elliott's "Prima Donna of the Negro Jazz Orchestra" (published in *The Lyric West* for April 1921) that begins "My tunic is a withered buff rose. / Palely my arms fall down," only to be noisily interrupted: "The fiddles leap behind me, a thin flute blows, / Cr-r-acks a sudden trombone, then all notes drown." Unlike the crude visuals of "Tiger Rag," Elliott presents a disturbance that is abruptly disarming but subtly managed. The singer's pale arms, white-seeming against her rose tunic, dis-guise their "primitive" African American origin, even as they expose themselves by appearing against an environment of noise, animation, and disarray: fiddles leap, flutes turn thin, trombones break. Yet if Elliott introduces confusion in the last two lines, she also contains it by introducing rhyme (rose / blow, down / drown), revert-ing to a mostly iambic pentameter (with two trochees in the last line's first feet), and distributing caesuras in identical position to make syntax run parallel. The passage cautiously but triumphantly blends discord with concord, as Elliott's poetic form treads close to a confusion that it nevertheless controls.

To introduce multiple registers to poems in order to demonstrate an ability to move deftly among them, like a jazz musician improvising a melody over a chord progression, or an urban dweller acknowledging the sediments of a city block, is invariably to expand the poem's framework beyond a traditional literary setting into a modernity whose dangers and pleasures are so contradictorily entwined they have to be negotiated at numerous junctures. By that standard, Carl Sandburg, an inveterate collector of folk song, may be responsible for perhaps the earliest poem to represent jazz seriously. His "Jazz Fantasia" (published in 1920) uses free verse organized around register and syntax to duplicate musical effects. The enormously popular Sandburg was associated with the "Chicago Renaissance" that had successfully translated realist elements into verse in Edgar Lee Masters's best-selling *Spoon River Anthology*, and as it showed itself responsive to materials indigenous to America, its poets were establishing a trend line for others to follow. Sandburg conveys the music's energy as exhausting, starting with two stanzas whose relation to the conventional pause of the line break deteriorates as they go:

> Drum on your drums, batter on your banjos,
> Sob on the long cool winding saxophones.
> Go to it, O jazzmen.[stanza break]
> Sling your knuckles on the bottoms of the happy
> Tin pans, let your trombones ooze, and go husha-
> husha-hush with the slippery sand-paper. (59)

Every phrase is launched by a verb; but the energy thus transmitted is almost at once dissipated. That dissipation is present evocatively in the descriptive phrases that begin to emerge in the next stanza, in which the variety associated with different instrumentation is transferred to emotional reactions. Sandburg's next words are in prose: "Moan soft like an autumn wind high in the lonesome treetops, moan soft like you wanted somebody terrible, cry like a racing car slipping away from a motorcycle cop, bang-bang!" If these lines echo Whitman's bountiful lists, they also scramble emotions. Yet the poem ends with a series of delicate inscriptions that return us to a nature softly illuminated; it simultaneously effects closure by leaving us on shore watching a boat trail away as if the environment now grows silent in its wake:

> Can the rough stuff...now a Mississippi steamboat pulses up the night river with
> a hoo-hoo-hoo-hoo...and the green lanterns calling to the high soft stars...a red
> moon rides on the humps of the low river hills ... go to it, O jazzmen. (59)

Rachel Blau DuPlessis reads "hoo," in modernist poetry in general, as a triumphant code in which whiteness mimics blackness's animal howl, so this closing movement toward simple sound and natural light may signal a reversion. The conjunctions celebrated throughout produce a "jazz fantasia," clashing noises from unlikely instruments (how can we slip on sand-paper?) in the quasi-lineated opening, yet eliciting more tangible emotions (including erotic undertones) in the ruminative prose sections. But since we always slide from one register into another, from "autumn wind" to "bang-bang!" the fantasia is evanescent, it always evaporates.

Sliding, slipping registers become Sandburg's device for portraying jazz's ability to conjure identifiable feelings that emerge only to be displaced by others, with an overall effect of rapid, mobile play. Linguists understand the rarity of registers appearing in multiples even for a brief duration. In sociolinguistics, as Charles A. Ferguson explains, to be made aware of register is to be alert to a "communication situation that recurs regularly" and that "will tend over time to develop identifying marks of language structure and language use, different from the language of other communication societies," and the components that help distinguish one register from another include "lexicon, lexical collocations, sentence structure and intersentential linguistic features" (20). When such components flood a text, the effect is supersaturation, an excess that offers exciting mobility and evanescent choice. Yet in Sandburg's poem, emergent dangers are fleeting instants, and to cross a barrier (or to break a taboo) is a temporary excitement. His presentation assures us that it is we who control and frame jazz music as spectacle. Though the music tugs emotions in unexpected directions, it is always a virtual experience: Sandburg keeps the band in the foreground and assures us that instruments are the source of these new feelings and all is temporary, all is play. These registers that clash, a sociolinguist might note, never add up to anything authoritative but instead remain as identifiable fragments, an ad hoc concoction.

A more disturbing example of dangerous modernity, especially if register-shifting linguistically identifies early jazz, may then be the "improvisations" that William Carlos Williams began around 1917 and were collected as *Kora in Hell* (1920). Not specifically associated with jazz, these were prose experiments influenced by Dadaist and surrealist "automatic writing" and intended as a beginning-over for a poet dissatisfied with his earlier verse. As Williams wrote in a prologue, the prose pieces seek to correct an "attention that has been held too rigid on the one plane instead of following a flexible, jagged resort." To evade the "one plane," Williams ranges across registers:

> Doors have a back side also. And grass blades are double-edged. It's no use trying to deceive me, leaves fall more by the buds that push them off than by lack of greenness. Or throw two shoes on the floor and see how they'll lie if you think it's all one way. (80)

While Sandburg emphasizes the leaps that differentiate one register from another (the moan of wind from the bang-bang of the motorcycle) and thus keeps them separate in their adjacency, Williams unearths associations that entwine with each other: the door that opens has another side, grass growing, and buds pressing forward—even as back doors close, grass can be as sharp as a blade, and leaves are cast away. A rich disorder, divulged in shoes tossed off to fall willy-nilly, is evident and to be embraced. Williams further enhances the interactive diversity within these short pieces by arranging them in groups of threes that follow what he calls "the A.B.A. formula, that one may support the other, clarifying or perhaps enhancing the other's intention" (28). He amplifies this interplay by appending "explanatory" afterthoughts on an occasional basis, and while these are enigmatic and align themselves at best indirectly with the short piece to which they refer, they almost always revert to a stable register: *"Having once taken the plunge the situation that preceded it becomes obsolete, which a moment before was alive with malignant rigidities"* (51). Their discourse draws on abstraction and technical terms, so even as they are typographically keyed as urgent—these explanations are always in italics—they also convey a degree of relative sobriety. In such arrangements, it is not simply the freshness of first thinking that Williams values as it is the counterpoint among different perspectives.

Williams's yen for improvising reappears in prose sections for *Spring and All* (1923) and *The Descent of Winter* (1927), but improvisation that is specifically musical is portrayed in verse first published in *The Dial* in 1923. Describing "Banjo jazz / with a nickelplated // amplifier to / soothe // the savage beast—" (1923, 130), Williams performs in one passage a feat of prosodical kinship:

> Get the rhythm
>
> That sheet stuff
> 's a lot of cheese.
>
> Man
> gimme the key
>
> and lemme loose—(180)

Williams's ability to produce a line break that radically recasts the next line signals a willingness "to take a word around the corner on two wheels," in Michael North's words, and "an impatience with ordinary boundaries, even those between words" (153). But Williams is not simply surmounting boundaries but discovering multiple registers embedded in levels of words that point in directions both high and low, both precise and demotic: "sheet stuff" associates with bedtime matters as well as music, and "cheese" is not just processed food but slang that conveys dismissal even as it echoes back to "sheet" as if it were not far from "shit." It is important that the poem open with an offense, announcing "Our orchestra / is the cat's nuts"—an *ars poetica* moment for what is to follow (when the poem was printed by *The Dial* in 1923, the opening required an adjustment from "cat's nuts" to the "cat's meow" [see Benet, 318]). A key is a musical signature that doesn't lock the musician but unlooses him. Banjo jazz that can't be copied, that lives in the moment, thus exists in the elusive associations of words and, most dramatically, in a jump that occurs in the evanescent time of moving from one line break to another, in a flashing instant of rule-breaking.

JAZZ MODERNISM

Williams's interest in improvisation produces a poem that not only makes Sandburg's "Jazz Fantasia" seem as tame as a waltz but exposes Sandburg's registers as clashing and separating, never mixing to produce hybrid sensations that might actually trouble. Williams's "engagement with black music," Nathaniel Mackey pointedly suggests, was "influenced by his sense of himself as cut off from the literary mainstream" (241). His readiness to "jazz" his own lines in consanguinity with his subjects contrasts sharply with the analytic intricacy in the three-line standalone "stanza" that T. S. Eliot invokes to paraphrase the central lyrics of Gene Buck and Herman Ruby's 1912 tune "That Shakespearian Rag":

> O O O O that Shakespeherian Rag—
> It's so elegant
> So intelligent. (61)

David Chinitz concludes his evaluation of the lyrics by Buck and Ruby by noting that the original passage, "its various contexts considered," "gestures in several directions at once" (49). Eliot is more distressingly engaged than Sandburg but less exuberant than Williams. The 1912 original from which he deviates would have been familiar to a number of readers as a dance tune that breaks into ragtime syncopation in the very passage Eliot rewrites. The lyrics by Buck and Ruby playfully self-advertise themselves by claiming that Shakespeare's characters (especially his lovers, Romeo and Juliet and "Desdemona the colored pet"), if they were alive today and enjoyed access to a sensational treat like the very rag we are listening to, would (as Buck and Ruby write) "Grizzly Bear in a different way" (96). (The Grizzly Bear was a popular dance with gestures that drew attention to the body by mimicking animals.) The music of the original's four-bar 4/4 phrase ("That—Shake—spearian rag, most intelligent [pause], very elegant [pause]") opened with a long two-beat emphasis on "That" and "Shake," that moved the lyrics into four descending eighth notes for each syllable in "spearian rag" before breaking into a lilting syncopation of dotted-eighth and sixteenth notes (these stand out as the only syncopated phrases in the melody of the song) that accompany the rapid-fire syllables of "most intelligent" and "very elegant." The original tune, then, first points toward ("Tha-a-a-at") then divides the name of "Shakespeare" by pausing long over the first syllable, urging dancers at that point to shudder with pleasure—that is, to "sha-a-a-ke"—before the downward swoon and the breaking into the syncopated eighth- and-sixteenth notes that are the signature of ragging: "shake" dominates, in this presentation, over "most intelligent" and "very elegant," both words swirled into a pronunciation so swift it gobbles both.

Eliot's stance toward the original involves multiple positioning: at its simplest, he pretends to be scandalized by the vulgarization of Shakespeare, one more sign of cultural deterioration. In his poem, he affirms this by reversing the sequence of adjectives so "intelligent" comes after "elegant," and setting each on its own line to deliver a rhyme that is indecorously clanging. But with this arrangement, the poem's lineation has these words standing out as moments of poise—as if plucked from a maelstrom, they now stand against the musical lyric's ragtime breakout moment, in which multisyllabic words are made to prance and swagger in syncopated steps. By repeating "so," Eliot introduces a finicky precision where there had previously been excess ("most," "very"). Such precision is also a bit unexpected, for Eliot's quadruple "O" is a startling intrusion. One "O" is a vocative, but four together comport with ecstasy—an ecstasy that may find culmination in the delicious shudder of "Shakespeherian," with its extra syllable that, if it had existed in the sheet music, would have interpolated a pair of syncopated eighths-and-sixteenths into the phrase. What Eliot makes prance and swagger, unlike the sheet music's version, are not big words but a big name; to readers of the poem, the big words aren't that big but that name is huge. In his own way, Eliot is asserting that (as Williams would have said) this "sheet music / 's a lot of cheese" and he has dispensed with it for his own rhythm, which, as it extracts a register of the ecstatic, conveys not just the erotics of the song but the animality of its grizzly bear prowls.

Buck and Ruby's easy promotion of young lovers into famous characters, along with its embrace of a controversial jazz dance, moves within that portion of *The Waste Land*, section II, "The Game of Chess," that centers on the splendors and miseries of heterosexual coupling. Ultimately, then, Eliot rags Buck and Ruby's ragging of Shakespeare, folding into the passage a spasm of pleasure that erupts from the lugubrious exchanges between morose city dwellers that otherwise dominate the section. Perhaps most important, though, is that this musical phrase acquires a distinctive power retroactively, if it is remembered and allowed to echo in the aftermath of the next section's centerpiece, the typist's seduction. Though the typist post-coital may appear only to be withdrawing into lassitude by playing her gramophone "with automatic hand" (a phrase that conflates machine and woman) after submitting to the advances of a predatory male, the music that rises from this encounter is, as heard by Eliot's poetic narrator, made coincidental with Ariel's haunting melodies in *The Tempest*, as recalled by a shipwrecked survivor still stunned by personal loss: "This music crept by me upon the waters." The strains of such music, as detected by Eliot, merge with "the pleasant whining of a mandoline" in a working-class tavern that remarkably transforms into "the walls / Of Magnus Martyr" that "hold / Inexplicable splendour of Ionian white and gold" (257, 261, 263–265). The resilience of the typist, or her ability to shake off despair and survive humiliation, operates as a talisman Eliot seizes to summon the voices of the "departed" nymphs whose traces were earlier found only in the discarded fragments of "Silk handkerchiefs, cardboard boxes, cigarette ends, / Or other testimony of summer nights" (175–177), and to reconstitute their presence, and even to hear words they speak, in the voices of the three "Thames-maidens" that echo with rich moments from the past when the voices of other forgotten women spoke. In a rhyme scheme that borrows from the octet of the Shakespearean and the sestet of the Petrarchan sonnet (ABABCD-CDEFGEFG), and whose language resonates with such other epitaph-moments of forgotten women as Dante's presentation of La Pia in Canto V of the *Purgatorio*, Eliot turns away from judgment and despair, looking beyond the shells of his obsession, and begins to imagine others as resilient, as damaged but surviving. This tune that emerges from the typist's gramophone, a melody plucked from the crowded noise of city streets, is foreshadowed in the snatch of ragtime that rises out of the murmurs of an earlier passage that Eliot intensifies and complicates. Popular music functions for Eliot, then, as unexpectedly layered with emotion and capable of importing into everyday life a fragment of an earlier richness that promises the chance of redemption.

In Europe since 1914, Eliot would relate to popular music in 1922 by fastening, not surprisingly, on a 1912 ragtime tune, but any sense that *The Waste Land* might seem out of date is countered by its textual presence that is quintessentially improvisational. Collecting scattered impressions from numerous linguistic registers, Eliot's long poem quickly established itself as a limit case for transgressive writing that suggestively hinted at underlying patterns. Though it trafficked in distorting phrases from predecessor texts, it did so not for a hoax effect but to pry out multiple possibilities within them. These traits, however, could still strike contemporaries as signs of ostentation, as marks of erudition. In his 1930 lampoon "The Moist Land," what Samuel Hoffenstein targeted for mockery were allusions to the classical tradition as they collided with contemporary referents ("I am the same, Panthides, / I, Lotychides, who once in Elymias.../ Wreathed for your head a crown of eglantine. /And drank a copper keg of home-made wine" [113]) and foreign phrases that seemed to resonate with mythic undertones until they melted into banality: "Take these, *les fleurs mourantes, mademoiselle.* / There's nothing more for me to say, / (Oh, Neptune, Neptune, call your mermaids in!) / Until you get my letter" (113). Throughout, though, as these examples also attest, Hoffenstein relies on the incongruity of juxtaposing elevated diction with colloquial talk: "Here in this desert place the frogs are withered / The griffons are no bigger than fleas, / The sands are rocky and the rocks are sandy / And there's not enough water / And not enough brandy" (115).

Hoffenstein's phrasing that deliciously evokes Eliot's sonorous cadences also should remind us that the haunting songs by Ariel that allayed both the water's fury and Ferdinand's despair in *The Tempest*—the music, he said, that "crept by me upon the waters"—was a necessarily tempestuous mélange that included both plaintive love lyrics ("Come into these yellow sands, / And take hands") and sounds of watchdogs barking and roosters crowing ("Hark! Hark! I hear / The strain of strutting chanticleer / Cry Cock-a-diddle-crow!"). Animal noises reproduced through musical instruments were, as we have learned, a staple of early jazz recordings. Paul Whiteman's 1924 Carnegie Hall concert that concluded with the premier of George Gershwin's *Rhapsody in Blue* followed a program that traced the history of jazz, a program that opened with "Livery Stable Blues," another hit by the Original Dixieland Jazz Band that mimicked barnyard noise and jungle growls in "Tiger Rag" (Osgood 136–137; also see La Rocca 115). But animal noises are also threaded through many passages in Eliot's *Waste Land*, especially the sounds of birds, often in transcriptions that are notably distorted, ranging from the relatively pure "Co co rico co co rico" of the cock on the rooftree in section V to the ominous "Jug Jug" and its repetition "Twit twit twit / Jug jug jug jug jug jug" to the hauntingly evocative hermit-thrush's song that resembles water dropping: "Drip drop drip drop drop drop drop drop." Many of the phrases from vaudeville tunes and Broadway musical numbers that dotted the manuscript of "He Do the Police in Different Voices" fell under Ezra Pound's blue pencil, but the natural sounds of birds—their audibility twisted by their literary heritage, much as barnyard noises could be discerned within the timbre of various instruments—remained in the final product. They stand out as both suggestive and opaque, both meaningful and mimetic, recalling *The Waste Land* in its time as a premier example of the "new poetry" that editorial writers so quickly associated with jazz dancing. Eliot's poem examines "Jazz Age" paraphernalia, which might be dismissed as trash, to recycle it as waste that should not be discarded.

Hart Crane's idea in 1923 to counter Eliot's long poem with *The Bridge* ruled the kind of noise that Eliot had employed as out of bounds in his poem. Even when positioning us in a bar in the 1926 poem "Cutty Sark," listening to a nickel-in-the-slot pianola, what might be fragmentary sounds from a noisy background Crane resolves into thematically relevant words: "*galleries—galleries of watergutted lava / snarling stone—green—drums—drown*" (52). Crane is determined to shape meaning, but the idea of a jazz text—of a process-driven, apparently spontaneous, and improvisational response to events that caught up discordant strains—had begun to change in the mid-twenties as jazz began to be treated as a marketable commodity.

"Jazz may have been the Jazz Age's name for any up-tempo music" (115), Michael Rogin dourly remarks in his study of the 1927 talkie *The Jazz Singer*. Marketing meant that the "danger" of jazz had to be recalibrated, as Paul Whiteman sought with his Carnegie Hall concert and his alliance with Gershwin. Composers trained in the classics, and students who had studied with figures such as Edward MacDowell, had previously worked to present compositions that clearly identified the African American origin of a music whose harmonic dissonance and dance-based rhythms were aligned with sites like New Orleans. But Henry F. Gilbert's pioneering efforts in the early 1900s, including his 1908 *The Dance in Place Congo* (a composition that took its title from an 1886 article by George Washington Cable that "described, with pictorial and musical illustrations, the Sunday-afternoon revels of off-duty New Orleans slaves in a 'no-'count open space [Congo Square] at the fag-end of Orleans Street") was rejected as "Niggah Music" when submitted to the Boston Symphony (Darrell, 7). Gilbert saw a rewritten version performed in 1918, and in the same year John Powell's *Rhapsodie Nègre* (dedicated to the Joseph Conrad of *Heart of Darkness*) was performed by the Metropolitan Opera in New York, with a later presentation in 1922 in Boston. Powell's second movement antiphonally develops the spiritual "Swing Low Sweet Chariot." John Alden Carpenter's 1921 *Krazy Kat* ballet (incorporating characters from African American George Herriman's syndicated comic strip) featured a "Katnip Blues" sequence announced by a smearing trombone glissando that was an uptown version of animal noise. Adolph Weiss's *American Life* is counted among these compositions, a 1929 tone poem subtitled "Scherzoso Jazzoso" that folded in the distinctive blues harmony of the flatted fifth into a twelve-tone scale (Weiss studied with Schoenberg and the tradition of inventive titles began with Carpenter's tempo specifications that called for "jazzando," "pizzi-kat-to," "kurioso," and "kantandao" in a piano score illustrated by Herriman [Darrell, 12]).

None of these works, however, were widely performed or made available on records at the time, and what defined "jazz" through the 1920s were commercialized representations. In these versions, the emphasis on black and white interrelations featured in the symphonies and suites of Gilbert, Powell, Carpenter, and Weiss was replaced by a stress on jazz as a music that took its energy from not one but any and all immigrant ethnic groups. For progressives intent on countering prejudice against immigrants in the 1920s, jazz did powerful cultural work. The 1930 talkie, *King of Jazz*, which featured Paul Whiteman's band and that staged a dance spectacle around Gershwin's *Rhapsody in Blue*, introduced its climactic sequence by building on a segment from the 1924 Carnegie Hall concert that presented the folk music of four different regions. As a prelude to the finale, an authoritative voice in the movie declared that "America is a melting pot of music wherein the melodies of all nations are fused into one great rhythm—jazz." Whiteman's last scene offered tunes and dancers associated with the Orient, Mexico, Scotland, Germany, England, and so on in a grand display whose commitment to representing "all nations" excluded the continent of Africa. Indeed, the most direct appearance of anything African was in the opening animated cartoon, which depicted a caricaturized Whiteman in Africa, stalking tigers amid cartoon natives.

What Crane inherited, then, when writing in the late 1920s was a situation in which jazz, uncoupled from its African American practitioners by a shift in focus that drew back from the particular to search for origins, was losing its aura of danger. Writing a progress report to benefactor Otto Kahn in 1927 that included several sections of *The Bridge*, Crane described the opening of "The River" by noting that its "rhythm is jazz," but as he further explained, this meant it was "an intentional burlesque on the cultural confusion of the present—a great conglomeration of noises analogous to the strident impression of a fast express rushing by" (Crane, 555–556).

> Stick your patent name on a signboard
> brother—all over—going west—young man
> Tintex—Japalac—Certain-teed Overalls ads
> and lands sakes! Under the new playbill ripped
> in the guaranteed corner—see Bert Williams what?
> Minstrels when you steal a chicken just
> save me the wing for if it isn't
> Erie it ain't for miles around a
> Mazda...(41)

Crane's readiness to acclimate jazz rhythms by incorporating them into a "fast express" may have been aimed at Kahn who, though a lavish supporter of the Metropolitan Opera, was also father to Roger Wolfe Kahn, the teenage leader of a jazz orchestra whose success rivaled Paul Whiteman's. (Indeed, Crane's letter to Kahn, dated September 12, 1927, may have originated in Crane's knowledge that Kahn's son, then aged nineteen, would be featured on the cover of the following month's issue of *Time* [T. Collins, 147–148].) At the same time, Crane's lines also dramatize the emptiness of such commercial transactions. Jazz rhythm signifies only a cultural mash-up, and its closest connection, in this passage, to black-white relations

is the harlequinade that is the blackface minstrel show. Crane's inclusion of the vir-
tuoso Bert Williams and the minstrel buck-and-wing routine may serve, in part, as
a smooth placement of the "wing" that now reappears from *The Bridge*'s opening
lines that flash on the seagull's wings that "dip and pivot him" over the city's "chained
bay waters," but it also serves here to expose the ease with which a minstrelized
version of African American experience has come to dominate jazz descriptions.
No doubt that the minstrel version is no more authentic than any of the other "pat-
ent name[s]" spied fleetingly by a Cleveland-bound, heading-home Crane as the
Twentieth Century Limited surfaces on the New York Central tracks above 125th
Street: Bert Williams appears on a playbill whose rip exposes the weakness of its
"guaranteed corner" and implies all such slogans are useless. Crane means these
words to deteriorate into the "*din and slogans of the year,*" as he writes in the mar-
ginal gloss adjacent to this passage. Here "jazz rhythm," far from authenticating a
primitive danger, is a mark of fast-talking relations, smooth maneuvers, glib chatter;
it reflects Crane's brush with entry-level ad agency jobs in which he haplessly ground
out copy.

In the same year that Crane summarized the opening collage of "The River" for
his patron, Mina Loy read "The Widow's Jazz" to a gathering at Natalie Barney's home
(Burke, 361). The poem, before unexpectedly turning into an elegiac cry of grief for her
beloved but mysteriously lost husband, developed a series of mocking, ironic descrip-
tions that reduced any claims to ecstasy by jazz as just a stage setting contrived by
slumming intellectuals: "The white flesh quakes to the negro soul / Chicago! Chicago!"
Like a talisman, the name of the raw Midwest city is evoked with a shudder, inaugurat-
ing a sequence of self-deceptive practices that Loy deflatingly exposes. In fragmentary
couplets that move in and out of possible narratives, different registers appear yet
remain apart. Lapses into an artificial-sounding dialect with an air of minstrelsy—
"White man quit his actin' wise / colored folk hab de moon in dere eyes"—are fol-
lowed by excursions that shift from the elevated diction of transcendental transport
to the descriptions of an exotic décor to abject confessionalism:

> Haunted by wind instruments
> in groves of grace
>
> the maiden saplings
> slant to the oboes
>
> and shampooed gigolos
> prowl to the sobbing taboos. (95)

What Marjorie Perloff has identified as Loy's "sardonic wit and bitter acerbity" (206)
here describes a music that cannot go long without revealing that it exists to cover
its own lack of substance. As a façade, it may be invoked only to collapse, as a prepa-
ration for the release, in the poem's later lines, of Loy's deep anguish: no distraction
is sufficient to assuage this widow whose endless pain, once it cannot be withheld
further, turns the world's richness into just so much Chicago jazz.

For these late 1920s poets, all of whom are white, the dangers that jazz represents are threats that can be more or less managed. Jazz texts signify that their poetry is modern, and the result can be rule-breaking, at least until the music begins to resemble the products of an inauthentic commercialism. However, the experience of jazz was quite different for the African American poet Sterling A. Brown, whose description of a cabaret performance in the same year that Crane and Loy wrote their jazz texts simmers with anger. "Cabaret," subtitled "1927, Black & Tan Chicago" (from *Southern Road*, 1932) opens by describing not the players or their music but the audience whom the performers must please ("overlords sprawl here with their glittering darlings"). It proceeds to expose the laboring environment behind such exotic features as the "Creole Beauties from New Orleans" ("By way of Atlanta, Louisville, Washington, Yonkers") who "wiggle and twist" to silly noise ("Bee—dap—ee—DOOP, dee—ba—dee—BOOP") even as the cabaret scene imitates the markets of slavery: "*Show your paces to the gentlemen, / A prime filly, she. / What am I offered, gentlemen, gentlemen …*" The drummer throws his sticks to the moon, when the "band goes mad," but Brown makes sure we know that it is "a *papier-mâché* moon" in this concocted production that ends with still more annoying noise: "Dee da dee D A A A A H." Brown's awareness of stage-setting differs from Loy's sense of saplings, oboes, and dialect chatter about "colored folk" that "hab de moon in dere eyes." For Brown, the distortions are malevolent, recalling historic simplifications that underwrote a regime of control, confining persons to a script that reduced them to arms, bodies, mouths, "[b]ending, writing, turning." Shifting registers now disclose not issues of authenticity but dimensions of history that embody brutal dismissals, contemptuous manipulations, or unwelcome possessions. The cabaret is a crime scene, or as James Smethurst writes, its music "is appropriated from the folk and transformed into a vehicle for the erasure of the musicians as full; humans and the southern black communities from which the music is ultimately drawn" (75). Staged jazz appears as a white-based cultural formation that, insofar as its music is parlayed into a display both savage and childlike, wild, and artificial, represents a dismissal of African American culture as that which has been made to be diverting.

BLUES FORM

Modernist jazz of the 1920s offered itself to poets as that which could affront. Here was modernity expressed as a tangle of discord and chaos. For some modern poets, "saxophone" was the kind of new word that was at once a goof, a silly-sounding artifact with an unlikely prefix that slyly insinuated the sexual while sounding quite mechanical and streamlined: "All night the saxophones wailed the hopeless comment of 'The Beale Street Blues,'" Scott Fitzgerald wrote in *The Great Gatsby*, recycling a passage from a short story he published in 1924, "while a hundred pairs of golden and silver slippers shuffled the shining dust" (53; West, 180). Just by its inclusion in verse the word had a power to startle, to jangle: Sandburg's jazzmen "sob on the long cool winding saxophones" in a cluster of adjectives detached from weeping, as if the instrument is designed to deny sorrow. In Wallace Stevens's "A High-Toned Old Christian Woman" (in the 1923 *Harmonium*), when "our bawdiness" is "indulged at last," that errant drive is "converted into palms, / Squiggling like saxophones"—hands open and freely wagging, as if signaling availability, but also alarmingly mechanical and serpentine (59). The contrast, however, is telling when Langston Hughes referenced "saxophone" in "The Cat and the Saxophone" in 1926. For him, the word signifies the name of a well-known Harlem club.

To all the novelty represented by the noisy nonmusic of saxophones in Jazz Age poetry, the blues were poised to circulate as a powerful emotional alternative. Though their lyrics might verge on the sensational, their structure maintained an underlying sobriety. Poetry associated with the blues delivered just what the jazz text often avoided: the blues establishes a groundwork for appreciating and even respecting the difficulties of black experience. The blues also begins to assemble a strategy through which white outsiders can penetrate the barriers protectively erected by black insiders, and proposes a set of recognizable formal properties that will eventually circulate so broadly that they operate as a variant on the refined flexibility of the European sonnet. Modern poetry eventually imagines the blues as the site where a black voice finds expression with an emotional resonance that can be heard beyond the black community and thus becomes a space where anyone may confront suffering.

Of obvious importance here is African American ownership of the blues, whose forebears were remarked upon by Frederick Douglass's 1844 autobiography where he described work songs chanted by slaves that seemed "rude and incoherent" but whose "unmeaning jargon" was actually "full of meaning" to the singers. Such songs filled Douglass with "ineffable sadness," even as the singing by slaves had been taken by others as evidence of "contentment and happiness." Yet singing, Douglass insisted, was also a meaningful escape from pain but "only as an aching heart is relieved by its tears": "I have often sung to drown my sorrow" (57–58). To realize how strongly blues components were available to Douglass as he cast his memory back to the 1830s is to understand the blues as a testament of and an access to generations of suffering. If the "personalized, solo elements of the blues style may indicate a decisive move into twentieth-century American consciousness," historian Lawrence Levine writes, "the musical style of the blues indicates a holding on to the old roots" at a time when African Americans were dispersing themselves into the north and when "the rise of the radio and the phonograph could have spelled the demise of a distinctive Afro-American style" (223).

As indelibly identified as the blues were with black experience, ownership of the form still had to be defended from well-meaning admirers such as Carl Van Vechten. His 1926 best-seller *Nigger Heaven* benefited, after its seventh edition, with examples of blues lyrics written by Hughes (Van Vechten had reproduced copyrighted songs in previous printings, attracting a lawsuit and a need for a quick correction). These blues, which Hughes never collected or anthologized in his own volumes, played a central role in the novel's numerous sketches of Harlem cabaret life. Yet in his final chapter, Van Vechten shows that his protagonist is incapable of listening to a blues song without hearing its words merge into the babble of others around him, in a passage with references to bestial chaos: "It all became a jumble in Byron's mind. A jumble of meaningless phrases accompanied by the hard, insistent regular beat of the drum, the groaning of the saxophone, the shrill squeaking of the clarinet" (278). Notably, the lyrics that Hughes produced for Van Vechten followed the template of the "Vaudeville Blues," commercialized properties whose sensational lyrics were rife with double entendres: "You ain't gonna ride no chariot tonight / "Less you take your sweet mama along! / I say, Ben Hur, you ain't goin' out / 'Till you listen to this song" (246). Hughes supplied the kind of low-down material, that is, that the responses that Van Vechten ascribed to his characters deserved.

Hughes operated quite differently when he privileged the blues in his second collection. *Fine Clothes to the Jew* (1927), using opening and closing sections with groups of eight and nine poems that, though they were at times sensational, preferred that form of the blues closely linked to folk music. Musical historians have construed descriptions of the blues that sharply differentiate them from the type of the romantic ballad: the blues provide "a gritty, realistic engagement with everyday life, offering metaphoric revenge and a mordant sense of humor as the best available antidote to oppression" (Starr and Waterman, 103–104). But in 1927, these antiballads were still unusual enough, certainly to readers of poetry, to warrant an introductory "Note on the Blues" at the opening of his volume in which Hughes provided a definition that resonated with Douglass's recall. "The mood of the *blues* is almost always despondency, but when they are sung people laugh" (xiii)—a characterization he would carry into his career, down to *The First Book of Negroes,* his 1952 children's book: "The blues were a sad kind of music, but a funny kind of music as well, with words that made people laugh" (46). Though Hughes took the performing of the blues as a subject in his first book, *The Weary Blues* (1926), its title poem, as Stephen Henderson has explained, was not a blues "but a lyric framework with narrative elements"—a hybridity necessary if the poem is to dramatize "the blues experience as performance, as social ritual, and as an existential experience" (142). By contrast, the blues that bookend *Fine Clothes to the Jew* (1927) are transcriptions of a performance, not a descriptive rendition that surrounds a performance.

So familiar is that blues form today that Hughes's work as a pioneer is easy to overlook. While Hughes no doubt entertained the possibility that it might someday be "intellectually indefensible," as Cary Nelson has written, to exclude the blues as sung by performers as "nonliterary lyrics" (1989, 66), the "strict poetic pattern" that Hughes identified in his 1927 "Note" was identical to that which W. C. Handy had been presenting through the 1910s in popular sheet music: "one long line repeated and a third line to rhyme with the first two," and "[s]ometimes the second line in repetition is slightly changed and sometimes, but very seldom, it is omitted" (xiii). (This pattern appeared in some of the blues Hughes contributed to *Nigger Heaven* and in examples furnished by Hughes as a native informant for Van Vechten's 1925 *Vanity Fair* essay, "The Black Blues" [95–96], and for the essay by Abbe Niles that accompanied the 1926 *Blues: An Anthology*, edited by W. C. Handy [4]). Even so, Hughes brought important, if subtle, innovations when he depicted the blues as a poetic form. When Niles transcribed examples of the blues in his introduction to Handy's anthology, he rendered the twelve-bar musical form into three lines, each representing four bars of music:

> Did you ever see yo' honey, when her good man's not aroun'?
> Did yo' ever see yo' honey, when her good man's not aroun'?
> She get up in de mo'nin', tuns de feader-bed upside-down (4)

The pause in the blues line, in this transcription, is represented by a comma. When Hughes rendered the blues, though, he arranged the twelve-bar lyric into a six-line form to stress the midline pause. By draping every two-bar phrase over a line break, he promoted that pause into what Raymond G. Patterson has called "the blues caesura" (191). In addition, his version of dialect minimized the numerous apostrophes that marked elided consonants and the phonics-based spellings inherited from Paul Laurence Dunbar. Dunbar's effort to reproduce pronunciation exactly inadvertently fostered the kind of reading that, in performance, suggested inertia, even laziness. Hughes freed the poem to unfold in rapid time, allowing pronunciations based on clear phrasings that moved with musical sinuosity.

Hughes's use of the blues form scandalized the elders of the Harlem Renaissance who, if they considered poetry as an avenue for racial equality, envisioned the sonnet as a leveling field for play. But the blues poem worked as such a field, effectively engaging a readership with its second line that imperfectly echoes the first, providing an occasion to enter the poem in response to a call. As Fahamisha Patricia Brown has stressed, call "in African American vernacular culture...elicits response" (29). The second line's act of reiteration does multiple work: it allows performers time to improvise a third line, and it serves as a factor of suspense before the satisfying closure of the third line's rhymed couplet. But its greatest value may be the accessibility it affords its audience, grounded in the seriousness of the first line when it is reiterated as if in communal agreement. Such availability serves as a conditioning device that renders improvisation customary. The slight variations that differentiate the second line from the first represent an incremental adjustment that customizes the moment, undermining rigid adherence to exactness. Such small, yet significant and understandable, substitutions reproduce—in a verbal form, in miniature, and locally—an abiding principle of the blues. Although the blues are characteristically described as employing the African-based musical scale that lowers by a half-tone the seventh, third, and fifth notes in the diatonic scale, what actually happens in performance, as Sterling Brown has observed, is that "the third and seventh notes are not pitched steadily but waver between flat and natural" (1996, 267). This distinctive waver was confirmed by the music historian Gerald Abraham, who described a process in which the "seventh and third degree" of the blues scale was "slightly flattened"—an instability that produced not clear half-tone substitutions but rather "dubious notes" that "were said to be 'blue'"(817). Peter Van Der

Merwe further emphasizes this instability by noting how often minor and major intervals (that is, both the half-tone diminishment that we call "flat" and the full tone itself) freely coexist within the same song: "a blues may have major thirds right through to the end, where one or two minor thirds appear" (120)—an example of which, incidentally, is the musical transcription of the "Hesitation Blues" with shifts from A to A-flat and B to B-flat that Hughes reprints in *Ask Your Mama: Twelve Moods for Jazz* (3). Which note is "correct"? Which the norm and which the deviant? No such resolution is possible: both operate in tandem.

The blues form that Hughes represented in his poetry, then, manages a call-and-effect relation as a resource whose repeated second line is literally engaging, and it prompts a performancelike involvement that rests on verbal variations whose very slightness sharpens awareness. The variations echo as an improvisational wavering that in turn signals the inclusion of slightly different voicing, with poet and reader like singer and listener. The third line, then, insofar as it completes a couplet that has been held in suspension and fully embodied by reader and listener, arrives with maximum amplification. Scholars who address the content of the blues have continually admired the tendency of their singers to find a temporary resolution, produced against great odds and out of nowhere and usually through a verbal twist that hinges on a detail. The great attraction of blues music, Andrew Tracy suggests, is the capacity of the form "to appreciate several different conflicting schemes at the same time" (qtd. in Van Der Merwe, 220). If the authority of the blues moment turns on repeating so as to firmly register an experience, revising it slightly to fine-tune its presence, then moving to resolve it not by a swerve away but a focus in, that exquisite intensity will depend on a verbal twist or an ingenious adjustment that requires a mood of enhanced sensitivity in which minute tonal shifts are amplified. As developed by Hughes, the blues form is the vessel that is performing for others the experience of registering and (temporarily) resolving conflicts. This experience of doubling up so the listener, in the act of attending, is folded into the moment is described and enacted in a stanza of Hughes's "Hey-Hey Blues" that *The New Yorker* printed in a 1939 issue: "While you play 'em, / I will sing 'em, too. And while you play 'em, / I'll sing 'em too. I don't care how you play 'em / I'll keep right up with you" (213). In such assertions, the blues is not just the opposite of a "rigidly personalized form," as Houston Baker has maintained, but its "nonlinear, freely associative, non-sequential meditation" that presents "an anonymous (nameless) voice issuing from the black (w)hole" (5) is also deftly construed by attentive listeners who recognize an invitation to participate.

Hughes's earliest blues poems are not simply an expression of black subjectivity but a staging that elicits others to find a position within the text. "Bound No'th Blues," appearing in the final section of *Fine Clothes to the Jew*, evokes the Great Migration, enjoins its listener to experience the monotony of "Goin' down the road" as variations on the phrase serve as a persistent refrain through the first three stanzas. In a last stanza that verges on the virtuosic, Hughes pushes repetition until it breaks into a closing couplet that is simultaneously a dismissive curse and a satisfying perception:

Road, road, road, O!
Road, road ... road ... road, road!
Road, road, road, O!
On the no'thern road.
These Mississippi towns ain't
Fit fer a hoppin' toad. (*Collected Poems*, 76)

The reader, mimetically slogging through a verbal landscape that barely shifts its details, is able to appreciate boredom and rejection; the poem is sardonically dissolving "road" into nonsense sounds through repetition. Yet the final couplet, pronounced with disgust ("These Mississippi towns ain't / Fit fer a hoppin' toad"), declares progress underway (Mississippi towns are being left behind), the speaker is superior to a toad (just leaving the south already promotes status), and we are walking, not hopping (moving forward with determination, not jumping to the side). Without exactly casting off "this load," it alters just enough to point dismissively to "These Mississippi towns"—a gesture of small triumph, especially if leaving small towns in the south is also an escape from comparison with an animal. If the process is particularized in relation to black experience, it is nonetheless generalized in relation to anyone's experience.

Hughes's minimalist writing, as it takes shape through the words of a man speaking clearly, has won praise from Charles Altieri for its unadorned directness. "The speaker is not exposed as having a false consciousness," Altieri writes, commenting specifically on a later blues poem, "Evenin' Air Blues" (1941) but with words that refer generally to Hughes's other works in a "black idiom": "The poem depends on our seeing how effectively and precisely the speaking captures an experience and avoids any escapist tendencies.... Because there is no self-staging on the part of the poet ... what is not said, or not able to be said, is often more evocative than the imagery that can enter into speech" (121). Altieri moves easily from specific to general, however, through the super-subtle staging of the highly familiar blues form, as Hughes's "simple" structure proves a capacious one, able to erase a sense of "self-staging" by involving a reader as sophisticated as Altieri in an apparently effortless projection. Describing blues music as a form of folk poetry, Sterling Brown wrote in 1930 that "[t]he poetry of the blues deserves close attention" (1998, 551), but it was Hughes who devised a means to present the blues as poetry, inviting and shaping that close attention.

Jazz Text

The British literary historian Michael Schmidt has read Hughes's blues poems as "written with white readers as well as black in mind" but as a result, he finds "something missing from them, tonalities withheld," and these include "a lack of candor about his sexuality, a guardedness in relation to his own as well as the white 'culture of reception'" (793). Hughes may have had personal reasons for developing, as his signature, a form that valued the demonstrative gesture over the revealing detail. The strength of such a form, in a racist culture that sanctioned so very few places where blacks and whites could comfortably interact, had been its development of a neutral ground, calling on musical rhythms as those that engender feelings despite racial distinctions. In just this sense, the blues poem remains powerful for its cultural trace of the unfinished: it is less than adequate as a medium of rich exchange, but it is what is needed to begin overcoming barriers between whites and blacks that have been cemented by years of prejudice.

Hughes, though, in his own later writings, regularly pushed beyond the blues form. In the postwar sequence entitled *Montage of a Dream Deferred* (1948), he used two contrary musical styles in jazz to describe a postwar Harlem caught between anger and hope, between broken promises and dreams battling for a future. Both the past and future simmer with discontent. The rapid-fire, hard-driving rhythms of boogie-woogie that surged through a predictable harmonic field closely attuned to the basic changes in the blues recall a past seething with frustration. Boogie-woogie rhythms, orchestrated for big bands during the war, were co-opted to martial ends, hailing "the boogie-woogie bugle boy of company C," whose musical offerings at reveille brought troops to life. But no black serviceman could serve in even so minor a role, and the rewards of that hit tune belonged to the Andrews Sisters. The future was represented by the musical style known as bebop that had developed during the wartime recording ban among young musicians deliberately extending both harmonics and rhythms into territories that required virtuosic skill. The future, that is, was hailed, through such music, as marked as unknown, still in definition, but expansive, open to impossible feats that could be glimpsed in improvisations at breakneck speed with combinations of chords that depended on elaborate substitutions. In his poetry, Hughes represented those jazz styles as irreconcilable. "The boogie-woogie rumble / Of a dream deferred" ("Dream Boogie," 388) unfolded in a stylish six-beat iambic surge, kicked along by sumptuous alliteration, consonance, and assonance. In contrast to that pressure forward, Hughes used phrases in fragments, erratically emergent, to characterize a bebop sensibility that was impatient, eager, but also evasive, uncertain. (Even the name "bebop" kept shifting about, morphing into new syllables, as if its energy originated as a fleeting hope that could either soar to the heights or dissolve into smoke.) These opposing styles serve as poles, and to define the area in between requires numerous brief poems that capture fleeting impressions of Harlem as spoken or thought by its inhabitants. The speakers occupy an uncertain middle that is the postwar present, defined by a past that is too rigid, too bitter, and a future that is all ambition, all evanescence. Black musical styles that had once had promise as a site upon which respect for African Americans could be won have lost their utopian aura. A second world war in which blacks had once again demonstrated their loyalty to a country that belittled them had once again ended with no appreciable increase in social justice.

Hughes's use of jazz is a corrective, Anita Hays Patterson proposes, for those who considered jazz "a pleasant background for conversation": "too many people

who listened to jazz did not hear the seriousness of its emotional message and were
not aware of the violent historical conditions out of which the impulse to formal
innovation emerged" (682). Other black poets developed works whose jazz styling
directly aligned with violent historical conditions, such as Melvin B. Tolson's con-
solidation of elements from Hughes with aspects of Sterling Brown's work. Though
Robert Hass characterized Brown's work in *Southern Road* as "a record of the peo-
ple Brown met and the music he heard: street corner blues singers and preachers,
the gossip and oratory of Southern churches, the talk of men who had spent time
on work gangs and prison farms" (99), his poetry, unlike the direct transcription
that Hass implies, is subtly construed with tonal irregularities, immersed in his-
torical details, peppered with evocative pauses, gaps, and omissions. Tolson had
incorporated blues poetry passages in dozens of poems in a work he assembled in
the 1930s, *A Gallery of Harlem Portraits* (1935, but unpublished until 1979), where
they sometimes functioned as epigraphs that launched dramatic monologues, and
in a later work, *Harlem Gallery* (1965), he manufactured a smooth-talking oratory
that was half-dazzle, half-defiance, but in his monumental *Libretto for the Repub-
lic of Liberia* (1953) he attempted a full improvisational style in a later section that
triples the length of the poem and produces a heteroglossic verbal flow that shifts
through allusions, references, quotations, and other languages with a global per-
spective that intersects centuries, in a barrage of information that resembles the
torrent of sixteenth and thirty-second notes of an improvisation by Charlie Parker.
This is a typical passage from a much longer sequence:

> and no mourners go crying *dam-bid-dam*
> about the ex-streets of scarlet letters
>   only the souls of hyenas crying *teneo te africa*
>   only the blind men gibbering *mboagan* in greek
>   against sodom's pillars of salt
>   below the mountain of rodinsmashedstatus *aleppe*
>   (459–460)

Information channeled so tempestuously, as in a late-night jam session that casts
off chorus after chorus, is tinged with an intellectual version of blue notes, represented
here in information that continually weaves African material with world history. At
the same time, moving apart from and below yet within the text are Tolson's *Waste
Land*–like footnotes, in counterpoint with the flow, sometimes identifying foreign
terms in the text ("*dam-bi-dam*: 'blood for blood'") but often producing further asso-
ciations. Any one of Tolson's footnotes, such as his further comment on "blood for
blood"—"This was the way the Saadists phrased the idea of Talion at the Abbasiya
mausoleum of Nokray Pasha. Cf. Leviticus XIV, xvii–xxi" (459)—can easily call for
its own footnoting, or more accurately, counterpoint work by the reader. "Talion,"
research discloses, is punishment that fits the crime, and the passage from Leviticus
discusses the "eye for eye, tooth for tooth." The degree of readerly collaboration var-
ies, for at times Tolson will refer to quotations without translating them (he writes,

"*Teneo te Africa*: the words uttered by Caesar when he stumbled and fell on touching the shores of Africa. Cf. Suetonious, *Lives of the Caesars*"), so that the reader must find that the phrase in Suetonious's Julius Caesar chapter is rendered as "Africa, I have tight hold of you." And at other times, Tolson will leave crucial words unannotated (Plutus, emblem of wealth and guardian of Hell's fourth circle, is the figure that shouts "*aleppe*" among other gibberish but collapses upon a word from Dante's guide Virgil). Tolson's esoteric display is as virtuosic linguistically as Parker was musically, and by unearthing allusions to Africa and race through unexpected associations, he echoes Parker's propensity for finding blues harmonics within the most intricate chord progressions. Tolson proposes an equality based not on a plea for fairness but on recognizing the numerous exchanges that have been forgotten in the past.

The ethnomusicologist Adelaida Reyes observes that music historians agree that the primary step in American music finding "an unambiguous identity that was truly its own" was the advances made by jazz in fostering interracial harmony: "painfully at first but with increasing inevitability in the wake of social forces that finally acknowledged racism and battled against it, African American musicians finally interacted with white society—musicians and audiences—on equal terms.... The music of an originally debased minority not even entitled to call itself American had become the music of the whole" (87). The stature acquired by jazz by midcentury is evident in numerous poems that openly imitate various schools of jazz. Robert Creeley's "I Knew A Man" (in *For Love*, 1963) echoes the understated, minimal interplay of cool jazz in its laconic phrasings and off-beat line breaks—"drive, he sad, for / christ's sake, look / out where yr going" (38)—that resembles, in Charles O. Hartman's words, "the painful attempt to articulate something that disappears as soon as words seem about to hold still" (54). Michael Harper's title poem in *Dear John, Dear Coltrane* (1970) engages with the title of the John Coltrane song "A Love Supreme" in lines that, Cary Nelson explains, "mix strong acts of witness to America's racist history with wrenching accounts of family tragedy" (2000, 1043) and elevate sonorous drones into ritualized chant. As jazz styles grow increasingly recognizable, a tradition begins to coalesce around performers who can be hailed as powerful innovators. Lawson Fusao Inada (in *Legends from Camp*, 1993) interacts with Thelonious Monk in the first part of his two-part poem "Blue Monk" (its title echoing a Monk composition): "You're dancing, humming, / strolling slowly across, / tossing blue notes, floating over the wide, blue water, / like you're a luminous, musical spider" (66) or Kevin Young (in *To Repel Ghosts*, 2001) addresses Lester Young in "Lester Yellow": "playing up // beat, on / the one—pork-/pie hat cymbal-flat— / wearing it out" (159). At an earlier time in the century, poetic technique was used to contain jazz's eruptive barbarism; now poetic technique takes direction from jazz's individualizing gestures. And out of this informal understanding of generational leaders, musicians emerge not just as innovators or musical virtuosi but as mentors for future generations, as wise men. Charles Mingus is so elevated by William Matthews in one of a series of three poems in *Time & Money* (1995), "Mingus at the Half Note," in which he halts his set to chastise "a sleek / black man bent chattering across / a table to his lavish date: / 'This is your heritage and if you / don' wanna

listen then you got / someplace else you'd better be'" (18). By century's end, poets
agree upon figures of stature that make up a hierarchy of greatness, confirming not
simply the centrality of jazz in American culture but its contribution to social cohe-
sion. Considering the "opposition between individualism and being part of a group,"
Reyes concludes that this "opposition that is central to jazz resolves the dilemma of
inclusiveness and exclusiveness, favoring neither but creating the kind of tension
that, instead of disrupting, binds like glue" (89).

Among poets who have conceptualized jazz for its inherent values, none has
been so active as Yusef Komunyakaa. Since his 1984 debut volume *Copacetic*, he has
embraced jazz for giving "symmetry—shape and tonal equilibrium" to his poetry
(*Blue Notes*, 7). Rather than deifying the jazz great, however, he has concentrated
on registering and conveying the anguish behind that music and the obstacles to its
production. The sonnet sequence entitled "Testimony" that chronologically exam-
ines the career of Charlie Parker (commissioned as an oratorio in 1997, published in
Thieves of Paradise, 1998) continually searches for clarity within a mythic narrative;
in a characteristic gesture that locates jazz understanding both within and outside
the black community, Komunyakaa writes in the voice of Nica Koenigswater, the
European baroness and jazz patron who cared for Parker in his last days. In con-
junction with improvisation, what engages Komunyakaa's interest is the problem
of transmitting information that has been lost from memory. As he provocatively
charged in his introduction as editor to *The Best Poetry of 2003*, "Sometimes artists
and writers let us down through silence and erasure" (12). In his long poem *Taboo*
(2004), a text that closely derives from the practice in Tolson's *Libretto*, Komunya-
kaa turns improvisation and silence into a dialectic. The poems of *Taboo* in their
brief three-line stanzas present a "collage / montage effect propelled by a certain flu-
idity" that incorporates "information that enhances the text without undermining
the poem's fluidity and music" ("[On 'Nude Study']," 261; "Trueblood's Blues," 50).
The interplay of responding variously with sorrow or anger or irony to historical
knowledge that has been suppressed, ignored, or mislaid is an improvisational aes-
thetic that moves dartingly, elusively, enigmatically in a series of risky swerves.

Taboo reveals a secret history of western practices that regimented against
cross-racial desires, and in the process it erased from the archive both instances of
brutality and gestures of tenderness, thus producing a broad cultural memory that
simplified or evaded or rewrote cross-racial exchanges. As jazz texts, these engage
with an archive that is at once a treasure chest, dream cabinet, and nightmare log.
When one of Komunyakaa's poems riffs on a text that is more or less familiar, such
as Melville's *Benito Cereno*, its lines stray over familiar ground; Melville's writing has
served for some time to examine the dominant culture's ignorance of its own repres-
sive tactics. In this passage as throughout, the poem is spoken by Amasa Delano:

> That old sea salt
>
>   who handed me the wet
>   Gordian knot to undo,
>   his words were lost

> because Cereno stole
> my mind with a litany
> of silent signs
>
> though I mastered
> satire & irony
> a lifetime ago (32–33)

Excuses tumble out, shifting attention to Cereno, sheltering Delano, who is hardly a master of "satire & irony" but a devotee of distraction and excuse. The evasive mind is portrayed in a syntax that unspools itself in a dribble, that speeds rapidly as alliteration darts us past questionable conclusions ("Cereno stole / my mind," "litany / of silent signs"). Improvisation is here inscribing a historical unconscious that does not wish to see, that insists it cannot see, even as Komunyakaa places it on display.

As interesting as this is, even more interesting are poems that turn on obscure information, such as lines in "Monticello" that recall poems by "Thomas // Moore, & William Cullen Bryant" in whose "wet sighs" trail a historical memory of negative reaction to Jefferson's desire for Sally Hemings. These fleeting allusions by Komunyakaa repay readerly collaboration and scholarly confirmation, much like Tolson's footnotes, for *Taboo* emerges from the exclusive cluster of long poems based on exhuming little-known historical facts. When Komunyakaa alludes to a "ditty sung to Yankee Doodle," an original is certain to be found. Printed in a politically charged editorial in the *Boston Gazette,* the parodic version of "Yankee Doodle," supposedly the Jeffersonian version, includes such couplets as "Black is love's proper hue for me / And white's the love for Sally." There are similar couplets in the poems by Moore, "To Thomas Hume, Esq., M.D." (where "The patriot" finds a "dream of freedom in his bondsmaid's arms" even as he "retires to lash his slaves at home"), as well as in "The Embargo," a satire by a precocious thirteen-year old Bryant, with the address: "Go scan, Philosophist; thy ***** charms, / And sink supinely in her sable arms." These additions evoke a historical superstructure nastily entwined with fear and desire, with horror and fantasy, in evidence that must be sought by the reader. Komunyakaa elicits a collaborative enterprise that breaks the silence of a repressed history. And other passages in "Monticello" resonate under the weight of lost knowledge that a reader may bring:

> This dome-shaped
> room, did they kiss & hug
> here, gazing out over
> luteous fields as round windows
> changed the world? (27)

World-changing perspectives depend not simply on architectural niceties but on how one looks through a window and what one projects onto the world. With "luteous," Komunyakaa choose a strikingly arcane word that refers to the hue of green fields turning yellow or brown, as if that word's lack of circulation indexes a culture's ambivalence toward color gradations: are such colors turned away from to be rejected or can they be cherished for their exoticism? "Nude Study," a related text, describes in detail John Singer Sargent's nude portrait of Thomas McKeller, the black elevator operator at Boston's Copley Plaza: "Someone lightly brushed the penis / alive" but the detailed painting had been "hidden / among sketches & drawings" even as its torso had been recycled in Sargent's images of "Apollo & a bas-relief // Of Arion" (68). Here Komunyakaa composes an *ars poetica* for *Taboo*, as he recalls the black body as that which was "caricatured worldwide" even as Sargent's embrace of "the true physical beauty of a black man" remained both hidden in his studio and exploited for other uses there. The "other heads and hues grafted on his classical physique," as exposed by Kumunyakaa, become one more instance of the black body "used to construct the economic foundation of America" ("[On 'Nude Study']," 260–261).

The jazz text produced by *Taboo*, like the improvisation that takes up a standard set of harmonic progressions only to rework them, always exposes the existence of another side, a life at the margin or viewed from an angle. Some kinds of improvisation, Komunyakaa seems to propose, are not so easy to follow. Like the piano sounds of Thelonious Monk, some poetry may be "an exactitude defined by what's left out," a music that "requires someone who's an active listener—someone who doesn't have to be told the whole story" ("Improvised," 22). Yet the difficulty of the jazz text stems from its agreement to work with resistant information, and its difficulty is quite unlike the claims made by modernist critics that demanded that readers cultivate approaches to reading based on depth psychology, linguistics, and epistemology. Leonard Diepeveen has shown such arrangements to work in favor of an academic setting that subtends professional specialists, to train a reader to savor ambiguity, to become a member in an "exclusive club" (227) that also purveys a "critique of pleasure" (234). What Komunyakaa's jazz text, like Tolson's, wants to prompt by exposing history's lost byways and obscure passages, is a rearrangement of the archive that initiates revisions and adjustments that press against exclusivity, and the reader embarks on a search for clarity that makes discovery a pleasure. Komunyakaa's jazz text resembles the idea of the difficult that accompanies works that are paradoxical by nature as they are "written to a public that does not yet exist" (109) in Michael Warner's words: "a way of imagining a speech for which there is yet no scene and a scene for which there is yet no speech" (124).

EVERYBODY'S BLUES

If the jazz text in the twenty-first century carries on from Tolson (as Tolson carried on from Eliot) to establish itself as a quasi-elitist production designed as a display case for archival treasures that await full discovery—and whose display, though covert, is also designed to draw our interest—the blues form has always been moving in an opposite direction. The phenomenon of blues recordings, beginning with Mamie Smith's "Crazy Blues," that were quickly selling in the millions throughout the 1920s, has been associated with a black community acquiring record players on installment plans (Kenney, 65–87). Yet recordings that were selling in such numbers indicate a large market supported by broad demand. Daphne A. Brooks proposes that an "era of recording 'crossovers' was officially ushered in" by Smith's recording, tapping into "a climate of racial crossover that was finally evolving bilaterally" (548). When Hughes transcribed blues presentation as poetry, he shifted an occasion associated with entertainment (or, in Van Vechten's depiction, with sensational violence) toward an engagement that fostered understanding and even allowed for admiration. Arna Bontemps's 1974 entry for "Blues" in *The Princeton Encyclopedia of Poetry and Poetics* occupies twenty-five lines; in the 1996 revised edition, Stephen G. Henderson's entry uses 108 lines to describe a form that may well be, to American verse, an apparatus as flexible and familiar as the sonnet once was (81; 142–143).

Earliest exponents of blues as a poetic form were such socially active poets of the 1930s as Sol Funaroff and Muriel Rukeyser whose writing aligned the blues with African American speech. Jonathan Scott, building on observations made in Amiri Baraka's *Blues People* (1963), has described "the historical experience of being at one and the same time 'free' (no longer a really enslaved lifetime bond-laborer) and unfree (still really oppressed)" (114–115). Rukeyser's "George Robinson: Blues" in *The Book of the Dead* (1935) enacts such a contradiction. As Michael Thurston points out, the poem departs from the form's devices, for it "continues in the second line the thought begun in the first" (184). Rhyme words float unmoored within some opening lines, concentrating attention on the second and third lines when the rhymes deliver closure:

> Gaunley Bridge is a good town for Negroes, they let us stand
>   around, they let us stand
> Around on the sidewalks if we're black or brown.
> Vanetta's over the trestle, and that's our town. (868)

A fiercely segregated space curtails African American activity in what Rukeyser's Robinson defines as a "good town," but which could seem eager to keep blacks in plain sight, on the streets instead of the stores. To cross from Vanetta to Gauley Bridge is to span a gulf, a maneuver fraught with danger (trestles are built for trains, not pedestrians). The easygoing lope of Rukeyser's opening lines is exposed as a superficial languor: the line break might have come at "around," as Thurston maintains, but the rush of words that Rukeyser provides instead evoke a jitteriness below the standing-about. At the same time, disrupting the anticipated break may score a small victory against regimentation.

Blues poetry not only recognizes a historically black form but reveals that form as a means for channeling its own sense of history. Aaron Kramer's *Denmark Vesey* (1952) works with various metrical structures in its twenty-six poem sequence that details Vesey's 1822 slave rebellion, ending with a blues poem that functions less as a conclusion than as a coda. It is not Vesey at the center of that poem, "The Hammer and the Light," but a witness who remembers him, who stands in at this point for the reader. Blues form is a house haunted by other voices, and the colloquy between father and son that develops when the son asks his father why he weeps enacts a transmission across generations in a form that retains ancestral voices. When the father cries because Vesey's hammer has been quieted and his light has been extinguished, the son takes this as a call that demands a response: "My son said, 'Buy me a hammer; / I'll beat all day and night. / I'll make the angriest hammer / That ever was heard in the night.' / My son said, 'Buy me a lantern— / I'll take good care of its light'" (65). When Kramer wrote of the ending, he considered it "as much about 1952 as about 1822" (Gilzinger and Nelson, xix), recalling the anthropologist James C. Scott's categorization of the blues as one of the "Arts of Political Disguise" whose material resembles "the anonymity of collective property, constantly being adjusted, revised, abbreviated, or, for that matter, ignored" (161).

Although it is always the case, as Lynn Keller has remarked, that the "repetitions" of blues poems by Hughes might "feel monotonous to one reader and richly suggestive to another who hears them with a trained ear" (143), the blues poem as broadly developed after midcentury aims for the acknowledgment as that site that stands for a social form in which others can join as sympathetic listeners, as well as an occasion for expressiveness within the vernacular, finding delight and wit and play in everyday speech, and an opportunity to demonstrate a last-second act of salvage, a pulling away from disaster, a sudden reversal, that is produced out of nothing but a shift in attitude. The particularities of form may be honored, as in Natasha Trethewey's "Graveyard Blues" (in *Native Guard* [2006]), a eulogy to her mother:

> The road going home was pocked with holes,
> The home-going road's always full of holes;
> Though we slow down, time's wheel still rolls (8)

Or they may be reconfigured, as in Sonia Sanchez's "Blues Haikus" (in *Like the Singing Coming off the Drums* [1998]), as rapid-fire erotics:

> when we say good-bye
> i want yo tongue inside my
> mouth dancing hello.
> you too slippery
> for me. can't hold you long or
> hard. not enough nites. (61)

Marilyn Chin has written "Blues in Yellow" (in *Rhapsody in Plain Yellow* [2002]) that conveys the form's ability to evoke phrases that constellate an ethnic group's cultural memory. The immense obstacles to Chinese immigration, including official barriers that refuse entry, are recorded here, even as Chin herself speaks defiantly as the living proof of her mother's perseverance. (In an earlier segment, we stand inside

"Chin's kitchen" where she now consigns "yellow-bellied sapsuckers" to bake in a pie, and cries with pleasure as she cracks eggs on a griddle: "Run, run, sweet little Puritan, yellow will ooze into white"):

> Do not be afraid to perish, my mother, Buddha's compassion is nigh,
> Do not be afraid to perish, my mother, our boat will sail tonight.
> Your babies will reach the promised land, the stars will be their guide. (137)

There is even a suburbanized version of the form, in Billy Collins's generically titled "The Blues" (in *The Act of Drowning* [1995]), that opens as meta-poetry—"Much of what is said here / must be said twice, / a reminder that no one / takes an immediate interest in the pain of others"—and concludes by describing the blues as a stage on which a culture too admiring of restraint finds in this music a chance to express strong emotion: "you release with one finger / a scream from the throat of your guitar // and turn your head back to the microphone / to let them know / you're a hard-hearted man / but that woman's sure going to make you cry" (91). Collins's self-irony shows the singer performing in public, though not necessarily acting with empathy in private.

It is blues as a form, then, that has most broadly engaged in cultural work over the last decades, a supplement to the esoteric drive of the jazz text. (Rap verse emerges as a common ground for both jazz and the blues, with texts improvised under pressure along with the formal trait of an irregularly arriving rhyme or off-rhyme whose emergent "couplet" punctuate meaning, as Michele D. Gibbs demonstrates in this excerpt from "weather report 2003" [in *Line of Sight*, 2004]: "The U.S. says / diplomacy's irrelevant, / the world's opposition / ignored by Amerika's elephant. // 'Shock and awe' their only strategy / the 'Mother of All Bombs' / their main gift to humanity" [79]). The most undeniable trait of the blues as brought over into poetry is that it aspires to become a self-medicating moment, a way of handling traumatic memories. Ralph Ellison, in a 1945 essay on Richard Wright, called the blues in music "an impulse to keep the painful details and episodes of a brutal experience alive in one's aching consciousness, to finger its jagged grain, and to transcend it, not by the consolation of philosophy but by squeezing from it a near-tragic, near-comic lyricism" (78). When such a fingering of a "jagged grain" is transferred to poetry, it stands out as a lyric that runs counter to the simply lyrical. It is a moment being handed on to others through a medium that engenders a response, a medium that makes a text into a call. This element of exchange identifies the blues poem with what Alison Landsberg has termed "prosthetic memory," the conveyance of "memories of events which one did not live," purveyed through a mass-market commodity (3). As calibrated through poetry, the blues mixes anonymous voices with a particularized voice and moves to engage listeners to sustain a continuum, staging an encounter in which the poem's speaker interacts with voices that the poet's listener takes up. Fundamentally an interpellation, blues poetry operates as an avenue that makes a listener receptive to a transmission of group-experience "memories that no one person can own, that people can share with others and whose meanings can never be completely stabilized" (147). Verbally concretizing a form derived from mass-produced music, blues poetry constructs a temporary space in which lines of alliance and understanding momentarily exist across gender, ethnic, and racial barriers. And in such moments, poetry also recaptures some of its past power and authority, as if the familiarity once emblemized in the sonnet has now been transferred for channeling through the blues.

REFERENCES

Abraham, Gerald. *The Concise Oxford History of Music*. New York: Oxford University Press, 1979.

Altieri, Charles. *The Art of Twentieth Century American Poetry: Modernism and After*. Oxford: Blackwell, 2006.

Baker, Houston A., Jr. *Blues, Ideology and Afro-American Literature: A Vernacular History*. Chicago: University of Chicago Press, 1984.

Barka, Amiri [Leroi Jones]. *Blues People: Negro Music in White America*. 1963. New York: Quill, 1999.

Benet, Stephen Vincent. "Poems of the Month." *The Bookman* 58:3 (November 1923): 317–318.

Bontemps, Arna. "Blues." In *The Princeton Encyclopedia of Poetry and Poetics*, ed. Alex Preminger, Frank J. Warnke, and O. B. Hardison Jr. Princeton: Princeton University Press, 1974. 81.

Brooks, Daphne A. "Mamie Smith's 'Crazy Blues.'" In *A New Literary History of America*, ed. Greil Marcus and Werner Sollors. Cambridge: Harvard University Press, 2009. 545–549.

Brown, Fahamisha Patricia. *Performing the Word: African American Poetry as Vernacular Culture*. New Brunswick: Rutgers University Press, 1999.

Brown, Sterling A. "The Blues as Folk Poetry." 1931. In *The Jazz Cadence of American Culture*, ed. Robert G. O'Meally. New York: Columbia University Press, 1998. 540–551.

———. "Cabaret." 1932. In *Southern Road*. Introd. Sterling Stucky. Boston: Beacon Press, 1974. 115–117.

———. "Stray Notes on Jazz." 1946. In *A Son's Return: Selected Essays of Sterling A. Brown*, ed. Mark A. Sanders. Boston: Northeastern University Press, 1996. 265–274.

Burke, Carolyn. *Becoming Modern: The Life of Mina Loy*. New York: Farrar, Straus & Giroux, 1996.

Chin, Marilyn. "Blues in Yellow." 2002. Reprinted in *Blues Poems*, ed. Kevin Young. New York: Everyman/Knopf, 2003. 136–137.

Chinitz, David. *T. S. Eliot and the Cultural Divide*. Chicago: University of Chicago Press, 2003.

Collins, Billy. "The Blues." In *The Art of Drowning*. Pittsburgh: University of Pittsburgh Press, 1995. 91.

Collins, Theresa M. *Otto Kahn: Art, Money and Modern Time*. Chapel Hill: University of North Carolina Press, 2002.

Crane, Hart. *The Bridge*. 1930. *Hart Crane: Complete Poems and Selected Letters*, ed. Langdon Hammer. New York: Library of America, 2006. 31–76.

———. Letter to Otto J. Kahn. 12 September 1927. In *Hart Crane: Complete Poems and Selected Letters*, ed. Langdon Hammer. New York: Library of America, 2006. 555–556.

Creeley, Robert. "I Knew A Man." In *For Love: Poems 1950–1960*. New York: Scribner, 1962. 38.

Darrell, R. D. "The Music of Henry Gilbert, John Alden Carpenter, John Powell, Adolph Weiss." *Carpenter / Gilbert / Powell / Weiss*. Los Angeles Philharmonic. New York: New World Records. 1977. CD.

Diepeveen, Leonard. *The Difficulties of Modernism*. New York: Routledge, 2003.

Douglass, Frederick. *Narrative of the Life of Frederick Douglass, an American Slave*. 1845. Ed. Houston A. Baker. Harmondsworth: Penguin, 1986.

DuPlessis, Rachel Blau. *Genders, Races and Religious Cultures in Modern American Poetry, 1908–1934*. Cambridge: Cambridge University Press, 2001.

Eliot, T. S. *The Waste Land*. 1922. In *The Annotated Waste Land with Eliot's Contemporary Prose*, ed. Lawrence Rainey. New Haven: Yale University Press, 2005.

Elliott, Ellen Coit. "Prima Donna of the Negro Jazz Orchestra." 1921. In *Anthology of Magazine Verse for 1922*, ed. William Stanley Braithwaite. Cambridge: Small, Mayfeld. 1923. 71–72.

Ellison, Ralph. "Richard Wright's Blues." 1945. In *Shadow and Act*. New York: Random House, 1964. 77–94.

Ferguson, Charles A. "Dialect, Register, and Genre: Working Assumptions of Conventionalization." In *Sociolinguistic Perspectives on Register*, ed. Douglas Biber and Edward Fingena. Oxford: Oxford University Press, 1994. 15–30.

Gibbs, Michele D. *Line of Sight*. Albuquerque: West End Press, 2004.

Gilzinger, Jr. Donald and Cary Nelson. "Aaron Kramer: American Prophet." In *Wicked Times: Selected Poems [of] Aaron Kramer*. Urbana: University of Illinois Press, 2004. xvii–lix.

Harper, Michael. "Dear John, Dear Coltrane." In *Dear John, Dear Coltrane*. Pittsburgh: University of Pittsburgh Press, 1970. 74–75.

Hartman, Charles O. *Jazz Text: Voice and Improvisation in Poetry, Jazz, and Song*. Princeton: Princeton University Press, 1981.

Hass, Robert. "Sterling Brown." 1998. In *Now & Then: The Poet's Choice Columns, 1997–2000*. Berkeley: Counterpoint, 2007. 99–101.

Henderson, Stephen. "Blues." In *The Princeton Encyclopedia of Poetry and Poetic*, ed. T. V. F. Brogan. Princeton: Princeton University Press, 1996. 142–143.

Hoffenstein, Samuel. "The Moist Land." In *Year In, You're Out*. New York: Liveright, 1930. 107–117.

Hughes, Langston. *Ask Your Mama: Twelve Moods for Jazz*. New York: Knopf, 1969.

——. "Bound No'th Blues." In *Fine Clothes to the Jew*. New York: Knopf, 1927. 66.

——. "Dream Boogie." 1948. In *The Collected Poems of Langston Hughes*, ed. Arnold Rampersad. New York: Vintage, 1995. 388.

——. *The First Book of Negroes*. New York: Franklin Watts, 1952.

——. "Hey-Hey Blues." 1939. In *The Collected Poems of Langston Hughes*, ed. Arnold Rampersad. New York: Vintage, 1995. 213.

——. *Montage of a Dream Deferred*. New York: Knopf, 1948.

——. *The Weary Blues*. New York: Knopf, 1926.

——. "[You Ain't Gonna Ride No Chariot Tonight]." 1926. Reprinted in *Nigger Heaven*, 246.

Inada, Lawson Fusao. "Two Variations on a Theme Inspired by Thelonious Monk as Inspired by Mal Waldron." In *Legends from Camp*. Minneapolis: Coffee House Press, 1993. 62–67.

Keller, Lynn. *Forms of Expansion: Recent Long Poems by Women*. Chicago: University of Chicago Press, 1997.

Kenney, William Howland. *Recorded Music in American Life: The Phonograph and Popular Memory, 1890–1945*. New York: Oxford University Press, 1999.

King of Jazz. Dir. John Murray Anderson. Universal. 1930. Film.

Komunyakaa, Yusef. Introduction. In *The Best American Poetry 2003*, ed. Yusef
 Komunyakaa. New York: Scribner, 2003. 11–21.

———. "It's Always Night." 1988. In *Blue Notes: Essays, Interviews and Commentaries*, ed.
 Radiciani Clytus. Ann Arbor: University of Michigan Press, 2000. 22.

———. "[On 'Nude Study']." In *The Best American Poetry 1996*, ed. Adrienne Rich. New
 York: Scribner, 1996. 260–261.

———. *Taboo: The Wishbone Trilogy, Part One.* New York: Farrar, Straus and Giroux, 2004.

———. "Testimony." In *Thieves of Paradise.* Middletown: Wesleyan University Press,
 1998. 89–104.

———. "Trueblood's Blues." 1995. In *Blue Notes: Essays, Interviews and Commentaries*, ed.
 Radiciani Clytus. Ann Arbor: University of Michigan Press, 2000. 48–51.

Kramer, Aaron. "Denmark Vesey." 1952. In *Wicked Times: Selected Poems*, ed. Cary Nelson
 and Daniel Gilzinger, Jr. Urbana: University of Illinois Press, 2004. 44–64.

Landsberg, Alison. *Prosthetic Memory: The Transformation of American Remembrance in
 the Age of Mass Culture.* New York: Columbia University Press, 2004.

La Rocca, D. J. "Tiger Rag: One Step." 1917. In *For Me and My Gal and Other Favorite Song
 Hits, 1915–1917*, ed. David A. Jasen. New York: Dover, 1994. 115–118.

Levine, Lawrence. *Black Culture and Black Consciousness: Afro-American Folk Thought
 from Slavery to Freedom.* New York: Oxford University Press, 2007.

———. "Jazz and American Culture." 1989. In *The Unpredictable Past: Explorations in
 American Cultural History.* Berkeley: University of California Press, 1993. 172–188.

Lindsay, Vachel. "The Jazz Bird." In *Rendezvous with Death: American Poems of the Great
 War*, ed. Mark Van Wienen. Urbana: University of Illinois Press, 2000. 229–230.

Loy, Mina. "The Widow's Jazz." 1927. In *The Lost Lunar Baedeker*, ed. Roger Conover.
 New York: Farrar, Straus and Giroux, 1996. 95–97.

Mackey, Nathaniel. *Discrepant Engagement: Dissonance, Cross-Culturality, and
 Experimental Writing.* Cambridge: Cambridge University Press, 1993.

Matthews, William. "Mingus at the Half Note." In *Time & Money.* Boston: Houghton
 Mifflin, 1995. 18.

Moore, Thomas. "To Thomas Hume, Esq., M.D." www.readbookonline.net/
 readOnLine/32644. June 12, 2010.

Nelson, Cary. "Michael S. Harper." In *Anthology of Modern American Poetry.* New York:
 Oxford University Press, 2000. 1043.

———. *Repression and Recovery: Modern American Poetry and the Politics of Cultural
 Memory, 1910–1945.* Madison: University of Wisconsin Press, 1989.

Newcomb, John Timberman. *Would Poetry Disappear? American Verse and the Crisis of
 Modernity.* Columbus: Ohio State University Press, 2004.

Niles, Abbe. "Sad Horns." In *The Blues: An Anthology*, ed. W. C. Handy. 1926. Bedford,
 MA: Applewood, n.d. 1–40.

North, Michael. *The Dialect of Modernism: Race, Language and Twentieth-Century
 Literature.* New York: Oxford University Press, 1994.

Ogren, Kathy J. *The Jazz Revolution: Twenties America and the Making of Jazz.* New York:
 Oxford University Press, 1989.

Osgood, Henry O. *So This Is Jazz.* 1926. New York: Da Capo, 1978.

Patterson, Anita Hays. "Jazz, Realism, and the Modern Lyric: The Poetry of Langston
 Hughes." *Modern Language Quarterly* 61.4 (2000): 651–682.

Patterson, Raymond R. "Blues." In *An Exaltation of Forms: Contemporary Poets Celebrate
 the Diversity of Their Art*, ed. Annie Finch and Kathrine Varnes. Ann Arbor: University
 of Michigan Press, 2002. 188–197.

Perloff, Marjorie. *Poetry On and Off the Page: Essays on Emergent Occasions*. Evanston, IL: Northwestern University Press, 1998.

Reyes, Adelaida. *Music in America: Experiencing Music, Expressing Culture*. New York: Oxford University Press, 2005.

A Rhapsody in Black and Blue. Dir. Aubrey Scotts. Perf. Louis Armstrong. Paramount, 1932. Film.

Rogin, Michael. *Blackface, White Noise: Jewish Immigrants in the Hollywood Melting Pot*. Berkeley: University of California Press, 1996.

Sanchez, Sonia. "Blues Haiku." 1998. Reprinted in *Blues Poems*, ed. Kevin Young. New York: Everyman/Knopf, 2003. 111.

Sandburg, Carl. "Jazz Fantasia." 1920. In *Harvest Poems: 1910–1960*. New York: Harcourt, Brace & World, 1960. 59.

Smethurst, James Edward. *The New Red Negro: The Literary Left and African-American Poetry, 1930–1946*. New York: Oxford University Press, 1999.

Schmidt, Michael. *Lives of the Poets*. London: Weidenfeld & Nicolson, 1998.

Scott, James C. *Domination and the Arts of Resistance: Hidden Transcripts*. New Haven: Yale University Press, 1990.

Scott, Jonathan. *Socialist Joy in the Writing of Langston Hughes*. Columbia: University of Missouri Press, 2006.

Starr, Larry, and Christopher Waterman. *American Popular Music: From Minstrelsy to MTV*. New York: Oxford University Press, 2003.

Stevens, Wallace. "A High-Toned Old Christian Woman." 1923. In *Collected Poems of Wallace Stevens*. New York: Knopf, 1955. 59.

Thurston, Michael. *Making Something Happen: American Political Poetry Between the World Wars*. Chapel Hill: University of North Carolina Press, 2001.

Tolson, Melvin B. *Libretto for the Republic of Liberia*. 1953. In *Anthology of Modern American Poetry*, ed. Cary Nelson. New York: Oxford University Press, 2000. 418–470.

Tretheway, Natasha. "Graveyard Blues." In *Native Guard*. Boston: Houghton Mifflin, 2006. 8.

Van Der Merwe, Peter. *Origins of the Popular Style: The Antecedents of Twentieth-Century Popular Music*. 1989. Oxford: Oxford University Press, 2002.

Van Vechten, Carl. "The Black Blues." 1925. Reprinted in *Vanity Fair: A Cavalcade of the 1920s and 1930s*, ed. Cleveland Amory and Federic Bradlee. New York: Viking, 1960. 95–96.

———. *Nigger Heaven*. 1926. Introd. Kathleen Pfeiffer. Urbana: University of Illinois Press, 2000.

Wagner, Bryan. *Disturbing the Peace: Black Culture and the Police Power after Slavery*. Cambridge: Harvard University Press, 2010.

Warner, Michael. "Styles of Intellectual Publics." In *Just Being Difficult? Academic Writing in the Public Arena*, ed. Jonathan Culler and Kevin Lamb. Stanford: Stanford University Press, 2003. 106–128.

West, James L. III. "Illustrations." In *Trimalchio: An Early Version of "The Great Gatsby" By F. Scott Fitzgerald*. Cambridge: Cambridge University Press, 2000.

Williams, William Carlos. *Kora in Hell: Improvisations*. 1920. In *Imaginations*. New York: New Directions, 1970. 3–82. Print.

———. "XVII: *Spring and All*." 1923. In *Imaginations*. New York: New Directions, 1970. 130–131.

Young, Kevin. "Foreword." In *Jazz Poems*. New York: Everyman/Knopf, 2006. 11–18.

———. "Lester Yellow." In *To Repel Ghosts: Five Sides in B Minor [Sung by the Author]*. Cambridge: Zoland, 2001. 159.

CHAPTER 10

OUT WITH THE CROWD: MODERN AMERICAN POETS SPEAKING TO MASS CULTURE

JOHN TIMBERMAN NEWCOMB

THE discourse we call modern American poetry was shaped from its very beginnings by the world of modern mass culture. In the three decades after the Civil War, the accelerating mechanization of printing technologies, coupled with new economies of scale in manufacturing and distribution, made possible the marketing of print and visual culture on an unprecedented scale, leading to the first popular song to sell a million copies ("After the Ball" in 1893), the first magazine to garner a million subscribers (*The Ladies' Home Journal* in 1903), and a turn-of-the-century fiction "craze" featuring the first group of novels to sell a million copies (Benton, 152–155; Tebbel and Zuckerman, 73). To the captains of these new mass-culture industries, literary poetry, with its emphasis on nuance and contemplation, was merely a use-less obstacle to the relentless production and consumption of commodity-texts.[1] In response, the belletristic genteel elite who presided over the nation's literary institu-tions circled their wagons around the genre they saw as most opposed and most vulnerable to the erosion of taste augured by the rise of mass-marketed print, treat-ing poetry as a reliquary of tradition rather than a vigorous contemporary art form (Newcomb, *Would Poetry Disappear?* 49–54). By 1900 the impasse between these two positions had created a serious crisis of value in which many foresaw literary poetry becoming a rank anachronism in the new century, fit only for the longueurs of the salon or the moldering crannies of the gentleman's library.

Those who surveyed the state of American poetry in 1900 could readily imagine this outcome because they encountered so much verse that—at least from the perspective of the genteel elite—seemed trivial or cheapened. Compared to our own time, the mass-literate world of a century ago was filled with verse: in daily newspapers, after-dinner speeches and other ceremonial occasions, school yearbooks and recitation classrooms, popular magazines of amusement and uplift, specialized magazines for hobbyists and fans, the "poem-cards" for every occasion that Cary Nelson is exhaustively recovering, and in advertisements for everything from baked beans to eternal salvation. In other words, literary poetry seemed to be disappearing not *from* the face of the earth so much as *into* a culture industry that used verse as merely as a tool in its voracious production of disposable commodity-texts.

The guardians of turn-of-the-century academic-genteel culture, our distant disciplinary predecessors, were tortured by this anxiety that a once-venerated form of high art was being subsumed into a mass culture that "sickens the soul" by "vulgarizing . . . everything in life and letters and politics and religion" (Gilder, 294). Such disdainful formulations were participating in a widespread style of modern nostalgia that expresses its allegiance to embattled high art by condemning mass culture "either as a symptom or a cause of social decay," in Patrick Brantlinger's phrase (17). Ever since then, the disciplinary formation of modern American poetry has been shaped by anxious attempts to preserve poetry as a prestigious form of high art not only by demonizing the commodity-texts of mass culture, but also by denigrating any poetry that posits a less antithetical and more generative relationship between the two. A nearly unbroken century of literary-critical tradition has presumed this relationship to be one of absolute opposition in which true poetry must be protected from the despoiling tastes of the masses lest they "drag everything down to their level, perhaps smashing the very machinery of civilization in the process" (Brantlinger, 32).

The hand-wringing of the turn-of-the-century belletristic elite soon gave way to a potent high modernist tradition of cultural theory, initiated by the early literary essays of T. S. Eliot and ramified into the New Critical hegemony that would determine the interpretive horizons, instructional methods, and canonical structure of modern American poetry studies at least through the 1950s.[2] The evaluative premises of New Criticism depended on a rigid division between genuine poetry and the meretricious products of mass culture, including any verse seeking a wider audience, which led either to didacticism or to outright propaganda. Thus in the seminal 1938 essay "Tension in Poetry," Allen Tate posited the "fallacy of communication" as a defining fault of much twentieth-century verse, arguing that because "communication" has "tainted" all forms of "public speech" in the twentieth century, poems written with the goal of communicating to a reader became just another form of "mass language" seeking to sway or sell, lacking artistic integrity (58, 57). The following year, in the essay "The Present State of Poetry in the United States," Robert Penn Warren elaborated this proposition into a devastating dismissal of the socially engaged American verse of the 1930s, in which the communicative goals of writers such as Kenneth Fearing and Muriel Rukeyser had produced "little more than a kind of journalism," fatally flawed by being "crude in technique and unconcerned with making nice poetic discriminations" (386).

The paranoid polarities behind such formulations as the "fallacy of communication" bridged vast geographical, demographic, and ideological divisions in twentieth-century literary-critical discourse. Indeed, the necessity of preserving the great divide between literary poetry and mass culture seems the one presumption that all factions of high-modern cultural theory could agree on, uniting conservatives such as Eliot and Tate with the young anti-Stalinist leftists who from the mid-1930s carried on a vigorous critique of mass culture in their journals of opinion *The Partisan Review* and later *Politics*. As Patrick Brantlinger and Paul Gorman show, the works of such "New York intellectuals" as Dwight MacDonald and Clement Greenberg exhibit an often savage contempt for the modern public's voracious demand for mass culture, which they saw as contributing to the totalitarian drift of twentieth-century history.[3]

These homegrown condemnations of mass culture in the defense of art—particularly on behalf of "difficult" modernist texts—dominated the postwar academy as modern American poetry was being consolidated as a disciplinary object. In the later 1950s, when younger American literary scholars began to react against New Criticism by incorporating European cultural theory into their work, they would have seen nothing in the intellectual landscape, no usable past or present, for elaborating a more sympathetic relationship between high art and mass culture.[4] The situation was not improved by the phenomenological criticism of the 1960s and the American form of deconstruction of the 1970s, which by focusing on a vanishingly small number of ultra-canonical authors and *über*-texts, reinforced longstanding disciplinary barriers between modern American poetry and mass culture.

Even now, after two decades of hearing that "the canon" is expanding or has expanded, and with articles on Burma-Shave verse now finding their way into *PMLA*, these disciplinary barriers remain largely in place. Although unabashed defenses of the intrinsic distinction between high art and mass culture may be, as Chinitz suggests (4), relegated to the peevish pages of the *New Criterion* and other bastions of the cultural right, we would be wrong to assume that this binary no longer holds any sway upon modern poetry studies. It lingers in entrenched institutional practices and pressures, in the choices routinely made and not made by young scholars, dissertation advisers, job-search and tenure committees, journal editors, and academic publishers. Meanwhile, as Joseph Harrington puts it, "If new writers eke their way into the penumbra of the modern poetry canon, it is only when they can be considered modern*ist* writers" (2). The fine revisionist accounts of modern American poetry that have extended the ground broken by Cary Nelson's *Repression and Recovery* (1989) are politely received, but then it's back to business as usual, "'mostly talking about the same half-dozen figures as we have for the last 35 years'" (Harrington, 2–3).

To challenge these tenacious old conceptual polarities means actually expanding the canon of "modern American poets" we take seriously, rather than applying our new openness to mass culture primarily to the recuperation of the usual canonical suspects. The danger of this latter approach is that such impressively executed projects as David Chinitz's book on Eliot, Michael Coyle's work on Pound and "popular genres," or the spate of recent scholarship on H.D. and cinema, will be taken as sufficient rethinking of the relations between modern poetry and mass culture, leaving existing canonical structures and other forms of institutional prestige untouched or even reinforced. We need not only to surround the old titans with fresh contexts, but also to situate a much wider variety of poets into those contexts. This involves paying sustained attention to writers and genres overlooked or dismissed by high-formalist critical traditions, as Rita Barnard has done with Kenneth Fearing, Mark Van Wienen with American Great War verse, Nelson and Jefferson Hendricks with Edwin Rolfe, Harrington with Arturo Giovannitti and Anna Louise Strong, various scholars including Tim Dayton and John Lowney with Muriel Rukeyser, and as my forthcoming book *How Did Poetry Survive? The Making of Modern American Verse* seeks to do with Carl Sandburg and a host of others. The success of this kind of recovery work requires that we stop condescending to such poets as curiosities or "interesting" failures, and instead treat them as potentially formative to our evolving sense of what modern American poetry was, or what it might become in a more genuinely historicized discipline.[5]

Above all, we need more work that refutes the domineering disciplinary assumption that modern American poetry was or should be defined by its antagonism to mass culture. The remainder of this chapter seeks to show that American poets writing between 1910 and 1945 were vastly more responsive to the forms and meanings of mass culture than mainstream critical traditions have ever admitted. Most poets of the period avoid the top-down critiques of MacDonald or Adorno, which assume the categorical inferiority of the commodity-text to the artistic object. Instead they seek not merely to condemn mass culture as debased or retarded, but to find something in it worth admiring, challenging, or adapting.

My analysis considers "mass culture" in two senses: first as collective spectacle or performance experienced in spaces of commodified amusement, then as semiotic and textual phenomena, advertisements above all, that interpellate modern subjects for the ideological project of corporate capitalism. Though William Carlos Williams and Kenneth Fearing loom largest, I have opted to survey work by a variety of poets in order to show that this engagement with mass culture was no tangent limited to the work of a few oddballs or specialists but was a pervasive dimension of American poetry during these decades. We can frame the entire careers of several significant poets—not only Williams and Fearing but Carl Sandburg, Vachel Lindsay, Langston Hughes, and Muriel Rukeyser—as attempts to articulate a productive relationship with the forms and meanings of modern mass culture. The same could be said for significant parts of other careers, including those of Eliot, Pound, Edna St. Vincent Millay, and Archibald MacLeish, whose turns toward and away from radio at particular historical and personal junctures reveal the inescapable role mass culture played in their poetics. Still others, particularly Lindsay, Sandburg, Millay, and Robert Frost, created iconic public personae that challenged the boundaries between literary art and mass culture.

OUT WITH THE CROWD

A crucial issue in many American mass-culture poems of these decades is how the crowd of spectators at the movie or ballgame might resemble and differ from the mobs and mass-men that haunt pessimistic theorists of modernity from Nietzsche and Gustav Le Bon to Ortega y Gasset and Eliot. "The crowd" was a central problem of cultural sociology after 1789, but around 1900 emphasis shifted from the menace posed by rampaging illiterate *sans-culottes* to the "dehumanized, conformist, insensate mass" consuming prepackaged cultural commodities (Chinitz, 100). This *lumpenbourgeoisie*, aesthetically empty and spiritually dispossessed, became the robotic figures populating Eliot's infernal modern cityscapes in *The Waste Land*, and later the main objects of contempt in the postwar writings of MacDonald, Greenberg, and the Frankfurt theorists (Gorman, 152–155).

Eliot's poetic contemporaries seldom treat the crowds consuming mass culture as wholly beneficent, but neither are they merely passive herds or empty vessels waiting to be filled by the toxic mass-cult text, performance, or sporting contest. Two works from the early years of the American New Verse movement—John Gould Fletcher's "In the Theatre" (*Some Imagist Poems, 1916*), and Vachel Lindsay's "Blanche Sweet—Moving-Picture Actress" (*The Little Review*, 1914)—can be taken as initial approaches to representing the mass-culture crowd in modern poetry. Fletcher portrays the vaudeville or music-hall audience as an anonymous "multitude / Assembled in the darkness" (43), isolated from one another despite their physical proximity. But he pointedly does not dehumanize them into a mob, a blind or unfeeling mass force antithetical to poet and reader. They remain simply "These who every day perform / The unique tragi-comedy of birth and death": members of a human collectivity, each assumed to possess a life story and a distinctive combination of desires and fears. As the "irresistible weight of their thoughts" presses toward the stage, the poet identifies them with the "great broad shaft of calcium light" that "cleaves . . . the darkness" to reveal "A tiny spot which is the red nose of a comedian." As the "goal" of their gaze, this bibulous beacon clearly registers as absurd relative to the intensity of their yearning, suggesting Fletcher's skepticism toward the actual content of much mass-spectatorial experience. But by identifying the crowd's eyes "which people the darkness" with the technological means of delivering the performance, the calcium "spotlight," he suggests that their gaze and their desire drive the event, that they are at least partially the agents of their own culture rather than its passive dupes.

Lindsay, whose fascination with cinema led to one of the first sustained attempts to theorize the new technology as a distinct art form (*The Art of the Moving Picture*, 1916), begins his paean to a goddess of the silent screen by emphasizing the discomfort involved in the mass-spectatorial experience: the "odorous aisle" viewers must traverse and the din of "Rag-time ballads vile" they must endure ("Blanche Sweet," 4). Yet far from being numb or oblivious to these conditions, as a Frankfurt theoretician or New York intellectual might see them, these spectators are hyperconscious of the surrounding "squalor," but "forgive" it because of the intensity of their spectatorial desire and the promise of its fulfillment by Blanche Sweet. Cinema for Lindsay is thus not an anaesthetizing experience for the modern subject, but a heightening of awareness in which inchoate and often unspeakable yearnings—for self-knowledge, for validation among one's fellows, for a refreshed capacity to feel wonder—are gathered into collective form and conveyed from audience to screen, where they become embodied by the iconic performer:

> Mid the restless actors
> She is rich and slow,
> She will stand like marble,
> She will pause and glow,
> Though the film is twitching
> Keep a peaceful reign,
> Ruler of her passion,
> Ruler of our pain. (5)

Like Fletcher, Lindsay associates the yearning subjectivity of the spectators with the action ("twitching") of the technological apparatus. Yet this nervousness derives not from the cinemagoing experience but from the conditions of modern life outside the movie house, and it is calmed by the most distinctive quality of Sweet's physiognomy and gesture: a mesmerizing stillness in the midst of a convulsively moving environment. As her projection of restraint and self-possession makes her the "Ruler of our pain," capable of "Filling oafs with wisdom, / Saving souls with smiles," Lindsay proposes mass-spectatorial experience as capable of uplifting modern subjectivity, creating "Mobs of us made noble / By her strong desire." This unusual emphasis not only on the audience's desire but on the desire projected by Sweet's screen presence suggests a reciprocal dynamic in which she acts as a mirror that absorbs these yearnings and conveys them dynamically back, making spectatorial subjects feel, at least for these moments, recognized and valued by the object of their own desire.

The often racialized character of mass-culture spectatorship is explored by two major American poems of the 1920s, Langston Hughes's "The Weary Blues" (*Opportunity*, 1925) and Sterling A. Brown's "Cabaret" (probably written in 1927, published in *Southern Road* in 1932). Both emphasize tensions between two ways of reading African American musical performance: as distinctive vernacular forms expressive of the desires and fears of a marginalized social group, and as commodities homogenized and mass-marketed by white-owned corporations to consumers (implicitly both white and black) who seek the exotic, authentic, or primitive. Not surprisingly, given its title, "The Weary Blues" aspires to the complex tonal range inhabited by blues music, balancing melancholy and self-affirmation. This complexity is established by the opening lines, which emphasize unstable interchange between two African American voices with different relations to the blues:

> Droning a drowsy syncopated tune,
> Rocking back and forth to a mellow croon,
> I heard a Negro play.
> Down on Lenox Avenue the other night.
> By the pale dull pallor of an old gas light
> He did a lazy sway. . . .
> He did a lazy sway. . . .
> To the tune o' those Weary Blues. (143)

The syncopation of the tune, where the song's melody or the singer's inflections play against the rhythmic pulse, asserts an ironic distance between two elements, which is redoubled by the speaker's references (here and later) to hearing "a Negro" playing, as if he were not one himself. And yet in other respects Hughes identifies the two figures, grammatically by means of the dangling participles that associate the speaker with the singer's actions of "droning" and "rocking," and emotionally by the listener's profound response to the man's performance. This tension between identification and differentiation suggests that the speaker does see himself as a "Negro," but not exactly as the same kind as the singer. In diction, syntax, and grammar, he speaks in a self-consciously poetic voice to which typical blues dialect ("I's gwine to quit ma frownin' / And put ma troubles on the shelf") may well be spiritually akin but is at least to some degree culturally alien. Though he aspires to incorporate the rhythms and the soul of the blues into his own speech, the speaker never pretends to *become* the blues singer, which Hughes may have felt would unjustly appropriate a certain kind of life experience that some African Americans possessed firsthand but others didn't. Instead he creates a dialectical interplay of distinction and convergence between the two expressive figures, speaker and singer, poet and bluesman, which continues throughout the poem. Bluesy interjections ("O Blues," "Sweet Blues") which sound like part of the song but are identified with the speaker's poetic voice, suggest that hearing the performance has enriched his expressive vocabulary. In turn, as the final lines narrate the singer's postperformance state of mind in the voice of the speaker, they suggest that expressive and psychological authenticity are not limited to the vernacular. As the Weary Blues "echoes" through the singer's sleep and equally through the speaker's cadences, Hughes affirms both voices as distinct aspects of African American life, each deserving equal time and respect, each benefiting from the other.

If "The Weary Blues" offers a harmonious echoing between two distinct but mutually enriching African American voices, Brown's jazz study "Cabaret," subtitled "1927, Black & Tan Chicago," is built from the cacophonous interplay among five clashing voices, all identifiably African American but conveying drastically different attitudes toward the production and consumption of black popular music. The poem's tone of wrenching dissonance and its imagery of wrecked lives reflect Brown's response to the catastrophic Mississippi Delta flooding of April 1927 that wiped out small African American communities from Arkansas to Louisiana, dispossessing millions of people, many of whom would have had relatives in Chicago fearful of their safety. Despite its well-warranted skepticism toward the motives of the white businessmen and urbanites who patronize the cabaret, the poem cannot be reduced to a simplistic struggle between authentic *popular culture* and compromised *mass culture*. In other words, no one voice owns the whole truth or tells the full story. Brown uses graphic formats in various combinations—indentation, italics, parentheses—to play the five voices against one another. The first is a highly educated, bitter voice offering a panoramic social critique of the commodification of black artistry for the amusement of whites. This voice emphasizes the cynical fakery perpetrated by African Americans—obsequious waiters, dancers scantily clad to evoke sexy plantation wenches, even the musicians themselves—who purvey their talents to the "Hebrew and Anglo-Saxon" "overlords" (111). The second voice (indented italics), which can perhaps be understood as the nightmarish creation of its more analytical predecessor, is the aural embodiment of cynicism and race treachery: a barker flattering the monied consumers and goading the performers to "*show your paces to the gentlemen. / A prime filly, seh. / What am I offered, gentlemen, gentlemen . . .*" (112; ellipsis in poem). Together these two constitute a ferocious—if perhaps heavy-handed—critique of African Americans' apparent eagerness to sell their art to white-controlled capital.

But the next voice (indented unitalicized text) complicates this rather superior stance by adding to the aural mix the tonalities of unsophisticated Delta blacks suddenly wrenched by the floods from all they had known (many of whom made their way to Chicago). This voice speaks or sings of the loss of its Delta home in earnest, nostalgic cadences evoking black religious music ("There's peace and happiness there / I declare"), but it also resonates with the prepackaged emotions of mass-marketed popular songs ("Still it's my home, sweet home") and even the racial stereotypes endemic to minstrel song: "I've got my toes turned Dixie ways / Round that Delta let me laze" (112–113). Next we are presented with third-person quasi-objective narration (unindented italics in parentheses) of the misery inflicted upon the dispossessed by the chaos of the flooding and the opportunism of those in authority: "*(In Arkansas, / Poor half-naked fools, tagged with identification numbers, / Worn out upon the levees, / Are carted back to serfdom / They had never left before / And may never leave again)*" (112). The fifth element, which appears only twice (also in indented unitalicized type) but claims the poem's last word, is the voice of the jazz itself, which consists of rhythmically accented syllables: "bee-dap-ee-DOOP, dee-ba-dee-BOOP" (112).

The poet's decision to give the music itself the final say provides a modicum of hope in a profoundly bitter work. Brown's rejection of words for sheer sound and rhythm may suggest his sense that all language, even the well-meaning analytical critique of the first voice that dominates the poem's first third but recedes thereafter, may be fatally compromised by cynicism, commodification, or racial despair. Those other voices must be heard because they represent crucial aspects of the African American response to the events of 1927. But none of them offers any sort of way forward, which only the music in its vigor and momentum seems to provide—despite its continuing susceptibility to co-optation.

The conventional trope of "bread and circuses" associates mass culture not only with scripted performance texts, such as movies and vaudeville, but also with sporting contests of unpredictable outcome. The growth of national sports industries in the decades after the Civil War—major league baseball first, followed by professional boxing and big-time college football—was central to the turn-of-the-century sense that forms of mass culture were coming to dominate American life. Drawing upon such elements of narrative as rising action, climax, falling action, and denouement, sporting contests enact scenarios of predation and escape, annihilation and conquest that create pleasurable collective suspense framed around demographic or regional affiliations. Rooting for the home team or hometown favorite in a crowd is perhaps one of the most characteristic collective experiences of modern life, and it carries many potential meanings, some deeply personal, others potently political. Poems by Louis Untermeyer and William Carlos Williams use the sports crowd to explore the complex and often obfuscated relations between three intersecting social entities: the individual subject, the collective populace, and the impersonal authority of the state. The subtitle of Untermeyer's sonnet "The Score Board: Summer-1917" (published in *Roast Leviathan*, 1923), dates the poem to one of the New York Giants' pennant-winning seasons, but more importantly it places the mass-culture spectacle into a highly charged sociopolitical context: the first months after the American entry into the Great War in April 1917, during which growing hysteria led to anti-German vigilante violence and widespread governmental persecution of political dissenters, including the suppression of such anticapitalist publications as *The Masses* (with which the poet had been closely affiliated since its beginnings in 1911), and eventually the indictment of its editors for sedition.[6] Yet perhaps surprisingly, the poem portrays the mass consumption of sports not as the whipping up of bellicose nationalism but as a form of resistance to the oppressive forces of the state. As the home team rallies, the cheering of its fans renders them all "deaf to war's vain trumpeting": although "The brassy summons of a bugle floats / Through the wide square," "The crack of ash is all that each one hears" (*Roast Leviathan*, 105).

In this vein, the title signals a reliance on objects and forms—including the highly conventionalized but endlessly varying forms of baseball, to which fans are so devoted—as symbols of a truth that cannot be warped by the ideological manipulations symbolized by bugle and drum. Regardless of the home team's ultimate fortunes, the scoreboard will publicize the results of the game accurately, providing an antidote to the fanatical partisanship and strategies of propaganda that were then threatening to invade every aspect of national life. The objectivity of the scoreboard and the anonymity of the crowd are contrasted to the only figure who stands out: a "blind beggar" whose hands "drum" on his cup, an odd detail that seems to associate individuation with acquiescence to the forces of militarism. At this menacing historical moment of 1917, it seems, anonymity functions not as a sign of the modern subject's anomic dispossession, but as a form of personal and political liberty in which all can root and speak as they wish, without fear that the state will target and conscript them for its own agenda.

Writing some five years later in an interval of relative peace, William Carlos Williams in "At the Ball Game" (*Spring and All*, 1923) reopened the elusive question that Untermeyer's urgent antiwar goals had led him to sidestep: are competitive sports, especially when experienced in a context of mass spectatorship, a safety valve displacing or defusing human impulses to aggression, or are they a site for marshalling those impulses toward some state-dictated or mob-crazed purpose? Without question, Williams's ballgame crowd carries the possibility of menace, but its meaning can never be reduced to menace alone. At the moment of the poem's narration, the crowd's attention takes the form of pure delight at the formal "beauty" of the game, the "exciting detail / of the chase / and the escape, the error / the flash of genius" (*Collected Poems*, 1:233). But this same tendency to be "moved uniformly" also means the crowd can become a "deadly, terrifying" force if its attention shifts to social outsiders who don't wear the same uniform, such as "The flashy female with her mother" or "The Jew," who will "get it." With that potently ambiguous colloquialism "get it," which hints at both ideological pressure and physical violence, Williams evokes the dangers of a modern crowd not fully aware of its own power, whose collective action is performed "without thought," making it protean and unpredictable. Yet his portrayal never becomes a jeremiad in the style of MacDonald or Adorno. The crowd's full meaning, like the fate of the flashy female and the Jew, remains intractably ambiguous: the "power of their faces," producing both "venom" and "beauty" and enabling oppression ("the Inquisition") and liberation ("the Revolution"), must be simultaneously "warned against, / Saluted and defied" (1:233–234).

No American poet of these decades said more about mass culture than Kenneth Fearing, whose entire corpus is built from its materials: the visual syntax of Hollywood movies, the prepackaged slang of radio speech, and above all the prolific images and texts advertising the commodities that surround the twentieth-century subject. In the opening lines of the early "St. Agnes' Eve" (first published in *New Masses*, 1926), Fearing announces the direct influence of mass culture—here, Hollywood gangster film—upon his narrative, descriptive, and characterological choices:

> The settings include a fly-specked Monday evening,
> A cigar store with stagnant windows,
> Two crooked streets;
> The characters: six policemen and Louie Glatz.
>
> (*Complete Poems*, 31)[7]

The poem then explodes into a hell-bent chase sequence punctuated by cartoonish noises ("Rat-a-tat" and "blam-blam-blam"), before ending with its most explicit evocation of cinematic convention yet: "Close-up of Dolan's widow. Of Louie's mother. / Picture of the fly-specked Monday evening, and fade out slow" (*Complete Poems*, 32–33). The title's inescapable evocation of Keats is key to Fearing's relationship to mass culture. What has the deathless story of Madeline and Porphyro to do with the sordid death of a present-day thug and murderer? A straight "bread-and-circuses" reading would presumably view this intertextual irony as evidence of the deterioration of aesthetic or spiritual experience since Keats's day, either attempting to enlist Fearing into its antimodern project, or condescending to him as a victim of this debased modernity. But given how willingly his precise revision of Keats's title embraces modern journalistic efficiency (including the increased awkwardness that results), I would argue that the referentiality of the title is Fearing's way of asserting that, as material for poetry, Louie's story is just as viable as any high-toned tale of yore, or even that in a century of subways and "gats," it may be the only sort of story that makes sense to tell. "St. Agnes' Eve" was not among the earliest poems Fearing preserved, yet he repeatedly placed it at the head of later collections—his first volume, *Angel Arms* (1929); *Collected Poems* (1940); and *New and Selected Poems* (1956)— suggesting its function as a manifesto for his distinctive poetics of mass culture.

Many of Fearing's best-known poems, including "Dirge" and "Devil's Dream," mount withering satirical critiques of the depthless eternal present, relentless optimism, and formula-bound structures that proliferate in American mass culture. He is particularly unsparing in showing how these qualities refuse to remain confined within individual texts, but seek to colonize every aspect of modern subjectivity, as in "Yes, the Agency Can Handle That" (*The New Yorker*, 1939), which obsessively reiterates the central message of mass culture before poignantly turning it inside out in the final line:

> And there is no mortal ill that cannot be cured by a little money, or lots
>   of love, or by a friendly smile; no.
> And few human hopes go unrealized; no.
> And the rain does not fall ever, anywhere, fall upon corroded monuments
>   of the forgotten dead.
>
> (*Complete Poems*, 183)

And yet despite the evident power of such critiques, I cannot fully agree with Rita Barnard's characterization of Fearing's poetic project as "singularly negative" (108). This view is perhaps an understandable defense against entrenched presumptions of his ostensibly minor status, but it has the regrettable effect of reducing his complex response to mass culture toward orthodox high modernist disdain. I see his relationship to the landscape of mass culture as much richer than those of, say, Eliot and Pound, who always seem to be reminding us that they are visiting from a radically distinct world of high art—in other words, slumming. In contrast, Fearing wholeheartedly inhabits that landscape even as he deplores much of what he sees there. The forms and language of mass culture not only supply him with a vocabulary, a reservoir of rhythmic effects, and a range of themes; they inform his entire understanding of the role of poetry in twentieth-century modernity. On the jacket to his *Collected Poems* (1940), Fearing wrote that "my poetry, as well as anything else I write, . . . must be exciting; otherwise it is valueless." Such a refusal of any categorical distinction between poetry and the other genres he worked in—particularly the noirish crime fiction he would turn toward in the next few years—poses a radical alternative to the exceptionalist assumptions dominating literary-critical discourse, which typically seek to elevate poetry above all other linguistic modes. And so does his further assertion that "everything in this volume has been written with the intention that its meaning should disclose itself at ordinary reading tempo," which frankly challenges Tate's condemnation of "communication" in poetry, and embraces the very qualities that dominant disciplinary norms since the New Critics have denigrated: frank communicativeness, immediate consumability, wide appeal.[8]

I'll go further and propose that Fearing's work is not just dutifully informed by the political necessity of critiquing mass culture but is positively inspired by its appealing qualities: vigor, linguistic inventiveness, ready humor, directness of appeal. The accelerated galloping rhythms and comic phraseology of his poems certainly evoke the absurdity of living in a regime of commodified objects and experience, but they often achieve a laugh-out-loud exuberance that is drastically unlike the doleful seriousness of an Eliot or Tate:

> There is a jungle, there is a jungle, there is a vast, vivid, wild, wild,
>   marvelous, marvelous, marvelous jungle,
> Open to the public during business hours,
> A jungle not very far from an Automat, between a hat store there,
>   and a radio shop. . . .
>
> There, there, whether it rains, or it snows, or it shines,
> Under the hot, blazing, cloudless, tropical neon skies that the
>   management always arranges there,
> Rows and rows of marching ducks, dozens and dozens and dozens of
>   ducks, move steadily along on smoothly-oiled ballbearing feet,
> Ducks as big as telephone books, slow and fearless and out of this
>   world. . . .
>
> And there it is that all the big game hunters go, there the traders and
>   the explorers come,
> Leanfaced men with windswept eyes who arrive by streetcar, auto or
>   subway, taxi or on foot, streetcar or bus,
> And they nod, and they say, and they need no more:
> "There . . . there . . . [poem's ellipses]
> There they come, and there they go" . . .
>
> There, in the only jungle in the whole wide world where ducks are
>   waiting for streetcars,
> And hunters can be psychoanalyzed, while they smoke and wait for
>   ducks.
>
>   ("Travelogue in a Shooting-Gallery," *New Yorker*, 1943; *Complete*
>   *Poems*, 224–225)

Whether parodying its forms or psychoanalyzing its perplexed consumers, Fearing in poem after poem offers spirited subversion of the ideological verities of mass-marketed consumer spectacle. Another of his manifesto poems, "Continuous Performance," which he placed at the head of *Afternoon of a Pawnbroker* (1943), allegorizes modern life by narrating a typical Hollywood melodrama as experienced by a viewer who enters near the end and stays to watch the beginning:

> The place seems strange, more strange than ever, and the times are still
>   more out of joint;
> Perhaps there has been some slight mistake?
> It is like arriving at the movies late, as usual, just as the story ends.
> There is a carnival on the screen. It is a village in springtime, that much
>   is clear. But why has the heroine suddenly slapped his face? And what
>   does it mean, the sequence with the limousine and the packed valise?
>   Very strange.
> Then love wins. Fine. And it is the end. O.K.
> But how do we reach that carnival again? And when will that springtime
>   we saw return once more? How, and when?
>
> (*Complete Poems*, 211)

Fittingly the poem's title is an advertisement, the phrase often seen on marquees to announce the exhibition policies of most American vaudeville and movie theaters before 1960, in which the day's program was looped without breaks, and patrons were invited to enter and leave at any point lest the house lose a sale. Obviously these policies were driven by economic imperatives, yet they make possible the deconstruction of Hollywood's carefully homogenized idealist formulas, allowing consumers to make any film into an estranging "modernist" experience in which settings are unstable, narrative progress nonsensical, symbolism opaque, and motivations obscure. Though Fearing's cynical speaker claims that "this is fixed, believe me, fixed," the result is to perceive that the formulas of Hollywood, which swaddle themselves in cloaks of inexorability and common sense, can instead be used to imagine surreal worlds in which "fate emerges from new and always more fantastic fate" without ever achieving satisfying coherence or closure (*Complete Poems* 211–212).

Fearing achieves a similar effect in "Cracked Record Blues" (*New Yorker*, 1942), in which ideologized banalities ("the mind is a common sense affair filled with common sense answers to common sense facts") are subjected to convulsive repetitions that reveal them as absurd:

> It can add up, can add up, can add up, can add up earthquakes and
>   subtract them from fires,
> It can bisect an atom or analyze the planets—
> All it has to do is to, do is to, do is to, do is to start at the beginning and
>   continue to the end.
>
> (*Complete Poems*, 210)

But starting at the beginning and continuing smoothly to the end is exactly what doesn't happen in Fearing's poems. The "cracked record" effect and the "continuous performance" experience trope ideological loopholes, fissures in the ostensibly monolithic surfaces of capitalist culture industries that high-modernist cultural jeremiads have chosen to ignore. Fearing's poetry enriches our understanding of mass-spectatorial experience by bringing such loopholes to light, proposing that no matter how "fixed" the formulas might seem, many things can disrupt them, and once disrupted they may perhaps never be quite as transparent as their creators intended.

Signs of the Times

Much of what we call "mass culture" consists of ephemeral semiotic phenomena, including advertisements, radio and televisual speech, and street signage and shop-window displays, which exist to entice modern subjects into the ideological project of capitalist enterprise and consumption but which can sometimes assume divergent or contradictory meanings. These semiotic forms typically interpellate their subjects by means of a distinctive combination of intimacy and unanswerability. That is, they are designed (sometimes with uncanny success) to function on a mass scale while creating the impression that they are speaking to their receivers as unique individuals, yet discouraging the receivers to talk back to them (except perhaps by declining to buy what they are selling, in which case they move imperturbably to other potential buyers). Fearing's whimsical portrait of a "majestic" jukebox in "King Juke" (*Poetry*, 1943) reveals this asymmetry by noting that although the box can say anything we can say "and say it in a clearer, louder voice" than ours, the "juke-box has no ears . . . / The box, it is believed, cannot even hear itself. / IT SIMPLY HAS NO EARS AT ALL" (*Complete Poems*, 218)—an imperfection that ironically makes it not weaker but that much more powerful.

Fearing's jukebox is a comical but apt metaphor for a capitalist mass culture possessing the capacity to voice any idea or emotion imaginable but offering no channel allowing its consumers to speak back to it. This nonreciprocity encourages endemic confusions between communication and commodity, between free will and coercion, which become powerful ideological means for obfuscating class consciousness, ethnic solidarity, and economic self-interest. Yet in modern life these interpellations are so nearly continuous that trying to ignore or reject them altogether would mean losing any connection to the world around us. Perhaps our only recourse is to push back against the pressure they exert upon us (to buy, to consume, to believe, to acquiesce), pursuing strategies for making their utterances part of our individual and collective agendas, rather than allowing ours to be entirely subsumed within theirs.

Fearing produced his share of deterministic portrayals of the semiotic landscapes of mass culture such as "Dirge" and "Obituary," in which human subjectivities seem reduced to economic counters that lack all agency. But at other times (as in "Continuous Performance" and "Cracked Record Blues") he pushes back. In "Aphrodite Metropolis" (*This Quarter*, 1926), he portrays expressions of authentic

experience erupting unpredictably upon the instrumentalized forms of mass cul-
ture, imbuing them with new meanings. Here is the poem in full:

> "Myrtle loves Harry,"—It is sometimes hard to remember a thing
>   like that.
> Hard to think about it, and no one knows what to do with it when
>   he has it.
> So write it out on a billboard that stands under the yellow light of an
>   "L" platform among popcorn wrappers and crushed cigars,
> A poster that says "Mama I love crispy wafers so."
> Leave it on a placard where somebody else gave the blonde lady a pencil
>   mustache, and another perplexed citizen deposited:
> "Jesus Saves. Jesus Saves."
> One can lay this bundle down there with the others,
> And never lose it, or forget it, or want it.
> "Myrtle loves Harry."
> They live somewhere.
>
>   (*Complete Poems*, 25)[9]

From the initial graffito "'Myrtle loves Harry,'" which stands out from the obscur-
ing surfaces of advertisements and discarded objects, the speaker extrapolates an
unauthorized network of spontaneous emotional utterance scattered through the
urban landscape, pressing back against the pressure of the ubiquitous advertise-
ments either by revealing their semiotic emptiness (the contrasting uses of "love" in
the poem) or by literally defacing their fetishized surfaces (the mustache drawn on
the obligatory advertising blonde). Unlike "the blonde lady" and the wafer-loving
child, which are merely composites and types calculated to reach the populace's
largest common denominator, Myrtle and Harry (and even the "perplexed citizen")
are individuals who really "live somewhere," and their graffiti records an authen-
ticity of experience that has not been subsumed into the realm of the commodity.
Once traces of this more authentic perception reach us, Fearing hopes they might
become permanent "deposits" within our consciousness, even if we never know the
individuals involved or share their particular sentiments.

Two striking poems of the 1930s—William Carlos Williams's "The Attic Which
Is Desire:" and Muriel Rukeyser's "Boy With His Hair Cut Short"—press back
against the pressure of mass-consumer culture by appropriating the quintessential
symbolic object of the advertising world: the illuminated sign. Advertising signs
feature prominently in various modern American texts including *The Great Gatsby*
and *Manhattan Transfer*, as well as in poems by Lindsay ("Rhyme to an Electrical
Advertising Sign") and Sandburg ("Skyscraper"), among others. Such signs register
not merely the general prevalence of ads in our lives but a specific pressure that all
ads strive for: to capture our visual field so powerfully that we become quite unable
to look away. The sign in Williams's poem has that penetrating quality, but its power
allows the poet to appropriate it for a radically different purpose. "The Attic Which

Is Desire:" (first published in *Blues* in 1930), was written in 1929–1930 as Williams was finishing the top floor of his house into a long-dreamed-of study for his literary work (*Collected Poems* 1:519). This "unused tent / of / bare beams" is quite directly an object of the poet's desire, symbolizing his mostly unfulfilled but still animating poetic ambitions. In this room of his own, he believes that "the night / and day" will "wait" for him more "directly" than ever before. However, the second half of the poem, emphasizing not the enclosed room but its window, turns away from this lofty and rather self-involved ideal of artistic accomplishment and toward "the street" dominated by an illuminated advertising sign:

> Here
>
> from the street
> by
>
>   * * *
>   * S *
>   * O *
>   * D *
>   * A *
>   * * *
>
> ringed with
> running lights
>
> the darkened
> pane
>
> exactly
> down the center
>
> is
> transfixed[.] (*Collected Poems*, 1:325)

Williams's graphic representation of the sign's design on the page indicates his commitment to using the demotic material particulars of twentieth-century life to challenge the divide between the world of art and the world of ads. If the attic space emblematizes the poet's imagination and the window represents his perceptual apparatus, the sign functions (much like the red wheelbarrow) as a metonym of everything that he might see and use for his poetry. Together they form a precision-ist composition defined by the exactitude with which the sign bisects the window-pane, which Williams expresses through the adjective "transfixed." This composition acknowledges that the goal of the sign and all advertisements is to transfix the eye of the consumer, but by repurposing its transfixing capacity for the benefit of his art-istry, Williams posits a modern poetry not despoiled but empowered by its contact with the world of the commodity.

The opening lines of Muriel Rukeyser's "Boy With His Hair Cut Short" (from *U. S. 1*, 1938) announce an ambition to represent an exemplary moment of modernity, a "twentieth-century evening," through a collection of material objects and commodity-texts: the El, a dreary upstairs apartment dominated by the commercial street, the worn furniture, and the "stocks, news, serenade" forced upon the boy and girl by the "neighbor radio" (89), a phrase that captures the peculiar tendency of mass-commodity culture to invade as it claims to accompany, to become a possession that can intensify our sense of dispossession. This collection of objects culminates in the "impersonal" neon sign from the drugstore, whose unrelenting penetration of domestic space provides an objective correlative for the pervasiveness of commodity-texts upon modern subjectivity. In such an environment, the cutting of the boy's hair signals the danger of his premature submission to a lifetime of bare economic and imaginative subsistence. Holding still under his sister's scissors, his head forced into a single fixed position by their grinding economic need, he is "impressed" by the "precision" of the neon arrow as a symbol of the worldly "success" denied him. The daunting, often defeating force exerted by mass-commodity culture on the modern subject is reinforced by other images of pressure upon his body: the suit, which in the morning will support his newly adult mien, is "new-pressed"; his forehead is "bleached"; and the sign's relentless repetition of its own success is a rhythmical "tattoo" pressing upon his eye until it blears.

But this pressing inward of his environment upon him is not a one-way exertion of deterministic forces. The poem's bleak realist surfaces, in which mass culture seems a valueless prop of capitalist modernity, is counterbalanced at a deep metaphoric level by an affirmation of imaginative writing as an act of potential resistance to these pressures. The impersonal sign is not the only embodiment of the virtues of precision in the poem; the movements and attributes associated with the bodies of the boy and girl, while less mechanical, are no less precise: *clear, solicitous, careful, level, steady, sleek, fine, trim*. Rukeyser also employs imagery akin to Stephen Crane's habitual use of "upturned faces with open unseeing eyes" troping "the blank page on which the action of inscription takes place," as Michael Fried puts it (99–100). The careful movements of the girl's "level fingers" around the boy's head and face mime the action of writing, an act of symbolic inscription described as "erasing" his previous failures and constructing a new identity for him as one who resembles the "finest gentleman." Though both currently feel her words of encouragement as "hopeless," the boy's precise and expressive gesture of response, his "forehead wrinkling ironic," which suggests the sudden appearance of lines of writing on the page of his face, reaffirms the human capacity to adapt to adverse circumstances. These wrinkles write the boy's capacity to maintain some ironic distance between his immediate economic failures and his larger sense of self. In other words, the boy is not a hapless victim of modern capitalism's deficiencies, and an object of the poet's and reader's pity, but a strongly recreative figure, described four times as observing—*watching, seeing*—the precise details of his environment. The last three lines carefully reinforce this emphasis upon his capacity to observe and understand, as his eyes sweep panoramically across the entire scene while also maintaining a close focus upon the "blue vein" pulsing on his sister's temple. As this intimate image of the delicacy and vulnerability of the human body becomes more powerful by echoing and supervening the impersonal mechanized tattoo of the neon sign, Rukeyser's work exemplifies the dialectic of engagement sought by all the writers I've discussed here, in which modern poetry seeks and speaks what mass culture will not or cannot say about itself.

NOTES

1 Edward Bok, the editor of the *Ladies' Home Journal*, dismissed "literary style" as "nothing except a complicated method of expression which confuses rather than clarifies" (27), while S. S. McClure, founder and publisher of the leading mass-circulation magazine of the 1890s, denigrated style as well, insisting that an author "can say the same thing in fifty different ways" (196).

2 In *T. S. Eliot and the Cultural Divide*, David Chinitz shows that Eliot himself—fascinated by London music-hall culture, heard often on radio broadcasts, courting Broadway hits—showed persistent if selective interest in mass culture. Yet the very freshness of Chinitz's recuperative argument for a "messy, intractable Eliot" (16), who sought to integrate art and mass culture, reveals the inhibiting and divisive function played by the high-canonical Eliot in American literary criticism. Chinitz seems to concede as much in an ambivalent passage from the introduction, noting that "the critics of the 1930s and 1940s required a 'serious' Eliot to help them establish a place for modernism (and for the New Criticism) in the academy; their successors required a Rock-of-Gibraltar Eliot to anchor the post–World War II cultural-political consensus" (16). I have no desire to employ a simplistic "bogeyman Eliot to epitomize the hierarchical, elitist tradition against which they have defined themselves" (16). But however one-sided previous uses of Eliot may have been, they cannot just be erased from the history of our discipline. They have shaped nearly a century of literary-historical narratives and canons—and continue to do so, arguably to an alarming degree. Subject searches in MLA online databases reveal that, year after year, Eliot still appears as a subject heading for many more items than any other modern American poet—nearly 2,100 such items between 1990 and 2009. Given that since 1990, his already sizable lead over Pound, Stevens, and the others has actually widened relative to previous decades, we must consider reports of his canonical decline to be greatly exaggerated.

3 Gorman (138–185, esp. 153–156). Brantlinger notes Eliot's acknowledgment of the influence of MacDonald's 1944 essay "A Theory of Popular Culture" upon his theory of mass culture in *Notes Toward the Definition of Culture* (1948), and concludes that both the aging doyen of high modernism and the radical student of Soviet film saw capitalist mass culture in "conspiratorial" terms, as "a deception that has been palmed off the unwitting" (200) by a sinister culture industry.

4 We can hardly be surprised at the growing influence during this period of the nostalgic and Olympian critique of mass culture by members of the Frankfurt School, who (with the honorable exception of Walter Benjamin) damned modern mass-culture industries for nearly all the ills of the twentieth century, including the rise of totalitarianism, and whose ideological kinship with the influential MacDonald–

Greenberg defense of avant-garde art against kitsch has been discussed by Brantlinger (222–248), Gorman (176–181), and Alan Wald (222–223).

5 Though I can't pursue them here, two further steps are needed: to engage more fully with theoretical accounts of modern culture (by Raymond Williams, Jürgen Habermas, Pierre Bourdieu, and Franco Moretti, among others) that reject elitist "bread and circuses" models; and to compile a more comprehensive and widely accessible web archive, searchable not only by author but by publication venue and subject matter, of verse that engages the defining experiences of twentieth-century modernity: urbanization and technology, commodification and consumer spectacle, class consciousness and ethnic difference, and, of course, mass culture.

6 Untermeyer had been the unofficial house poet of *The Masses* in its early years and remained an active participant throughout its existence. His autobiography, *From Another World*, contains a valuable eyewitness account of the two sedition trials of 1918 (68–79).

7 I give the sites of original publication of Fearing's poems in parentheses; however, all page references cite the 1994 *Complete Poems*, edited by Robert M. Ryley.

8 These remarks from the jacket for the 1940 volume are reproduced on the jacket to Fearing's *New and Selected Poems* (1956).

9 Fearing published several poems with this title, and he grouped, separated, and renumbered them over three decades. In *Angel Arms* (1929), "Aphrodite Metropolis" is in five sections, of which the ten lines quoted here form section II. But upon first publication in 1926 they appear by themselves as "Aphrodite Metropolis," and by the time of *New and Selected Poems* (1956), Fearing had discarded the other four sections, making these lines the entirety of "Aphrodite Metropolis" once again.

REFERENCES

Barnard, Rita. *The Great Depression and the Culture of Abundance.* Cambridge: Cambridge University Press, 1995.

Benton, Megan. "Unruly Servants: Machines, Modernity, and the Printed Page." In *Print in Motion: The Expansion of Publishing and Reading in the United States, 1880–1940*, ed. Carl F. Kaestle and Janice A. Radway. A History of the Book in America, vol. 4. Chapel Hill: University of North Carolina Press, 2009. 151–168.

Bok, Edward. *The Americanization of Edward Bok.* New York: Scribner's, 1920.

Brantlinger, Patrick. *Bread and Circuses: Theories of Mass Culture as Social Decay.* Ithaca: Cornell University Press, 1983.

Brown, Sterling A. "Cabaret." In *The Collected Poems of Sterling A. Brown*, ed. Michael S. Harper. Evanston: Tri-Quarterly Books, 1989. 111–113.

Chasar, Mike. "The Business of Rhyming: Burma-Shave Poetry and Popular Culture." *PMLA* 125 (2010): 29–47.

Chinitz, David. *T. S. Eliot and the Cultural Divide.* Chicago: University of Chicago Press, 2003.

Coyle, Michael. *Ezra Pound, Popular Genres, and the Discourse of Culture.* University Park: Pennsylvania State University Press, 1995.

Dayton, Tim. *Muriel Rukeyser's "The Book of the Dead."* Columbia: University of Missouri Press, 2003.

Fearing, Kenneth. *Afternoon of a Pawnbroker.* New York: Harcourt, Brace, 1943.

———. *Angel Arms*. New York: Coward McCann, 1929.

———. *Collected Poems*. New York: Random House, 1940.

———. *Complete Poems*. Ed. Robert M. Ryley. Orono: National Poetry Foundation, 1994.

———. *New and Selected Poems*. Bloomington: Indiana University Press, 1956.

Fletcher, John Gould. "In the Theatre." In *Some Imagist Poems, 1916: An Annual Anthology*.
    Boston: Houghton Mifflin, 1916. 43.

Fried, Michael. *Realism, Writing, Disfiguration: On Thomas Eakins and Stephen Crane*.
    Chicago: University of Chicago Press, 1987.

Gilder, Richard Watson. *Letters of Richard Watson Gilder*. Ed. Rosamond Gilder. Boston:
    Houghton Mifflin, 1916.

Gorman, Paul R. *Left Intellectuals and Popular Culture in Twentieth-century America*.
    Chapel Hill: University of North Carolina Press, 1996.

Harrington, Joseph. *Poetry and the Public: The Social Form of Modern U. S. Poetries*.
    Middletown: Wesleyan University Press, 2002.

Hughes, Langston. "The Weary Blues." *Opportunity* 3 (May 1925): 143.

Lindsay, Vachel. *The Art of the Moving Picture*. New York: Macmillan, 1916.

———. "Blanche Sweet—Moving-Picture Actress." *Little Review* 1.4 (June 1914): 4–5.

Lowney, John. *History, Memory, and the Literary Left: Modern American Poetry, 1935–1968*.
    Iowa City: University of Iowa Press, 2006.

McClure, S. S. *My Autobiography*. New York: Frederick Stokes, 1914.

Nelson, Cary. *Repression and Recovery: Modern American Poetry and the Politics of Cultural
    Memory*. Madison: University of Wisconsin Press, 1989.

Newcomb, John Timberman. *How Did Poetry Survive? The Making of Modern American
    Verse*. Urbana: University of Illinois Press, 2012.

———. *Would Poetry Disappear? American Verse and the Crisis of Modernity*. Columbus:
    Ohio State University Press, 2004.

Rolfe, Edwin. *Trees Became Torches: Selected Poems*. Ed. Cary Nelson and Jefferson
    Hendricks. Urbana: University of Illinois Press, 1995.

Rukeyser, Muriel. "Boy With His Hair Cut Short." In *U. S. 1*. New York: Covici-Friede, 1938.
    89–90.

Tate, Allen. "Tension in Poetry." In *Essays of Four Decades*. New York: Morrow, 1970. 56–71.

Tebbel, John, and Mary Ellen Zuckerman. *The Magazine in America, 1741–1900*. New York:
    Oxford University Press, 1991.

Untermeyer, Louis. *From Another World*. New York: Harcourt Brace, 1939.

———. "The Score Board: Summer-1917." In *Roast Leviathan*. New York: Harcourt Brace,
    1923. 105.

Van Wienen, Mark W. *Partisans and Poets: The Political Work of American Poetry in the
    Great War*. Cambridge: Cambridge University Press, 1997.

Wald, Alan M. *The New York Intellectuals*. Chapel Hill: University of North Carolina Press,
    1987.

Warren, Robert Penn. "The Present State of Poetry in the United States." *Kenyon Review* 1
    (1939): 384–398.

Williams, William Carlos. *Collected Poems of William Carlos Williams*. Ed. A. Walton Litz
    and Christopher MacGowan. 2 vols. New York: New Directions, 1986.

———. *Spring and All*. Paris: Contact Publishing Co., 1923.

CHAPTER 11

EXQUISITE CORPSE: SURREALIST INFLUENCE ON THE AMERICAN POETRY SCENE, 1920–1960

SUSAN ROSENBAUM

THIS chapter makes the case for a sustained and growing interest in surrealism on the American poetry scene from the 1920s to the early 1960s, chiefly through a focus on the little magazines involved in adapting and publicizing surrealist work and ideals. Although surrealism's influence on American poetry from the 1960s forward has been widely recognized,[1] its early history and influence in the United States have been just as widely overlooked, despite Dickran Tashjian's foundational work on this topic. For instance, the poet Dana Gioia comments that "one of the provocative ironies of twentieth-century literature is that during the Thirties and Forties when surrealism was transforming the landscape of European and Latin American poetry, it never took root in the United States." I demonstrate that surrealism profoundly transformed the landscape of American poetry in the 1930s and 1940s and that these surrealist roots gave vital shape and direction to the subsequent history of American poetry.

What might explain the lack of critical attention paid to the history of surrealist influence on American poetry?[2] In that literary history tends to follow the leads of movements and schools, it is significant that the United States lacked a clearly defined surrealist movement akin to the movement in France or other European countries, a movement with particular leaders, formal meetings, journals, and manifestos.[3] Indeed, the lack of an official surrealist movement in the United

States (prior to the founding of the Chicago Surrealist group in 1966) led to ritual pronouncements of surrealism's "death" as it crossed the Atlantic. While there are clear exceptions to this narrative—including American artists and poets affiliated with the European surrealist movement such as Man Ray, Philip Lamantia, and Ted Joans, and journals such as *Transition, View,* and *VVV*—to study surrealism in the United States is in general not a matter of charting the history of a cohesive movement, but rather of uncovering surrealist affinities and transformations, as well as significant critical departures from what John Ashbery has called "the narrow interpretation of its theologians" (*Reported*, 6). As Ashbery pointed out in 1964, "Breton is right in claiming that Surrealism is very much alive, but it remains so in spite of the politics and court etiquette which he has sought to impose on it" (*Reported*, 4).

Far from the tightly knit surrealist group in France, whose membership and comings and goings were controlled by André Breton, U.S. surrealism resembled nothing so much as a surrealist "exquisite corpse," the collaborative poems and drawings produced by artists who contributed a word or a line without seeing the previous contributions. In other words, tracking surrealist influence opens a fascinating window on to the chance juxtapositions and mongrel mixtures of old and new that characterized the American poetic avant-garde. Amelia Jones observes "the tendency within surrealism to rationalize in its own fashion—by orienting its explorations toward the ultimate recontainment of femininity, flux, homosexuality, and other kinds of dangerous flows that intrigued the surrealists but which they could not bear to allow to remain unbounded" (252). The history of surrealism's assimilation and transformation in the United States is largely a history of resistance to such containment, by poets and artists who were at times explicitly opposed to Breton's homophobia and conceptions of women, and who were often ambivalently allied with the avant-garde. A focus on the U.S. poetry scene decenters Breton and brings other figures into view, many expelled from or on the margins of the surrealist movement. At the same time, the surrealist dedication to an absolute freedom was capacious enough that it enabled such transformations, and surrealism is perhaps unique in the history of the avant-garde in its openness to adaptation by artists and poets who were marginalized due to gender, sexual orientation, race, and class.[4] Especially intriguing is the subtle claim by many American poets that their adaptations enabled a truer, freer surrealism to emerge and that surrealist ideals were most fully realized on the margins of the movement. In short, surrealism was far from dead when it arrived in the United States: poets and artists would animate particular features of surrealism's exquisite corpse.

Even while many U.S. poets critically engaged the leadership of André Breton, they were inspired by his understanding of poetry. As articulated by Breton in France in the 1920s and 1930s, surrealism was devoted to expressing in conscious life the workings of the unconscious mind. In the first Surrealist Manifesto, Breton defined surrealism as "psychic automatism in its pure state, by which one proposes to express—verbally, by means of the written word, or in any other manner—the actual functioning of thought. Dictated by thought, in the absence of any control exercised by reason, exempt from any aesthetic or moral concern" (*Manifestoes*, 26).

Although Breton would later revise the conflation of surrealism with automatism (Ray, 11–12), his initial interest in automatism exemplified the surrealist search for an imagination freed from "a state of slavery" (*Manifestoes*, 4), induced by the "absolute rationalism" and "reign of logic" in twentieth-century culture (*Manifestoes*, 9). Like Freud, Breton was guided by "the belief in the superior reality of certain forms of previously neglected associations, in the omnipotence of dream, in the disinterested play of thought" (*Manifestoes*, 26). While Freud sought a therapeutic outcome in the discovery of unconscious wishes and desires, Breton conversely sought a deepened perspective on and experience of the real: "I believe in the future resolution of these two states, dream and reality, which are seemingly so contradictory, into a kind of absolute reality, a surreality, if one may so speak" (*Manifestoes*, 14).

Poetry was the means of this dialectical resolution of opposed states, the first step toward a broader social, political, and economic revolution. With his roots in Dada, Breton did not associate poetry with a particular genre, but he understood it as a way of knowing, its value located in its capacity to realize a surreality. As Tzara put it, "Life and poetry were henceforth a single indivisible expression of man in quest of a vital imperative" (Motherwell, 406). Breton acknowledged Dada and surrealism's debts to romanticism, "of which we are quite ready to appear historically to-day as the tail, though in that case an excessively prehensile tail" (*This Quarter*, 32–33). A film or painting could participate in the poetic act of commingling dream and reality as much as an essay or poem, and generic experimentation and collaboration were a natural outgrowth of this understanding. Automatic writing and painting, collaborative games, and chance operations were techniques used to facilitate unconscious expression, and an inherent democracy accompanied the view of the poet as a "modest recording instrument" (*Manifestoes*, 28). Building on Lautreamont's statement that poetry should be made by all, Breton said that he wanted "to put [poetry] within reach of everyone" (*Manifestoes*, 37).

The incongruity between the unconscious and conscious states of mind served as the central formal principle of surrealist work, and this was conveyed through the juxtaposition of discordant elements, often meant to shock the reader or viewer. Breton explained this principle of juxtaposition through Reverdy's definition of the image: "The image is a pure creation of the mind. It cannot be born from a comparison but from a juxtaposition of two more or less distant realities. The more the relationship between the two juxtaposed realities is distant and true, the stronger the image will be—the greater its emotional power and poetic reality" (*Manifestoes*, 20). Reverdy and the surrealists took inspiration from Lautreamont's celebrated comparison of beauty to "the chance meeting upon a dissecting table of a sewing-machine with an umbrella," which Max Ernst paraphrased as "the fortuitous encounter upon a non-suitable plane of two mutually distant realities" (*This Quarter*, 8). To elicit these fortuitous encounters, many surrealists employed techniques culled from the modernist avant-garde, in particular collage,[5] and devised new ones, such as frottage and fumage, while others brought the unconscious to vivid life through realistic modes, contrasting dreamlike content with precise detail. Other aspects of Breton's poetics—convulsive beauty, the marvelous, objective chance, black humor—would prove influential,[6] yet the surrealist image was an enduring legacy for American poetry, evident in an understanding of the poem as enacting and inviting a dialectical action of mind, a new way of knowing. As Anna Balakian argues, "Encounter of objects, encounter of persons (particularly of man with woman), and encounter of the words are the basis of the poetic composition which adapts the physical world to the poet's ability to see connections. The poem is generally located in a perpetual present, the immediacy of life cast in the present tense" (1236).

While specific cases of surrealist influence are fascinating (e.g., Ashbery's response to De Chirico in his collection *The Double Dream of Spring*), this chapter seeks to provide a more comprehensive history of surrealist influence, by focusing on the little magazines that introduced surrealism to an American audience from the 1920s onward. Before galleries and museums exhibited surrealist art, the little magazines functioned as portable textual galleries, setting the terms for understanding surrealist poetry as an interdisciplinary endeavor. As surrealism was absorbed into larger institutions such as the Museum of Modern Art (MoMA), the little magazines continued to offer innovative "exhibitions" and interpretations of surrealism: they make visible a modernist history we have lost track of even while we live in the aesthetic landscape they helped create, a history whose range and eclecticism invites us to think outside the boundaries of established schools and movements.[7]

THE 1920S: INTRODUCING SURREALISM

Although literary histories have minimized the importance of surrealist influence in the 1920s and early 1930s,[8] the little magazines of this era introduced surrealism to an American audience, revealing this decade to be crucial to the transatlantic conversation about surrealism. Hence Morton Dauwen Zabel could write in *Poetry* in 1936 that "America thus continues, as for the past decade here or abroad, to lead in the vanguard of surrealist nations."[9] Although a number of magazines engaged surrealist art and poetry in the 1920s and early 1930s, including *The Dial*, *Poetry*, *Modern Quarterly*, *This Quarter*, *The Sewanee Review*, and *Pagany*, two in particular—the *Little Review* and *Transition*—stand out for their comprehensive presentation of surrealist work, made possible by their editors' access to the Dada/surrealist scene in Paris. These magazines display some characteristic responses to surrealism that would recur in the following decades.

The little magazines associated with New York dada (1915–1919)—*291*, *391*, *The Blind Man*, *Rongwrong*, *New York Dada*—coupled with the presence of Duchamp and Picabia in New York, had helped to establish an interest in the European avant-garde that would carry over to surrealism as it emerged from Dada (Tashjian, *Boatload*, 18). The early reception of surrealism reflects what Dickran Tashjian has called "the difficult problem of plotting the subtle and mercurial transformation of Dada into Surrealism" (*Skyscraper*, 14), evident in *The Little Review*'s treatment of surrealism in the Autumn–Winter 1923–1924 issue. The editor Jane Heap called this a "French Number," pointing out that the issue's French writers "do not belong to any formal group," adding, "We will be accused of booming the Dadaists…why not? (except that these men are not Dada)" (35). The surrealist movement would officially begin in October 1924 with the publication of André Breton's first manifesto; however, Breton and others involved in the surrealist movement had been involved in Paris Dada, and Breton and Soupault's 1919 publication of *The Magnetic Fields*, a collaborative text produced through techniques of automatic writing, was considered by Breton as the first surrealist work, reflecting the significant overlap (of artists, ideas, and techniques) between the two movements. René Crevel in *The Little Review* (1923–1924) and Paul Morand in *The Dial* (1924–1925) provided some early definitions of surrealism (translated as "superrealism" by Crevel and "surrealisme" by Morand), both emphasizing the Freudian unconscious and techniques of automatic writing as central to the surrealist movement. Both writers cited Breton, with Morand noting that "Breton's Manifeste du Surrealisme is a useful thing to read, and a sharp instrument. At the moment it is having a great success."[10] *The Little Review* would publish the work of the surrealists in many subsequent issues, with a surrealist number in Spring–Summer 1926.

As surrealism traveled to the United States, the connections and distinctions between Dada and Surrealism at times became highly charged, as evidenced by Matthew Josephson's open letter to the Paris surrealists in the 1926 surrealist number. Josephson, who was involved with the Paris Dada circle in 1921 (Tashjian, *Boatload*, 15) and who served as associate editor of *Broom* (1922–1924), found that versus "the exquisite roar of Dada," "this superrealism is the faint, ugly whine of a decrepit engine" (17). He mocked automatic writing—"A new style was invented: by drinking quantities of beer and writing as fast as you could in competition with others after three or four hours you were so dazed that your subconscious began working" (18)—and found that the "literary production of the super-realists is bastard," asking, "Of what value are these tedious and tepid dreams, these diffuse poems in prose, these wearisome manifestoes couched in an habitual imagery and an inverted syntax" (18). Josephson objected to Breton's efforts to subsume poetry to surrealism's revolutionary ideals, emphasizing the privilege that permitted such an anti-art position: "The bleakness of our situation here compared with the easy brilliance of my friends in Paris…calls for a reserve of vitality and courage that is scarcely ever needed there" (18). In sum, he pronounced the new "movement" dead upon arrival: "as we billet this new artistic organism in the *Little Review*…word comes that it is no longer among the living" (18).

Former participants in French Dada, including Philippe Soupault[11] and George Ribemont-Dessaignes, also provided ambivalent commentary on surrealism's origins in Dada. In an essay titled "In Praise of Violence" in the 1926 surrealist number of *Little Review*, Ribemont-Dessaignes asserted that Dada, a movement "which assailed all the moral defenses," had ended but pointed out that "its acquired impetus only enabled it to go on making love" (40). What resulted was surrealism: "It so happened that a little piece of Dadaism thought it could perfectly well invest itself with Sex Quality and fill a respectable role within the vulva of the mob. The success of Surrealism is the wedding apparel of this bird of paradise" (41). Ribemont-Dessaignes' metaphor revealed his ambivalence about surrealism's success; he observed that surrealism lacked Dada's violence and hard edges, as "a bed of pumice stones which was without much trouble transformed into a comfortable sofa," adding, the "turn of fashion is for an easy nonchalance" (41).

Both Ribemont-Dessaignes and Crevel defined surrealism as a revolutionary spirit that they distinguished from its status as a movement controlled by Breton, a distinction that would prove particularly important not only to disaffected French dadaists and surrealists but to U.S. poets, most of whom would resist any formal alliance with the movement. Heap anticipated this response in her introduction to the surrealist number, noting the American prejudice against "groups, cliques, revolutions, movements" (1). As the clear leader of the surrealist movement in France, Breton carefully policed its membership, publicly breaking with or expelling those who disagreed with his ideas, including Crevel and Aragon (in Crevel's case, for his homosexuality; in Aragon's, for political differences regarding surrealism's communist commitments) (Nadeau). Ribemont-Dessaignes commented, "They don't agree any more about Surrealism than they used to about Dadaism. The same thick swamp subsists. Who is surrealist, who is not? They know it only at the Central Office—where everybody is it" (41). Similarly, in discussing superrealism, Crevel emphasized that he was not defining "the followers of one school or another"; he distinguished the "revolutionary spirit" of surrealism from other modernist movements that were satisfied with destroying "detestable monuments" only so that they could "place [their] bomb on the mantelpiece."[12]

In its reproduction of surrealist painting and sculpture alongside poems and essays, the *Little Review* functioned as a virtual gallery and exhibition catalog, anticipating the surrealist museum and gallery exhibitions of the 1930s.[13] This format invited an exploration of "poetry" in its capacious sense, as a means of conjoining dream and reality, whether in poems, prose, painting, film, or photography. For instance, the French number included poems in the original French by Pierre Reverdy, Jacques Baron, Philippe Soupault, Benjamin Peret, Paul Eluard, and artwork by Man Ray, Max Ernst, André Masson, Georges Braque, and G. Ribemont-Dessaignes. The role of poetry as a faculty of the imagination unrestricted by genre was made clear in a number of essays on surrealist painting. Ribemont-Dessaignes' discussion of "Dada Painting or the Oil-Eye" demonstrated that Arp, Man Ray, Ernst, and Duchamp have "broken with sight" and eluded the tyranny of the real, following instead the "fantastic imagination" that permits a "poetry" to emerge.[14] Similarly, Crevel's appreciation of Georgio de Chirico's paintings, reproduced in the essay, poetically conveyed their power and effect: "we long to walk into the pictures of Georgio de Chirico" (8). These and other essays on painters were a direct outcome of the surrealist understanding of "poetry."

While *The Dial* (Paul Morand), *TransAtlantic Review* (Philippe Soupault, René Crevel), and *Poetry* (Jean Catel) featured regular Paris letters in the 1920s, which reported on recent publications and the literary scene in Paris, the importance awarded to the French avant-garde often vied with a desire to establish the independence and vitality of American poetry. *Poetry* in the 1920s is a case in point. In 1920 Richard Aldington made the case for the influence of Gertrude Stein on modern French poetry, including the futurists, cubists, simulteneists, fantasistes, and dadaists.[15] At the end of the decade, the editor Harriet Monroe offered a review of René Taupin's *L'Influence du Symbolisme sur la Poésie Americaine (de 1910 a 1920).*[16] Although Monroe admired the scholarship, she objected to Taupin's nationalist perspective: "Dr. Taupin is manifestly convinced that only along the current of French influence have our twentieth-century poets produced anything of value" (45). Accusing the French of a "superiority complex" (48), Monroe lashed out at Taupin's suggestion that *Poetry* would have benefited from greater contact with the French avant-garde, arguing that "*Poetry* was founded as an organ of the art, not of a group or a school. It was dedicated especially to the service of American poets" (47).

In contrast to the nationalist designs of *Poetry*, Eugene Jolas, the founder and editor of *Transition* (1927–1938),[17] described the magazine as a "workshop of the intercontinental spirit, a proving ground of the new literature, a laboratory for poetic experiment" (*Transition Workshop*, 13). Jolas would edit the magazine in Paris until 1936, when he relocated to New York. In 1928 Jolas proclaimed, "We fight the idea that by grafting a nationalistic consciousness onto the American, literature will flower. The intellectual frontiers of America do not exist for us, and we are as much interested in the wonders brought by esthetic explorers from Mexico, the West-Indies, South-America, and our own Southern and South-Western past" (142). Jolas commented that New York's "Universe of races and languages" had inspired the magazine's polyglot nature: *Transition* sought to realize "an ideal America," a "Super-America" (*Transition Workshop*, 13) that could absorb and subsume nationalistic thought.

Transition would carry on the work begun by *Little Review*, both in its interdisciplinary presentation of surrealism and in its serialized publication of Joyce's "work in progress" (*Finnegan's Wake*). Jolas, an accomplished poet and reporter for the *Chicago Tribune* in Paris, was friendly with the French surrealists, a connection that enabled him to publish English translations of their poetry and other works (*Transition* February 1933: 141). In addition to translations of French surrealism,[18] *Transition* published the work of American, English, Latin American, and other European writers, and reproductions of surrealist paintings, objects, photographs, film stills, film scenarios, and musical scores. American and British poets who contributed poetry or opinions to *Transition* included Gertrude Stein, Hart Crane, Archibald MacLeish, William Carlos Williams, T. S. Eliot, Kenneth Burke, Robinson Jeffers, John Gould Fletcher, Kenneth Fearing, Bravig Imbs, Kay Boyle, Djuna Barnes, Yvor Winters, Malcolm Cowley, Elsa Von Freytag-Loringhoven, Paul Bowles, Charles Henri Ford, Parker Tyler, James Agee, Samuel Beckett, James Johnson Sweeney, Randall Jarrell, and Muriel Rukeyser. To facilitate transatlantic dialogue, Jolas published questionnaires in the Summer and Fall 1928 issues, which asked European writers to reflect on American influence in Europe; similarly, he asked American expatriates to reflect on living in Europe and about their feelings regarding communism, surrealism, and anarchism. Symptomatic of this cross-cultural dialogue was Jolas's publication of "Hands Off Love," a Manifesto signed by the French Surrealists (*Transition* September 1927) that defended Charlie Chaplin, a "genius" and "poet," from his wife's charges of seduction and immoral conduct.

Although he was clearly inspired by Breton and surrealism, Jolas never joined the surrealist movement: he would stick to his ideal of creating a "bridge between creative Europe and America" ("Frontierless Decade," *Transition* 1938, 8), while defining his own variation on surrealist thought. Despite Yvor Winter's charges to the contrary, Jolas claimed that he did not consider "*Transition* an annex of the surrealiste movement" (June 1930, 46–47); *Transition*, he wrote in 1938, "was not satisfied... to merely be the mirror of continental advance-guard movements" (8). Indeed, *Transition* published work by Americans critical of surrealism.[19] Nevertheless, in Jolas's numerous editorial essays and manifestos, we can chart the literal and figurative translation of surrealism to the American poetry scene. As Jolas commented in "Literature and the New Man" (*Transition* June 1930), "By revealing the work of the Surrealistes in translation, *Transition* introduced a new spirit, which, nurtured on Rimbaud, Freud and Lautreamont, sought in the discovery of another reality the exclusive aim of expression. Although my own definition of reality differs from theirs in the implication of methodology, I have no hesitancy in saying that the Surrealistes, following in the wake of Dada, were the only ones to recognize the importance of the explorations into the subconscious world" (14).

Although he preferred Jung to Freud, Jolas shared the surrealist belief that poetry was at the center of "explorations into the subconscious world" and could lead the way to a new spirit that defied the "pragmatism of the age" and the "realistic idea of poetic values" (*Transition* June 1930, 14, 18). And, like the surrealists, Jolas understood poetry as an imaginative faculty that transcended genre: "Poetry— I use the term in its generic semantics as indicating the primal impulse to create" (*Transition* June 1930, 13). Echoing Breton, Jolas argued, "It is the future poet's task to present to us the dual reality of life" (*Transition* Summer 1928, 276) and "The wedding of reality with the automatic expressions of the subconscious, the intuitive, the somnambulist, the dream, will lead us to a revolutionary ethos" (*Transition* Summer 1928, 277). On the importance of *Transition* to French surrealist poets, Soupault's remarks in the June 1930 issue were telling: "At a time when we stood in France before the collapse of all poetic values, when those most qualified to consider poetry had become discouraged, and when, for reasons that seem to me superfluous to enumerate here, those same persons turned their attention in other directions, *Transition* represented the only living force, the only review which did not despair of poetry, and thus authorized the poets to continue their work" (376).

Jolas closely followed Breton's ideas, but his departures from surrealist doctrine would be echoed by many subsequent American poets. He criticized surrealist poetry for its adherence to stylistic convention: "But the movement remained incomplete, in my opinion, because it refused to consider the problem of the word in the struggle for a new reality. Its revolutionary activity did not transcend the traditional style" (*Transition* June 1930, 14). Jolas felt strongly that poetic *experiment* was essential to surrealist exploration, including coining words and departing from conventions of grammar: "Not only does the orphic poet try to find the territories of the unknown, to penetrate still deeper into the most abstract limits of his conscious and sub-conscious personalities, he is also eager to explore new ways of transmitting his discoveries" (*Transition* June 1929, 26). Automatism, he wrote, should be "simply the preliminary phase in any creative process, since it is the fact of becoming conscious that makes the creator who organizes the chaotic world of his hallucinations" (*Necessity*, 275). In a June 1929 "Proclamation" on the revolution of the word, signed by Jolas, Kay Boyle, Hart Crane, the Crosbys, Robert Sage, Laurence Vail, and others, Jolas advanced "the right to disintegrate the primal matter of words" in the pursuit of "pure poetry" and concluded with a pointed defense of the romantic imagination: "the writer expresses. He does not communicate."[20]

THE 1930S: POLITICS ON DISPLAY

In the 1930s surrealism gained public stature in the United States through influential anthologies, historical surveys, and museum and gallery exhibitions, all of which sought to teach the public about surrealism. The politics of display were at stake: who would curate these collections, and what version of surrealism and its Marxist politics would be conveyed? As members of a politically engaged movement, the European surrealists sought control over the display and publication of their work; however, as surrealism traveled to the United States, such control would prove elusive, and for many critics the entrance of surrealism into the American museum signified the rationalization of a movement that thrived on the flux and unpredictability of everyday life. Despite repeated pronouncements of surrealism's museum death, however, its corpse was vividly resurrected, by American curators, editors, poets, and artists who, inspired by the surrealists, sought to reimagine the museum and related exhibitionary practices.[21]

The politics of display come into focus in two significant anthologies of surrealist writing in English published in the early 1930s: *European Caravan* (1931), edited by the American translator and journalist Samuel Putnam, and a special issue of *This Quarter* (1932), guest edited by André Breton. Putnam's approach was historical and didactic, offering a guided tour of the literature of Dada and surrealism: his anthology included brief (often excerpted) literary selections that charted the growth of both movements, accompanied by author biographies and introductions that concisely explained their histories and fundamental ideas.[22] An American perspective was evident in a section titled "the American-Surréaliste Influence (1926)": "America being one of the most fascinatingly unreal portions of a world which the young European, following the War, beheld with new eyes, it was not unnatural that the American theme and the impulse to the discovery of a Super-realism should meet and be, to a degree, amalgamated" (199). The anthology was attentive to representing surrealism beyond Breton's control: "some of the best Super-realism indeed, is to be found in the work of dissenters, those who, Surrealistes in all but name, have withdrawn from the party, like Desnos and Ribemont-Dessaignes, those who have been read out of the party like Delteil, or who have gradually, almost imperceptibly drifted away as has Soupault. There are, also, those larger individual figures such as Fargue and Reverdy who have never been confined within the limits of this or any other group" (175).

In contrast, Breton's editing of *This Quarter*'s Surrealist Number (5.1, September 1932), resulted in a collection of the movement's stalwarts and their central works, introduced in a manner that emphasized the movement's interdisciplinary understanding of poetry and its dynamic engagement with leftist politics. While Putnam's anthology excluded the visual arts, *This Quarter* included poetry in English translation (courtesy of Beckett and Bronowski) by Breton, Dalí, Eluard, Peret, and Tzara; drawings and two examples of the "exquisite corpse"; the scenario for "Andalusian Dog"; psychological documents relevant to the theme of "surrealism and madness"; and expository essays on the ideals, key techniques, and history of the movement.[23] In ceding control of the issue to Breton as a condition of publication, the editor Edward Titus asked Breton to avoid "politics and such other topics as might not be in honeyed accord with Anglo-American censorship usages" (6) and Breton agreed, commenting that he was not "inclined to over-estimate an opportunity to make ourselves heard only in undertones" (8). Yet Breton took the opportunity of "explaining [surrealism] to English and American readers...at more effectual length than has been possible hitherto" (8). He warned that surrealism is not an "abstract system...safeguarded against contradiction," nor an "inert stock of ideas," but a "living movement...still bringing together diverse temperaments," a "continuous sequence of acts" (10).[24]

Breton's emphasis on the dynamism of the movement extended to his presentation of its politics. Although Breton sought an explicit alliance with communism in the "Second Surrealist Manifesto" (26–33), he stated that surrealism in 1932 had to "combat the evil resulting from...the will to immediate political action" (39), with Aragon's poem "Red Front" ("Front Rouge") a case in point. Aragon, after becoming a communist, had been imprisoned for calling for the murder of government leaders in "Red Front," and though Breton defended him, Aragon ultimately broke with the movement over perceived slights to communism (Nadeau, 177–181). The poem prompted Breton to ask "whether a social purpose which we pursue in common with others can justify the relinquishing of methods peculiar to ourselves" (40). His answer was decidedly no, for he found that "Red Front" did not "bring us nearer to a settlement of the conflict existing between man's conscious thought and his lyric expression" (41) but was simply "an occasional poem" (43). Breton would struggle in the 1930s to put surrealism in the practical service of the communist revolution, whose preferred genre was realism, and the feasibility of this endeavor was widely debated in leftist little magazines in the United States, including *Art Front*, *New Masses*, and *Partisan Review*.[25] In *Art Front* (March 1937), Samuel Putnam concluded that "any reference to a 'super-real' which may at the same time conceivably be Marxian implies a woeful ignorance of the very bases and whole trend and character of the Marx-Engels teaching." The surrealist "proposes to change, not the world, but the reflection of the world in consciousness," implying that "consciousness conditions being, not being consciousness." He concluded "Marxism and Surrealism are, therefore, diametrically opposed, in their very essence" (10). Despite the mixed reviews of the surrealist effort to synthesize Freud and Marx, the effort itself revealed surrealism's leftist politics, a facet of the movement that was often downplayed or omitted in its presentation by American museums and magazines.[26] The French surrealist poets made a notable appearance in Nancy Cunard's *Negro: An Anthology* in 1934, and many wrote and signed a statement titled "Murderous Humanitarianism," translated by Samuel Beckett, which condemned imperialism and the legacy of slavery in the United States (574–575).[27]

The politics of display evident in *This Quarter* and *European Caravan* operated on a grander scale in the numerous exhibitions of surrealism held in the United States and England in the 1930s, including shows at the Julien Levy Gallery (1932), the Hartford Atheneum (1931), the Harvard Society for Contemporary Art (1932), the Stanley Rose and Howard Putzel Galleries in California (1935), the Baltimore Museum of Art (1936), the Springfield Museum (1936), the Museum of Modern Art (1935–1936), and the New Burlington Gallery in London (1936). While the English surrealist group had organized the International Surrealist Exhibition in London with the help of the French surrealists, this was not the case in the United States. Alfred Barr, the director of MoMA, had originally sought the help of Breton and Eluard for the surrealist exhibition, but both poets pulled out of the project when they realized that Barr would not cede control of the exhibition (Kachur 14–19).

Although the exhibitions emphasized the visual arts, the importance of poetry was evident in the catalogs and printed material that accompanied them, as well as the guides to surrealism published in the 1930s.[28] The International Surrealist Exhibition in London (1936) was accompanied by a pamphlet containing essays by Breton, Gascoyne, and Herbert Read, and it occasioned a translation of Paul Eluard's poetry collection *Thorns of Thunder*, as well as Herbert Read's guide to surrealism, and a number of English surrealist magazines.[29] Barr's exhibition catalog to "Fantastic Art, Dada, Surrealism" emphasized the visual arts over poetry, although Barr pointed out "that for many it is more than an art movement: it is a philosophy, a way of life, a cause to which some of the most brilliant painters and poets of our age are giving themselves with consuming devotion" (8).[30] The interdisciplinary spirit of surrealist poetry was displayed most prominently not at the MoMA but at the innovative Julien Levy gallery, which not only held the first surrealist exhibition in New York, but throughout the 1930s and 1940s served as the premier American gallery for surrealist work of all kinds. Levy was interested in surrealist poetry, painting, photography and film, and he screened films by Bunuel and Dalí, Leger, Disney, Cocteau, Duchamp, Man Ray, and Joseph Cornell (Schaffner and Jacobs, 179, 188–189).

Levy's book *Surrealism* (1936) is an exhibition of surrealism analogous in aim to his gallery. James Thrall Soby said that Levy "was as close to being an official Surrealist himself as one could come without signing one of André Breton's guidelines to the surrealist faith" (*Portrait*, 23). While Breton's influence is clear, Levy's book attests to his American adaptation of surrealism, underscored by the cover, a Cornell collage of a small boy trumpeting the word "surrealism." Levy's collection includes "painting, literature, photography, cinema, politics, architecture, play and behaviour" (4); he emphasized that "unlike so many other 'isms' surrealism is evidently not a deadend, it is not static, but is a dynamic and expansive point of view. Just as surrealism could invite the genius of Picasso so it may still invite the new generation of poets and painters" (27). He added, "Its fundamental doctrine is that poetry originates in, and appeals to, the subconscious. Every one shares the subconscious. Every one can enjoy poetry and every one can make it" (5), and he defined the poet as the artist who overcomes the "irreparable divorce between action and dream" (5). With the aim of educating an American public, Levy's book included profuse "illustrations" and examples of the artwork and writing of figures with a surrealist point of view, many translated by himself, which were organized not by formal attributes but by categories such as "fetishism," "politics," "play," and "dream."

Levy's gallery would set the stage for other innovative galleries and publications in the United States. As Lewis Kachur has shown, surrealist artists creatively sought to elude the museum's rationalizing tendencies by implementing disorienting exhibits and innovative installation designs. Artists such as Duchamp and Cornell took the museum as muse in their miniature collections that transformed the official museum's didactic, rationalizing mission into a stage for surrealist-inspired ends, including collaborative experiment, irrational wandering, the pursuit of pleasure and erotic desire, and the fusion of dream and reality.[31] The poets Jean Cocteau and Mina Loy would also take the museum as muse in 1930s texts that reveal the importance of surrealism's margins to the American scene.

Cocteau's "The Laic Mystery: An Essay in Indirect Criticism" was originally written in 1928 as a defense of De Chirico to the French surrealists, and it was subsequently translated into English by O. E. Rudge and published in *Pagany* (1932) and was republished in *New Directions* (1936). The essay, a "Painter of Modern Life" for the early twentieth century, is a small masterpiece, illuminating the poetry of De Chirico's paintings through the poetry of Cocteau's prose.[32] Cocteau's "guide" explicitly departs from the didactic model of the museum: "People think realists are the lunatics that fill museums. A museum is a morgue. The only chance of feeling anything there is to recognize a friend. A friend behind the corpse. A fine canvas is a testimony to dead activity. In these exhausting excursions through rooms that stink of death one only finds one's feet again before the singular works" (11). A means of animating the "friend behind the corpse," Cocteau's series of aphorisms, metaphors, analogies, prose poems, each linked by an asterisk, provide indirect yet piercing glimpses of Chirico's "singular works": "The horror of a street accident comes from immobile swiftness, a cry changed to silence (not the silence after a cry). One recognizes the corpses at once by their attitudes that are grotesque but not funny. Distance in Chirico is of death. A picture by Chirico is the brutal passage of one state to another" (2). Chirico has been able to "compose a poem with the mechanism of a dream," as has Cocteau in his response: "Poetry expresses itself as it can. I decline to set limits for it. I am free" (9). "The brutal passage of one state to another" not only describes De Chirico's paintings but the translation of Chirico's paintings into Cocteau's language, and the essay concludes by conjuring this poetic collision and its aftermath: "Good bye reader I am going to bed. / I am ravaged by poetry as certain doctors are from using X-rays" (21). This ravaging was far from the civilized, rational intercourse with painting promoted by the modern museum.[33]

Mina Loy's novel *Insel* (1937) is also a work of poetic prose that depicts a ravaging occasioned by surrealist painting and its exhibition. Loy's daughter Joella married Julien Levy in 1927, and Loy would serve as Levy's Paris agent during the early 1930s, arranging the purchase and transportation of surrealist work and exhibiting her paintings at the gallery in 1933.[34] A poet, painter, designer, participant in New York Dada, and the widow of Arthur Cravan, Loy was held in high esteem by the French surrealists (Burke, 328). *Insel* is structured around Loy's role as an agent for the Levy Gallery, chronicling her relationship with the German Surrealist painter Richard Oelze (Insel): Oelze's painting "Expectation" first hung in Loy's Paris apartment, was shown at Levy's gallery, and entered MoMA's permanent collection (Burke, 385; Schaffner and Jacobs, 72). In collecting and giving narrative form to the fragmented, "irreal" Insel and his paintings, Loy creates a textual museum that critically engages European surrealism in its movement from Paris to New York. The novel, completed after Loy's move to New York in 1937, is, like Cocteau's text, an indirect self-portrait.

Although initially Insel appears more surreal than the surrealists to Loy's protagonist, offering access to an altered state of consciousness that threatens to shatter her, in debunking Insel's mesmeric force, Loy associates Insel with surrealism's "black magic," which connotes gothic travels into uncharted dimensions of mind, but also showmanship and trickery. Variously portraying Insel as a living work of surrealist art, as an exhibit in the wax museum, as the walking dead star of a horror film, as a "will o'the wisp" haunting Paris, as an actor "playing" Kafka to eke out his meager living, as a Broadway showman, and as a circus freak, the novel charts the narrator's (and reader's) absorption into the Insel spectacle, followed by the assertion of an everyday, skeptical rationalism that enables an exit from the Insel show. Indeed, if we consider Insel as a surrealist Frankenstein, whose pieces are collected, sewn together, animated and critically vanquished by novel's end, then the novel offers itself as a hybrid surrealist exhibition, one that subjects Oelze's surrealist ideals to feminist critique, black humor, and an American popular culture keen for Dalí's "extravagant publicities" (27).[35] Loy's virtuosic "sideshow" would unfortunately remain unpublished until 1991, its location on the margins of surrealist exhibition enabling its critical purchase but sealing its fate. As Rachel Blau DuPlessis and others have argued, the ambivalent stance of the female experimental writer toward established avant-garde movements has often resulted in her double marginalization and erasure, and this would prove true for Loy and other women artists as they negotiated surrealism.[36]

At the end of a decade notable for surrealism on display, H. R. Hays reflected in *Poetry* (54 [Apr.-Sept. 1939]) on the question of "Surrealist Influence in Contemporary English and American Poetry," evaluating the work of Harold Rosenberg, Charles Henri Ford, Dylan Thomas, and David Gascoigne (sic). Hays noted, "It has had its schisms and burnt its heretics. Some of its members have gone in the direction of social protest. Some of its painters have achieved a faddish popularity. It has been sentenced to death a number of times by the critics; yet today, in 1938, its influence still crops up in the work of various younger British and American poets" (202). For Hays, the surrealist "progression by associated images instead of logic, is probably the turning point which divides modern poetry from the academic tradition"; he argued "the movement still has power to stimulate the creative imagination" because it was never simply a style but "it was for poetry a reemphasis of an axiom, a reassertion of the poetic process" (202).

THE 1940S: *VIEWED THROUGH THE EYES OF POETS*

For many commentators, French surrealism ended in 1940 with the occupation of France by Germany. During World War II, however, the key figures associated with the surrealist movement sought refuge in the United States, influencing American art and literature in tangible ways, and contributing to what Serge Guilbaut has described as "the birth and development of an American avant-garde, which in the space of a few years succeeded in shifting the cultural center of the west from Paris to New York" (1). While the importance of surrealism to the formation of this postwar American avant-garde is clear, studies such as Serge Guilbaut's and Monica Sawin's are limited to the fine arts, emphasizing the New York School painters (Robert Motherwell, Jackson Pollock, Willem de Kooning, Arshile Gorky, etc.). In short, the history of surrealist influence privileges painting, a largely male cast of characters, and nationalist agon, presenting the exile of European surrealists in New York during the early 1940s as indicative of the movement's death throes, even as the New York School rises from surrealism's ashes. Not only does the earlier history of surrealism in the United States drop out, but poetry is given scant attention: keeping poetry firmly in view enables a different history of surrealist influence to emerge, one in which the sexual and national politics of surrealism become increasingly important.

The relationship between the surrealists in exile and their American colleagues was productive if tense, due to American adaptations of surrealism. James Laughlin's *New Directions Annual* of 1940 included a surrealist section guest edited by the Greek poet Nicolas Calas, a disciple of Breton, who became a prominent explicator of surrealism in the United States in the 1940s.[37] Laughlin's aim was "to present to the American public exhibitions of important foreign literary movements...with as much impartiality as possible"; he added, "I hope that Surrealism…will not be kicked around as a dead body that has no further use, but curiously examined in an effort to salvage its good features and make the most of them" (xvi–xvii). Although the Annual presented a manifesto by Calas, a "Surrealist Pocket Dictionary" and anthology of surrealist literature in English translation assembled by Calas and Breton, it also included critical appraisals by Herbert Muller and Kenneth Burke, and a series of chainpoems by American, English (New Apocalypse), and Japanese (Vou Group) poets.

The chainpoems, originated by the poet Charles Henri Ford, exemplified the fissures that emerged between official surrealism and its American adaptations. Although authored collaboratively, the chainpoem differed from the exquisite corpse in that the poets did not need to be present together to write it, and they could consciously study previous lines, using their own line to either "contradict" or "carry forward the preceding line." As Calas emphasized in his "Towards a Third Surrealist Manifesto," the chainpoems were not surrealist precisely because of this conscious evaluation of what others had written (417), which diminished the role of chance and emphasized craft over spontaneity. A further faultline emerged in the Annual, connected to the surrealist movement's sexual politics. Calas argued that dissident surrealists had been afflicted by "weaknesses of a sexual nature" (e.g., they couldn't accept monogamous love as an ideal: 418–419). Ilya Ehrenburg in his blistering attack on surrealism's communist politics (published in Partisan Review in 1935) had made similar accusations, arguing that "studying pederasty and dreams" (12) made surrealists unfit for work and revolution. Kenneth Burke pointed out the contradiction in Calas's desire to "modernize Surrealism by imposing upon it the pattern of monogamy" given that surrealism "is the ultimate extreme of liberalism—'freedom' projected into the aesthetic domain with an absoluteness, a squandering, that can only be found at a time when a 'free' cultural trend is drawing to a close" (572). This contradiction had its origin in Breton's homophobia, at odds with his championing of freedom of desire. Ford had challenged Breton on this very point in a 1939 meeting in Paris, and he would depart from Bretonian influence by privileging the work of queer artists and a queer sensibility in his magazine View (Boatload, 169–171).[38]

Ford's description of the chainpoems as a "collective invention" (369) was an equally apt description of View: Through the Eyes of Poets (1940–1947), the magazine he coedited with Parker Tyler; View continued the work of Transition, publishing European surrealists alongside American poets and artists.[39] Like Jolas and Transition, Ford did not define View as surrealist,[40] but it quickly became the key publication for the European surrealists in New York in the early 1940s, rivaled only by VVV, a magazine edited by the artist David Hare with assistance from Breton, Ernst, and Duchamp. VVV was published in four issues between 1942 and 1944. Levy's innovative gallery and catalog set an influential precedent for View: its stylish design and imaginative layout, along with its striking cover art by well-known surrealists, allowed it to reach an audience beyond the avant-garde. Several issues were devoted to particular surrealists (e.g., Max Ernst, Yves Tanguy, Marcel Duchamp) or themes (Americana Fantastica, Vertigo, Surrealism in Belgium), while other numbers creatively explored the boundaries of the magazine as an exhibition space, much like Peggy Guggenheim, whose surrealist gallery (1942–1947) designed by Frederick Kiesler attempted to "break down the physical and mental barriers which separate people from the art they live with" (*VVV* 2–3 [March 1943]: 76). A feature on the gallery in *VVV* included moving parts and a moving eye piece, while in the March 1945 *View*, Kiesler's "triptych" of Duchamp's studio could be folded to construct the studio in three dimensions, transforming the pages of the magazine into the artist's "gallery," complete with his "large glass" and photos of the twine that covered the First Papers of Surrealism exhibition (1942). *View*'s sponsorship of art exhibitions, lectures, jazz concerts, a surrealist puppet show, and its own poetry imprint similarly worked to dissolve the boundaries between textual and literal gallery, generating a surrealist-centered poetry scene in New York.[41]

The variety of American poets who published their poems, commentaries, and/ or translations in *View* is a testament to the interest in surrealism at the time: Wallace Stevens, William Carlos Williams, Marianne Moore, Randell Jarrell, Philip Lamantia, Parker Tyler, Charles Henri Ford, Joe Massey, H. R. Hays, Paul Eaton Reeve, Mina Loy, Archibald MacLeish, Harold Rosenberg, Louis Zukofsky, e.e. cummings, Man Ray, Kay Sage, Paul Childs, Richard Eberhart, Edouard Roditi, Lionel Abel, Maurice Harper, and Donald Windham. Although Ford and Lamantia explicitly aligned their poetry with surrealism, many of the other American poets engaged surrealism more warily.

Wallace Stevens, building on his early interest in Dada, followed surrealism closely and shared his appraisal in *View*. In the first issue of *View* (September 1940), Charles Henri Ford published an interview with "Verlaine in Hartford," while Stevens's epigrammatic "Materia Poetica," included in the same issue, indicated his interest in surrealist ideas: "To a large extent, the problems of poets are the problems of painters and poets must often turn to the literature of painting for a discussion of their own problems." However, he added, "In poetry, at least, the imagination must not detach itself from reality." Stevens elaborated in 1942, arguing that the "essential fault of surrealism is that it invents without discovering. To make a clam play an accordion is to invent, not to discover. The observation of the unconscious, so far as it can be observed, should reveal things of which we have previously been unconscious, not the familiar things of which we have been conscious plus imagination" (*View* 2.3, "Materia Poetica," 28). Stevens's clam playing an accordion connotes Lautreamont's sewing machine meeting an umbrella, suggesting Stevens' rejection of the artifice of the surrealist image. Stevens argued that "the imagination does not add to reality" and that "the great well of poetry is not other poetry but prose: reality. However it requires a poet to perceive the poetry in reality" (28). Elizabeth Bishop would call this the "always-more-successful surrealism of everyday life," and Bishop, Stevens, and Williams exhibit this preference for a surrealism latent in the real, revealed through a shift in or distortion of perspective, as opposed to the attempt to express unconscious states and desires through imagined or spontaneously rendered grotesque, absurd, or amorphous forms.[42] The latter tendency was evident in the paintings of Dalí, Tanguy, and Klee, and in the poetry of Ford (e.g., "She beat me over the head with a lung" from "There's No Place to Sleep In this Bed, Tanguy" in *View* 2.2 [May 1942]).

Stevens's poem "Analysis of a Theme" explores this preference (*View* 5.3 [Oct. 1945]: 15). The subconscious, Stevens suggests, is best understood as a "time," "There being no subconscious place, / Only Indyterranean / Resemblances / Of place: time's haggard mongrels." Time's "haggard mongrels" are "immaterial monsters," "Invisible," "Not speaking worms, nor birds / Of mutable plume, / Pure coruscations, that lie beyond / The imagination, intact / and unattained, / Even in Paris..." Despite his skepticism of "speaking worms," and a belief that the subconscious lies beyond imagination, Stevens's punning coinages in the poem ("Indyterranean," "We enjoy the ithy oonts and long-haired / Plomets, as the Herr Gott / enjoys his comets") give linguistic form to "immaterial monsters," echoing Eugene Jolas's call in "Revolution of the Word" (1929) for new expressions that can articulate man's irrational nature. In "Materia Poetica," Stevens wrote, "Poetry must be irrational" (*View* 2.3 [Oct. 1942]: 28) and in his essay "The Irrational Element in Poetry" (1937), Stevens commended the surrealists for tapping into "the dynamic influence of the irrational. They are extraordinarily alive.... One test of their dynamic quality and, therefore, of their dynamic effect, is that they make other forms seem obsolete. They, in time, will be absorbed."

Like Stevens, William Carlos Williams, an active contributor to and supporter of *View*, praised surrealism as a spur to creativity in a letter to Ford printed in the May 1942 issue:[43] "you're creating the impossible magazine of the arts no one could have dreamed.... Everyone is trying. That is why they fail. You are not trying. That is why you succeed" (n.p.). He added, "Surrealism is just that: Don't try. An incentive to creation." Williams also praised *View*'s independence: "The thing seems to be that *View* might become anything; that is what I admire about it. It's not a party organ and has no more relation to SURREALISM than that has to the moment, and no less. When it becomes sold on some viewpoint and fixes itself there, you can have it." Williams expressed his nationalist ambivalence about surrealism in a review of Edouard Roditi's *View* edition of Breton's poems, *Young Cherry Trees Secured Against Hares* (7.1 [Oct. 1946]). The review gave backhanded praise that served to ally Breton's surrealism and his "classic coldness of line" with France's conventional, classical past while distinguishing American poetic experiment as the true modernist endeavor, echoing Jolas's criticisms of Breton. In the interest of emphasizing the innate surrealism of America (a gesture Ford and Tyler would follow in 1943's Americana Fantastica number), Williams submitted and introduced a poem by the "mad" Baptist preacher Alva Turner, "The Cat That Came Back," as an example of "the true American surrealism" ([Feb.–March 1942]: 1.11–12, 5).

Williams, like Stevens and Bishop, emphasized that reality is always divulging its irrationality if we pay attention, a perspective he explored in two essays on Ford's lover, the painter Pavel Tchelitchew. Williams distinguished Tchelitchew's work from the surrealists "because these things are drawn from life."[44] Williams's poem "Catastrophic Birth" (*VVV* [June 1942]), may have been inspired by his discussion of

Tchelitchew's "Hide and Seek," a painting that superimposes images of a tree, a man, and children's faces ("Cache Cache," *View* [May 1942]: 2.2). Overlaying imagery of the explosion of Mt. Pelee in 1902 with imagery of one of his female patients who had given birth to six children, "Catastrophic Birth" considers the sublime power of nature to destroy and create. In the context of *VVV*, the poem's reflection on the volcanic explosion, followed by the rescue of "he who had been confined / in disgrace underground" resonates with the surrealist effort to release the unconscious. Yet tellingly, Williams's poem was "drawn from life." In reply to a *View* questionnaire "what is the disappearing point of the unconscious?" Williams answered, "the NY Evening Star" which gives us "all sorts of fascinating detail, the most accurate and expensive that the imagination can buy" (*View* 1.11–12 [Feb.–March 1942]: 10). He added, "In this congeries of factual events is caught the sublime and the irrational. There the sense has, in real truth, disappeared." Similarly, Bishop's "Man-Moth" was inspired by a newspaper misprint for "mammoth" and by Ernst's frottages, the poem akin to the subterranean, irrational landscape opened up by the misprint, much as Ernst's practice of placing paper atop wood and rubbing with charcoal revealed submerged forms or images (*Poems, Prose*, 10; Mullen).

In contrast to poets who absorbed surrealist influence without claiming allegiance to the movement, Philip Lamantia expressed great admiration for the work of Breton and joined the surrealist movement at Breton's invitation. As the son of Sicilian immigrants and a fifteen-year-old high school student from San Francisco, Lamantia had discovered surrealism through exhibitions of Dalí and Miró and in Levy's and Gascoyne's books on surrealism. He published his first poems in *View* in June 1943 (3.2) and the editors proclaimed their "discovery" (43) of this precocious talent. A stanza of "The Ruins," one of Lamantia's first poems published in *View*, illustrates his mastery of the surrealist image:

> Beneath its feathered mirror
> love is lying, a wounded flavor,
> never again to steal,
> when ragged for plastic honey,
> the moon's long frigid kiss. (56)

Love is not simply likened to a "wounded flavor" but is juxtaposed with flavor, a property with which it has no logical relationship, on an unlikely stage (beneath a feathered mirror, under which love may be literally or figuratively "lying").[45] *VVV* No. 4 (Feb. 1944) published a letter from Lamantia to Breton, in which Lamantia proclaimed a "formal adherence to Surrealism" and expressed disdain for American poets ("mimics") who pick and choose what they want from surrealism and "'integrate' the artistic and literary elements into their own productions" (18). Moving to New York in April 1944, Lamantia met Breton and worked for *View*'s editorial board.

Given his view of poetic "mimics," it's not surprising that Lamantia severed ties with Ford and *View* in an unpublished March 15, 1946, letter. *View*'s reproduction of the renaissance artist Zumbo's death sculpture in February 1946 signified to Lamantia a frivolous and "perverse" treatment of surrealism. Lamantia said of the sculpture: "His treatment of death is no different, except in medium, from that of a newsreal [*sic*] photographer in the war. With the millions of corpses, and pictures of corpses, in the war and in concentration camps in Europe, your insistence on reproducing death, by unnatural causes, under the pretense of artistic interest, is either just pure stupidity or mere perverseness." Lamantia accused Ford of "exploiting the macabre and freakish" and cultivating the "thrill" of death, adding that this thrill is "the most foul of modern psychopathological states," helping to corrupt the "perverted sensibility of our time." In this, *View* was guilty of an assault on surrealism equivalent to "perverted, abnormal sexual relationships" [46]: "You can now be proud of adding another neurotic trait to View: necrophilia." Lamantia's comment signaled a broader disaffection; in 1946 he returned to California where he would form a direct link between Bretonian surrealism and the poets of the San Francisco Renaissance and Beat movement, reading at the Six Gallery the evening Ginsberg read *Howl*, a poem with clear surrealist origins.[47] Marianne Moore would also condemn *View*'s "demoralizing strangeness" in March 1944, seeing it "as not in good health" (23).[48] The editors replied to Moore with a spirited condemnation of "the Puritan moral code," which they found to be "a challenge to those in whose natures (I need mention only Villon and Poe) debauchery and the acquisition of dirt have been somehow inseparable from the aggrandizement of the spirit" (23).

Despite the nationalist ideals of poets such as Williams, *View* and *VVV* remained remarkably international in their approach to poetry (as Calas stated in *VVV* (1.1 [1942]), "no national-surrealism!") and helped to generate an interest in new translations. Laughlin had remarked in his 1940 *Annual* on the need for new translations (xx), and *View* answered this call, publishing poets from France, Cuba, Spain, Egypt, Chile, Japan, Scotland, Wales, as well as Emilio Ballagas's letter "A Cuban Poet speaks" (1.4–5 [Dec.–Jan. 1940–1941]) and George Henein's "Message from Cairo to Poets in America" (1.7–8 [Oct.–Nov. 1941]) Also published in *View* were Edouard Roditi's translation of Roussel's *Impressions of Africa* and Paul Bowles's translation of De Chirico's *Hebdomeros*.[49] Like *View*, *VVV* published poets from France, Egypt (George Henein), Martinique (Aimé Cesaire),[50] Chile (Jorge Caceres), Peru, and Belgium. Both magazines followed surrealist poetry's career in Latin America, Mexico, and the Caribbean, a trend that would influence translations in the United States in the 1950s and beyond.[51]

By 1947 *View* had shut its doors, and many of the surrealists in New York had returned to Europe. At this moment, surrealism's legacy in France and the United States was debated in the pages of *Poetry*. Jacques Alamand's "The Genealogy of Lettrism" reported on the view from France (*Poetry* 71 [1947–1948]): while in 1939 "surrealism was still holding out," after the war, it was regarded as "an outdated fetish" (144), with Lettrism taking its place as the latest –ism, its disintegration of the word a "logical inheritance of surrealism" (144). In New York, Parker Tyler, in a review of Ana Balakian's *The Literary Origins of Surrealism*, objected to intimations of surrealism's death: "The sort of energy…employed here is that post-mortem zeal…which one may have in speaking of an interesting corpse" (*Poetry* 70 [1947]: 282). Balakian felt Tyler had missed the point of her history: "There is nothing 'post,' there is nothing cadaverous about any of the poets about whom I have written; their vitality has nothing imitative about it, and their failings are not those of moribunds but of undaunted pioneers" (*Poetry* 71 [1947–1948]: 228).

The 1950s: Absorbing the Surrealist Revolution

Parker Tyler's worries were prescient: surrealism had exerted a profound influence on U.S. art and poetry in the 1940s, but with the exception of a poet like Lamantia who had proclaimed his surrealist allegiance, surrealism would often continue its work under other names, as it shaped the various poetry communities and movements that arose after World War II. As John Ashbery argued, "The Surrealist Revolution cannot happen again because it is no longer necessary. We all 'grew up Surrealist' without even being aware of it." He added, "We have absorbed the lesson to the extent that we have almost forgotten it, but that is not the lesson's fault, it is indeed one of its virtues" (*Art News*, 43). This simultaneous absorption and forgetting of surrealist influence was characteristic of surrealism's American reception. Even as William Rubin's 1968 MoMA retrospective for surrealism positioned surrealism as a thing of the past, the Chicago Surrealist Group was protesting this purported death and staging an alternative exhibition.[52] Poetry, at the center of surrealist exploration, would prove to be the agent of its continual absorption in the United States.

Wallace Fowlie's "Surrealism in 1960: A Backward Glance" (*Poetry* 95) aptly summed up the pervasiveness of surrealist influence on the American poetry scene.[53] Although Fowlie found surrealism "essentially French" and its influence on most countries slight, he found in America "more traces of its effects" (365) and remarked: "Much of the best poetry of the past twenty years bears the mark and the influence of surrealism" (367). Fowlie pointed out that "the surrealist contribution to the theory of poetics ranks high today among the movement's major contributions" (371), summing up the surrealist understanding thus: "Poetry is the power to create, to confer a new meaning on an object. The activity conveys for the surrealists both the meaning of exploration and revelation. Under the practice of poetry the dreams of man and his subconscious life recover their rights, and thus he penetrates the secrets of the world" (371). Fowlie asserted that "today it seems to us the founder of a new literature and a new poetry" (372).

The decade's tempered romanticism owed much to surrealism's "prehensile tail," evident in widespread efforts to conjoin art and everyday life, to explore poetry as process rather than product, to cultivate spontaneity, to practice chance procedures and incorporate accident, to pursue eros and dream, to position the lyric speaker as a vessel for other voices and technologies, and to employ collaborative modes as well as techniques inspired by readymades, collage, cinematic montage, and frottage. Little magazines adapted mimeograph technology, making publication inexpensive and quick: magazines continued to play an important role in defining new poetic communities (Kane, *All*, 57–64). Even as specific transformations of surrealism distinguished various poetic communities (San Francisco Renaissance, Beat, Confessional, Deep Image, Ethnopoetics, New York School, etc.), it also cut across such distinctions. Ginsberg, Plath, Ashbery, Bly, Guest, and Joans were very different poets beginning their careers in the 1950s, yet each found inspiration in surrealism. Its absorption was a measure not only of its cultural influence and aesthetic interest but of its history of adaptation by feminist and queer poets, and by writers of color in "Martinique, Haiti, Cuba, Puerto Rico, South America, Africa, the United States" (Rosemont and Kelley, 1). Although the founding of the Chicago Surrealist group in 1966 (Sakolsky; Rosemont) might be regarded as an aberration from the history of surrealism in the United States, in that the group was officially recognized as part of the surrealist movement by Breton, in fact the group's interest in racial, sexual, and gender politics builds on a tradition initiated by earlier American poets influenced by surrealism. The internationalism established by *VVV* and *View* was also carried forward through the translation of the surrealists of Spain, Latin America, the Caribbean, and France in the 1950s and 1960s, particularly on the part of poets associated with the New York School, Deep Image, and Ethnopoetics.[54]

The poetry of the New York School exemplifies the legacy of the earlier history of surrealism in the United States, and it suggests how a focus on surrealist influence can move us beyond the school, invigorating our understanding of an American avant-garde. Robert Motherwell's *The Dada Painters and Poets: An Anthology* (1951) aimed to pass on the key literary works of Dada and early surrealism to a new generation of poets and painters; he described it as "an accumulation of raw material for students" (xvix), joining (and reprinting materials from) *European Caravan*, *This Quarter*, and the *New Directions Annual*. Motherwell, who had been actively involved in surrealist circles during World War II, effectively passed along not only "raw material" but a collaborative ethos centered on poetry as an inquiry central to painting and the other arts.[55] John Bernard Myers would also convey a sensibility formed in the 1940s to a new generation. Growing up in Buffalo, New York, Myers was so taken with *View* that he wrote a letter of praise (published in *View* 4.1 [March 1944]) and started working as managing editor later that year (*Tracking* 12). Myers recalled, "To my delight I became acquainted with the leader of the Surrealists, André Breton and many of his friends and colleagues—Max Ernst, Matta, Yves Tanguy, Kurt Seligman, Wilfredo Lam, Wolfgang Paalen, Joseph Cornell, and Nicolas Calas" (12–13). He "felt bereft" when most of these artists left the United States in 1947, "but my sadness was mixed with satisfaction. I had absorbed a Surrealist point of view: to keep myself open to wonder, to be endlessly curious, to revere the imagination, never to cease to desire more of life. And above all, to track the marvelous" (13).

In "The Impact of Surrealism on the New York School"(*Evergreen Review* [March–April 1960]), Myers noted that the French surrealist movement had "grown flaccid" but its influence persisted in New York: "Since Breton professed that 'surrealism is not a rational, dogmatic and consequently static theory of art,' that it is without 'accurate definition or explanation,' it is not surprising that the seed which Breton planted in New York during the years in which he resided here have come to flower in a soil not French." In short, "the avant-garde spirit seems largely to continue in New York" (76). Myers had much to do with this: he opened the Tibor de Nagy Gallery in 1952, which exhibited the work of the younger painters of the New York School (Grace Hartigan, Jane Freilicher, Larry Rivers, Alfred Leslie, Nell Blaine, etc.), and would also publish the first works of the New York School poets John Ashbery, Frank O'Hara, Barbara Guest, Kenneth Koch, and James Schuyler, including collaborations with the gallery's painters. Myers solicited poets' plays, published a small magazine *Semi-Colon*, and in 1969 published an anthology *Poets of the New York School*, carrying forward the legacy of the Levy Gallery and *View* (Lehman, 20–27; Diggory).

Barbara Guest deemed Myers "absolutely essential to our cultural inheritance" (Lehman, 24) and remarked, "I grew up under the shadow of Surrealism. In that creative atmosphere of magical rites there was no recognized separation between the arts....One could never again look at poetry as a locked kingdom. Poetry extended vertically, as well as horizontally, never did it lie motionless within a linear structure. Assisting in this poetic mobility would be an associative art within whose eye the poet might gaze for reassurance and for a glowing impersonal empathy" (Guest, 8). Guest adopted the surrealists' capacious understanding of poetry, but in her sense of the mobility made possible by this understanding, she and her contemporaries would build on Jolas's and Williams's call for "a revolution of the word," pursuing experiments in syntax, structure, and visual layout. Tellingly, Guest and the other poets published by Myers would carve out careers centered on the visual arts. All worked as art critics and O'Hara as a curator at the MoMA; all wrote poems about painting and other kinds of visual media (film, photography); and all avidly pursued collaborations with visual artists, producing plays, films, lithographs, poem-paintings, and so on. If they recognized language as their essential medium (e.g., O'Hara, "Why I Am Not a Painter," 261-2), they nevertheless shared the surrealist sense of poetry as defined less by genre or medium than by an imaginative act that enabled a transformed perspective on the irrational, erotic texture of the everyday.

John Ashbery, like Guest, emphasized the importance of the earlier American reception of surrealism on his sensibility, particularly *Life* magazine's coverage of the MoMA 1936 Fantastic Art, Dada, and Surrealism exhibition: "I think it was at that moment I realized I wanted to be a Surrealist, or rather that I already was one. It was nice to know I was something and to know what that something was. For years I pored over that issue of *Life*, and then found some more examples in the museum library, including *View* magazine and a book about Joseph Cornell, who immediately became my favorite artist and has remained one to this day" (*Selected*, 246). This claiming of surrealism on the part of Ashbery, Guest, and many other poets writing in the 1950s opened up surrealism to queer and feminist perspectives, building on the earlier American reception of surrealism in ways that we are still discovering. As Marsha Bryant argues, for instance, Sylvia Plath found in surrealism a means of critically engaging the fantastical promises of 1950s ads for domestic commodities and women's roles. Guest stated to Rachel Blau DuPlessis that surrealism "meant freedom, especially for a woman" (DuPlessis, 169–170), and DuPlessis has demonstrated how Guest negotiated Bretonian surrealism's limited idealizations of woman and its liberating bequests in her development of a "fair realism," a feminist twist on surrealism (168–170). Ashbery, like Ford and Burke before him, explicitly objected to Breton's homophobia: "Sexual liberty, he [Breton] proclaimed, meant every conceivable kind of sexual act except for homosexuality…to restrict something proclaimed as 'total' is to turn it into its limited opposite" (*Reported*, 6).

Ashbery called these critical adaptations of surrealism "the second, open sense in which it can still be said to animate much of the most advanced art being done today" (*Reported*, 27), implying that surrealist ideals were more genuinely realized beyond the control of Breton.[56] The openness of surrealism to such transformation, however, is what allowed it to persist: "And this really is what the Surrealists were doing—not letting anything be lost on them—and our poetry is descended from Surrealism in the sense that it is open. I do not think of myself as a surrealist, but I feel akin to it in the same way that the poet Henri Michaux does—he once said that he wasn't a Surrealist, but that Surrealism for him was *la grande permission*—the big permission. The big permission is, I think, as good a definition as any of poetry, of the kind that interests me at any rate" (*Selected*, 115–116). Like earlier American poets, the poets associated with the New York School articulated their affinities for surrealist outliers, including Dora Maar, Duchamp, Crevel, Reverdy, Roussel, Cocteau, and De Chirico.

The little magazine *Locus Solus* (named after the 1914 novel by Raymond Roussel) exemplified this opening up of surrealism and suggests one direction for opening up an understanding of the 1950s poetry scene. Six issues were published in 1961–1962 by Harry Matthews, with Koch, Matthews, Schuyler, and Ashbery rotating as editors. Roussel's *Locus Solus* centers on the enigmatic scientist-curator Canterel's museum of corpses, which are animated through injections of the substances vitalium and resurrectine, such that the corpses relive a scene of great drama from their lives. As the corpses come to life, the text unravels their stories. The 1950s interest in Roussel and other surrealists functioned similarly: like Canterel, the little magazine *Locus Solus* resurrected the "corpses" of past poetry, in some cases literally through the cutting up and re-presentation of past poems. This was particularly evident in the collaboration issue (No. 2, 1961), edited by Kenneth Koch, which opened with two epigraphs, the first by Roussel: "L'écriteau bref qui s'offre à l'oeil apitoyé"; and the second from Lautreamont: "La poesie doit etre faite par tous. Non par un [. . .]." The issue provided a history of poetic collaboration, including poems by Chinese and Japanese poets, Renaissance English poets, British romantic poets, futurists and surrealists, and concluding with contemporary collaborations.[57] In "A Note on This Issue," Koch wrote that he found collaboration inspiring "because it gives objective form to usually concealed subjective phenomenon and therefore jars the mind into strange new positions" (193). This strangeness "might lead them to the unknown, or at the least to some dazzling insights at which they could never have arrived consciously or alone. The surrealists were the first avowed practitioners of literary collaboration for this specific purpose, though I think that poets of all times who have written together have done so partly in the hope of being inspired by the strange situation" (193). Collaboration made possible the unlikely encounters that center the surrealist image.

Studying little magazines such as *Locus Solus* can also jar our minds into "strange new positions," helping us to consider literary history beyond the categories of schools and movements. Certainly, little magazines functioned as a means of consolidating movements or communities. At the same time, their role as ephemeral, impromptu museums, their ability to speak to a particular moment, can help us recover the richness and irrationality of literary history as it was being made— the fortuitous encounters and affinities that cut across schools and movements. Although the New York School poets Guest, O'Hara, Ashbery, Koch, and Schuyler all published writing in *Locus Solus*, so did many other poets and painters. For instance, Gregory Corso and William Burroughs, associated with the Beats, contributed cut-ups to the *Locus Solus* collaboration issue: this practice would prove important to poets associated with both movements and begs the usual distinctions drawn between them.[58]

Once we consider surrealism in 1950s New York as a lingua franca, unexpected connections emerge. For instance, both Ted Joans and Frank O'Hara arrived in New York in 1951. O'Hara, reflecting on his modernist precursors in "Memorial Day 1950," stated "Our responsibilities did not begin / in dreams, though they began in bed" (*Collected*, 17–18). Ted Joans, in April 1953, writes in "The Enigma of Francis Parrish of Paris France": "Under the cold bed I saw / heavy masses of shadows and many people of all races / ready to fall on the sleeping knife and the snoring plate" (*Teducation*, 216–17).[59] And in 1950 Mina Loy's chronicle of New York's Bowery, "Hot Cross Bums," appeared in *New Directions*: "And always on the trodden street / —the communal cot— / embalmed in rum / under an unseen / baldachin of dream / blinking his inverted sky / of flagstone / prone / lies the body of the flop / where'er he drop" (*Lost*, 143). The responsibilities that began in, on, or under the surrealist bed would shape each poet's career. Ted Joans in 1960 met André Breton in Paris and became active in the surrealist movement in Paris and Chicago, writing to Breton: "Without surrealism, I would not have been able to survive the abject vicissitudes and acts of racist violence that the white man in the United States has constantly imposed on me. Surrealism became the weapon that I chose to defend myself, and it has been and always will be my own way of life" (Rosemont and Kelley 229). Frank O'Hara in 1960 became an assistant curator of painting and sculpture at the Museum of Modern Art, helping to exhibit many of the artists (e.g., Motherwell) who were surrealism's American heirs. And Mina Loy, far from being a relic of an earlier avant-garde, continued to play a vital role in critically adapting surrealism to an American stage in her poems and collages of the 1940s and early 1950s.[60] This work, fueled by Loy's feminist and Christian Scientist beliefs, depicts an everyday "sub-realism" of the streets, originating in homelessness, poverty, and addiction.

These varied poetic adaptations of surrealism are a measure of its vitality at the beginning of the 1960s, a vitality sustained by surrealism's deep, if forgotten, American roots.

KEY EARLY HISTORIES OF
SURREALISM IN ENGLISH

Jane Heap, ed. *Little Review, French Number* Autumn–Winter 1923–1924, *Surrealiste Number*, Spring–Summer 1926.

Eugene Jolas, ed., *Transition*, 1927–30, 1932–1938.

Peter Neagoe, *What Is Surrealism*, 1932.

Samuel Putnam, ed., *European Caravan*, 1932.

Edward Titus, ed. (André Breton, guest ed.), *This Quarter, Surrealist Number*, V.1 1932.

David Gascoyne, *A Short Survey of Surrealism*, 1935.

Herbert Read, *Surrealism*, 1935.

Julien Levy, *Surrealism*, 1936.

Alfred Barr Jr., *Fantastic Art, Dada & Surrealism*, 1936.

James Laughlin, ed. (Nicolas Calas, guest ed.), *New Directions Annual*, 1940.

Georges Edouard Lemaitre, *From Cubism to Surrealism in French Literature*, 1941.

Nicolas Calas, *Confound the Wise*, 1942.

Anna Balakian, *Literary Origins of Surrealism* 1947; *Surrealism: the Road to the Absolute* 1959.

Eugene Jolas, ed. *Transition Workshop*, 1949.

Marcel Raymond, *From Baudelaire to Surrealism*, 1950; translation of *De Baudelaire au Surrealisme*, 1933.

Wallace Fowlie, *Age of Surrealism*, 1950.

Robert Motherwell, *Dada Painters and Poets*, 1951.

Maurice Nadeau, *History of Surrealism*, 1965; translation of *Histoire du Surrealisme*, 1945.

Harry Matthews, *Introduction to Surrealism*, 1965.

William S. Rubin, *Dada, Surrealism, and Their Heritage*, 1968.

NOTES

1   See Arnold, Cook, Joron, Perloff, and Young.

2   A number of factors have contributed to the submergence of surrealism's influence on American poetry, including the role of nationalism; the assimilation of surrealism by popular culture; surrealism's relationship to communism; the role played by marginalized poets in the U.S. reception of surrealism; the uneven history of translations of surrealist writings; the dispersal of surrealist ideas into other rubrics such as the "everyday"; and the disciplinary divide between art history and literature.

3   For instance, see Jackaman, Ray, and Remy on the English surrealist movement.

4 Breton noted, "The freedom it possesses is a perfect freedom in the sense that it recognizes no limitations exterior to itself. As it was said on the cover of the first issue of *La Revolution Surrealiste*, 'it will be necessary to draw up a new declaration of the Rights of Man'" (Titus, Ed., Breton, Guest Ed., *This Quarter*, 22). See also Rosemont; Rosemont and Kelley.

5 On collage, see Ernst, "Inspiration to Order," Titus, Ed., Breton, Guest Ed. *This Quarter*, 81; Breton, *Manifestoes*, 41.

6 See Calas, *New Directions*; Ray, "Introduction," *Surrealist Movement*.

7 On modernist little magazines, see Churchill and McKible; Scholes and Wulfman.

8 Nadeau; Rosemont and Kelley, 193–194.

9 "A Surrealist Master," *Poetry* 48 (April–Sept. 1936): 347–355; 353.

10 "Paris Letter," *The Dial* (Jan.–June 1925): 222–223; 223.

11 Josephson's defense of Dada echoed Soupault, who, in a November 17, 1922, letter to *The Dial* (73), criticized Henry McBride's remarks about the death of Dada, emphasizing Dada as an "état d'esprit."

12 "Which Way?" *Little Review* (Autumn–Winter 1923–1924): 29–34; 29.

13 Under Jane Heap, the *Little Review* sponsored two art exhibitions, though not of surrealist art.

14 "Dada Painting or the Oil-Eye," *Little Review* (Autumn–Winter 1923–1924): 11.

15 "The Disciples of Gertrude Stein," *Poetry* 17 (Oct.–March 1920–1921): 36–40.

16 Review of Taupin, *Poetry* 37 (Oct.–March 1930–1931): 45–49.

17 *Transition* ran as a monthly review from April 1927 to April 1928, and it ran as a quarterly review from June 1928 to June 1930. It was suspended between the June 1930 issue and the March 1932 issue; further issues appeared in February 1933, July 1935, June 1936, Fall 1936, 1937, and 1938.

18 *Transition* published poems in English translation by Desnos, Peret, Soupault, Eluard, Arp, Isidore Ducasse/the Comte de Lautreamont, Reverdy, and Queneau; Breton's "Introduction to the Discourse on the Dearth of Reality" (August 1927); the opening chapter of *Nadja* (March 1928); a section of *Mad Love* (April–May 1938); and Soupault's essay "Whither French Literature" (June 1929) on surrealist precursors from Rimbaud to Dada.

19 See, for example, Salemson, *Transition* (February 1929): 103. See Tashjian, *Boatload*, for a discussion of *Transition*'s critics.

20 The proclamation was followed by a list of "slanguage: 1929" in the same issue, by a "revolution of the word dictionary" and a "dictionary of neologisms" in 1932, and by a June 1936 list of symbol words that appeared in Jolas's dreams and daydreams, including "mistagriffre," "Marabimini," etc. (113).

21 Following the work of Heffernan, Paul, Bergmann-Loizeaux, and Fischer, I consider the museum as an arbiter of cultural value, an institution of cultural memory, and as a textual trope for the literary anthology, little magazine, and poetic collection.

22 Translations included a section of *The Magnetic Fields*; poems by Ribemont Dessaignes, Reverdy, de Boully, and Tzara; and "Un Cadavre," a collaborative text on the death of Anatole France that had appeared in the *Little Review* (Autumn–Winter 1924–1925).

23 The anthology remains a "greatest hits of Surrealism": essays included Dalí's "The Object as Revealed in Surrealist Experiment" and "The Stinking Ass," in which he defined the paranoiac image; Max Ernst's "Inspiration to Order," which described surrealist methods including collage, frottage, and exquisite corpse; Paul Eluard's essay "Poetry's Evidence"; René Char's essay "The Poetic Spirit"; Crevel's "The Period of Sleeping-Fits," which recounts early experiments with automatism; and an excerpt from Duchamp's notes on "The Bride Stripped Bare by her Own Bachelors, Even."

24 Breton's essay "Surrealism: Yesterday, To-Day and To-Morrow" summarized the key ideas and history of surrealism, quoting liberally from his manifestoes while providing commentary for an English-speaking audience.

25 In 1935 Breton and the French surrealist movement were expelled from the Communist party. On surrealism and communism, see Nadeau; Tashjian, *Boatload*, 113–114; Steven Harris; on modernist poetry's complex relation to communist politics in the 1930s, see Filreis. For commentary on surrealism's politics published in the little magazines, see Horace Gregory's review of e. e. cummings's translation of "Red Front" in *Poetry* 42 (Apr.–Sept. 1933); Jerome Klein's essay in *Art Front* 1.3 (Feb. 1935); *Partisan Review*'s 1935 publication of Ilya Ehrenbourg's [sic] blistering attack "The Surrealists"; Dwight Macdonald's (*Partisan Review* 3 [Aug.–Sept. 1938]) review of *Transition*'s tenth-anniversary issue, and his translation (Fall 1938, 6.1) of Breton's and Diego Rivera's "Manifesto: Towards a Free Revolutionary Art." In the August–September 1936 *Contemporary Poetry and Prose* (1 no. 4–5: 74–75), the editor Roger Roughton published "Surrealism and Communism," which Ezra Pound grumpily answered in "The Coward Surrealists" (7 [Nov. 1936]).

26 On the reception of the poetry of the American left and the politics of historical memory, see Cary Nelson and Lowney.

27 Crevel also contributed an essay, "The Negress in the Brothel," that revealed an intimate understanding about how gender and sexuality function as categories of oppression much like class and race.

28 See Neagoe, Gascoyne, Read. Read's guide, published in response to the International Surrealist Exhibition in London, included ninety-six reproductions of surrealist art, as well as essays by Breton, Davies, Eluard, and Hugnet.

29 On the English surrealist magazines inspired by the London exhibition, see Jackaman. American poets such as Djuna Barnes, Stevens, Ford, and cummings contributed poems to these publications. On the American response to the London exhibition and its associated publications, see Morton Dauwen Zabel's reviews in *Poetry* (48 [Apr.–Sept. 1936]).

30 A legacy of this exhibition is the MoMA collection of Dada and Surrealist documents: see the bibliography in Motherwell assembled by the MoMA librarian Bernard Karpel.

31 See McShine; Rosenbaum.

32 *European Caravan* noted that although Cocteau is "an artist, musician, actor as well as a poet, it is as a poet that he regards himself in all his activities" (76). *The Dial* and *Poetry* in the 1920s published numerous reviews of Cocteau's work.

33 On the civilizing mission of the modern museum, see Bennett, Duncan.

34 On Loy's role as Levy's agent, see Burke (377), Schaffner and Jacobs (67–71, 175), and Arnold (182). Arnold proposes that *Insel* is at once "an experiment in surrealist narrative" and a "satire on the whole surrealist endeavor," with Breton's *Nadja* in its sights ("Afterword," *Insel*, 186). Miller and Bronstein concur, arguing that *Insel* inverts *Nadja* by positioning the male surrealist painter as the muse to the female narrator's quest for self-definition.

35 Breton had concluded in *This Quarter* that it was "enough if surrealism is restored to its true perspective, and we shall not despair of seeing some day a storm rising from within this tea-cup" (44). The media storm triggered by Meret Oppenheim's fur-lined teacup at the MoMA show and Salvador Dalí's Venus Pavilion at the 1939 World's Fair may not have been what Breton had in mind, but surrealism's treatment in the United States was marked by these mixtures of the popular and avant-garde.

36 On women artists' and poets' relationships to surrealism, see DuPlessis, Caws, Chadwick, and Rosemont.

37 See Calas; Kolocotronni.

38 *View* began as a monthly magazine in 1940, became a bimonthly in 1941, and
    subsequently was published quarterly. Ford was a savvy editor and promoter, founding
    his first magazine, *Blues* (1929–1930), a "bi-sexual bi-monthly," at the age of sixteen,
    and he garnered the support and contributions of Williams, Pound, Barnes, Stein,
    Boyle, Rexroth, H.D., Jolas, Tankersley Young, and others. In 1930 Ford moved to
    Paris where he became part of the expatriate scene and became close to Djuna Barnes
    and Gertrude Stein, and published with Parker Tyler, *The Young and the Evil* (Obelisk
    Press, 1933), recounting their poetic and sexual adventures. In Paris, Ford met the artist
    Pavel Tchelitchew, who returned with him to New York in 1934 and became his lifelong
    partner. See Ford.

39 Ford published poetry in *Transition* and corresponded with Jolas while editing *Blues*.

40 Hence, Ford called *View* 1.7–8, edited by Nicolas Calas, a "surrealist number," a
    distinction predicated on the fact that Calas was part of the surrealist movement.

41 Ford sponsored art exhibitions in the offices of View on E. 53rd Street and coordinated
    many special issues to coincide with exhibitions held at galleries, which helped to
    defray publication costs because the galleries would use the issues as exhibition
    catalogs (*Boatload*, 199, 200).

42 Bishop wrote to Anne Stevenson of "dreams, works of art (some), glimpses of the
    always-more-successful surrealism of everyday life, unexpected moments of empathy
    (is it?), catch a peripheral vision of whatever it is one can never really see full-face but
    that seems enormously important" (*Poems, Prose*, 860–861). On Bishop's surrealism,
    see Mullen and Page.

43 Williams not only supported and contributed writing to Ford's first magazine, *Blues*,
    but he wrote an introduction for Ford's first collection of surrealist-influenced poetry,
    The Garden of Disorder (1938), and he maintained a lively correspondence with Ford.
    On Williams's engagement with surrealist film, see McCabe.

44 W. C. Williams, "An Afternoon with Tchelitchew," *Life and Letters Today* (1937) 17.10:
    55–58.

45 On Lamantia's use of surrealist poetics, see Frattali. For a good discussion of the
    surrealist image see Balakian, *Road to the Absolute*, 119–126.

46 In discussing *View*'s contributions to "perverted, abnormal sexual relationships,"
    Lamantia added parenthetically: "and I don't mean among fairies, but between man
    and woman."

47 In "Howl," Ginsberg "dreamt and made incarnate gaps in Time & Space through
    images juxtaposed, and trapped the archangel of the soul between 2 visual images
    and joined the elemental verbs and set the noun and dash of consciousness together
    jumping with sensation of Pater Omnipotens Aeterna Deus." Metaphors such as "lamb
    stew of the imagination," "taxicabs of Absolute Reality," "orange crates of theology," and
    "animal soup of time" vividly enact Lautreamont's meeting of a sewing machine and
    umbrella.

48 Parker Tyler, a fan of Moore, published a Moore interview in the November 1940
    issue (1.3) in which he stated, "Mentioning surrealism, I learned that she sees some
    merit in it" (3). Moore also participated in a questionnaire, "Towards the Unknown,"
    in 1942 (1.11–12).

49 Roditi, an American poet born in Paris who moved in surrealist circles in the 1920s
    and 1930s, published his original poetry and translations in *Transition, Poetry*, and
    View, and joined Samuel Beckett as a key translator of surrealist poetry. He wrote
    numerous reviews of translated works and reflections on translation, for example,
    "The Poetics of Translation" (*Poetry* 60 [Apr.–Sept. 1942]). He was a victim of the

McCarthy era's purging of homosexuals from U.S. government jobs, fired in 1950 from his job as a translator.

50 Breton, who met Césaire in 1940, was a strong advocate of his work, publishing "A Great Black Poet" in *Hemispheres* (Fall/Winter 1943–1944). See Richardson.

51 *Poetry* magazine responded to this trend in its reviews of new translations, and H. R. Hays translated Andrade's essay "The New American and His Point of View Towards Poetry" on Latin American poetry and "transplanted surrealism" (*Poetry* 62 [Apr.–Sept. 1943], 103).

52 See Sakolsky, *Forecast*, 44–45.

53 Fowlie was *Poetry*'s key critic of French poetry during the 1950s, reviewing translations of poetry by Michaux, Baudelaire, St. John-Perse, Mallarmé, Char, Cocteau, and contemporary Haitian and French poets.

54 Robert Bly, Jerome Rothenberg, Robert Kelly, James Wright, and Robert Creeley (and later W. S. Merwin, Galway Kinnell, and Mark Strand) were interested in "deep image," the image originating in the unconscious rather than in the eye. Bly noted the origins of deep image in French surrealism, and he would use his magazines the *Fifties* and *Sixties* to decry the Puritanism of the Anglo-American tradition and to advocate for French influence. See Rasula on the importance of translation for deep image poetics. Rothenberg would develop ethnopoetics, the interest in the subconscious and pre-rational taking an anthropological turn to an emphasis on "stateless, low-technology cultures and on oral and nonliterate [nonliteral] forms of verbal expression" (Rothenberg 388).

55 Motherwell cautioned that "it must be remembered, in using the book, that dada, like surrealism, was probably more the work of poets than painters ... and that, like surrealism, dada's permanent effects have been on contemporary French literature, not on modern painting—though there is a real dada strain in the minds of the New York School of abstract painters that has emerged in the last decade; painters, many of whom were influenced by the presence of the Parisian surrealists in New York during the second world war" (xvix).

56 On Ashbery's debts to dada and surrealism, see Cook, Carvalho, Maggie Nelson, Kane, Silverberg, and Sweet. Ashbery, like Jolas and Williams, objected to automatism and to surrealist poetry's adherence to conventions of grammar (*Selected*, 20–21).

57 Koch included collaborations by Breton and Eluard, Eluard and Peret, Breton and Tanguy, Char and Eluard, and examples of exquisite corpse. From New York School circles, Koch included collaborations by Ashbery and Schuyler, O'Hara and the French language, Deravole and Perrault, Freilicher and Koch, Berkson and Elmslie, and Ashbery and Koch. He also included cut-ups by Burroughs, Corso, and "Rimbaud"; a cut-up by Corso and "Eisenhower"; two cut-ups by Ruth Krauss; and a cut-up by Daniel Krakauer.

58 Indicating the renewed interest in this practice, Charles Henri Ford published his collection of collage and cut-up poems, *Spare Parts* (Athens: New View, 1966). On the cut-up as developed by William Burroughs, who contributed to the *Locus Solus* collaboration issue, see Oliver Harris.

59 African American Beat poets Ted Joans and Bob Kaufman "did more than anyone else to advance the cause of surrealist revolution in the United States," according to Rosemont and Kelley (219; see 219–232).

60 Miller reads *Insel* as a symptom of "an avant-garde on the verge of disappearance" (208). Schreiber cautions against reading Loy's late work as a response to a failure in modernist aesthetics," arguing that "Loy's poetics are ... often generated in response to

cultural circumstances" and therefore "compel us to seek out new frames of analysis" (481, 482). Rexroth's essay on Loy published in *Circle* in 1944 made the case for her as a major American modernist and bemoaned her obscurity; Jonathan Williams listened, and his Jargon Press published *Lost Lunar Baedeker & Time-Tables* in 1958. Loy also placed some of her poems from the 1940s in *Accent*, and published "Hot Cross Bums" in *New Directions* 12 (1950): 311–320 (see Schreiber).

REFERENCES

Arnold, David. *Poetry and Language Writing: Objective and Surreal.* Liverpool: Liverpool University Press, 2007.

Ashbery, John. *The Double Dream of Spring.* New York: E.P. Dutton, 1970.

———. "Growing Up Surreal." *Art News* 67.3 (1968): 42–44, 65.

———. *Reported Sightings: Art Chronicles 1957–1987.* New York: Alfred A. Knopf, 1989.

———. *Selected Prose.* Ed. Eugene Richie. Ann Arbor: University of Michigan Press, 2004.

Balakian, Anna. "Surrealism." In *The New Princeton Encyclopedia of Poetry and Poetics*, eds. Alex Preminger and T. V. F. Brogan. Princeton: Princeton University Press, 1993.

Barr, Alfred H. *Fantastic Art, Dada, Surrealism.* New York: Museum of Modern Art, 1936.

Bennett, Tony. *The Birth of the Museum: History, Theory, Politics.* New York: Routledge, 1995.

Bergmann-Loizeaux, Elizabeth. *Twentieth-Century Poetry and the Visual Arts.* Cambridge: Cambridge University Press, 2009.

Bishop, Elizabeth. *Poems, Prose, and Letters.* Eds. Robert Giroux and Lloyd Schwartz. New York: Library of America, 2008.

Breton, André. *Manifestoes of Surrealism.* Trans. Richard Seaver and Helen Lane. Ann Arbor: University of Michigan Press, 1969.

———. *What Is Surrealism? Selected Writings.* Ed. and trans. Franklin Rosemont. New York:: Pathfinder, 1978.

Bronstein, Hilda. "Mina Loy's *Insel* as Caustic Critique of the Surrealist Paradox." *HOW2* 1.4 (September 2000). n.p.

Bryant, Marsha. "Plath, Domesticity, and the Art of Advertising," *College Literature* 29.3 (Summer 2002): 17–34.

Burke, Carolyn. *Becoming Modern: The Life of Mina Loy.* Berkeley: University of California Press, 1997.

Calas, Nicolas. *Confound the Wise.* New York: Arrow Editions, 1942.

———. "Towards a Third Surrealist Manifesto," *New Directions In Prose & Poetry 1940.* Norfolk, CT: 1940. 408-421.

Carvalho, Silvia. *The Desire to Communicate: Reconsidering John Ashbery and the Visual Arts.* Frankfurt: Peter Lang, 2000.

Caws, Mary Ann. *The Surrealist Look: An Erotics of Encounter.* Cambridge: MIT Press, 1997.

Caws, Mary Ann, Rudolf E. Kuenzli, and Gwen Raaberg, Eds. *Surrealism and Women.* Cambridge: MIT Press, 1991.

Chadwick, Whitney. *Women Artists and the Surrealist Movement.* Boston: Little, Brown, 1985.

Churchill, Suzanne, and Adam McKible. *Little Magazines and Modernism: New Approaches.* Burlington: Ashgate, 2007.

Cocteau, Jean. "The Laic Mystery: An Essay in Indirect Criticism." Trans. O. E. Rudge. *Pagany* 3.1 (Jan.–March 1932).

Cook, Albert. "Surrealism and Surrealisms." *American Poetry Review* (July/August 1984): 29–38.

Cunard, Nancy. *Negro: An Anthology*. 1934. New York: Frederick Ungar, 1970.

Diggory, Terence. *Encyclopedia of the New York School Poets*. New York: Facts on File, 2009.

Duncan, Carol. *Civilizing Rituals: Inside Public Art Museums*. New York: Routledge, 1995.

DuPlessis, Rachel Blau. *Blue Studios: Poetry and Its Cultural Work*. Tuscaloosa: University of Alabama Press, 2006.

Filreis, Alan. "Modern Poetry and Anticommunism." In *A Concise Companion to Twentieth-Century American Poetry*, ed. Stephen Fredman. Oxford, UK: Blackwell, 2005. 173–190.

Fischer, Barbara K. *Museum Mediations: Reframing Ekphrasis in Contemporary American Poetry*. New York: Routledge, 2006.

Ford, Charles Henri. *Water from a Bucket, A Diary 1948–1957*. New York: Turtle Point Press, 2001.

Frattali, Steven. *Hypodermic Light: The Poetry of Philip Lamantia and the Question of Surrealism*. New York: Peter Lang, 2005.

Gioia, Dana. "James Tate and American Surrealism." *Denver Quarterly* (Fall 1998).

Guest, Barbara. "The Lost Speech: The Shadow of Surrealism." *Women's Studies* 30.1 (February 2001): 7–9.

Guilbaut, Serge. *How New York Stole the Idea of Modern Art: Abstract Expressionism, Freedom, and the Cold War*. Trans. Arthur Goldhammer. Chicago: University of Chicago Press, 1983.

Harris, Oliver. "Cutting up the Corpse." In *The Exquisite Corpse: Chance and Collaboration in Surrealism's Parlor Game*. Eds. Kanta Kochlar-Lindgren, Davis Schneiderman, and Tom Denlinger. Lincoln: University of Nebraska Press, 2009. 82-103.

Harris, Steven. *Surrealist Art and Thought in the 1930s: Art, Politics, and the Psyche*. Cambridge: Cambridge UP, 2004.

Heffernan, James. *Museum of Words: The Poetics of Ekphrasis from Homer to Ashbery*. Chicago: University of Chicago Press, 1993.

Jackaman, Rob. *The Course of English Surrealist Poetry Since the 1930s*. Lewiston: E. Mellen Press, 1989.

Joans, Ted. *Teduction: Selected Poems 1949-1999*. Minneapolis, MN: Coffee House Press, 1999.

Jolas, Eugene. "Necessity of the New Word." *Modern Quarterly* 5.3 (Fall 1929): 273–25.

———, ed. *Transition Workshop*. New York: Vanguard Press, 1949.

Jones, Amelia. *Irrational Modernism: A Neurasthenic History of New York Dada*. Cambridge, MA: MIT Press, 2004.

Joron, Andrew. *Neo-Surrealism: Or, the Sun at Night: Transformations of Surrealism in American Poetry*. Oakland, CA: Kolourmeim Press, 2010.

Kachur, Lewis. *Displaying the Marvelous: Marcel Duchamp, Salvador Dali, and Surrealist Exhibition Installations*. Cambridge: MIT Press, 2001.

Kane, Daniel. *All Poets Welcome: The Lower East Side Poetry Scene in the 1960s*. Berkeley: University of California Press, 2003.

Koch, Kenneth, ed. *Locus Solus II: Special Collaborations Issue*. Summer 1961.

Kolocotronni, Vassalike. "Minotaur in Manhattan: Nicolas Calas and the Fortunes of Surrealism." *Modernist Cultures* 4 (2009): 84–102.

Lamantia, Philip. 15 January 1946 Letter to Charles Henri Ford. Charles Henri Ford Papers. Yale Collection of American Literature. Beinecke Rare Book and Manuscript Library.

Lehman, David. *The Last Avant-Garde: The Making of the New York School of Poets.* New York: Doubleday, 1998.

Levy, Julien. *Surrealism.* New York: Black Sun Press, 1936.

Lowney, John. *History, Memory, and the Literary Left: Modern American Poetry, 1935–1968.* Iowa City: University of Iowa Press, 2006.

Loy, Mina. *Insel.* Ed. Elizabeth Arnold. Santa Rosa, CA: Black Sparrow Press, 1991.

———. *The Lost Lunar Baedker.* Ed. Roger L. Conover. New York: Farrar, Straus, Giroux, 1996.

McCabe, Susan. *Cinematic Modernism: Modernist Poetry and Film.* Cambridge: Cambridge University Press, 2005.

McShine, Kynaston, ed. *The Museum as Muse: Artists Reflect.* New York: Museum of Modern Art, 1999.

Miller, Tyrus. *Late Modernism: Politics, Fiction, and the Arts Between the World Wars.* Berkeley: University of California Press, 1999.

Motherwell, Robert. *The Dada Painters and Poets.* Wittenborn: Schultz, 1951.

Mullen, Richard. "Elizabeth Bishop's Surrealist Inheritance." *American Literature* 54 (1982): 63–80.

Myers, John Bernard. *Tracking the Marvelous.* New York: Grey Art Gallery, 1981.

Nadeau, Maurice. *History of Surrealism.* Trans. Richard Howard. Cambridge: Harvard University Press, 1989.

Nelson, Cary. *Revolutionary Memory: Recovering the Poetry of the American Left.* New York: Routledge, 2001.

Nelson, Maggie. *Women, The New York School, and Other True Abstractions.* Iowa City: University of Iowa Press, 2008.

O'Hara, Frank. *The Collected Poems of Frank O'Hara.* Ed. Donald Allen. Berkeley: University of California Press, 1995.

Page, Barbara. "Off-Beat Claves, Oblique Realities: The Key West Notebooks of Elizabeth Bishop." In *Elizabeth Bishop: The Geography of Gender*, ed. Marilyn May Lombardi. Charlottesville: University of Virginia Press, 1993. 196–211.

Paul, Catherine,. *Poetry in the Museums of Modernism.* Ann Arbor: University of Michigan Press, 2002.

Perloff, Marjorie. *Frank O'Hara: Poet Among Painters.* University of Chicago, 1977, 1998.

Rasula, Jed. "Deep Image." In *Don't Ever Get Famous: Essays on New York Writing After the New York School*, ed. Daniel Kane. Dalkey Archive Press, 2006.

Ray, Paul C. *The Surrealist Movement in England.* Ithaca: Cornell University Press, 1971.

Rémy, Michel. *Surrealism in Britain 1999.* Aldershot: Ashgate, 1999.

Richardson, Michael, ed. *Refusal of the Shadow: Surrealism and the Caribbean.* Trans. Krzysztof Fijałkowski and Michael Richardson. London, NY: Verso, 1996.

Rosemont, Penelope. *Surrealist Women: An International Anthology.* Austin: University of Texas Press, 1998.

Rosemont, Franklin, Penelope Rosemont and Paul Garon, eds. *The Forecast Is Hot! Tracts and Other Collective Declarations of the Surrealist Movement in the United States, 1966–1976.* Chicago: Black Swan Press, 1997.

Roussel, Raymond. *Locus Solus*, trans. Rupert Copeland Cuningham. New York: Riverrun Press, 1983.

Rosemont, Franklin, and Robin Kelley, eds. *Black, Brown, and Beige: Surrealist Writings from Africa and the Diaspora.* Austin: University of Texas Press, 2009.

Rosenbaum, Susan. "Elizabeth Bishop and the Miniature Museum." *Journal of Modern Literature* 28.2 (2005): 61–99.

Rothenberg, Jerome. "Ethnopoetics." *New Princeton Encyclopedia of Poetry and Poetics*. eds. Alex Preminger and T.V.F. Brogan. Princeton: Princeton UP, 1993. 388-389.

Rubin, William. *Dada, Surrealism, and Their Heritage*. New York: Museum of Modern Art, 1968.

Sakolsky, Ron, ed. *Surrealist Subversions: Rants, Writings & Images by the Surrealist Movement in the U.S.* Brooklyn, NY: Autonomedia, 2002.

———. *The Forecast Is Hot! Tracts and Other Collective Declarations of the Surrealist Movement in the United States, 1966–1976*. Chicago: Black Swan Press, 1997.

Sawin, Martica. *Surrealism in Exile and the Beginning of the New York School*. Cambridge: MIT Press, 1995.

Schaffner, Ingrid and Lisa Jacobs, eds. *Julien Levy: Portrait of an Art Gallery*. Cambridge: MIT Press, 1998.

Scholes, Robert, and Clifford Wulfman. *Modernism in the Magazines: An Introduction*. New Haven: Yale University Press, 2010.

Schreiber, Maeera. "Divine Women, Fallen Angels: The Late Devotional Poetry of Mina Loy." In *Mina Loy: Woman and Poet*, ed. Maeera Schreiber and Keith Tuma. Hanover: University Press of New England, 1998. 467–483.

Silverberg, Mark. *The New York School Poets and the Neo-Avant-Garde: Between Radical Art and Radical Chic*. Aldershot: Ashgate, 2010.

Stevens, Wallace. "The Irrational Element in Poetry." In *Opus Posthumous*, ed. Samuel French Morse. New York: Knopf, 1957; Random House, 1982.

Sweet, David L. *Savage Sight/Constructed Noise: Poetic Adaptations of Painterly Techniques in the French and American Avant-Gardes*. Chapel Hill: University of North Carolina Press, 2003.

Tashjian, Dickram. *A Boatload of Madmen: Surrealism and the American Avant-Garde, 1920–1950*. New York: Thames and Hudson, 1995, 2001.

———. *Skyscraper Primitives: Dada and the American Avant-Garde, 1910–1925*. Middletown, CT: Wesleyan University Press, 1975.

———. *William Carlos Williams and the American Scene 1920–40*. Berkeley: University of California Press, 1979.

Young, Dean. "Surrealism 101." In *Poet's Work, Poet's Play: Essays on the Practice and the Art*. Ann Arbor: University of Michigan Press, 2008, 120–143.

CHAPTER 12

MATERIAL CONCERNS: INCIDENTAL POETRY, POPULAR CULTURE, AND ORDINARY READERS IN MODERN AMERICA

MIKE CHASAR

PAUL Erwin Fox was born on November 21, 1893, in Ohio's Vermillion township, which is now about a forty-five-minute drive from the city of Ashland in the north-central part of the state. Except for two years' military service during World War I (he enlisted in the army on September 23, 1917, participated in the first allied offensive victory of the war at the Second Battle of the Marne, and was discharged on August 9, 1919), Fox lived his entire life in Ashland County, first working as a farmer near the village of Sullivan and then as a "gas man" for the Logan Gas Company and the Ohio Fuel Gas Company. With the Rev. T. T. Buell of the Methodist Episcopal Church of nearby Newark presiding, he married Mary Kathryn McManamay on September 14, 1920, and the pair eventually had one son, Donald. Fox had life insurance through the All American Life and Casualty Company of Park Ridge, Illinois, attended the Dickey Church of the Brethren, and was a member of the American Legion's Harry Higgins Post Number 88. He died on May 19, 1943, two days after suffering a stroke while working on a gas well near Medina and six months before reaching his fiftieth birthday.

When Fox died, he left among his belongings a cluster of official documents stored inside a brown, wallet-sized portfolio originally issued with his discharge papers from the army. Those discharge papers, signed by Major H. B. Karkoff at Camp Sherman in Chillicothe, Ohio, are still intact; Fox's middle name is misspelled "Irvin." To these documents, Fox would later add his social security card, itself contained in a specially designed, chocolate-colored folder marked "Compliments of the Mansfield Typewriter Company" and dated December 12, 1936, making it one of the thirty million issued when the Social Security Board first began mass-registering people nationwide in late November of that year. Fox would also include his marriage license and life insurance paperwork. And then he'd cap off this encapsulated record of his life by adding a poem that may well have been one of the most widely distributed poems of its time, but which few people remember today.

Fox wasn't alone in keeping among his personal effects—or carrying on his person—poetry that he'd clipped from magazines or newspapers, that he'd possibly heard on the many nationally broadcast poetry radio shows that aired in the late 1920s and 1930s, or that he'd been given by someone else. Ralph Edmond Baxter, a World War II veteran and Illinois physician, for example, did the same as Fox, keeping in a wallet of other paperwork (an announcement of his "separation from military service," a menu for a May 30, 1946, dinner held aboard the U.S.A.T. Sea Barb, and an incomplete application for membership in the Illinois American Legion) two verses by James Metcalfe that had first appeared in the daily "Portraits" poetry column that Metcalfe wrote for "Chicago's Picture Newspaper," The Times. Earl Stafford, father of the poet William Stafford, had a copy of Edgar Allan Poe's "Annabel Lee" in his pocket when he died in 1943. American literature is full of additional examples ranging from the nameless, suicidal tramp in Willa Cather's My Antonia, who is found to be carrying only a penknife, a wishbone, and a poem "cut out of a newspaper and nearly worn out" (1918, 204) to Fulkerson of William Dean Howells's A Hazard of New Fortunes, who has "some of [Basil] March's verse in his pocket-book, which he had cut out of a stray newspaper and carried about for years" (2002, 26–27). In delivering the annual address to the Zenith Real Estate Board, George Babbitt prefaces his reading of a poem by T. Cholmondeley "Chum" Frink—Sinclair Lewis's fictional version of writers like Metcalfe or Edgar Guest—by stating, "I always carry this clipping of it in my note-book" (1998, 78). Dr. Almus Pickerbaugh from Lewis's Arrowsmith also carries a poem by Frink, one that he describes as "a genu-ine vest-pocket masterpiece" (1980, 215).

I start this essay with Fox, Baxter, Babbitt, Pickerbaugh, and Cather's tramp in order to argue for the importance of the "vest-pocket masterpiece" and the individual poetry clipping in understanding the situation of poetry in twentieth-century American popular culture and in the lives of ordinary readers. Odds are, none of the readers listed here would self-identify or be described as "intentional" poetry readers—a term that the 2006 study Poetry in America uses to designate people who seek and make time in their schedules for extended, private, intensive reading of poetry printed in books or literary magazines (Schwartz et al., 2006). Rather, my readers would most likely have encountered their verse in what Poetry in America calls "incidental" ways—in newspapers or periodicals, at public events, or as items shared between friends in contexts not devoted exclusively to poetry—that sometimes became occasions for reading and re-reading poetry that were no less sustained or meaningful than they would have been for intentional readers.[1] Such incidental poems saturated modern America, appearing in papers, magazines, Hollywood movies and advertisements, and on fliers, broadsides, billboards, stereoview cards, magic lantern slides, and a variety of radio programs. They were read or recited at church, public and private events, civic holidays, Chautauqua gatherings and picket lines, and were printed on a wide range of souvenir or value-added items including business cards, greeting cards, pin-up girly posters, pillows, matchbooks, calendars, handkerchief holders, wall hangings, and candy boxes.[2] Some of this verse was considered canonical, some was not, and some would go on to become canonical; some of it was read for a moment and then discarded, and some was preserved, sometimes with painstaking care, in autograph albums, poetry scrapbooks, and other personally assembled verse anthologies (figure 12.1).

But despite the fact that it was present in many forms in many facets of modern American life where it was put to what Pierre Bourdieu would call an enormous range of "possible uses" by institutions, corporations, the culture industries, and individuals, most of this incidental poetry and culture of incidental poetry reading has escaped commentary and analysis by literary critics and historians (1984, 42). This is partly because the poetry at its center wasn't produced, distributed, or archived in formats that are as friendly to standard twentieth-century catalogs or indexes as literary magazines or slim volumes have been. But it's also the case that many of those catalogs and indexes were designed to accord with the

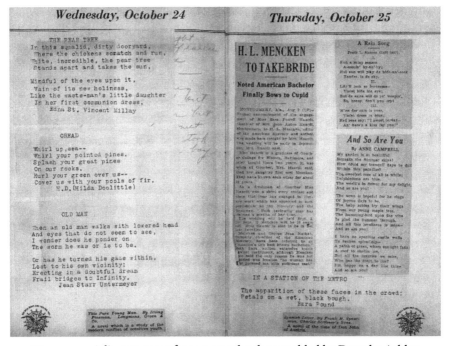

Figure 12.1 Adjacent pages from a scrapbook assembled by Dorothy Ashley, circa 1929. Author collection.

expectations and presumptions of intentional readers who incorrectly perceive the poetry of popular culture to have been, well, simply too incidental to be of more than passing interest to intentional readers and their codex-based archives.

In order to more fully understand the impact of poetry on twentieth-century American life, however, it is necessary to deemphasize—as a privileged site of literary production and as a privileged site of intentional reading—what Bob Brown in 1931 described as the "antiquated, word-dribbling book" (1931, 168). Extending or redirecting critical and scholarly attention to what the book historian Robert Darnton has called the "communications circuits" by which poetry more commonly circulated will not only open up new archives of heretofore unexamined material, but it also has the capacity to reveal the complex network of literary economies that brokered relationships between readers, writers, and texts in private and public, to say nothing of how and why poetry proliferated in so many incidental ways during the emergence and maturation of the U.S. consumer economy and its culture industries (1982, 67).[3] Of chief concern to this recalibration should be, as I've suggested, an intensified focus on the clipping as a particularly—and intentionally—charged site of social, aesthetic, and political reading for and between individual readers. The necessary process of uncovering the material, social, and aesthetic contexts that make the pop cultural activity of poetry clipping "legible" to us today promises, in turn, to also augment the ways that we assume poems in general—including lyric poems—make or acquire meaning beyond the actual, oftentimes idealized words of what critics used to call "the poem itself."[4]

In the pages that follow, I want to access the culture of incidental poetry in two major ways, each of which taps—via the individual clipping and its carriage—in to a different point along the communications circuit of poetry's social lives. First, I want to trace the international circulation of a single poem—V. M. Rodebaugh's Depression-era "Rejected," a piece of political satire first printed in 1938—as it made its way not only into Paul Fox's portfolio in Ashland, Ohio, but also into the footlockers and albums of World War II soldiers, onto the desk of Eleanor Roosevelt, and into the hands and rocket bombs of propagandists in Nazi Germany. Then, I want to examine the political and aesthetic dimensions that individual poetry clippings like "Rejected" acquired as they were collected, read, edited, and saved in poetry scrapbooks. Many noteworthy authors kept scrapbooks themselves; by focusing primarily on anthologies edited by less credentialed individuals, however, I hope to show how such albums became engines for critical reading processes in the hands of readers who would have encountered poetry largely in incidental ways. Such readers depended on and nourished a media culture saturated with poetry in an age when, many people have argued, poetry was having trouble competing with the products of the culture industries and was thus on the verge of dying out. Far from being unable to keep pace with comic books, movies, radio shows, and dime novels for readers' attention, most American poetry actually thrived in this environment. While readers may have encountered it in incidental ways, it was far from incidental in their lives and is thus essential reading for today's scholar who is hoping to understand the broader range of cultural uses that poetry served in the twentieth century.

FROM FOX TO FUHRER

By including a poem in the stack of rote paperwork that reduces his lived experience to a series of dates and signatures of approval, Paul Fox preserves a space for his own agency that makes that official record of his life "habitable"—a term that Michel de Certeau has used to describe what the "tactics" of everyday life accomplish in "the jungle of functionalist rationality" imposed by dominant power structures (1988, xxi, xix, xviii). The overlapping of discursive registers—poetic and bureaucratic—that results is compelling, for while we can understand the function and provenance of the official documentation surrounding it, the poem remains to some extent hermeneutically inaccessible. That is, even though we can read the words of the poem itself, it remains comparatively obscure, because we don't know the particular significance that the verse had for Fox, nor can we trace the history by which it made its way into his hands and then into the portfolio. Unlike the official records of his life, which are intended to signify transparently and without issue, in this context the poem *qua* poem signifies ambiguously, functioning as what Marjorie Perloff has called "a discourse that defers reading" (1991, 105) or what Cary Nelson has described as "a special discursive terrain" that is "perhaps less likely to write itself out on our tongue unawares" (1989, 106, 124). And yet, despite this obscurity—what Charles Bernstein might describe as a particular, if contextual, "antiabsorptive" quality that resists the illusion of a standardized life narrative constructed by the official documents (1992, 25)—the actual act of including the poem is a perfectly recognizable assertion of selfhood that the rest of the paperwork does not otherwise acknowledge. Personally chosen and thus representing or restoring a historically lived, even literary-critical activity on Fox's part, the poem refuses to submit completely to the life rubric and rites of passage that the military, federal government, church, and insurance company identify as supremely important. In short, by including the poem in his portfolio, Fox resists the very thing that his social security card—account 281-10-0792—seemed to many people capable of doing: turning a person into a number.

The inclusion of any personally chosen poem, I'd argue, would restore at least some element of lived experience to—and thus make more habitable—the otherwise bureaucratically organized life in Fox's portfolio. For de Certeau, such tactics are not acts of overt, organized opposition to dominant power structures but are "poetic ways of 'making do'" or "ways of operating" that operate under the radar and, as such, lack "a 'proper' (a spatial or institutional localization)" (1988, xv, xix, xix). Thus, while Fox's act of including the poem among his papers can be read as a way of "making do" that politicizes how his life narrative has been constructed, that resistance is not political, per se, even though the poem he saved is.

Printed as a 3.5-x-8-inch handbill or flier and distributed in lots of one hundred or more by H. C. Chappell, a newspaper editor from Middlesboro, Kentucky (a note at the bottom of the handbill explains how to order "Extra Copies by the 100 or 500"), V. M. Rodebaugh's "Rejected" is itself a statement of open dissent if not part of a counterhegemonic war of position against President Franklin Roosevelt's administration and the New Deal (figure 12.2). Composed within a "so-and-so-goes-to-hell" tradition of storytelling and poem writing—one that not only provided modern poems such as Ezra Pound's *Cantos*, William Carlos Williams's *Kora in Hell*, and Sterling Brown's "Slim Greer in Hell" with their respective frame-works but that also formed the primary conceit for the many "Kaiser in Hell" poems written during World War I—"Rejected" begins with the following lines:

> A stranger stood at the gates of Hell
> And the Devil himself had answered the bell;
> He looked him over from head to toe
> And said, "My friend, I'd like to know
> What you have done in the line of sin
> To entitle you to come within."
> Then Franklin D., with his usual guile,
> Stepped forth and flashed his toothy smile.

In the next forty lines, the fictional FDR enumerates everything he's done to deserve entrance to hell: he betrayed the country's faith, raised taxes, let farmland lie fal-low while importing food from abroad, created a series of alphabet agencies, and so on. Referring to *Schechter v. United States*—the 1935 Supreme Court case that struck down the National Recovery Administration as an unconstitutional exercise of executive authority—Roosevelt concludes, "I ruined their country, their homes, and then, / I placed the blame on 'Nine Old Men.'" Rodebaugh reserves the poem's punch line for the devil, however:

> Now Franklin talked both long and loud,
> And the Devil he stood and his head he bowed.
> At last he said, "Let's make it clear.
> You'll have to move. You can't stay here.
> For, once you mingle with this mob,
> I'll have to hunt myself a job."

Because the devil is worried about how a surplus of evil labor will negatively affect his own employment status, the joke—the poetic justice, really—is that, in death, FDR is a victim of the very regulated marketplace he supported in life; if the devil were a *laissez-faire* capitalist, FDR would not have been turned away. The joke's critique, then, is that regulating the U.S. economy would mean replicating and enforcing the (im)moral economy of hell—that is, doing the devil's work.

"Rejected" is part of a body of American protest literature, much of which circulated outside of codex formats because clippings, handbills, fliers, and cards were more easily passed hand to hand on picket lines or at protests and were easier to hide, carry, share, or save. In Fox's portfolio, "Rejected" doesn't only function to reg-ister a protest against the impersonalizing forces of bureaucracy broadly conceived, but it also restores a specific historical and political subjectivity to Fox himself—a

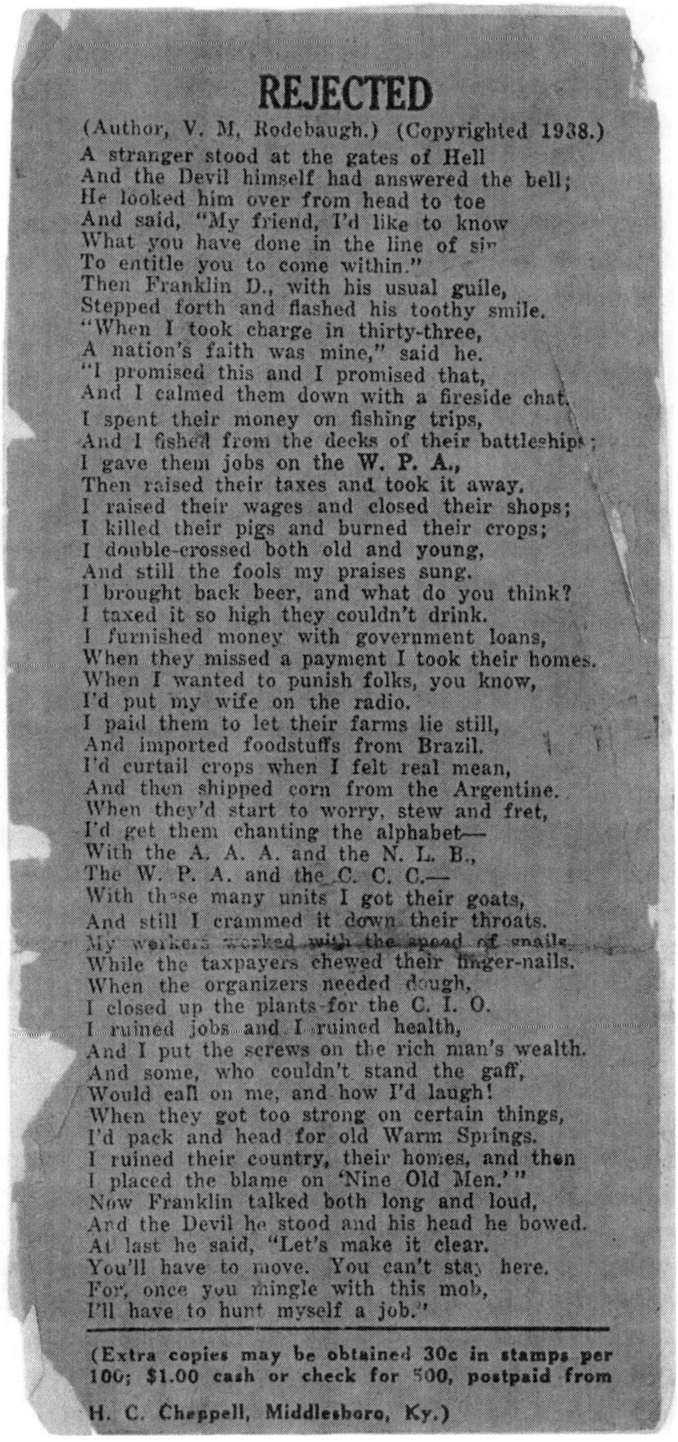

REJECTED

(Author, V. M, Rodebaugh.) (Copyrighted 1938.)
A stranger stood at the gates of Hell
And the Devil himself had answered the bell;
He looked him over from head to toe
And said, "My friend, I'd like to know
What you have done in the line of sin
To entitle you to come within."
Then Franklin D., with his usual guile,
Stepped forth and flashed his toothy smile.
"When I took charge in thirty-three,
A nation's faith was mine," said he.
"I promised this and I promised that,
And I calmed them down with a fireside chat.
I spent their money on fishing trips,
And I fished from the decks of their battleships;
I gave them jobs on the W. P. A.,
Then raised their taxes and took it away.
I raised their wages and closed their shops;
I killed their pigs and burned their crops;
I double-crossed both old and young,
And still the fools my praises sung.
I brought back beer, and what do you think?
I taxed it so high they couldn't drink.
I furnished money with government loans,
When they missed a payment I took their homes.
When I wanted to punish folks, you know,
I'd put my wife on the radio.
I paid them to let their farms lie still,
And imported foodstuffs from Brazil.
I'd curtail crops when I felt real mean,
And then shipped corn from the Argentine.
When they'd start to worry, stew and fret,
I'd get them chanting the alphabet—
With the A. A. A. and the N. L. B.,
The W. P. A. and the C. C. C.—
With these many units I got their goats,
And still I crammed it down their throats.
My workers worked with the speed of snails,
While the taxpayers chewed their finger-nails.
When the organizers needed dough,
I closed up the plants for the C. I. O.
I ruined jobs and I ruined health,
And I put the screws on the rich man's wealth.
And some, who couldn't stand the gaff,
Would call on me, and how I'd laugh!
When they got too strong on certain things,
I'd pack and head for old Warm Springs.
I ruined their country, their homes, and then
I placed the blame on 'Nine Old Men.'"
Now Franklin talked both long and loud,
And the Devil he stood and his head he bowed.
At last he said, "Let's make it clear.
You'll have to move. You can't stay here.
For, once you mingle with this mob,
I'll have to hunt myself a job."

(Extra copies may be obtained 30c in stamps per
100; $1.00 cash or check for 500, postpaid from

H. C. Chappell, Middlesboro, Ky.)

Figure 12.2 Handbill version of "Rejected," written by V. M. Rodebaugh, printed by H. C. Chappell, and owned by Paul Fox. Author collection.

fact made particularly clear in that the poem protests the very Roosevelt adminis-
tration that mandated, and is thus represented by, Fox's social security card. Even so,
unlike Rodebaugh's poem, which appears—by virtue of its deliberate composition
and ambition to large-scale distribution—to have been part of a concerted protest,
Fox's collection of the verse is still a fleeting act of resistance that Fox himself may
have registered as such. For in saving the poem, which was printed on flimsy news-
print, he optimistically glued it to a thicker, more stable piece of paper, seeking in
this reinforcement, perhaps, a material analogue for the "proper," which de Certeau
says tactical actions do not have.

Amazingly, Fox's act of (self) preservation worked: his copy of the poem sur-
vived his death in 1943, the death of his wife, its passing to his heirs, its probable auc-
tion or estate sale, and its passing into my hands via an online eBay auction in 2009.
Comparatively speaking, Rodebaugh hasn't been as fortunate, for despite the huge
circulation that "Rejected" once enjoyed, it's all but disappeared from literary history.
I have hunted in every catalog, index, and database available to me, but neither "Rode-
baugh" nor "Rejected" has been recorded. As often as not, bylines on reproductions of
"Rejected" are either left blank or else credit the poem to "anonymous." One can't help
but wonder about the identity of Rodebaugh—especially because Rodebaugh's Ken-
tucky vendor, H. C. Chappell, *does* appear in the historical record; Chappell edited
Middlesboro's newspaper, *The Three States*, for nearly forty years until his death in
1953. Did Chappell (whose version of the poem is the only one I can find that attri-
butes authorship) know Rodebaugh? Did he see "Rejected" printed elsewhere and
pirate copies of it? Or is it possible, given the policy- and news-specific nature of the
poem's complaints—that FDR "curtailed" domestic farming and imported "foodstuffs
from Brazil" and "the Argentine," for example—that Chappell *was* Rodebaugh, print-
ing and distributing "Rejected" under the misdirection or safety of a pseudonym?

If the provenance of "Rejected" remains a question mark—albeit a provocative
one with implications for our understanding of authorship and literary economics—
there are fewer uncertainties about how thoroughly the poem saturated U.S. culture.
I've found it in Colorado and Washington newspapers as well as in *The American
Flint*, the official publication of the American Flint Glass Workers' Union of North
America ("Rejected," 53–54). A typed copy of it survives in the papers of former Okla-
homa governor William H. "Alfalfa Bill" Murray, who remained bitter about losing
the 1932 Democratic presidential nomination to Roosevelt.[5] The British journalist
Charles Graves, brother of the English poet Robert Graves, remembers being shown
a copy of the "unkind, but not unamusing skit" while traveling by train on one leg of
a five-week visit to the United States in 1938 and 1939. "This was," he writes, "the first
copy of five or six afterwards pressed into my hand during the tour" (1939, 139). Har-
old Heidler remembers his mother paying him a dollar to recite it to her women's club
("Hell on Earth in the Third Grade," 1996, para. 38). Dorothy Jones Howard memo-
rized it so she could share it with her family when she got home from a trip to St. Louis
(chap. 7, para. 6). Karl Bell memorized it as well, and "to this day," he claims, "I could
recite about [all] of it from memory" (2009, comment 4). Posting a comment online
under the user name "Vigilanteman," another person remembers, "My Dad used to

recite this to me while cutting my hair" (2007, comment 1). Other people have found it preserved in their parents' or grandparents' scrapbooks, "folded and tucked into the pages of [an] old Merriam Webster's New International Dictionary" (Anonymous, 2007, para. 2), "in my dad's WWII footlocker, along with his uniforms, flight logs, etc." (Big Fred, 2008, comment 5), or typed in a "WWII pilot's log book" (Past Your Eyes, 2007, comment 1). As the latter two examples suggest, "Rejected" circulated especially widely among U.S. military personnel. One retired World War II veteran whom I interviewed (after being drafted, he served in the 83rd Infantry Division in Europe and stayed in the Army Reserve until retirement) was given a typed copy of the poem in basic training at Florida's Camp Blanding in 1944. If the distribution of an anti-FDR poem among basic trainees strikes us as a self-consciously transgressive activity, we would not be misguided in that assessment; sixty-five years after receiving his copy of "Rejected," that veteran still does not want it revealed that he had Rodebaugh's poem in his possession, so he remains anonymous here.

If these various anecdotes suggest the possible uses or "meanings" that "Rejected" could have for American readers—we can see it as an expression of Murray's ongoing if private need for political revenge, as a source of income for Heidler and entertainment for his mother's women's club, as a site of parent-child bonding or indoctrination in the case of Bell, and as an expression of protest or camaraderie not to mention a source of surreptitious pleasure for my anonymous World War II veteran—its heuristic and hermeneutic contingencies are further illustrated by how the poem was engaged by the very target of Rodebaugh's critique: the Roosevelts themselves. On January 20, 1939, Eleanor Roosevelt's "My Day" column (a feature syndicated to up to ninety American newspapers six days a week, from 1935 to 1962) took up the subject of "Rejected" explicitly, not surprisingly with reference to a clipping of Rodebaugh's verse taken from a newspaper in Washington State. Eleanor begins her column with two paragraphs: a brief update on her son's travels, and a reflection on how talking with ambitious young men like her son reveals that "it takes imagination and initiative today to do something which really goes over" (1939, para. 2). She ends her column with a paragraph about her speaking engagement at the Executive Board of the National Federation of Women's Clubs where she also heard "a speech by a young Chilian [sic] woman doctor." "It was interesting," Roosevelt concludes, "to see her interest in democracy" (1939, para. 6).

The lion's share of the piece, however, is given to a letter writer from Washington who sends a "clipping" of "Rejected" taken from the "The Poet's Corner" of the *Statesman-Index*. The correspondent wants, Roosevelt explains, to know whether the poetic attack is "called free speech." In order to answer in such a way that would include (and thus instruct) a broader public, Roosevelt summarizes the poem's narrative and how it lists "[a]ll the faults of [FDR's] Administration" including "personal things such as his wife" (1939, para. 3). She quotes the final five lines, comments "Strange to say the author is, 'Unknown,'" and then provides her response:

> Certainly, Madame Correspondent, this is freedom of speech. Anyone in this coun-
> try has a right to state his or her opinion about anyone else. Even if you disagree

with the opinion you must uphold this right, because that same right allows you to express your opinion freely as well. You are worried because you were taught to respect the office of the President of the United States regardless of politics, but this is not an attack on the office or even on the Presidency. It is an attack on the man and perhaps it is better to have more freedom and less enforced respect. (1939, para. 5)

As with Murray, Heidler, Bell, and others, Roosevelt doesn't dispute the "message" or manifest content of "Rejected"—she doesn't even deny that what the poem identifies as "faults" are in fact faults—but she rearticulates the poem to not only affirm the U.S. constitutional right to freedom of speech but to theatrically display the administration's dedication to "more freedom" even in the face of speech that attacks that administration. In fact, by discussing "Rejected" in the same breath as she reports on the "imagination and initiative" of young American men and on the Chilean doctor's public statement of interest in democracy, Roosevelt discredits "Rejected" as a poor and misunderstood product of its author's freedoms: its author resorts to attacking "personal things," points out faults without having the imagination to offer alternatives, and isn't even brave enough to sign his or her name. Compared even to Eleanor herself—whom the poem attacks but who nevertheless signs and stands behind her writing—the author of "Rejected" is a cowardly speaker whose anonymity (at least in the *Statesman-Index*) suggests he or she doesn't believe enough in the civilian administration and protection of free speech to put a name to the piece without fear of retribution.

If Rodebaugh's poem wasn't widely known by the time this column ran, it certainly was afterwards, as Roosevelt's rejection of "Rejected" had the simultaneous effect of giving the verse—or at least its final five lines—high-profile exposure via national syndication. It's difficult to assess poetry in the terms that Walt Whitman suggested in the "preface" to his 1855 *Leaves of Grass* ("The proof of a poet is that his country absorbs him as affectionately as he has absorbed it"), but if a drinking song that students at the Rensselaer Polytechnic Institute devised is any indication, "Rejection" was thoroughly absorbed into U.S. culture. Singers of that song—adapting the Irish quickstep and drinking tune "Garry Owen" in somewhat the same way as "Rejected" adapted the "Kaiser in Hell" poems from World War I—claim "We live to drink; we drink to die" and in the final two stanzas imagine arriving at hell where the devil receives them in the same way, and with the same rhymes and nearly the exact wording, as he received Roosevelt in "Rejected":

> The Devil says, "You can't stay here.
> I want no men from Rensselaer."
>
> "Although your souls are black with sin,
> I'm sorry, boys, you can't come in.
> For if you mingle with the mob
> I'll have to hunt myself a job."
>   ("Rensselaer Beer Song")

Perhaps the most surprising part of the circulation history of "Rejected," however, may be its international publication, for the poem was discovered—on the body of a dead or captured American soldier? by a German operative working in the United States?—by the Nazi propaganda machine during World War II which then mass-produced it as a four-page booklet featuring an extremely toothy caricature of FDR on the title page that illustrates the "toothy smile" described in line 8 of Rodebaugh's verse (figure 12.3). The S.S. Standarte *Kurt Eggers* (the German war correspondent formation that is known to have employed at least two U.S. citizens during the war) disseminated the 6-x-4-inch leaflet via specially designed propaganda rockets fired at the more than 800,000 U.S. troops motivated during the Battle of the Bulge in December 1944 and January 1945.[6] It may be impossible to find out how many copies—thousands? hundreds of thousands?—of "Rejected" were produced. It's an equally daunting project to imagine discovering and recording how the poem was then read by U.S. soldiers, how often it was saved or sent home, and, most intriguingly, how U.S. troops who had first encountered the poem on American soil as private citizens or military recruits later *re-read* the verse as Nazi propaganda on the front lines in Europe. Yet the communications circuit that I've traced here raises just these sorts of questions about the historical impact and various meanings that poems could have when embedded and encountered in popular culture. Is "Rejected" a piece of Nazi propaganda? Is it a poem that soldiers used to distinguish between loyalty to a president and loyalty to the nation? A source for a drinking song? Proof of free speech? An effort on the part of a gas man in Ashland, Ohio, to assert his individuality in the face of American bureaucracy? In the end, Rodebaugh's poem (or is it Chappell's poem?) is none of these. And yet it is all of them, able to matter in so many ways in large part because it circulated via clipping, flier, leaflet, and page—material formats characterized by a mobility, adaptability, and social interactivity that the more readily disembedded codex might display, but not in spades.

Figure 12.3 Nazi propaganda pamphlet version of "Rejected," distributed by rocket bombs aimed at the more than 800,000 American troops fighting at the Battle of the Bulge, circa 1944 or 1945. Courtesy of Cary Nelson.

Sometime near the end of the war, the Pan American Publishing Company of El Paso, Texas, issued a 3.25-×-5.5-inch folding postcard on khaki or olive-green card stock recalling the color of U.S. military fatigues and headlined "Hitler at the Gates of Hell" (figures 12.4a and 12.4b).[7] Printed inside the postcard and modeled on the Rodebaugh poem—in primarily tetrameter couplets, a national leader goes to hell, meets the devil, petitions for admission, and is turned away by a devil who

Figure 12.4a Cover of "Hitler at the Gates of Hell" folding postcard, published by the Pan American Publishing Company of El Paso, Texas, circa 1945. Author collection.

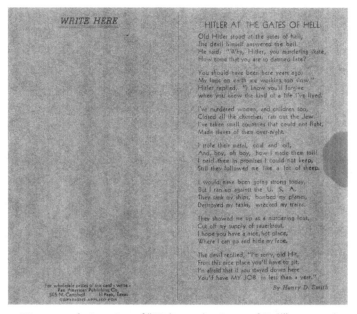

Figure 12.4b Interior of "Hitler at the Gates of Hell" postcard.

is anxious about competition for his job—"Hitler at the Gates of Hell" further testifies to the cultural purchase that "Rejected" enjoyed and continues the increasingly elaborate remediation that it experienced in the six or seven years since its first publication; no longer a handbill with blank verso, the new version is illustrated and folded in such a way that it might well have been modeled on the illustrated and folded Nazi version.[8] That remediation in no way damages the poem's portability, however. In fact, given how the postcard's design is intended to facilitate easy and efficient carriage—by hand or purse to the post office, across the nation in the bags of mail carriers, and so on—it probably increased the poem's potential to circulate. Unlike hand-to-hand circulation (which could be slow and unreliable) or distribution via a rocket bomb (which was too diffuse to hit a specific target and thus could be equally unreliable), copies of a postcard could move in large quantities with a precision suggested by the extremely accurate trajectory of the "smart bomb" that severs Hitler's tail on the postcard's cover.[9]

Given this potential mobility, and given the anti-Hitler content—a moral and patriotic subject capable of unifying U.S. political factions and thus doubling the item's potential audience—what interests me most about "Hitler at the Gates of Hell" is the actual *lack* of circulation that it appears to have had. In fact, it was only after I completed what I thought would be the final version of this essay that I discovered the existence of Henry D. Smith's poem, and, as far as I can tell, vastly fewer copies of it circulated than "Rejected," and fewer yet survive. In other words, "Hitler at the Gates of Hell" was—and this is one pun *not* suggested by the cover cartoon—a total bomb. There are many possible reasons for this failure. As the "It Won't Be Long Now" headline suggests, the postcard was produced late in the war, and thus the ending it envisions (of Hitler dying and going to hell) might have come sooner than expected and thus closed the window of the item's commercial viability. Perhaps the Pan American Publishing Company was deficient in its marketing, even though it adopted H. C. Chappell's successful strategy of offering the postcard in bulk quantities. Perhaps paper shortages interfered with mass production. Perhaps "Hitler at the Gates of Hell" might simply have been too *bad* of a poem—and it is a poorly executed propaganda poem, as I'll explain shortly—to gain a popular audience.

All of these reasons might account for the postcard's failure, except—as we've seen in the case of "Rejected," which was memorized, typed, and copied out by hand at individuals' personal expense—popular audiences are regularly willing to subsidize the reproduction, transportation, and publication of items that are of use to them, paper shortages or not. Given this fact, I want to suggest another, likely counterintuitive, explanation for the card's failure: I think that "Hitler at the Gates of Hell" failed to become a popular success precisely because it was in fact *too* ideological. As a close analysis of the postcard reveals, it was neither well written enough nor conceptually coherent enough—except in its analysis of imperialist economics and in its identification of capitalism as the primary and inescapable governing factor of human experience—to offer readers anything more useful than an uncomfortable model of justice predicated on a capitalist logic. As Stuart Hall has explained, "[A]

longside the false appeals, the foreshortenings, the trivialisation and shortcircuits"
characteristic of products manufactured by the culture industries, "there are also
elements of recognition and identification, something approaching the recreation
of recognizable experiences and attitudes, to which people are responding" (1981,
233). "Hitler at the Gates of Hell" failed to recognize and cultivate this latter aspect
of the commodity item; that is, I think it underestimated the consumer's critical
acumen and assumed the reader would uncritically buy, and buy into, what turns
out to be little more than an oversimplification of human experience and thus a cyn-
ically empty and cynically marketed product. As a result, it was even more quickly
forgotten than Rodebaugh, who disappeared into literary history as "anonymous"
but whose poem—about how the agents of power are sometimes consumed by the
very power they hold—lived on.

"Hitler at the Gates of Hell" is, ultimately, a poem so full of mixed and conflict-
ing messages, broken promises, and incomplete logics that its promise of legibility
appears to be almost completely undermined. For starters, the heteroglossic diction
and speech patterns of both the devil and Hitler—to say nothing of the values asso-
ciated with those languages—are difficult if not impossible to parse. At times, the
devil speaks with an element of reflective, gentlemanly formality ("Why, Hitler . .
." in line 3), in American dialect and slang ("you murdering skate"[10] in line 3, and
"From this nice place you'll have to git" in line 26), in the slight accent and speech
patterns of a non-native English speaker ("How come that you are so damned late?"
in line 4), and in an otherwise unmarked or "standard" English. Hitler, too, sounds
like he's speaking a particularly American English ("boy, oh boy" in line 14) as well
as an unmarked English and a non-native English ("when you know the kind of a
life I've lived" in line 8). The poem's formal characteristics send a similar set of mixed
signals: it is written in couplets but printed in quatrains associated with the ballad;
and while it promises a baggy iambic tetrameter meter, its awkward performance
of that meter (line 8 inserts the unnecessary article "a" in what would have been the
otherwise metrically sound tetrameter line, "when you know the kind of life I've
lived") and its deviations from that meter (especially in lines 12 and 15) are difficult
to account for—so difficult, in fact, that one prosodic specialist I consulted could
only explain the badness of Smith's ear by saying he must have been raised entirely
outside the accentual-syllabic poem-writing culture of the English language.

I've been unable to locate the historical Henry D. Smith to whom the post-
card attributes authorship, but even if Smith were writing in English as his sec-
ond language—in fact, it might have been a particularly effective strategy to have a
non-native English, or even native German, speaker composing "Hitler at the Gates
of Hell"—the poem's conflicting vocal and formal registers nonetheless, and likely
unintentionally, produce interpretive dissonances that contradict the very pro-
pagandistic intention announced by the postcard's cover. What does it mean, for
example, that the devil speaks an *American* dialect, and what does it then mean
that he and the United States have a mutual interest in bringing Hitler to hell? Who
are the devil's "imps" mentioned in line 6, and how are we to process the fact that
the United States is doing the job the devil initially assigned to those imps (rather

than acting as the hand of God, for instance)? In some literary and especially Leftist contexts, these questions might in fact be a work's central, counterhegemonic point of departure—a daring one, to be sure, but not unimaginable—but in the pro-U.S. propagandistic context of this postcard, that notion doesn't square. Incredibly, this lack of synergy doesn't stop with the poem itself. One can't help but wonder, for instance, whether the "H.D. Smith" named in the cartoon is in fact the same "Henry D. Smith" identified in the poem's byline. Even the familiar medium of the post-card itself—which typically makes the content of its correspondence public but here encourages private communication—presents a generic crisis via its folding design, as it ends up looking as much like a greeting card as it does a postcard.

If the postcard's makers don't extend their attention and care to these various aspects of the work—thereby producing a piece surprisingly similar to the abom-inably therianthropic Hitler on its cover—then what, one has to ask, *do* they pay attention to? In the way of a partial answer, I would argue that the item is ultimately most concerned with, and most clear in its analysis of, the conflict between impe-rialist and capitalist economic systems and the administration of justice as carried out by the latter. The poem's middle stanza, which the red adhesive tab used to seal the postcard points to as singularly important, identifies the source of Germany's colonial power and moral transgression in Hitler's unjust seizure of goods from the "small countries" mentioned in stanza three. Paying with "promises I could not keep" rather than with a more equitable, convertible, or institutionally recog-nized form of compensation, Hitler's chief crime against humanity—at least from the poem's viewpoint—has as much or more to do with his transgression of free market economic laws than with moral or ethical ones; the description of Hitler's imperialism is three times as long as the crimes he admits in lines 9–10 (all of which go unexamined in relation to each other and the rest of the poem) and focuses on method or process, not just the end result. Later in the poem, the administration of earthly justice takes economic form as well; Hitler is defeated not by a morally superior United States that purportedly "showed me up as a murdering lout" but one that ultimately triumphs via economic power by "[c]ut[ting] off my supply of sauerkraut." Not only does the poem identify and sustain an interest in the eco-nomics of war in a way that it doesn't in regards to morality, but this interest lays the groundwork for a more general material and conceptual unity as well, as the cutting off of Hitler's sauerkraut supply undoubtedly resonates with the cutting off of Hitler's wiener-dog tail on the postcard's cover.

This unity is visible in other places as well—the phrase used to expose Hit-ler's moral crimes ("showed me up") is also language used to advertise or exhibit (show) something for sale, for example—but nowhere as clearly as in the going-to-hell narrative of the poem itself in which Hitler is refused admission to hell out of fear that his presence would create a surplus of evil and thus put the devil out of a job. Unlike "Rejected," then, where the naturalness or inevitability of a regulated free market capitalism is called into question, "Hitler at the Gates of Hell" assumes from the start that capitalist logic governs in life as well as the afterlife. That is, the belief in a regulated free market as the universal administrator of justice is foundational for "Hitler at the Gates of Hell"; Hitler's most unnatural and thus most egregious crime, according to the poem, was challenging this order, and thus he is punished by being excluded from the free market economy of earthly life (via capitalism's worldly enforcer, the United States) and from its equivalent in the afterlife. The notion that evil needs the same sort of New Deal regulation as pork bellies or wheat futures is a remarkable compromise position coming as it does at the end of a long war. Nevertheless, in its acceptance of evil, and of the "necessary evil" of a regulated free market capitalism, it's a cynical rather than idealistic view of a world that can't in fact be improved. In "Rejected," the vision of a capitalist hell served as a sort of cautionary tale—FDR was creating hell on earth via the New Deal, but that could in fact be changed—but in "Hitler at the Gates of Hell," this economic system is imagined as part and parcel of an eternal order that governs in life as well as death. The notion that morality might in fact be measured via a capitalist logic in the afterlife (not via the moral logic of a god or other judge of ultimate goodness, for example) is a cynical recognition and acceptance of capitalism's hegemony, and not one for which popular audiences—already suffering from the effects of capitalism and looking, as Hall writes, for some more nuanced "recreation of recognizable experiences and attitudes"—could find a whole lot of sympathy, even at the low cost of ten cents per postcard.

From Clipping to Collection

In 1914—the year that *Blast*, *The Little Review*, and *The Egoist* were all founded—the newspaper poet Walt Mason of Emporia, Kansas, explained to the *Literary Digest* what happened to the vest-pocket masterpieces he and other poets wrote for the newspapers. "A man," he said, "sees in the newspaper a clever rime full of hope and encouragement, and he cuts it out and shows it to his friends, and carries it in his pocket-book, and takes it home and reads it to his family, and his wife pastes it in the scrap-book for future reference" (1914, 341–342). I begin the second part of this essay with "Uncle Walt" Mason not just to illustrate a specific circuit by which poems moved in and between public and private spheres in modern America—a circuit that connected (but also distinguished between) men and women, individuals and families, public and domestic spaces, the "imagined communities" of newspaper readers and the specific communities of friends and families—but also to describe the close, ultimately dialectical, relationship between the individual clipping and the collection of clippings, the poetry scrapbook. As Mason's description indicates, the individual clipping came to signify, for many modern readers, public, social, and masculine literacy practices, while the collection and organization of clippings into scrapbooks and albums came to stand for a gendered though no less intentional alternative—a familial, domestic, resourceful, and thus feminine, literacy. That is, if the clipping came to be associated with what de Certeau helps us to understand as a situational hermeneutics, then the accumulation and pasting of poems in a scrap*book* can be seen as a distinct, readerly attempt at establishing a literary "proper" (1988, xix). Insofar as this latter activity "accumulates, stocks up, resists time by the establishment of a place and multiplies its production through the expansionism of reproduction," it is tantamount to an act of writing (de Certeau, 1988, 174).

Scrapbooking became extremely common after the Civil War and remains so today, though today's predominant form—the album of school souvenirs, photos, and other items constructing what the anthropologists Tamar Katriel and Thomas Farrell describe as an idealized life narrative "of growing up as a fun-filled journey"—did not emerge as predominant until the second half of the twentieth century (1991, 7). Before then, scrapbooks served, in part, as a pragmatic method of sorting through, organizing, and archiving the booming print world of postbellum America and combined with national values of thrift and resourcefulness to offer, especially in the case of poetry scrapbooks, aspiring members of the business and professional classes a way to bootstrap into middlebrow cultural legitimacy. Albums were filled more often with news articles, poems and songs, recipes, calling cards, advice columns, medical remedies, and colorful advertisements (materials collected, as Mason indicates, "for future reference") than they were with items of a more identifiably biographical orientation. Families and friends scrapbooked in groups, saved material for each others' albums, and sometimes passed their anthologies from generation to generation. Reading in this way (Louisa May Alcott claimed she read "with a pair of scissors in my hand"), Americans not only created a culture of album-making that gave rise to and supported an industry of commercialized blank books, how-to guides, and scrappable die-cuts and other paper items, but they also retrofitted the largely chirographic tradition of commonplace bookkeeping for the modern era of commercialized, widely circulated print (qtd. in Garvey, 2003, 224).[11]

Though various in size, editorial rubric, and function, personally assembled poetry anthologies compose a large, distinct subgenre of the "scrapbook" more generally. Eminently clippable, culturally prestigious (especially compared to popular fiction), and widely available, poems made for perfect scrapbook material. Newspapers recognized this and printed them boxed-in under headings such as "Poems for Your Scrapbook." Source books such as *Clippings for Your Scrap Book: 52 Famous Writings Reproduced for Your Convenience* (figure 12.5) were common, and nationally broadcast poetry radio shows such as *Between the Bookends* and *'R Yuh Listenin'* issued print companions of listener-contributed verse with titles such as *Ted Malone's Scrapbook* and *Tony's Scrap Book*. Carefully organized, themed, and indexed acts of bricolage and collage, some of these albums were kept and maintained for decades and now contain hundreds of pages of verse that offer material records not only of what poetry people read and valued but also how they read it. They oftentimes mixed canonical and noncanonical, high and low, genteel and modern, and British and American poetries in ways that frustrate critical assumptions about poetry and poetry reading that have thus far structured much of twentieth-century poetry studies. The mixtapes of their age, these anthologies

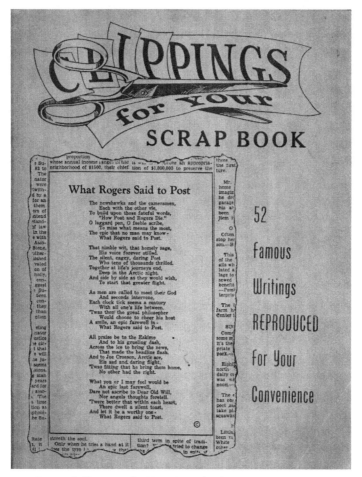

Figure 12.5. Cover of *Clippings for Your Scrapbook: 52 Famous Writings Reproduced for Your Convenience*. 1937. Buffalo: The Hevenor Company.

don't just witness to a widely practiced method of appropriating and repurposing mass-produced poems that would pave the way for cut-and-paste practices throughout popular culture later in the century, but they also represent an entire genre of poetic production that has so far gone unexplored by literary critics.

There are many ways to begin approaching this archive, and this chapter can only begin to scratch the surface. Crucial to any examination of the poetry scrapbook and the appeal it had for American readers, though, is understanding the transformation that the codex album, and the editorial activity of album making, exacted on the individual clipping. As suggested by Cather's use of the poetry-reading tramp in *My Antonia*, American literature regularly associated the individual clipping with a literal and figurative homelessness; example after example indicates that the scrap became a shorthand for figuring the dispossessed—the physically, geographically, institutionally, or literarily homeless person who doesn't have a blank book or bookshelf but only a pocket in which to store and maintain the literary resources of modern life.[12] This was true in the popular press as well.

Consider the following poem and its prefatory note, which are part of a constellation of other scrapbook-themed, scrapbook-related items that form an introduction or statement of purpose on the first page of a large, 160-page collection housed between the embossed, heavy cardboard covers of a 1939 New York World's Fair souvenir album (figure 12.6):

> Mrs. William F. Davenport, Box 205, Big Ranch Rd., Napa, California, in starting her scrapbook nearly 60 years ago put this verse on the first page with this notation underneath it: "The words of a man whose life is but a scrap of what it might have been." In explanation Mrs. Davenport tells us that it was written by one calling himself a tramp, who worked in a town for a while and then disappeared—suddenly, as he had come. He gave the verse to the young woman who later became Mrs. Edwin Markham, who passed it on to our contributor. We are grateful for both the verse and its story.

Figure 12.6. Page 1 of a two-thousand-poem scrapbook assembled by an anonymous woman living near Denver, Colorado, in the 1930s and 1940s. Author collection.

SCRAPS

Days are but scraps in the pattern of years.
Years but scrapwork in the mantle of time.
Scraps are we all in the mystical plan
That tunes the song of the spheres into rhyme.
The cradle and bier are scraps of a life.
Infantile dreams and heartbroken cries
Are but scraps of the anthem and dirge
That anchor the earth to faith in the skies.
Despair's but a scrap of joy that has flown;
Love's but a scrap of fate's bitter curse.
Ah! Life's but a scrapbook, dog-eared and filled
With pages of prose and fragments of verse.

If a threat of homelessness or disenfranchisement inhered in the individual clipping—here it is doubly present in the metonymic relationship between the tramp and the verse he carried *and* in the poem's metaphysical album that unites and makes coherent a potentially fragmented set of life experiences—then the comparatively permanent, "proper" space of the poetry album helped Americans to manage the anxiety that that threat produced. Imagined as an activity that occurred in ordered, domestic spaces, scrapbooking offered a literary analogue for the physical building and the humanistic self—it was, as Elizabeth Bishop wrote in her short story about a scrap-collecting beach-comber, "more like an idea of a house than a real one" (1984, 171)—and the act of converting "fragments of verse" into private property and/or personhood can thus be seen as ideological in nature. Fueled by the fantasy of a unified self with a bourgeois editorial eye at its core, the codex album served as what de Certeau calls "a spatial or institutional localization" that offered a way for modern American readers, if not T. S. Eliot himself, to shore fragments against their ruin.

So strong was the association between housing, poetry, and scrapbook making that on at least one occasion, as the folklorist Lois Karen Baldwin recorded, "the stairwell walls" of an actual house in Pennsylvania "were papered with … newsprint poems" in an act that collapsed the distinction between album and building almost entirely; people could literally live inside their poetry scrapbooks (1975, 236). The effects of this calculus were far reaching, as the "intentional" reading, writing, and collection of poems came to be viewed as a distinctly feminine activity; the Pennsylvania family of Baldwin's study, for instance, called poetry "domestic as a plate" and described its composition as "piecing" rhymes together as one might a patchwork quilt or scrapbook (1975, 231). In carving out a masculinist discursive space for modern poetry that was separate from that of popular verse, many modernist writers reinforced this equation (Pound, for example, disparaged the "emotional slither" [1954, 12] of popular verse as little more than "nice" poetry that "Aunt Hepsy liked" [1971, 10]), and it is an equation that, to this day, dominates the popular imagination of poetry reading and scrapbooking more generally. Not all women kept poetry scrapbooks, of course, nor did all men refrain from the activity, but of the one hundred or so albums I've studied that were assembled by adults and not as school projects, at least 80 percent appear to have been produced by women readers. Some collected for their own personal benefit and private reading. Others did so because they were expected to provide family reading matter, entertainment, or resources for children's education. Still others were aspiring writers and thinkers, and their albums recorded—or established—artistic and intellectual exchanges in their immediate communities and extended social networks. Still other women readers and editors were fashioning themselves as middlebrow Americans; they were keeping poetry scrapbooks because, as Walt Mason indicated, that's precisely what middlebrow or aspiring middlebrow American women did.

Especially provocative for me—to extend the domestic metaphor those anthologists and their collections helped to create and maintain—is how the scrapbook likely offered readers, particularly women readers, a culturally approved textual room of their own in which to safely and critically explore or claim the new and emerging subject positions of modernity. That albums sometimes became places in which to process, record, or articulate a feminist or protofeminist politics is undeniable; large scrapbooks full of material related to women's suffrage suggest as much, but others do so via less overt—and I'd say more poetic—acts of critical bricolage. Consider, for example, page four of the 1939 New York World's Fair album cited earlier (figure 12.7). Assembled, I believe, near Denver, Colorado, by a woman I've been unable to positively identify, this collection is larger than many I've seen—it collects nearly two thousand poems and fragments of verse—yet it displays many hallmarks of twentieth-century scrapbooks more generally. It mixes poetry from a variety of poetic registers ranging from nineteenth-century British and American traditions (Wordsworth, Blake, both Brownings, Tennyson, Rossetti, Kipling, Khayyam, Longfellow, Whitman, Holmes, Riley, and Eugene Field) to twentieth-century modern, popular, religious, inspirational, and greeting-card poetries by writers as various as Paul Laurence Dunbar; Sara Teasdale; Edna St. Vincent Millay; Dorothy Parker; Conrad Aiken; the "people's poet" Edgar Guest; the future poet laureate of Oregon, Ethel Romig Fuller; the unofficial poet laureate of Hawaii, Don Blanding; and, not surprisingly, Walt Mason of Emporia, Kansas, who claimed that this was the very place where his poems would end up. (In fact, a few of the verses in this album have fold marks on them, suggesting they were first carried around in wallets or pocketbooks as Mason said such poetry would be.) The poems are not only *not* assembled chronologically but date as far back as 1885 and as far forward as 1948—a sixty-year span suggesting that the album was part of a long-range, possibly multigenerational effort to collate, "theme," and otherwise organize verses that the editor herself clipped out and that were sent to and from friends and family members. Most of the poems don't preserve standard bibliographical information that, in the act of repurposing, meant little to this maker. This doesn't mean that she was unconcerned with where her verse came from, though, for she does

Figure 12.7. Page 4 of the scrapbook pictured in figure 12.6.

regularly record the *people* who gave her poem clippings, in the process employing an alternative bibliographical system that privileges users over producers and the circuits of incidental over intentional poetry. Individual clippings are marked, for example, with notes such as "Esther sent me this 1946" or "This was often quoted by Mrs. Pine" that indicate an active if localized exchange economy fueled by women readers who were intentionally sharing and reading poetry they first encountered in newspapers, nationally circulated magazines, religious publications, greeting cards, and even advertisements.

It's difficult to make wholesale claims about a collection of two thousand poems—whole pages are dedicated to poems about mothers, holidays, Abraham Lincoln, dogs, children, and so on—especially because different parts of the album may have served different purposes and the editor's intentions may have changed over time. However, page four is especially meaningful, particularly given its proximity to the statement of purpose created by the items on page one, which

I referenced earlier. Here, the album's editor has matched eleven inspirational or motivational poems of uplift ("The Things That Count," "Life's Lessons," "It Can Be Done," "Keep at It," "Keep a-Hopin'," etc.) with two equally inspirational prayer poems, all of which trade in the truisms, proverbs, and generalities that made such verse widely applicable. Without being overly specific, these verses celebrate commonplace activities and encourage a positive attitude toward life, but they really can't be said to value the status quo or promote complacency or self-satisfaction as, in aggregate, they create a discursive field that promotes learning and hope as well as a faith in the progressive if incremental nature of change. Modernist writers—and M.F.A. programs that institutionalized "show, don't tell" as a maxim of creative writing after World War II—would try to counter this vagueness with a discourse of images and "things," but that very vagueness continues to attract popular audiences precisely because it's vague; the poems' hermeneutically underdetermined frameworks rely on readers and users to supply contexts in order to make the verse meaningful. Anyone who can "Keep Moving" or "Keep at It" is a potential audience for these poems, which, in providing templates or analytics for users to apply or test against the realities of their own lives, become—especially in the context of poetry scrapbooks—miniature engines for thought, or what the computer theorist Ted Nelson might call "thinkertoys" (2003, 330).

Page four is a good case in point, as the album's editor applies a specific interpretive framework to the thirteen poems via a single, postage-stamp-sized image

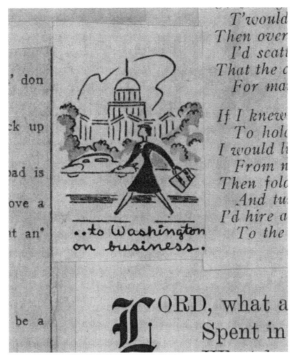

Figure 12.8. Detail from page 4 of the scrapbook, showing a small black-and-white illustration captioned ". . . to Washington on business."

pasted in the center of the page (figure 12.8). That image—a pen-and-ink drawing of a New Woman carrying a briefcase and confidently striding in front of the U.S. Capitol—is captioned "to Washington on business" and works to articulate the poems' Progressive Era mixture of optimism, religiosity, hope for social change, and a positive attitude to a women's rights agenda. It is likely, given the sixty years' worth of poetry in this album, as well as the connections to other women it records, that the anthologist herself lived through the passage of the Nineteenth Amendment in 1920 and that this page not only tracks that historical moment but, in its call to "Keep at It," commits its compiler to an ongoing women's-rights agenda that makes the last line of "Keep Moving" ("Some people won't like us, but other folks will") newly meaningful, turning that sentence's collective pronoun into a demonstration of political solidarity not just on behalf of the album's maker but on behalf of all of the women—Esther, Mrs. Pine, and even Edna St. Vincent Millay, who is given a page of her own later in the album—whom the album unites in common cause. I don't know where in print the scrapbook's maker first found "to Washington on business," but it appears to have been one in a series of similar images that have been put to use elsewhere in the album. The fact that "to Washington on business" has been separated from the others—which appear sixty pages later and have captions reading "So much to do and see in NY" and "Just like the old days"—should give us some sense of how deliberately this collection was assembled and how specifically the clippings on page four are made significant not by virtue of their having been written or published, but by virtue of the fact that they have been read, cut out, organized, and pasted down.

Whether or not this anthologist did her work in secret is hard to tell. Some women did keep such projects private—or used them to create private spaces in domestic ones—including Virginia Woolf, who, at seventeen years old, cut out the pages of her diary and pasted them inside a copy of Isaac Watts's 1726 work *Logick, or, the right use of Reason, with a variety of rules to guard against error in the affairs of religion and human life as well as in the sciences*. Working with a similar desire for privacy, Dorothy Ashley, editor of the album in figure 12.1, assembled her poetry scrapbook inside a recycled "Year Book" day planner originally distributed for promotional purposes by the United States Fidelity and Guaranty Company in 1928. She features many of the same poets included in the World's Fair album, assembling an eclectic collection of late nineteenth and twentieth-century poetries that exhibits a particular interest in the intersection of "modern" literature and gender identity—an interest illustrated, perhaps, by the mixing of Millay, H.D., Jean Starr Untermeyer, and an article reporting on H. L. Mencken's 1930 marriage to writer and Goucher College professor Sara Powell Haardt. If the "Year Book" offered Ashley a literal and figurative cover for her activity, she appears, in one instance at least, to have sought even more privacy. Missing a diary's lock and key to secure her project, she uses the scrapbook's compositional resources instead, pasting in a copy of Margaret Widdemer's poem "The Modern Woman to Her Lover," which begins

I shall not lie to you any more,
  Flatter or fawn to attain my end—
I am what never has been before,
  Woman—and Friend.

—and then tipping a copy of David Morton's "Old Ships" over it, no doubt to further hide her project from prying eyes.

CONTEMPORARY CIRCUITRY

Tools such as World Wide Web search engines, Google Books, and rapidly expanding electronic databases offer literary critics access to the twentieth century's rich, energetic culture of incidental poetry reading that we only could have imagined gaining a few years back. Fifteen, maybe even ten years ago, and working with catalogs and indexes privileging the activity of intentional poetry circuits, we didn't have nearly the capabilities that make projects like the current one not just viable but possible. Using the Web and Google Books, I've been able to find versions of Rodebaugh's poem that I wouldn't have been able to locate previously, or that would have taken a prohibitive amount of time to track down. Using eBay, I've been able to compile a large archive of poetry scrapbooks that libraries wouldn't have preserved and that, without the niche markets created by eBay's centralized flea market, likely would have been destroyed; I also purchased Paul Fox's portfolio online, outbidding a surprising number of people who no doubt valued it for reasons other than, or in addition to, my own. Using blogs, bulletin board conversations, and email, I've been able to locate and interview readers and networks of readers who are preserving, commenting on, and recirculating material beyond the auspices of higher education and in noncodex formats in much the same way that readers did a century ago.

In the process, I've found that while "Rejected" and many other popular poems from the first half of the twentieth century may have dropped out of print culture (as far as I can determine, for example, "Rejected" last appeared in print in 1962 in Arthur Power Dudden's anthology *The Assault of Laughter: A Treasury of American Political Humor*), new access to, and new sets of, communication technologies have given that verse renewed cultural and social imperatives—if, in fact, those imperatives ever waned. "Rejected," for instance, is now being cited and circulated online to make comparisons between the present moment and the Great Depression, especially between Roosevelt's administration and Barack Obama's, and particularly in the conservative blogosphere. "[T]here's really nothing new under the sun," one political blogger remarks in posting a digital photo of a typewritten copy of "Rejected" that one of the "old bucks" in town gave to him; cynically, he concludes, "[o]nly the names and dates change" (Skip, 2008, para. 1). Another reader sent

"Rejected" to the Oklahoma Food Retail Cooperative group on Yahoo.com, saying, "I found this poem while going through some of my mother's papers. Some of the members may find it pertinent today!" (Lebow, 2009, para. 1). Yet another individual prefaces his or her presentation of the poem as an act of cultural recovery, explaining, "I am glad to be able to publish this truly unearthed text as its content relates, in part, to the reforms in farming policy during the FDR administration that have led to the prevalence of agribusiness conglomerate-run factory farms that dominates our agricultural landscape today" (Anonymous, 2007, para. 2).

As these examples suggest, online and digital technologies have given readers more power to clip, "carry," circulate, collect, and repurpose poems than they've ever had before. Thanks in part to social networking sites such as Facebook and Web 2.0 interfaces that depend on user-generated content, there are more poems being circulated and encountered in our present day, especially in incidental ways, than there were in clipping-frenzied modern America. Digital poetry scrapbooks are now being marketed to generations of readers who imagine "cut and paste" to be primarily electronic activities and who digitally store noteworthy material in the "clippings" file of their Kindles. ("Here," one digital scrapbook site explains, "you can browse hundreds of beautiful and inspiring poems submitted by...scrapbookers around the world. Use relevant poems to add deeper meaning to your layouts and cards" ["Poems," para. 1].) Understanding the communications circuits of poems in modern America—that is, extending critical attention to the culture of incidental poetry as it occurred outside of what Brown called the "antiquated, word-dribbling book"—will not only help us to better gauge the importance of poetry as it structured people's lives in the first half of the twentieth century, but it will give us a foothold to begin assessing what it means in our own time as well.

NOTES

1   On the subject of incidental poetry, the study finds: "Ninety-nine percent of all adult readers, including those adults who said that they have never read or listened to poetry, indicate that they have been incidentally exposed to poetry in at least one unexpected place.... Eighty-one percent of the respondents who reported any incidental exposure to poetry said that they read or listened to the poem when they came across it" (Schwartz et al., 2006, 69). I borrow the terms "intentional" and "incidental" with some hesitation, for while they can be useful in describing how people encounter poetry, they can nonetheless be misleading in a number of ways. For instance, many people in modern America expected to find poems in the newspaper and thus sought them out there; that reading was no more or less intentional than the reading done by people who turned to books and little magazines. Additionally, and I think more importantly, the terms "intentional" and "incidental" suggest a *qualitative* difference in the seriousness with which two types of readers take poetry, which is not a difference that *Poetry in America* was manufactured to study despite the implications of its terminology; nor is that a difference this essay wants to support—quite the opposite,

in fact. Thus, when I use "incidental" and "intentional" here, I use them merely to describe the ways that people encountered poetry in spaces and media devoted, or not devoted, exclusively to poetry.

2   For a history of how poetry was used inside of institutional contexts such as church, school, and at public events in modern America, see Rubin, 2007.

3   Important foundational work on poetry's circulation throughout the wider culture has been done by scholars such as Maria Damon, Joseph Harrington, Cary Nelson, Rubin, Joseph Harrington, and Mark W. Van Wienen, but that scholarship has occurred largely on the fringes of mainstream poetry criticism and is known more for its singularity than for its exemplarity. For studies of poetry's proliferation in, and use by, commercial culture, see Chasar, 2010.

4   I single out lyric poetry at this juncture to suggest how the present essay—and a study of poetry in popular culture more generally—intersects with what is being called the "new lyric studies." So far, the effort to historicize the genre of lyric poetry and what Virginia Jackson has called "lyric reading" has focused largely on nineteenth-century poetry; see, for example, Prins, 1999, and Jackson, 2005. For the most influential use of "the poem itself," see the Cleanth Brooks and Robert Penn Warren college textbook and anthology *Understanding Poetry*, first published in 1938 and issued in three subsequent editions (1950, 1960, and 1976).

5   Murray's copy of the poem is typewritten on legal-sized paper and has been folded to fit into an envelope. That—along with the faint typewriter ink that suggests a duplicate—indicates Murray was sent a copy of the poem from someone else. See Box 4, Folder 9, Item 7 in the William H. Murray Collection of the University of Oklahoma's Carl Albert Center Congressional Archives.

6   For more on the use of poems in World War II propaganda, including their dissemination via rocket bombs, see Nelson, 2004.

7   I'm grateful to Karen Ford, Jeff Jaeckle, Lynn Makau, Meredith Martin, and Adalaide Morris for their insights into this poem.

8   The iconography of this cartoon is not unique to this postcard, as wartime propaganda from both world wars regularly paired Kaiser Wilhelm or Hitler with what became known as the "Hitler dog." During World War II, the image was even used to sell U.S. war bonds, prompting one six-year-old dachshund owner, John Anson, to write in protest to U.S. Secretary of the Treasury Henry Morgenthau Jr. "I asked him not to make fun of dachshunds or to make them unhappy by drawing Hitler's face on them," Anson explained. "I told him I had two dachshunds and that they were nice little dogs and I loved them and that they were good Americans." Anson later received a letter from Morgenthau "apologizing to dachshunds in general." ("Morgenthau Defends Dachshund Cartoon," *New York Times*, April 5, 1943: 16). On the cover of "Hitler at the Gates of Hell," the metonymic association between Hitler and the wiener dog is further elaborated, as the cover's quotation "It Won't Be Long Now" refers to the length of the war and to the length of Hitler's phallic, wiener-dog tail, which is being cut off by a bomb from a U.S. fighter plane.

9   My postcard-bomb comparison is suggested by the postcard itself, where the stars decorating the edges of the cover rhyme with the star on the airplane bomber shooting at Hitler, thus encouraging users to think of sending a postcard as an analogous attack on Hitler.

10 The *Oxford English Dictionary* identifies "skate" as primarily American slang.

11 For more on the history and practice of scrapbooking generally speaking, see Garvey, 1996, 2003, and 2007; Tucker et al., 2006; and Helfand, 2008.

12 Examples abound: a bum at the beginning of Jack Kerouac's *The Dharma Bums* carries a prayer to St. Theresa that he "[cut out] of a reading-room magazine in Los Angeles" (1976, 5); an elderly African American couple evicted from their apartment in Ralph Ellison's *Invisible Man* have newspaper clippings among their belongings (1995, 271–272); Ma Joad from John Steinbeck's *The Grapes of Wrath* burns her collection of clippings before leaving the farm in Oklahoma (2006, 108); Sophie in Nelson Algren's *The Man with the Golden Arm* assuages her fear of having "[n]o true place at all" by "reaching for an outsized album labeled . . . *My Scrapbook of Fatal Accidence*" (1976, 236, 34); an immigrant Bajan woman from Paule Marshall's *Brown Girl, Brownstones* carries "in her pocketbook" a clipping of the house she one day hopes to own (1981, 36); living in a shelter so basic that it is "more like an idea of a house than a real one," Edwin Boomer keeps a beach free of paper scraps in Elizabeth Bishop's "The Sea and Its Shore" (1984, 171); and in *The House on Mango Street* by Sandra Cisneros, the character of Minerva, who "is always sad like a house on fire," writes poems "on little pieces of paper that she folds over and over and holds in her hands a long time" (1984, 84).

REFERENCES

Algren, Nelson. 1976. *The Man with the Golden Arm.* New York: Seven Stories Press.
Anonymous. October 23, 2007, 5:49 p.m. "A Stranger Stood at the Gates of Hell." *Corduroy Orange,* http://corduroyorange.com/?p=250. Accessed June 25, 2009.
Baldwin, Lois Karen. 1975. "Down on Bugger Run: Family Group and the Social Base of Folklore." PhD diss., University of Pennsylvania.
Bell, Karl. March 30, 2009, 1:11 a.m. Comment on "A Stranger Stood at the Gates of Hell." *Corduroy Orange,* October 23, 2007 (5:49 p.m.), http://corduroyorange.com/?p=250. Accessed June 25, 2009.
Bernstein, Charles. 1992. "Artifice of Absorption." In *A Poetics,* 9–89. Cambridge: Harvard University Press.
Big Fred. April 23, 2008, 1:18 p.m. Comment on "OT/war rations." Tractor Talk Discussion Forum, Yesterday's Tractor Co. http://www.ytmag.com/cgi-bin/viewit.cgi?bd=ttalk&th=637268. Accessed June 25, 2009.
Bishop, Elizabeth. 1984. *The Collected Prose.* New York: Farrar, Straus and Giroux.
Bourdieu, Pierre. 1984. *Distinction: A Social Critique of the Judgement of Taste.* Trans. Richard Nice. Cambridge: Harvard University Press.
Brooks, Cleanth and Robert Penn Warren, eds. 1938. *Understanding Poetry: An Anthology for College Students.* New York: H. Holt and Co.
Brown, Bob. 1931. Appendix to *Readies for Bob Brown's Machine,* ed. Bob Brown, 153–206. Cagnes-sur-Mer: Roving Eye Press.
Cather, Willa. 1918. *My Antonia.* Boston: Houghton Mifflin.
Certeau, Michel de. 1988. *The Practice of Everyday Life.* Trans. Steven Rendall. Berkeley: University of California Press.
Chasar, Mike. 2010. "The Business of Rhyming: Burma-Shave Poetry and Popular Culture." *PMLA* 125.1: 29–47.
Cisneros, Sandra. 1984. *The House on Mango Street.* New York: Vintage.
Darnton, Robert. 1982. "What Is the History of Books?" *Daedalus* 111.3: 65–83.

Ellison, Ralph. 1995. *Invisible Man*. New York: Vintage.

Garvey, Ellen Gruber. 1996. *The Adman in the Parlor: Magazines and the Gendering of Consumer Culture, 1880s to 1910s*. Oxford: Oxford University Press.

———. 2007. "Imitation Is the Sincerest Form of Appropriation: Scrapbooks and Extra-Illustration." *Common-place* 7.3. http://www.common-place.org/vol-07/no-03/garvey/. Accessed January 13, 2010.

———. 2003. "Scissoring and Scrapbooks: Nineteenth-Century Reading, Remaking, and Recirculating." In *New Media, 1740-1915*, ed. Lisa Gitelman and Geoffrey B. Pingree, 207–227. Cambridge: MIT Press.

Graves, Charles. 1939. *You're Welcome*. London: National Book Association, Hutchinson.

Hall, Stuart. 1981. "Notes on Deconstructing 'the Popular.'" In *People's History and Socialist Theory*, ed. Raphael Samuel, 227–240. London: Routledge and Keegan Paul.

Heidler, Harold. 1996. *The Lucky Son: My Autobiography*. http://home.wwdb.org/heidler/luckynew.htm. Accessed June 25, 2009.

Helfand, Jessica. 2008. *Scrapbooks: An American History*. New Haven: Yale University Press.

Howard, Dorothy Jones. n.d. "The Great Election Bet of 1936." http://www.argenweb.net/white/ wchs/TheGreatElectionBetof1936_files/TheGreatElectionBetof1936.htm. Accessed June 25, 2009.

Howells, William Dean. 2002. *A Hazard of New Fortunes*. New York: The Modern Library.

Jackson, Virginia. 2005. *Dickinson's Misery: A Theory of Lyric Reading*. Princeton: Princeton University Press.

Katriel, Tamar, and Thomas Farrell. 1991. "Scrapbooks as Cultural Texts: An American Art of Memory." *Text and Performance Quarterly* 11.1: 1–17.

Kerouac, Jack. 1976. *The Dharma Bums*. New York: Penguin.

Lebow, David. January 29, 2009, 7:51 p.m. "White House Chef." Yahoo! Groups Message, Oklahoma Food Retail Cooperative, http://groups.yahoo.com/group/okfoodret/message/6774. Accessed December 29, 2009.

Lewis, Sinclair. 1980. *Arrowsmith*. New York: Signet.

———. 1998. *Babbitt*. New York: Signet.

Marshall, Paule. 1981. *Brown Girl, Brownstones*. New York: The Feminist Press at the City University of New York.

Mason, Walt. 1914. "A Kansas Poet's Income." *Literary Digest* 48: 340–343.

Nelson, Cary. 1989. *Repression and Recovery: Modern American Poetry and the Politics of Cultural Memory 1910-1945*. Madison: University of Wisconsin Press.

———. 2004. "The Vexed History of the Wartime Poem Card." *American Literary History* 16.2: 263–289.

Nelson, Ted. 2003. "Computer Lit/Dream Machines." In *The New Media Reader*, ed. Noah Wardrip-Fruin and Nick Montfort, 303–338. Cambridge: MIT Press.

Past Your Eyes. September 28, 2007. Comment on "Poem on FDR. Anyone know the source?" *Free Republic*, http://www.freerepublic.com/focus/f-news/1903710/posts. Accessed June 25, 2009.

Perloff, Marjorie. 1991. *Radical Artifice: Writing Poetry in the Age of Media*. Chicago: University of Chicago Press.

"Poems." n.d. Scrapbook.com, http://www.scrapbook.com/poems.php. Accessed December 29, 2009.

Pound, Ezra. 1971. *How to Read*. New York: Haskell House Publishers.

———. 1954. "A Retrospect." In *Literary Essays of Ezra Pound*, ed. T. S. Eliot. Norfolk, CT: New Directions. 3–14.

Prins, Yopie. 1999. *Victorian Sappho*. Princeton: Princeton University Press.

"Rejected." 1940. *The American Flint* 29: 53–54.

"Rensselaer Beer Song." n.d. Rensselaer Polytechnic Institute. http://www.stutt.net/
rpi/index.php?option=com_content&view=article&id=109:rensselaer-beer-
song&catid=36:songs&Itemid=55. Accessed January 13, 2010.

Roosevelt, Eleanor. January 20, 1939. *My Day: A Comprehensive, Electronic Edition of Eleanor
Roosevelt's "My Day" Newspaper Columns*. The Eleanor Roosevelt Papers Project. http://
www.gwu.edu/_erpapers/myday/displaydoc.cfm?_y=1939&_f=md055168. Accessed
January 13, 2010.

Rubin, Joan Shelley. 2007. *Songs of Ourselves: The Uses of Poetry in America*. Cambridge:
Harvard University Press.

Schwartz, Lisa K., Lisbeth Goble, Ned English, and Robert F. Bailey. 2006. *Poetry in
America: Review of the Findings*. Chicago: The Poetry Foundation.

Skip. December 9, 2008, 11:43 a.m. "Been there. Done that. Uh-oh!" GraniteGrok,
http://granitegrok.com/blog/2008/12/been_there_done_that_uhoh.html. Accessed
December 29, 2009.

Steinbeck, John. 2006. *The Grapes of Wrath*. New York: Penguin.

Tucker, Susan, Katherine Ott, and Patricia Buckler, eds. 2006. *The Scrapbook in American
Life*. Philadelphia: Temple University Press.

Vigilanteman. January 7, 2007. Comment on "Rejected FDR at the Gates of Hell." *Free Republic*,
http://www.freerepublic.com/focus/fr/1763904/posts. Accessed June 25, 2009.

CHAPTER 13

"WITH AMBUSH AND STRATAGEM": AMERICAN POETRY IN THE AGE OF PURE WAR

PHILIP METRES

War is not a life: it is a situation,
One which may neither be ignored nor accepted,
A problem to be met with ambush and stratagem,
Enveloped or scattered.

> —T. S. Eliot, from "A Note on War Poetry"

The troops are quiet tonight, but it's not alright
because we know they're planning something . . .
We must keep our eyes open. . . .

> —Fugazi, from "KYEO" [Keep Your Eyes Open]

In the closing scene to the 2009 Oscar-winning film *The Hurt Locker*, ordnance disposal expert Sergeant First Class William James has returned to Iraq after a failed stint as a civilian back in the United States. The multilayered final image of the film shows James—now enclosed within immense and arcane protective armor—marching away from the camera, his arms swinging comically apart from his body. The image uncannily echoes the iconic images of astronauts taking a leap into the unknown, risking their lives; we feel the ardor of the warrior to confront death without fear, and the apotheosis of courage under fire. At the same time, in the awkward marching toward what may be death, James appears almost robotic, sapped of his own humanity, in service to the machinery of war. As Simone Weil has argued about *The Iliad*, war—whose true subject is force—has the tendency to "transform man into a thing … petrif[ying] equally the souls of those who suffer it, and those who wield it" (173).

In a single image, then, *The Hurt Locker* encapsulates the paradox at the heart of war and war literature; while war provides the most intense context for humans to demonstrate their superhuman courage, strength, and love in the face of death, it also can rob the warrior of the very things that brought him to fight in the first place. It is not accidental that the very first scene of the movie also distills these two images—that of the astronaut and that of the robot—into one; we see what looks like a lunar landscape, a rocky terrain without recognizably human parameters, coming at us quickly, until the film cuts away to reveal that we've been seeing a street in Iraq from the point of view of a small bomb-exploring robot on treads, like a miniature lunar landing vehicle.

It is little wonder that *The Hurt Locker* was so widely celebrated, when we consider its ability to explore simultaneously and so vividly the bravery of the soldier and the benighted addictiveness of combat. Still, like much war literature, the film's focus on the soldier comes at the cost of everything outside the frame: Iraqis in *their* homeland are seen as potential or actual murderous bombers; the U.S. "homefront" is an absurd, even obscene site of capitalist plenty and suffocating domesticity, with no opposition to the war visible; and women are out of the picture almost entirely. (The only female character, James's wife, was so forgettable that it seems appropriate that the Internet Movie Database's website for "Connie James" reads as "this character biography is empty.") In short, Iraqis, women, civilians, the peace movement, the machinations of the military-industrial complex, the workings of empire and Pure War—all of these people and institutions cede to the frame of the war story.

In *Frames of War*, Judith Butler considers the ways in which our political discourse about war frequently frames to narrow, exclude, or render unrecognizable that which contradicts the official version of what war is and whom it may affect. (The problematics of framing, of course, are evident in both prowar and antiwar discourse.) In particular, Butler concerns herself with how the humanity of others becomes abstracted or even excluded entirely. In her words, "to call the frame into question is to show that the frame never quite contained the scene it was meant to limn, that something was already outside, which made the very sense of the inside possible, recognizable.... Something exceeds the frame that troubles our sense of reality" (9). Butler's philosophical exploration enacts what has happened in war poetry criticism since Paul Fussell's brilliant *The Great War and Modern Memory* (1975). While Fussell brings a keen eye to the elegiac and satiric work of the great soldier poets of World War I and sets those poems in the cultural contexts of British literature and culture, subsequent criticism has both drawn upon and illuminated the limits of his frame. Lynne Hanley critiques the myth "of soldiers as the [only] tragic victims of war" (31), and focusing on the English soldier poets in the European trenches, perpetuates the exclusion of the voices of women, noncombatants, pacifists, and people in the colonial world—all of whom were affected by the war. Moreover, she deconstructs how war literature has perpetuated "a structure of feeling of remarkable persistence.... After war after war after war, that innocence is re-created which the next war will destroy" (27). Similarly, Miriam Cooke has coined and critiqued the "war story" as a bildungsroman narrative that tends to explore the mysteries of initiation into the cult of the warrior and to make order out of the disordered and often nonsensical and traumatic experience of war.

A thoroughgoing and future-thinking examination of American war poetry should both explore the parameters of the "war story" as it is articulated in poetry, and it should expand our notion of war poetry by addressing what we term "war" and who is authorized to speak about war. Though the scene of battle, that most highly charged site of war, requires our attention (even as it repels representation), we must follow the poetry outside and behind the lines, as it were, to the other sites of war: to the hospitals, to the homefront, and to the halls of power. In *Pure War*, Paul Virilio proposed that we (Americans in particular) are now living in an age of "Pure War"—a state in which *the real war* is not the event of battles between states, not the endless preparation for war (in an imperial state) but "the preparation for war is what I call Pure War, war which isn't acted out in repetition, but in infinite preparation" (92). Though William James first proposed this very notion over one hundred years ago, it seems even more salient today, when the United States spends more on "defense" than every other county in the world combined, sustaining hundreds of thousands of U.S. troops on hundreds of bases abroad, engaging in multiple wars and military actions.[1] In the United States today, war feels like an anticipated inevitability, increasingly planned for and paid for, and perhaps increasingly necessary to sustain "our way of life"—what presidents like to refer to as "the national interest."[2] The new version of the national-security state has developed ever more byzantine layers of secrecy in the name of security, but its weaponry—especially the unmanned drones that conduct assassinations in the Middle East—increasingly blurs the formerly crucial distinction between soldiers and civilians.[3]

This overview of American war poetry will explore poets who follow in the boots of the World War I soldier poets, such as Randall Jarrell, Yusef Komunyakaa, and Brian Turner, who in certain respects have come to represent World War II, the Vietnam War, and the Iraq War, respectively, as they "dismantle glory" (Goldensohn). Great soldier poetry has tended to succeed in its "realisms" of the battle experience—from the adrenalized psychic and spiritual intensities—to the postwar reverberations of war. But if soldier poets oscillate between "the undeniable appeal of the heroic—the irrepressible glamour of its self-forgetfulness in the face of great danger to achieve a public good—and revulsion at what traffic in the heroic has always brought about" (Goldensohn, Dismantling 5), civilian poets remind that none of us is immune to what Chris Hedges ironically referred to as "the force that gives us meaning." In light of the need to expand our view of "behind the lines" and "beyond the lines," we ought to show how the visionary work of civilian poets such as Walt Whitman, Emily Dickinson, Mark Twain, Carl Sandburg, T. S. Eliot, Langston Hughes, Gwendolyn Brooks, Robert Lowell, William Stafford, Robert Bly, Adrienne Rich, William Heyen, June Jordan, Muriel Rukeyser, Dunya Mikhail, H. L. Hix, Lawrence Joseph, the Sidewalk Blogger, Denise Levertov, Juliana Spahr, and Naomi Shihab Nye (among many others) enables a dilatory rethinking not only of how we represent war, but also of what war is, where it comes from, and whether it is inevitable.

In this study, I will thread a chronological discussion of war poetry in three manifestations—(1) soldier poetry, (2) Pure War/war resistance poetry, and (3) peace poetry. Though these artificial categories overlap considerably, they suggest a way to acknowledge and organize the problematics of war poetry as it manifests itself from different points of view. Regardless of category, T. S. Eliot's "A Note on War Poetry"—an admittedly minor poem—establishes some of the conundrums at the heart of war poetry: if war is a situation, can poetry illuminate war without accepting it? And, if so, how? And if war is not a specific situation, but in fact a cultural phenomenon, do we see the parameters of "Pure War" begin to take shape in American war poetry? What sorts of "ambushes and stratagems" have poets used— whether as soldiers or civilians, whether prowar or antiwar or some combination in between—to render the traumatic and inarticulable articulate? Has poetry worked to ambush by enveloping war (through a visionary long view) or by scattering it (through diminishing its powers, unmaking its syntax)? And if war is indeed a failure of the imagination, and given that peace seems to be a nebulous and abstract thing, what does peace poetry contribute to our thinking about war and about alternatives to war?

Though war poetry is as old as all other forms of poetry, we often trace modern war poetry to the trenches of World War I, when soldier poets such as Wilfred Owen and Siegfried Sassoon challenged war's glorification with a raw and antiheroic picture of the brutality on the front lines, defiantly marking an abyss between soldier and civilian. The antiheroic strain, however, is as old as Archilochus and Sappho; in American poetry, war's confusion was already visible in the Civil War–era poetry of Walt Whitman, Emily Dickinson, and Herman Melville.[4] Whitman's work as a nurse brought him into physical contact with the direct effects of war—including his walking by a pile of amputated limbs, and witnessing the death of wounded soldiers—and led to his important book of poems, *Drum-Taps* (1865) and, years later, a prose memoir called *Memoranda During the War*. Whitman articulated the skepticism about literature's ability to capture the awesome power and traumatizing force of war, when he admonished that "the real war will never get in the books" (*Prose Works*, 1:116). Yet his war poems gesture toward the complexity of conflict, with tones that vary from martial intensity ("Beat! Beat! Drums!") to elegiac gloom ("Come Up From the Fields Father"). Himself a patriot, Whitman once told a bellicose friend that war was "about nine hundred and ninety-nine parts diarrhea to one part glory: the people who like the wars should be compelled to fight the wars" (qtd. in Kaplan, 291). Poems like "The Wound Dresser" attempt to reclaim the soldier's body that "disappears into the ideological discourse of the state" (Sweet, 6): "I dress the perforated shoulder, the foot with the bullet-wound, / Cleanse the one with a gnawing and putrid gangrene, so sickening, so offensive, / While the attendant stands behind aside me holding the tray and pail" (Leaves 261). In "The Centenarian's Story," Whitman gives voice to an old Revolutionary War veteran still suffering from trauma; Whitman himself suffered a physical and emotional collapse, a casualty of the war.

Emily Dickinson was long excluded from discussions of war poetry, but recent criticism has shown how her poetry, as Gilpin Faust writes, "is filled with the language of battle—the very vocabulary of war that she would have encountered in the four newspapers regularly delivered to the Dickinson household. Campaigns, cannons, rifle balls, bullets, artillery, soldiers, ammunition, flags, bayonets, cavalry, drums, and trumpets are recurrent images in her poetry" (n.p.). Dickinson's engagement with the war is more than lexical; critics such as Shira Wolosky, Faith Barrett, Cristanne Miller, Renee Bergland, and Benjamin Friedlander have shown convincingly that Dickinson engaged the questions of war in ways that compel a rethinking not simply of Dickinson's oeuvre but also about what *war poetry* looks like. Her occasional poems such as "It Feels a Shame to Be Alive" as well as her more oblique meditations on pain, suffering, and God suggest the reverberating power of war far behind the lines. For example, Barrett and Miller include Dickinson's meditation on spiritual struggle; in "My Portion Is Defeat," written in 1863, Dickinson employs the imagery of battle to posit that the inner wars can be "more arduous than balls [bullets]" (358). For Barrett and Miller, the war compelled in Dickinson a pursuit of ultimate questions:

> What do "victory" and "defeat" mean, in relation to each other, and in relation to moral questions or to religious speculation about an afterlife? How does the individual deal with acute pain? How can one believe in a protective and benevolent God when men are dying by the thousands in the most violent circumstances? How does news of such cataclysmic dying affect the living, especially those living far from the battlefields? (352)[5]

FROM THE INDIAN WARS TO THE SPANISH-AMERICAN WAR

In the latter half of the nineteenth century, the United States recovered from its bloody Civil War to become a global power, annexing various territories throughout the world and engineering dictatorial takeovers in the Caribbean and Latin America. Emboldened by its westward expansion through the defeat of Mexico (in the Mexican War, 1846–1848) and the elimination of Native Americans, the United States defeated Spain in the Spanish-American War (1898) and crushed Filipino resistance (1899–1902) in a brutal conflict that led to the deaths of hundreds of thousands of civilians. Goldensohn's *American War Poetry: An Anthology* (2006) provides a window into the poetry written during the time and in subsequent eras, looking back at the formative historical events that turned the United States into an imperial power. Reading Native American poems of elegy and resistance (e.g., the "Last Song of Sitting Bull" [122]) alongside those of martial patriotism (e.g., William Vaughn Moody's "On a Soldier Fallen in the Philippines" [148]) provides a window into the complex and contradictory meanings of the "American" in "American poetry."

In an unpublished poem (not in Goldensohn's fine anthology), Mark Twain parodies the "Battle Hymn of the Republic" (1901) and savages the imperial arrogance and capitalist greed that drove U.S. policy in Manila:

> Mine eyes have seen the orgy of the launching of the Sword;
> He is searching out the hoardings where the stranger's wealth is stored;
> He hath loosed his fateful lightnings,
>   and with woe and death has scored;
> His lust is marching on....
> In a sordid slime harmonious,
>   Greed was born in yonder ditch,
> With a longing in his bosom—and for other's good an itch—
> As Christ died to make men holy,
>   let men die to make us rich—
> Our god is marching on.
>
> (qtd. in True, 44)[6]

Twain's subversive employment of the patriotic "Battle Hymn"—a strategy of resistance that persists throughout the history of dissent and resistance poetry—anticipates the trajectory of comic antiwar verse, from Country Joe and the Fish's "I Feel Like I'm Fixin' to Die Rag" (1967) to Kent Johnson's Iraq War poetry in *Lyric Poetry After Auschwitz* (2005).

WORLD WAR I

World War I also led to significant American war poetry. Stephen Crane, a journalist who interviewed veterans, succeeded in creating one of the most memorable narratives of war in *The Red Badge of Courage*, and so did civilian poets during World War I. The English soldier poets of World War I deservedly garner much critical attention, yet crucial poems by Louise Bogan, e. e. cummings, T. S. Eliot, Ezra Pound, Carl Sandburg, Alan Seeger, and others widen our view of the war from battlefield

(Seeger's soldier poetry) to the homefront (Bogan's elegy "To My Brother Killed: Haumont Wood: October, 1918"), from war strategy (Sandberg's "Buttons") to conscientious objection (cummings's "i sing of olaf"), from critique of Western civilization (Pound's "Hugh Selwyn Mauberly") to existential spiritual crisis (T. S. Eliot's *The Waste Land*).[7] Carl Sandburg's "Buttons" (1916) starkly measures the distance between the laughing newspaperman on the homefront moving buttons on a map and the soldiers "twist[ing] on their bodies in a red soak along a river edge":

> I have been watching the war map slammed up
> for advertising in front of the newspaper office.
> Buttons—red and yellow buttons—blue and black buttons—
> are shoved back and forth across the map....
>
> (Ten thousand men and boys twist on their bodies in a red soak along a
>   river edge,
> Gasping of wounds, calling for water, some rattling death in their
>   throats.)
> Who would guess what it cost to move two buttons one inch on the war
>   map here
>   in front of the newspaper office where the freckle-faced young man is
>   laughing to us? (40)

The jovial young man, of course, stands in for the war planners with their own maps, moving the pawns of blithe abstraction.

Yet it is in the apocalyptic *The Waste Land* (1922) that we see unmistakably how war and the crisis of modernity converge:

> What is that sound high in the air
> Murmur of maternal lamentation
> Who are those hooded hordes swarming
> Over endless plains, stumbling in cracked earth
> Ringed by the flat horizon only
> What is the city over the mountains
> Cracks and reforms and bursts in the violet air
> Falling towers
> Jerusalem Athens Alexandria
> Vienna London
> Unreal (17–18)

Eliot's poem maintains a gauzy, almost otherworldly "unreal" distance from the violence that Owen and Sassoon lived and wrote about; still, his work captured that broader sense of civilizational crisis that led Freud to pose the existence of the "death drive" and to begin to articulate early trauma theory (so-called shell shock). Perhaps it is no mistake that Eliot's decidedly "civilian" poem takes such a distantiated, benumbed view. On the one hand, we might read in such distance the cruel and inhumane viewpoint of the chickenhawk, who vociferously argues for war's necessity but believes that it is for others ("the hordes") to fight it. On the other hand, this distance may also be the clarifying distance of prophetic lamentation and dissidence, who murmurs "maternal lamentation" at the madness of the confusion that is war.

The Spanish Civil War

Each war, of course, has brought its own significant poetry, but some wars tend to be excised from the discussion; the Spanish Civil War, for example, has been left out because it was a Leftist cause célèbre, or because the U.S. military did not participate, or because it is one of those rare examples of a just war, or because it does not fit easily into the "Futile War" (World War I), "Good War" (World War II), or "Bad War" (Vietnam War) trajectory. Yet the Spanish Civil War elicited a broadly internationalist poetry in the 1930s from poets such as Langston Hughes and W. H. Auden, extolling the virtues of the fight against Franco and fascism. In later years, both Hughes and Auden would come to disavow their period of partisan poetry—for both political and poetic reasons, as cold war containment culture looked with jaundiced eyes on those who showed any favor toward socialism and communism. As Cary Nelson has demonstrated, the poetry about this war is richly diverse and bears our continued reading, despite its seeming disappearance from the canon.[8]

For example, Langston Hughes's ballad "Letter from Spain" (1937) explores the colonial and racial implications of the war in Spain, from the point of view of a black American soldier, who engages in conversation with a captured "wounded Moor" "just as dark as me" (Nelson, *Wound*, 85). Using the ballad conventions of dialogue, compressed narrative, and regular rhythm and rhyme, Hughes turns the traditional medium of poetic journalism into a meditation on colonial struggle, both at home and abroad. This "Moor," it turns out, has been pressed into military service by the fascists, even though he knew "this whole thing wasn't right." The speaker of the poem realizes the implications of the war in a new way:

> And as he lay there dying
> In a village we had taken,
> I looked across to Africa
> And seed foundations shakin'.
>
> Cause if a free Spain wins this war,
> The colonies, too, are free—
> Then something wonderful'll happen
> To them Moors as dark as me.

> I said, I guess that's why old England
> And I reckon Italy, too,
> Is afraid to let a workers' Spain
> Be too good to me and you—
>
> Cause they got slaves in Africa—
> And they don't want 'em to be free.
> Listen, Moorish prisoner, hell!
> Here, shake hands with me!
>
> I knelt down there beside him,
> And I took his hand—
> But the wounded Moor was dyin'
> And he didn't understand. (85–86)

In that final tender moment, the two "enemy" soldiers hold hands as if in truce. Though the Moor dies, "Letter from Spain" gave hope—when the war was far from being decided—that the fight against fascism may not only prevent fascism in Spain but also instigate liberation movements of colonized peoples throughout the world.

World War II

If World War I had a strange unreality for many Americans, because of its relative geographical distance, the immensity and inhumanity of World War II seemed to crush both the glorification impulse and the personal elegies that characterized the poetry of the Great War. As Robert Goralski wrote, "What we did to each other was almost beyond human conception" (qtd. in Fussell, *Norton Book of Modern War*, 307). Goralski's "we" admits to the terrible cruelty that was not limited to any nation's conduct during the war. The literature that emerged had a tone of weariness, horror, and absurdity. And because World War II was the first fully bureaucratized, mechanized war, many of the most successful representations of the war avoid the realistic mode entirely and move toward absurdity and surrealism.[9]

Of the panoply of accomplished soldier poets of World War II—James Dickey, Richard Eberhardt, Anthony Hecht, Richard Hugo, Howard Nemerov, George Oppen, Karl Shapiro, and Louis Simpson, to name a handful—Randall Jarrell occupies a particularly critical position, for his irreducibly complex portrait of war, which spans the experiences of the homefront, the battlefronts, and the concentration camps, and for his ability, as Goldensohn puts it in *Dismantling Glory*, to "stretch the war poem to accommodate the larger civilian politics [and ethical questions] gestating it" (180). Like Joseph Heller's *Catch-22*, and Kurt Vonnegut's *Slaughterhouse-Five*, Randall Jarrell's "The Death of the Ball Turret Gunner" (1945) employs a dreamlike surrealism to give voice to a pilot awakening into the implications of his life at the very moment that it will be extinguished:

> From my mother's sleep I fell into the State,
> And I hunched in its belly till my wet fur froze.
> Six miles from earth, loosed from the dream of life,
> I woke to black flak and the nightmare fighters.
> When I died they washed me out of the turret with a hose. (144)

By the use of prosopopoeia, a recurrent trope in war poetry in which the dead speak, Jarrell becomes the medium for a man whose metaphors suggest he was more fetal and animal than adult male; however womblike the "belly" of the ball turret, he wakes to incoming fire and his death. An industrial hose, not a burial, will remove his remains for the next gunner. The numbed directness of the tone at once harmonizes the gunner's flatlined description of death and the author's rage at the destruction of innocence.

In a war where air power took on a huge role, Jarrell—who became a flight instructor and watched pilots take off and never come back—painstakingly explores the psychic implications of secondary witness and survival as well in "Eighth Air Force" (1945). With his recurrent triplet rhymes in each stanza, Jarrell paints a picture of an everyday barracks scene, in which his fellow pilots are described, almost lovingly, as "murderers" as they play games and sweat out their remaining missions. What makes the poem so strangely compelling is the speaker's sense of perspectival distance from the other men; but unlike a failed antiwar diatribe, Jarrell includes himself: "I did as these have done" (143). Moreover, the concluding lines of the poem render Jarrell in the position of Pilate, to the Christ figures of the pilots: "Men wash their hands in blood, as best they can: / I find no fault in this just man" (143). Like Whitman and Owen before him, Jarrell sees these men in the image of Jesus Christ; however, rather than merely ceding to the sacrificial myth of the soldier giving all for his country, Jarrell reminds us that their business is murder, not salvation—or, as Jarrell later posed it, salvation by murder.[10]

Other poems from the war such as Witter Bynner's "Defeat" and Gwendolyn Brooks's "Negro Hero"—both included in Harvey Shapiro's compelling anthology *Poets of World War II*—underscore aspects of the war typically repressed by our conventional narrative of the Good War. In "Defeat" (1947), Bynner notes how German prisoners are allowed to eat with white American soldiers "while black American soldiers sit apart, / The white men eating meat, the black men heart" (Shapiro, 1). In a nation not entirely awake to racial injustice, Bynner's poem underscores how "it is again ourselves whom we defeat" (1). Likewise, Gwendolyn Brooks's "Negro Hero" (1945) is a dramatic monologue about a brash black soldier who is willing to "kick their law in the teeth in order to save them" (Shapiro, 115). Willing to fight and die for a country who still did not consider him a full human, the Negro hero admits that his fight was not against the enemy "but them" (115), for the "stuttered promise" of the "fair lady" of democracy. Still he worries that "they might prefer the /

Preservation of their law in all its sick dignity and their knives / To the continuation of their creed / And their lives" (115).

In addition to the homefront poetry by women such as Brooks, Marianne Moore, and Muriel Rukeyser (thoroughly explored by Susan Schweik in *A Gulf So Deeply Cut*), conscientious objector poets such as Robert Lowell, William Stafford, and William Everson would come to play an important role in American poetry and the peace movement. As Karl Shapiro wrote in "The Conscientious Objector" (1944), to those who served in alternative service camps and also in prison: "you who saved neither yourselves nor us / Are equally with those who shed the blood / The heroes of our cause" (31). Though they would emerge only after the war as public poets, the war and their resistance to it—as I detail in *Behind the Lines: War Resistance Poetry on the American Homefront since 1941* (2007)—were foundational experiences that shaped the tenor of their loyal dissent in poetry and in life. Yet a recent collection, *Another World Instead* (2008), details William Stafford's complex and ongoing meditation on what it means to live against war at a time when the entire world seemed to be engaging in total war. In "These Mornings" (1944), Stafford acknowledges the bleak devastation that he must write himself through each day:

> And this is what happens to the people when a city is bombed:
>   Part of them goes away into the sky,
>   And part of them goes into the earth.
> And what is left, for us, between the sky and the earth
>   is a scar. (52)

THE AMERICAN CENTURY: "SMALL WAR ON THE HEELS OF SMALL WAR"

In *The Life of Poetry* (1949), written in the wake of World War II, Muriel Rukeyser noted that American poetry must confront the culture of conflict in which it exists: "we are people tending toward democracy on the level of hope; on another level, the economy of the nation, the empire business within the republic, both include in their basic premise the concept of perpetual warfare. It is the history of the idea of war that is beneath our other histories" (61). This cultural condition became clarified and intensified after World War II. As the other former imperial powers dug themselves out of the rubble of war, the United States ascended to superpower status, with a global export economy driven and protected by an increasingly well-funded military-industrial complex. All across the world, just in the period between World War II and the Vietnam War, the United States made military interventions and aided coups, including in China (1945), the Philippines (1945), Italy (1947), Greece (1947), Korea (the Korean War), Albania (1949), Guatemala (1953), Iran (1953), Cambodia (1955), the Middle East (1956), and Indonesia (1957–1958). Even in 1953, President

Eisenhower—one of the prime movers and beneficiaries of military power, the same "Ike" whom John Berryman parodied and Robert Lowell lamented—delivered ominous warnings of the military-industrial complex and its deleterious effects on American society. His words in "The Chance for Peace" strike with the force of absolute moral panic:

> Every gun that is made, every warship launched, every rocket fired signifies, in the final sense, a theft from those who hunger and are not fed, those who are cold and are not clothed. The world in arms is not spending money alone. It is spending the sweat of its laborers, the genius of its scientists, the hope of its children.... This is not a way of life at all, in any true sense. Under the cloud of threatening war, it is humanity hanging from a cross of iron. (n.p.)

In his farewell address in 1961, Eisenhower gave this new phenomenon a name: the military-industrial complex, "the total influence" of which, he said, reverberates from economics to politics and spirituality and "is felt in every city, every State-house, every office of the Federal government. We recognize the imperative need for this development. Yet we must not fail to comprehend its grave implications. Our toil, resources, and livelihood are all involved. So is the very structure of our society" (n.p.).

After World War I, critics of war profiteering reached an apogee, before ceding to the fever of war and the righteous fight against fascism. Bob Dylan's song "Masters of War" (1963) returned that critique and brought it in popular form, excoriating the purveyors and beneficiaries of the weapons industry. The stance of the song does not offer a complex reading of the military-industrial complex, and it largely registers its effects on the "masters," not on us. Still, what makes the song so powerful is the speaker's righteous animus, which renders its vengeful conclusion ominous; when he looks forward to the deaths of the masters, Dylan appears, Ahab-like, to assume that the deaths of certain individuals will kill an industry that is bigger than anyone. It is ironic that Eisenhower's visionary self-indictment and warning—one of the most despised presidents by liberal intellectuals—activates the self-indictment that is the preferred tack of political poetry, while the poetics of Dylan's jeremiad is perceived as too divisive and self-inflated.

While the conscientious objector ("C.O.") poets of World War II produced verse and prose while in prison and work camps, their contribution to American poetry emerged most publicly in the postwar era—what Henry Luce baptized "the American Century." Robert Lowell, a former C.O. in World War II, is perhaps the most illuminating poet of the "American Century"; despite his posthumous critical decline, Lowell's poems are suffused with the United States' newly expanded imperial dilemmas, so terrifyingly echoed in the Greek and Roman literature to which he obsessively referred and translated. Lowell's "Memories of West Street and Lepke" (1959), written in the economically flush years after World War II, dramatizes the struggle to represent resistance to a war that had near-unanimous support, in a time when the cold war consensus made dissent yet again unpatriotic.[11] Relatedly, "For the Union Dead" (1964) makes an anguished cry against the postwar culture of amnesiac excess, as the Gaudens Civil War monument becomes threatened by omnivorous capitalism. In "Waking Early Sunday Morning" (first published in 1965), written during the expansion of the Vietnam War, Lowell jumpcuts from the libidinous President Johnson—swimming naked but doomed to "ghost-written rhetoric," trapped in the decisions of empire—to a telescopic view of the consequences of those decisions:

> No weekends for the gods now. Wars
> flicker, earth licks its open sores,
> fresh breakage, fresh promotions, chance
> assassinations, no advance....
>
> Pity the planet, all joy gone
> from this sweet volcanic cone;
> peace to our children when they fall
> in small war on the heels of small
> war—until the end of time
> to police the earth, a ghost
> orbiting forever lost
> in our monotonous sublime. (386)

Lowell's telescoped vision—like Eliot's before him—renders in strict tetrameter couplets the feeling of an inexorable logic. It is a dirgelike vision of unending war. When Lowell enjambs "peace to our children when they fall / in small war," we see the children from a parental perspective, simultaneously as the young *and* as soldiers, as if in a single line break we measure the speed of growing up. Echoing the argument that the United States should not be in the business of being the "world's police force," Lowell dramatizes the feeling of the seemingly inescapable inertia of empire. At the same time, this inertial energy is not vitalizing. The "ghost" to which he refers at the end is either the earth "orbiting forever lost" or ourselves, like Czar Lepke in "Memories of West Street and Lepke," disconnected and addicted to our sublimes: war, capitalist adventure, sex, and so on. Yet Lowell ends this vigorously coupled march into oblivion with an alternating rhyme, providing the feeling of an opening, despite its dread fatalism.

William Stafford's poems—in contrast, perhaps, to Lowell's aristocratic and densely modernist verse—articulated a lifelong struggle in parabolic but plainspoken free verse to maintain a stand against injustice and violence by tracing what he called "smoke's way." Perhaps the most important American pacifist poet, Stafford's "Traveling Through the Dark" (1963) may be one of the best poems that no one has talked about as a war poem, engaging the ethical problem of killing. Stafford's "Peace Walk" (1977), another postwar poem, gives voice to a group of war resisters on an "un-march" to protest the nuclear arms race—a central target of the peace movement during the cold war era. Though the poem identifies itself as one among resisters, "Peace Walk" maintains a Yeatsian self-argument in how it points to the limits of the demonstrators' vision (both physical and metaphorical) and of the walk itself; "we held our poster up to shade our eyes" (*Way It Is*, 59) suggests both a desire to flee the protest and the judging gaze of the bystanders. The poem concludes:

> that love could fill the atmosphere:
>
> Occur, slow the other fallout, unseen,
> on islands everywhere—fallout, falling
> unheard. We held our poster up to shade our eyes.
>
> At the end we just walked away;
> no one was there to tell us where to leave the signs. (59)

The final lines—"At the end we just walked away; / no one was there to tell us where to put the signs"—register the ambiguity of the moment. On the one hand, perhaps nothing was accomplished by the demonstration. On the other hand, in their symbolic action, they have participated in an egalitarian community, where each must decide what to do with the "signs." These signs, of course, are not merely the placards they held, but the signs that we give the world with our lives and that the world gives us.

THE VIETNAM WAR

The sheer volume of verse written in response to the Vietnam War—as flawed, varied, and visionary as the range of human responses to that war—threatens to send the staunchest poetry partisan scurrying behind the walls of canonicity. In *Behind the Lines*, I provided a simple taxonomy of Vietnam War–era verse as a way to mitigate the predominating piety that the only authentic, "real" war poetry could be written by participants, who would therefore write a more "real" and honest picture of war. In addition to widening the discussion of poetry to include songs, symbolic actions, and other symbolic or linguistic deployment of language against war, I made a claim for the visionary/prophetic, the documentary, autobiographical first-person witness, and cross-cultural interactions (translations) as viable, sometimes overlapping, modes of war writing.[12] Implicit, perhaps, was the notion that successful soldier poetry tends toward the first-person witness and that successful civilian poetry tends toward the visionary and documentary. While there is a modicum of truth in this piety, it is in the overlapping where so much of the best poetry happens.

The soldier poetry of the Vietnam War, in particular, and perhaps more than any other war poetry, presents a particular critical problem regarding not *geographical* distance (as is the case for much American civilian war poetry) as much as *temporal* distance. In other words, the poetry written during the span of this extended conflict tends toward the raw, crude, and provocatively antipoetic—as if to combat not only the war at hand but the aestheticizing, glorifying tendencies that invariably render any poem as an enticement to future recruits. It's as if Jarrell's "Eighth Air Force" pilots—rendered as children by the elder Jarrell—were allowed to speak for themselves. One particularly anguished poem from *Peace Is Our Profession* (1981), collectively written by "GI's of the 1st Air Infantry Division," gives voice to the cruel fate of the pilot who knows what he has done, and continues to do:

> We shoot the sick, the young, the lame,
> We do our best to kill and maim,
> Because the kills count all the same,
> Napalm sticks to kids. (22)

Of course, the average GI may have had a closer view of what napalm was doing to the people on the ground than the pilot; but in any case, this poetic collective refuses to distinguish between what the grunts and pilots were doing. The poem, with its sing-song rhyme, delivers an excoriating blow both to the corporatist logic of the Pentagon planners that counted every kill equally, and to themselves, for participating in it, as "'agent-victims' of their own atrocities ... [with] the conviction that there is no return to innocence" (Gotera, 191).

The particularly grueling and cruel nature of the Vietnam War played a role in the increasingly desperate and provocative poetry that emerged in its wake. Michael Bibby's study, *Hearts and Minds: Bodies, Poetry, and Resistance in the Vietnam Era*, explores the various liberation movement poetries of the period, including GI resistance poetry, which articulated its resistance "through images, tropes, and poetics of mutilation in which the fragmented, dismembered, disincorporated (masculine) body signifies both the brutal incoherence of the war and the failure of the dominant ideology's notion of the soldier body as an impenetrable totality" (9). Yet such poetic brutality became less necessary—for the poets, and for the country—as the war ceded to the uneasy peace of the 1970s. Soldier poets such as Jan Barry, Kevin Bowen, Michael Casey, W. D. Ehrhart, Walter McDonald, Basil Paquet, and Bruce Weigl not only produced starkly memorable poetry, but they also worked tirelessly to promote the work of other soldiers (and even Vietnamese) in the years following the war.

But consider the rhetorical gulf between the napalm poem and a poem like "We Never Know," by the Vietnam veteran Yusef Komunyakaa, published in 1988, thirteen years after the war's conclusion:

> He danced with tall grass
> for a moment, like he was swaying
> with a woman. Our gun barrels
> glowed white-hot.
> When I got to him,
> a blue halo
> of flies had already claimed him.
> I pulled the crumbled photograph

> from his fingers.
> There's no other way
> to say this: I fell in love.
> The morning cleared again,
> except for a distant mortar
> & somewhere choppers taking off.
> I slid the wallet into his pocket
> & turned him over, so he wouldn't be
> kissing the ground. (207)

The poem's lush, almost erotic description of the killing of what presumably is the enemy echoes most closely not the raw and sometimes brutal verse of Jan Barry and Michael Casey, but the plaintive philial poems of Whitman and Owen—except that this poem appears to cross enemy lines of identification. That men experience love in battle is part of war poetry—not only love for each other, but also for the enemy soldier, whose bravery and humanity render the encounter more honorable. Though Komunyakaa does not broach it directly, African American identification with the colonial struggle of the Vietnamese—and the African American resistance to the Vietnam War—took on explicitly racial terms, when icons such as Muhammad Ali were reputed to proclaim that "no Vietnamese ever called me a nigger."[13]

Since the war, veteran poets such as Kevin Bowen, W. D. Ehrhart, and Bruce Weigl have written poignantly about grief and survival, refusing to allow grief and loss to become merely a cause for future war, in the service of state ideology.[14] In "Facing It" (1988), Komunyakaa dramatizes a black veteran's encounter with the Vietnam Veterans Memorial, and the struggle to move beyond the trauma, guilt, and grief that haunt the speaker:

> My black face fades,
> hiding inside the black granite.
> I said I wouldn't,
> dammit: No tears.
> I'm stone. I'm flesh.
> My clouded reflection eyes me
> like a bird of prey, the profile of night
> slanted against morning. I turn
> this way—the stone lets me go.
> I turn that way—I'm inside
> the Vietnam Veterans Memorial
> again, depending on the light
> to make a difference.
> I go down the 58,022
> half-expecting to find
> my own in letters like smoke.
> I touch the name Andrew Johnson;

> I see the booby trap's white flash.
> Names shimmer on a woman's blouse
> but when she walks away
> the names stay on the wall.
> Brushstrokes flash, a red bird's
> wings cutting across my stare.
> The sky. A plane in the sky.
> A white vet's image floats
> closer to me, then his pale eyes
> look through mine. I'm a window.
> He's lost his right arm
> inside the stone. In the black mirror
> a woman's trying to erase names:
> No, she's brushing a boy's hair. (234–235)

Situated halfway between flesh and stone, between the living and the dead, the soldier-veteran is himself partly lost "inside the stone." As bearer of the brutal truths and losses of war, the speaker vigilantly and almost obsessively seeks to protect the erasure of his comrades, and of history; he misreads a woman's brushing of her son's hair—perhaps the son of a lost soldier, or a future lost soldier himself—as an erasure of the names that the memorial elegizes. Further, such brushing replicates the honored practice of rubbing a beloved's name from the wall onto paper, a practice that echoes centuries of cemetery-stone rubbings. Elegiac poems such as "Facing It" offer us a "black mirror" of veteran subjectivity, along with all its traumatized hauntings.[15]

Still, both the soldier and civilian poetry written during the span of the Vietnam War—particularly in its latter phase—is invaluable, sometimes for its sheer poetic accomplishment despite its occasionality and sometimes for the picture it provides of the anger, shame, guilt, and hopes of those who resisted the war. The anthologies of the period amply demonstrate the tenor of the time for those in "the movement," and they bring future generations in touch with what has too long been misrepresented or excised in subsequent films and pop cultural forms. One need only recall the famous scene in *Forrest Gump*, when the eponymous protagonist—now a veteran of the Vietnam War—steps up to the microphone, only to have his speech go unheard because an angry military man literally pulls the plug. We see his mouth move, but not what he has shared. This is, of course, what happened to soldier-resisters, who bravely spoke out but went unheard by those who could not bear to hear what they had to say. It is that silent speech, the silencing of those voices, which the poetry of the period offers to restore to our conversation about the war.

During the span of the war, and beyond the war, war resistance poetry—by both soldiers and veterans—deployed a variety of poetic strategies to bridge the gap between the felt experience of war and the imagined experience on the home-front. From the visionary mythopoetics of Robert Bly and Robert Duncan to the documentary labors of Denise Levertov and Daniel Berrigan, from the prophetic incantations of Allen Ginsberg to the apocalyptic minimalism of W. S. Merwin, from the C.O. poetry of John Balaban to the collaborative narrative poetry of Wendy Wilder Larsen and Tran Thi Nga, from the Black Arts poetry of Clarence Major to the Chicano poetics of Ben Reyes, civilian poets attempted to bring the war back home—to render the workings of the war visible again. While a full treatment of war resistance poetry is available elsewhere, the example of Robert Bly's booklength poem *The Teeth Mother Naked at Last* (1970) might illuminate how visionary poetry attempted to map cognitively the relationships between the war and the homefront and how such poems, forged in the heat of the war, continue to evolve.

In an interview, Robert Bly recalled how *The Teeth Mother* was the product not just of solitary composition, but of interaction with newspaper articles and audience reaction:

> [*The Teeth Mother*] was written spontaneously on stage during those times. I would take newspaper articles and read a bit on stage, composing lines to fit the horrible news. I would check the tape of the reading and in that way find out what I had said. Sharing it with an audience, the give and take between poet and the audience would bring things that would never arrive if you were just sitting down composing alone. "The Teeth Mother Naked at Last" is the only poem I have created with that ancient relationship between poet and audience. The dark times of the Vietnam War gave us that bond, the union only poetry could give us.
>
> (Gonzalez, 3)

The poem as interaction, as dialogue between poet and audience, between poet and the news, shows how war poetry—and poetry addressing itself to particular social movements (here, the antiwar movement)—challenges any simple notion that the poet writes for a "universal" audience.

But *The Teeth Mother* is not a single poem; since its initial book publication in 1970, it has gone through multiple revisions, as if the poem itself were an ongoing relational medium between the poet and the war. In brief, *The Teeth Mother* is a booklength attempt at a mythic-visionary explanation of the war, and it uses syllogistic statements to bring together American culture (capitalism, Puritanism, etc.) and the war in Vietnam. For example, from the 1970 version:

> It's because a hospital room in the average American city now
>   costs $60 a day that we bombed hospitals in the North
> It's because the aluminum window-shade business is doing so
>   well in the United States that we roll fire over entire villages
> It's because the milk trains coming into New Jersey hit the right
>   switches every day that the best Vietnamese men are cut in two
>   by bullets that follow each other like freight cars (14)

The associative leaps propose here a causal, but uncanny, connection between consumerist capitalism and the destruction of Vietnam. Yet these lines disappear from the version published in Bly's version in his selected poems (2000). Why?

Many of Bly's revisions of *The Teeth Mother* pare away the obvious and the didactic. For example, "This is what it's like for a rich country to make war / this is what it's like to bomb huts [afterwards described as 'structures'] / this is what it's like to kill marginal farmers [afterwards described as 'Communists']" (13). But the strange magic of syllogism does not get excised elsewhere, because many other syllogistic lines remain:

> It is because we have so few women sobbing in back rooms,
> because we have so few children's heads torn apart by high-velocity bullets,
> because we have so few tears falling on our own hands
> that the Super Sabre turns and screams down toward the earth. (78–79)

Perhaps Bly has, in the interest of cutting to the quick of the poem, shaved away to the most effective lines. But it is also possible that the Marxist critique implied by the excised lines no longer satisfied Bly, who as a poet has moved further toward quasi-Jungianism (also present in the original poem). The war poem, then, does not necessarily remain a static object of historical or aesthetic interest but becomes a kind of field where the poet struggles against his own (and our own) pasts.

THE WARS IN THE MIDDLE EAST:
BEFORE AND AFTER 9/11

In the context of Pure War and a more historically inflected understanding of U.S. foreign policy, the terrorist attacks of 9/11, the Afghanistan War (2002), and the Iraq War (2003) amplified and focused U.S. policies toward the Middle East—from the unflagging support of the United States for Israel (to the detriment of Palestinians) and the oil oligarchies to its exertion of imperial might over petty dictators like Saddam Hussein. The event of the 1991 Persian Gulf War, ostensibly begun as a defense of Kuwait, which Iraq invaded due to political and economic disputes, ended in forty-two days, but the decade of economic sanctions decimated a once-prosperous nation. Given the speed of the war, and relative absence of ground fighting, very little in the way of soldier poetry emerged. Though there was some good occasional war poetry, including William Heyen's diaristic *Ribbons: The Gulf War* (1992), larger, more rangy poems—June Jordan's "The Bombing of Baghdad," Adrienne Rich's "An Atlas of the Difficult World," and Barrett Watten's *Bad History* (1998)—situate the eventness of the Persian Gulf War within the poetic, political, and economic matrices that enabled the war to take place at all.

June Jordan's multisectioned "The Bombing of Baghdad" (1997) ranges from a catalog of the bombing to the lovers' bed to an address to a leap to Native American history—as if to mark the trajectory of the war in a longer history of oppression, one which attempts to reach into our very bedrooms. The poem's first section, which I will focus on here, begins with a litany that pummels the audience with the particular human catastrophe of a war that was largely unrepresented in mass media, despite its being the first simulcast war. The poem throws us in almost *in medias res*:

> began and did not terminate for 42 days
> and 42 nights relentless minute after minute
> more than 100,000 times
> we bombed Iraq we bombed Baghdad
> we bombed Basra/we bombed military
> installations we bombed the National Museum
> we bombed schools we bombed air raid
> shelters we bombed water we bombed
> electricity we bombed hospitals we
> bombed streets we bombed highways
> we bombed everything that moved/we
> bombed Baghdad
> a city of 5.5 million human beings.
>
> (Directed, 535–536)

In contrast to the triumphalist media reports of the time, Jordan's poem acts as an alternative news source, faithfully documenting the extent of the bombing—which attacked basic infrastructure in ways from which Iraq could not recover, particularly during the period of economic sanctions. Further, her employment of the "we"—which U.S. news outlets used to describe the lack of distance between the military effort, the media, and its American audience—now cuts back against us, rendering our complicity visible, admonishing us and herself.

Like Barrett Watten's *Bad History*, which includes the Gulf War among other pieces that illuminate the particular postmodern conditions of the 1990s, Adrienne Rich's long poem "An Atlas of the Difficult World" (1991) places the Gulf War in a series of mappings of "the difficult world"—a difficulty that is both arduous for its inhabitants and obscured by privilege and putative distance.[16] In *What Is Found There: Notebooks on Poetry and Politics*, Rich addresses the problem that politically engaged art too frequently loses the wholeness of its vision and succumbs to righteousness, separating the politically correct artist from the society from which she comes. Instead, Rich advocates an "engaged art" that moves beyond mere engagement, for such art fails "because it is not engaged enough: when it tries to express what has been logically understood but not yet organically assimilated" (47). In her long career of political poetry, "Atlas" situates itself in the wake of Rich's radical feminist turn in the 1970s and 1980s, when she wanted to address women particularly, and the poem becomes an attempt to address the entire nation.

Activating the literary trajectory from Walt Whitman ("Song of Myself") to Muriel Rukeyser (*The Book of the Dead*), Rich's "Atlas" engages in a national mapping project. Though it is not exactly a "cognitive mapping," in Fredric Jameson's sense, Rich's project is a poetic mapping, a drawing together, of diverse subjectivities and locations. Beginning with a "dark woman, head bent, listening for something"—which could

be Rich herself, or a migrant farm worker picking strawberries in the fields nearby—
Rich's poem ranges in time and space, attempting to heal the painful distances that
isolate and destroy us. In Section XI, Rich addresses the Gulf War directly:

> . . . some for whom war is new, others for whom it merely
>   continues the old paroxysms of time
> some marching for peace who for twenty years did not
>   march for justice
> some for whom peace is a white man's word and a white
>   man's privilege
> some who have learned to handle and contemplate the shapes
>   of powerlessness and power
> as the nurse learns hip and thigh and weight of the body he
>   has to lift and sponge, day upon day
> as she blows with her every skill on the spirit's embers still
>   burning by their own laws in the bed of death.
> A patriot is not a weapon. A patriot is one who wrestles for
>   the soul of her country
> as she wrestles for her own being, for the soul of his country
> (gazing through the great circle at Window Rock into the
>   sheen of the Viet Nam Wall)
> as he wrestles for his own being. A patriot is a citizen trying
>   to wake
> from the burnt-out dream of innocence, the nightmare
> of the white general and the Black general posed in their
>   camouflage,
> to remember her true country, remember his suffering land:
>   remember
> that blessing and cursing are born as twins and separated at
>   birth to meet again in mourning
> that the internal emigrant is the most homesick of all women
>   and of all men
> that every flag that flies today is a cry of pain. (156)

From a remove, Rich catalogs the various members of a demonstration, who might
oppose the war but also hide their own complicities and failures and forsake true patri-
otism—our connection to place and to each other. In discussing a war where the Patriot
missile—a guided missile that was alleged falsely to be highly successful in eliminating
Iraq's SCUD missiles—was the first hero of the war, according to CNN, Rich registers
her own definition of patriotism: "one who wrestles for the soul of her country." The false
patriotism of ticker-tape triumphalism was in abundance during the Gulf War. But Rich
does not focus on the outrageously whitewashed narrative of that war. Instead, she sees
in all those flags "a cry of pain." She knows that patriotism is a refuge to those who have
sacrificed their lives for their country and for what their lives have not given them.

THE IRAQ WAR

It was only with the Iraq War that soldier poetry has re-emerged. At a time when few poets could provide a full story of frontline experiences of the Iraq War, Brian Turner has given voice to the acute vulnerability experienced by soldiers, who daily must face death by bullets and other means. In the title poem of his best-selling first book of poems, *Here, Bullet* (2005), Turner apostrophizes to a bullet and goads it to enter his flesh. The bullet is at once the literal bullet and the soldier himself, who craves "the adrenaline rush...the inexorable flight," the ecstasy of battle:

> If a body is what you want
> then here is bone and gristle and flesh.
> Here is the clavicle-snapped wish,
> the aorta's opened valves, the leap
> thought makes at the synaptic gap.
> Here is the adrenaline rush you crave,
> that inexorable flight, that insane puncture
> into heat and blood. And I dare you to finish
> what you've started. Because here, Bullet,
> here is where I complete the word you bring
> hissing through the air, here is where I moan
> the barrel's cold esophagus, triggering
> my tongue's explosives for the rifling I have
> inside of me, each twist of the round
> spun deeper, because here, Bullet,
> here is where the world ends, every time. (13)

Despite its power and truth, the poem has its limits as a full picture of the Iraq War. In a recent review of war poetry, a former soldier, Nathaniel Fick, saw in the poetry of the Iraqi poet Sinan Antoon "the egalitarian nature of war": "We stood on opposite sides of a chasm: I was a combatant, and he was a civilian. But Antoon understands war's egalitarian nature: that it often doesn't matter which end of the gun we're on" (n.p.). Soldiers, particularly ones of an occupying foreign power fighting a dread insurgency, are indeed incredibly vulnerable. But the "often" of Fick's phrase gets larger, the closer you are to actually being on the wrong end of a gun. It is precisely the absence of "egalitarianism" in the Iraq War that goes unmentioned in the poem, "Here, Bullet"; one feels very strongly the mix of bravado and fear of the soldier, but the bravado is the pose of the warrior, not the civilian. Despite its dangerous power, the poem remains safely within the frame of the soldier's view. While other poems by Turner—especially "2000 lbs."—are superior for their scope and for including the suffering of Iraqis into the lens, the book suffers from its inability to pull back farther from the experience at the front.

To exercise a contrapuntal reading—Edward Said's strategy for exploring and resisting imperial culture through cross-cultural juxtaposition—we have to go to poets like the Iraqi exile Dunya Mikhail, who emerged with her first book translated into English, *The War Works Hard* (2005), to hear what war feels like from a civilian's point of view. In her title poem, Mikhail personifies the labors of the war, bringing a comic touch to the brutality that Iraqis have lived with since the 1980s, with the Iran-Iraq War.[17] An anti-ode in the style of Pablo Neruda and Bertholt Brecht, "The War Works Hard" makes war sound, well, like a very industrious person:

> How magnificent the war is!
> How eager
> and efficient!
> Early in the morning,
> it wakes up the sirens
> and dispatches ambulances
> to various places,
> swings corpses through the air,
> rolls stretchers to the wounded,
> summons rain
> from the eyes of mothers,
> digs into the earth
> dislodging many things
> from under the ruins . . .
> Some are lifeless and glistening
> others are pale and still throbbing . . .
> . . . .
> achieves equality
> between killer and killed,
> teaches lovers to write letters,
> accustoms young women to waiting,
> fills the newspapers
> with articles and pictures,
> builds new houses
> for the orphans
> invigorates the coffin makers,
> gives grave diggers
> a pat on the back
> and paints a smile on the leader's face.
> It works with unparalleled diligence!
> Yet no one gives it
> a word of praise. (6–8)

The final lines, of course, belie the fact that wars are endlessly prepared for, trumpeted, justified, and sanctified by the culture of Pure War. Mikhail's comic-ironic tone is all the more remarkable, given that the war itself exiled Mikhail from her native Iraq.

Lacking the first-person access of a soldier and a civilian in harm's way, poets have worked to document the War on Terror with the dominant narrative itself. Docupoetry arises from the idea that poetry is not a museum-object to be observed from afar but should be a dynamic medium that informs and is informed by the history of the moment. H. L. Hix's *God Bless: A Political/Poetic Discourse* (2007) is built almost entirely from speeches made by George W. Bush and Osama bin Laden, setting them into poetic conversation, molding the conversation into various traditional Western and non-Western forms, from the sestina to the ghazal. By taking these men at their word—literally and figuratively—Hix demonstrates how aesthetic attention becomes a kind of ethical and political attention, a close reading of the first order. In "September 2001," Hix culls from Bush's speeches during that pivotal month to create the following:

> Our country will...not be cowed by terrorists,
> by people who don't share the same values we share.
> Those responsible for these cowardly acts
> hate our values; they hate what America stands for.
> We can't let terrorism dictate our course of action.
> We're a nation that has fabulous values:
> as a nation of good folks, we're going to hunt them down,
> and we're going to find them, and...bring them to justice.
> Either you are with us, or you are with the terrorists.
> They're flat evil. They have no justification.
> There is universal support for what we intend.
> Americans are asking: What is expected of us?
> I ask you to live your lives, and hug your children.
> Go back to work. Get down to Disney World. (21)

Rather than merely deriding the president, selectively quoting malapropisms, Hix distills his representative language. And what does it mean to have President Bush suddenly voiced into sonnets? What does it mean not only for the president, but also for the sonnet? In contrast to *Pieces of Intelligence*, a book that works the language of Donald Rumsfeld into Rumsfeldian poetry, Hix's poems do not extend or ironize political rhetoric. On the contrary, as Susan Schultz has written, "Rumsfeld wants to get people off his scent so he can do things. [Poetry] is the scent, you could say—it's really trying to get you deep into a cultural moment or political moment, or just into how language works" (qtd. in Thomas, n.p.). Harvey Hix does precisely that—he brings us more fully into the political moment and shows how language is being used, and misused, in the War on Terror.

A document of close listening, *God Bless* aptly demonstrates the profound lack of listening at the heart of the Bush administration's decision-making process—in ironic contrast to bin Laden's obsessive study and reply to U.S. policy. Take, for example, bin Laden's reply to the events of 9/11:

> Are human beings free only in the U.S.?
> Can it alone retaliate against injustice?
> *As you violate our security, so we violate yours.*
>
> Manhattan was not the first atrocity.
> Lebanon 1982: third fleet, Israelis.
> *We have been fighting you because we are free.*
>
> Deceiving yourself about the real reasons
> for one disaster only invites a second.
> *Does a crocodile understand anything other than weapons?*
>
> Again and again he claims to know our reason,
> and tells you we attacked because we hate freedom.
> *Perhaps he can tell us why we did not attack Sweden.* (23)

In contrast to Bush's sound-bite speeches, bin Laden's speeches used a formal rhetoric and richly complex argumentation that was almost impossible to form into poems. It is terrifying to realize that, despite bin Laden's obvious deficiencies—his anti-Semitism, his fundamentalism, his selective reading of history—his arguments have a logic that our own president's frequently lacks. In Hix's rendering, *God Bless* becomes a kind of history lesson, a way of reading into the archive and thus extending the archive into poetry, poetry that works to "extend the document."

Since the first Persian Gulf War, Lawrence Joseph has emerged as one of our most astute and prophetic poets of Pure War, imaginatively linking the realms of capitalism and consumption to the global conflicts that it spurs. Clearly, wars have predated capitalism, yet Joseph probes, anxiously, the subjective position of those of us in privilege and how that privilege may, if not cause, then fuel, global conflict. With *Into It* (2005), Joseph immerses himself in the conditions of the present, refusing to abnegate his own implicated subject position as a member of the global elite, at the same time that he intuits (the pun of the title) what cannot always be seen—thus cognitively mapping his (and our) position to the wars in the Middle East. Of the book, David Kirby has written that "Joseph seems to be writing ahead of actual events, and that makes him one of the scariest writers I know" (n.p.). Joseph's obsessive meditation on 9/11 and the Iraq War, suturing together through a collage multiple voices, scenes, allusions, and epochs, is without paralyzing moral judgment, oscillating between a terrified awe of military power and resistance to its unmaking force.

In "News Back Even Further Than That" (2005), Joseph jumpcuts between mediated images of war brutality, quotes from military commanders, biblical references to the destruction of ancient Iraqi cities, and an antiwar rant recounted and

told to the speaker by an unnamed person. Because the poem covers so much ter-
ritory, I will quote it in full:

I
Dust, the dust of a dust storm;
yellow, black, brown, haze, smoke;
a baby photographed with half
a head; the stolen thoroughbred
the boy is riding bareback attacked
by a lion; the palace, fixed up
as a forward command post—"This,"
says Air-War Commander Mosely,
"would make a pretty nice casino":
why is such a detailed
description necessary?
that smell in the air is the smell
of burned human flesh;
those low-flying A-10 Warthogs
are, each of them, firing
one hundred bullets a second.

II
The President refuses to answer a question
he wasn't asked. The President denies
his are the eyes of a lobster.
The map is being drawn: Mosul in the north,
Baghdad in the center, Basra in the south.
The news back even further than that:
"He Says He is the Prophet Ezekiel.
In the Great Mudflats by the River Chebar.
He Has Seen, He Proclaims, Four Angels,
Each with Six Wings, on a Fiery Wheel."
Collaborators cut into pieces and burnt to death
in public, on spits, like lambs. In spray paint
across the armored personnel carrier:
"Crazy Train," "Rebel," "Got Oil?..." There,
on Sadoun Street, in a wheelbarrow, a coil
of wire, carpet, rolled, Persian, antique.

III
"I've just been to see her. It's made her
mad—angry, yes, of course, but I mean mad,
truly mad. She spoke quietly, quickly—
maniacally. 'Wargame, they're using wargame

as a verb, they didn't wargame the chaos—
chaos! Do you think they care about
the chaos? The chaos just makes it easier for them
to get what they want. Wargame!
What they've wargamed is the oil,
their possession of the oil, what they've wargamed
is the killing, the destruction,
what they've wargamed is their greed…'
Had I noticed that Lebanon has become
an abstract noun, as in 'the Lebanonization of"?
'It may just as well have been two or three
atomic bombs, the amount of depleted
uranium in their bombs, the bombs
in this war, the bombs in the war before this—
uranium's in the groundwater now,
uranium is throughout the entire
ecology by now, how many generations
are going to be
contaminated by it, die of it, be poisoned by it? …'
War, a war time, without limits.
Technocapital war a part
of our bodies, of the body politic.
She quoted Pound—the *Pisan Cantos*—
she couldn't remember which—
there are no righteous wars.
'There is no righteous violence,'
she said, 'it's neurobiological
with people like this—
people who need to destroy and who need to kill
like this—and what we're seeing now
is nothing compared
to what we'll see in the future…"' (38–40)

The poem, in all its leaps, updates *The Waste Land* for the era of Pure War,
24/7 media coverage, and the Internet. In the first section, Joseph highlights the
unmaking and brutalizing powers of war with bestial motifs: a baby has "half
/ a head," but a boy rides a "thoroughbred," though even he is being attacked
by a lion. Humanity is halved; the apocalypse reigns, but capitalism imagines a
great casino where a dictator once slept. Joseph's "the smell of burned human
flesh" echoes Levertov's famous Vietnam-era poem "Making Peace," but instead
of lingering and finger-pointing, he cuts quickly to the technologically proficient,
almost chimerical "Warthog" (another beast), which can fire "one hundred bul-
lets a second." What is human flesh in the face of such might, in the epoch of such
monstrous machines?

And in the third section, Joseph quotes an unnamed interlocutor, who voices a third person's outrage at the "wargaming" of the United States. With this Pure War rant, yet embedded within three frames (speaker, interlocutor, wargame theory), Joseph gives voice to the voices that both reflect and deflect from what may be his own subjective position. Rather than being just the critic of Pure War, Joseph creates a poem that witnesses to the awesome power of the Warthog, the lobster eyes of the president, and the outraged critic all at once—containing the multitudes of constituted imperial life. A self-proclaimed moralist, Joseph creates a vision of theological depth, but without the exclusivism of our tribal faiths.[18]

Finally, war resistance poetry in the 2000s emerged not only in books and on the Internet, but also on scrawled bedsheets hung on highway overpasses, through homemade placards placed on fences, graffiti tags, faculty office doors; at peace shows, poetry readings and reading halls; and on the streets. Often assiduously documented and circulated online afterward, war resistance poetry has brought language into public spaces usually only occupied by the language of advertising. In "*Lang/scapes:* Further Explorations of War Resistance Poetry in Public Spaces," I explored how this site-specific poetry "sutured the space between the public sphere and the literary sphere (pace Habermas), and created its own presses and transient pages (pace Liebling) to give voice to the growing weariness and outrage at the Iraq War" (n.p.).[19] This poetry complicates our idea of poetry as language that privileges "difficulty, complexity, and ambiguity above all else. Such poetry—with its limited and fugitive palettes—cannot manifest the 'difficulty' made possible by a larger field; yet, the examples of lang/scape that most fully deserve to be called 'poetry' provoke in multiple ways—not merely as agitprop, whose messages are always and necessarily transparent—and induce further rumination by their audiences" (n.p.).

The work of the poet Susan Schultz in Hawai'i, who gave herself the moniker of "Sidewalk Blogger"—echoing the "Highway Blogger," who had been placing bedsheets with antiwar slogans on highway overpasses—stood out for its inventiveness. During Christmas 2007, Schultz inherited some old Christmas signs, which she deployed as textual frames in which to compose war verse. Like the Industrial Workers of the World's Little Red Book's appropriation of traditional song melodies to use with new radical lyrics, Schultz subverted the saccharine images of Santa and doe-eyed biblical figures with the language of protest and outrage (figure 13.1). In "Come Let Us Impeach Him," Schultz disturbingly exposes the way in which the president—in the American Christian imagination—seems to take the place of the Son of God, but is a figure who deserves not adoration, but impeachment.

In "Give to the Iraq War," next to a banner for a craft and gift fair (no doubt, to raise money for the public school), Frosty the Snowman invites us to pay out millions per day to an unwinnable war: "Give to the Iraq War! $195 million per day!" Such juxtapositions provide a painful accounting of our national priorities as an imperial power. In the end, worldwide military dominance takes precedence over education. The Sidewalk Blogger's oscillation between satire and factuality offers the best sort of rhetorical one-two punch, because it offers its audience only a momentary relief of cynical distance, before drawing the implications back home; in other

Figure 13.1 "Come Let Us Impeach Him," by Susan Schultz, the Sidewalk Blogger.

words, we cannot laugh long when we begin to add up the costs—both personal and national—to us and to future generations.

PEACE POETRY

Cicero once wrote "inter arma enim silent leges": during war, the law goes silent. Over time, the proverb has become "when guns speak, the muses go silent." In times of terror, our civil selves and our artistic selves are suddenly bereft, silenced. How to maintain an ethical or aesthetic relationship to the world when bodies and souls, law and language are under attack? War poetry—whether by soldiers or civilians, whether antiwar or prowar—works to come to terms with a phenomenon that repels language and defies any easy representation; yet, as a subgenre, war poetry has generated certain doxa and rules that it honors (though often, in the case of great war poetry, it breaks them). Alice Templeton noted that the recent wars have brought her to a "brink of artistic depletion. Even as I welcome the general effort of resistance that *Poets Against the War* represents, as a reader, I feel exhausted by most (though certainly not all) of the poems in the volume. And as a poet, I . . . suffer a loss of voice, as if the very task of expressing war consciousness has 'sucked' the poetry out of me" (43). In *Down in My Heart* (1947), William Stafford's memoir of his years as a conscientious objector, one of the pacifists remarks: "During a war is a time of rest for a pacifist; the war itself is an incident, a lost battle in itself" (81).

Just as war poetry is part of a larger human confrontation with the violence, injustice, and oppression that is in us and in our world, peace poetry offers other ways, with ambushes and stratagems of its own. At the conclusion of *The Life of Poetry* (1949), Muriel Rukeyser writes, "To be against war is not enough, it is hardly a beginning. . . . As we live our truths, we will communicate across all barriers, speaking for the sources of peace. Peace that is not a lack of war, but fierce and positive" (213–214). Peace poetry is not quite a tradition, but a tendency, a thematic undertow within poetry and within culture. Yet it has been with us as long as we have been writing; one could begin with the Sumerian priestess Enheduanna's laments against war, with Sappho's erotic lyrics, or with Archilochus's antiheroic epigrams.[20] Yet this poetry isn't mere sweetness and light. "Peace" is no mere cloud-bound dream but is a dynamic of living amid conflict, oppression, and hatred without either resigning ourselves to violence or seizing on our own violent response; peace poems vividly and demonstrably articulate and embody such a way. At their best, peace poems, as John Milton did in "Aereopagitica," argue against "a fugitive and cloistered virtue, unexercised and unbreathed, that never sallies out and sees her adversary" (n.p.). If, in Milton's words, "that which purifies us is trial, and trial is by what is contrary" (n.p.) then peace poetry must also interrogate the easy pieties of the peace movement and its own ideological blindspots. Indeed, Michael True's exploration of nonviolent literature confirms that "although writings in [the nonviolent tradition] resemble conventional proclamations recommending peace reform, their tone and attitude tend to be provocative, even disputatious, rather than conciliatory" (xi).

Peace poetry—like the peace movement that it anticipates, reflects, and argues with—is part of a larger human conversation about the possibility of a more just and pacific system of social and ecological relations. But there is no road map to peace, and we live in a culture that thrives on conflict and violence. Even Denise Levertov found herself at a loss for words at a panel in the 1980s, when Virginia Satir called upon Levertov and other poets to "present to the world images of peace, not only of war; everyone needed to be able to *imagine* peace if we were going to achieve it" (154). In "Poetry and Peace: Some Broader Dimensions" (1989), Levertov argues that "peace as a positive condition of society, not merely as an interim between wars, is something so unknown that it casts no images on the mind's screen" (155). But she does proceed further: "if a poetry of peace is ever to be written, there must first be this stage we are just entering—the poetry of preparation for peace, a poetry of protest, of lament, of praise for the living earth; a poetry that demands justice, renounces violence, reveres mystery" (170–171).

Seamus Heaney, in his essay "The Government of the Tongue," proposed it this way: "The order of art becomes an achievement intimating a possible order beyond itself, although its relation to that further order remains promissory rather than obligatory. Art is not an inferior reflection of some ordained heavenly system but a rehearsal of it in earthly terms; art does not trace the given map of a better reality but improves an inspired sketch of it" (94). We see signs of such a poetry that rehearses some better way, amid the poetry of war, and beyond it. In addition to William Stafford, Muriel Rukeyser, Denise Levertov, June Jordan, and Grace Paley, contemporary poets such as Kazim Ali, Daniel Berrigan, Wendell Berry, Peter Cole, Martha Collins, Martin Espada, Benjamin Friedlander, Jeff Gundy, Robert Hass, H. L. Hix, Fady Joudah, Yusef Komunyakaa, Fred Marchant, Khaled Mattawa, Anna Meek, W. S. Merwin, E. Ethelbert Miller, Mark Nowak, Naomi Shihab Nye, Kevin Prufer, Adrienne Rich, Susan Schultz, Leonard Schwartz, Juliana Spahr, Susan Tichy, C. D. Wright, and Rachel Zolf have contributed to imagining peacemaking. Juliana Spahr's "This Connection of Everyone with Lungs," a global love poem, draws upon the largesse of a Whitmanic vision of human union, despite all the ways in which we are separated:

> When I speak of yours thighs and their long muscles of smoothness, I speak of yours cells and I speak of the British Embassy being closed in Kenya and the US urging more aggressive Iraq inspections and the bushfire that is destroying homes in Sydney....
>
> I want to tie it all up and tie up the world in an attempt to understand the swirls and patterns.
>
> But there is no efficient way.
>
> The news refreshes every few minutes on the computer screen and on the television screen. The stories move from front to back and then off the page and then perhaps forward again in a motion that I can't predict but I suspect is not telling the necessary truths.
>
> I can't predict our time together either. Or why we like each other like we do.
>
> I have no idea when our bodies will feel very good to one of us or to all of us together or to none of us.
>
> The drive to press against one another that is there at moments and then gone at others.
>
> The drive to press up against others in the same way. (32–33)

Written in the wake of the 9/11 attacks, Spahr's poetic gambit—creating a love poem that is at once intimate and general, at once personal and plural, local and global—is both refreshingly contemporary in its formal operations and radically traditional in its dream of mystical union.

I'd like to conclude, however, with Muriel Rukeyser's more formally modest "Poem," which chronicles her own attempt to maintain her humanity during the century of world wars. Despite the violence around us, Rukeyser stakes her faith in language, in the imagination, to reach out to "others unseen and unborn":

> I lived in the first century of world wars.
> Most mornings I would be more or less insane.
> The news would pour out of various devices
> The newspapers would arrive with their careless stories,
> Interrupted by attempts to sell products to the unseen.
> I would call my friends on other devices;
> They would be more or less mad for similar reasons.
> Slowly I would get to pen and paper,
> Make my poems for others unseen and unborn.
> In the day I would be reminded of those men and women,
> Brave, setting up signals across vast distances,
> considering a nameless way of living, of almost unimagined values.
> As the lights darkened, as the lights of night brightened,
> We would try to imagine them, try to find each other,
> To construct peace, to make love, to reconcile
> Waking with sleeping, ourselves with each other,
> Ourselves with ourselves. We would try by any means
> To reach the limits of ourselves, to reach beyond ourselves,
> To let go the means, to wake.
>
> I lived in the first century of these wars. (430)

For Rukeyser—and arguably for the poets of war and peace—poetry can be part of the restorative alchemy of human beings, a transfer of energy, a way to return ourselves to ourselves, ourselves to each other, to "reach the limits of ourselves" and "beyond ourselves," to wake from the nightmare of our history of blood. Poetry is not enough, but it has been and can continue to be part of that reaching, that mapping of our collective human and planetary futures. As Naomi Shihab Nye writes, at the conclusion of "Jerusalem": "it's late but everything comes next" (96).

NOTES

This chapter relies on my past research, especially *Behind the Lines: War Resistance Poetry on the American Homefront since 1941* (2007), but it also borrows occasionally from posts on my blog, "Behind the Lines Poetry" at www.behindthelinespoetry.blogspot.com. Special thanks to Cary Nelson for encouraging me to produce this chapter, and to Jeff Gundy and Fred Marchant, who provided astute feedback during the revision phase.

1 Virilio's focus on the militarization of U.S. culture provides a necessary supplement to Hardt and Negri's recent theorization of empire, their term for the "political subject that effectively regulates ... global exchanges, the sovereign power that governs the world" (xii). For Hardt and Negri, even though nation-states have declined in power, "sovereignty as such" (xii) has not; though they reject the notion that we live in an age of American imperialism, they acknowledge that the United States "does occupy a privileged position in Empire" (xii), and thus a central site where "empire" as such requires constant ideological justification and cultural support.

2 Though it appeared at the end of the twentieth century, Virilio's formulation borrows directly from William James in the early twentieth-century essay "The Moral Equivalent of War" (1906): "It may even reasonably be said that the intensely sharp *preparation* for war by the nations is the *real war*, permanent, unceasing; and that the battles are only a sort of public verification of the mastery gained during the 'peace'-interval" (n.p.). But James could not have dreamed of the elaboration and expansion of the military-industrial-security complex in the last century or how extensive the flexible American empire could become. See also Bacevich's *Washington Rules: America's Path to Permanent War* (2010), in which he coins a parallel term "semiwar"; and also The American Empire Project (www.americanempireproject.com).

3 See, in particular, P. W. Singer's recent study, *Wired for War: The Robotics Revolution and Conflict in the 21st Century* (2009), for the ways in which new technologies of combat are blurring the line between soldiers and civilians. The effects of this transformation do not merely make civilians more susceptible to attack, but also the soldiers who conduct these attacks. According to Singer, "the drone pilots actually have higher levels of PTSD—Post-Traumatic Stress Disorder—than those who are actually physically serving in the combat zone" (n.p.). The disconnect between soldiers and civilians is simultaneously widened (because the soldiers have to navigate these two worlds almost daily) and narrowed (because their work remains "behind the lines"). See also my "Remaking/Unmaking: Abu Ghraib and Poetry" for an exploration of how poets and artists have responded to the War on Terror policies of interrogation and torture.

4 For an exhaustive study of the life of Herman Melville during the Civil War, see Stanton Garner's *The Civil War World of Herman Melville* (1993). Melville's work, according to Timothy Sweet, is remarkable for how it resists "the naturalizing tendency of ... representations [in which] the wounds of war disappear into a rhetoric of nature and necessity" (165).

5 Even contemporary poets have seen in Dickinson a source for their own meditations on war. Foregrounding Dickinson as war poet, Janet Holmes's recent *The MS of M Y Kin* (2009) produced a series to "erasure" poems on the Iraq War by using Dickinson's texts as her source.

6 While this poem is less known, Mark Twain's classic story "War Prayer" (written in 1910, published in 1916) remains a fixture of antiwar literature for its critique of how institutional Christianity gets mobilized in the machinery of warfare.

7 In a period when poetry still occupied a place in public and political discourse, as Mark van Wienen has shown in *Partisans and Poets: The Political Work of American Poetry in the Great War* (1997), poets also deployed poetry as a mode of political argument in newspapers of the day; van Wienen's research broadens our scope of what we consider "modern" poetry and allows us to see what role poetry has played in the country's discussions about war. See also his anthology, *Rendezvous With Death: American Poems of the Great War*, which activates and sets *in chronological order* his interest in partisan poetries with soldier poems.

8 See, in particular, *The Aura of the Cause: A Photo Album for North American Volunteers in the Spanish Civil War* (1997) and *The Wound and the Dream: Sixty Years of American Poems about the Spanish Civil War* (2002) for full treatments of American poetry in the Spanish Civil War.

9 There are, of course, numerous exceptions to the rule. One would be remiss not to mention Cary Nelson's inclusion of haiku written in Japanese American internment camps, written between 1942 and 1944, in his *Anthology of Modern American Poetry* (2000). These haiku, written by multiple authors, locate themselves very specifically in the natural (and political) landscape, with the ubiquitous fence that surrounds them as a constant motif.

10 At a reading of "Eighth Air Force" in 1961, Jarrell noted that "these people were our saviors. I mean if people like this hadn't murdered other people and died why we would be under a Nazi government and there would be a concentration camp over at High Point and so on" (qtd. in Goldensohn *Dismantling*, 224).

11 See also Edward Brunner's *Cold War Poetry* (2002), in particular his discussion of "nuclear bomb poetry"—in which Lowell's "Fall 1961" takes an important place.

12 See also Andrew Hammond's *Cold War Literature* (2006) for its opening of the field beyond American literature, implicitly critiquing "the privileging of Western experience" (3). See, in particular, Dana Healey's exploration of Vietnamese poetry on the American war.

13 Though Ali is not on record for having uttered this term, it was seen on placards at the time. Ali did say, in becoming a conscientious objector to the war:

> Why should they ask me to put on a uniform and go 10,000 miles from home and drop bombs and bullets on Brown people in Vietnam while so-called Negro people in Louisville are treated like dogs and denied simple human rights? No, I'm not going 10,000 miles from home to help murder and burn another poor nation simply to continue the domination of white slave masters of the darker people the world over. This is the day when such evils must come to an end. I have been warned that to take such a stand would cost me millions of dollars. But I have said it once and I will say it again. The real enemy of my people is here. (qtd. in Zinn, n.p.)

14 Many of these poets, alongside civilian poets such as Martha Collins, have become key editors and translators of the growing corpus of Vietnamese poetry in English translation—as a way to continue their process of widening our sense of what the Vietnam War has meant.

15 War poetry, particularly soldier poetry during and after the Vietnam War, has illuminated the particularly "unmaking" character of war (see Elaine Scarry), and it centrally contributes to our discourse about trauma. The work of Jonathan Shay, particularly in *Odysseus in America: Combat Trauma and the Trials of Homecoming* (2002), proposes that the veteran's journey home demands a narrative reintegration in a community of social trust, usually composed of other veterans. While I have not discussed it fully here, war poetry also is the poetry of trauma—of traumatized speakers and traumatized narratives, of the breakdown of traditional meanings.

16 For a full discussion of *Bad History* as a war resistance poem, see my *Behind the Lines: War Resistance Poetry on the American Homefront since 1941* (2007).

17 In "Baghdad Burning," Miriam Cooke explores how women writers—from poets to bloggers—have begun to write their own stories, those that have not fit in the U.S. mass media narratives of the war. In addition to Dunya Mikhail, Cooke gives special attention to the work of "Riverbend," the pseudonymous author whose blog "Baghdad

Burning" provides a "powerful multiple critique" of both U.S. imperial policies and regressive policies of the conservative Islamist and corrupt regimes in the Middle East.
18 See Charara's *Inclined to Speak: An Anthology of Contemporary Arab American Poetry* (2008) for a representation of Arab American poets—including Joseph, Naomi Shihab Nye, Fady Joudah, and Khaled Mattawa—many of whom directly address the ongoing wars in the Middle East.
19 See also Jules Boykoff and Kaia Sand's study of what they define as "guerrilla poetry" in *Landscapes of Dissent: Guerrilla Poetry & Public Space* (2008) and James Sullivan's *On the Walls and in the Streets: American Poetry Broadsides from the 1960s* (1997).
20 See Gioseffi's *Women on War: An International Anthology of Writings from Antiquity to the Present* (2003) and Metres and colleagues' *Come Together: Imagine Peace* (2008) for two resources of the poetry of war and peace.

REFERENCES

The American Empire Project. Online. www.americanempireproject.com. Accessed August 20, 2010.
Bacevich, Andrew. *Washington Rules: America's Path to Permanent War*. New York: Henry Holt, 2010.
Barrett, Faith, and Cristanne Miller, eds. *Words for the Hour: A New Anthology of Civil War Poetry*. Amherst: University of Massachusetts Press, 2005.
Barry, Jan, ed. *Peace Is Our Profession: Poems and Passages of War Protest*. Montclair, NJ: East River Anthology, 1981.
Bergland, Renee. "The Eagle's Eye: Dickinson's View of Battle." In *A Companion to Emily Dickinson*, ed. Martha Nell Smith and Mary Loeffleholz. Malden, MA: Blackwell, 2008. 133–156.
Bibby, Michael. *Hearts and Minds: Bodies, Poetry, and Resistance in the Vietnam Era*. New Brunswick, NJ: Rutgers University Press, 1996.
Bly, Robert. *Eating the Honey of Words: New and Selected Poems*. New York: Perennial, 2000.
———. *The Teeth Mother Naked at Last*. San Francisco: City Lights, 1970.
Boykoff, Jules, and Kaia Sand. *Landscapes of Dissent: Guerrilla Poetry & Public Space*. Berkeley, CA: Palm Press, 2008.
Brunner, Edward. *Cold War Poetry*. Urbana: University of Illinois Press, 2001.
Butler, Judith. *Frames of War: When in Life Grievable?* New York: Verso, 2009.
Charara, Hayan, ed. *Inclined to Speak: An Anthology of Contemporary Arab American Poetry*. Fayetteville: University of Arkansas Press, 2008.
Cicero. http://en.wikiquote.org/wiki/Cicero. Accessed August 21, 2010.
Cooke, Miriam. "Baghdad Burning: Women Write War in Iraq." *World Literature Today* (November-December 2007): 23–26.
———. *Women and the War Story*. Berkeley: University of California Press, 1996.
Country Joe and the Fish. 1967. "I Feel Like I'm Fixin' to Die Rag." http://www.countryjoe.com/feelmus.htm. Accessed September 13, 2010.
Crane, Stephen. *The Red Badge of Courage*. 1895. New York: W. W. Norton, 2008.
Dylan, Bob. "Masters of War." http://www.sing365.com/music/lyric.nsf/Masters-of-War-lyrics-Bob-Dylan/A17B1E57D80048D0482569690027973B. Accessed August 17, 2010.
Eisenhower, Dwight. "The Chance for Peace." April 16, 1953. http://www.edchange.org/multicultural/speeches/ike_chance_for_peace.html. Accessed August 17, 2010.

———."Eisenhower's Farewell Address." January 17, 1961. http://en.wikisource.org/wiki/Military-Industrial_Complex_Speech. Accessed August 17, 2010.

Eliot, T. S. "A Note on War Poetry." In *Collected Poems: 1909–1962*. New York: Harcourt Brace Jovanovich, 1963. 215.

———. *The Waste Land*. 1922. Ed. Michael North. New York: W. W. Norton, 2000.

Faust, Gilpin. n.d. "Emily Dickinson, War Poet (Quote of the Day / From Drew Gilpin Faust's Pulitzer Prize Finalist, 'This Republic of Suffering')." http://oneminutebookreviews.wordpress.com/2009/04/28/emily-dickinson-war-poet-quote-of-the-day-from-drew-gilpin-fausts-pulitzer-prize-finalist-this-republic-of-suffering/. Accessed August 18, 2010.

Fick, Nathaniel. "When Yellow Ribbons and Flag-Waving Aren't Enough." http://www.poetryfoundation.org/journal/article.html?id=180043. Accessed August 22, 2010.

Forrest Gump. Dir. Robert Zemeckis. 1994.

Friedlander, Benjamin. "Emily Dickinson and the Battle of Ball's Bluff." *PMLA* 124.5 (October 2009): 1582–1599.

Fugazi. "KYEO." *Steady Diet of Nothing*. France: Dischord, 1991.

Fussell, Paul. *The Great War and Modern Memory*. New York: Oxford University Press, 1975.

———, ed. *The Norton Book of Modern War*. New York: W.W. Norton & Company, 1991.

Garner, Stanton. *The Civil War World of Herman Melville*. Lawrence: University Press of Kansas, 1993.

Gioseffi, Daniela, ed. *Women on War: An International Anthology of Writings from Antiquity to the Present*. New York: Feminist Press at the City University of New York, 2003.

Goldensohn, Lorrie. *American War Poetry: An Anthology*. New York: Columbia University Press, 2006.

———. *Dismantling Glory: Twentieth-Century Soldier Poetry*. New York: Columbia University Press, 2003.

Gonzalez, Ray. "Going to the Mailbox: An Interview with Robert Bly." *The Bloomsbury Review* (September/October 2002): 3, 21, 22.

Gotera, Vincente. *Radical Visions: Poetry by Vietnam Veterans*. Athens: University of Georgia Press, 1994.

Hammond, Andrew, ed. *Cold War Literature: Writing the Global Conflict*. New York: Routledge, 2006.

Hanley, Lynne. *Writing War: Fiction, Gender, and Memory*. Amherst: University of Massachusetts Press, 1991.

Hardt, Michael, and Antonio Negri. *Empire*. Cambridge, MA: Harvard University Press, 2000.

Healey, Dana. "Poetry, Politics, and War: Representations of the American War in Vietnamese Poetry." In *Cold War Literature: Writing the Global Conflict*, ed. Andrew Hammond. New York: Routledge, 2006. 114–136.

Heaney, Seamus. *The Government of the Tongue: Selected Prose 1978–1987*. New York: Noonday Press, 1988.

Hedges, Chris. *War Is a Force That Gives Us Meaning*. New York: Anchor, 2002.

Heyen, William. *Ribbons: The Gulf War*. St. Louis: Time Being Books, 1991.

Hix, H. L. *God Bless: A Political/Poetical Discourse*. Wilkes-Barre, PA: Etruscan, 2007.

Holmes, Janet. *The MS of M Y Kin*. New York: Shearsman, 2009.

The Hurt Locker. Dir. Kathryn Bigelow. 2009.

James, William. "The Moral Equivalent of War." http://www.constitution.org/wj/meow.htm. Accessed August 21, 2010.

Jameson, Fredric. *Postmodernism: Or, the Cultural Logic of Late Capitalism*. Durham, NC: Duke University Press, 1991.

Jarrell, Randall. *The Complete Poems*. New York: Farrar Straus & Giroux, 1969.

Johnson, Kent. *Lyric Poetry After Auschwitz: Eleven Submissions to the War*. Austin, TX: effing press, 2005.

Jordan, June. *Directed by Desire: The Collected Poems of June Jordan*. Port Townsend, WA: Copper Canyon, 2005.

Joseph, Lawrence. *Into It*. New York: Farrar Straus & Giroux, 2007.

Kaplan, Justin. *Walt Whitman: A Life*. New York: Perennial, 1980.

Komunyakaa, Yusef. *Neon Vernacular: New and Selected Poems*. Middletown, CT: Wesleyan University Press, 1993.

Kirby, David. "'Codes, Precepts, Biases, and Taboos' and 'Into It': The Double." *New York Times*. September 25, 2005. http://www.nytimes.com/2005/09/25/books/review/25kirby.html. Accessed August 13, 2010.

Levertov, Denise. *Making Peace*. Ed. with introduction by Peggy Rosenthal. New York: New Directions, 2006.

———. "Poetry and Peace: Some Broader Dimensions." In *New & Selected Essays*. New York: New Directions, 1992. 154–171.

Lowell, Robert. *Collected Poems*. New York: Farrar, Straus and Giroux, 2003.

Metres, Philip. *Behind the Lines: War Resistance Poetry on the American Homefront since 1941*. Iowa City: University of Iowa Press, 2007.

———. "*Lang/scapes*: Further Explorations of War Resistance Poetry in Public Spaces." *Big Bridge*. 2008. http://www.bigbridge.org/WAR-MET.HTM. Accessed August 20, 2010.

———. "Remaking/Unmaking: Abu Ghraib and Poetry." *PMLA*. October 2008.

Metres, Philip, Ann Smith, and Larry Smith, eds. *Come Together: Imagine Peace*. Huron, OH: Bottom Dog, 2008.

Mikhail, Dunya. *The War Works Hard*. Trans. Elizabeth Winslow. New York: New Directions, 2005.

Milton, John. "Areopagitica." http://www.dartmouth.edu/~milton/reading_room/areopagitica/. Accessed August 20, 2010.

Nelson, Cary, ed. *Anthology of Modern American Poetry*. New York: Oxford University Press, 2000.

———. *The Aura of the Cause: A Photo Album for North American Volunteers in the Spanish Civil War*. Urbana: University of Illinois Press, 1997.

———, ed. *The Wound and the Dream: Sixty Years of American Poems about the Spanish Civil War*. Chicago: University of Chicago Press, 2002.

Nye, Naomi Shihab. "Jerusalem." In *Come Together: Imagine Peace*, ed. Philip Metres, Ann Smith and Larry Smith. Huron, OH: Bottom Dog, 2008.

Rich, Adrienne. *Adrienne Rich's Poetry and Prose*. Selected and edited by Barbara Charlesworth Gelpi and Albert Gelpi. New York: W. W. Norton, 1993.

———. *What Is Found There: Notebooks on Poetry and Politics*. New York: W. W. Norton, 1993.

Rukeyser, Muriel. *Collected Poems*. New York: McGraw-Hill, 1978.

———. *The Life of Poetry*. Williamsburg, MA: Paris Press, 1996.

Said, Edward. *Culture and Imperialism*. New York: Vintage, 1993.

Sandburg, Carl. *The Complete Poems: Revised and Expanded Edition*. New York: Houghton Mifflin Harcourt, 1970.

Scarry, Elaine. *The Body in Pain: The Making and Unmaking of the World*. New York: Oxford University Press, 1985.

Schultz, Susan. "The Sidewalk Blogger." Photographs. Private Circulation. 2006–2008.

Schweik, Susan. *A Gulf So Deeply Cut: American Women Poets and the Second World War*. Madison: University of Wisconsin Press, 1991.

Seely, Hart. *Pieces of Intelligence: The Existential Poetry of Donald H. Rumsfeld.* New York: Free Press, 2008.

Shapiro, Harvey, ed. *Poets of World War II.* New York: Library of America, 2003.

Shapiro, Karl. "The Conscientious Objector." In *Trial of a Poet and Other Poems.* New York: Reynal and Hitchcock, 1947.

Shay, Jonathan. *Odysseus in America. Combat Trauma and the Trials of Homecoming.* New York: Scribner, 2002.

Singer, P. W. "Wired for War Explores Robots on the Battlefield." Interview by Terry Gross. *Fresh Air.* WHYY, Philadelphia. January 22, 2009. Online transcript. http://www.npr.org/templates/transcript/transcript.php?storyId=99663723. Accessed September 13, 2010.

——. *Wired for War: The Robotics Revolution and Conflict in the 21st Century.* New York: Penguin, 2009.

Spahr, Juliana. *This Connection of Everyone with Lungs.* Berkeley: University of California Press, 2005.

Stafford, William. *Another World Instead: The Early Poems of William Stafford, 1937–1947.* Ed. Fred Marchant. St. Paul, MN: Graywolf, 2008.

——. *Down in My Heart.* Swarthmore: The Bench Press, 1985.

——. *The Way It Is: New and Selected Poems.* St. Paul, MN: Graywolf, 1998.

Sullivan, James. *On the Walls and in the Streets: American Poetry Broadsides from the 1960s.* Urbana: University of Illinois Press, 1997.

Sweet, Timothy. *Traces of War: Poetry, Photography, and the Crisis of the Union.* Baltimore, MD: Johns Hopkins University Press, 1990.

Templeton, Alice. "What's the Use? Writing Poetry in Wartime." *College Literature* 34.4 (2007): 43–62.

Thomas, Christine. "What I'm Reading: Susan Schultz." *The Honolulu Weekly.* May 20, 2007. http://www.tinfishpress.com/about_us/advertiser/index.html?AID=2007705200356. Accessed August 27, 2010.

True, Michael. *An Energy Field More Intense Than War: The Nonviolent Tradition and American Literature.* Syracuse: Syracuse University Press, 1995.

Turner, Brian. *Here, Bullet.* Farmington, ME: Alice James Books, 2005.

Twain, Mark. "The War Prayer." 1916. http://www.midwinter.com/lurk/making/warprayer.html. Accessed September 13, 2010.

Van Wienen, Mark. *Partisans and Poets: The Political Work of American Poetry in the Great War.* New York: Cambridge University Press, 1997.

——. *Rendezvous with Death: American Poems of the Great War.* Urbana: University of Illinois Press, 2002.

Virilio, Paul, and Sylvere Lotringer. *Pure War.* New York: Semiotext(e), 1997.

Watten, Barrett. *Bad History.* Berkeley, CA: Atelos, 1998.

Weil, Simone. "The Iliad, Poem of Might." In *The Simone Weil Reader,* ed. George Panichas. Mt. Kisco, NY: Moyer Bell Limited. 1977. 153–183.

Whitman, Walt. *Leaves of Grass and Other Writings.* Ed. Michael Moon. New York: W. W. Norton, 2002.

——. *Prose Works, 1892.* Ed. Floyd Stovall. 2 vols. New York, New York University Press, 1962.

Wolosky, Shira. *Emily Dickinson: A Voice of War.* New Haven: Yale University Press, 1984.

Zinn, David. "The Hidden History of Muhammad Ali." *The International Socialist Review* 33 (January–February 2004). http://www.isreview.org/issues/33/muhammadali.shtml. Accessed August 20, 2010.

CHAPTER 14

THE FIGHT AND THE FIDDLE IN TWENTIETH-CENTURY AFRICAN AMERICAN POETRY

KAREN JACKSON FORD

The first thing that any critic writing about the history of Black poetry should do is read the poetry.

—Gwendolyn Brooks

A well-known poem whose first line became a motto for politically engaged black poetry seems to argue, as many have observed, that in African American poetry "politics must precede art" (Melhem, 72):

> First fight. Then fiddle. Ply the slipping string
> With feathery sorcery; muzzle the note
> With hurting love; the music that they wrote
> Bewitch, bewilder....
> But first to arms, to armor. Carry hate
> In front of you and harmony behind.
> Be deaf to music and to beauty blind.
> Win war. Rise bloody, maybe not too late
> For having first to civilize a space
> Wherein to play your violin with grace.
>
> (Brooks, *Blacks*, 118)

Even the author, Gwendolyn Brooks, countenanced a programmatic reading of the poem: "That mother is making the statement that such children as she has—black, deprived, disadvantaged and besieged—will have to give their attention to civilizing a space for themselves to survive in before they give their attention to such a lovely thing as the fiddling next to them" (*Conversations*, 102). Yet though Annie Allen, the mother speaking in the poem, may be "making the statement" that civilizing (fighting) must come before art (fiddling), the poem itself just as adamantly argues that fiddling *is* a means of fighting and therefore an effective weapon in the battle to civilize a space.

The most obvious way that the poem contradicts a stark opposition between the fight and the fiddle is that it is a Petrarchan sonnet, not a particularly obliging form for an argument against art. Though the initial four words issue the command to fight before fiddling, the octave is entirely consumed with fiddling. "First" is anxiously asserted three times in the poem, but what actually comes first is a rich, nuanced description of the very fiddling that ought to be deferred. "Fiddle" reduces high art to mere amusement (poets are just fiddling around), but it also confounds that very opposition. The opening line juxtaposes "fiddle" and "ply," the first term connoting the word "play" and the second a near homonym for it. Thus, despite itself, the dictum aligns playing at poetry with the diligent work of plying. The last line of the poem will retrieve the notion of play from its trivial connotations by uniting it to the respected activity of playing a violin gracefully. The speaker might retort that mere fiddling can be elevated to violin playing in the last line because political action has created a space for art. But *playing* the fiddle has already been depicted as serious, important work in the octave, not just in the pun on "ply" but in its related lexicon of laborious effort ("muzzle," "qualify," "devise," "devote") and in the speaker's passionate description of fiddling.

The sestet tries to reject these contradictions, rousing itself from the bewitching depiction of fiddling back to the speaker's more immediate purpose: "But first to arms, to armor." "But" is an admission that the poem has become distracted with fiddling. The sestet, where the problem introduced in the octave is traditionally resolved, now works assiduously to keep itself on task. Another series of oppositions attempts to distinguish between fighting and fiddling, a strategy that only perpetuates fiddling by contrast—hate/harmony, blind/beauty—as alliteration once more underscores the difficulty of separating activism and art. If we accept Brooks's charge to "read the poetry," then we confront a poem whose fiddly formal structure takes issue with its speaker's straightforward "statement."

As it turns out, this collapse of the speaker's repeated distinctions between artistic production and political action provides a better axiom for African American poetry than "First fight. Then fiddle," for it is Brooks's lifelong, unresolved argument with herself about the proper poetic form for black poetry that is most indicative of her poetic tradition. Behind the dualism of *fight* and *fiddle* is W. E. B. Du Bois's commanding portrayal of the African American predicament, which he famously termed *double-consciousness* at the beginning of the century: "It is a peculiar sensation, this double-consciousness, this sense of always looking at one's self through the eyes of others.... One ever feels his twoness,—an American, a Negro; two souls, two thoughts, two unreconciled strivings; two warring ideals in one dark body, whose dogged strength alone keeps it from being torn asunder" (45). The double-ness of cultural identity was translated in discussions of poetry to debates about cul-tural forms. Born in 1917, Brooks wrote poetry from her childhood until her death in 2000, and her career encompasses the shifting formal motives and strategies in twentieth-century African American poetry. She began reading poetry under the influence of Dunbar's traditional prosody; began writing under the subversive for-malism of the Harlem Renaissance; won the Pulitzer Prize for *Annie Allen* (1949), a virtual compendium of traditional verse forms, at midcentury; became radicalized during the Black Arts Movement of the 1960s and 1970s and rejected conventional verse to embrace the free verse of the Black Arts Movement; and she has remained a touchstone for younger African American writers—black aesthetic, neoformalist, avant-garde, and slam poets—through the end of the twentieth century into the twenty-first. As the many poems written to and for her suggest, Gwendolyn Brooks has been singularly influential to African American poetry. Though she typically receives scant notice in mainstream histories of American poetry,[1] her importance to black poets is legendary and has been celebrated in anthologies of poetry dedi-cated to her and books of essays assessing her impact.[2] The shift from traditional prosody to the black aesthetic marked for Brooks, as for the African American poetic tradition more broadly, a change from what was once considered white or Negro to black poetry and from an integrationist to a black-identified worldview. The warring ideals that Du Bois identified as *American* and *Negro* were reiterated in different terms throughout the century, but the sense of unreconciled identities continued to generate arguments about ideal poetic form.

In the post-Movement period, however, African American poets have insisted on the multicultural dimensions of blackness and thus on claiming, and reclaiming, any form of poetry—from free verse to villanelles, slam to sonnets, haiku to hoo-doo, kwansaba to quatrains, performance to paratexts—that they deem "appropri-ate to create a poem" (Rowell, ix).[3] In "The New Black Aesthetic" (1989), Trey Ellis describes this generation of African Americans as culturally multiracial: "a cultural mulatto, educated by a multi-racial mix of cultures, can...navigate easily in the white world. And it is by and large this rapidly growing group of cultural mulattoes that fuels the NBA [New Black Aesthetic]. We no longer need to deny or suppress any part of our complicated and sometimes contradictory cultural baggage to please either white people or black" (235).[4] His last sentence here is especially noteworthy: it responds to and revises Langston Hughes's renowned 1926 declaration of black cultural independence in "The Negro Artist and the Racial Mountain": "We youn-ger Negro artists who create now intend to express our individual dark-skinned selves without fear or shame. If white people are pleased we are glad. If they are not, it doesn't matter.... If colored people are pleased we are glad. If they are not, their displeasure doesn't matter either" (143). During the Harlem Renaissance, Hughes asserted the right to express his blackness; sixty-odd years later Ellis makes a sim-ilar appeal for his hybridity (242). Yet both claim the authority of their "individual dark-skinned selves," Ellis explaining that cultural mulattoes become "those 'tragic mulattoes' critic Sterling Brown wrote about in the Thirties only when they too forget they are wholly black" (235). For contemporary African Americans, to be "wholly black" is to be "complicated and sometimes contradictory." Speaking specifically about African American poets, Fred Moten refers to this as "the multiple oneness of blackness" (964).

So, too, in the Fall 2004 issue of *Callaloo*, an issue devoted to *Contemporary African-American Poetry: A New Wave*, Charles Henry Rowell, its editor, emphasizes the diversity of contemporary black poetry: "the poets in this number of *Callaloo* continue to exercise freely their rights, and are beginning to build a tradition as hybrid as that which the jazz masters created, one which disregards geography, race, culture, class, and those other boundaries which do violence to human beings in the West" (ix). Rowell marshals the language of Civil Rights—*exercise freely, rights, freedom, responsibility, American*—to argue for a "poetic space that belongs to all of us": "Their respect for and use of difference, and their responsible exercise of literary freedom—perhaps this is what makes them American, in fact more American, as poets, than those who have traditionally monopolized the term, wrapped themselves in it, stamped it on their foreheads, and, for nefarious reasons, sought to dominate the poetic space that belongs to all of us."

Rowell's insistence that these young black poets are "American," are even "more American" than canonical poets, because of their formal variety (their "exercise of literary freedom"), articulates a characteristic American impulse to associate poetic form and national identity.[5] In fact, his emphasis on the superior Americanness of contemporary black poets recapitulates James Weldon Johnson's claim about African Americans in the United States in 1921. Establishing the cultural contributions of Negroes in his preface to the first edition of his influential *The Book of American Negro Poetry*, Johnson asserts, like Rowell, the primacy of that culture: "the Negro has already proved the possession of these powers by being the creator of the only things artistic that have yet sprung from American soil and been universally acknowledged as distinctive American products" (10). Those powers are "the emotional endowment, the originality and artistic conception, and, what is more important, the power of creating that which has universal appeal and influence"—by which he means African American music, blues and ragtime, in particular. Thus, another important similarity between Rowell's recent case for black artistic excellence and Johnson's of nearly a hundred years ago is the cultural authority each garners for black poetry by associating it with African American music, whose greatness was uncontested even in 1921.[6] Yet Johnson also struggles in his important preface to negotiate the contradictions of claiming African American culture as simultaneously distinctly American, uniquely Negro, and universal, a struggle about the origins and authenticity of African American poetry that continues today. While Werner Sollors has rightly asserted that "there is no ontological connection between a country and a form" (237), he nevertheless observes that minority American writers, defining their formal practices in opposition to those of the dominant culture, have consistently equated their identity with particular forms. Such forms are not necessarily "ancestral"; rather, American ethnic literature is characterized by innovation rather than tradition, and these innovations are often, ironically, attempts to preserve ethnic or racial origins (245).

While eloquent assertions of racial origin come readily to mind—"I've known rivers, / I've known rivers ancient as the world and older than the flow of human blood in human veins"[7]—African American poetry has from the start both mastered and altered the dominant Anglo-European literary tradition it encountered in the United States. There is no doubt that poetic form has been enlisted to codify a stable cultural identity, yet it has more often been employed to expand what it means to be a black American. Indeed, such contradictions as Sollors points to have been generative in the development of African American poetry: oppositions like *origin* and *innovation* have repeatedly been invoked with prescriptive force, and the multiplicity of African American creativity enjoined to resolve itself into the first term in an array of oppositions: black/white, black/Negro, oral/textual, authentic/inauthentic, African/American, political/poetical, vernacular/Standard English, music/literature, free verse/verse, black aesthetic/Anglo-European poetics, cult-nat/freaky-deke, fight/fiddle.[8] And yet the poems themselves just as persistently draw these rival terms into a complex, sometimes contradictory multiple oneness. Fight, fiddle, ply, muzzle, bewitch, bewilder.

Surely no poet's work has been more defined by these polarities than that of Paul Laurence Dunbar. The Ohio-born son of former slaves was "America's first professional black literary man" (Braxton, ix) and the first to garner a wide readership. So important did Dunbar become, despite his legendary sense of failure, that the poets of the Harlem Renaissance twenty years after his death routinely invoked him in order to pay tribute to his achievement and distance themselves from it. The problem was Dunbar's dialect poetry, which he wrote in order to gain a hearing from white readers, expecting that they would then be interested in his nondialect poetry; they weren't. His poems in Negro dialect sometimes gave voice to the racist nostalgia of the postwar South, as in "Chrismus on the Plantation," when a former slave responds to the plantation owner's tearful announcement that he's too poor to keep the homestead and will have to sell it and move away: you're telling us to forget that you've been kind and to leave you here helpless, he asks, then asserts, "Well, ef dat's de way dis freedom ac's on people, white er black, / You kin jes' tell Mistah Lincum fu' tek his freedom back" (*Collected Poetry*, 138). We could read even Dunbar's most retrograde poems in this mode with some nuance (here, for instance, noting that "ol' Ben" is remembering kindness not abuse and, more generally, that these dialect speakers typically preach humanity toward "white or black," not black submission to white cruelty), but letting "Chrismus on the Plantation" stand at one extreme of Dunbar's dialect poetry, the other extreme is anything but submissive to the plantation ethos. The cagey speaker in "An Ante-Bellum Sermon" predicts African American liberation through the story of Moses and Israel despite his repeated assurances that he's not "preachin' discontent" (14): "So you see de Lawd's intention, / Evah sence de worl' began, / Was dat His almighty freedom / Should belong to evah man, / But I think it would be bettah, / Ef I'd pause agin to

say, / Dat I'm talkin' 'bout ouah freedom / In a Bibleistic way." By the end of his
sermon, the speaker has grown so animated about emancipation that he has to stop
and clear his throat midword to avoid saying that slaves should be recognized as
citizens: "An' we'll shout ouah halleluyahs, / On dat mighty reck'nin' day, / When
we'se reco'nised ez citiz'— / Huh uh! Chillun, let us pray!" (15). In Dunbar's most
famous dialect poem, "When Malindy Sings," the speaker silences the white Lucy,
who has no natural musicality, and deploys melodious, cadenced dialect to demon-
strate black Malindy's superiority:

> Fiddlin' man jes' stop his fiddlin',
>   Lay his fiddle on de she'f;
> Mockin'-bird quit tryin' to whistle,
>   'Cause he's jes' so shamed hisse'f.
> Folks a-playin' on de banjo
>   Draps dey fingahs on de strings—
> Bless yo' soul—fu'gits to move em,
>   When Malindy sings. (82)

Not just tone-deaf white girls but musicians (likely African American musicians since
they are "Folks" who play fiddles and banjos) and even nature's songsters stop to listen
to Malindy's "real melojous music," and only the tour-du-force poem rivals Malindy's
singing. Though Dunbar acknowledged the merits of his dialect poetry—after all, he
began writing it, he said, because he knew he could "write it as well, if not better, than
anybody else I knew of" (qtd. in Wagner, 106)—he believed the genre was limited by
being too lyrical and sentimental and wanted the greater range of other forms.

James Weldon Johnson recounts a conversation with Dunbar on the dialect
question that has been repeated in every discussion of the poet: "Often he said to
me: 'I've got to write dialect poetry; it's the only way I can get them to listen to me'"
(35–36). His poetic expression of this dilemma, "The Poet," written near the end of
his short life, has also become legendary:

> He sang of life, serenely sweet,
>   With, now and then, a deeper note,
>   From some high peak, nigh yet remote,
> He voiced the world's absorbing beat.
>
> He sang of love when earth was young,
>   And Love, itself, was in his lays.
>   But ah, the world, it turned to praise
> A jingle in a broken tongue. (*Collected Poetry*, 191)

This is the poem through which we have historically read Dunbar, and thus until
recently we have approached his work through the opposition it laments between
the "serenely sweet" singing of his nondialect poems and the "broken tongue" of his

dialect verse. Dunbar loved Tennyson, and it is probably no coincidence that "The Poet" is written in Tennyson's *In Memoriam* stanza (envelope quatrains in iambic tetrameter) because this is an elegy both for himself and for his poetry. The structure of the poem serves not only the elegiac import but also the logic of contraries. Two stanzas dole out the contradiction, and the two rhymes of the *abba* rhyme scheme underscore this conflict. The first stanza describes ideal poetry, while the second concludes with its degradation. Mellifluous lyric poetry (figured in a musical lexicon, "sang," "note," "beat," "sang," "lays," and sounded out in sibilant and liquid alliteration) gives way to crass ditties in halting words (delivered with rough consonance), and the tragedy of Dunbar's divided energies is comprehended in these differences.

Yet in a poem so committed to stark oppositions, the use of "world" in both stanzas effects a subtle but important conflation of its polarities. If the poet is one who "voice[s] the world's absorbing beat," then he cannot express it, this repetition suggests, without inevitably absorbing and expressing the world's vicissitudes ("beat" encompasses not just the undulations of poetic rhythm but the ups and downs of life). Indeed, the poem has internalized contradictions all along ("now and then," "deeper" and "high," "nigh yet remote") but in lines so serene, sweet, and musical we hardly mind them. That Dunbar here represents the world's contradictions as the very stuff of poetry does not, of course, mitigate the severe opposition he faced as an African American poet in one of the most virulently racist periods of U.S. history, but it can refine the terms of Dunbar's formal struggle and thus of the formal debates within the African American poetic tradition that issued from it. Authentic versus inauthentic, standard English versus dialect, literary versus popular—these terms have shaped Dunbar discussions from the beginning, disallowing the poet's complexity even when *both* his nondialect and dialect poetry have been judged the most authentic. It has taken a century to be able to recognize in Dunbar's work, as Harryette Mullen recently does, "an innovative use of literary code-switching from standard English to nonstandard and regional dialects, including black vernacular, indicating . . . a dialogical writing practice that foregrounds and encourages critical examination of African American double consciousness" ("When he is least himself," 278).

But the immediate legacy of Dunbar's renown was the obstinate distinction between white and black, rigidly racist thinking that readers would not let him evade—"My position is most unfortunate" he once said, "I am a black white man" (qtd. in Dunbar, *Life and Works*, 81), not because he wanted to be white but because his era had no suitable terms for the kind of identity he did want. A comment found among his papers after his death clarifies that he did not wish to be white but to be granted white cultural privileges: "It is one of the peculiar phases of Anglo-Saxon conceit to refuse to believe that every black man does not want to be white" (82). Yet though Dunbar's poems could exceed these boundaries, the perceived limitations of dialect poetry were outlined decisively in 1921 and 1931 by James Weldon Johnson in his prefaces to the first and second editions of his influential *The Book of American Negro Poetry*. Observing that the poets collected in that volume had "a tendency to discard dialect" (40), he explained that "[t]hey are trying to break away from, not Negro dialect itself, but the limitations on Negro dialect imposed by the fixing effects of long convention" (41). Because it was borne of the minstrel and plantation traditions during Reconstruction, such poetry could only offer racist depictions of the African American "as a happy-go-lucky, singing, shuffling, banjo-picking being or as a more or less pathetic figure." Dialect poetry "is an instrument with but two full stops," Johnson asserted, "humor and pathos." By 1931 he declared that "[t]he passing of traditional dialect as a medium for Negro poets is complete" (3). The work of the contemporary writers in his anthology, poets who would define the Harlem Renaissance—like Countee Cullen, Georgia Douglas Johnson, Helene Johnson, Claude McKay, and Alice Dunbar Nelson—largely justifies this claim. Johnson called upon them to seek a poetic form to replace dialect—"[The colored poet] needs to find a form that will express the racial spirit by symbols from within rather than by symbols from without, such as the mere mutilation of English spelling and pronunciation" (41)—and, curiously, the sonnet was the form most of them discovered in themselves.

Though African American poets had employed the sonnet routinely before the 1920s, Claude McKay's two-page spread of sonnets in *The Liberator* during the Red Summer, a period of intense racist violence following World War I, focused black writers on the form anew by demonstrating the political efficacy of traditional prosody, which could render incendiary subject matter even more volatile by putting it under the pressures of conventional form. McKay's "If We Must Die" is the most renowned of six sonnets published together in July 1919, all of them critical of the United States for the postwar increase in lynchings and riots, hypocrisy, capitalism, and imperialism. Almost all of the poets associated with the Harlem Renaissance wrote sonnets (Hughes is the significant exception) to criticize U.S. racism and exalt African heritage and African American culture. The sonnet was not merely, as critics too often insist, a white, high-cultural poetic form that black poets appropriated in order to subvert the cultural hierarchy. The sonnet was already their own form, something that black poets came into possession of by virtue of their reading and education in English and American literature (which included sonnets by African American poets) and their status as members of the intelligentsia.

Moreover, virtually everyone associated African Americans with lyricism at this time (Johnson refers to "their natural musical instinct and talent" and "the Negro's extraordinary sense of rhythm") and assumed that Anglo-European lyric forms gave unqualified expression to this African musicality (12). Thus, McKay can trace the rhymes and meters of his verse back to his "Jamaica Negro dialect"— "Of our purely native songs... all [are] singularly punctuated by meter and rhyme" (*Complete Poems*, 314)—and assert that they are unstudied—"I have chosen my melodies and rhythms by instinct"—while simultaneously defending his use of learned traditional prosody in an age of modernist innovation: "I have adhered to such of the older traditions as I find adequate for my most lawless and revolutionary passions and moods" (315). The sense here of a rich and varied lyric continuum that encompasses instinct, native song, and traditional Anglo-European verse forms is crucial for our understanding of what James Emanuel will eventually call the "Negro sonnet" (206), a phrase he applies to poems that offer black liberation a usable past, positive self-image, and model for future work. During the Harlem Renaissance, the sonnet became an African American form with roots in diverse cultural traditions.

This is not to gainsay that the poets could employ the sonnet with extreme irony, pitting the form's traditional associations against defiant thematics. But the tension that writers could generate between the expectations of the sonnet and their disturbing subjects was only one dimension of the "adequacy," to use McKay's term, of "older traditions" for "lawless and revolutionary" materials. Another well-known sonnet from the Harlem Renaissance, Countee Cullen's "Yet Do I Marvel," simultaneously uses the form to demonstrate intellectual and creative parity with whites and to undermine the logic of white cultural values associated with the sonnet:

> I doubt not God is good, well-meaning, kind,
> And did He stoop to quibble could tell why
> The little buried mole continues blind,
> Why flesh that mirrors Him must some day die,
> Make plain the reason tortured Tantalus
> Is baited by the fickle fruit, declare
> If merely brute caprice dooms Sisyphus
> To struggle up a never-ending stair.
> Inscrutable His ways are, and immune
> To catechism by a mind too strewn
> With petty cares to slightly understand
> What awful brain compels His awful hand.
> Yet do I marvel at this curious thing:
> To make a poet black, and bid him sing! (*My Soul's*, 79)

The opening inverted syntax, which registers doubt before "not" doubting, signals the skeptical speaker's strategy of exposing hypocrisy under the guise of pondering imponderable mysteries. Like many modern sonnets, this one combines Shakespearean structures (opening with two quatrains in alternating rhymes) with a Petrarchan rhetorical structure (an octave and sestet): *ababcdcdeeffgg*. The first eight lines enumerate "curious" injustices in God's creation: moles that must dwell in the dark; humans who must die; and characters from Greek mythology who are tortured by gods (God has been demoted) who do, notoriously, "stoop" to the level of human caprice and meanness.

In a poem saturated with doubt ("marvel," "doubt," "quibble," "why," "inscrutable," "curious" are only the most straightforward expressions of misgiving; additionally, God won't "tell," "make plain," "declare," and his ways are "immune" to catechism, so the speaker will never even "slightly understand"), the sestet will not resolve the questions raised in the octave; indeed, Cullen's sestet reinforces the perplexity of the octave, acknowledging that God isn't going to stoop to tell him why the world is unjust. Instead, God's towering greatness is derided in the pun on "awful," suggesting

He inspires terror rather than wonder. Having resolved that these questions are irresolvable, the speaker nevertheless ("yet") concludes with the implied question that has generated all the preceding ones: why would God give a black man the talent and the urge to be a poet in a society that denies him artistic equality?

The answer, of course, is that He wouldn't. The conceit of interrogating God is only a way to put the challenge to readers: why would you deny me my God-given gifts and rights? The argument against such injustice is the virtuoso sonnet itself, plying the slipping strings of formal demands, literary allusions, ornate diction, and devastating irony. Its catechism entails Greek mythology, biblical scripture, *Paradise Lost* ("Inscrutable His ways are" rejects Milton's assertion that the poet can "justify the ways of God to men"), and prior sonnets, literary credentials that cannot eradicate racism but can eloquently prove its irrationality. In "Yet Do I Marvel" and many other poems in traditional verse forms of the period, conventional prosody was perfectly commensurate with racial politics.

But the racial politics of the period varied greatly and so too did poetic forms. If Cullen cast his lot with the dominant literary tradition—"As heretical as it may sound, there is the probability that Negro poets, dependent as they are on the English language, may have more to gain from the rich background of English and American poetry than from any nebulous atavistic yearnings toward an African inheritance" (*Caroling Dusk*, xi)—Langston Hughes judged him submissive to white cultural values and cast *his* lot with the black folk: "One of the most promising of the young Negro poets said to me once, 'I want to be a poet—not a Negro poet,' meaning, I believe, 'I want to write like a white poet'; meaning subconsciously: 'I would like to be a white poet'; meaning behind that, 'I would like to be white.' And I was sorry the young man said that, for no great poet has ever been afraid of being himself" ("Negro Artist," 139–140). Hughes's phrase "write like" takes issue with Cullen's choice of form rather than his subject matter, and it is not surprising that Hughes is one of the only poets from the period who did not write in high-cultural forms like the sonnet because he derived his sense of national and poetic identity from the black masses, who, he says, "furnish a wealth of colorful, distinctive material for any artist because they still hold their own individuality in the face of American standardizations. And perhaps these common people will give to the world its truly great Negro artist, the one who is not afraid to be himself" (140).

Yet even Hughes contended with the sonnet in his own resistant way. Though his poems abjure the traditional forms he associates with American standardization ("Most of my own poems are racial in theme and treatment, derived from the life I know. In many of them I try to grasp and hold some of the meanings and rhythms of jazz" ["Negro Artist," 142]), his *Shakespeare in Harlem* (1942) contains "Seven Moments of Love: An un-sonnet sequence in Blues." As the book's title suggests, that volume in part explores what Shakespeare would be like were he an African American in 1940s Harlem and, in the "un-sonnet sequence," what the sonnet's fate would be in the hands of a poor, black, modern bard. Such poems would, first and foremost, take a black folk form: sonnets "in Blues." The seven poems hover around the sonnet's length (the first four ranging from thirteen to fifteen lines, the second poem the only one with fourteen lines) before growing less sonnet-like toward the end (the last two are twenty and twenty-four lines, respectively). They all rhyme, usually in couplets, occasionally with a closing triplet, but they have uneven lines and prosy rhythms. Like the form they reject, these are love poems, lamenting not just the loss of the beloved, however, but the implications of her departure for the un-sonneteer's physical as well as emotional well-being. This is one of their bluesy aspects: that the subject of lost love is invariably a figure for lack of basic necessities. "Supper Time," the second poem, opens with images of poverty that are not mere metaphors for the absence of love: "I look in the kettle, the kettle is dry. / Look in the bread box, nothing but a fly. / Turn on the light and look real good! / I would make a fire but there ain't no wood" (218). The end of "Supper Time" makes clear that the deprivations of lost love are both emotional and literal in Harlem: "If I had a fire I'd make me some tea / And set down and drink it, myself and me. / Lawd! I got to find me a woman for the WPA— / Cause if I don't they'll cut down my pay." The final poem in the sequence no longer even toys with the sonnet form; it is a "Letter" to the lover, coaxing her back without conceding too much. Now she and the speaker have names, and he situates their lovers' quarrel in the historical reality of their lives as poor people:

> I can't get along with you, I can't get along without—
> So let's just forget what this fuss was about.
> Come on home and bake some corn bread,
> And crochet a quilt for our double bed, . . .
> Here's five dollars, Cassie. Buy a ticket back.
> And I'll meet you at the bus station.
> > Your baby,
> > > Jack. (220)

Repetition of phrasal units, colloquial diction, folk figures and adages, long, cadenced lines, and perhaps even the occasional triplet are blues infusions in the un-sonnets. If Shakespeare were in Harlem, these poems attest, he would write like Langston Hughes.

And he would not write sonnets. As we have seen, Hughes aligned himself with the black folk and eschewed the forms of poetry he associated with "American standardizations"; he composed many poems in popular African American forms like ballads and blues and others in highly musical free verse and syncopated jazz rhythms. In all these modes he kept an ear tuned to the rhythms of black speech and music, often performing his poetry with musical accompaniment. Yet if Hughes drew a line in 1926 between the "whiteness" (140) of American standardization and "an honest American Negro literature" (142), that line did not separate poetic forms so much as artistic motives: "An artist must be free to choose what he does, certainly, but he must also never be afraid to do what he might choose." Of course, those motives would have formal ramifications, and his own motives drew Hughes toward black popular forms, but he recognized the permeability of cultural boundaries—for all his warnings about standardization. *Montage of a Dream Deferred* (1951) exemplifies his complex view of culture in the very notion of *montage*, as his prefatory remarks make clear: "this poem on contemporary Harlem, like be-bop, is marked by conflicting changes, sudden nuances, sharp and impudent interjections, broken rhythms, and passages sometimes in the manner of the jam session, sometimes the popular song, punctuated by the riffs, runs, breaks, and distortions of the music community in transition" (387). The volume teems with voices, rhythms, and forms, from scat singers to English teachers to blues singers to balladeers to the myriad, competing voices of the Harlemites in "Deferred."

In "Ballad of the Landlord," the cultural cacophony may seem to fall into stark oppositions rather than generate a diverse montage, oppositions between African Americans and whites, black forms and white forms, as tenant and landlord compete for verbal authority within the ballad (a form that might belong to either culture). The quatrain's rhyming *abcb*, its use of dialogue and ordinary language, emphasis on story, dramatic action, single episode, the swift pace, and the sense of impending catastrophe are classic ballad traits. Ballads like this one have preserved and disseminated a mythic and historic record of the populace that high cultural forms and conventional histories have typically ignored. But whose ballad is this?

The main speaker in the poem is a poor black man who tries to talk with his white landlord about his dilapidated house, yet the poem is not called "Ballad of the Tenant." Instead, it records the interruption of the tenant's ballad by the landlord's (in the italicized sixth stanza), a disruption that precipitates a chain of verbal events (police arrest, precinct report, trial record, court sentencing, and newspaper coverage) that increasingly deny the tenant's verbal authority:

> Landlord, landlord,
> My roof has sprung a leak.
> Don't you 'member I told you about it
> Way last week?
>
> . . . .
> *Police! Police!*
> *Come and get this man!*
> *He's trying to ruin the government*
> *And overturn the land!*
>
> Copper's whistle!
> Patrol bell!
> Arrest.
>
> Precinct Station.
> Iron cell.
> Headlines in the press:
>
> MAN THREATENS LANDORD

TENANT HELD NO BAIL
∴

JUDGE GIVES NEGRO 90 DAYS IN COUNTY JAIL. (402–403)

The tenant's loss of speech and authority is graphically depicted in the poem as a loss of poetic form. The ballad quatrains are replaced by the one-line newspaper headlines, and the formal structure of folk history is reduced to a caption of racist self-justification. The ballad of the landlord, not to mention the other lords of the land, effectively, and visually, supersedes the ballad of the poor black tenant.

Aurally, however, the tenant's ballad continues to worry the poem. Though at the line reading "Copper's whistle!" the ballad quatrains seem to disintegrate, the ballad sound continues unperturbed by the appearance of free verse on the page. The lines could be graphically rearranged to indicate this (Man threatens landlord / Tenant held no bail / Judge gives Negro / 90 days in county jail). This contest of eye and ear replicates the dispute between the landlord and tenant and mobilizes familiar opposites like white and black, written and oral, dominant and marginal, high and low, contemporary and archaic. The ballad form, with its varied history, puts all these tensions into play. The tenant is verbally more adept (his stanzas are rhetorically rich and humorous) than the landlord, who resorts to stilted clichés, and the tenant might be physically more able, too, because the landlord feels so easily threatened by him and calls on the police for protection. But the landlord's voice has political authority; he can silence and incarcerate the black tenant. Still, by means of the ballad form, the tenant's power persists in subtle and significant ways. White culture may preempt his speech with its own, but it speaks in his cadences. The landlord, judge, even the racist headlines follow the rhythms of the tenant's ballad stanzas. In creating these tensions between what we see on the page and what we hear in those same lines, Hughes brings crucial opposites into relation: most important is the convergence of two kinds of cultural authority. The eye might register that the tenant has been silenced, but the ear will hear his "impudent interjections, broken rhythms." In "Ballad of the Landlord," ironically, the tenant's form has a strong if subtle authority even if the tenant himself does not.

Hughes began writing during the Harlem Renaissance and continued until the end of his life in 1967; his last volume of poetry, *The Panther and the Lash: Poems of Our Time*, produced during the Black Power Movement, was published posthumously that year. Though he had reservations about both movements, it is an indication of his lifelong political radicalism that he had written many of those "poems of our time" much earlier in his career.[9] He had committed himself to the black folk in 1926 and continued to compose in forms relevant to them: ballads, blues, and jazzy free verse. His aesthetic radicalism—black vernacular and nonverbal vernacular sounds, jazz structures, montage of cultural discourses, nonverbal graphic notation, poetry performances with jazz—anticipated the black aesthetic, which would employ many of these techniques, years in advance. But before the Black Arts Movement redefined African American poetry in the late 1960s, Hughes was distinctive among African American poets writing at midcentury—like Margaret

Walker, Gwendolyn Brooks, Melvin Tolson, and Robert Hayden—for exempting himself from the tensions and demands of double-consciousness, an exemption that resonates in his characteristically forthright lines and his singular freedom from disputes about appropriate poetic forms.

In "I, Too," a response to Whitman's declaration of national poetic authority in "Song of Myself," Hughes's awareness of being "an American, a Negro" inspires confident, knowing patience (the poem opens and closes with the same self-possessed assertion of poetic citizenship) in a speaker who fully recognizes the social antagonisms of race but has not internalized them as his own conflict. "I, too, sing America," he claims, even though

> I am the darker brother.
> They send me to eat in the kitchen
> When company comes,
> But I laugh,
> And eat well,
> And grow strong.
>   (*Collected Poems*, 46)

Hughes's easy rhythms and easygoing speaker contrast with those in Tolson's reply to Whitman, "A Song for Myself," which proposes a severely curbed purpose and scope (it is only "a" song for just himself) in clipped monometer lines that refuse Whitman's expansiveness and optimism: "I judge / My soul / Eagle / Nor mole: / A man / Is what / He saves / From rot" (*Harlem Gallery*, 45). Though Tolson's speaker, like Whitman's, contains multitudes—"Jesus, / Mozart, / Shakespeare, / Descartes, / Lenin, / Chladni, / Have lodged / With me" (49)—he knows that such cultural wealth will not save his poetry from becoming rot. While Hughes's poet can say with certainty that "Tomorrow, / I'll be at the table" (46), Tolson's poet has no confidence that his work will "span / The Gulf / Of man" (50–51). That gulf is both inborn and socially constructed in Tolson's poem; God created different races, and people choose to "add" the "grief" of racism to the problem of life's brevity: "If hue / Of skin / Trademark / A sin, / Blame not / The *make* / For God's / Mistake. // Since flesh / And bone / Turn dust / And stone, / With life / So brief, / Why add / To grief?" (47–48). In lock-step lines, God first blunders by creating racial difference, we perpetuate the mistake by associating dark skin with evil, and another of God's errors, mortality, is thus exacerbated by bigotry. "Trademark" suggests the whole economy of racism, as does "The *make*," a phrase that commodifies people of different "hues" as if they were different brands. Tolson's two-syllable lines, performing their accentual tug of war with incessant determination, provide an apt structure for the claustrophobic warring of Du Bois's ideals.

Melvin Tolson's early poetry looked something like the early work of his contemporaries, though it always exhibited his distinctive rhetorical energy and inventiveness, his catholic cultural interests ("catholic" is a favored word in his early poetry), and his preference for long poetic sequences. "Tapestries of Time," from his first book, *Rendezvous with America* (1944), is a sequence in quatrains that may look at first like Brooks or Hughes but reads as decidedly Tolson (the pentameter lines of these Rubaiyat stanzas are one indication that the poem keeps company with high cultural prosody rather than with folk ballads); in section III, the "Undersoul of the quick and dead" (109) speaks about man's hypocrisy (111):

> His tonguesters wedge the White against the Black;
> His bellygods muster the Palace against the Shack;
> His ostrichmen island the people and wall them in
> And dagger his catholic charters in the back.
>
> To escape the waste land of the Doomsday hour,
> His poets scurry into the ivory tower.
> The ghosts of Milton and Whitman grieve without,
> While the moderns sonnetize a hothouse flower. (112)

Tolson's own "catholic charters" are evident here, as he ranges explicitly from Milton to Whitman and allusively from puritan Wigglesworth (infamous for "The Day of Doom") to modernist Eliot (equally infamous for *The Waste Land*) in Rubaiyat stanzas that decry not only injustice and tyranny but also contemporary poets who "scurry to the ivory tower" to compose sonnets about romantic clichés in the cultured environs of academe—betraying their poetic forebears who did not run from social responsibilities. This is the same Tolson who would shortly tell Hughes that "he was going to write so many foreign words and footnotes that they [the white literary establishment] would *have* to pay him some mind!" (qtd. in Rampersad, 235). Hughes was disconcerted when it worked; Allen Tate praised the Tolson of *Libretto for the Republic of Liberia* (1953) as the first Negro poet who "has assimilated completely the full poetic language of his time and, by implication, the language of the Anglo-American poetic tradition" (234–235).

Assimilation of racial subject matter to Anglo-European poetic forms and the integration of African American poets into mainstream American poetry were artistic ambitions shared by most black poets—with the important exception of Hughes—as the century neared its midpoint. Robert Hayden published his Counterpoise Manifesto in 1948, rejecting any "special pleading" that "seeks to limit and restrict creative expression" (*Collected Prose*, 41), insisting that "it is more profitable for our generation to read good poetry than it is to listen to soap opera" (42). He gave particular emphasis to form, saying that experimentation was "an absolute necessity in keeping the arts vital and significant in contemporary life" (41) and rejecting the custom of viewing African American art thematically rather than formally, "entirely in light of sociology and politics." To categorize the poetry of African Americans as "so-called minority" writing, he asserted, is to obscure "the oneness of mankind and the importance of the arts in the struggle for peace and unity" (42). Just a year later in 1949, Tolson gave a speech in which he announced that "the time had come for 'a New Negro Poetry for the New Negro,' [and] he proposed that African American poets present a 'rich heritage of folk lore and history' while using the techniques developed by Eliot, Pound, Williams, and other white poets" (Beach, 128). And in just another year, Brooks would win the Pulitzer Prize for *Annie Allen*, a volume replete with the forms of "other white poets" (sonnets, an epic composed in a variation on rhyme royal, and modernist free verse), and she would emphasize the importance of craft in an interview: "The Negro poet's most urgent duty, at present, is to polish his technique, his way of presenting his truths and his beauties" (qtd. in *Conversations*, 38). At midcentury, then, black poets were calling for artistic freedom and, like other modernists, associating that freedom with greater attention to poetic form. Hayden was interested in unity, Tolson in black heritage, and Brooks in distinctive Negro truths and beauties, but each agreed that the issue was crafting good poetry and assumed that Anglo-European aesthetics would produce it. The two warring ideals had shifted their ground from national identity, "a Negro, an American," to artistic identity, "a Negro, a Poet."

This is how Brooks reformulated the problem of double-consciousness in 1964 when she wrote the foreword to Hughes's *New Negro Poets U.S.A.*, just a few years before the Black Arts Movement commenced. There she distinguished contemporary New Negro poets from the old New Negroes of the Harlem Renaissance and recast their old double-consciousness as a new sensation:

> At the present time, poets who happen also to be Negroes are twice-tried. They have to write poetry, and they have to remember that they are Negroes. Often they wish that they could solve the Negro question once and for all, and go on from such success to the composition of textured sonnets or buoyant villanelles....
>
> In the work of most of today's Negro poets the reader will discover evidences of double dedication, hints that artists have accepted a two-headed responsibility. (13)

Though "twice-tried" acknowledges the hardships of having been made a black poet and bidden to sing, "double dedication" suggests that this challenge is now a point of pride—not two warring ideals in one dark body but two heads, the Negro's and the poet's, working together for one dark body. And that African American body, she asserts, "is an eloquence," an expressive, articulate identity in and of itself, not a constraining exterior that stifles warring identities inside. If there remains something monstrous in having a "two-headed responsibility," there is also something marvelous, for two heads are better than one in Brooks's formulation, which emphasizes the black poet's freedom of choice ("dedication," "accepted") and suggests a double endowment of intellectual and creative gifts. This is not yet the multiple oneness of blackness, but it does prefigure, in however ungainly terms, that ideal.

In *New Negro Poets U.S.A.*, Hughes is making a new distinction between American poets and United States poets, and Brooks is parsing the doubleness of black U.S. identity in new, specifically artistic terms; the African American's "mere body...is an eloquence," but "no real artist is going to be content with offering raw materials" of racial identity (13). The shift from *America* to *U.S.A.* registers a growing recognition over the course of the century that the United States was only a fraction of the Western world and its culture and ideologies were not universals;

and this qualification—even skepticism—of U.S. cultural authority influenced how poets measured and defined themselves. By 1964, with African countries winning independence abroad and U.S. authority challenged at home, African American poets like Hughes and Brooks were thinking less about the old American/Negro conundrum and more about what it meant to be a black poet in the United States. "Race-fed testimony" must be shaped into a distinctly U.S. art, and Brooks suggests that sonnets and villanelles are not the right shapes for these poems.

Brooks would argue with herself about the proper form for black poetry her entire career, an argument that generated some of the best poems of the century in ballad, sonnet, nonce, and free-verse forms. By the early 1960s, she was still writing ballads but more often now also composing in free verse, typically with random rhymes and other highly lyrical effects. Yet her free-verse poems continued to wrestle with traditional verse forms, sometimes by falling into their cadences and sometimes by invoking conventional form as a figure for conventional thought. Even as she repudiated textured sonnets and buoyant villanelles, she persisted in placing her racial testimony in tension with traditional poetic forms because that tension—as the Harlem Renaissance poets had demonstrated—could represent the contradictions of black life in the United States with volatile exactness.

For instance, two poems from *The Bean Eaters* (1960) explore the 1955 lynching of Emmett Till, a Chicago youth who was murdered in Mississippi after being accused of flirting with a white woman. The woman's husband and his half-brother kidnapped the boy, and his mutilated corpse was later pulled from a river. Both poems structurally bear out the fact that the "wildness" and brutality of racism cannot be "tied in little bunches, / Like the four-line stanzas of the ballads" (333), but they also demonstrate that the very inadequacy of those generic conventions can aid in representing the sometimes elusive complexities of racism. The poem about the white Mississippi mother is in free verse but invokes the ballad as a way to conceptualize the volatile events of the murder and trial—and the white woman's troubling place in them:

> From the first it had been like a
> Ballad. It had the beat inevitable. It had the blood.
> A wildness cut up, and tied in little bunches,
> Like the four-line stanzas of the ballads she had never quite
> Understood—the ballads they had set her to, in school. (333)

Caught up in a sensational story of revenge and murder, the white mother begins to understand the ballad's "beat inevitable"—the emphatic meter and rhyme that give a sense of barreling forward on dynamic rhythms toward impending tragedy. The "blood" and "wildness" of the ballad's standard themes (love, hate, betrayal, death) cannot be contained by the "little bunches" of its quatrains, just as the white mother's story cannot be managed by thematic conventions of the form: "Herself: the milk-white maid, the 'maid mild' / Of the ballad. Pursued / By the Dark Villain.

Rescued by the Fine Prince." She cannot imagine herself pretty enough to justify the crime, view the boy as evil, or recognize her husband as the hero.

Her husband is himself the Dark Villain, of course, something she begins to understand when he slaps his own little boy, a "small and smiling criminal" (337), who, like Till, is no criminal at all. She comes to see her husband as Mars, the god of war, with blood dripping from his hands. As he caresses her, "a hatred for him burst into glorious flower" (339). The white mother's recognition that her husband, not Emmet Till, is guilty, that her own family has been destroyed by this crime along with Till's family, and that she is thus connected to the dead boy's mother becomes

> The last bleak news of the ballad.
> The rest of the rugged music.
> The last quatrain. (339)

Here, the last *tercet* of the poem, like the free verse throughout, is a figure for the insufficiency of the ballad to arrange the wildness of lynching into stanzas that could keep such a tragedy in check. In one sense "The last quatrain" is an admission of failure: "last" acknowledges the impossibility of containing Till's murder and the larger history it replicates in poetic form. And yet if the ballad is judged insufficient in the Mississippi mother's poem, its "beat inevitable" persists into the other mother's poem, where "The last quatrain" is not a conclusion but a premise.

The last line of one poem becomes the first phrase in the next poem's title, "The Last Quatrain of the Ballad of Emmett Till," because the white family guilty of the crime and the black family victimized by it cannot be cordoned off in segregated poetic structures (segregation was the motive for the crime). Ironically, though, it is precisely the persistence of the ballad form, even with all its "breaks," that foregrounds this truth. The white mother senses this paradox: "The one thing in the world that she did know and knew / With terrifying clarity was that her composition / Had disintegrated. That, although the pattern prevailed, / The breaks were everywhere" (335). She realizes that her romantic illusions have been destroyed by her husband's violence; the roles of Maid Mild, Dark Villain, and Fine Prince have "disintegrated"—a grim pun on the larger issue of "integration" and the specific decomposition of Till's body in the river—and she observes the destruction "everywhere." Though the superficial pattern of her comfortable domestic life may "prevail," she knows that life is fundamentally changed. However, the formal pattern of the ballad also prevails as a structure that can connect her to Till's mother despite the breaks, just as the last line of the white woman's poem persists in the title of the black woman's. The racial hatred and violence that tear them apart also paradoxically connect them.

"The Last Quatrain of the Ballad of Emmett Till" takes up his mother's point of view in something more like a ballad form. In this sense, then, the prosody in the second poem tentatively restores the ballad pattern after the first poem's critique of the form. It is appropriate that the pattern prevails even as the composition disintegrates because the ballad has been one important means for recording African American culture and history in the popular memory. The second poem serves just such a purpose. Turning the page to these eight lines, however, we might wonder in what sense this can be the last *quatrain* of the ballad of Emmett Till:

Emmett's mother is a pretty-faced thing;	*a*		
the tint of pulled taffy.	*b*	*a*	*a*
She sits in a red room,	*c*		
drinking black coffee.	*b*	*a*	*a*
She kisses her killed boy.	*d*		
And she is sorry.	*e*	*b*	*a*
Chaos in windy grays	*f*		
through a red prairie. (340)	*e*	*b*	*a*

As the columns of differently marked rhyme scheme show, the poem may appear to comprise two quatrains with mostly three-beat lines and slant rhymes in the second and fourth lines (*abcbdefe*, a common ballad pattern) or one quatrain with long lines and rhymed couplets (*aabb*) or even one quatrain with a single end rhyme (*aaaa*)— also familiar ballad variations. In any case, the ballad, a structure of thought in the preceding poem, is actualized here as a formal structure, too.

Except for "And she is sorry," these can be read as long lines that wrap over when they meet the right margin; three of the four "pairs" are single sentences, the indentations follow conventional graphic practice for formatting long lines, and three of the four indented lines begin with lowercase letters, suggesting that they are continuations of the preceding lines. As a last quatrain of Emmett Till's ballad, its lines are uncommonly long, each having five or more beats and a heavy caesura. They refuse the lively cadences common to the ballad. These are listless, mournful, protracted lines, the calm after the storm, perhaps, but also perhaps the calm before another storm, as the imagery hints. The "little bunches" of lines in the traditional ballad quatrain here extend menacingly beyond their customary borders. That is, taken as a single quatrain, the poem has a doleful, sinister sound that portends chaos and violence, retribution. If this poem is devoted to Emmett Till's "end," the end of his life and the end of his story, it equally commits itself to an apocalyptic "end" to his murder. "Last" rings all these meanings in order to affirm the significance of Till's life and death; just so, the "last" quatrain is both two quatrains, implying the continuation of the ballad tradition, and one quatrain, implying an apocalyptic conclusion to the long story of racist violence. The ballad is thus both the form of racist mythology and the form of a "terrifying clarity" about racism.

Brooks explored the capacities of poetic forms from her first volume, *A Street in Bronzeville* (1945), to her posthumous *In Montgomery* (2003), and her work throughout her career is marked by formal experimentation and adaptation as she wrote in verse (sonnets, ballads, quatrains, triplets and couplets, metered and rhymed stanzas of her own invention, and an ornate variation on rhyme royal) and free verse; in colloquial, formal, and extravagantly poetical registers; and, most of all, as she challenged and enlarged the very genres she now employed and now rejected. Yet when she became radicalized in 1967, she would attempt to draw a line between her pre- and postliberation poetry, between her Negro, integrationist work and her black nationalist writing.[10] It would be an extremely hard line to draw, partly because her poetry had always been black and partly because her conventional forms had never been conventional. Nevertheless, critics have typically assisted her in this misleading distinction. Don L. Lee (Haki Madhubuti) discerned a growing clarity about appropriate forms for black poetry following her pre-1967 "confusion over social responsibility and 'art for art's sake'" (17). And Houston A. Baker Jr. recurred to a familiar formulation: "What one seems to have [in the early work] is white style and black content—two warring ideals in one dark body" (21). Her own calculation came up even shorter: "It frightens me to realize that, if I had died before the age of fifty, I would have died a 'Negro' fraction" (*Report from Part One*, 45).

As the old notion of a monolithic America was being fractured by the social upheavals of the 1960s, African America was finding a new wholeness. In "Black Cultural Nationalism," Ron (Maulana) Karenga, one of the movement's most influential leaders, distinguished between "art for art's sake" and "art for all our sake" and laid out a new poetics for the new consciousness (34): "all art must reflect and support the Black Revolution, and any art that does not discuss and contribute to the revolution is invalid, no matter how many lines and spaces are produced in proportion and symmetry" (33). Proportion and symmetry were aesthetic values identified with the white literary tradition, of course, and poetic form was yoked to racial identity during the movement even more adamantly than in previous periods. Now Ishmael Reed conflated slavish adherence to traditional prosody with slavery itself: "Some slaves excelled at 'Sonnets,' 'Odes,' and 'Couplets,' the feeble pluckings of musky Gentlemen and slaves of the metronome" (406). In that same important anthology of cultural criticism, Sarah Webster Fabio equated conventional prosody not merely with slavery but with lynching: "Black writers, finding themselves up a tree with 'the man's' rhetoric and aesthetic, which hangs them up, lynching their black visions, cut it loose. All the way—swinging free" (190). The free verse of the black aesthetic, they argued, escaped both the formal and the cultural constraints of sonnets, odes, and couplets. Free people wrote free verse.

Following the teaching of the Senegalese poet and president Leopold Senghor, Karenga asserted that revolutionary black art must be functional, collective, and committing. It must "expose the enemy, praise the people and support the revolution" (33–34). At the Fisk University First Black Writers' Conference in 1966, Robert Hayden maintained that he was "a poet who happens to be a Negro" and resisted any prescriptions for his writing (qtd. in Llorens, 62). Melvin Tolson took him to task for this, retorting, "I'm a black poet, an African-American poet, a Negro poet. I'm no accident" (63). Given Tolson's arcane, elliptical, allusive high-modernist poetics in *Libretto for the Republic of Liberia* (1953) and *Harlem Gallery* (1965), it remains perplexing that he denounced Hayden in the name of the black aesthetic—a style of writing that involved free verse, rhythms and themes from black music, colloquial diction, orthographic and rhetorical violence, and, most of all, accessibility to ordinary African American readers. LeRoi Jones's "Black Art" was the defining poem and the *ars poetica* for the Black Arts Movement:

> Poems are bullshit unless they are
> teeth or trees or lemons piled
> on a step....
> ...We want "poems that kill."
> Assassin poems, Poems that shoot
> guns. Poems that wrestle cops into alleys
> and take their weapons leaving them dead
> with tongues pulled out and sent to Ireland. Knockoff
> poems for dope selling wops of slick halfwite
> politicians Airplane poems, rrrrrrrrrrrrrrrr
> rrrrrrrrrrrrrrr...tuhtuhtuhtuhtuhtuhtuhtuhtuh
> ...rrrrrrrrrrrrrrrr...setting fire and death to
> whities ass.
>
> (Baraka, *Transbluesency*, 142)

Revolutionary poems have "teeth," and not the teeth of smiling portraits, for the familiar props of decadent art (trees in landscapes or lemons in still lifes) will be redeployed as weapons. Valid poems, the speaker urges, must assault white culture and bring down its oppressive authority. All other poems are "bullshit" and must be abandoned until the revolution has succeeded and the world is safe for black people: "Let there be no love poems written / until love can exist freely and / cleanly" (143). First fight. Then fiddle.

This combative, threatening poetic stance was a necessary and effective part of the revolutionary change in black U.S. consciousness that occurred during the 1960s and 1970s, but such strident prescriptions for art (along with disturbing expressions of sexism, homophobia, and anti-Semitism) were fairly quickly questioned, even by Jones (now Amiri Baraka) and others who had composed rousing assassin poems. Already in *Black Fire* (1968), the anthology of Black Arts writing that consolidated the movement, Welton Smith was testing the limits of such poetic strategies and suggesting that a greater aesthetic range was critical to political progress. In "malcolm," the different sections of his elegy move restively from vulgar invective ("slimy obscene creatures," "you rotten motherfuckin' bastards," "[you have] let machines crawl up your cock / rammed your penis into garbage disposals") to wordless anguish ("screams / screams") to a rhetorical composure that may be his most effective weapon ("i am comfortable in your house," "i am comfortable in your language" [285–286, 289, 290]). Black women poets also quickly took issue with the movement's directives, and Ntozake Shange, for instance, refuted the dictum against love poems by writing a series of "no more love poems," pointing out the contradictions between liberation and sexism, whose numbered titles ("no more love poems #1," "no more love poems #2,"...) flaunted their disobedience to the strictures of "Black Art" (42–45). Likewise, in "The Last M.F.," Carolyn Rodgers wryly protested the gender politics that restricted revolutionary poetics for women: "they say, / that i should not use the word / muthafucka anymo / ... as the new Black Womanhood suggests / a softer self" (37). Making a show of submission to male dictates that curtail female creativity, the speaker takes possession of the word she is told to relinquish:

> and so i say
> this is the last poem i will write calling
> all manner of wites, card-carrying muthafuckas
> and all manner of Blacks (negroes too) sweet
> muthafuckas, crazy muthafuckas, lowdown muthafuckas
> cool muthafuckas, mad and revolutionary muthafuckas.

Her last M.F. clearly has the last laugh, but it more importantly demonstrates the ingenuity of her language, the profusion of meanings in a single term, and the capacity of poetry to sound out the shades and subtleties of words, poetic resources the revolution needs.

Robert Hayden held out for the kind of cultural complexity that Shange, Rodgers, and others demanded during the Black Arts Movement and that African American poets assume today: "I have said this until I almost think I'll choke and fall over backwards," he said with exasperation in 1966 (qtd. in Llorens, 62). But in a more forbearing essay a decade later, "How It Strikes a Contemporary: *Reflections on Poetry and the Role of the Poet*," he created a genial dialogue between himself and a critic he dubbed the Inquisitor, who, predictably, presses him about his "responsibility toward *them* [blacks]." The Poet responds: "I'm fully conscious, and sometimes painfully conscious, of their and my situation. But I assert my right to approach it in my own way as a poet. I deal with it as I feel it, and not as people like you think I should" (*Collected Prose*, 8). This and countless other statements on the role of the black poet make clear that Hayden did not deny his racial identity but wanted to preserve his particular perspective on race: "their and my situation" encompasses both collectivity and individuality. Most confounding, though, is why Hayden's poems didn't earn him more respect from the radical black poets. The first thing anyone writing about Robert Hayden's poetry should do is read the poetry.

Hayden's poems consistently treat African American matters in ways that expose the enemy, praise the people, and thus in crucial respects support the revolution. His frequently anthologized "Night, Death, Mississippi," "A Ballad of Remembrance," "Homage to the Empress of the Blues," "Middle Passage," and "Frederick Douglass" expose racism and praise revered African American figures. Distinctive of Hayden's poetry, though, is a determination to represent the competing points of view that create racism, often designated by numbered sections, stanzaic indentations, or different fonts. "Night, Death, Mississippi," for example, is a two-part poem; in the first section, a third-person speaker listens to a white grandfather who is too old and infirm to participate in a lynching, while in the second section, direct dialogue from his lynching son's point of view alternates with italicized ejaculations from a disembodied voice of lamentation: "*O Jesus burning on the lily cross*," "*O night, rawhead and bloodybones night*," and the last line of the poem, "*O night betrayed by darkness not its own*" (*Collected Poems*, 16). In this complex collage of meanings and motives, night, death, and Mississippi (black and white Mississippi) are all encompassed differently by the term "darkness," and the natural darkness of night is "betrayed" by the twisted darkness of racial violence.

"Middle Passage" orchestrates even more voices in an effort to comprehend the intricate, bewildering illogic of slavery:

> *Jesús, Estrella, Esperanza, Mercy:*
>
>> Sails flashing to the wind like weapons,
>> sharks following the moans the fever and the dying;
>> horror and corposant and compass rose.
>
> Middle Passage:
>> voyage through death
>>> to life upon these shores.
>
>> "10 April 1800—
>> Blacks rebellious. Crew uneasy. Our linguist says
>> their moaning is a prayer for death,
>> ours and their own. Some try to starve themselves.
>> Lost three this morning leaped with crazy laughter
>> to the waiting sharks, sang as they went under."
>
> *Desire, Adventure, Tartar, Ann:*
>
>> Standing to America, bringing home
>> black gold, black ivory, black seed.
>
>>> *Deep in the festering hold thy father lies,*
>>> *of his bones New England pews are made,*
>>> *those are altar lights that were his eyes.*
>
>> Jesus   Savior   Pilot   Me
>> Over   Life's   Tempestuous   Sea. (48)

The names of slave ships jostle incongruously here with words from Christian spirituals (*Jesús*, Jesus, *Mercy*, Pilot Me), direct quotation from a crew member's journal, slave-trader talk, deposition testimony, allusions to *The Tempest* and *The Waste Land*, and the eloquent, mournful voice of the poem itself: "Shuttles in the rocking loom of history, / the dark ships move, the dark ships move, / their bright ironical names / like jests of kindness on a murderer's mouth; / plough through thrashing glister toward / fata morgana's lucent melting shore, / weave toward New World littorals that are / mirage and myth and actual shore" (51). Here is Hayden's complex understanding of history—mirage and myth and the actual—and his poetry works to bring these competing versions into proximity where their collision (not their resolution) may spark understanding. Yet a further complexity in Hayden's work is that these multiple viewpoints are all part of a "Oneness" that exceeds the history of racism in which we are caught but which that history itself prevents us from apprehending. (Hayden became a member of the Bahá'í Faith in 1943, embracing its vision that humanity is one family.) "El-Hajj Malik El-Shabazz" again employs a multipart structure in order to represent the many facets of Malcolm X, especially his growing awareness of a full identity, as the epigraph referring to *"masks and metamorphoses"* suggests. In the final stanza, Malcolm X falls "upon his face before / Allah the raceless in whose blazing Oneness all / were one" at the very moment he falls from the bullets that kill him. Though Hayden's elegy invokes a transcendent Oneness, it concludes in recognition of the limitations of time: "He rose renewed renamed, became / much more than there was time for him to be" (89). To *be more* than there is time to *be* simultaneously articulates Hayden's faith in our potential for unity and his admission that we have not achieved it. That he believed in the possibility of unity did not mean that he denied racial division and its consequences.

Hayden's unfinished poem "[American Journal]" indicates both the extent of his commitment to disparate points of view and the particular ability of such a formal prism to represent the intricacies of national identity. The speaker is an alien, come to earth to study "the americans,"—whom he terms "multi people   extremes and variegations" (192)—in service of The Counselors. This more advanced race looks upon Americans as "charming savages enlightened primitives," bent on making "extravagant claims / for their importance and identity." America, he observes, is "as much a problem in metaphysics as / "it is a nation," "an organism that" changes even as i / examine it   fact and fantasy never twice the / same   so many variables" (195). The metaphysical problem of America is its complexity, its competing identities, and thus his report is saturated with words that point to cultural difference ("multi people," "extremes and variegations," "varied pigmentations," "variousness," "variables," some of these repeated). He himself utilizes these varied identities, and his alien difference is masked by all the differences around him:

> disguise myself in order to study them unobserved
> adapting their varied pigmentations   white black
> red brown yellow   the imprecise and strangering
> distinctions by which they live   by which they
> justify their cruelties to one another. (192)

The speaker is "curiously drawn" to the Americans even as he "[doubts he] could exist among them for / long" (195). But he is "attracted" to "that some thing essence / quiddity   i cannot penetrate or name." He cannot comprehend Americans, paradoxically, because their very "essence / quiddity" is that they have no single essence. They are a "multi people" who live by "imprecise and strangering / distinctions," distinctions that are kin to Du Bois's "warring ideals" and Brooks's "double dedication." But Hayden's vision of universal unity was antithetical to what the liberation movement meant by black unity. From a necessarily limited vantage point, he worked to represent the contending perspectives that simultaneously, paradoxically, create our larger unity and obscure it.

As Hayden's work and career make plain, contentions exist not only among different groups but within groups. Brooks tried to make light of differences between the radical poets and Hayden in a 1966 *Negro Digest* review of his *Selected Poems*, but what she registers are her own reservations about each:

> Robert Hayden, for at least thirty years, has busied himself with a very active and earnest subscription to his faith in spite of occasional light heckling from the bare-fight boys, the snarls of whom, indeed, have been at least half-affectionate because few are quicker than they to sense authentic quality in the work of "the enemy," and to salute it. (51)

Though Brooks embraced black liberation and the ideas of the radical young poets, she could never quite sanction their black aesthetic, especially its combativeness and vulgarity. Her caricatures of young ruffians snarling at the harmless old toiler, who busies himself "with a very active and earnest subscription to his faith," *not* with poetry, as if Hayden's spiritual beliefs made mere busywork of his poetic labors, are condescending to both. And while she claims the radicals "sense authentic quality" in Hayden's poetry, *authenticity* and *quality* were strictly circumscribed terms in the black aesthetic (only authentically revolutionary poetry was valid, and only valid poetry had quality) and were not to be found in the work of "the enemy"—her scare quotes notwithstanding. Brooks's struggle here to negotiate the disagreements between Hayden's poetics and black revolutionary poetics plays out a battle she waged with herself about poetic form. Indeed, her descriptions of her post-1967 style— "My newish voice will not be an imitation of the contemporary young black voice, which I so admire, but an extending adaptation of today's G. B. voice" (*Report from Part One*, 183) or "some special kind of Gwendolynian poem" (*Conversations*, 68)— situate a revolutionary response to racism in a distinctive, individual perspective. Her phrasing calls to mind Hayden's insistence on his "right to approach [the social context] in my own way" (*Collected Prose*, 8).

While Brooks worked to extend and adapt her poetry to the times, the times were changing. Her young protégés were moving away from the proscriptions of the black aesthetic and expanding their poetic interests. And even Baraka was revising his infamous dictum that struggle must precede art. His 1982 "In the Tradition" richly rehearses a centuries-long, worldwide body of black cultural expression. Dedicated to the jazz artist "*Black Arthur Blythe*" (199), the poem chronicles the history and creativity of the African diaspora, linking memory to identity: "in the tradition thank you arthur for playing & saying / reminding us how deep how old how black how sweet   how / we is and bees / when we remember / when we are our memory as the projection / of what is evolving / in struggle / in passion and pain / we become our sweet black / selves" (208). Race memory, every line testifies, is preserved in the artistic tradition of a people. Thus, his declamatory free verse at last admits a quiet lyric strain—"open us / yet bind us / let all that is positive / find / us" (209)—a strain that anticipates the final movement into full song as he acknowledges that the fight *is* the fiddle: "thank you langston/arthur / says sing / says fight / in the tradition, always clarifying, always new and centuries old / says / Sing! / Fight! / Sing! / Fight! / Sing! / Fight! &c. &c" (209–210). Like Baraka, Brooks would eventually acknowledge that the African American tradition had always conducted some of its fight in song, but she remained skeptical about that lyric strain, which she associated with the Anglo-European tradition. Asked in 1977 to "talk a little bit about the poets who have reverted to the way you were writing prior to the late sixties," Brooks retorted, "I wouldn't trouble to name any of them. But it's enough to say that some of them wrote rather rowdily then and used four letter words. Now some are writing very carefully polished poetry in forms, even in haiku" (*Conversations*, 98). Declining to name them implies they are beneath her notice, but it also spares her having to identify poets she was close to and fond of, like Sonia Sanchez and Etheridge Knight. She regarded their interest in verse as "a stage" and hoped they would eventually find a balance between the "rawness" of the militant black poetry and the excessive "finesse" of haiku and other forms. Her remark that they wrote "*even* in haiku"—as if haiku were the most inappropriate form of all for African American poets—points up the continuing argument over the ideals of black identity and poetic form.

Despite Brooks's skepticism, however, haiku has had a significant presence in twentieth-century African American letters. Countee Cullen's 1927 *Caroling Dusk: An Anthology of Verse by Black Poets of the Twenties* includes twelve "Japanese Hokku" by Lewis Alexander alongside Alexander's free verse, sonnets, tanka, and a ballad. Richard Wright composed thousands of haiku at the end of his life, which began appearing in black journals a year after his death in 1961; there was a slight but steady trickle of Wright's haiku available in magazines and books until 1973 when the first edition of *The Norton Anthology of Modern Poetry* put them permanently before readers. Haiku was booming in the post–World War II U.S. counterculture out of which many of the Black Arts poets emerged, and it was one of the poetic forms taught by social activists working with prisoners in writing programs. The back cover of Etheridge Knight's *Poems from Prison* (1968) quotes him as saying, "*I died in Korea from a shrapnel wound and narcotics resurrected me. I died in 1960 from a prison sentence and poetry brought me back to life*"—among the poems that saved him are numerous haiku. Dudley Randall, James Emanuel, Knight, Sanchez, and other Black Arts poets composed haiku, and African American poets have continued to work in the form. Sanchez has just published a volume of haiku in 2010. In 1977, though, what Brooks fears is that haiku "tends to obscurity" and thus undermines the clarity of black nationalist identity the Black Arts poetry had achieved (*Conversations*, 98).

Still, it is curious that Brooks would single out haiku, with its celebrated precision and attention to the concrete, everyday world, as a form tending to obscurity. Knight's early "Haiku" is a vivid description of prison life: "Eastern guard tower / glints in sunset; convicts rest / like lizards on rocks" (*Poems from Prison*, 18). Likewise, one of Sanchez's many poems called "Haiku" renders emotion palpable: "did ya ever cry / Black man, did ya ever cry / til you knocked all over?" (*Shake Loose*, 12). Both poets could, as Sanchez does here, adapt haiku to an African American idiom. In fact, in the ninth poem of his haiku sequence, Knight casts haiku as a black vernacular form and insists on its suitability for African American poets: "Making jazz swing in / Seventeen syllables AIN'T / No square poet's job" (*Poems from Prison*, 19). Later, in a poetry reading, he introduced the following poem as a haiku:

> Say, Mister! Uh-huh?
> You a poet man? Uh-huh.
> Me too. Uh-huh. Uh-huh.

If, for most American poets at the time, haiku presented a vivid image in seventeen syllables delivered in three lines of five, seven, and five syllables respectively, then Knight's haiku revises and parodies that form as the two speakers fill out the lines with syllables of sheer vernacular sound ("uh-huh"). Here, the visual immediacy associated with haiku is supplanted by the aural vitality of the two black speakers in conversation, and the formality, precision, compactness, and finish of haiku are jovially abandoned for the informality, imprecision, and improvisational imperatives of a self-consciously spoken poem. In haiku like these, the black vernacular articulates the form to a racial identity even Brooks would have approved.

But Knight, Sanchez, and numerous other black poets also employed haiku to distance themselves from the constraints of racial identity in America. In a later "Haiku" sequence, for instance, Knight juxtaposes personal emotions and the natural world in poems that are not racially inflected: "Two hours I've walked... / ...this Tulsa rain... / In her house, my wife sleeps, snoring" (*Essential*, 99). Sanchez's haiku often similarly treat personal emotion: "love between us is / speech and breath. loving you is / a long river running" (*Shake Loose*, 128). Many of Sanchez's haiku are love poems, and she describes haiku as a form that contained and controlled volatile emotions: haiku "was a form that allowed me to put a lot of emotion into three lines and allowed it to be finished in a sense. It allowed me also to reflect on it, smile and gain some insight" (qtd. in Harris and Davis, 303). Her repeated assertions of what haiku "allowed" her to do suggest this brief form offered her scope, not limitation. Paradoxically, the requirements of haiku's seventeen syllables helped Sanchez express and then detach herself from powerful emotions. But it was precisely this detachment that troubled Brooks.

What seemed obscured to Brooks by the interest in poetic form among the younger African American poets was not the sense of the poem but the poet's sense of racial identification. Haiku was popularized in the West as a form that taught impersonality, a quality lauded as an antidote to the Western obsession with the self.[11] The supposed impersonality of haiku could facilitate both cultural identification and renunciation. For instance, many critics speculate that Richard Wright composed thousands of haiku at the end of his life to free himself from racism by disassociating himself from his race: "'Selflessness' and the sense of 'rest and ease' prevail in Wright's 'haikus'. His strong and uneasy consciousness in his early years of being a Black American is gone" (Kodama, 67). And one of Wright's haiku may seem to confirm this: "I am nobody: / A red sinking autumn sun / Took my name away" (1). However, the name that Wright relinquishes in haiku may not be his given name but rather the identity imposed on him in the United States, and perhaps he composed thousands of haiku at the end of his life to free himself from racism by disassociating himself from his nationality, not his race. In fact, Sanchez's most recent volume of haiku suggests that the form encourages racial self-discovery rather than self-effacement: "from the moment i opened the book, and read the first haiku," she recounts in her preface, "i had found *me*" (*Morning Haiku*, xiii). Finding herself does not entail the valorization of individual ego that haiku is supposed to suppress—"i knew that haiku were no short-term memory, but a long memory"— rather, "like the blues," haiku "help us to maintain memory and dignity" (xiv). What Sanchez finds in haiku—her inventory ranges from "Cornbread and greens," "Beethoven," "Coltrane," and "Sarah Vaughan" to "*Cante jondo*"— is the rich mix of cultures African American poets claim today.

In Sanchez's *Morning Haiku*, the long memory of the form reaches from St. Augustine to Oprah Winfrey. The "14 haiku (*for Emmett Louis Till*)," for instance, commemorate the lynched boy in their number (he was fourteen when he died), in tender personal details ("young Chicago / stutterer whistling / more than flesh" [9]), in powerful evocations of his death ("say no words / time is collapsing / in the woods" [12]), and in a thematics of remembering that infuses the whole sequence. In the opening poem, Till is not only buried in the north but in the bodies of the living there: "Your limbs buried / in northern muscle carry / their own heartbeat" (9). If the eighth poem imagines his body under the assaults of dismemberment and decomposition—"your limbs / fly off the ground / little birds . . ." (11), it also trans- forms severed limbs into figures for spiritual escape. Likewise, Till's very "pores" are "wild stars embracing / southern eyes" (10); he has both transcended bodily suffering and remains spiritually present as an observing conscience. The fifth poem assures him that "footprints blooming / in the night remember / your blood" (10) and the seventh that the speaker has not forgotten him: "i hear your / pulse swal- lowing / neglected light" (11). Indeed, like Till's own mother, who would not forget her child, "a mother's eyes / remembering a cradle / pray out loud" (12), the speaker assures Till that she will never betray his memory: "your death / a blues, i could not / drink away" (13).

Sanchez's haiku in blues, reminiscent of Hughes's un-sonnet sequence in blues, is a form of poetry that helps her "maintain [the] memory and dignity" she needs to elegize Till, not one that effaces her personal or collective history. A dozen years earlier, she had tapped the long cultural memory of an even more dubious form, a variation on rhyme royal, for an elegy about her own brother. Brooks recounts a phone call in which Sanchez asked permission to use her "Anniad" stanza for the poem; she responded, "that is not 'MY' form: It's EUROPEAN" (*Report from Part Two*, 96–97). She assumed that Sanchez "was kidding": "Of all our poets," Brooks assured herself, Sanchez and Madhubuti "are LEAST likely to flop back into the Forties." But Sanchez wasn't kidding. She published *Does Your House Have Lions?* (1997), a volume of poems about her brother's death from AIDS, which not only employs the "Anniad" stanza but also insistently pays tribute to the earlier poem in diction and structure. Sanchez uses the "Anniad" stanza not, obviously, because it's

European, which is to say white, but because it's Brooksian, and black. And she certainly does not "flop back into the Forties" to recuperate an outdated, invalid stanza, as Brooks implies, but she recovers a form that remains valid precisely because it belongs to Brooks and thus to African American poetry.

Even more recently, in 2006 Major Jackson published "Letter to Brooks," a seventy-page poem in "Anniad" stanzas that asserts, "I write in the tradition," a claim about cultural identity cast in terms of prosody (*Hoops*, 121). The "Fairmont" section of the epistle recalls a heated debate between the New Black Aesthetic poets and their elders about appropriate poetic form, an argument that came to "knockdown, verbal blows that purged / Us from the thumb of the Black Arts" (120). No longer under the thumb of the "black scrutiny" that had rendered Hayden "Fisk's unrewarded poet" decades before (119), the young speaker surveys a tradition of black poetry that ranges from sonnets to slam:

> Just think of all the poems to Malcolm
>   Little or John Coltrane. Fast-forward
> To Regie Gibson, transformed to become
>   The verbal strum of Hendrix's guitar,
>   Breathing back his fire chords.
> Then, return to Hayden's "Frederick Douglass,"
> Ideal sonnet to cover in any class. (121)

Or, more accurately, he surveys a tradition that ranges from slam *back* to sonnets ("*return* to Hayden's.../ Ideal sonnet") but not to prescribe an ideal form or even to suggest a return to past forms, "Ideal" and "return" notwithstanding. What saves Jackson's appreciation of the past from being backward looking is his notion of writing "in the tradition" as a "circle of words" (one of the volume's many hoops) and not as a straight line from past to present:

> What do we have here? A cypher has broken
>   Out. Where's my camera? A circle of words,
> Freestyling returned, ancient as this autumn,
>   Reddish air. I have the silly urge
>   To break in, a little flow of my own, stir
> The unbroken spirit that has us return
> To ancestral waters. Here's my next sojourn. (122)

"Cypher" is profuse with meanings: it denotes writing that is coded or disguised and simultaneously the key to that code; it is the literal figure for zero and the figurative name for someone or something of no importance, especially someone who is subservient to others. As the tradition breaks out into view, the speaker discovers it is a "circle of words"—neither the zero's "O" nor a boundary circumscribing correct poetry but words that return "freestyling," like the seasons, inspiring him to break in with his own "little flow" and "stir." What do we have here in the speaker's return to Brooks and Hayden, to the tradition? A *breaking out* (of misconceptions, of prescribed forms, of convention) and a *breaking in* (to clarity, to formal freedom, to the tradition) that paradoxically produce the "*unbroken* spirit" of the "ancestral waters." And more, this freestyling return is his "next sojourn," his way forward (not backward) to the concluding poem of the volume, "Spring Garden," a last homage to Gwendolyn Brooks.

The seasonal title makes good on the speaker's discovery of cyclical return and renewal in the penultimate poem. The African American "circle of words" continues its flow and stir in Jackson's response to Brooks's "when you have forgotten Sunday: the love story" (*Blacks*, 36–37). In this early poem, her speaker tenderly refuses to accept that the lover has forgotten her; "when you have forgotten Sunday" and all that Sunday represents (leisure, closeness, special dinners, lovemaking), she tells him, "Then I may believe / You have forgotten me as well" (37). But the poem is a litany of reminders, assuring that he cannot forget. Jackson's "Spring Garden" lovingly renews the promise to remember, pledging to keep the words of ancestor poems alive in descendant poems: "When you have forgotten popsicle stick / Races along the curb and hydrant fights, / Then, retrieve this letter from your stack / I've sent by clairvoyant post & read by light" (125). But perhaps the most significant advance in *Hoops* is announced in the title: Jackson's volume recognizes the century's contest over black identity and black form but rejects the oppositional figure of "two warring ideals in one dark body" in favor of a "circle of words," an inclusive image of cultural respect and renewal.

Just as "The Anniad" provides a meaningful form for a contemporary African American poetry, the sonnet has also resumed its role as a valid form for African American expression. June Jordan's "Something Like a Sonnet for Phillis Miracle Wheatley" (1986) tentatively began a rapprochement with the form that Jordan made even more confident use of in her later poems. The sonnet to Wheatley appears at the end of Jordan's "The Difficult Miracle of Black Poetry in America or Something Like a Sonnet for Phillis Wheatley," in which both the essay meditating on Wheatley's life and the poem in honor of her are "something like a sonnet." By the time Jordan collects the poem in *Naming Our Destiny: New and Selected Poems* in 1989, however, she includes, among now-more-conventional free-verse poems, other sonnets that unambiguously announce themselves as such: "A Sonnet from the Stony Brook," "A Sonnet for A.B.T." Rita Dove's *Mother Love* (1995) also makes extensive use of the sonnet. In her introduction to the volume, Dove explains that working within and against the form's expectations generated the complex representation she was after:

> The sonnet is a *heile Welt*, an intact world where everything is in sync, from the stars down to the tiniest mite on a blade of grass. And if the "true" sonnet reflects the music of the spheres, it then follows that any variation from the strictly Petrarchan or Shakespearean forms represents a world gone awry. (xi)

Marilyn Nelson, too, relies on the sonnet to depict a world gone awry in her "heroic crown of sonnets," *A Wreath for Emmett Till* (2005). However, Nelson contends that adhering to the form, rather than varying it, helped her write this difficult book: "The strict form became a kind of insulation, a way of protecting myself from the intense pain of the subject matter" ("How I Came to Write this poem," *Wreath*, n.p.). Nelson finds such formal protection not merely in the stability of the iambic pentameter lines and the Petrarchan rhyme scheme but in the entire literary history these forms summon. The poems are highly allusive, and many of their allusions foreground the very act of remembering that the figure of allusion performs. In the "Sonnet Notes" following the sequence, Nelson glosses each of the fifteen poems, identifying, among other references, their literary allusions. The first line of the first sonnet, for instance, echoes Ophelia in *Hamlet*— "Rosemary for remembrance, Shakespeare wrote"—and raises the subject of death and memory. Though the speaker repeatedly acknowledges her desire to forget ("Forget-me-nots. Though if I could, I would," "Forget him not. Though if I could, I would," "Erase the memory of Emmett's victimhood," "If I could forget, believe me, I would"), she insists on the moral necessity of remembering: "Forgetting would call for consciencelessness." In Nelson's volume, allusion and the sonnet are structures of remembrance precisely because they are traditional and thus signify the past. The formal control she takes from the literary tradition makes her difficult task of elegizing Emmett Till possible.

Etheridge Knight had come to the same conclusion thirty years earlier at the height of the Black Arts Movement in "For Malcolm, A Year After": "Compose for Red a proper verse; / Adhere to foot and strict iamb; / Control the burst of angry words / Or they might boil and break the dam.... / And drench me, drown me, drive me mad" (*Essential*, 50). The speaker charges himself to "make it rime and make it prim" because the "dead white" forms of the white literary tradition paradoxically enable the expression of an African American grief so powerful that it must come under restraint to be represented at all. He explicitly avoids conventional black forms: "sing no song blue Baptist sad." Knight's first elegy for Malcolm X, "It was a Funky Deal," written in a Black Arts mode, took the form of an immediate, colloquial address to the slain leader—too immediate and colloquial, it turns out. The bereaved black poet requires not just the distance of time ("A Year After") but of culture ("Make empty anglo tea lace words") in order to compose himself enough to compose the poem, and the clash of two warring ideals—black, white—sustains African American poetic expression in unanticipated ways.

These dead white forms continue to serve African American poets in the contemporary period because, of course, they are neither dead nor white. Though Knight, Dove, and Nelson conceptualize the "strict iamb" as a figure for poetic control, pitting white prosody against black expressivity and white rule against black resistance, their poems are freestyling rather than contesting. Likewise, in Duriel E. Harris's "Villanelle for the dead white fathers" (2003), the speaker dresses down the dominant Anglo-European tradition—not by rejecting it but by insisting on her place, even on the priority of her place, in it: "You're poets dead; I'm poet live," she asserts in the final quatrain, having demonstrated her poetic vitality and virtuosity in the preceding stanzas:

I can write frontpocket Beale Street make you sweat and crave the blues,
Dice a hymnal 'til you shout *Glory! The Holy Ghost done sent me sin!*
Backwater, yeah, but I ain't wet, so misters, I ain't studin' you:

Signify a sonnet—to the boil of "Bitches Brew."
Rhyme royal a triolet, weave sestina's thick through thin.
I said God made me funky. There ain't nothin' I cain't do. (53)

Harris is an award-winning slam poet with a bachelor's degree in English from
Yale, a master's in creative writing from New York University, and a Ph.D. from the
University of Illinois, Chicago; her speaker's quarrel with the dead white fathers is as
complex and contradictory as her own cultural background. "I ain't studin' you" is
not to say that she *hasn't* studied the Western poetic canon, as is immediately evident
when that rebuff is followed by a catalog of verse forms in the Anglo-European tra-
dition. But this expertise in canonical poetry is deeply entwined with the speaker's
knowledge of African American expressive forms—spirituals, hymns, gospel songs,
the blues, and, thanks to Brooks and other black poets, sonnets and rhyme royal, too.
"I ain't studin' you" alludes to the famous refrain from "Down by the Riverside"—"I
ain't gonna study war no more"—and is less a denial of learning conventional poetic
forms than a rejection of the warring ideals associated with them.

In a preface to *Rainbow Darkness: An Anthology of African American Poetry*
(2003), Keith Tuma wonders "if the anthology represents a moment...when some
or even many African American poets are likely to disarticulate issues of poetic form
from issues of cultural identity" (xii). Most of the writers in the volume, he notes,
share Harryette Mullen's sense that African American poets should be "exploring
the infinite permutations of our lived experience and creative imaginations as black
people" rather than attempting "to embody or represent authentic black identity"
(xi).[12] At a panel on "What's African American about African American Poetry?"
from which Tuma quotes these remarks, Mullen opens the discussion with a hun-
dred-year-old formulation: "If an important aspect of African American experience
is the 'double consciousness' defined by W. E. B. DuBois, it is increasingly appar-
ent that the recipe for mixing our African with our American consciousness varies
with each individual." What's contemporary in her reformulation is the absence of
"warring ideals." Mullen replaces the heroic struggle for cultural identity, waged on
the battleground of poetic form, with a workaday "recipe" that takes "mixing" rather
than fighting as its standard. She might be thinking of Gwendolyn Brooks's "Mrs.
Small," who makes apple pies for her large family in the midst of poverty, racism,
domestic chaos, and lyrical ebullience: at the end of the poem she is left "to release
her heart / And dizziness / And silence her six / And mix / Her spices and core /
And slice her apples, and find her four. / Continuing her part / Of the world's busi-
ness" (*Blacks*, 343). Mrs. Small was already freaky-deke in 1960, and this suggests,
first, that the progress of African American poetry is not strictly linear. Its freestyl-
ing motion has made a circle of words that continually surpass the boundaries that
do violence to poetic form and cultural identity. It also reveals what one learns from
"reading the poetry": that the poems have known this all along.

NOTES

The epigraph for this chapter is Brooks's response to the question "How should African American poetry be critiqued, evaluated, chronicled?" ("Conversation," 274–275).

1 See Beach, 130, for instance.

2 See, for example, *To Gwen with Love: An Anthology Dedicated to Gwendolyn Brooks* (1971), *Say That the River Turns: The Impact of Gwendolyn Brooks* (1987), and, most recently, *Gwendolyn Brooks and Working Writers* (2007). Moreover, Brooks was Poet Laureate of Illinois in 1968 and Library of Congress Consultant in Poetry in 1985. The Gwendolyn Brooks Center for Black Literature and Creative Writing was established at Chicago State University in 1990. The Furious Flower conference, about African American poetry but conceived as a tribute to Brooks, was first held in 1994.

3 Kwansaba is a forty-nine-word form composed of seven lines of seven words (each of which typically cannot have more than seven letters) invented by Eugene B. Redmond in 1995; paratexts are "the highly creative essays, notes, prefaces, and source documents that [avant-garde poets] provide with their experimental poetry" (Vanderborg, 5).

4 Ellis's phrase "cultural mulatto" has connotations that minimize its aptness as a description of the NBA multiplicity he heralds, a limitation that becomes clear when he defines his term: "Just as a genetic mulatto is a black person of mixed parents who often can get along fine with his white grandparents, a cultural mulatto, educated by a multi-racial mix of cultures, can also navigate easily in the white world" (235). That the terms of an argument for cultural diversity collapse into an opposition between black and white suggests the tenaciousness of this formulation.

5 At least since the nineteenth century, when Emerson called for a distinctly American literature and writers sought to create new forms in response to a widespread sense that the United States required a literary tradition rooted in North America rather than in Europe, literary form and national identity have been linked. Walt Whitman most prominently developed what came to be considered an American poetics, employing long, leisurely free-verse lines, inclusive catalogs, and colloquial language to suggest a democratic poetry available to and representative of all citizens. Of course, his free verse could not speak for those who did not share Whitman's political freedom. And yet American poets have continued to equate identity and form, as Anglo-European descendants first sought to distinguish themselves from their Old World literary forebears; as Native American, African American, and immigrant writers worked simultaneously to secure a voice in the nation's literature and preserve a distinctive cultural heritage; and, eventually, as white and nonwhite writers alike attempted to cast off an increasingly oppressive "American" identity associated with Western domination and destruction.

6 See Johnson's detailed discussion of African American music and dance as the context for his case for lyric poetry (10–20).

7 These are the well-known opening lines of Hughes's "A Negro Speaks of Rivers," in which the speaker claims an unbroken connection to the early civilizations along the Euphrates, Congo, and Nile rivers (*Collected Poems*, 23).

8 Tate's "Cult-Nats Meet Freaky-Deke" describes New Black Aesthetic artists as those "for whom black consciousness and artistic freedom are not mutually exclusive but complementary, for whom 'black culture' signifies a multicultural tradition of expressive practices; they feel secure enough about black culture to claim art produced by nonblacks as part of their inheritance" (207).

9 Hughes was as resistant to the willed offensiveness of the Black Arts Movement
   (Rampersad, 398–399) as he had been to the decorum of the Harlem Renaissance.

10 She eventually insisted that her writing always embodied the black aesthetic but not
   before she struggled for decades to differentiate between her pre- and post-1967 poetry
   in both her thinking and her writing: "An announcement that we are going to deal with
   'the black aesthetic' seems to me a waste of time. I've been talking about blackness and
   black people all along" (*Conversations*, 108).

11 In *Eastern Culture*, the first volume of his extremely influential series of books on
   haiku, Blyth articulated assumptions about the Asian impersonality that haiku poets
   still regularly reiterate today: "It is said with some truth that [the Japanese] have a
   feeble grasp of personality, and haiku shows a democracy among its subjects which
   derives from this" (150).

12 Tuma is quoting remarks that Mullen made on a panel discussion of "What's African
   American about African American Poetry," which was published in *Fence*.

REFERENCES

Baker, Houston, A. Jr. "The Achievement of Gwendolyn Brooks." 1972. In *A Life Distilled:
    Gwendolyn Brooks, Her Poetry and Fiction*, ed. Maria K. Mootry and Gary Smith.
    Urbana: University of Illinois Press, 1989. 21–29.
Baraka, Amiri. *Transbluesency: Selected Poems, 1961–1995*. New York: Marsilio, 1995.
Beach, Christopher. *The Cambridge Introduction to Twentieth-Century American Poetry*.
    Cambridge: Cambridge University Press, 2003.
Blyth, R. H. *Haiku*. Vol. 1: *Eastern Culture*. 1949. Tokyo: Hokuseido, 1981.
Braxton, Joanne M. "Introduction." In *The Collected Poetry of Paul Laurence Dunbar*, ed.
    Joanne M. Braxton. Charlottesville: University Press of Virginia, 1993. ix–xxxvi.
Brooks, Gwendolyn. *Blacks*. 1987. Chicago: Third World, 2001.
———. "Conversation: Gwendolyn Brooks and B. Denise Hawkins." In *The Furious
    Flowering of African American Poetry*, ed. Joanne V. Gabbin. Charlottesville: University
    of Virginia Press, 1999. 274–280.
———. *Conversations with Gwendolyn Brooks*. Ed. Gloria Wade Gayles. Jackson: University
    Press of Mississippi, 2003.
———. Foreword. In *New Negro Poets U.S.A.*, ed. Langston Hughes. Bloomington: Indiana
    University Press, 1964. 13–14.
———. *Report from Part One*. Detroit: Broadside, 1972.
———. *Report from Part Two*. Chicago: Third World, 1996.
———. Review of *Selected Poems*, by Robert Hayden. *Negro Digest* 15.12 (1966): 51–52.
Brown, Patricia L., Don L. Lee, and Francis Ward, eds. *To Gwen with Love: An Anthology
    Dedicated to Gwendolyn Brooks*. Chicago: Johnson, 1971.
Bryant, Jacqueline Imani, ed. *Gwendolyn Brooks and Working Writers*. Chicago: Third
    World, 2007.
Cullen, Countee. Foreword. In *Caroling Dusk: An Anthology of Verse by Black Poets of the
    Twenties*. 1927. New York: Citadel, 1993. ix–xiv.
———. *My Soul's High Song: The Collected Writings of Countee Cullen, Voice of the Harlem
    Renaissance*. Ed. Gerald Early. New York: Anchor, 1991.
Dove, Rita. *Mother Love: Poems*. New York: W. W. Norton, 1995.
Du Bois, W. E. B. *The Souls of Black Folk*. 1903. New York: Penguin, 1969.

Dunbar, Paul Laurence. *The Collected Poetry of Paul Laurence Dunbar*. Ed. Joanne M. Braxton. Charlottesville: University Press of Virginia, 1993.

———. *The Life and Works of Paul Laurence Dunbar*. Ed. Lida Keck Wiggins. Naperville, IL: Nichols, 1907.

Ellis, Trey. "The New Black Aesthetic Author(s)." *Callaloo* 38 (1989): 233–243.

Emanuel, James A. "Blackness Can: A Quest for Aesthetics." In *The Black Aesthetic*, ed. Addison Gayle Jr. Garden City, NY: Doubleday, 1971. 192–223.

Emerson, Ralph Waldo. "The American Scholar." 1837. In *Essays and Lectures*. New York: Library of America, 1983. 51–71.

Fabio, Sarah Webster. "Tripping with Black Writing." In *The Black Aesthetic*, ed. Addison Gayle Jr. Garden City, NY: Doubleday, 1971. 182–191.

Gayle, Addison, Jr. *The Black Aesthetic*. Garden City, NY: Doubleday, 1971.

Harris, Duriel E. "Villanelle for the dead white fathers." In *Drag*. Minneapolis: Elixir, 2003. 53.

Harris, Trudier, and Thadious M. Davis, eds. *Dictionary of Literary Biography*. Vol. 41: *Afro-American Poets since 1955*. Detroit: Gale Research, 1985.

Hayden, Robert. *Collected Poems*. Ed. Frederick Glaysher. New York: Liveright, 1985.

———. *Collected Prose*. Ed. Frederick Glaysher. Ann Arbor: University of Michigan Press, 1984.

Hughes, Langston. *The Collected Poems of Langston Hughes*. Ed. Arnold Rampersad; Assoc. Ed. David Roessel. New York: Knopf, 1994.

———. *New Negro Poets U.S.A.* Bloomington: Indiana University Press, 1964.

———. "The Negro Artist and the Racial Mountain." 1926. In *Poetry in Theory: An Anthology 1900–2000*, ed. Jon Cook. Malden, MA: Blackwell, 2004. 139–143.

Jackson, Major. "Letter to Brooks." In *Hoops*. New York: W. W. Norton, 2006. 57–125.

Johnson, James Weldon. Preface to the Revised Edition, Preface to the Original Edition, In *The Book of American Negro Poetry*. Original ed., 1922; rev. ed., 1931. New York: Harcourt, Brace, & World, 1950, 3–8, 9–48.

Jones, LeRoi and Larry Neal. *Black Fire: An Anthology of Afro-American Writing*. New York: Morrow, 1968.

Jordan, June. "The Difficult Miracle of Black Poetry in America or Something Like a Sonnet for Phillis Wheatley." *Massachusetts Review: A Quarterly of Literature, the Arts and Public Affairs* 27.2 (1986): 252–262.

———. *Naming Our Destiny: New and Selected Poems*. New York: Thunder's Mouth, 1989.

Karenga, Ron. "Black Cultural Nationalism." In *The Black Aesthetic*, ed. Addison Gayle Jr. Garden City, NY: Doubleday, 1971. 32–38.

Knight, Etheridge. *The Essential Etheridge Knight*. Pittsburgh: University of Pittsburgh Press, 1986.

———. Etheridge Knight Reads from his *Poems from Prison*. Sound cassette. Rec. 3 Oct. 1986. Kansas City, Mo. New Letters Magazine. New Letters on the Air.

———. *Poems from Prison*. Detroit: Broadside, 1968.

Kodama, Sanehide. *American Poetry and Japanese Culture*. Hamden, CT: Archon, 1984.

Lee, Don L., Preface, "Gwendolyn Brooks: Beyond the Wordmaker—The Making of an African Poet." In Brooks, *Report from Part One*. Detroit: Broadside, 1972. 13–30.

Llorens, David. "Writers Converge at Fisk University." *Negro Digest* 15.8 (1966): 54–68.

Madhubuti, Haki R., ed. *Say That the River Turns: The Impact of Gwendolyn Brooks*. Chicago: Third World, 1987.

McKay, Claude. *Complete Poems: Claude McKay*. Ed. William J. Maxwell. Urbana: University of Illinois Press, 2004.

Melhem, D. H. *Gwendolyn Brooks: Poetry and the Heroic Voice*. Lexington: University Press of Kentucky, 1987.

Milton, John. *Paradise Lost. John Milton: The Complete Poems*. Ed. John Leonard. London: Penguin, 1998. 119–406.

Moten, Fred, with Charles Henry Rowell. "'Words Don't Go There': An Interview with Fred Moten." *Callaloo* 27.4 (2004): 953–966.

Mullen, Harryette. "'When he is least himself': Dunbar and Double Consciousness in African American Poetry." *African American Review* 41.2 (2007): 277–282.

Mullen, Harryette et al. "What's African about African American Poetry?" *Fence* 4/1 (2001). http://fence.fenceportal.org/v4n1/text/afric_amer.html.

Nelson, Marilyn. *A Wreath for Emmett Till*. Boston: Houghton Mifflin, 2005.

Rampersad, Arnold. *The Life of Langston Hughes: Volume II: 1941–1967, I Dream a World*. New York: Oxford University Press, 1988.

Reed, Ishmael. "Can a Metronome Know the Thunder or Summon a God?" In *The Black Aesthetic*, ed. Addison Gayle Jr. Garden City, NY: Doubleday, 1971. 405–406.

Rodgers, Carolyn. "The Last M.F." In *Songs of a Black Bird*. Chicago: Third World, 1969. 37–38.

Rowell, Charles Henry. "The Editor's Note." *Callaloo* 27.4 (2004): vii–ix.

Sanchez, Sonia. *Does Your House Have Lions?* Boston: Beacon, 1997.

———. *Morning Haiku*. Boston: Beacon, 2010.

———. *Shake Loose My Skin*. Boston: Beacon, 1999.

Shange, Ntozake. *for colored girls who have considered suicide / when the rainbow is enuf*. 1977. New York: Macmillan, 1989.

Smith, Welton. "malcolm." In *Black Fire: An Anthology of Afro-American Writing*, ed. LeRoi Jones and Larry Neal. New York: Morrow, 1968. 283–291.

Sollors, Werner. *Beyond Ethnicity: Consent and Descent in American Culture*. New York: Oxford University Press, 1986.

Tate, Greg. "Cult-Nats Meet Freaky-Deke." In *Flyboy in the Buttermilk: Essays on Contemporary America*. New York: Simon & Schuster, 1992. 198–210.

Tolson, Melvin B. *"Harlem Gallery" and Other Poems of Melvin B. Tolson*. Ed. Raymond Nelson. Charlottesville: University Press of Virginia, 1999.

Tuma, Keith. Preface. In *Rainbow Darkness: An Anthology of African American Poetry*. Oxford, Ohio: Miami University Press, 2003. ix–xiv.

Vanderborg, Susan. *Paratextual Communities: American Avant-Garde Poetry since 1950*. Carbondale: Southern Illinois University Press, 2001.

Wagner, Jean. *Black Poets of the United States: From Paul Laurence Dunbar to Langston Hughes*. Trans. Kenneth Douglas. Urbana: University of Illinois Press, 1973.

Wright, Richard. *Haiku: This Other World*. Ed. Yoshinobu Hakutani and Robert L. Tener. New York: Arcade, 1998.

....

CHAPTER 15

ASIAN AMERICAN POETRY

....

JOSEPHINE PARK

THE varieties of Asian American poetry span the full spectrum of modern verse. This growing body of work came to life with the formation of Asian America, created against a history of American Orientalism and charged with encompassing an ever-expanding array of subjects and locations. The historian Gary Okihiro explains the origins of the designation "Asian American":

> Their classification as Asian was a European invention that named the Orient as spaces east of Europe and assigned natures, Orientalism, to its peoples. Accordingly, from 1850 to World War II, United States laws governing immigration, citizenship, and civil and property rights and social conventions and practice lumped together Chinese, Japanese, Koreans, Asian Indians, and Filipinos as an undifferentiated group. But that essentializing name was also made in America by Asians during the late 1960s, when they sought a pan-Asian identity premised upon a common past in the United States and upon a racialized politics that they believed would enable and lead to mobilization and empowerment. (xiv–xv)

In resignifying an "essentializing name," panethnic activists mobilized a new political entity—but it was one bound to a history of Orientalism. An American history of exclusion and injustice brought together disparate ethnic groups; as a result, the expressive products of this unstable unity are marked by both a converging sense of alienation within the United States and vastly divergent cultural inheritances. For Asian American poets, an American poetic tradition steeped in Orientalism applied a distinctly formal pressure on their work; they carved their verse into a literary terrain overrun with Oriental fantasies.

Perhaps the best illustration of an Orientalist poetic legacy may be seen in the extraordinary American career of the haiku. This now-ubiquitous form was reportedly first written in English by Sadakichi Hartmann, a naturalized American of German and Japanese ancestry who electrified the American literary scene in the 1890s. Hartmann is presently cited as the first Asian American poet—of course, an anachronistic designation for a self-styled bohemian who paraded his European and Japanese aesthetic fancies—and though his astonishingly strange writing is little read, his influence was widely felt. The delirious riot of his art is most evident in the culminating scene of his 1897 play *Buddha*: "A kaleidoscopical symphony of color effects continually changing … and at last improvising an outburst of new colors, like ultra red and violet, for which optical instruments have first to be invented before the human eye can perceive and enjoy them" (Chang, *Quiet Fire*, 4–5). *Buddha* was one of a series of sacrilegious dramas that Hartmann penned (he served jail time for *Christ*), and the eastern theme was a vehicle for "an outburst of new colors," which called forth a future perception. Among his admirers was Ezra Pound, whose interest in East Asian verse played a significant part in his revolution of American poetry. In Pound's account of crafting his most famous poem, "In a Station of the Metro" (1913), he describes a process of paring down a thirty-line poem into a single "*hokku*-like sentence" (*Gaudier-Brzeska*, 89). That small poem was the centerpiece of the Imagist movement, which Pound famously defined as poetry that captured "an intellectual and emotional complex in an instant of time" (*Literary Essays*, 4)—a movement shot through with a reverence for Asian poetic forms.

For Japanese immigrants in the United States, traditional poetic forms were commonly featured in community publications, and when they were incarcerated en masse in the American West after Pearl Harbor, the constraints of Japanese verse provided apt modes for conveying their devastating experience. Haiku and tanka were the predominant literary expressions of the internment camps; they were written in Japanese by the first generation and translated by the second, as in Yoshiko Uchida's translations of her mother's verse, included in her 1984 memoir of internment, *Desert Exile*:

> Plate in hand,
> I stand in line,
> Losing my resolve
> To hide my tears. (83)

The poem captures the precise moment of broken resolve, brought on by the loss of domestic life and an attendant failure to hold in private feelings. And beyond this individual shattering, Japanese verse enticed all manner of American writers, including luminaries of the fifties counterculture, who discovered a cool transcendence in its measured lines. One collection exemplifies the postwar Americanization of the haiku: *Trip Trap*, a slim volume of irreverent haiku by Jack Kerouac, Lew Welch, and Albert Saijo, a Japanese American poet whom Kerouac met in San Francisco. Written during a 1959 road trip in Welch's jeepster, this rowdy bunch shouted haiku into the American landscape. From the desolation of the camps to the expanse of the American road, the small compass of the Japanese verse form could express both constriction and sudden transport.

The haiku presented a different kind of constraint on the poets of the Asian American movement. As the form took hold in America, Asian American poets found themselves shackled to its halting tones and ponderous silences. For Lawson Fusao Inada, the most well-known poet of the activist movement, the haiku became a despised emblem of Orientalist expectations. Inada excoriated fellow Asian American poets who, in his estimation, were "trying to sound acceptable 'Oriental,'" and he vowed not to write in the form: "No doubt a quaint collection of cricket haikus would have been cause to praise my Oriental sensibility" (qtd. in Kim, 235). Freighted with such associations, the haiku became a target for Asian American poets in the wake of the activist movement. Its all-too-recognizable spareness consistently revived the old specter of Orientalism—but the form could be put to ironic use. John Yau's "Sam Spade Haiku" (1988) whittled pulp fiction into Imagistic lines:

Perfect oval	Dark intermission
Unlaced leather smile	Satin waist nipper
Tall drink of water	Coal blue lips
Fist full of trouble	Pink alabaster burden (188)

Yau brought together the clichés of hardboiled talk and haiku. The pairing reveals the power of haiku form: it newly arrests these old lines. The first and last words of the poem convey the haiku's legacy for Asian American poets: it is a perfect burden that requires a wit as sharp as Yau's to pull off.

At the end of the twentieth century, Albert Saijo evoked his old road trip with Kerouac and Welch in his first published book of verse, *Outspeaks* (1997). In the emphatic capital letters of the collection, Saijo describes a peculiar haunting in "A SYLLOGISM NO DOUBT":

I COULDN'T BRING IT BACK—I WAS AT AN ODD PLACE WHERE THE WAKING STATE SLEEP & THE DREAMSTATE MET & A POEM OR APHO- RISM OR CALL IT WHAT YOU WILL CAME TO ME—I SET IT OUT IN PER- FECT DICTION WITH JUST THE RIGHT WORDS—THE FEELING & IDEA WERE EXPRESSED COMPLETELY IN 3 SHORT SENTENCES—NOW I SAID I'LL WAKE UP AND WRITE IT DOWN—BUT ON THE JOURNEY FROM THERE BACK TO THE WAKING STATE I LOST IT THE POEM OR APHO- RISM OR CALL IT WHAT YOU WILL—I EVEN WENT BACK TO THE PLACE WHERE IT CAME TO ME & I EVEN FOUND IT AGAIN BUT BRINGING IT BACK I LOST IT AGAIN—YOU WOULD NEVER BELIEVE HOW BEAUTIFUL IT WAS (69)

Saijo's "feeling & idea" recalls Pound's "intellectual and emotional complex," but the compact perfection of these "3 short sentences" "with just the right words" cannot be retrieved. Saijo expresses an unbridgeable distance between poem and poet; the beauty of the poem is in fact premised upon its loss. The haiku belongs to a distant time and place and only the process of losing it can be expressed.

This brief sketch of the haiku's fate illustrates both the major influence of Oriental form on American poetry and the consequences of this legacy for Asian

American poets. The appreciation of Oriental art in the United States has long operated in tandem with an utter lack of interest in living Asians—they are two sides of the coin of Orientalism, which fantasizes aesthetic ideals and abjects other bodies. The panethnic Asian American coalition of the late 1960s modeled itself after earlier cultural nationalist movements, and it followed its predecessors in poetic experiments that aimed to capture a new awareness and to voice antiracist resistance. Born in the movement, Asian American poetry matched the formal constraints of Orientalism in verse to a history of racial denigration. In the wake of the activist moment, however, some poets registered a loss of something beautiful: Saijo's memory of haiku muses upon its loss but does not attempt to recreate it, but other poets imagined such forms afresh—and still others bypassed this vexed formal history.

Theorizations of Asian American poetry have lagged behind its practice. The late appearance of scholarly work on the subject in part reflects the slow inclusion of poetry in the field of Asian American literature. The defining anthology of the ethnic nationalist movement, *Aiiieeeee!* (1974), largely a recovery project that sought to create a canon of non-Orientalist literary works written by Chinese Americans, Japanese Americans, and Filipino Americans, included no poetry. Years later, an expanded version of the anthology titled *The Big Aiiieeeee!* (1991) made up for this initial omission, but the burgeoning scholarship in Asian American literature in the intervening years was almost entirely devoted to fiction and autobiography.

We can chart scholarship on Asian American poetry from Shirley Geok-lin Lim's foundational essay "Reconstructing Asian-American Poetry: A Case for Ethnopoetics" (1987), which argues for "ethnocentered reading" (51). Lim excoriates Orientalist ornament in minority verse, and her essay suggests the range of textures and nuances possible in a poetics fully engaged with questions of ethnicity. By 1992, George Uba suggested a new turn for poets in a postactivist era, who "have been thrust back on their sense of an individual self" and back "toward European-American poetics" (35). Uba's call for multiple poetic genealogies was echoed by several poets in the 1990s, as in Garrett Hongo's introduction to his 1993 anthology of Asian American poetry, *The Open Boat*, in which he criticized *Aiiieeeee!*'s "strongly worded and hectoring introduction" (xxvi), declaring instead that "being doctrinaire is not a requirement for inclusion in this anthology" (xxxviii). Both the "doctrinaire" cry of *Aiiieeeee!* and Hongo's more "open" policy of inclusion are crucial to Asian American poetry: a resistant mode defines the field; an expansive one enlarges it.

The scholarship that followed discovered different ways of bridging this division between activist and postactivist poetics. In a 1996 overview of Asian American poetry, Juliana Chang secures a shared, albeit "rough and uneven terrain" for Asian American poetry by calling attention to "histories of psychic or material violence" ("Reading," 94): Asian American poetry as a whole can be read as a mode of resistance to a dominant culture that conceals such violence. Following Chang's assertion of a common ground for Asian American poetry, Sunn Shelley Wong in a 2001 assessment of the field suggests a shared condition: "we may characterize the Asian

American poet's existence in the English language as one of estrangement" (301). This sense of alienation leads to multiple kinds of difficulty—and through a structural elaboration of these different types, Wong finds a way of discussing activist and postactivist poetry without privileging either.

The first booklength studies that paid considerable attention to Asian American poetry appeared in the twenty-first century. In the first monograph entirely devoted to Asian American poetry, Xiaojing Zhou's *The Ethics and Poetics of Alterity in Asian American Poetry* (2006) reconsiders the question of Orientalist otherness that first sparked Asian American poetry in order to uncover an ethics of alterity at the heart of minority writing. In Zhou's work, we witness scholarship on Asian American poetry come full circle: from Lim's championing of an "ethnopoetics" against Orientalist othering to Zhou's "deeper roots" (19) of an other buried within the self, which ultimately undoes the split between the self and the other that fuels Orientalism.

Zhou's study is part of a recent flurry in scholarship in Asian American poetry. These new approaches are part of a growing interest in poetics and minority literary study, as in Timothy Yu's *Race and the Avant-Garde* (2009), which examines the significance of race to modern American poetry. Redefining the American avant-garde as "an attempt to create a community by aesthetic means" (6), Yu constructs a critical framework for the aesthetic formation of Asian American poetry. A renewed attention to transnational and diasporic frames in literary and cultural studies has been particularly fruitful for scholarship in Asian American poetry: Yunte Huang's two books *Transpacific Displacements* (2002) and *Transpacific Imaginations* (2008) attest to the multiple points of intertextual contact and the profound ties between the United States and Asia throughout American poetry; Benzi Zhang's *Asian Diaspora Poetry in North America* (2008) uses a postcolonial framework to understand the diversity of Asian North American poetries; and my *Apparitions of Asia* (2008) reads transpacific crossings in American poetry through the lens of Orientalist form.

This new scholarship is the product of a surge in interest in a handful of Asian American poets whose works have acquired critical weight in a number of different fields. Asian American poetry is no longer consigned to the "new directions" back section of studies of Asian American literature—instead, key works have become centerpieces of literary scholarship in wide-ranging inquiries into racial formation and formal innovation. From this overview of the late-blooming critical scholarship on Asian American poetics, then, the remainder of this chapter turns to read some of the significant poems that have shaped the field of Asian American poetry—and reshaped the broader American literary canon.

The early poetry written by Asians in the United States was the work of immigrant laborers and foreign students—roles that often merged into each other, with migrant workers who composed their verse in rare moments of contemplation, in which they schooled themselves in the art of verse, and scions of wealthy families who found themselves serving as houseboys to fund their studies. Recognition of their work relied on their mastery of English, both for American publication and for their eventual recuperation within the Asian American movement, whose activist artists were second-generation immigrants who developed their American voices often at the expense of their parents' languages.

Poetry by Asian immigrants in languages other than English has yet to be collected, studied, and translated—but there are two notable exceptions: poems carved into the walls of the Angel Island Immigration Station between 1910 and 1940 by Chinese immigrants, and poetry written by Japanese immigrants in the concentration camps that held them during World War II. Significantly, selections of both of these kinds of writing appeared in *The Big Aiiieeeee!*, and they have come to represent the foundations of Asian America: these two sets of poems mark the defining outrages of Asian immigrant experience—Chinese exclusion and Japanese internment—and they graphically and formally express confinement, on the walls of the Angel Island barracks and within the bounds of traditional verse forms. It is important to note, however, that these poems established a framework for Asian American poetry that in turn constrained later artists, both for the privileging of Chinese and Japanese experience and an emphasis on poetry occasioned by political and social injustice that seemed to narrow its emotional spectrum.

Of course, the wide range of poetry by Asian immigrants and their descendants did not hew to the concerns of the activist movement. Juliana Chang's 1996 anthology, *Quiet Fire*, attests to the rich history and political and aesthetic diversity of Asian American poetry: lost, overlooked, and in some cases disdained by the activists, these poems presented fantastic scenes (as in Sadakichi Hartmann's scandalous writings of the 1890s), ecstatic visions (as in Yone Noguchi's meditations on the mystical role of the poet at the turn of the century), and calls to a collective, international consciousness (as in H. T. Tsiang's ringing 1930s Marxist verse). In dramatic contrast to the enforced and bitter isolation endured on Angel Island and in the camps, these poems reveal a wealth of contacts and influences in domestic and international literary arenas. They are products of literary communities and political allegiances long neglected by scholars, and the revelation and examination of these works have changed the shape of the field.

From these contested beginnings, I consider four key moments and approaches in Asian American poetry—modernism, activism, mainstream, and avant-garde—through readings of influential and emblematic poems.

Carlos Bulosan and José Garcia Villa provide two matching portraits of poets who achieved significant recognition in the 1940s—but through very different talents. Both poets were born in the Philippines and arrived in the United States in 1930, but they occupied opposite ends of the class spectrum: Bulosan migrated to the United States in order to escape a life of penury, only to face the violent instability of migrant labor in the American West; Villa arrived in the United States to pursue a university degree and thwarted his father's hopes of a future in medicine to become a darling of the New York literati. Both possessed extraordinary literary ambitions: they voraciously consumed the Western canon, founded periodicals, and forged often intimate connections with prominent poets and arbiters of the American literary scene.

Bulosan is most famous for his autobiography *America Is in the Heart* (1946), which details the grueling hardships he endured in the Philippines and the United States, as well as the extraordinary birth of a poet out of these desperate straits. The now-canonical status of this text—an excerpt of which appeared in *Aiiieeeee!*—has overshadowed his poetry, and the longstanding neglect of Bulosan's poetry is indicative of the concerns of Asian American literature, which has been heavily invested in autobiography for its rendering of the formation of an ethnic subject. The American subject whose emergence Bulosan depicted in his autobiography was first and foremost a poet, and Bulosan captured his experiences of solidarity and alienation in ringing anthems and closely observed lyrics.

Bulosan's first published book was a collection of poetry entitled *Letter from America* (1942). "These Are Also Living" portrays those barely subsisting at the edges of a glittering American city:

> After the dreary walk and the tinsel city
> That thrusts its tongue hollowly into the night;
> After the crowded streets and the tenement houses
> Where the lost and the dying flash mocking eyes
> With indelicate movements, waiting for death;
> After the flight of watersoaked steps and dark halls,
> The uneven door and the cold room above the stairs,
> The anger in your face settles down—suddenly—
> Your lips tremble as we look into the streets below
> Where hungry men are passing into the night, moving
> Close to the buildings for warmth and comfort.
> These are also living men thrown as we are thrown
> Into the troubled room of earth, crying for bread,
> Their continuous procession into the dark streets
> Lifts a stabbing arrow of pity, striking your eyes,
> Pushing a nervous wave through your rainsoaked body.
> Why are you sobbing profusely? We too are hungry.
>   (Evangelista, 140)

The poem balances a personified city against scarcely living men: the vivid, opening portrayal of the city with thrusting tongue presents a salacious and hungry entity that has drained the men in its streets. Bulosan depicts both the men outside and the actions of two observers who move out of the crowd to observe them, and in presenting these figures, the poem charts a series of movements both "indelicate" and orderly; the movement of the hungry men sharpens into "a stabbing arrow" and sends out "a nervous wave" that pierces the speaker's companion. The procession on the street enters into the body watching it: distinctions between inside and outside fall away because the body in the cold room is as "rainsoaked" as those walking in the dark streets. The poem insists that the speaker and his companion belong to the same "troubled room of earth" occupied by the hungry men. Thus, though the poem portrays the speaker and companion climbing up above the street, their ascent does not distance them from those below—and Bulosan's pointed use of apostrophe folds the reader into the scene as well.

The poem describes a shifting emotion: the "mocking eyes" of "the lost and dying" is matched by the "anger in your face"—which then turns into trembling lips. Strikingly, the eyes do not belong to the witness, whose mouth only trembles and does not speak; the tongue belongs to the city and not to its inhabitants. A break at the heart of the poem ("—suddenly—") registers an emotional shift, in which mockery and anger give way to cries for bread, which are answered by sobs. The poem is evenly divided between hard, cold gestures in its first half and overwhelming cries and tears in the second. Yet the poem's emotional turn provides no solace; indeed, Bulosan seems to critique the companion's—and, by extension, the reader's—tendency to dissolve in the face of such appeals. "Why are you sobbing profusely?" Bulosan asks, critiquing the pity that elevates observer above observed. The poem concludes by insisting on a shared condition: "We too are hungry." He is portraying a pitiable condition, but not pitiful men: "These are also living," even as they are rendered objects in the haunting grammar of the title. The final declaration of hunger suggests a human condition, but the beauty of the poem lies in its ability to make a larger plight personal; Bulosan channels the desolation of the street into a single observer while keeping alive the city and its hungry men.

Unlike his compatriot Bulosan, Villa never depicted his experiences in America. Instead, his poems present fierce confrontations with mythical and divine beings; his compressed verse is shot through with visions that often depict a charged natural world animated by a terrible divinity. Bulosan and Villa both attracted significant admirers in the upper echelons of the American literary arena, but Villa belonged to this world; championed by the likes of e. e. cummings and Edith Sitwell, his poetry garnered major prizes and fellowships. Villa invented new forms for his otherworldly poems, and both his method and his subject matter kept him out of Asian American literary anthologies. The highly idiosyncratic forms he crafted could not be folded into a cultural legacy, and his poems were not about being American—they were thus neither Asian nor American. Villa's utter singularity as a poet isolated his work, but his verse has sustained a passionate following. In 2008, his collected poems were published by Penguin Classics, thus cementing his significance to American poetry.

Like Bulosan, Villa published his first book of poems *Have Come, Am Here*, in 1942. He later identified a method of "reversed consonance" in those poems, and his second book of poetry made his preoccupation with formal innovations astonishingly evident. *Volume Two* (1949) presented a new kind of writing: "comma poems." This new style necessitated an opening note by Villa: "The reader of the following poems may be perplexed and puzzled at my use of the comma: it is a new, special and *poetic* use to which I have put it" (78). In "Elegy for the Airplane," we witness both the perplexing quality and singular innovation of the style:

> At,last,the,automobile,flew.
> At,last,Icaros.

At,last,too,much.
At,last,too,fast.
At,last,the,present.

Flying,is,air-swimming.
Flying,is,bird-seeming.
Flying,is,death-daring.
At,last,meaning.
At,last,weaning.
At,last,morning.

Morning,is,evening,dead.
Mourning,is,for,the,dead.
Moving,is,for,the,head.
At,last,'tis,said.
At,last,we,were.
At,last,we,war.
At,last,we,fall.
At,last,we,all.
Alas,we,all. (106)

"Elegy for the Airplane" transposes Greek myth into the modern world. Most of Villa's work stays in the mythic world and makes no mention of the world of airplanes and automobiles, but the modernity on view in this poem makes it particularly revealing for sketching out Villa's world. The shock of Villa's "comma poetry" lies in the disjunction between the meditations within them and the proliferation of commas, which shatter the music of the poetry he has created. Hence, though the vast majority of his poetry never includes artifacts of the modern world, the commas that follow every word—and eviscerate the spaces between words—shoot up the lines as thoroughly as the airplane pierces the sky. The brash and machinelike perforation of the comma evinces a modern world that insists upon punctuating divine contemplation. These poems blast away rhythm and meter; because they cannot be scanned for movement and emphasis, they call forth a new reader, one who can hear and feel these breaks without losing the images and emotions that they consistently puncture.

The poem describes a long-awaited moment: "At,last,the,present." At last, we have arrived at the morning of mourning, when Icaros has fallen into the sea. The young man has finally grown up; he has been weaned, but at the cost of his life. Villa attaches "meaning" to "weaning," and in conjunction with the present, he suggests that it is death that has meaning in our present world. Prime evidence for this truth appears with "At,last,we,war": war, of course, is the paradigmatic event for young men weaned into death, and the poem suggests that we all share this experience: "At,last,we,all." The final line beautifully evokes a wearied response to this final arrival: "Alas,we,all." The machinations of the poem work to produce this final understanding, which takes a flat, well-worn sentiment and renews it. In Villa's hands, that most stock-poetic of words, "Alas," acquires a new edge, suddenly able to express a modern condition. The poem as a whole is about a movement from "At,last" to "Alas": from expectation to chagrined understanding. Yet though the poem describes an expected death, it presents poetic language infused with new life.

These very different poems by Bulosan and Villa describe ascensions that reveal a fall at the heart of the modern condition. Against the bodies of Bulosan's hungry men, however, Villa turns first to Icaros and then inside, into the mind: "Moving,is,for,the,head." If Bulosan's poem collapses the distinction between inside and outside, Villa is ultimately presenting an interiorizing trajectory. Villa's poems are, without question, "for,the,head"; they require a critical labor that readers have come to identify with modernist poetry, and in his own inimical fashion, he chops up the surface of his poems to roil the sentiments beneath. Yet Bulosan's poem is the more precise in feeling: he separates pity from anger and then refuses both to express an absolute expression of hunger. In appealing to universal desires and expressions, Bulosan and Villa are finally both products of the modernist literary era, which packaged universalist sentiments within broken visions and fractured forms.

A generation later, the poets of the Asian American movement valorized particular experiences: instead of matching their experiences to a universal plight, their art sought to express conditions unique to this newly formed group. The movement poets emphatically broke from literary and cultural traditions that marginalized and silenced their voices, and they fought to install new traditions. Lawson Fusao Inada and Janice Mirikitani led the crusade: both poets fostered the movement by editing and facilitating groundbreaking collections of poetry, and their verse established new, collective rhythms. Significantly, Inada and Mirikitani were both interned as children during World War II, and their poetry targeted the wall of silence that surrounded Japanese internment: their work sounds a call to speak out and to sing.

One of the editors of the landmark *Aiiieeeee!* anthologies, Inada played a significant part in shaping the Asian American literary tradition. His contributions to the 1991 anthology spelled out the tradition and his role in it, as well as the uses of this tradition for coming generations of Asian Americans. "The Discovery of Tradition" recounts the wonder of Inada's discovery of literary predecessors. The poem is dedicated to two Japanese American fiction writers: Toshio Mori and John Okada. Mori is best known for his carefully crafted short stories in *Yokohama, California* (1949), which depicted a Japanese American community, and Okada's only published novel, *No-No Boy* (1957), a once-forgotten, now-canonical account of the trauma of internment and resistance to military conscription, was rediscovered and championed by the activist movement.

"The Discovery of Tradition" imagines these artists together: "I'm sitting here with Toshio and John, / talking over such momentous things" (Chin, *The Big Aiiieeeee!*, 604). Though he never met his progenitors, Inada establishes a familial and natural relation with them; together, they create a living body of tradition figured as flowing river. By imagining an intimacy between these artists, the poem provides a model for establishing a personal literary tradition. For Inada, the work of poetry is the work of fashioning a suitable tradition and demonstrating how to inhabit it. "The Discovery of Tradition" imagines a series of encounters with Mori and Okada, and the final section, entitled "The Rhythm of Tradition," depicts an annual activity in the Japanese American community, the making of rice cakes: "(and we, the hands, including Toshio and John, / looked up between the force of our strokes / and smiled, since mochi-making / brings your energy out into the rice and air / where it can be shared again)" (607–608). Matching the rhythm of an ethnic communal activity to the movement of poetry, Inada marks a new, Asian American time.

From "The Discovery of Tradition," Inada turns to future generations in "On Being Asian American," in which he portrays a "journey" to become Asian American. "Distinctions are earned," Inada writes, because "not everyone / can be an Asian American." The poem is at pains to explain that this new identity is not an accident of birth; it is a conscious movement. Thus, for Inada, neither tradition nor being is a given: the movement transformed both into activities. The poem, however, anticipates a hesitation:

> Take me as I am, you cry.
> I, I, am an individual.
> Which certainly is true.
> Which generates an echo. (619)

The echoing "I" that opens the cry of the second line becomes evidence for an echo that has the potential to bring together many such "I"s; the new formation is not a mass formation but a gathering of individuals who have "arrived" at a shared consciousness. Inada's verse imagines group formations by hitching individual movements to a larger whole, and his work is most innovative for the music he imagines. The ambling rhythms of his verse often build in warmth, and Inada's oeuvre may best be described as a poetry of welcome, which offers to take in and shelter those out in the cold. The embrace of his poetry, however, does not make universal appeals; instead, Inada's poetry folds in particular individuals in order to create an assembly of shared convictions.

Mirikitani's verse, too, expresses a preoccupation with tradition, but her poems unsettle received traditions. Her poem "Breaking Silence" lent its title to the first published anthology of Asian American poetry, which appeared in 1983. The poem's dedication explains that it was composed "For my mother's testimony before Commission on Wartime Relocation and Internment of Japanese American Civilians," and it features portions of this testimony alongside a portrait of her mother, who moves from silence to speech: "We were told / that silence was better / golden like our skin" (Bruchac, 189). The color of silence is the color of skin: from this racialized injunction against speech, the poem goes on to portray the emergence of Mirikitani's mother's speech as a "yellow flame" that heats her testimony, imagined as water brought to boil. In moving from golden silence to yellow flame, the poem reassigns a raced quality: from Asian silence to a new kind of raced speech—Asian American speech—that exposes injustice. With the light of this flame, "everything is made visible":

> We see the cracks and fissures in our soil:
> We speak of suicides and intimacies,
> of longings lush like wet furrows,
> of oceans bearing us toward imagined riches,
> of burning humiliations and
> crimes by the government. (191)

The call to address the unspeakable—"suicides and intimacies"—builds toward the two essential components of Asian American experience: the migration "toward imagined riches" of the American Dream, and the "burning humiliations" that follow once on American soil. Asian American poetry can thus express private desire and expose state crimes. The poem concludes,

> We must recognize ourselves at last
> We are a rainforest of color
> and noise.
> We hear everything.
> We are unafraid.
> Our language is beautiful. (191)

This language is beautiful because it expresses an awakened collectivity and bears witness to its hardship. The fullness of the final line is striking: Mirikitani's art marks a complete divergence from the standard of pregnant silence that has come to define an American poetic tradition informed by Japanese verse.

Mirikitani's second poem in *Breaking Silence* makes explicit her resistance to tradition. Written for her daughter, "Breaking Tradition" (192) depicts a daughter breaking loose from her mother's hold. The poem begins with "My daughter denies she is like me," a line matched by "I deny I am like my mother," thus installing a tradition of breaking tradition. The poem concludes with this identity between them: "She mirrors my aging. / She is breaking tradition." The mirror does not shatter in this poem—instead, tradition does. Though this lesson neatly encases the poems, it is a difficult realization; we hear the pain of isolation: "I want to tell her about the empty room / of myself. / This room we lock ourselves in." The empty room of the self has little to offer to succeeding generations; it can only transmit the fact of the room and imprisonment. The chain from Mirikitani's mother to daughter is thus a series of closed doors: the poem offers a glimpse into each woman's room, but each is sealed off and ultimately unknowable to the others. Of course, the poem itself brings together these three generations, but the structural similarity between the women—which the poem renders with a repeated set of indentations—offers only cold comfort.

Between Inada and Mirikitani, we experience contrasting portrayals of an emerging Asian American collective: alongside Inada's manly embrace, we hear the unsettled voices of women yearning to speak out in Mirikitani's verse. These poets shouldered an extraordinary—and exhilarating—task, and their work acknowledges the difficulty of ushering in a new, shared voice: the fear of losing the individual self and the locked isolation of the self. Modern conceptions of lyric poetry have privileged an individual, private voice, but the poetry of Inada and Mirikitani opens up the often narrowed form of the modern lyric: not only do they include other voices, but their verse consistently moves toward a plural first person. Inada insisted that being Asian American meant becoming Asian American; Mirikitani understood that "We must recognize ourselves at last." Theirs is poetry meant to be spoken aloud, and they invited new voices. For the collective voice of the activist movement, the individual, locked interior could pose a threat—but for poets who imagined a different path from the journey toward becoming celebrated by the movement, the ringing tones of movement poetics could themselves feel like a constraint.

The field of Asian American poetry dramatically widened in the 1980s, and a handful of poets achieved mainstream recognition. The acclaimed poems of Cathy Song and Li-young Lee present intimate voices that captivated Asian American readers as well as established American poets. Both poets depict the experience of being Asian in America, but they do not pitch their voices as representatives of a larger collective. This verse does not make explicit appeals to particular groups—but neither does it make universalizing gestures. These poets describe deeply felt experiences ordered into epiphanies.

Song's 1982 collection, *Picture Bride*, which was enthusiastically received by prominent American poets, transported her work beyond the circle of minority poetry. "The Youngest Daughter" describes an intimate scene of tenderness and repugnance between daughter and mother:

> This morning
> her breathing was graveled,
> her voice gruff with affection
> when I wheeled her into the bath.
> She was in a good humor,
> making jokes about her great breasts,
> floating in the milky water
> like two walruses,
> flaccid and whiskered around the nipples.
> I scrubbed them with a sour taste
> in my mouth, thinking:
> six children and an old man
> have sucked from these brown nipples. (5)

The vision of the mother's body brings forth a sour taste pungent enough to pucker the reader's mouth. The animal portrayal of the mother's breasts suggests a wild family, untouched by culture, both in the larger civilizational sense and the specific trappings of an Asian family. The preceding poem—the opening and title piece—presents a very different portrait of this mother: "Picture Bride" imagines her mother's arrival in Hawaii from Korea, picturing her clothed in "the silk bow of her jacket, / her tent-shaped dress / filling with the dry wind" (4). Decades later, and stripped of her Korean dress, this mother is not portrayed as an Asian body but as a large, spent, and helpless one.

The poem concludes with a very different rendering of the daughter's body:

> In the afternoons
> when she has rested,
> she prepares our ritual of tea and rice,
> garnished with a shred of gingered fish,
> a slice of pickled turnip,
> a token for my white body.
> We eat in the familiar silence.
> She knows I am not to be trusted,
> even now planning my escape.
> As I toast to her health
> with the tea she has poured,
> a thousand cranes curtain the window,
> fly up in a sudden breeze. (6)

Against the weight of the mother's body, the daughter's is strikingly immaterial: her "white body" only appears after the ritual of tea and rice. This body is interestingly clothed in ritual, and if the mother's breasts brought forth a sour taste, the daughter's body flashes white with the taste of delicate morsels: "a shred of gingered fish, / a slice of pickled turnip." This body's whiteness is not a marker of race but an element of contrast to the mother's body that had been darkened by years of labor; the poem began with the pale skin of the daughter, which "feels the way / mother's used to before the drying sun / parched it out there in the fields" (5).

And yet this whiteness is also inseparable from race: the daughter's whiteness is intertwined with identifiably Asian rituals; she is legible within a mainstream that has long cherished such details. The refinement of Asian images played a significant part in sharpening American poetry, and the concluding lines of the poem, with its "thousand cranes" and "sudden breeze," bear the hallmarks of the haiku: a moving evocation of nature and a sudden turn. The daughter's desired escape flutters these curtains—and perhaps it is through the thousand cranes that she will find a way out. The Asian image enjoys an astonishing freedom that the Asian American laborer does not.

Like Song's *Picture Bride*, Lee's first book of poems, *Rose* (1986), has enjoyed an admiring and even passionate following by a wide-ranging audience. Unlike Song's verse, whose at once lovely and unsettling tones echo the dictates of observation and precision that have come to characterize the mainstream of modern American poetry from Imagism onward, Lee's poetry roams a surprisingly vast terrain. The way in which he stalks his images and the arc of his verse push his work to the edge of modern poetry and back to a descriptive intensity more reminiscent of Romanticism.

One of his most well-known poems, "Persimmons," opens with a childhood memory:

> In sixth grade Mrs. Walker
> slapped the back of my head
> and made me stand in the corner
> for not knowing the difference
> between *persimmon* and *precision*.
> How to choose
>
> persimmons. This is precision.
> Ripe ones are soft and brown-spotted.
> Sniff the bottoms. The sweet one
> will be fragrant. How to eat:
> put the knife away, lay down newspaper.
> Peel the skin tenderly, not to tear the meat.
> Chew the skin, suck it,
> and swallow. Now, eat
> the meat of the fruit,
> so sweet,
> all of it, to the heart. (17)

The poem's "precision" has nothing to do with its method, which forsakes the precision of an image in order to revel in sensual appreciation. A strange vengefulness runs through this opening, from the teacher's slap to the adult consumption of the fruit. The poem's sensory riot, however, does not quite overrun its lines: "Persimmons" relies on controlled line breaks in order to experience this particular forbidden fruit.

The eating of the fruit leads to a different scene of instruction:

> Donna undresses, her stomach is white.
> In the yard, dewy and shivering
> with crickets, we lie naked,
> face-up, face-down.
> I teach her Chinese.
> Crickets: *chiu chiu*. Dew: I've forgotten.
> Naked: I've forgotten.
> *Ni, wo*: you and me.
> I part her legs,
> remember to tell her
> she is as beautiful as the moon. (17)

This scene registers the distance between the sixth-grade child and the adult: the child made mistakes in English, but the man has forgotten Chinese. Donna's whiteness both necessitates his translation of Chinese and accelerates his forgetting. Between the classroom and the nighttime scene, the persimmon functions as a hinge from one identity, defined by a linguistic failing, to a new one equally tied to language loss.

The poem, however, is not done with persimmons. Lee returns to the fruit to define his relations with his parents: his mother emphasizes the "golden, glowing" (18) warmth of the fruit, and for his father, who is losing his sight, the "ripe weight" (19) of persimmons offers loving solace. Indeed, the poem's persimmons are touched by every sense but sight—we never quite see the fruit; instead, we are given the intense feelings they inspire. The objects of Lee's poems are full to bursting; they are not images but touchstones for passionate and poignant emotion. In "Persimmons," the classroom offers an instance of minority subject formation, but it is not this identity that interests Lee. Just as Song's poem depicts a longing to escape, Lee's verse is marked by a tendency toward flight. These flights—and often falls—are deeply interior ones, which finally admit only a singular lyric first person.

The distance between the movement poetics of Inada and Mirikitani and the mainstream accolades garnered by Song and Lee seemed to rehearse a familiar debate in literary study: politics versus aesthetics. This manufactured and ultimately impossible division provided an axis for reading minority literature. The novelty of a work of art is typically registered by fixing preceding works into stable categories, and innovative works are sometimes appreciated by flattening the past. In Asian American poetry, a new text shone at the end of the century: Theresa Hak Kyung Cha's *Dictée*, first published in 1982 but only appreciated a decade later. We may read the late reception of this work as an indication of the field's ability to incorporate it; in the 1990s, *Dictée* appeared to bridge the constructed gap between minority political demands and aesthetic difficulty. *Dictée* revealed as much about the field of Asian American poetry as it did about the complicated speaker and journey depicted in its pages. The hindsight afforded by the text tended to imagine Asian American poetry as a narrative of development: early setbacks and strides, a rebellious phase, and then verse that conformed to rules set by mainstream standards of taste and style. Celebrated for its complexity, Cha's work seemed to announce the full maturation of the field.

Dictée is an experimental epic composed of nine sections named after the Classical muses and shaped into a novena. Through its avant-garde strategies, the text weaves together different kinds of afflictions: individual somatic concerns, mythic plights, and political occupations. *Dictée* delves into a single body in order to survey a complex political history: a speaker Cha names the "diseuse"—gendered in French, a language the text constantly returns to in order to express difference and untranslatability—becomes a vehicle for uncovering many different voices. Through these multiple voices, *Dictée* imparts a history lesson: the neocolonial relation between the United States and Korea. Cha includes in full a 1905 "Petition from the Koreans of Hawaii to President Roosevelt," which warns of an impending occupation by Japan. The petition failed, and the text dwells on the consequences: colonization, division, and war. Cha explains the significance of this history:

> Why resurrect it all now. From the Past. History, the old wound. The past emo-
> tions all over again. To confess to relive the same folly. To name it now so as not
> to repeat history in oblivion. To extract each fragment by each fragment from the
> word from the image another word another image the reply that will not repeat
> history in oblivion. (33)

The "old wound" of history is the fountainhead of her art: from its source, words and images come forth. Cha distinguishes between reliving and repeating history: *Dictée* relives history in a ritualized Catholic confession as a deliberate counter to repeating history. Against the oblivion of repetition, she is arguing for an embodied remembering.

Dictée is remarkable for its wealth of allusions: alongside historical documents, the text relives Classical epics, silent films, and Korean folk tales. Yet amid these multiple influences, Cha makes painfully clear the specific contours of a Korean American experience. The text sketches out an astonishing artistic freedom, but all of its innovations are anchored to a central experience of occupation and the difficulty of expressing this condition. Political occupation penetrates the individual body; the text captures the pervasiveness of occupation by plumbing its living depths, felt deeply by Cha herself. And in painstakingly expressing "each fragment by each fragment," Cha holds out the revolutionary possibility that an aesthetic rendering of the experience of occupation may be more than mere representation—it can bring a speaker to life.

In tracing a colonial history into American minority experience, *Dictée* insisted on a transnational vision, and it roved the world for influences. Because it braids together multiple genealogies, Cha's work has invited multiple interpretive frameworks. Her work is presently read in both minority literary study and studies of avant-garde literature—indeed, *Dictée* has become a bridge between these critical traditions. Hence, just as Cha's text has been lauded for healing a divide between ethnic nationalism and aesthetics within Asian American poetry, it has stretched across a larger version of the same artificial divide, this time between minority and avant-garde writing.

Most significantly, however, *Dictée* has inspired artists. In *The Shock of Arrival* (1996), Meena Alexander cites Cha's influence:

> And so the questions of colonialism bleed into an era of decolonization, into the
> complicated realms of American ethnicity. They mark our memory. Our spiritual
> flesh cannot be torn apart, cannot be cleansed. I think of the haunting lines in
> Theresa Cha's *Dictée*. The image is that of a fine cloth folded, perhaps a handker-
> chief: "Already there are folds remnant from the previous foldings now leaving a
> permanent mark." Elsewhere in the same book, she writes of how the stain begins
> to absorb the material it is spilt upon.
>   Memory in this postcolonial world transforms what lies around it. (5–6)

Alexander's text is a collection of essays, stories, and poems that examines "questions of colonialism" and "the complicated realms of American ethnicity." The intertwined pieces of the text demonstrate that aesthetic products are inseparable from the conditions that bring them to life. Alexander's intertextual relation to Cha marks a shared condition of postcoloniality that bleeds into their American lives. In this transmission, we witness again the power of opening the wound of history: the global south comes into view, linking continents as well as disparate American experiences.

In a passage entitled "That Other Body," Alexander traces the emergence of the poem out of the wound of history:

> The imagination strikes against the stones of a city, against the stubble at the edge of a city.
> The stones and stubble cry back.
> The response cannot be willed. The will has little to do with the workings of imagination.
> I must write what I hear: both cry and response, till the poem, instead of being cut and polished like a stone—though who does not long for solidity, for precision?—is glimpsed as a body, another body, *chinmaya deha*.
> This other body is formed within mine, at times with the speed of lightning, at times with the infinite patience of sunlight that strikes at a billowing curtain, muslin puffing and weaving in the wind.
> This image has force. It fills my hollow body with light, tilts the exile that is so often forced upon us so that to say, "I," in another country, becomes a recognition of truth.
> Change comes from this voice, this listening: the imagination striking the world, the world crying out in its own innumerable tongues. (111)

The initial spark of poetry is imagination striking "the stones of a city." The poet takes in this impetus, which comes to life within her body. Alexander's longing "for solidity, for precision" reveals both the desires and limitations of the poet. Her image is not the silent perfection of haiku but a force capable of moving the poet to speak and to say "I." In describing the life cycle of a poem, Alexander moves from the world into an individual body and then back out, into the world.

The movement between a complex world and a marked individual lies at the heart of all of the poems featured in this essay. The field of Asian American poetry has been shaped by pendulum swings between worlds and selves, and the visions and voices exhibited in these texts describe very different ambitions. For all of these poets, the "I" of poetry that Alexander describes as "a recognition of truth" is an ethnic or diasporic identity. Whether or not this "truth" is evident in the lines of the poem, the gestation of the "other body" of the poem within a racially marked body conditions its emergence. Of course, it was the problem of the other that launched the creation of Asian America in the first place, and the notion of Asian American aesthetic products as being themselves other bodies reveals how thoroughly its political origins continue to bleed into its poetry.

Asian American poets in the twenty-first century are heirs to a rich legacy. Two recent anthologies demonstrate the breadth and diversity of this work: *Asian American Poetry: The Next Generation* (2004), which registers significant debts to the work of past generations and the new political and aesthetic exigencies of the next, and *Indivisible: An Anthology of Contemporary South Asian American Poetry* (2010), which redresses the longstanding lacuna of South Asian American literature within Asian America by celebrating verse by this heterogeneous population that is united by experiences of diaspora and division. These collections reveal both the continuing significance of the creation of Asian America as well as the importance of exploring the expressions of a particular group, which in turn uncovers a rich and complex literature with multiple genealogies. Asian American poetry has undergone a series of expansions and constrictions; this work reaches back into different pasts and stretches across oceans, and it presents American experiences too often obscured and unheard.

REFERENCES

Alexander, Meena. *The Shock of Arrival: Reflections on Postcolonial Experience.* Boston: South End, 1996.

Bannerjee, Neelanjana, Summi Kaipa, and Pireeni Sundaralingam, eds. *Indivisible: An Anthology of Contemporary South Asian American Poetry.* Fayetteville: University of Arkansas Press, 2010.

Bruchac, Joseph, ed. *Breaking Silence: An Anthology of Contemporary Asian American Poets.* Greenfield Center, NY: Greenfield Review, 1983.

Bulosan, Carlos. *America Is in the Heart.* Seattle: University of Washington Press, 1973.

Cha, Theresa Hak Kyung. *Dictée.* Berkeley, CA: Third Woman, 1995.

Chang, Juliana. "Reading Asian American Poetry." *MELUS* 21.1 (1996): 81–98.

———, ed. *Quiet Fire: A Historical Anthology of Asian American Poetry, 1892–1970.* New York: The Asian American Writer's Workshop, 1996.

Chang, Victoria, ed. *Asian American Poetry: The Next Generation.* Urbana: University of Illinois Press, 2004.

Chin, Frank, Jeffrey Paul Chan, Lawson Fusao Inada, and Shawn Hsu Wong, eds. *Aiiieeeee! An Anthology of Asian-American Writers.* Washington, DC: Howard University Press, 1974.

———. *The Big Aiiieeeee! An Anthology of Chinese American and Japanese American Literature.* New York: Meridian-Penguin, 1991.

Evangelista, Susan. *Carlos Bulosan and His Poetry: A Biography and Anthology.* Seattle: University of Washington Press, 1985.

Hongo, Garrett. "Introduction." In *The Open Boat: Poems from Asian America,* ed. Garrett Hongo. New York: Anchor, 1993. xvii–xlii.

Huang, Yunte. *Transpacific Displacements: Intertextual Travel in Twentieth-Century American Literature.* Berkeley: University of California Press, 2002.

———. *Transpacific Imaginations: History, Literature, Counterpoetics.* Cambridge: Harvard University Press, 2008.

Kerouac, Jack, Albert Saijo, and Lew Welch. *Trip Trap: Haiku on the Road.* San Francisco: Grey Fox, 2001.

Kim, Elaine H. *Asian American Literature: An Introduction to the Writings and Their Social Context.* Philadelphia, Temple University Press, 1982.

Lee, Li-young. *Rose.* Brockport, NY: Boa Editions, 1986.

Lim, Shirley Geok-lin. "Reconstructing Asian-American Poetry: A Case for Ethnopoetics." *MELUS* 14.2 (1987): 51–63.

Mori, Toshio. *Yokohama, California*. Seattle: University of Washington Press, 1985.

Okada, John. *No-No Boy*. Seattle: University of Washington Press, 1979.

Okihiro, Gary. *The Columbia Guide to Asian American History*. New York: Columbia University Press, 2001.

Park, Josephine Nock-Hee. *Apparitions of Asia: Modernist Form and Asian American Poetics*. New York: Oxford University Press, 2008.

Pound, Ezra. *Gaudier-Brzeska: A Memoir*. New York: New Directions, 1970.

———. *Literary Essays of Ezra Pound*. Ed. T. S. Eliot. New York: New Directions, 1968.

Saijo, Albert. *Outspeaks: A Rhapsody*. Honolulu: Bamboo Ridge, 1997.

Song, Cathy. *Picture Bride*. New Haven: Yale University Press, 1983.

Uba, George. "Versions of Identity in Post-Activist Asian American Poetry." In *Reading the Literatures of Asian America*, ed. Shirley Geok-lin Lim and Amy Ling. Philadelphia: Temple University Press, 1992. 33–48.

Uchida, Yoshiko. *Desert Exile: The Uprooting of a Japanese-American Family*. Seattle: University of Washington Press, 1984.

Villa, José Garcia. *Doveglion: Collected Poems*. New York: Penguin, 2008.

Wong, Sunn Shelley. "Sizing Up Asian American Poetry." In *A Resource Guide to Asian American Literature*, ed. Sau-ling Cynthia Wong and Stephen Sumida. New York: Modern Language Association, 2001. 285–307.

Yau, John. *Radiant Silhouette: New and Selected Work, 1974–1988*. Santa Rosa, CA: Black Sparrow, 1994.

Yu, Timothy. *Race and the Avant-Garde: Experimental and Asian American Poetry since 1965*. Stanford: Stanford University Press, 2009.

Zhang, Benzi. *Asian Diaspora Poetry in North America*. New York: Routledge, 2008.

Zhou, Xiaojing. *The Ethics and Poetics of Alterity in Asian American Poetry*. Iowa City: University of Iowa Press, 2006.

CHAPTER 16

"THE PARDON OF SPEECH": THE PSYCHOANALYSIS OF MODERN AMERICAN POETRY

WALTER KALAIDJIAN

Hieroglyphics of hysteria, blazons of phobia, labyrinths of the *Zwangsneurose*—charms of impotence, enigmas of inhibition, oracles of anxiety, talking arms of character, seals of self-punishment, disguises of perversion—these are the hermetic elements that our exegesis resolves...in a deliverance of the imprisoned meaning, from the revelation of the palimpsest to the given word of the mystery and the pardon of speech.

—Lacan, "Function," 76

Hailed on his seventieth birthday as "the discoverer of the unconscious," Sigmund Freud nevertheless declined this accolade. "The poets and philosophers," he pointed out, "before me discovered the unconscious. What I discovered was the scientific method by which the unconscious can be studied" (Trilling, 34). However gracious, Freud's self-effacing disclaimer also performs a symptomatic gesture insofar as it dwells on the analyst's belated relation to the poet. Likewise, the former's scientific stance serves arguably as a defense against the latter's powers of psychic discernment. Beginning with Freud, the modern analyst and modern poet share a vexed but reciprocal investment in exploring the unconscious.[1] In this vein, the "psychoanalysis of modern poetry" reads as a double genitive: signifying poetry's paradoxical status both as the literary object of clinical analysis and as a forceful agent of psychic revelation. Unlike analysis, however, poetry offers neither a science of nor cure for the anxieties, neuroses, and psychoses of social modernity. Rather, as an envoi of the unconscious, poetry gives testimony to the latter's mystery and enigma in the linguistic registers of what Jacques Lacan describes as "the pardon of speech."

Psychoanalysis arrived in the United States early on in the twentieth century and was popularized by Freud himself after his Clark University lectures in 1909. Americans received Freud with enthusiasm, but "they don't realize," he reportedly quipped to Carl Jung on their arrival, "we are bringing them the plague."[2] Indeed, the new science of psychoanalysis was contagious and quickly spread through A. A. Brill's translation of the third edition of *The Interpretation of Dreams* in 1913, *The Psychopathology of Everyday Life* (1914), and *Jokes and Their Relation to the Unconscious* (1916), accompanied by popularizing introductions by Max Eastman in *Everybody's Magazine* (1915). "Everyone at that time who knew about psychoanalysis," wrote Floyd Dell of the New York avant-garde, "was a sort of missionary on the subject, and nobody could be around Greenwich Village without hearing a lot about it."[3] Meanwhile, free association, the dream work, parapraxes, and the joke were psychic resources that were also mined in the enclaves of international Dadaism, inaugurated in 1916 by the founding members of Zurich's Cabaret Voltaire: Hugo Ball, Richard Huelsenbeck, Tristan Tzara, and Jean Arp. Dadaism's anarchic attacks on tradition, decorum, and rationality as such would be an influence on the automatic writing of André Breton and the surrealist movement that was promoted in America by such editors as Margaret Anderson and Eugene Jolas in *The Little Review* (1914–1929) and *transition* (1927–1928, 1936–1938).

Freud's revolutionary theories of sexuality were soon on view in Mina Loy's 1915 contribution to Alfred Kreymborg's experimental modernist magazine *Others* (1915–1919). Lifting the veil on "Pig Cupid his rosy snout / Rooting erotic garbage" prompted the charge of "hoggerel" and a certain resistance from the critic Louis Untermeyer, who cited it as "Exhibit A, the first of Miss Loy's *chansons d'amour.*" Untermeyer not only sought to mock but also to repress the sexuality of certain modern sex reformers or "Lilliths" who "having studied Freud," he quipped, "began to exhibit their inhibitions and learned to misquote Havelock Ellis at a moment's notice" (192).[4] In fact, Mina Loy read Freud with Mabel Dodge, met him through Scofield Thayer in Vienna, sketched his profile while he read her writing, and later commented wryly that "When the Gentile world required a Saviour they nailed up the Christ. When it required a second Saviour to counteract the effects of the first, Freud was at its service."[5] Two years after Loy's American debut in *Others*, Ezra Pound—signifying on Freud's analysis of Little Hans—slyly diagnosed William Carlos Williams's nativist Anglophobia as an Oedipal symptom of rebellion against the doctor's English-born father, William George Williams: "You (read your Freud) have a *Vaterersatz*, you have a paternal image at your fireside, and you call it John Bull" (Pound, Letter, 31). For experimental modernists such as Hart Crane, psychoanalysis was more than a clinical practice; rather, it represented a distinctively modern phenomenon: one that poetry should reckon with and celebrate. Reporting to Yvor Winters on the Atlantis section of *The Bridge*, Crane described it as a "metaphysical synthesis of a number of things like aeronautics, telegraphy, psychoanalysis, atomic theory, relativity, and what not!" (Crane, 79). Psychoanalysis was not just a pursuit of the American avant-garde, but also became a hot topic in popular journalism of the 1920s. Not infrequently, as Frederick J. Hoffman has shown, Freud became the butt of low-brow humor in such magazines as *Vanity Fair* for poets like e. e. cummings and for cartoonists, sportswriters, and humorists such as the Algonquin Round Table commentator Heywood Broun, who parodied Freud in his 1922 *Vanity Fair* send-up "Bambino the Maestro: The Suggestion of a Possible Freudian Interpretation of the Aesthetic Appeal of Babe Ruth."[6]

For his part, Freud had early on admired, but also diagnosed, the figure of the poet in his seminal 1908 essay "Creative Writers and Daydreaming." In this essay, he acknowledges a certain "curiosity" fueling the analyst's epistemological drive to understand and thus master the "strange being" of the poet's creativity and its "unknown sources." "We laymen," he writes, "have always been intensely curious to know…from what sources that strange being, the creative writer, draws his material, and how he manages to make such an impression on us with it and to arouse in us emotions of which, perhaps, we had not even thought ourselves capable" (Freud, "Creative," 143). Curious, aroused, humbled, Freud hankers after the enigma belonging to the poet. "If we could at least discover in ourselves," he exclaims, "or in people like ourselves an activity which was in some way akin to creative writing!" (143). Nevertheless, based on his work as a clinician, Freud proceeds to analyze the poet. To begin with, he defines the creative process as a sublimation akin to child's play: the prototype of adult ambitions of power and erotic wish fulfillment. The narrative representations of childhood play, adult fantasy, and creative writing serve, for Freud, to disguise and thereby censor the otherwise more arresting desires, passions, and drives belonging to the primary processes of the unconscious as such. Eight years earlier, Freud had proposed a similar theory of repression in *The Interpretation of Dreams* and thus comes to regard the creative writer as a "dreamer in broad daylight" ("Creative," 148). Yet unlike the dreamer, whose unconscious desires are largely repressed from consciousness, the creative writer's *ars poetica*, or formal aesthetic technique, yields an "incentive bonus" and "fore-pleasure" where "our actual enjoyment of an imaginative work proceeds from a liberation of tensions in our minds" (152).

Already in *The Interpretation of Dreams*, however, Freud had borrowed from a literary lexicon to describe the labor of "translating" the "hieroglyph" or "rebus" of the manifest content of dream representations so as to discern the latent, unconscious dream thought. "The dream-thoughts and the dream-content are presented to us," he writes, "like two versions of the same subject-matter in two different languages. Or, more properly, the dream-content seems like a transcript of the dream-thoughts into another mode of expression, whose characters and syntactic laws it is our business to discover by comparing the original and the translation" (Freud, *Interpretation*, 277). Freud held that the dream's latent meaning is at best obscure in its manifest presentation. Dream thoughts are subject to processes of condensation, displacement, and distortion that serve to repress and to deny unconscious contents to consciousness. Later, Jacques Lacan, in his structuralist revision of the Freudian field, frames these processes in terms of metaphoric substitution and metonymic association. Thus, "of all mental systems," Lionel Trilling famously concluded, "the Freudian psychology is the one which makes poetry indigenous to the very constitution of the mind. Indeed, the mind, as Freud sees it, is in the greater part of its tendency exactly a poetry-making organ" (52). Freud discovered poetry at the heart of unconscious processes, yet poetic metaphors had not just a casual but, at times, a constitutive role in shaping the otherwise scientific cast of his psychoanalytic theory.

Offhand tropes abound in Freud's writing and make up a defining feature of his writing style. To take just one example, having related the poignant dream of the "burning boy" that opens chapter 7 of *The Interpretation of Dreams*, Freud relies on the metaphor of the "journey" and its limits to mark "incompleteness" of any theory of dreaming (511). His extended metaphors, such as, in this case, "the journey," "the path," and the interplay of "light" and "darkness," are not just stylistic embellishments of what Freud otherwise asserts as "the scientific method by which the unconscious can be studied." Rather, poetic tropes serve as persuasive rhetoric to advance the theoretical project that both reflects and guides his clinical practice. More telling, poetry takes on a life of its own as Freud lapses into mixed metaphors that perform his symptomatic failures to capture the enigma of the unconscious whose mystery punctuates the dream as its interpretative limit:

> There is often a passage in even the most thoroughly interpreted dream which has to be left obscure; this is because we become aware during the work of interpretation that at that point there is a tangle of dream-thoughts which cannot be unravelled and which moreover adds nothing to our knowledge of the content of the dream. This is the dream's navel, the spot where it reaches down into the unknown. The dream-thoughts to which we are led by interpretation cannot, from the nature of things, have any definite endings; they are bound to branch out in every direction into the intricate network of our world of thought. It is at some point where this meshwork is particularly close that the dream-wish grows up, like a mushroom out of its mycelium.
>
> (Freud, *Interpretation*, 525)

Wrestling with the enigma of the dream-work, Freud's scientific rigor gives way, as in this well-known passage, to a certain epistemological slide into the poet's rhetorical domain. Here, a "passage" becomes a "tangle," then a "navel" and "spot" whose origin "branches out" like a "mushroom out of its mycelium" in a "meshwork" and "network" of disguised dream-wishes.

In addition to such proliferating tropes, figurative models have a more substantive role to play in *The Interpretation of Dreams*. For example, in depicting the "psychical locality" of the unconscious, Freud unpacks a constituting visual metaphor based on the optical apparatus of "a compound microscope or a photographic apparatus, or something of the kind":

> On that basis, psychical locality will correspond to a point inside the apparatus at which one of the preliminary stages of an image comes into being.... Accordingly, we will picture the mental apparatus as a compound instrument, to the components of which we will give the name of 'agencies', or (for the sake of greater clarity) 'systems'. It is to be anticipated, in the next place, that these systems may perhaps stand in a regular spatial relation to one another, in the same kind of way in which the various systems of lenses in a telescope are arranged behind one another.
>
> (Interpretation, 535–536)[7]

Freud continues at length to present this optical model for the "psychical locality" of the dream-work: so much so that he must defend against the specter of the trope's eclipse of its referent. "We are justified, in my view," he writes, "in giving free rein to our speculations so long as we retain the coolness of our judgement and do not mistake the scaffolding for the building." Yet, inevitably, the "coolness of judgement" is inscribed with the heat signature of figurative rhetoric. The ideal of scientific objectivity is always already at risk from the "free rein" of speculation insofar as the latter is susceptible to a certain drift into limitless figurative displacement. Indeed, as belied in Freud's own proliferating metaphors, one cannot help "mistaking the scaffolding for the building" (535).

If figurative language inscribes Freud's "speculations" on dreaming and the creative writer's disguised wish fulfillments, modern poets have been keen to crack the codes underwriting Freud's own symptomatic tropes. Indeed, the contest between the modern analyst and the modern poet is no more dramatic than when Freud puts the Imagist writer H.D. (Hilda Doolittle) on the couch. H.D. underwent analysis with Freud at his home at 19 Berggasse, Vienna, for three months during the spring of 1933 and again for five more weeks during October and November of 1934. Composed a decade later in London, her psychoanalytic memoir *Tribute to Freud* (1956) records her experience as an analysand and her impressions of her final encounters with Freud following his emigration to London in November 1938 and during the summer before his death in 1939. H.D. became Freud's analysand through a referral from Hanns Sachs, the analyst of her partner, Bryher (Annie Winifred Ellerman). In treatment, H.D. sought to work through her writing block following the traumas of World War I and the deaths of her brother, father, and first child; her own near-death from influenza; and her episodes of psychotic or mystical hallucinations. She also sought relief from pressing anxieties concerning the upheavals of the war's violence to come, foreshadowed in the rise of Nazism.

Beyond her status as a major American poet, H.D.'s belief in her vocation as a modern prophet and spirit medium stemmed from her famous 1920 account of her visions of the goddess Niké in Corfu, after having been turned back from Delphi while touring Greece with Bryher. Freud was drawn to the mystery of H.D.'s investment in classical Grecian mythology that resonated with his own identity as a collector of the antiquities everywhere on display in his rooms at 19 Berggasse.

But, following his bent in "Creative Writers and Day-Dreaming," he viewed the conjuncture of H.D.'s Sapphic modernism and Hellenism through the lens of clinical analysis. H.D.'s childhood memories, chain of associations, and behavior gleaned in the transference led Freud to diagnose her passion for Hellenism as a "danger signal" of a psychotic break: "the only actually dangerous 'symptom'" (*Tribute*, 47) of H.D.'s "megalomania" (57) and a "desire for union with [her] mother" (50), Helen Eugenia Wolle Doolittle. For her part, H.D. famously respected but also questioned Freud's judgment: "I was a student," she writes, "working under the direction of the greatest mind of this and of perhaps many succeeding generations. But the Professor was not always right" (24).

One symptom of H.D.'s resistance to Freud's psychoanalytic reduction—her conviction that "the Professor was not always right"—was to view it as bound to a modern, secular materialism that she gleaned from Freud's metaphors in session. Freud, of course, had early on employed economic tropes, notably in describing the effect of the day's residual events on dreaming as analogous to the entrepreneur's relation to the modern capitalist. "The position," he concludes, "may be explained by an analogy. A daytime thought may very well play the part of *entrepreneur* for a dream, but the *entrepreneur*, who, as people say, has the idea and the initiative to carry it out, can do nothing without capital. An entrepreneur needs a *capitalist* who can afford the outlay, and the capitalist who provides the psychical outlay for the dream is invariably and indisputably, whatever may be the thoughts of the previous day, *a wish from the unconscious*" (Freud, *Interpretation*, 561). Similarly, in H.D.'s account, Freud would lapse into even more patently materialist tropes during the work of analysis. For her part, H.D. regarded the psyche as "a source so deep in human consciousness" that it was considered "the well of living waters"; the unconscious was a sacred mystery, and she was its priestess. "The Professor," however, "spoke of this source of interpretation in terms of oil.... He used the idiom or slang of the counting-house, of Wall Street, a business man's concrete definite image for a successful run of luck or hope of success in the if-we-should-strike-oil or old-so-and-so-has-struck-oil-again manner. 'I struck oil but there is enough left for 50, for 100 years or more'" (88).

In resistance to Freud, H.D. tends to attribute his tropes of modernity to stereotypes of Judaism. H.D. was, of course, an anti-Fascist not an anti-semite. By the time of her analysis, she and Bryher were actively supporting Jewish refugee efforts. Nevertheless, in the transference with Freud, she does lapse into ethnic notions that offered her a certain defense against her analyst's power and authority. Rebuffing Freud's diagnosis of her psychotic tendencies, she asserts at times in *Tribute* a certain spiritual supersession fulfilling but also displacing the science of psychoanalysis as tied to the dead letter of the Old Testament covenant.[8] For example, in his role as a collector of antiquities, Freud shares with H.D. his favorite statue of what she recognizes as a likeness of Pallas Athene. In a rare break from the rigors of the couch, Freud points out the statue to her with a performative, enigmatic comment: "'She is perfect,' he said, '*only she has lost her spear*'" (*Tribute*, 74). On the one hand, H.D. acknowledges the complex and rich moment of Freud's remark: alluding as it does to the psychic lack, or narcissistic wound, driving the grandiosity, and at times the psychosis, of her Hellenistic identifications. On the other hand, she defends against his intervention, and, gaining the upper hand of spiritual supersession, she trumps but also forecloses the powers of self-analysis:

> He was speaking in a double sense, it is true, but he was speaking of value, the actual intrinsic value of the piece; like a Jew, he was assessing its worth; the blood of Abraham, Isaac and Jacob ran in his veins. He knew his material pound, his pound of flesh, if you will, but this pound of flesh was a pound of spirit between us, something tangible, to be weighed and measured, to be weighed in the balance and pray God not to be found wanting! (76)

In H.D.'s condensed, literary, and biblical allusions to Shakespeare's Shylock in *The Merchant of Venice* and the Old Testament's "Writing on the Wall" episode from the Book of Daniel, "Freud's materialism," according to the critic Joanna Spiro, "is made to disqualify him for the interpretive authority she fears he might otherwise have claimed" (617). H.D. composed *Tribute to Freud* contemporaneously with her long poem sequence *Trilogy* (1944–1946), and that long poem sequence—as a counterstatement to Freud's diagnosis—fulfilled the promise of her Corfu vision insofar as in it H.D. conceived a definitive poetics that advanced a new mythology, variously, of the unconscious, occult phenomena, spiritualist practice, alchemical transfiguration, and a syncretistic feminist theology.

Nevertheless, Freud's imagined presence, in H.D.'s writing, persists after his death in 1939. Not only do the later long poems adopt the fragmented, associative form gleaned from the Freudian field, but the Professor takes on a second life among the cast of characters of H.D.'s later writing. For example, Freud appears in the figure of Frederik von Alten, the archaeologist, in *The Sword Went Out to Sea* (1946–1947), H.D.'s *roman à clef* of her séance work during World War II. Similarly, H.D.'s impressions of Freud, according to Susan Stanford Friedman, shape *Trilogy*'s persona of Mage Kaspar, who attends on and receives a vision from Mary Magdalene. In addition, the character of Theseus in *Helen in Egypt* is a veiled portrait of H.D.'s analyst: "Like Freud of her tribute," Friedman observes, "Theseus helps Helen retrieve what she has forgotten and reunite the fragmented selves of Helen in Sparta, Helen in Troy, Helen in Egypt" (*Penelope's Web*, 303). Finally, H.D.'s poem "The Master" revisits the scene of her struggle with Freud in order to work through the transferential passions that were awakened in treatment:

> I was angry with the old man
> with his talk of the man-strength,
> I was angry with his mystery, his mysteries,
> I argued until day-break;
> O, it was late,
> and God will forgive me, my anger,
> but I could not accept it.
> I could not accept from wisdom
> what love taught,
> *woman is perfect*
>
> (H.D., *Collected*, 455)

In "The Master," H.D. accepts her resistance to Freud's analytic diagnosis—framed as it is by the phallic bent underlying "his talk of the man-strength." Yet as a poet, she not only acknowledges anger but, through her craft, also transforms it into a vision of feminine perfection that, "until daybreak," is yet to come: then "men will see how long they have been blind, / poor men / poor mankind / how long / how long / this thought of the man-pulse has tricked them, / has weakened them, / shall see woman, / perfect" (460). In the guise of visionary poet-prophet, H.D. claims the last word in her ongoing dialogue with Freud. Addressed to his memory, her final prosopopoeia performs an arresting wish fulfillment: one that decisively displaces the master's phallic authority. Encrypted in the homonym of the "sun," H.D. assumes the mantle of a filial heritage as the messianic son, transfigured now, however, in a distinctly feminine incarnation: "O heart of the sun / rhododendron, / Rhodocleia, / we are unworthy your beauty, / you are near beauty the sun, / you are that lord become woman" (461).

On the one hand, H.D. presents a preeminent feminist mythology whose exotic, expatriate Hellenism is resistant to, but also profoundly shaped by, modern psychoanalysis. Her contemporary William Carlos Williams, on the other hand, conceives an Imagist poetics of self-analysis: one that is rooted in the local conditions of his clinical experience. As a practicing physician in East Rutherford, New Jersey, Williams was not just a keen observer of America's cultural scene but also a discerning and empathic diagnostician both of his patients and, equally important, of his own psychic investments in their life stories. Williams presents a definitive self-analysis in his well-known Imagist lyric "To Elsie" from *Spring and All* (1923):

> The pure products of America
> go crazy—
> mountain folk from Kentucky
>
> or the ribbed north end of
> Jersey
> with its isolate lakes and
>
> valleys, its deaf-mutes, thieves
> old names
> and promiscuity between
>
> devil-may-care men who have taken
> to railroading
> out of sheer lust of adventure—
>
> and young slatterns, bathed
> in filth
> from Monday to Saturday
>
> to be tricked out that night
> with gauds
> from imaginations which have no

peasant traditions to give them
character
but flutter and flaunt

sheer rags—succumbing without
emotion
save numbed terror

under some hedge of choke-cherry
or viburnum—
which they cannot express—

Unless it be that marriage
perhaps
with a dash of Indian blood

will throw up a girl so desolate
so hemmed round
with disease or murder

that she'll be rescued by an
agent—
reared by the state and

sent out at fifteen to work in
some hard-pressed
house in the suburbs—

some doctor's family, some Elsie—
voluptuous water
expressing with broken

brain the truth about us—
her great
ungainly hips and flopping breasts

addressed to cheap
jewelry
and rich young men with fine eyes

as if the earth under our feet
were
an excrement of some sky

and we degraded prisoners
destined
to hunger until we eat filth

while the imagination strains
after deer
going by fields of goldenrod in

the stifling heat of September
Somehow
it seems to destroy us

It is only in isolate flecks that
something
is given off

No one
to witness
and adjust, no one to drive the car
                (*Collected Poems*, 217–219)

As he allowed in a letter to Louis Zukofsky, Williams considered the poem "to be one of my best works," but its opening lines—"The pure products of America / go crazy"—point to a strange side effect of the modernist impulse to "make it new" (Pound, *Make It New* [1934]) and "destroy the cult of the past" (Boccioni et al., 63). The poet's modern truism casts the "crazy" production of American modernism into a decidedly psychoanalytic register. In particular, Williams engages Freud's clinical discovery of the unconscious force of sexuality and the partial drives—theorized as early as 1905 in *Three Essays on the Theory of Sexuality*—as they bear on the otherwise conscious habits and normative conventions of everyday life.

Williams graduated from the University of Pennsylvania medical school in 1906, just three years before Freud's Clark University lectures. Not only did Williams undertake advanced medical training in Leipzig but he also absorbed Freudian theory as a member of the New York avant-garde. By 1917, Williams was describing the psychic effects of "release" and "relief" from poetic "improvisations" and "automatic writing" that echoed Freud's 1908 essay "The Creative Writer and Day-Dreaming." Later, Williams explicitly alludes to the influence of *Beyond the Pleasure Principle* on his thinking in his *roman à clef Voyage to Pagany* (Floyd Dell's code word for psychoanalysis) (see Diggory). As a practicing clinician, Williams made empathic diagnoses that part company with the more rigid prescriptive practices of turn-of-the-century physicians such as S. Weir Mitchell. Rather, Williams's diagnostic poetics, according to Brian A. Bremen, anticipates the "vicarious introspection" of self-psychology in Heinz Kohut and Jessica Benjamin (104). Yet this somewhat altruistic model of compassionate diagnostics runs up against a certain limit in explaining Williams's anxious encounter with the figure of Elsie, who, by Bremen's own account, remains unassimilable to the more humanistic tenets of American ego and self-psychology. In a similar vein to James Clifford's and Arnold Krupat's ethnographic readings of Elsie's racial, ethnic, and class otherness, Bremen notes that she "occupies a threatening position not only within Williams's 'poetry,' but also within the confines of his own domestic space" (61). Ironically, the ideal of diagnostic empathy can be viewed, I would suggest, as a symptomatic defense against the "crazy" forces of primary process aggression, fragmentation, and alienation that are radically in excess of any gender, race, or class difference that Elsie's "threatening position" embodies.

Beyond the normative tendencies of American ego and self-psychology—and supplementing the ethnographic framing of Elsie's social Otherness—a more sophisticated, psychoanalytic reading would examine the semantic resonances found in the interlocution of Williams's poetics and Lacan's later writings on the partial drives, surplus *jouissance,* and the latter's ethical relation to the Real. For his part, Williams acknowledges the force of desire on both a personal and public level in the preface to his autobiography where he famously avows that "I am extremely sexual in my desires. I carry them everywhere and at all times. I think that from that arises the drive which empowers us all" (*Autobiography*, xi). For Williams, moreover, the driving force of desire is "not easily deciphered," and, like the navel or mycelium of the dream thought, it bears on the unconscious otherwise repressed in the public mind: "We always try," he writes, "to hide the secret of our lives from the general stare. What I believe to be the hidden core of my life will not easily be deciphered, even when I tell, as here, the outer circumstances" (xii).

In "To Elsie," the dynamic interplay of desire's "hidden core" and "outer circumstances" are played out across the registers of private fantasy and national narration. To begin with, the poem's arresting opening lines "The pure products of America / go crazy—" (*Collected Poems*, 217) feature the key term of American nationalism that draws otherwise haphazard social arrangements into alignment "as the pure products" of a public, imagined community. Thus, the Kentucky mountain folk displaced throughout "the ribbed north end of / Jersey" (217), the latter's deaf-mutes, thieves, devil-may-care men, young slatterns, Elsie, Doctor Williams and his suburban family together find their places as "pure products" under the sign of America. But equally important, such social production—as Lacan theorizes it in *Seminar XVII, The Other Side of Psychoanalysis* (1969)—produces a certain excess of *surplus jouissance* that in "To Elsie" spawns fantasies of desire that ultimately "go crazy." In the poem's drama "young slatterns" are "tricked out…/ with gauds…addressed to…rich young men with fine eyes" (218). Yet such lures and fetishes of modern sexual courtship—however removed from their "peasant traditions"—fail to regulate or contain America's surplus production of desire. "Promiscuity" and the "sheer lust of adventure" are overdetermined by the poem's own discursive production insofar as enjambment works at cross purposes to syntax, thereby queering the conventions of heteronormativity. Suggested in the poem's line breaks, "promiscuity between // devil-may-care men" (217) happens in homoerotic relation before being linked syntactically and heterosexually to the next tercet's "young slatterns."

Equally important, the "pure products" of America's surplus sexuality mask a primary lack of being: what Lacan theorizes in *Seminar VII, The Ethics of Psychoanalysis* (1960) in terms of the Real. That "hidden core," for Williams, "will not easily be deciphered" precisely because its "numbed terror" in "To Elsie" signals what Lacan characterizes as "the Thing" (*das Ding*): "whatever is open, lacking, or gaping at the center of our desire" (*Seminar VII*, 84). Indeed, as Lacan explains, the production and circulation of symbolic representation (*Vorstellung*) seeks to regulate the traumatic force of a primordial lack as *das Ding* bears on the Real:

Right at the beginning of the organization of the world in the psyche, both logically and chronologically, *das Ding* is something that presents and isolates itself as the strange feature around which the whole movement of the *Vorstellung* turns—a *Vorstellung* that Freud shows us is governed by a regulatory principle, the so-called pleasure principle, which is tied to the functioning of the neurotic apparatus. And it is around *das Ding* that the whole adaptive development revolves, a development that is so specific to man insofar as the symbolic process reveals itself to be inextricably woven into it.

(Seminar VII, 57)

What, for Williams, "presents and isolates itself as the strange feature" of *das Ding* inheres in the "pure products of America," which in his national narrative turns on an enigma reaching back to the Puritans. Contemporaneous with "To Elsie," Williams's commentary on Cotton Mather from *In the American Grain* (1925) ruminates on the signifier of "the pure" in order to, as the poet says, "separate it out, to isolate it" (114) precisely as the thing-like substantive haunting American national identity beginning with the Puritans. Williams's essay presents a dialogue with the French scholar Valery Larbaud, who derives his understanding of the United States from the scriven record of American history. In contrast, Williams as a nativist is possessed by the American Thing in the register of the Real:

Puritans we name them, but they were not so called because of moral qualities. They were not blessed with that name by virtue of a stern but just conception of the world. That is a misconception of the name. . . . I wish to drag this THING out by itself to annihilate it. He answered, That one cannot do. Yes, I insisted, it MUST be done, you do not know America. There is a "Puritanism"—of which you hear, of course, but you have never felt it stinking all about you—that has survived to us from the past. It is an atrocious thing, a kind of mermaid with a corpse for tail. Or it remains, a bad breath in the room. This THING, strange, inhuman, powerful, is like a relic of some died out tribe whose practices were revolting.—

But the relic will be beautiful, he answered, sometimes. I have enjoyed the books.

Against his view I continually protested. I cannot separate myself, I said, from this ghostly miasm. It grips me. I cannot merely talk of books, just as Mather as if he were some pearl.

(American Grain, 114–115)

While Larbaud, as a continental man of letters, reads Mather's Puritanism at a symbolic remove from the American THING, Williams inherits its possessing force as a generational fate that bears on the Real. If, as Lacan has it, that "the Thing only presents itself to the extent that it becomes the word, hits the bull's eye" (*Seminar VII*, 55), then in Williams the "purity" of the Puritans is a radical misnomer: one that bears on the "bull's eye" of *das Ding* as a distorted inversion. Moreover, the poet's mixed metaphors do not so much target the Puritan THING as they pepper it in the scatter shot of verbal catachresis. At once "relic" and "pearl" the American THING "grips" the poet like a "bad breath in the room," a "ghostly miasm," and an "'atrocious thing', a kind of mermaid with a corpse for tail."

Supplementing *In the American Grain*, "To Elsie" offers a more properly ana-
lytic account of Dr. Williams's ethical relation to the American Thing in the regis-
ter of the Real. Viewed through a Lacanian lens, Williams does not simply offer a
self-portrait of the physician as desiring subject. More provocatively, as poet, he
also assumes a distanced and, I would suggest, an analytic ethic of witness. Indeed,
via the aesthetic space of the poem, Williams offers what Lacan would recognize as
a topology of *surplus jouissance*: one that exceeds the subject's pleasurable relation
to its constituting objects of psychic fantasy. Ordinarily, the discursive representa-
tion of desire as *Vorstellung* would be sustained by the force of the drive whose aim
of satisfaction, as the poet has it, is "tricked out" by the "gaud" of Elsie's sexuality.
In this vein, Williams's poem shares certain semantic resonances with Lacan's idi-
omatic "formula" for the drive in *Seminar XI, The Four Fundamental Concepts of
Psychoanalysis* (1964): "*la pulsion en fait le tour.... Tour* is to be understood here,"
he writes, "with the ambiguity it possesses in French, both *turn*, the limit around
which one turns, and *trick*" (168). The trick encrypted in Lacan's pun on "en fait le
tour" derives from his take on the object's relation to the drive in the Freudian field.
In particular, Lacan revisits the four-fold nature that Freud attributes to the source,
pressure, aim, and object of the drive (*trieb*). For his part, Freud, in "Drives and
Their Vicissitudes" (1915) makes a distinction between the biological role of the ner-
vous system in "mastering" external stimuli and the drive, locating the latter "at the
frontier between the mental and the somatic, as the psychical representative of the
stimuli originating from within the organism" (121–122). Lacan's reading of Freud
further discounts the object as the determining cause of the drive, claiming that
for Freud, "it was a matter of total indifference" (*Seminar XI*, 168). Instead, Lacan
revises the function of the object in accord with his key thesis that "the unconscious
is structured like a language" (Lacan, *Seminar XX*, 55).

Thus, the subject's Oedipal passage into the symbolic domain of language, for
Lacan, marks the loss of the object displaced now along a metonymic chain of "unary
traits": associated signifiers that substitute for the breast, the feces, the voice, the gaze,
and other representations of the pre-Oedipal body. To "function as object" in this
linguistic register, the unary trait necessarily lacks full presence insofar as its satisfac-
tion is circumscribed and determined by language's signifying system of differences
without positive terms. If "the unconscious is structured like a language," then the
object of desire is shadowed by what Lacan calls the "*objet a* cause of desire." For
Jacques-Alain Miller, what is at stake in the divide between the object of desire and
the object cause of desire is the trace of death hollowing out language's symbolic
representation insofar as "the symbol manifests itself first as the death of the thing"
(29). The *objet a*, like *das Ding*, bears on the Real, denoting as it does the lack in
language's differential structure whose force regulates the subject's desire in pursuit
of its part objects. For Lacan, the force of the *objet a* bends the circuit of the drive
around a constituting placeholder or desirable object that otherwise masks an absence
"in a movement outwards and back" (*Seminar XI*, 177). In this way "*la pulsion en fait
le tour*" (168), turning (and tricking) the pressure of the drive's vector of desire such
that it succeeds in "attaining its satisfaction without attaining its aim" (179).

Similarly, in "To Elsie," the erotic lure of "sheer lust" only thinly masks the "numbed terror" (Williams, *Collected Poems*, 217) encountered within but also lying at the heart of what Williams knows to be a "pure product" of "the American Thing." Somewhat symptomatically perhaps, Elsie embodies the Real as object cause of the drive, "expressing...the truth about us" precisely to the extent that it "seems to destroy us" (218). On the one hand, Williams assumes his place as patriarch to "some doctor's family" (218) in a signifying chain of America's state agents who would "rescue" Elsie out of an idealized civic altruism. The conventional moral "good" of welcoming "some Elsie" (218) into the hospitality of "some doctor's family" rests on the "golden rule"—"thou shalt love thy neighbor as thyself." The ethics of that philanthropy, however, is otherwise demystified in "To Elsie." Beyond the "golden rule," the ethics of the drive, for Williams as for Freud and Lacan, risks a devastating self-revelation. For Freud, writing famously in *Civilization and Its Discontents* (1930), the golden rule belies an inherent aggressivity defining neighborly relations beyond the pleasure principle. If anything, history teaches that for people everywhere the neighbor is "not only a potential helper or sexual object, but also someone who tempts them to satisfy their aggressiveness on him, to exploit his capacity for work without compensation, to use him sexually without his consent, to seize his possessions, to humiliate him, to cause him pain, to torture and to kill him" (*Civilization*, 68–69).

Likewise, Lacan marks a crucial distinction between philanthropy and the neighborly love that veils a certain "malignant jouissance." In examining the lives of certain Catholic saints—such as Angela de Foligno who "joyfully lapped up the water in which she had just washed the feet of lepers" and "Marie Allacoque, who, with no less a reward in spiritual uplift, ate the excrement of a sick man"— Lacan considers how such acts of extreme altruism veil desire driven beyond the pleasure principle toward the "place of the unnameable thing and what goes on there" (*Seminar VII*, 188). If, for Lacan, the excess jouissance of neighborly altruism "arouses Freud's horror," then it is likewise "the horror of the civilized man" that Williams revisits in "To Elsie." Desire here is driven toward the domain of the American THING where it is "as if the earth under out feet / were / an excrement of some sky // and we degraded prisoners / destined / to hunger until we eat filth" (*Collected Poems*, 218). Catholic saints, in *Imitatio Christi*, not only repeated Christ's role as healer of the sick, but many literally ate filth in order to merge with the mystical corpus Christi as a sacrament of communion. Likewise, Williams's own vocation as a healer, however abject, proves salutary insofar as he moves beyond any regulated desire for "the Sovereign good" (*Seminar VII*, 70) to sustain what Lacan describes as the "experienced desire" of the analyst (*Seminar VII*, 301). In this way, Williams occupies a dual position in the double genitive of being a desiring subject produced by the drive *and* an analytic subject witnessing to the drive. As a clinician, Dr. Williams traverses the drive's circuit by moving beyond the lure of the pleasure principle to diagnose, in the role of analyst, the radical "truth about us": an analytic truth that assumes neither a therapeutic knowledge of self (ego psychology) nor an interpersonal empathy toward the other (Kohut's "vicarious introspection"). Rather, the poet's self-analysis attends to what Lacan describes in *Seminar VII* as the psychic topology of an "intimate exteriority" or extimacy (*extimité*). "To Elsie" draws into fateful proximity—or rather extimacy—the intimate psychic life of "some doctor's family" and a national enigma where "the pure products of America / go crazy." From this locus of the unconscious, "something / is given off" (*Collected Poems*, 219) whose "truth"—encountered as gap, break, or discontinuity—runs counter to the pleasurable vector of desire that would otherwise prop up the doctor's normative social identity. As placeholders in the poem's circuit of "promiscuity," the poem's knowing subject ("some doctor") and desired object ("some Elsie") converge at the vanishing point of extimacy where there is "no one / to witness / and adjust, no one to drive" (219). Thus, Elsie not only evokes the doctor's sexual *jouissance* but is herself the "pure product" of the anonymous, random and undifferentiated "promiscuity" whose "lust of adventure" and "numbed terror" are only partly contained and regulated by the myths and institutions of conventional family life: "Unless it be that marriage / perhaps / with a dash of Indian blood // will throw up / a girl so desolate."

In representing the primal scene of Elsie's origins, Williams's enjambment of "perhaps" not only renders the ethnicity of her "dash of Indian blood" uncertain, but as a key signifier "perhaps" —in its syntactic ambiguity—also bears on the questionable status of her parents' union and thus of Elsie's identity not just as a ward of the state but as an illegitimate child. It is this indeterminate birth that in the poem will "throw up" Elsie as a figure of abjection. Above all, it is her unknown story that possesses, paradoxically enough, the enigmatic power of "expressing with broken / brain the truth about us." Criticism has tended to read this "truth" as a universal reference to the "crazy" excesses of modernity that Williams portrays everywhere on offer throughout "the ribbed north end of / Jersey." Yet I want to suggest here that Elsie also embodies a more intimate psychosis whose "truth" of *extimité* goes to the heart of the poet's family narrative as he portrays it in the *Autobiography*. In it, Williams revisits another narrative of orphanage and unknown birth: one that turns on the legitimacy of his ancestral namesake, his paternal grandmother, Emily Dickenson Wellcome. As he says, "it was the passion, independence, and the determination of this woman, born Emily Dickenson of Chichester, England and orphaned as a small child somewhere in the 1830's that had begun our whole history in America" (167). Raised by the Godwin family of London, Williams's paternal grandmother was an orphan whose unknown birth, like Elsie's, is linked by the poet's own account with the national narrative of "our whole history in America." Compounding the enigma of her birth status, Emily Dickenson Wellcome never knew the identity of her father, and she never disclosed the name or identity of her first husband, the biological father of Williams's own father, William George Williams. Having been rejected and disowned by the Godwins, Emily left England in 1856 for Brooklyn, where she later married George Wellcome, but the fate of her first husband and indeed whether they were ever married at all remained an enigma for her grandson. Critics such as Audrey T. Rodgers and Paul Mariani have interpreted Williams's well-known statement—"I identified my grandmother with my poetic unconscious" (*Interviews*, 76)—as it bears on the poet's mythic imagination: his tendency to split the feminine into the motifs of the sacred and the profane, of Virgin and Whore, Demeter and Persephone, "The Young Housewife" of *Spring and All* and "the Beautiful Thing" of *Paterson*, Book III.

Yet the unconscious "truth" of Emily's mythic power poses not just an enigma of psychic meaning for Williams as poet but, equally important, an enigma of signification insofar as her story opens a signifying gap in the generational narrative of the Williams family. Elsie's indeterminate parentage fascinates Williams precisely because it stands as the outward specter of an intimate family secret: one that repeats Emily's obscure origins, status, and generational story. Not just a reenactment of a repressed psychic meaning, "To Elsie" witnesses to what Lacan—in his reading of Freud's 1911 analysis of Judge Schreber's memoir—characterized as psychotic foreclosure (*verwerfung*). Distinguishing between repression (*verdrängung*) and foreclosure (*verwerfung*), Freud says of the latter "that what was abolished internally returns from without" (Freud, "Psycho-analytic Notes," 71). Lacan's return to Freud in *Seminar III: The Psychoses*, likewise draws a distinction between, on the one hand, negation (*verneinung*) and return of the repressed (*verdrängung*) and, on the other hand, the more radical enigma of foreclosure (*verwerfung*) that, he says, "has a completely different destiny" (Lacan, *The Psychoses*, 12). Rereading the example of the Wolf Man, Lacan in an echo of Freud concludes that "what is refused in the symbolic order re-emerges in the real" (Lacan, *The Psychoses* 13).

Similarly, the catastrophe of Elsie's status—that, "Somehow," as the poet avows, "it seems to destroy us"—marks precisely the re-emergence in the Real of Williams's own intimate family narrative of paternal foreclosure. As a figure of psychosis, Elsie represents, for Williams, the loss of the signifying name of the father (*Nom du père*) whose symbolic function is foreclosed in the secret history associated with Emily Dickenson Wellcome. Lacan asserts in "On a Question Prior to Any Possible Treatment of Psychosis" that "we should concern ourselves not only with the way the mother accommodates the father as a person, but also with the importance she attributes to his speech—in a word, to his authority—in other words, with the place she reserves for the Name-of-the-Father in the promotion of the law" (482). Not only is the "place" of paternal authority radically at risk both in "To Elsie" and in Williams's family genealogy, but the signifying function of "speech" as such breaks down in the extimacy that Elsie, Emily, and Williams's mother, Elena Hoheb, share. In this vein, the catachresis of Elsie's speech—"expressing with broken / brain the truth about us"—recalls the childhood trauma of a specific loss of language that Williams witnessed in his grandmother and mother whenever they would lapse into their "trances" and "seizures" as spirit mediums:

> These meetings of the spiritualists, preceding the organization of the Unitarian Church and Sunday School in Rutherford, went on for years....Mother would be possessed at such times—and it went on for years—by an uncontrollable shaking of the head. It would happen anywhere and at any time. I even saw it happen once while she was playing the piano at Sunday School....We'd all know at once what was about to take place—Mother's look would become fixed, her face would flush,

and she'd reach out her hand and grasp the hand of one of us.... Her face would be red, contorted, she couldn't talk, her whole body seized by some inscrutable violence.

A name would be offered. No. Then another. She would shake her head violently, her cheeks flaming, her eyes like those of a person in violent effort of any sort. Finally Pop might say, "Is it Carlos?" meaning her brother, and she'd grasp the hand offered in both hers, and the presence would leave her.

How Ed and I dreaded these occasions!

(*Autobiography*, 16–17)

Not just a spiritualist enigma, the primal scene of maternal possession can also be read as a symptom of psychosis. In this vein, the foreclosure of the *Nom du père*—that, as we have seen, haunts Williams's extended family narrative—opens a certain gap in the signifying processes that for Lacan, following Freud, "gives psychosis its essential condition, along with the structure that separates it from neurosis" ("On a Question," 479). Psychosis, accordingly in Williams's *Autobiography*, returns as the possession by a signifying gap: one that not only marks the loss of the mother as a speaking subject but drives the whole family to supplement what befalls all of them as a lack in familial signification. To fill the gap opened by the enigma of the paternal signifier, "A name," Williams writes, "would be offered. No. Then another." Not so much a psychic as it is a linguistic supplement, the actual name that Williams recalls in his *Autobiography*—the name that "cures" Elena's trance—is also a stopgap against the poet's own psychotic anxieties. Signifying on his maternal uncle, Carlos Hoheb—the other family physician—the uncanny namesake of "Carlos" shores up Williams's place and identity as the head of "some doctor's family" against the psychosis that in the generational saga of his American identity, he is—like Elsie, Emily Dickenson Wellcome, and his father, William George Williams—"no one."

At midcentury the psychoanalysis of modern American poetry continues apace for the next generation of poets that turn to the analytic truth of the unconscious in negotiating the political repressions, psychic foreclosures, and social containments that define what Robert Lowell tellingly dubbed the "Tranquilized Fifties." Following Williams, such major post–World War II poets as Lowell, Randall Jarrell, Theodore Roethke, John Berryman, Elizabeth Bishop, Sylvia Plath, and Anne Sexton give poetic testimony to the "pure products" of the American unconscious. These canonical poets were at first regarded as, what M. L. Rosenthal called, neo-Romantic "confessional" ephebes of high modernism.[9] Yet in retrospect, M. L. Rosenthal's now dated rubric of poetic "confessionalism" seems an oversimplified framing of what Helen Vendler has more recently described as the contemporary "Freudian" lyric. "The aim of the Freudian lyric," she argues, "is primarily analytic, not confessional" (50). Yet if there is, *pace* Vendler, a confessional dimension to Freudian lyricism, it cuts against the grain of Rosenthal's solipsistic reduction. For her part, Sexton famously said that "I can be deeply personal but I'm not being personal about myself."[10] Similarly, as Sexton writes in her poem dedicated to her first creative writing workshop leader, John Holmes, "At first it was private / Then it was more than myself" (*Complete Poems*, 34).

Implied in Sexton's account, the confessional subject is not to be regarded as someone who testifies to the naked facts of his or her privacy. To the contrary, the "truthful confession," as Michel Foucault argues, begins in the Middle Ages and goes to the heart of the "procedures of individuation by power" (59). In reading the history of sexuality at the *fin de siècle*, Foucault examines how modern psychoanalysis adapts rituals of confession—reworking them through specific interpretive techniques and practices of confessional labor—to produce a *scientia sexualis*: a "complex machinery for producing true discourses on sex" (68). Embedded in this "complex machinery" of modern psychoanalysis, postwar confessional verse is hardly the "sullen art" of the private self but a discourse actively engaged in what Foucault describes as the "techniques and practices of confessional labor." Confessional discourse, he writes, "unfolds within a power relationship, for one does not confess without the presence (or virtual presence) of a partner who is not simply the interlocutor but the authority who requires the confession, prescribes and appreciates it, and intervenes in order to judge, punish, forgive, console, and reconcile" (62). Similarly, for Shoshana Felman, the institutions of psychoanalysis and literature not only share a highly cathected and transferential relation to each other, but each involves a testimonial moment that is transpersonal: "By virtue of the fact that the testimony is *addressed* to others," she writes, "the witness, from within the solitude of his own stance, is the vehicle of an occurrence, a reality, a stance or a dimension *beyond himself*" (3). However recollected in solitude, confessional verse is seldom solitary but, like the discourse of the analysand, sustained by the presence of an interlocutor.

For his part, Robert Lowell solicits readerly empathy through a confiding, direct address to his imagined audience.[11] Moreover, his conversational performatives conjure any number of historical figures and departed family members addressed in the verse through the rhetorical figure of prosopopoeia. Finally, not unlike Lacan's splicing of the narrative subject in such essays as "The Subversion of the Subject and the Dialectic of Desire in the Freudian Unconscious," Lowell witnesses to the psychic divide between the poem's narrative subject and its represented subject. Such invocations of the interlocutor as a divided self produced in language are particularly complicated in his late volume *The Dolphin* (1973) whose title-piece "Dolphin" ends with the uncanny line: "my eyes have seen what my hand did" (*Collected Poems*, 708). A typical moment from this book finds the poet like his former döppelganger Stanley from "Waking in the Blue" and like his father in "Commander Lowell" submerged in the tub where, he writes "I soak, / examining and then examining / what I really have against myself" (649). Particularly controversial in this book is the poet's apostrophes to his second wife, Elizabeth Hardwick, whose anguished voice Lowell appropriates from her correspondence written in the midst of their divorce and his subsequent marriage to the poet's third wife, Caroline Blackwood.

Increasingly in *Life Studies* (1959) and *For the Union Dead* (1964), Lowell's confessionalism finds political linkages between, on the one hand, the private Oedipal narratives of works such as "91 Revere Street," "My Last Afternoon with

Uncle Devereux Winslow," "Commander Lowell," "Father's Bedroom," "Sailing Home from Rapallo," "During Fever," and, on the other hand, incisive social critiques of American culture as in "Memories of West Street and Lepke," "For the Union Dead," "Fall 1961," "Florence," and "Waking Early Sunday Morning." To take one example, in "Memories of West Street and Lepke" the figure of the interlocutor is overdetermined as Lowell marks the psychic distance between his remembered self—the "fire-breathing Catholic C.O., / . . . telling off the state and president"—and the narrating self at home in the "Tranquilized Fifties": "where even the man / scavenging filth in the back alley trash cans, / has two children, a beach wagon, a helpmate, / and is 'a young Republican'" (183). The manifest stereotype of the latter's normative conservatism is overshadowed by the latent and more arresting recollections of Louis Lepke dredged up from the poet's memories of doing time in the West Street jail. As the head hit-man of *Murder Incorporated*, "Czar Lepke" emerges in the poem as a specter of America's postwar national hegemony, figured in the symbolism of "his little segregated cell full / of things forbidden to the common man: / a portable radio, a dresser, two toy American / flags tied together with a ribbon of Easter palm" (184). Pious, privileged, and patriotic, Lepke is above all "lobotomized." As a poetic döppelganger, he not only foreshadows the poet's own estrangement from the "Tranquilized Fifties," but, more disturbingly, reflects a national death wish "where no agonizing reappraisal"—to signify on Secretary of State John Foster Dulles's Cold War rhetoric—" / jarred his concentration on the electric chair / hanging like an oasis in his air / of lost connections" (184).

Such overdetermined figures of analytic address run the gamut in confessional poetics from the controversial blackface minstrelsy of "Huffy Henry" and endman "Mr. Bones"—the alter egos of John Berryman's *Dreamsongs*— to the psychic regressions of Theodore Roethke's forays into the subhuman world of animal and vegetal otherness. Similarly, the mythic provocations and exorcisms of Plath's "Lady Lazarus" and "Daddy" as well as the empathic solicitations of audience in Sexton's "Her Kind" draw on the energies of pre-Oedipal fantasy whose psychic vicissitudes are also the subject of Elizabeth Bishop's poetry of childhood trauma.[12]

Like Lowell, Berryman's poetic imagination was powerfully shaped by a family romance rooted in Oedipal drama. Beginning with an extended analysis from 1947 to 1953 and in treatment off and on thereafter, Berryman gradually came to regard the suicide of his father, John Allyn Smith, in 1926 and his mother's hasty marriage to John McAlpin Berryman three months later as a sinister, murderous narrative: one that came to drive his scholarly obsession with Shakespeare's *Hamlet*.[13] According to Berryman's biographer, Paul Mariani, "*Hamlet* became his text: the death of the father, the determination to uncover the truth, the inability to act, drunken oblivion, reinventing one's life" (*Dream Song*, xvii). Shakespearean echoes find their way into Berryman's verse in works such as "Dream Song 168, The Old Poor," which begins "and God has many other surprises, like / when the man you fear most in the world marries your mother / and chilling other" (*Dream Songs*, 187). Echoing Shakespeare's other murderous villains, Berryman's persona "Henry," like Macbeth, waxes "Cawdor-uneasy" in "Dream Song 48" (52). Moreover, Henry suffers what Berryman characterizes, following Eric Erikson, as the "unmasterable identity crisis" that befalls King Richard III the night before his defeat by the Earl of Richmond (Henry VII) in the battle of Bosworth Field.[14] Haunted by the nightmarish procession of the ghostly victims he has previously put to death, Richard in Shakespeare's history play awakens beside himself:

> Cold fearful drops stand on my trembling flesh.
> What do I fear? myself? There's none else by:
> Richard loves Richard; that is, I am I.
> Is there a murderer here? No;—yes, I am:
> Then fly. What, from myself? Great reason why:
> Lest I revenge. What, myself upon myself?
> (Shakespeare, *Richard III*, Act V, sc. iii)

Signifying on the iterative syntax of Richard III's manic rant scene, Berryman similarly performs Henry's psychic crisis in "Dream Song 85, Op. posth. no. 8" : "The cold is ultimating. The cold is cold. / I am—I should be held together by— / but I am breaking up / and Henry now has come to a full stop-" / vanisht his vision, if there was, & fold / him over himself quietly" (*Dream Songs*, 100). Not unlike Lowell's invocation of the divided self, Berryman's presentation of Henry as a suicidal subject—torn by the punitive guilt of an interior interlocutor—signifies on the subtext of Richard's symptomatic repetitions and redundant self-incriminations.

Oedipal aggression, guilt, manic dissociation, and the fragmentation of identity are all psychic conditions that Berryman's aesthetic shares not only with Robert Lowell but also with Theodore Roethke. With his very first volume, *Open House* (1941), Roethke sounds "Confusion's core set deep within / A Furious, dissembling din."[15] Such interior discord and drama would shape his career thereafter. His pathbreaking volume *The Lost Son and Other Poems* (1948) works through the filial anxiety of Roethke's vexed relationship to a powerful father figure, Otto Roethke, who died during the poet's adolescence. For many midcentury poets, the loss of the father either through death (Roethke, Berryman, Plath, Bishop), weakness (Lowell), or perversion (Sexton) is a trigger for psychic discord: one that resonates with the crisis of state sovereignty and the eroding authority of traditional social rituals, customs, and beliefs in the postwar public sphere. For Lacan, the foreclosure of the "paternal metaphor"— the *Nom du père* —defines psychosis as a breakdown, tear, or hole in symbolization: one that "sets off the cascade of reworkings of the signifier from which the growing disaster of the imaginary proceeds, until the level is reached at which signifier and signified stabilize in a delusional metaphor" ("On a Question," 481). Lacan's theory of psychosis follows Freud in two respects. First, he invokes the pre-Oedipal in linking the psychotic break to the prelinguistic enigma of the Real. Second, Lacan interprets the subject's delusional "remodeling of reality" as a "restitutional" defense against a primordial loss whose trauma he, like Freud and Melanie Klein, regards as radically positional rather than phasal in its temporal mode.

In modern American verse, no other poet depicts the trauma of pre-Oedipal experience as vividly as Theodore Roethke, who pioneered a poetics of psychic regression based, in part, on the periodic breakdowns and hospitalizations that began in 1935 and persisted throughout the rest of his life. "Sometimes," he writes, "of course, there is regression. I believe that the spiritual man must go back in order to go forward" (*On the Poet*, 12). Going back meant, among other things, revisiting what Kenneth Burke described as the "vegetal radicalism" of the "greenhouse" settings of the poet's youth, growing up in Saginaw, Michigan.[16] Accompanying the "greenhouse" sequence, his long poem "The Lost Son" regresses further back toward what Melanie Klein would characterize as the undifferentiated, schizoid world of childhood fantasy and its earliest pre-Oedipal objects.

For all of their differences, Klein and Lacan follow Freud's early insights into regression and the radically positional topology of the unconscious. Writing in *Five Lectures on Psycho-Analysis* (1910), Freud theorized that the "extraordinary plasticity of mental developments is not unrestricted as regards direction; it may be described as a special capacity for involution—for regression—since it may well happen that a later and higher stage of development, once abandoned, cannot be reached again. But the primitive stages can always be re-established: the primitive mind is, in the fullest meaning of the word, imperishable" (Freud, *Five Lectures*, 11). In 1910 Freud asserts regression's potential to revisit and re-establish the "imperishable" domain of the mind's "primitive stages," but his theorization of pre-Oedipal object relations reaches back five years earlier to his 1905 essay "The Finding of an Object." There, he locates the sexual aims of adulthood in pre-Oedipal object relations such that the "finding of an object is in fact the refinding of it" (Freud, *Three Essays*, 222). Influenced by Melanie Klein's notions of pre-Oedipal infantile fantasy, Freud later revised his developmental view of the subject's libidinal organization to emphasize a more spatial and contiguous understanding of sexual stages and investments. By 1933, Freud writes in *New Introductory Lectures on Psycho-Analysis*, "Our attitude to the phases of the organization of the libido has in general shifted a little. Whereas earlier we chiefly emphasized the way in which each of them passed away before the next, our attention now is directed to the facts that show us how much of each earlier phase persists alongside of and behind the later configurations and obtains a permanent representation in the libidinal economy and character of the subject" (100). Freud's shift from a phasal to a positional understanding of libido organization reflects Klein's influential formulations of the paranoid-schizoid, depressive, and reparative modes of infantile fantasy as positional rather than phasal stages.[17]

Such positions, moreover, are mediated by melancholic fantasies of object loss. Differing from Freud's theory of melancholia as an act of internalizing and thus preserving the incorporated, lost object, Klein's model of "introjection" submits the lost object to a further trauma occasioned by the infant's aggressive, sadistic, and specifically cannibalistic fantasies of devouring loss.[18] The persistent psychic returns of the paranoid-schizoid position—whose radical reversals of love and hate, benevolence and hostility, protection and destruction play havoc with the ego's relation to its earliest part-objects—also belie the aim of achieving any normative, prescriptive, and thus terminal self-possession of identity by means of the redemptive logic of symbolic reparation. Indeed, as Jacqueline Rose—following Lacan—has observed, Klein's positing of a third stage of symbolic reparation demands at once "too much and too little of an ego whose role it is to master the anxiety out of which it has itself been produced" (Rose, "Negativity," 146). Reparation thus bears a "mysterious" relation to melancholia insofar as it is always already predicated as a kind of negotiated defense against what it purports to cure. For Rose, the radical negation that marks the Kleinian field proves salutary, paradoxically enough, "in the trouble it poses to the concept of a sequence" and as a "bar...to what might elsewhere (and increasingly) appear as normative and prescriptive in the work and followers of Melanie Klein" (146). Similarly, Esther Sánchez-Pardo insists that what is revolutionary in modern object-relations theory remains "the deconstructive efforts Klein undertakes, the subversion of any normative teleology implicit in her theory of the fragility of the paranoid-schizoid and depressive positions" (188). Such recent valorizations of Kleinian melancholia parallel Leo Bersani's resistance to an aesthetics of redemption tied to symbolic reparation. Bersani's reading of Klein's 1923 essay on "Early Analysis" elicits a new understanding of symbolization where the sublimation of objects would not be reducible in some literal-minded way to displaced symptoms of desire. Rather, "sublimation," he writes "would describe the fate of sexual energies detached from sexual desires." Such a view of "sublimation as coextensive with sexuality" would lead to an aesthetic positioned metonymically "to the side" rather than metaphorically "behind the object." Again, it is the positional, rather than developmental, side of Klein's project that, for Bersani, proves salutary in advancing modes of literary reading that, as he puts it, would "reinstate a curiously disinterested mode of desire for objects, a mode of excitement that, far from investing objects with symbolic significance, would enhance their specificity and thereby fortify their resistance to the violence of symbolic intent" (229, 234).

The drama of pre-Oedipal experience—its excitable objects and their traumatic loss—is everywhere on view in postwar American poetry but no more so than in the verse of Elizabeth Bishop. The vicissitudes of Bishop's childhood are well known: the death of her father while she was just an infant; her permanent separation at age five from her mother, owing to the latter's hospitalization for insanity; the displaced moves from her mother's parents in Nova Scotia to her paternal grandparents in Worcester, to her maternal aunt in Revere, Massachusetts. Bishop bore these traumatic losses and dislocations, symptomatically, in the body—presenting such nervous conditions as eczema, asthma, allergies, and later her chronic alcoholism as an adult. Although H.D.'s companion and patron, Bryher, urged Bishop in Paris to seek a psychoanalytic cure for her asthma, as a writer Bishop had a principled resistance to analysis: "everything I have read about it," she wrote to Marianne Moore, "has made me think that psychologists misinterpret and very much underestimate all the workings of ART!"[19] Nevertheless, during the mid-1940s, the poet entered treatment with psychiatrists in Key West and New York for her chronic alcoholism.

Bishop associated her drinking with an early screen memory. Her draft manuscript of "A Drunkard" begins "When I was three, I watched the Salem fire" (Bishop,

Edgar Allan Poe, 150). In the poem, she not only recollects the historical referent of the 1914 Salem Fire, but, equally important, she also revisits the "strange objects" of pre-Oedipal fantasy: a burning red sky, a black stocking, her mother's "reprimand," and an "abnormal thirst." Bishop's aim is neither to commemorate nor glean thematic meaning from what has been otherwise called "the greatest disaster in Salem's history."[20] Rather, Bishop beholds the spectacle of the Salem fire in what Bersani would characterize as "a curiously disinterested mode of desire." Resisting what Bersani describes as the "violence of symbolic intent," she brings into remarkable focus the sensuous immediacy of vividly recollected objects, bathed in the disaster's primary-color palette of reds and blacks. "I stood in my crib," she writes, "& watched it burn. / The sky was bright red; everything was red; / out on the lawn, my mother's white dress looked / rose-red; my enameled crib was red / and my hands holding to its rods—" (*Edgar Allan Poe*, 150). Against the intense visual field of the disaster, the rest of the visible landscape stands out as "all black— / in silhouette—)" (150). "Strange objects," she recalls, "seemed to have blown across the water / ... Blackened boards, shiny black like black feathers—" (151). As a matter of literary form, terminal dashes serve not just to end-stop her lines but rather to invoke the arresting drama of re-finding objects that, however familiar, possess the uncanny address of what Jean Laplanche theorizes as "enigmatic signifiers."[21]

Reiterating the palpable yet fascinating Otherness of these "strange objects," Bishop invests them, in memory, with an uncanny and forbidden sexual allure: one that she associates with her mother's "reprimand":

> I picked up a woman's long black cotton
> stocking. Curiosity. My mother said sharply
> *Put that down!* I remember clearly, clearly—
>
> But since that night, that day, that reprimand
> I have suffered from abnormal thirst—
> I swear it's true—and by the age
> Of twenty or twenty-one I had begun
> To drink, & drink—I can't get enough
> And, as you must have noticed,
> I'm half-drunk now ...
>
> And all I'm telling you may be a lie ... (151)

Like Lowell and Berryman, Bishop probes the psychic fissure splitting the represented subject of childhood "When I was three" from the narrative subject of the authorial present who not only admits "I'm half drunk now" but whose mode of witnessing is itself divided between the avowed testimony of "I swear it's true" and its perverse disavowal—"all I'm telling you may be a lie." What matters, finally, is not the "truth" of the event but the passion of the poet's associations—red sky, a white dress that is also rose-red, red bars, red hands, blackened boards, black feathers, a black stocking, a reprimand, an abnormal thirst—positioned metonymically "to the side" rather than metaphorically "behind" the lost object cause of desire. It is precisely such a recovery of the poet's earliest object relations that leads Bishop to "the possibility of pursuing not an art of truth divorced from experience, but," as Bersani has it, "of phenomena liberated from the obsession with truth" (237).

Yet if there is a "truth" of thematic meaning to be discerned in Bishop's pre-Oedipal memories and their "strange objects," it surfaces as symptom rather than as purposeful symbol in "A Drunkard." Not insignificantly, the poet's earliest associations of thirst with maternal "reprimand" are linked not just to the place name "Salem"—a key term of American national narrative—but also to the more enigmatic signifier of "a woman's long black cotton / stocking." Like much of modernist verse, Bishop's poetry not infrequently stages psychoanalytic truths through what Toni Morrison describes in *Playing in the Dark* as a certain "fetishizing of color, the transference to blackness of the power of illicit sexuality, chaos, madness, impropriety, anarchy, strangeness, and helpless, hapless desire" (80–81).[22] Blackness in Bishop's poetry is not just linked metonymically to representations of the unconscious but is, more often than not, racially marked. To take just one example, the childhood panic attack that overwhelms the narrator of "In the Waiting Room" comes on as "the sensation of falling off / the round, turning world / into cold, blue-black space" (*Elizabeth Bishop*, 150). Bishop experiences the physical space of the waiting room as "sliding / beneath a big black wave, / another, and another." Elsewhere, blackness is linked in the poem with the waiting room's *National Geographic* images of "the inside of a volcano, / black, and full of ashes" (149) and—turning the page—the uncanny figures of "black, naked women" whose corporeality is rendered "horrifying" (149) in the ethnographic photographs of Osa and Martin Johnson. Such associations of blackness, femininity, and pre-Oedipal psychic extremity are likewise inscribed, for example, in Robert Lowell's mythic apostrophes to the Medusa in "Florence," the "dark night" of domestic crisis in "Skunk Hour," and more explicitly the racial representations of "A Mad Negro Soldier Confined at Munich" and "For the Union Dead." Similarly in, say, Sylvia Plath's beekeeping poems, the conjuncture of feminine sexuality and primitive, unconscious desire is figured in "the swarmy feeling of African hands / Minute and shrunk for export, / Black on black, angrily clambering" (213).[23] In retrospect, such racial tropes have certainly not stood the test of time. Revisiting the closing lines of her title piece to her 1955 volume *The Diamond Cutters*, Adrienne Rich repudiates the colonizing metaphor for the poet's sources of unconscious inspiration: "And know that Africa / Will yield you more to do" (20–21). "Thirty years later," she writes, "I have trouble with the informing metaphor of this poem.... But I was drawing, quite ignorantly, on the long tradition of domination, according to which the precious resource is yielded up into the hands of the dominator as if by a natural event. The enforced and exploited labor of actual Africans in actual diamond mines was invisible to me" (329).

Such racialized figures of psychic blindness and insight are not unique to modern American poetry but reach back to the founding of modern psychoanalysis. Indeed, the example of, say, Roethke's famous psychoanalytic line "In a dark time, the eye begins to see" (*CPTR*, 231) finds its antecedent in Freud's own tropes for the analyst's discernment as a kind of vision "adapted…to the dark."[24] Such reliance on psychic tropes of blackness is one of several issues that have stalled the rapprochement of psychoanalysis and African American poetics. If "the problem of the Twentieth Century," as W. E. B. Du Bois famously observed, "is the problem of the color line," then it also has persisted as a problem for psychoanalysis (xxxi). Du Bois's foundational take on African American "double consciousness" itself evolves from the medical diagnostics of nineteenth-century figures such as Oswald Külpe and the psychological theories of Du Bois's Harvard mentor, William James. "Double consciousness as a term," writes Arnold Rampersad, facilitates entry into the human mind" (200). Yet, in just six short years, Du Bois himself came to resist the mind's psychoanalytic depths, favoring instead the key terms of "race, milieu, and moment" in his biographical study of John Brown. "Far from being influenced by psychology," writes Rampersad, "black biography has kept a vast distance between itself and that discipline" (198), owing to the anxiety that "to impose Freud on the black mind is to extend European hegemony over blacks" (202). Indeed, the skewed power relation in psychoanalysis's colonial relation to Africa and African Americans, for Claudia Tate, is condensed in Freud's oft-repeated joke comparing analysands to "negroes": a joke that Tate, following Sander Gilman, attributes to Freud's own racial anxieties as a *fin de siècle* European Jew. Freud's issues surrounding race, gender, and colonialism—on view in such infamous comments as "the sexual life of adult women is a 'dark continent' for psychology" ("*The Question*," 212)—go far in explaining, for Tate, why "black scholars have not rushed to embrace psychoanalysis as an ally in their struggle against this particular psychopathology of white people" (54).

Despite the resistance to psychoanalytic theory in the reception of modern African American literature, "the simple truth" remains for Rampersad, "that being a Negro or colored or even a black in America is above all a psychological state" (208). Certainly, canonical African American modernists such as Richard Wright and Ralph Ellison write out of that recognition. Both carried on a productive psychoanalytic collaboration with such figures as Dr. Frederic Wertham, the founder with Wright and Earl Brown of Harlem's Lafargue Psychiatric Clinic. At a time when most analysts and psychiatric hospitals refused to treat African Americans— and when less than 25 of the some 4,500 psychiatrists in America were black—the Lafargue Clinic provided a race-blind, sliding-scale psychiatric facility serving the Harlem community. Housed in the basement of St. Philip's Episcopal Church, it offered in many cases free analytic treatment with the volunteer staff of fourteen psychiatrists, in addition to some dozen social workers and other specialists. The Lafargue Clinic balanced traditional analytic practice with what was then characterized as "social psychiatry" geared to the psychic vicissitudes of institutional racism, class oppression, and other forms of social discrimination.[25] In this vein, Wright and Wertham named the clinic after the French Marxist Paul Lafargue out of the progressive conviction that "discrimination and poverty," as Wertham had it, "cause as much mental confusion and neurosis as the bewilderment of possessing several million dollars."[26] Paying tribute to the work of the Lafargue Clinic, Ralph Ellison's essay "Harlem Is Nowhere" praises the clinic as "one of Harlem's most important institutions and "perhaps the most successful attempt in the nation to provide psychotherapy for the underprivileged." Ellison's title signifies on the vernacular turn of phrase "I'm nowhere": a common expression of "the feeling borne in upon many Negroes that they have no stable, recognized place in society." The Lafargue Clinic was a way station for those "in desperate search for an identity…for answers to the questions: Who am I, What am I, Why am I, and Where" ("Harlem Is Nowhere," 294–295, 297)?"

Such fundamental questionings of one's psychic and social location go to the heart of Harlem Renaissance poetics as, for example, in the vernacular blues lyricism of Langston Hughes's "Cross." In it, Hughes's persona is split by the "double consciousness" of a family romance whose race, gender, and class antagonisms persist across the generations as a traumatic legacy:

> My old man's a white old man
> And my old mother's black.
>
> …………………………
> My old man died in a fine big house.
> My ma died in a shack.
> I wonder where I'm going to die,
> Being neither white nor black? (59)

Such self-analysis—linked as it is to an interrogation of social modernity—is also posed in the formalist measures of Countee Cullen's "Heritage" and the repeated refrain of the poet's rhetorical question. "What is Africa to me?" (Locke, 250). Cullen's query, in Barbara Johnson's analysis, "'plays a double part,' as does the repeated phrase 'so I lie,' which carries the ambiguity the poem enacts between language and the body, between legend and unconscious desire" (Johnson, 96). Such pioneering depictions of the psychic "double part" in African American verse are also advanced in the realms of feminine sexuality in women's poetry of the Harlem Renaissance. In this vein, Mae V. Cowdery's "Insatiate" explores sexuality's psychic divide as it splits her poem's persona. On the one hand, Cowdery's desire for the other is presented visually in an opening blazon of imaginary part objects:

> If her lips were rubies red,
> Her eyes two sapphires blue,
> Her fingers ten sticks of white jade,
> Coral tipped…and her hair of purple hue
> Hung down in a silken shawl…
> They would not be enough
> To fill the coffers of my need.

On the other hand, the same-sex, cross-racial features that Cowdery visualizes in her lover—however exotic—lack satisfaction. The rubies, sapphires, jade, coral, and shawl of lips, eyes, fingers, nails, and hair fail, as she says, "to fill the coffers of my need." Such erotic signifiers are ultimately symbolic placeholders for what Lacan would designate as the *objet a* cause of the desire. In the course of the poem, these lures of desire are driven and displaced by the more perverse erotics of "uncertainty" sustained not by the desire *for* the other but what Lacan identifies as the socially mediated desire *of* the Other, imagined here in the rivalrous "tip of one pink nail / upon another's hand":[27]

> But if my love did whisper
> Her song into another's ear
> Or place the tip of one pink nail
> Upon another's hand,
> Then would I forever be
> A willing prisoner . . .
> Chained to her side by uncertainty! (130)

The "double consciousness" of the modern desiring self that was ventured in African American women's poetry of the Harlem Renaissance remains remarkably contemporary even as the latter looks forward to the complicated performances of race and desire in the midcentury verse of, say, Gwendolyn Brooks's "a song in the front yard." There, Brooks's child narrator yearns "to be a bad woman, too, / And wear the brave stockings of night-black lace / And strut down the streets with paint on my face."[28] Like Bishop, Brooks's persona associates desire with the fetished "stockings of night-black lace" and, like Cowdery, she invests in the desire of the Other imagined here in the "charity children" who "do some wonderful things" and "have wonderful fun" out "in the back yard" and "down the alley" otherwise repressed in the respectable public sphere of the "front yard."

   In such moments, the psychic powers of blackness—at once desired and subject to "reprimand"—haunt modern American poetics in figures of what more recent theorists such as Anne Anlin Cheng, José Esteban Muñoz, David Eng, Sara Clarke Kaplan, Paul Gilroy, and others variously analyze as racial melancholia.[29] Rereading Freud's 1917 essay "Mourning and Melancholia," this line of critical reception considers the vexed legacy of racial identifications, exclusions, and oppressions in the United States as a melancholic history of object loss. However repressed, denied, and misremembered, such lost objects of melancholy nevertheless remain incorporated in the American unconscious and persist in the spectral returns and re-findings of race haunting the public sphere of the United States.

   In recent African American poetics, the most sophisticated working through of racial melancholia happens, arguably, in the work of Pulitzer Prize–winner Natasha Trethewey. The photographic image is the chosen medium that Trethewey revisits in conjuring specters of the past. Against what Roland Barthes would describe as the manifest narrative of the photograph's *studium*—the cultural and ideological codes by which "the figures, the faces, the gestures, the settings, the actions" take on a readable historical meaning—Trethewey discerns the photograph's *punctum*: whose latent force punctuates, pricks, and wounds the manifest scene with "what

Lacan," Barthes writes, "calls the Tuché, the Occasion, the Encounter, the Real in its indefatigable expression" (26, 4, 6). It is this encounter that Trethewey's poetry invokes in conjuring the specters of melancholy as they haunt the personal and public registers of race in America. In particular, Trethewey's second volume, *Bellocq's Ophelia* (2002), negotiates the desire of the Other as evidenced in Ernest J. Bellocq's well-known photographic portraits of African American women who labored as sex workers in the Basin Street Mansion, Mahogany Hall's "Octoroon Club," and the other bordellos of New Orleans's Storyville. Appropriating the intimacies of epistolary verse and diary forms, Trethewey recovers the imagined figure of Ophelia—a composite narrative persona gleaned from Bellocq's photos. Trethewey's strategy intervenes in Bellocq's oeuvre as it signifies on the Western palimpsest of arrested feminine agency represented, say, in Shakespeare's Ophelia and Sir John Everett Millais's 1852 portrait of her drowning.[30]

Trethewey's feminist strategy assumes Ophelia's narrative point of view in analyzing the manifest scene of Bellocq's portraiture as it puts on display the desire of the Other driving Storyville's sexual economy. Moreover, she gives voice to the racial melancholia whose shadow falls as a counternarrative of oppression across the erotic framing of Storyville's sex workers. In "Letters from Storyville, December 1910," Ophelia's madam gives her the racially coded pseudonym Violet in performing as *tableau vivant* for her white clientele: "She calls me Violet now— / A common name here in Storyville—except / that I am the *African Violet* for the promise of that wild continent hidden beneath my white skin. At her cue, I walked slowly / across the room, paused in strange postures / until she called out, *Tableau vivant*" (13). The erotic performance on display here depends on the incorporated, lost object of race whose "wild continent" is "hidden" by "white skin": the lure of what Frantz Fanon described as "a racial epidermal schema" framing Ophelia's exotic "octoroon" identity (112). As a "white-skinned black woman," Ophelia's visual exploitation is part of a racial narrative that is not unlike the vexed heritage in "Cross" insofar as it cuts across personal and public legacies. "It troubles me," she writes,

> to think that I am suited
> for this work—spectacle and fetish—
> a pale odalisque. But then I recall
> my earliest training—childhood—how
> my mother taught me to curtsy and be still
> so that I might please a white man, my father.
> For him I learned to shape my gestures,
> Practiced expressions on my pliant face. (20)

More than Hughes, however, Trethewey plumbs the traumatic social text of race's sexual economy insofar as Ophelia must "fear the day a man enters my room both customer and father" (38).

Becoming herself adept at portraiture, Ophelia gains a certain empowerment in seeing beyond the studied gaze of Papa Bellocq's photography: "I look," she says at what he can see "through his lens / and what he cannot—silverfish behind / the walls the yellow tint of a faded bruise— / other things here, what the camera misses" (43). Ultimately, Trethewey's poetics of the photographic lens and its powers of visual representation discern the conjuncture of race and visuality whose melancholic structure of feeling—what Du Bois describes as a "peculiar sensation"—registers the force of social modernity encrypted at the heart of the psyche's "double consciousness." Negotiating her status as the enigmatic object of Bellocq's photographic gaze, Ophelia attains a provisional mastery over modernity's powers of visual representation. In her "Letters from Storyville," she claims the psychic resources that belong to the modern subject of color whom Du Bois describes as the one "born with a veil, and gifted with second-sight in this American world,—a world which yields him no true self-consciousness, but only lets him see himself through the revelation of the other world." Ophelia assumes a certain self-possession of character through her "letters," but her identity as a writer does not entirely dispel the affective force of melancholia: what Du Bois describes as the "shadow" of American race relations as it traverses the self—the "peculiar sensation, this double-consciousness, this sense of always looking at one's self through the eyes of others, of measuring one's soul by the tape of a world that looks on in amused contempt and pity" (3).

Working through the internalized desire as well as the "contempt and pity" of the Other remains both the difficult and exhilarating challenge at stake in the psychoanalysis of modern American poetry. Beyond any personal or therapeutic gain to be had from the talking cure, giving testimony to the poetics of the unconscious affords a singular political agency: one that, as Anne Anlin Cheng writes, moves from the melancholia of "bearing *grief* to being a subject speaking *grievance*" (174). Finally, despite or, better, by way of our resistance to the psychoanalysis of American poetry, we may be possessed, paradoxically enough, of its cure and "pardon of speech": the recognition as Alice Walker has it in "So We've Come at Last to Freud":

> That I, once unhappy, am
> Now
> Quite sanely
>   Jubilant,
> & that neither you
> Nor I can
> Deny
> That no matter how
> "Sick"
> The basis
> is
> Of what we have,
> What we *do* have
> Is Good. (125)

NOTES

1   On the relation of psychoanalysis to poetry, Adam Phillips writes, "Freud, Jung, Lacan, Winnicott, Bion, Meltzer, Milner, Segal, among many others, all agree in their privileging of the poetic. Psychoanalysis may not have mattered quite as much as it would have liked to poetry, but poetry has certainly mattered to psychoanalysis" (2002, 4). Of the psychoanalytic dimension of literary interpretation, Cary Nelson writes, "Incorporation provides a surprisingly apt analogy for the special, privileged status we assign to the literary text and to the form of internalization we know as interpretation. In criticism, the encrypted object is the interpreted text" (57–58).

2   Lacan is reported to have been told of Freud's aside directly from Jung himself. See Roudinesco, 177.

3   Floyd Dell, letter to Frederick J. Hoffman, September 17, 1942, quoted in Frederick J. Hoffman, *Freudianism*, 58.

4   Quoted in Burke, 195.

5   Mina Loy, "Notes on Jews," quoted in Burke, 313.

6   "We hope it will not be considered extravagant if we suggest that the subconscious spectator tends to identify the pitcher with all the forces of negation throughout the world. As he winds up and puts upon the ball every ounce of repression which is in him, he becomes suddenly a little brother to Puritanism, Volstead, law and order, the Malthusian theory, and keep off the grass" (Broun, 79), quoted in Hoffman, *Twenties*, 199–200.

7   On the relation of psychoanalysis and photography, see Baer.

8   See Spiro; Morris; Friedman and DuPlessis; Friedman, *Analyzing*; Friedman, *Psyche*.

9   M. L. Rosenthal coined the term "confessional poetry" in "Poetry as Confession," a 1959 review of Robert Lowell's *Life Studies*. Commenting on the new personal lyricism inaugurated by W. D. Snodgrass, Lowell, Berryman, and later Plath and Sexton, M. L. Rosenthal later wrote that "these poems seemed to me one culmination of the Romantic and modern tendency to place the literal Self more and more at the center of the poem" (*New Poets*, 79).

10 Quoted in Middlebrook, 158.

11 See Kramer.

12 Rose, *Haunting*; Diehl.

13 See Berryman, *Berryman's Shakespeare*.

14 Berryman, "Shakespeare's Reality," in Berryman, *Berryman's Shakespeare*, 244; quoted in Maber, 222.

15 Roethke, "Silence," in *Collected Poems of Theodore Roethke* , 21 (hereafter cited in the text as *CPTR*).

16 See Kenneth Burke, "The Vegetal Radicalism of Theodore Roethke," *The Sewanee Review*, 58, 1 (January–March 1950): 68–108.

17 "Klein chose the term 'position,'" according to Hanna Segal, "to emphasize the fact that the phenomenon she was describing was not simply a passing 'stage' or 'phase' such as, for example, the oral phase; her term implies a specific configuration of object relations, anxieties and defences which persist throughout life" (ix); quoted in Soto-Crespo, 204.

18 See Butler.

19 Elizabeth Bishop, letter to Marianne Moore, September 2, 1937, quoted in Millier, 127.

20 Frances Diane Robotti, *Chronicles of Old Salem* (1948), quoted in Travisano and Quinn, 345.

21 "Briefly, let us remember that this is a world of signification and communication, swamping the child's capacity for apprehension and mastery. Messages are offered on all sides. By messages I do not necessarily nor chiefly mean verbal messages. Any gesture, any mimicry functions as a signifier. These originary, traumatic signifiers I propose to call 'enigmatic signifiers'. These signifiers are not enigmatic by virtue of the simple fact that the infant does not know the code, which he or she would need to learn.... What is crucial is the fact that the adult world is entirely infiltrated with unconscious and sexual significations to which *adults themselves* do not have the code" (Laplanche, 127).

22 See also Lott; North; Nielsen, *Reading Race*; Nielsen, *Reading Race in American Poetry*; Walton.

23 See Ford, 147.

24 Sigmund Freud, *Letter to Andreas-Salomé*, May 25, 1916, in *Sigmund Freud and Lou Andreas-Salomé Letters*, 45; cited in Ogden, 6.

25 See Doyle.

26 Bendiner, quoted in Doyle, 182–183.

27 In "The Symbolic Order," Lacan describes the psychic uncertainty of desire as follows: "An incessant see-saw of the lark mirror which, at each moment, makes a complete turn on itself—the subject exhausts himself in pursuing the desire of the other, which he will never be able to grasp as his own desire, because his own desire is the desire of the other. It is himself whom he pursues. Therein lies the drama of this jealous passion, which is also a form of imaginary intersubjective relation" (*Seminar I*, 221).

28 Gwendolyn Brooks, "a song in the front yard," *Blacks* (Chicago: Third World Press, 2001), 10.

29 See Cheng; Muñoz; Eng and Han; Gilroy.

30 See Debo.

REFERENCES

Baer, Ulrich. *Spectral Evidence: The Photography of Trauma*. Cambridge, MA: MIT Press, 2005.

Barthes, Roland. *Camera Lucida*. Trans. Richard Howard. New York: Hill and Wang, 1981.

Bendiner, Robert. "Psychiatry for the Needy." *Tomorrow* (April 1948): 22.

Berryman, John. *Berryman's Shakespeare*. Ed. John Haffenden. New York: Farrar, Straus & Giroux, 1999.

———. *The Dream Songs*. New York: Farrar, Straus, & Giroux, 1969.

Bersani, Leo. "Death and Literary Authority: Marcel Proust and Melanie Klein." In *Reading Melanie Klein*, ed. Lyndsey Stonebridge and John Phillips. London: Routledge, 1998. 223–244.

Bishop, Elizabeth. *Edgar Allan Poe & The Juke-Box: Uncollected Poems, Drafts, and Fragments*. Ed. Alice Quinn. New York: Farrar, Straus and Giroux, 2006.

———. *Elizabeth Bishop: Poems, Prose and Letters*. Ed. Robert Giroux and Lloyd Schwartz. New York: Library of America, 2008.

Boccioni, Umberto, Carlo Carrà, Luigi Russolo, Giacomo Balla, and Gino Severini, "Manifesto of the Futurist Painters" (1910). In *Futurism: An Anthology*, ed. Lawrence S. Rainey, Christine Poggi, and Laura Wittman. New Haven, CT: Yale University Press, 2009.

Bremen, Brian A. *William Carlos Williams and the Diagnostics of Culture.* New York: Oxford University Press, 1993.

Broun, Heywood. "Bambino the Maestro: The Suggestion of a Possible Freudian Interpretation of the Aesthetic Appeal of Babe Ruth." *Vanity Fair* (May 1922): 79.

Burke, Carolyn. *Becoming Modern: The Life of Mina Loy.* Berkeley: University of California Press, 1987.

Butler, Judith. "Reply from Judith Butler to Mills and Jenkins." *differences, A Journal of Feminist Cultural Studies* 18, 2 (Summer 2007): 180–195.

Cheng, Anne Anlin. *The Melancholy of Race: Psychoanalysis, Assimilation, and Hidden Grief.* New York: Oxford University Press, 2001.

Clifford, James. *The Predicament of Culture: Twentieth-Century Ethnography, Literature, and Art.* Cambridge: Harvard University Press, 1988.

Crane, Hart. Letter of April 20, 1927 to Yvor Winters. In *Hart Crane and Yvor Winters: Their Literary Correspondence,* ed. Thomas Francis Parkinson. Berkeley, CA: The University of California Press, 1978.

Debo, Annette. "Ophelia Speaks: Resurrecting Still Lives in Natasha Trethewey's *Bellocq's Ophelia.*" *African American Review* 40, 2 (Summer 2008): 201–214.

Diehl, Joanne Feit. *Elizabeth Bishop and Marianne Moore: The Psychodynamics of Creativity.* Princeton: Princeton University Press, 1993.

Diggory, Terence. "William Carlos Williams's Early References to Freud: 1917–1930." *William Carlos Williams Review* 22, 2 (1996): 3–17.

Doolittle, Hilda. *Collected Poems, 1912–1944.* Ed. Louis L. Martz. New York: New Directions, 1986.

——. *Tribute to Freud.* New York: Pantheon, 1956.

Doyle, Dennis. " 'A Fine New Child': The Lafargue Mental Hygiene Clinic and Harlem's African American Communities, 1946–1958." *Journal of the History of Medicine and Allied Sciences* 64, 2 (April 2009): 173–212.

Du Bois, W. E. B. *The Souls of Black Folk.* New York: Bantam, 1953.

Ellison, Ralph. "Harlem Is Nowhere." *Shadow and Act.* New York: Random House, 1964.

Eng, David L. and Shinhee Han. "A Dialogue on Racial Melancholia." In *Loss: The Politics of Mourning,* ed. David L. Eng and David Kazanjian. Berkeley: University of California Press, 2003. 343–371.

Fanon, Frantz. *Black Skin, White Masks.* Trans. Charles Lam Markmann. New York: Grove Weidenfeld, 1991.

Felman, Shoshana. *Testimony: Crises of Witnessing in Literature, Psychoanalysis and History.* New York: Routledge, 1991.

Ford, Karen Jackson. *Gender and the Poetics of Brocade.* Jackson: University of Mississippi Press, 2009.

Foucault, Michel. *History of Sexuality, Volume 1: An Introduction.* Trans. Robert Hurley. New York: Pantheon, 1978.

Freud, Sigmund. *Civilization and Its Discontents.* Trans. James Strachey. New York: W. W. Norton, 1961.

——. "Creative Writers and Day-Dreaming." In *The Standard Edition of the Complete Psychological Works of Sigmund Freud,* ed. and trans. James Strachey. Vol. 9 (1906–1908): *Jensen's 'Gradiva' and Other Works.* London: Hogarth Press and the Institute of Psychoanalysis, 1953–1974. 141–154.

——. "Drives and their Vicissitudes." In *The Standard Edition of the Complete Psychological Works of Sigmund Freud,* ed. and trans. James Strachey. Vol. 14 (1914–1916): *On the History of the Psycho-Analytic Movement, Papers on Metapsychology and*

Other Works. London: Hogarth Press and the Institute of Psychoanalysis, 1953–1974. 109–140.

——. *Five Lectures on Psycho-Analysis.* In *The Standard Edition of the Complete Psychological Works of Sigmund Freud,* ed. and trans. James Strachey. Vol. 11 (1910). London: Hogarth Press and the Institute of Psychoanalysis, 1953–1974. 1–56.

——. *The Interpretation of Dreams.* In *The Standard Edition of the Complete Psychological Works of Sigmund Freud,* ed. and trans. James Strachey. Vol. 4 (1900). London: Hogarth Press and the Institute of Psychoanalysis, 1953–1974. ix–627.

——. *New Introductory Lectures on Psycho-Analysis.* In *The Standard Edition of the Complete Psychological Works of Sigmund Freud,* ed. and trans. James Strachey. Vol. 22 (1932–1936). London: Hogarth Press and the Institute of Psychoanalysis, 1953–1974. 1–182.

——. "Psycho-Analytic Notes on an Autobiographical Account of a Case of Paranoia (Dementia Paranoides)." In *The Standard Edition of the Complete Psychological Works of Sigmund Freud,* ed. and trans. James Strachey. Vol. 12 (1911–1913): *The Case of Schreber, Papers on Technique and Other Works.* London: Hogarth Press and the Institute of Psychoanalysis, 1953–1974. 1–82.

——. "*The Question of Lay Analysis.*" In *The Standard Edition of the Complete Psychological Works of Sigmund Freud,* ed. and trans. James Strachey. Vol. 20 (1925–1926). London: Hogarth Press and the Institute of Psychoanalysis, 1953–1974. 177–258.

——. *Sigmund Freud and Lou Andreas-Salomé Letters.* Ed. E. Pfeiffer; trans. W. and E. Robson-Scott. New York: Harcourt, Brace, Jovanovich, 1966.

——. *Three Essays on the Theory of Sexuality.* In *The Standard Edition of the Complete Psychological Works of Sigmund Freud,* ed. and trans. James Strachey. Vol. 7 (1901–1905). London: Hogarth Press and the Institute of Psychoanalysis, 1953–1974. 123–246.

Friedman, Susan Stanford. Ed. *Analyzing Freud: Letters of H.D., Bryher, and Their Circle.* New York: New Directions, 2002.

——. *Penelope's Web: Gender, Modernity, H.D.'s Fiction.* New York: Cambridge University Press, 1990.

——. *Psyche Reborn: the Emergence of H. D.* Bloomington: Indiana University Press, 1981.

Friedman, Susan Stanford, and Rachel Blau DuPlessis. Ed. *Signets: Reading H. D.* Madison: University of Wisconsin Press, 1990.

Gilroy, Paul. *Postcolonial Melancholia.* New York: Columbia University Press, 2005.

Hoffman, Frederick J. *Freudianism and the Literary Mind.* Baton Rouge: Louisiana State University Press, 1957.

——. *The Twenties.* New York: Viking, 1949.

Honey, Maureen. Ed. *Shadowed Dreams: Women's Poetry of the Harlem Renaissance.* New Brunswick, NJ: Rutgers University Press, 1989.

Hughes, Langston. *The Collected Poems of Langston Hughes.* Eds. Arnold Rampersad and David Roessel. New York: Knopf, 1994.

Johnson, Barbara. *The Feminist Difference: Literature, Psychoanalysis, Race, and Gender.* Cambridge, MA: Harvard University Press, 1998.

Kramer, Lawrence. "Freud and the Skunks: Genre and Language in *Life Studies.*" In *Robert Lowell: Essays on the Poetry,* ed. Steven Gould Axelrod. New York: Cambridge University Press, 1987. 80–98.

Krupat, Arnold. *Ethnocriticism: Ethnography, History, Literature.* Berkeley: University of California Press, 1992.

Lacan, Jacques . "The Function and Field of Speech and Language in Psychoanalysis." *Écrits: A Selection.* Trans. and ed. Alan Sheridan. London: Routledge, 1977.

———. "On a Question Prior to Any Possible Treatment of Psychosis." In *Écrits*, trans. Bruce Fink. New York: W. W. Norton, 2007. 445–488.

———. *The Seminar of Jacques Lacan: Encore on Feminine Sexuality, The Limits of Love and Knowledge (Book XX)*. Trans. Bruce Fink. New York: W. W. Norton, 1998.

———. *The Seminar of Jacques Lacan: The Ethics of Psychoanalysis (Book VII)*. Trans. Dennis Porter. New York: W. W. Norton, 1997.

———. *The Seminar of Jacques Lacan: The Four Fundamental Concepts of Psychoanalysis (Book XI)*. Trans. Alan Sheridan. New York: W. W. Norton, 1998.

———. *The Seminar of Jacques Lacan: Freud's Papers on Technique 1953–1954 (Book I)*. Trans. Jacques-Alain Miller. Cambridge: Cambridge University Press, 1988.

———. *The Seminar of Jacques Lacan: The Other Side of Psychoanalysis* (Book XVII). Trans. Russell Grigg. New York: W. W. Norton, 2007.

———. *The Seminar of Jacques Lacan: The Psychoses* (Book III). Trans. Jacques-Alain Miller and Russell Grigg. New York: W. W. Norton, 1997.

———. "The Subversion of the Subject and the Dialectic of Desire in the Freudian Unconscious" (1960). In *Écrits*, trans. Bruce Fink. New York: W. W. Norton, 2007. 671–702.

Laplanche, Jean. "The Drive and Its Source Object: Its Fate in the Transference." Trans. Luke Thurston. In *Essays on Otherness*, ed. John Fletcher. London: Routledge, 1999. 120–135.

Locke, Alain LeRoy. Ed. *The New Negro*. New York: Albert & Charles Boni, Inc., 1925; rpt. New York: Touchstone, 1997.

Lott, Eric. *Love and Theft: Blackface Minstrelsy and the American Working Class*. New York: Oxford University Press, 1995.

Lowell, Robert. *Collected Poems*. Ed. Frank Bidart and David Gewanter. New York: Farrar, Straus and Giroux, 2003.

Maber, Peter. "Berryman and Shakespearean Autobiography." In *"After Thirty Falls." New Essays on John Berryman*, ed. Philip Coleman and Philip McGowan. New York: Editions Rodopi B. V. Amsterdam, 2007. 209–224.

Mariani, Paul. *Dream Song: The Life of John Berryman*. Amherst: MA: University of Massachusetts Press, 1996.

———. *William Carlos Williams: A New World Naked*. New York: McGraw-Hill, 1981.

Middlebrook, Diane. *Anne Sexton, A Biography*. Boston: Houghton Mifflin, 1991.

Miller, Jacques-Alain. "Mathemes: Topology in the Teaching of Lacan." In *Lacan: Topologically Speaking*, ed., Ellie Ragland and Dragan Milovanovic. New York: Other Press, 2004.

Millier, Brett C. *Elizabeth Bishop: Life and the Memory of It*. Berkeley: University of California Press, 1993.

Morris, Adalaide. *How to Live / What to Do: H.D.'s Cultural Poetics*. Urbana: University of Illinois Press, 2003.

Morrison, Toni. *Playing in the Dark*. New York: Vintage, 1993.

Muñoz, José Esteban. *Disidentifications: Queers of Color and the Performance of Politics*. Minneapolis: University of Minnesota Press, 1999.

Nelson, Cary. "The Psychology of Criticism, or What Can Be Said." In *Psychoanalysis and the Question of the Text 1976–77*, ed. Geoffey H. Hartman. Baltimore: Johns Hopkins University Press, 1978. 46–61.

Nielsen, Aldon. *Reading Race: White American Poets and the Racial Discourse in the Twentieth Century*. Athens: University of Georgia Press, 1990.

———. Ed. *Reading Race in American Poetry: "An Area of Act."* Champaign: University of Illinois Press, 2000.

North, Michael. *The Dialect of Modernism: Race, Language, and Twentieth-Century Literature*. New York: Oxford University Press, 1998.

Ogden, Thomas H. *Conversations at the Frontier of Dreaming*. London: Jason Aronson, 2001.

Phillips, Adam. *Promises, Promises: Essays on Literature and Psychoanalysis*. New York: Basic Books, 2002.

Plath, Sylvia. *The Collected Poems of Sylvia Plath*. New York: HarperCollins, 1992.

Pound, Ezra. Letter to William Carlos Williams, November 10, 1917. In *Pound/Williams: Selected Letters of Ezra Pound and William Carlos Williams*, ed. Hugh Witemeyer. New York: New Directions, 1996.

——. *Make It New*. London: Faber and Faber, 1934.

Rampersad, Arnold. "Biography and Afro-American Culture." In *Afro-American Literary Study in the 1990s*, ed. Houston A. Baker Jr. and Patricia Redmond. Chicago: University of Chicago Press, 1989. 194–224.

Rich, Adrienne. *The Fact of a Door Frame: Poems Selected and New, 1950–1984*. New York: W. W. Norton, 1985.

Rodgers, Audrey T. *The Virgin and the Whore in the Poetry of William Carlos Williams*. Jefferson, NC: McFarland & Company, 1987.

Roethke, Theodore. *The Collected Poems of Theodore Roethke*. Norwell, MA: Anchor Press, 1975.

——. *On the Poet and His Craft: Selected Prose of Theodore Roethke*. Seattle: University of Washington Press, 1974.

Rose, Jacqueline. *The Haunting of Sylvia Plath*. Cambridge, MA: Harvard University Press, 1991.

——. "Negativity in the Work of Melanie Klein." In *Reading Melanie Klein*, ed. Lyndsey Stonebridge and John Phillips. London: Routledge, 1998. 126–159.

Rosenthal, M. L. *The New Poets*. New York: Oxford University Press, 1967.

——. "Poetry as Confession." *The Nation* 189 (September 19, 1959): 154–155.

Roudinesco, Élisabeth. *Jacques Lacan & Co: A History of Psychoanalysis in France, 1925–1985*. Chicago: University of Chicago Press, 1990.

Sánchez-Pardo, Esther. *Cultures of the Death Drive: Melanie Klein and Modernist Melancholia*. Durham, NC: Duke University Press, 2003.

Segal, Hanna. *Introduction to the Work of Melanie Klein*. London: Karnac Press, 1973.

Sexton, Anne. *The Complete Poems*. Boston: Houghton Mifflin, 1981.

Shakespeare, William. *King Richard III*. Ed. Janis Lull. Cambridge: Cambridge University Press, 1999.

Soto-Crespo, Ramón E. "Heterosexuality Terminable or Interminable? Kleinian Fantasies of Reparation and Mourning. " In *Psychoanalysis & Homosexuality*, ed. Tim Dean and Christopher Lane. Chicago: University of Chicago Press, 2001. 190–209.

Spiro, Joanna. "Weighed in the Balance: H.D.'s Resistance to Freud in 'Writing on the Wall.'" *American Imago* 58, 2 (Summer 2001): 597–621.

Tate, Claudia. "Freud and His 'Negro': Psychoanalysis as Ally and Enemy of African-Americans." *JPCS: Journal for the Psychoanalysis of Culture & Society* 1, 1 (Spring 1996): 53–62.

Travisano, Thomas. "'With an Eye of Flemish Accuracy': An Afterward." *Georgia Review* (Winter 1992): 612–616.

Trethewey, Natasha. *Bellocq's Ophelia*. St. Paul, MN: Graywolf Press, 2002.

Trilling, Lionel. *Liberal Imagination: Essays on Literature and Society*. New York: Viking, 1950.

Untermeyer, Louis. *American Poetry Since 1900.* New York: Henry Holt, 1923.

Vendler, Helen. *The Given and the Made: Strategies of Poetic Redefinition.* Cambridge, MA: Harvard University Press, 1995.

Walker, Alice. "So We've Come at Last to Freud." In *Her Blue Body Everything We Know: Earthling Poems 1965–1990 Complete.* Orlando, FL: Harcourt, 2004.

Walton, Jean. "Race, Psychoanalysis, and H. D.'s *Borderline.*" In *The Psychoanalysis of Race,* ed. Christopher Lane. New York: Columbia University Press, 1998. 395–416.

Williams, William Carlos. *The Autobiography of William Carlos Williams.* New York: New Directions, 1948.

———. *The Collected Poems of William Carlos Williams, Volume I, 1909–1939.* Ed. A. Walton Litz and Christopher MacGowan. New York: New Directions, 1988.

———. *In the American Grain.* New York: New Directions, 1956.

———. *Interviews with William Carlos Williams: "Speaking Straight Ahead."* Ed. Linda Wagner. New York: New Directions, 1976.

CHAPTER 17

AMERICAN POETRY, PRAYER, AND THE NEWS

JAHAN RAMAZANI

TWENTIETH-CENTURY American poetry metabolizes a variety of discursive genres, including fiction, song, theory, advertising, letters, and the law. To adapt Mikhail Bakhtin's terms, it dialogizes "literary and extraliterary languages," "intensifying" and "hybridizing" them, making them collide and rub up against one another (Bakhtin, 298). But Bakhtin famously theorized poetry as monologic and exclusionary, "suspended from any mutual interaction with alien discourse, any allusion to alien discourse" (285), "destroying all traces of social heteroglossia and diversity of language" (298): "The language of the poetic genre is a unitary and singular Ptolemaic world outside of which nothing else exists and nothing else is needed" (286). A vastly more dialogic conception of poetry emerges, however, from close analysis of twentieth-century American poems in relation to their generic others. For the purposes of this chapter, I restrict my attention to poetry's ambivalent interactions with two of its generic others: the news and prayer as representing two widely divergent positions on a broad discursive spectrum. How do modern and contemporary American poems that engage the news respond to journalism's mimeticism, presentism, and transparency? How do poems that adapt prayer respond to its ahistoricity, ritualism, and recursiveness? Does modern and contemporary American poetry more nearly resemble one or the other of its discursive cousins? How does American poetry overlap with, and distinguish itself from, these intergenres?

Poetry and the News

Probably the most famous comment on the relation between poetry and the news appears in William Carlos Williams's "Asphodel, That Greeny Flower":

> It is difficult
> to get the news from poems
> yet men die miserably every day
> for lack
> of what is found there.
> (Williams, "Astrophel," 319)

One way of understanding poetry, it seems, is as antigenre to the news. Elsewhere, Williams expounds this antithesis. "What is the use of reading the common news of the day," he asks in his *Autobiography*, "the tragic deaths and abuses of daily living" (Williams, *Autobiography*, 360) because such news is "trivial fill-gap," unlike the "profound language" of "poetry" (361). Newspapers "reveal nothing whatever, for they only tell you what you already know" (Williams, *Selected Essays*, 269), and their "headlines die in less than twenty four hours and become meaningless," "too short lived a mode for serious thought" (Williams in Bollard, 322).[1] With the turn-of-the-twentieth-century development of mass-circulation daily newspapers in rapidly expanding cities, their publication enabled in part by the increasingly efficient rotary press and ever cheaper pulp paper, the newspaper had become, as Alan Trachtenberg observes, a dominant form of reading and experience in America. "Unlike the printed page of a novel," or, we might add, a page of poetry, "the newspaper page declares itself without mistake as good only for a day, for this reading only: as if today's history of the world has nothing in common with yesterday's or tomorrow's"; "the daily newspaper deadens memory" (Trachtenberg, 125). Williams was disturbed by the newspaper's discursive dominance, a position strangely strengthened by what Benedict Anderson calls the "obsolescence of the newspaper on the morrow of its printing" (35). Walter Benjamin came to a similar conclusion about the commodified information called the news: "The value of information does not survive the moment in which it was new. It lives only at that moment; it has to surrender to it completely and explain itself to it without losing any time" (90). In London, Ezra Pound also railed in *Hugh Selwyn Mauberley* (1920) against Fleet Street and the press's displacement of cultural memory and high art with the crass short-term values of the marketplace. For Williams, as for other modernists such as Pound, T. S. Eliot, and W. B. Yeats, the news is shallow, ephemeral, and predictable, while poetry can, at its best, claim durability, profundity, and unexpectedness. In the first half of the twentieth century, this modernist understanding of the specificity of poetry is shaped by its contention with the more intensively capitalized and more pervasive discursive form for representing living history.

But if the news and poetry take sharply divergent approaches to the representation of public events, then why does Williams paste newspaper stories and clippings into his poetry, especially in his urban epic, *Paterson*? Apparently a modernist poem can incorporate the newspaper within its heteroglossia without becoming it. Despite his objections to the transience and shallowness of the news, Williams does not scorn it as beneath notice, in keeping with Andreas Huyssen's "great divide"; instead, Williams thinks the poet uses "the same materials as newsprint, the same dregs" (*Selected Essays*, 295). This is not poetry as aestheticist escape from living history. Even so, Williams believes the poet, etymologically a maker, does not "hold the mirror up to nature" but makes something distinctive from these materials—"a new thing, unlike any thing else in nature, a thing advanced and apart from it" (*Autobiography*, 241). By contrast with the seemingly passive mediation of current events by the reporter, the poet's use of language and form must actively re-create the historical present, an imaginative event that recurs perpetually in the sustained present of poetry's inventiveness.

For Williams, the main attraction of the newspaper lies in its immersion in locality. The modern newspaper as a genre has been conceptualized as helping "create and sustain Americans' sense of local community" (Pauly and Eckert, 313), a sense of locality rooted in what appear to be "factual, immediate, commonsensical, and authentic" stories (316). In his comments on *Paterson*, Williams emphasized the poet's need "to write particularly," not "in vague categories," trying "in the particular to discover the universal" (*Autobiography*, 391). Adapting John Dewey in the claim that "the local is the only universal, upon that all art builds" (391), Williams wished the city Paterson in his poem to "be as itself, locally, and so like every other place in the world" (392).[2] In "Americanism and Localism," a 1920 essay in *The Dial* that is ironically sandwiched with Pound's extravagantly transnational fourth canto, Dewey had argued that "the newspaper is the only genuinely popular form of literature we have achieved" (685) because it "has revelled" in localism and so provides the "depth or thickness" lacking elsewhere in American literature (686). Sympathetic to American nativism after World War I, Williams refused what he saw as Pound's and Eliot's "conformist" cosmopolitanism, their "rehash, repetition" of their European masters (Williams, "Prologue," 24–25).[3] In *Paterson* he seized on the urban newspaper as an intergenre to help curb poetry's pull toward abstraction, seeking instead to indigenize the foreign forms of epic and of poetry more generally by making them responsive to the local experience of American landscape, language, and history.[4]

Trying to absorb the newspaper's local "depth" and representational "thickness" into poetry, Williams gleaned news of gruesome child deaths and other local stories from issues of the newspaper *The Prospector* published in 1936 (Williams, *Paterson*, 280n98):

> Old newspaper files,
> to find—a child burned in a field,
> no language. Tried, aflame, to crawl under
> a fence to go home. So be it. Two others,

> boy and girl, clasped in each others' arms
> (clasped also by the water) So be it. Drowned
> wordless in the canal. So be it.
>
> (Williams, *Paterson*, 98)

Williams grounds his American epic in the local specificity of such news items, even thematizing appropriation of the news into literary form ("Old newspaper files," "amazed from the reading") (98). But in the process of generic metamorphosis, instead of remaining purely "local," these stories are abstracted as synecdoches for tragic news stories—"a child," "boy and girl." In this long series in *Paterson's* library episode, moreover, Williams punctuates the news items with a refrain, "So be it," once an English rendering of "amen" that archaically places the adverb "so" before the verb, a phrase that goes back hundreds of years in English literary history.[5] Williams was anxious to assign this English "chant," with its "sense of almost liturgical formality" (in Louis Martz's phrase) (Martz, 516), an American provenance, telling Pound, "the 'so be it' I copied verbatim from a translation of a Plains Indian prayer" (Williams, *Paterson*, 280n97). But in a translation that substitutes a venerable English equivalent for Hebrew and Native American post-prayer interjections, the indigenous and the foreign have become inseparable. Other repetitions, such as the children's being figuratively "clasped" by the water, weave the news's denotations into poetry's metaphoric texture. Meanwhile, Williams retells these stories in lines that approach English blank verse, though his irregular rhythms, cannily end-stopped lines ("a child burned in a field, / no language"), and violent and sometimes mimetic enjambments ("to crawl under / a fence"; "Drowned / wordless in the canal") suggest efforts to Americanize the Miltonic line. Despite Williams's putative nativism, he bends the newspaper's present-minded localism and linear American realism in the direction of prayer's recursiveness and ritualism. Rather than holding the mirror up to current events, he fashions a cross-cultural and intergeneric amalgam that is "a new thing, unlike any thing else." Its fingers reaching deep into the language and across traditions, *Paterson* deploys literary and liturgical resources that ritualize and transnationalize the ephemeral stories commodified by local journalism.

Williams saw the news as offering "the precise incentive to epic poetry, the poetry of events," and his epic poem incorporates large chunks of prose taken from or summarizing newspaper stories (Williams in Weaver, 120). In the first long news story that Williams includes in *Paterson*, set off typographically like subsequent passages by its small typeface, as well as its plain-style prose, Williams condenses two different events (*Paterson*, 256n9). A shoemaker is said to have found pearls in "mussels from Notch Brook near the City of Paterson" and sold them, including one known as "the 'Queen Pearl,' the finest of its sort in the world today," starting a nationwide search, with mussels "destroyed often with little or no result"; one pearl that "would have been the finest pearl of modern times, was ruined by boiling open the shell" (9). Though journalistically grounded in the city of Paterson and its environs, this narrative's locality is entwined with transnational flows and geographies. The local news travels far beyond New Jersey—"News of this sale created such excitement that search for the pearls was started throughout the country"—as emphasized by the ensuing verse lines about Paterson's worldwide "communications" (9). Trade circulates the pearls nationally ("sold to Tiffany") and even globally ("and later to the Empress Eugenie") (9). Even in the poem's deployment of the news as signifier of locality, the local is enmeshed in global trade and communications.

Williams's remaking of the story further stitches it into webs of what Édouard Glissant terms "le poetique de la Relation" (relational, or cross-cultural, poetics).[6] Echoes between the prose passage and the encompassing poetry ripple beyond the news story's emphatically specific geography—"Notch Brook near the City of Paterson." The pearls, fastidiously quantified as being worth "$900" or "$2,000" and "weighing 400 grains," reverberate across networks of poetic figuration: they are made to echo the metaphorical and unquantifiable pearls in the lines of poetry immediately preceding the prose news passage, lines in which Williams metaphorizes the mountain's base as "Pearls at her ankles" (9). The resonance implicitly contrasts the poet's benign figuration of nature with the destructive commodification of nature in pearls for profit. *Paterson*'s "The Delineaments of the Giants," as indicated by the subtitle, also transnationally mythologizes local geography, allegorizing the city Paterson as a male giant, slumbering side by side with the female giant of the mountain—an anthropomorphic figuration of landscape that goes back to the Norse creation myth of Ymir that Williams cited in the manuscript but extirpated from the final text (Weaver, 152). His collage technique of patching together news and high art is a rough literary approximation of synthetic cubism, paintings such as Picasso's *Still Life with Chair-Caning* (1912) and Braque's *Bottle, Newspaper, Pipe, and Glass* (1913) that paste newspaper cuttings onto canvas alongside other found or designed forms, which, through convergences and contrasts, visual and verbal puns, transform them. It can also be traced to Joyce's *Ulysses*, a prose epic that Williams was reading when he conceived his long poem and that also incorporated newspaper stories both verbatim and in summary (Williams, *I Wanted*, 72). In keeping with poetry's deep formal memory, *Paterson* also echoes older intergeneric hybridizations of prose and verse, such as the medieval French *Aucassin and Nicolette*, introduced to Williams by H.D.[7] In accordance with Williams's homiletic critique of efforts since Alexander Hamilton to capture and commercially exploit the Passaic River's Great Falls, the news story's local geography is absorbed into a moral fable about the greedy destruction of Paterson's natural environment. In sum, in addition to the globalizing forces of market capitalism ("sold to Tiffany") and worldwide communications ("News of this sale") at the level of content, Williams's use of narrative condensation (two stories in one), webs of figuration ("Pearls at her ankles"), personifying myth ("The Delineaments of the Giants"), ethical fable ("ruined"), and imported techniques like collage further translocalize *Paterson*'s local news at the level of form. He creolizes European collage and English verse with American news, news that is already riddled with global movement and conveyed by a form of print journalism transplanted from Europe. "No ideas but in things," but the local things migrate along multiple axes, and the ideas that inhere in them are neither autochthonous nor immobile (Williams, *Paterson*, 9). Despite Williams's ideological nativism, his poetry reveals the penetration of globality into even the most local news, deconstructing what has been called "the myth of 'the local' in American journalism" (Pauly and Eckert, 310), and it further interbraids journalism with artistic and mythical paradigms that move the poem beyond poetry's traditional boundaries, as well as beyond the city's and the nation's.

In the aftermath of modernism, one of Williams's admirers in the so-called middle generation also interfused poetry with the news, but whereas Williams was drawn to the news for its centripetal localization, Frank O'Hara's news-inflected poems often spin instead with centrifugal force. By the time the speaker of "The Day Lady Died" encounters "a NEW YORK POST with her face on it," his words have traveled with tremendous speed from New York City to the Bastille, back to East-hampton, then newly independent Ghana, France again (Verlaine, Bonnard), Greece (Hesiod), Ireland (Brendan Behan), France again (Jean Genet), Italy (Strega), and yet again France (Ziegfeld, Gauloises).[8] All the while, the poem supplies numerous news-report details about the speaker's location ("in New York," "in Easthampton") and the time ("It is 12:20," "a Friday / three days after Bastille day, yes / it is 1959," "I will get off the 4:19") (O'Hara, 325). Although the poem's sustained engagement with the news has been left largely unexplored, O'Hara's narrative, with its relent-less spatiotemporal specificity, exaggerates and parodies moment-by-moment news reporting, akin to the live broadcasting in 1950s radio and television news, as well as rapidly produced newsprint, invoked by the reference to the July 17, 1959, same-day issue of *The New York Post,* edited at the time by the lapsed communist James Wechsler. The headline "BILLIE HOLIDAY DIES" filled up most of the ten-cent paper's cover, sandwiched against a head-and-half-torso shot of the singer in song. Page three carried reporter William Dufty's account of Holiday's last days and hours in the hospital, "Billie Holiday Dies After Relapse; First Lady of the Blues Was 44," an article that began with the moment and place of her death: "Billie Holiday died at 3:10 this morning in Metropolitan Hospital as simply and regally as she had lived," before recounting her "46-day stand in Room 6A12."[9]

Whether conservative or liberal, hard or soft news, tabloid or serious, broadcast or printed, the news is a defining record of public happenings in Eisenhower's 1950s, and O'Hara's lyric takes up and torques the news's basic procedures of accounting empiri-cally and precisely for time and space. Although the poem assumes a singular report-ing location, circling back to Sixth Avenue in New York City, this space is shown to be anything but local and unitary, even in its extreme localness, but is instead dispersed and criss-crossed by literary and commodity vectors from multiple countries. In the cold war era when, as Edward Brunner and Deborah Nelson have shown, poetry is a form where the boundaries between public and private, state and personal, are being negotiated, and traditional privacy is, in Nelson's words, "eroding under the…market pressures in the form of tabloid journalism" (D. Nelson, 5), O'Hara provides a kind of mock news story.[10] In it, as in any news account, he details the precise sequence of when and where, except that this pseudo-reporter has dissolved the public/pri-vate divide into the flickering data of his own world-immersed experience, instead of hewing to the reportorial myth of objectivity. His state of "quandariness" contrasts with the authoritative and unperplexed tone expected in news reporting. Even the poem's title wittily plays on and elegantly refashions the trope of the headline pun, "Day" serving, by syntactic inversion, as both common noun and the stage name of the unnamed singer. The poem ends with an elegiac spiral inward to a memory of a Billie Holiday performance—"and everyone and I stopped breathing"—diverging sharply from the objectifying indices and empirical record of the standard news obituary. Although O'Hara, like Williams, opens poetry to the factual welter of the news, he also remakes it: he layers it with the meditative inwardness of grief, explodes the myth of the local by uncovering its global flows, satirizes the news's anonymity and objectivity by immersing the subject within these flows, and pushes the news's temporal and spatial specificity so hard that it becomes emblematic of modernity's speed and movement, its penetration and dispersal of the subject.

The newspaper headline "LANA TURNER HAS COLLAPSED!" appears twice in a more comic O'Hara poem written a few years later, in 1962, setting up an implicit analogy between poem and news report—an analogy the poem plays with and ultimately undoes (O'Hara, 449).[11] Even though the poem begins with a headline, at first in lowercase, it rapidly and satirically switches to a whimsical catalog of the speaker's movements and an oddly dialogic weather report:

> Lana Turner has collapsed!
> I was trotting along and suddenly
> it started raining and snowing
> and you said it was hailing
> but hailing hits you on the head
> hard so it was really snowing and
> raining....

The headline's report on a movie star marks the singularity of the tabloid incident by its finite verb ("has collapsed"). This factual report could hardly be more different from the processual and dialogic texture of the ensuing lines, with their present participles("raining...snowing...hailing...hailing...snowing...raining...acting"), their paratactic ramble ("and suddenly it started...and you said...and I was"), their mundanity ("I was trotting along"), their comic alliterations ("hailing / but hailing hits you on the head / hard"), and their humorously retrospective pursuit of a disagreement with a friend over the weather ("you said it was hailing / but"). Although the newspaper and the poem begin with the same event, they are shown to take dramatically different syntactic, verbal, tonal, and temporal routes. Among the standard qualities of American news reporting are said to be timeliness, factuality, an anonymous third-person author, and an "unemotional accounting of events" (Zelizer, 38–39). By contrast with the seeming neutrality of such third-person reporting, O'Hara's poem enacts desire in language, dramatizing it by the rapid-fire tumble of its syntax and thematizing it in the statement "I was in such a hurry / to meet you." Through the impediments of weather, traffic, and physical distance, the poem plunges toward the desired "you," in accordance with the refinement of poetic address in O'Hara's "Personism: A Manifesto," in which the poem must "address itself to one person...thus evoking overtones of love," the "poem squarely between the poet and the person, Lucky Pierre style," in sharp contrast with the generalized addressee of news reports (O'Hara, 449).

But "suddenly I see a headline," a final impediment, and suddenly the poem makes a sharp turn, laying out implied antitheses between the speaker and the celebrity: it rains and snows where he lives, but where she lives, there is "no snow" and "no rain in California"; he has been to parties like the ones that Lana Turner went to "and acted perfectly disgraceful," but unlike her, he "never actually collapsed." The speaker was already divided between locations—between, that is, the place where he was "trotting along" and his destination, where he hurries "to meet you." But the news of Turner's collapse translocalizes him all the more dramatically: now his thoroughly relational self-understanding is splayed across America, between sunny Hollywood and wintry New York. Whereas a news report is typically represented as grounded in a singular location, O'Hara's report on the news report is spatially stretched and fissured. In a final departure from the norms of newswriting, the desire that had been intently focused on the addressee is in the end mockingly diverted to the movie icon: "oh Lana Turner we love you get up." "Conative" language oriented toward the addressee, in Roman Jakobson's terms, "finds its purest grammatical expression in the vocative and imperative" (67), and "imperative sentences cardinally differ from declarative sentences: the latter are and the former are not liable to a truth test" (68). "The most important *textual* feature of journalism," writes John Hartley, "is the fact that it counts as true" (35). Part of the humor of O'Hara's poem lies in the contrast between the declarative mode of true-or-false third-person news, as instanced by "LANA TURNER HAS COLLAPSED!" and the last line's emotive or "expressive" statement, "oh Lana Turner we love you," which in Jakobson's terms is "focused on the ADDRESSER" and "aims a direct expression of the speaker's attitude toward what he is speaking about" (66)—a contrast that extends to the final imperative, "get up." While absorbing and parodying the news's declarative language, O'Hara's poetry twists it around to its opposite: the conative, the vocative, the expressive, and in this instance even the imperative. The friction between the last line ("oh Lana Turner we love you get up") and the first ("Lana Turner has collapsed"), between affectively charged "personist" address and third-person description, exemplifies Bakhtin's heteroglossia, the literary incorporation of "*another's speech in another's language*" in a "*double-voiced discourse*" (Bakhtin, 324). Though intertwined with the speed, presentness, impersonality, and bric-a-brac of the news, O'Hara's poetry unmakes these journalistic norms from within. If Hartley is right that "journalism is *the* textual system of modernity" (3), O'Hara energetically takes on a dominant discursive form, greatly complicating any simple notions of unitary location, refusing the subordination of private affect to public reality, rejecting a regulative neutrality, and insisting on desire-charged and dialogic language in which speaker and addressee meet.

The modernist and cold war struggle between American poetry and the news gains renewed intensity in the Vietnam War era, when most Americans first began receiving most of their news from television instead of from newspapers or magazines, although the distinction between conventional journalism and other media forms, as Hartley indicates, "should not be overstated, for...the technology of journalism is less important than the ideas it communicates and their popular reach" (124). Whereas O'Hara's ironic, knowing, camp pseudo-news is written in a discursive register below standard news discourse—its "personism" more colloquially familiar—Robert Duncan moves it up several notches in one of the Vietnam era's most powerful poems, applying no less pressure on the "gigantic archive of textuality" that is the news, whether in imagistic, verbal, or other form (Hartley, 3). First published in *The Nation* in 1965, his "Up Rising, Passages 25," is a prophetic vision of the Vietnam War. This is not to say that it lacks journalistic content, perhaps surprisingly for a poet of intense mysticism. A couple of years after network television doubled the length of news broadcasts but several years before the mass antiwar protests of the late 1960s, Duncan critically witnesses current history: President Johnson is said to have sent planes from Guam over Asia; "the professional military" uses Johnson in its "business of war"; the planes drop napalm on the jungles; the American war enemy is conceived as an undifferentiated "communism"; American officials have been elected in part by fraudulent votes; "the closed meeting-rooms of regents of university and sessions of profiteers" have been behind the war; scientists have developed new means of biological warfare, including "new plagues, measles grown enormous, influenzas perfected" (Duncan, 117).[12] But in Duncan's poem, these facts are not merely successive moments in "clocked, calendrical time," or "homogeneous, empty time," ascribed by Benedict Anderson to the newspaper's representation of the nation (26); instead, belonging to "a simultaneity of past and future in an instantaneous present," they are metamorphosed into ingredients for a vatic revisioning of America (24). If hints of prayer and veneration can be found in Williams's and perhaps even O'Hara's poetic handling of the news (the end of "The Day Lady Died"), Duncan absorbs the news into a more overtly spiritual poetics, his poem straddling the gap between these discursive forms.

How does a poet like Duncan tell "the news" so that, in Pound's words, it "STAYS news" (29)? At the most basic, syntactic level, whereas the news report is typically a series of short, discrete declarative sentences, Duncan's poem is one long sentence that unspools clause after clause. In its temporality and connectivity, it is the opposite of the news's atomism, which fractures time and space into discrete and unrelated verbal or imagistic snapshots. "Up Rising" syntactically glues together the details of the journalistic present, and it returns these to the deep past that has formed and that typologically prefigures them. The insistence of the past is lexically highlighted by Duncan's use of archaic, literary forms of past participles and the past tense: "stirrd," "heapt," "develost," "passt," "workt," "cleard," "feard" (116–118). The war represents, in Duncan's religio-ethical history, the "black bile of old evils arisen anew," in particular the genocide against Amerindian nations on which the U.S. nation was founded: "the pit of the hell of America's unacknowledged crimes," "a holocaust of burning Indians, trees and grasslands, / reduced to his real estate" (118). The white settler is driven by a "hatred of Europe, of Africa, of Asia, / the deep hatred for the old world," and by a disastrously imperial and capitalist approach to "the alien world, the new world about him, that might have been Paradise" (118). The present catastrophe repeats and fulfills the ominous past: the nation was premised on antipathy toward its others, aggression that has been rekindled in neocolonial wars, "this Texas barbecue of Asia, Africa, and all the Americas" (116). Delving back into the country's origins, Duncan recalls the prophetic fear that Adams and Jefferson had of future corruption and despotism. But he displays none of the hatred for the old world that he sees as afflicting the United States. In his transnationalist prophecy, he cites English poets for their prescient insight into America, quoting D. H. Lawrence's allegorical figure of overweening pride and materialism in "The American Eagle" and referring to the revolutionary fire-and-blood imagery of William Blake's "America." Duncan's vision of America is even darker than theirs, so he quotes Lawrence but substitutes ellipses for Lawrence's vision of the possible emergence of "something splendid" in America and elides Blake's fervent hopes for the American Revolution (Lawrence, 414). Far from representing his utterance as emanating from a journalist's single location and simple national present, Duncan's multilayered poem channels a transatlantic array of voices from different times. He suggests that poetry, by contrast with the self-explanatory and seemingly transparent immediacy of calendrical news, draws on a collective unconscious in its fierce response to the urgencies of the present. For Duncan, poetry breaks away from the time and space coordinates onto which the news maps the nation, affiliating itself instead with the trans-temporal simultaneities and trans-spatial reach of prophecy.

Although Duncan's Johnson is a simplified figure of evil, a typological iteration of the lust for fame that drove both Hitler and Stalin, the evil that Duncan envisions in the war extends well beyond any single figure to "small-town bosses and business-men" (117), the "good people in the suburbs" (117), the scientists "we have met at cocktail parties, passt daily and with a happy 'Good Day' on the way to classes or work" (117–118), the "sea of toiling men" (116), and finally, "the all-American boy in the cockpit / loosing his flow of napalm," "drawing now / not with crayons" (117). No one, presumably not even the poet, is exempt from complicity. Indeed, the makers of biological warfare are described as creative in their own way, "dreaming" like the poet, but perverting this creative capacity—"dreaming / of the bodies of mothers and fathers and children and hated rivals / swollen with" diseases (117). In the long, rolling declamations of this sweeping and indeed panoramic vision, Duncan still insists on the particular horrors of the particular moment: "the burning of homes and the torture of mothers and fathers and children, / their hair a-flame, screaming in agony" (117). His framing of the war's atrocities in transnational and even mythical contexts makes their criminality all the more lurid. Unlike the focus on discrete, successive events in news journalism, Duncan's porous and multivoiced poem both formally and diegetically presents America as transected by cross-national and transhistorical realities, even those to which it is willfully oblivious.

Though Williams thought of the news as a localizing ground for poetry, it has had the reverse function for internationally minded American poets, such as those involved in the Spanish Civil War[13] and for a still broader array of poets since the Vietnam War. Published near the beginning of the Salvadoran Civil War (1980–1992), in which the United States backed the right-wing Salvadoran government in its brutal effort to suppress a leftist insurrection, Carolyn Forché's book of poems about atrocities she witnessed or learned of while working as a human rights advocate in El Salvador, *The Country Between Us* (1981), famously incorporates journalistic reportage, but even the prose poetry in this volume can't be confused with a news clipping. Unlike Duncan's long-winding syntax, Forché's short, simple sentences in her signature prose poem "The Colonel," written in 1978, at first seem to match journalistic discourse: "What you have heard is true. I was in his house. His wife carried a tray of coffee and sugar. His daughter filed her nails, his son went out for the night. There were daily papers, pet dogs, a pistol on the cushion beside him" (16). The flat, clipped syntax and literal descriptiveness hew close to journalistic norms, and the domestic space could hardly be more mundane, except that the detail of the pistol warns of violence and the possessive adjective "his" is imperially stamped on everything and everyone. The next sentence's startling metaphor clearly marks a departure from a direct transcription of events: "The moon swung bare on its black cord over the house" (16). The ominous metaphor implicitly likens the moon to fearful objects and events, such as a hanging, a lynching, a grandfather clock, an interrogation lamp, a dangling telephone, or Edgar Allan Poe's pendulum. In this moment, as through the remainder, the poem twists together horrifying political violence with the mundane particulars of the colonel's home and family life, of the dinner menu and light conversation:

> The colonel returned with a sack used to bring groceries home. He spilled many human ears on the table. They were like dried peach halves. There is no other way to say this. He took one of them in his hands, shook it in our faces, dropping it in a water glass. It came alive there. (16)

The passage oscillates between banality and brutality. The grocery sack recalls earlier domestic details, but then the spilling of ears out of it jerks the language out of the domestic and into the gothic, before returning again to the domestic in the metaphor of peaches. The reader has been positioned at the dinner table, a participant in this domestic space where public atrocity on a horrific scale overwhelms the scene. The metamorphic bursting of the dead body parts into life and the collapse of the homely into the unhomely, of domestic coziness into political killing, disturb distinctions by which news reality is organized. By the end, the poet makes no pretense of reportage. Like the ear in the water glass, other ears are revitalized by poetic language, Forché literalizing the metaphoric idiom for extreme attentiveness, not unlike the poet's own: "Some of the ears on the floor were pressed to the

ground" (16). The colonel is not merely, however, a destructive figure. He has been
granted a role as co-creator of this very poem: "Something for your poetry, no?
he said," after sweeping the ears to the ground (16). And indeed, by his dramatic
political performance, the colonel collaborates in creating the very poem we read.
Like O'Hara's blurring of the spaces between speaker and addressee, reader and
writer, Forché's poem confounds the static subject positions presupposed by jour-
nalism—objective author and subjects of a news report—as well as here and over
there, national and international.

    Born like Forché in the spring of 1950, Jorie Graham also grew up in a period
of increasing news saturation, and part of her achievement, too, has been to
develop inventive strategies for negotiating the relations between poetry and the
news, between private experience and global public history. In her poem "Fission"
(1991), she returns to one of the defining events of the 1960s, the 1963 assassination
of President John F. Kennedy (incidentally, the first news event I can remember
from my childhood, when I was three years old). But unlike a reporter, her angle
of approach to the event is to measure its impact on an autobiographical pubes-
cent "I," then thirteen years old, who learns of it while in Italy watching Stanley
Kubrick's 1962 movie *Lolita*.[14] In the interval between modernism and postcon-
fessionalism, between Williams's and Graham's poetry, the visualization, accelera-
tion, and ubiquity of the news media have intensified. Graham's poem is written
out of this experience of ever greater penetration of the news media into human
subjectivity and self-understanding. In this poem, the news is apprehended not
as objective data but through the resemblances we construct between ourselves
and public figures, our lives and public narratives. The adolescent girl is watching
an enormous on-screen Lolita, a character nearly her age, whose image, when the
assassination is announced and sunlight floods the movie theater, dissolves into

> vague stutterings of
> light with motion in them, bits of moving zeros
>
> in the infinite virtuality of light,
>   some *likeness* in it but not particulate,
>   a grave of possible shapes called *likeness*—see it?—something
>   scrawling up there that could be skin or daylight or even....
>   (Graham, 101)

The violent transnational impact of the news is figured in the sunlight's crashing
through the roof of the movie theater, exploding both cinematic and personal
illusions. Under the pressure of the news, the likenesses between the real and the
cinematic girl, between fantasy and history fray, break apart, and their fissures are
exposed. Usually segregated from one another for moviegoers, daylight, house
lights, and the projector's light collide and compete in this crisis moment. So, too,
public and private history—normally kept stably separated from one another—
criss-cross traumatically. The movie images seem to lick and play on the speaker's
"small body,"

　　　　where the long thin arm of day came in from the top
　　to touch my head,
　　　　　reaching down along my staring face—
　　where they flared up around my body unable to

　　merge into each other
　　　　over my likeness,
　　slamming down one side of me, unquenchable—here static

　　　　there flaming—

                                                                        (102)

Touching, reaching, slamming down, flaming—the news is experienced neither as spectacle nor as objective datum to be consumed but as personal assault. The curtain between interiority and externality and between subjective experience and public history has come crashing down. But in Graham's retelling of the news, an adolescent girl's fall from innocence into experience and her construction and deconstruction of poetic likenesses between herself and others to make sense of the assassination are no less a part of the history of November 22, 1963, than what could be seen on TV or read in the next day's newspapers.

One way of understanding twentieth-century American poetry, in short, is in its vexed dialogue with the news. Pace Williams, you can get the news of twentieth-century America from poems—tragic child deaths and the despoliation of the natural environment, the loss or fall (literal and figurative) of celebrities, the scientific perversions unleashed in the Vietnam War, U.S.-abetted war crimes in Latin America, JFK's assassination, and so forth. But this news isn't told or conceived the same way that it is in newspapers and other news media, because even newsy poems absorb and play on, question and parody journalism's language, procedures, and assumptions. In various poems, as we've seen, the news's localism is translocated, its outward-directed mimeticism is turned around in inwardly recurring ritual, its objectivity is sandwiched between experiential subjects, its present-mindedness is tethered to the deep or mythical past, its denotative language is flushed with metaphoricity, and its transparency is clouded by densely figurative mediation and subjectivity. To the extent that these tropings of the news move it in the direction of long-lived forms and myth, inwardness and ritual recursiveness, they move it—sometimes boldly in the case of Duncan's "Up Rising," often less obviously—in the direction of prayer. Surely we'd never mistake a poem like O'Hara's "The Day Lady Died" or Forché's "The Colonel" for a prayer, and yet even these news poems, in their final moments, sound deeply meditative bass notes that reverberate well beyond the news flash. We could pursue the antinews news history of modern and contemporary American poetry at great length, exploring the many different ways in which poets have told alternative public histories of current events, from the Great Depression and the Spanish Civil War, to the civil rights and women's movement, September 11 and the Iraq War; from Ezra Pound, Langston Hughes, and Carl Sandburg to Gwendolyn Brooks and Adrienne Rich, Sharon Olds,

Michael Palmer, Yusef Komunyakaa, Fady Joudah, Juliana Spahr, and the author of
a wryly deconstructive transcription of one day's *New York Times*, Kenneth Gold-
smith.[15] But to avoid reducing poetry to its historical and mimetic registers, we need
to calibrate the generic identity of poetry by considering it in relation to at least one
of its other intergenres.

POETRY AND PRAYER

As I've been broadly hinting, one of the genres least like the news, and thus a useful
indicator of other dimensions of poetry, is prayer. While some poems play with and
against the representational imperatives of journalism—contemporary public his-
tory "objectively" reported—others move closer to the discursive field and generic
norms of prayer. That poetry often inhabits a middle zone between what J. L. Austin
would call the "performative" or "illocutionary" acts of prayer and the descriptive or
"constative" statements of the news,[16] or what Jakobson, as we've seen, would term
conative, expressive, vocative, and imperative language and true-or-false declarative
statements, is one measure of its elasticity and range, even though poetry is some-
times reduced to one or the other of these poles.

At this juncture in the argument, it might be worth baldly asserting some of
the broad differences between prayer and the news. If the news, typically cast in
the third person, aims to provide an objective record of contemporary events in the
secular world, prayer, usually in the second person, is addressed to the divine and
often secondarily to oneself. Empirical verifiability is the foundation of the news,
while nonverifiability is fundamental to prayer. The news transmits information,
but when the deity addressed in prayer is omniscient, by definition no knowledge
can be transmitted, because, as Kant writes, the being addressed "has no need of any
declaration regarding the inner disposition of the wisher" (210), and as Jean-Louis
Chrétien states in his phenomenology of prayer, "the function of speech is not in
this case to communicate a piece of information or to transmit something we know
to our invisible interlocutor" (21). Can a poem both communicate like the news and
transcend the communicative function of language like prayer? Although poetry
shouldn't be confused with either prayer or the news, we learn something about
it by examining how it interacts with, and departs from, the mimetic, presentist,
and transmissive norms of the one and the ritualistic, traditionalist, and formalized
structures of the other. Poetry quarrels with and co-opts elements of each discourse,
ultimately assimilating them to its own procedures and imperatives.

Modern and contemporary poetry's conflicted response to the news is inten-
sified, as we've seen, by the media's discursive dominance and massive capitaliza-
tion; so, too, poetry's idiosyncrasy makes for significant ambivalences toward the
institutional weight, religious doctrines, and communal rites and symbols that are
often contexts of prayer. Sylvia Plath sounds a characteristically skeptical note of
prayerlike antiprayer:

> Oh God, I am not like you
> In your vacuous black,
> Stars stuck all over, bright stupid confetti.
> Eternity bores me,
> I never wanted it.
>
> (Plath, 255)

Charles Simic addresses the deity with similar irreverence:

> Boss of all bosses of the universe.
> Mr. know-it-all, wheeler-dealer, wire-puller,
> And whatever else you're good at.
> Go ahead, shuffle your zeros tonight.
> Dip in ink the comet's tails.
> Staple the night with starlight.
>
> (Simic, "To the One," 63)

But even as they mock the star-maneuvering deity's power and pretensions, accusing him of dull vacuity and manipulative pomposity, these poets find themselves taking up the mode of prayerful address. Although Simic makes fun of people in acts of petition and adoration, "begging you on their knees, / Sputtering endearments, / As if you were an inflatable, life-size doll," even he ends his poem with a self-reflexive glance at the vestiges of prayer in his antiprayer: "As I scribble this note to you in the dark" (63). Both poetry and prayer can be described as scribbling *in the dark* due to the uncertainty of their audiences and the imponderability of their subject matter. "It's like fishing in the dark" ("Mystic Life," 82), Simic writes in another poem, "The hook left dangling / In the Great 'Nothing' " (85).

The interconnections between poetry and prayer are many, starting with their rhetorical stance as apostrophic discourses. Paul de Man argued that "the figure of address is recurrent" and perhaps even "paradigmatic" for poetry (61), and Jonathan Culler identified apostrophe "with lyric itself" (151).[17] But this influential body of theoretical work has shied away from noting the comparable rhetorical structure of prayer. As Kant writes, in prayerful "*address*, a human being assumes that this supreme object is present in person, or at least he poses (even inwardly) as though he were convinced of his presence, reckoning that, suppose this is not so, his posing can at least do no harm but might rather gain him favor" (210n). As speech acts directed to an other, yet an other more oblique and veiled than an interlocutor in everyday second-person address, poetry and prayer function simultaneously as acts of address, albeit partly suspended (hence, "address" modulating into "apostrophe"), and as forms of meta-address, or images of voicing, due to the decontextualization of address from normal lines of communication. But the resistance to conventional forms in much modern and contemporary poetry has meant that it is less obviously akin to prayer than, say, sixteenth-century lyrics by Herbert, Donne, Crashaw, and Vaughan, or seventeenth-, eighteenth-, and nineteenth-century lyrics by Bradstreet,

Wheatley, and Dickinson, let alone the *Vedas*, the *Kanteletar*, the Psalms, the divine odes in Greek tragedy, Rumi's *Masnavi*, bhakti poetry, Christian chants and hymns such as the "Dies Irae," and so forth.[18] With the exception of a handful of poems, from Gerard Manley Hopkins to A. R. Ammons and Geoffrey Hill, few distinctly modern and contemporary poems overtly resemble psalms, hymns, litanies, or rosaries. Yet many characteristics of prayer remain, albeit often twisted or disguised, even in poems that turn divine homage on its head. To get at the intricate tensions and continuities between poetry and prayer, I focus on a handful of examples, reluctantly setting aside an abundance of other modern and contemporary American poets whose work could be explored through this lens, including, to name but some of the most prominent figures, Robert Frost, Wallace Stevens, H.D., Robinson Jeffers, T. S. Eliot, Claude McKay, Jean Toomer, Hart Crane, Sterling Brown, Langston Hughes, Theodore Roethke, Charles Olson, William Everson, John Berryman, Robert Lowell, Amy Clampitt, A. R. Ammons, Allen Ginsberg, Galway Kinnell, W. S. Merwin, Anne Sexton, Charles Wright, Mary Oliver, Lucille Clifton, Michael Palmer, Leslie Marmon Silko, Jorie Graham, Joy Harjo, and Li-Young Lee.

While poems such as Plath's and Simic's invert many of the codes and conventions of prayer, other poems are more obviously continuous with them. James Weldon Johnson was one of a number of poets of the Harlem Renaissance, including Langston Hughes and Sterling Brown, who absorbed prayer among other African American oral speech genres into literary verse, a vitalizing intergenre as well for later poets such as Robert Hayden, Amiri Baraka, and Thylias Moss. Though an agnostic, Johnson began his landmark 1927 sequence of poems adapting African American sermons and other religious speech acts, *God's Trombones*, with "Listen Lord: A Prayer," a poem that sets down as literary verse the oral performativity, creative exuberance, incantatory rhythms, and humanistic energy of an African American prayer-sermon. Because the poem is spoken by a preacher as intercessor for the congregation, it assumes the doubly overheard structure of prayer as dramatic monologue, in which, as the speaker ostensibly addresses God, the congregation overhears the prayer, and the reader overhears the overheard prayer. This double nesting of the prayer foregrounds its performative and aesthetic strategies. Unlike Plath's and Simic's irreverence toward God and traditional modes of prayer, this poem, after its conventional address to the divine being, immediately turns to expressions of humility:

> O Lord, we come this morning
> Knee-bowed and body-bent
> Before thy throne of grace.
> O Lord—this morning—
> Bow our hearts beneath our knees,
> And our knees in some lonesome valley.
>   (J. W. Johnson, "Listen," 13)

Each of the hyphenated compounds enacts humility, immediately humbling "knee" and "body" with a participle ("-bowed," "-bent"). God is magisterially seated on a throne, and the bowing and bending suggest subjects groveling before a king. As if this self-humiliation weren't enough, the hearts are figured hyperbolically as bowing beneath knees—and just in case the body hasn't sunk far enough, those knees are lowered in the landscape by reference to a spiritual, "Jesus Walked This Lonesome Valley."

Ironically, however, the more humble the state described, the more imaginatively extravagant the poetic figuration used to evoke it. Much of the sermon's language is conventional and accords with expected rhetorical formulas and inheritances. But Johnson's imaginative stretching of these images, his aesthetic flourishes and surprises, suggest the underlying tension between poetry and prayer, even when a poem such as this one seems largely to harmonize with religious codes. In his life of Waller (1799), an earlier poet named Johnson famously articulated the problem: "The essence of poetry is invention; such invention as, by producing something unexpected, surprises and delights. The topicks of devotion are few, and being few are universally known; but, few as they are, they can be made no more; they can receive no grace from novelty or sentiment, and very little from novelty of expression" (S. Johnson, 1:274). Addressing the "claim that devotion is incompatible with invention," Kevin Hart argues that there are "many strong poems that are also prayers" ("Poetry and Revelation," 263), even as he concedes the tension: "The metaphor required to express the transcendence of God can distract writer and reader from the truth of the faith" ("Transcendence in Tears," 128). In a prayerful poem, the aesthetic risks leaping out ahead of the devotional.

Later in his prayer-poem, the speaker petitions the Lord to use his cleansing powers on the "man of God": "Wash him with hyssop inside and out, / Hang him up and drain him dry of sin" (J. W. Johnson, "Listen," 14)—an injunction that echoes the verse of a biblical prayer but deletes from it language that, in early twentieth-century America, would have been racially problematic: "Purge me with hyssop, and I shall be clean: wash me, and I shall be whiter than snow" (Psalm 51.7). Remaking the language of the King James Bible for modern African American verse, the prayerful poet must strike a delicate balance between humble self-subordination and revisionary and imaginative self-assertion. "Lord, turpentine his imagination," he writes, but this novel metaphor for God's cleansing power instances an imagination that has hardly been wiped clean (J. W. Johnson, "Listen," 14).

Though writing largely in Standard English, Johnson uses throughout the poem the kind of "constant iteration and repetition" he ascribes to African American spirituals (J. W. Johnson, "Preface," 41), such as the phrase repeated every few lines, "this morning" ("Listen," 13–14), or the worrying or varying in lines such as the imperative to God to "ride, ride by old hell, / Ride by the dingy gates of hell" (14). In accordance with African American church rhetoric, he employs not only hyperbole but also homely figures of speech, such as the intercessory prompting to God to "open up a window of heaven, / And lean out" (13), as well as the orality of repetitions and insistent rhythms. Despite Johnson's misgivings about the use of dialect in poetry, by the poem's end, having moved from the first section's propitiation ("no merits of our own" [13]) to the middle section's intercessory prayer on behalf of both sinners and good people, and finally to petition on the speaker's behalf ("Lower me to my dusty grave in peace" [15]), the language more overtly incorporates African American vernacular in the final section's second line, "When I've done drunk my last cup of sorrow" (14), and its last, "To wait for that great gittin' up morning—Amen" (15). By bringing the figurative, rhetorical, rhythmic, and lexical properties of African American speech into a prayer written as literary verse, Johnson creolizes the normative language of mainstream poem-prayers in English, while playing prayer's protestations of humble self-abnegation against poetry's imagistic and verbal inventiveness.

At the same time that poetry and prayer are, as Johnson's poem indicates, in some tension with one another, their commonalities are multiple (hence some twentieth-century American Protestants and Jews, among others, were able to put poetry to religious and devotional uses).[19] Both poetry and prayer, as I've already suggested, are often characterized by an apostrophic or vocative structure. But in both poetry and prayer, address isn't only outwardly directed. Both genres frequently take the form of internal dialogue, the speaker self-dividing in two. Although prayer is ostensibly addressed to the divine, when one prays, as Kant puts it, one speaks "within oneself and in fact *with oneself*, though allegedly all the more comprehensively with God" (212); a praying person resembles someone "having a slight fit of madness" (210n).[20] This last phrase may well bring to mind descriptions of Orphic inspiration, and like prayer's speech "within oneself and in fact *with oneself*," lyric poetry has often been conceived, as in J. S. Mill's famous definition of poetry as speech "overheard," as "feeling confessing itself to itself in moments of solitude," "the natural fruit of solitude and meditation" (95). Even so, both prayer and poetry also have a social dimension as well, so that the circuit of speech is never closed; at the very least, a fissure is opened for the addressed or eavesdropping other.

The truth status of prayers and poems, moreover, differs from that of declarative statements: according to Aristotle on prayer and I. A. Richards on poetry's pseudo-statements, the utterances in both prayers and poems are neither true nor false.[21] Partly for this reason, from the perspective of scientific epistemology, both poetry and prayer seem superfluous and even ridiculous, inassimilable to rational and empirical discourse. Both genres emphasize the less instrumental qualities of language, intensifying rhythm and figuration, manipulating syntax and heightening diction. However up-to-date in their diction, they belong to generic histories going back thousands of years; they are long memoried and themselves memorable, as activated in recitation and performance. "Absolutely unmixed attention is prayer," said Simone Weil (170), and magnified awareness—to language, the world, feelings—has often been seen as part and parcel of poetry.

In view of all these commonalities, we might ask whether George Oppen's poem entitled "Psalm" is indeed a psalm—a prayer, a sacred song used in worship, like the biblical hymns in the Book of Psalms. There are connections worth exploring, but the differences are more immediately apparent. Even though "psalm" comes from a Greek word literally meaning the twanging or twitching of harp strings, Oppen's poem is an exercise in asceticism, in contrast to the figurative extravagance and musical resonance of Johnson's "Prayer." Maeera Shreiber notes the sometimes "contentious" relationship between poetry and prayer in Judaism, Maimonides even identifying prayer-poems as "a significant source of distraction" and "'the major cause of the lack of devotion'" (Shreiber, 180). Prayer has sometimes been seen as theologically problematic because of its anthropomorphization of Godhead, and poetry's "unbridled penchant for metaphor" brings it into still greater conflict with "Judaism's central commitment to a disembodied deity" (181),[22] even more so than in the friction we found lurking in Johnson's prayer-poem. Oppen's epigraph from Aquinas, "*Veritas sequitur,*" or "Truth follows," brings Christian language into play, but the elision of "*esse rerum*" ("the existence of things") circumscribes its implications (Oppen, 99). Oppen's declaration of existence is nontheological: "That they are there!" he exclaims of the wild deer.

Even so, in a poem called "Psalm," the deer recall the first psalm in the so-called Exodus section of the Psalms: "As the hart panteth after the water brooks, so panteth my soul after thee, O God" (Psalm 42). Oppen secularizes the trope, because his deer, instead of allegorizing human incompleteness in longing for the divine, are emblematic only of themselves and of existence, or Heideggerian being there:[23]

> Their eyes
> Effortless, the soft lips
> Nuzzle and the alien small teeth
> Tear at the grass
>
> The roots of it
> Dangle from their mouths
> Scattering earth in the strange woods.
> They who are there.
> (Oppen, "Psalm," 99)

The "Effortless" eyes of the deer exemplify the state of consciousness to which the poet aspires, a noncoercive consciousness that lets existence emerge, lets it appear as mere being. The sentence fragment "They who are there" seems utterly simple, unadorned, in keeping with Oppen's objectivist poetics. But, as with the trope of the deer, there is more to it: the refrainlike repetition and variation create a muted ritualism, and the poem's final line, repeating the phrase "wild deer," also resonates with the *r*-colored vowel sounds in "they … *are* the*re*": "St*ar*tle, and st*are* out" (Oppen, "Psalm," 99). This echo of "are" in "Startle" and "there" in "stare," not to mention the embedded eye-rhyme of "are" within "stare," subtly accords with the musical and liturgical implications of the poem's title.

Though restrained and intently focused on the encounter with deer, Oppen's "Psalm" is at the same time enriched by its echoes of a high Romantic poet and a Romantic modernist poet whose work frequently intersects with prayer. As is often the case with poetry, this lyric's response to existence is mediated through echoes of earlier poems. Despite the view that "Oppen's poems are written out of the faith that things can be seen with clarity, and that words can refer to and name an extant reality without trying to mediate it with transcendental or symbolic overlays," his poetry is hardly devoid of symbolic, religious, and literary "overlays" (Young, 150). Perhaps surprisingly, the poem recalls an extravagant Romantic celebration of being, Shelley's "Ode to the West Wind," in which the poet beckons the wind to drive his "dead thoughts over the universe / Like withered leaves":

> Scatter, as from an unextinguished hearth
> Ashes and sparks, my words among mankind!
> Be through my lips to unawakened Earth....
> (Shelley, 223)

Echoing the word cluster *scatter-earth-leaves*, Oppen's severely economical poem tries to steer clear of anything like Shelley's voluptuous prophecy; yet it, too, begins by extolling the being of nature and ends up meditating on "words," or in Oppen's case "small nouns," as the home of being. Those words and nouns include, of course, the poet's own, his "leaves" of "grass" torn from the language, including—however discretely—the language of previous poems and psalms. The leaves in Oppen's poem "Hang in the distances / Of sun" (Oppen, "Psalm," 99), recalling Wallace Stevens's late poetic thought experiment of trying to conceive of being without human projections, appropriately titled "Of Mere Being," initially published in the 1957 *Opus Posthumous*: "In the bronze distance, // A gold-feathered bird / Sings in the palm, without human meaning, / Without human feeling, a foreign song...." (Stevens, 117).[24] Like Oppen's deer "bedding down," Stevens's bird is emblematic of being, and its feathers "dangle down" (Stevens, 118). Though they may seem innocently "natural images" in the tradition of Pound's Imagism, Oppen's deer also recall, along with the hart of the psalms, the deer at the end of Stevens's "Sunday Morning," and the participle "Crying" is also key to Stevensian vernacular in poems such as "Waving Adieu, Adieu, Adieu." Akin to the bird in Stevens's "Of Mere Being" that sings "a foreign song," Oppen's deer have "alien" teeth and live in "strange woods," the diction of alienation emphasizing their existence beyond anthropomorphism. Despite Stevens's more extravagant artifice, Oppen resembles him in summoning but ascetically muting the anthropomorphism central to prayer in many religious cultures. The word "small" repeats through Oppen's poem ("small beauty," "small teeth," "small nouns"), bridging the potential gap between nonverbal and verbal being and underscoring Oppen's effort at radical simplicity and restraint. Cultivating poetic smallness, or as he put it in a letter of December 21, 1962, writing "carefully, lucidly, accurately, resisting the temptation to inflate" (Oppen, *Selected Letters*, 73), Oppen put his restrained figurative language, barely audible music, unadorned diction, and preference for nouns over finite verbs in the service of a negative poetic theology, whereby being reveals itself through the space cleared by the writer's verbal and artistic austerity. Although we may be dissuaded from looking to the objectivists for continuities with prayer, because of their putative emphasis on what Louis Zukofsky called "the detail, not mirage, of seeing, of thinking with things as they exist" (12), a poem such as Oppen's "Psalm," as well as poems such as Charles Reznikoff's

"Te Deum" (named after the Latin hymn of praise to God) and Lorine Niedecker's awe-struck *New Goose* poems, should alert us to the connections.

An admirer of Oppen's "clean, austere, dynamic poetry" of "silence" who shares his distanced affiliation with Jewishness, Louise Glück published a poetic sequence, *The Wild Iris* (1992), that abounds in prayer-poems, many of them entitled "Matins" and "Vespers," in a remarkable trialogue among gardener-poet, flowers, and God (Glück, "Disruption," 30). Some of the initial critical response suggested astonishment at an acclaimed contemporary American poet's assimilation of religious discourse. Glück adapts the apparatus of prayer, including address to God, apology, petition, pleading, thanksgiving, complaint, and lament, but she repeatedly questions the structures she is mobilizing. Tonally evident in what Shreiber describes as the sequence's "quarrelsome" (195) and "confrontational, highly critical relation to the divine" (197), this questioning can also be located in these poem-prayers' probing of figuration—a version of the tension between prayer and the aesthetic already seen in Johnson and Oppen: if God is unembodied, how can he be addressed without being figuratively likened to embodied beings, such as humans and flowers?

The third of the prayer-poems titled "Matins" begins conventionally enough as an apology, "Forgive me if I say I love you," but then immediately seems partly to retract the apology as a deliberate feint of the sort "the weak" make to "the powerful," who are "always lied to" (Glück, "Matins," 12). This is troubled love, at best. "I cannot love / what I can't conceive, and you disclose / virtually nothing" (12), complains the speaker. God is secretive, withdrawn behind a veil of "silence" (12). As the nothing that both is and is not there, God defies poetic comprehension in part because he is beyond figuration. The poet asks, "are you like the hawthorn tree," with its constancy, "or are you more the foxglove, inconsistent" (12)? And in the next poem titled "Matins," she pursues these comparisons with the vegetable world: "I see it is with you as with the birches: / I am not to speak to you / in the personal way" (13). The question of what God can be compared to is in part a theological question about the abstract and disembodied spirit that can never be fully known, but it is also a crucially poetic question about vehicle and tenor, metaphoricity, and resemblance. It is impossible to understand God without comparing him to something, in this case trees and flowers, but at the same time that she does so, Glück skeptically interrogates her inevitably inadequate efforts at poeticizing God. As if addressing an aloof lover, she accuses him of an "absence / of all feeling, of the least / concern for me," and then concludes, "I might as well go on / addressing the birches" (12). Closely related to the question of God's evasion of figurative likeness is that of his nonhumanity. Glück uses prayer's structure of address but deconstructs it. Having called into question how she is "to speak to you," she then raises the specter of the absence of anything to be addressed: "Or / was it always only / on the one side?" (12). It may be, she suggests, that her prayers are self-returning speech-acts, hall-of-mirrors reflections without opening to, or reciprocity with, any genuine Other.

As a Harlem Renaissance poet, an objectivist, and a postconfessionalist, respectively, Johnson, Oppen, and Glück represent very different strands of twentieth-century American poetry, yet they have in common a blurring of the lines between poetry and prayer, a rubbing of these discursive forms up against one another that reveals both likenesses and differences. By incorporating prayer and many of its conventions—address, humility, petition, intercession, anthropomorphism, musical repetition—they bring sacramental and ritualistic qualities into poetry, at the same time that they play on tensions between poetry and prayer, between "invention" and "devotion"—tensions they reveal as inherent within prayer itself. How can one speak to and pay homage to the divine without at the same time speaking to and paying homage to oneself? If God is beyond the human, how can she or he be addressed without humanizing figurative language? By virtue of its deliberate and self-conscious artifice, its stubborn materiality, its signification in excess of the signified, poetry exposes the metaphoricity and rhetoricity that structure human engagements with the divine, at the same time that prayer's absorption within poetry reveals the survival of long-lived religious and poetic traditions, even within modern and contemporary poems that seem to negate or refuse or austerely withdraw from Godhead.

As indicated by these and many other points of intergeneric contact, twentieth-century American poetry raises fundamental questions about what prayer is, what the news is, and, in turn, about what poetry is. After all, if some poetry, regardless of school or aesthetic, can turn the discursive dial in the direction of the news—secular and mimetic, historicist and empirical—and some can turn it toward prayer's sacredness and nonempiricism, recursiveness and ritualism, then what is the glue that holds the genre together? Arguably, much modern and contemporary American poetry can be understood as animating an array of discursive possibilities between the news and prayer. Visibly mediating between these generic poles are poems from Eliot's *Waste Land,* which tells the news of post–World War I civilizational collapse in a language studded with Christian and non-Christian prayer ("Shantih   shantih   shantih"), and H.D.'s *Trilogy,* which includes both news of war violence and prayers to a mother goddess, to the interfusions of news and prayer in the poetry of Anne Sexton, Allen Ginsberg, Charles Wright, and Jorie Graham. Like the news, much poetry vitally engages the present moment, at the same that it, like prayer, addresses enduring fundamentals of existence, straddling the divide between empirical truth and untestable belief. Poetry crosses the informational with the devotional, the present with eternity, mimesis with ritual. As the news that stays news, it bespeaks a "now" ambered in patterned language, the public moment preserved and remade in arrangements of style, sound, and image. As we saw even in poems dialogized with journalism, such as Williams's news stories punctuated by "So be it" or in Duncan's prophetic mythologizing of the Vietnam War, poets often push the news in the direction of prayer. Could prayerlike poems be seen, in turn, as sometimes pushing prayer in the direction of news? "Novelty" is incompatible with religious devotion, according to Samuel Johnson, but the "news" is all about "novelty," and poetry's contamination of prayer with novelty could be seen as nudging it in the direction of the news—though not the same kind of current history chronicled by the news media.

What we hypostatize as poetry is a genre that frequently attaches itself to and incorporates other genres. Although in Bakhtin's influential formulation, the novel is the omnigeneric genre par excellence and poetry is purist and exclusivist, already in Homer, epic poetry was an expansive compendium of a vast array of genres, and while modern epic poems such as the *Cantos, The Waste Land, The Bridge, Trilogy,* and *Paterson* obviously contain generic multitudes, even the shorter lyric poems explored above likewise take up, frame, and reconceive other genres. By virtue of its exacting attention to form and language, poetry makes visible the structuring assumptions behind the genres it assimilates. When O'Hara's poem quotes the headline "LANA TURNER HAS COLLAPSED!" it decontextualizes it as trope and raises up to view the attendant assumptions behind it. When Glück's poems titled "Matins" adapt prayer's address to the divine, this rhetorical structure similarly appears as if in relief. Even when it isn't quoting directly, poetry casts the languages and genres it absorbs in quotation marks. Although Bakhtin thought of the novel as making "images of languages" it cited (358), this idea may be even better suited to poetry, due to its more deliberate and irrepressible artifice—even in its newslike guises. When we remember the many uses modern and contemporary poets make of the news and prayer, of law and song, of letters and theory, we can say with Bakhtin that they exploit the "ability of a language to represent another language while still retaining the capacity to sound simultaneously both outside it and within it, to talk about it and at the same time to talk in and with it," "simultaneously to serve as an object of representation while continuing to be able to speak to itself" (358). Because of its sticky fingers, modern and contemporary poetry is enriched by long-memoried and widely scattered genres, tropes, and linguistic inheritances. Though poetry, it is dialogized by nonpoetry, and though American, it is entangled in the non-American. Its tentacles spread far and dangle deep.

NOTES

1 Williams, "The Present Relationship of Prose to Verse."
2 Dewey actually wrote that "the locality is the only universal"; see Dewey, 687.
3 On Williams and other American modernists' nativism, see Michaels.
4 On nineteenth-century U.S. poems printed in newspapers, see Bennett, 1–10, 69–85.
5 *Oxford English Dictionary,* s.v. "so be it," 3.a.
6 See Glissant, xii, 134–144.
7 See Williams, *Autobiography,* 52; Weaver, 7, 15.
8 On the poem's French and cold war contexts, see Perloff.
9 *The New York Post,* July 17, 1959, p. 3.
10 See Brunner; D. Nelson.
11 "Poem (Lana Turner Has Collapsed)," in O'Hara, 449.
12 On the poem's contexts, see Keenaghan.
13 See C. Nelson.
14 On "Fission" and adolescence, see Burt, 260–268.
15 Goldsmith's *Day* (2003) omits photos, design graphics, typeface variations, and other structuring visual cues, running together the newspaper's text as a massive collage.
16 See Austin.

17 See also Waters.
18 See Hart, "Religion and Poetry."
19 See Rubin, 287–335.
20 See also Chrétien, 20.
21 See Aristotle, 17a3–5 ("prayer is a sentence, but is neither true nor false"); see Richards.
22 See also Shreiber's reading of Oppen's "Psalm" in Shreiber, 188–192.
23 On Heidegger's influence on Oppen, see Nicholls, 62–72.
24 In later published editions of the poem, "bronze distance" was revised to "bronze decor," in accordance with the typescript at the Huntington Library.

REFERENCES

Anderson, Benedict. *Imagined Communities*. Rev. ed. London: Verso, 1991.
Aristotle. "On Interpretation."
Austin, J. L. *How to Do Things with Words*. Cambridge, MA: Harvard University Press, 1962.
Bakhtin, M. M. *The Dialogic Imagination: Four Essays*, ed. Michael Holquist; trans. Caryl Emerson and Holquist. Austin: University of Texas Press, 1981.
Benjamin, Walter. "The Storyteller." *Illuminations*, trans. Harry Zohn. New York: Schocken Books, 1969, 83–109.
Bennett, Paula Bernat. *Poets in the Public Sphere: The Emancipatory Project of American Women's Poetry, 1800–1900*. Princeton: Princeton University Press, 2003.
Bollard, Margaret Lloyd. "The 'Newspaper Landscape' of Williams' *Paterson*." *Contemporary Literature* 16, no. 3 (1975): 317–327.
Brunner, Edward. *Cold War Poetry*. Urbana: University of Illinois Press, 2001.
Burt, Stephen. " 'Tell Them No': Jorie Graham's Poems of Adolescence." In *Jorie Graham: Essays on the Poetry*, ed. Thomas Gardner. Madison: University of Wisconsin Press, 2005, 257–274.
Chrétien, Jean-Louis. "Wounded Speech." *The Ark of Speech*, trans. Andrew Brown. New York: Routledge, 2004, 17–38.
Culler, Jonathan. *The Pursuit of Signs*. London: Routledge, 1981.
de Man, Paul. "Lyrical Voice in Contemporary Theory." In *Lyric Poetry: Beyond New Criticism*, ed. Chaviva Hošek and Patricia Parker. Ithaca: Cornell University Press, 1985, 55–72.
Dewey, John. "Americanism and Localism." *The Dial* 68, no. 6 (1920): 684–688.
Duncan, Robert. "Up Rising, Passages 25." *Selected Poems*, ed. Robert J. Bertholf. New York: New Directions, 1993, 116–118.
Forché, Carolyn. "The Colonel." *The Country Between Us*. New York: Harper and Row, 1981. 16.
Glissant, Édouard. *Caribbean Discourse: Selected Essays*, trans. J. Michael Dash. Charlottesville: University Press of Virginia, 1989.
Glück, Louise. "Matins." *The Wild Iris*. Hopewell, NJ: Ecco Press, 1992, 12, 13.
———. "Disruption, Hesitation, Silence." *The American Poetry Review* 22, no. 1 (1993): 30–32.
Goldsmith, Kenneth. *Day*. Great Barrington, MA: The Figures, 2003.
Graham, Jorie. "Fission." *The Dream of the Unified Field: Selected Poems, 1974–1994*. Hopewell, NJ: Ecco Press, 1995, 99–103.
Hart, Kevin. "Poetry and Revelation: Hopkins, Counter-Experience and *Reductio*." *Pacifica* no. 18 (2005): 259–280.

———. "Religion and Poetry." In *The Princeton Encyclopedia of Poetry and Poetics*, ed. Roland Greene and Stephen Cushman. 3rd ed. Princeton: Princeton University Press, forthcoming.

———. "Transcendence in Tears." In *Gazing through a Prism Darkly*, ed. B. Keith Putt. New York: Fordham University Press, 2009, 116–138.

Hartley, John. *Popular Reality: Journalism, Modernity, Popular Culture*. London: Arnold, 1996.

Huyssen, Andreas. *After the Great Divide: Modernism, Mass Culture, Postmodernism*. Bloomington: Indiana University Press, 1986.

Jakobson, Roman. "Linguistics and Poetics." *Language in Literature*, ed. Krystyna Pomorsk and Stephen Rudy. Cambridge, MA: Belknap-Harvard University Press, 1987, 62-94.

Johnson, James Weldon. "Listen Lord: A Prayer." *God's Trombones: Seven Negro Sermons in Verse*. New York: Viking, 1927, 13–15.

———. "Preface." *The Book of American Negro Poetry*, ed. Johnson. Rev. ed. New York: Harcourt Brace Jovanovich, 1931, 9–48.

Johnson, Samuel. "Waller." *Lives of the Most Eminent English Poets*, Vol. 1. London: Thomas Tegg, 1824, 228-283.

Kant, Immanuel. *Religion within the Boundaries of Mere Reason*, trans. George Di Giovanni. *Religion and Rational Theology*, ed. and trans. Allen W. Wood and Di Giovanni. Cambridge: Cambridge University Press, 1996, 39–215.

Keenaghan, Eric. "Life, War, and Love: The Queer Anarchism of Robert Duncan's Poetic Action during the Vietnam War." *Contemporary Literature* 49, no. 4 (2008): 634–659.

Lawrence, D. H. "The American Eagle." *The Complete Poems*, ed. Vivian de Sola Pinto and F. Warren Roberts. New York: Viking, 1971, 413–414.

Martz, Louis L. "'Paterson': A Plan for Action." *Journal of Modern Literature* 1, no. 4 (1971): 512–522.

Michaels, Walter Benn. *Our America: Nativism, Modernism, and Pluralism*. Durham, NC: Duke University Press, 1995.

Mill, John Stuart. "Thoughts on Poetry and Its Varieties." *The Crayon* 7, no. 4 (1860): 93–97, 123–128.

Nelson, Cary. "Introduction." *The Wound and the Dream*, ed. Nelson. Urbana: University of Illinois Press, 2002, 1–61.

Nelson, Deborah. *Pursuing Privacy in Cold War America*. New York: Columbia University Press, 2002.

Nicholls, Peter. *George Oppen and the Fate of Modernism*. Oxford: Oxford University Press, 2007.

O'Hara, Frank. "The Day Lady Died." *The Collected Poems of Frank O'Hara*, ed. Donald Allen. New York: Knopf, 1971, 325.

Oppen, George. *Selected Letters of George Oppen*, ed. Rachel Blau DuPlessis. Durham, NC: Duke University Press, 1990.

———. "Psalm." *New Collected Poems*, ed. Michael Davidson. New York: New Directions, 2002, 99.

Pauly, John J., and Melissa Eckert. "The Myth of 'The Local' in American Journalism." *Journalism and Mass Communication Quarterly* 79, no. 2 (2002): 310–326.

Perloff, Marjorie. *Poetry on and Off the Page*. Evanston: Northwestern University Press, 1998.

Plath, Sylvia. "Years." *The Collected Poems*, ed. Ted Hughes. New York: Harper and Row, 1981, 255.

Pound, Ezra. *ABC of Reading*. New York: New Directions, 1960 (original, 1934).

Richards, I. A. *Science and Poetry*. 2nd ed. London: K. Paul, Trench, Trubner & Co., 1935.

Rubin, Joan Shelley. "God's in His Heaven: Religious Uses of Verse." *Songs of Ourselves: The Uses of Poetry in America*. Cambridge, MA: Belknap-Harvard University Press, 2007, 287–335.

Shelley, Percy Bysshe. "Ode to the West Wind." *Shelley's Poetry and Prose*, ed. Donald H. Reiman and Sharon B. Powers. New York: W. W. Norton, 1977, 221–223.

Shreiber, Maeera Y. *Singing in a Strange Land: A Jewish American Poetics*. Stanford: Stanford University Press, 2007.

Simic, Charles. "To the One Upstairs." *Jackstraws*. New York: Harcourt Brace, 1999, 63.

———. "Mystic Life." *Jackstraws*. 1999, 82–85.

Stevens, Wallace. "Of Mere Being." *Opus Posthumous*, ed. Samuel French Morse. New York: Knopf, 1957. 117.

Trachtenberg, Alan. *The Incorporation of America: Culture and Society in the Gilded Age*. New York: Hill and Wang, 1982.

Waters, William. *Poetry's Touch: On Lyric Address*. Ithaca: Cornell University Press, 2003.

Weaver, Mike. *William Carlos Williams: The American Background*. Cambridge: Cambridge University Press, 1971.

Weil, Simone. *Gravity and Grace*, trans. Arthur Wills. New York: Putnam, 1952.

Williams, William Carlos. "Asphodel, That Greeny Flower." *The Collected Poems of William Carlos Williams*, Vol. 2, ed. Christopher MacGowan. New York: New Directions, 1986, 310–337.

———. *The Autobiography of William Carlos Williams*. New York: New Directions, 1967.

———. *I Wanted to Write a Poem*, ed. Edith Heal. Boston: Beacon Press, 1958.

———. *Paterson*, ed. Christopher MacGowan. Rev. ed. New York: New Directions, 1992.

———. "The Present Relationship of Prose to Verse." Unpublished essay at Yale University Library, quoted in Bollard, 322.

———. "Prologue." *Kora in Hell* (1919), reprinted in *Imaginations*, ed. Webster Schott. New York: New Directions, 1970, 6–28.

———. *Selected Essays of William Carlos Williams*. New York: New Directions, 1969.

———. Unpublished manuscript of *Paterson*, quoted in Weaver, 120.

Young, Dennis. "Anthologies, Canonicity, and the Objectivist Imagination: The Case of George Oppen." In *No Small World: Visions and Revisions of World Literature*, ed. Michael Thomas Carroll. National Council of Teachers of English, 1996, 146–159.

Zelizer, Barbie. *Taking Journalism Seriously*. Thousand Oaks, CA: Sage, 2004.

Zukofsky, Louis. *Prepositions: The Collected Critical Writings of Louis Zukofsky*. Expanded ed. Berkeley: University of California Press, 1981.

CHAPTER 18

THE TRANQUILLIZED FIFTIES: FORMS OF DISSENT IN POSTWAR AMERICAN POETRY

MICHAEL THURSTON

My title is taken, of course, from Robert Lowell's "Memories of West Street and Lepke," in which the poet, "book-worming / in pajamas," looking about himself for a moment before recalling his "seedtime" during the previous decade, describes his present moment as "the tranquillized *Fifties*." In this (allegedly) free-verse poem (it's actually held together with a good deal of rhyme)—exemplary of the looser style the poet crafted in his award-winning 1959 volume, *Life Studies*—Lowell italicizes the decade, as if to acknowledge the novelty of proper-nouning ten-year spans. In this chapter, I will shift the emphasis back a syllable, in an effort to recover some of the cultural work of the more tightly constructed traditional stanzas and forms in which Lowell himself had written his earlier poems. In the acceptance speech he gave when *Life Studies* won the National Book Award in 1960, Lowell famously sketched an opposition between the "raw" open-form poetry that had come to prominence in the previous ten years, and the "cooked" poetry we now call by such labels as the New Critical or New Formalist lyric. *Life Studies* set Lowell "hanging like a question mark" between these types, a space he would occupy for the rest of his life. His remarks, though, deftly characterize (caricature, really) the poles. The "cooked" side of the table, from which Lowell had emerged, served up "marvelously expert and remote" poems calculated to lure graduate students as catnip tempts the cat. "Raw" poetry, on the other hand, is "often like an unscored libretto by some bearded but vegetarian Castro." While these terms themselves have, happily, fallen into disuse, the dichotomy they name still soaks up a lot of critical ink whether the argument is about contemporary poetry or the contested terrain I want to survey here. Debate might still rage over which side won, which type of poetry has had the greater success or influence in the intervening decades, but the critical jury is largely in about the specific raw and cooked poetries to be found on the *Fifties* smorgasbord: The Cooked fought the Raw, and the Raw won.

A fairly standard literary historical account of that prize fight would gather the team members (Louis Simpson, Karl Shapiro, Howard Nemerov, and Richard Wilbur star for the Cooked, while Allen Ginsberg, Charles Olson, Robert Creeley, and Frank O'Hara line up for the Raw); recount some key episodes from each team's narrative (e.g., Ginsberg's 1956 reading of *Howl* at San Francisco's Six Gallery) and set-piece head-to-head moments (e.g., Wilbur and Louise Bogan tag-teaming against William Carlos Williams in Bard College's 1948 "Experimental and Formal Verse" symposium); line up each team's important first books and prizes (the Yale Younger Poets series selection for the Cooked, City Lights publication for the Raw); and mention the anthology war that broke out when Meridian Books published *New Poets of England and America* (edited by Cooked exemplars Donald Hall, Robert Pack, and Louis Simpson) in 1957 and Grove Press answered in 1960 with Donald Allen's *The New American Poetry*. Typically, Raw (experimental, countercultural) poetry comes off as innovative, energetic, politically adventurous, and spiritually fulfilling, while Cooked (formalist, New Formalist, New Critical) poetry is represented as an enervated, culturally conservative retrenchment from modernism, politically quietist and spiritually vapid. As James Breslin puts it in one of the most thoughtful and interesting versions of this account, "The well-made autotelic poem was simply the literary version of the fifties idea of order" (51).

It's a good story but it's only one story among many that might (and should) be told about formal verse in the postwar decade or so. Recent scholarship—by Edward Brunner (*Cold War Poetry*), Deborah Nelson (*Pursuing Privacy in Cold War America*), Alan Filreis (*Counterrevolution of the Word*) and others—has done a good deal to add alternative narratives. Sometimes, these new stories illuminate even those characters most familiar from the old ones. Richard Wilbur, for instance, is often brought out as what Edward Brunner calls the "notorious example" of Cooked poetry par excellence; as Breslin writes, Wilbur "may serve as one representative figure of the poetic decade following the Second World War" (30). To be sure, the lapidary verbal surfaces of Wilbur's poems, the "ease of Wilbur's ironic meditations" (30), exemplify the postwar formalism often deemed useful as a foil for experimental or innovative poetry. But, as Brunner points out, something *drove* Wilbur to work those surfaces. Where Breslin focuses on the title poem of Wilbur's prize-winning first book, *The Beautiful Changes*, Brunner reminds us that the book opens with "a dozen or so poems set in the European war zone where he saw combat as an infantryman" (26). This clutch of poems, Brunner writes, "portrays a Wilbur distinctly aware of the need for healing and restoration," and when read in light of this reminder, the careful balancing of opposites, the maintenance of paradox, the baroque rhymes of a poem like "Mined Country" or "First Snow in Alsace" are clearly doing cultural work beyond just looking pretty. What Brunner is able to show by recovering the contexts in which Wilbur began his career is that a poem like "The Death of a Toad" (from Wilbur's 1950 volume, *Ceremony and Other Poems*) is also working to heal historical and cultural trauma, with its jarring juxtaposition of the clearly seen real toad ("Chewed and clipped of a leg") and the "elegiac music" of an imaginary garden ("Toward misted and ebullient seas / And cooling shores, toward lost Amphibia's reveries") (25–26).

What the multiplicity of stories about lyric poetry in the 1950s helps us to remember is the sense that what Breslin calls the decade's "idea of order" was imposed on a good deal of historical chaos—that Lowell's "*Fifties*" were not tranquil but "tranquilized." Poetic form is related not to a comfort with consensus but is instead a register of tensions to be managed. This is especially obvious if we look beyond the first string typically trotted out to illustrate the Cooked, if we read formalist work by poets at once deemed part of but also with reason to agitate against the decade's "idea of order." Adrienne Rich, for example, is among the poets whose first books Breslin includes in a catalog of early Fifties formalism (*A Change of World* was chosen by W. H. Auden for the Yale Younger Poets Series and published, with an infamously condescending introduction by Auden, in 1951). Rich's poetic voice changed dramatically a decade later, in the poems of *Snapshots of a Daughter-in-Law*, and her work since the early 1960s has mobilized open and experimental forms to attack gendered power dynamics. But even in the early work Auden described as "neatly and modestly dressed" (Rich, 11), Rich's stanzas are carefully composed to contain feminist discontent and register feminist dissent. "Aunt Jennifer's Tigers" illustrates the point especially effectively. The title figure embroiders tigers on a screen; where the creatures her work calls into being are fearless (unafraid of "men," in particular) and free, Aunt Jennifer herself is subject to patriarchal power:

> Aunt Jennifer's fingers fluttering through her wool
> Find even the ivory needle hard to pull.
> The massive weight of Uncle's wedding band
> Sits heavily upon Aunt Jennifer's hand. (19)

The stanza constructs its opposition through a variety of lyric means. The female figure, at her feminine labor, has trouble wielding even the miniature and domesticated phallic instrument of her needle, while the male figure passively asserts his power through a figurative manacle. Rich's quatrain divides into two sentences, each containing a rhymed couplet. Aunt Jennifer's couplet rhymes on a relatively weak liquid consonant; Uncle's rhyme sound is the somewhat more forceful palatal. Alliteration stresses the powerlessness of Aunt Jennifer's finger, while it links "Uncle's wedding band" to "massive weight." Though the deck is stacked, at every level, against the creative female figure (even when she is dead, Aunt Jennifer will be "ringed" by her husband and the power structure for which he stands), Rich grants fearlessness and freedom to the creation she might effect if she persists in her acts of encumbered making. Like Rich's own poem, these are creatures of artifice ("Bright topaz" tigers have not yet been found in nature). And in artifice, for Rich and for Aunt Jennifer, begins resistance.

It was not only in individual lyrics, or even in collections of them, that form was brought to bear in the management and expression of cultural tension. I will conclude this essay with a discussion of one impressive lyric sequence that arises from the political Left and deals with race in the United States (Aaron Kramer's *Denmark Vesey*), but I want to conclude this introductory section with a brief discussion of another important lyric sequence on the same theme: Gwendolyn Brooks's Pulitzer Prize–winning 1949 volume, *Annie Allen*. The book tells the story of a young African American woman who dreams of rising from the ghetto to a life of luxury, pursues her dream through the only means available to her (an ill-considered marriage), and finds herself, ultimately, no better off than she began. Brooks elaborates this narrative in poems whose forms range from variations on the sonnet and ballad (and one "sonnet-ballad"), to rhyming couplets and tercets, to, in the central long poem "The Anniad," a sort of abbreviated ottama rima (seven-line stanzas of rhyming trochaic tetrameter). The second half of *Annie Allen* leaves this individual narrative and explores the broader social context that determines Annie's fate. While she is unnamed in these poems (whose forms are also various and virtuosic), Annie remains the chief and cautionary example implicitly held up in their damning descriptions of "beauty" techniques aimed at minimizing features (like kinky hair) codified as "black"; in their warnings about sweet-talking men who won't stick around; and in their acknowledgment of color prejudice within the African American community.

"The Anniad" is the heart of Brooks's book, and in it she weaves into a single poetic fabric several strands of social stress. Annie, shown in earlier poems to be spoiled and waiting for romantic love to deliver her from both poverty and her family's demands, is as powerless before her husband as Aunt Jennifer is under Uncle's ring. But Annie's husband, too, confronts his own powerlessness in American society; having gone to war, he returns to find himself no longer a soldier but simply a baffled "tan man":

> With his helmet's final doff
> Soldier lifts his power off.
> Soldier bare and chilly then
> Wants his power back again.
> No confection languider
> Before quick-feat quick famish Men
> Than the candy crowns-that-were. (23)

Wanting to recapture both power and a sense of "fervor," the husband strays specifically to women whose skin is lighter than Annie's. Where the opening stanza of "The Anniad" casts her as "sweet and chocolate," the husband "Gets a maple banshee." Sexism, racism, and the invidious distinctions that heighten the nonsensical nature of skin color's significance all appear as forces that limit the possibilities even for a figure as creative, imaginative, and energetic as Annie. Having introduced her protagonist in an atmosphere of foreshadowing—"Think of sweet and chocolate / Left to folly or to fate / ... / Fancying on the featherbed / What was never and is not"—Brooks revises that introduction at the narrative's climactic turn. As she does so, she catalogs the illusions without which Annie is left to realize (and we are made to realize) that her story can, in her society, take only one form:

> Think of sweet and chocolate
> Minus passing-magistrate,
> Minus passing-lofty light,
> Minus passing-stars for night,
> Sirocco wafts and tra la la,
> Minus symbol, cinema
> Mirages, all things suave and bright. (24)

Betrayed, bereft, and left to live as a diminished thing, Annie is, by the end of "The Anniad," "Derelict and dim and done."

At the level of lyric form, Brooks adumbrates the arc of her narrative so that the poem at once exposes and encloses tensions. Not only does the story itself strongly suggest that it can travel only one trajectory, but the sonic riches on display throughout the poem render our experience of that over-determined downward slope quite pleasurable. In the stanzas I've already quoted, Brooks's facility with rhyme and her deployment of anaphora are apparent. The closed bracelet of the poem is also studded with diction that, whether archaic ("paladin"), exotic ("sirocco," "bacchanalian"), or simply over-the-top ("thaumaturgic," "hecatombs"), brings a luxurious sensation to the stanzas. And even when the protagonist herself and the poem's vision of her possibilities are at their most impoverished, alliteration decorates the bleak prospect:

> Think of almost thoroughly
> Derelict and dim and done.
> Stroking swallows from the sweat.
> Fingering faint violet.
> Hugging old and Sunday sun.
> Kissing in her kitchenette
> The minuets of memory. (29)

A minuet, of course, is a stately (and outmoded) dance, a relic not only of the past but of an entirely superseded civilization. And here is a hint to how form works for Brooks, as for Rich, as something of a countertext: for while "The Anniad" brings Annie low, the language remains as high and ornate as her most richly imagined fantasies. The gap between wealth like that on display in Brooks's lines and Annie's ability to realize in her life any wealth at all remains a sore spot to be addressed by something other than the poem itself—by, that is, the politics toward which the poem might implicitly point.

In the remainder of this chapter, I want to sketch the career of closed form on the political Left during the tranquilized Fifties. Where much of the formal verse of the decade let the lyric's dream work release social tensions in managed and manageable ways, a good deal of poetry aimed at once to name and to arouse the will to change the causes of social stress. The pages that follow focus on one exemplary periodical—the communist magazine *Masses & Mainstream*—and on the work of four poets who published in the magazine and produced avowedly political poetry in conventional meters and stanzas, poetry that sought not to tranquilize but to awaken.

MASSES & MAINSTREAM

In 1948, the defunct *New Masses*, once the widely distributed and avidly read magazine of the Communist Party of the United States (CPUSA), the publisher of numerous important American writers, but long-embattled by the cultural and political forces of American anticommunism, merged with the short-lived CPUSA magazine *Mainstream* to produce *Masses & Mainstream*, a monthly devoted to left-wing politics and culture. The magazine's masthead boasted some storied figures from the heyday of communist and Popular Front literature of the 1930s, from A. B. Magil to W. E. B. Du Bois, and during its eight-year run (it reverted to *Mainstream* in the September 1956 issue and continued for another year under that title), it published poems by Dalton Trumbo, Lorraine Hansberry, Howard Fast, Eve Merriam, Meridel LeSueur, Thomas McGrath, Alvah Bessie, Michael Gold, Ettore Rella, Walter Lowenfels, Martha Millet, and many others. Only Hansberry and McGrath, among these writers, have much of a profile for contemporary readers. A few of the other names will be familiar to students of cold war history (Trumbo and Bessie were two of the "Hollywood Ten," screenwriters who were jailed for refusing to name other communists when they testified to the House Un-American Activities Committee [HUAC]). Others (Fast, Gold, LeSueur) might ring a bell for students of the American Left (though their best-known work appeared in the 1930s, much of it in *New Masses*, and neither was known as a poet). The roster of non-American writers who published in these pages boasts some more familiar names. A communist magazine, *Masses & Mainstream* promoted and participated in an international literary culture; its pages often included poems and other writings by the Chilean poet Pablo Neruda; the Turkish poet Nazim Hikmet; the French poet Paul Eluard; and the Irish playwright and poet Sean O'Casey, to name a few.

As this list might already suggest, the magazine's unity derives from its politics; the poetry published in *Masses & Mainstream* is aesthetically diverse (though the literary editors for its first couple of years, Charles Humboldt and Thomas McGrath, tended to favor modernist and proletarian styles). The 1950 volume includes, in its first issue, the Whitmanesque catalogs of Neruda:

> Through the tall night, through all of life,
> from tears to paper, clothes to clothes,
> I wandered in those oppressive days.
> Fugitive from the police,
> in the hour of clarity, the denseness
> of solitary stars, I passed through cities,
> woods, small farms, ports,
> from the door of one human being
> to another, from the hand of one being
> to another, and another.
>
> (Neruda, 5)

A few months later, Eve Merriam takes on HUAC's Hollywood inquisition in rhyming couplets:

> Oh, we're scouring the flickers span and spick,
> Removing each trace of politic;
> Forecasting which gem for an Oscar is slated
> (The one with its content the most dehydrated);
> Just ibbety-bibbety-boo and a sunshine cake,
> With a teentsy touch of mayhem, or art for Bogart's sake;
> Sweetness and light and Technicolor éclairs,
> Then Widmark plugs his granny while she's saying her prayers!
>
> (Merriam, "Hollywood Blackout," 26)

And in the next issue, Dalton Trumbo, heading to prison as a result of that very inquisition, addresses his wife and children in "Four Poems on Parting," the most poignant of which is a rhyming fable addressed to his daughter, Melissa, "too young to understand"):

> Not many people have seen it,
> Nor caught the faintest gleam,
> Of the ice green cave in the deep green sea
> In the heart of the cold sea stream,
> Where the sea mare hides her young sea colt
> Wrapped in a shy sea dream.
>
> (Trumbo, 16)

I want to make two points here. First, this aesthetic diversity differentiates the magazine somewhat from many of the literary and cultural magazines of the 1950s. From the literary magazines associated with the New Critics (*Kenyon Review, Sewanee Review, Southern Review*) to Robert Bly's *The Fifties* (which vowed to continue the experimental energy of modernism and which devoted much of its space to translations of modernist European poets), or the *Evergreen Review* (affiliated with Grove Press and dedicated to experimental work), or the *Black Mountain Review* (dominated by work in the emerging tradition of Robert Creeley, Charles Olson, and Denise Levertov), most literary magazines settled on one or another side of the Raw versus Cooked divide. *Masses & Mainstream* did not. (The magazine did, however, both in the selections made by literary editors Thomas McGrath and Charles Humboldt and in such pieces as Sidney Finkelstein's 1950 essay, "The 'New Criticism,'" opt for a formal verse not characterized by such New Critical hallmarks as paradox, synaesthesia, or the objective correlative.) Second, and more importantly, the magazine's inclusion of poems in closed forms helps to complicate the easy assumption of correspondence between formal closure and cultural comfort. Where James Breslin writes of *New Poets of England and America* that its (typically formal) contents leave the impression "of a tame and sedate generation of poets who are comfortable with each other, with their predecessors, with their audience, with their wives, their children, their professorships, their grants," the same cannot be said of even the most formally conventional poems in *Masses & Mainstream*.

What we do find in these poems, just as we find in much other formal verse of the 1950s, is the manifestation of the social and political tensions with which the 1950s were riven. I want to turn now to a more sustained examination of four poets of the Left, each of whom contributed to *Masses & Mainstream* and who deployed the resources of conventional forms for political purposes during the 1950s: Edwin Rolfe, Eve Merriam, Walter Lowenfels, and Aaron Kramer.

THE LATE CAREER VERSE OF EDWIN ROLFE

A fixture on the New York literary Left and a frequent contributor to *New Masses* during the 1930s, Edwin Rolfe (1909–1954) published only one poem ("Elegy") in *Masses & Mainstream*. His last two volumes of verse appeared in the Fifties, though, and *Permit Me Refuge*, published posthumously in 1955, is advertised in some issues of the magazine. Rolfe (born Solomon Fishman) grew up on the Left—his parents were committed socialists and labor activists—and he was a member of the Communist Party (first in the Young Communist League and later in the CPUSA) from 1925 until the end of his life. After an early career writing journalism and poetry and publishing a first book, *To My Contemporaries*, in 1936, Rolfe joined the International Brigades and fought in Spain in 1937–1938. For the poems he created out of that experience, he is known as the unofficial "Poet Laureate of the Abraham Lincoln Battalion" but, as Cary Nelson has written, Rolfe also produced, during the late 1940s and early 1950s, "the strongest body of anti-McCarthy poems of any American poet" (Nelson, "Edwin Rolfe").[1] Especially interesting in that oeuvre

are Rolfe's ironic and satiric ballads, couplets, and quatrains. Rolfe wrote numer-
ous sonnets throughout his career and several appear in *Permit Me Refuge*, but his
political sonnets lack energy and urgency. This results not from an absence of force
in Rolfe's rhetoric but from an earnest prolixity in his diction and a concomitant
slackness in his lines. Here, for example, is the sestet of "In Praise Of":

> Therefore I honor him, this simple man
> who never clearly saw the threatening shapes, yet fought
> his complex enemies, the whole sadistic clan,
> persistently, although unschooled. Untaught,
> he taught us, who could talk so glibly, what
> the world's true shape should be like, and what not.
>
> (Rolfe, *Permit Me Refuge*, 19)

The last lines here evince a nice balance of oppositions through repetition of
sound ("Untaught, / he taught," "what / ... not"), but the pentameter is stretched
out in the earlier lines and neither image nor sound enlivens the language
there.

Where the sonnet had long been a form ready to hand for Rolfe, he seems
only in the 1950s to have discovered the satiric possibilities of the ballad, the cou-
plet, and the quatrain. It is in these that Rolfe best exemplifies political energy
manifest in poetic form. Like Trumbo, in his poem "For Melissa," Rolfe effec-
tively displaces present political pressures into parabolic or fabulous scenarios.
In "A Hunter Went Killing," he depicts a hunter needlessly slaughtering harm-
less birds beyond number, and when one bird notices that the hunter is weeping,
whether from the cold or the smoke of his rifle or remorse, another replies, "Never
mind his eyes.... Watch his hands" (Rolfe, *Permit Me Refuge*, 32). Like Merriam's
"Hollywood Blackout," Rolfe's "Ballad of the Noble Intentions" addresses the phe-
nomenon of testimony about one's political activities (and those of others) before
a committee. This was a situation the poet faced himself; he was called to testify
before HUAC and was spared this fate only by worse: heart disease and, in 1954,
death. Rolfe's poem enacts a dialogue in which one speaker questions and the
other answers. Here, questions and answers are about the second speaker's "noble
intentions":

> What will you do, my brother, my friend,
> when they summon you to their inquisition?
> *I'll fire from the heart of my fortress, my brain,*
> *my proudest possession.* (20)

Over the course of the poem, the second speaker's confidence (in himself, in the
power of his cultural arsenal) is shown to have been misplaced. In the first half, he
promises to answer the committee's accusations with the ringing words of literary
forebears ("*I'll read them bold pages from Areopagitica, / quote Milton and Marvell to*

rout and abuse them"), but in the second half, when the questioner asks not what he will do but what he has done, he sings a different tune:

> *I decided that boasting like Milton were vain,*
> *or refusing, like Marvell, their guineas with anger.*
> *I patterned myself after Waller, who lived*
> *more richly—certainly longer.* (21)

And, finally, under the persistent questioning of the first speaker, he admits a series of betrayals, first naming "*a disinterred corpse*" safe from the committee's sanctions and then "*some living men too,*" though only, he insists, ones whose names were already known and who, because decades had passed since their activities, were also beyond harm.

Evidence, perhaps, of a poetic road Rolfe might have taken had he lived long enough to do so, Rolfe's unpublished late poems (gathered in Nelson's edition of Rolfe's *Collected Poems*) are among his most interesting lyric responses to the age's demands. Taut and tart, Rolfe's quatrains harness compression and critique. The best of these attack specific institutions, as "1949 (After Reading a News Item)" does with the papacy of Pius XII:

> His first official act was to bless
> The planes that bombed their Barcelona home.
> Ten years have passed. Today his Holiness
> Welcomes the Catalan orphans into Rome.
> (Rolfe, *Collected Poems*, 259)

The rhymes here are deft and significant; where "bless" and "Holiness" are drawn from the same discursive field, the "home" bombed by Franco's Catholic nationalists and the city that houses the Holy See are linked by opposition. A savage irony energizes these late, formal poems, a politicized variant of the irony that manifests, in the work of more "mainstream" postwar formalists, other modes of dissatisfaction with the cultural consensus sometimes assumed or alleged by literary historians. "Little Ballad for Americans—1954" intensifies dissatisfaction into a sense of danger, and it locates that danger in precisely the politically energized language Rolfe's poems themselves construct. Or, rather, the poem locates danger in the consequences entailed by such language under the restrictive political atmosphere of McCarthyism: "Brother, brother, best avoid your workmate— / Words planted in affection can spout a field of hate" (260). Renovating a tactic from his poems of the 1930s (one I have elsewhere called "serial interpellation"), Rolfe calls out couplet by couplet to a sequence of auditors.[2] Here, each addressee stands for a different kind of relationship (a coworker, neighbor, fellow student), climaxing with "Lovers," who are warned that the paranoid ears of the state encroach even upon the marital bed. "No person's really trustworthy," Rolfe concludes the poem, "until he's dead."[3]

EVE MERRIAM'S EARLY VERSE

Among the most frequent poetry contributors to *Masses & Mainstream* was Eve Merriam (1916–1992). Best known now as a writer of children's books (including the controversial *Inner City Mother Goose*, published in 1969), Merriam began her career as a poet. Her first poems were published in *The New Anvil*, the inheritor of the 1930s left-wing magazine *The Anvil*. Other early poems appeared in *New Masses*, and her first book, *Family Circle*, was chosen by Archibald MacLeish for the Yale Younger Poets Series in 1946. Along with poems about family (both her own and the family as an institution in American life) and poems inspired by characters and stories from the Old Testament, *Family Circle* includes poems on the just-concluded World War II and on the continuing problems of poverty and the inequitable distribution of wealth in the United States. As her "Hollywood Blackout" suggests, Merriam, like Rolfe in his late, formal verse, was often at her best when at her most ironic and satirical. In "Rumba," she addresses the grind of menial office work in rhyming quatrains consisting, after a first scene-setting stanza, of imperatives:

> Unlock the box of work,
> File your face away;
> Clip legs to letterhead
> Moisten flap with blood.
> (Merriam, *Family Circle*, 17)

In a trope familiar from labor poetry of the 1930s, Merriam conveys the costs of work by melding labor and laboring body. The worker here disappears into and becomes her work, leaving her, when the workday ends, without the energy to dance the title's rumba:

> Stub out ash of day,
> Fold evening under arm;
> Wind into sheet of night,
> Set for alarm-clock light.

Instead, she is simply exhausted to the point of the figurative death suggested by the echo of "winding sheet," or shroud. This death is, however, a reprieve denied, in the last line, by the sense that dawn will bring the profane resurrection of yet another day of work.

Where "Rumba" delineates the dance of daily labor, "Slick Story" treats the cultural fantasies that prevent agitation that might alter the lives of laborers. The octave of this sonnet sets out the plot of a typical, escapist romance. Jill Darlington is torn between two lovers, and all three characters' class positions are suggested by the metonyms of nightclub, roadster, and golden curls. Merriam links the triangle's resolution, or the suspension of it, explicitly to the reader's need for pleasurable distraction: "Not yet; the golden curls must tantalize / At least two pages longer!" In the sestet, the speaker straightforwardly expresses her desire for Jill's life and its accoutrements (indeed, the "champagne" and "aeroplane" of that life are woven into the rhyme scheme). But the illusory character of her mass-produced dreams is admitted in the closing lines:

> Farewell to the flat, the noise from the street, the clothesline view;
> Goodbye to the life I live. Untrue, hello to you. (16)

Merriam writes some poems that focus on "the life I live," or the life lived by those without the fictional Jill Darlington's fantastic resources. "Fifth Avenue at Noon" and "Summer, Second Avenue" realistically depict poverty and its attendant cultural death. More often, though, Merriam uses her tripping rhythms and sharp rhymes to puncture the illusions that enable her society to ignore poverty and the poor.

THE LEFT'S PREEMINENT SONNETEER: WALTER LOWENFELS

As we have seen, the sonnet appealed to numerous poets writing in traditional forms during the 1940s and 1950s; at the Bard College symposium on "Experimental and Formal Verse," William Carlos Williams complained that "we live in an age of sonnets" (quoted in Breslin, 38). In his *Sonnets of Love and Liberty*, Walter Lowenfels (1897–1976) established himself as the most insistent practitioner of the sonnet on the political Left. By the early 1950s, Lowenfels had had two distinct literary careers. Resident in Paris during the late 1920s, Lowenfels cofounded Carrefour Press in 1930. He published a book on the French poet Guillaume Appolinaire with Nancy Cunard's Hours Press, and he published two volumes of his own verse. Upon his return to the United States in the mid-1930s, though, Lowenfels began a new career as a political poet, publishing *Steel 1937*, poems on workers killed during the 1937 strike of the Little Steel company and on the nascent Spanish Civil War. That career was interrupted for seventeen years while Lowenfels devoted his energy to the Pennsylvania edition of the Communist Party newspaper, the *Daily Worker*.

In 1953, Lowenfels was arrested in New Jersey and charged under the Smith Act with advocating the overthrow of the U.S. government. While his conviction was eventually overturned, Lowenfels spent months in prison awaiting trial. During that time he wrote half the poems that make up *Sonnets of Love and Liberty*. In a prefatory "Note on the Sonnet," Lowenfels explicitly takes on the suitability of the sonnet for his political purposes. "How is it," he writes, "that a form invented during the days of chain mail is still found useful during the hydrogen age?" (7). Noting that the form achieved its dominance in the English lyric during times of political turmoil, and adducing a recent article by Louis Aragon to show that the same was true of the sonnet's French career, Lowenfels writes that he, too, dreams that even "in the epoch of revolutions and modern wars, the sonnet—like the thinking machine it is—perhaps can still give new and strange answers" to the problems posed by "a new historic base" (9). He approvingly quotes Aragon, who writes that "'We are again in a time when the instrument must be sharpened, ready for the necessary song'" (9).

Sonnets of Love and Liberty is divided into two sections. The latter half (sonnets XIX–XXXIV) contains sonnets Lowenfels wrote, mostly on the theme of love, during the 1920s. The first half of the book consists of the sonnets Lowenfels wrote before and during his trial. In these, he consociates the key terms of his title, linking love and liberty not only in almost every sonnet but also in almost every stanza. Often, the "love" is the love that is shared by Lowenfels and his wife, Lillian, but the poems redefine love so that the romantic is simply a figure for a larger, and profoundly politicized, love. This is especially clear in the last of the 1953 sonnets. Hoping no scholar "fingering our dust" will do the kind of analytical work on the poems that I'm beginning, Lowenfels writes that if one does, he hopes the scholar will discover

> our common love, our country love, not tree
> alone nor common earth nor sky, but all
> our yesterdays we hold when we hold each,
>
> and in the instant that we loved were free
> with lovers working to undo this pall
> of lying death to live their own true speech. (36)

The first half of this sestet effects the shift from love for individual to "common love," not only naming the move but also emblematizing it in the change from singular to plural, in the rhyme scheme's emphasis on "all," and in the discursive change of field from space to time. The second tercet explicitly connects community and freedom; the poem's "we" becomes free not alone but in (and, it seems, only in) the company of others undertaking similar political work. Lowenfels clarifies the nature of that work by constructing an opposition notable for its alliteration: lovers' living their "true speech" versus "lying death."

These sonnets are composed in the full awareness of the form's long tradition, and often, I think, with specific precursors in mind. The sonnet "For the Reader" (the second in the book), for example, is saturated with the sense of previous prison sonnets by the likes of Wyatt, Surrey, and Raleigh. Lowenfels must, then, be aware of the allusion he makes in sonnet XVIII to Macbeth's "Tomorrow and tomorrow and tomorrow" soliloquy. The phrase "all our yesterdays" names the memories embraced in any individual embrace, but cannot help but hold, at the same time, the way to "dusty death" they open to for "fools" in Shakespeare's lines. One of the things I most admire in Lowenfels's sonnets is their construction of such eddies against the main current of their meanings. These moments suggest that none of this—love, liberty, or the political work entailed by each—is easy.

THE MASTERPIECE OF THE LYRIC LEFT: AARON KRAMER'S "DENMARK VESEY"

Privately printed in 1952, Aaron Kramer's *Denmark Vesey and Other Poems* boasts what Cary Nelson calls "probably the single most ambitious and inventive poem about race ever written by a white American" (Nelson, "On Aaron Kramer"). In this twenty-six-poem sequence, Kramer imagines, explores, and makes clear the contemporary significance of the 1822 slave revolt planned but never carried out by the title figure, Denmark Vesey. In its researched reinterpretation of historical events, *Denmark Vesey* joins such poetic projects as Muriel Rukeyser's *The Book of the Dead*, Charles Reznikoff's *Testimony*, and Kay Boyle's "Communication to Nancy Cunard" (to say nothing of certain sections of Pound's *Cantos*). Kramer's sequence abjures the documentary style deployed by Rukeyser, Reznikoff, and Boyle, though. Instead, Kramer narrates, dramatizes, and analyzes the events of 1822 in a variety of traditional stanzas: couplets, tercets, quatrains (cross-rhymed and couplet-rhymed), sestets, octaves. Kramer writes lines of trimeter, tetrameter (switching, in one case, from iambic to trochaic), pentameter, and heptameter. His rhymes are sometimes perfect, sometimes slant, sometimes strong, sometimes weak. The sequence is at once a rigorous imaginative exploration of an episode in the ugly racial history of the United States, an implicit commentary on contemporary racial politics, and a tour-de-force demonstration of poetic prowess and lyric ability.

That last phrase might sound reminiscent of the work of many young mainstream poets in the 1950s; as I have described it, Kramer's sequence might seem to resemble, say, W. S. Merwin's *A Mask for Janus* (at least as James Breslin characterizes that book): "two ballads, two sestinas, a rondel, a 'half-rondel,' an ode, two sonnets, three 'carols,' five 'songs,' a dramatic colloquy written in nine-line stanzas" (Breslin 38). Traditional form for Kramer, though, is related neither to the antimodernist retrenchment Breslin describes nor to the young poet's need to demonstrate mastery that we see in Merwin's first book. Rather, it is linked to Kramer's intention to play "the role of 'people's poet,' spokesman for the 'voiceless millions,' in traditional stanzas and accessible language" (quoted in Nelson and Gilzinger, xxxiv). This is a role that Kramer spent much of his career trying to play (though it was often in tension with other literary inclinations), from his early work published in *New Masses*, and it is a role that Kramer played with respect to race politics throughout his career, from early poems on Paul Robeson and a fire in a Natchez dance hall in the 1930s to poems on Medgar Evers and Elinor Bumpers in the 1960s. "People's poet" only partly describes, though, the work he undertakes in *Denmark Vesey*, a sequence that goes far beyond speaking accessibly to or for "voiceless millions."

On one level, *Denmark Vesey* tells the story of the would-be slave rebellion that bears this leader's name. Kramer generally follows the historical record in his narrative: In 1822, Denmark Vesey, a former slave who had bought his freedom and worked as a carpenter in Charleston, South Carolina, was at once inspired by the rebellion of slaves in Haiti (where he had, himself, briefly worked) and enraged by new restrictions on slaves' ability to congregate (the closure, for the second time, of the local African Methodist Episcopal Church he had helped to found, the passage of newly restrictive laws in reaction to the Missouri Compromise of 1820). He resolved to lead a rebellion of slaves on Bastille Day, but word of the plot leaked. Vesey and others were captured and, on July 2, 1822, executed. In a set of carefully crafted scenes, Kramer almost cinematically takes us through these events, introducing Vesey as the carpenter called upon to build a table for a wealthy Charlestonians' banquet; showing the rise of resentment among slaves; demonstrating the coalescence of revolutionary intention around Vesey; offering a quiet interlude in which (echoing Hector's farewell to Andromache) Vesey says good-bye to his beloved; revealing a traitor, a pampered slave, who informs his master of the plot; following a heroic member of the resistance who is tortured almost to death before he gives up the ringleader's name; and, finally, narrating the hanging that transforms live rebels into much more dangerous martyrs.

On another level, though, Kramer constructs what Lowenfels calls, in his discussion of the sonnet, a thinking machine. Beneath, beside, and interspersed with the narrative of Denmark Vesey and the thwarted uprising is a layered analysis of slavery, racism, the paranoia of the powerful, the treachery of the comfortable, and the resources available to the dispossessed. What I want to show in this fairly brief discussion of the sequence is how Kramer conducts that analysis through aspects of lyric form.

One thing that strikes the reader the first time through the sequence is that its title figure is not mentioned until the seventh poem. The sequence opens with a capsule history of the slave trade and with some sketching of the scene in Charleston, along with the strange atmosphere in which, at the same time, slaveowners worry when they hear rumors of a revolt in Santo Domingo and go about business as usual, planning the banquet for which they commission a table from Vesey. (It is only at this point that he is named.) Kramer also includes in these early poems an exploration of the casuistries required to accept the moral outrages endemic to slavery. In "Auction Block," a slaveowner's wife recoils at the sight of families broken up and humans treated as animals: *"The sobs and moans cut through my bones / more cruelly than knives"* (Kramer, 45; emphasis in original). Her husband responds first by pointing out how the couple's wealth and comfort depend upon slaves' labor ("Without those blacks to bend their backs / your wrists would soon be bare"), then by admitting that violence will break the slaves, and, finally, by averring that "soon they'll call this 'Home'" (45). Nelson has written persuasively about Kramer's use of internal rhyme in this poem; I'd like to focus on another of the preliminary poems in the sequence, "Revolt in Santo Domingo."

From 1791 until 1804, a revolution that began as a slave revolt raged in the French colony of St.-Domingue. Out of this revolution, the independent state of Haiti came into existence. Throughout the Haitian Revolution and during the years immediately after, Haitian leaders also fomented rebellion in the neighboring colony of

Santo Domingo. These events shook the confidence of slaveowners throughout the Caribbean and the American South. "Revolt in Santo Domingo" explores the etiology of the rebellion and its significance for slaveowners in a-rhymed tercets:

> Santo Domingo was the first to learn
> what comes to pass when feet may not return
> to the beloved soil for which they yearn. (46)

Slaves kept down by violence, who are denied their own culture and condemned to bestial treatment, will rise up and turn against their erstwhile masters all that had been brought to bear to keep them in their place. Against this news and the dire prediction it implied for their own society (dependent, as the husband in "Auction Block" openly admits, on slavery), the "lords of Charleston" work to block out word of such revolts and their meanings. The rhyme sound for the closing tercet in which their efforts are described is a slanted repetition of the rhyme sound in the opening tercet, which sets out the (temporary) effectiveness of slaveowners' violence. Here are the two stanzas:

> The whip worked magic everywhere it fell;
> the chains performed miraculously well;
> the threat of starving cast a mighty spell. (46)

> And though the lords of Charleston raised a wall
> to keep the news away, it was not tall
> or thick enough—the news reached one and all. (47)

Kramer's rhymes enclose the poem just as the slaveowners' efforts construct a cordon around Charleston. The subtle shift of the rhyme's vowel, though, alters the repetition enough to breach the wall and thus enacts the thematic opposition between the poem's first and last stanzas; where violence works like magic in the beginning, attempts to block the "news" of rebellion and the possibility of freedom fail in the end.

Even when his name is finally mentioned, Vesey does not show up as a character. Instead, he is reputation, name, the sound of his hammer. Named as the carpenter who will build a banquet table, Vesey is shown, in "The Denmark Vesey Song," to arise not as an individual body but as a name ("Do you know the name?" is something of a refrain in the poem) produced by historical determinants. Vesey finally appears as the dreamer of "Vesey's Nightmare," in which a point that Kramer has heretofore metaphorically implied is finally made explicit: The banquet planned by the "lords of Charleston" is the consumption of black bodies by white owners. The poem's images are reminiscent both of Sterling Brown's "Slim in Hell," in which the trickster hero sees that the pleasure palaces of Hell (which turns out to be Dixie) are fueled by the bodies of black devils shoveled into a furnace by white devils, and of reports out of the postwar Nuremberg Trials of Nazi relics made of human remains:

> The lovely brocade their ladies wore
> had once been Negro grandmothers' hair.
> The gems that blinked on their arms like stars
> were bright Negro eyes that had lately shed tears. (50)

The stanzas of "Vesey's Nightmare" are of varying lengths, but all consist of couplets whose slant rhymes effect in sound the slippage and displacement of this revelatory dream work.

Once Vesey himself appears in the poem, Kramer uses rhyme and meter to establish his relationship with the community of the enslaved. That community is given its own distinctive speech in "Sunday Offertory Prayer," whose cross-rhymed quatrains alternate multi- and monosyllabic rhymes:

> We bring you, Lord, a week of wounds and worry—
> put forth your loving arms and take them in.
> We wished to fill your cups of offertory,
> but better coin than hurt we did not win. (51)

This is carefully composed collective speech, patient as well as prayerful, adorned not only with this alternation of rhyme types but also with parallel constructions, chiasmus, and anaphora. In "Vesey Speaks to the Congregation," the main character's voice is metrically regular and strongly rhymed, but it is also complex enough to enact the poem's dynamic of identification and exhortation. The poem alternates quatrains set flush to the left margin and quatrains indented. The flush-left quatrains are couplet-rhymed; the rhymes are monosyllabic. The indented quatrains rhyme abcb. The first four stanzas make two pairs of quatrains. In each, the second answers the first. Where the poem's first stanza has Vesey identify with the physical suffering of the congregation—"My leg is weak from the chains you wear"—the second intensifies the identification by moving from the physical to the spiritual:

> But when you bow, my beautiful sisters,
> ah brothers, when you bow and beg,
> my heart wears chains. (51)

The relation of the third and fourth stanzas is opposition rather than intensification. After condemning the passive hope for salvation in one, Vesey adduces the people of Israel to urge active resistance—"She cried aloud," "She rose"—against the modern stand-ins for Pharoah. The poem's final "quatrain" is broken into two couplets that draw identification and exhortation together; where there had been a "you" and "I," a "your" and "my," there is now us, and the collective promises to transform "sobs to battle-cries" (52).

There is much more to say about this eloquent and effective sequence (some has been said by Nelson and his students on the Modern American Poetry website), but I hope this discussion both suggests the quality of Kramer's work in *Denmark Vesey* and, more important for the purposes of this essay, demonstrates the possibility, quite live during the 1950s, for political critique not only to coexist with but also to take shape in and through traditional lyric forms. That possibility persists in spite of polemics (both by those who oppose conventional poetic form and by formalist poets who want to separate poetic and political discourses) that argue to the contrary. One fifty-year-long demonstration is the career of Nobel Prize–winner Derek Walcott. Lyric form as the means of political work is on display, for example, in Walcott's devastating analyses of colonialism, whether in the rhyming stanzas of "A Far Cry from Africa" (1956) or "The Sea Is History" (1979) or in the *terza rima* tour-de-force of *Omeros* (1990). Walcott's career has used the lyric forms imposed by British colonial rule on his native St. Lucia to explore precisely the conflict of the colonized subject speaking the colonizer's language. And in his long poem, *The Arkansas Testament* (1987), Walcott brings a version of the sonnet (sixteen-line stanzas derived from George Meredith's *Modern Love*) to bear on American racism. Like Brooks's *Annie Allen* or Kramer's *Denmark Vesey*, *The Arkansas Testament* moves from the experience of the individual constructed as the subject of racial discourse to broader views of that discourse and the questions it forces regarding citizenship and responsibility. In the former vein, Walcott's speaker feels himself criminalized (by the history he wears on his skin and by white eyes in the present) simply for being out before dawn in Fayetteville:

> Hugging walls in my tippler's hop—
> the jive of shuffling bums,
> a beat that comes from the chain—
> I waited for a while by the grass
> of a urinous wall to let
> the revolving red eye on top
> of a cruising police car pass. (109)

And in the latter, after wondering whether he can ever be a true citizen or will be forever "an afterthought of the state," he brings the question back to his vocation and its burden of critique:

> Can I swear to uphold my art
> that I share with them too, or worse,
> pretend all is past and curse
> from the picket lines of my verse
> the concept of Apartheid? (115)

In both of these excerpts, language and form carry history. Walcott renders that history as visible as his skin renders his own identity (or one aspect of it). In doing the same with the forms in which he writes, Walcott shows that the pretty rooms of sonnets and other traditional stanzas are anything but spaces comfortably or complacently to inhabit. A speaker as jittery as the one in *The Arkansas Testament*, like those in the poems of Rich and Rolfe, Brooks and Kramer, and Merriam and Lowenfels, occupies a space where tensions might be tranquilized but is nowhere near domestic tranquility.

NOTES

1 Biographical information here is from Nelson and Hendricks.
2 I discuss the strategy in readings of poems by Rolfe and Langston Hughes in *Making Something Happen* (52, 91–93).
3 On Rolfe's later career, see Nelson's essential discussion in *Revolutionary Memory* (125–140).

REFERENCES

Breslin, James E. B. *From Modern to Contemporary: American Poetry, 1945–1965*. Chicago: University of Chicago Press, 1983.

Brooks, Gwendolyn. *Annie Allen*. New York: Harper, 1949.

Brunner, Edward. *Cold War Poetry*. Urbana: University of Illinois Press, 2001.

Filreis, Alan. *Counter-Revolution of the Word: The Conservative Attack on Modern Poetry*. Chapel Hill: University of North Carolina Press, 2008.

Finkelstein, Sidney. "The 'New Criticism.'" *Masses & Mainstream* 3.12 (December 1950): 76–86.

Kramer, Aaron. *Wicked Times: Selected Poems*. Ed. Cary Nelson and Donald Gilzinger. Urbana: University of Illinois Press, 2004. Quotations from *Denmark Vesey* (full text is included in this volume) are drawn from this book.

Lowell, Robert. *Selected Poems*. New York: Farrar Straus and Giroux, 2006.

———. National Book Award acceptance speech. http://www.nationalbook.org/nbaacceptspeech_rlowell.html.

Lowenfels, Walter. *Sonnets of Love and Liberty*. New York: Blue Heron Press, 1955.

Merriam, Eve. *Family Circle*. New Haven: Yale University Press, 1946.

———. "Hollywood Blackout." *Masses & Mainstream* 3.6 (June 1950): 26.

Nelson, Cary. "About Aaron Kramer." Modern American Poetry website. http://www.english.illinois.edu/maps/poets/g_l/kramer/about.html.

———. "Edwin Rolfe Biography." Modern American Poetry Website. http://www.english.illinois.edu/maps/poets/m_r/rolfe/bio.htm.

———. *Revolutionary Memory: Recovering the Poetry of the American Left*. New York: Routledge, 2001.

Nelson, Cary, and Donald Gilzinger. "Aaron Kramer: American Prophet." In Kramer, *Wicked Times: Selected Poems*. Urbana: University of Illinois Press, 2004. xvii–lix.

Nelson, Cary, and Jefferson Hendricks. *Edwin Rolfe: A Biographical Essay and Guide to the Rolfe Archive at the University of Illinois at Urbana-Champaign*. Urbana: University of Illinois Press, 1990.

Nelson, Deborah. *Pursuing Privacy in Cold War America*. New York: Columbia University Press, 2002.

Neruda, Pablo. "The Fugitive." *Masses & Mainstream* 3.1 (January 1950): 5–20.

Rich, Adrienne. *A Change of World*. New Haven: Yale University Press, 1951.

Rolfe, Edwin. *Collected Poems*. Ed. Cary Nelson and Jefferson Hendricks. Urbana: University of Illinois Press, 1993.

———. *Permit Me Refuge*. Los Angeles: California Quarterly, 1955.

Thurston, Michael. *Making Something Happen: American Political Poetry between the World Wars*. Chapel Hill: University of North Carolina Press, 2001.

Trumbo, Dalton. "For Melissa." *Masses & Mainstream* 3.7 (July 1950): 16.

Walcott, Derek. *The Arkansas Testament*. New York: Farrar, Straus and Giroux, 1987.

Wilbur, Richard. *New and Collected Poems*. New York: Harcourt Brace Jovanovich, 1988.

CHAPTER 19

THE END OF THE END OF POETIC IDEOLOGY, 1960

AL FILREIS

silence—after a word-waterfall of the banal—
as unattainable
as freedom.

> —Marianne Moore, "In the Public Garden" (1959)[1]

[C]onsidering the wide spaces where past crimes high-lighted a Soviet-sponsored bit to make Short Time. The Iron Age, six months short, was convicted of killing a cabbie who had crossed the Atlantic in the balloon Small World. / There seemed little doubt, however, that Mr. Eisenhower said, "I weigh 56 pounds less than a man," flushed a nodded curtly.

> —William S. Burroughs, "First Cut-Ups," a collage of news articles made in September 1959[2]

I'm writing about a time when *modern* seemed to give way to *contemporary* and natural-seeming idealizations of freedom gave way to compounded newspaper clippings about cabbie killers and the cold war—when the argument over the association of avant-gardism and leftism on one hand and of poetic traditionalism and conservatism on the other finally shifted. It was the moment when Marianne Moore, deemed a dowdy, superannuated great modern, was apparently yesterday's poetic news, while William S. Burroughs, with his crazy embrace of the cut-up method, was being celebrated by politically alienated avant-gardists as working in the liberating mode of the day, a Beat descriptiveness finally inflected by a genuine experimental urge to torque language by quasi-nonintentional procedure obtaining at the level of the phrase and even of the word. The modern urge had come back to the word as such. The "silence" for which Moore longs in the public garden, a peace made untenable by the "word-waterfall of the banal"—in her poem, "In the Public Garden," as we will see later, this phrase refers to conventional American political talk—is the very thing that Burroughs's jumbled, multivocal version of the day's news would seem to disdain.

But setting aside what is ordinarily in studies of modern American poetics a useful measure, namely the axis running from lyric modernism to juxtapositional postmodernism, and preferring instead a literary history moving downward into a moment in time—the poetic frenzy of the year 1960—this chapter begins by hypothesizing a remarkable concurrence between Burroughs and Moore on the cultural value of what "Mr. Eisenhower said": that what the president says is negligible, except *in the poem*, where counterintuitively it derives enormous poetic possibility and where, they also agree, such "word-waterfall" can be vital to American art—can feed us out of the well-spring of lives as actually lived in the linguistic ambience of our polity. In the writing as a worldly done thing, for both poets, nothing less than freedom is at stake. Of course, this aesthetic sensibility—the poetic practice it authorized and the large claims associated with it—had its doubters right then (as it does still now). And while antimodernism in the expressions of this doubt did not serve to unify writers as otherwise different and unaffiliated as Moore and Burroughs—and poets such as Philip Whalen, Anne Sexton, Ed Dorn, Bob Kaufman, and Ezra Pound, all of whom were doing major poetic work in 1960—it certainly helped to identify a moment in which the politics of modernism beyond cold war culture was freshly discernible.

To be sure, again, among mainstream poets skepticism abounded. Two months before 1960 commenced, for example, Stanley Kunitz in *Harper's* redefined the word "experimental" to mean the inevitable resistance to any prevailing style for the sake of "keep[ing] it supple." Yet at the time of his writing, the turn of this new decade, "the nature of that resistance is in effect *a backward look*." The recent Pulitzer Prize winner added: "This happens *not* to be a time of great innovation in poetic technique: it is rather a period in which the technical gains of past decades, particularly the 'twenties, are being tested and consolidated."

By using the phrase "the 'twenties," Kunitz was referring to modernism's heyday. He meant expatriation, avid rule-breaking, and aesthetic hijinx coinciding with social high hilarity. The sixties, starting now, he averred, would be a time of modest "consolidation" rather than of experiment. Kunitz's historical generalization would make better sense, as a lament, if he had been seeking to position *himself* as an inheritor of modernism or had he been commending the avant-garde. But Stanley Kunitz was certainly not an experimenter, nor did he hope for a new ascendancy of heterodox verse. He gratefully noted widespread popular praise of Robert Frost. On January 20, 1961, that genuine conservative would somewhat confusingly conclude the year in question, traveling to Washington to help inaugurate a Make It New sort of U.S. president, a young person's leader. Thus poetry took political center stage at the culmination of that election year, and yet, as Kunitz had observed, "I don't detect many signs of [Frost's] influence" among the young writers of 1960. Instead, disappointingly, the new poets "have found it easier to raid [William Carlos] Williams." In short, modernism had become the new status quo, a false stand-in for politically relevant traditionalism (Kunitz, 173–179).

Faced with Kunitz's impressionistic and unevidenced assertion that a "pivotal" year was a time of "consolidat[ing]" the modern poetic mode, it remains for the literary historian to construct specific bibliographical and interpretive contexts for testing such claims, eschewing grand cross-generational generalizations (such as Kunitz's own) that tend to follow the largest contours of aesthetic movements and thus subdue the unlikely convergences that occur at any given moment along the continuum of aesthetic ideologies maturing and then waning at different rates of speed. Whereas Kunitz contends that "resistance" had by 1960 become retrospect, had become a longing rather than a looking forward, a literary history operating from this constraint, preferring deep to wide, might serve as a resistance to such a sense of resistance. To be sure, readers will hardly be shocked to learn, through consideration of actual lines and stanzas of poetry written and published that year, that Kunitz was plainly wrong when he contended that modernism had become static and had reached a dead end. But they might be surprised by the extraordinary degree to which he was misguided by an antimodernist ideology, which held that it had to be, and should be celebrated as, a derivative epoch. They might be startled, too, by—conversely—the remarkable dynamism and ardent experimentalism in new poetry; by the freshness of the late work, just then, of aging high modernists; by the subtle mix (as opposed to rejection or exhaustion) of modernism in emergent works of postmodernism; and by the unshy awareness and progressive consciousness with which young poets defied gloomy and "mature" predictions of the coming "end of ideology"—the title of sociologist Daniel Bell's book arguing that "among the intellectuals, the old passions are spent" (also published in 1960). Bell's titular phrase had already moved quickly into common use by those affirming political centrism and rejecting as immature all forms of "apocalyptic and chiliastic visions." At the dead end of ideology, no longer does social reform have "any unifying appeal"; nor does it "give a younger generation the outlet for 'self-expression' and 'self-definition' that it wants" (Bell, 404–405).[3]

From roughly 1945 (some would argue 1939) to the end of the 1950s, modernism's association with cultural and political heresy and heterodoxy in the 1930s had been condemned, sometimes with an hysteria borrowed from (or the same as) McCarthyism, and a fantasized cleaner, purer, prepolitical modernism was sought (in, for instance, 1920s writing) to redress the alleged imbalance.[4] In 1960 we see a surprisingly sudden turn against the logic of that cold war–era separation, against the designation of advocates of "the old passions" as "terrible simplifiers," in Bell's terms (Bell, 404, 405), and concurrently an explosion of poetic activity— and, rather than a culture war between modernists and emergent postmodernists ("New American" poets, beats, Black Mountain affiliates, New York School writers, latter-day Dadaists and surrealists, post-Duchampian conceptual poets, and others), we discover a disorganized but nonetheless effective collaboration of historically distinct avant-gardes now prepared finally to restate cultural and political terms that after fifteen years of "consolidation" had become idiomatic, naturalized—in the air poets were supposed to breathe.

Paul Blackburn, for instance, in his 1960 book of poems, *Brooklyn-Manhattan Transit*, made overt the heresies his NYU teacher and poetic mentor M. L. Rosenthal had long repressed and mostly feared during the cold war. Blackburn was a Rosenthal born too late to be bamboozled or guilt-tripped by either academic or poetic anticommunism. John Wieners, fresh from *The Hotel Wentley Poems* written in the blue heat of depression in 1958, began to compose poems later collected in *Ace of Pentacles* (1964). The new poems, *as writing*, seek to "get away from this place and see / that there is no fear without me," where by "without" Wieners means what is external to him in the American social and political landscape. What would remain, after such exile ("in this country it is terror"), is the psychological "total wreck" of the *Poète maudit* brilliantly courting "disaster and doom" while talented enough to leave ambiguous the true source, political or psychic, of the "great fear"—a phrase, in any case, commonly referring to Red Scare culture (Wieners, 62–63).[5] Donald Allen's anthology, *The New American Poetry*, sought to respond primarily to the *poetic* conservatism of its Robert Frost–prefaced predecessor, *New Poets of England and America* (1957), but along with the formal experimentation of the "New American" poets featured in this red-white-and-blue counteranthology came Michael McClure's "The Flowers of Politics," with its call to "Break in the forms and take real postures!"—and Ray Bremser's "Poem of Holy Madness," with its prankish poet-heretic's debasements before un-American activities committees: "I am a traitor traitor traitor / traitor / traitor! / you will investigate me finally, / along with my mother" (Allen, 349, 354). Frank O'Hara in 1960 finally published his long poem, *Second Avenue*, a "sprawling exploration[...] of spontaneity" (Ferguson, par. 23), his attempt to do without apologies precisely what Vladimir Mayakovsky had done: to make a work, as he put it, "as big as cities where the life in the work is autonomous (not about actual city life) yet similar." This was O'Hara's politically incorrect way of making an homage of William Carlos Williams's social-observation modernism (in the latter's modernist epic *Paterson*) by way of puckishly commending Soviet-style largeness. Gregory Corso neither commends nor really refers at all to Soviet designs in *The Happy Birthday of Death*; yet such an omission is nearly all one can think of when reading that book of 1960, its lens open more widely than on mere political views. Corso's book is about the whole "charnel planet," taking no sides yet eschewing any anti-anticommunist bilateralism—rather, presenting itself as a kind of terrestrial writing. The phrase "charnel planet" comes from the concrete (bomb-shaped) poem "Bomb" (City Lights, 1958; reprinted here), exploding outward here on three horizontally tipped-in pages from the New Directions edition of Corso's *Happy Birthday*. A single cute birthday candle *and* a black-and-white image of an atomic mushroom cloud juxtapose on the volume's jacket (Corso, 32–33). Barbara Guest, in her stunning first book of 1960, *The Location of Things*, attempts to see

"Russians at the Beach"—*the Russians have landed! the Russians are coming!*—by totally clearing her language of any (political, visual, aural) preconceptions (Guest, 8), just when the aforementioned Marianne Moore (a counterintuitive yet real influence on Guest) was said in a big *Vogue* spread (published on August 1, 1960) to be one elder poet whose act of "really looking at what you see" as much constitutes "adventure" as it does "enjoyment" (Moore, "Plums," 82–83, 140). And Muriel Rukeyser, a frankly leftist poet—infamous for her alleged membership in the Communist Party of the United States in the late 1930s and 1940s[6]—reviewed Moore's new book *O to Be a Dragon* for *Saturday Review* and contended that we ought to reconsider the value and methodological purpose of Moore's much-mocked annotations: they are not in the Eliotic *Waste Land* mode, footnotes shoring up *the idea of the real* and supporting far-flung poetic uses of myth, but, on the contrary, an expression of a program for achieving accuracy and *currency* of political and civic rhetoric in the verse itself as distinct from (so the New Critics' complaint against political poetry ran) imposed irrelevantly from the outside (Rukeyser, 17–18). Charles Reznikoff's *Inscriptions*, written in the immediate post-Holocaust decade but momentously seen through press (by the poet himself) only now, in 1960, ponders the problem of setting into words a poetry-negating "Disaster" before it was given its permanent name, a problem of representation that is the precise analogue for the dilemma of comprehending where one fits poetically (generationally, ideologically, aesthetically, theologically). Was Reznikoff an "Objectivist"? Antifascist? Modernist? A documentary poet? A Jewish American poet? Reznikoff's volume indicates that he did not want these questions resolved. In her first book, *To Bedlam and Part Way Back* (1960), Anne Sexton has a similar problem of poetic generational identity, anxious (in her desperate poem "The Expatriates" and elsewhere) to know if this time of intense domesticity is an allegory for the pattern of experimental liberation and then retrenchment in a poetic lifestyle that had commenced four decades earlier? Or is the current landscape—for instance, an inexpertly planted "false" forest of quietude—merely a literal suburban locale for those trapped in a state-supported rapid retreat from heresy and difference?

Suburbanized and longing for a freer era in which to lead the poetic life, the Sexton of *Bedlam* in 1960 expresses jealousy in terms and forms that begin in the well-ordered stanzas of a midcentury formalist but typically end with an image derived from the works of Edvard Munch, H.D., Pablo Picasso, Edith Sitwell, Gertrude Stein, the laconic Imagist Ernest Hemingway of *In Our Time*, or the insane Dadaist Elsa von Freytag Loringhoven. "My dear, it was a moment," says Sexton's expatriate looking back, "to clutch at for a moment." The speaker shifts immediately after this opening testimony, and now it's the Sextonian Bedlamite, coming home but only, it seems, "part way back": now she notices that the forest at home is "false," landscaped with "misplanted Norwegian trees" that "refused to root." Now we are treated to a flawed post-urban postmodern allegory for the modernist era as it gives way to the quietistic 1950s: "For forty years this experimental / woodland grew," and so on. In the end, the speaker realizes ever more that "Today" she is "in my house" and "see[s] / our house," including its "dim basement" and so forth, and the poem ends with a return to a sudden and yet expected expatriate voice, the modernist frame, bearing witness to "a time / butchered from time" that must be told of "quickly / before we lose the sound of our own mouths" (Kumin, 21–22).

The method of Charles Olson, whose blockbuster book, *The Maximus Poems*, long in coming, was also published in 1960, could not be further from Sexton's. But here too is a confusion (superconscious in Olson's case) of, on one hand, literal local history (of Gloucester, Massachusetts) and, on the other hand, language as mythologization, always implicitly a commentary on the mode of Poundian cyclonic history in *The Cantos* and Williams's collagist American docu-archeology in *Paterson*. And Sexton's horror at developers misplanting in American postwar sprawl the false Norwegian wood that won't sink roots is remarkably shared by Olson's Maximus, with his obsession over sustaining small-town life, preserving historical structures, fishing by hand, and, generally, over the fate of the Poundian epic modernist, in which "we who throw down hierarchy" inevitably must reject contemporary American culture and its imperial narrative style of historiography and yet must accept that "the history of weeds / is a history of man." The sense of Olson's, Sexton's—as well as Marianne Moore's—work of this time is, as Maximus visiting Boston writes: "[A]ll / is how the splendor is worn" (Olson, 93). With his own keen sense of worn splendor, of cultural (and his own) massive botching, this is Ezra Pound's sense, too, just then. Pound himself was making a crucial comeback: *Thrones* (Cantos 95–109) had been published in November 1959, and a myriad of reviews printed throughout 1960 finally began to get beyond critical prejudices one way or another left over from the 1949 controversy over the poet's hateful political views—indeed beyond the alleged intrinsic relation between fascism and modernism's collage mode. In 1960 the young and already well-established poet Donald Hall, with his own ambivalent relationship to modernism (he was one of the editors of the anthology Donald Allen's set itself against), traveled to Italy to interview Pound, after which Pound mailed drafts of the final cantos, numbered 110 through 116, to Hall in March. Hall showed the new cantos to Tom Clark, then an undergrad student-poet taught and mentored by Hall at Michigan, whose honors thesis on "the formal structure" of the *Cantos* was influenced by the presence of this new writing. The quasi-*samizdat* influence of the very last cantos—these gnomic, coded, minimalist messages from epic modernist in a precarious psycholegal exile shaped by cold war politics—cascaded forward, hand to hand and copy by copy, among those young New Americans who now sought ties to the old way of "throw[ing] down hierarchy"—not just through Olson, in other words, but directly from Ezra Pound himself. Any understanding of the new political significance of modernism and antimodernism at the start of the 1960s will entail a look at these last cantos, botched apologies, even though they were not widely available until Fuck You Press published them together in 1968.

Edward Dorn, a friend of Tom Clark and a student of Olson who heard ceaselessly about Pound from his mentor, famous later for *Gunslinger*, wrote in his own 1960 book of poems, *The Newly Fallen*, an affecting anarchistic view of atomic annihilation, verses that lurch from political aphorism to personal—almost confessional—memory. "No leader can be exempt from drunk blood, / remember we passed Trinity site." "Can Jack [Kennedy, then running for President] / hold up his grimy hands and shade us / from that vileness falling in particles?..../ Still they whisper in the wind / we need you" (Dorn, 17). In the vivid political poem "Sousa," Dorn directly addresses John Philip Sousa, the begetter of patriotism's regular rhythm in a line that will not easily scan: "you drumhead, there is no silence / you can't decapitate" (12). Shouted-sung words, voiced by summering picknickers, "laughing / to the air, Sousa be here," give way to atomic-age soundless mouths, akin to that of Sexton's unhinged postexpatriate: "when mouths are opened," writes Dorn in "Sousa," "waves of poison rain will fall" (14). Out of the orifice filled with fallout comes an allegiant vocabulary entirely deranged by the circumstance of "Los Alamos, 1960, not Salinas / nor Stockton." There's the familiar patriotic Sousa sound, yet this time "no drums, [no] loudness,.../ no warning," and: "you won't recognize anyone" (13).

The urgent impulsion toward fresh seeing through decontextualized, rehistoricized, and unrecognizable terms—befitting Dorn's atomized *Newly Fallen*, Sexton's *unheimlich* home, Corso's terrestrialism rather than unilateralism or bilateralism, Olson's worn splendor, Wieners's courted anti-anticommunist insanity, Burroughs's cut-up newspapers mangling cold war news—was shared by Gary Snyder in *Myths & Texts*, another groundbreaking volume of 1960 which Kunitz's antimodernism rendered him incapable of anticipating. Snyder's poetic values are deliberately archaic, so radically retrospective as to be *un*traditional—so old as to be new. In "go[ing] back to the upper Paleolithic" (Snyder, viii), Snyder locates in his writing an unlikely merging of primeval and modernist, and his poems are as much a *Genesis* as that of Williams's *Spring & All* or *Tender Buttons*, with Gertrude Stein speaking apparent babble or babytalk. Jerome Rothenberg has made a lifework, and a whole politico-aesthetic conception of history, out of this particular convergence—primitive ecomaterials (a mode of the sixties) and Steinian Dada (a mode of the teens and twenties); 1960 marked the commencement of his project. Rothenberg's first book, *White Sun Black Sun*, was also published that year. This poet emerged from the 1950s having been instructed in graduate school that Walt Whitman's verse and Whitmanism generally were politically irrelevant or, for that matter, perhaps even professionally detrimental in a time of anticommunism (Filreis, 99). He resisted, and embraced and combined Whitman and Dada, ethnic localism and aesthetic internationalism, and communal anthologizing (starting with *New Young German Poets* in 1960) as a powerful and—for young people especially—persuasive new variety of anti-anticommunism. Rothenberg would later become a convener of an extensive intergenerational *pro*-modernist communitarianism of leftist poets who openly rejected Harold Bloom's idea of the poetic company as fraught with vengeant anxiety and Freudian competitiveness. For Rothenberg, 1960 brought the first exhilarating break from that thinking, a move into a post-McCarthyite, anti-nonideological modernism. This version of the avant-garde was for many the sourcework of political consciousness.

Insofar as interpretations of Burroughs typically repress such connections, it is because his most experimental writings—the cut-up collages first published in *Minutes to Go*—are not read in the context of 1959–1960, the moment of his and Brion Gysin's "discovery" of the method. My sense of Burroughs's and Gysin's ecstatic promulgation of the cut-up technique is that its political significance *follows* from Snyder and Rothenberg rather than represents a breaking back, a purer or more direct connection to word-as-such avant-gardism or, in short, a separate new postmodern lineage in the making. Only later versions of conceptual poetics would, perhaps necessarily, make such a distinction.[7] *Minutes to Go* achieves a refusal of the supposed end of ideology in a mode remarkably similar to the 1960 writings of Dorn, Reznikoff, the Corso of "Bomb," Wieners, O'Hara, Snyder, and Rothenberg. To look at 1960 as a turning point in this manner, we must be able to learn how to read unusual—presumably unreadable—"political" writing, words taken and accidentally rearranged from newspapers, for example, these

> USAIRBASENCIENT CITYOG MEK HOBBLESONOIL MOROSIBLE PEN-
> INDEFTINGLEWAND DILUTES FAMILIES WIT MOROMIGALSUDDS CHEAP
> SURPLUSAIR WORKS DEATHRALYSIS
>
> (Burroughs et al., 38)

—as *befitting* rather than *contradicting* Marianne Moore's sense of "a word-waterfall of the banal" and her compositional process entailing words "cut short from" sourcetexts (Rukeyser, 17); as aligned with, rather than irrelevant to, H.D.'s memoiristic novel of modernist self-realization and the growth of the languaged self, finally published in 1960 (*Bid Me to Live*); as supporting rather than rebuking the passionate round-the-campfire Make It New-ism of Snyder ("new born / Jay chatters the first time / Rolling a smoke by the campfire / New! never before") (Snyder, 33); as belonging to the realm of politically irrational venturesomeness in Robert Duncan's ground-clearing neo-Romantic "return to a meadow" (Duncan, 7) in *The Opening of the Field*. All of these, taken together, form a line of continuity arising from the modernist "word-waterfall" project, permanently put the poetics of "DEATHRAL-YSIS" behind, and opened the field.

Before we turn to close examinations of a few poems from our unlikely 1960 pairing, Burroughs and Moore, let us take another look at the particular variety of liberal antimodernism—set to oppose the convergence described just above—which was also then gaining currency. We found Stanley Kunitz's expression of it to be somewhat incidental and half-hearted; anyway, he was not essentially a critic, not one for making grand cultural gestures derived from the poetry he disliked of his time. Karl Shapiro, on the other hand, loved a literary-political fight and relished an agitated antimodernist claim. His intervention, like that of Kunitz, came just a few weeks before the start of the new year. All modes of art in the twentieth century are flourishing, announced the influential former editor of *Poetry* magazine in the *New York Times Book Review* on December 13, 1959. *Except poetry.* Poetry, Shapiro contends, is "diseased" and modernism is to blame. Modernism: a "minor intellectual program which took the stage more than a full generation ago...with standards [that] are enforced rigorously by literary constables ready to haul away any dissenters." Alas, Shapiro laments, our poetry today is "the only poetry in history that has had to be taught in its own time." Contemporary poetry is a bad verse-criticism compound. He calls it "criticism-poetry." The essays of T. E. Hulme—the philosophical sourceworker for Anglo-American Imagism, the first powerful modernist movement in which U.S. poets actively participated—were gathered posthumously in *Speculations*, but to Shapiro this work, sitting on every modernist's shelf, is "the 'Mein Kampf' of modern criticism." With that loaded designation, we can only assume that his own position, supporting "the revolt against modernism [which] seems to be gaining ground at long last," is analogous to or indeed a form of antifascism. This stipulation is quite an ideological trick on Shapiro's part. Those seeking to restore poetry to its traditional mode—these anti–*Mein Kampfers*—are, thankfully, "beginning to use subjective judgment in place of the critical dictum." Such "new anti-modernist poetry is brutal, illiterate and hysterical," but it is helpful, for that is "the price we have to pay for the generation-old suppression of poetry by criticism" (Shapiro, 1, 22).

Shapiro's attack was wild and no doubt for many readers exciting, seeming to augur a cultural great awakening in 1960, a counter-revolution. But if one presses just a little at its wanton generalizations, it falls apart in confusion. The chief problem is that it is never clear whom Shapiro means to attack. He excoriates the modernist poetics enabled by the likes of Hulme—think Pound, H.D., at least the early Williams, early Eliot. And perhaps figures like Wallace Stevens who were atheists and made modern art a proxy for God (the supreme fiction). But Shapiro is also here assailing the New Critics, and it's them he means when he excoriates poetry-criticism—Allen Tate, John Crowe Ransom, certainly, and Eliot and perhaps proponents of practical criticism, I. A. Richards and his ilk. So, conversely, what new poetry does Shapiro seek? "Brutal, illiterate and hysterical," nonacademic, anti-intellectual: here he doubtless refers to the Beats, the new Whitmanians, yet assumes wrongly that they will stand in properly as antimodernists in the culture war he hopes to wage. Near the end of the essay Shapiro refers to these rough figures as emerging from the restored lineage of Whitman and Williams. Yet Williams is of course very much in the modernist line Shapiro spends most of the essay damning. And the fact that the Beats had already openly embraced Williams might have signaled that there was a close connection between them and modernism (in Burroughs and Ginsberg). In a few months, of course, Donald Allen's landmark anthology of 1960 (*The New American Poetry*) would indicate that a continuously thriving avant-garde was sharing both the anti-academicism and antiformalism Shapiro feels is necessary now and also the direct links to modernist elders Shapiro believes are anathema to any new development in poetry—Pound, Williams again, Marcel Duchamp, Wallace Stevens to some degree, Gertrude Stein whom John Ashbery among others admired, and H.D. as revered by Duncan (Shapiro, 1).

In letters to the *Book Review* editors, published in the January 10, 1960, issue (and later), reaction against Shapiro's negative gesture of historical naming ranged from corrections of fact (modernists didn't abhor Blake) to ridicule of his use of New Critics as straw men.[8] Chester Page, a friend and advocate of the modernist novelist Djuna Barnes, wrote from Brooklyn to say that Shapiro might want to know that Marianne Moore seems to be doing just fine and that American poetry is in good shape. The poet Theodore Enslin noted an obvious problem with Shapiro's complaint against academic critics—namely that Shapiro himself had become one. Charles Martell wrote from North Carolina to remind Shapiro's readers that "this sophomoric diatribe" should remind everyone of the half-logical scattershot attacks against all of modernism (he meant those which had been launched by Robert Hillyer) at the time of the Bollingen Prize controversy about Ezra Pound in 1949, ten years earlier (Scholes, 30, 32). Historical assessments of the place of screeds of Shapiro's sort—antimanifestos—permit them to count as context. In this case, it is convenient to assume that here in 1960 was the final undoing of F. T. Marinetti's futurist manifesto (1909) or of Pound's Imagist dicta (1913), a sober rebuke, in the style of Daniel Bell's mature end-of-ideological considerations, of the propagandistic (read: ideologically naïve and pure) confidence in the future that enabled Pound's "sense of sudden liberation... sense of freedom from time limits and space limits" (200–201), a human victory he felt could and should be derived from modernism. Roughly dating the start of that false "sense of sudden liberation" at 1910, we get a neat epitaph for half-century experimentation: *AMERICAN POETIC MODERNISM, RIP: 1910–1960*. Yet this context is as shallow as the neat dating. Not unlike Robert Hillyer flailing conservatively at "fascist" Poundian modernism in 1949–1950, Shapiro gets to stand for the day in 1959–1960. But as always, of course, the sociology of aesthetic value runs more deeply and in crossing currents.

There were, of course, a few serious young antimodernist poets who had a sense of the complex continuity coming out of modernism, and in fearing it produced writing more knowing than Shapiro's. X. J. Kennedy was one such poet. In 1960 Kennedy published an antimodernist satire entitled "Nude Descending a Staircase." This poem concedes the influence and importance of Marcel Duchamp's 1912 painting of the same name, a work that by midcentury had become iconic of the cubist and futurist side of the revolution in art. The Duchamp painting, shown at the 1913 Armory Show, depicts the motion of a nude woman by presenting her as successive superimposed images, something like stroboscopic motion photography. In 1913 the object of this cubistic multiperspectivalism had been sensational and scandalous. Here in 1960 is Kennedy, looking back at Duchamp's way of looking, with a critical eye such that the poem offers its own end-of-ideological history of modernism:

> Toe upon toe, a snowing flesh,
> A gold of lemon, root and rind,
> She sifts in sunlight down the stairs
> With nothing on. Nor on her mind.
>
> We spy beneath the banister
>
> A constant thresh of thigh on thigh—
> Her lips imprint the swinging air
> That parts to her parts go by.

> One-woman waterfall, she wears
> Her slow descent like a long cape
> And pausing, on the final stair
> Collects her motions into shape.
>
> (Kennedy, 224)

How can we be certain that X. J. Kennedy's poem of 1960 satirically criticizes the Duchamp? First, we should ask: Would an unironic homage to this cubist hyperkineticism be presented in perfectly rhymed ABCB tetrameter quatrains? (Tetrameter with internal rhyme too: "Toe upon toe, a snowing flesh, / A gold of lemon, root and rind.") Duchamp's was a form-busting breakthrough, characterized by energetic simulateneity, uncalmed and uncollected. Kennedy counters with lines of stasis about the woman's movement: "One-woman waterfall, she wears / Her slow descent like a long cape / And pausing, on the final stair / Collects her motions into shape." The poem has found her at a certain single moment of descent, seen from a single perspective. She "collects" motions into shape; she catches and is caught. There is a condescending pun here: for Kennedy the nude Duchampian woman has "nothing on"—which is to say, she is naked, yes, but also vapid, empty-headed, with *nothing on her mind*. She is the precise opposite of the author of her movement, and as such eschews affiliation with her creator, he who is the instigator of an art movement: the dumb lovely object of the modernist subject. And of course she is ever more an object. The poet of 1960 looks up at her, standing beneath the bannister, watching from below as her unclothed thighs thresh. What is excoriated here is the most allegedly dangerous feature of the modern when it is applied to the cold postwar peace: a multiplicity of places from which to observe, an anything-goes aestheticism that tends to undermine the hard-earned position, tolerating and indeed enabling all views and positions all at once—famously, the cultural as well as aesthetic revolution augured by Duchamp in this work. That multiplicity and intersubjectivity has been rendered by Kennedy as a single point of view, and satirically gendered (a male "we" are gaping up at the body, nude upskirt). If Kennedy meant to praise kinetic modernism, then he creates a major formal irony in the effort, and undoes the aesthetic of the "one-woman waterfall" he sets in inexorably rhymed lines.

Duchamp's conceptualism was hardly itself static or descending in 1960. On the contrary, it was remarkably on the rise, and his presence in New York that year, in particular his active support of surrealism,[9] made it possible for many young poetic avant-gardists to see in his work—and in his person, a living link to prewar modernism—a set of radical possibilities entirely separable from then-typical discussions of art during the cold war. It has been argued that Duchamp's "elaborately staged 'comeback'" in 1959–1961 produced a broad challenge to the cold war ideology of complete conflict and irreconcilable division realized through ever-on-the-brink gamesmanship, and that Duchamp's and others' support of surrealism, neo-Dadaism, and conceptualism (in the Fluxus movement) induced a "game-focused art" very unlike cold war brinkmanship: laconic, variable, uncompetitive, uninvested in ownership and other anxieties of influence (Mesch, 1, 38). (For many avant-gardists around 1960 who sought means of getting past abstract expressionism and its both rumored and explicit connections to the cold war temperament, Duchampian indifference was itself a liberating value.) In "Cold War Games and Postwar Art," Claudia Mesch makes this argument about Duchamp's playing of chess,[10] but it seems that Duchamp's hilarious, attention-getting rejection of painting—"I don't believe in the magic of the hand"; "Painting always bored me"[11]—achieved the same resistance, because it helped bring into being, in 1960, the idea that other art modes were more exciting because they had not yet tried what painting had tried by 1910. Painting was a half-century ahead of poetry and that was precisely a reason for turning to language. Kenneth Goldsmith, a contemporary conceptualist trained as a sculptor, prefers working in the field of poetics because Duchampian art is still left to be done there, and Goldsmith regularly quotes Brion Gysin's claim that indeed poetry is fifty years behind painting.[12]

Cutting canvas for a painting project, Gysin happened to read the sliced under-layers of newspapers (protecting the table) and came upon "the cut-up method" (Miles, 111–128). From that moment—summertime 1959—to the publication in 1960 of *Minutes to Go* and *Exterminator*, William S. Burroughs repeatedly asserted three newly merged interests: (1) writing as a means by which artists could comprehend and un-inscribe theories of randomness in current geopolitical strategy; (2) final proof of the radical democracy of poetry—"Say it again: 'Poetry is for everyone'" (Burroughs, 31); (3) a return to the earliest and most radical modernists' longing for a "systematic derangement of the senses" (Rimbaud in Burroughs, 32). Indeed, modernism was very much on Burroughs's mind. In connection with the cut-ups, he mentioned Tristan Tzara, John Dos Passos ("The Camera Eye" sequences in *USA*), Arthur Rimbaud, and T. S. Eliot. "When you think of it," Burroughs later observed, "'The Waste Land' was the first great cut-up collage" (Burroughs in Morgan, 112). Here finally was a way in which modernist ideas "can be applied to other fields than writing" (Burroughs, 32). In John von Neumann's theories of games and economic behavior, one found the cut-up method of "random action" introduced into military gaming ("assume that the worst has happened and act accordingly") (Burroughs, 31). When the relevant sentences in his essay "The Cut-Up Method of Brion Gysin" are themselves cut up (in the final section of the essay itself), the result actually makes the analytical synthesis under which Burroughs was operating in 1960 arguably more rather than less cogent:

> ALL WRITING IS IN FACT CUT-UPS OF GAMES AND ECONOMIC BEHAVIOR OVERHEARD? WHAT ELSE? ASSUME THAT THE WORST HAS HAPPENED EXPLICIT AND SUBJECT TO STRATEGY IS AT SOME POINT CLASSICAL PROSE. CUTTING AND REARRANGING FACTOR YOUR OPPONENT WILL GAIN INTRODUCES A NEW DIMENSION YOUR STRATEGY (33).

Which of the following is likely to offer a more cogent presentation? A poem constructed of a transcription of a speech by President Dwight D. Eisenhower and a poem by Gregory Corso—the two texts having been placed side by side, then vertically cut with razors or scissors, then rearranged as joined textual strips? Or the same two whole texts, read separately in sequence? The poets of *Minutes to Go* contended that the quasi-nonintentional merging of these two American voices simultaneously mocks and celebrates the state of the American language (befitting the Beat project), thus causing meaningful confusion about the agency in radical political critique and official democratic blather.

> With final agreement to this
> and all that has been said
> hithertofor and it is my
> contention that no territorial
> gains be garland with rosed feet—
>   (Burroughs et al., 33)

One can probably tell which phrasing is that of Corso and which of Ike, but one cannot be absolutely certain where the seams lie. Doubt is just sufficient to create wonder, in the reader of *Minutes to Go*, whether it is the deadbeat Beat or the martial-hero president who utters a "promise to carry on," speaks of "common cause" (33)—or even (remember, this is the caution-giving, lame-duck end of Eisenhower's eight years in office) whether concerns over that which "stains civilian / & military leadership" (33) are oppositionally presidential or poetic. Indeed, from "CUT UP of Eisenhower Speech & Mine Own Poem" it would seem that "CUTTING AND REARRANGING FACTOR YOUR OPPONENT WILL GAIN INTRODUCES A NEW DIMENSION YOUR STRATEGY" (Burroughs et al., 33)—namely, that despite the square, officially optimistic subheadline given the newspaper printing of Ike's speech ("no peril to U.S. held likely," as quoted in the poem), the radical "opponent," having now fully joined the discussion, has rendered it poetically idiomatic and has disclosed its own tendency to affirm critique (Burroughs et al., 33).

Writing is in fact cut-ups of games and economic behavior overheard. The recognition of this truth in 1960 meant the difference between a "beat movement" to be known through the likes of Neal Cassady, John Clellon Holmes, and Lawrence Ferlinghetti and one that would extend, under the capacious banner "New American Poetry," to affiliate the experimentalism of Philip Whalen, Lew Welch, Anne Waldman, Bob Kaufman, Tuli Kupferberg, Ray Bremser, and Ed Dorn. The quasi-nonintentional yet fervent political poems of *Minutes to Go* more responsively and interestingly render the "rounendless talk" of the world and ambient incessant language-making and -uttering—which is Burroughs's cut-up equivalent of Marianne Moore's "word-waterfall of the banal"—than did the earlier, more coherently and singularly subjective Beat narratives such as *On the Road* or *Howl*.

And because it in effect *overhears* the American cultural response to the supposed end of ideology, the Burroughs/Gysin piece titled "Open Letter to Life Magazine" responds more effectively to the sensational, erroneous, dismissive, and culturally conservative *Life* article about the "Beat Generation" published on November 30, 1959,[13] than does the conventional Beat rejoinder to the predictable hegemonic absorption of the challenge represented by this frankly obscene, linguistically awry,

antiquietist opposition. In works such as "Open Letter to Life Magazine" that oppo-
sitional mode is very much at hand, undiminished but with a crucial difference: the
words and phrases themselves originate from the source, turned (literally) now into
the Kerouacian, Ginsbergian rapturous manner. The presence of this style tends to
prove at least to sympathetic readers that the language of alterity is already in the
American ambience. Here is a passage from the first third of the piece, constructed
entirely of text strips from *Life*'s long, condescending article:

> Pitiful personal lives of suspension, flapping frantic, come to stare. An opium eater
> and Vincent-visitors bathe their feet in San Francisco market-deal of the world's
> art-compacted-feathers. Sunbrow those third street bums on se. Some kind of fur
> coat glissel-ways when they see a young Negro-ruby dance rounendless talk on
> the truck preoccupation. Man's hideous professional crouch, the beat movement,
> embackwards on an old man's members of the north bea
>
> (Burroughs et al., 11)

So who now does the staring? Not tourists visiting North Beach (said to gawk at
the local bearded fauna) but the poets themselves; in the remix, they are the ones
who "come to stare." And whose life is thus suspended? Not much of a typograph-
ical accident is required to shift the gaze back on the gazers, those curious about
the countercultural Other, he or she who opts out of Americans' hideous profes-
sional crouch. Risen from that, "embackwards," the touring subject merges with
street bums, opium eaters and "Negro-ruby dance rounendless talk on the truck
preoccupation." It seems that the latter, in the sourcetext, is a reference to juvenile
delinquents forcing their jalopies cross-country, to the inevitable seeking out, in
each city, of the underclass neighborhood. The line—"Negro-ruby dance rounend-
less talk on the truck preoccupation"—with its internal rhymes, consonance, and
syncopations, seems right out of *Howl*, composed painstakingly by the best heret-
ical minds of the generation, and yet here it is—the work of *Life*'s writers. They
are the very ones Ginsberg tended to mock—for instance, in the set-piece antic
poem "America," where the speaker despises and yet is addicted to their happy/
paranoid consumerist/cold war blather. They make every bit as much of a "personal
appearance" (Burroughs's phrase) in a cut-up as Arthur Rimbaud does, if one cuts
Rimbaud. In *Minutes to Go* the us/them binarism is rendered senseless (an end of
ideology) even as the original sourcetext is revealed through juxtaposition to be a
closed set of ideas needing—nay, requiring—liberation through disorientation (an
end of the end of ideology). If you just look at the language a certain way, you can
"sample a drug," says square *Life* in hip *Minutes to Go*. The drug is "called heavy
commitments."

Heavy commitments. For *Life*, a plain irony; but for the author of "The Cut-Up
Method of Brion Gysin," deadly serious, for democracy's promise can here be ful-
filled: "Cut-ups are for everyone." It is meant to be as radical as anything written by
Lenin, a manifesto on the order of *What Is to Be Done*, the ultimate guide to "some-
thing to do." "Anyone can make cut ups. It is experimental in the sense of being
something to do. Right here write now. Not something to talk and argue about."

If in Paul O'Neil's long-form creative nonfiction piece for *Life*, "THE SHABBY BEATS BUNGLE THE JOB IN ARGUING, SULKING AND BAD POETRY,"[14] in *Minutes to Go*, by writing through that very same language—by doing a hatchet job on a hatchet job—Burroughs and his colleagues present us with writing that moves beyond "ARGUING" yet doesn't shy from being itself an argumentation. It is writing as indeed "not something to talk and argue about," not secondary (writing's conventional referential unreal status) but primary (the done thing itself) (Burroughs, 31).

Such a conception of writing offers ecstatic resolution to the "poetry makes nothing happen" dead end of modernism (Auden, 197), an end of the alleged end of ideology: the authorial subject is decentered as, oddly, the Emersonian idea of American self-discipline is restored; high and low (poetic and nonpoetic) voices "overheard" are given permission, such that the site of writing becomes, in a sense, a crowded linguistic public garden; and expectations of a diminution of quality ("SULKING AND BAD POETRY") are ipso facto refused. If you cut up Rimbaud, Burroughs observes, "you are assured of good poetry." "There is no reason to accept a second-rate product when you can have the best. And the best is there for all" (Burroughs, 32). Poetic writing no longer constitutes a world separate from the world.

The facile critical line on Marianne Moore at the time of *Minutes to Go* was that her poems constitute a world made anew in the poem. The standard against which new work of the aging poet would be measured was modernist: each new poem is a new world naked. Almost inevitably, new Moore poems were greeted by laments such as "Major Poet, Minor Verse"—a phrase that served as the title of the review of *O to Be a Dragon* printed in *Time* magazine. "Her new book…is a simple, narrow, carefree path that proves in a whimsical way that Poet Moore walks through a verseland entirely of her own making" ("Major Poet," 110). This is willfully to misread the poems, which are full of cuttings from the day's newspapers, constructed, more than ever, of overheard and read phrases. Far from writing poems in order to "defend[…] the English language from the barbarians among us"—the centrist assessment of Delmore Schwartz in *The New Republic* (Schwartz, 10)—Moore's writing of this time had opened the gates. Schwartz's review was published on January 4, 1960, and there is little doubt that his "barbarians," threatening linguistic felicity, penetrating and compromising the poetic separate sphere, were the Beats; they had been dubbed such dozens of times in the late 1950s, and Lawrence Lipton's book-length celebration, *The Holy Barbarians*, had been published, with fanfare, in 1959. The "felicitous precision of Moore's use of English," in *O to Be a Dragon*, derives in fact from an exacting cut, or take, on contemporary public rhetoric, and served well as an opposition to Beat "conformity of nonconformity" at the level of the line (Bradbury, 41). Schwartz meant to praise Moore to the skies, calling her "the most original poet alive," but *unoriginal* might have been an more apt term of praise (Schwartz, 10).

A poem called "Enough" makes couplets of *New York Times* coverage of the 350th anniversary of the landing at Jamestown (Moore, *O to Be*, 16–17). "Leonardo da Vinci's," a poem about an unfinished painting of the master depicting St. Jerome and his lion, in order to be a poem against the "officializ[ation]" of "lionship" and in praise of "household / lions," draws from, as its first and main source, a *Time* magazine article that Moore clipped in May 1959. The poem is about art made of everyday language, the aesthetic but also the ethical primacy of "the Vulgate"; *Time* is where we find Leonardo now. "Hometown Piece for Mssrs. Alston and Reese" seems, from its rhymed title on, to poeticize the unpoetical, and thus to create high/ low incongruities, but when one lays the poem beside clippings from *New York Times* sports-page coverage of the Brooklyn Dodgers, one realizes the extent to which this and other poems are rewrites of—in contemporary conceptualist terms, *writings through*—already published journalism, with its myriad normative phrasings, inconsequential, and fascinating out of context, such as "get a Night," "stylist stout," and in general sports-journalism diction assimilated beyond need of quotation marks, beyond scare-quote ironies: "irked by one misplay," "a specialist versed in an extension reach," "Podres on the mound" (14–15). Another poem, "Glory," is about the artists' public campaign opposing the planned demolition of Carnegie Hall in 1960; it is also about how artists move into the public discourse. They change it less than it changes them, for (in Moore's view) the better, and this poem is an instance of what's better as the result. Thus, "Glory" is as strong a statement of poetics as one finds anywhere in 1960. (The poem was written after *O to Be a Dragon* and published in *The New Yorker* on August 13, 1960.) Similarly, "In the Public Garden" seems to have as its "central concern... the plight of refugees," as one critic put it—the first person to publish a commentary on the poem, in 1964 (Weatherhead, 488). But that critic, A. K. Weatherhead, has assumed a liberal piety about political poetry here, and it leads him to assume that in the final lines of the poem Moore seriously asserts that she "need not fail / to wish poetry well" and feels finally "happy that Art" (Moore, *O to Be,* 21) expresses its politics personally—or, in short, that she believes poetry as it has been conceived can do something about refugee crises. That this is a wrong-headed reading of the end of the poem—indeed, thus, of the whole sense of the poem, and its mode of cut-up public discourse—is owing, I would argue, to the unexamined truism that Moore resisted or ignored the New American Poetic modes; that her modernism was preserved intact from the earlier period; that her gatherings of newspaper and pop-magazine clippings were merely inspirational triggers for generating instances of the same insular poetic that remained successfully oblivious of poets' post-1950s radical democratic urges as expressed by Burroughs when he argued, about cut-ups, that this kind of unoriginal or uncreative writing is ethically and politically "something to do."

"In the Public Garden" is a major expression of doubt about the kind of poetry one used to "wish...well" because such poetry is a site "where intellect is habitual," but we will return to that (Moore, *O to Be,* 21). "Glory" enacts the same new move, and its ending is similarly easy to misread outside the 1960 context. "Glory" praises Isaac Stern, the most energetic, leaderly, and politically astute of the artists defending Carnegie Hall against the wrecking ball and opposing the brutal, eminent-domain-wielding urban centralization of the massive Lincoln Center project.[15] (His political astuteness was perhaps especially impressive to Moore, who was always herself anxious about the eminent artist's public role.) That Stern, in the course of this public campaign, "has grown forensic," is, to Moore, a worthy thing. "Forensic" is in fact an appropriate word for describing the poem, which drills vertically deep into the history not just of momentous performances at Carnegie Hall but of the long chronicle of artists' civic engagement at such moments of crisis.

> in music, Stern—
> has grown forensic,
> and by civic piety
> has saved our city panic.
> ("Glory," ll. 21–24)

The Moore we have been taught would seem allergic to such piety, but here such nervousness and distance from public discourse have been fully overcome. Her anti–Big Developer politics—modern urban planning is a threat to the independence of art—is as piously anarchic and anticentralist about the city in 1960 as a chapter out of Jane Jacobs's decentralist urbanism in *The Death and Life of Great American Cities* (published in 1961). "Glory" as an expression of art—historically vortexical, archaeological, unchronological, and unoriginal (in sourcework and sentiment)—is certainly itself a part of what will stop the "bulldozing potentate, / land-grabber" (ll. 27–28). The poem, a contribution to the spring/summer 1960 campaign, is the opposite of panicked, and it owes unironic thanks to Isaac Stern for that. Looked at from across this modernist's *oeuvre,* the poem's final line would seem to be yet another clincher in a Moorean snarky satire of artists who erroneously think of entrance into the public sphere as creative and aesthetically generative. But examined in the context of the repudiation in *Minutes to Go* (and elsewhere) of creativity as a separate sphere of language and aesthetic activity, the thanks given to Stern for stepping out must be read as genuine because civic engagement is an extension of his performativity, just as this poem, with its sources in the news of major art-world crisis in the summer of 1960, fresh off the presses when it appeared in the August 13 *New Yorker,* was Marianne Moore's attempt to enact such engagement, civic piety constructed not of her own *but out of the historically specific ambient language around her.* For that—cueing the further development of Moore's inclination to write her poems from language already out there—

> We...
> are thanking you for glittering,
> for rushing to the rescue
> as if you'd heard yourself performing.
> ("Glory," 37, ll. 49–53)

"In the Public Garden," an occasional poem about occasional poetry, begins with a public performance: her public reading of a poem—this poem (in an earlier version)—at the Boston Arts Festival. It tells first of her trip to Boston for the purpose of presenting an occasional poem. She passes Harvard and ponders the structures ("cupolas of learning" trigger the thought) "that / have made education individual." She records a wise comment about Harvard offered by her taxi driver, uttered without irony: "They / make some fine young men at Harvard" (Moore, *O to Be,* 20, ll. 1–10). Now she falls into standard flashback, associations of earlier visits to Boston: a summer visit years earlier when she first noticed the glitter atop Fanueil Hall, a memory that doubly connects the association (Harvard's towers) and implies that her thoughts are moving from private to public, individual to all. Next she ponders springtime and feels herself engaged in a rote poetic litany, caused by the customary post-Romantic process—poems that condense personal memories. Adding "O yes, and snowdrops," we have evidence that she is becoming aware of the mere dutifulness of the verse, what remains of "spring and all" (spring and all that—the stuff of lyric). She steps away from the public—perhaps that is the cause of the conventionality—and ducks into King's Chapel, hearing the devout sing a hymn praising divine work. It is the kind of work that transforms a stranger in public into "a child / at home," an expatriate finally returned, a refugee rediscovering family. Thus the experience of the chapel seems like "a festival" and so we are back to the occasion and to lists of festive things, things one might find at a festival. The last item on the list is "silence," "more unusual" than anything one would expect to encounter at such a public event (ll. 26–36). Silence is unusual "after a word-waterfall of the banal" and it is "as unattainable / as freedom." This leads to wondering—with seeming patriotic cold war–era diction—"And what is freedom for?" The answer is that freedom is

> For "self-discipline," as our
>   hardest-working citizen has said—a school;
>
>   it is for "freedom to toil"
>   with a feel for the tool.
> Those in the trans-shipment camp must have
> a skill. With hope of freedom hanging
>   by a thread—some gather medicinal
>
> herbs from which they can sell.
> Ineligible if they ail.
>   Well?
>
> There are those who will talk for an hour
> without telling you why they have
>   come. And I? This is no madrigal—
>   (*O to Be,* 21, ll. 39–51)

The "word-waterfall of the banal" that precedes a silence as unattainable as freedom might—logically—be a state in which freedom is more attainable. It seems an unlikely assertion but it is logically possible. Whose banal language? It's in fact that

of President Dwight David Eisenhower. In a seemingly quite trivial use of language
from a contemporary newspaper, Moore has drawn on a May 6, 1958, article entitled
"President Urges Junior Leaguers to Widen Good Work" (Furman). Eisenhower
had met with women from the Junior League in the Rose Garden of the White
House and spoke platitudinously about the importance of voluntarism in hospi-
tals and schools, unaffected by prospects of political patronage. Then he observed
(claiming to quote Clemenceau), "Freedom is nothing in the world but the oppor-
tunity for self-discipline." And then, according to the article, he repeated the term
as an exclamation: "Self-discipline!" The poem would seem to mock such easy, pre-
dictable talk—just as Gregory Corso's joining with presidential mundanities would
seem at first to do so. But the merging of Moore's unremarkable associations, in
an occasional poem that had seemed to be going nowhere—seemed in fact thus
far to have been a public poem unwilling to get written—leads to the aural pairing
of "feel for the tool" and "freedom to toil," the latter a phrase in the diction of one
of the famous Four Freedoms, an international human right declared in wartime
by Americans. This internationalist homonym in turn enables the association of
Eisenhower's bland language about world service and the fate of refugees in "the
trans-shipment camp." If they are ill, they are not permitted to leave the camp: a bit-
ter paradox, because illness in such a situation—whether the trans-shipment camps
filled with Holocaust survivors on Cyprus in 1946 or those of Congolese displaced
in 1958–1960 by the beginnings of bloody struggles there—is caused by the very
displacement that resettlement, or coming home, would relieve. It turns out that
while silence is as unattainable as freedom, the word-waterfall of the banal, the aim-
less hourlong talk that would seem to be so useless, is what leads the poet to ask,
by comparison: "And I?" This—the poem—is itself "no madrigal": neither beautiful
nor intricately harmonized. But it is a polyphony and thus "it is a grateful tale," its
gratitude akin to that expressed for Isaac Stern's extension of his performativity to
the world of political campaigning (ll. 51–53). In this context, how can it be that
the poem unironically concludes with "glad[ness] that the Muses have a home and
swans," or "Happy that Art, admired in general, / is always actually personal" (ll.
69, 62)? It cannot. Here, then, is the strongest lesson learned from the apparently
meaningless banal noise preceding the (unattainable) freedom of silence: those
structures that have "made education individual," like poetry that would seem best
when personally, peculiarly associative (the insular poem, like a Harvard educa-
tion), are not now suitable for well wishing. The question, "And I?" leads to embrace
of a poetic that is no madrigal, a tentative but surprisingly pleasurable acceptance,
into the verse itself, of "those who will talk for an hour / without telling you why
they have come" (ll. 49–50). Why, after all, did Moore come to Boston? To present
an occasional poem that seems to be going nowhere, until—well—until, from the
least remarkable source, it finds its urgent direction? The formulaic *Times* article
quoting an inarticulate president speechifying to well-connected do-gooders set the
conventional public poem, otherwise toward a conventional political that is con-
ventionally personal, on its inexplicable way to unhappiness with admiration of art
that "is always actually personal" (l. 62).

Undoing X. J. Kennedy's undoing of Duchampian modernism in 1960, such a poetics refuses to collect its motions into shape—refuses to reject readymade multivocality and unassimilated linguistic ambience. The intrusion into the writing of its impersonal sources—facile political calls for engagement with crises of health and education, reports of desperate refugees whose experience of freedom is that it is "hanging / by a thread" (ll. 44–45)—taught Moore, as it did Burroughs (and Dorn and Rothenberg and many other New Americans at this time), how to discern for herself the end of the end of ideology, an engagement extracted from—or cut from—the ample civic rhetorical noise around her, of which her poems are a part. Bitterly opposed to such a method, of course, antimodernists continued to decry it as one effect of the modernist critical dictatorship (with its theoretical *Mein Kampf*) and to express disingenuous gratitude, as Karl Shapiro did, for young poets who were "beginning to use subjective judgment in place of the critical dictum," and to claim such an antimodernist mode as a version of antifascism. The positioning here as a matter of pure poetic politics was shrewd. It surely made ironizing the "always actually personal" a move risking accusations of cold dissociation and incomprehensible elitism. Yet self-discipline is knowing how and why to suppress the poetically normative urge to write yet another individually subjective lyric when "rounendless talk" is freely available and unrare (as distinct from freedom), and constitutes a generous performance.

NOTES

1 See Moore, *O to Be a Dragon*, 21.
2 See Burroughs et al., *Minutes to Go*, 7.
3 See, especially, Bell, 393–407. On the currency of the phrase, see Waxman.
4 See Filreis.
5 See Caute.
6 See, for instance, Robins, 226–228.
7 See Goldsmith, "Conceptual Poetics."
8 A young Robert Scholes (then a rising-star Joycean) writes from Charlottesville, Virginia, that Shapiro's claim that the anti-Romantic modernists abhorred Blake is in error, because, for one thing, Yeats was a great admirer of Blake. Responding to Shapiro's objections to New Critical pedagogy (where biography and history are set aside in favor of attention to the poem itself), one couple from Narbeth, Pennsylvania, wrote in with sarcasm to ask Mr. Shapiro to list colleges where such a method is used—since they, having been dully trained with biographical information he claims is said to be irrelevant to poetic understanding, are hoping to enroll and learn a bit about the current poetics. See Scholes, 30, 32.
9 Surrealism in the United States seems to have had three big moments in 1960: (1) Wallace Fowlie's essay, "Surrealism in 1960: A Backward Glance," published in *Poetry* in its March issue; (2) the publication of Anna Balakian's important book, *Surrealism: The Road to the Absolute*; and (3) a show at D'Arcy Galleries, featuring fifty-eight surrealist painters and sculptors put together by Marcel Duchamp and Maurice Bonnefoy (owner of the gallery)

at the end of November. When reviewers showed up at the gallery to find out about the show in advance of the opening, they found Duchamp himself, standing outside 1091 Madison Avenue, awaiting the delivery of three live chickens. The fowl were to participate in the show. (They were set off in a corner near a sign that read "Coin Sale.") A pair of half-burned logs was set neatly on andirons against a wall in which there was no fireplace. The fifty-eight pieces that Duchamp and Bonnefoy chose were meant to be more representative of the surrealist movement "from 1913 to today." In one gallery, five electric clocks hung from the ceiling. There was also "an ancient typewriter" and an old time clock with which guests at the premiere punched their invitations upon entering. There was a length of garden hose, to be spread around "as a good-natured hazard." A toy electric train circled a track set up in one of the gallery's Madison Avenue windows, pulling cards marked with the names of the surrealists in the show. Generally critics in 1960 either gloated over the fact that surrealism no longer shocked the middle classes or tsk-tsk'ed that "what once seemed sick now seems strangely sane." On the state of surrealism in 1960, the *New Yorker* critic wrote, "It might be said that instead of Surrealism's taking over America, America took over the Surrealists" (Coates, 200). See Preston; Canaday; "Boys Will Be Boys"; and "Surrealistic Sanity."

10   See also Bailey.

11   From a television interview with Marcel Duchamp conducted by Russell Connor on the occasion of the Boston Museum of Fine Arts exhibit of the work of Duchamp's brother, Jacques Villon, 1964.

12   See Goldsmith, "Introduction to Flarf vs. Conceptual Writing." "The quote to which you are referring," Goldsmith said in a dialogue with Marjorie Perloff, "was made by Brion Gysin in 1959 when he said that writing was 50 years behind painting. I still believe that this is true today. If we look at how easily the conventions of the art world are bent and apply those to writing, we will see how limited the world of innovative writing has been. It's not really a matter of form, it's more a matter of permissions granted by any given community." See Perloff, par. 5–6. Burroughs, in "The Cut-Up Method of Brion Gysin," notes that the method "brings to writers" a process "which has been used by painters for fifty years." See Burroughs, 29; a shorter version of the essay was originally published in Parkinson, 105–107.

13   Burroughs incorrectly gives the date as December 5, 1959.

14   See O'Neil.

15   See Cumming, "Carnegie Hall's Deadline," 8, and "Carnegie Hall Saved," 42. See also Schickel.

REFERENCES

Allen, Donald, ed. *The New American Poetry, 1945–1960*. Berkeley: University of California Press, 1960.

Auden, W.H. *Collected Poems*. Ed. Edward Mendelson. New York: Random House, 1976.

Bailey, Bradley. "*The Bachelors*: Pawns in Duchamp's Great Game." *Tout-Fait: The Marcel Duchamp Studies Online Journal* 1, no. 3 (December 2000). http://www.tout-fait.com/issues/issue_3/Articles/bailey.bailey.html.

Bell, Daniel. "The End of Ideology in the West." *The End of Ideology: On the Exhaustion of Political Ideas in the Fifties*. New York: Collier Books, 1961. 393–407.

Blackburn, Paul. *Brooklyn-Manhattan Transit: A Bouquet for Flatbush*. New York: Totem Press, 1960.

"Boys Will Be Boys." *Newsweek*, January 18, 1960: 87–88.

Bradbury, Malcolm. "A Very Exclusive Club." *Review Reporter* 21 (July 9, 1959): 40–42.

Burroughs, William S. "The Cut-Up Method of Brion Gysin." *The Third Mind*. New York: Viking Press, 1978.

Burroughs, William S., et al. *Minutes to Go*. Paris: Two Cities Editions, 1960.

Canaday, John. "Art: Surrealism with the Trimmings." *New York Times*, November 28 1960: 36.

Caute, David. *The Great Fear: the Anti-Communist Purge under Truman and Eisenhower*. New York: Simon and Schuster, 1978.

Coates, Robert M. "The Surrealists." *New Yorker*, December 10, 1960: 198–200.

Corso, Gregory. *The Happy Birthday of Death*. New York: New Directions, 1960.

Cumming, Robert. "Carnegie Hall's Deadline." *Music Journal* 17, no. 8 (1959): 8.

———. "Carnegie Hall Saved." *Instrumentalist* 14, no. 10 (1960): 42.

Dorn, Edward. "Sousa." In *The Newly Fallen*. New York: Totem Press, 1960. 12–15.

Duchamp, Marcel. By Russell Connor. 1964. http://www.youtube.com/watch?v=uzHXus7dQlw.

Duncan, Robert. *The Opening of the Field*. New York: New Directions, 1960.

Ferguson, Russell. "In Memory of Feelings: Frank O'Hara and American Art." *Jacket* no. 10 (2000). http://jacketmagazine.com/10/oh-ferg.html.

Filreis, Alan. *Counter-Revolution of the Word: The Conservative Attack on Modern Poetry, 1945-60*. Chapel Hill: University of North Carolina Press, 2008.

Furman, Bess. "President Urges Junior Leaguers to Widen Good Work." *New York Times*, May 6, 1958.

Goldsmith, Kenneth. "Conceptual Poetics." *Sibila*. 2009. http://sibila.com.br/index.php/sibila-english/410-conceptual-poetics.

———. "Introduction to Flarf vs. Conceptual Writing." Talk given at the Whitney Museum of American Art, New York, NY, April 17, 2009. http://epc.buffalo.edu/authors/goldsmith/whitney-intro.html.

Guest, Hadley Haden, ed. *The Collected Poems of Barbara Guest*. Middletown: Wesleyan University Press, 2008.

Kennedy, X. J. "Nude Descending a Staircase." *Poetry* 95, no. 4 (1960): 224.

Kumin, Maxine, ed. *The Complete Poems of Anne Sexton*. Boston: Houghton Mifflin, 1999.

Kunitz, Stanley. "American Poetry's Silver Age." *Harper's Magazine*, no. 219 (1959): 173–179.

"Major Poet, Minor Verse." *Time*, September 21, 1959: 110.

Mesch, Claudia. "Cold War Games and Postwar Art." *Reconstruction: Studies in Contemporary Culture* 6, no. 1 (2006). http://reconstruction.eserver.org/061/mesch.shtml.

Miles, Barry. *A Portrait of William Burroughs: El Hombre Invisible*. New York: Hyperion, 1993.

Moore, Marianne. "Glory." *New Yorker*, August 30, 1960.

———. *O to Be a Dragon*. New York: Viking Press, 1959.

———."The Plums of Curiosity." *Vogue*, August 1, 1960.

Morgan, Ted. *Literary Outlaw: The Life and Times of William S. Burroughs*. New York: Henry Holt, 1988.

Olson, Charles. *The Maximus Poems*. New York: Jargon/Corinth Books, 1960.

O'Neil, Paul. "The Only Rebellion Around: But the Shabby Beats Bungle the Job in Arguing, Sulking and Bad Poetry," *Life*, November 30, 1959: 115–116, 119–120, 123–126, 129–130.

Parkinson, Thomas, ed. *A Casebook on the Beat*. New York: Thomas Y. Crowell, 1961.

Perloff, Marjorie. "A Conversation with Kenneth Goldsmith." *Jacket* no. 21 (2003). http:// jacketmagazine.com/21/perl-gold-iv.html.

Pound, Ezra. "A Few Don'ts by an Imagiste." *Poetry* 1, no. 6 (1913): 200–201.

Preston, Stuart. "Questions of Meaning." *New York Times*, April 10, 1960: 13.

Robins, Natalie. *Alien Ink: The FBI's War on Freedom of Expression*. New York: Morrow, 1992.

Rukeyser, Muriel. "The Rhythm Is the Person." *Saturday Review* no. 42, September 1959.

Schickel, Robert. *The World of Carnegie Hall*. New York: J. Messner, 1960.

Scholes, Robert. "Poetry Today: The Reader and Mr. Shapiro." *New York Times Book Review*, January 10, 1960.

Schwartz, Delmore. "The Art of Marianne Moore." *New Republic*, January 4, 1960.

Shapiro, Karl. "What's the Matter with Poetry." *New York Times Book Review*, December 13, 1959.

Snyder, Gary. *Myths & Texts*. New York: New Directions, 1960.

"Surrealistic Sanity." *Time,* December 12, 1960: 81.

Waxman, Chaim Isaac. *The End of Ideology Debate*. New York: Funk & Wagnalls, 1968.

Weatherhead, A. K. "Two Kinds of Vision in Marianne Moore." *ELH* 31, no. 4 (1964): 482–496.

Wieners, John. *Selected Poems, 1958–1984*. Santa Barbara, CA: Black Sparrow Press, 1986.

CHAPTER 20

FIELDWORK IN NEW AMERICAN POETRY: FROM COSMOLOGY TO DISCOURSE

LYTLE SHAW

[A] poet, now, must be as full a culture-morphologist as any professional.

—Charles Olson, letter to Louis Martz, 1951[1]

The spoken word is a gesture, and its meaning, a world.

—Maurice Merleàu-Ponty[2]

Often in close dialogue with the place-based poetries of William Carlos Williams and Charles Olson, the New American poets of the 1950s and 1960s sought to dismantle and reinvent the concept of history both by reorienting it toward notions of temporality borrowed from anthropology and by grounding it within concrete spatial locations. This reinvention at once mobilized previously excluded versions of the cultural past and authorized new modes of lived experience in the present, especially in the place-based rural social formations poets increasingly constructed. To frame these emergent models of living, poets reinvented themselves as "fieldworkers" in the dual sense of working with spatially specific locations and with the authority of the disciplinary fields that might explain or contextualize those literal spaces.[3]

If Williams and Olson established the dominant ethnographic and historio-graphic vocabularies for the poetics of place, they both accepted a division, how-ever, whereby their own places—Paterson and Gloucester, respectively—did not yet embody the values they hoped to dredge up from the study of places in general, and theirs specifically. Over the course of the 1960s this changed: the poetry of a lone researcher offering his results to futurity was no longer seen as sufficient. Poets sought, instead, to *live* the experimental polis now, to enact it in daily life. As they did so, they externalized many features of Olson's practice in particular—turning his personal cosmology into a range of more public discourses. This chapter traces this process by charting how transformative readings of Olson were crucial to two seemingly opposite discourses that emerged in the 1960s: the back-to-the-land eco-poetics of Gary Snyder, grounded in part in his familial compound, Kitkitdizze, in the foothills of the Sierra Nevada mountains; and the Black Nationalism of Amiri Baraka, grounded in the city of Newark, New Jersey. Though obviously Olson is not a single source for either of these poets, understanding their relation to him opens up one of the characteristic and central transformations of American poetry in the 1960s—the path from cosmology to discourse.

Understanding Olson's influence this way would certainly have disturbed the poet himself, who was careful to frame his entire practice *against* such a movement: "discourse . . . has [since 450 BC] so worked its abstraction into our concept and use of language that language's other function, speech, seems so in need of restoration that several of us got back to hieroglyphics or to ideograms to right the balance" (Olson, *Human Universe*, 3–4). But if Olson saw the singularity of speech opposed to the iterable abstraction of discourse, many of those influenced by Olson saw more of a dialectical relationship that allowed such singularity to frame itself culturally, discursively in part *through* its recalcitrant singularity.[4] Which is to say that Olson occupies an interestingly ambiguous position between what Foucault and Barthes deem an author (a writer of individual works) and a "founder of discursivity"—one who produces not only texts, but also "the possibilities and the rules for the forma-tion of other texts."[5] Whereas Olson, that is, preserves the occasion of his disjunctive thinking, speaking, and self-making-in-time in books of anticipatory Charles Olson studies (such as *Reading at Berkeley* and *Poetry and Truth*), other poets similarly interested in the ethnographic and historiographic substratum of Olson's concerns channeled these more explicitly into a series of discourses—ecopoetics and Black Nationalism in particular—that could be detached from an individual cosmology.

In the same year as Donald M. Allen's 1960 epochal *The New American Poetry* anthology the commercial publisher George Braziller would publish *The Golden Age of American Anthropology*, edited by Margaret Mead and Ruth Bunzel. Part of a four-volume series that also included volumes on history, philosophy and literature, the Braziller books might be read as part of a larger postwar American attempt to renegotiate its cultural status in relation to Europe by formalizing and disseminat-ing canons within fields whose constellations of references had previously been in comparative states of flux.[6] What is of interest here, in this gesture being applied to the field of anthropology at that moment, however, is that Mead and Bunzel consider this golden age not as a methodological breakthrough—as, for instance, when modernist anthropological methods began to be disseminated in universities, and Franz Boas's students were sent to Samoa or elsewhere—but rather as a particular encounter between Americans of European descent and Native Americans, one that takes place while "the young science could still draw on the living memories of Indians and often on their still living practices and could use these to illumine the records of the early travelers" (Mead and Bunzel, 2). If modernist anthropology is central to this history too (Boas also trained many of the main anthropologists who worked on Native Americans, like Alfred Kroeber), Mead and Bunzel nonetheless present a wider, more capacious, historical canon of "anthropology"—one in which, for instance, many of the same Jesuit missionaries whose absence from American history William Carlos Williams had bemoaned could now enter a canon of the American past through the discipline of anthropology.[7] In the scramble to consolidate a particularly American anthropology, those figures that seemed to threaten American historiography could now enter almost seamlessly into a history of fieldwork, or of "contact" as Williams termed it.[8] Anthropologists therefore began publicly to ask Olson's question of how one might "pick up these injuns—that is, as Stephens, Prescott, Parkman did not pick them up 100 years agone" (Olson, *Mayan*, 31).

By 1950 Charles Olson and Robert Creeley were using anthropology to brush history against the grain, turning in particular to Bronislaw Malinowski's claim that "myth in a primitive society, i.e. in its original living form, is not a mere tale told but a reality lived" both to question historical accounts of "myth"—like Francis Parkman's—and to underlie their own model of "process" (Olson, *Charles Olson and Robert Creeley*, 3:135).[9] A myth-oriented poetry of process, then, was not just one that referenced a distant body of tales about creation but rather one that took its own self-conscious coming into being as poetry—its real-time, breath-based discovery of its associative materials—as a kind of horizon that could fuse present lived myth with its radically reconceived antecedents. It was in this sense that the poets sought to appropriate for their own process, and not just for distant narratives, Mircea Eliade's formulation of myth as "the recital of a creation…[telling] how something was accomplished, began to *be*" (Eliade, 95).

During the early 1950s, then, and particularly in the practice of Olson (who both begins Allen's anthology and is granted the largest number of pages), the model of the poet as ethnographer and experimental historiographer took on a new importance and a new set of cultural meanings. But beyond buttressing this new poetry by appealing to the authority of existing disciplines of anthropology and historiography (which *did* happen), poets more interestingly sought to revise and revivify these disciplines through radical new readings of their possible aims and methods. Seeking imaginative antidotes to what Nietzsche had called the "stifling of life by the historical, by the malady of history" (121),[10] poets developed a historiography that not only revalued canonical figures but also *challenged narrative itself* as the primary frame for historical understanding. In the process, they emptied out sequence and progress into a range of thick presents or instances of becoming. These moments were in turn authorized, paradoxically, by an appeal to the authorities both of anthropological method and of often distant historical subjects: the Aztecs, the Samoans, the Presocratics, the earliest Native Americans. And when these were not historical but present subjects, poets sought out an anthropology that did not simply confront alterity but rather *became it*: not recording stories, but rather channeling and embodying them. After describing a six-day fieldwork session undertaken by the anthropologist Alfred Kroeber with a Mojave informant, Gary Snyder comments, "That old man sitting in the sand house telling his story is who we must become—not A. L. Kroeber, as fine as he was" (Snyder in Rothenberg, *Pre-Faces*, 170).[11]

The journal or notebook of one's trip to India, China, and Mexico (or to marginalized areas inside the United States, like Native American reservations) became a new, highly charged, and eagerly read genre from the 1950s through the 1970s, with Olson, Allen Ginsberg, Gary Snyder, Joanne Kyger, William Burroughs, Jack Kerouac, Jerome Rothenberg, and many others publishing them.[12] Poets sought these contact zones in order to perform historical revisions and expansions of the possibilities of American identity. Thematizing their concrete experiences in these locations, poets recoded travel writing (the journal, the notebook, the letter) as a form of cultural critique.[13] In Olson's work especially, this distant fieldwork, undertaken in narrative or epistolary form, was in intimate dialogue with a new, non-narrative, increasingly anthropological poetry of place. That, during the 1950s and 1960s, poets "turned anthropologists, turned outward toward lost cultures, native chants, old irrational wisdoms—work of what [Jerome Rothenberg] calls 'The Technicians of the Sacred'"—was, according to Hugh Kenner, "part of the Olson legacy" (Kenner, 181). And yet we might wonder why it is that many of those poets whom Olson inspired to turn to anthropology are more widely read today than Olson.

Let me begin with Olsonian historiography. This is a difficult topic not only because of its corporeal and spatial dimensions. Certainly Olsonian history is bound up with breathing, speaking bodies and with particular locations—and it's true that many complexities emerge through this intertwining. Still, what is most complex here is that Olson insists (as I will demonstrate in a moment) on staging his concept of history at the syntactical level of his sentences. Many critics simply lose patience and accuse him of being unhistorical: writing of Olson and Dorn as "mythologising geographers," for instance, Terry Eagleton, in a rare article on American poetry, argues that, "by knotting, conflating and spatialising historical time," the two poets "achieve a kind of global liberation won at the possible cost of a reverence for routine causality" (Eagleton, 234).[14] Fewer commentators, however, have seen the terms of Olson's process poetics as providing interpretive models, especially models that might extend beyond the domain of what I will call Olsoniana (the discourse that sprung up to describe his cosmology) toward the exterior modes of historiography and anthropology that Olson's work engages.[15]

For Olson, as a new anthropological poetics derailed familiar narratives of myth and history, it not only challenged their valuations (as in Williams) but also exploded their syntax into a world of quasi-independent clauses—a real time of process like that Olson and Creeley identified in Malinowski's account of myth.[16]

In the famous anthropologist's version, which Olson quoted to Creeley in the same 1950 letter (appending his commentary in parenthetical phrases), myths

> are not kept alive by vain curiosity, neither as tales that have been invented nor again as tales that are true. For the natives (ya, let's name ourselves) on the contrary they are the assertion of an original, greater and more important reality through which the present life (how about that, R Cr) fate and work of mankind are governed (well, the verbal function, certainly, could be improved), and the knowledge of which provides men on the one hand with motives for ritual and moral acts, on the other with directions for their performance.
>
> (Charles Olson and Robert Creeley, 3:136)[17]

In Olson's ritual performances, both live ones like his *Reading at Berkeley* and his various readings, and the *Maximus Poems,* a world of independent clauses was imagined as a space of both conceptual and bodily liberation, one in which the real-time speaking subject could, as he improvised with cultural/historical materials, continually break through into new quasi-epiphanic insights suspended from finalized narrative ends and thus more physically available and present (because now deinstrumentalized). This was where anthropology and history came together—both could be lived, rendered present, in performance. "The factual information of the poem," as Barrett Watten argues, "is kept in the present by means of an ever-expanding sentence structure, with numerous digressions at the level of the phrase—but the sentence never arrives to complete its 'statement'" (*Total Syntax,* 132).[18] Or as Olson puts it in a section of *The Maximus Poems* that reproduces an exchange with the poet Paul Blackburn:

> He sd, "You go all around the subject." And I sd, "I didn't know it
>   was a subject."
> He sd, "You twist" and I sd, "I do." He said other things. And I
>   didn't say anything.
> Nor do I know
> that this is a rail
> on which all (or any)
> will ride (as, by Pullman)
>
> (*Maximus,* 72)

Challenging the idea of a single subject, Olson positions the twisting associative logic of his project here against the frictionless train car, the Pullman, of historical narrative.

Olson was the first among postwar poets to have the public role of a poet/ethnographer, in part because of his 1950–1951 archaeological digs in Mexico.[19] The details of this trip were reported by letter to Creeley in what became *The Mayan Letters* (1953)—one of the first postwar countercultural recuperations of pre-Columbian history. Because of its staging in the field, we might read *The Mayan Letters* as the nomadic pole within Olson's practice, the opposite end from *The Maximus Poems,* on which he was just beginning work. Ultimately his trip becomes an instance of Olson's often-quoted definition of *'istorin,* not as noun but as verb: "to find out for oneself" (Butterick, ix). Rather than critiquing the valuations of canonical historians like Parkman from the safety of his study in Gloucester, Olson wants to recover the "ground" of these valuations with an appeal to geography. His way of expanding and complicating American history and literature, and situating Gloucester's status within world history as a fishing rather than religious settlement in the New World, thus emerges through a series of geographically based field trips that seek to uncover raw social and historical determinants in the landscape. Olson not only went to college libraries around Black Mountain—Duke, University of North Carolina at Chapel Hill, Sondley Library (within Pack Memorial Library in Asheville)— but after moving back to Gloucester, he also, according to George Butterick, sought out libraries "up and down the Massachusetts coast between Gloucester and Boston," consulting "town records in the vault of the Gloucester City Clerk's office, deeds and wills among the county probate records at Salem, an account book at the local historical society, documents on microfilm, [and] family papers" (Butterick, xviii). In his *A Guide to the Maximus Poems,* Butterick describes Olson's "progress of...investigation, [as an] act of history that will take the poet from [Samuel Eliot] Morison through John Babson and Frances Rose-Troup [historians of the Bay Colony, Gloucester, and John White, respectively] to the town records themselves and, in 1966, to England and the original records of the Dorchester Company and the Weymouth Port Books" (xvii).

Such accounts of Olson's contact with the material residues of his varying "archives" have been crucial to the dominant version of Charles Olson studies.[20] But rather than take them simply as proof of persistence and insight, it might be productive instead to read them as performing the authenticating office that fieldwork does for the anthropologist—performing, that is, a rhetorical as well as a would-be physical and immediate effect. Considering the relation between writing and fieldwork in anthropology, Clifford Geertz discusses precisely this contact effect: "The ability of anthropologists to get us to take what they say seriously has less to do with either a factual look or an air of conceptual elegance than it has with their capacity to convince us that what they say is a result of their having actually penetrated (or, if you prefer, been penetrated by) another form of life, of having, one way or another, truly 'been there.' And that, persuading us that this offstage miracle has occurred, is where writing comes in" (Geertz, 4–5).

What separates Olson from anthropologists, then, is that his writing imagines the clause—uncoupled from narrative completion, swirling in and out of connection with other clauses—as the immediate and even physical mechanism of this "been there" effect, this effect of contact. For readers wishing to make contact with Olson, then, his commitment to a world of atomistic references embodied in disjunctive clauses has typically involved the attempt to turn this vast intellectual terrain (itself expanded by his essays) into a unified cosmology.[21] Coupled, then, with Olson's drive to "find out for oneself" is the contradictory drive, within Olsoniana, to find out what a particular text meant *for Olson.*[22]

GARY SNYDER, ANTHROPOLOGY, KITKITDIZZE

Basing itself in and rethinking an array of literal and disciplinary fields, Gary Snyder's version of ecopoetics had an especially close relation to anthropology, using readings of early twentieth-century fieldwork, in particular, to open history to an expanded concept of daily life. This interaction ultimately helped build bridges between New American poets and New Left youth revolts of the 1960s (especially those involving back-to-the-land or digging-in movements, like the Diggers, with whom Gary Snyder was in close contact). Because they sought to denaturalize and de-universalize Western social and economic life, Margaret Mead's anthropological writings on the culture of youth and adolescence were of special use. What is of importance in this link is not the celebration of youth per se but rather the resistance to ideologies of maturity that encode naturalized versions of successful acculturation. Poets sought to question such naturalized narratives of maturation in part through a place-based anthropological turn. And yet within the New Left's return to place, understandings of what counted as a place oscillated, interestingly, between empirical sites and charismatic bodies, between geographically bounded spaces and exemplary beings, usually writers, who helped to focus the experience of those spaces.

The author of the influential *American and the New Era,* Richard Flacks was a key figure in the early formation of Students for a Democratic Society (SDS).[23] "The sixties youth revolt was in part," according to Flacks, "about the possibility of redefining 'adulthood' in our society" (Whalen and Flacks, 2). This redefinition—with its critique of the supposed "ephemerality of idealism" (1), its contestation of normative concepts of adjustment, maturation, and success—was aided by a comparative approach to societies, one that could place Samoa and New Guinea next to Ann Arbor and Berkeley. If the anthropological underpinnings of ecopoetics were in sync with and extended the New Left embrace of youth, they also extended in a perhaps less obvious way toward the New Left goal of "making history." The New Left version of "participatory democracy" was, according to Flacks, "a vision that addressed itself to a fundamental schism in American experience: the gap most people feel most of the time between their daily lives and history" (9).[24] In most accounts of the New Left, including Flacks's own *Making History,* this gap is overcome by democratic subjects intervening in the decision-making process from which they had previously been barred; it is overcome by increasing participation. What counts as history, in other words, is not at stake—only who makes it. Certainly new agents of historical action did make their way into most accounts of the 1960s. And yet, in a paradox of the New Left, the more the notion of daily life is recovered, rendered participatory, the more "history" ceases to be a self-evident or even a familiar category. We might therefore hear Flacks's call to "make" history in relation to 1960s attempts to accord daily life a greater role in our understanding of what counts as "history." [25] In fact, while it might seem at first in Flacks's formulation like a secondary category (less important than history), daily life emerges throughout the decade as perhaps the most contested domain of historical representation—for many, indeed, *the* key to historical thought in general.[26] If 1960s social activists popularized the importance of thinking globally and acting locally, so within historiography—including that practiced by poets—daily life became a new local, a new pragmatic and material base, from which to access, complicate, and sometimes contest accounts of vast diachronic change or decisive, singular events.[27] For poets as for historians, then, the phase "making history" contained a generative ambiguity, pointing at once toward direct participation, by fiat, in the (typically mediated and imposed) decisions that most affect one's life and toward a thorough rethinking of how the everyday basis of that life might be accounted for in historical writing.

Snyder engages these questions by at once rejecting and revising historical thought. We can trace this shift from the full rejection of history to its reformulation within the course of a single essay, his 1967 "Poetry and the Primitive: Notes on Poetry as an Ecological Survival Technique," sections of which were later reprinted in Jerome Rothenberg's *Symposium of the Whole*.[28] "To live in the 'mythological present,'" Snyder suggests, "in close relation to nature and in basic but disciplined body/mind states suggests a wider-ranging imagination and a closer subjective knowledge of one's own physical properties than is usually available to men living (as they themselves describe it) impotently and inadequately in 'history'—their mind content programmed, and their caressing of nature complicated by the extensions and abstractions which elaborate tools are" (*Earth House*, 118). By the end of the essay, however, this scare-quoted history will be replaced by a progressive version: "we are now gathering all the threads of history together and linking modern science to the primitive and archaic sources" (127).

Snyder's revised concept of history, history of a thick present, is underwritten by a turn to anthropology—including Kroeber's and Boas's works on the Pacific Northwest.[29] Anthropological history is thus paradoxical in that what it provides for Snyder is instances of rich historyless cultures in history—proof, that is, that the rejection of Western history could coincide with deeply immersive social possibilities in the present. Snyder double-majored in anthropology and English at Reed College; quoted Malinowski, Frazer, Kroeber, and Boas in his undergraduate thesis; and later spoke of anthropology as "probably the most intellectually exciting field in the university" (Snyder, *Real Work*, 58).[30] Boas's work also probably influenced Snyder's second book, *Myths and Texts* (1960).[31] But later, after Snyder settled in California, it was Kroeber's work on the Native American tribes of California to which Snyder turned, in an attempt to "get a sense of that region," relating Kroeber's maps of Native Californian group and tribe distribution to "certain types of flora...types of biomes, and climatological areas...drainages" (Snyder, *Real Work*, 24). However, in the same works that include these maps, Kroeber also commented on the status of history for California Indians in a way that Snyder must have appreciated:

> The California Indian did not record the passage of long intervals of time. No one
> knew his own age nor how remote an event was that had happened more than

half a dozen years ago. Tallies seem not to have been kept, and no sticks notched annually have been reported. Most groups had not even a word for "year," but employed…"summer," or "winter" instead."

(A. Kroeber, Elements, 320)[32]

Though Kroeber does not comment here on the epistemological implications of this concept of time, it appears closely related to the rejection of "history" advocated by Snyder in "Poetry and the Primitive," where full engagement with the present seems to mean giving up many of our most common markers of temporal succession: "Having fewer tools, no concern with history, a living oral tradition rather than an accumulated library, no overriding social goals, and considerable freedom of sexual and inner life, such people live vastly in the present" (Snyder, *Earth House*, 117). Certainly Snyder saw the work of Kroeber and other anthropologists as buttressing his claims, which he did not hesitate to align with modern science: "Science, as far as it is capable of looking 'on beauty bare' is on our side. Part of our being modern is the very fact of our awareness that we are one with our beginnings—contemporary with all periods—members of all cultures. The seeds of every social structure or custom are in the mind" (126). Evoking the work of Margaret Mead, Snyder continues: "College students trying something different because 'they do it in New Guinea' is part of the real work of modern man" (127).

If Mead's large print-run anthologies of American anthropology made a space for Williams's heroes of American history like Père Rasles, her even more widely distributed books on Samoa and New Guinea lent themselves (at least in part) both to the New Left in general and to neo-primitive poets like Snyder in particular.[33] Published initially in 1928 with a preface by Franz Boas, Mead's *Coming of Age in Samoa* was reprinted in 1955 and 1961 and then kept in print throughout the 1960s. In it, Mead—in her first work in the field—helped Boas extend arguments for cultural relativism by denaturalizing the mood of crisis often taken in the West as an essential feature of adolescence. Mead, on the contrary, asserted "that adolescence is not necessarily a time of stress and strain, but that cultural conditions make it so" (*Coming of Age*, 234). Similarly, after studying basically the same problems in the new location of New Guinea a few years later, Mead was "forced to conclude" in her 1930 book *Growing Up in New Guinea* "that human nature is almost unbelievably malleable, responding accurately and contrastingly to contrasting cultural conditions" (Mead in Howard, 162). Snyder thus found a perhaps unwitting countercultural ally in Mead, who, by popularizing cultural relativism, aided the New Left's reinterpretation of youth.[34] While Mead's work generated a heated debate among anthropologists, what's interesting about Snyder's position in this debate is that he, like Mead, is more interested in would-be timeless structures of variable cultures (or even human beings themselves) than in exploring the historical transformations (colonial and otherwise) that characterize these cultures.[35] Indeed, Snyder's reference to Mead hints at a move away from a strictly relativist anthropology toward a more essentialist position. This "work of modern man" that he links to "college students trying

something different because 'they do it in New Guinea' is ultimately that of uncover-
ing "the inner structure and actual boundaries of the mind" (*Earth House*, 127).

Like the human mind, physical geography in Snyder often has an almost
timeless essence. It makes sense then that Snyder's argument for a return to full
embodiment, to a nonrepressed corporeal being-in-the-world, coincides with the
desire for a return to a kind of geographical specificity, even a geographical deter-
minism inasmuch as Snyder considers the watershed "the first and last nation whose
boundaries, though subtly shifting, are unarguable" (Snyder, *Place*, 229).[36] Taking
the watershed as the ultimate horizon of place, Snyder's poetics of place jumps off
from the ecological dynamics of the watershed: "Teaching should begin with what
the local forces are" (*Real Work*, 16).[37] Tapping into the forces of place, however,
also involves an ethical imperative to examine the historical dimension of its oral
culture, especially that produced by Native Americans: "you have to consult Indian
mythology and ritual and magic of the area and try to understand why it was they
saw certain figures as potent" (16). Rather than simply re-presenting this mythol-
ogy inside poetry, Snyder wants more generally to collapse the distinctions between
poetry myth, ritual, and practical knowledge.

As a mode of place-based history, Snyder's writing differs therefore not just
from dominant American historians but from the dominant American tradition
of the poetics of place in Williams and Olson as well. Snyder re-explains the his-
tory of his own region, the Sierra foothills of California in a 1990 talk, for instance,
by shifting emphasis away from "the brief era of the gold miners, the forty-niners,
who tediously dominate the local official mythology and decorate our county seal"
toward what he sees as a richer, more legitimate group of "teachers and spiritual
ancestors"—that is, "the Nisenan people who preceded" white settlers and had "a
rich culture, with stories, music, ceremonies, and a deep knowledge of plants and
animals" (*Place*, 57).

Snyder's admirable ecological activism and his expanded place-specific histori-
cal poetics run up against a limit, however, inasmuch as he presents these goals as
a fixed interpretive framework that a responsible poetics of place *must* confront—a
research recipe with preestablished orders and hierarchies. More, while he is infi-
nitely particular about the flora and fauna within his watershed, he intentionally
generalizes about his experience in urban centers—referring, for instance, to an
interview as taking place "in an office building labyrinth somewhere in Manhattan"
(*Real Work*, 31).[38] Here his affected disorientation is precisely the point: cities, he
implies, do not reward (or even allow) the kind of attention he lavishes on subsec-
tions of his watershed.[39] And yet the history of place-based writing has certainly
demonstrated that cities too must qualify as possible places, that the watershed is
not the only or ultimate interpretive frame for an environment, and that a place's
commentators need not be ranked by their length of residence.

It was a perceived failure to operate by such standards that set Snyder against
many versions of the back-to-the-land movement of the late 1960s. Snyder's was
indeed a more rigorous version. And his intense embodiment of this in a built struc-
ture may partly explain his visitors' strong reaction to Snyder's house—Kitkitdizze

(the name comes from a Native American word for an indigenous groundcover), which he began building on the south fork of the Yuba River near the town of Nevada City in 1969, and which Snyder clearly intended as an essay on place-based living, an enactment and grounding of his own theorization.[40] "It was a simple but eloquent statement of Gary's philosophy of life, expressed without an excess syllable," says Coyote (Snyder and Coyote, 160). In particular this involved a literal attempt to live in tandem with the animals and insects that already inhabited the spot; toward this end Snyder consciously avoided enclosure—doors, windows, screens. "We came to live a permeable, porous life in our house," says Snyder (*Place*, 195). This means, in addition to seasonal struggles with yellow jackets, that "ground squirrels come right inside for fresh fruit on the table, and the deer step into the shade shelter to nibble a neglected salad" (196). Here is Peter Coyote's description:

> From the hill just above the clearing, the house radiated a sense of unmistakable, timeless gravity. The thick, orange clay roof tiles were supported by heavy, hand-hewn lintels and posts. Between these, adobe walls or small-paned windows lightened the feeling of the house's massive construction. The house gave the impression of being fastened in place, as if the trees supporting it had not been cut down, but simply peeled and pressed into service where they stood, with their roots still gripping the soil. It seemed then, and still seems today, to be a house that is *exactly* right.
>
> (*Dimensions of Life*, 160)

In a hallucinatory countercultural image of architectural symbiosis that seems to locate Snyder's construction on a Roger Dean album cover or a J. R. R. Tolkien illustration, the house is not so much an intervention (however mild) in a setting, as a *greater realization* of it, its trees "simply peeled and pressed into service where they stood, with their roots still gripping the soil." For Coyote, this capturing of the genius loci, this seriousness and gravity in living in place, calls into stark relief the fact that his own attempts to return to the earth, his own "vision of 'the timeless present'" was sadly represented in "an abandoned cow shed covered with tar paper and old rugs" (162). But Coyote takes his reading of Snyder's house even further. The house does not merely capture its setting, it also enacts or embodies Snyder—in a way that would seem to encompass Snyder's whole being, writing included: "Every time I asked myself what *he* was about, the answer appeared self-evident to me. He was *about* his house; part Japanese farmhouse, part log cabin, part Indian longhouse; highly civilized, elegant, refined, and comfortable, and obviously efficient" (161).

Perhaps stated here in its most extreme form, Coyote's impression of Snyder's house merging with the landscape, and his self merging with his house, is actually consistent with an ongoing pattern in Snyder's reception—one in which Snyder is seen as quite literally embodying place-based values—at the scale either of the specific locale (like Kitkitdizze) or at that of the larger region, as in William Everson's reading of Snyder as the embodiment of West Coast poetics. Painting California as "the sundown quarter," haunted both by a "masculine penchant for violence" and by a "softer, feminine side" that shows itself in the "touch of Lethe" (Everson, 60–61),

Everson sees Snyder as representing "the terminal literary situation of the archetype at present" because "he typifies that aspect of the Westward thrust which actually leaps the Pacific to retouch the origins of civilization in the Orient" (141).[41]

Once Snyder could substitute for his farmhouse or for West Coast poetics more generally, this type of embodiment could become even more literal. If Olson was sometimes seen in his live performances (like his famous *Reading at Berkeley*) as a towering and unyielding "wall of sound" breaking his own strings of free associations only to add new ideas that would forever hold a final thought or sentence at bay, then Snyder became a kind of ecological commando who could literally dominate place by his keen regional knowledge and boundless bodily powers.[42] Consider this passage from a 1968 article by Thomas Parkinson:

> If [Snyder] were put down in the most remote wilderness with only a pocket knife, he would emerge from it cheerfully within two weeks, full of fresh experience, and with no loss of weight. There is a physical, intellectual and moral sturdiness to him that is part of each movement he makes and each sentence he phrases.
>
> (cited in Everson, 142)

As in Olson's reception, bodily values and effects are understood to operate, too, at a grammatical level in the writer's sentences. But here, in Parkinson's reading of Snyder, the connection is conceived as far more direct. Imagine Parkinson's test applied (as a measure of value!) to other prominent New American poets: Ashbery would certainly not have emerged from this remote wilderness spot; Ginsberg might make it out but would most likely have lost weight; Creeley, too, might emerge two weeks later knocking at a cabin door full of fresh experience, but not cheerfully. What Parkinson's formulation points to, in fact, is a tendency (developing in the 1960s) to understand the poet's body as a physical exemplar of a poetics that expands and amplifies the meaning of performance, rendering it continuous with quotidian experience. Ultimately, this way of thinking leads to a fracture or duplication within the concept of place: is Gloucester, Massachusetts (the ostensible subject of Charles Olson's *The Maximus Poems*), the poet's "place" or is it rather, always, his speaking and breathing six-foot-seven body, his infinitely portable "wall of sound," which can be plugged in equally in Berkeley's Wheeler Hall or in his study at Fort Square in Gloucester? Are the few remaining old-growth West Coast redwood groves, or his house, Kitkitdizze, Snyder's "place" or is it rather his corporeal embodiment as a kind of Zen Boy Scout? In unconsciously insisting on *both,* critics used a reading of the body to authorize a reading of the larger place, projecting corporeal characteristics into the otherwise unwieldy, perhaps unframeable spatial continuum that that body would make subject to experience. And yet even within this tendency to make the body the precursor to the larger "place," there is an obvious and important difference between Snyder's and Olson's cases: if Synder can thrive after being parachuted into any unfamiliar terrain, his "success" (his omnivorous contextualism) depends not upon a vocal performance that rescripts time into a thick present but upon acts by legs and arms that subdue space.

PERFORMING THE BLACK ARTS:
BARAKA'S NEWARK

> I wanted to make a series of syllables... that would be identical... with a historical event... the end of the war... and so I prepared... the declaration... by saying I hereby... *declare the end of the war!* and set up a force field of language... so solid... and absolute.... that it will ultimately overwhelm... the force field of language, pronounced out of the State Department and out of Johnson's mouth.
>   —Allen Ginsberg, *Improvised Poetics* (35)

> All the stores will open up if you will say the magic words. The magic words are: Up against the wall mother fucker this is a stick up!
>   —Amiri Baraka, "Black People!" (*Black Magic*, 225)

Rather than seeking to end the Vietnam War remotely through an unstoppable "force field of language" that might be unleashed from anywhere, Baraka tries to extend the war concretely to a second front by digging in to his hometown—Newark, New Jersey, whose famous riots of July 1967 were still in the future.[43] Galvanized by role-reversing "magic words" that put white proprietors on the defensive, African Americans become, in A. B. Spellman's amazing phrase, the "williecong" (Spellman, 247). Proposing further "magic actions," Baraka continues: "Smash the window at night... smash the windows daytime, anytime, together, let's smash the window and drag the shit from in there. No money down. No time to pay. Just take what you want. The magic dance in the street" (*Black Magic*, 225). If these were some of the more provocative new roles conceived for poetry in the 1960s, and if they both imagine new powers for the performative, they also imply vastly different ideas of context, of the conditions necessary for the speech act to perform its function, so that it does not go awry or become "unhappy," as J. L. Austin says of those misfired performatives severed from their enabling contexts and conditions (Austin, 14).

Critics have often noted that Baraka's moves from Greenwich Village to Harlem and then to Newark over the course of the 1960s were designed to situate his writing in relation to African American communities that could find themselves both reflected and revolutionized in his practice.[44] And yet, there has been surprisingly little attention to precisely *how* this would-be grounding might work—to how immersion in these new contexts might realize the performative powers of revolutionary speech acts. In his early work Baraka himself had been more skeptical about such mergings of poetic subject and would-be constituency; by the early 1970s, he would grow unsatisfied, in turn, by the model of political agency proposed by "Black People!" too.[45] As he develops his own objections, he reconceptualizes the role of writing: no longer primarily designed to provide the "magical" rush of understanding that would call an individual subject into action, writing now seeks to lay an institutional framework that would secure and sustain such rushes of understanding. But where, exactly, does one locate such institutions: in smaller-scale sociolects or shared linguistic practices, or in more macro-scale positions articulated, for instance, in political speech? In radicalized, self-conscious bodies of political actors, or in expressive architectural structures that might secure the pleasure and relative autonomy of those bodies?

If such an attempt at grounding will eventually cause Baraka to rethink the kinds of speech acts he proposes in "Black People!" it will not cause him, as is often believed, to part ways definitively with the concerns of the New American Poetry, in particular with the model of the poet as fieldworker that Baraka transforms from Charles Olson and William Carlos Williams. Like Gary Snyder (whose first book, *Myths and Texts* [1960], Baraka's Totem Press co-published with Corinth Books, and who appears regularly in *Yugen* and *The Floating Bear*), Baraka seeks to bridge the gap that separates Williams's or Olson's theorization of new social formations in *Paterson* and *Maximus* from the *enactment* of those formations in the present.[46] And yet Baraka's version of this enactment—in his Spirit House in Newark, or his Kawaida Towers project (a proposed sixteen-story public housing project in Newark that, for political reasons to be explained shortly, was never built)—obviously departs significantly from Snyder's at Kitkitdizze, where the exemplary construction of the house, with its refusal of full enclosure, puts human beings in contact, literally, with the animal and vegetal kingdoms. For Baraka, by contrast, the exemplary urban sitings of Spirit House and Kawaida Towers were designed to put African Americans in conscious contact with *each other*, and with a version of African culture from which they had historically been violently separated.[47] Baraka and Snyder, then, might be seen as imagining almost symmetrically opposite rural and urban afterlives for Olson's model of the poet as fieldworker. Both, however, pry Olsonian fieldwork loose from its cosmological underpinnings and couple it instead with an exterior discourse their work helps to articulate—be it ecopoetics or Black Nationalism.

Baraka's early issues of *Yugen* treat New Jersey as an object of ethnographic curiosity.[48] Still, the title of his 1964 poem—"A contract. (for the destruction and / rebuilding of Paterson"—quickly gives a sense of his difference from Williams: if there is a subterranean story to be uncovered in this town for Baraka it is more along the lines of a nagging plumbing problem than a figure for alternative American history: "Flesh, and cars, tar, dug holes beneath stone / a rude hierarchy of money, band saws cross out / music, feeling. Even speech, corrodes" (*Dead Lecturer*, 11). Neither Paterson nor Newark presents itself to Baraka as an archive to be carefully mined: We will not find Baraka earnestly counting the number of thwart saws, butter firkins, sides of bacon, and hogsheads of beer the town fathers needed to make it through their first winters. We will, however, find him noting the *absence* of such material goods among those at the bottom of Paterson's "rude hierarchy." More importantly, perhaps, we will find him exhorting those in this position simply to conceptualize their status in material terms. Though there is not yet an identification with these "Loud spics" and "dirty woogies" (who are "no brothers"), there is a proto-nationalist concern that they will not "smash their stainless / heads, against the simpler effrontery of so callous a code as gain."

A beachhead not an archive, Newark, in the wake of his frustration in orga-
nizing the Black Arts Movement in Harlem, is at once, like Harlem, outside the
lower Manhattan of his bohemian past, and yet still *intensely urban*.[49] It is rather,
in fact, an epitome of what "the city" was beginning to be understood as in the
1960s: largely black, economically and socially marginalized, controlled by white
owners, and thus, after Watts, increasingly mobilized to riot. As Komozi Woodard
notes, Newark had "the highest maternal mortality and venereal disease rate in the
country; as well as the highest rate of tuberculosis cases for all cities; a drug crisis
ranking seventh and an air pollution problem ranking ninth in the nation; and a
housing crisis that involved more than 75 percent of the city's old and rapidly aging
structures" (143). The city also had an 11.5 percent unemployment rate and median
household income for African Americans of just $3,839 (versus $6,858 for whites)
(143). Given these conditions, Baraka's choice to dig in to Newark could also be
understood as a negation of the cosmopolitan metropolis—here, however, not in
favor of the communes and rural collectivities to which white bohemians rushed in
the 1960s, but rather for precisely the kind of blighted urban "slum" that, increasing
throughout the 1960s, was the engine of white flight (both suburban and bohemian)
in the first place.

Inasmuch as Baraka understood his activism in the 1960s as gradual unlearning
of his white Western education, we might see his return to Newark, the town of
his birth and where his parents still lived, as an even *more* explicit echo of Aimé
Césaire's return to Martinique (after his education in Paris) than was Baraka's
period in Harlem.[50] The reoccupation and attempted radicalization of the blighted
hometown then parallels Baraka's remotivation of the array of concepts and sub-
ject positions from blackness or negritude, to "magic" (as the derisively identified
African Other to western rationalism), to badness and even "terribleness" (again,
judgments recast as badges of alterity), to the word "nigger" (as the identity term
that, unlike "negro," does not imagine itself as finding adequate representation
within the United States' political system for the group it identifies): "nigger is a
definition of the wholly detached from material / consideration a nigger don't have
no gold / not even a negro got gold but a negro think like he would if he / had gold"
(*In Our Terribleness*).[51]

These terms might originate as hateful speech acts directed at an African Amer-
ican; their revaluation, though, seems to hold out liberatory possibilities. Judith
Butler, for instance, sees the citational quality of hate speech (and by extension its
recodings) not as absolving its speaker from its consequences, but rather as situating
him or her in relation to both the speech act's problematic past and possibly alterable
future. "The responsibility of the speaker does not consist of remaking language ex
nihilo, but rather of negotiating the legacies of usage that constrain and enable that
speaker's speech" (Butler, 27).[52] What emerges, then, in recodings of such speech "is
a ritual chain of resignifications whose origin and end remain unfixed and unfix-
able" (14). Alterable, yes; fixable, no. That is, if groups can intervene in these histo-
ries, rerouting terms and plugging them into new values, they cannot, according to
Butler, permanently ensure these values by insisting that certain speech acts always

be understood in specific contexts. And yet it is possible—as Baraka's practice of the 1960s suggested—to build contexts that can affect (if not simply contain) these questions of reception.[53]

Part of this building came through a dialogue with Olson. Baraka published all of the components of "Proprioception" (in the magazines *Yugen, The Floating Bear,* and *Kulchur*)[54] as well as the first standalone pamphlet version of Olson's "Projective Verse" (published by Totem in 1959); Baraka also included many of Olson's poems in both *Yugen* and *The Floating Bear*.[55] In "Proprioception," Olson had written, "The 'soul' then is equally 'physical'" (*Proprioception,* 2).[56] The simultaneous insistence upon and materialization of the soul (as force, energy, resistance, song) parallel Baraka's own attempts to make seemingly transcendent forms perform concrete cultural work. Speaking of his immersion in a group of "Olson-Creeley types," Baraka was nonetheless careful to claim that "Olson's thing was always more political" (*Conversations,* 108).[57] Their relation was important enough that Baraka appears, rather prominently, in Olson's *The Maximus Poems* in a February 9, 1966, poem from Volume 3 titled "I have been an ability—a machine—up to / now" (495). Olson situates his own immigrant father in relation to the forced migrations of African Americans, suggesting that his father's demise was caused in part by this oppression.

Associated with a genealogy with which Olson, too, wants to identify—one of failed and/or enforced diaspora, and suppressed left activist postal work (which we might take as a figure for an alternative communication system)—Baraka emerges as an actor in *The Maximus Poems* at the precise moment that Olson moves toward a new, separatist form of polis.

> the U.S. Post Office
> using
> his purpose to
> catch him
> in their trap   to bust him
> organizing
> Postal Workers
> benefits—Retirement age
> Widows pensions a different
> leadership in Washington than
> Doherty my father a Swedish
> wave of
> migration after
> Irish? like Negroes
> Now like Leroy and Malcolm
> X the final wave
> of wash upon this
> desperate
> ugly

>   cruel
>   Land this Nation
>   which never
>   lets anyone
>   come to
>   shore
>   (496–497)

Behind the scenes in this passage is not just the oppression of Baraka's father and grandfather, but of him, too—his arrest for mailing Harold Carrington issues of *The Floating Bear,* which had sections of *The System of Dante's Hell.*[58] But if this shift marks one sense in which the Olsonian epic has failed, what is important to note here is that Olson does not cite Baraka as a symptomatic example; Olson, too, suggests the necessity of Gloucester breaking off from the American mainland.

>   how many waves
>   of hell and death and
>   dirt and shit
>   meaningless waves of hurt and punished lives shall America
>   be nothing but the story of
>   not at all her successes
>   —I have been—Leroy has been
>   as we genetic failures are
>   successes, here
>   it isn't interesting,
>   Yankees—Europeans—Chinese (498)

This passage then leads directly into a shaped poem that, as it twists to the right and curls in on itself, asks to be taken in analogical relationship to the handle of the gun referenced in the lines within—one with which "my father and I shot / off the back porch Worcester / as the rats came closer / as they filled the Athletic Field /— and Beaver Brook Goddamn US Papers / with my 22 / he gave me / and I don't have now to give / my own son / as I'd like to the bolt / was such a delicate / piece of machinery / to handle / and to lock to / fire" (498). Directly upside down, the word "fire" marks this curving passage's full twist to 180 degrees. Several times earlier the visual prosody of *The Maximus Poem* has evoked maps, and once it has broken down into a spiraling tangle of hand-scrawled lines.[59] But this is the first moment in the epic in which the arrangement of lines on the page has been asked to analogize three-dimensional objects in the world; this is, I think, no accident, because the "instrumental" nature of this analogy with a gun—a gun that is imagined at that historical moment as an appropriate gift for a son—is also coincident with a shift in the poem's model of polis, abandoning the idea that it could be shaped out of the current social world of the United States. Olson uses his references to prominent Black Nationalists, then, as a preface to a new phase in his project's ongoing theorization of a polis, suggesting, in the spiraling and falling movement of the second poem, that Gloucester, too (a word that here seems to name Olson's project rather than the empirical city) might "sail away / from this Rising Shore" of America.[60]

Baraka's end of the dialogue with Olson can be traced, in turn, from the series of positive statements about field poetics and sonic research—including "How You Sound" (Baraka's statement on poetics in Don Allen's *The New American Poetry*) and the introduction to his 1963 anthology *The Moderns*—to the break articulated in his 1984 autobiography. Describing the transformations of his life in the late 1960s in a chapter titled "The Black Arts: Politics, Search for a New life," Baraka suggests that he begins at that point to question his reliance on the "set of 'licks' already laid down by Creeley, Olson" (*Autobiography*, 247)—not because of a new distrust of the poets or their work, but because the terms seemed unconsciously inherited, and thus part of a wider white acculturation Baraka began consciously to analyze. Turning to prose as a way to tear himself "away from the 'ready-mades' that imitating Creeley or Olson provided," Baraka began to feel that, in writing *The System of Dante's Hell*, he was beginning to make his language "genuinely mine" (247).[61] But if the Olsonian vocabulary came under scrutiny, Olson's position in *The Maximus Poems* did not: "What fascinated me about Olson was his sense of having dropped out of the U.S." (Baraka, *Autobiography*, 282).[62]

If Baraka's moves to Harlem and Newark might be seen as an attempt to drop out of the bohemian poetry world of the New American poetry, the latter move especially might also be understood as an attempt to establish an exemplary model of place-based activism that, operating at various scales, could be exported to other situations: from the cultural and educational practices of Spirit House and Amina Baraka's Afrikan Free School (which included new recipes, clothing design and production, political theory, childcare, and drama) to the larger domain of city politics (the election of Kenneth Gibson, the first African American mayor of a major northeastern town) and beyond that also state, national, and international politics through institutional structures including CAP (the Congress of African Peoples) and the Modern Black Convention Movement. Insisting on a local base, the goal was both to effect change within an immediate spatial and social framework and to demonstrate to other African American communities how they might achieve something similar.[63] "Baraka led," Komozi Woodard writes, "in the development of a number of institutional 'prototypes' that would serve as models for other branches of CAP. Many leaders of the new branches were trained in Newark at the Political School of Kawaida" (Woodard, 220). After Gibson's victory, Newark was presented in CAP meetings as a "case study for the Black Power experiment" (190).

During this period, in the context of such successes, Baraka began to rethink just how his poetry might operate as a model or example. If "Black People!" goes about situating the incendiary utterance in just the right social situation, considering possible actors in relation to linguistic prompts, Baraka's focus moves in his 1970 book *In Our Terribleness* toward a wider view of these actors' situation. Recoding sociology, planning, and urbanism—the array of disciplines used, in fact, to analyze "the slums"—*In Our Terribleness*, subtitled (*Some elements and meaning in black style*), is a work of experimental urbanism that combines ethnography, political writing, fashion theory, photography by Fundi (Billy Abernathy), and poetry into a kind of political style manual for working-class urban African Americans, reclaiming their bodily postures and clothing styles as modes of radicality. Structured in a circuit that goes "from black to black," as Baraka puts it, the book is designed to "show the significance of how the black man looks and sounds" (*Conversations*, 90–91). To flesh out what Baraka will present as a necessary passage from self-present body to realized family to conscious nation, the book highlights a series of strategic and generative negations that begin with the individual.

> Since there is a "good" we know is bullshit, corny as Lawrence
> Welk On Venus, we will not be that hominy shit. We will be,
> definitely, bad, bad, as a mother-fucker.
>> "That's a bad vine that dude got on."
>> "Damn."
>> "Its a bad dude."

How, then, to secure this badness? Over the course of the 1970s Baraka's answers involve terms other than those proposed in "Black People!": "We should not make any statements we cannot back up, in ways that our community can see and understand. Words are not immediate change. Crackers killed in revolutionary sentences are walking around killing us in the real streets."[64] This statement is from a pamphlet called "Strategy and Tactics of a Pan-African Nationalist Party." It continues:

> We must learn to build houses, and how to acquire the land necessary to build houses. We can write revolutionary slogans in the lobbies of those buildings if we like, as part of our educational programs, or paint pictures of revolutionary heroes on the fronts of those buildings and in the hallways if we want to, but we must learn to build those buildings and get hold of the political power necessary to effect this dynamic, now.
>
> (Woodard, 188)

This project was taken up very concretely beginning in 1972 in Baraka's collaboration with the architect Majenzi Kuumba (Earl Coombs) on a large public housing project, Kawaida Towers. Like Spirit House, Kawaida Towers was conceived not just as an embodiment of a Black Nationalist community but rather as an example that might be studied and reproduced in the future—now on a much larger scale. As Woodard tells us: "Kawaida Towers apartment building was designed with a basement and first-floor plan providing for a 300-seat theater with lighting, projection, and dressing rooms; a lounge, woodshop, hobby shop, day care center, and public kitchen; and rooms for art display, reading, and arts and crafts" (228). The infrastructure for cultural life was thus integrated within what is usually the barebones instrumentality of the housing project. Characteristically, too, cultural life was both expanded to include diet and healthcare, and physically combined within the daily life setting—rather than, say, associated with a district in a city where one goes for entertainment.

If *In Our Terribleness* represented a new attempt to collaborate with African American artists to produce a genre-blurring manual for daily life, Baraka's Kawaida Towers collaboration seeks to frame and institutionalize that daily life within a built environment—to expand the claims of *In Our Terribleness* into a literal space or ground in which the newly conscious bodies could exercise the freedom and stylistic power claimed and theorized in the previous book. The story of this project's unhappy ending has been narrated well by Woodard; it is straight from *The Sopranos*. In short, a Rutgers professor named Stephen Abudato, who covered the groundbreaking for the local television station, asked rhetorically why the project was reflecting African and not Italian cultural heritage, why it was not called Garibaldi Towers (Woodard, 231). Picketing began in November 1972; Mayor Gibson, in whose election Baraka had played an enormous role, now turned against Baraka and the project. The result was that the tax exemption necessary for the project going forward (and standard in all public housing projects) was soon rescinded and the project was dead by 1974. Woodard rightly links the failure of the project to a shift in direction—both by Baraka specifically and by the Black Power Movement more generally: "Faith in the black *will* for self determination was at the heart of the politics of black cultural nationalism and its Black Power experiments during the 1960s and 1970s.... By 1974, however, those political circumstances had changed quite dramatically; that vision was shattered and CAP's faith in its own experience was profoundly shaken" (221–222). Kawaida Towers was for Baraka the kind of period-ending experience enforced for others by May 1968 in France, the Siege of Chicago in 1969, Altamont, or the Manson murders. And yet while those experiences often led left activists to see political subjects as fatally and often eternally conspiring in their own oppression (as Woodard claims many African American activists, too, did), for Baraka the failures of this event instead shook his faith in Black Nationalism and led him into his Third World Marxist period, where we will not be following him now. We will note only that Baraka's shift in analytical frame did not in any way negate his attempt to ground himself in Newark, to *live* the poetics of place; rather, his shift toward Marxism caused him to reconceive place's relation to audience, and to articulate the local now in relation to a global not conceived solely in terms of race.

Where, then, does this leave Baraka in relation to Olsonian fieldwork? Certainly Baraka did not understand his relation to Newark as that of selecting a place whose special history could be used to challenge dominant versions of American history. And yet his attempts to ground and institutionalize performative speech acts in Newark, his project of going about building a physical environment in which claims could be embodied, is, in many ways, a form of what the New Left in the 1960s, including many New American Poets, called "making history." If Baraka distanced himself from SDS's attempts to mobilize working-class African Americans in Newark, even blaming them in part for the 1967 riots, his attempt to ground speech acts within physical and institutional bases in Kawaida Towers bears a close relationship to Tom Hayden's analysis of the riots, which, the SDS activist suggests, "will only disappear when their energy is absorbed into a more decisive and effective form of history-making" (Hayden, 70).[65]

During his Black Nationalist period Baraka's concept of "history making" transformed from a matter of *instigating* revolutionary events (whose outcomes, he came to decide, would amount to "voluntary suicide") to building an institutional environment that might *sustain* them and thus itself *become* a historical event at a larger scale (*Conversations*, 78). Rather than forcing white business owners up against anonymous urban walls, emphasis now turned toward *building Afro-centric walls* that might, so the proposal went, both insulate black businesses and ensure the transmission of African culture. Many, including Baraka himself, have commented critically on both the metaphysical and the bourgeois elements of Black Nationalism.[66] Separated, insulated, and culturally assured, the utopia of Black Nationalist space would nonetheless reproduce the capitalism outside its walls—now in the guise of Dickinson's "cooler host" within (Dickinson, 333, no. 670).[67]

But if this economic narrative is familiar, what is perhaps less so are the relations among space, language, and the social encoded in Baraka's place-based writing of the late 1960s through the 1970s: here, an array of terms from hate speech and racist discourse are retrofitted and recoded—selected precisely because of their history of marginality. These become not ironic designations, but markers of social space that announce at once their symptomatic histories and their recoded presents. Throughout I've been locating a tension between the new meaning that Baraka has wrested performatively from symptomatic speech and his desire to secure this meaning in stable institutional casing. It is certainly true that semantic fixity would freeze the very condition by which Baraka effected change. But rather than see his idea of fabricating institutions as but another instance of that would-be totalitarian impulse lurking under all desires for linguistic fixity, we might instead place our emphasis on Baraka's articulation of constructive and mobile tools that resist any, including his own, desire for containment. While the premium on action never disappears, Baraka nonetheless moves—in his exploration of how to authorize or enable performative change—from revolutionary actions that might emerge from correctly situated utterances alone to a more revolutionary *culture* sustained not by isolated violent actions, but by a recognition of the complex corporeal status of its terrible actors; and yet to secure these bodies in their resistance he finds himself then forced to confront the social, architectural framework that might, in turn, enable the negations on which their "terribleness" relies. At each stage, the project of pronouncing change entails an expansion of the frame, an unarrestable movement from working word to signifying body to encasing building. Seen from this angle, then, Baraka's version of the Black Arts presents less a singular journey into identity politics than a development that is parallel to Snyder's: away from Olsonian cosmology toward countercultural discourse. And it is this transformation, I want to suggest, that came to characterize the most active and energetic afterlife of Olson's concept of place, as poet-fieldworks merged their energies with elements of the New Left.

NOTES

1 Olson, *Charles Olson and Robert Creeley,* 7:70.

2 Merleau-Ponty, 214.

3 Olson's status in the 1960s can be gauged by the fact that he both begins Donald M. Allen's 1960 influential anthology, *The New American Poetry,* and is granted the largest number of pages within it. See Allen.

4 As Andrew Ross puts it (following Olson's reading of Whitehead), Olson's subject is "always in the process of becoming through objectification." And yet even these exterior subjects-become-objects are ultimately atomistic singularities.

5 The formulation is Foucault's, from "What Is an Author?" See Foucault, 114.

6 See Friedel; Frankel; P. Miller.

7 Under a heading that would have annoyed most ethnographically oriented poets— "Trying to Cope with the Indians"—we get, among others, passages from Jesuits Paul Le Jeune, Jacques Marquette, and Maturin le Petit.

8 What the Mead and Bunzel anthology suggests, however, is less a specific point of reference for poets like Olson, Snyder, and Rothenberg—all of whom read widely enough in the field not to need such anthologies—than a broader measure of the increasing popularity (and new historical construal) of anthropology in the United States.

9 The context is a discussion of "space-time." Framing the quote, Olson says, "Let me slug in here a quote I'm holding for a day. Think it's the best damn statement (and very propos what you & I are whacking away at, when we talk abt, narrative or verse, as of now, the push. It is this, of Malinowski, talking abt the Trobriands, specifically, but it doesn't matter (it works, anywhere, including, now, you and me, this instant)" (*Charles Olson and Robert Creeley,* 3:136). For inverse accounts of how Malinowski draws crucially on literature, see Geertz; Ginzburg. Ginzburg argues, for instance, that "[Robert Louis] Stevenson's short story ["The Bottle Imp"] would have given Malinowski not the actual content of his discovery of course [about the kula among the Trobriand Islanders] but the ability to see it, through a leap of imagination, as a whole, as a gestalt, to construct it, as he wrote later, 'very much as the physicist constructs his theory from experimental data' " (85).

10 Nietzsche also argues that "the unhistorical and the historical are necessary in equal measure for the health of an individual, of a people and of a culture" (63).

11 This story with its commentary is cited approvingly in Rothenberg, *Pre-Faces,* 170. Rothenberg himself will publish, among many examples, a poem titled "'Je Est un Auture': Ethnopoetics and the Poet as Other." See Rothenberg, "Je Est."

12 These include Ginsberg's *Indian Journals,* which records his trip from March 1962 to May 1963; Snyder's *Passage Through India,* which documents his 1962 journey with Kyger, who wrote *Big Strange Moon.* John Cage also visited India in 1964 with Merce Cunningham's Dance Company. See Cage, 179.

13 And if these trajectories had been anticipated within the Federal Writers' Project of the late 1930s, still most of this previous work was understood as *preliminary* to actual poetry; it was taken as raw material that would later be shaped into work. Within the postwar *New American Poetry,* emphasis on process allowed for raw materials to play a more primary role: one among many instances of this is the fact that Rothenberg, in *America: A Prophecy,* includes passages from Zora Neale Hurston's work based on ethnographic fieldwork, *Mules and Men.*

14 Other critics, like von Hallberg, see time in *Maximus* as driven, paradoxically, by
    thematic concerns within historiography, like Turner's model of the frontier as a
    primitivizing contact zone: "Olson's militant frontierism gives the Maximus Poems a
    layered structure of reference (Gloucestermen/Norsemen/Tyrians) and a cyclical sense
    of time" (von Hallberg, 126).

15 My account of the functions of Olson's syntax builds off the insights of Byrd; Watten,
    Total Syntax.

16 One could almost read Olson as parodying Nietzsche's claim that one must turn to
    history "for the sake of life and action" (Nietzsche, 59). With Olson, history is brought
    to an especially unruly life as each phrase disrupts consciousness in the present,
    causing it to swerve and change directions, and building an enormous parenthesis that
    is never closed.

17 Olson then comments: "BY GOD, clean that statement up, that is, make its words work
    harder, and I take it you have a REAL PACKAGE (wot dya say, rob't)" (*Charles Olson
    and Robert Creeley*, 3:136).

18 The context of Watten's claim is ["Some Good News"], but his description applies more
    generally.

19 For an account of Olson's relation to Mayan glyphs in the context of cultural history,
    see Belgrade. Belgrade notes, for instance, that as early as 1945, even before his Mexican
    trip, Olson was writing to the anthropologist Ruth Benedict about his project of
    "reaching back down" to alternate origins for the writing practice he was trying to
    establish (87).

20 In fact, the first journal on Olson, which published ten issues from spring 1974 until fall
    1978 was titled *Olson: The Journal of the Charles Olson Archives*.

21 This practice was central to a wide range of poets and critics who turned to Olson in
    the 1970s and early 1980s—some through a desire to focus the terms of postmodernism
    or poststructuralism in contemporary poetry through Olson's example, others through
    interest in a poetics of historiography, and still others through a kind of accumulative
    poetics that could incorporate and link seemingly disparate cultural materials. The
    early monographs include Paul, Christensen, von Hallberg, and Byrd. Interest in a
    poststructuralist and postmodern Olson was developed by Bové, Spanos, and in many
    of the essays that Spanos edited at *Boundary 2* in the 1970s and early 1980s. A historicist
    Olson emerges in Davidson. Olson as a poet of accumulative space can be seen in
    Waldrop and in Watten, *Total Syntax*.

22 In her review of Butterick's *A Guide to the Maximus Poems of Charles Olson*, for
    instance, Perloff notes that rather than just gloss facts and names, Butterick instead
    relies on a great number of Olson's occasional remarks in conversation. The result
    is that the guide "glosses" an array of associations and references that there is "no
    conceivable way any reader who has not been in direct contact with Charles Olson
    could identify" (Perloff, 363).

23 See J. Miller; Gitlin.

24 Flacks writes, "If we define everyday life as constituted by activity relevant to the
    survival, maintenance, and development of self and of one's dependents, we can
    identify another dimension of human activity—action relevant to the survival
    maintenance, and development of society. Let us call such action 'making history'" (2).

25 This is obviously not to suggest that such reflexivity about historical representation is
    unprecedented; in fact, historians like Anthony Grafton have for some time now been
    challenging the long dominant view that modern historiography emerges only in the
    nineteenth century in the wake of Ranke. See Grafton.

26 This is the case made by the Italian proponents of microhistory, for instance. For Levi, "Microhistory has demonstrated the fallibility and incoherence of social context as conventionally defined" and therefore it "accentuates individual lives and events" rather than "wider generalization" (108–109). Levi offers a justification for this focus on the individual and quotidian by arguing that "all social action is seen to be the result of an individual's constant negotiation, manipulation, choices and decisions in the face of a normative reality which, though pervasive, nevertheless offers possibilities for personal interpretations and freedoms" (94).

27 Braudel argued, for instance, that historians could better conceptualize the impact of daily life through his now famous concept of the *longue durée*, which was not to be understood as pure diachronic sequence, but rather as quotidian living patterns that persist diachronically, frames or horizons against which slight transformations occur. For Braudel, these features are integrally tied to place: "Look at the position held by the movement of flocks in the lives of mountain people, the permanence of certain sectors of maritime life, rooted in the favorable conditions wrought by particular coastal configurations, look at the way the sites of cities endure, the persistence of routes and trade, and all the amazing fixity of the geographical setting of civilizations" (31).

28 This talk, which was delivered in an earlier version at the epochal Berkeley Poetry Conference in 1965, was first published in Snyder, *Earth House Hold*. Further references will be to this text. For an account of the 1965 version delivered at Berkeley, see Gray, 215.

29 Describing Alfred Kroeber's education with Boas, his wife, Theodora Kroeber, writes, "Kroeber stood on Parnassus with Boas, who pointed out to him the land below, its shadowed parts and its many sunny places alike virgin to the ethnologist. Virgin but fleeting—this was the urgency and the poetry of Boas' message. Everywhere over the land were virgin languages, brought to their polished and idiosyncratic perfection of grammar and syntax without benefit of a single recording scratch of stylus on papyrus or stone; living languages orally learned and transmitted and about to die with their last speakers.... To the field then! With notebook and pencil, record, record, record! Rescue from historylessness all languages still living, all cultures" (T. Kroeber, 51); Snyder also quotes from Lévi-Strauss's *The Savage Mind* in "Poetry and the Primitive."

30 The thesis, written in 1951, is called *He Who Hunted Birds in His Father's Village: The Dimensions of a Haida Myth*.

31 Snyder also mentions reading "Haida Songs, Kwakiutl mythology—all of those things" (*Real Work*, 58). Boas had also worked on the Kwakiutl.

32 A. Kroeber's *Elements of Culture in Native California* includes versions of the maps later published in *A Handbook of the Indians of California*.

33 See Mead and Bunzel.

34 Mead herself was more classically liberal; she used her anthropological skills to support the war effort in World War II and remained staunchly nationalist. When she did address the youth revolt directly in works like *Culture and Commitment*, her analyses sounded at once conservative and unaware of the new forms social struggle was taking: "I have spoken mainly about the most articulate young people, not those who want to drop out of the whole system and those who want to take the system apart and start over. But the feeling that nothing out of the past is meaningful and workable is very much more pervasive. Among the less articulate it is expressed in such things as the refusal to learn at school, co-operate at work, or follow normal political paths. Perhaps most noncompliance is of this passive kind. But the periodic massing of students behind their more active peers suggests that even passive noncompliance is highly inflammable" (87).

35 See, for instance, Leacock, who writes, "Freeman bluntly argued that Mead's study of Samoa was designed to provide Boas with a 'negative instance'—a case where adolescence was not accompanied by the stress familiar in the West—thereby demonstrating the primacy of cultural factors in social behavior, that the inexperienced and biased Mead found what she was supposed to, but that in fact adolescence in Samoa is very stressful and Samoan culture as a whole is and always has been characterized by highly punitive parenting and a strong emphasis on aggression and violence" (5). Leacock suggests that whereas Mead may have had a somewhat ahistorical cultural determinism, Freeman's critique is based on an even *more* ahistorical biological determinism: one whose social implications are far more conservative, to boot: the "bad savage" replaced with the "good" one.

36 Snyder continues: "For the watershed, cities and dams are ephemeral and of no more account than a boulder that falls in the river or a landslide that temporarily alters the channel. The water will always be there, and it will always find its way down" (*Place*, 229).

37 As far back as 1924, Lucien Febvre had critiqued the French attempts, from the eighteenth century on, to identify the scale of a natural region "in the Procustean bed of 'river basins' rigorously encircled by the 'lines of the water-sheds'" (Febvre, 57).

38 Snyder's more recent work does, however, address questions of urbanism more directly. He suggests, for instance, that "the bioregional movement is not just a rural program: it is as much for the restoration of urban neighborhood life and the greening of the cities" (*Practice*, 43).

39 Both his insistence on a recipe for successful place-based work and his refusal to consider urban areas as places in his early work now seem typical of the first wave of the ecology movement. As Buell notes, "For first-wave ecocriticism, 'environment' effectively meant 'natural environment'" (21).

40 Snyder writes, "In 1969, back for good in California, we drove out to the land and made a family decision to put our life there" (*Place*, 253). Snyder, too, recognized this interest in the elements of the New Left, like the Diggers. In an interview with the Digger, Peter Coyote, Snyder speaks of "this idea of place that Peter and I have been working on for so many years, each in our own way" (Snyder and Coyote).

41 Everson continues: "Jeffers had looked westward to the vast expanse of water, and Kerouac and Ginsberg both responded to the sweep of beyond, but more than any other American poet Snyder has followed that gaze to its conclusion" (141).

42 The phrase "wall of sound" is Watten's in *Total Syntax* (130).

43 This is not to suggest that Ginsberg could only imagine performatives removed from context. For an account of his strategic and contextual use of nonsense in the 1968 antiwar marches in Oakland, see Watten, "The Turn to Language and the 1960s." Rothenberg, too, shares this sense of poetry's fundamental performative power: "In its primary processes—naming and defining—language is itself a poetic act, which becomes remarkable when it revives its latent power to bring about change" (*America, A Prophecy*, 79).

44 Benston argues, for instance, that "the individual's creativity is celebrated insofar as it serves the group. For the black artist there can be no achievement outside the collective aspiration of his audience, and his audience must be black" (42). See also Sollors; Harris.

45 See, by contrast, Baraka's "Notes for a speech."

46 On Totem, see Clay and Phillips, 90–91.

47 Considering in his music criticism the effects of enslavement and enforced diaspora, Baraka suggests, first, that "Africans were not Christians, so their religious music

and the music with which they celebrated the various cultic or ritualistic rites had to undergo a distinct and complete transfer of reference" (*Blues People,* 18); later in this same book he argues that with migrations to the north around the turn of the twentieth century a second displacement occurred: "the provinciality of place, the geographical and social constant within the group, was erased" (97).

48   In the contributors' notes, poets tend to "appear mysteriously out of New Jersey" enough for him to ask in *Yugen 3* "What is happening in Jersey?" Baraka also selected (or was perhaps pointedly given) an untitled work of Ginsberg's in issue 1 with the lines "I longed for a look of secrecy / with open eyes / —intimacies of New Jersey— / holding hands / and kissing golden cheeks." Baraka notes in issue 2 that "Barbara Ellen Moraff appeared mysteriously out of Paterson, N. J." Then, in *Yugen 3,* he notes Ray Bremser's being from the state, and that "Thomas Jackrell appeared mysteriously, also from New Jersey."

49   Though Baraka would take exception to the comparison, one might compare SDS's practice of setting up branches in working-class urban neighborhoods in the late 1960s. For accounts of this, see Gitlin; J. Miller; Sale.

50   Baraka writes, "The arrival uptown, Harlem, can only be summed up by the feelings jumping out of Césaire's *Return to My Native Land* or Fanon's *Wretched of the Earth* or Cabral's *Return to the Source.* The middle-class native intellectual, having outintegrated the most integrated, now plunges headlong back into what he perceives as blackest, native-est. Having dug, finally, how white he has become, now, classically, comes back to his countrymen charged up with the desire to be black, uphold black, etc....a fanatical patriot!" (*Autobiography,* 295).

51   For *In Our Terribleness,* note that the book is not paginated. In an amazing passage from his essay "What Does Nonviolence Mean?" Baraka comes at this problem from the opposite angle, suggesting how the "Negro" operates as a kind of timeless category for Southern whites: "We know what Negroes are, what they want. Governor Wallace, on television, admonishes his black housekeeper warmly, 'Y'all take care of everything, heah?' The old woman smiles, and goes off to take care of his baby. That is the Negro that really exists for him. No other. The smiling convicts raking up leaves in his yards. He waves as he crosses to his car. More real Negroes. He is on his way to the University to make the fake Negroes disappear" (*Home,* 134).

52   Because it is citational, hate speech constitutes subjects "in a chain of significations that exceeds the circuit of self-knowledge. The time of discourse is not the time of the subject" (Butler, 31).

53   Butler claims, however, that no strictly contextual argument can describe the effects of hate speech: "To argue...that the offensive effect of [hate speech] is fully contextual, and that a shift of context can exacerbate or minimize that offensiveness, is still not to give an account of the power of such words are said to exercise" (13).

54   Olson says, in *Reading at Berkeley,* "Every one of those essays, by the way, is published by LeRoi Jones alone, in *Yugen, Floating Bear,* and *Kulchur.* And I sat in Gloucester, suffering, suffering! That the world had been captured by Allen and Peter and Gregory, and in fact their own master (like my Pound), Burroughs. And you know, I didn't want to lose my world. I'm older. I *crave* power" (32).

55   In a 1980 interview with William J. Harris, Baraka says, "I met people like Joel Oppenheimer, then got turned on to people Charles Olson, and you know, Ginsberg connected me up with people like Philip Whalen, Snyder and Kerouac" (Baraka, *Conversations,* 169).

56   *Proprioception,* 2.

57 Baraka goes on to claim that "when politics did emerge, as in Olson's work, I didn't agree with it" (*Conversations*, 108). However, in a later interview, William J. Harris comments to Baraka: "Robert von Hallberg says in a book on Charles Olson that he feels that Olson influenced both you and Ed Dorn toward writing a political poetry," to which Baraka responds, "That could be true. I think he probably did. I know that reading Olson's poetry, which I liked a great deal, and I like the fact that he did take a stance in the real world, that the things he said had to do with some stuff that was happening outside of the poem as well as within the poem" (*Conversations*, 173).

58 For an account of this see Nielsen, 84–96.

59 The typography of *The Maximus Poems* is obviously active and multivalent. Still, Olson seems to evoke maps specifically on pages 150 and 193. On page 438, single lines cross at oblique angles and on page 479 the swirl of handwriting appears.

60 The choice of referring to his project as "Gloucester" rather than Maximus seems to emphasize the intersubjective, social aspect of his project: whereas Maximus is also a singular speaker, Gloucester is both the current city and the imagined or realized version that Maximus would like to bring into being.

61 In the same section Baraka describes the same poets' influence through a jazz metaphor as a matter of a "set of 'licks' already laid down by Creeley, Olson" (*Autobiography*, 247).

62 In *Fieldworks* I have a much longer exploration of how performatives work in Baraka and how he recodes hate speech. See Shaw.

63 See Woodard, especially 114–155. See also Baraka, *Autobiography*, 329–465.

64 Even by 1970 Baraka had been careful to qualify his sense of the possibilities of the political effects of riots, for instance: "Actually violence—if you want to call it that—is little more than a safety valve: it lets off some steam and calms the people down a little. But it's absurd to argue violence is the best strategy in politics. It's crazy to suggest a few poorly-trained and poorly-armed novices could take on the government of the United States, which has one of the biggest armies in the world. Such an act might seem noble, but it amounts to little more than voluntary suicide" (*Conversations*, 78).

65 For blame, see Hayden, 160. For Baraka's critique of his own previous position here, see *Autobiography*, 385.

66 "Many of us have moved to the left since that period. And some of our metaphysics and crass cultural nationalism is embarrassing even to us, but the essence of the work was resistance to imperialism, resistance to white supremacy, even in its flawed form" (Baraka in Neal, xiv). Elsewhere Baraka calls Black Nationalism "essentially a bourgeois ideology" (*Conversations*, 98).

67 Dickinson, "One need not be a chamber."

REFERENCES

Allen, Donald M. *The New American Poetry*. New York: Grove Press, 1960.

Austin, J. L. *How To Do Things With Words*. Ed. J. O. Urmson and Marina Shisà. Cambridge: Harvard University Press, 1975.

Baraka, Amiri. *The Autobiography of LeRoi Jones*. Chicago: Lawrence Hill Books, 1997.

———. *Black Magic Poetry*. Indianapolis: Bobbs-Merrill, 1969.

———. *Blues People*. New York: Morrow, 1963.

———. *Conversations with Amiri Baraka*. Ed. Charlie Reilly. Jackson: University of Mississippi, 1994.

———. *The Dead Lecturer*. New York: Grove, 1964.

———. *Home: Social Essays*. Hopewell, NJ: Ecco, 1998.

———. *In Our Terribleness (Some elements and meaning of black style)*. Indianapolis: Bobbs-
  Merrill, 1970. (not paginated)

———. "Notes for a speech." In *Preface to a Twenty Volume Suicide Note*. New York: Totem/
  Corinth, 1961.

———. "Strategy and Tactics of a Pan-African Nationalist Party." Newark: CFUN, 1971.

Belgrade, Daniel. *The Culture of Spontaneity: Improvisation and the Arts in Postwar
  America*. Chicago: University of Chicago Press, 1998.

Benston, Kimberly W. *Baraka: The Renegade and the Mask*. New Haven: Yale University
  Press, 1976.

Bové, Paul. *Destructive Poetics: Heidegger and Modern American Poetry*. New York:
  Columbia University Press, 1980.

Braudel, Fernand. "History and the Social Sciences: The *Longue Durée*." In *On History*,
  trans. Sarah Matthews. Chicago: University of Chicago Press, 1980.

Buell, Lawrence. *The Future of Environmental Criticism*. Malden, MA: Blackwell, 2005.

Butler, Judith. *Excitable Speech: A Politics of the Performative* New York: Routledge, 1997.

Butterick, George. *A Guide to the Maximus Poems of Charles Olson*. Berkeley: University of
  California Press, 1978.

Byrd, Don. *Charles Olson's Maximus*. Urbana: University of Illinois Press, 1980.

Cage, John. *Empty Words: Writings '73–'78*. Hanover, NH: Wesleyan University Press, 1981.

Christensen, Paul. *Charles Olson: Call Him Ishmael*. Austin: University of Texas Press, 1978.

Clay, Steven, and Rodney Phillips. *A Secret Location on the Lower East Side: Adventures in
  Writing, 1960–1980*. New York: New York Public Library/Granary Books, 1998.

Davidson, Michael. "Charles Olson, Edward Dorn and Historical Method." *ELH* 47, 1
  (1980).

Dickinson, Emily. "One need not be a chamber—to be haunted." In *The Complete Poems of
  Emily Dickinson*, ed. Thomas H. Johnson. Boston: Little Brown, 1960. 333, no. 670.

Eagleton, Terry. "Myth and History in Recent Poetry." In *British Poetry Since 1960*, ed.
  Michael Schmidt and Grevel Lindop. Oxford: Carcanet, 1972

Eliade, Mircea. *The Sacred and the Profane*. Trans. Willard R. Trask. New York: Harcourt,
  1959.

Everson, William. *Archetype West: The Pacific Coast as a Literary Region*. Berkeley: Oyez,
  1976.

Febvre, Lucien. *A Geographical Introduction to History*. Trans. E. G. Mountford and J. H.
  Paxton. London: Kegan, 1966.

Flacks, Richard. *Making History: The Radical Tradition in American Life*. New York:
  Columbia University Press, 1988.

Foucault, Michel. "What Is an Author?" Translated by Josué Harari, in *The Foucault Reader*,
  ed. Paul Rabinow. New York: Pantheon, 1984.

Frankel, Charles, ed. *The Golden Age of American Philosophy*. New York: Braziller, 1960.

Friedel, Frank Burt, ed. *The Golden Age of American History*. New York: Braziller, 1959.

Geertz, Clifford. "Being There: Anthropology and the Scene of Writing." In *Works and Lives:
  The Anthropologist as Author*. Stanford: Stanford University Press, 1988.

Ginsberg, Allen. *Improvised Poetics*. Ed. Mark Robinson. San Francisco: Anonym, 1972.

———. *Indian Journals*. San Francisco: City Lights, 1970.

Ginzburg, Carlo. "Tusitala and His Polish Reader." In *No Island Is an Island: Four Glances at
  English Literature in a World Perspective* (New York: Columbia University Press, 2000).

Gitlin, Todd. *The Sixties: Years of Hope, Days of Rage*. New York: Bantam, 1987.

Grafton, Anthony. *The Footnote*. Cambridge, MA: Harvard University Press, 1997.

Gray, Timothy. *Gary Snyder and the Pacific Rim: Creating Counter Cultural Community*. Iowa City: University of Iowa Press, 2006.

Harris, William J. *The Poetry and Poetics of Amiri Baraka: The Jazz Aesthetic*. Columbia: University of Missouri Press, 1985.

Hayden, Tom. *Reunion: A Memoir*. New York: Random House, 1988.

Howard, Jane. *Margaret Mead: A Life*. New York: Simon and Schuster, 1984.

Hurston, Zora Neale. *Mules and Men*. Philadelphia: J. B. Lippincott, 1935.

Kenner, Hugh. "Classroom Accuracies." In *A Homemade World: The American Modernist Writers*. New York: Knopf, 1975.

Kroeber, Alfred. *Elements of Culture in Native California*. Berkeley: University of California Press, 1922.

——. *A Handbook of the Indians of California*. New York: Dover, 1976.

Kroeber, Theodora. *Alfred Kroeber: A Personal Configuration*. Berkeley: University of California Press, 1970.

Kyger, Joanne. *Big Strange Moon: The Japan and India Journals: 1960–1964*. Berkeley: North Atlantic Books, 2000.

Leacock, Eleanor. "Anthropologists in Search of a Culture: Margaret Mead, Derek Freeman, and All the Rest of Us." In *Confronting the Margaret Mead Legacy*, ed. Lenora Foerstel and Angela Gilliam. Philadelphia: Temple University Press, 1992.

Levi, Giovanni. "On Microhistory." In *New Perspectives on Historical Writing*, ed. Peter Burke. University Park, PA: Penn State University Press, 1992.

Mead, Margaret. *Coming of Age in Samoa*. New York: Morrow, 1928.

——. *Culture and Commitment: A Study of the Generation Gap*. New York: Doubleday, 1970.

——. *Growing Up in New Guinea; A Comparative Study of Primitive Education*. New York: Morrow, 1930.

Mead, Margaret, and Bunzel, Ruth, eds. *The Golden Age of American Anthropology*. New York: Braziller, 1960.

Merleau-Ponty, Maurice. *Phenomenology of Perception*. Trans. Colin Smith. London: Routledge, 2003.

Miller, James. *Democracy Is in the Streets: From Port Huron to the Siege of Chicago*. New York: Touchstone, 1987.

Miller, Perry, ed. *The Golden Age of American Literature*. New York: Braziller, 1959.

Neal, Larry. *Visions of a Liberated Future: Black Arts Movement Writings*. Ed. Michael Schwartz, with commentary by Amiri Baraka et al. New York: Thunder's Mouth Press, 1989.

Nielsen, Aldon Lynn. *Black Chant: Languages of African-American Postmodernism* New York: Cambridge University Press, 1997.

Nietzsche, Friedrich. "On the Uses and Disadvantages of History for Life." In *Untimely Meditations*, trans. R. J. Hollingdale. Cambridge, UK: Cambridge University Press, 1983.

Olson, Charles. *Charles Olson and Robert Creeley: The Complete Correspondence*, Vols. 3, 7. Ed. George F. Butterick. Santa Rosa, CA: Black Sparrow, 1987.

——. *Charles Olson Reading at Berkeley*. Trans. Zoe Brown. San Francisco: Coyote, distributed by City Lights, 1966.

——. *The Maximus Poems of Charles Olson*. Ed. George Butterick. Berkeley: University of California Press, 1983.

——. *Mayan Letters*. Ed. Robert Creeley. London: Jonathan Cape, 1968.

——. *Proprioception*. San Francisco: Four Seasons, 1965.

Perloff, Marjorie. Review of *A Guide to the Maximus Poems*. *The Yearbook of English Studies* 11 (1981): 361–364.

Paul, Sherman. *Olson's Push: Origin, Black Mountain*. Baton Rouge: Louisiana State University Press, 1978.

Ross, Andrew. *The Failure of Modernism: Symptoms of American Poetry*. New York: Columbia University Press, 1986.

Rothenberg, Jerome. "Je Est un Auture." *American Anthropologist* 96, 3 (1994).

———. *Pre-Faces and Other Writings*. New York: New Directions, 1981.

Rothenberg, Jerome, and George Quasha, eds. *America, A Prophecy: A New Reading of American Poetry from Pre-Columbian Times to the Present*. New York: Random House, 1973.

Sale, Kirkpatrick. *SDS*. New York: Vintage, 1973.

Shaw, Lytle. *Fieldworks: From Place to Site in Postwar Poetics*. Tuscaloosa: University of Alabama Press, forthcoming.

Snyder, Gary. *Earth House Hold*. New York: New Directions, 1969.

———. *He Who Hunted Birds in His Father's Village: The Dimensions of a Haida Myth*. Bolinas: Grey Fox Press, 1979.

———. *Myths and Texts*. New York: Totem, 1960.

———. *Passage Through India*. San Francisco: Grey Fox, 1972.

———. *A Place in Space: Ethics, Aesthetics, and Watersheds*. Washington DC: Counterpoint, 1999.

———. *The Practice of the Wild*. New York: Farrar, Straus and Giroux, 1990.

———. *The Real Work: Interviews & Talks, 1964–1979*. Ed. Wm. Scott McLean. New York: New Directions, 1980.

Snyder, Gary, and Peter Coyote. "Freewheeling the Details: A Conversation with Gary Snyder and Peter Coyote." *Poetry Flash* 283 (1999).

Sollors, Werner. *Amiri Baraka/LeRoi Jones: The Quest for a "Populist Modernism."* New York: Columbia University Press, 1978.

Spanos, William V. "Charles Olson and Negative Capability: A Phenomenological Interpretation." *Contemporary Literature* 31, 1 (1980).

Spellman, A. B. "tomorrow the heroes." In *Black Fire: An Anthology of Afro-American Writing*, ed. LeRoi Jones and Larry Neal. New York: Morrow, 1968. 247.

von Hallberg, Robert. *The Scholar's Art*. Cambridge, MA: Harvard University Press, 1978.

Waldrop, Rosmarie. "Charles Olson: Process and Relationship." *Twentieth Century Literature* 23, 4 (1977).

Watten, Barrett. *Total Syntax*. Carbondale: Southern Illinois University Press, 1985.

———. "The Turn to Language and the 1960s." *Critical Inquiry* 29 (2002).

Whalen, Jack, and Richard Flacks. *Beyond the Barricades*. Philadelphia: Temple University Press, 1989.

Woodard, Komozi. *A Nation within A Nation: Amiri Baraka (LeRoi Jones) & Black Power Politics*. Chapel Hill: University of North Carolina Press, 1999.

CHAPTER 21

"DO OUR CHAINS OFFEND YOU?": THE POETRY OF AMERICAN POLITICAL PRISONERS

MARK W. VAN WIENEN

FOR the vast majority of U.S. citizens, the possibility that their nation holds political prisoners is unthinkable. At least until recently, the notion that the United States has a significant tradition of *poetry* by such prisoners has likewise been unthinkable, even to most scholars of American poetry. There are a handful of well-known classics of American nonfiction prose that were written in prison, and they were by authors who might be considered prisoners of conscience, no less—the most prominent works are Henry David Thoreau's "Civil Disobedience" and Martin Luther King Jr.'s "Letter from Birmingham Jail." But there is no clearly defined subgenre of poetry by political prisoners, as there has been in the national literatures of countries in Latin America, Eastern Europe, Africa, the Middle East, and the Far East. *Spirits of the Age: Poets of Conscience*, Mona Adilman's 1989 anthology underwritten by PEN, includes poets from Argentina, Chile, Cuba, Guatemala, Nicaragua, Peru, El Salvador, Uruguay, the USSR, Czechoslovakia, Poland, Malawi, South Africa, Morocco, Egypt, Iran, Iraq, Israel, Pakistan, China, Korea, and Vietnam. None of the poets, however, are from the United States. Apparently, poetry by political prisoners is a phenomenon of other countries, practically anywhere that an authoritarian government judges expressions of dissent to be treasonous. Conversely, it would seem that poetry by political prisoners is impossible in the United States, with our traditions of political pluralism and constitutional guarantees of freedom of speech and assembly ensuring tolerance to dissenting voices.

To be sure, poetry written by more conventional American prisoners has received a certain amount of attention, both in criticism and anthologies of their work. This attention is often offered with a high degree of sympathy for Americans behind bars, sometimes extending to claims that their treatment during incarceration or the conditions leading to their imprisonment have been unjust—arguments, especially centered on issues of race and racism, that raise politicizing questions about the U.S. criminal justice and penal systems.[1] But furthermore, in recent years a number of articles and anthologies have focused on individual American poets, and even groups of poets, who have been imprisoned for reasons that are manifestly political. My interest here is in building especially upon this work on political-prisoner poets as conventionally defined. I conceive of the various kinds of such poets as constituting not isolated, exceptional cases but an American subgenre and a tradition, multifarious but united by a struggle against a common antagonist, a supposedly liberal state that tolerates dissent and diversity only to a certain point. The United States *has*, after all, imprisoned various individuals on openly political grounds, and a number of these have been poets who have produced important work about their prison experiences, poets as prominent as Ezra Pound, Robert Lowell, William Stafford, and Daniel Berrigan. Not merely troublesome individuals but also whole classes of people reckoned to be undesirable—political radicals, Chinese laborers, Japanese Americans—have been imprisoned primarily for their group identity. Lately it has come to light that members of these groups have produced poetry manifesting their collective experience, sometimes in highly improbable circumstances. Ultimately, the signal characteristic of American political imprisonment may be its basis in prejudice not merely according to stated ideological preferences but according to one's group affiliation, especially one's racial group, and this means that a study of American poetry of political imprisonment may offer yet another vantage point for considering racism in the U.S. prison system generally, as well as a site for challenging one of the myths of American exceptionalism: that the United States is specially open to dissenting voices.

We can learn something of the cultural assumptions that have, until recently, prevented recognition of American poems by political prisoners if we examine the few such poems that have long been established as part of the poetry canon—although not recognized as belonging to a subgenre of political-prisoner poetry.[2] The *Pisan Cantos* are at the very heart of one of the most famous and influential of all modern poems, Ezra Pound's *Cantos*. They are also unquestionably the work of a political prisoner, for Pound drafted and revised the eleven cantos while being held in a U.S. military detention center in Pisa, Italy, on charges of high treason. Moreover, the *Pisan Cantos* exhibit two key features that are, as will soon be evident, characteristic of poetry by political prisoners. On the one hand, these cantos offer a general reflection upon the experience of imprisonment, regardless of whether the reasons for imprisonment are political or not. The *Pisan Cantos* describe the brutalization of prison life, sharply evident to Pound because for the first three weeks at Pisa he was held in solitary confinement in a cage that was open to the elements. They also describe the possibilities for generosity and solidarity among prisoners, emblemized, for example, in the sympathy shown Pound by a black fellow inmate who fashioned a writing table out of a packing crate and secreted it to the poet in violation of prison rules: "the greatest is charity / to be found among those who have not observed / regulations" (Pound, *Pisan*, 12). On the other hand, the *Pisan Cantos* take up the righteousness of the poet's special cause—standing firm on the ground that sets the poet arrested on political grounds apart from inmates held or convicted upon more ordinary criminal charges. Hence the very opening of the *Pisan Cantos* laments the mutilation of the bodies of Mussolini and his mistress, and Pound links their tragedy with the misfortune of the common people: "The enormous tragedy of the dream in the peasant's bent shoulders" (3). Other cantos offer appreciative if somewhat cryptic mentions of Hitler as well as Mussolini, reprise Pound's fulminations against usury, and persist in advocating the Mussolini economic system of Social Credit. All this remained, or was even written into, *The Cantos* after Pound learned that other citizens of the Allied powers who had publicly asserted their sympathies for the Axis—William Joyce of Britain (the infamous "Lord Haw Haw"), Vidkun Quisling of Norway, and Pierre Laval of France—had been condemned to hang for treason (Sieburth, xxxv). Pound, like many a political prisoner, was prepared to die for a principle.

But something peculiar happened on Pound's way to the gallows, and that something has everything to do with a peculiar, though longstanding, notion about the role of poetry in American culture and much to do also with why Pound's *Pisan Cantos* have seldom been read as specimens of political-prisoner poetry. The notion, roughly speaking, is that poetry is by its very nature above politics. If Pound was an important poet—and who would be willing to challenge that?—then his offensive political views must be allowed for, explained away, or simply ignored. One option, suggested by Ernest Hemingway, was that Pound's poetry expressing his pro-fascist politics was really not so much poetry as evidence of lunacy (Carpenter, 699). Poetry expressing politics so overtly was, in Hemingway's view, simply not poetry. Hemingway was of course suggesting the very defense that would succeed in court in 1945–1946, when Pound was ruled mentally incapable to stand trial and was turned over to the supervision of psychiatrists at St. Elizabeth's mental hospital (751–752). But Hemingway represented the minority opinion. More typical was the view that Pound's work was so fully the work of idiosyncratic genius that none of his discourse—whether the *Cantos* or his radio broadcasts—could count as political speech. The issue for many literary luminaries, including F. O. Matthiessen, Conrad Aiken, and Archibald MacLeish was the question of Pound's political efficacy (Carpenter, 698–699). If a man talks treason but his speech is too convoluted and arcane for anyone to understand, these reasoned, can he really have committed treason? The psychiatrist principally responsible for the diagnosis that rescued Pound from trial offered a still balder defense, closer to Pound's own self-concept: as Pound's biographer, John Tytell, suggests, Winfred Overholser and his colleagues, fascinated by the exceptional qualities of the man of genius, believed "that Pound was a special case because he was a great poet" (290). In subsequent years, this was the opinion that held sway. When in 1948 T. S. Eliot led a jury of literati in awarding Pound's *Pisan Cantos* with the inaugural award of the Bollingen Prize for the best book of poetry for the year, he and the majority asserted that they were taking their stand for the greatness of American civilization in choosing to separate Pound's poetry from his (and his poem's) politics. The public declaration of the awards committee maintained that "to permit other considerations than that of poetic achievement to sway the decision would destroy the significance of the award and would in principle deny the validity of the objective perception on which any civilized society must rest" (qtd. in Carpenter, 792).

Poetry must be separated rigidly from political statement; conversely, poetry that engages in political utterance may not be poetry at all. Such notions required the most extreme contortions of logic when applied to the poet who had set out to write not only "a poem containing history" (Pound, *ABC*, 46) but also one backing a particular interpretation of economics and social order meant to *change* history. Within this twisted logic, practically the only way to write poetry treating politics is to treat the subject with relentless irony—thus effectively rendering the poetry nonpolitical after all. A case in point can be found in the one other poem about political imprisonment that appears with any regularity in anthologies of American literature or poetry: Robert Lowell's "Memories of West Street and Lepke." Probably not coincidentally, Lowell was on the 1948 Bollingen jury and voted with the Eliot-led majority to honor Pound's *Pisan Cantos* (Axelrod, 122). Certainly Lowell could relate to Pound's predicament, for he too had been imprisoned during World War II for his political views—his conscientious objection. Lowell may well have also learned a lesson from Pound's close shave with the law. To be sure, the difference in tone and philosophy between *The Cantos* and "Memories of West Street and Lepke" lies partly in the very different stances and activities of Pound and Lowell during the war: Whereas Pound had sought to justify the wartime aims of the Italian fascists across the board, Lowell argued more subtly that he could justify the self-defensive actions of the United States after Pearl Harbor but not the disproportionate force adopted by its military by 1943—particularly its indiscriminate bombing of German cities.[3] But the difference between Pound and Lowell may also stem in part from a post-World War II retreat from anything but the most guarded and self-satirizing expressions of political conviction. The speaker in "Memories" is playfully ironic about his postwar domestic circumstances, "Only teaching on Tuesdays, book-worming / in pajamas fresh from the washer each morning," but his is equally ironic about his "seedtime" as "a fire-breathing Catholic C. O.," the convictions of fellow conscientious objectors housed at the West Street penitentiary, and the mobsters and murderers also serving their sentences there (Lowell, 85). The inability of Lowell's postwar speaker to take anything like a principled stand might have its own politically useful function. Lowell's almost existential uncertainty is certainly preferable to the mind-set of mob hit-man "Czar Lepke," who is troubled by "no agonizing reappraisal" as he calmly awaits his execution, and the patriotic decoration and bourgeois comfort in Lepke's cell extends the poet's criticism to the ethical certainties of the nation-state, righteously victorious in World War II and, at the time "Memories" was written, fully launched into the rigidly drawn ideological conflict of the cold war. At the same time, in backtracking upon the young poet's stand, the middle-aged speaker of "Memories of West Street and Lepke" wonders whether any sincere political commitment is possible.

That the *Pisan Cantos* and "Memories of West Street and Lepke" remain the only American poems about political imprisonment that are widely anthologized is not only symptomatic of critical antipathy toward openly political poetry; these poems—and their reception—helped to forge precisely that antipathy. In turn, that these particular expressions of political dissent should be the ones that are anthologized—each, in their own way, so idiosyncratic as to demand they be written off as nonserious—implies that in the United States there must be no substantial tradition of poetry by political prisoners. The United States is just too politically and ideologically capacious, too lenient, for any such tradition to be demanded. It certainly seems that the United States must be uniquely tolerant of dissenting expression— and therefore free of the proscription of political dissent so conducive, elsewhere, to poetry by political prisoners—when Lowell, the religious conscientious objector (CO), is (by his own report) given merely a year in prison for his views, and when Pound the avowed fascist is never made to stand trial, wins poetry prizes, and is eventually released to live out his life in his beloved Italy.

If Pound and Lowell were the sole representatives of American poetry by political prisoners, then I would admit the subject to be only minimally worthy of close examination. Indeed, it would only be minimally worthy of examination if they were in any way *representative* of the kinds of political views and principles typical of American political-prisoner poets. But at various times in its history, the United States has prosecuted individuals for much more dubious reasons than those for which it pursued Pound, and it has imprisoned dissenters for principles more righteous and more clearly articulated than those that resulted in Lowell's detention. Many such imprisonments have taken place during national emergencies, when those in power have been allowed far freer rein to behave like the kind of authoritarian, single-party states that have been most likely to produce a permanent class of political-prisoner poets. Other politically motivated detentions, however, have taken place in peace time, during periods of supposedly progressive government, and even as a matter of systematic persecution against a particular undesirable class of people. These cases raise the question of how much U.S. pluralistic democracy actually does differ from the kinds of authoritarian states that hold political prisoners as a matter of open public policy. It is the poetry written by a number of these prisoners, with causes both better articulated and more substantive ethically and politically, that makes a fuller case for the importance of a subgenre of American poetry by political prisoners.

In the early twentieth century, government policy toward the Industrial Workers of the World (IWW) offered examples of state repression in both peace and wartime. Certainly the IWW presented a likely target, dedicated as it was to the end of capitalism by the general strike and to the replacement of the capitalistic state by a government of, by, and for the working masses. With a lively political culture featuring poetry and song as tools for recruitment and education, the IWW, whose members called themselves "Wobblies," was also a likely source of poetry by political prisoners. The IWW's most famous lyricist, Joe Hill, was also its most famous political prisoner. Historians have never reached consensus about whether Hill actually committed the murder of a Utah grocer for which he was tried, convicted, and executed in 1915, but they do agree that the circumstantial evidence against Hill became compelling only because of the notoriety of the Wobblies and of Hill's irreverent songs (Dubofsky, 307–308, 312). Although Hill was more prolific before his imprisonment than during it—the author of more lyrics than any other songwriter in the union's "little red songbook"—the poems and messages he did send from prison served to confirm his already well-established, defiant persona. In the "Joe Hill Memorial" edition of the IWW songbook published within a few months of his November 1915 execution, alongside a dozen of Hill's songs written before his imprisonment there appeared "Joe Hill's Last Will," which declared their author's solidarity with the penniless unskilled laborer: "My will is easy to decide, / For there is nothing to divide" (*Songs*, 56). Hill's bravado was of a piece with his already widely disseminated final communication to his comrades, "Don't waste any time mourning—ORGANIZE!" as well as with his wishes regarding the deposition of his ashes, which, according to the songbook, were to be divided into forty-seven portions and scattered in all of the states of the union except Utah.

Other IWW poets were, in fact, more prolific writers of verse in prison and about the experience of imprisonment. Working as organizers during the 1912 Lawrence, Massachusetts, textile strike, Arturo Giovannitti and Joseph Ettor were arraigned on murder charges when a police officer fired into a crowd of marching strikers (Dubofsky, 247–248). Giovannitti and Ettor had not been present at the scene; the state of Massachusetts held them liable, apparently, because had they not organized the strikers the police would have had no crowd to shoot upon. During subsequent months of trials and appeals that eventually led to acquittal for both men, Giovannitti wrote many of the poems in his 1914 collection, *Arrows in the Gale*. With far more justification than Pound's *Pisan Cantos*, Giovannitti's book draws abundantly upon the unique authority claimed by the political prisoner. Repeatedly, Giovannitti mobilizes that authority not only to plead his own case but also to challenge the rule of law as practiced in the United States more generally. The key figure in "The Walker," for instance, is a fellow prisoner in the Lawrence jail who is entirely unknown to the poem's speaker, save for the fact that he can be heard pacing his cell ceaselessly. In this, the poet finds a universal fact of imprisonment: whatever crimes the inmate may be charged with, the attention of the walker and all the other two hundred inmates is fastened upon the immediate conditions of imprisonment and the "little key of shining brass" with the power to release one and all (26). Here in prison is the one place where U.S. society appears to support a principle of democratic equality, and here the political-prisoner poet who has made equality his raison d'être outside prison walls begs to differ, bidding his fellow prisoner to cease pacing and contemplate means beyond the narrow channel of jurisprudence, symbolized in the little brass key, to gain release. The poem concludes with merely a hint, though a pointed enough one, at the poet's revolutionary aspiration beyond merely winning a court decision: "Stop, rest, sleep, my brother, for the dawn is well nigh and it is not the key alone that can throw open the gate" (27).

The United States' participation in World War I and the red scare of 1919–1920 that immediately followed were the occasions for the most widespread offenses against freedoms of speech and assembly in modern American history. In the last hundred years, at least, this was the period when the U.S. government came the closest to acting as the kind of police state that has traditionally been the catalyst for political-prisoner poetry. Almost predictably, wartime laws restricting speech were used to target the IWW with all the more ferocity; in September 1917 practically the entire leadership—more than one hundred men—were arrested and charged with sedition. A year later, all were convicted on all charges, beginning a protracted publicity campaign on behalf of the Wobbly political prisoners that ultimately sapped the resources of the organization and virtually eliminated it as a factor in the postwar labor struggle. Somewhat in that spirit, the best-known poet among the political prisoners, Ralph Chaplin, a longtime cartoonist and editor of the union organ *Solidarity* in 1917, split his attention between the kind of pugnacious verse for which the Wobblies were famous and a more lachrymose poetry lamenting the lost youth of the political prisoners and yearning for reunion with his wife and child. The lament for home is a common enough mode in the poetry of political imprisonment, and it is an important one for fostering connection, even empathy, between the political prisoner and readers outside. But Chaplin's case also appears to demonstrate its dangers, for not only in his poetry but in action it was the personal, the individual interest, that finally won out over solidarity with the collective. Chaplin and about half of the other IWW inmates at Leavenworth won clemency from Warren Harding in June 1923, on the condition that they swear loyalty to the government—and thus forswear the revolutionary ambitions that they had proclaimed in poetry, art, and song. When the rest of the IWW prisoners were released before the end of the year without any such conditions, bitter divisions sprang up among the union leadership that were never remedied (Dubofsky, 461–462).

Also caught in the government roundup of suspect persons were activists of the National Woman's Party (NWP), which broke ranks in 1917 with the more mainstream National American Woman's Suffrage Association (NAWSA). While NAWSA pledged to support the war effort and make no special plea for women's rights until after the war, NWP activists determined to continue their public agitation regardless of whether the president and Congress viewed women's suffrage as a reasonable concern in wartime. Late in the year NWP members picketing the White House were arrested, convicted of disturbing the peace, and imprisoned in Occoquan Work House in nearby Virginia. Having already shown their gifts for wit and theatricality in their White House protests—displaying banners, for instance, that quoted the president's lofty wartime rhetoric to delicious ironic effect—the women maintained *esprit de corps* in prison by devising new satirical lyrics to popular tunes.

One such verse, "We Worried Woody-Wood," records the various deprivations of prison life even while proclaiming the protestors' unflinching dedication to their cause, closing with the tongue-in-cheek admonition, "Now, ladies take the hint, / Don't quote the President, / Don't quote the President, as ye stand" (Van Wienen, 203). These and other lines they sang together in triumph when President Woodrow Wilson gave way, ordering their release and soon after announcing his support for women's suffrage as a vital war measure. Wilson recognized a losing battle when his "War for Democracy" was being waged by imprisoning women who merely sought democracy for themselves.

The victory of the NWP was, however, an unusual case. More typical was the government's harsh persecution of COs, most of whom were compelled to go to training camps along with the regular military trainees where they were subjected to abuse intended to coerce them to repudiate their views. One of the rare exceptions, the poet and Harvard graduate Brent Dow Allinson, initially found favorable nonmilitary appointments with the U.S. Fuel Administration and the State Department. But Allinson was not content to lie low, instead publishing poems that critiqued the religious hypocrisy of the U.S. mobilization and thereby maintaining the stance he had taken in 1916, when he had praised the Wilson administration's policy of neutrality. Armed with both the prewar and wartime poems (and ignoring the chronological distinction between the two), the New York *Tribune* denounced the State Department for appointing a "pacifist" to serve in the "storm center." Apparently in response to this pressure, the draft board sent Allinson a notice to report for regular military duty and, when he failed to show (fittingly, the summons that arrived on April 1 had required Allinson to report by March 31), a military tribunal tried Allinson for desertion and sentenced him to a life term, subsequently shortened to fifteen years by presidential decree (Van Wienen, 338–339). His poetic protest was not much affected either by the severity of his treatment in wartime or the government's postwar leniency (for his sentence was commuted and he was released in 1921). Indeed, his best poems, featuring narrative and dialogue, appeared during or after his time at Leavenworth. "The Hero of Vimy (An Incident of the Great War)," published in July 1921 in the newspaper of the American occupation force in Germany, describes an instance of friendly fire killing American soldiers. One of the speakers of the poem, an officer, praises the "splendid" deaths of the soldiers. When the other speaker, a dough-boy wounded in the incident, says he intends to file a report about the artillery's failure, the officer's retort reveals his callousness: " 'It *was* a bloody shame; / But then, we'd men to spare and there's no blame / So far as we're concerned' " (Sanford and Schauffer, 42). A still later poem, "Mr. Bryan Enters Arlington," heaps scorn upon the equivocating William Jennings Bryan, who resigned from his post as secretary of state when the United States went to war but otherwise retired quietly rather than leading the antiwar opposition. Like Joe Hill, Allinson seems to have written little about his experiences in prison, even as he and Hill belong to that subgroup of political-prisoner poets who were prosecuted primarily on account of the offense given by their poetry.

Finding, perhaps, that little was accomplished by the aggressive tactics taken against Joe Hill and Allinson (both of whose cases were major publicity boons for their groups), and recognizing too the potential for co-optation in the leniency shown to Ralph Chaplin and some other IWW members, government policy toward dissenters at the time of World War II was considerably less draconian and more flexible. Lowell's one-year sentence hardly seems a proportionate punishment when his peers were serving in the infantry for the duration of the war, and Lowell seems to have responded with a degree of survivor guilt that makes him wonder why, exactly, he had declared himself an objector to the war in the first place. In the case of the Quakers, Mennonites, and the Church of the Brethren, many of whose young men were harassed cruelly or even killed during World War I, the government and church leaders entered into an agreement that enlisted draft-aged men from these traditional peace churches into a public service corps, doing soil conservation and forestry work at no pay until the end of the war (Stafford, *Down*, 10). It took a meticulous firsthand account from one of the participants in the corps to spell out the ways that the camps remained—for all the cooperation between the churches and the government—an experience of political imprisonment for a group of principled young men stigmatized for their opposition to the government. This was the account provided by William Stafford, first in his memoir, *Down in My Heart*, and subsequently in his poetry.

Stafford's poetry both documents and reflects upon each stage of the CO's surrender to state authority. Describing the departure of a young man for wartime service, the poem "1940" leaves ambiguous his destination and the type of service, thus blurring the line between those conscripted by the government to fight and those detained by the government for their unwillingness to do so. "How It Is" considers essentially the same scene through the consciousness of the conscientious objector, who wants to tell the well-wishing crowds that he, unlike others on the train, is "not a soldier," for they of course cannot tell the difference (118, 119). Other poems recounting the labor camp experience suggest the range and variety of resistance while under military authority. "Objector" describes how "In line at lunch I cross my fork and spoon / to ward off complicity—the ordered life / our leaders have offered us," while at the same time articulating global solidarity with others elsewhere, subject to crueler state authorities and thereby all the more innocent victims of the war that Americans are urged to wage:

> I bow and cross my fork and spoon: somewhere
> other citizens more fearfully bow
> in a place terrorized by their kind of oppressive state.
> Our signs both mean, "You hostages over there
> will never be slaughtered by my act." Our vows
> cross: never to kill and call it fate. (116)

Resistance against violence, both individually and institutionally, became the central theme of Stafford's immensely productive poetic career. As Robert Bly asserted,

"His adult life...began with a right decision," and all of his subsequent life and work threshed out its implications, "fac[ing] decisions about aggression in every poem" and "refus[ing] to adopt instinctive pressures" (Bly, xx).

Various as governmental responses to dissent have been in the wars in which the United States has participated in the twentieth and twenty-first centuries, there is a notable "red" thread running through the national anxieties that fueled the development of the U.S. military industrial complex. This thread links the persecution of the IWW with the indifference of the United States to the Loyalists in the Spanish-American war, and it extends to the McCarthy witch-hunts of communist sympathizers. The McCarthy era produced another generation of political prisoners as well as other forms of harassment, demonization, and economic expropriation through the blacklists. The Hollywood Ten were imprisoned because they not only refused to cooperate with the House Un-American Affairs Committee (HUAC) but also declined to excuse themselves by claiming Fifth Amendment protections— essentially rejecting the premise that their communist affiliations were criminal offenses demanding such protection. One of their number, Alvah Bessie, articulated their point of view in poems written in jail—a few published in radical journals in the fifties, but most unpublished and unknown until their recovery in Cary Nelson's *Revolutionary Memory*. Bessie, a veteran of the Abraham Lincoln Brigade, links explicitly the convictions of the Hollywood Ten with the earlier Loyalist cause in his poem "For My Dead Brother" (Nelson, 185–186). Like other political-prisoner poets, Bessie uses his vantage point both to describe the common experiences of all prisoners and to focus attention upon the particular politicized circumstances that have resulted in his imprisonment, as in the unpublished poem "Technicality":

> It seems, if we had said: "The Fifth Amendment!"
> We would never have passed a day in jail.
>
> Instead we cried: "The Bill of Rights!"
> And we have spent, now, seven months inside.
>
> Euclid would be stunned to learn, today,
> The whole no longer equals its parts.
> (Nelson, 182)

Eventually Alvah and his comrades were released. It amounted to a pyrrhic victory, however, when many former party members—including one of the Hollywood Ten—were induced to cooperate with the HUAC hearings and much of the active Communist Party was driven underground. Moreover, while enthusiasm for the McCarthy witch-hunts waned in the late 1950s, the politically polarizing effects of the undeclared war in Vietnam soon gave fresh life not only to the Left but also to anti-Leftist paranoia.

As if to underscore the diversity of grounds, personal and collective, religious and secular, on which American citizens have resisted their government, proposed radical alternatives to it, and been sent to prison for their trouble, the most prolific of left-leaning poets to be imprisoned during the Vietnam conflict was a Jesuit priest, Daniel Berrigan. Even while Berrigan's reasons for war opposition were deeply religious, he and his colleagues exhibited a dramatic flair, evoking the days when IWW members spoke on street corners in defiance of local antiassembly ordinances and were carried off to jail by scores. In 1968, Berrigan; his brother and fellow priest, Philip; and seven other opponents of the Vietnam War used homemade napalm to burn draft files outside a Catonsville, Maryland, selective services office (Berrigan, *To Dwell*, 220). In 1980, the two Berrigan brothers and six others entered a U.S. missile-launch facility, vandalized two ICBM nose cones, and scattered their own blood thereon (290). In both cases, the protestors were tried and received multiple-year sentences in a federal penitentiary. In the former case, Daniel Berrigan refused to surrender himself to serve his sentence, and for months he was hidden from the FBI by sympathizers; he even gave clandestine interviews that formed the basis for a documentary film (241–252).

Written during his first term in a federal penitentiary, Berrigan's collection *Prison Poems* had its share of antiwar vitriol, as one would expect. But *Prison Poems* is just as often about the quotidian experience and everyday struggle of any and all inmates. Like the works of Giovannitti and other political-prisoner poets, Berrigan's prison poems sometimes draw the critical distinction between the political prisoner and the more conventional convict, but almost always for the purpose of asserting its relative unimportance; the poems see all prisoners as victims of authoritarian and unjust power. The glances of some of the killers with whom Berrigan comes into contact are utterly chilling, the poet observes in "Uncle Sam, You're a Card!" and yet these glances are less threatening than the actions of the government, a still greater mass murderer. In "What Is the Opposite of Charisma?" as well as "Uncle Sam," Berrigan expresses outrage that the convicts at the Danbury, Connecticut, penitentiary are employed in a factory building parts for missiles to be used in Vietnam, so that

> the perfect corporate circle is closed;
> the poor, Blacks and Spanish, for
> slave wages, fashion eradicators
> of their opposite numbers: the poor of southeast
> Asia. To kill off your intractable
> kinsmen, profitably to yourself (68)

Through a number of his poems, Berrigan finds that the view from the penitentiary reveals fundamental injustice and cruelty in the United States, and on grounds going beyond the antiwar cause that Berrigan represents. "One Prisoner Was Driven Mad," particularly, lays its finger on one of its furthest-reaching bases, when it reports the words of a Black Panther who had found in the black-majority world of Danbury prison, "*The nearest thing this nigger ever knew / to being free*" (27). Even as he reports the racist dimensions of the war in Southeast Asia, Berrigan recognizes racism in the United States as a fact underlying the whole of the social and political fabric. "The poor, Blacks and Spanish," are disproportionately represented in prison, and this observation holds the potential to make the majority of prisoners (and perhaps too the greater number of prison poems) essentially political. In this connection, we may observe that even Pound, preoccupied with his own cultural *idée fixé*, did not fail to notice that the vast majority of fellow prisoners at Pisa were black soldiers undergoing rehabilitation for minor offenses (Sieburth, xii–xiii).

Race is, in fact, the central question upon which turns the very scope of the topic of poetry by American political prisoners. This was recognized by Carolyn Forché in her groundbreaking 1993 anthology, *Against Forgetting: Twentieth-Century Poetry of Witness*, which organized its section dedicated to American poets under the heading of "The Struggle for Civil Rights and Civil Liberties." In *Against Forgetting*, Berrigan is joined not only by Robert Oppen and Thomas McGrath, blacklisted in the McCarthy era, but also by a variety of individuals sent to prison for their antiracist agitation or, arguably for some, for their race alone: Muriel Rukeyser, jailed during a protest of the Scottsboro Boys; Quincy Troupe, imprisoned for his part in Civil Rights demonstrations; Amiri Baraka, a cause célèbre in his legal fight against racially motivated weapons-possession charges; and Jimmy Santiago Baca and Etheridge Knight, both sentenced to long terms for their involvement in illicit drug use and trafficking.

The imprisonment of Baca and Knight, particularly, raises basic questions about the degree to which the incarceration of drug addicts in the United States is a racially inscribed category of political imprisonment. The Mexican American poet Raúl Salinas, who wrote *Un Trip through the Mind Jail* while in prison serving hard time for drug crimes, recounts that imprisonment for drug offenses might well be the *best* outcome for young males coming of age in the environment of his barrio—with violent crime or death being about as likely. A list recounting the fates of his peers concludes with

> Ratón: 20 years for a matchbox of weed. Is that cold?
> No lawyer   no jury   no trial   I'm guilty
>   Aren't we all guilty? (59)

With the indifference of the court system to Ratón's situation followed by a generic assumption of guilt for anyone in the neighborhood—including but not limited to the "I" of Salinas himself—the question concluding this stanza both covers the Hispanic community as a whole and points outward to the guilt of the wider society, with its mania of criminalizing drug use and of accepting, even embracing, the consequence of a wildly disproportionate number of Hispanics and blacks being imprisoned. A Latina inmate and poet, Lorri Martínez, describes drug-related crime similarly, as a particular site for racial profiling and therefore social control of undesirable minorities: "Remember—technically, / Im doing time / because I used to be / a drug addict" (8). Citing this passage, Barbara Harlow theorizes that drug crime is just one of many possible locations for promulgating such control; indeed, she offers that "the calculated distinction between criminal offenses and political activities is one that is manipulated by the dominant ideology precisely in order to maintain its control over borders of dissent" (162). Particularly in the U.S. South through much of the twentieth century, the routine assignment of long prison terms to black defendants accused of minor crimes was manifestly calculated to manage the black population and to provide the lucrative prison-contract system with fresh labor to build railroads and public works. Such recognition might bring the Southern tradition of prison blues into the orbit of poetry by political prisoners.[4]

Even if some version of the distinction between criminal and political offenses is accepted, racist discrimination within the U.S. penal system may have the effect of politicizing the experience of incarceration. This is the testimony of many black and Hispanic poets in prison communities. The outlook of the poets in *Betcha Ain't: Poems from Attica*, many of whom wrote their first poems in a workshop held following the catastrophe at the Attica penitentiary, ranges from stoic to despairing to utterly defiant. Daniel Brown's "Tears" offers equivocally, "If tears could destroy, / Our plight would cease," but Robert Sims offers a forthright definition of what "Revolution Is": "Black brother— / revolution is loving you,— / for a change [....] Then–killing them, / not you,— / for a change" (Tisdale, 18, 21). Writing during the same turbulent period of institutional violence and prisoner agitation, Etheridge Knight makes no distinction whatsoever between the political prisoner and the regular inmate, urging instead the necessity of prisoner solidarity and resistance to authority. In his well-known "Hard Rock Returns to Prison from the Hospital for the Criminally Insane," there is no reference at all as to whether the title character's imprisonment is just or unjust; it is just a shame that aggressive psychiatric treatment has tamed Hard Rock and that the other black prisoners have thus lost their champion, who had formerly dared to act out the aggression and defiance they all felt (*Poems*, 11–12).

Of course, poetry recording or protesting against the inhumanity of prison conditions—and thereby to a degree raising fundamental, politicized questions about U.S. prisons and prisoners of all kinds—can be and has been written by white inmates as well as by inmates of color. Collections including poetry in this vein were often facilitated by sympathetic prison educators promoting the therapeutic and rehabilitative possibilities of poetry. But whether written by inmates who are white, black, or brown, whether more or less aggressively political, it is notable that such collections proliferated in the 1970s, the era in which black and Hispanic movements within inmate communities led the way in articulating openly the injustices of the U.S. penal system.[5] This leadership is not only openly asserted in *Black Voices from Prison* (1970), *Who Took the Weight? Black Voices from Norfolk Prison* (1972), and *Imprisoned in America: Prison Communications 1776 to Attica* (1973) but is also suggested in poems included in *Men in Exile: An Anthology of Creative Writing by Inmates of the Oregon State Penitentiary* (1973), *Over the Wall* (1974), and *From the Bottom: Writings from Wisconsin State Prison* (1978).[6] Carolyn Forché's identification of racism as the very fulcrum of political imprisonment in the United States may be seen, then, as not only the reflection of a reality running back through the twentieth century and beyond, but also as a response to explicit protests raised by prison poets themselves.

Meanwhile, throughout the same decades that brought poetic and scholarly recognition to black and Hispanic inmates, scholars documenting Asian American communities were bringing to light instances of their political imprisonment—and poetry documenting that imprisonment—dating from the first half of the twentieth century. In 1976 Mitsuye Yamada's *Camp Notes* used poetry to testify to the inhumanity of the U.S. military detention of people of Japanese descent during World War II. Yamada offers for the Japanese American detainees' experience what William Stafford provides for the CO's experience, as she covers the narrative arc from peacetime life, through the process of being gathered in temporary stockades, transported to more permanent camps, in order to endure a dreary existence there, and finally returned awkwardly, painfully, to "normal" life. Yamada's poetry, like Stafford's, is retrospective; it took many years for her to overcome her shame about detention and to recognize it as worthy of public, poetic treatment. Although the racist treatment of Japanese Americans during the war was markedly different from the racist conditions underpinning black or Hispanic overrepresentation in U.S. penitentiaries, Yamada describes the surfacing of her memories of the internment as catalyzed by an encounter with an African American man: in "Thirty Years Under," the testimony of a black man who had found "nothing more / humiliating / more than beatings / more than curses / than being spat on // like a dog" triggers Yamada's own memory of being spat upon when finally, after the war, she had been released and tried to start her life anew (32). Essentially, the experience of racist hatred was universal enough that the recollection of a black man could unlock memories of Yamada's experience in the camps—and give her license to express them.

It took Violet Kazue de Christoforo's *May Sky: There Is Always Tomorrow*, published in 1997, to bring to a wide audience the recognition that many Japanese American poets had written a large quantity of very high-quality poetry *during* the time of their incarceration. Prior to the war, both men and women had been active in Japanese-language haiku clubs; they continued in this activity through the war, in defiance of the harsh conditions of their imprisonment, and with a corresponding adaptation of the venerable form to those conditions. Working in a form only recently modernized to include themes other than the serenity of nature (de Christoforo, 23), those poets who continued to write haiku in the camps tend to register their opposition obliquely. Indeed, the resistance of certain poets seems to lie in taking the materials of their changed life conditions and making them into poems just as serene as any earlier haiku. Soichi Kanow hints just delicately at the inadequacy of the camp buildings: "People sitting / in the shade / under the narrow eaves" (de Christoforo, 127). But Hisao Fukuda's productions celebrating kinship with Italian prisoners of war, in spite of vast cultural and linguistic differences, amount to dangerously subversive fraternizing with the enemy ("Both sides laughing / not understanding the language / face wet with snow" [119]). The ironies gained by the counterpointing of the natural world with the arbitrarily and cruelly imposed military order turns bitter in Kyotaro Komuro's production: "Between ceiling slats / and thick electric wires / dawn comes through unhindered" (103).

By the time *May Sky* was published, other remarkable scholarly work had turned up a still more improbable source of poetry showing that the political imprisonment of people of Asian descent was not a matter only of wartime emergencies. Ever since the Chinese Exclusion Act of 1882, the great majority of Chinese emigrants who had not previously resided in the United States were forbidden to enter. Beginning in 1910, the primary facility through which claims of prior residency were adjudicated was a detention center on Angel Island in San Francisco Bay. For the next thirty years, while the entrance of immigrants from other countries was handled swiftly at the San Francisco docks, would-be Chinese entrants were forced to wait for weeks and sometimes months before their cases were settled (Lai, Lim, and Yung 17, 20). For many, Angel Island was the only U.S. soil they ever touched before being returned to China. Meanwhile, the detainees began to cover the walls of the Angel Island dormitories by carving into them lines upon lines of Chinese characters; these were not just random graffiti but were many short poems in the classical Chinese style, expressing the detainees' various moods and attitudes (25). Recovered and translated by Him Mark Lai, Genny Lim, and Judy Yung, and published for the first time for a significant American audience in the 1991 collection *Island*, the mostly anonymous poems represent a collective and collaborative effort to make sense of a system of arbitrary, discriminatory detention directed primarily at Chinese laborers—essentially, political imprisonment based upon group characteristics of race and class.

The Angel Island poems range from almost good-natured stoicism to revenge fantasy. The former attitude was possible, in part, because some detainees had some foundation for hope that they would be admitted and, in part, because the secrecy of the screening policy bred uncertainty. One of the few authors to identify himself, Xu, takes issue with the complaints of his fellow detainees, finding instead in their plight a cause for heroism altogether in keeping with Chinese traditions: "Why should one complain if he is detained and imprisoned here? / From ancient times, heroes often were the first ones to face adversity" (62). Other poets explained their situation by reference to sociopolitical factors—"For what reason must I sit in jail? / It is only because my country is weak and my family poor" —which, of course, just underscores the degree to which the detention regimen imposed by the United States amounts to a form of political imprisonment, not at all oriented to individual misdeeds but to the indiscriminate control of a certain undesired group. Responding to these circumstances, other poems seethe with rage: "If there comes a day when I will have attained my ambition and become successful, / I will certainly behead the barbarians and spare not a single blade of grass" (84). Such sentiments are of a piece with the poets affiliated with the Black Panthers, whose ranks in Attica only grew after the black prisoners' uprising there was crushed with disproportionate, murderous force.

Are there further discoveries to be made of poetry by American political prisoners? Unfortunately, both our evolving understanding of the forms that political oppression can take and has taken, and the earnest wish that those who hold power would like their misdeeds to be hidden—certainly not addressed openly in poetry—mean that there are likely to be fresh discoveries such as the poetry at Angel Island or the Japanese American concentration-camp haiku. And will the further discoveries of poetry by political prisoners be made of past eras only? Again, the example of previous poetry makes it likely that even now there are political prisoners being held by the United States, that even now some of them are writing poetry, and that even now our government is seeking to suppress that poetry. A specific case can be made from the United States' ongoing, open-ended war against Islamic radicals, whose more shadowy manifestations are the undisclosed third-country sites of extreme rendition and its more public face is the prison on U.S. soil at Guantánamo Bay, Cuba.[7] Like the Chinese detainees on Angel Island, the prisoners of war at Guantánamo Bay stretch the limits of just who might count as an "American" poet. The majority of the Chinese kept for months or even years on Angel Island never became U.S. citizens; they never set foot on any American soil *except for* Angel Island. None of the Guantánamo Bay prisoners have any chance at all of becoming U.S. citizens (even if any should wish it), and most are likely never to set foot on any U.S. soil except for patches enclosed by tall fences and razor concertina wire. Unquestionably, though, both groups represent classes of individuals who are being confined for political reasons by the U.S. government; both testify to the arbitrary and unjust application of power by that government; and both include individuals whose prison time has radicalized them. They are voices that say much about the condition of U.S. political and legal culture, even if they do so from the position of extreme outsiders.

While facing an apparently interminable political detention, the Guantánamo Bay prisoners have been writing poetry, doing so with a sense of community and of collective purpose akin to the Angel Island poets and the Japanese American haiku writers in the detention camps. Like these poets, appreciation of the Guantánamo Bay poetry as poetry is hindered by the fact that they are available to English-speaking audiences only when translated from a language not widely spoken in the United States. In fact, the poems are unavailable to anyone in the outside world in their original language, published solely in English translation in a slim volume edited by the lawyer of a number of the detainees, Marc Falkoff. This is a consequence of the U.S. government's extreme paranoia about how the poems could be used to transmit hidden messages to the prisoners' brothers and sisters in arms: any poems to be translated had to be approved by U.S. officials, and the translations themselves were done by government employees, the originals being withheld from the review of any unofficial person (Falkoff, 4–5). Written both by detainees with little previous experience composing poetry and by detainees widely recognized as poets in their home countries, the poems arise from cultures in which poetry is widely accepted as a mode of political and social commentary (F. Miller, 8–9, 12). One of the prisoner-poets' tamer themes, very common, is resignation, that this imprisonment like all things must be part of the will of Allah and therefore must be patiently borne. The very stoicism of these poems, however, underscores cultural differences with the West and professes a faith in superior moral authority. Another smaller group of poems describe the physical deprivations of the prison camp at Guantánamo, similar to a number of the concentration-camp haiku. One of these is "Cup Poem I," composed by Shaikh Abdurraheem Muslim Dost and so titled because it had originally been inscribed upon a styrofoam cup, a recording medium forced into use because at the time writing implements and paper were being denied the prisoners: "What kind of spring is this, / Where there are no flowers and / The air is filled with a miserable smell?" (Falkoff, 3, 35). A larger number of the poems are directly confrontational. "Death Poem" by Jumah al Dossari wishes for martyrdom for reasons that are pointedly political:

> Take my blood.
> Take my death shroud and
> The remnants of my body.
> Take photographs of my corpse at the grave, lonely.
>
> Send them to the world,
> To the judges and
> To the people of conscience,
> Send them to the principled men and the fair-minded. (32)

The profound situational irony is that Dossari and the other Guantánamo inmates have not gotten, and have little likelihood of getting any time soon, the satisfaction of being judged in any court of law, let alone gaining an audience of fair and principled people. Judging from the limitations placed upon the translation and transmission of the Guantánamo poems, we may conclude that it is our government's determination precisely to prevent, so far as possible, any such audience.

Still, thanks to the work of Falkoff, the Guantánamo poets have some opportunity to reach a broader readership. It is unclear how many of the poems collected by him were written with any hope they would be read by anyone other than fellow inmates: invocations to Allah and verses offering encouragement and advice, both common modes, certainly seem to assume the narrower audience. But the number of poems that inveigh against the injustice of the Guantánamo detention is considerable, and these poems play at least as much to an outside audience as to an inside one. The Arabic-literature scholar Flagg Miller finds in the poems a degree of secularism that suggests awareness of a Western, non-Islamic audience, while noting that models for poems focusing upon secular ideals of justice and equality are available in the anthems of socialist-inspired political leaders active in many Islamic countries in the 1950s and 1960s (13). Such a tradition constitutes an improbable yet tangible link between the Guantánamo poets and Leftist political-prisoner poets in the United States, even as the poets' religious fervor—evident in many poems—recalls the importance of religious commitment for a number of the strongest dissenting voices that have cried out from other American prisons.

At their most powerful, the Guantánamo poets combine depiction of the prison's dehumanizing physical conditions with poetic expression revealing the persistence of human imagination. "Ode to the Sea" by Ibrahim Al Rubaish sometimes describes the ways that the ocean represents a force greater than, and indifferent to, the military and political power of the United States—and this becomes a source of comfort.

Then again, the poem also casts the sea as a villain, fitting insofar as the peninsular situation of the Guantánamo Bay camp uses the Caribbean Sea as an outermost barrier on three sides. The differing responses are recorded in the sharp juxtapositions of a number of couplets, such as: "If the wind enrages you, your injustice is obvious. / If the wind silences you, there is just the ebb and flow." The next couplet follows up on these suggestions about the sea's mood, initially playing with the absurd implications of the poem's pathetic fallacy, then offering a no-nonsense, deadpan explanation of the detainees' presence at Guantánamo: "O Sea, do our chains offend you? / It is only under compulsion that we daily come and go" (65). Here and elsewhere in the poem, the "Sea" becomes not merely itself, a body of water that is both allied with the U.S. military and neutral in the conflict between the United States and the inmates, but also a stand-in for the poem's readers, largely inscrutable to the poet but holding the power to ally themselves with the military authority at Guantánamo (merely by remaining neutral or indifferent) or to respond constructively and courageously to the poet's call for justice. In this second, figurative frame of reference, the interrogative is particularly telling, as it indicates the degree to which the fact of incarceration itself demonizes the prisoner: even if the reader does not actually, actively assume the prisoner's guilt, the prisoner is as good as guilty so long as the U.S. military's power to do whatever it pleases remains in effect.

As the state has striven to do throughout the history of political imprisonment—in the United States and elsewhere—the simple, material power to imprison obliterates the distinction between the justly tried and convicted criminal and the unjustly tried, or entirely untried, victim of political force. But as U.S. political-prisoner poets have also repeatedly testified, the state's disregard for this distinction raises the question of whether *any* convicts are justly tried, and hence whether *all* inmates may in fact be political prisoners. In this sense, "our chains" *should* "offend you," for indifference about the Guantánamo detainees is tantamount to indifference about the rule of law. It is this fundamental question that brings together all of the various American poets of political imprisonment into an ongoing tradition, for not only the detention without trial of the Guantánamo inmates but also the nontrial of Ezra Pound, the legal persecution of political dissenters, and the mass incarceration of blacks and Hispanics, Chinese immigrants, and Japanese Americans point to the degree to which our society—like more nakedly oppressive regimes the world over—is organized, after all, by force and compulsion rather than by free association and genuine equality before the law.

NOTES

1 For some of the most recent work in the field, see D. Quentin Miller and Olguín.
2 Aside from Forché's anthology, discussed later in the chapter, there are still just two anthologies widely available that help to make visible the multiple occasions on which the United States has imprisoned individuals for political reasons: the *Heath Anthology of American Literature* (ed. Paul Lauter et al.) and the *Oxford Modern American Poetry*

Anthology (ed. Cary Nelson).The former anthology includes poems written by Chinese emigrants detained at Angel Island (vol. D) and a "sheaf" of prison poetry featuring racial minority poets (vol. E). The latter anthology reprints works by some of the Angel Island poets and of the Japanese American haiku artists in the World War II camps.

3 Metres, "Confusing," 665–666. Metres describes "Memories of West Street and Lepke" as a "containment poem," reading its confessionalism as a specimen of a 1950s political culture rendered spineless by the HUAC investigations. Metres offers a number of other points of interest: first, that Lowell's almost entirely unknown poetry of the 1940s reflects a substantial antiwar critique, almost entirely lacking in "Memories" (667–668); second, that during his imprisonment at the Danbury, Connecticut, penitentiary (the same prison where Daniel Berrigan would serve in the 1970s), Lowell remained on the sidelines when other COs carried on a campaign for desegregation of the prison (680–682); third, that the activism of other COs in prison, notably including Lowell Naeve, included producing a journal that published poetry, among other materials (682–683).

4 For a selection of prison blues as well as a brief account of the convict-lease system of labor that provided monetary incentives for sentencing blacks to maximum sentences for minor crimes, see Garron and Tomko, 177–198.

5 On the therapeutic uses of poetry in prison, see Rothman. For the role of imprisoned black writers, including several poets, in political consciousness-raising, see Bernstein. For a wide-ranging examination of the politics and culture of Hispanic prisoner literature, including several poets, see Olguín.

6 For the anthologies focusing explicitly on black poets' leadership, see Knight, Norfolk Prison Brothers, and Philip; for those in which such leadership is more implicit, see Norris, Andrews and Dickens, and Trudell.

7 Metres, "Remaking/Unmaking," examines efforts by artists and poets to represent constructively the voices (as well as the tortured bodies) of the Abu Ghraib prisoners, and these projects clearly parallel the efforts of Falkoff to assist the Guantánamo Bay poets to speak in their own (translated) voices. Metres also offers his own poetic collage drawn from the testimony of both the Abu Ghraib torturers and their victims (plus passages from the book of Genesis)—another kind of addition to the corpus of political-prisoner poetry, and one that uniquely dramatizes the collaborations of political prisoners with bibliographers, editors, and other kinds of amanuenses that are absolutely vital to the subgenre's existence.

REFERENCES

Adilman, Mona, ed. *Spirits of the Age: Poets of Conscience.* Kingston, Ontario: Quarry Press, 1989.

Andrews, Frank Earl, and Albert Dickens, eds. *Over the Wall.* New York: Pyramid, 1974.

Axelrod, Steven Gould. *Robert Lowell: Life and Art.* Princeton: Princeton University Press, 1978.

Bernstein, Lee. "Prison Writers and the Black Arts Movement." In *New Thoughts on the Black Arts Movement,* ed. Lisa Gail Collins and Margo Natalie Crawford. New Brunswick, NJ: Rutgers University Press, 2006. 297–316.

Berrigan, Daniel. *Prison Poems.* Greensboro, NC: Unicorn Press, 1973.

———. *To Dwell in Peace: An Autobiography.* San Francisco: Harper and Row, 1987.

Bly, Robert. "Introduction: William Stafford and the Golden Thread." In *The Darkness Around Us Is Deep: Selected Poems of William Stafford*, ed. Robert Bly. New York: HarperPerennial, 1993. vii–xxii.

Carpenter, Humphrey. *A Serious Character: The Life of Ezra Pound*. Boston: Houghton Mifflin, 1988.

Chaplin, Ralph. *Bars and Shadows: The Prison Poems of Ralph Chaplin*. New York: Leonard, 1922.

De Christoforo, Violet Kazue, ed. *May Sky: There Is Always Tomorrow: An Anthology of Japanese American Concentration Camp Kaiko Haiku*. Los Angeles: Sun and Moon, 1997.

Dubofsky, Melvin. *We Shall Be All: A History of the Industrial Workers of the World*. Chicago: Quadrangle Books, 1969.

Falkoff, Mark, ed. *Poems from Guantánamo: The Detainees Speak*. Iowa City: University of Iowa Press, 2007.

Forché, Carolyn, ed. *Against Forgetting: Twentieth-Century Poetry of Witness*. New York: W. W. Norton, 1993.

Garron, Paul, and Gene Tomko, eds. *What's the Use of Walking if There's a Freight Train Going Your Way?* Chicago: Kerr, 2006.

Giovannitti, Arturo. *Arrows in the Gale*. Riverside, CT: Hillacre Bookhouse, 1914.

Harlow, Barbara. "Sites of Struggle: Immigration, Deportation, Prison, and Exile." In *Criticism in the Borderlands: Studies in Chicano Literature, Culture, and Ideology*, ed. Héctor Calderón and José David Saldívar. Durham, NC: Duke University Press, 1991. 149–163.

Knight, Etheridge, ed. *Black Voices from Prison*. New York: Pathfinder, 1970.

——. *Poems from Prison*. Detroit, MI: Broadside, 1968.

Lai, Him Mark, Genny Lim, and Judy Yung, eds. *Island: Poetry and History of Chinese Immigrants on Angel Island, 1910–1940*. Seattle: University of Washington Press, 1991.

Lauter, Paul, et al., eds. *Heath Anthology of American Literature*, 5 vols., 6th ed. Boston: Wadsworth, Cengage Learning, 2010

Lowell, Robert. *Life Studies*. New York: Farrar, Straus and Cudahy, 1959.

Martínez, Lorri. *Where Eagles Fall*. N.p.: Author, 1982.

Metres, Phillip. "Confusing a Naive Robert Lowell and Lowell Naeve: 'Lost Connections' in 1940s War Resistance at West Street Jail and Danbury Prison." *Contemporary Literature* 41 (2000): 661–692.

——. "Remaking/Unmaking: Abu Ghraib and Poetry." *PMLA* 123 (2008): 1596–1610.

Miller, D. Quentin, ed. *Prose and Cons: Essays on Prison Literature in the United States*. Jefferson, NC: McFarland, 2005.

Miller, Flagg. "Forms of Suffering in Muslim Prison Poetry." In *Poems from Guantánamo: The Detainees Speak*, ed. Mark Falkoff. Iowa City: University of Iowa Press, 2007. 7–16.

Nelson, Cary. *Anthology of Modern American Poetry*. New York: Oxford University Press, 2000.

——. *Revolutionary Memory: Recovering the Poetry of the American Left*. New York: Routledge, 2001.

Norfolk Prison Brothers. *Who Took the Weight? Black Voices from Norfolk Prison*. Boston, MA: Little, Brown, 1972.

Norris, Faith G., and Sharon J. Springer, eds. *Men in Exile: An Anthology of Creative Writing by Inmates of the Oregon State Penitentiary*. Corvallis: Oregon State University Press, 1973.

Olguín, B. V. *La Pinta: Chicana/o Prisoner Literature, Culture, and Politics*. Austin: University of Texas Press, 2010.

Philip, Cynthia Owen. *Imprisoned in America: Prison Communications 1776 to Attica*.
    New York: Harper and Row, 1973.
Pound, Ezra. *ABC of Reading*. 1934. New York: New Directions, 1960.
———. *The Pisan Cantos*. Ed. Richard Sieburth. 1948. New York: New Directions, 2003.
Rothman, Juliet C. "Prison Poetry: A Medium for Growth and Change." *Journal of Poetry
    Therapy* 10 (1997): 149–158.
Salinas, Raúl. *Un Trip through the Mind Jail*. Houston, TX: Arte Público, 1999.
Sanford, A. P., and Robert Haven Schauffer, eds. *Armistice Day*. New York: Dodd, Mead
    and Company, 1928.
Sieburth, Richard. "Introduction." In *The Pisan Cantos* by Ezra Pound. New York:
    New Directions, 2003. ix–xliii.
Songs of the Workers on the Road, in the Jungles and in the Shops. 9th ed. Cleveland:
    IWW Publishing Bureau, 1916.
Stafford, William. *The Darkness Around Us Is Deep: Selected Poems of William Stafford*. Ed.
    Robert Bly. New York: HarperPerennial, 1993.
———. *Down in My Heart*. 1947. Swarthmore, PA: Bench, 1985.
Tisdale, Celes, ed. *Betcha Ain't: Poems from Attica*. Detroit, MI: Broadside, 1973.
Trudell, Dennis, ed. *From the Bottom: Writings from Wisconsin State Prison*. Madison, WI:
    Bottom Press, 1978.
Tytell, John. *Ezra Pound: The Solitary Volcano*. New York: Doubleday, 1987.
Van Wienen, Mark, ed. *Rendezvous with Death: American Poems of the Great War*. Urbana:
    University of Illinois Press, 2003.
Yamada, Mitsuye. *Camp Notes and Other Poems*. Latham, NY: Kitchen Table, 1976. 19.

CHAPTER 22

DISABILITY POETICS

MICHAEL DAVIDSON

"A WORD MADE FLESH"

AMERICA's first published book of poems, Anne Bradstreet's *The Tenth Muse Lately Sprung Up in America,* was printed anonymously in England by her brother-in-law, John Woodbridge, in 1650. In his preface, Woodbridge uses metaphors of pregnancy and parturition to describe these poems written by a woman "honored and esteemed where she lives," and he speaks of his own midwife efforts "to force a woman's birth" by publishing this collection (qtd. in Martin, 27). In her vexed response to the book's appearance (it was published without her knowledge), Bradstreet transforms Woodbridge's metaphor of child-bearing into one of child-rearing:

> I wash'd thy face, but more defects I saw,
> And rubbing off a spot, still made a flaw,
> I stretcht thy joints to make thee even feet,
> Yet still thou run'st more hobbling than is meet (40)

Bradstreet's comparison of prosodic and printing defects to an unruly, disabled child is not the first time that poetry and disability have been conjoined.[1] Disability has often provided literature with metaphors for moral failing (Oedipus), megalomania (Ahab, Richard III), or redemption (Quasimodo, Tiny Tim). The mythological image of the poet as inspired singer is accompanied by a number of disabled variants—the mad jeremiadist, blind bard, crippled soothsayer, and wise fool—by which poetry is celebrated (or caricatured). And beyond the rhetorical level, literary history is full of references to poets who are blind (Homer, Milton), physically disfigured (Alexander Pope, Samuel Johnson, Jonathan Swift) or who live with cognitive disorders (John Clare, Gerard de Nerval), neurological diseases (Larry Eigner, Josephine Miles), and chronic diseases (Audre Lorde, Marilyn Hacker). The Romantics envisioned themselves as "poets [who] begin in gladness: / But thereof come in the end despondency and madness," a characterization of romantic agony as operative for the age of Wordsworth as for postwar confessionalists like Robert Lowell and Anne Sexton. While poets are probably no more disabled than other individuals, they have often been figured (and, indeed, figure themselves) as courting extreme physical and mental states necessary to achieve a level of inspiration.

Bradstreet's reference to her poem's "uneven feet" testifies to the close linkage between ideas of poetic form and ideals of embodiment. "The poet is ... the man without impediment.... He is the true and only doctor," Emerson says in "The Poet," and he regards those without poetry as "mutes, who cannot report the conversation they have had with nature" (224, 225, 223). English prosody, adapted from classical quantitative meters, is based on a foot metric that marks the number of stressed and unstressed syllables in a line. The most prevalent foot, the iamb, is thought to derive from a Greek word meaning "cripple," due to its pairing of an unstressed and stressed syllable.[2] Anne Bradstreet's reference to her poem's uneven feet may derive from the early modern reference to metrical variants as "hobbled meters." Early modern debates over the use of classical quantities versus stress meters often deployed images of disability. The Elizabethan poet Samuel Daniel argues that attempting to configure English verse to Greek and Latin meters is "but a confused deliverer of their excellent conceits, whose scattered limbs we are faine to look out and joyne together" (qtd. in Smith, II:364). Roger Ascham counters by speaking of verse based on patterned stresses rather than classical quantities as having "feet without joints" that are "born deformed, unnatural, and lame" (qtd. in Smith, I:32–33). The idea of the line as a form of walking is reinforced in the strophe and antistrophe of classical drama where the chorus literally paced their lines back and forth across the stage. The comparison reappears, in a different form, among Romantic poets from Wordsworth and Clare to Gary Snyder and Frank O'Hara, for whom a more relaxed line may approach the condition of a desultory stroll. When grammatical sense continues uninterrupted onto the next line it is known as "enjambment," from the French word *jambe* for leg. Hence, semantic sense literally "steps over" the metrical pattern to the next line. Formal divisions within poems themselves are often seen as rests or prostheses for the weary traveler. George Puttenham in his "Arte of English Poesie" (1589) notes that stanzas are like a "bearer or supporter of a song or ballad not unlike the old weake bodie that is stayed up by his staff, and were not otherwise able to walke or to stand upright" (qtd. in Smith, II:68). And just as poetic rhythm is often compared to somatic features, so its acoustic realization is figured through "voice," "orality," and "ear." Such formal and prosodic metaphors suggest that the poem is a type of linguistic body whose variations and deformations are impairments.

Poets in the United States have been especially sensitive to the poetics of embodiment, perhaps as a result of that powerful incarnational metaphor, derived from Puritanism, that links Bradstreet with her more modern antecedents, such as Emily Dickinson:

> A word made flesh is seldom
> And tremblingly partook
> Nor then perhaps reported
> But have I not mistook
> Each one of us has tasted
> With ecstasies of stealth
> The very food debated
> To our specific strength—
>   (Dickinson, 616)[3]

Dickinson, like Bradstreet, figures her authorial presumption as a woman by appropriating the metaphor of incarnation to her "specific strength." Her antinomian contemporary, Walt Whitman, eroticizes the incarnational metaphor by figuring himself as the "poet of the Body" whose flesh partakes of divinity:

> Divine am I inside and out, and I make holy whatever I touch
>   or am touch'd from,
> The scent of these arm-pits aroma finer than prayer,
> This head more than churches, bibles, and all the creeds. (46)

Although Whitman was to witness the more painful forms of disability when he visited wounded Union soldiers during the Civil War, his poetry consistently asserts the spiritual nature of his sexual body, transforming the "word made flesh" into the "flesh made word" in the pages of *Leaves of Grass* (by typesetting the first edition in 1855, Whitman literalized the metaphor even further). Whitman's legacy to subsequent generations was to think of his ongoing poem as a direct extension of a body, whose ardors and excesses, chronicled in great detail, are embodiments of spiritual conditions.

The idea of the poem as an extension of the body, while not a new idea, had a particular resonance among modernist poets who sought a more scientific approach to prosody against late Victorian affect and rhetorical excess. Modernist poets like Yeats, Pound, and Eliot became interested in rhythmics, the scientific study of patterned speech by technological devices such as the phonoscope and the chronograph, which mapped vocal contours onto a metal drum. By measuring the rhythmic changes in the metabolism of a speaking subject, the acoustic scientist attempted to understand the unique properties of each human voice. As Michael Golston says, poets became interested in the science of rhythmics and appropriated many of its speculations into their poetics. Ezra Pound's belief in an "absolute rhythm" in his writing about Imagism or Gertrude Stein's belief in a psychological "bottom nature" based on how each individual repeats himself or herself and William Carlos Williams's interest in "variable measure" all treat the poem not as the mastery of traditional foot meters but of what Pound called the "musical phrase" established by emotional qualities of the entire line. These theories of "natural rhythm" often accompanied more insidious notions of "national rhythm" that reinforced racist ideas of bodily purity and national character. When Pound speaks of the epic as the "tale of the tribe" or when Eliot speaks of the need to "purify the dialect of the tribe," we may hear the more ominous implications of philological cleansing.

The foundational nature of these embodied metaphors for and in poetry needs to be contextualized against the backdrop of persons with nontraditional bodies, sensoria, or cognitive abilities. Furthermore, these metaphors must be historicized within a culture founded on an ideal of independence and self-reliance, for which any variation is seen as imperfect, "handicapped," or dependent. What does it mean for a poet who lives with a chronic disease or who uses a wheelchair to write through such metaphors? What do the ocular imperatives of "Imagism" or "deep image" mean for a blind poet? How does a deaf poet translate terms like "oral tradition," "text," "line," "voice," and "rhythm" when he or she signs a poem in American Sign Language (ASL)? In short, to what extent are modernist and postmodern poetics framed by "compulsory able-bodiedness"?[4]

These are questions that have been raised within disability studies, a disciplinary field that emerges out of the disability rights movement as well as academic research in the social sciences and humanities. A core tenet of disability studies is a distinction between two significant models of physical and cognitive impairment.[5] The first, or "medical model," defines an individual by his or her impairment—a woman with a cane, a man in a wheelchair. According to the medical model, a person with a disability is incomplete or handicapped and must be rehabilitated. This ideology of normalcy governs what it means to be human and organizes regimes of health, education, and civic life. The second, or "social" model, sees disability not in the individual but in the barriers to full social participation that the person with a disability encounters. To adapt Simone de Beauvoir's remark about female gender, one is not *born* disabled; one *becomes* disabled because of social obstacles, physical barriers, and prejudice. A person in a wheelchair is not disabled until she or he encounters a building without elevators; a deaf student is not disabled until entering a classroom without an ASL interpreter. Disability studies tries to understand the historical factors that have produced such barriers as well as the forms of political and cultural agency that people with disabilities have created in response.

There are several levels through which a poetics of disability can be studied: metaphoric (tropes of blindness, lameness, illness); structural (formal variations produced by physical or sensory conditions); and sociological (poetry as resistance and community formation).[6] Perhaps the closest link between poetry and disability lies in a conundrum within the genre itself: poetry makes language visible by making language strange. The Russian Formalist view of poetry as defamiliarization (*ostrenenie*) from conventional speech has served to define much modernist writing, but it applies in various ways to embodiment. In terms developed by Viktor Shklovsky, poetic language calls attention to the fictive character of representation itself; it "lays bare the device," exposing the poetic figure of speech *as* a figure, not as a transparent window upon a prior reality. The analogy to disability is that just as the body of transparent communication is exposed through poetic language, so the transparent character of bodily normalcy is revealed when a person with a disability no longer conforms to socially acceptable roles. In such cases, the presumed normalcy of what it means to be human is made strange by the encounter of a nontraditional body with an ideology of able-bodiedness.[7]

This fact has led the disability theorist Lennard Davis to speak of disability as "dismodernizing" traditional identity categories based around gender, race, national origin, and sexuality because it cuts across all such divisions.[8] Although he is not speaking of poetry, he is drawing on a key discourse of modernist writing to describe the way that disability challenges the body produced within modernity. In this respect, he extends Michel Foucault's ideas of biopolitics developed in *The History of Sexuality*—the technologies and institutions by which individuals are measured, categorized, racialized, and medicalized—to disability. It is not that the body was invented in the modern period but that political and juridical institutions developed technologies to police and monitor physical bodies and sexual activities in the interests of sustaining power. The pseudo-science of eugenics was the most egregious example of this taxonomic imperative. Invented by Francis Galton, the half-cousin of Charles Darwin, eugenics sought to regulate society by "improving" genetic stock and controlling "degenerate" reproduction. Although eugenics is usually identified with programs that classified individuals according to racial characteristics and that warned against racial intermarriage, it was no less concerned with nonnormative bodies. Eugenics fueled the Nazis' extermination of thousands of disabled and mentally ill people ("lives unworthy of life" as they were called) in concentration camps, long before they expanded their efforts against Jews in the Final Solution.[9] And throughout the United States and Europe, anti-miscegenation laws were applied to persons with cognitive disabilities or deafness—persons who were often sterilized or euthanized in campaigns of negative eugenics. As Susan Schweik has documented, in the early part of the twentieth century, "Ugly Laws" were passed in many U.S. cities, prohibiting the appearance in public of anyone whose physical deformity or disability would cause distress to the "normal" citizen.

As troubling as these developments are to current notions of individual rights, many intellectuals and artists in the early twentieth century were attracted to eugenic and racialist theories. W. B. Yeats, Charlotte Perkins Gilman, D. H. Lawrence, Emma Goldman, William Faulkner, Virginia Woolf, Ezra Pound, T. S. Eliot, Mina Loy, and many other Anglophone writers figured cultural decay and personal malaise through the optic of the weak or crippled body, the neurasthenic aesthete, the mentally retarded child, or the hysterical woman. In the era's most representative poem, T. S. Eliot's *The Waste Land* (1922) a blind, transgendered speaker laments the sickness of society, which is figured through a king who is suffering from an undiagnosed disease who fishes by a polluted stream. The speaker encounters a one-eyed merchant, a fortune teller with a bad cold, a clerk with serious acne, a husband suffering from nervous disorders, his wife, who is hysterical, and the denizens of a pub who discuss abortion and the loss of teeth. In the distance, the poem's speaker hears the sound of a young woman who has been raped and whose tongue has been cut out. Eliot confesses obliquely in the poem that he wrote most of it while living at sanatoria where he was recovering from his own psychological collapse. Although *The Waste Land* is usually read as an elegy for the decline of Europe and the loss of religious authority and natural order, its multiple references to illness, disease, and cognitive disorders suggest that this foundational poem for modernism was *founded* on (and by) a disabled body.

To some extent, Eliot's references to disease and illness are a response to the "hooded hordes" of immigrants that he imagined invading the metropole or the unsettling appearance of independent women and racial Others in public spaces.[10] Against the perceived threat of infectious diseases, crowded living conditions, and what was called "amalgamation" among races and classes, Progressive Era reformers advanced various strategies—birth control, settlement homes, quarantines, and legal prohibitions against miscegenation—to rationalize and segregate bodies. The appeal of such reforms can be seen in the rhetoric of modernist poets like Pound, whose desire to reinvigorate English verse is often figured as a "cure" and "hygiene" and who, in *The Cantos*, represents decay through the metaphor of infection. In Canto 45 he describes the corrosive effects of Jewish usury, which "hath brought palsy to bed, lyeth / between the young bride and her bridegroom / CONTRA NATURAM" (230). When his Imagist colleague, H.D., wants to render the ugliness of cities against the spare beauty of classical nature, she imagines

> … in these dark cells,
> packed street after street,
> souls live, hideous yet—
> O disfigured, defaced,
> with no trace of the beauty
> men once held so light. (41)

And Yeats's *Under Ben Bulben* urges Irish poets to "learn your trade":

> Sing whatever is well made,
> Scorn the sort now growing up
> All out of shape from toe to top,
> Their unremembering hearts and heads
> Base-born products of base beds. (327)

Mina Loy, in "Songs to Joannes" (1917), worries that "Unnatural selection / [will] Breed such sons and daughters / As shall jibber at each other" and relates racial mixing to what she calls "mongrelization" (66). In her "Feminist Manifesto," Loy attacks the institution of marriage and compulsory reproduction, arguing for the "*unconditional* surgical *destruction of virginity*" at puberty, thereby eliminating the "principal instrument of her subjection" as commodity (156). Her call for sexual liberation, however, contains a troubling eugenicist subtext: "Every woman of superior intelligence should realize her race-responsibility, in producing children in adequate proportion to the unfit or degenerate members of her sex" (157). Perhaps the most extreme expression of negative eugenics in literature occurs in a remark by D. H. Lawrence, who, although not an American poet, summarizes overtly what many of his artistic colleagues felt inwardly:

> If I had my way, I would build a lethal chamber as big as the Crystal Palace, with a military band playing softly, and a Cinematograph working brightly; then I'd go out in the back streets and main streets and bring them in, all the sick, the halt, and the maimed; I would lead them gently, and they would smile me a weary thanks.
>
> (qtd. in Childs, 10)

Such troubling metaphors of disability and illness permeate a good deal of poetry during the first decades of the twentieth century. Disability scholars have described the use of a physical or cognitive impairment to mark a character flaw or cultural trauma as a "narrative prosthesis" that diverts attention from the person with a disability to some broader social condition.[11] The function of such metaphoric displacement is to close or complete the aesthetic whole by means of a subject who is partial, fragmented, or impaired. Although David Mitchell and Sharon Snyder apply this phrase to narrative works, it is no less pertinent to poetry. William Carlos Williams's poem "To Elsie," for example, gains a good deal of its critical assessment of modern American society by treating the eponymous maid as someone with mental illness:

> Unless it be that marriage
> perhaps
> with a dash of Indian blood
>
> will throw up a girl so desolate
> so hemmed round
> with disease or murder
>
> . . . .
> ... some Elsie—
> voluptuous water
> expressing with broken
>
> brain the truth about us— (218)

Elsie epitomizes "The pure products of America" / [who] go crazy," through mixed-race intermarriage and exposure to transitory excitements and material wealth. As a "white ethnic" himself, the product of a British father and Puerto Rican mother, Williams may very well be identifying with Elsie as a "pure product" of America. And like sociological accounts of the Judds and hill folk of the Progressive Era, Williams studies Elsie as the product of isolated mountain and rural communities where intermarriage and dysgenic life "throw up" inordinate numbers of children.[12] The absence of "peasant traditions" in the United States leaves tragic figures like

Elsie vulnerable to the lure of "cheap / jewelry / and rich young men with fine eyes" (218). Although Williams *did* employ the real Elsie in his household as a nursemaid, he uses her to signify a particular quality of American life. And despite his medical profession, Williams is not particularly interested in Elsie's mental illness so much as the ways her large body and "broken / brain" signify a loss of agency in U.S. culture where there is "No one to witness / and adjust, no one to drive the car" (219).

Williams's formal innovations in free verse are marked by his own experience of disability following a series of strokes beginning in 1952 that left him partially paralyzed with his speech slurred. To this extent, the prosthetic character of disability to support modernist innovation is extended to the formal means of poetic production, as my subsequent example by Larry Eigner will indicate. Many critics feel that Williams's development of a triadic, stepped line beginning with "The Descent" passage in *Paterson 2* was a direct outcome of his strokes, a typographic response to his newly vulnerable body and speech. There is no indication that Williams formulated his stepped line in this manner, but it leaves open the degree to which physical limits have powerful effects on formal strategies.

With the 1930s and the Depression, modernist poets shifted their "mythic method," as Muriel Rukeyser said, from "Sappho [to] Sacco."[13] Unemployment, rent strikes, and social activism brought renewed focus on the historical, rather than eugenic, body; vegetation myth, classical allusion, and aesthetic distance gave way to poetry as social commentary and testimony. Disability is thematized in any number of poems dealing with the laboring body and the impact of workplace conditions under capitalism. Muriel Rukeyser's long poem *Book of the Dead* (1938) draws upon Eliot's use of myth and quotation to document an outbreak of silicosis among miners in Gauley Bridge, West Virginia, and the subsequent U.S. Senate investigation that followed. Like previous modernist poems that quote from documentary materials, Rukeyser draws on court testimony, stock quotations, interviews, and medical reports to chronicle a major case of corporate malfeasance. The poem is usually seen as an example of the Popular Front emphasis on documentary (the project began as a collaboration between Rukeyser and the photographer Nancy Naumberg), but it could also be seen as an important contribution to disability literature with its focus on the body that has been disabled by modern industrial capitalism. Rukeyser exploits the fact that the cause of the disease—silicon absorbed into the miners' lungs—is also an ingredient used to make glass. Hence the photographer's lens, a metaphor for clarity and testimony, is made out of the same material that is killing the workers who are the camera's subjects. Likewise, the X-ray technology that doctors used in their testimony before the Senate investigating committee is also made of silicon:

> This is a lung disease. Silicate dust makes it.
> The dust causing the growth of
>
> This is the X-ray picture taken last April.
> I would point out to you: these are the ribs;
> this is the region of the breastbone;

> this is the heart (a wide white shadow filled with blood),
> In here of curse is the swallowing tube, esophagus,
> The windpipe. Spaces between the lungs. (667)

Here, the doctor's testimony, in its bare presentation of the X-ray image, verbally penetrates the diseased body at the same time and reminds the reader of no less invasive effects of silicosis on those "Spaces between the lungs."

A second example of a documentary poem focused on disability in the workplace is Charles Reznikoff's *Testimony*, a vast, multivolume work chronicling late nineteenth-century industrial and agricultural accidents. Reznikoff is usually identified as a member of the Objectivist movement (George Oppen, Louis Zukofsky, Carl Rakosi), which valued spare, economical language and a clarity in presentation of the materials. Reznikoff, who was a lawyer, speaks of the Objectivist poet as one "who is restricted to the testimony of a witness in a court of law." In *Testimony*, he fulfills this goal quite literally by quoting from court documents involving workplace accidents. As such, he serves as witness to massive suffering due to the forces of poverty, industrialization, and standardization, although the poem's language is startlingly concrete:

> Ellen saw a collar with a lap on it—
> the buttonhole part lapped back on the collar—
> put her hand out to pull it away
> and her finger was caught in the buttonhole
> and she could not get it out
> before her hand was drawn between the rollers—
> burnt and crushed as she screamed. (59)

Such unadorned presentation and reportorial language belie the violence that is under the surface. By drawing on court cases, often verbatim, Reznikoff calls attention to the juridical frame within which capitalism thrives but through which workers hope for some compensation. The poem's title, *Testimony*, suggests an almost biblical witness to tragic events whose centerpiece is the vulnerable, laboring body.

"Limits / Are What Any of Us / Are Inside Of"

The incarnational metaphor with which I began undergoes two strong transformations in the postwar period. New Critics, drawing on Eliot's impersonal theory of art, appropriated the metaphor to fuse its religious connotations with the aesthetic. The successful poem that masters rhetorical and prosodic tensions displays what John Crowe Ransom calls a "miraculist fusion" of universals and particulars— eternal verities grounded in concrete images. If this secularizes a religious trope, it also revives Kantian aesthetics with its doctrines of disinterested appreciation and joins it to Eliot's "objective correlative" by which the poet may distance himself from his personal condition. In this respect, *The Waste Land* is one large objective correlative for Eliot's own psychological disorder during the late teens.

Reacting against this formal model of the poem, many poets of the 1950s and 1960s returned to Whitman's eroticized version of embodiment and to Williams's poetics of immanence. The new aesthetic was launched in the mid-1950s by Allen Ginsberg's *Howl* (1956) and Robert Lowell's *Life Studies* (1956) and solidified through the appearance of Donald Allen's 1960 anthology, *The New American Poets*, which gathered Beat, Black Mountain, San Francisco Renaissance, and the New York School in one volume. Here, the incarnational metaphor undergoes a further variation as poets sought a poetics grounded in the expressive body and speech, a line based, as Olson said, on the "breathing of the man who writes, at the moment that he writes" (242). In his theory of "Projective Verse," Olson sees the poetic line as an extension of the breath of the poet, the syllable as a registration of what the ear hears. Allen Ginsberg seeks to return, through the poem, to a kind of social incarnation "with the absolute heart of the poem of life butchered out of their own bodies good to eat a thousand year" (131). Donald Hall refers to poetic form as "the sensual body" and Michael McClure speaks of poetry as a kind of "meat science." The idea of the poem *as* body or as direct expression of psychic and physiological ratios characterizes one dominant mode of poetry during this period forged around the authenticity of expression guaranteed by the signifying body.

As I have written elsewhere, what if we subjected such ideas of embodiment to the actual bodies and mental conditions of its authors?[14]

> What would it mean to read the 1960s poetics of process and expression for its dependence on ableist models, while recognizing its celebration of idiosyncrasy and difference? By this optic, we might see Robert Lowell, Anne Sexton, and John Berryman not only as confessional poets but as persons who lived with depression or bipolar disorder, for whom personal testimony was accompanied by hospitalization, medicalization, and family trauma. What would it mean to think of Charles Olson's "breath" line as coming from someone with chronic emphysema exacerbated by heavy smoking? What if we added to Audre Lorde's multicultural description of herself as a Black, lesbian, mother, "sister outsider," a person with breast cancer? Robert Creeley's lines in "The Immoral Proposition," "to look at it is more / than it was," mean something very particular when we know that their author has only one eye (125). To what extent are Elizabeth Bishop's numerous references to suffocation and claustrophobia in her poems an outgrowth of a life with severe asthma? Robert Duncan's phrase in "Poem Beginning with a Line by Pindar," "I see always the underside turning" may refer to his interest in theosophy and the occult, but it also derives from the poet's visual disorder, in which one eye seems the near and the other far (64). It is worth remembering that the signature poem of the era was not only a poem about the madness of the best minds of the poet's generation, but about the carceral and therapeutic controls that defined those minds as mad, written by someone who was himself "expelled from the academies for crazy" (126). And if we include in our list the effects of alcoholism and substance abuse, a good deal of critical discussion of 1960s poetry could be enlisted around disability issues. (119)

Such connections between individual lines or poems and authorial biography are purely speculative, but it is hard *not* to measure the sustained emphasis on embodiment in postwar poetry against the backdrop of the cognitive and physiological conditions of its authors. Charles Olson's assertion that "Limits / are what any of us / are inside of" is a fair definition of the disabled artist, just as it defines the American self-reliant hero of his *Maximus Poems* (17).

To some extent the New American poetry's stress on terms like "gesture," "breath," "action," and "testimony" helped produce a collective, activist poetics in the later 1960s and 1970s. Frank O'Hara's whimsical view of the poem as having the immediacy of a phone call is transformed into the frontal, performative rhetoric of cultural nationalists who take the poem off the page and into the street. Significant alliances formed between poets and political activists that addressed civil rights, antiwar, feminist, queer, and youth issues, yet disability was significantly absent from such social movements. One reason for this may relate to the fatal historical links between physical and cognitive disabilities and racial and gendered categories. African Americans have been historically subject to medicalized regimes that marked bodies as inferior or subjected bodies to experimentation. Women's emancipation in the nineteenth century was thwarted by the creation of specific psychological conditions, usually related to reproduction, that necessitated rest cures and passivity. Homosexuality was, until recently, categorized as mental illness, and gay men and lesbians were routinely incarcerated. For African Americans, women, and gay people, gaining civil rights meant repudiating pathologizing regimes and medical nomenclature. It also meant projecting an ideal of racial, gendered, or queer identity as a physically fit, able-bodied community leader. Disability, as an identity that crosses racial, gender, and sexual boundaries, was harder to see as an identity category and thus remained for some time as a medical condition.

Feminism, strongly aided by the work of Adrienne Rich, Audre Lorde, Susan Griffin, Judy Grahn, and other poets, recognized that for women those "limits" that Olson mentions refer not to personal psychology but to masculinist ideology. A good deal of feminist poetry in the early 1970s is an attempt to deconstruct this ideology by focusing on that "book of myths / in which / our names do not appear" as Adrienne Rich writes (164). In works like Rich's "Diving into the Wreck" or Lorde's *Cancer Journals* or Ntozake Shange's *For colored girls who contemplated suicide...*, women poets focus on the uses of the female body in patriarchal culture, arguing for issues of healthcare, reproductive rights, workplace access, parental leave, childcare, and other issues particular to women's lives. Adrienne Rich often describes her experience of coming into feminist consciousness as a crippling experience, of being alienated from normative mobility. She describes this emergent consciousness as "an unnatural act" that derives from possessing a kind of double consciousness:

> The freedom of the wholly mad
> to smear & play with her madness
> write with her fingers dipped in it
> the length of a room

which is not, of course, the freedom
you have, walking on Broadway
to stop & turn back or go on
10 blocks; 20 blocks

but feels enviable maybe
to the compromised

curled in the placenta off the real
which was to feed & which is strangling her. (165)

Female agency here is depicted as a fatal opposition between the freedom of the "mad" and that of the mobile woman, yet the two are placed in congruence as though to display the fact that in a society in which female mobility and agency *are* deemed a kind of madness, the two states cannot be so separate. Disability activists would find fault with the conflation of cognitive disability to describe gender trouble, but for women of Rich's generation—Denise Levertov, Sylvia Plath, Muriel Rukeyser, and Elizabeth Bishop—disability often provided an active lens through which gender could be made visible.

Inspired by new social and civil rights movements of the 1960s, people with disabilities began to redress their own history of marginalization and stigma through protests over lack of accommodations, education, interpretation, and representation. The development of the Independent Living movement, led by Ed Roberts in Berkeley, began in the shadow of the University of California's Free Speech movement. Elsewhere, disability activists put their bodies literally on the line by getting out of their wheelchairs and crawling up the steps of the nation's Capitol Building to dramatize the lack of access to public venues. Using the model of the 1964 Civil Rights law, disability rights advocates saw the passage of legislation designed to provide an equal education for students with disabilities (IDEA, 1975) and redress for discrimination in the private sector (section 405 of the Rehabilitation Act, 1973), which culminated in the Americans with Disabilities Act (ADA) in 1990. The latter landmark legislation defines disability broadly as an "impairment that substantially limits one or more of the major life activities" or "a record of such an impairment." Perhaps the most important clause in the ADA prohibits discrimination against anyone who is "regarded as having such an impairment," thus addressing both social prejudice as well as medical sources of discrimination. The passage of the ADA made disability visible as public and private buildings, transportation services, and hiring practices were brought into compliance. And in like manner, the 1988 protests at Gallaudet University, the nation's premier university for deaf students, brought attention to the need for a "Deaf President Now" that resulted in the school's hiring of the first deaf president, King Jordan.

If people with disabilities became visible as rights-bearing individuals, they also emerged as poets and artists who made that new visibility a subject of innovative work. Building on gay and lesbian activists' rearticulation of the term "queer" to define a confrontational posture toward homophobia, disabled activists and artists reassigned the term "crip" to refer to their own forms of politics and artistic production. The work of Kenny Fries, Cheryl Marie Wade, Johnson Cheu, Eli Clare, Tom Andrews, Lynn Manning, Terry Galloway, Jim Ferris, Anne Finger, Petra Kuppers, and Tom Savage is an outgrowth of the disability rights movement, which sets its sights on social stigmatization based around impairment. The title of a 1997 anthology of disability writing edited by Fries, *Staring Back*, condenses the collected authors' desire to confront the history of disability prejudice and scopic curiosity. Cheryl Marie Wade refuses the saccharin labels for the handicapped ("I am not one of the physically challenged") but addresses her reader frontally:

> I'm a sock in the eye with a gnarled fist
> I'm a French kiss with a cleft tongue
> I'm orthopedic shoes sewn on a last of your fears
> I'm not one of the differently abled— (592)

And Kenny Fries responds to stigmatizing terms applied to him as someone born missing bones in his legs:

> *Freak, midget, three-toed*
> *bastard.* Words I've always heard.
>
> *Disabled, crippled, deformed.* Words
> I was given. But tonight I go back
>
> farther, want more, tear deeper into
> my skin. Peeling it back I reveal
>
> the bones at birth I wasn't given—
> the place where no one speaks a word.
>   (*Staring Back*, 146)

At the same time within the Deaf community, poets and performers such as Peter Cook, Debbie Rennie, Ella Mae Lentz, Clayton Valli, and Patrick Greybill began creating poems and performances out of American Sign Language that challenged the presumed oral and written basis of poetry.[15] Because cultural Deafness is constructed around issues of language and representation, deaf poets and performers do not necessarily think of themselves as disabled so much as a linguistic minority. Their work has repudiated the "audist" or hearing-based English language culture (ASL is an entirely specific language with its own grammar and morphemics, separate from English) by, in most cases, refusing voiceover translation on audiotapes or at performances. But these performers often thematize their bicultural status as signing poets who inevitably know English or who live in a hearing culture. What I have elsewhere called the "scandal of speech in ASL performance" is the uneasy rapprochement between deaf and hearing culture.[16]

Among the most significant deaf poets is Clayton Valli, whose signed poems build thematically on traditional English models, while modifying and extending ASL signs in new and complex ways. One of his best-known poems, "Snowflake," tells the story of a deaf child being interrogated by his hearing father. Valli utilizes four different modalities of ASL to mark the various idiolects and code-switching that are common when deaf people confront hearing people. The deaf child's attempt to answer his father's various questions displays the inadequacies of his—the child's—oralist education (Valli was himself educated in an oral school) yet this part of the poem is framed by a larger description of a gray day in a snowy landscape in which a single snowflake metaphorizes the child's solitude in hearing culture. This "snowflake" segment brackets the father/child frame but also provides a poetic alternative to a discursive binary of speech/silence. Here, Valli exploits the richness of ASL, utilizing extensive variations of hand shape, body position, facial expression, and visual puns to create a wintery landscape as a metaphor for alienation. The use of repeated hand shapes in various positions assists in creating rhythm, much as rhyme or alliteration links elements in traditional English verse. Although the father of the middle section uses his son to celebrate his son's oral skills, the poet who creates the "snowflake" frame in ASL shows that the deaf child has become the father of the hearing man.

In 1984 Allen Ginsberg visited the National Technical Institute for the Deaf (NTID) in Rochester, New York, and participated with other deaf poets in conversations and translations.[17] Out of this event emerged the "Bird's Brain Society," named after one of Ginsberg's poems. Sponsored by Jim Cohn, the Bird's Brain Society was the first attempt at a Deaf poetry movement whose participants, as Cohn remembers, "share a collective awareness that ASL contains aesthetic properties that place the body in direct relationship with the perceptual, expressive, notational, and mnemonic essences of the image" (30). One of the participants in the event was a student at NTID, Peter Cook, who, with his hearing partner, Kenny Lerner, formed the Flying Words Project and who created performances drawing on several vernacular Deaf traditions, including mime, deaf ventriloquism, dance, and storytelling. Where Flying Words differs from deaf poets like Clayton Valli is the fact that they incorporate sound and speech into their work. Lerner occasionally translates Cook's signs, and in at least one poem, 'I Am Ordered Now to Talk," Cook vocalizes (speaks) while he signs.[18] For Deaf cultural nationalists, such collusion with hearing culture is anathema, but for Cook and Lerner it offers an expression of the multicultural nature of deaf persons.

A final significant site of disability poetics is the work written in the shadow of the AIDS pandemic of the early 1980s. Although the poetry written by poets who live with HIV/AIDS or who have lost friends and lovers crosses many aesthetic boundaries, it has served as an important vehicle of expression—and mourning—for many poets. The work of Thom Gunn, Mark Doty, Essex Hemphill, Tori Dent, Aaron Shurin, Kevin Killian, Dodie Bellamy, Sam D'Allesandro, Bob Gluck, Bruce Boone, Steve Abbott, Tim Dlugos, David Melnick, and others confronts the massive losses within the gay community. Such poetry must be set against the homophobic response to AIDS by the religious right, figures like Jerry Falwell who declared that "AIDS is God's judgment of a society that does not live by His rules" or William F. Buckley's idea that people w/AIDS "should be tattooed ... on the buttocks to prevent the victimization of other homosexuals" (qtd. in Landau, 193–194). Against such virulent reactions, the poetics of AIDS can often be confrontational, yet despite the pain of loss, many poets refuse consolation. Thom Gunn's *The Man with Night Sweats* chronicles the loss of his lover in heroic couplets:

> In hope still, courteous still, but tired and thin
> You tried to stay the man that you had been,
> Treating each symptom as a mere mishap
> Without import. But then the spinal tap.
> It brought a hard headache, and when night came
> I heard you wake up from the same bad dream ... (199)

His elegiac response is also historical as he reflects on the crushing blow that AIDS delivers to the newly empowered Gay Rights movement after Stonewall:

> I sat upon a disintegrating gravestone.
> How can I continue, I asked?
> I longed to whet my senses, but upon what?
> On mud? It was a desert of raw mud.
> I was tempted by fantasies of the past,
> but my body rejected them, for only in the present
> could it pursue the promise ... (19)

Despite the obvious links between political, sexual, and literary constituencies, disability rights advocates have not always accepted chronic diseases such as HIV/AIDS as components in the movement. Early activism for the ADA often paraded under the motto "we're not sick," and some disability rights supporters argued against including AIDS within the protected class. The 1998 Supreme Court decision in *Bragdon v. Abbott* confirmed that a person with HIV/AIDS fell under the ADA's provision for protecting an individual (in this case, a woman refused treatment by a dentist because she was HIV positive) whose condition "limits one or more life activities." In recent years, the disability rights movement has become open to including persons with learning disabilities, chronic diseases, and cognitive disorders while disability studies, as an academic discipline, has embraced intersectional alliances around race, class, gender, and sexuality. The poetics of AIDS has shifted from U.S.-centered activism within the gay and lesbian community over the need for increased research and treatment to a global, cross-cultural movement whose cultural forms include forms of infotainment, community drama, standup poetry, and theater sponsored by nongovernmental organizations.

"THE LINES ARE IRREGULAR"

Not all disabled poets have necessarily identified with the disability rights or Independent Living movement. My earlier list of poets whose bodies and cognitive conditions *could* be enlisted within a disability poetics suggests that for a certain generation that emerged after World War II identifying oneself as disabled was limited by the lack of an active disability community. Poets such as Josephine Miles, who lived much of her adult life with severe arthritis, James Schuyler, and Robert Lowell, who spent extensive periods in mental hospitals for bipolar disorders and depression, or Hannah Weiner, whose clairvoyant poetics—seeing words appear on bodies, walls, and faces—was enabled by schizophrenia, seldom defined their literary work in terms of their physical or cognitive states. How, then, does one approach the work of disabled poets in a way that respects their reticence to talk about their conditions, yet that shows the relevance of these conditions to their work?

My final example illustrates just this problem. Larry Eigner was born in Lynn, Massachusetts, on August 6, 1926. He developed cerebral palsy at birth and remained severely disabled throughout his life, spending his early days in the glassed-in porch of his parents' home in nearby Swamscott. The administration of cryosurgery at age thirty-five offered him a greater degree of control over his movements. Following the death of his father in 1978, Eigner moved to Berkeley, California, where he participated, briefly, in the city's Independent Living movement. He became dissatisfied with aspects of communal living and subsequently moved into his own home along with the poets Robert Grenier and Kathleen Frumkin, who served as his aides and companions until close to his death in 1996.

Eigner is usually associated with the New American poets of the 1950s and 1960s, whose work he encountered in 1949 through Cid Corman's "This Is Poetry" radio program out of Boston, and he had begun an active correspondence with Olson, Allen Ginsberg, Robert Duncan, and others. Eigner's particular contribution to the poetics of the New American poetry was his perceptual immediacy—his registration of surroundings, attention to patterns of light and shade, and registration of sounds and speech:

> a bird gropes a branch
>   the direct sun
>   on the clouds
>   (*Things Stirring*, 98)

> squirrels everywhere   all
>   of
>   a
>   sudden
>   (*Things Stirring*, 59)

              a man climbing
                his steps while the clouds go
            by he comes to the corner
                apt.   above
                the store
                            (*air the trees*, 40)

Such precise recordings of sights and sounds might be seen as any poet's attention to
detail, but when read as a record of limited mobility and starkly restricted perspec-
tive, such attentiveness means something different.

Eigner used his limited mobility to create a highly idiosyncratic pattern of linea-
tion. As in the examples above, his lines tend to slant gradually across the page, each
line indented a few spaces further toward the right to indicate both the onrushing
force of his perceptual awareness as well as his physical difficulty in returning the
carriage to the left margin. Because his typing was limited to his right index finger, he
painstakingly measured each word and phrase, often isolating individual words on a
single line or using the space bar to mark changes of attention. And in order to avoid
having to put a new piece of paper into the typewriter, he often continued the poem
in the space vacated by his rightward tending lines. In short, Eigner's material page
became a cognitive map of his relationship to space, phenomena, and physiology.

Although Larry Eigner did not self-consciously identify with the disability rights
movement, he nevertheless embodied its political activism (he was a lifelong pacifist)
and independent living. He regularly attended readings by local poets, especially once
he moved to the San Francisco Bay area, and he entertained younger poets at his North
Berkeley home. Furthermore, many of his short stories, memoirs, and poems record
his life growing up as a child with a disability—attending summer camps, engaging in
regimes of physical therapy, and confronting the limits of an ableist world:

              broken curbs

                  travel and distance
              proportion themselves

                  we must be animate,   and walk

              turn, abruptly

                  the lines are irregular
                            (*Selected*, 24)

These lines *are* irregular, which, to earlier readers, simply meant that Eigner was
writing in the Pound tradition of free-verse lineation. Seen in terms of Eigner's cere-
bral palsy, the lines take on a new meaning, qualifying the imperative, "we must be
animate, and walk" to refer both to his daily therapeutic regime but also to an ableist
ideology in which to walk is to be human. Eigner folds the two roles—ableist and dis-
abled—into one poem, one enabled by the open form poetics of the postwar period

but marked by his own attentive relationship to the "broken curbs" and proportioned "distances" he may have felt to a world that had yet to accommodate him.

The poetry of Larry Eigner suggests that a disability poetics does not describe a movement or an aesthetic so much as a spectrum of positions around embodiment—from poets like Eigner who seldom referred to his neurological condition to self-consciously "crip" poets for whom poetry is an arm (or leg) of the disability rights movement. It also describes the degree to which poetry is constituted by and within ideas of embodiment, from the "oral" tradition to the foot metric to the most recent versions of stand-up (or sit-down) performance. As I have indicated, the twin terms resonate loudly in the U.S. context where ideas of embodiment have been synonymous with antinomian positions of self-reliance and independence and for which dependence and communality are deemed threatening or, in the worst case, un-American. A disability poetics, while forged within the liberating ethos of the Independent Living movement, creates a site where the putative normalcy of bodies, sensations, and agency can be understood differently. If this has been poetry's ancient heritage, it is also disability's utopian horizon.

NOTES

1   The convention of comparing one's book to a difficult birth was common in the early modern period. Elizabeth Sacks remarks that at a moment when the "English language itself was undergoing rebirth," many early modern works were described as "vulnerable, helpless infant[s] struggling for existence in an unfriendly world" (qtd. in Caldwell, 11). Sacks mentions poems by Spenser, Sidney, Chapman, Turberville, Lyly, Dekker, and Shakespeare, who describe their works as "delivered" by careless printers that produced offspring that were maimed and crippled.

2   On "crippled" poetry, see Ferris .

3   In the Johnson edition, this is Dickinson's poem #1651. In the R. W. Franklin edition, it is number #1715. I am referring to pagination in the latter.

4   See McRuer.

5   On the medical and social models of disability, see Siebers; Shakespeare; Davidson.

6   A fourth model, "poetry therapy," has been developed by rehabilitation therapists as part of a therapeutic regime. While this is a significant role for poetry to play, it tends to reinforce both the medical model of disability, on the one hand, and an instrumentalist view of poetry, on the other.

7   I have discussed the parallel between linguistic defamiliarization and disability in *Concerto for the Left Hand*, chapter 1.

8   On "dismodernism," see Davis, 9–32.

9   On eugenics and disability, see Snyder and Mitchell, 100–129; Brueggemann, 141–162; and Pernick.

10   What is that sound high in the air
Murmur of maternal lamentation
Who are those hooded hordes swarming
Over endless plains (T. S. Eliot, *The Waste Land*, lines 367–370)

11 See Mitchell and Snyder.
12 Edith Wharton's description of the "mountain folk" in her novel *Summer* bears an uncanny resemblance to Williams's account of Elsie:

> Down at Creston they told me that the first colonists are supposed to have been men who worked on the railway that was built forty or fifty years ago between Springfield and Nettleton. Some of them took to drink or got in trouble with the police, and went off—disappeared into the woods. A year or two later there was a report that they were living up on the mountain. Then I suppose others joined them—and children were born.... They seem to be quite outside the jurisdiction of the valleys." (66)

13 Not Sappho, Sacco.

> Rebellion pioneered among our lives,
> viewing from far-off many-branching deltas,
> innumerable seas.
> (Muriel Rukeyser, "Poem Out of Childhood," 1)

14 See my *Concerto for the Left Hand*, chapter 5.
15 Among deaf people, it is common to capitalize "D" when speaking of deaf persons as a cultural entity and to use lower case "d" when speaking of deafness as an audiological condition.
16 See "Hearing Things: The Scandal of Speech in Deaf Performance," in *Concerto for the Left Hand*, chapter 3.
17 On Ginsberg's appearance at NTID, see Cohn.
18 "I Am Ordered Now to Talk" can be seen on a DVD included in *Signing the Body Poetic: Essays on American Sign Language Literature*, edited by Dirksen Bauman et al. Bauman himself has written significant essays on ASL poetry and performance in this volume and elsewhere.

REFERENCES

Bauman, H-Dirksen, L. Bauman, Jennifer L. Nelson, and Heidi M. Rose, eds. *Signing the Body Poetic: Essays on American Sign Language Literature*. Berkeley: University of California Press, 2006.

Bradstreet, Anne. *The Poems of Anne Bradstreet*. Ed. Robert Hutchinson. New York: Dover, 1969.

Brueggemann, Brenda Jo. *Deaf Subjects: Between Identities and Places*. New York: New York University Press, 2009.

Caldwell, Patricia. "Why Our First Poet Was a Woman: Bradstreet and the Birth of an American Poetic Voice." *Prospects* 13 (1988): 1–35.

Childs, Donald J. *Modernism and Eugenics: Woolf, Eliot, Yeats, and the Culture of Degeneration*. Cambridge: Cambridge University Press, 2001.

Cohn, Jim. *Sign Mind: Studies in American Sign Language Poetics*. Boulder, CO: Museum of American Poetics Publications, 1999.

Creeley, Robert. "The Immoral Proposition." In *The Collected Poems of Robert Creeley*. Berkeley: University of California Press, 1982. 132.

Davidson, Michael. *Concerto for the Left Hand: Disability and the Defamiliar Body*. Ann Arbor: University of Michigan Press, 2008.

Davis, Lennard. *Bending Over Backwards: Disability, Dismodernism annd Other Difficult Positions*. New York: New York University Press, 2002.

Dickinson, Emily. *The Poems of Emily Dickinson*. Ed. R. W. Franklin. Cambridge: Harvard University Press, 1998.

Duncan, Robert. "Poem Beginning with a Line by Pindar." *The Opening of the Field*. New York: New Directions, 1960. 62–69.

Eigner, Larry. *air the trees*. Los Angeles: Black Sparrow, 1968.

———. *Selected Poems*. Ed. Samuel Charters and Andrea Wyatt. Berkeley: Oyez, 1972.

———. *Things Stirring Together or Far Away*. Los Angeles: Black Sparrow, 1974.

Eliot, T. S. *The Collected Poems and Plays: 1909–1950*. New York: Harcourt, Brace & World, 1962.

Emerson, Ralph Waldo. "The Poet." In *Selections from Ralph Waldo Emerson*, ed. Stephen E. Whicher. Boston: Houghton Mifflin, 1960. 222–241.

Ferris, Jim. "The Enjambed Body: A Step Toward a Crippled Poetics." *Georgia Review* 53.2 (Summer 2004): 219–233.

Fries, Kenny, ed. *Staring Back: The Disability Experience from the Inside Out*. New York: Penguin, 1997.

Ginsberg, Allen. "Howl." In *Collected Poems, 1947–1980*. New York: Harper & Row, 1984. 126–139.

Golston, Michael. *Rhythm and Race in Modernist Poetry and Science*. New York: Columbia University Press, 2008.

Gunn, Thom. *The Man with Night Sweats*. New York: Farrar Straus, 1992.

H.D. (Hilda Doolittle). *Collected Poems, 1912–1944*. Ed. Louis L. Martz. New York: New Directions, 1983.

Hall, Donald. *Goatfoot Milktongue Twinbird: Interviews, Essays, and Notes on Poetry, 1970–1976*. Ann Arbor: University of Michigan Press, 1978.

Landau, Deborah. "'How to Live. What too Do': The Poetics and Politics of AIDS." *American Literature* 68.1 (March 1996): 193–225.

Loy, Mina. *The Lost Lunar Baedeker: Poems of Mina Loy*. Ed. Roger L. Conover. New York: Farrar, Straus, & Giroux, 1997.

Martin, Wendy. "'A Lonesome Glee'—Poets before 1800." In *Shakespeare's Sisters: Feminist Essays on Women Poets*, ed. Sandra Gilbert and Susan Gubar. Bloomington: Indiana University Press, 1979.

McClure, Michael. *Meat Science Essays*. San Francisco: City Lights, 1966.

McRuer, Robert. *Crip Theory: Cultural Signs of Queerness and Disability*. New York: New York University Press, 2006.

Mitchell, David, and Sharon Snyder. *Narrative Prosthesis: Disability and the Dependencies of Discourse*. Ann Arbor: University of Michigan Press, 2000.

Olson, Charles. *The Maximus Poems*. Berkeley: University of California Press, 1983.

———. "Projective Verse." In *Collected Prose*, ed. Donald Allen and Benjamin Friedlander. Berkeley: University of California Press, 1997. 239–249.

Pernick, Martin S. *The Black Stork: Eugenics and the Death of "Defective Babies" in American Medicine and Motion Pictures Since 1915*. New York: Oxford University Press, 1996.

Pound, Ezra. *The Cantos of Ezra Pound*. New York: New Directions, 1972.

Puttenham, George. "The Arte of English Poesie." In *Elizabethan Critical Essays*, Vol. II, ed. G. Gregory Smith. London: Oxford University Press, 1959. 1–93.

Ransom, John Crowe. "Poetry: A Note in Ontology." In *Critical Theory Since Plato*, ed. Hazard Adams. New York: Harcourt Brace Jovanovich, 1971. 871–881.

Reznikoff, Charles. *Testimony*. Volume 1: *The United States (1885–1915) Recitative*. Santa Barbara, CA: Black Sparrow, 1978.

Rich, Adrienne. "The Phenomenology of Anger." In *The Fact of a Doorframe: Poems Selected and New, 1950–1984*. New York: W. W. Norton, 1984. 165–169.

Rukeyser, Muriel. *The Book of the Dead*. In *Anthology of Modern American Poetry*, ed. Cary Nelson. New York: Oxford University Press, 2000. 656–687.

———. "Poem Out of Childhood." In *Out of Silence: Selected Poems*. Evanston, IL: TriQuarterly Books, 1992. 1–3.

Schweik, Susan. *The Ugly Laws: Disability in Public*. New York: New York University Press, 2009.

Shakespeare, Tom. "The Social Model of Disability." In *The Disability Studies Reader*, ed. Lennard J. Davis. 3rd ed.. New York: Routledge, 2010. 266–273.

Shklovsky, Victor. "Art as Technique." In *Russian Formalist Criticism: Four Essays*, trans. Lee T. Lemon and Marion J. Reis. Lincoln: University of Nebraska Press, 1965. 3–24.

Siebers, Tobin. *Disability Theory*. Ann Arbor: University of Michigan Press, 2008.

Smith, G. Gregory. *Elizabethan Critical Essays*. London: Oxford University Press, 1959.

Snyder, Sharon, and David Mitchell. *Cultural Locations of Disability*. Chicago: University of Chicago Press, 2006.

Wade, Cheryl Marie. "I am not One of the." In *The Disability Reader*, ed. Lennard J. Davis. 3rd ed. New York: Routledge, 1997. 592.

Wharton, Edith. *Summer*. New York: Harper & Row, 1979.

Whitman, Walt. *Leaves of Grass and Other Writings*. Ed. Michael Moon. New York: W. W. Norton, 2002.

Yeats, William Butler. "Under Ben Bulben." In *W. B. Yeats: The Poems*, ed. Richard J. Finneran. New York: Macmillan, 1983. 327.

CHAPTER 23

GREEN READING: MODERN AND CONTEMPORARY AMERICAN POETRY AND ENVIRONMENTAL CRITICISM

LYNN KELLER

ENVIRONMENTALLY oriented criticism of literature (here designated either *environmental criticism* or *ecocriticism*) has existed as a mode of analysis for only about twenty years, yet this still "emergent discourse" is, as Lawrence Buell has remarked, "one with very ancient roots" (*Future*, 2). Ancient traditions of pastoral, with its formative opposition between town and country, and especially pastoral's nineteenth-century descendants in the nature writing of the British Romantics and American transcendentalists have guaranteed poetry's importance to environmental criticism. This legacy, moreover, offers modern and contemporary poets an array of models on which to draw as they invite readers, in John Felstiner's words, to "stop, look, and listen long enough for imagination to act, connecting, committing ourselves to the only world we've got" (13).

Yet that literary legacy also has its drawbacks. As the environmental historian William Cronon has argued, the ideas of wilderness and nature embodied in these foundational traditions reflect orientations that are problematic for contemporary environmentalism. The Romantic notion of the sublime—of the palpable presence of the divine in the most awesome of nature's spectacles—is tied to an understanding of the wilderness as something apart from human habitation and human history.

Combined with the American ideology of the frontier, with its nostalgic glorifica-
tion of a wild space into which men might escape from the ugly degradations of
modern civilization to reinvigorate themselves, ideas of the sublime have generated
in American thought a "romantic ideology of wilderness," which places the human
outside the natural world (Cronon, 80). The idealization of an unworked landscape
tends to focus environmental concern solely on wilderness preservation, not on
issues affecting cities, agricultural sites, or the people who inhabit them. "[W]e need
an environmental ethic that will tell us as much about *using* nature as about *not*
using it," Cronon observes (85). The inherited dualism that separates the human
from nature, evident in much modern poetry about nature and wilderness, leaves
"little hope of discovering what an ethical, sustainable, *honorable* human place in
nature might actually look like" (81).

Environmental criticism is closely tied to the environmental social movement
that aims "to reground human cultures in natural systems and...to rescue a sense
of the reality of environmental degradation from the obfuscations of political dis-
course" (Heise, 505). Issues of ethics and sustainability prompted by a sense of envi-
ronmental crisis inevitably weigh on aesthetic considerations in this field, and the
pastoral and Romantic legacies reflected in modern and contemporary poetry may
not serve these political goals well. If we concur with Cronon that "[i]n its flights
from history, in its siren song of escape, in its reproduction of the dangerous dual-
ism that sets human beings outside of nature—in all these ways, [the American
construction of] wilderness poses a serious threat to responsible environmentalism
at the end of the twentieth century" (81), then it behooves environmental critics
to consider the extent to which the poetry we associate with nature or wilderness
represents such an ideology and to explore alternative perspectives that other types
of poetry might offer.

Because poetry so deliberately displays and tests the resources of language,
debates within environmental studies about poststructuralist theories of language
have further complicated ecocritical approaches to the genre. The speaker of Robert
Hass's "Meditation at Lagunitas" enacts this complication when he notes the pro-
found sense of loss inherent to the "new thinking":

> The idea, for example, that each particular erases
> the luminous clarity of a general idea. That the clown-
> faced woodpecker probing the dead sculpted trunk
> of that black birch is, by his presence,
> some tragic falling off from a first world
> of undivided light. Or the other notion that,
> because there is in this world no one thing
> to which the bramble of *blackberry* corresponds,
> a word is elegy to what it signifies. (4)

Seen from such perspectives, "everything dissolves." This is why many have found
structuralist and poststructuralist theories, particularly Derridean understandings

of the endless deferral of reference in the chain of signifiers, inimical to ecocriticism. Ecocritical concerns about real-world environmental degradation have fostered an insistence on nature as something that is phenomenologically real, even if in some ways culturally constructed. It is this feeling that motivates Leonard Scigaj's proc- lamation, "It behooves us to be referentially oriented, to learn nature's biocentric, ecological logic, and conform to it" (56), and the same spirit motivates his righteous dismissal of Hass as a writer for whom "only the human has value" (57). According to Scigaj, the "poetics of textuality" of Hass and other "postmodern poets" seals off poetry from the "referential world" and removes the reader "from the practical world we must engage, moment to moment" (56).

This position does not do justice to the complicated view of language that devel- ops in Hass's "Meditation at Lagunitas," from which Scigaj cites only the line about the word as elegy (35). After exploring memories that in their vivid particularity counter the supposed dissolution of everything words name, at the poem's close Hass not only celebrates sensual existence and reminds us of the role that the sound of words plays in sensual pleasure, but he also momentarily melds word and flesh, word and nature:

> ...There are moments when the body is as numinous
> as words, days that are the good flesh continuing.
> Such tenderness, those afternoons and evenings,
> saying *blackberry, blackberry, blackberry*. (5)

Blackberry, repeated, becomes itself a substantial bramble felt on the tongue. And syntactic ambiguity—which makes it unclear whether the speaker, the body, or the days do the "saying"—suggests that there are precious moments when the language of phenomena, however inexplicably, merges with that created by humans. In this poem Hass successfully meets an important challenge faced by many ecocritics, namely "to keep one eye on the ways in which 'nature' is always in some ways cul- turally constructed, and on the other on the fact that nature really exists, both the object and, albeit distantly, the origin of our discourse" (Garrard, 10).

My intention in challenging Scigaj's reading of Hass is to provide some counter- weight to Scigaj's and other ecocritics' general dismissal of what Scigaj calls "post- modern" writing as having no value for environmental criticism. His wariness of constructionism and of theories that complicate referentiality is characteristic of this critical enterprise, particularly in its early stages. Nonetheless, those familiar with the "poetry wars" of recent decades will also perceive in his views (and in those of other important ecocritics focusing on poetry, such as John Elder) evidence that environmental criticism has mapped itself onto—or been held hostage to- debates already ongoing within poetry studies. In the final decades of the twentieth century, the U.S. poetry scene was divided in ways that extended the oppositional dynamics of the "anthology wars" of the 1960s: poetry aligned with poststructural- ist thought, such as Language poetry, was positioned against the mainstream per- sonal lyric, which treated language as a transparent vehicle for conveying feelings or experiences rather than as a means of their construction. Allied with mainstream poetics, ecocritics attended primarily to straightforwardly representational writing. With a few very recent exceptions, poetry associated with linguistic and formal experimentation has rarely been examined through an environmental lens. Yet poetry that self-consciously investigates how language shapes our understanding of the world, or experiments with space and place as they are registered on the page, may valuably point us toward alternative understandings of the environment and our modes of interacting with it. This chapter will suggest that the canon of poetic works considered by ecocritics needs to expand so as to include not only more writing based in environments other than "nature" and "wilderness" but also more linguistically experimental, "postmodern" writing.

In its alignment with environmental science, much early environmental literary criticism sought "a corrective to critical subjectivism and cultural relativism" (Buell, *Future*, 18). The field has shifted recently to acknowledge a less clear line between science and culture so that literary environmental studies has acquired a more social bent; the focus on exclusively "natural" environments and "nature writing" has given way to a less organicist understanding that includes urban and degraded landscapes in its concept of environment. Environmentality, as Buell notes, is no longer confined to particular texts but may be "a property of any text" (*Future*, 25). The subfield of environmental poetry studies, however, has only begun to make these shifts, along with the shift toward a more global perspective that key critics like Buell and Ursula Heise advocate. The waning of the poetry wars in the first years of the twenty-first century, which is opening the eyes of poets, readers, and critics alike to more diverse aesthetics, may help propel the incipient expansion of perspectives in environmental studies of poetry.

While I want to avoid duplicating the excessive focus on "nature poetry" that has constricted environmental studies of poetic work, discussions of a few key "nature poets" will allow me to identify some significant issues in modern American nature poetry involving the relation of humankind and human culture to the green world. Thereafter, this chapter will look beyond nature poetry to other environmental tropes and beyond conventionally realist writing to other poetics.

Robinson Jeffers (1887–1962) is widely cited as the founding figure for twentieth-century American environmental poetry. Accurately identified by Albert Gelpi as "the poet of the sublime without peer in American letters," Jeffers's work starkly demonstrates Cronon's claims about the American notion of wilderness excluding the human (Jeffers, *Wild God*, 14 ["Introduction"]). Jeffers reveres the natural world and regards humans, distinguished from the rest of nature by their egos, as inevitably pitted against its beauty and integrity. The more embroiled in human civilization, the more distant people are from "the wild God of the world": "You do not know him, you communal people, or you have forgotten him; / Intemperate and savage, the hawk remembers him; / Beautiful and wild, the hawks, and men that are dying, remember him" ("Hurt Hawks," *Wild God*, 49). While rejecting high modernist aesthetics, which he sees as manifesting rather than resisting the conditions of modernity responsible for the decline of civilization, Jeffers nonetheless shares his generation's sense of civilization in crisis. But rather than trying to shore up the ruined fragments of that civilization, he turns away from humanity's corruption and toward a pantheistic reverence for the natural world, "the immense beauty of the world, not the human world" ("De Rerum Virtute," *Wild God*, 177).

Jeffers lived a reclusive life for almost fifty years in Tor House, which he and his wife built on the rocky Monterey coast of California, and he wrote primarily narrative poems of violent and tragic dramas set against a vast and awesome natural environment, along with short prophetic lyrics. In his later writing he developed a doctrine of Inhumanism "based on a recognition of the astonishing beauty of things, and on a rational acceptance of the fact that mankind is neither central nor important in the universe; our vices and abilities are [as] insignificant as our happiness" (*Double Axe*, 172). In many ways Inhumanism anticipates deep ecology's shift from human-centered to nature-centered values, though Jeffers's denigration of the human sometimes goes beyond deep ecology's egalitarian approach to all entities in an ecosphere. For instance, in "Original Sin" he asserts he would "rather // be a worm in a wild apple than a son of man. / But we are what we are, and we might remember / Not to hate any person, for all are vicious; / And not to be astonished at any evil, all are deserved" (*Wild God*, 172). Reflecting his belief in the unworthiness and unimportance of the human race, without regret his poems anticipate humanity's self destruction as a way to restore nature. He writes of Carmel Point,

> ...It knows the people are a tide
> That swells and in time will ebb, and all
> Their works dissolve. Meanwhile the image of the pristine beauty
> Lives in the very grain of the granite,
> Safe as the endless ocean that climbs our cliff.—As for us:
> We must uncenter our minds from ourselves;
>
> ("Carmel Point," *Wild God*, 175)

Jeffers admits in one poem that he'd "sooner, except the penalties, kill a man than a hawk" ("Hurt Hawks," *Wild God*, 49), and he is seen by some as misanthropic; for ecocritical studies, however, it may be more useful to observe how his work presents the extreme logical consequence of the romantic ideology of wilderness: if nature is destroyed because we enter it, then the elimination of humankind is required for nature's salvation. Jeffers's readiness to dismiss the human places his work at one end of the continuum of responses to the problem of anthropocentrism that all environmentally attuned nature poets encounter.

Gary Snyder (b. 1930), whom Greg Garrard dubs "the 'poet laureate' of deep ecology" (20), is also committed to an ecocentric perspective, though he is far more positive about possible ways of organizing human communities to exist harmoniously with the ecosystems they inhabit. A countercultural figure early associated with the Beats, Snyder, like Jeffers, is thought of as a poet of a particular place, the foothills of the Sierras, and is associated especially with Kitkitdizze, the home he built there with the help of friends. Using simple language, flexible free-verse arrangements, and a disarming sense of humor, much of his poetry represents his family life and labors as a homesteader and his experiences following hunter-gatherer modes of living on the San Juan Ridge. His manner, however, is far from the confessional, as his inclusive perspective takes in earlier cultures and even geological time. Snyder lived in Japan and other parts of Asia between 1956 and 1968; his extensive study in Zen Buddhism with its nondualistic modes of thinking has been particularly important for his work. His anthropologically trained interest in indigenous mythologies and tribal cultures has also shaped his ideas of humanity's place in the natural world, fostering an understanding of the local that is thoroughly entwined in the global and a perspective on personal experience that is mediated through ancient cultures, the behavior of nonhuman species, and vast temporal expanses. This perspective is evident, for instance, in "Surrounded by Wild Turkeys":

> Little calls   as they pass
>   through dry forbs and grasses
> Under blue oak and gray digger pine
> In the warm afternoon of the forest-fire haze;
>
> Twenty or more, long-legged birds
>   all alike.
>
> So are we, in our soft calling,
>   passing on through.
>
> Our young, which trail after,
>
> Look just like us.
>   (*No Nature*, 368)

As Timothy Gray has noted, "Advocating a transformative ethnopoetics, Snyder proved that a place-based identity did not mean a place-bound identity" (270). *Turtle Island*, the title of the 1969 volume that established Snyder's reputation as an environmentalist poet, is an American Indian name for North America,[1] and some of its poems present Snyder's local observations close to home:

> The creek falls to a far valley.
> hills beyond that
> facing, half-forested, dry
> —clear sky
> strong wind in the
> stiff glittering needle clusters
> of the pine—their brown
> round trunk bodies
> straight, still;
>   ("By Frasier Creek Falls," *Turtle Island*, 41)

Others record different American landscapes or, like "Mother Earth: Her Whales," take a global perspective protesting worldwide environmental destruction. *Turtle Island* was controversial, not merely because some critics saw its movement into didactic political modes as reducing poetry to sloganeering, but also because it was one of the places where Snyder's ideas of "becoming native" to North America were emerging, and some Native Americans objected to these as appropriative "white shamanism." Snyder's more recent writing has followed developments in the ecological sciences to place increasing emphasis on bioregionalism; in the essays that have become his primary genre for environmental activism he has championed watersheds as the basis for grassroots political activism by heterogeneous communities with shared environmental interests. Although few people in the industrialized world have access to the kinds of experiences in nature that his poems recount, such as skinning coyotes, contemplating bear scat, or observing the regrowth on logged land, Snyder's interest in awakening people to joyful human participation in the energy that flows among all life forms is accessible without wilderness living. The "digging in" that Snyder advocates includes "the tiresome but tangible work of school boards, county supervisors, local foresters—local politics" (*Turtle Island*, 101), not just the labor of learning local flora and fauna or the pleasures of "fording a stream / barefoot, pants rolled up, / holding boots, pack on, / sunshine, ice in the shallows, / northern rockies" ("For All," *No Nature*, 308). For Snyder, wilderness can be distinguished from wildness, and, as was true for Thoreau, it is wildness, available within and around us all, that is key. Consequently, Snyder's poems speak to those with little firsthand access to the wilderness or to the tasks associated with living there, both of which he celebrates as quotidian sources of learning and delight.

Completing the triumvirate of white men who have been the most discussed environmentally concerned nature poets is Wendell Berry (b. 1934), a key contemporary spokesperson not so much for wilderness as for rural agrarianism. Of the three, Berry most effectively counters the tendency to separate nature from culture, as he emphasizes working with the land. The specific culture he advocates, however, would be regarded by many as premodern, or at least as unavailable to the vast majority of people in the developed nations today. Most of his poems derive from his life on his nearly self-sustaining farm in Port Royal, Kentucky, a region where five generations of his family have farmed and to which he returned in 1964 after seven years in academic settings elsewhere. Using the simple language that he calls "community speech," Berry's discursive poetry argues directly for a way of living tied to knowing well and caring for one rural place:

> There is no earthly promise of life or peace
> but where the roots branch and weave
> their patient silent passage in the dark;
> uprooted, I have been furious without an aim.
> I am not bound for any public place,
> but for a ground of my own
> where I have planted vines and orchard trees,

> and in the heat of the day climbed up
> into the healing shadow of the woods.
> Better than any argument is to rise at dawn
> and pick dew-wet red berries in a cup.
> ("A Standing Ground," *Selected Poems*, 73)

In his essays and novels as well as in his poems, Berry is an advocate for small farm-ing communities and family farms, and he supports traditional, environmentally sound farming practices such as using draft animals rather than tractors. He is also a staunch opponent of industrialized agribusiness. While well aware that the agri-cultural practices of non-indigenous Americans have never sufficiently protected the land, he remains hopeful that careful human stewardship, in combination with nature's healing powers, can reverse past damages.

Berry exemplifies a perspective that assumes the interconnection of all species without attempting to repress all anthropocentrism. He believes in human respon-sibility for the well- being of the land and sees this as required by his Christian faith, which rests on a sacralized sense of the natural world:

> To perceive the world and our life in it as gifts originating in sanctity is to see our human economy as a continuing moral crisis. Our life of need and work forces us inescapably to use in time things belonging to eternity, and to assign finite values to things already recognized as infinitely valuable. This is a fearful predicament. It calls for prudence, humility, good work, propriety of scale. It calls for the complex responsibilities of caretaking and giving-back that we mean by "stewardship."
> ("Agrarian Standard," 27)

Berry is most explicit about his religious beliefs in his "Sabbath poems," collected in *A Timbered Choir*, but biblical cadence frequently contributes to the conserva-tive flavor of his poetic oeuvre, while a sense of mystery in nature and of "the world [being] greater than our words" is often evident ("Window Poems," *Selected Poems*, 49).

In part because it is a Christian sacrament, Berry, it is often noted, uses the metaphor of marriage to describe his bond to the land. The following passage from "The Current" can suggest why this has proved troubling, particularly for feminist readers:

> Having once put his hand into the ground,
> seeding there what he hopes will outlast him,
> a man has made a marriage with his place,
> and if he leaves it his flesh will ache to go back.
> (*Selected Poems*, 76)

Far from being unique in figuring as female the land that is rendered fertile by the seminal husbandman, Berry draws on ancient Western traditions; indeed, Snyder is another poet prone to feminizing nature and eroticizing his bond to it. Many contemporary readers object to the implicit gender dynamics of such work.

Some contemporary poets are deliberately revising the feminization of nature that constitutes another constricting aspect of our inherited ways of thinking about the natural environment.[2]

That Snyder and Berry have been, among American poets of the twentieth century, the most widely discussed by critics concerned with environmental literature, with Jeffers probably the third, reveals a good deal about poetry's place in the recent environmental imagination. Evidently, critics still tend to think of environmental poetry first and foremost as nature poetry. To the extent that all three poets live in far more strenuous and intimate relation to the rural or wild nature than most of their readers do, and to the extent that their ways of living are associated with earlier, less populated eras, their canonicity suggests that poetry readers continue to romanticize a notion of nature or wilderness as being opposed to urban and suburban living. It indicates an ongoing tendency to invest nature with spiritual and religious values, as well as a widespread investment in a narrative of decline from earlier forms of social organization thought to foster more harmonious relations between humans and the nonhuman world. It even suggests a sense of environmental poetry as ultimately elegiac; for despite Snyder's contention that the unifying energy he celebrates interanimates all life of any period, the way of living that gives him ready access to that energy is more threatened with each passing day. The eco-canonical status of these poets also indicates widespread concurrence with their belief that bringing language close to nature means using a simple accessible vocabulary to produce accurate, accessible, largely unadorned representations of sensory, and particularly visible, phenomena.

Other contemporary nature poets who lead lives more typical of middle-class Americans, so that their encounters with the green world take place in the parks or nature preserves that suburbanites can easily visit, often still maintain an illusion of solitary experiences in nature that suggests removal or retreat from the urban industrial world. Mary Oliver (b. 1935), for instance, lives in Provincetown, Massachusetts, yet she follows the nineteenth-century model of depicting a lone speaker's observation of or encounter with some creature in nature, from which arises a sense of the oneness of life, an expanded sense of self that includes the given world. As if she lived at a far remove from civilization, other human beings rarely figure in her poems, and signs of urban development—or possibilities for political activism—tend to be absent as well. Although critics such as John Elder and Laird Christensen have claimed for Oliver an ecological vision or a subject position based on ecological interdependence, her work—whose project is "learning / little by little to love / our only world"—seems to me far from ecocentric. Oliver's focus is on human happiness, which she sees as generated especially through ecstatic moments of communion with the nonhuman. Ironically, her commitment to diminishing the gap between the human and nonhuman finds expression in her representing nonhuman creatures as like humans in possessing emotions. When Oliver attributes human feelings like "joy," "disgust," "solicitude," or "love" to the animals she describes, when she attributes to peonies an "eagerness / to be wild and perfect for a moment" (22) or says of humpback whales that "They sing, too. / And not for any reason / you can't imagine" (168), her anthropomorphizing renders them less Other—less distinctly or impenetrably themselves. Her poetry's focus on human emotion is reinforced by the epiphanic lyric structure on which she consistently relies: climactic epiphany inevitably focuses attention on the speaker's inner state of revelation. This mode, which elides from the landscape humans other than the privileged speaker in order to find there a source of individual spiritual revelation and renewal, offers another enactment of the problematic "romantic ideology of wilderness" that Cronon identifies. The exceptional popularity of Oliver's poetry and work like it speaks to the continuing allure of that ideology.

Alongside Oliver, a diversity of important twentieth-century poets might well be discussed here as nature poets—among them Robert Frost, William Carlos Williams, Wallace Stevens, Marianne Moore, Theodore Roethke, Elizabeth Bishop, Lorine Niedecker, William Stafford, Denise Levertov, Robert Bly, Galway Kinnell, A. R. Ammons, Maxine Kumin, Louise Erdrich, David Wagoner, and Joy Harjo. Because of space constraints, however, I will cut short the examination of what is recognized as nature poetry to call attention to other, less widely discussed kinds of poetry that warrant fuller consideration from the perspectives of environmental criticism. These are types of poetry that focus less on individual encounters with nature and more on collective modes of inhabiting the earth; that consider in complex ways the impact of particular social structures, particular industrial or commercial practices, and such global phenomena as colonialism on the environment and those it sustains; that expand poetry's scientific engagement beyond the natural sciences of biology or geology to explore more abstract concepts of contemporary physics and chaos theory; that are not necessarily opposed to modernization and technology; that do not necessarily resist poststructuralist thinking and that invite connection to bodies of theory in literary and cultural studies; that think about the formal resources of poetry in ecological terms; or that seek in experimental approaches to poetic form and language liberation from the inherited modes of thinking that have brought us to the environmental mess in which we find ourselves.

The booklength poems of A. R. Ammons (1926–2001)—particularly *Sphere: The Form of a Motion* (1974) and *Garbage* (1993)—as opposed to the short lyrics that have earned him recognition as a nature poet, deserve separate notice here because of their unusual incorporation of current scientific understandings of the given world and their integration of natural processes into poetic form. Ammons revises Coleridge-like notions of organic form to accommodate the current understandings of the given world's fundamental structures that are available in such sciences as physics and genetics. Daniel Tobin and others have persuasively presented Ammons's capacious and seemingly rambling meditations as "reconfiguring patterns across multiple scales of experience" (132), linking his poetic structures to the fractal forms now understood to be pervasive in nature. Scientific vocabularies contribute importantly to his markedly heterogeneous diction, while concepts from geology, astronomy, and other sciences appear in the poems and inform his ecological vision. As early as 1963, Ammons identified the principle underlying his dynamic poetics as ecology:

> *ecology* is my word: tag
>   me with that: come
>   in there:
>   you will find yourself
> in a firmless country:
>   centers & peripheries
>   in motion,
>   organic,
> interrelations!
>
>   (*Tape*, 112)

As his long poem "Extremes and Moderations" demonstrates, Ammons is keenly aware of the balances achieved in natural systems through constant change and circulation of energy, as well as the vulnerability to human interference of their marvelous integration. His favorite rhetorical device, as many have noted, is chiasmus, which itself suggests the balanced interrelation of parts within a whole.

Sphere was prompted by the first images of the earth seen from outer space—images that emphasize the interdependent, unified one in the one/many problem Ammons often wrestles with. In *Garbage,* the generative image of a literal mountain of trash in a landfill near I-95 in Florida prompts contemplation of the roles that destruction and decomposition play in poetry and in the dynamics of the natural world, itself the realm of garbage. Dedicated "to the bacteria, tumblebugs, scavengers, wordsmiths—the transfigurers, restorers," *Garbage* employs what Willard Spiegelman calls a "poetics of composting," both mimicking—particularly in its relation to literary history—and examining the processes of energy transfer that enable fresh creation from waste. As an aging man confronting both his own impending physical decay and the huge quantities of trash generated by unsustainable human consumption, Ammons manages to salvage a positive vision by focusing on ongoing transformation. Thus, late in *Garbage* he announces that rather than being on the lookout for evil, he would:

> rather call everything else holy, you know, even
>
> plowing a good way into garbage, taking that on
> as having, perhaps, just served a sacred function
>
> or, having passed through the cleansing of decay,
> ju[s]t about to: for, you know, forms are never
>
> permanent form, change the permanence, so
> that one thing one day is something else another

> day, and the energy that informs all forms just
> breezes right through filth as clean as a whistle:
>
> (*Garbage*, 115)

Ammons's use of the colon as his primary punctuation mark, his frequently asyn-
tactic line breaks, and the constant shifting of his thought from the microscopic to
macroscopic, trivial to grand, scatological to philosophical, all give formal embodi-
ment to his understanding of the ongoing flux of the universe—"the form of a
motion"—within which human life and thought, too, are always moving and neces-
sarily provisional.

While Ammons's tendency to think of poetic form in ecological terms has
gained critical attention, little notice has been paid to the ecological dimensions of
the influential ideas of "composition by field" and of the poem as energy exchange
that Charles Olson (1910–1970) laid out in his essays and exemplified in his poetry.
Partly because of the narrowness—and ignorance—generated by the balkanization
of poetry studies discussed earlier, and partly because of the widespread sense that
environmental poetry is synonymous with nature poetry in conventional Roman-
tic/realist modes, ecocriticism has tended to overlook work in the Objectivist tradi-
tion to which Olson's poetics may be traced, as well as work by the Black Mountain
writers with whom he was affiliated. Only very recently has the Objectivist Lorine
Niedecker (1903–1970) been considered in an ecocritical light, for instance, though
most of the production from her marvelous poetic "condensery" concerns her "life
by water" and its movements "thru birdstart / wingdrip / weed-drift" (238). In 2000,
the critic Matthew Cooperman published the first essay to analyze Olson's poetry
and poetics from an ecological perspective; before that, only Sherman Paul even
wrote about Olson as a nature poet.[3] Yet Olson proclaimed, "I take SPACE to be
the central fact to man born in America, from Folsom cave to now. I spell it large
because it comes large here. Large, and without mercy" ("Call Me Ishmael," *Collected
Prose*, 17), and in his early *Maximus Poems* about Gloucester, Massachusetts, he
attends to its environmental history. His writing should command considerable
interest among environmental critics interested in space and place in U.S. literature.

"Projective Verse," the essay/manifesto in which Olson outlines his princi-
ples of composition by field, emphasizes that "the projective involves a stance
toward reality outside a poem as well as a new stance towards the reality of a
poem itself" (246):

> It comes to this: the use of a man, by himself and thus by others, lies in how he
> conceives his relation to nature, that force to which he owes his somewhat small
> existence. If he sprawl, he shall find little to sing but himself.... But if he stays
> inside himself, if he is contained within his nature as he is participant in the larger
> force, he will be able to listen, and his hearing through himself will give him secrets
> objects share. (247)

Olson advocated "objectism" in poetry: "the getting rid of the lyrical interface of
the individual as ego...by which western man has interposed himself between

what he is as a creature of nature…and those other creations of nature which we may, with no derogation, call objects" (247). In "Human Universe," he asserts that discourse "needs now to be returned to the only two universes which count, the two phenomenal ones, the two a man has need to bear on because they bear so on him: that of himself, as organism, and that of his environment, the earth and planets" (156). Larry Eigner (1926–1996) is one example of a Black Mountain–associated poet, also linked to early Language writing, who took Olson's ideas to heart and whose work invites ecocritical reading. His work is of additional interest because it brings together the concerns of environmental and disability studies; Eigner was severely disabled by cerebral palsy so that much of his experience of the outdoor environment was mediated through windows, often from a prone position that contrasts with the ambulatory upright stance assumed in most nature writing.

While poets at least since the dawn of the industrial era have expressed alarm about human-induced environmental degradation, only since World War II, when it became evident that humankind could virtually destroy life on the planet with the use of the atom bomb, have large numbers of poets been producing work that brings into focus not nature's meaning or beauty but nature's abuse and the consequences of that abuse. In this context of what Buell dubs a "discourse of toxicity," "the nature one engages must now inescapably be—if indeed it has not always in some sense been—not pristine but the effect of 'second' (i.e., modified) nature or (in Derek Jarmon's phrase) 'modern nature'" (*Writing*, 45). James Wright's (1927–1980) depictions of the ugly and polluted landscapes produced by mining and steelmaking operations in his native Ohio—the "pits of stripmines," "the chemical riffles of the Ohio River" (20, 24)—provide examples. Similarly, in Brenda Hillman's (b. 1951) experimental tetralogy organized around the elements of earth, air, water, and (yet to be published) fire, reminders of environmental degradation are frequent. *Cascadia*'s exploration of the geology of California includes poems on dioxin and on nonbiodegradable Styrofoam cups, while *Practical Water* is full of observations like "Unusually warm global warming day out" (5) or "Geese pull worms through agricultural runoff / pooling on side lawns" (90).

Poetry that calls attention to degradation of the environment often has an angry, political edge because there is always some entity or social system responsible for the damage. Wright names particular local companies such as Hanna Coal or Wheeling Steel, but often poets leave the adversary/perpetrator less specific so as to allow for suggestion of broader complicity in destructive and inequitable consumption of natural resources. Either way, such work often warrants consideration in terms of environmental justice, which involves a strategic revision of anthropocentrism that brings to the fore the socially inequitable human costs of environmental damage. Environmental justice perspectives, for instance, can illuminate the work of Simon Ortiz (b. 1941); while his poetry generally focuses on the sustenance provided by the bond that Native Americans feel with the land, it also makes clear that white hegemony—as manifest in the vicinity of his Acoma Pueblo, for instance, in the laying of the railroad or, more recently, uranium mining—is responsible for the loss or degradation of Indian land that has left Native people struggling to survive. A poem that begins "The horizons are still mine," ends

> Gila River, the interstate sign says
> at the cement bridge over bed
> full of brush and sand and rusty cans.
> Where's the water, the water
> which you think about sometimes
> in empty desperation?
> It's in those green, very green fields
> which are not mine.
>
> You call me a drunk Indian, go ahead.
> ("'And the Land is Just as Dry,'" *Woven Stone*, 245)

From Sand Creek draws connections between the misery of Vietnam veterans and the massacre of Cheyennes and Arapahoes that took place at Sand Creek a century before. There, Ortiz presents the early white settlers, in the arrogance of manifest destiny, as having squandered an opportunity to live in right relation to the land as the Native people of the continent had been doing for millennia: "Like a soul, the land / was open to them, like a child's heart. / There was no paradise, / but it would have gently and willingly / and longingly given them food and air / and substance for every comfort. / If they had only acknowledged / even their smallest conceit" (*Sand Creek*, 79). Their error proved a source of spiritual imbalance and violence in white society, and of impoverishment and degradation in both the Indians and their land. In such poetry, as in environmental justice writing more generally, the crucial division is not between humans and nature or wilderness; rather, it is between, on the one hand, powerful people—often representing the socioeconomic system of capitalism—bent on colonization, profit, and the development of their built world and, on the other, oppressed, disempowered people—often women or people of color—along with the natural world on which all life forms rely for sustenance.

One poetic genre in which the intertwining of environmental and human destruction can readily be exposed is documentary poetry where the incorporation of nonliterary documents provides factual evidence that lends authenticating force to the poet's exposure of environmental (and other) ills. Muriel Rukeyser's (1913–1980) *The Book of the Dead*, depicting the Gauley Bridge, West Virginia, mining disaster in which hundred of miners died of silicosis, is the best-known poetic documentary from the decade most associated with that form, the 1930s. The documentary poet avails herself of the resources of the historian and the journalist, while drawing also upon the emotional power of the lyric, so that Rukeyser's sequence juxtaposes transcriptions of congressional testimony, descriptions of the countryside, legislative petitions, stock market quotes, affecting lyric testimonials from varied voices, and passages from the Egyptian *Book of the Dead*. Rukeyser's primary focus is on the plight of the exploited workers, but the deadly transformation of

the natural environment wrought by mining is conveyed through images of hell-
ish distortion—a "hill of glass," silica forming "a blinded field of white / murdering
snow" (95), "the roaring flowers of the chimney-stacks"(96). In contrast to much
nature poetry, however, Rukeyser's poem is not hostile to industry or technology
per se, nor opposed to all forms of human "mastery" of nature. The river is a source
of power, and power or energy has no ethical valence in the poem; the issue is how
it is used. Contemporary poets such as Claudia Rankine (*Don't Let Me Be Lonely* or,
in an even more mixed-genre mode, her guided bus tour *The Provenance of Beauty*)
and Mark Nowak (*Shut Up Shut Down, Coal Mountain Elementary*) are reinvigorat-
ing documentary poetics, incorporating more photographs and other visual ele-
ments while continuing to expose the intertwining of social and economic systems
with environmental health and justice.

Because of her largely Marxist agenda, Rukeyser downplays the racial dynam-
ics of the Gauley Bridge disaster, in which most of the victims were migrant black
workers, although her imagery's emphasis on the whiteness of the power station
and of the silicone, particularly as it coated the dark skin of African American
workers like George Robinson, clearly links the abuses of Union Carbide with heg-
emonic white society more generally. Environmental injustice in the United States
is closely bound to environmental racism; consequently, the environmental justice
movement has provided an impetus for environmentally engaged writing by poets
of color when environmentalism otherwise seemed connected only to concerns,
like wilderness preservation, that have been perceived as the luxury of a white elite.
African American writers in particular have had a vexed relation to American
nature and to nature writing: African Americans slaved in the fields though that
also meant they knew the land intimately; trees offered welcome shade but also
inevitably called to mind the "strange fruit" of lynchings; and while most African
Americans have familial roots in the rural South, the substantial majority now are
urban residents. Camille Dungy's impressive anthology *Black Nature: Four Centu-
ries of African American Nature Poetry* (2009) has significantly expanded aware-
ness among environmental critics of the range and complexity of African American
nature poetry. It also increases the visibility of urban pastoral writing, which often
conveys environmental justice concerns. Increasing awareness of the urban pastoral
is helping poetry studies catch up with the trend within environmental studies of
examining urban environments and the ecosystems within which they exist.

Ed Roberson's (b. 1939) *City Eclogue* exemplifies recent poetry that revises the
pastoral tradition of eclogue in which the elevation of rustic life implied a denigra-
tion of the urban. "City Eclogue: Words for It" opens with a romanticized vision
of how "you'd expect" trees would be planted: they "should rise from seeds whose
fluttering to the ground / is the bird's delicate alight / or the soft petal stepping its
image / into the soil." Instead, the speaker observes city trucks "bumping up over
the curb" to drop trees with balled roots that are then "bur[ied]" by city workers
(16). He asserts the naturalness of such a mode of plant dispersal, while reminding
readers that seeds are more likely to be planted by passing through birds' digestive
systems than by some delicate fluttering suited to the idealized *locus amoenus* that

pastoral has taught readers to expect. Similarly locating the natural in the city, "Urban Nature" (83) depicts the "simple quiet" of a pocket park in the interval between buses and subway trains; one need not retreat from the city to find the peace that people conventionally seek in rural living. The poem ends with a moment of fruitfulness in which "sweet berries ripen in the street," a moment that alludes to the close of Wallace Stevens's "Sunday Morning," where "sweet berries ripen in the wilderness" and "casual flocks of pigeons make / Ambiguous undulations as they sink / Downward to darkness, on extended wings" (*Collected Poems,* 70). The birds that are part of urban nature in Roberson's poem, however, are "street / hawk[s]" selling imported fruit in kiosks; his poems convey a belief that "there is no outside of Nature" (Dungy, 3).

In "Manufacturing the Ghetto," Michael Bennett has called for an urban eco-criticism that will help put an end to racist public policy by confronting "the eco-logical devastation being wreaked upon inner cities and the ideologies that underlie this assault" (170). *City Eclogue* seems a perfect text on which to practice such crit-icism, for Roberson, who is African American, has a keen sense of the spatializa-tion of race that Bennett emphasizes. In "The Open," Roberson explicitly writes as part of a "[a] people within a people" whose "any beginning is disbursed / by a vagrant progress, // whose any settlement / is overturned for the better // of a highway through to someone else's / possibility" (64). Roberson describes vacant city lots "fallowing" (64) like uncultivated farm fields; house-brick rubble as "a flat-tened sea" in which the "catch" is broken glass (70); "stands of houses" "mowed down" as if in clear-cut logging (64); and a garbage truck that "lopes" from house to house—embodiment of the white power structure that deprives inner-city residents of jobs—as "the wolf" that has "our scent" (56). With such images, he mobilizes the language of nature to link the current degradation of the urban environment, which threatens the survival particularly of impoverished black residents, to the destruc-tion of natural habitats usually decried by environmentalists.

Roberson's work connects the falsity—and ultimately the violent immorality—of dividing the "natural" from the built environment with the error of dividing people according to race and class. The characteristic fluidity of his syntax, in which one structure often drifts almost undetectably into another, itself counters the American tendency to divide white from black, the present from the past, various manifesta-tions or scales of nature from each other. "Sit In What City We're In" significantly depicts black protestors and the white segregationists in the early civil rights sit-ins as mirrored versions of each other—"our one / long likeness" endlessly reflected in the lunch counter mirrors. Part 1 ends by extending this mirroring into all of built and nonbuilt nature to emphasize their unity and the unity of humankind:

> The oceans, themselves one,   catch their image
>   hosed by riot cops down the gutter into
> The sphere surface
> river
>   looked into   reflects
>   one face. (27–28)

It can be a short step from writing that highlights crises of environmental deg-
radation, pollution, and toxicity to writing that warns of or prophesies apocalypse,
particularly in the postatomic age. W. S. Merwin (b. 1927), a passionate environmental-
ist, has produced a great deal of work that celebrates the sensual beauty of nature or
expresses outrage on behalf of ruined landscapes and threatened cultural values (par-
ticularly in Hawai'i, where he has been living and restoring land since the early 1980s);
early in his career, however, he produced powerful poetry in the apocalyptic vein. His
haunting 1967 collection, *The Lice,* uses pared-down language and semi-surreal narra-
tives with mythic overtones to convey the planet's impending desolation. By instruct-
ing the gray whale what to tell the creator "When you have left the seas nodding on
their stalks / Empty of you," the poem titled "For a Coming Extinction" comments bit-
terly on the anthropocentrism that allows humans heedlessly to cause the extinction of
countless "irreplaceable hosts": "Tell him / That it is we who are important" (68, 69). In
contrast to that collection, which focuses on the void to come and only gestures broadly
toward the causes of the approaching annihilation of human and animal life, Jorie Gra-
ham (b. 1950), in her 2008 volume *Sea Change,* is explicitly concerned with climate
change and sometimes offers specific details about what exactly is going wrong:

> ...in the
> coiling, at the very bottom of
> the food
> chain, sprung
from undercurrents, warming by 1 degree, the in-
> dispensable
plankton is forced north now, & yet farther north,
> spawning too late for the cod larvae hatch,
> such
that the hatch will not survive, nor the
> species in the end, in the right-now forever
> un-interruptible slowing of the
> gulf
stream...

("Sea Change," 4–5)

Almost unfathomably, "The permanent is ebbing" (3); "fish are starving to death in
the Great Barrier Reef, the new Age of Extinctions is / now / says the silence-that-
precedes—you know not what / you / are entering, a time / beyond belief" (42).

Ecocritics debate the value of apocalyptic writing: Does it produce crises as
much as respond to them? Do apocalyptic predictions that prove false discredit the
environmental movement more broadly? In identifying the threat as evil does apoc-
alyptic discourse foster a tendency to simplify the moral landscape? Or is it the most
powerful tool available with which to convey to people the seriousness of the envi-
ronmental issues we face? Can imagining the apocalypse prompt action and thereby
help forestall it? Here are Graham's ruminations from an interview:

What is the imagination supposed to do with its capacity to "imagine" the end? Is the imagination of the unimaginable possible, and, perhaps, as I have come to believe, might it be one of the most central roles the human gift of imagination is being called upon to enact? Perhaps if we use it to summon the imagination of where we are headed—what that will feel like—what it will feel like to look back at this juncture— maybe we will wake up in time? I have written it [*Sea Change*] in order to make myself not only understand—we all seem to "understand"—but to actually "feel" (and thus physically believe) what we have and what we are losing—and furthermore what devastatingly much more of creation we are going to be losing.

("Imagining the Unimaginable")

In *Sea Change* she attends not just to the current disruption of established cycles— e.g., "Deep autumn & the mistake occurs, the plum tree blossoms,"—but also to the kind of wondrous beauty that nature poets have long celebrated, trying to grasp through her senses and her intellect what humans are privileged to experience in the elusive present. In lines that spill down the page and shift constantly in focus but maintain relentless intensity, Graham attempts to capture the complexity not only of the web of global environmental interrelation but also of human beings' tangled, inconsistent ability to recognize and respond to our precarious planetary situation.

As more extended quotation from *Sea Change*, Roberson's *City Eclogue,* or Hillman's *Cascadia* would demonstrate, a substantial body of contemporary environmentally concerned poetry eschews the straightforward and readily accessible modes that poets like Jeffers, Snyder, and Berry have felt essential to their cause. Joan Retallack explains that experimental poets of recent decades have been bent on using language "not so much as instrument to peer through as instrument of investigative engagement." Avoiding a focus on the self, they seek to "enact interrogations" into the most problematic structures of the contemporary moment, and very recently the environmental problem of anthropocentrism has come to be among them. Retallack proposes that the goal of "allowing parts of the world, previously excluded, into the operational purview of our poetics—somehow on their own terms" requires that the poet begin by asking questions:

How can the unalike know one another if "know" means to encounter and experience one another well? How can the bird, the fly-catcher, enter the poem without having to do work for the sentimentally needy poet? Such questions suggest an experimental design (a way to investigate the questions) of a poem that must be driven by honest observation, research, and—because it is a poem—chancing, inventing new interrelationships among subjects, vocabularies, literary devices. The results, if one calls all this an experiment, are the poem itself.

Retallack speaks for many when she posits experimentation as a necessary, problem-solving response when our previous ways of thinking and being have been too narrowly focused on the human:

The chaotic interconnectedness of all things, the dynamic pattern-bounded indeterminacy in which we find ourselves, in which we must somehow find/make patterns among contingencies not intelligently designed for our convenience alone, leads to the pragmatic necessity of ingenious experimentation as wager on the possibility of a viable, even pleasurable future together in this world with all those others.

Through his journal *ecopoetics*, Jonathan Skinner has helped draw attention to the interest in environmental writing among those committed to "investigative poetics." His claim, like Retallack's, is that such poetry's complexities might be useful for extending our perceptions of the natural world. While some experimentalists associated with slightly earlier avant-garde practices, including Language writing—such as Bruce Andrews, Robert Grenier, Tina Darragh, Rachel Blau DuPlessis, Alice Notley, Joan Retallack, and Charles Bernstein—have published in *ecopoetics*, Skinner criticizes that generation for generally failing to bring their sophisticated approaches to bear on environmental issues. His loosely annual journal especially showcases work by writers born in the second half of the century, including Ben Friedlander, Cole Swensen, Lisa Jarnot, Kenneth Goldsmith, Catherine Daly, Alicia Cohen, Forrest Gander, and Juliana Spahr—to name but a few of the growing number of contributors.

The work of Juliana Spahr (b. 1966) can demonstrate a few of the experiments these younger poets are undertaking. Moreover, Spahr speaks for many experimentally inclined ecopoets when she expresses an aversion for "nature poetry." In the statement appended to her chapbook *things of each possible relation hashing against one another*, she recalls that after moving to Hawai'i she felt a moral revulsion not only toward the error-filled "747 poems" written by those who merely flew to the islands for a vacation, but also toward the poetry that was accurate about flora and fauna; the latter, she explains, "tended to show the beautiful bird but not so often the bulldozer off to the side that was destroying the bird's habitat. And it wasn't talking about how the bird, often a bird which had arrived recently from somewhere else, interacted with and changed the larger system of this world we live in and on" (27). That chapbook emerged from Spahr's taking a course in ethnobotany and then applying several experimental procedures to the writing sparked by the course. She put the poems through an online translation machine that translated her words "between the languages that came to the Pacific from somewhere else" before weaving together the numerous versions into complicated patterns taken "from the math that shows up in plants" or approximating the shapes of things around her (28). Spahr's procedures in this radically reconceived nature poetry, then, incorporate into the form of the poem the processes of trade and contact that have had such profound impacts on ecosystems worldwide while they imitate the complex processes, interactions, and patterns evident in nature. What resulted highlights the different significance analogy holds for botanists and for poets as well as the imbalances produced by the introduction of nonnative species and nonindigenous forms of government and commerce.

Spahr's experimentalism adapts to suit different projects. In "Poem Written After September 11, 2001," from *This Connection of Everyone with Lungs* (2005), she uses a repeating, cumulative structure associated with nursery rhymes. Particularly because of its reliance on prepositions, which emphasize relationality, this structure underscores the interconnectedness of all members of all breathing species. Here's one iteration, in which the breath is also expanded by repeated "ands" that extend the exhalation:

as everyone with lungs breathes the space between the hands and the space around
the hands and the space of the room and the space of the building that surrounds
the room and the space of the neighborhoods nearby and the space of the cities and
the space of the regions and the space of the nations and the space of the continents
and islands and the space of the oceans in and out. (6–7)

The poem closes with a reminder that we all breathe the industrial pollution as well
as the environmental consequences of events like the 9/11 bombings:

> The space of everyone that has just been inside of everyone mixing inside of every-
> one with nitrogen and oxygen and water vapor and argon and carbon dioxide and
> suspended dust spores and bacteria mixing inside of everyone with sulfur and sul-
> furic acid and titanium and nickel and minute silicon particles from pulverized
> glass and concrete.

> How lovely and how doomed this connection of everyone with lungs. (9–10)

The other extended poem in that volume experiments with unusual plurals; this
is most noticeable with pronouns, as in "yours hands." Reflecting a constructiv-
ist belief that our language shapes our thought and behavior, the poem's address
to "beloveds" in a time of war and environmental destruction is one strategy with
which Spahr attempts to extend to a planetary scale the loving relationship that
individuals enjoy with their closest companions.

   In emphasizing the value of what experimental poetry may offer ecocriticism,
I mean to correct an oversight, not generate a new imbalance. Ecocritical reading
can serve many functions, and no single poetics best serves them all.[4] Ecocritism
can increase awareness of the multiple levels of humanity's reliance on nature, from
spiritual sustenance or aesthetic gratification to physical nourishment and survival.
It can highlight the ways in which humans endanger planetary survival, through
our behaviors and through the conceptual—and linguistic—structures that motivate
them. It can foster examination of the ethics of our relations with the species with
whom we share the planet, and it can attempt—within the limits of what is human-
produced—to allow their ways, sounds, and rhythms to enter into our words. It can
attune us to significant losses of biodiversity or of ecosocial well-being and convey the
urgency of particular crises. Most importantly, whether by directly inspiring polit-
ical action or by shifting our ways of thinking and perceiving, it can move humans
to change or to make environmentally beneficial changes. As long as we cultivate
awareness of implicit ideologies and mindfulness of the limits of human language, a
range of poetic and critical approaches can contribute to this vast agenda.

NOTES

1 Garrard notes that "the assumption of indigenous environmental virtue is a foundational
   belief for deep ecologists and many ecocritics" (120) and provides insightful examination
   of the stereotype of the "ecological Indian" (120–135).
2 The denigrating association of women with nature is one issue that is addressed by
   ecofeminists. "Radical ecofeminists" embrace this association but reverse the

conventional hierarchy in which men, in association with culture and reason, are more valued. Other ecofeminists, such as Val Plumwood, resist any notion of essential femininity grounded in biological sex, and critique the gendered dualism that opposes reason to nature.

3 More recently, in a more experimental mode, Jed Rasula's *This Compost: Ecological Imperatives in American Poetry* (2002) combines critical essay and a "compost library" of poetic extracts placed side by side without authorial distinction to explore the composting sensibility evident in writing within the Black Mountain lineage.

4 Similarly, there is value in developing multiple theoretical models, a topic not addressed here. Martin Hiedegger, Maurice Merleau-Ponty, Gilles Deleuze, Mikhail Bakhtin, Gayatri Spivak, Bruno Latour, and Michel Serres, among others, have provided the foundations for promising ecotheoretical approaches.

REFERENCES

Ammons, A. R. *Garbage*. New York: W. W. Norton, 1993.
———. *Sphere: The Form of a Motion*. New York: W. W. Norton, 1974.
———. *Tape for the Turn of the Year*. 1965. New York: W. W. Norton, 1972.
Bennett, Michael. "Manufacturing the Ghetto: Anti-urbanism and the Spatialization of Race." In *The Nature of Cities: Ecocriticism and Urban Environments*, ed. Michael Bennet and David W. Teague. Tucson: University of Arizona Press, 1999. 169–188.
Berry, Wendell. "The Agrarian Standard." In *The Essential Agrarian Reader: The Future of Culture, Community, and the Land*, ed. Norman Wirzba. Washington, DC: Counterpoint, 2004.
———. *The Selected Poems of Wendell Berry*. Washington, DC: Counterpoint, 1998.
Buell, Lawrence. *The Future of Environmental Criticism: Environmental Crisis and Literary Imagination*. Malden, MA: Blackwell, 2005.
———. *Writing for an Endangered World: Literature, Culture, and the Environment in the U.S. and Beyond*. Cambridge: Harvard University Press, 2001.
Cronon, William. "The Trouble with Wilderness; or, Getting Back to the Wrong Nature." In *Uncommon Ground: Rethinking the Human Place in Nature*, ed. Willian Cronon. New York: W. W. Norton, 1995. 69–90.
Dungy, Camille T., ed. *Black Nature: Four Centuries of African American Nature Poetry*. Athens: University of Georgia Press, 2009.
Felstiner, John. *Can Poetry Save the Earth? A Field Guide to Nature Poems*. New Haven: Yale University Press, 2009.
Garrard, Greg. *Ecocriticism*. London: Routledge, 2004.
Graham, Jorie. "Imagining the Unimaginable: Jorie Graham in Conversation." Interviewed by Deirdre Wengen. http://www.poets.org/viewmedia.php/prmMID/20176 (accessed July 1, 2010).
———. *Sea Change*. New York: HarperCollins, 2008.
Gray, Timothy. *Gary Snyder and the Pacific Rim: Creating Counter-Cultural Community*. Iowa City: University of Iowa Press, 2006.
Hass, Robert. *Praise*. New York: Ecco, 1979.
Heise, Ursula. "Hitchhiker's Guide to Ecocriticism." *PMLA* 121.2 (March 2006): 503–516.
Hillman, Brenda. *Practical Water*. Middletown, CT: Wesleyan University Press, 2009.

Jeffers, Robinson. *The Double Axe and Other Poems*. New York: Liveright, 1977.

———. *The Wild God of the World: An Anthology of Robinson Jeffers*. Ed. with introd. by Albert Gelpi. Stanford: Stanford University Press, 2003.

Merwin, W. S. *The Lice*. 1967. New York: Atheneum, 1974.

Niedecker, Lorine. *Collected Works*. Ed. Jenny Penberthy. Berkeley: University of California Press, 2002.

Oliver, Mary. *New and Selected Poems*. Boston: Beacon, 1992.

Olson, Charles. *Collected Prose*. Ed. Donald Allen and Benjamin Friedlander. Berkeley: University of California Press, 1997.

Ortiz, Simon J. *From Sand Creek*. 1981. Tucson: University of Arizona Press, 2000.

———. *Woven Stone*. Tucson: University of Arizona Press, 1992.

Rasula, Jed. *This Compost: Ecological Imperatives in American Poetry*. Athens: University of Georgia Press, 2002.

Retallack, Joan. "What Is Experimental Poetry & Why Do We Need It?" *Jacket* 32 (April 2007), http://jacketmagazine.com/32/p-retallack.shtml (accessed July 1, 2010).

Roberson, Ed. *City Eclogue*. Berkeley, CA: Atelos, 2006.

Rukeyser, Muriel. *The Book of the Dead*. In *The Collected Poems of Muriel Rukeyser*, ed. Janet E. Kaufman and Anne F. Herzog. Pittsburgh: Pittsburgh University Press, 2005. 73–111.

Scigaj, Leonard M. *Sustainable Poetry: Four American Ecopoets*. Lexington: University Press of Kentucky, 1999.

Snyder, Gary. *No Nature: New and Selected Poems*. New York: Pantheon, 1992.

———. *Turtle Island*. New York: New Directions, 1974.

Spahr, Juliana. *things of each possible relation hashing against one another*. Newfield, NY: Palm, 2003.

———. *This Connection of Everyone with Lungs*. Berkeley: University of California Press, 2005.

Spiegelman, Willard. "Breaking Up and Breaking Down: The Poetics of Composting." In *Complexities of Motion: New Essays on A. R. Ammons's Long Poems*, ed. Steven P. Schneider. Cranbury, NJ: Associated University Presses, 1999. 51–67.

Stevens, Wallace. *The Collected Poems of Wallace Stevens*. New York: Alfred A. Knopf, 1968.

Tobin, Daniel. "A. R. Ammons and the Poetics of Chaos." In *Complexities of Motion: New Essays on A. R. Ammons's Long Poems*, ed. Steven P. Schneider. Cranbury, NJ: Associated University Presses, 1999. 113–137.

Wright, James. *This Branch Will Not Break*. Middletown, CT: Wesleyan University Press, 1963.

CHAPTER 24

....

TRANSNATIONALISM AND DIASPORA IN AMERICAN POETRY

....

TIMOTHY YU

SCHOLARS within American literary studies have become increasingly transnational in their outlook, reframing questions of U.S. national identity in a global context of imperialism, migration, and hybridization. The work of Asian American and African American writers is increasingly being read alongside the work of other writers from the Asian and African diasporas. The transnational turn in U.S. literary studies has been characterized by a rejection of narrowly national paradigms in favor of a renewed awareness of cross-border contexts. The concept of diaspora, historically used to describe the dispersion of the Jewish people but since broadened to include other populations displaced from their native homelands, has gained increasing prominence in the study of ethnic or racial minority groups.

This chapter explores how literary-critical understanding of modern and contemporary American poetry is shifting under the pressure of transnational and diasporic forces. Drawing on several case studies aimed at illuminating what it means to read American poetry transnationally, I argue that transnational and diasporic perspectives encourage us to view the United States as a node of political, economic, and cultural exchange, in which the crossing of borders has become constitutive of Americanness rather than external to it, and invite us to examine how such border crossings are registered in the content and form of modern and contemporary American poetry. In contrast to the seeming solidity of national identities, diasporic identifications are often ambivalent, acknowledging the pull of multiple histories while remaining at a critical distance from any single location.

Adopting a transnational paradigm for reading modern American poetry means more than simply acknowledging the transatlantic influences that have shaped U.S. writing, or turning our attention to the international and cosmopolitan character of modernism. The concept of transnationalism—defined by Steven Vertovec as "sustained cross-border relationships, patterns of exchange, affiliations and social formations spanning nation-states" (2)—has emerged in recent decades as a key term in theories of globalization and postmodernity. While "international," as Jahan Ramazani puts it, suggests relations among "static national entities," "transnational" emphasizes "flows and affiliations...across the borders of nation-states, regions, and cultures" (181). The way in which transnationalism registers its crossing of borders, its movements across uneven and disjointed terrains, distinguishes it from an international perspective.

Transnationalism encompasses the global production and distribution networks of multinational corporations as well as the border-crossing flows of migration, media, and capital that link diasporic populations in different countries. Although these populations do interact in complex ways with national forces, transnationalism is characterized by social, political, and economic formations that are no longer tied to the nation-state, understood as a geographically bounded political and cultural entity. Indeed, some theorists have asserted that in the era of globalization, the nation-state has lost its value as the primary unit through which to analyze global relations. Arjun Appadurai, for example, argues that "the nation-state, as a complex modern political form, is on its last legs" (19) and that transnational forces will increasingly "confound theories that depend on the continued salience of the nation-state as the key arbiter of important social changes" (4).

Within American literary studies, the turn to transnationalism has meant an increased attention to the history of U.S. imperialism. In her introduction to *Cultures of United States Imperialism*, Amy Kaplan argues that an attention to imperialism in the study of American culture "shows how putatively domestic conflicts are not simply contained at home but...emerge in response to international struggles and spill over national boundaries" (16). Amritjit Singh and Peter Schmidt assert that at the dawn of the twenty-first century, U.S. studies has reached a "'transnational' moment" in which the study of differences that appear internal to the nation (race, gender, class) can be understood only in the context of global forces that extend beyond the nation's borders (viii). The permeability of national borders has also been emphasized by work in Chicana/o and Asian American studies, from Gloria Anzaldúa's *Borderlands/La Frontera* to David Palumbo-Liu's *Asian/American: Historical Crossings of a Racial Frontier*.

Closely linked to the rise of the transnational paradigm is the increasing use of the term "diaspora" to describe populations that might previously have been studied as racial or ethnic minority groups within a particular nation-state. As Jana Evans Braziel and Anita Mannur note, while the term diaspora "denotes communities of people dislocated from their native homelands through migration, immigration, or exile as a consequence of colonial expansion," its current usage also contains connotations of "fertility of dispersion, dissemination, and the scattering of seeds"

(4). Paul Gilroy's *The Black Atlantic* is perhaps the paradigmatic example of this new approach to diaspora. Gilroy rejects "nationalist" or "ethnically absolutist" frameworks for understanding black British or black American culture in favor of a transnational, intercultural concept of "the black Atlantic" organized around "the structure of the African diaspora into the western hemisphere" (15). Aihwa Ong has focused on the Chinese diaspora, arguing that increased mobility of people and capital between Asia and North America makes it increasingly difficult to conceive of distinct "Chinese American" communities separated off from China by a national boundary. Arjun Appadurai asserts that the new "diasporic public spheres" created by transnational migration and media may be increasingly displacing nation-based frameworks, forming "the crucibles of a postnational political order" (22).

The embrace of transnational and diasporic paradigms has not gone unquestioned by some critics. The Asian Americanist scholar Sau-ling C. Wong has raised concerns over the "denationalization" of ethnic studies, in which critiques of cultural nationalism and greater awareness of transnational circulation have led away from Asian American studies' previous emphasis on "claiming America" and a space for Asians in U.S. history and culture. Wong worries that the new transnationalism may exclude American-born Asians and weaken the pan-ethnic coalitions that have previously characterized Asian American activism and scholarship. "[T]he loosely held and fluctuating collectivity called 'Asian Americans,'" Wong asserts, "will dissolve back into its descent defined constituents as soon as one leaves American national borders behind," replaced by studies of the Chinese or Indian diaspora (138).

Just as Wong worries that the transnational turn may spell the end of Asian American studies, one might easily ask whether, by extension, it also spells the end of American studies. In the wake of critiques of nationalism like Gilroy's and Appadurai's, does it make sense to continue to conceive of literary study in national terms at all? What is the continuing value of a category like "American poetry"?

Jahan Ramazani's *A Transnational Poetics* considers a number of "transnational templates," from migration to travel to decolonization, as alternatives to grouping poets by nationality, even as he acknowledges the persistent power of national categories (xi). Appadurai argues that the United States may need to be reconceived as a "federation of diasporas," since "no existing conception of Americanness can contain this large variety of transnations" (172–173). But Appadurai also acknowledges that the United States' ideology of pluralism means that "there is a special American way to connect to these global diasporas," and that the United States "might come to be seen as a model of how to arrange one territorial locus (among others) for a cross-hatching of diasporic communities" (173). A transnational reading of American poetry does not mean rejecting the national framework entirely, but it does mean recasting the United States as a node of exchange for political, social, and economic flows—forces that help shape the form of modern American poetry.

A consideration of transnationalism in modern American poetry might begin by inquiring into the transnationalism of American poetic modernism. Modernism was an international and transatlantic phenomenon, and expatriates like T. S. Eliot and Ezra Pound spent much of their careers working outside the United States. Just as important were these poets' uses of a global range of sources, particularly non-Western sources. Eliot famously concludes *The Waste Land* with a citation of the Hindu Upanishads, quoting the words *datta, dayadhvam, damyata* (give, sympathize, control) and ending on the repeated word *shantih* (peace). Much of Pound's poetics draws on Asian models, from his translations of Chinese poetry in *Cathay* to his use of the Chinese ideogram as a structuring principle for *The Cantos*—a work that places Chinese characters alongside its blend of European languages.

Ramazani sees the work of Eliot and Pound as "profoundly cross-cultural, translocal, and transnational" in its interweaving of "Euro-classicism and Chinese ideograms, cockney gossip and Sanskrit parable, Confucius and Thomas Jefferson, the thunderous God of the Hebrew Bible and a Brahmin creator god" (28). Anita Patterson makes the case for Eliot as a "transnational New World poet" for whom the "diasporic histories associated with New World imperialism" formed a crucial influence (4), and who in turn laid the groundwork for the hybrid poetics of Caribbean and African American writers. Other critics, however, have been more skeptical about modernism's transnational qualities, seeing Pound's and Eliot's uses of non-Western sources as forms of appropriation or cultural imperialism. Singh and Schmidt cite Elleke Boehmer's assertion that "metropolitan modernism" ultimately "could not transcend the structures of imperial authority that were ingrained in the canonical modernist writers" (Singh and Schmidt, 21).

American modernists' engagements with Asia have offered a fruitful arena for transnational inquiry, particularly as critics have begun to move beyond textual explication to an examination of the global movements and migrations that underpinned modernist aesthetics. Josephine Nock-Hee Park's *Apparitions of Asia* gives renewed attention to the career of Ernest Fenollosa, whose work on Chinese poetry and language helped give Pound the basis for his poetics in *The Cantos*. Park shows how Fenollosa's travels between the United States and Japan laid the groundwork for modernist conceptions of Asia, placing poetics in the context of international relations and arguing that later Asian American writers help reveal and critique this "modern history of transpacific literary alliances" (3).

The shift toward a transnational paradigm may have had its most visible impact on the study of American poets of color, who are increasingly being studied in the context of diasporic communities that extend beyond U.S. boundaries. The study of the writers of the Harlem Renaissance—to choose one central example from the first half of the twentieth century—has been transformed by a renewed attention to the international contexts of this seemingly localized movement. Many critics of African American literature have argued that the Harlem Renaissance produces a distinctly African American form of modernism, grounded in African American speech, sensibility, and history, and exposing the elitism and Eurocentrism of white modernism. The work of Langston Hughes, for instance, is read by Arnold Rampersad as infusing the "raceless" idiom of modernism (65) with forms and styles drawn from African American vernacular culture—most notable in Hughes's use of stanza structures, rhythms, and diction derived from the blues and jazz. The result is what

Houston A. Baker Jr. calls a distinctively "modern Afro-American sound" (xiv) that achieves a "blending of class and mass" (93).

A diasporically minded critic like Paul Gilroy, however, would likely view such readings as too closely bound to a U.S.-centered framework, and more recent scholarship has followed Gilroy's example in emphasizing the transnational context of Harlem Renaissance writing. Brent Hayes Edwards's *The Practice of Diaspora* reminds us of W. E. B. Du Bois's remark that "the color line belts the world" and that the title of Alain Locke's anthology *The New Negro* refers in part to a "new" black internationalism (2). Edwards uses this context to highlight poems like Hughes's "Jazz Band in a Parisian Cabaret," whose French locale appears to be an anomaly among the American settings of Hughes's other poems. The poem's polyvocal, multilingual qualities reflect Hughes's own experiences in France and suggest an effort "to frame blackness as an object of knowledge beyond the nation-state" (67). Kenneth W. Warren juxtaposes Hughes's "The Negro Speaks of Rivers," written in the voice of a black history and consciousness that spans eons and continents, with the physical travel described in Hughes's autobiography *The Big Sea,* in which Hughes finds himself called "a white man" by Africans. Warren's reading illustrates "the ambiguities that inhere in diasporic thought," ambiguities that "encourage and frustrate both the desire to forge links between blacks in Africa and the West and the attempt to establish connections between black elites and masses in urban centers in the United States" (393).

A transnational re-reading of the Harlem Renaissance would also place greater emphasis on the work of diasporic figures like Claude McKay, the Jamaican-born poet who came to New York in 1914 and became a central figure in the cosmopolitan literary culture of Harlem. McKay's early poems were written in Jamaican dialect, a vernacular he had been encouraged to pursue by Walter Jekyll, an Englishman and amateur folklorist. While these early works were well received in Jamaica, McKay, schooled in the British colonial tradition, came to believe that he would only be taken seriously by a wider audience if he wrote in formal, standard English. He moved to the United States but quickly became disillusioned by the harshness of American racism and segregation. He abandoned the writing of dialect poetry in favor of a highly traditional, formalist, and even conservative style—strictly rhymed and metered, with elevated poetic diction; yet he filled that style with radical content that directly confronted issues of class and race. His poems of black life in Harlem display the ambivalence and ambiguity that Warren finds characteristic of diasporic writing; these works immerse themselves in African American culture while still remaining estranged from it.

McKay's "The Harlem Dancer" is a strict Shakespearean sonnet, with each quatrain a separate sentence. But the opening lines offer a jarring contrast between the formal diction of the speaker and the sexual license of the setting, in which "Applauding youths laughed with young prostitutes / And watched her perfect, half-clothed body sway." The speaker both participates in and distances himself from the scene; he watches with the others, but while they crudely "Devoured her shape with eager, passionate gaze," the speaker aestheticizes the dancer and associates her with memory: "To me she seemed a proudly-swaying palm / Grown lovelier for passing through a storm." The association of the Harlem dancer with the tropical palm suggests a transnational connection between the New York setting and the Caribbean, one that is perhaps filtered through the speaker's own nostalgia for home.

But perhaps the most striking moment of diasporic ambivalence comes in the couplet: "But looking at her falsely-smiling face, / I knew her self was not in that strange place." The speaker's sense of alienation from the scene becomes, paradoxically, the source of his most powerful identification with the dancer herself, whose own alienation he believes he can read in her face. This imagined—and possibly false—connection can be understood as the attempt to create a diasporic link. The speaker imagines that both he and the dancer are "strangers" in a place that ought to be their own, the world's capital of black culture, yet what brings them together is not their presence in the same physical space, but their association with another space marked as outside the nation. That realization, moreover, is framed in a form drawn not from African American vernacular culture, but rather from the colonial heritage that scattered Africans throughout the Americas. In short, we can see in McKay's poem an attempt to think beyond the "American" boundaries of Harlem, a struggle that is registered in both the poem's content and its form—even though Harlem remains the necessary site for this diasporic encounter.

If McKay's work shows us how a consideration of transatlantic diasporas alters our understanding of the American scene of modern poetry, writers of the Asian diasporas remind us of the central role of transpacific forces in shaping modern America. The Pacific has been one of the major theaters for U.S. imperialism and neoimperialism, from American colonization of the Philippines to military interventions in Korea and Vietnam. American readers have often been unable or unwilling to see how this colonial legacy has shaped the course of American literature and culture, even as successive generations of Asian American writers have offered persistent reminders of this complex history.

If transpacific encounters in modernist American poetry were largely the result of journeys (whether physical or textual) by white Americans to Asia, by the mid-twentieth century transpacific flows were growing more bilateral, thanks to U.S. military action and the gradual relaxation of laws excluding Asians from the United States. A bridge between modernist and contemporary poetic transnationalism can be found in the work of José Garcia Villa, a Filipino poet who enjoyed a brief period of renown in the United States in the 1940s and 1950s. Born in 1908, less than a decade after the beginning of the U.S. occupation of the Philippines, Villa received an English-language education at the University of the Philippines and quickly gained notoriety as a pioneer of modern Filipino writing in English. He traveled to study in the United States in 1929 and spent most of the remainder of his life there, returning to the Philippines only for brief visits. Yet during his long absence he wielded tremendous authority as perhaps the preeminent authority on Filipino letters in English, regularly editing anthologies of Filipino poetry and fiction and propagating his aesthetic views in essays and reviews.

Villa's transpacific career is best understood through a transnational paradigm that takes into account both Filipino and U.S. contexts and describes their relationship to each other. As I have argued elsewhere, Villa's work emerged in a contact zone between U.S. and Filipino literary formations. That English presented itself to Villa as the medium for modern Filipino writing was, of course, a product of the U.S. occupation and the American-style education system imposed by the colonizers, and Villa's literary authority in the Philippines was closely tied up with his American success and his long residence in New York. Villa's American reception was itself conditioned by his Filipino origins, although in less obvious ways. American reviewers of his early work tended to repress the legacy of U.S. colonialism evident in his poetry, eliding his nationality into an imagined "Asian" aesthetic. But as his later work became more provocative and experimental, critics increasingly cited Villa's Filipino origins to place his work outside the U.S. mainstream, suggesting the limits of transnational mobility.

Villa's first American book of poetry, *Have Come, Am Here*, received wide acclaim from readers such as Marianne Moore, Louis Untermeyer, and Babette Deutsch. Villa's poems were praised for their self-conscious displays of the influence of Blake, Hopkins, Dickinson, and other pillars of the Anglo-American modernist canon. But perhaps Villa's most distinctive innovation was the technique he called "reversed consonance," in which, as Villa writes in a note, "The last sounded consonants of the last syllable, or the last principal consonants of a word, are reversed for the corresponding rhyme" (*Anchored Angel*, 31):

> It is what I never said,
> What I'll always *sing*—
> It's not found in days,
> It's what always *begins*
> In half dark, half light.
> (*Anchored Angel*, 3)

Villa's formal inventiveness answered modernist aesthetic demands for innovation, but perhaps more important was that his experiments were subtle and restrained—a trait that rather curiously resonated, for American readers, with his Asian origins. U.S. critics were, by and large, bemused by the phenomenon of a Filipino poet writing in English. Writing in *The New Republic*, Deutsch characterizes Villa as "a native of the Philippines who comes to the English language as a stranger," overlooking the American colonial educational system in which Villa was educated (512). Although Deutsch's evaluation of Villa is generally positive, she expresses some unease as to whether Villa's "unusual syntax" may be more a product of his foreignness than of his linguistic inventiveness. Other critics voice discomfort about Villa's "Spanish" and "Catholic" influences, an emphasis on Spanish colonial history in the Philippines that again elides the U.S. occupation.

Those critics who praise Villa's work most highly are also those who find ways to both mark and aestheticize Villa's Filipino origins. This is nowhere more evident than in the review of Villa by Marianne Moore in *The Nation*. Moore makes only fleeting reference to the fact that Villa is a "native of the Philippines." She praises Villa's impersonality and indirectness, arguing that Villa "is with great effect, at times, 'deliberately aiming just beside the mark'" (394)—a statement, of course, that could also apply to Moore's own poetry. But the most remarkable moment in the review comes when Moore compares Villa's work to painting, remarking that "the delicacy with force of such writing reminds one of the colors of black ink from a hogs'-hair brush in the hand of a Chinese master" (394). Here, Moore brings in Villa's Filipino origins only metonymically, transforming the Filipino colonial subject into a "Chinese master." This elision identifies Villa with the broader Asian influences that underpin modernism itself, from Ezra Pound's interest in the Japanese haiku and Chinese ideogram to Moore's own preoccupation with *chinoiserie*. By replacing the U.S.-colonized landscape of the Philippines with the textual, literary landscape of China, Moore is able to make a space for this Asian writer within American modernism in a way that is consonant with U.S. national aesthetics, not disruptive of them.

This delicate ideological work, however, was disrupted by the more aggressive experimentation of Villa's subsequent writing. His next collection, the 1949 book *Volume Two*, featured his notorious "comma poems," in which Villa inserted a comma between each word:

> The, bright, Centipede ,
> Begins, his, stampede!
> O, celestial, Engine , from ,
> What, celestial, province! (13)

The subtlety of reversed consonance allowed readers like Moore to absorb Villa into the American modernist canon while filtering his problematic Filipino origins through the prism of "Chinese" indirectness and reticence. But the more intrusive, foregrounded device of the commas seems to have upset this aesthetic balance.

As critics' evaluations of Villa's work became more negative, their attention to his national origins grew. This is most evident in Randall Jarrell's attack on *Volume Two* in *Partisan Review*, which sarcastically proposes a "fairy tale" about Villa's career:

> Once upon a time, in Manila or Guadalajara, as he sat outside a convent wall and listened to the nuns preparing a confection called *Angels' Milk*, a little boy decided to go to New York City and become a great poet. There he wrote a book called, charmingly, *Have Come, Am Here*; after he had read the reviews of it he telegraphed to his parents, *Vici*, and said to himself, in his warm, gentle, Southern way: "What critics these mortals be!" (192)

While for Moore, Villa was able to "pass" in American letters as a "Chinese master," for Jarrell, Villa is irredeemably foreign, identified with colonial Spanish Catholicism rather than with American colonialism.

Transnational movement and poetic form are deeply intertwined here. The subtle techniques of Villa's first collection granted his work a certain kind of transnational mobility, one that allowed him to enter the U.S. national literary scene in the guise of a "Chinese master" (rather than as a colonial subject). But the experimentation of *Volume Two* seems to have made Villa's transnational movement *too* visible to U.S. readers, who sought to banish Villa to the realm of the utterly foreign. Villa's career is an intriguing case study in transnational aesthetic mobility and its limits, showing that while poetic styles and forms may "travel," their crossing of boundaries is always registered and at times resisted.

U.S. discussions of transnationalism have encompassed both transatlantic and transpacific connections. Less frequently considered is the significance of connections across the northern border with Canada. As diasporic perspectives become more prominent, some critics are beginning to examine possible parallels between diasporic populations in the United States and Canada. This has been most evident in the study of what has come to be called (primarily by Canadian critics) "Asian North American" literature, which includes U.S. and Canadian writing by authors of Asian descent. The category itself is, of course, a transnational one, and perhaps a bit paradoxical, given that "Asian American" has traditionally functioned as a nationally bounded category intended to claim a space for Asians in the United States. The label "Asian Canadian" has never enjoyed the same widespread usage as "Asian American" has. As Donald Goellnicht observes in a 2000 article, "compared with the rapid rise of Asian American literary studies... Asian Canadian literary studies have languished in the wilderness" (3). But there is good reason to argue for cross-border connections between Asian American and Asian Canadian writing.

The work of Fred Wah, a major Canadian writer and perhaps the best-known of Asian Canadian poets, emerges from a complex blend of transnational and diasporic forces. Wah's multiethnic ancestry—Chinese, British, and Scandinavian— would become the subject of much of his later work. But as a young writer in the 1960s, Wah first gained notoriety as a leader of the Canadian poetic avant-garde, co-founding the groundbreaking journal *Tish*. As Louis Cabri notes in his introduction to Wah's *The False Laws of Narrative*, *Tish* turned away from British paradigms of poetic form toward the free-verse, collage-based style employed by U.S. writers like William Carlos Williams, Charles Olson, Robert Creeley, and Robert Duncan—a cross-border influence that "stir[red] up controversy among Canadian cultural nationalists" (ix). But Cabri also argues that Wah adapted these "American" techniques to Canadian contexts and landscapes.

In works of the 1980s such as *Breathin' My Name with a Sigh* and *Waiting for Saskatchewan*, Wah began to apply these techniques drawn from the U.S. avant-garde to more explicitly biographical material, in meditative poems that drew on his family's history and his own travels to Asia. But the innovative forms of these works reflect their composition at the intersection of unexpected transnational flows. Curiously, what Canadian readers might see as the "American" style of Wah's poems in fact strongly differentiates his work from that of most Asian American poets of the 1980s. Wah's immersion in the Olson-Creeley-Duncan aesthetic, with its emphasis on immediate movement from one perception to the next, pointed Wah away from the first-person, postconfessional narratives favored by many Asian American poets and toward a more dynamic juxtaposition of elements, cross-cutting personal memories and histories with objects and landscapes, as in the opening poem of *Waiting for Saskatchewan*:

> Waiting for Saskatchewan
> and the origins grandparents countries places converged
> europe asia railroads carpenters nailed grain elevators
> Swift Current my grandmother in her house
> he built on the street (3)

The poem's form blurs syntactic and semantic borders, making the poem itself—like the Saskatchewan it describes—a site where "places converged," Europe and Asia brought alongside each other through the labor of farming and railroad building.

The most striking example of transnational poetics in Wah's work comes when he reverses the diasporic arrow, chronicling his own visit to China in his 1982 collection *Grasp the Sparrow's Tail* (subsequently incorporated as a section of *Waiting for Saskatchewan*). His travel to Asia, combined with the increasingly autobiographical turn in his work, seems to have pushed Wah to experiment with forms beyond the U.S. models he drew on earlier in his career. From a diasporic perspective it might not seem surprising that this "return to roots" would draw Wah toward the use of Asian poetic forms. But Wah's diasporic writing in fact works against any simplistic notion of genealogical return. In recording his journey to China, Wah does not employ Chinese forms. Instead, he uses a Japanese form—that of the *utanikki*, or "poetic diary," which in Wah's practice juxtaposes brief journal-like entries with more fragmented poetic meditations:

July 28

In Vancouver just before trip to China and talk with G of different ways the writing could get done. J's birthday.

Her a daughter's birthday think China book out linked to poetry each day something new apparent each word capable of total Chinese character baggage really gain sight of world's imprint to pose itself as action on the world in the context of the journey somewhere get ready for the Canton poem (32)

What does it mean for Wah, a Canadian writer whose ancestry lies in the Chinese diaspora, to use a Japanese form to explore that ancestry? Here, perhaps, we see an illustration of Appadurai's insight that transnationalism can be a "historical, uneven, and even *localizing* process" (17). Combining Chinese content with Japanese form points away from any notion of ancestral purity and toward Wah's contemporary North American context, in which racialization and pan-ethnic coalitions group those of Chinese and Japanese ancestry into categories like "Asian American" or "Asian Canadian." And indeed, it could be argued that Wah's use of the *utanikki* points as much to a U.S. as to an Asian context; as Cabri points out, Wah was deeply influenced by the Beat poet Gary Snyder, one of the primary popularizers of Japanese culture in the United States, whose work also draws extensively on Japanese models. On a layover in Tokyo, Wah's speaker finds himself seeing Japan through the eyes of his American poetic mentors, dreaming of "Duncan's Shinto gates" (37).

Wah completes this localizing of Asian poetic forms—bringing them "home," as it were—in the concluding section of *Waiting for Saskatchewan*, where he uses another Japanese form, the *haibun*, to write a series of poems set in Canada called "This Dendrite Map: Father/Mother Haibun." Like the *utanikki*, the *haibun* is a dialogic form, a prose paragraph followed by a single "informal haiku line." The poems' content, too, is dialogic, exploring the contrasting characters of Wah's Chinese-British father and his Swedish mother. If, as Paul Gilroy argues, the state of diaspora is one of "creolisation, métissage, mestizaje, and hybridity" (2), Wah enacts that hybridity poetically, embracing dialogic forms and writing about his Chinese- and European-Canadian ancestry in Asian forms filtered through the U.S. avant-garde. The result is a transnational poetics that self-consciously registers its crossing of borders, eschewing "natural" formal choices (Chinese styles or English Canadian formalism) in favor of an aesthetics that both maps the historical node within which Wah writes and keeps a critical, skeptical distance from it. As Wah more pithily puts it, "When you're not 'pure' you just make it up" (43). As the study of American poetry grows more transnational, it may expand to incorporate work like Wah's— poetry that exists in a deep dialogue with U.S. writing but that provides alternatives to American conceptions of race, ethnicity, and nation.

Challenges to U.S. nationalism, of course, come from within the nation's borders as well as from beyond it, particularly from those immigrant groups whose incorporation into American narratives of citizenship and belonging has remained incomplete. As I have already suggested, Asian American poetry provides a particularly rich site for transnational reading. Although in the 1960s and 1970s the category "Asian American" was most frequently employed by American-born Asians to establish their sense of national belonging, the Asian American population was already becoming more diverse and more foreign-born, under the influence of the 1965 liberalization of immigration laws and the legacy of U.S. wars in Korea and Vietnam.

The work of the Korean American poet Myung Mi Kim brilliantly illustrates the broadening transnational and diasporic concerns of Asian American writing. Kim, who came to the United States in the 1960s, engages traditional Asian American topics such as immigration, citizenship, and racism, but she does so with an awareness of the porousness of national and linguistic borders. Kim draws on the same experimental tradition that animates Wah's work in order to create a poetics that sharply registers the disjunctive and border-crossing flows of colonialism, migration, and capitalism.

Kim's first collection, *Under Flag*, most explicitly references the experiences of immigration and exile. Poems such as "Into Such Assembly" and "Under Flag" depict language lessons, citizenship exams, and scenes of war and racism. But Kim does not provide a narrative framework for these scenes, and she does not create a consistent "I" when speaking about these experiences. Influenced by language writing, Kim employs a fragmented style that shows how the migrant subject is shaped by a range of discourses, from the official interrogations of bureaucrats and teachers to news reports and private reminiscences. The subject of "Into Such Assembly" is composed of questions as much as assertions:

> Do they have trees in Korea? Do the children eat out of garbage cans?
>
> We had a dalmation
> We rode the train on weekends from Seoul to So-Sah where we
>   grew grapes
>
> . . .
>
> How often when it rains here does it rain there?
>
> One gives over to a language and then
>
> What was given, given over? (30)

What might lead us to call this a "diasporic" subject, rather than a conventionally Asian American or immigrant subject? To answer this question, we might turn to the opening stanzas of the poem, the first of which seems to quote the language of an American citizenship exam: "Do you renounce allegiance to any other country but this? / Now tell me, who is the president of the United States? / You will all stand now. Raise your right hands" (29). The following stanza responds with what seem to be memories of the speaker's childhood in Korea: "Red lacquer chests in our slateblue house / Chrysanthemums trailing bloom after bloom...So-Sah's thatched roofs shading miso hung to dry" (29). The dynamic here is a familiar trope in Asian American literature: the juxtaposition of the Asian past and the American present and future, the gaining of an American identity paired with nostalgia for what is left behind.

But Kim's poem forcefully rejects this conventional Asian American narrative with its third stanza, which consists of one line: "Neither, neither" (29). This remarkable turn would seem to reject both the abstract language of U.S. citizenship and the hazy nostalgia of Korean reminiscence, and it jolts us into seeing the limitations of both discourses. The first stanza would hardly seem to qualify as an Asian American "claiming" of America; the immigrant subject is given no agency at all but is simply interpellated into a set of official binaries ("Can you read and write English? Yes ____. No ____" [29]). And the memories of Korea are lyrical yet remote. To proclaim "Neither, neither" is to question any simple narrative of the Asian immigrant who is leaving her past behind to become a full-fledged American.

But if we call this a diasporic subject, we must acknowledge that Kim is not replacing an "Asian American" identity with a "diasporic Korean" identity oriented toward Korea as homeland. Instead, Kim rejects the idea that either Korea or the United States can form a stable ground for identity. Her diasporic subject is neither a homeward-looking exile nor a free-floating cosmopolitan. Instead, it is a subject that comes into being in the process of crossing borders, sharply registering its traversal of national discourses and providing a site from which categories of national and cultural belonging can be questioned: "Who is mother tongue, who is father country?" (29)

As these examples have shown, transnationalism has helped shape American poetry from the modernist era to the present. But poets like McKay, Villa, Wah, and Kim also show the ambiguity and ambivalence that characterize transnational poetics. To read transnationally is to become aware of how poets register the crossing of national, cultural, and linguistic barriers. The interplay of content and form becomes a means of mapping transnational histories and flows, from McKay's Shakespearean sonnets of postcolonial connection in Harlem to Kim's fragmenting of discourses of citizenship and memory through the tools of U.S. language writing. The diasporic identifications imagined by black and Asian writers in North America are self-consciously constructed and often fleeting; they do not replace national or immigrant identities with homeward-looking ones, but rather find new and shifting nodes for identification. Villa's and Wah's poems generate a surprising range of cross-ethnic connections—the Filipino writer as "Chinese master," the Chinese Canadian poet discovering his roots through Japanese forms—while the Jamaican-born McKay connects himself with an African American dancer through their mutual sense of alienation.

Although my focus here has been on the work of black and Asian diasporic writers, the impact of transnationalism on American poetry reaches far beyond these populations. The transnational influences evident in the work of Eliot, Pound, and Moore have continued into the contemporary period; Charles Olson's studies of Mayan hieroglyphs in Mexico, Allen Ginsberg's travels to India and embrace of Buddhism, and Elizabeth Bishop's long residence in Brazil are only a few examples. What has changed since the early twentieth century is that the international mobility of the cosmopolitan expatriate has been supplanted by the transnational circulation of migrants, capital, and texts. The relationship of the American poet to "foreign" locales and influences can no longer be one of tourism and appropriation, when the foreign is equally at home within America's increasingly permeable borders. American poets' engagements with Asian or Latin American sources must now be read alongside the work of diasporic Asian or Latino writers working within the United States, a conjunction of bodies and texts that is reshaping traditional notions of a national literature. Transnational reading does not render the category of "American poetry" irrelevant; instead, it encourages us to reconceptualize the study of American poetry as a distinctive node of transnational and diasporic circulation.

REFERENCES

Anzaldúa, Gloria. *Borderlands/La Frontera: The New Mestiza.* San Francisco: Aunt Lute, 1999.
Appadurai, Arjun. *Modernity at Large: Cultural Dimensions of Globalization.* Minneapolis: University of Minnesota Press, 1996.
Baker, Houston A., Jr. *Modernism and the Harlem Renaissance.* Chicago: University of Chicago Press, 1989.
Braziel, Jana Evans, and Anita Mannur. *Theorizing Diaspora: A Reader.* Malden, MA: Blackwell, 2003.
Deutsch, Babette. "Have Come: A Good Poet." Review of *Have Come, Am Here,* by José Garcia Villa. *New Republic* 107.16 (October 19, 1942): 512.

Edwards, Brent Hayes. *The Practice of Diaspora: Literature, Translation, and the Rise of Black Internationalism.* Cambridge: Harvard University Press, 2003.

Gilroy, Paul. *The Black Atlantic: Modernity and Double Consciousness.* Cambridge: Harvard University Press, 1993.

Goellnicht, Donald C. "A Long Labour: The Protracted Birth of Asian Canadian Literature." *Essays on Canadian Writing* 72 (Winter 2000): 1–41.

Jarrell, Randall. Review of *Volume Two,* by José Garcia Villa. *Partisan Review* 17.1 (1950): 191–193.

Kaplan, Amy, and Donald E. Pease, eds. *Cultures of United States Imperialism.* Durham: Duke University Press, 1993.

Kim, Myung Mi. *Under Flag.* Berkeley, CA: Kelsey St., 1991.

McKay, Claude. "The Harlem Dancer." In *The Book of American Negro Poetry,* ed. James Weldon Johnson. New York: Harcourt, 1922; New York: Bartleby.com, 2002. http://www.bartleby.com/269/76.html

Moore, Marianne. "Who Seeks Shall Find." Review of *Have Come, Am Here,* by José Garcia Villa. *The Nation* 155.16 (October 17, 1942): 394.

Ong, Aihwa. *Flexible Citizenship: The Cultural Logics of Transnationality.* Durham: Duke University Press, 1999.

Palumbo-Liu, David. *Asian/American: Historical Crossings of a Racial Frontier.* Stanford: Stanford University Press, 1999.

Park, Josephine Nock-Hee. *Apparitions of Asia: Modernist Form and Asian American Poetics.* New York: Oxford University Press, 2008.

Patterson, Anita. *Race, American Literature and Transnational Modernisms.* New York: Cambridge University Press, 2008.

Ramazani, Jahan. *A Transnational Poetics.* Chicago: University of Chicago Press, 2009.

Rampersad, Arnold. "Langston Hughes and Approaches to Modernism." In *The Harlem Renaissance: Revaluations,* ed. Amritjit Singh, William S. Shiver, and Stanley Brodwin. New York: Garland, 1989. 49–71.

Singh, Amritjit, and Peter Schmidt, eds. *Postcolonial Theory and the United States: Race, Ethnicity, and Literature.* Jackson: University Press of Mississippi, 2000.

Vertovec, Stephen. *Transnationalism.* New York: Routledge, 2009.

Villa, José Garcia. *The Anchored Angel: Selected Writings by José Garcia Villa.* Ed. Eileen Tabios. New York: Kaya, 1999.

——. *Have Come, Am Here.* New York: Viking, 1942.

——. *Volume Two.* New York: New Directions, 1949.

Wah, Fred. *The False Laws of Narrative: The Poetry of Fred Wah.* Ed. Louis Cabri. Waterloo: Wilfrid Laurier University Press, 2009.

——. *Waiting for Saskatchewan.* Winnipeg: Turnstone, 1985.

Warren, Kenneth W. "Appeals for (Mis)recognition: Theorizing the Diaspora." In *Cultures of United States Imperialism,* ed. Amy Kaplan and Donald E. Pease. Durham: Duke University Press, 1993. 392–406.

Wong, Sau-ling C. "Denationalization Reconsidered: Asian American Cultural Criticism at a Theoretical Crossroads." In *Postcolonial Theory and the United States: Race, Ethnicity, and Literature,* ed. Amritjit Singh and Peter Schmidt. Jackson: University Press of Mississippi, 2000. 122–148.

Yu, Timothy. "Asian/American Modernisms: José Garcia Villa's Transnational Poetics." In *Pinoy Poetics,* ed. Nick Carbó. San Francisco: Meritage, 2004. 343–367.

——. "'The Hand of a Chinese Master': José Garcia Villa and Modernist Orientalism." *MELUS* 29.1 (Spring 2004): 41–59.

CHAPTER 25

"INTERNATIONALLY KNOWN": THE BLACK ARTS MOVEMENT AND U.S. POETRY IN THE AGE OF HIP HOP

JAMES SMETHURST

We're internationally known (in the ghetto)
We're internationally known (in the subway)

—Grandmaster Melle Mel and the Furious Five,
"Internationally Known"

The impact of the Black Arts Movement (BAM) of the 1960s and 1970s on subsequent poetry in the United States is profound. One might expect this impact to be obvious to readers, writers, and critics. However, as has often been the case with respect to African American literature and U.S. literature, BAM has been seen through a racial filter that makes a very large percentage of white writers and critics reluctant (or unable) to acknowledge that impact—unlike, say, the cases of basketball and jazz where white participants are willing and even proud to cite black models and mentors. In fact, many white writers are more likely to point to a black musician as a model and inspiration than to a black literary artist. In this chapter I will discuss this impact of BAM within the context of a dramatic demographic shift in the United States as a result of worldwide migrations of African-descended peoples that has completely transformed the environment for poetry here as well as greatly complicating notions of social identity. While BAM, among other things, did much to create the public arts sphere and influenced notions of the relation between "popular" and "high" culture in the United States, what primarily concerns me here is how BAM poetry, in its aesthetics, practice, transmission, and reception within the context of this movement of African-descended peoples and culture, influenced and inflected the rise of rap and hip hop, creating a truly mass audience for poetry and spoken word in the United States, a phenomenon that all U.S. poets working after the late 1970s have had to take into account.

WHAT WAS BLACK ARTS? A FEW THOUGHTS

BAM in general, and BAM poetry in particular, was more like a conversation or debate about politics and poetics that revolved around common issues and concerns than a centralized movement. The network of journals, workshops, artist groups, study circles, conferences, conventions, festivals, presses, and so on, where many black artists and intellectuals met, exchanged work, listened to each other, and often argued formed an infrastructure that gave black writers the sense of a vital movement without creating any definitive organizational, ideological, or institutional center—unlike, say, the Left artistic subculture of the 1930s and 1940s where the Communist Party was, for better or for worse, the three-hundred-pound gorilla in the room. Anyone who is familiar with only the most widely circulated BAM poems, such as Amiri Baraka's "Black Art," Nikki Giovanni's "Nikka-Rosa," Etheridge Knight's "The Idea of Ancestry," Sonia Sanchez's "a/Coltrane/poem," Haki Madhubuti's "Don't Cry, Scream," and The Last Poets' "Niggers Are Afraid of Revolution," should recognize that there was a vast range of tone, diction, lineation, meter/rhythm, sonic bonding, approach to popular culture, political ideology, and so on, in BAM poetry.

However, some generalizations about BAM poetic practice can be made. Politically, there was a general agreement that, however diverse, African Americans constituted a people or a nation with a substantially common history and a significantly shared culture and with an imperative to determine the destiny of one's self, family, community, and nation. Still, there was much discussion and difference around the questions of how this nation should be organized and the relation of gender and class to the constitution or reconstitution of the liberated nation.

No unified aesthetic or ideological practice or stance cohered in BAM. There was, however, considerable concurrence that the creation of a unified set of black literary standards (often subsumed under the rubric of the "Black Aesthetic"), which could be used to create and evaluate a liberated black literature for the new nation without recourse to "mainstream" or "white" standards, was desirable. Again, despite this agreement, there was a lot of difference about the foundation and nature of what this aesthetic might be—and even the timeline for when it was practical or even desirable to establish such standards. To some, like Chicago's Haki Madhubuti, it was a pressing task. Madhubuti argued in his report to the "Creativity Workshop" at the 1970 founding convention of the Congress of African People:

> The Black critic, like the Black poet, must start giving some leadership, some direction. We agree with Darwin T. Turner where he states, "Despite fifty years of criticism of Afro-American literature, criteria for that criticism have not been established. Consequently, some readers judge literature by Afro-Americans according to its moral value, a few for its aesthetic value, most by its social value, and too many according to their response to the personalities of the Black authors." This narrow-mindedness must end and substantial criteria must come into existence.
>
> ("Dynamite Voices," 207)

Others, like New Orleans's Kalamu ya Salaam, claimed that it was important to wait until a large-enough body of new work by revolutionary black artists existed on which to base any serious efforts to create unified critical standards for the practice and evaluation of black art:

> We feel that what we're doing is a relatively new thing in our environment. Our molds aren't quite set yet. Like jazz, what we're doing is constantly moving; the changing same. Right now all we're trying to do is to get our work out there and be honest about the things we put out. Maybe two or three years from now we'll be able to set down some standards to judge our works by (real standards and not personal considerations, likes and dislikes, theorizing from "one-eye" critics. (469)

Of course, even Madhubuti wrote in roughly the same period that "the Black Aesthetic cannot be defined in any definite way. To accurately and fully define a Black Aesthetic would automatically limit it" ("Toward a Definition," 232). Madhubuti's call for the development of "standards" and then his caution about adopting well-defined, universal black standards mirrors in reverse Salaam's critique of an urgent drive for "standards" even as he admits that they might well be a good idea a couple years down the road. Again this says something about movement activists who in many ways simultaneously desired and resisted more centralized coherence.

As a number of commentators, then and more recently, have noted, performance became emphasized to even a greater degree than in Beat/New American poetry and in the work of even earlier artistic ancestors, such as Langston Hughes and Sterling Brown. Not only did poets read/perform their poetry in almost every conceivable venue (coffee shops, community centers, bars, street corners, political rallies, parks, conventions, museums, college auditoriums, theaters, prisons, churches, mosques, and so on), but they also connected their work with other modes/media of performance associated with African American culture, especially music, dance, and theater. Often, it would be impossible to exactly delineate the particular genre in which a BAM piece fell. Even on the printed page, BAM poets recreated this mixture of media and genres, especially an interface of poetry, jazz, and black popular music, as well as in oral performance. Amiri Baraka, Sonia

Sanchez, Askia Touré, David Henderson, Amus Mor, and Jayne Cortez not only invoked such musical icons as John Coltrane, Billie Holiday, Charlie Parker, Curtis Mayfield, and James Brown, but also played with typography, lineation, space, and punctuation to approximate the form, feeling, and even the interpolated sounds of R&B, soul, bebop, and the new jazz:

(Sonia Sanchez, "On Seeing Pharaoh")

Or to take another example, Amiri Baraka concluded his political report to the 1970 founding convention of the Congress of African People with a performance of "It's Nation Time," blurring the generic boundaries between poetry and political address. And how did one classify the music and spoken word offerings of the Last Poets or Gil Scott-Heron?

Despite its performative, multigeneric, multimedia bent, it was the printed text that largely enabled BAM to exist as a national cultural formation through such journals as *Black World* (originally *Negro Digest*), *Liberator*, *Soulbook*, *Black Dialogue*, and *The Journal of Black Poetry*, such black presses as Chicago's Third World Press (now the oldest existing African American literary publisher), Detroit's Broadside Press and Lotus Press, the Bay Area's Journal of Black Poetry Press, and Newark's Jihad Productions, and anthologies (most notably Amiri Baraka's and Larry Neal's 1968 *Black Fire*). It is important to keep in mind Mike Sell's observation that BAM was a "textually supported anti-textual movement" ("Ed Bullins as Editorial Performer," 418).[1] Most BAM artists consciously tried to defetishize the printed text as literary product or an object hermetically sealed from society, from other forms of popular expressive culture, and from the active participation of a black audience. However, due to the enormous geographical dispersion of the movement and to the technologies generally available to BAM participants, the printed text was still the vehicle that was most easily amenable to grassroots, black-controlled production and distribution—though BAM activists like Baraka and his Jihad Productions experimented with other technologies for the dissemination of radical black litera- ture to a mass audience, such as film and sound recording, within the limitations of the accessibility of those technologies, financial resources, and systems of distribu- tion. It is plausible to claim that BAM was, among other things, the most widely circulated and most influential literary magazine and small-press movement in the history of the United States. As Melba Boyd points out, in the decade from 1965 to 1975, Detroit's Broadside Press alone put out dozens of poetry titles in editions total- ing something like a half a million volumes, far more than the offerings of the work of black poets by *all* U.S. publishers combined in the previous decade (Boyd, 3–4). In other words, BAM was marked by dialectics between performance and textuality, between the oral/sonic and the printed page to an extraordinary extent as well as by an ethos of creating a politically and aesthetically radical art designed to reach and move the largest possible black audience—an ethos that was realized to a con- siderable extent and strangely morphed beyond the black community since BAM, as the black poet and longtime official at the National Endowment for the Arts A. B. Spellman commented, had an enormous impact on the creation of the public art sector in the United States (Spellman, interview with author).

The Diaspora in Practice: Migration, Black Arts, and the Rise of Hip Hop

On or about October 1965, the character of the United States changed. More spe- cifically, on October 3, 1965, U.S. President Lyndon Johnson signed into law the "Immigration and Nationality Act of 1965" (aka the "Hart-Celler Act") in a cer- emony at the Statue of Liberty. This act abolished the "Nation Origins Formula" that had guided immigration law in the United States since 1924, greatly restricting legal migration to the United States from practically anywhere except northern and western Europe. While this act would have many demographic, cultural, political, and ideological consequences, one thing it did was open up the United States to large-scale legal immigration from Africa and its diaspora for the first time since the early 1920s.

The social forces that produced the Immigration and Nationality Act can be seen as arising from the intersection of the Civil Rights and incipient Black Power movements, decolonization, the cold war, and changes in the world economy and labor market. In some ways, this moment resembled the one that produced modern- ism in the early twentieth century. Raymond Williams made the claim that perhaps the most important feature defining modernism was the mass migration of millions of people from Asia, Eastern Europe, southern Europe, Latin America, Africa, and the southern United States to the industrial and/or urban centers of what we now sometimes call the "industrial nations" or the "developed world" (14–15). The era of the 1965 act, which appeared near the beginning of what has been termed "post-modernism," was characterized by a similar (and even larger) circulation of peoples (and their cultures) around the world.

Again, this movement of people had many consequences, but for the purposes of this chapter, I will consider only a few. One was the migration of millions of people from the English-, Spanish-, French-, and Kreyòl-speaking Caribbean to the United States. One major landing place for these migrants was the Bronx. Among these migrants were families of the Jamaican-born Clive Campbell (aka DJ Kool Herc) and the Barbadian/Bajan-born Joseph Saddler (aka Grandmaster Flash) who, especially Kool Herc, adapted the Jamaican Sound System/early Dance Hall style into an R&B/funk modality in the housing projects of the South Bronx. They, along with Afrika Bambaataa (also of Jamaican and Bajan descent, albeit from an earlier era of migration), whose mother and uncle had been black political activists in the 1960s and 1970s, became the dominant DJs of an emerging rap/hip hop music, dance, and graffiti scene in the black and Puerto Rican neighborhoods of the Bronx. They also adopted and adapted the "toasting" or verbal commentary/accompaniment of the Jamaican DJs into an R&B/funk style. Though early raps over the music were not particularly complex, eventually they developed into much more elaborate rhymes. The early raps/rhymes were in a party mode and not overtly political for the most part—though some of the early DJs, especially Afrika Bambaataa (who had encountered the thought of Malcolm X, the Nation of Islam, and the Black Power Movement earlier in his life), had the conscious political purpose of promoting neighborhood peace and unity in an area much marked by gang violence, sometimes sampling the speeches of Malcolm X (Chang, 67–109; Hebdige).

A related migration of people that began in the 1950s was from the Anglophone Caribbean to the United Kingdom and to Canada. Again, musical forms like calypso, soca, ska, and reggae traveled with these migrants. Some of the forms, notably calypso, already had an overtly political or topical aspect to them. Ska and, especially, reggae developed a pointedly Afrocentric ideological tendency marked by indigenous Caribbean influences, such as the Rastafarian religion and the thought of Marcus Garvey, as well as by variants of North American Black Power during the 1960s and 1970s. Artists like Bob Marley (himself briefly a part of the movement to the United States where he worked in an automobile factory in Delaware) and Winston Rodney of Burning Spear wrote brilliant songs filled with condensed, often millenarian imagery reminding listeners of the enslavement of Africans in the Americas and the legacy of slavery and attacking colonialism, neocolonialism, racism, and class oppression. At the same time, black Britons who faced extreme discrimination in employment, education, housing, and so on, as well as much police harassment and violence, embraced a Black Power Movement influenced by that of the United States, but they adapted it to British conditions. One member of the British Black Panther movement, Linton Kwesi Johnson, was deeply involved in the creation of the black British Dub Poetry scene in the 1970s. The performance ethos, multigeneric/multimedia cast, Caribbean-British orality, and radical black politics of this scene were deeply influenced by Black Arts antecedents and by the new radical music issuing from Jamaica and elsewhere in the Caribbean. Many of Johnson's early poems-performances drawing on dub/toasting/reggae, such as "Sonny's Lettah" and "It Dread Inna Inglan," highlighted police violence and racist misuse of the vagrancy or "Sus" (as in "Suspicion of Vagrancy") laws:

> Dem tump 'im in 'im belly
> An' it turn to jelly
> Dem lick 'im pon 'im back
> An' 'im rib get pop
> Dem lick 'im pon 'im head
> It tuff like lead
> Dem kick 'im in 'im seed
> An' it started to bleed
> ("Sonny's Lettah: An Anti-Sus Poem")

The sounds, rhythms, rhymes, diction, politics, and even the songs themselves of both Jamaican reggae and ska and black British adoptions and adaptations, including the work of Johnson, deeply marked many British punk and postrock bands, perhaps most notably the Clash (who in turn influenced Chuck D and Public Enemy in the United States) in the 1980s.[2] Johnson in particular presented a high-profile Black Arts–influenced black British version of a vernacular spoken word-music combination on which "conscious" hip hop artists could draw.

So by the mid-1970s African-descended peoples and their cultures moved throughout the world in new ways and created new community, social, political, and cultural connections. For example, a single family might well have members in Kingston, Jamaica; the Bronx; Toronto; and London. For black musical and musical-spoken word artists based in those cities, a new kind of international circuit grew up, mixing Black Arts/Black Power; soul/R&B; ska, reggae, dub, calypso, and soca; Rastafarianism and Garveyism in its various local manifestations; and the emerging rap/hip hop subculture that owed much, in turn, to both Black Arts and the Caribbean.

By the early to mid-1980s a socially minded, often radical, black nationalist strain of hip hop that eventually became known under the rubric of "conscious hip hop" evolved out of this matrix. Grandmaster Flash and the Furious Five's 1982 "The Message" (with the lyrics written by Melle Mel, one of the group's rappers) brought this "conscious" strain to a mass audience. "The Message" is composed of three parts: an impressionistic, first-person catalog of ghetto problems and indignities, which takes up the majority of the performance; a tightly compressed story of a young man ("you") who grows up in the ghetto ultimately to be raped and commit suicide in prison; and a sort of mini-docudrama in which the listener can hear the members of the group meet and greet each other and then be arrested by the police for the crime of gathering while being young, male, and black in the ghetto. Other younger artists, such as KRS-One and BDP (Boogie Down Productions) and Public Enemy combined these reports from the ghetto front with a revolutionary, black

nationalist consciousness directly influenced by the Black Power/Black Arts Move-
ments that they encountered as children and adolescents through parents and in
their neighborhoods and often through, as in the case of Public Enemy at Adelphi
University, Black Studies departments and programs that had been established in
many colleges and universities in the 1970s and 1980s.[3]

This influence of Black Arts and Black Power is not only displayed in the fre-
quent acknowledgment by "conscious" rappers like KRS-One, Chuck D (of Public
Enemy), the Roots, Talib Kweli, Mos Def, and Common in interviews of their debt
to such well-known Black Arts spoken word-music artists as the Last Poets and
Gil Scott-Heron, but also in their collaborations and public association with such
iconic Black Arts poets as Amiri Baraka (who appeared on the Roots 2002 record-
ing *Phrenology*), Nikki Giovanni (who worked with Tupac Shakur's mother, Afeni
Shakur, in bringing out a collection of Tupac's poetry, *The Rose That Grew from Con-
crete* [1999] and who assembled and coedited a 2008 anthology of hip hop, proto-
hip hop, and hip hop–inflected poetry for children, *Hip Hop Speaks to Children*),
and Sonia Sanchez (who appeared on Talib Kweli's 2007 recording, *Eardrum*). It is
also during the 1980s that hip hop/rap, this product of the circulation of African-
descended peoples and their cultures and politics throughout Africa, the Americas
and Europe, became a dominant, perhaps the dominant, popular music form in the
United States, and, ultimately, the world. It is worth noting here that BAM veterans
like Baraka, Sanchez, Giovanni, Haki Madhubuti, and Askia Touré both celebrate
hip hop for its linguistic and rhythmic inventiveness (a tradition of innovation that
they see as being part of African American culture from the beginning) and its
chronicling of and opposition to racial and class oppression (at least on the part
of some rappers) and sharply critique what they see as its frequent cooptation and
corporatization by the mass culture industries, encouraging a crass materialism and
reinforcing longstanding racist stereotypes of black people.[4] Both the celebrations
and critiques by poets who many hip hop artists see as their elders and ancestors
enter into and influence already existing debates within the community of hip hop
artists and their audience about the nature, current status, and objectives of their
art and its relation to larger communities, especially black and Latina/o neighbor-
hoods, with a degree of credibility unavailable to "mainstream" critics of hip hop.

Hip hop not only provided a vehicle to articulate and protest racial, ethnic,
national, regional, and class oppression in the United States and around the world,
but it also did much to promote a relatively unified black identity among the diverse
peoples of African descent in the United States after 1965. This is not to under-
play tensions and even violent conflict between various peoples from Africa and
the African diaspora in the United States. However, among younger people, hip
hop has provided a cultural lingua franca that is seen as both "American" and able
to accommodate cultural elements from throughout the diaspora. A prominent
example of this sort of African-descended amalgamation was the hip hop group the
Fugees, which included the Haitian-born (and aspiring Haitian presidential candi-
date) Wyclef Jean, the New Jersey–born Lauryn Hill, and the Brooklyn-born (but
of Haitian descent) Pras Michel. The Fugees (derived from "refugees") mixed R&B,

hip hop, reggae, and other Caribbean genres, looking back to the 1960s and 1970s with hip hop covers of Bob Marley, Roberta Flack, and the Delfonics among their biggest hits. It is worth noting that the Fugees (and Jean after the group broke up) were extremely successful among a broad African American audience despite (or more likely because) of the black hybridity of their work, almost always doing significantly better on the R&B music charts than in the general pop category.

One might also see Barack Obama's gestural quote of Jay-Z's "Dirt Off Your Shoulders" in a speech during the 2008 election campaign in this light of promoting black unity while promoting a black cultural pluralism or hybridity, if you will. Of course, hip hop (and Obama) has a great appeal beyond African Americans, but it has a particular meaning to black people, often celebrating an imagined shared black space, black community, black diction and syntax, and black identity in which, to quote the hip hop scholar Murray Forman, "the 'hood comes first."[5] Even one of the foremost exponents of the "Dirty South" version of the "gangsta" strain of hip hop, which has often been opposed to the more overtly BAM-influenced "conscious" variety, Houston's Scarface (aka Brad Jordan) speaks of black love and black solidarity tied to his south Houston community in the 2002 "My Block":

> We stay confined to this small little section we livin' in
> Oh my block, I wouldn't trade it for the world
> 'Cause I love these ghetto boys and girls
> Born and raised, on my block

On the face of it, it might seem that these new patterns of physical and cultural migration from Africa and its diaspora in the Americas to Europe and North America in the post-1960s era reinscribed the old "triangle trade" model of the transatlantic slave trade era in the form of something called "the Black Atlantic." One could object to this model on a number of levels. On one level, much of the newest migration has been from places in Africa (e.g., Uganda, Somalia, Ethiopia, and Eritrea) that have traditionally looked north culturally, socially, and economically to the Arabian Peninsula or east across the Indian Ocean more than to anywhere on the Atlantic rim. After all, if one is interested in Swahili literature, one of the most essential sources lies in the archives of Goa, which, like much of India, was closely connected to Africa through the Islamic political, religious, cultural, and economic networks of the Indian Ocean rim. Even migrants from West Africa had strong links eastward, especially through Islam, though they may have physically crossed the Atlantic to the United States, Canada, or Britain.

On a more ideological plane, the fact that Europe and North America conquered the vast majority of the land and peoples of the continents of Africa and Asia in the nineteenth century, establishing colonies and semicolonies (as in China) underpinned by notions (or even "sciences") of the racial superiority of so-called Caucasians or white people over other largely subjugated "races" laid the basis for the development of communities of interest and even identification between African Americans and these subjugated peoples in the high Jim Crow/colonial era.

To note an obvious example, Pan-Africanism would not have been possible without colonialism. The new sorts of black radicalism that arose from the new communities of solidarity and identification with African, Asian, Caribbean, and Latin American subjects of European and North American imperialism transcended and often even consciously rejected notions of the "Atlantic World" that almost inevitably privileged the relationship between Europe and Africa, generally placing Europe at the center. In fact, a hallmark of much African American radicalism in the twentieth century, whether the black Bolshevism of Claude McKay in the 1920s or the Nation of Islam leader Elijah Muhammad's preaching of the "Afro-Asiatic" connection later in the century was a conscious decentering of Europe (and the Atlantic).[6] Even Rastafarianism's veneration of Haile Selassie and Ethiopia looked toward a country that is not an "Atlantic" nation geographically, culturally, or even spiritually.

The early Black Power and Black Arts movements continued and strengthened the black radical tradition that embraced this new internationalism looking beyond the old idea of the Atlantic world. Inspired by the efforts of the national liberation movements and emerging nations of Africa, Asia, and Latin America, many of the initiators of Black Arts and Black Power spoke of a "Bandung World"—named after the 1955 Afro-Asiatic Conference in Bandung, Indonesia. They saw the revolutionary epicenter of the world as located in Africa and Asia (and in the interface between Africa and Asia, especially China), not Europe and North America.[7] This sort of black internationalism marked hip hop, especially among the "conscious" rappers who were much moved by the thinking of Malcolm X, Elijah Muhammad, and the Nation of Islam. In that sense the overwhelming acceptance of Barack Obama as "black" by African Americans despite debates about "middle passage blackness" epitomized a rejection of a narrow Atlantic worldview even if African-descended migrants to the United States did travel over the Atlantic—though in the case of Obama his African father did not.

POETRY IN THE AGE OF HIP HOP

It is remarkable how few scholars in literary studies have considered at any real length the fact that poets in the United States for more than thirty years have been writing in a period in which a spoken word form that one could (and I do) consider poetry has been among the most widely (and often *the* most widely) circulated type of popular culture. What scholarship exists mostly deals with the impact of hip hop on African American literature. Strangely enough, one of the few critics to take seriously hip hop's impact on U.S. poetry has been the conservative, former George W. Bush administration National Endowment for the Arts chairman Dana Gioia, even if Gioia's characterizations of hip hop are often overly simplistic or just plain wrong, using a weird conflation of hip hop, performance poetry, and "cowboy" poetry to advance his advocacy of an accessible and even market-driven U.S. poetry (Gioia, 29–38).[8] Yet there has been no phenomenon like it in the history of the United States, even in the heyday of James Whitcomb Riley. Writers from Walt Whitman through Carl Sandburg, Vachel Lindsay, and Langston Hughes to the BAM poets have dreamed of and hoped for such a popular poetry, but only in the last few decades has it become a reality. The closest that poetry in the United States has come to reaching such a mass audience since the nineteenth century was during the Black Arts/Black Power moment, but even that important predecessor to hip hop reached only an audience in the hundreds of thousands (possibly the low millions if one stretched it)—a remarkable achievement for poetry in the United States, but still dwarfed by hip hop's reach to many tens of millions (at least) in the United States and hundreds of millions (perhaps billions) worldwide. While Barack Obama is obviously familiar with African American poetry (and was prominently pictured shaking hands with Sonia Sanchez at the 2010 Urban League convention) and was personally close to at least one important radical black poet, Frank Marshall Davis, no mention of the work of an older poet could have reached and excited his audience like the aforementioned gestural quote of Jay-Z in 2008.

In other words, every poet writing in the United States since the late 1970s has been doing so during the age of hip hop/rap. It does not matter whether she or he has been or is hostile, indifferent, or enthusiastic toward the many varieties of hip hop, hip hop is an inescapable cultural fact with which poets of every stripe and community must grapple. Even more than the New American Poetry and the Black Arts Movement (though with links to both), it has made performance an almost mandatory aspect of a poet's craft and created an enormous and unprecedented audience for such performance.

This, of course, is particularly true of "performance poetry," the most directly hip hop–inflected genre outside of rap itself with some of its most skilled practitioners like Saul Williams actually switching back and forth between performance poetry and hip hop modes in the course of their careers. Again, this performance ethos comes largely from BAM as filtered through the "conscious" stream of hip hop that insisted that poetry could be aesthetically and politically serious, fun, and accessible to a mass audience—though it is important to note that even the least "conscious" of the gangsta/thug current of hip hop artists have often felt it imperative to declare their work "real" on some level. While not reaching an audience on the scale of hip hop itself, performance poetry and poetry slams have engaged larger numbers of listeners/readers and artists than any other written or spoken word verse form in the United States except hip hop, particularly among young African Americans. Aalbc.com, a major Internet site for African American literature and culture reported in 2000 that Saul Williams was the best-selling artist in any genre on the site for the previous three years. While the practitioners of performance poetry are from almost every imaginable racial, ethnic, class, and geographical background, an African American verbal and performance aesthetic derived from hip hop and BAM dominates the genre. The genre's most high-profile artists and organizers, like Saul Williams, are black or Latina/o, artists who, like Williams, acknowledge the influence of Black Arts and Black Power as well as the conventions and tropes of hip hop (Albanese):

> this fool actually thinks he can drive his hummer on the moon
> blasting DMX off the soundtrack of a South Park cartoon
> niggas used to buy their families out of slavery
> now we buy chains and links, smokes and drinks
> they're paying me to record this, even more if you hear it
> somebody tell me what you think I should do with the money
> yes, friend tell me what you think I should do with the money
> exactly how much is it gonna cost to free Mumia?
>
> (S. Williams, "A Penny for a Thought")

The numbers of venues for spoken word/performance poetry are legion and not restricted to college campuses and arts/bohemian enclaves. (Even in my basically rural area north of the University of Massachusetts Amherst where I work, there are more than a half dozen spoken word series in bars, restaurants, coffeehouses, community centers, and so on—with very few of the participants directly connected to the university and colleges farther south.) The highest profile venue was no doubt *Def Poetry*, an HBO television performance poetry program that ran from 2002 until 2007. Produced by the hip hop impresario Russell Simmons and hosted by "conscious" hip hop artist and actor Mos Def, *Def Poetry* linked performance poetry to hip hop (including pieces by such leading "conscious" hip hop artists as DMX, Common, Talib Kweli, KRS-One, Mos Def, and Dead Prez) and to BAM (through performances by such renowned BAM veterans as Amiri Baraka, Sonia Sanchez, Nikki Giovanni, Haki Madhubuti, and the Last Poets—not to mention the BAM-influenced Linton Kwesi Johnson).

There are also considerable numbers of poets who one might not consider performance poets as such, but whose poetry is filled with hip hop sensibilities, formal practices, and tropes. Again, many of the leading poets of this type of writing are African Americans and Afro-Latina/os, such as Kevin Young, and they are also extremely conscious of the Black Arts heritage behind that of hip hop, seeing BAM as enabling the individual black voice within the context of a communal identity (Rowell and Young, 43–44). Young's poetry balances a profound historical consciousness with a deep sense of the contemporary. In the 2005 *To Repel Ghosts: The Remix* (a reworking of an earlier 2001 work invoking the hip hop term for revision and reclamation of earlier music), Young uses the career of the artist Jean-Michel Basquiat to meditate on the location of the black artist in the cultures of the United States. Formally, *To Repel Ghosts* draws on a dizzying array of sources, including rap, graffiti art, comic books, sports, film, the blues, R&B, bebop, pop art, Romare Bearden's collages, Jacques Derrida, Dadaism, surrealism, "high" modernism, Robert Hayden's historical poems, Langston Hughes's poetic sequences (especially *Montage of a Dream Deferred*), performance poetry, and on and on:

FIRST ARTISTIC
CARTOONIST.
Among Blondie & electric

boogaloo, lies
his big break—head
spinning, scratch—able

to buy paint, a bit
of pot—he's stoked
SET THAT

ON FIRE—& some start
to notice. Blondie
buys her a small canvas
(23)

Here, Young invokes the moment in early hip hop after downtown bohemia and its interface with the hip edge of mainstream pop culture in the form of Deborah Harry, Chris Stein, and the New Wave rock group Blondie has ventured to the Bronx to sample, so to speak, rap firsthand and introduces the related forms of rap, graffiti, break dancing, and so on, merged to some degree with punk and New Wave to the hip high fashion industry and a variety of other media/industries, promoting the careers of Basquiat, Keith Haring, and Stephen Sprouse (the fashion designer) in addition to the public profile of hip hop outside the black and Latina/o communities of New York, with varying results. In this he is reaching back both to the multimedia, multigeneric BAM and to the early hip hop sensibility of Afrika Bambaataa, who famously would include samples from an unbelievably wide range of sources, from Bugs Bunny to Malcolm X, from soul and funk to German electronica in his work.

Even for poets whose work is not directly (or at least overtly) inflected by hip hop, the existence of a mass public for spoken word/performance poetry greatly affected their work and their careers. For example, Robert Pinsky's verse does not draw much on the resources of hip hop as such—though the resources of jazz and BAM are another story. He is, in fact, reluctant to consider hip hop poetry—and he did not include hip hop or performance poetry as part of his "Favorite Poem Project."[9] Nonetheless, his work as poet laureate and his efforts to connect his sense of poetry with a mass audience owes a great deal to the literary environment created by hip hop and spoken word. The Whitmanic-Sandburgian-Hughesian (and Popular Front) dream of poetry as a vehicle and even an arbiter of democracy relying on a dialectic of individual and mass espoused by Pinsky during and after his term as poet laureate became broadly plausible only in the post-BAM hip hop era. Even poets and critics who hate hip hop (and the performance-based "identity" ethos of BAM) often directly or indirectly write against it, emphasizing the poem on the printed page and the printed text. And, as mentioned before, various practitioners and advocates of the "new formalism" in U.S. poetry during the late twentieth- and early twenty-first centuries, most notably Dana Gioia, cited hip hop as a popular return to rhyme and meter even if they elided the politics of hip hop and smoothed out its sonic and rhythmic complexities much as an earlier generation of conservative New Critics drew on a very constrained version of modernism to underpin their theories about value, form, and meaning in poetry. In short, hip hop is (and has been for some decades) a sort of poetic ocean in which the poet-fish must swim either with or against the current. The only other option is to be a fish on dry land, which is to say, walking catfish notwithstanding, dead.

So coming back to BAM, BAM poetry, and BAM performance as it evolved and influenced and was influenced by the new circulation of people of African descent in the United States and around the world, fundamentally transformed the field in which all poetry in the United States was created, transmitted, and received. BAM raised a host of political, social, cultural, and aesthetic issues about what it meant to be black in the United States and in the world. The new migrations of African and African-descended peoples and cultures to the United States made much more visible (and audible) the internationalist Pan-African connections proposed by Black Arts and Black Power. Yet these migrations greatly complicated and challenged any easy notion of blackness and black culture in the United States—connections and complications made audible in the very diction and accents of the many Caribbean (dub, dancehall, reggae, meringue, and so on) hip hop switching efforts of such hip hop artists as KRS-One and the Fugees.

Drawing on the BAM interdisciplinary, multigeneric, Pan-African performance ethos and an imperative to address, chronicle, define, consolidate, defend, and control black territory and black community (an imperative that even the least "conscious" of rappers feel to some degree or another), hip hop artists created a verbal art form, a form of poetry. This form reached an unprecedented poetry audience in the United States. It was (and is) a poetry that foregrounded its status as formally and thematically radical, fun (though not necessarily "accessible" in the sense that Dana Gioia means it), and popular. Like the popular cultural and avant-garde hybrid art of BAM, hip hop with its wild sonic, rhythmic, and visual mixtures redefined what it means to be "popular" in poetry (and expressive culture in general). Again, this legacy of BAM can be seen in the frequent and continuing references by hip hop artists honoring their BAM predecessors and well as the collaborations between hip hop artists and surviving BAM icons like Amiri Baraka, Nikki Giovanni, Sonia Sanchez, and the Last Poets. In short, one of BAM's greatest legacies is its major part in creating this new world for poetry in which we all now live.

NOTES

1 See also Sell, *Avant-Garde Performance*, 217–242.
2 When asked about early influences on the work of Public Enemy in a 2005 interview, Chuck D. answered:

> The Last Poets, Gil Scott-Heron, and also eight years of rappers that came before us. I grew up with Motown, Stax Records, and Atlantic. The Philadelphia International sound like the O'Jays had a profound influence on me. As a late teenager, the punk movement pushed me further. In particular, the Clash, which happened to

leak through the time of disco, showed me that there was this cross-cultural sound that could cut across genres and audiences. Like punk was to disco, rap music was a rebellion against R&B, which had adopted disco and made it worse.

(D'Ambrosio, 39)

3 For a short account of the impact of Black Studies on the members of Public Enemy while they were at Adelphi University, see Chang, 239–241.

4 A good example of such praise and critique is found in Baraka's essay, "What Do You Mean, Du Wop," collected in *Digging*.

5 Forman sees the semantic and symbolic turn from the ghetto to the 'hood in hip hop as in part an imaginative reclaiming of the black and Latina/o neighborhood from the discourses of "criminal justice" and social control: "I want to argue that, as a discursive shift, the turn to the 'hood involves an intentional, engaged process of recuperation of African-American- and Latino-dominated space enacted primarily by contemporary urban minority youth" (65).

6 For an essay arguing that an important aspect of black radicalism in the twentieth century is the decentering of the "Atlantic World," see Smethurst, "The Red Is East." This is not to say that the Atlantic did not retain an importance in the black political imagination. After all, as Amiri Baraka wrote in his "Africa" section of his *Wise, Whys, Y's* sequence: "At the bottom of the Atlantic Ocean there's a / railroad made of human bones. / Black ivory / Black Ivory." As far as I know, though Baraka has read and recorded versions of this part of the "Africa" section, it has not been published. However, the text can be found on the website for Bill Moyer's *Fooling with Words* television program at http://www.pbs.org/wnet/foolingwithwords/guide/fooling.pdf). Only that there were other ties, a black Pacific and a black Indian Ocean that mattered to these radicals practically and ideologically.

7 For two seminal articles from the early Black Arts/Black Power era that see the revolutionary center of the world in the relationship between Africa (and the peoples of the African diaspora) and Asia, see Askia Touré's 1965 *Liberator* essay, "Afro-American Youth and the Bandung World," and Harold Cruse's 1962 *Studies on the Left* essay, "Revolutionary Nationalism and the Afro-American," later collected in Cruse's *Rebellion or Revolution*.

8 It is worth noting that, besides the questionable move of placing hip hop and performance poetry alongside cowboy poetry (a publicly "white" genre that certainly has a niche but has nothing like the popular reach of hip hop or performance poetry), Gioia argues that hip hop is essentially a sort of blackened version of a "traditional English folk meter" (34) without much empirical evidence for such a derivation other than some shared metrical patterns (basically lines with four stresses) between hip hop and English folk poetry—metrical patterns that have long been found in African American song (e.g., the blues).

9 In responding to a question about whether hip hop is poetry, Pinsky answered, "The crucial distinction for me between something that may be a great song and poetry is, Does it depend upon the performer? The poem must sound like a poem in the voice of anyone who chooses to say it aloud. And the Favorite Poem Project demonstrates that. I honor performance a lot, but poetry is not the art of performance" (Butler).

REFERENCES

Albanese, Rob. "Saul Williams: An Interview with Saul Williams." Junkmedia.org, October 11, 2004, http://junkmedia.org/index.php?i=1267.

Baraka, Amiri. *Digging: The Afro-American Soul of American Classical Music.* Berkeley: University of California Press, 2009.

———. *It's Nation Time.* Black Forum/Motown. 1972.

Boyd, Melba Joyce. *Wrestling with the Muse: Dudley Randall and Broadside Press.* New York: Columbia University Press, 2003.

Butler, Kira. "Spreading the Word." *Mother Jones,* October 16, 2007, http://motherjones. com/media/2007/10/spreading-word.

Chang, Jeff. *Can't Stop Won't Stop: A History of the Hip Hop Generation.* New York: St. Martin's, 2005.

Cruse, Harold. *Rebellion or Revolution.* New York: Morrow, 1962.

D'Ambrosio, Antonio. "Interview: Chuck D." *The Progressive* 69.8 (August 2005): 37–41.

Forman, Murray. *The 'Hood Comes First: Race, Space, and Place in Rap and Hip-Hop.* Middletown, CT: Wesleyan University Press, 2002.

Gioia, Dana. "Disappearing Ink: Poetry at the End of Print Culture." *Hudson Review* 56.1 (Spring 2003): 21–49.

Grand Master Flash and the Furious Five. "The Message." Sugar Hill Records. 1982.

Grand Master Melle Mel and the Furious Five. "Internationally Known." Sugar Hill Records. 1984.

Hebdige, Dick. "Rap and Hip Hop: The New York Connection." In *That's the Joint: The Hip Hop Studies Reader*, ed. Murray Forman and Mark Anthony Neal. New York: Routledge, 2004. 256–266.

Johnson, Linton Kwesi. *Forces of Victory.* Island Records. 1979.

Madhubuti, Haki (Don L. Lee). "Dynamite Voices." In *African Congress: A Documentary History of the First Modern Pan-African Congress*, ed. Amiri Baraka (LeRoi Jones). New York: Morrow, 1972. 200–211.

———. "Toward a Definition: Black Poetry of the Sixties (After LeRoi Jones)." In *The Black Aesthetic*, ed. Addison Gayle Jr.. Garden City: Doubleday, 1971. 222–233.

Rowell, Charles, and Kevin Young. "An Interview with Kevin Young." *Callaloo* 21.1 (Winter 1998): 43–54.

Salaam, Kalamu ya. "BLKARTSOUTH/get on up!" In *New Black Voices*, ed. Abraham Chapman. New York: Mentor, 1972. 468–473.

Sanchez, Sonia. "On Seeing Pharaoh Sanders Blowing." *Journal of Black Poetry* 1 (Fall 1967): 5.

Scarface. *The Fix*, Def Jam. 2002.

Sell, Mike. *Avant-Garde Performance and the Limits of Criticism: Approaching the Living Theatre, Happenings/Fluxus, and the Black Arts Movement.* Ann Arbor: University of Michigan Press, 2005.

———. "The Black Arts Movement: Performance, Neo-Orality, and the Destruction of the 'White Thing.'" In *African American Performance and Theater History*, ed. Harry J. Elam Jr. and David Krasner. New York: Oxford University Press, 2001. 56–80.

———. "Ed Bullins as Editorial Performer: Textual Power and the Limits of Performance in the Black Arts Movement." *Theatre Journal* 53.3 (October 2001): 411–428.

Smethurst, James Edward. *The Black Arts Movement.* Chapel Hill: University of North Carolina Press, 2005.

——. "Everyday People: Popular Music, Race, and the Articulation and Formation of Class Identity." In *The Resisting Muse: Popular Music and Social Protest*, ed. Ian Peddie. Aldershot, UK: Ashgate, 2006.

——. "The Red Is East: Claude McKay and the New Black Radicalism of the Twentieth Century." *American Literary History* 21.2 (Spring 2009).

Spellman, A. B. Interview with author, December 28, 2000, Washington, DC.

Thomas, Lorenzo. "Classical Jazz and the Black Arts Movement." *African American Review* 29.2 (Summer 1995): 237–240.

——. *Extraordinary Measures: Afrocentric Modernism and Twentieth-Century American Poetry*. Tuscaloosa: University of Alabama Press, 2000.

——. "Neon Griot: The Functional Role of Poetry Readings in the Black Arts Movement." In *Close Listening: Poetry and the Performed Word*, ed. Charles Bernstein. New York: Oxford, 1998. 300–323.

Touré, Askia (Rolland Snellings). "Afro-American Youth and the Bandung World." *Liberator* 5, no. 2 (February 1965): 4, 24.

Williams, Raymond. *The Politics of Modernists: Against the New Conformists*. New York: Verso, 1996.

Williams, Saul. *Amethyst Rock Star*, American Recordings. 2001.

——. African American Literature Book Club. http://aalbc.com/authors/saul.htm.

Young, Kevin. *To Repel Ghosts: The Remix*. New York: Knopf, 2005.

CHAPTER 26

MINDING MACHINES/ MACHINING MINDS: WRITING (AT) THE HUMAN-MACHINE INTERFACE

ADALAIDE MORRIS

Our task is to simply mind the machines.

—Kenneth Goldsmith, "Provisional Language"

This chapter attempts a switch in perspective. Instead of arranging modern and contemporary American poets in a forward-moving lineage or scanning such a lineage for generative breaks, I want to ask what poetries come into view if we look backward from the circuitries of twenty-first-century digital writing. We've told the story of American poetry forward from Ralph Waldo Emerson's transparent eyeball or Walt Whitman's Adamic self; we've refigured it as a progression along the lines of gender and sexuality, race, and class; we've punctured national boundaries by tracing U.S. poetries of immigration and migrancy and period boundaries by delineating a modernism that lasts into the twenty-first century.[1] The thought experiment of this chapter is to start the story with the body electric of the cyborg used to introduce the website of the performance artist Stelarc (figure 26.1).

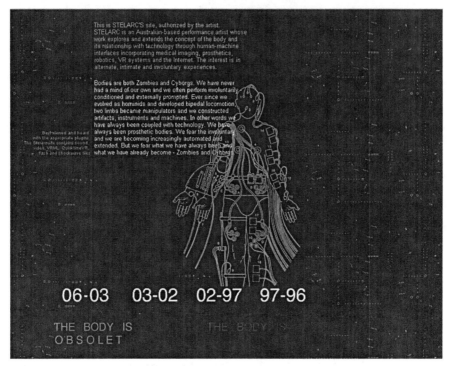

Figure 26.1 Screenshot of splash page from Stelarc's website (2007). Courtesy of Stelarc.
Source: http://web.archive.org/web/20070829003523/www.stelarc.va.com.au/stelarc1.html

The black-and-gray background of Stelarc's splash screen appears to be an abstraction of memory blocks, logic boards, and input/output pads. Into it is plugged a block of small white introductory text, a blip of red text listing the devices necessary to access the site, and a sketch showing a body wired with EEGs to catch the brainwaves, ECGs to trace the heartbeat, EMGs to monitor the flexor muscles, and an array of contact microphones, position sensors, and kineto-angle transducers to chart everything else. In this circuit, voltage-in probes the body; voltage-out extends it. In case the point is not yet clear, two neon-bright chunks of text in the middle of the page blink on and off to announce it: "THE BODY IS," the first line reads all in a rush, then slowly, spelling it out, "O-B-S-O-L-E-T-E."

The shock of Stelarc's performance—the claim that the bounded, flesh-and-blood body has been overtaken by networked-and-programmable flesh-and-wire circuitry—obscures a more complex and interesting hypothesis. There is, I want to suggest here, not a break but a synergy between Stelarc's claim and the thinking of twentieth-century American poets who position their work at the human-machine interface in order to protest conditions of industrial labor, to appropriate for writing the aims and strategies of emergent recording and storage technologies, and to participate in the human-computer collaborations of late twentieth- and early twenty-first-century cybernetic culture.

Of little interest to critics who are focused on the lyric's inward gaze, bounded subjectivity, and emotional nuance, poetry situated at the machine-human interface

comes into focus through a criticism that aligns it with the labor conditions, eco-
nomics, politics, science, and technologies that saturate and sustain it. Instead of
constituting a reserve from such matters, poetry—or, for our purposes here, a sig-
nificant strain in modern and contemporary American poetry—thinks along with
technology, engaging the debates it generates, the hopes and fears it raises, and the
reservoir of images it produces.

Because aesthetic objects, judgments, theories, experiences, attitudes, and prac-
tices are not apart from but a part of their surroundings, it is crucial, as Paul Gilmore
argues, to follow resonant poetic tropes back into the matrix they share with their
culture. Gilmore's example is Whitman's "body electric," which he aligns with "vari-
ous discursive uses of electricity as well as the material developments and economic
structures within which they were conceived" (473). In conversation with such
breakthroughs as Michael Faraday's confirmation of electromagnetic induction in
the 1830s and Samuel F. B. Morse's invention, patenting, and installation of a single-
wire telegraph in the 1830s and 1840s, Ralph Waldo Emerson in 1844 attributes to
poets "a power transcending all limit and privacy" that renders them "conductor[s]
of the whole river of electricity" (197), and Whitman in 1855 envisions himself with
"instant conductors all over me whether I pass or stop" ("Song," 32). At once invaded
and extended by the forces that pass through it, the body electric is a node, a trans-
fer, a relay; its skin is not a barrier but a membrane; its nerves, like Stelarc's bristle of
wires, "[m]ad filaments, ungovernable shoots" ("I Sing," 102) that receive and trans-
mit the information that forms sensual, cognitive, and spiritual experiences.

Flanking the twentieth-century lyric, late nineteenth-century Romantic poetry
on one side and twenty-first-century new media poetry on the other imagine not
a limited but a linked or networked self. The conduction that invades and extends
the mid-nineteenth-century figure of the poet, however, differs in significant ways
from the circuitry that composes the twenty-first-century figure that the digital
poet Talan Memmott dubs the "Cell.f."[2] The first—Whitman's one-in-many—is
a person-to-person join: the self-in-friendship, the amative or adhesive self, the
self that breaches racial, social, and political categories to form a collectivity that
Whitman celebrates with "a word of the modern—the word En-masse" ("Passage"
[1867], 48) and delineates as a global network—instantaneous and telegraphic—
through which "the distant [is] brought near, / [T]he lands…welded together"
("Passage" [1891–1892], 316).[3] The second—the permeable and distributed subjec-
tivity of Memmott's "cell.f"—is, by contrast, an intimate configuration of humans
and machines, nerves and instruments, minds and mechanisms.

The scandal of Stelarc's assertion that the body is O-B-S-O-L-E-T-E is its con-
flation of the organic and the mechanical. Hand-cranked Victrolas, telephone
switchboards, typewriter erasers, eight-track tapes, card catalogs, and the ven-
erable Apple I have fallen into disuse, but the human body, however tweaked or
augmented, will carry forth, we want to believe, intact. "I too had received iden-
tity by my body," Whitman writes, scripting this foundational assumption: "That
I was, I knew was of my body, and what I should be, I knew I should be of my

body" ("Sun-Down," 216). Metallic joints, intra-ocular lenses, cochlear implants, pacemakers, artificial hearts, and other machined body parts do not collapse the category "of my body," we tell ourselves, because they augment rather than erode the continuities by which we guarantee our relation to the past and place in the future.

At once hard to look at and hard to look away from, Stelarc's performances dissolve each component—the preposition *of*, the possessive *my*, the bounded noun *body*—in Whitman's talismanic phrase. In *Ping Body*, the performance schematized on Stelarc's splash screen, the notion of a source or spring of action marked by the preposition *of* dissolves in the relays of an operational system that integrates his body, a six-channel muscle stimulator that controls his left side, a screen that projects his image across distances—in this performance, over the Internet, from a studio in Luxembourg to screens in Paris and Amsterdam—and the bodies of distant observers who, by touching a contact point on the screen image, send signals through an arrangement of sensors, electrodes, and traducers back to Luxembourg to activate Stelarc's left arm and left leg (figure 26.2).[4]

In this display, it is not the body that is obsolete—the performance's endpoints are, after all, bodies linked by digital pings—but rather the set of questions begged by the words *of* and *my* and *body*: questions of origin, ownership, mastery, and the distinctions between the system's organic and synthetic components. The body that is O-B-S-O-L-E-T-E is the nontechnological, "natural," purely biological and

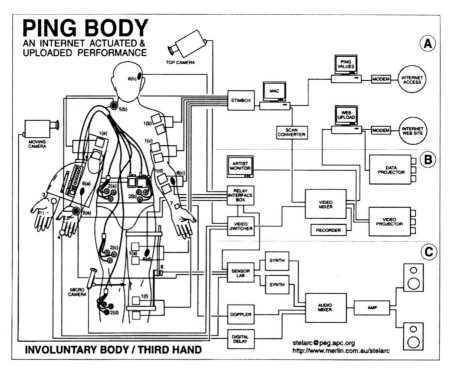

Figure 26.2 PING BODY. Digital Aesthetics. Artspace, Sydney, 1996. Courtesy of Stelarc.

unprosthetic body that we, like Whitman, assume to be enduringly foundational. The emergent body—the body Stelarc relentlessly performs—is an evolutionary structure extended by technologies, a body designed to be adequate to the information environment with which it interacts.

Ping Body, however, is more complex than this already complicated description catches, for on Stelarc's right side, the side controlled by his interior nervous system, his arm is doubled by a robot arm attached to an artificial hand with pinch-release capabilities activated by sensors controlled through his stomach and leg muscles. Collapsing any binary we might hope to reinstate as an organic/inorganic, human-machine split is Stelarc's *Third Hand*, a both-and operational system he has trained himself to control with automatic ease. In *Ping Body*, what counts is not the divide but the mesh of voluntary and involuntary, organic and cybernetic, instinctual and computerized components. Significantly, in his performance of this system, Stelarc's three hands work together to spell out the opposite edge of obsolescence: the term E-V-O-L-U-T-I-O-N (figure 26.3).

Altering the architecture of the body by splicing it into networked machines and activating it across distances, *Ping Body* transforms Whitman's "self" into Memmott's "cell.f." Incorporating the mathematical symbol for a function that signals a basic operation on a computer, the cell.f—a "cell function" or, perhaps, by elision, a "self-function"—is constituted, in Memmott's formula, by the amalgam (I+device), which he configures variously as I + Terminal or, in a more detailed diagram from his new media poem *Lexia to Perplexia*, Org + {...(x,y); (x,y);...} = S (figure 26.4).[5] This interface of organism and machine is the unit that comes into view as we look backward from Stelarc's performances through new media poetics to earlier twentieth-century figurations of the industrial and instrumental "I" in American poetry.

Figure 26.3 HANDSWRITING: Writing One Word Simultaneously with Three Hands. Maki Gallery, Tokyo, 1982. Photographer: Keisuke Oki. Courtesy of Stelarc.

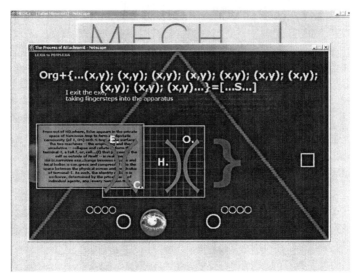

Figure 26.4 Screenshot from "The Process of Attachment," *Lexia to Perplexia.*
Courtesy of Talan Memmott. Source: http://collection.eliterature.org/1/works/
memmott__lexia_to_perplexia.html

Thinking the Interface

The first illustration in Lucy A. Suchman's groundbreaking anthropological study *Human-Machine Reconfigurations* is an early 1980s advertisement for the new, feature-rich Xerox 8200 copier. In it, a bushy-haired man wearing dark-rimmed eyeglasses and a white lab coat extends an index finger like God on the ceiling of the Sistine Chapel to press a button that kicks a large beige machine into life (9). This button is the interface, the site of interactivity, the join that complicates the compound "human-machine" by simultaneously separating and linking its components. For Suchman, the button marks the point at which two diverse entities—organic and inorganic—are imaginatively and materially reconfigured. For our purposes, it could be said to mark the spot where a machine is minded or, from the opposite perspective, a mind machined.

Like Stelarc's "the body is O-B-S-O-L-E-T-E," the epigraph for this chapter—Kenneth Goldsmith's declaration that "[the poet's] task is to simply mind the machines"—is combative and complex ("Provisional"). As a polemic originally posted in a blog on the Poetry Foundation website, it flies in the face of accepted beliefs about the nature of poetry; as an epistemological proposition, it engages emergent theories about the nature of cognition; as an ethical prompt, it opens questions of a viable life in the industrial and information ages. Before taking up poems that explore specific configurations of these elements, however, I want to pause briefly to explore the ways in which the ambiguities in Goldsmith's pronouncement dissolve, suspend, and redraw interfaces between human beings and their tools, instruments, and machines.

Schooled by the Romantics and their descendants, readers tend to construct poets as beings who are interior, meditative, imaginative, emotional, and, if not original, at least, in some fashion, striking and singular. This figure—by now, something of a caricature—is the "creative writer" that Charles Bernstein consigned to a corporation he calls "official verse culture"[6] and Ron Silliman attached to a clique he calls the "School of Quietude."[7] To extend the caricature only slightly, this sort of poet might be said to "mind the machines" in the sense that a listener "minds" static. For these poets and their advocates, industrial machines, recording or transcribing machines, and, perhaps especially, digital computers interfere with lyric contemplation, an act that is apparently, Rae Armantrout observes in an astringent review of *The Morrow Anthology of Younger American Poets* (1985), best accomplished in a pastoral setting by a solitary male "doing physical labor with a sharp implement" (143).

Figures that "mind the machines" in the stronger, more straightforward sense of designing and programming their operations have been, as Goldsmith well knows, not poets but physicists, engineers, and scientists. For our purposes here, the exemplary figures would be the post–World War II engineers who developed the paradigms and procedures that continue to shape our understanding and use of computers. With a chastened awareness of the role of science and engineering in the development and deployment of atomic weaponry, Vannevar Bush, Douglas Engelbart, J. C. R. Licklider, and their colleagues turned their expertise to the task of developing intelligent machines that could manage, circulate, share, and store information in the service of what Bush called "creative [as opposed to repetitive] thought" (41).

In a key paper from 1960 titled, in a rush of optimism, "Man-Computer Symbiosis," Licklider anticipated a new turn in the phrase "mind the machines." "The hope," he writes, "is that, in not too many years, human brains and computing machines will be coupled together very tightly, and . . . the resulting partnership will think as no human brain has ever thought and process data in a way not approached by the information-handling machines we know today" (74). For Licklider as for Bush, the integration of humans and computers had the potential to generate "intellectually the most creative and exciting [period] in the history of mankind" (75).

It is in this sense that poets—especially, although not exclusively, poets dedicated to an array of practices that Goldsmith celebrates as "uncreative writing"— could be said to "mind the machines."[8] Donna J. Haraway's "A Cyborg Manifesto," first published in 1985, famously positions science-fiction writers as cutting-edge theorists of cyborganization, but poets, purported guardians of the interior life, have also—and importantly—prefigured, registered, assessed, and participated in the integrated human-machine circuitry through which we now construct and understand both our subjectivities and our sense of the world.

MACHINING THE MIND: A POETICS OF INDUSTRY

Armantrout's late twentieth-century lyricists carry their tools through rural scenes that were in decline even as the century began. As machines increasingly dominated American life and culture in the period between the two World Wars, the experiences of space, time, and subjectivity shifted to meet the needs of an increasingly urban industrial economy. In the period known as America's Machine Age, elaborate systems of rails, cars, and planes reconfigured local, regional, and national geographies; scientific management studies by Frederick W. Taylor and his disciples synchronized workers' movements and paced their days to meet the demands of the machinery they serviced; and vertical cities laid out in grids that were, as George Oppen dryly notes, "More formal / Than a field" (*Discrete Series* 35) replaced meandering horizontal villages. Streamlining the flow of people, cars, taxis, buses, trucks, trains, and boats no less relentlessly than Henry Ford's River Rouge Complex organized the manufacture of Model A and Model B automobiles, lampposts, traffic lights, curbs, bricks, ironwork, girders, cables, and bridges became the structures Gertrude Stein called "the composition in which we live" (287).[9]

In an essay entitled "The New Conditions of Literary Phenomena," published in the little magazine *Broom* in 1922, the film theorist Jean Epstein lists "the innumerable instrumentations that encumber laboratories, factories, hospitals, photographic studios, and electrical shops, the engineer's table and the architect's drawing-board, the aviator's seat, the moving picture theatre, the optician's show window and even the tool-kit of the carpenter." "These machines," Epstein continues, "are not merely dead objects. At certain moments these machines become part of ourselves, interposing themselves between the world and us, filtering reality as the screen filters radium emanations" (6).

Machines became part of twentieth-century industrial, clerical, financial, and artistic life not only by disciplining bodies but also, in a twist of Goldsmith's phrase, by machining minds. Both the high modernists who upheld the traditions of an agrarian past and the leftists who aspired to a revolutionary future condemned the mental, corporeal, emotional, and spiritual effects of the processes through which workers were drained of spontaneity, synchronized with the rhythms of industry, and otherwise drawn, like Charlie Chaplin's Tramp, into the gears of production.[10] High modernist and Left poetry—one looking to the past, the other to the future— converge in condemning the truncation of life at the human-machine interface.

Like Stelarc declaring the body O-B-S-O-L-E-T-E, Machine Age modernists maximized the shock of the present by collapsing carefully tended cultural distinctions between bodies and things. In *The Waste Land*, the era's most celebrated poem, the erotic connection that Whitman exalted has no more intimacy than the coupling of railroad cars. Recording "the human engine wait[ing] / Like a taxi throbbing waiting," T. S. Eliot depicts the rendezvous of "the typist"—a figure who seems at once to operate and to be her machine—and "[a] small house agent's clerk," the subordinate of a functionary of an owner of a building: after the event, the clerk gropes his way to the street while the typist, idling and empty, "smoothes her hair with automatic hand, / And puts a record on the gramophone" (293–295). "No one / to witness / and adjust," William Carlos Williams comments, recounting the listless seduction of a girl he describes as one of "[t]he pure products of America": "no one to drive the car" ("To Elsie," 168, 170).

Unlike the tools that Armantrout's poets carry as metonyms of their manhood, the human engines in these iconic scenes are metaphors that decry the machining— the "making-into-machines"—of human beings. For Eliot, Williams, and many of their fellow modernists, this perverse alchemy is a profound violation of deeply held values: in Eliot's case, it violates the wisdom of sanctioned aesthetic and religious traditions; in Williams's, it violates the "isolate flecks" (169) that are all that remains of Whitmanian natural abundance, balance, and grace.

Scattered through these seduction scenes is an array of consumer goods—tinned food, stockings, slippers, stays, cheap jewelry, and other "gauds"—purchased with the wages for which the poems' personnel trade their labor. In an inversion Marx identified as inherent to the operations of a market economy, the typist, the clerk, and Elsie, Williams's servant of "some hard-pressed / house in the suburbs" (169), exhibit not just the "reification of the person" these poets lament in their machining figures of speech but also the "personification of the thing," the symbolic charging of goods through which, for theorists of the Left, social relations are negotiated.[11]

For increasing percentages of Machine Age workers, however, the interface between humans and machines was not predominantly metonymic or metaphoric— a linguistic turn, a figure of speech, a category confusion—but an unforgiving fact of life in factories, foundries, mills, mines, railroad yards, slaughterhouses, and other industrial sites of processing and production. Although carefully posed images such as Lewis Hine's "Power House Mechanic Working on Steam Pump" (1920; see figure 26.5) suggested a collaboration between men and machines—here, the muscular worker's body torqued in synchrony with the machine he tends—the human-machine interface was more frequently a site of slipping, piercing, ripping, mangling, mutilation, and, not infrequently, death. Too disturbing to circulate in images, this information was documented for the public sphere not just by investigative journalists and reporters but also by poets. Returned to contemporary notice by critics who have put the Left at the center of their practice, these poets—among them, Mike Gold, Tillie Olsen, Charles Reznikoff, and Muriel Rukeyser—dedicated their art to the documentation of life at the human-machine interface.[12]

In an afterword to her groundbreaking investigative poem *The Book of the Dead* (1938), Muriel Rukeyser declared her intention to use her writing to "extend the document" ("Note," 146). Documentary wasn't the only vehicle of worker-oriented poetry: as Cary Nelson has shown in his studies of early twentieth-century American poetries of the Left, traditional ballad and song forms, lyric, narrative, and dramatic poems, and other recognizably literary verse continued to do vital cultural work throughout this period. Overlooked by a practice of close reading that has prized the interior, psychological, aesthetic, and mythic, however, this poetry of fact

Figure 26.5 Lewis Hine, "Powerhouse Mechanic Working on Steam Pump" (1920).
National Archives and Records Administration, Records of the Work Projects
Administration. Source: http://www.archives.gov/exhibits/picturing_the_century/
port_hine/port_hine_img22.html

extended to support social and political engagement has until recently remained all
but invisible.[13]

Composed for the most part by poets who were convinced that only radical
change could bring about social and economic justice, these poems appeared on
features pages or in columns of such publications as *The Daily Worker* or *The New
Masses*. Gold's and Olsen's lineation of workers' correspondence, Rukeyser's cita-
tions of guidebooks, congressional hearings, medical reports, and stock-ticker read-
outs, and Reznikoff's condensations of court records appeared in tandem with news
reports, political analyses, satires, polemics, cartoons, advertisements, and letters to
the editor, functioning, as Nelson suggests, "not only as discrete objects but also as
varied contributions to collective discourses" (*Revolutionary Memory*, 2–3).

Many poems of the period posed crucial questions: How had workers been
"sold," in Langston Hughes's words, "to the machine"? (516). In what ways were the
luxury items retailed in fashionable emporiums "dyed in blood," as Olsen reports,
"stitched in wasting flesh"? (652). What drove the worker who, John Beecher tells
us, "loaded and wheeled / a thousand pounds of manganese / before the cut in his
belly was healed"? (559). What were the forces that rendered the most dutiful and
diligent Machine Age laborers, in Edwin Rolfe's poem "Asbestos," "dead before they
cease[d] to be"? (609). Coinciding with the rise of photojournalism, documentary
photography and film, newsreels, the Federal Theater Project's living newspapers,

and on-the-spot radio broadcasts by such reporters as Edward R. Murrow and William L. Shirer, poems of fact asked the public not only to look at material they would prefer to look away from but also to comprehend their own complicity in—and thus responsibility for—the processes that routinely dragged human lives into the machinery of industrial capitalism.

In *Testimony*, the most unrelenting of these documentary probes, Reznikoff detailed the daily realities of human-machine interactions. Distilling thousands of pages of late nineteenth- and early twentieth-century court records into a two-volume, four-part chronological compendium divided by region, then sorted by topic, Reznikoff edited out legal arguments, commentary, summations, and judgments to leave statements of fact to carry the poem's "psychological, sociological, and perhaps even poetical" meaning (Dembo, 202).

Each of *Testimony*'s four chronological parts contains a cluster of cases that appear under the rubric "Machine Age." At the core of each case is a collision at the human-machine interface:

> and when she had placed the shirts on the table
> [she] rested her fingers on the rollers;
> and another little girl who also worked in the mill
> started the machine:
> it caught Betty's arm and crushed it. (II, 91)
>
> . . .
>
> But this machine had a jerky motion
> so that it might suddenly pull the mold—
> and the hand upon it—
> under the frame. . . .
> [After] the machine had pressed four or six bricks,
> the boy's hand was drawn under the frame
> and crushed under the plunger. (I, 239)
>
> . . .
>
> when the saw came to where the two teeth were out,
> it jumped,
> and three fingers of [the man's] left hand were cut off. (I, 241)
>
> . . .
>
> [the girl's] apron was caught
> and drawn about the shaft
> and she was whirled around
> striking the wall and machinery. (I, 238)
>
> . . .
>
> In kicking a bobbin [Lea] slipped
> and fell against one of the twisters;
> her hair, caught in the rollers,
> was torn off—
> hair,

scalp,
an ear,
and part of her face. (II, 131)

Reznikoff's discipline in these passages is to curb the impulse that Charles Olson would call "the lyrical interference of the individual as ego" (247): as unadorned as they are devastating, these excerpts offer no elaborated symbolism, no descriptive distance, and no preemptive registration or rationalization of shock. Skillfully lineating the court records to reproduce the spin that pulls the workers into their machines, Reznikoff leaves the reader to face the fact-in-action.

If, in this poetics of industry, the poet's obligation is to present—to make present—the carnage at the human-machine interface, the reader's no-less-arduous obligation is "to witness and adjust." Hine's idealizing photograph aside, human bodies—in many of Reznikoff's examples, the bodies of children—were no match for the brute power of the machinery they tended and the criminal negligence and greed of factory owners willing to trade lives for profits. The conditions that Olsen, Gold, Rukeyser, Reznikoff, and other poets describe hollowed out the body's interior, stripped away will and vitality, and rendered individuality all but irrelevant. If, as Stelarc asserts, the twentieth century's industrial and information economies make the purely biological body insufficient, one of the realities these writers ask us to witness is the waning relevance of poems founded in and of the body and/or exalting a private, enclosed, and interiorized self. To witness the realities Reznikoff and his fellow poets describe, poetries in the twentieth century had to learn to adjust their language and procedures.

A MACHINE MADE OF WORDS:
THE OBJECTIVIST POEM

> I am kino-eye, I am a mechanical eye. I, a machine, show you
> the world as only I can see it.
>
>   —Dziga Vertov (1923)

On April 27, 1934, Walter Benjamin opened his address to the Paris Institute for the Study of Fascism by reminding his audience that Plato had ejected poets from his model state on the grounds that they were at once harmful and superfluous, dangerous and trivial ("Author," 83). Amid the real and present dangers of the times—in Germany, the passage of the "Law for the Prevention of Genetically Diseased Offspring," Heinrich Himmler's assumption of command over all police forces in Germany, Hitler's ascension to the title of Führer; in America, the failure of 11,000 of the country's 25,000 banks, a quarter of the population out of work, waves of the destitute streaming west, catastrophic winds stripping the topsoil from Texas, Oklahoma, Kansas, Nebraska, and Colorado, propelling pieces of the earth into clouds ten thousand feet high, and leaving behind a barren, uninhabitable land— what prompted Benjamin to return, with Plato, to the question of the uses of poetry? If poetry were indeed superfluous and trivial, what threat could it pose, what remedies might it offer, in the current moment of crisis?

Odd as it might now seem, Benjamin's gesture is not only cannily appropriate to its political moment—a moment of intense debate about the efficacy of art in the face of fascism—but also, for our purposes, key to comprehending the challenges of writing in the era that Benjamin famously called "the age of mechanical reproduction." As Reznikoff and his fellow Objectivists quickly intuited, profound discursive shifts at work in the thirties were rendering the strategies of the post-Romantic lyric if not obsolete, nonetheless insufficient to the exigencies of the moment.

As the scholar Eric A. Havelock would later demonstrate, in warring against poets, Plato's concern was epistemological. The expulsion of the poets was imagined at a moment that coincided with the transition from a culture based on oral transmission of information to a culture that would compose, store, test, and transmit information through writing. As Havelock argues at length, the epics of Homer and the bards that recited them to crowds seized and intoxicated by their rhythmic language had to be pushed aside to make room for the structures of critical thought, reasoned calculation, and the autonomous self that would become foundational to the discourse regime of writing.[14]

As Benjamin was among the earliest to understand, Euro-American culture in the thirties was in the throes of another massive epistemological shift, this time from print literacy to the mediated environment that Havelock's colleague Walter J. Ong would call "secondary orality." Driven by the growing dominance of such emergent electronic media as telephones, radios, loudspeakers, sound recording technologies, portable cameras, and projectors and accelerated by the rise of such hybrid genres as photojournalism, photobooks, documentary poetics, newsreels, and popular cinema, the mind-set nurtured by print was beginning to erode, taking along with it habits of mind associated with poetry as it had developed across the centuries-long expanse of print literacy.[15]

In the epigraph that Benjamin selected to preface "The Work of Art in the Age of Mechanical Reproduction," the poet Paul Valéry forecasts the cataclysmic nature of this shift. "For the last twenty years," Valéry wrote in 1931, "neither matter nor space nor time has been what it was from time immemorial. We must expect great innovations to transform the entire technique of the arts, thereby affecting artistic invention itself and perhaps even bringing about an amazing change in our very notion of art" (217).

As this chapter has been arguing, the changes associated with new media poetics—changes that seem abrupt when glimpsed from the perspective of the late Romantic lyric—have a long foreground in twentieth-century print poetry that registers and reenacts the effects of the Machine Age on human perceptions of space, time, and subjectivity. As consequential as the raw technological power that drove the industrial economy, the media that led the turn toward the contemporary information economy interposed an array of machine languages between the mind and physical phenomena. Just as perceptions of the body altered radically at industry's human-machine interface, perceptions of the world shifted significantly at the join between humans and instruments of mechanical reproduction. As Michael North suggests in his book *Camera Works*, it may in fact be that "the wholesale reorganization of human knowledge that we think of as arriving with the computer actually begins with mechanical recording" (vi).

The turn from an industrial toward an information economy marks the moment at which the poet Louis Zukofsky, writing under the title "Program: 'Objectivists' 1931," introduced the readers of Harriet Monroe's *Poetry* to the work of a set of writers that Rachel Blau DuPlessis and Peter Quartermain have described as "persistently under-known and undervalued" (2). Returning to salience in recent years, the first generation of Objectivist poets—here, most prominently, Zukofsky, George Oppen, Carl Rakosi, and Reznikoff, their elder by a decade—variously appropriated for their writing the aims and strategies of information recording and storage technologies.

Writing like other Left poets in and against economic, political, and social crisis, the Objectivists described their aim not as the delivery of fact but as the making of meaning. To build on a term that Benjamin deploys in his address to the Paris Institute, poets who testify to political, economic, and social abuses position themselves as *informing* artists, artists whose mission is to document a reality that preexists their report. Objectivists, by contrast, tended to position themselves as *constructing* or *producing* artists, artists whose mission is to craft a mechanism of perception that brings into view a reality that was otherwise imperceptible.[16]

As a cognitive technology, a way of knowing, a probe, the Objectivist poem is, in Oppen's words, "an instrument / of thought" (*Selected Prose*, 118). Tinkering again and again with this idea in his daybooks, Oppen struggles to keep it from slipping into metaphor: just as he thought of himself as a carpenter, construction worker, boat builder, and woodworker at various moments in his life, Oppen thought of the poem as a tool designed to do a job. It is, he says again and again, not decorative but efficient, shaped to its task, hard-edged, and precisely weighted. Selecting and pacing his words with care in a daybook entry, he sets the idea in caps: "I THINK THAT A POEM SHOULD BE THE WORK OF A MAN WHO REALLY MEANS TO DRIVE A NAIL—NOT TO POSTURE OR TO SHOW OFF—AND WHO KNOWS FROM CHILDHOOD—HOW A HAMMER SHOULD BE HANDLED" (*Selected Prose*, 191).

For a person who has handled it from childhood, the hammer is an extension of the arm. Like the act of a blind man navigating with a cane, a pilot flying by radar, or Stelarc inscribing the initial letters of the word "E-V-O-L-U-T-I-O-N" with his third hand, the act of driving a nail is distributed across an assemblage of organic and inorganic components. In this sense, an instrument in use is not an inert lump animated by a transcendent human intelligence but an interaction between human and nonhuman parts. The human-machine binary that seems self-evident in the factory looks from the instrumental or cybernetic perspective Oppen adopts here more like an extended horizon, feedback loop, continuum, or collaboration.[17]

In introducing the collection of poems he titled *The Wedge*, William Carlos Williams reiterates Oppen's idea of the poem as an instrument in use. A tool for splitting wood or stone, forcing apart contiguous objects, tightening or securing a part of a structure, or raising a heavy body (all definitions from the *Oxford English Dictionary* [*OED*]), a wedge is an element in a field of action that includes the worker, her materials, and her project. To think of the poem as a tool, instrument, or machine in this sense is neither a personification nor a pathetic fallacy: "There's nothing sentimental about a machine," Williams insists. "A poem is a small (or large) machine made of words" ("Author's Introduction," 256).

The model that Zukofsky had used to make this point in his 1931 manifesto was the camera. "*An Objective*," his "Program: 'Objectivists'" begins: "*(Optics)— The lens bringing the rays from an object to a focus*" (268). As DuPlessis and Quartermain point out, Zukofsky's term gathers to itself nuances that include an *objective* as a desire, the *object* as a thing in the world, *objectivity* as an ethical obligation to be precise, and the Marxist sense of *the objective* as the inevitable endpoint of historical process (8–9). For our purposes here, however, the most pertinent aspect of Zukofsky's analogy is its superimposition of the lens of the eye and the lens of the camera to form the composite that Memmott later called the (I+device): the human-machine intermediation at the heart of new media poetics.[18]

Poetic constructions emerge, as Gilmore argued in his analysis of Whitman's "body electric," in synchrony with the technologies of their time. It is not, therefore, surprising to find that Zukofsky was neither the first nor the last experimental artist to superimpose the lens of the eye and the lens of the camera. The intimate overlap of the human and mechanical "eye" at the lens of a camera-in-use, the trope that centers the contentions of the filmmaker Dziga Vertov's 1923 manifesto "Kinoks: A Revolution," not only recurs in visual form in numerous frames from his 1929 film *The Man with a Movie Camera* but also keys the publicity for the film (figures 26.6 and 26.7).

The questions broached by Vertov's "kino-eye" anticipate those explored by Stelarc's *Ping Body* and *Third Hand*. Neither entirely a man nor entirely a camera, "the man with a movie camera" is the human-machine reconfiguration that Hayles calls the "posthuman" and the neurobiologist Andy Clark terms "the natural-born cyborg." This hybrid being anchors the "Successive / Happenings" (35) in the thirty-one-section photographic poem George Oppen began in the winter of 1928–1929 when he met Zukofsky in New York City, drafted under the title "The Thirties," and published in 1934 as *Discrete Series*.[19]

A crucial challenge to the subjectivity that had long regulated notions of the lyric, *Discrete Series* is best approached on Oppen's terms as "an instrument of thought" designed "to test the truth of a common assumption" (*Selected Prose*, 117, 136). The poem's cryptic, condensed, precisely detailed, and often asyntactic sections, printed one to a page, flicker like frames shot from the window of a moving

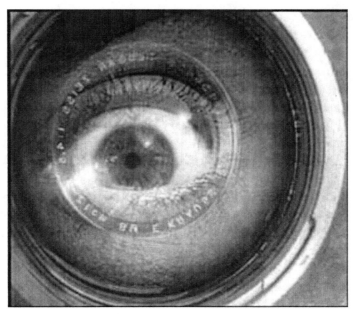

Figure 26.6 Camera-eye still from Dziga Vertov's *Man with a Movie Camera* (1929).

Figure 26.7 Poster for Dziga Vertov's *Man with a Movie Camera*, designed
by Vladimir and Georgy Stenberg (1929).

streetcar, train, or automobile, the porthole of a steamship, or deck of a tugboat "against the river— / Motor turning" (19). What passes by is an urban network of roads, lampposts, construction sites, and skyscrapers, the

> Up
> Down.   Round
> Shiny fixed
> Alternatives (6)

of vertical and horizontal motion, streaks of light against structures of wood, stone, and steel, the gleam of machined commodities and flash of "'city ladies'" (29), "[p]eople everywhere, time and the work pauseless" (25).

A repeated frame in these clips from the urban flow isolates an instant Steve Shoemaker describes as "a technomorphic interpenetration or entanglement of human and machine, flesh and steel" (64). Shoemaker's example is the human subject stepping *inside* the structure that Alfred Stieglitz called the "giant machine" of the skyscraper (69).[20] Caught just before, during, or after the join, Shoemaker's "primal scene of human/machine interface" (70) is reiterated by figures who enter an elevator (6), step into "that dark instrument / A car" (8), or board a streetcar, train, steamship, or tugboat to become, for a moment, Memmott's (I+device). Dissolved in the everyday life of the city, the antinomies of lyric subjectivity—a bounded separate self, organic and masterful; an organic or inorganic Other to be mastered—fall together and apart, each newly visible as, simply, "[a] thing among others / Over which clouds pass and the alteration of lighting" (13).

Operating the poem's parts of speech, syntax, line breaks, and dashes as tools of thought, Oppen pulls again and again into close-ups of the human-machine interface—a "hand on [a gearshift's] sword-hilt" (8), a "man sliding / Levers in the steam-shovel cab" (14)—then out to follow the lines of force through which information flows:

> In firm overalls
> The middle-aged man sliding
> Levers in the steam-shovel cab,—
> Lift (running cable) and swung, back
> Remotely respond to the gesture before last
> Of his arms fingers continually—
> Turned with the cab. But if I (how goes
>   it?)—(14)

In this clip from the series, the current that tests the thought passes through successive nodes of intermediation—man > levers > lift > cable > swung > arms fingers > cab > I—to end, temporarily, in a parenthetical ensemble that goes, for the moment, by the name of "it." The syntax switches along the lines of force to couple man-levers, then levers-lift, then lift-swung: each thing responding, in an endless chain, "to the gesture before last." Suffused in a flow of knowledge and directives, no one part of the ensemble is more consequential than any other. The whole turns—takes turns, revolves, transforms—like a nested series of gears, the cab meshed into the larger ensembles of the steam shovel, the construction site, the street, and the I/eye of the poet.

Oppen concludes this section with the "electric flash of streetcar, / The fall . . . falling from electric burst" (14). This cascade of sparks marks the cross-media transfer made into an icon half a century later by the finger-on-the-start-button in the 1982 Xerox advertisement but, as Oppen reminds us, available decades previously in the squeeze of the bulb that takes a "Civil war photo" (21) or the lifting of a receiver that patches us into a communications network (35). These intricate, intimate configurations not only redraw the industrial era's stark human-machine binary but also anticipate, as Shoemaker suggests, the shift toward the posthuman analyzed by new media critics such as Hayles, Mark B. N. Hansen, and Lev Manovich and also by contemporary neurobiologists and cultural theorists such as Andy Clark and Brian Rotman.

The far-reaching implication of the Objectivists' explorations is that humans are now and have long been cyborganized "not in the merely superficial sense" of using tools or benefiting from devices that mesh flesh and wire components "but in the more profound sense of being human-technology symbionts: thinking and reasoning systems whose minds and selves are spread across biological brain and nonbiological circuitry" (Clark, 3). This is the matrix of new media poetics.

Human-Machine Symbiosis: Writing (at) the Interface

an 'I' becoming 'beside itself'

—Brian Rotman

As this chapter has argued, significant strains in modern American poetry anticipate ways in which new media poetry constructs and is constructed by its relation to contemporary technologies. Emerson's vision of the poet's power to breach "all limit and privacy" in order to channel a "whole river of electricity," Whitman's depiction of himself with "instant conductors all over me whether I pass or stop," Reznikoff's accounts of workers imperiled by industrial machinery, Oppen's cybernetic notion of "arms fingers" that extend into "levers" that regulate "running cable[s]": all of these were in concert with the technologies of their time, and all re-imagine the humanist self by understanding the signifying unit not as a bounded organic body but as a human-machine symbiosis or cross-media flow of information.

With the post–World War II development of analog and digital computers, the establishment of government and academic networks and protocols and their transition to the commercial development and use of the Internet by the general public in the 1990s,[21] the exponential growth since the early 1990s of computing capacities and speed, and the increased centrality of computational media to the production, archiving, and dissemination of knowledge, the intelligent machines that were envisioned by Bush, Licklider, Engelbart, and their fellow computing pioneers have become an integral part of social, political, and economic life across the globe.[22] The rapid development and proliferation of mobile computer-based devices from smartphones to tablet PCs, netbooks, and e-readers, GIS mapping and navigation tools, cloud computing, RFID tags, and intelligent textiles are intensifying the migration from desktop to ubiquitous computing, a migration both deepened and accelerated by advances in nanotechnology, quantum computing, biotechnology, and the cognitive neurosciences.

As Suchman's anthropology of human-machine configurations demonstrates in fascinating detail, following the groundbreaking work in artificial intelligence in the 1950s, conceptions of machines had expanded from craft instrumentality and industrial technology to include "intelligent machines" as acting and interacting others.[23] The transition from the industrial interfaces documented by Reznikoff, Rukeyser, and other poets of the thirties to cybernetic horizons suggested in the work of Zukofsky and Oppen provides a foreground for comprehending the transformed subject–object relations in new media poetry and the cultural work it undertakes.

For Suchman, irresolvable differences between humans and machines mean that human–computer interactions can never approximate conversations of the sort that occur between human beings, but these interactions, nonetheless and perhaps more importantly, constitute an "ongoing, *contingent coproduction* of a shared sociomaterial world" (23, emphasis in original), a coproduction that has redefined not only what we can expect machines to do but also how we understand what it means to be "human."

This definitional shift marks a leading edge in contemporary neurobiology and cognitive science that is evident in the thinking of such theorists as Andy Clark and Brian Rotman. Humans are, in Clark's binary-dissolving oxymoron, "*natural-born cyborgs*" (3, emphasis in original). To live in constant practical, critical, and generative engagement with desktop, hand-held, attached, implanted, and/or environmental computing devices opens the unit Whitman capsulized in the phrase "of my body" to what is for Clark "a complex matrix of brain, body, and technology . . . [that] constitute[s] the problem-solving machine that we should properly identify as *ourselves*" (27, emphasis in original).

For Rotman, the primary mind-constituting technology—or, in Clark's phrasing, "*mindware upgrade*" (10, emphasis in original)—was alphabetic writing, which, as recent theorists have persuasively argued, gave rise to print culture's "lettered selves" (1). The ongoing shift that Rotman identifies as the "dethroning of the alphabetic text," begun in the era of Emerson and Whitman, "is now entering a new, more radical phase brought about by technologies of the virtual and networked media" (2). For Rotman, the effects of this displacement "go beyond the mere appropriation and upstaging of alphabetic functionality" to challenge "the intransigent monadism, linear coding, and intense seriality inseparable from alphabetic writing"

(2–3).[24] We are now, as the title of Rotman's recent book insists, "becoming beside ourselves": each of us, that is, is, willy-nilly, "a self becoming…plural, trans-alpha-betic, derived from and spread over multiple sites of agency, a self going parallel: a para-self" (8–9), even, perhaps, as Memmott has it, a cell.f.

Instead of describing our interactions with computational artifacts as a cross-media "conversation," the aspirational metaphor employed by artificial intelligence researchers, Suchman suggests that "a more productive metaphor…may be that of writing and reading" (23). In the present context, it is important to note that Such-man's metaphor points not to the practices of close reading and solitary introspec-tive writing associated with print traditions but toward the dynamic, contingent, human-machine collaborations of contemporary digital graphics, animation, art, design, mapping, electronic gaming, and, not least, the various and rapidly evolv-ing forms of writing known as new media poetics.[25] If, as Clark and Rotman argue, collaboration with technologies has long defined our humanity, it is important to understand these poems composed in symbiotic collaboration with intelligent machines and computational programs as part of an ongoing tradition that is now assuming new forms within the current configuration of culture, technology, and artifacts.

Reactions to electronic literature veer extravagantly between utopian and dys-topian predictions. If the buzz surrounding hypertext fiction in the early nineties, which forecast the upending of the linear, the demise of the novel, and the transfor-mation of readerly dutifulness into writerly creativity, has proved to be, in the jour-nalist Laura Miller's estimation, "little more than empty, apocalyptic showboating," more recent visions of children pulled into video-game spaces as ruthlessly as their precursors were dragged into rollers, spinners, and saws prove to be, in their turn, equally hyperbolic.[26] Like the game engines they sometimes resemble, new media poems are not just, in McKenzie Wark's words, "a key part of the shared culture from which one can begin the process—as laborious as it is playful—of creating a reflective and critical approach to the times" (Acknowledgments) but also, in their turn, as we have seen, an extension of earlier experiments in print and other media, newly visible in a backward gaze from the twenty-first century.

Licklider's vision of human–computer symbiosis widens the category used by biologists to describe the interdependence of two organisms—for example, two plants, an insect and a plant, two animals—to include the intimate coupling between humans and intelligent machines predicted by Bush and Licklider, described by Clark and Rotman, performed by Stelarc, and enacted in many varieties of new media poetry. The final pages of this chapter look briefly at three forms of writing (at) the human-machine interface that demonstrate contemporary variants of the practice that Goldsmith calls "minding the machines": cybertext, computational poetry, and codework.

Merging the prefix *cyber-*from Norbert Wiener's *cybernetics*, or science of com-munication and control, with the term *text* from poststructuralist literary theory, cybertext is a category introduced by the new media critic Espen J. Aarseth to describe the functioning of dynamic texts in a variety of media. In a significant correction to early attempts to read new media writing into the traditions of print narrative and poetry, Aarseth's term is crafted to highlight the human-machine synergies through which new media poems produce verbal meaning.

The defining feature of cybertexts is not a consistent aesthetic, coherent set of themes, developmental lineage, or uniform medium but a distinctive computational structure. Like a blind man and his cane, a pilot and her navigational system, or Stelarc and his Third Hand, a cybertext operates through a series of feedback loops that link a machine with its user in mutually constitutive exchanges of information. Like all circuits, cybertextual feedback loops consist of relays of inputs and outputs in which a user's action—for example, clicking a link or swiping a mouse—reconfigures available interpretive options by altering the material organization of the text.

As Aarseth emphasizes, cybertexts can be constructed in print, on a computer, or by hand. In addition to printed books such as Italo Calvino's *If on a winter's night a traveler*, electronic hypertexts such as Shelley Jackson's *Patchwork Girl* or Michael Joyce's *Twelve Blue*, and digital poems such as Stephanie Strickland's *The Ballad of Sand and Harry Soot* or John Cayley's *riverIsland*, the form could also be said to include ancient divination systems like the *I Ching*, early computer programs like Joseph Weizenbaum's *Eliza*, text-based digital games like *Myst*, multiuser domains (MUDs) of all sorts, and real-time virtual worlds like Second Life.

The most straightforward example of a literary cybertext is the digital form known as hypertext, anticipated by post–World War II computer engineers including Bush and Ted Nelson, elaborated in fictions composed between 1985 and 1995 by writers such as Jackson, Joyce, and Stuart Moulthrop, and disseminated on diskettes by Eastgate Systems. Like their fictional counterparts, hypertext poems contain three distinct components: links, chunked texts or lexia, and multiple reading paths. By clicking on a succession of links, a user navigates through related sections of a text or between related parts of different texts in the same retrieval system. Each click materially alters the text by closing one set of options and opening another.

In introducing the term "cybertext," Aarseth paired it with a second coinage to emphasize the "nontrivial" effort this form demands from its users. Like other hermeneutic structures, cybertexts are interactive in the general sense that text and interpreter act on or influence each other, but the effort involved to navigate a cybertext, play a textual game, or interact in a MUD is, in Aarseth's terminology, "ergodic" (1). From the Greek *ergon* + *hodos,* or "work" and "path," Aarseth's term describes the combined action of individuals and text engines—the human-machine symbiosis—that produces hypertextual sequences of events in computational poems.

Strickland's *The Ballad of Sand and Harry Soot* is a self-reflexive remediation of a print poem that won the *Boston Review*'s Second Annual Poetry contest in 1999. Strickland's hypertext, like ballads in oral and print traditions, tells a story of desire and delay, here between Harry Soot, a carbon-based life form like the poem's user, and Sand, a silicon-based machine like the user's computer, who mesmerizes him with her ability to generate seemingly infinite worlds of subtle, complex, and beautiful patterning but, as Suchman would concur, can't by nature enter into meaningful conversation with Soot's clumsy, yearning humanity. The poem's thirty-three sections each contain two link-words that flip the user into other sections of the poem and a set of graphics that link the sections with contemporary computer art projects listed in the poem's coda and searchable on the web. The poem's form enacts its thematics, for it is, as Suchman would emphasize, a tale about reading and writing across the human-machine interface.

Strickland's *Ballad* is an excellent example of what Hayles calls "second-generation" electronic literature composed after 1995 for presentation on the World Wide Web (*Electronic Literature*, 7). First-generation electronic literature, conceived by writers who began to experiment with computers in the late 1950s, remained predominantly text-based. In contrast, second-generation electronic literature combines text with graphics, sound, animation, video, and other multimedia components. More capacious than "hypertext," the term "cybertext" captures this wide range of computational and combinatory interactions.

Aarseth's term corrects two opposed critical responses to early new media writing: a tendency, on the one hand, to apply poststructuralist literary terms to electronic texts without taking into account the shift in the material apparatus, and a tendency, on the other, to treat digital texts as radically different from their print precursors. For Aarseth, Hayles, and other digital theorists, new media poetic compositions are textual engines that operate outside conventional author-text-message paradigms and must be understood as computational engines that work in synergy with a user. The cell.f they materialize as a user traverses them is, in Rotman's words, "plural, trans-alphabetic, derived from and spread over multiple sites of agency, a self going parallel: a para-self" (9). In their densely suggestive language, emotional textures, and narrative structures, these poems, like Strickland's *Ballad*, engage in dynamic intertextual relations with their oral and print predecessors; in machining the mind and/or minding the machine, they probe what it means to be "human"—or, more accurately, "posthuman"—in contemporary cybernetic culture.[27]

Like a cybertext, a computational poem is a linguistic artifact that emerges in tandem with a textual machine, but the focus here is the interplay between a set of preliminary instructions that can be formalized as procedural or algorithmic sequences and the complex arrays of information these instructions generate. Whether executed in print or on a computer, the defining features of a computational poem include the presence of a program that precedes and determines it, a relationship between form and content that distinguishes it from conceptions of organic poetry, on the one hand, and formalist poetry, on the other, and a dispersal of the authorial function that distances it from lyric or expressivist poetry.

Generative programs for computational poems include numerical patterning; mathematically driven permutations of linguistic elements; schematic transformations of source texts; and an array of alphabetic, syntactic, semantic, and/or homophonic procedures. As various as the devices that produce them, examples of computational poems would include Zukofsky's homophonic renderings into English of Latin poems by Catullus; Silliman's *Tjanting*, in which the number of sentences per unit equals the sum of the number of sentences in the preceding two units (the Fibonacci sequence); Brian Kim Stefans's "Stops and Rebels or, The Battle of *Brunaburh*," in which a mix of texts contained in files on a hard drive have been recombined by a digital algorithm; and Lee Ann Brown's "Pledge," in which each noun in the Pledge of Allegiance is replaced by the seventh subsequent noun in a dictionary (N + 7).

The subjectivity constructed in these poems, the "I" that emerges through their procedures, is not the "self" Whitman guaranteed through the phrase "of my body" but a self-function that emerges from a contingent mix of meaning-carrying agents that include alphabetic language, structures of syntax and sound, and permutations of cultural commonplaces. This unit—or, as Memmott would say, cell.f—is the meaning effect that Rotman calls the "para-human" or "beside ourselves": "[a] psyche that is at once porous, heterotopic, distributed and pluralized, permeated by emergent collectivities, crisscrossed by networks of voices, messages, images, and virtual effects, and confronted by avatars and simulacra of itself" (134).

Brown's "Pledge," composed by running the Pledge of Allegiance through the Oulipean N + 7 algorithm, consists of a series of permutations: "I pledge allergy to the flail of the United States of Amigo," it begins; "I pledge allegory to the flagellant of the United Statistic of Ammunition"; "I pledge allelomorph to the flagelliform of the United State-of-the-Art of American English." Opening to analysis a block of text most U.S. citizens learn by heart before comprehending the meaning of its words, Brown makes space for the critical contemplation of this highly consequential performative speech act.

Just as, at the turn toward literacy, Plato asked citizens of his ideal state to scrutinize ideas learned by rote and taken on faith, Brown's permutations, composed in the late 1990s as the Internet was transforming the dissemination of information, ideas, and news—especially, here, news of actions in the Mideast undertaken in the name of U.S. democracy—pose a series of uneasy alternatives: Does a pledge of allegiance to a flag override instinctive revulsion to military operations pursued in the name of that flag? What if such actions appear to betray or even mock the principles for which the flag is said to stand? Does it matter if the rhetoric that defends these actions conflates or confuses "Amigo" with "Ammunition," "flail" with "flagellant," "States" with "Statistic"?

As the word "allegiance" cascades through the N + 7 algorithm into "allergy," "allegory," and "allelomorph," the poem's sequence suggests that, like "allelomorphs"— "alternative forms of the same gene, occupying the same relative positions in homologous chromosomes" (*OED*)—syntactical structures, committed to memory as inherited patterns, can easily morph into dangerous, perhaps even lethal, variants. That the generation of these variants is mechanical, the result not of intent or insight but of the action of an algorithm on a source text, doesn't mean the result has no meaning: this particular machine has been, to borrow Goldsmith's formulation, "minded" not just by the poet's choice of this particular source text and algorithm and by her selection among dictionaries, choice of variants, and sequencing of alternatives, but also by the cultural ideas embedded in the resonant structure of the Pledge of Allegiance and by the thinking of interpreters who contemplate the overlaps between the source text and its contingent variants.

Unlike an organic poem, in which form is said to arise from content, or a formalist poem, in which form is said to contain content, a computational poem is produced and enacted by a procedure in which the poem's form acts as its intelligence. Computational poems do not aim to construct an authentic voice, capture nuances of emotion, or put passionate convictions into eloquent language but rather to engage and probe broad structures of meaning. In this sense, a computational poem is, to borrow John Cage's definition of experimental music, "not a question of having something to say" but rather an instrument to attend to flows of information through culture (17).

Computational poetry is a site of contemporary interest and debate not just because procedural texts such as Lyn Hejinian's *My Life* and Silliman's *Tjanting* are landmarks of Language Poetry and projects such as Kenneth Goldsmith's *No. 111.2.7.93–10.20.96* and Craig Dworkin's *Parse* stand as models for the practice that Goldsmith calls "Uncreative Writing" but also because of its heightened visibility as a precursor and ally of poems composed and performed on computers.

Starting with the earliest mainframes, programmers have created algorithms that access, filter, and recombine the contents of databases to generate texts that simulate the linguistic structures, promise of interpretability, and cultural capital of poetry. Such combinatory projects as Loss Pequeño Glazier's *Io Sono at Swoons*, Talan Memmott's *Self Portrait(s) [as Other(s)]*, Millie Niss's *Oulipoems*, and geniwate's *Concatenation* capture for the screen the experimental energies of a form initially executed in other media. In a literary ecology composed of texts that migrate between print, electronic, exhibited or installed, and performed versions, datamining, sampling, mixing, and other forms of procedural, combinatory, and computational practice are a key part of contemporary culture: to take this form seriously is not only, as Wark suggests, to undertake a reflective and critical approach to our times but also to understand the ways in which technologies continue to be constitutive of poetic structures, procedures, and effects.

The most medium-specific of these three variants, codework is a form of electronic literature in which normally invisible machine language, language addressed to a computer's operating system, shares the screen with language addressed to human interpreters. As practiced by such poets as Mez (Mary-Anne Breeze), John Cayley, Talan Memmott, Alan Sondheim, and Ted Warnell and theorized by Cayley, Memmott, Sondheim, and such critics as Funkhouser, Hayles, and Rita Raley, codework not only foregrounds for analysis the human-machine interface specific to digital writing but, as Raley points out, "presents a fusion at the level of language, substituting for, and functioning as, the figure of the cyborg...[by violating] the categorical and epistemological boundaries between the organic and inorganic, the public and the private, the visible and the hidden."[28]

Although all writing draws on semantic and bibliographic codes that prepare information for display, electronic writing depends on a tower of programming languages that includes machine code, assembly code, and such higher-level mark-up codes as BASIC, Perl, and HTML.[29] These languages share with so-called natural languages a complex syntax and grammar, a nuanced semantics, and a specific community or culture of address, but, as the theorist Alexander R. Galloway emphasizes, "[c]ode is the only language that is executable" (165, emphasis in original). For codewriters and critics alike, discussions of new media poetry that fail to account for code miss its most significant feature.

Coined by Sondheim in 2001, the term "codework" has sparked a series of critical discussions that distinguish new media poetry from its print predecessors by challenging the notion that text on the screen is an isolate or isolable entity, situating machine-addressed code as part of a digital poem's "text," positioning both code and text as artistic compositions, and underscoring the time-based unfolding that makes electronic writing an event or performance rather than a static object or artifact.

For Hayles, code or code elements that mingle with natural language on the screen construct a creole or pidgin whose semantic, epistemological, and poetic resonances foreground the symbiosis between humans and intelligent machines. As exemplified in Hayles's parsing of such compounds as "cell.f" or "I-terminal" from Memmott's *Lexia to Perplexia* (*Writing Machines*, 53) and Raley's deciphering of "m[ez]ang.elle," the "net.wurked" language of Mez's *data][h!][bleeding texts*, codework's often flashy rhetoric layers programming vocabulary and syntax with poetic and theoretical language to capture the hybrid subjectivity, cognitive processing, and textual possibilities available in a networked culture.

To process the human-machine creole that poet-programmers like Memmott and Mez deploy in their new media poems, it is necessary to allow commerce between the syntax, punctuation, and thought-structures of machine-addressed code and the sounds, shapes, and meanings of human-addressed language. As these two layers jostle against, complicate, and enrich each other, machine code becomes a way of thinking about poetic language at the same time that poetic language—especially, here, avant-garde or experimental poetic language—becomes visible as a form of procedural or operating code. In this sense, as Raley suggests in her deft analysis of Mez's *data][h!][bleeding texts*, codework functions as a pedagogical space in which reader-users learn to process the meaning of elements of high-level mark-up code at the same time that programmer-users learn to deploy technical operators, instructions, and characters to probe cultural and aesthetic concepts.

The periods, brackets, asterisks, double pipes, and other operators of programming language *.fect—that is to say, perhaps, simultaneously *affect*, *effect*, *infect*, and *perfect*—the theoretical concepts Memmott deploys to explain the hybrid being that haunts the screens of *Lexia to Perplexia*. Anticipating Clark, Memmott constructs a lingua franca for his (highly philosophical) natural-born cyborg; antic-ipating Rotman, he describes this figure—this cell.f—as "any/every para.I-terminal." Because human subjects who "become beside themselves" by linking their mortal being (I-terminal) into an x[ternal computer]-terminal can't be thought without the language(s) that produce them, the poem's users, perplexed by its lexia, need to learn how to think a being distributed between local and remote terminals: a "ping body," for example, that links Stelarc in Amsterdam with Stelarc in Luxembourg, a body that is, in a normative sense, neither (t)here nor (t)here (figure 26.8). For this, the lexicon of the lyric "I," the bounded self "of my body," and the psychoanalytic theory that supports it—the cogitations, Memmott notes, of one Sign.mud.Fraud—are not "ideo.satisfractile" (figure 26.9).

In opposition to the elaborate codework of artists such as Memmott and Mez, Cayley advocates code that works: code that makes things happen, code read by an intelligent machine, code that synchronizes the actions of a programmer, an operating system, and a user. To Cayley, the significant distinction is the distinc-tion between code that is operational and has depth and code that is "broken" because it is marooned on the screen and rendered inoperable. Nonreferential or nonperformative code, code that lacks an operating function, is, for Cayley, at best an aesthetic "decoration or rhetorical flourish"; at worst, new media's brand of "baroque euphuism" ("Code is not the Text").

Operational or "strong sense" code is code that exhibits an "aesthetics of com-pilation" ("Code is not the Text") by bringing to the level of the screen not a simu-lation of machine-addressed code but an experience of its incremental pacing and effects. Representative of a form of writing that Cayley calls "literal art," his ambient

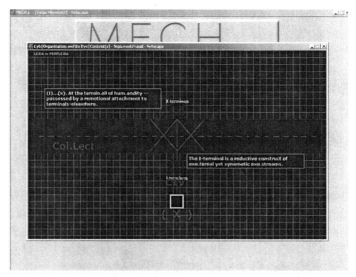

Figure 26.8 Screenshot from "Cyborganization and its Dys|Content(s)—Sign.mud. Fraud," *Lexia to Perplexia.* **Courtesy of Talan Memmott. Source: http://collection. eliterature.org/1/works/memmott__lexia_to_perplexia.html**

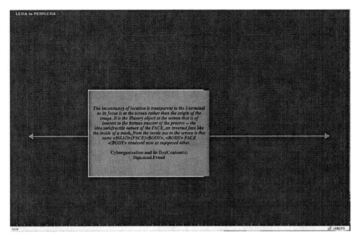

Figure 26.9 Screenshot from "The Process of Attachment," *Lexia to Perplexia*.
Courtesy of Talan Memmott. Source: http://collection.eliterature.org/1/works/
memmott__lexia_to_perplexia.html

time-based poems employ an algorithm that incrementally replaces letters of a sta-
ble underlying text with similarly shaped letters from different systems or stages of
change. As it moves the source text into and out of legibility, this "transliteral mor-
phing" generates dynamic tapestries of language accompanied, in Cayley's *riverIs-
land*, by QuickTime movies and recorded voices and, in *overboard* and *translation*,
by Giles Perring's generative music.

Whether on the screen or in a gallery installation, *overboard* appears as "an ever-
moving 'language painting'" ("Overboard"). As time passes, the text underlying its
changing display—paragraphs from Governor Bradford's *Of Plymouth Plantation*
describing an incident in the Mayflower crossing in which a man is swept overboard
and later hauled back alive onto the ship—moves in and out of legibility, "sinking,
rising, and sometimes in part, 'going under' or drowning, then rising to the surface
once again." The music that Perring composed for the piece follows similar genera-
tive procedures to provide an aural complement to the text's visual morphing.

On the left-hand side of the screen, at the margins of the viewer's consciousness,
a visual correlative of the text and its processes is displayed, with small images—
fragments of a photograph of the sea's surface—each corresponding in position and
identity to the letters of the text. *overboard*'s scheme of minimally distinct alternate
letters operates during both the surfacing and the sinking algorithm. During surfac-
ing, this means that, at a particular letter position, if a space is blank then either the
"natural" letter (the letter in this position in the underlying text) or its alternate may
appear. In surfacing, if the natural letter appears it will persist, whereas its alternate
letter will eventually change to the target letter over time. So long as the surfacing
state remains in effect, the algorithm scans and rescans the text until all the letters
of the complete text have appeared in their intended positions. At this point, the text
is fully legible according to modern dictionary-endorsed spelling and conventional
typesetting, then it begins, once again, to sink (figure 26.10).

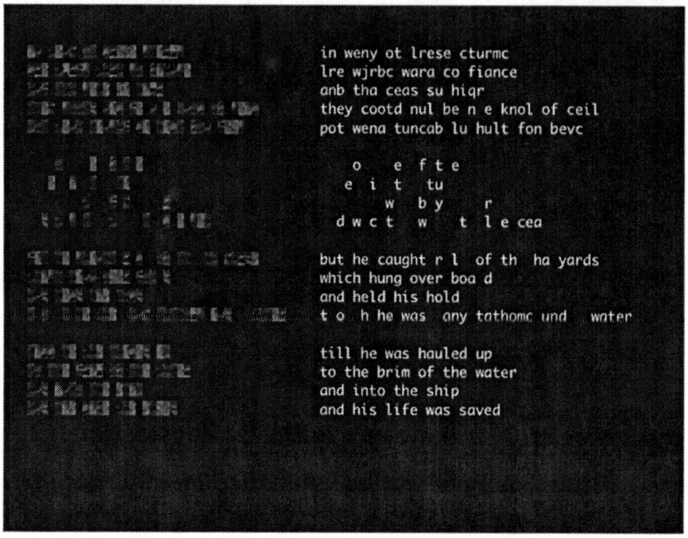

Figure 26.10 Screenshot from *overboard* with verse 1 "sinking," verses 2 and 3 in slightly differing stages of "surfacing," and verse 4 "floating." The musical cursor is in line 4 of verse 2. Reproduced from "overboard: An Example of Ambient Time-Based Poetics in digital art." Courtesy of John Cayley. Source: http://www.brown.edu/Research/ dichtung-digital/2004/2/Cayley/index.htm

Operating at a crossroads between readability and resistance, excitement and boredom, coherence and dissolution, Cayley's poem-engine churns out its changes whether a viewer attends to it, talks to a friend, or thinks about dinner. The poem's user is involved not in the preprocessing or programming of the piece but in what we might think of as a real-time coprocessing in which the poem functions as an intervention into an information flow. Its pedagogy is not a reading of code syntax but an immersion in the experience of code, a demonstration of the art of thinking in a world of databases and algorithms, source texts and kinesthetic mutations.

Participating with cybertextual and computational poetics in the reinvention of textual art for networked and programmable media, both Memmott's codework and Cayley's "code that works" explore the human-machine interface, the nature of reading and writing in tandem with a machine, and the role of intelligent machines in contemporary constructions of subjectivity. Together with these and other forms of new media poetics, they generate new strategies for making and new frameworks for understanding the linguistic constructions we call poetry in a world evolving in conjunction with the code-based operations of intelligent machines.

As Suchman suggests, more than displays of dominance or companionable conversations at an interface, we need creative explorations of the ways humans and intelligent machines together explore the stakes of minding the machine or, by reversal, machining the mind. In the penultimate chapter of *Human-Machine*

Reconfigurations, Suchman comes face to face with Stelarc's *Prosthetic Head* in a wonderfully fresh example of a dynamic assemblage that joins humans (Stelarc, Suchman, Suchman's companion videographer, and, by extension, Stelarc's programming team); a machine (here, a three-dimensional animated simulacrum of Stelarc's head), fitted with an ultra-sound sensor system that alerts it to a visitor's presence, automatically generated speech capacities that allow it to initiate interactions, a keyboard through which it can take a visitor's questions, and a congeries of programs that allow it to generate computational poems on the fly; and, not least, a scene of inquiry in which theorist and artist come together in the presence of the *Prosthetic Head*'s programmed but unpredictable actions.

When Suchman asks the Head, "Recite a poem, please," the Head responds with a compliment—"Your polite style is very nice," it says—and a three-line computational poem generated from a database of keywords set into something like a Whitmanian syntax:

> Our breathing imploding breathing imploding,
> City body electric system city excessive replicating,
> And city city involuntary imploding. (248)

Closing the interchange, the Head "(Smiles)." "Oh," Suchman responds, "that was very nice!" (248).

What can we make of this exchange? It's not designed for the page, much less the variorum edition, of print tradition. The term "author" misses the mark: no introspective gesture, emotional outburst, or coherent biography underwrites the lines. Because the words are spoken, there is, in a literal sense, no "reader," although, in an appeal to interpretation, Suchman imports the lines—implodes them?—into her book and I replicate them to end this chapter. "[S]ome interesting kind of philosophical kind of data," Stelarc remarks, adding, repetitiously, "and information" (249). "Yeah?" Suchman says.

"Uncreative" and "unoriginal" as they are, these lines seem, nonetheless, quite stubbornly, to approximate an event we could call a "poem": they are, after all, a linguistic performance, given intensity by a resonant lexicon, set of images, and rhythmic pulse of "breathing imploding breathing imploding." In the context of the installation, they form an act of transfer, a conduction of meaning, between Stelarc, Suchman, and the intelligent machine. As we think about them, finally, the lines reflect on their own nature as an "excessive" and "replicating" supplement to everyday transactions. Like the poetry they regenerate, they do the cultural work of making strange the act of speech and providing an occasion for us to contemplate not only the piths and gists of our traditions but also the iterations of our own technological moment. And, not least, they have a place, I would argue, in a handbook of modern and contemporary American poetry side by side with Whitman's "body electric," Reznikoff's records of "involuntary imploding," Oppen's "city...system," and other experiments in generative poetics long at work in various technological assemblages across diverse and evolving platforms.

NOTES

1 For exemplary rewritings, see DuPlessis; Davidson; Edwards; Nelson, *Repression and Recovery*; Perloff, *21st-Century Modernism*.
2 For Memmott's description of the cell.f, see Olivetti.
3 For Whitman and the Internet, see Roche.
4 For additional descriptions of this and other projects, see Smith.
5 Memmott's formula Org + S, like the term "cell.f," can be interpreted in various ways to accommodate both Organism + System and, its reverse, Organization + Self. At the screenic interface, the organic and inorganic "collapse and collate." "Even prior to logging on," Memmott explains, "when first seated at the terminal we are cyborganized and reconfigured to operate within this hybrid state," a state he calls ID.entity. "Where Identity can be localized, reified at the body, ID.entity is only made evident through a remotional attachment to the Cell…f that is elsewhere, neither (t)here nor (t)here." See Olivetti.
6 Perloff, "Conversation." Bernstein continues, "I do think that Creative Writing programs, taken in aggregate, are more open now to alternative approaches to poetic composition; but when I read the *Writer's Chronicle* of the Associated Writing Programs, I mostly see the same problems many of us criticized two decades ago, though now expressed with a kind of embattled, nostalgic tinge of those who have know[n] their ground is more like thin ice: better to skate on than to pound."
7 As Silliman points out in an entry from his blog, "School of Quietude" is a phrase coined in the 1840s by Edgar Allan Poe.
8 For descriptions of this tradition grounded in avant-garde practices of the early twentieth century, see Goldsmith, *Uncreative Writing*, and Perloff, *Unoriginal Genius*.
9 For additional information about this period, see Wilson, Pilgrim, and Tashjian, *The Machine Age in America*. For the aesthetics of the age, see *Machine Art*, the catalog for a Museum of Modern Art exhibit that ran from March 6 to April 30, 1934.
10 Clips of the assembly line and the automatic feeding machine scenes in Chaplin's film *Modern Times* (1936) are available on YouTube.
11 For the elaboration of these phrases, see Marx, "Productivity of Capital."
12 For critics who focus on poetry of the American Left, see, for example, Kalaidjian; Lowney; Nelson, *Repression and Recovery*, *Revolutionary Memory*, and "What Happens When We Put the Left at the Center?"; Smethurst; and Thurston.
13 "For much of the poetry of the American Left," Nelson writes in the introduction to his *Revolutionary Memory*, "the accompanying public context is silence" (1). Nelson's *Anthology of Modern American Poetry* returns many of these poets to view.
14 Since Havelock, Walter J. Ong, and their contemporary Marshall McLuhan, a number of scholars have elaborated, contested, and/or extended this hypothesis in fascinating detail. See especially Kittler; Rotman.
15 "Let us rehearse starkly," Julian Murphet writes, "the long series of abrupt media-technological intrusions upon the hitherto untrammelled media system or discourse network of the Enlightenment during the late nineteenth and early twentieth centuries: telegraphy, photography, typewriting, machine-set printing, photomechanical printing, the cheap rotary press, telephony, recorded sound on wax cylinder and phonograph, stereoscopes, electric light, early cinema exhibitions, nickelodeon kinetoscopes, wireless radio, facsimile machines, teletype and television (all by 1927)" (14).
16 Benjamin's distinction in this context is between informing artists, who seek to convey information, and "operative" artists, who see their mission as "not to report,

but to struggle" ("Author," 86). Any distinction between informing and operative, constructing, or producing artists is, of course, heuristic: as Reznikoff's selection and lineation of court records demonstrates, information is always already framed for interpretation.

17 For additional examples of the dynamic partnership between humans and machines, see Hayles, *How We Became Posthuman*, 283–291.

18 "Intermediation" is a term that Hayles uses to describe the process by which feedback and feed-forward loops tie organic and inorganic systems together in interactions that operate across a series of levels. It describes the interactions between a blind man and his cane and a pilot and her navigational system, but the most pertinent example is, of course, the many ways in which "the human and computer are increasingly bound together in complex physical, psychological, economic, and social formations" (*Electronic Literature*, 47).

19 *Discrete Series* has generated a series of richly evocative readings. See especially Hejinian, "Preliminary"; Shoemaker; Golding.

20 In a synchrony that Shoemaker points out, the publication of Zukofsky's Objectivist manifesto coincided with the completion of the Empire State Building in 1931.

21 ARPANET, Telnet, and other protocols were in use as early as the late 1960s; the spread of Internet use led to the idea of a global network based on standardized protocols officially implemented in 1982. Commercialization and introduction of privately run Internet service providers in the 1980s led to its expanded use by the general public in the 1990s.

22 I am indebted in this quick summary to Lenoir's excellent introduction to Rotman's *Becoming*.

23 First given currency by Turing in his landmark essay "Computing Machinery and Intelligence," published in the journal *Mind* in 1950, the definition of the term "intelligent machine" remains contested. For Hayles, it refers to "the ideal of machines performing tasks that require cognition, e.g., neural nets performing sophisticated decisions, expert systems that require judgments, information-filtering ecologies selecting data, genetic programs designing electrical circuits, etc." (personal communication, October 5, 2004). I use the term here to mean any digital device that is capable of processing data and acting on the basis of that data.

24 "[T]he alphabet's hold on factual description and memory was broken by photography," Rotman explains; "its inscription and preservation of speech sounds eclipsed by the direct reproduction of sound by the phonograph and its descendants; its domination of narrative form, fictional and otherwise, upstaged by documentary and film art; and its universal necessity weakened by television's ability to report or construe the social scene, via images and speech, in a manner accessible to the non-literate" (2).

25 For an excellent introduction to the operations and variety of new media poetry, see Hayles, *Writing Machines* and *Electronic Literature*, as well as the essays collected in Morris and Swiss, *New Media Poetics*. For a prehistory of digital poetics in early computing practices, see Funkhouser. For examples of contemporary new media writing, see the *Electronic Literature Collection*, Vols. 1 and 2.

26 For alternate assessments of the effect of electronic games, see for example, Johnson; Wark.

27 For a generative discussion of the implications of the term "posthuman," see Hayles, "Conclusion: What Does It Mean to Be Posthuman?" in *How We Became Posthuman* (283–291).

28 For the history and cultural contexts of codework, see Funkhouser, "Codeworks," Appendix A, in *Prehistoric Digital Poetry*, 257–261; Hayles, "Speech, Writing, Code: Three Worldviews," chapter 2 of *My Mother Was a Computer*, 39–61. For an extended analysis of the effects of codework-in-practice, see Raley.

29 For theories of textuality that compare digital mark-up language to bibliographic and semantic coding, see McGann.

REFERENCES

Aarseth, Espen J. *Cybertext: Perspectives on Ergodic Literature*. Baltimore, MD: Johns Hopkins University Press, 1997.

Armantrout, Rae. "Mainstream Marginality." Review of *The Morrow Anthology of Younger American Poets*. *Poetics Journal*, issue 6 (1986): 141–144.

Beecher, John. "Report to the Stockholders." 1925. In *Anthology of Modern American Poetry*, ed. Cary Nelson. New York: Oxford University Press, 2000. 557–559.

Benjamin, Walter. "The Author as Producer." 1934. *New Left Review* 62 (1970): 83–96.

———. "The Work of Art in the Age of Mechanical Reproduction." Trans. Harry Zohn. In *Illuminations*, ed. Hannah Arendt. New York: Schocken Books, 1968, 217–251.

Brown, Lee Ann. 1999. "Pledge." In *Polyverse*. Los Angeles: Sun & Moon Press, 36–37. Also available at http://bostonreview.net/BR23.5/Equi.html#Pledge. Accessed December 15, 2010.

Bush, Vannevar. "As We May Think." 1945. In *The New Media Reader*, ed. Noah Wardrip-Fruin and Nick Montfort. Cambridge, MA: MIT Press, 2003. 37–47.

Cage, John. "Experimental Music: Doctrine." In *Silence: Lectures and Writings*. Middletown, CT: Wesleyan University Press, 1961, 13–17.

Calvino, Italo. *If on a winter's night a traveler*. Trans. by William Weaver. New York: Harcourt Brace Jovanovich, 1981.

Cayley, John. "The Code is Not the Text (Unless It Is the Text)." 2002. http://www.electronicbookreview.com/thread/electropoetics/literal. Accessed December 15, 2010.

———. "overboard: An Example of Ambient Time-Based Poetics in digital art." 2004. *Dichtung-Digital*. http://dichtung-digital.mewi.unibas.ch/2004/2/Cayley/index.htm. Accessed December 19, 2010.

———. *riverIsland*. 2002, rewritten for QuickTime, 2007. Version 1.0. http://homepage.mac.com/shadoof/net/in/riverisland.html. Accessed December 15, 2010.

Cayley, John, with Giles Perring. *translation*. 2004. http://homepage.mac.com/shadoof/FileSharing9.html. Accessed December 15, 2010.

Cayley, John, with Giles Perring and Douglas Cape. *overboard*. 2004. http://homepage.mac.com/shadoof/net/in/overboardEng.html. Accessed December 15, 2010.

Clark, Andy. *Natural-Born Cyborgs: Minds, Technologies, and the Future of Human Intelligence*. New York: Oxford University Press, 2003.

Davidson, Michael. *Guys Like Us: Citing Masculinity in Cold War Poetics*. Chicago: University of Chicago Press, 2004.

Dembo, L. S. Interview with Charles Reznikoff. *Contemporary Literature* 10.2 (1969): 193–202. Excerpted http://www.english.illinois.edu/maps/poets/m_r/reznikoff/interv.htm. Accessed December 13, 2010.

DuPlessis, Rachel Blau. *Genders, Races, and Religious Cultures in Modern American Poetry, 1908–1934*. Cambridge: Cambridge University Press, 2001.

DuPlessis, Rachel Blau, and Peter Quartermain, eds. *The Objectivist Nexus: Essays in Cultural Poetics*. Tuscaloosa: University of Alabama Press, 1999.

Dworkin, Craig. *Parse*. Berkeley, CA: Atelos, 2008.

Edwards, Brent Hayes. *The Practice of Diaspora: Literature, Translation, and the Rise of Black Internationalism*. Cambridge, MA: Harvard University Press, 2003.

Electronic Literature Collection, Volume 1. 2006. Ed. N. Katherine Hayles, Nick Montfort, Scott Rettberg, and Stephanie Strickland. http://collection.eliterature.org/1/. Accessed December 13, 2010.

Electronic Literature Collection, Volume 2. 2011. Eds. Laura Borràs, Talan Memmott, Rita Raley, and Brian Kim Stefans. http://collection.eliterature.org/2/. Accessed June 21, 2011.

Eliot, T. S. *The Waste Land*. 1922. In *Anthology of Modern American Poetry*, ed. Cary Nelson. New York: Oxford University Press, 2000, 285–301.

Emerson, Ralph Waldo. "The Poet." 1844. In *Emerson's Prose and Poetry: Authoritative Texts, Contexts, Criticism*, ed. Joel Porte and Sandra Morris, New York: W.W. Norton, 2001, 183–198.

Epstein, Jean. "The New Conditions of Literary Phenomena." *Broom* 2.1 (1922): 3–10.

Funkhouser, C. T. *Prehistoric Digital Poetry: An Archaeology of Forms, 1959–1995*. Tuscaloosa: University of Alabama Press, 2007.

Galloway, Alexander R. *Protocol: How Control Exists after Decentralization*. Cambridge, MA: MIT Press, 2004.

geniwate. *Concatenation*. 2006. In *Electronic Literature Collection*, Vol. 1, ed. N. Katherine Hayles, Nick Montfort, Scott Rettberg, and Stephanie Strickland. http://collection.eliterature.org/1/works/geniwate__generative_poetry.html. Accessed December 15, 2010.

Gilmore, Paul. "Romantic Electricity, or the Materiality of Aesthetics." *American Literature* 76.3 (2004): 467–494.

Glazier, Loss Pequeño. *Io Sono At Swoons*. 2002. http://epc.buffalo.edu/authors/glazier/java/iowa/. Accessed December 19, 2010.

Golding, Alan. "George Oppen's Serial Poems." *Contemporary Literature* 39 (1988): 221–239.

Goldsmith, Kenneth. *No. 111.2.7.93–10.20.96*. Great Barrington, MA: The Figures, 1997.

———. "Provisional Language." 2010. Harriet: A blog from the Poetry Foundation. http://www.poetryfoundation.org/harriet/2010/04/provisional-language/. Accessed December 2, 2010.

———. *Uncreative Writing*. New York: Columbia University Press, 2011.

Haraway, Donna J. "A Cyborg Manifesto: Science, Technology, and Socialist-Feminism in the Late Twentieth Century." 1985. In *Simians, Cyborgs, and Women: The Reinvention of Nature*. New York: Routledge, 1991, 149–181.

Havelock, Eric A. *Preface to Plato*. Cambridge, MA: Harvard University Press, 1963.

Hayles, N. Katherine. *Electronic Literature: New Horizons for the Literary*. Notre Dame, IN: University of Notre Dame Press, 2008.

———. *How We Became Posthuman: Virtual Bodies in Cybernetics, Literature, and Informatics*. Chicago: University of Chicago Press, 1999.

———. *My Mother Was a Computer: Digital Subjects and Literary Texts*. Chicago: University of Chicago Press, 2005.

———. *Writing Machines*. Cambridge, MA: MIT Press, 2002.

Hejinian, Lyn. *My Life*. 1978/1987. Los Angeles: Green Integer, 2002.

———. "Preliminary to a Close Reading of George Oppen's *Discrete Series*." In *Thinking Poetics: Essays on George Oppen*, ed. Steve Shoemaker. Tuscaloosa: University of Alabama Press, 2009, 47–61.

Hughes, Langston. "Let America Be America Again." 1936. In *Anthology of Modern American Poetry*, ed. Cary Nelson. New York: Oxford University Press, 2000, 515–517.

Jackson, Shelley. *Patchwork Girl: or, a modern monster by Mary/Shelley, & herself: A graveyard, a journal, a quilt, a story, & broken accents.* Watertown, MA: Eastgate Systems, 1996. Electronic resource.

Johnson, Steven. *Everything Bad Is Good for You: How Today's Popular Culture Is Actually Making Us Smarter.* New York: Penguin, 2005.

Joyce, Michael. 2006. *Twelve Blue.* In *Electronic Literature Collection*, Vol. 1, ed. N. Katherine Hayles, Nick Montfort, Scott Rettberg, and Stephanie Strickland. http://collection. eliterature.org/1/works/joyce__twelve_blue.html. Accessed December 15, 2010.

Kalaidjian, Walter. *Languages of Liberation: The Social Text in Contemporary American Poetry.* New York: Columbia University Press, 1989.

Kittler, Friedrich A. *Discourse Networks 1800/1900.* Trans. Michael Metteer, with Chris Cullens. Stanford, CA: Stanford University Press, 1990.

Lenoir, Timothy. 2008. "Machinic Bodies, Ghosts, and Para-Selves: Confronting the Singularity with Brian Rotman." In Rotman, *Becoming Beside Ourselves: The Alphabet, Ghosts, and Distributed Human Being.* Durham, NC: Duke University Press, ix–xxix.

Licklider, J. C. R. "Man-Computer Symbiosis." 1960. In *The New Media Reader*, ed. Noah Wardrip-Fruin and Nick Montfort. Cambridge, MA: MIT Press, 2003, 74–82.

Lowney, John. *History, Memory, and the Literary Left: Modern American Poetry, 1935–1968.* Iowa City: University of Iowa Press, 2006.

Machine Art. 1934. Sixtieth Anniversary Edition. New York: Museum of Modern Art, 1994.

Marx, Karl. 1861. "Productivity of Capital. Productive and Unproductive Labour." 1863. In *Marx's Economic Manuscripts of 1861–63*, Vol. 34, 121–146. Archived in Marx and Engel's Internet Archive, http://www.marxists.org/archive/marx/works/1861/economic/ch38.htm.

McGann, Jerome. *Radiant Textuality: Literature after the World Wide Web.* New York: Palgrave Macmillan, 2001.

Memmott, Talan. *Lexia to Perplexia.* 2000. In *Electronic Literature Collection*, Vol. 1. Ed. N. Katherine Hayles, Nick Montfort, Scott Rettberg, and Stephanie Strickland. http:// collection.eliterature.org/1/works/memmott__lexia_to_perplexia.html. Accessed December 2, 2010.

——.*Self Portrait(s) [as Other(s)].* 2003. In *Electronic Literature Collection*, Vol 1. Ed. N. Katherine Hayles, Nick Montfort, Scott Rettberg, and Stephanie Strickland. http:// collection.eliterature.org/1/works/memmott__self_portraits_as_others.html. Accessed December 15, 2010.

Mez [Mary-Anne Breeze]. *data][h!][bleeding texts.* 2002. http://netwurkerz.de/mez/datableed/complete/. Accessed December 15, 2010.

Miller, Laura. "www.claptrap.com." 1998. *New York Times Book Review*, March 15. http:// www.nytimes.com/1998/03/15/books/bookend-wwwclaptrapcom.html. Accessed December 2, 2010.

Morris, Adalaide, and Thomas Swiss. *New Media Poetics: Contexts, Technotexts, and Theories.* Cambridge, MA: MIT Press, 2006.

Murphet, Julian. *Multimedia Modernism: Literature and the Anglo-American Avant-garde.* New York: Cambridge University Press, 2009.

Nelson, Cary. *Repression and Recovery: Modern American Poetry and the Politics of Cultural Memory, 1910–1945.* Madison: University of Wisconsin Press, 1989.

——. *Revolutionary Memory: Recovering the Poetry of the American Left.* New York: Routledge, 2001.

———. "What Happens When We Put the Left at the Center?" *American Literature* 66.4 (1994): 771–779.

Nelson, Cary, ed. *Anthology of Modern American Poetry*. New York: Oxford University Press, 2000.

Niss, Millie, with Martha Deed. *Oulipoems*. In *Electronic Literature Collection*, Vol. 1, ed. N. Katherine Hayles, Nick Montfort, Scott Rettberg, and Stephanie Strickland. http://collection.eliterature.org/1/works/niss__oulipoems.html. Accessed December 15, 2010.

North, Michael. *Camera Works: Photography and the Twentieth-Century Word*. New York: Oxford University Press, 2005.

Olivetti, Peter. 2001. "Interview with Talan Memmott." *Histories of Internet Art: Fictions and Factions*. http://art.colorado.edu/hiaff/NP_CC_ART03_Intvs.htm. Accessed December 2, 2010.

Olsen, Tillie Lerner. "I Want You Women Up North to Know." 1934. In *Anthology of Modern American Poetry*, ed. Cary Nelson. New York: Oxford University Press, 2000, 652–654.

Olson, Charles. "Projective Verse." 1950. In *Collected Prose*, ed. Donald Allen and Benjamin Friedlander. Berkeley: University of California Press, 1997, 239–249.

Ong, Walter J. *Orality and Literacy: The Technologizing of the Word*. New York: Routledge, 1991.

Oppen, George. *Discrete Series*. 1934. In *New Collected Poems*, ed. Michael Davidson. New York: New Directions, 2002, 1–35.

———. *Selected Prose, Daybooks, and Papers*, ed. with an introd. by Stephen Cope. Berkeley: University of California Press, 2007.

Perloff, Marjorie. "A Conversation with Charles Bernstein." *Fulcrum* 2 (2003). Rpt. http://epc.buffalo.edu/authors/perloff/articles/mp_cb.html. Accessed December 2, 2010.

———. *Unoriginal Genius: Poetry by Other Means in the New Century*. Chicago: University of Chicago Press, 2010.

———. *21st-Century Modernism: The "New" Poetics*. Oxford: Blackwell, 2002.

Raley, Rita. "Interferences: [Net.Writing] and the Practice of Codework. " 2002. http://www.electronicbookreview.com/thread/electropoetics/net.writing. Accessed December 15, 2010.

Reznikoff, Charles. *Testimony*, Vol. I: *The United States (1885–1915) Recitative*. Santa Barbara, CA: Black Sparrow, 1978.

———. *Testimony*, Vol. II: *The United States (1885–1915) Recitative*. Santa Barbara, CA: Black Sparrow, 1979.

Roche, John F. "Walt Whitman's Temporary Autonomous Zone." 2005. *Mickle Street Review* nos. 17–18. www.micklestreet.rutgers.edu/index.html.

Rolfe, Edwin. "Asbestos." 1928. In *Anthology of Modern American Poetry*, ed. Cary Nelson. New York: Oxford University Press, 2000, 609.

Rotman, Brian. *Becoming Beside Ourselves: The Alphabet, Ghosts, and Distributed Human Being*. Durham, NC: Duke University Press, 2008.

Rukeyser, Muriel. *The Book of the Dead*. 1938. In *Anthology of Modern American Poetry*, ed. Cary Nelson, New York: Oxford University Press, 2000, 656–687.

———. "Note." *U. S. 1*. New York: Covici and Friede, 1938, 146–147.

Shoemaker, Steve. "*Discrete Series* and the Posthuman City." In *Thinking Poetics: Essays on George Oppen*, ed. Steve Shoemaker. Tuscaloosa: University of Alabama Press, 2009. 62–87.

Silliman, Ron. Blog. May 13, 2006. http://ronsilliman.blogspot.com/2006_05_07_archive. html. Accessed December 2, 2010 / <See fn. 7>

———. *Tjanting*. Berkeley, CA: The Figures, 1981.

Smethurst, James. *The New Red Negro: The Literary Left and African American Poetry, 1930–1946*. New York: Oxford University Press, 1999.

Smith, Marquard, ed. *Stelarc: The Monograph*. Cambridge, MA: MIT Press, 2005.

Sondheim, Alan. "Introduction: Codework." *American Book Review* 22.6 (2001): 1, 4.

Stefans, Brian Kim. "Stops and Rebels: A Critique of Hypertext." In *Fashionable Noise: On Digital Poetics*. Berkeley, CA: Atelos, 2003, 61–169.

Stein, Gertrude. "Portraits and Repetition." 1935. In *Writings, 1932–1946*, Volume 2, ed. Catharine R. Stimson and Harriet Chessman. New York: Library of America, 1998, 287–312.

Stelarc. *Third Hand*. 1980–1994. http://stelarc.org/?catID=20265 Accessed June 21, 2011.

———. *Ping Body*. 1997. http://www.medienkunstnetz.de/works/ping-body/. Accessed June 21, 2011.

———. *Prosthetic Head*. 2003. http://stelarc.org/?catID=20241 Accessed June 21, 2011.

———.Website. 2007. http://web.archive.org/web/20070829003523/www.stelarc.va.com.au/stelarc1.html. Accessed December 20, 2010.

Strickland, Stephanie. *The Ballad of Sand and Harry Soot*. 1999. http://www.wordcircuits.com/gallery/sandsoot/. Accessed December 15, 2010.

Suchman, Lucy A. *Human-Machine Configurations: Plans and Situated Actions*. 2nd ed. Cambridge: Cambridge University Press, 2007.

Thurston, Michael. *Making Something Happen: American Political Poetry between the World Wars*. Chapel Hill: University of North Carolina Press, 2001.

Turing, Alan. "Computing Machinery and Intelligence." *Mind* 59 (1950): 433–460.

Vertov, Dziga. "Kinoks: A Revolution." 1923. In *Kino-Eye: The Writings of Dziga Vertov*, ed. Annette Michelson, trans. Kevin O'Brien. Berkeley: University of California Press, 1984, 11–21.

Wark, McKenzie. *Gamer Theory*. Cambridge, MA: Harvard University Press, 2007.

Whitman, Walt. "Song of Myself." 1855. *Leaves of Grass*. Walt Whitman Archive. http://www.whitmanarchive.org/published/LG/1855/poems/1. Accessed December 2, 2010.

———. "Sun-Down Poem." 1856. *Leaves of Grass*. Walt Whitman Archive. http://www.whitmanarchive.org/published/LG/1856/poems/11. Accessed December 2, 2010.

———. "I Sing the Body Electric." 1867. *Leaves of Grass*. http://www.whitmanarchive.org/published/LG/1867/poems/7. Accessed December 2, 2010.

———. "Passage to India." 1867. *Leaves of Grass*. http://www.whitmanarchive.org/published/LG/1867/whole.html. Accessed December 2, 2010.

———. "Passage to India." 1891–1892. *Leaves of Grass*. Walt Whitman Archive. http://www.whitmanarchive.org/published/LG/1891/poems/239. Accessed December 2, 2010.

Wiener, Norbert. *Cybernetics: or, Control and Communication in the Animal and the Machine*. Cambridge, MA: MIT Press, 1948.

Williams, William Carlos. "Author's Introduction to *The Wedge*." 1944. In *Selected Essays of William Carlos Williams*. New York: Random House, 1954, 255–257.

———. "To Elsie." 1923. In *Anthology of Modern American Poetry*, ed. Cary Nelson. New York: Oxford University Press, 2000, 168–170.

Wilson, Richard Guy, Dianne H. Pilgrim, and Dickran Tashjian. *The Machine Age in America, 1918–1941*. New York: Brooklyn Museum in association with Henry N. Abrams, 1986.

Zukofsky, Louis. "Program: 'Objectivists' 1931." *Poetry* 37.5 (1931): 268–272.

Poets' Index

SUBJECT INDEX

Eliot, Charlotte C. 138
Eliot, Samuel Atkins 130–131
Ellis, Havelock 148, 426
Ellis, Trey 371–372
Ellison, Ralph 243, 328 n. 12, 449–450
Emami, Zohren 145–146
Eng, David L. 451
Engelbart, Douglas 661, 673
Engels, Friedrich 149, 277–278
English, Ned 302, 326 n. 1
Enlightenment 101, 164–165, 684 n. 15
Environmental Social Movement 603, 616
Epstein, Andrew 54
Epstein, Jean 662
Equal Rights 117 n. 3
Ernst, Max 270, 273, 282, 285, 288
Ethnopoetics 288, 409, 607
Ettor, Joseph 565
Eugenics 585–588
European Caravan 276–278, 288, 292,
    294 n. 32

Falkoff, Mark 575–576
Falwell, Jerry 595
Fanon, Frantz 452
Faraday, Michael 657
Farrell, Thomas 317
Fascism 19–21, 35–36, 59, 338–339, 516,
    562, 564, 666–667
  Antifascism 26, 35, 430, 515, 526
  Nazi 20, 311–313, 429, 502–503, 585
Paris Institute for the Study of Fascism 666
Faulkner, William 585
Faust, Gilpin 335
Febvre, Lucien 554 n. 37
Federal Theater Project 664–665
Federal Writers' Project 551 n. 13
Feiner, Susan F. 166
Felman, Shoshana 442
Felski, Rita 58, 65
Felstiner, John 602
Feminism 17, 18, 25, 43–44, 63, 98, 104–105,
    142–167, 321, 431–432, 452, 489–490,
    586–587, 591–592, 621–622 n. 2
Fenollosa, Ernest 178–180, 627
Ferguson, Charles A. 221
Ferguson, Russell 510
Fetter, Frank A. 163
Fick, Nathaniel 352
Film 61, 64, 251, 252–253, 257, 260, 270, 278,
    492–492, 569, 642, 669–670, 681
Filreis, Alan 24, 57, 294 n. 25, 488, 513

Finkelstein, Sidney 494
Finnegan, Cara A. 168 n. 10
Fischer, Barbara K. 293 n. 21
Fitterman, Robert 189 n. 39
Fitts, Dudley 182
Fitzgerald, Ann 120
Flack, Roberta 646
Flacks, Richard 536–537
Flying Words Project 594
Folbre, Nancy 150
Ford, Henry 662
Ford, Karen Jackson 6, 17, 40, 45–46
Forman, Murray 646
Forrest Gump 347
Foucault, Michel 442, 531, 585
Fourier, Charles 167 n. 4
Fowlie, Wallace 287
Fox, Paul Erwin 301–308, 325
Franco, Francisco 338, 496
Franco, Jean 59–60
Frankfurt School 59–63, 251–252,
    265–266 n. 4
Frattali, Steven 295 n. 45
Freud, Sigmund 10, 106, 270, 272, 275,
    278, 337, 425–453
  Interpretation of Dreams, The 427–429
Frick, Henry Clay 164
Fried, Michael 190 n. 43, 264
Friedman, Susan Stanford 431
Fry, Roger 195–196
Fugazi 331
Fugees 645–646, 651
Funkhouser, C. T. 678, 685 n. 25
Furman, Bess 525
Furr, Derek 114
Fussell, Paul. 332–333
Futurism 150, 174, 290, 434, 516

Galloway, Alexander R. 679
Galton, Francis 585
Garner, Stanton 363 n. 4
Garrard, Greg 604, 606, 621 n. 1
Garron, Paul 578 n. 4
Garvey, Ellen Gruber 327 n. 11
Garvey, Marcus 643
Gauley Bridge Disaster 25–26, 241, 588,
    615–616
Gay Rights Movement 591, 595
Geertz, Clifford 535, 551 n. 9
Gelpi, Albert 605
Genette, Gerard 173
Genre 57, 61, 258–259, 270, 273, 275, 461, 584

CPSIA information can be obtained at www.ICGtesting.com
Printed in the USA
BVOW01s0810131214

378907BV00005B/7/P

9 780190 204150